D0443156

Also by Paul Kennedy

The Rise and Fall of the Great Powers

PREPARING FOR THE TWENTY-FIRST CENTURY

PREPARING FOR THE TWENTY-FIRST CENTURY

Paul Kennedy

HarperCollins*PublishersLtd*

 For information address HarperCollins Publishers Ltd, Suite 2900, 55 Avenue Road, Toronto, Canada M5R 3L2.

First Edition

Canadian Cataloguing in Publication Data

Kennedy, Paul M., 1945–
Preparing for the twenty-first century

Includes bibliographical references and index.
ISBN 0-00-215690-3

1. Twenty-first century—Forecasts. I. Title.

CB161.K45 1993 303.49'09'05 C92-095388-3

---

93 94 95 96 97 98 99 AG 10 9 8 7 6 5 4 3 2 1

Book designed by Gloria Tso

To the Hamden under-fifteen
Boys' Soccer Team from their Coach

FOREWORD AND ACKNOWLEDGMENTS

THIS BOOK HAD ITS ORIGINS IN A DEBATE which took place between me and a large group of economists at the Brookings Institution in Washington in the spring of 1988, and which centered upon my newly published work *The Rise and Fall of the Great Powers.* In the course of a lively evening, one critic—not known to me—declared that he couldn't understand why such a fuss was being made about *Rise and Fall* by everyone. It was, after all, a very traditional sort of book, focusing upon the nation-state as the central actor in world affairs. Why hadn't I used my time better, to write about much more important and interesting issues, those forces for global change like population growth, the impact of technology, environmental damage, and migration, which were *trans*national in nature and threatened to affect the lives of us all, peasants as well as premiers?

I left it to others that evening to weigh in with opinions about why *Rise and Fall* might be of some pertinence, especially in the American presidential campaign of 1988, but I found my critic's comment sufficiently arousing to begin initial readings in subjects (global warming, demography, robotics, biotech) that were then totally foreign to me. Before long, I was making clippings of newspaper and journal articles upon those subjects and filing them away. After a further while, I realized that I had the makings of a new book, very different from *Rise and Fall* in its subject matter and structure and yet—as I explain in Chapter 1—closely related in its concerns and purpose. Both are an attempt to write what David Landes calls "large History." Whether the present work provokes the same interest as the previous study will be for the reader to say.

In the course of researching and preparing this book, I have become obliged to an embarrassingly large group of individuals, only a few of whom can be mentioned here. I am deeply indebted to Sheila Klein and Sue McClain, who once again typed repeated drafts of the manuscript with wonderful efficiency and dispatch. Old friends Gordon Lee and J. R. Jones read and commented on every aspect of the initial draft, then upon the revisions. Jonathan Spence, Richard Crockatt, David Stowe, W. H. McNeill, Paul Golob, André Malabré, James O'Sullivan, Bill Foltz, and Bill Cronon read and made notes on parts or all of this work. Kenneth Keller, Bill Nordhaus, and Maria Angulo tried to keep me from going too far wrong in my coverage of environmental issues.

I was also blessed by the assistance of a large number of Yale graduate students. For the past few years, Maarten Pereboom, Karen Donfried, Richard Drayton, Geoff Wawro, Kevin Smith, Fred Logevall, and Reynolds Salerno have successively grappled with the mountains of files, documents, correspondence, and other materials, reducing them to some order. David Rans did statistical analysis for me. My son John Kennedy took a summer off to reorganize and list the entire archive. Fred Logevall and Reynolds Salerno prepared the bibliography and checked the endnote references.

When, in the summer of 1990, it became clear that I was being overwhelmed by the sheer mass of literature upon the subjects I proposed to cover, I was rescued by a group of five research assistants, all Yale students. Zhikai Gao, with wonderful computing skills, organized a computer search of the literature held in the Sterling Library's extensive collections, providing the results to the rest of us. Tony Cahill investigated and prepared an extensive report on environmental issues. Gary Miller did the same on comparative education. Sameetah Agha reported on robotics, automation, high technology, and related issues, as well as advising on the developing world, Islam, India, and China. David Stowe was amazingly efficient in providing reports on demography, globalization, and biotech agriculture and also gave more general assistance. Without these five, the work would never have been completed. I remain, of course, solely responsible for all lingering errors, as well as for the general and specific arguments made in the text.

I am especially indebted to my literary agents, Bruce Hunter and Claire Smith, who have supported me throughout the project. Stuart Proffitt, my London editor at HarperCollins, has also been wonderfully supportive throughout this project, exchanging ideas and information, reading and gently criticizing the various drafts, and helping to give an overall shape to the work. I know the completed manuscript arrived later than he would have wished, but I hope he will find that the extensive revisions have been worthwhile.

My two greatest critics, Jason Epstein of Random House and my wife, Cath, deserve special mention. Being edited by the former is the literary equivalent of Marine Corps boot camp, but although the process of revision is a painful one, there is no doubt in my mind that the manuscript benefited immensely from Jason's line-by-line editing and from his insistence that the chapter themes be much more closely interrelated than they were in the first draft.

The manuscript was also vastly improved by the many amendments suggested by my wife; the Part Two chapters especially benefited from her advice.

This is dedicated to the Hamden under-fifteen Boys' Soccer Team, which I have had the pleasure of coaching for the past four years and hope to be with until they go to college. Coaching can be frustrating at times—usually when the team loses—but it is also a wonderful escape from one's books, files, and statistics. Some authors can be single-minded scholars. This one cannot; but I feel much the better, and much refreshed, for having been coach as well as professor during the writing of this work.

Paul Kennedy
Hamden/Branford, Connecticut
May 1992

CONTENTS

PART ONE: GENERAL TRENDS

PART TWO: REGIONAL IMPACTS

TABLES AND CHARTS

TABLES

CHARTS

PART 1

GENERAL TRENDS

1

PROLOGUE: OLD CHALLENGES AND NEW CHALLENGES

TWO HUNDRED YEARS AGO, AS THE EIGHTEENTH century was drawing to a close, observers of social and political trends in Europe were deeply troubled. A revolutionary tide, which had first surged in France in 1789, was spreading to neighboring states, bringing down regimes from Italy to the Netherlands. Instead of peaceful constitutional change to a more representative political system, here a revolution was feeding upon itself, producing demagogues, angry street mobs, violence, and a new pan-European war. As a consequence, authorities in nations as different as Georgian Britain and czarist Russia reacted by suppressing revolutionary tendencies. Moderate voices, as happens so often, found themselves scorned by the left and threatened by the right.

Although the French Revolution had specific causes—for example, worsening state finances during the 1780s—many felt that there were deeper reasons for these social upheavals. One such was obvious to anyone who visited Europe's crowded cities or noted the growing incidence of rural underemployment: it was the sheer press of human beings, all needing food, clothing, shelter, and work in societies not well equipped to meet those demands, at least on such a scale. Countryside hovels teemed with young children. Town authorities grappled with a rising tide of homeless vagrants. In the larger cities, a floating population of tens of thousands of unemployed slept on the ground overnight and poured into the streets the next day. Jails, pauper houses, foundling hospitals, and lunatic asylums were packed with human casualties who had not yet arrived at their common grave.

Concerned observers did not need statistics to know that their societies were experiencing a population boom. Had the data been available—the taking of a national census was only just being introduced around this time—the figures would have confirmed their judgment. The population of Europe (including Russia) had been about 100 million in 1650, was almost 170 million a century later, and by 1800 was well past 200 million.[1] The population of England and Wales grew by a mere 1 percent in the 1720s, by 4 percent in the 1750s, and by over 10 percent per decade as 1800 approached—and was still accelerating.[2] The major cities, swelled by the drift of population from the countryside, grew even faster. On the eve of the French Revolution, Paris had a total of between 600,000 and 700,000 people, including up to 100,000 vagrants—combustible materials for a social explosion. London's total was even larger, its 575,000 inhabitants of 1750 having become 900,000 by 1801, including a mass of the bustling street hawkers, pickpockets, urchins, and felons so well captured in contemporary prints. With more and more "have-nots" being born in a world of relatively few "haves," was it any wonder that the authorities were fearful and tightened up restrictions upon public assemblies, pamphleteering, "combinations" of workers, and other potentially subversive activities?

This late-eighteenth-century surge in population, which was also taking place in countries as far removed as China and America, had various causes. An inexplicable decline in the virulence of diseases like smallpox was one. So also was the increasing use of vaccination techniques. Improvements in food supply and diet, at least in parts of Western Europe, were another cause. In certain societies, women were marrying younger.[3] Whatever the exact combination of reasons, there were many more children in most parts of the world than there had been a century earlier. As the population expanded, it pressed upon existing resources.

The prospect of a growing mismatch between people and resources deeply troubled a learned and inquisitive English country curate named

Thomas Robert Malthus, who in 1798 committed his thoughts to paper in a work which has made him world-famous. In his *Essay on Population,* * Malthus focused upon what appeared to him the greatest problem facing the human species: "that the power of population is indefinitely greater than the power in the earth to produce subsistence for man."[4] This was so, he argued, because the populations of Britain, France, and America were doubling every twenty-five years whereas—although fresh land was also being opened up—there was no certainty that food supplies could increase at the same rate repeatedly. Indeed, while the output of farm produce might conceivably be doubled over the following twenty-five years, to suppose such a doubling could occur again, and again, and again was "contrary to all our knowledge of the qualities of land."[5] As Britain's population geometrically increased from 7 million† to 14 million over the next quarter century, and to 28 million over the following quarter century, and then to 56 million and 112 million, Malthus forecast there would be an ever greater gap between the people's food demands and the land's capacity to meet them. The result, he feared, would be increasing starvation and deprivation, mass deaths through famine and disease, and a rending of the social fabric.

It is not necessary here to follow all the debates between Malthus and his contemporaries, except to note that he had deliberately penned his *Essay* to contest the arguments of certain writers (Godwin, Condorcet) about the perfectibility of man. Those optimists had concluded that while things were troubled at the moment, the growth of human understanding, the capacity for self-improvement, and breakthroughs in knowledge would one day lead to a society that was much more equitable, free of crime and disease, free even of war.[6] The pessimistic Malthus, by contrast, felt that population growth meant that the human condition would worsen, with the existing gap between the "haves" and the "have-nots" exacerbated by the pressures upon the earth's resources.

This debate between optimists and pessimists has, in one form or

*More accurately, *An Essay on the Principle of Population as It Affects the Future Improvement of Society* (London, 1798). This is also known as Malthus's "first" essay on population, since it was rewritten in 1803 and there were later editions.

†It was actually larger, about 10 million, at this time.

another, been with us since then, and, this study will argue, it is even more pertinent today than when Malthus composed his *Essay.* As for that debate of two hundred years ago, the optimists were proved correct, although not necessarily for all the reasons they had advanced. While advocates of the perfectibility of man suffered frequent disappointments as the nineteenth and (especially) the twentieth centuries unfolded, Malthus's pessimistic, mathematical reasonings ignored a number of factors, so his forecast of "gigantic inevitable famine" was off the mark, at least as far as his native Britain was concerned. To be sure, the British Isles in the early nineteenth century felt some negative consequences of the population explosion: poverty in rural regions was widespread, and while millions decided to remain there, many more drifted into the towns and cities for work; sprawling slums of jerry-built houses, lacking water, light, heat, and sanitation, sprang up in the new manufacturing towns; hordes of children lacked adequate health care, nutrition, clothing, and education; gangs of unemployed agrarian workers attacked the new farming machines that had thrown them out of work; social protest was common, especially in years when poor harvests drove up the price of bread, and large-scale demonstrations (like the one held at Peterloo in 1819) were fiercely suppressed by authorities fearful of a Jacobin revolution.

Nevertheless, *three* developments permitted the British people to escape the fate Malthus predicted for them. The first was emigration: people left the British Isles in vast numbers, in search of better conditions elsewhere. While only slightly more than 200,000 emigrated in the 1820s, that figure trebled in the following decade and reached almost 2.5 million in the 1850s. Between 1815 and 1914, around 20 million Britons left the country,[7] a massive exodus relative to the overall population. (By 1900, the British population was about 41 million; without emigration, it would have been over 70 million.) More important than absolute numbers, however, was the fact that the British were not prevented by domestic or foreign authorities from migration. Apart from those who headed to the labor-hungry United States, millions also streamed to colonies rich in land and resources (in Canada, Australasia, southern Africa) and inhabited by peoples who could not long resist Western military technology. Existing communications—the long-range sailing ship, followed by the steamship and the railway—

permitted hundreds of thousands of families to cross the globe, in discomfort surely, but also in relative security. There was thus no need to linger in the hovels and slums of England or Scotland, borne down by the press of numbers.*

The second development was that just as Malthus was writing his *Essay,* there occurred significant improvements in British farming output—so significant, indeed, that the whole process was later called the Agricultural Revolution.[8] Far from being a sudden event (as the word "revolution" suggests), the process consisted of piecemeal improvements—rotation of crops, new breeding techniques, better estate management, new agricultural implements, introduction of the potato, enclosure of common lands and draining of wetlands, better publicity about these new farming methods, enhanced communications and access to markets—cumulatively raising the quantity and the quality of the food supply to the British nation, enhancing its well-being, reducing mortality rates, and also contributing to the population increase. In due course, the steadily expanding numbers of people could not fully be supplied from these augmented domestic sources; in that sense, Malthus was correct. However, by the third quarter of the nineteenth century, British demand for grains, meat, and other foodstuffs could be supplied from the farms established by earlier emigrants to North America, Australia, and elsewhere—such produce being transported in refrigerated steamships. Contrary to Malthus's forebodings, "the power in the earth" was able to match "the power of population," thanks to the ingenuity of his own countrymen.

The third and most important development was that just a decade or two before Malthus composed his *Essay,* Britain entered the first stages of the Industrial Revolution, that vast leap forward in productivity which followed from the substitution of mechanical devices for human skills, and of inanimate power (steam, then electricity) for animal and human strength.[9] Even in their early forms, power-driven looms could produce twenty times the output of a hand worker, while a power-driven "mule" (a spinning machine) had two hundred times the capacity of a spinning wheel. Moreover, the coal needed to fuel

*In the case of the Highland clearances, of course, the emigration was more involuntary than voluntary.

those machines and the manufactures flowing from the newly established factories in which the machines were grouped could be hauled by locomotives possessing the capacity of hundreds of packhorses. No earlier technological breakthroughs produced anything like the rise in output that flowed from the Industrial Revolution.

While the coming of steam power had many consequences, short-term and long-term, its greatest was to save at least parts of the human race from the dire results of the population explosion that so worried Malthus. The Industrial Revolution boosted productivity to such a degree that both national wealth and general purchasing power outran the rise in the numbers of people. During the nineteenth century as a whole, the British population grew *fourfold,* whereas the national product grew *fourteenfold.*[10]

This is not to say that the material benefits were immediate or, for that matter, evenly distributed. Industrialization brought early gains to the entrepreneurs, inventors, mill owners, and their financial backers who realized that the new methods of manufacture would lead to enhanced profits. But apart from the critical issue of providing jobs for the expanding populace, it did not greatly benefit the first or second generation of workers, who, suffering under awful conditions in factories and mines, were organized alongside their machines in a strict, time-driven system of labor unlike anything known previously. The difference clearly was between the short term and the long term. Only the later generations of workers gained from the general increase in prosperity that flowed from industrialization, for which their parents and grandparents paid so heavily. It was little wonder that Karl Marx—and Marx's followers elsewhere more recently—forecast that the proletarianization of a people would lead to a revolution against the classes in power, and did not foresee that things might improve over time. Marx—an angry critic of Malthus—was even worse at the art of prediction.

Because the new technology and system of production turned Britain into the workshop of the world, its people steadily became richer. With earnings from rising British exports—5 million pounds' worth of textile exports of the 1780s had been transformed into almost 40 million pounds' worth by the 1820s[11]—Britain was able to purchase the foodstuffs, raw materials, and other goods its population needed, and to transport those products more swiftly on more sophisticated ships. Possessing greater manufacturing efficiency than any other society at that time and enjoying ever-higher standards of living, many Britons became proponents of laissez-faire economics and of an "open" trading order in which national boundaries and ownership counted for less and less. Perhaps the great English economist Jevons best captured this mood when he exulted in 1865:

> The plains of North America and Russia are our cornfields; Chicago and Odessa our granaries; Canada and the Baltic are our timber forests; Australasia contains our sheep farms, and in Argentina and on the western prairies of North America are our herds of oxen; Peru sends her silver, and the gold of South Africa and Australia flows to London; the Hindus and the Chinese grow tea for us, and our coffee, sugar and spice plantations are all in the Indies. Spain and France are our vineyards and the Mediterranean our fruit garden, and our cotton grounds, which for long have occupied the Southern United States, are now being extended everywhere in the warm regions of the earth.[12]

In many ways, this was one of the great success stories of the human race, very different from, but as important as, the coming of representative government or the rise of religious tolerance. The Industrial Revolution, together with the earlier Scientific Revolution of detached research and inquiry, created a built-in upward spiral of economic growth and technological advance. New inventions, new manufacturing techniques, new forms of transport, and new capital tended to stimulate each other. For example, the creation of the large, iron-hulled steamship in the middle of the nineteenth century was both a product of the twin revolutions in science and industry and a means to improve global communications, food supply, migration, and so on. Since then, the interaction of technological change and industrial development has been unstoppable.[13]

Thus, "the power of population" was answered, not so much by "the power in the earth" itself, but by the power of technology—the capacity of the human mind to find new ways of doing things, to invent new devices, to organize production in improved forms, to quicken the pace of moving goods and ideas from one place to another, to stimulate fresh approaches to old problems. Malthus was absolutely correct to see that a doubling of a country's population every twenty-five years would involve a race between consumption and resources; but he missed the power of science and technology to create improvements in the transportation of people, goods, and services, to enhance agricultural output, and to stimulate breakthroughs in the manufacture of wares, so that fresh resources were harnessed and invented to meet the growing demands of a vigorous population. Moreover, the rising standards of living led to social changes—more years at school, improvements in the status of women, enhanced consumption, growing urbanization of the population—all of which tend to decrease the average number of children born per family. In other words, Britain went through a "demographic transition" that eventually led to a stabilization of the population, a century or more later. The geometric increase in numbers, it turned out, lasted only a few generations.

In sum, the British people escaped their Malthusian trap via three doors: migration, agricultural revolution, and industrialization. It is equally important to notice, however, that this escape was not very common. Certain countries—Belgium, Germany, the United States—imitated British practices and followed the upward spiral of increased productivity, wealth, and standards of living. However, many other countries were not so fortunate and, constrained either by internal or external forces, steadily lost ground. Ireland, disadvantaged in many ways (alien political control, lack of infrastructure, lack of coal, low per capita levels of consumption, depressed agriculture), was unable to solve "the central problem of the age . . . how to feed and clothe and employ generations of children outnumbering by far those of any earlier time."[14] By the 1840s, starvation and emigration had reduced population by about one-fifth.

India is another case in point, and much closer to Malthus's model. Its population also doubled and redoubled in the nineteenth century, but on a much less productive base. Furthermore, because the Indian states had been unable to resist Britain's East India Company militarily, their subjects could do little when British machine-made textiles—not only cheaper but of better quality than native cloth—poured into the country, driving out traditional domestic producers in the process.* The awful result, according to one calculation, was that whereas the British and Indian peoples had roughly similar per capita levels of industrialization at the onset of the Industrial Revolution (1750), India's level was only one-hundredth of the United Kingdom's by 1900.[15] Industrialization and modernization certainly caused problems in Western societies, but they paled in comparison with "the lot of those who increase their numbers without passing through an industrial revolution."[16]

There was, it is worth noting, another solution in Malthus's time to the problem of excess population, namely, internal unrest followed by external aggression. In France, popular discontents smashed an *ancien régime* that was less well structured than Britain in agriculture, industry, and commerce, and in its social framework and attitudes, to sustain rapid demographic growth. By the time the French Revolution's early hopes had been destroyed by terror, reaction, and then Bonapartism, an enormous number of young, energetic, and frustrated Frenchmen were being deployed in armies of occupation *outside* France, where many if not most of them died from combat or disease. Territorial conquest thus played its traditional role as a vent for overpopulation, social tensions, and political frustrations—although over the long run it could not compete with Britain's combination of technological innovation, economic growth, and colonial acquisitions.[17] Still, the record indicates that among the possible consequences of rapid population growth, social turbulence and territorial expansion are as plausible as any.

Those same interrelated issues—overpopulation, pressure upon the land, migration, and social instability on the one hand, and technology's power both to increase productivity and to displace traditional occupations on the other—still confront us today, with greater force than ever. In other words, we should see the demographic and economic conditions of the late eighteenth century as a metaphor for the challenges facing our present global society, two centuries after Malthus's ponderings. It is imperative, moreover, that we come to under-

*India imported a mere 1 million yards of cotton fabrics in 1814, but that figure had risen to 51 million yards by 1830 and to a staggering 995 million yards by 1870.

stand the *interconnectedness* of these issues in today's comparable dilemma. The real differences are not in the nature of our global problems, but in their greater intensity now compared with the late eighteenth century. The earth again confronts a population explosion, not in the developed societies of northwestern Europe but in the poverty-stricken regions of Africa, Central America, the Middle East, India, and China, involving *billions* rather than millions of people. At the same time, we are witnessing a knowledge explosion in an extraordinary number of fields of technology and production. In both respects, the impact is larger, and much more swiftly and widely felt. In the eighteenth century, the global population was adding another quarter of a billion people every seventy-five years; today, such an increase occurs every three years. Meanwhile, our integrated world of science and communications has immensely quickened the pace of technological change.

Although few, if any, of our political leaders appear willing to face the fact, the greatest test for human society as it confronts the twenty-first century is how to use "the power of technology" to meet the demands thrown up by "the power of population"; that is, how to find effective global solutions in order to free the poorer three-quarters of humankind from the growing Malthusian trap of malnutrition, starvation, resource depletion, unrest, enforced migration, and armed conflict—developments that will also endanger the richer nations, if less directly.

This problem is more sobering, because of the geographic disjunction between where the population pressures are and where the technological resources are. In late-eighteenth-century England, population explosion and technology explosion were occurring in the same society, and interacted with each other in ultimately beneficial ways: the increased population stimulated demand for food, and encouraged investment in agriculture; industrialization boosted national wealth, and that in turn led to increased purchases of textiles, kitchen goods, foodstuffs. The challenge posed by one of these great forces for change was thus answered by the other force. Increased demand was met by enhanced supply, demonstrating that a swift-growing population will not necessarily lead to lower per capita standards of living if its productivity is increasing at an equal or faster pace.

In today's world, however, there is no longer such a geographic overlap. The technology explosion is taking place overwhelmingly in economically advanced societies, many of which possess slow-growing or even declining populations. However, the demographic boom is occurring in countries with limited technological resources, very few scientists and skilled workers, inadequate investment in research and development, and few or no successful corporations; in many cases, their governing elites have no interest in technology, and cultural and ideological prejudices are much more tilted against change than they were in the England of the Industrial Revolution.

Even those differences of circumstance do not capture the full dimensions of the present global dilemma, since two further difficulties also need to be noted. The first is that population pressure in many developing countries is causing a depletion of local agricultural resources (overgrazing of the African savannahs, erosion of the Amazonian rain forests, salinization of the land from India to Kazakhstan) just when more farm output is needed. Even Malthus assumed that the food supply would continue to grow, albeit not at the same rate as the populace itself; presumably his writings would have been even gloomier had he conceived of possible decrease in "the power of the land" as occurs in Africa today. Secondly, there are indications that some of the "First" World's new technologies, far from rescuing the booming populations of the developing world, may harm poorer countries, by making redundant certain economic activities—just as the spinning jenny put Indian handloom weavers out of work on the other side of the globe. New scientific breakthroughs often create structural problems of transferring their benefits from the "haves" to the "have-nots" within that society; today's global community is presented with a far larger challenge, as advanced technologies threaten to undermine the economies of developing societies.

This book has many similarities to, and yet is very different from, *The Rise and Fall of the Great Powers.* To begin with, while the present study is not itself a historical work, it does rely upon the perspective of history, in that the developments analyzed here are not completely new. In both books, the reader is offered an analysis of broad-based forces for change that influence international events. Eschewing the historical detail of *Rise and Fall,* this study has shifted its focus somewhat, to consider the human race's encounter with technology, economic change, and population growth. Yet each in its way is an attempt to place world affairs in the largest possible context.

Secondly, while this work is not greatly concerned with military conflict, armed forces, the balance of power, and traditional ways of thinking about national security, it will argue that some of the newer forces for change bearing down upon our planet could cause instability and conflict in the future, and that governments and peoples need to reconsider their older definitions of what constitutes a threat to national and international security. Regardless of whether the Cold War is over or whether an end can be brought to Middle East rivalries, there now exist vast *non*military threats to the safety and well-being of the peoples of this planet which deserve attention.

Thirdly, because the focus here is upon transnational developments, less attention is paid to the nation-states themselves and to the diplomatic/alliance systems within which they traditionally operate. This does not mean that what decision-makers in Washington and Moscow do is unimportant, or that the future of specific territorial units like Japan and the European Community is insignificant, or that the global trends are such that it is irrelevant whether one lives in Switzerland or Chad. Different regions and countries of the globe are differently structured—in terms of geographic location, skill levels of the population, national resources, capital assets—and are either better or worse prepared to respond to the transnational challenges which all confront. Furthermore, structures within a certain country may mean that the impact of a new technology is more severe—or more beneficial—than in a nation with different structures; biotech farming, to give an obvious example, may be beneficial to a high-tech, food-importing country like Japan but potentially disastrous to developing nations like Ghana or Costa Rica that rely upon crop exports. Just where a people is located on this planet and how well endowed are its human and technological resources will greatly affect its prospects in the face of impending global transformations.

It is for that reason, therefore, that whereas the chapters in Part One analyze the dimensions of the transnational forces for change, those in Part Two examine the specific consequences for some of the most important parts of the globe—China and India, the developing nations, Europe, the erstwhile USSR, Japan, and the United States. Just as in Malthus's time, the various peoples of the globe are not poised along the same level starting line as they prepare to move out of one century into the next; and many of them are very badly handicapped indeed.

This suggests at first sight that History is, once again, producing its lists of winners and losers. Economic change and technological development, like wars or sporting tournaments, are usually not beneficial to all. Progress, welcomed by optimistic voices from the Enlightenment to our present age, benefits those groups or nations that are able to take advantage of the newer methods and science, just as it damages others that are less prepared technologically, culturally, and politically to respond to change. As with the Industrial Revolution in England, technological progress can have a trickle-down effect, so that the standards of living of all members of society improve over time; yet that was never a satisfactory explanation to the unemployed handloom weavers of 1795, nor is it likely to satisfy their equivalents in the world today.

In addition to attempting the tricky task of assessing potential winners and losers, this work also asks whether today's global forces for change are not moving us beyond our traditional guidelines into a remarkable new set of circumstances—one in which human social organizations may be unequal to the challenges posed by overpopulation, environmental damage, and technology-driven revolutions and where the issue of winners and losers may to some degree become irrelevant. If, for example, the continued abuse of the developing world's environment leads to global warming, or if there is a massive flood of economic refugees from the poorer to the richer parts of the world, everyone will suffer, in various ways. In sum, just as nation-state rivalries are being overtaken by bigger issues, we may have to think about the future on a far broader scale than has characterized thinking about international politics in the past. Even if Great Powers still seek to rise, or at least not to fall, their endeavors could well occur in a world so damaged as to render much of that effort pointless.

. . .

Because this work deals primarily with broad global trends, environmental issues, demographic patterns, and technological breakthroughs, it might appear that I pay insufficient attention to the intangible and nonmaterial dimensions of our human and social existence—to our spiritual and cultural values. This may be true of the general themes in Part One, but a careful reading of the regional case studies in Part Two will indicate how significant those dimensions are to understanding why different societies react differently to new challenges. In fact, the most important influence on a nation's responsiveness to change probably is its social attitudes, religious beliefs, and culture. Students of past civilizations that failed to adjust to the challenge of modernization point, in example after example, to the obstacles which hindered new developments: a distaste for industry and manufacture, a Mandarin suspicion of trade and enterprise, an ideological or religious opposition to Western, capitalist mores, power structures which favored courtiers, the bureaucracy, the military, and the church, and legal and taxation systems (or even outright plunder) that discriminated against entrepreneurs and in favor of officeholders.[18]

It has often been assumed by Western writers that these obstacles are characteristic of Oriental and African societies—in contrast to European societies, whose adoption of rationalism, scientific method, and experimentation led over time to their domination of the world.[19] With the extraordinary successes of Japan in recent decades in the fields of invention, design, manufacturing, and finance, that assumption looks more dubious than ever. Granted that certain regions of the world (New Guinea, the Kalahari Desert) pose natural obstacles to development, it nonetheless seems fair to assume that most peoples of the world, *if they so choose,* can respond positively to the challenge of change. But the very phrase "if they so choose" implies an adoption of those features that explain Holland's success in the seventeenth century and Japan's success in the late twentieth: the existence of a market economy, at least to the extent that merchants and entrepreneurs are not discriminated against, deterred, and preyed upon; the absence of rigid, doctrinal orthodoxy; the freedom to inquire, to dispute, to experiment; a belief in the possibilities of improvement; a concern for the practical rather than the abstract; a rationalism that defies mandarin codes, religious dogma, and traditional folklore. A society dominated by fundamentalist mullahs or by conservative land-owning barons is as unlikely to embrace change in the twentieth century as it was in the fifteenth.

Cultural obstacles to change are common in all societies, for the obvious reason that an impending transformation threatens existing habits, ways of life, beliefs, and social prejudices. They are as likely to occur in advanced societies as in underdeveloped ones. Indeed, countries (or elites within countries) which have passed their peak in world or regional affairs and are being overtaken economically by faster-growing nations often exhibit the greatest reluctance to change. The reasons are partly practical, but psychological and cultural as well. Having risen to the top under specific historical conditions, declining nations find it difficult to accept altered circumstances: that there are now different ways of organizing industry, educating the young, distributing resources, and making policy decisions—and that those new ways are more successful. To respond to change might mean altering one's own social priorities, educational system, patterns of consumption and saving, even basic beliefs about the relationship between the individual and society. Concerned Americans, struggling today with the issue of how to meet "the Japanese challenge," know how complicated and deep-rooted such cultural and social obstacles are.[20]

The structure of this book is relatively simple. The first part analyzes certain major forces for change bearing down upon our world and discusses the general implications of those transformations. Though this book is arranged in discrete chapters, I hope that the reader will see the interconnectedness of the population explosion and increased illegal migration, the robotics revolution and global labor demand, technology and shrinking national sovereignty. Since the global population explosion is so powerful in its implications, I examine it first; but I immediately follow it with an analysis of how new technologies (computers, satellites, information/communications) are globalizing world business and changing the way companies operate—this juxtaposition to show the gulf between developments in the overpopulated poor parts of the world and those in technologically advanced rich parts. I pursue the same theme in Chapter 4 (on biotech agriculture) and Chapter 5 (on robotics), which respectively explore why our contemporary agricultural revolution and industrial/technology revolution might aggravate the population explosion rather than—as in Malthus's England—mitigate it. Since all this points to the prospect of an ever-widening rift between rich and poor countries, Chapter 6 discusses the way in which widespread environmental damage, and in particular global warming, may compel developed societies, at last understanding the connectedness of demographic, environmental, and technological trends, to aid their poorer cousins. Part One concludes with a chapter exploring the extent to which transnational changes are affecting the position of the nation-state itself.

The second part of this book examines the different regions of the globe and their respective capacities to deal with newer challenges. I selected the countries/regions not only because of their importance but also because of their very different situations: Japan is increasingly seen as the leading technology-driven society; India and China, with over one-third of the world's population, grapple with the task of checking population growth and harnessing technology; smaller countries in the developing world (East Asia, Latin America, Muslim nations, and sub-Saharan Africa are examined here) show marked differences in their response to demographic and technological challenges; the erstwhile USSR confronts these global forces as its former unity disintegrates, whereas the European Community has to deal with transnational developments *and* strive after further integration; and finally, the United States, well equipped militarily, faces radically new challenges of a nonmilitary sort. Each chapter discusses, prospectively, a range of outcomes for the country or region in question.

The third and final part again switches focus, to reflect upon the most important question of all: if we are being challenged by major forces for change, how can a society best "prepare" itself for the coming twenty-first century? What characteristics, what strengths, are desirable for a people to possess in such fast-changing and unpredictable times? This seems a more sensible line of inquiry than to engage in the politically exciting but misleading question "Who will be number one in 2025 (or 2050)?" because it allows for the possibility that societies will adapt to change and focus upon the process of acquiring, or building upon, desirable characteristics. Whether the countries and regions concerned adapt and acquire those strengths remains, as ever, an open question. Human beings make their own history even if, as Marx reminded us, they do so under circumstances influenced by the past.

It is important to emphasize the time horizon that informs the present work. Some critics of my discussion of America's "relative decline" in *The Rise and Fall of the Great Powers* misread the text to conclude it referred to today rather than a generation hence. Similarly, those unconvinced by the potential of robots (Chapter 5) might fail to understand that the relatively few examples of today's automated factories may not be dissimilar from the few factory prototypes existing when Malthus penned his first *Essay*; the broader adoption was at least a generation away. In this book, because most demographic projections go to 2025, a range of about thirty years is assumed in discussing either transnational trends or a particular region's prospects. Estimates beyond that time are much more dubious. Moreover, the exercise is complicated by the fact that some of these forces for change are moving at a faster pace than others: for example, whereas the population of Norway will change only slowly, who can foresee how far the biotech revolution will take us in the next quarter century? Similarly, if great social convulsions (including wars) do break out early in the next century, how will they affect the fate of nations, or the speed of the transnational trends discussed here?

Preparing for the Twenty-first Century does not assume, therefore, that there is an ideal blueprint or marching plan which, if followed, will enable societies to grapple with the next few decades of enormous change. It *does* assume that the impending transformations—particularly the race between demography and technology—will affect some societies and classes more than others, in both positive and negative ways, simply because of the uneven pattern of change and of the human race's differentiated responses to it. Finally, it does not contend that change is, of itself, a good thing, but rather that it is likely to produce both beneficial *and* adverse consequences. Still, if we can at least understand the transformations bearing down upon our planet, we might be able to consider how best to prepare for them.

2

THE DEMOGRAPHIC EXPLOSION

THE EARTH, UNLIKE ITS NEIGHBORING planets, is covered with a film of matter called life. The film itself "is exceedingly thin, so thin that its weight can scarcely be more than one-billionth that of the planet which supports it. . . . [It is] so insignificant in size that it would be detectable only with the greatest difficulty by beings on other planets, and would certainly be unnoticeable to observers elsewhere in our galaxy. . . ."[1] Within that film, coexisting alongside plants, animals, insects, crops, and other organisms, is the human race. It assumed the form of *Homo sapiens* some half a million years ago, well after the emergence of many of the other members of the earth's film of life. But because of the human race's growth and its economic activities, it now risks endangering the delicate envelope of matter that makes this planet unique.

The *physical* impact of the human race's expansion upon the natural environment and in particular upon the earth's atmosphere is so critical an issue that a later chapter will be devoted to it.* This chapter will focus upon demographic change, its implications for human societies, and the range of outcomes that could result from the great regional disparities in population growth.

*See Chapter 6, "The Dangers to Our Natural Environment."

As will be seen, these regional disparities are the most critical aspect of all. Were the earth's population expanding and devouring resources at an equal pace across the planet, that would be serious enough. But that different peoples are experiencing very different demographic patterns—some expanding fast, some stagnant, some in absolute decline—is altogether more problematic. Such imbalances influence how the various races of the globe view one another; they affect international and domestic politics, the social fabric, and the politics of food, energy, and migration. Moreover, unlike certain other global developments treated in this book—global warming, for example, or production of biogenetically altered foodstuffs—the contours of the demographic explosion are already reasonably clear.

While there remains a *range* of estimates of what the earth's total population will be in the years 2025 and 2050, the raw figures are daunting, especially when placed in historical perspective. In 1825, as Malthus was making the final amendments to his original *Essay on Population,* about 1 billion human beings occupied the planet, the race having taken thousands of years to reach that total. By then, however, industrialization and modern medicine were permitting population to rise at an increasingly faster rate. In the following hundred years the world's population doubled to 2 billion, and in the following half century (from 1925 to 1976) it doubled again, to 4 billion. By 1990, the figure had advanced to 5.3 billion.[2] It is true that the increase has slowed in recent decades, because overall fertility rates are decreasing in many countries. Even among today's fast-expanding populations of the developing world, demographers expect average family sizes to decline in the future, as urbanization and other factors cause a demographic transition and numbers begin to stabilize. But that is decades away—*even if* those forecasts are correct—and since the globe's enlarging population continues to beget more people than those who die, the effect is like a giant supertanker at sea beginning to slow down. As it decelerates, it still has a considerable way to go before it stops. Before we reach what is termed "global replacement fertility" levels, which United Nations authorities believe may occur around 2045, the population supertanker will have moved a long way.

Just how far will that be? Because regional birth and death rates change over time, demographers use complex formulae to calculate

Chart 1. World Population Increase, 1750–2100
(*in billions*)

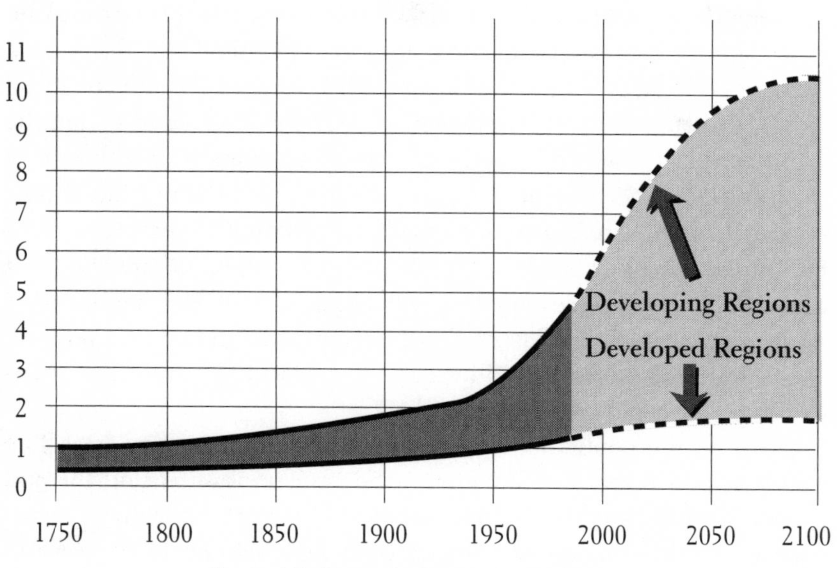

Source: *The Economist*, January 20, 1990, p. 19

these trends, and then offer three possible variants (high, middle, low). According to the middle one, by 2025—a year in which perhaps about half of the readers of this book may still be alive—the earth will contain a population of 8.5 billion people.[3] Even with the low variant of 7.6 billion, our population will have increased by almost one half. If the high variant is correct, the population will be nearly double what it is today, reaching 9.4 billion. One calculation, by the World Bank, suggests the total population of the earth may "stabilize" at between 10 and 11 billion people in the second half of the twenty-first century, but others have put the total as high as 14.5 billion.[4]

Another way of understanding these figures is to consider the increase in world population each year. In the 1950–55 period, the annual addition to world population was about 47 million—slightly more than the population of England and Wales today. In the 1985–90 period, the earth's enlarged population was adding about 88 million people annually—equal to the population of Mexico today. If future global fertility follows the high estimate, the years 1995–2000 could see annual increases of around 112 million—equal to the present Nigerian population.[5]

Mention of Mexico and Nigeria brings us to the crux of the problem: that these increases are taking place overwhelmingly in developing countries. In fact, between now and 2025, around 95 percent of all global population growth will take place in them. Concealed within the estimate that the world's "average" annual population growth rate in the years 1990–95 will be 1.7 percent lie some startling differences, ranging from Europe's small increase (0.22 percent per year) to Africa's far swifter rate of expansion (3.0 percent per year).[6] Perhaps the most dramatic way of expressing this difference is to note that in 1950 Africa's population was half of Europe's, by 1985 it had drawn level (at about 480 million each), and by 2025 it is expected to be three times Europe's (1.58 billion to 512 million).[7]

Why are the populations of certain countries growing so fast? The simple answer is that they are now in the same position as England and France were in Malthus's time—that is, they are basically agrarian societies in their first generation of enjoying a significant decrease in mortality rates. Historically, fertility rates in agrarian societies are usually very high, but so too are mortality rates, especially among the young. "Of 1,000 newborn children, 200 to 400 normally die within a year," and many of the others die before reaching the age of seven.[8] There was thus a reason for couples in preindustrial, agrarian societies to marry young and to have lots of children—on the twin assumption that each child would enhance the family labor force but that many of them would perish in their early years.

It is therefore easy to imagine what happens to the population of an agrarian society when mortality rates shrink, as they did in nineteenth-century Europe and are doing today, at a far faster rate, in large parts of the developing world: the total number of surviving human beings explodes within a few decades. In Tunisia, to take one example, the infant death rate (i.e., deaths before first birthday, per thousand live births) dropped from 138 to 59 between the years 1965–70 and the years 1985–90, and the child death rate (i.e., deaths of children under five, per thousand live births) dropped from 210 to 99 in the same period. Not surprisingly, Tunisia's overall population *doubled* in size in the three decades 1960–1990.[9] What also changes is the balance between old and young. In Kenya today, 52 percent of the population are less than fifteen, and only 2.8 percent are over sixty-five.

The irony is that this population explosion is chiefly the result of Western health practices, especially immunization and antibiotics, as well as the use of DDT to reduce mosquito-borne malaria. As mortality rates plunged after 1960, the number of children surviving infancy and early childhood quickly increased; in addition, populations began to enjoy increased average life expectancy because of improvements in food output. In retrospect, and especially with Europe's own nineteenth-century experience in mind, this demographic explosion was entirely predictable. Yesterday's perfectly natural wish to cut infant mortality in the developing world has resulted in today's unintended consequences, this time involving numbers far beyond those imagined by Malthus. For example, in the poorest and also the fastest-growing continent of all, Africa, which now contains about 650 million people, the total (as noted above) is forecast to increase almost threefold, to 1.58 billion, by 2025. Nigeria could expand from 113 to 301 million, Kenya from 25 to 77 million, Tanzania from 27 to 84 million, Zaire from 36 to 99 million, *without* corresponding increases in resources—indeed, with resources shrinking.[10]

Elsewhere in the developing world, the likely increases are almost as large. China's total may rise only (!) from today's 1.13 billion to about 1.5 billion in 2025, whereas the faster-growing population of India may reach the same total from today's 853 million. Given the approximate nature of these statistics and possible changes in both the birth and death rates of the two countries, it is conceivable that India might possess the world's largest population in 2025—for the first time in recorded history—and then eventually total 2 billion people. In addition to these demographic giants, other nations will contain unprecedently high populations by the third decade of the next century: Pakistan with 267 million, Indonesia with 263 million, Brazil with 245 million, Mexico with 150 million, Iran with 122 million.[11]

Behind these raw statistics lies the reality: human beings, each requiring daily two to three thousand calories and four and a half pounds of water, though getting much less except in reasonably well-off countries. The citizens of well-to-do societies get a glimpse of the poverty in which millions are forced to live in television broadcasts of famine in (say) Ethiopia, or in *National Geographic* magazine's photographs of slum cities in Latin America: the stricken landscape, the squalor, the attenuated limbs, the signs of disease, above all, the thousands and thousands of young children. If the sights are pitiful now, how will they seem when those regions possess three times as many human beings as today?

Of the twin manifestations of mass poverty, on the land and in the cities, the latter is of rising concern because of the tendency for the young and the mobile to abandon agricultural society. In 1985 about 32 percent of the population of the developing world lived in urban areas, but that figure is expected to rise to 40 percent by 2000 and to around 57 percent in 2025. Now 1.4 billion people are living in the urban areas of developing countries; there will be a crushing 4.1 billion in 2025. By that time Latin America will be the most urbanized region of the world, with nearly 85 percent of its population living in cities; in Africa the figure will be around 58 percent and in Asia about 53 percent. Even by the end of this present century, there will exist twenty megacities with populations of 11 million or more, of which seventeen will be in the developing world. Leading that list will be Mexico City, with an estimated 24.4 million in 2000, followed by São Paulo with 23.6 million, Calcutta with 16 million, Bombay with 15.4 million, and Shanghai with 14.7 million.

This trend involves not simply a question of numbers but also a potential change in our social and cultural assumptions about urban living. For thousands of years, cities (Nineveh, Tyre, Rome, Constantinople, Venice, Amsterdam, London, New York, Tokyo) were centers of wealth, creativity, and cultural activities, where the upper and middle classes resided, building fine houses, impressive boulevards, monuments, parks, concert halls. Many European cities such as Stockholm or Copenhagen, which remain attractive to their prosperous residents, will no doubt continue to function in that way; by contrast, Asian, Latin American, and Central American megacities of 20 million inhabitants have become increasingly centers of poverty and social collapse. Already, the sheer concentrations of people—143,000 per square mile in Lagos, Nigeria, and 130,000 per square mile in Djakarta, Indonesia, compared with New York's mere 11,400 per square mile—make it inconceivable that their inhabitants will enjoy the benefits offered by traditional European cities.[12]

Consider, for example, the burdens that will be placed on such cities' already inadequate (or nonexistent) housing, sanitation, transportation, food distribution, and communications systems if their populations double and treble in size. In many of these countries a disproportionate amount of the nation's limited wealth is owned by the governing elites, who will find it difficult to buy off the discontents of the fast-growing urban masses. How the crowded populations will be fed, especially in times of famine, and what will happen to the always sensitive relationship between city and country are not at all clear; but even if food is available, will it be possible to give these billions of young people decent health and education and, afterward, to provide new jobs at the rate needed to prevent mass unemployment and social unrest? The phenomenon is roughly similar to that crowd of 100,000 vagrants who roamed the streets of Paris in the 1780s, but today's numbers are fantastically larger. At present, the labor force in developing countries totals around 1.76 billion, but it will rise to more than 3.1 billion in 2025—implying a need for 38–40 million new jobs *every year.*[13] Over time, urbanization leads to a decline in the rate of population increase. But the real challenge comes in the next twenty to forty years, when urbanization in the developing world will exacerbate all of the problems associated with high population density, producing miserable living conditions for the vast majority of human beings at present in their infancy or soon to be born.

There remains one random—and tragic—factor which may significantly affect these statistical projections: the AIDS epidemic, which is especially prevalent in the continent of its origin, Africa. AIDS is caused by a human immunodeficiency virus (HIV) that weakens the body's immune systems and makes it unable to fight sicknesses. The problem in estimating the demographic impact of AIDS is that perhaps eight or nine years may pass before an HIV-infected person produces symptoms, after which point the fatality rate approaches 100 percent. The graph of an AIDS epidemic therefore looks something like an iceberg. "Those who have the disease are the part of the iceberg above the water. But the much larger and deadlier part of the iceberg is composed of those who are HIV-positive but who have not yet developed the disease."[14] There also exist many individuals who, aware or unaware of being infected, pass on the infection.

While the estimated number of AIDS cases in Africa in 1988 was only about 100,000, it was believed that that figure probably represented only 5 percent or less of those already HIV-infected. Death by AIDS could therefore total some 2 million Africans in the 1990s, yet even that sounds far too low an estimate, given the flood of recent reports on this problem. One, by the World Health Organization, calculates that as many as 25–30 percent of pregnant women in certain African countries tested HIV-positive, and offers evidence that entire families suffer from the disease.[15] Only recently, the World Health Organization abandoned its earlier estimate that 25–30 million people globally would be HIV-positive by 2000, raising the total to 40 million (including many more in Asia); fully 90 percent of AIDS victims would then be in developing countries, principally among the most impoverished.[16] A 1992 report, by Harvard epidemiologists, raised the total to 100 million, with more in Asia than Africa.

If there is no cure found for AIDS in the next few years, then Africa's high fertility rates could be checked by worsening mortality rates. One recent article on this subject reports that in contrast to the World Bank's assessment that the annual population growth in Central and East Africa may slow to 2.75 percent early in the next century, "some AIDS researchers predict growth as low as 1 percent, or even, on the bleakest of guesses, an absolute decline by the year 2010"; another talks of "more people dying than being born" in Uganda and neighboring states after 2000, and wonders whether it is wise to be pressing for increased population control![17] While that would represent a classic Malthusian check upon population expansion, it is worth noting that those estimates seem unduly bleak compared with earlier forecasts, in which demographic modelers had assumed that HIV prevalence rates in Africa would peak at somewhere between 20 and 30 percent of the adult population, implying that an AIDS epidemic might cut an initial population growth rate of (say) 3 percent down to nearly 2 percent per year.[18] Africa's overall population would still be growing rapidly, therefore, but in the midst of an appalling scene in which millions of people were dying of disease. Moreover, unlike most of the other afflictions that devastate Africa, AIDS strikes disproportionately among adults, that is, among the productive and (to some degree) educated parts of the population; it thus deals a severe economic blow to the societies in question, in addition to causing great human suffering.

Apart from the special horror of the AIDS epidemic, the chief problem remains: how can poor agrarian societies deal with excessively-rapid population growth? The Malthusian answer would be that, eventually, nature intervenes: increasing famine, a struggle to gain foodstuffs and resources, open conflict, war, and disease would reduce—perhaps drastically reduce—the size of the population. Yet, as we have seen, just as Malthus was composing his *Essay on Population* the Industrial Revolution was creating a medium-to-long-term escape for the fast-growing British population of his time: increased industrial productivity and urbanization led to increased per capita income, which gradually altered the life-styles and reproductive patterns of most families and slowed population growth.

Among the countries once crudely described as part of the "Third World," a few have recently imitated the pattern that occurred in Britain two centuries ago. These are the Newly Industrialized Economies (NIEs) of East Asia, like Singapore, Taiwan, and South Korea, and perhaps also some of their larger neighbors such as Malaysia. Partly stimulated by and partly in imitation of Japan's own fabulous economic growth, these East Asian states have achieved a fast, export-led expansion, with GNPs that in recent decades have grown by more than 10 percent each year (which implies a doubling every seven years). Although their annual growth rates are now 6 or 7 percent, that is considerably more than the global average, and the decline probably indicates that their economies are moving beyond their adolescent stage. With their own steel mills, shipyards, electronics firms, national airlines, and (in the case of Taiwan and South Korea) very considerable trade surpluses, they are becoming richer year by year, with per capita GNP fast approaching those of European countries such as Portugal, Spain, and Greece.

Moreover, as East Asian standards of living have increased, total fertility rates have tumbled,* in South Korea's case from 4.5 in 1965–70 to 2.0 in 1985–90, and in Singapore's case from 3.5 to 1.7 over the same period, so that several governments now have pro-natalist population policies as in some mature economies. Mortality rates have also dropped; infant death rates and average life expectancy levels are close to those of Europe and the United States. Unsurprisingly, the percentage of couples using contraceptives is much higher than in Africa or South Asia. In such other measures of an "advanced" society as male *and* female literacy levels, sanitation services, and so on, the East Asian economies are far removed from the desperate conditions of most other developing nations.[19] If trends continue, South Korea and Taiwan may be among the healthiest and richest nations in the world early next century.

Is not this, then, the solution to the problem—to encourage the rise of "trading states" throughout the developing world, on the assumption that they would enjoy the benefits that came to the Dutch and the British in centuries past, and now have come to Japan and Korea?[20] Yet as soon as that question is posed, one begins to see the difficulties. Previous and present trading states—Venice, the Dutch Republic, Britain, Japan, Singapore, Taiwan—were relatively small countries with a favorable geographical position, a skilled population, and an openness to foreign techniques and fashions. That can hardly be said of Zaire, Iran, Mali, Afghanistan, or Ethiopia, where a combination of structural and cultural hindrances at present blocks development.†

Furthermore, just as Britain's original industrial expansion was not achieved without cost, so also have there been considerable costs following the growth of Japan, Taiwan, and Korea. As we shall see later, atmospheric pollution, erosion of the forests and wetlands, surging demand for foodstuffs and raw materials, vast increases in CO_2 emissions, and the conversion of small coastal towns into giant shipyards and steel mills all cause environmental damage, not just in the industrial regions themselves but also abroad, as East Asian companies imi-

*A society's total fertility rate is an estimate of the number of children on average that a woman will have in that society.

†For an elaboration of this argument, see Chapter 10, "Winners and Losers in the Developing World."

tate their European and American equivalents in a relentless demand for ores, oil, gas, timber, and other materials from the developing world. As a nation like Korea reaches a European standard of living, it also consumes energy and foodstuffs at a European level. Given their relatively small size, the East Asian NIEs are not a major cause of global degradation, especially as compared with the resources consumed by the West. But if, for example, the per capita consumption of 1.2 billion Chinese reached that of Japan or the United States, the environmental damage would be colossal.

This issue of "population and economic growth" has led to considerable disagreement between demographers and economists. During the 1960s, it was common to suggest a negative correlation between demographic growth and economic development: more meant worse, because of the cost of raising children, the reduced amount of capital per head of population, and the diversion of investment from growth-related activities to meeting the increased social demands of a larger population.[21] In the early 1980s, a revisionist and pro-natalist school typified by Julian Simon's book *The Ultimate Resource* argued that "[i]n the longer run . . . per capita income is likely to be higher with a growing population than with a stationary one, both in more-developed and less-developed countries."[22] According to this viewpoint, while there may be short-term costs associated with looking after and educating lots of young children, over the longer term there will be a larger population of productive workers between fifteen and sixty-four years old. Given the ingenuity and inventiveness of human beings, the more of them there are, the better; if on average there are two or three really creative people in every hundred, better to have a population of 100 million than 1 million.

That population growth encourages economic expansion is true in some cases, but not in others. The chief weakness lies not in the argument per se, but in the context in which population growth occurs. Rates of population growth in many less developed countries today far exceed the moderate levels that the revisionist, pro-natalist school believes are conducive to economic expansion. Total fertility rates of 2.5 are one thing; Nigeria's 7.0, Syria's 7.8, and Rwanda's 8.3 are quite another.

In addition, it is increasingly clear that population growth affects the natural world and can affect the social order and international system. Not only does a demographic explosion hurt the masses of overcrowded and undernourished youngsters who compose that boom, but it does great damage in other spheres. Human activity and ecological damage will be discussed in more detail later, but the main outlines can be stated here. The overall consensus—with the exception of a few revisionists—is that the projected growth in the world's population cannot be sustained *with our current patterns and levels of consumption.* Unlike animals and birds, human beings destroy forests, burn fossil fuels, drain wetlands, pollute rivers and oceans, and ransack the earth for ores, oil, and other raw materials. It is therefore important whether the planet contains 4 billion people engaged in these activities, as it did in 1975, or 8 to 9 billion, as is likely in 2025.

With 95 percent of the anticipated population increase between now and 2025 expected to occur in developing countries, it might appear that the main problem is *there.* If the inhabitants of Africa, Central America, and other developing areas would temper their fast-breeding habits, the argument goes, they would not only require less of the earth's food, but would also cause less damage to its rain forests, water supply, and ecosystem in general. Moreover, because those activities contribute to global warming, the population explosion in the southern hemisphere threatens to affect more developed countries of the North.

Yet even if that is true, developed Northern regions place much greater stress per capita upon the earth's resources than do developing countries, simply because the former consume so much more. Thus, the consumption of oil in the United States—with only 4 percent of the world's population—equals one-quarter of total world annual production; in 1989, the United States consumed 6.3 billion barrels of oil, ten times the consumption of Britain or Canada, and hundreds of times that of most Third World countries, which make do on very little. The same imbalance in consumption is true of a range of other items, from paper to beef. According to one calculation, the average American baby represents twice the environmental damage of a Swedish child, three times that of an Italian, thirteen times that of a Brazilian, thirty-five times that of an Indian, and 280 (!) times that of a Chadian or Haitian because its level of consumption throughout its life will be so much greater.[23] That is not a comfortable statistic for anyone with a conscience.

From the viewpoint of environmentalists, therefore, the earth is under a twofold attack from human beings—the excessive demands and wasteful habits of affluent populations of developed countries, and the billions of new mouths born in the developing world who (very naturally) aspire to increase their own consumption levels. This in turn has led a number of environmentalist voices—the Worldwatch Institute, Greenpeace, the United Nations Population Fund—to portray the entire issue as a race against time. In their view, if we do nothing to stabilize the world's total population, curb the profligate use of energy, foodstuffs, and other raw materials, and control damage to the environment, as soon as possible, then before very long we will have so overpopulated and ransacked the earth that we will pay a heavy price for our collective neglect.[24]

This viewpoint, which challenges the assumption that growth is desirable and economic output is the most useful measure of a country's material success, has provoked counterattacks from many economists. In the optimists' opinion, natural resources are not an absolute amount that is steadily being depleted; rather, many resources are created through human inventiveness and labor, and technology has an infinite capacity for producing new resources. The scarcity of a commodity, such as petroleum, leads to the search for (and discovery of) fresh stocks and the creation of alternative forms of energy, alarm at the levels of world food production leads to significant increases in agricultural productivity from breakthroughs in biotechnology, and so on. Just as Malthus was incorrect in his predictions, so will today's doomsayers be proved wrong.[25]

Only time will tell which of these positions is more accurate, but the world's population was less than a billion when Malthus first wrote his *Essay;* now it is heading, at the least, toward 7 or 8 billion, perhaps to well over 10 billion. If the optimists are right, the world will simply contain many more prosperous people, even if that prosperity is unevenly distributed. If they are wrong, the human race as a whole could suffer more from a careless pursuit of economic growth than it may lose by modifying its present habits.

Even before the world is in a position to judge the outcome of this debate—in, say, 2025—it may be grappling with another potential consequence of the global population explosion: its impact upon national security. Traditionally, that concern focused upon the availability of military manpower; a declining population means fewer recruits for the armed forces, which, if rival nations enjoy a greater fertility rate, places the country in a state of relative strategical weakness.[26] Thus, a few years ago, NATO planners were warning that the West's declining age cohorts of fit young men would reduce the size of its armed forces. Not only have *perestroika* reforms and East-West arms accords made such fears seem irrelevant, but the NATO planners ignored the Soviet Union's own demographic problems. Even by the 1970s, differences emerged in total fertility rates between the nearly stagnant Russian population and the fast-growing populations of the southern republics, where a heady combination of local nationalism, the Muslim religion and way of life, ignorance of the Russian language, and a profound dislike of Moscow's control was alarming Soviet military manpower planners.[27] Now that those republics are independent, the immediate problem may have disappeared; but the larger issue, that some ethnic groups are growing much faster than their neighbors, remains.

Still, the problem of military manpower is probably less urgent than the other important implication of population change upon international security: the prospect of demographically driven social unrest, political instability, and regional wars. As noted earlier, behind many well-known historical upheavals—the outward thrust of the Vikings, the expansion of Elizabethan England, the French Revolution, Wilhelmine *Weltpolitik*, the turbulences that rack Central America and the Middle East today—the societies involved were experiencing population explosions, and often having difficulty in absorbing increasing numbers of energetic young men.[28] Sometimes the unfulfilled expectations of a new generation exploded into violence and revolution. In other instances, those energies were diverted by nimble and ambitious political leaders into *foreign* adventures and conquests.*

Those in developed countries who complain about the shrinking of their fertility rates—their "birth dearth"[29]—may wish to consider the places in the world nowadays experiencing the most serious unrest: Central America, South Africa, Southeast Asia, Afghanistan/Kashmir, the Middle East, Northern Ireland, the rimlands of the former USSR, the Horn of Africa. In all those regions, there exist fast-growing, youthful populations with pent-up social and economic expectations. It is surely no coincidence that the Palestinian *intifada*—"the war of stones" waged by teenage youth against the Israeli occupying forces—began in the Gaza Strip, with its population density of 4,206 persons per square mile (compared with 530 in Israel).[30] Obviously, ideological rivalries, racial and religious hatreds, and lots of other factors also contribute to these civil and regional wars. Nevertheless, the social effects of a population explosion appear to form the context within which such bitter struggles swiftly escalate. While this was as true in ancient Macedonia as in the Near East today, what has changed is the *momentum* of population growth, nowadays involving tens of millions of people rather than the thousands of Alexander the Great's day. What sort of future do we face if social turbulence increases at the same pace as the world's population?

While the demographic explosion (combined with reduced resources) is the greatest problem facing developing regions, many developed nations confront the opposite problem of stagnant or even negative population growth. These countries, with high standards of living and superior health care, now enjoy low mortality rates. To maintain a nation's overall size, a "replacement fertility" rate of approximately 2.1 children per woman is needed.† Current statistics from the United

*I use the words "often" and "sometimes" here because I'm not arguing that a population explosion *will* or *must* lead to instability or expansion. Other factors (nature of regime, geographic opportunity, state of economy) also play a role.

†This allows for the fact that a small number of girls die early, and that roughly half of births are male and thus excludable from reproduction calculations.

Nations Population Division indicate, however, that most developed nations have experienced lower fertility rates since the late 1960s; for example, Italy's rate has dropped from 2.5 to 1.5, and Spain's from 2.9 to 1.7.[31]

The most obvious cause of this decline is the changed position and expectations of women in Western societies, with larger numbers entering higher education, and then careers. Childbirth is delayed and the number of offspring reduced—something made possible by the availability of sophisticated methods of contraception. These trends interact with the effects of urbanization upon reproduction, especially in large cities. Whether because more sophisticated and career-ambitious couples tend to live in cities, or—more likely—because human beings find it hard to bring up children in cramped tenement housing where there is little place for their energies, urbanization leads over time to a reduction in fertility rates. But the key modifier is, indeed, "over time." Long before cities become the places in which those rates decline, they attract millions seeking employment, social improvement, and escape from the trials of an overpopulated, underresourced agricultural society.

The obvious implication arising from these different age structures is that whereas developing nations have the burden of supporting millions younger than fifteen, developed nations have to look after fast-increasing millions older than sixty-five. The reason for this is simple enough. The age structure of a swiftly growing society is a pyramid, as shown for Mexico in Chart 2, with the broad base representing the large numbers under twenty years old, and the narrow peak representing the small numbers of elderly. If a sharp reduction in the fertility rate takes place, the pyramid's base will become narrower, leaving a relatively smaller number of young people to sustain a relatively larger group of older ones.

Whereas in the poorest African countries only 2 or 3 percent of the population are over sixty-five, in the rich and healthy nations the proportion is far higher—Norway has 16.4 percent, for example, and Sweden 18.3 percent.[32] The average for richer countries* as a whole

*"Richer" here refers to the twenty-odd members of the Organization for Economic Cooperation and Development (OECD).

Chart 2. Age Structures

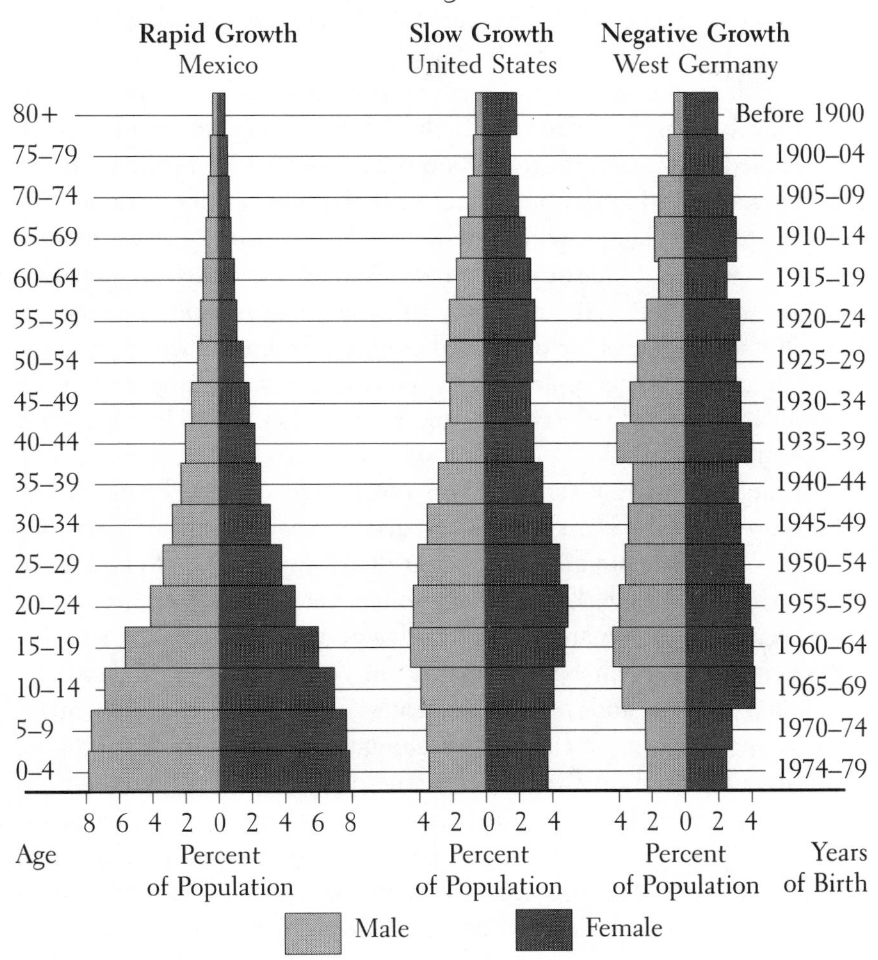

is steadily rising, partly because their total fertility rates are declining and partly because of improved health-care techniques for the elderly: by 2010 around 15.3 percent of their populations will be over sixty-five, and that figure will come close to 22 percent by 2040. This may one day pose an additional obstacle to international—or, rather, North-South—understanding, for as prosperous societies grapple with the problem of allocating more and more resources to the elderly, the rest of the globe begs for help dealing with the demands flowing from the boom in young children and infants.

Not all advanced economies are equally affected by the problem of excessively aging populations. In the United States, for example, the continued inflow of immigrants and the relatively high fertility rates of ethnic-minority families mean not only that overall population is expected to grow, but also that the bottom segments of the age-structure pyramid will not drastically narrow. And in Scandinavia, excellent maternity support systems appear to be stemming earlier declines in fertility rates. But other developed countries, such as Germany, Italy, and Japan, already grapple with the consequences of a large rise in the number of their elderly at the same time as their juvenile population is shrinking.

In macroeconomic terms, this is not a welcome development. On the whole, members of a population aged between fifteen and sixty-four tend to create wealth and place fewer demands upon health and social services. Old people, like the very young, tend to consume resources and place higher demands upon health and social services. Some of this financial burden can be anticipated (in richer societies, at least) by national savings and pensions schemes. Nevertheless, in countries where more and more expensive techniques are being used to prolong the lives of those *over seventy-five,* the question is whether these resources might better be invested elsewhere, such as in preventive medicine for the very young or improved educational facilities. Finally, there is the concern that the age structure and spending priorities of a country with a high "elderly dependency ratio" may be a drag upon overall production increases, weakening it relative to societies with a larger proportion of people at work and greater investment of resources in manufacturing and industry.

Still, the subject is too complex to say that all the consequences of this aging trend must be detrimental. A shrinking work force may stimulate a large investment in automation and other labor-saving devices, as in Japan at present.* An aging population may also save more, and thus increase aggregate national savings—although the evi-

*See Chapters 5 and 8.

dence here is not conclusive, since old people might also draw down their personal savings over time. A society with fewer youths is likely to have less crime and may be less prone to go to war, although it will also have fewer potential recruits for the armed services if it is threatened by external foes. How does one weigh the advantages against the disadvantages?

Ironically, all those consequences, negative and positive, will one day affect the peoples of the developing world, if they survive their present demographic explosion. Over the long run, the problem of aging populations in more developed and less developed countries is the same. The differences are in timing, and in scale. The median age of Europeans at present is 33.9 years; yet the median age of Mexico's population is projected to be 33.4 years by 2020. More dramatic still is the case of China, which for years has been trying to control its population growth by such vigorous means as the one-child policy. As a consequence of its relative success, "China in 2025 will have as big a share of over-sixties as Europe in 2010."[33] Whether both areas will have the same per capita resources to allocate to their over-sixties is a different question, especially when one considers the massive quantitative differences. About one-fifth of Italy's population in 2010 will be over sixty-five, or 11 million out of 55 million people. If China's population reaches 1.5 billion in 2025, then, by the same ratio, there will be 300 million elderly dependents, but there is no evidence that provision is being made to support such numbers.

So far, this issue of aging societies has been discussed almost exclusively as a cluster of practical and physical problems; but there is the further issue of deep-rooted cultural and racial anxieties, nicely described in one work as "the fear of population decline."[34] This phenomenon has a long history, including many examples from late-nineteenth-century Europe and the United States of writings and political movements agitating about the "decay" of the species, the fear that a certain race or culture will be overwhelmed in a sea of "lesser" peoples. Central to this anxiety is the belief that one's own racial and linguistic group has a special place in History, unique features within, and contributions to, world civilization, which must be preserved by the continued health and growth in population of the people in question. Should the fertility rate shrink, therefore, it is all too easy for cultural pessimists to proclaim that the nation is heading for decline and to agitate for methods to reverse the perceived "biological degeneracy."[35]

The usual consequence of these anxieties has been efforts to advance pro-natalist policies, encouraging women to have many more children. Such efforts range from punitive legislation (forbidding abortion and contraception), to more practical measures (child allowances, prenatal and natal care, ensuring release time for working women who are pregnant), to exhortions and propaganda (awarding medals and titles—"Heroine of the Soviet Union," for example—to mothers who bore five or, better still, ten children). These campaigns have been advocated by right and left, arch-patriotic conservatives urging the same pro-natalist policies as officials in certain socialist states, with only the liberal "middle" opposing attempts to interfere in a family's desire to choose its own size.[36]

The obverse side of this anxiety is, of course, a resentment against other peoples who reproduce at a much faster pace—the assumption being that, as in a Darwinian struggle, the faster-growing species will encroach upon, and eventually overwhelm, a population with static or declining numbers. Such fears are especially prevalent when there occurs differential growth of ethnic groups within the same country, since that (it is presumed) may eventually alter the economic and political balances. Israeli anxieties that the Arab population within Israel's own (enlarged) boundaries is growing faster than the Jewish population, the alteration in the Christian-Muslim population balance in Lebanon (to the Muslims' advantage), and tensions and apprehensions in places as far apart as Quebec and Fiji all remind us of the political dimensions of population decline. Occasionally, an understanding of these trends may also lead to positive results; to what extent, one wonders, was the South African government's decision to abandon apartheid influenced by its recognition of the whites' shrinking share of the total population, from one-fifth in 1951 to one-seventh in the early 1980s and to a projected one-ninth or one-eleventh by 2020?[37] Overall, however, there appear to have been many more examples of intransigence and conflict, rather than compromise, when a people has perceived it is in relative demographic decline.

• • •

There is one other response when a population explosion combines with a relative diminution of material resources: people can move out, to places where opportunities beckon. One form of migration is the drift of population from the countryside to the cities, as is happening in the developing world today. While that causes social problems in the cities themselves, most governments and their publics appear much more concerned about a very different form of migration, that from one country to another.

One reason for this concern is material. Because human beings (unlike migrating birds) require so much food, clothing, and shelter and demand many other items, migration always raises the issue of the allocation of resources. If food and land are plentiful, as in the Great Plains in nineteenth-century America, there may be less of a problem (except from the viewpoint of a Plains Indian); if the resources are believed to be more limited, as is felt in many European countries today, more migration will obviously raise the problem of providing for the immigrants. Moreover, large-scale immigration raises the fear of losing control of national boundaries and traditional sovereignty, the fear that an ethnically homogeneous or "pure" race will be altered through intermarriage, the fear not merely of foreign peoples but also of strange ways of life, religious norms, and cultural habits, of the newcomers encroaching upon the property, educational system, and social benefits owned and largely paid for by the natives. More recently, concern has been expressed that illegal immigration into (for example) the United States is responsible for outbreaks of old and new diseases—cholera, measles, AIDS—which place a further strain upon the health-care system as well as provoking new resentments against migrants. Finally, there is always the resident population's fear that if the immigration continues, they themselves may one day become a minority.

Much of the recent concern about uncontrolled migration has been expressed by European nations or by such European offshoots as Australia and the United States, which is very ironic historically. After all, several hundred years ago Europe itself was the source of the most important migratory movement in world history. Its first manifestations occurred centuries earlier, in such forms as the eastward expansion of Germanic settlers and the westward and southward conquests of the Iberian states.[38] But it was the Industrial Revolution in Europe, simultaneously sustaining massive growth in population *and* producing enhanced forms of transportation and weaponry, that really stimulated the continent's outward thrust. Between 1846 and 1890, people emigrated from Europe at an average rate of 377,000 per year, but between 1891 and 1910 emigration soared to an average rate of 911,000 per year. Indeed, between 1846 and 1930, over 50 million Europeans sought a new life overseas. Since the European populations *at home* were also expanding rapidly in this period, their share of total world population steadily increased; according to one calculation, "the Caucasian population was about 22 percent of the human species in 1800, and about 35 percent in 1930."[39] This was the demographic foundation of what would later be termed "the world revolution of Westernization."[40] Whether they liked it or not, other societies across the planet were compelled to respond to the expansion of Western man, his politics, ideas, and economics. Many of them, of course, fell under the direct political control of the European immigrants.

The basic difference today is that whereas that earlier migration went from the technologically advanced societies into less advanced societies,* contemporary migrations chiefly move from less developed societies toward Europe, North America, and Australasia. Given the global imbalances in population trends, this movement ought in principle to help all concerned. Migration from the less developed countries should lower population pressure and unemployment at home, while offsetting the economic problems of negative population growth and an aging work force in the developed countries. Why, then, should North America not allow the influx of millions of families from south of the Rio Grande; or labor-short Japan admit vast numbers of willing workers from Southeast Asia; or the European Community, with its graying populations, welcome the millions of unemployed of North Africa? Since most of Europe has a negative replacement fertility rate

*The great exception here was the United States, which, by the mid-nineteenth century at least, was clearly technologically more advanced than Ireland, Italy, Poland, Russia, and other societies from which its immigrants came.

and the populations of Algeria, Morocco, and Tunisia are expected to double over the next few decades, this seems—as *The Economist* put it, no doubt tongue-in-cheek—"the perfect match."[41]

The reason for *The Economist's* ironic comment on such migration flows is that its editors are well aware of how unpopular immigrants are in countries which lack America's "melting pot" traditions. During the boom years of the 1950s and 1960s, many European nations encouraged guest workers from southern Italy and Portugal, then Turkey, Yugoslavia, North Africa, and other less developed economies. Such guest workers not only provided the nonskilled labor in the factories and at the building sites but also the lower-paid jobs in health care, public transport, sanitation, and related fields. But the problem was that the host countries sought *labor* and got *people*: workers who, joined by their families, required housing and education and medical attention; people who conglomerated in a certain part of the city—usually the area with the cheapest housing—and brought to such districts their restaurants, shops, temples and mosques, foreign habits, foreign cooking, foreign skin. When the host economies slowed down in the late 1970s, it was impossible to return all these guest workers to their countries of origin; and many of them were still useful to their employers. By 1985, therefore, of the 30 million who had traveled to Europe to find work during the preceding decades, a full 5 million remained, whose families brought the total number of permanent immigrants to 13 million.

Although the laws of host countries officially ban discrimination, a nativist prejudice against immigrant communities clearly exists—in Britain against Indians and Pakistanis, in France against Algerians and Moroccans, in Germany against Turks, and in parts of the United States against Latin Americans and Asians. The root of these tensions lies in foreignness, or, to use another word, race. White Americans have no problem in welcoming to their shores many thousands of well-educated professionals from Scandinavia, Britain, and Germany, just as Australians welcomed British (as opposed to Chinese) immigrants, the European colonial states did not oppose the return of ex-settlers from Angola, Rhodesia, and Algeria (though British governments had a different response to Ugandans, Indians, and Hong Kong Chinese), the Germans had little difficulty in the immigration of former *Auslands-*

deutsche, and Israel actively embraces Jewish (but not Arab) immigrants.[42]

Given the political and social tensions that the *relatively limited* transnational migration has recently provoked, there is reason to be concerned should a massive surge in population occur from one country to another. In view of the imbalances in demographic trends between "have" and "have-not" societies, it seems unlikely that there will not be great waves of migration in the twenty-first century. The raw statistics alone suggest that conclusion. Australia, whose 1990 population of 16.7 million is expected to rise gently to 22.7 million by 2025, lies next to an Indonesia whose population is forecast to grow from 180 million to 263 million in the same period. The southern European states of Spain, Portugal, France, Italy, and Greece, whose combined populations are estimated to increase by a mere 5 million between 1990 and 2025, lie close to North African countries (Morocco, Algeria, Tunisia, Libya, Egypt) whose populations are forecast to grow by 108 million in those years. The United States' population is forecast to rise 25 percent by 2025, while its southern neighbors Mexico and Guatemala may grow 88 percent and 225 percent respectively in the same period.[43]

A recent study of "population and security" has suggested that because the territories of the globe are now divided among standing governments controlling their own boundaries, the amount of migration is (and will be) much less than it was a century ago.[44] While it is clear that nations nowadays make greater efforts to restrict immigration (and, in some cases, to prevent emigration), desperate migrants are unlikely to be deterred. Neither the U.S. Immigration and Naturalization Act of 1986 nor patrols along the Mexican border have stemmed the northward flow of migrants, which have again risen to well over a million each year. In July 1991, under pressure from a resentful home population, an embarrassed French government announced a series of stricter measures to reduce illegal migration, including chartering aircraft to deport the migrants; but with right-wing opposition leaders denouncing "the noise and the smell" of the 4 million mainly Arab immigrants, and government ministers themselves admitting the difficulty of accepting more newcomers when the country has a 9.5 percent unemployment rate, the controversy gave the impression that

France had *lost control* of its borders.[45] Furthermore, throughout Western Europe there is concern that the European Community, which permits internal migration and residency, will weaken a member nation's control over the inflow of population from other EC states and reduce its ability to check illegal immigrants. At present, as many as 15 million men, women, and children are living in camps as far apart as Central Europe and Southeast Asia, hoping for somewhere to go. While they, and those already on the move via Mexico and Turkey, may encounter obstacles, many of them are getting through. Often they are aided and sheltered by relations who have already made the trek. And they are increasingly stimulated, as we shall see, by the information revolution, which means that "[p]eople now, even if they are very poor, know how people live in other parts of the world," and will attempt to get there, by land, sea, or air.[46]

These push factors in the overpopulated developing world are compounded by the pull factor of population decline in the more developed societies. Today, as in the past, "billions of peasants and ex-peasants . . . are ready and eager to move into places vacated by wealthier, urbanized populations."[47] As the better-off families of the northern hemisphere individually decide that having only one or at the most two children is sufficient, they may not recognize that they are in a small way vacating future space (that is, jobs, parts of inner cities, shares of population, shares of market preferences) to faster-growing ethnic groups both inside and outside their national boundaries. But that, in fact, is what they are doing.

Enhanced efforts to control migration, therefore, are unlikely to succeed in the face of the momentous tilt in the global demographic balances. Perhaps the most compelling statistic of all is that while the industrial democracies accounted for more than one-fifth of the earth's population in 1950, that share had dropped to one-sixth by 1985 and is forecast to shrivel to less than one-tenth by 2025. By that time, only two of them (the United States and Japan) will be among the top twenty most populous countries, and the rest of the industrial democracies will almost all be regarded as "little countries."[48] This relative diminution of their share of world population presents the industrial democracies with their greatest dilemma over the next thirty years. If the developing world manages to raise its output and standards of living, the West's proportion of economic output, global power, and political influence will decline steadily, simply because of the force of numbers; which in turn has raised the interesting question of whether "Western values"—a liberal social culture, human rights, religious tolerance, democracy, market forces—will maintain their prevailing position in a world overwhelmingly peopled by societies which did not experience the rational scientific and liberal assumptions of the Enlightenment.[49] Yet if the developing world remains caught in its poverty trap, the more developed countries will come under siege from tens of millions of migrants and refugees eager to reside among the prosperous but aging populations of the democracies. Either way, the results are likely to be painful for the richest one-sixth of the earth's population that now enjoys a disproportionate five-sixths of its wealth.

This issue of global demographic imbalances between richer and poorer societies forms the backdrop to all of the other important forces for change that are taking place. There is little doubt that we are witnessing today, in major regions of the world, a population explosion analogous to—but hundreds of times bigger than—that which occurred in Malthus's England. Moreover, it is also occurring at a time of stupendous technological changes in the way we manufacture, grow things, trade, and communicate—changes which will now be examined, not only to consider them on their own terms, but also to see how they might mitigate or aggravate an impending demographic disaster.

3

THE COMMUNICATIONS AND FINANCIAL REVOLUTION AND THE RISE OF THE MULTINATIONAL CORPORATION

ANY ATTEMPT TO ESTIMATE WHETHER today's new technologies can solve an impending demographic crisis needs to be placed in context. The critical issues are which groups and individuals create, control, and have access to the new discoveries, and what are the general economic circumstances in which these scientific breakthroughs occur. This chapter will argue that the world economy is becoming much more integrated and much richer overall, although the creation and enjoyment of that wealth are very uneven. However, it will also argue that the main creators and controllers of technology have increasingly become large, multinational corporations with more global reach than global responsibility. Far from producing a solution to the gap between the world's "haves" and "have-nots," the changing structures of international business and investment may exacerbate them.

The tremendous expansion of the world economy in recent decades is the result of a number of interrelated causes. The most obvious, especially as compared with the troubled interwar years, is that after 1945 a system was set up by the major trading nations to ensure a reasonable degree of financial and economic stability and to restrict protectionist tendencies. With the U.S. dollar as the world currency, America became the "lender of last resort," as the City of London had been in the late nineteenth century, whereas there had been no such lender in the 1920s and 1930s. In addition, the postwar decades saw a remarkably long period of stability in Great Power relationships, at least to the extent that the world's most powerful nations have not gone to war with each other.

This stability, together with the need to rebuild economies after the ravages of World War II, led to an unprecedented rate of growth in world industrial output. Between 1953 and 1975, output grew on average at a remarkable 6 percent a year overall (4 percent per capita), and even in the 1973–80 period the average increase was 2.4 percent a year, which was very respectable by historical standards. Table 1 gives a sense of this dizzy rise, especially compared with the lackluster growth of world manufacturing industries in the inter-war years.

Table 1. Production of World Manufacturing Industries, 1900–80[1]

	Total Production	*Annual Growth Rate (%)*
1900	100.0	2.6
1913	172.4	4.3
1928	250.8	2.5
1938	311.4	2.2
1953	567.7	4.1
1963	950.1	5.3
1973	1730.6	6.2
1980	3041.6	2.4

These increases refer only to manufacturing. The growth in services such as advertising, banking, catering, and insurance was even greater, as such activities came to occupy an ever-increasing share of the GNP of most advanced economies (well over 70 percent in the United States). Agricultural trade, too, has grown steadily since 1945, as has the international demand for raw materials (especially oil). Given the decades of Great Power stability and the general growth in prosperity, tourism and travel boomed as well, becoming one of the world's greatest industries and employers. In consequence, the global economy grew more since 1945 than in all world history prior to World War II; in fact, world real GNP quadrupled—from 2 trillion to about 8 trillion U.S. dollars—from 1950 to 1980 alone.

Global economic growth has, however, been much more beneficial for the average inhabitant of an advanced industrial economy than for someone living in the developing world. By 1991 the per capita Gross Domestic Product of Switzerland had soared to $36,300, with Sweden ($32,600), Japan ($29,000), and Germany ($27,900) not far behind.* By contrast, India's per capita GDP languishes at a mere $360, and Nigeria's is only $278.[2] And there are, in Saharan and sub-Saharan Africa, as well as in South and Southeast Asia, dozens of countries with even lower average per capita GDPs.[3] The grotesqueness of this disparity in wealth—a citizen of Switzerland enjoys on average several hundred times the income of a native of Ethiopia—is mirrored in the differential rates of child mortality, life expectancy, and access to education. After nearly five decades of unprecedented global economic growth, the world heads toward the twenty-first century with *more than a billion people living in poverty*—an awful enough figure until one realizes that those billion are people "struggling to survive on less than $370 a year,"[4] not the billions of human beings who live in countries like Botswana or Guatemala where the per capita GDP is a relatively satisfactory $750 or a comfortable $1,000 each year—levels that would horrify inhabitants of the "First" World.

This uneven surge in global prosperity has occurred at the same time as—and has interacted with—the emergence of large multinational companies which are increasingly less attached to the particular interests and values of their country of origin. As they compete against rival firms for world market shares, they have developed a strategy of directing investment and production from one part of the earth to another, with the help of revolutionary communications and financial technologies that have created a global marketplace for goods and services. Already important in today's world, these corporations will be even more significant in the future, as Cold War trading barriers break down and the global economy becomes increasingly integrated.[5]

Companies with international rather than national interests are not new. They existed, in embryonic form, in the cosmopolitan private banks of the late nineteenth and early twentieth centuries, whose growth was assisted by the earlier "communications revolution" of the

*Followed by Austria ($24,800), the United States ($23,100), and Canada ($23,100). All figures are rounded to the nearest $100 and are at current exchange rates. Germany refers to West Germany only.

telegraph and by the absence of major Great Power coalition wars. The House of Rothschild in 1900, for example, had branches in Frankfurt, Vienna, Paris, and London in daily contact with one another. Lloyds of London before 1914 insured most of the German shipping industry and was prepared to pay out compensation for losses even in the event of an Anglo-German war. Again, earlier examples abound of multinational companies such as Lever Bros. (the forerunners of Unilever), with production facilities ranging from West Africa to India; or of major oil companies, scouring the globe for fresh sources of petroleum and switching the refined products from one market to another. Ford also went "global" when it decided to manufacture cars and trucks on both sides of the Atlantic.

But today's globalization is distinguished from those earlier examples by the sheer quantity and extent of the multinational firms in our expanded and integrated global economy. As noted above, they emerged in a postwar international economic order that reduced protectionism and encouraged a recovery of world trade, and were further stimulated in the 1970s by the United States' decision to abandon the gold standard, followed by a general liberalization of exchange controls, at first only in a few countries, later in many others. This not only provided more liquidity for world trade, but increased the flow of transnational capital investments, as companies invested abroad without constraints imposed by central banks.

Although this financial liberalization helped to expand world commerce, it also produced another effect: the increasing separation of financial flows from trade in manufactures and services. More and more, foreign-currency transactions took place not because a company was paying for foreign goods or investing in foreign assembly, but because investors were speculating in a particular currency or other financial instruments. This surge in global capital flows beyond those required to finance the boom in world industry and commerce is intimately connected with two further occurrences: the deregulation of world money markets, and the revolution in global communications as a result of new technologies. Without the vast increase in the power of computers, computer software, satellites, fiber-optic cables, and high-speed electronic transfers, global markets could not act as one, and economic and other information—politics, ideas, culture, revolutions, consumer trends—could not be delivered instantaneously to the more than 200,000 monitors connected into this global communications system. And all this, according to some pundits, may be only the initial phase.[6]

Except among black marketers and drug dealers, the physical handling of large amounts of currency notes is rapidly becoming redundant. Flows of paper have been replaced by electronic transactions that take place around the clock, picked up in one capital market when another shuts down for the night. From one major exchange to another—Tokyo, Hong Kong and Singapore, London, Frankfurt and Zurich, New York, Chicago, and Toronto—trading in yen futures or in General Motors stock goes on twenty-four hours a day and creates a single market. Daily foreign exchange flows amount to around *one trillion* dollars, and far outweigh the sums employed for the international purchase of goods and services or investments in overseas plants. Indeed, by the late 1980s, more than 90 percent of this trading in the world's foreign exchanges was unrelated to trade or capital investment.[7]

Within this system, and largely because of it, many successful companies are internationalizing themselves. Given a global market, competition among firms—whether automobile producers, aircraft manufacturers, pharmaceutical companies, makers of computer hardware, or publishing houses—is driving them to sell and produce in all of the major economic regions of the world. Not only does the company benefit from economies of scale, but it hopes to protect itself from the vagaries of currency fluctuations, differentiated economic growth, and political interference. A recession in Europe will be of less concern to a firm which also operates in booming East Asian markets than to one exclusively dependent upon European sales. A company interested in developing goods banned by certain bureaucracies (in the biotech industry especially) can switch its manufacture to parts of the world lacking such regulations. A multinational corporation, fretting at the "voluntary controls" imposed by governments to protect indigenous firms from open competition, can often get around those barriers by setting up plants *inside* the protected territory. Once a multinational breaches protectionist obstacles, it is likely to enjoy handsome profit opportunities, at least in the early years, in the newly accessible market.

Even research and product development is being shifted—from the United States to Switzerland, from Germany to California—when it suits a company's needs. For the same motives, large companies rush in to acquire small, innovative firms on the other side of the globe, to forestall preemption by their competitors.

A popular and somewhat shallow interpretation of these trends—put forward not coincidentally by people involved in international consulting and banking—is that the economic consequences of globalization can only be beneficial. In this interpretation, whereas government restrictions previously prevented the consumer from purchasing the best goods, free trade now permits individuals and companies to buy and sell on a world market. Moreover, not only firms but cities, regions, and countries will play a role in this process of global openness and competitiveness, at least if they understand the rules—that is, to invite investment and manufacturing, keep restrictions (including taxes) to a minimum, and provide a well-trained work force and modern infrastructure. If these rules are followed, the multinationals will flock to your door.[8] The result will be an upward surge in wealth creation, a development in which no one loses.

This optimistic interpretation also applauds the way in which the revolution in communications is influencing politics and society. In a world with more than 600 million television sets, viewers are as much consumers of news and ideas as they are of commercial goods. Thus governments of authoritarian states find it increasingly difficult to keep their people in ignorance. Chernobyl was swiftly photographed by a French *commercial* satellite, and then transmitted all over the world—including within the Soviet Union itself. The Chinese government's suppression of the students in Tiananmen Square and the outside world's shock at that event were immediately reported back *into* China by radio, television, and fax messages. As Communist regimes in Eastern Europe fell late in 1989, reports and pictures of each government's demise led to similar events in neighboring states.[9] In other words, just as television in the 1960s helped to shape American public perception and policy concerning civil rights and the Vietnam War, so the spread of the same technology around the world is leading to similar transformations of values.[10] Knowledge and openness, it is assumed, brings with it truth, honesty, fairness, and democracy.

Such a vision of a prosperous and harmonious world economic order, founded upon laissez-faire, twenty-four-hour-a-day trading, and all-pervasive television, seems breathtakingly naive in the light of this planet's demographic, environmental, and regional problems. Cheering references to the way in which the "discriminating consumer" can nowadays buy a Mont Blanc pen or a Vuitton suitcase without regard to that product's country of origin[11] recall Jevons's enthusiasm a century ago about the easy purchase of Argentine beef and Chinese tea.* In both cases, there is a failure to recognize that newer technologies may not benefit all, that the vast majority of the world's population may not be able to purchase the goods in question, and that profound changes both in economic production and in communications can bring disadvantages as well as advantages in their wake.

Since globalization has recently attracted immense publicity, it has become easier to identify which groups and interests are already being hurt by the process or are likely to be affected in the future: economic nationalists, interest groups and companies that wish to protect their domestic markets, workers whose jobs are made redundant when a multinational company moves its assembly and manufacturing elsewhere, and localities in which employment (especially of skilled labor) shrinks. There is, in addition, reason for concern about the volatility of the vast, computer-driven system of financial trading. Finally, since enthusiasts of globalization seem to focus overwhelmingly upon what it means for the "triad" of prosperous societies in North America, Europe, and Japan,[12] they devote less attention to the prospect of a further marginalization of four-fifths of the earth's population not well prepared for these new commercial and financial trends.

To today's economic nationalists, globalization threatens to undermine the assumed integrity of the nation-state as the central organizing unit of domestic and external affairs. The implications of this challenge will be further discussed in Chapter 7, but the general reason for this unease is clear: like illegal migration or global warming, the internationalization of manufacturing and finance erodes a people's capacity to control its own affairs. The idea that we are entering an era in which there will be no national products or technologies, no national corpora-

*See above, p. 9.

tions, and no national industries is bewildering to all who think in traditional terms. In the United States in particular, which for so long has possessed much more of a self-contained economy than, for example, the Netherlands or Britain, it must be unsettling to hear that "as almost every factor of production—money, technology, factories, and equipment—moves effortlessly across borders, the very idea of an American economy is becoming meaningless, as are the notions of an American corporation, American capital, American products, and American technology."[13] If products are no longer "American," what is the point of trying to measure the balance of merchandise trade, or the gap in U.S.-Japan commerce in high-technology goods? While the enthusiasts of globalization want national governments and their agencies to become invisible in the marketplace, many others are made uneasy by such a disappearance. The older ways are more familiar, more comforting—and besides, the people you know and can appeal to (Congress, Parliament, the Treasury) still seem to be in control of economic affairs.

These are not just theoretical concerns but practical, everyday ones, at least for businessmen and politicians struggling to protect certain interests from the effects of globalization. Examples here would be the attempts by Chrysler and Hyster (which makes forklift trucks) to reduce the competition from Japanese rivals by pressing for voluntary restraint agreements or special import duties because American manufacturing was being hurt by unfair foreign practices—a strategy which backfired when it was revealed that Hyster's own "American" forklift trucks contained more foreign parts than those they had identified as "Japanese," and that Chrysler cars contained the highest percentage of foreign-made parts of any made by the big three auto manufacturers.[14]

Consider also the problems that attend efforts by France and Italy to restrict the Japanese share of their home automobile market to a mere 2 percent or 5 percent. Such protectionism was possible when those two countries were still economically sovereign entities. The creation of a tariff-free Economic Community means, however, that Japanese automobiles assembled in Britain—with more than 80 percent local parts—cannot be excluded without a quarrel with the European Commission in Brussels. Nor is this the end of the dilemma, for if Japanese car makers export automobiles to the French and Italian markets from their *American* plants, protectionist politicians in Paris and Italy could find themselves in a dispute with the United States; and the U.S. Department of Commerce, better known for its "Japan-bashing," could be interceding in third markets on behalf of a Japanese company. While the Japanese firms might be operating according to what is now airily termed "the new logic of the global marketplace," these developments suggest that local polities and authorities are increasingly ceding control of their economic destiny. Indeed, the real "logic" of the borderless world is that nobody is in control—except, perhaps, the managers of multinational corporations, whose responsibility is to their shareholders, who, one might argue, have become the new sovereigns, investing in whatever company gives the highest returns.

If major corporations have largely broken free from their national roots, this is even more true of the fast-moving, twenty-four-hour-a-day, border-crossing, profit-hunting system of international finance, in which vast sums of capital—described by one investment authority as "the most purely rational thing there is"[15]—move in and out of a country or a stock according to perceptions of that entity's prospects.

Yet even if money is the most purely rational thing there is, it does not follow that it is immune to instability, panics, and financial flight. Forty years ago, foreign exchange ratios reflected the fundamentals of individual countries' trade balances, and most of the current exchanges that were made related to the flow of goods. Today, the daily volume of foreign exchange trading is *several hundred times* larger than the value of traded goods, and the relationship has altered. Across the world, millions of individual investors, companies, and banks speculate in currencies, many of them automatically following computer-generated indicators that reveal whether (say) the dollar is increasing or decreasing in value relative to other currencies. These players swiftly react to economic data such as the latest trade figures or a rise in interest rates, incidentally making it more difficult for governments and central banks to implement what may be necessary fiscal measures out of fear that international investors may find them unwelcome; a marked reduction in interest rates, judged by a government to be helpful to its country's industries and employment, may be ruled out or at least trimmed because of concern over its effect on the nation's currency. Still more do these investors react to political turbulence such as the threat of a war, or a political assassination. Were the event to be particularly serious—a major earthquake in Tokyo, or the death of the president of the United States—currency markets could be swiftly and seriously destabilized.

The ideological implications of this global system are debated more in Europe than in the laissez-faire United States. The reality nowadays is that any government which offends international finance's demand for unrestricted gain—by increasing personal taxes, for example, or by raising fees on financial transactions—will find its capital has fled and its currency weakened. From the difficulties of the Wilson government in the late 1960s, to the Mitterrand administration's failed attempt to "go it alone" in its economic policies of the early 1980s, to the experiences of innumerable regimes in the developing world, the message is clear: if you do not follow the rules of the market, your economy will suffer. But the market's message ignores important considerations. If, say, a French Socialist government is conscientiously attempting to provide better schools, health care, housing, and public utilities for its citizenry, by what means can it raise the necessary funds without alarming international investors who may be not at all interested in the well-being of those citizens but merely in their own profits? The rational market, by its very nature, is not concerned with social justice and fairness.

Political issues aside, there are practical problems in endowing a single currency—the U.S. dollar—with such an overwhelming responsibility within the international financial system. In the 1940s and 1950s, there was no alternative to that arrangement, which in any case rested upon firm foundations: the U.S. economy was strong, it enjoyed a national current-account surplus, and America was by far the world's largest creditor nation; its budgetary deficits were small, currencies were in fixed relation to one another (and to gold), and foreign-exchange dealings were controlled. There was thus much less room for volatility in the financial markets, at the same time as capital flows were relatively small. Today, none of those conditions applies. The American share of world assets is significantly smaller; the United States has run large current-account deficits for many years, covered by borrowing from abroad, which has made it an international debtor in a spectacularly brief period of time; the amount of speculative capital in the system is much larger and is under far less institutional control; and American political leadership has become used to huge budgetary and current-accounts deficits without having to face the discipline of the markets, which would be the fate of politicians in countries not benefiting from the special position of the U.S. dollar.

Orthodox economists offer many reasons why the present financial system will continue. As American deficits grow, foreigners simply hold more dollars. For various structural reasons, it is argued, no other currency can replace the dollar—at least not in the foreseeable future. Therefore, the position of the U.S. dollar remains "unassailable," according to the optimists.[16] History shows, however, that previous international monetary regimes—such as the one that revolved around the gold standard, the pound sterling, and the City of London prior to 1914—became ever more difficult to sustain when the hub economy itself began to lose its relative strength and competitiveness.[17] Current economic trends—the diminution of the American share of global assets, the rise of such other currencies as the yen and the ECU, the emergence of new financial centers, the increasing share of American national wealth needed for debt repayment—suggest that the post-1945 international monetary regime may also be drawing to a close, *without* an adequate successor system in view.

Ultimately, all these concerns are about credit. The system itself has to be believed in. If its credibility fails because more and more people become doubtful about American indebtedness or the value of the dollar or the volatility of the Tokyo stock market, those worries could explode in panic—especially when the system itself can rush hundreds of billions of dollars in and out of a currency in half a day's trading. Central banks and finance ministries have put emergency controls in place to avoid a financial "meltdown," but such controls have not yet been fully tested, and their very existence reflects fear on the part of those monitoring this vast, free-flowing flood of capital that people might one day cease to believe in the system.

• • •

What have these financial matters to do with preparing for the year 2025, and with the larger problems facing our global society? At first glance, the investment calculations of a multinational company's strategic planners and the daily maneuvers of Tokyo speculators may appear to overlap little with the challenges facing a West African groundnut producer or a Malaysian tin miner. If this is true, it means that the great gap between the rich and poor in today's world is increasing; how, indeed, will a technologically sophisticated, transnational, corporate culture, loyal to no government and beyond the reach of local regulation, coexist with the polyglot, hungry, and dissatisfied masses foreshadowed by a world population of 8 or 10 billion?[18] Moreover, if profound financial instability does occur as a consequence of the fast-flowing but irresponsible system of monetary exchanges, severe shocks to the international trading order are likely to depress developing world commodity prices—coffee, cocoa, ores—most of all. That was a lesson of the 1930s, and of the post-oil-shock 1970s. The continued dependence of developing countries upon such exports suggests that the same would be true today. Events in Central America may have little impact upon Wall Street, but Wall Street's actions could have serious consequences for the developing world.

Even within the industrial democracies themselves, the globalization of production, investment, and services has serious consequences. Until recently, many large companies still retained the characteristics of the typical post-1945 corporation: located in a particular region, the provider of jobs to its skilled blue-collar work force and to layers of managers, the provider also of philanthropic and social goods to the "company town." Although examples still exist of such localist and paternalist firms, many have been compelled by international competition to discard all such loyalties to the town, the region, or the country. "The United States," one prominent American executive observed, "does not have an automatic call on our resources. There is no mind-set that puts the country first."[19] In consequence, states, regions, cities, and townships have become "bidders" for the presence of a new factory, or, more often, the retention of an existing plant which a multinational company may be thinking of moving. If the community in question can offer enough inducements—tax concessions, operating subsidies, training grants—as did Danville, Illinois, in 1983 in a bid to win a new forklift assembly plant, it may succeed, at least for a while; if it does not make enough concessions, like Portland, Oregon, in the same bidding war, it will lose. If a union at one plant is willing to agree to the demands of the corporation—as did the General Motors workers in Arlington, Texas, thereby contributing to the closure of the firm's factory in Ypsilanti, Michigan, where the union was less cooperative—it may survive, until the next time.[20] Since communities and unions are bidding for the same jobs, it follows that one region's enhanced (or retained) employment means another region's rising unemployment. Winner or loser, it is clear that there is "uneven bargaining power" between communities and the globalized company.[21]

Within the developed world, globalization also affects the career expectations of individuals and the structure of employment generally. In the United States, which has opened itself to laissez-faire forces more readily than other industrial democracies, lawyers, biotechnology engineers, economics editors, software designers, and strategic planners are in demand because they contribute a high "added value" to whatever they are working upon. The demand for their services is international—the request for the software design, or legal brief, or "op-ed" commentary upon a diplomatic crisis may come from anywhere in the developed world—just as the means of communicating this knowledge (via Express Mail, or fax) are also international. Unlike the fast-food server, or the local policeman or schoolteacher, or the blue-collar worker, these creators and conveyors of high-added-value information are no longer linked to a regional or even a national economy. They have become functioning and prosperous parts of a borderless world—and, like the growing number of their equivalents in Europe, Japan, and Australasia, will remain so just as long as their education, skills, expertise, and inventiveness are in demand from distant consumers.

Much more important, in social and political terms, is the fate of the four-fifths of Americans who are not in such international demand. Skilled blue-collar employees—the core of the traditional high-per-capita-income U.S. work force, and the backbone of the Democratic Party—have lost jobs in the millions as American firms wilted under international competition or relocated industrial production to other countries with lower labor costs. During the 1980s, the United Auto Workers lost 500,000 members even as companies like General Motors were adding to employment abroad.[22] At the same time as high-paying blue-collar jobs were disappearing, millions of new jobs were being created across the United States. Unfortunately, the vast majority of those positions were low-paid casual or unprotected jobs requiring few skills and offering little opportunity, such as work in fast-food stores, gas stations, discount supermarkets, hotels, and cleaning and gardening services. An increasing majority of Americans have found their real standards of living—like the real level of national productivity—stagnating since the mid-1970s. Just as the gap between the upper one-fifth and lower four-fifths of global society has increased, so also, though less drastically, has the upper one-fifth in American society detached itself from the rest.

Although it is too early yet to be certain, these changes in American society—and in societies that go the "American way"—may also affect the debate on North-South relations. A family whose chief wage-earner has lost his job because the factory was moved to Mexico or Thailand is unlikely to be sympathetic to pleas for enhanced development aid to poorer countries. Employees who lack a college education and scramble to retain their low-paying positions as hospital janitors or office cleaners will resent the infiltration of immigrants (whether legal or illegal) willing to work longer hours and for less money. Politicians in constituencies suffering from factory closings by multinationals will be tempted—are already tempted—to push for greater protection of the home market, regardless of what that means for the developing world. Well-heeled professionals, who are college-educated, drive Volvos, contribute to Oxfam, and are sympathetic to environmental concerns, may increasingly recognize the need for unpopular reforms to counter worrying global trends; but that is unlikely to be true for most of their fellow citizens, who are finding it hard to preserve their standards of living.

The implications for the developing world of the financial and communications revolutions and the rise of the multinational corporations are even more sobering. So much of the breathlessly enthusiastic literature about the benefits of globalization focuses upon what is happening in

Europe, North America, and Japan, plus certain extensions of that triad (South Korea, Brazil, Australia). But little is said about the rest of the world. From the perspective of laissez-faire theory—from Adam Smith and Cobden to Kenichi Ohmae today[23]—such countries presumably become relevant only when they learn the lessons of the marketplace and possess those features which allow them to compete in the borderless world: a well-educated population, lots of engineers, designers and other professionals, a sophisticated financial structure, good communications, enormous deposits of knowledge (libraries, computers, laboratories), adequate capital and entrepreneurs, and perhaps a fledgling multinational corporation or two. If this has happened in South Korea, why can't it happen in every country of the world?

Chapter 10 argues that this beguiling theory is too abstract. Not merely would it require the ending of corrupt regimes, excess spending on the military, bureaucratic ineptitude, protection of special interests, lack of legal protection, religious fundamentalism, and all the other obstacles to commerce which exist in many countries in Central America, the Middle East, and sub-Saharan Africa. It would also involve a transformation of the dominant value systems in many developing world societies that are antithetical to the norms of Western rationalism, scientific inquiry, legal theory, and capitalism. Until such a profound change occurs, it is hard to foresee when Ethiopian-based or Philippine-based multinational companies, flush with funds and talented personnel, will begin to move into Japan or New England, making strategic acquisitions as they take *their* historic turn at the center of the global economic stage.

Accepting the logic of the global marketplace will also be difficult because of the structural obstacles that cramp many of today's developing nations. The idealized picture, in which hyperefficient multinational corporations compete to bring their latest products to discriminating consumers across the globe while governments become all but invisible, makes seductive reading; but it ignores the fact that what most poorer nations need is not simply the liberating effects of free-market economics, but also enormous investments in social improvement. In a predominantly agrarian, land-locked African country whose population is doubling every twenty-five years, the most urgent needs would appear to be family planning, environmental protection, health care, education, and basic infrastructure—which free-market, multinational corporations are not likely to be interested in financing. In other words, huge public funds are required—whether in Central Africa or Eastern Europe—before conditions become attractive to investment managers of Japanese and American companies. But how such public funds are to be provided is rarely if ever touched upon by the fans of globalization.

Moreover, if a developing country does manage to reconstitute itself on the East Asian model and enjoys a rise in foreign investment, production, exports, and standards of living, then it could in turn become steadily more susceptible to the relocation of branch plants and jobs as multinationals search for still cheaper regions for manufacture and assembly. According to borderless-world theories, this is not a problem; if the principles of supply and demand really work efficiently, deindustrialization and unemployment ought not to last for long: "In this interlinked economy, there is no such thing as absolute winners and losers. A loser becomes relatively attractive as its currency gets weaker and an unemployed work force emerges that is available at reasonable cost."[24] Just as an American automobile company would be willing to move assembly plants *back* to the United States if its currency and labor costs fell far enough, so would an obliging multinational return to (say) Malaysia or Brazil when it became cheap enough again. Such unimaginative reasoning does not consider whether the working populations and governments of newly industrializing countries are likely to remain complacent when multinational corporations move elsewhere, as happened to a large extent in northern England and the Ohio Valley. An angry native reaction and a backlash against being treated as the economic pawns of First World companies are equally plausible.

Poorer societies may come to resent cosmopolitan capitalism for two further reasons, both of them consequences of the financial/communications/multinational revolution. The first is the possibility that the transmission of information from one part of the globe to another via 1.5 billion radios and 600 million television sets may not necessarily lead to universal enthusiasm for the Western way of life, as some optimistic commentators have suggested. It is a remarkable technical and manufacturing achievement that as the 1980s ended, billions of people from the Inner Mongolian plain to the Andean mountains were able for the first time to see the world outside via television.[25] It is also true that the information revolution played a critical role in the demise of Communist societies that had visibly failed to keep up with the West.

Still, it is less certain that the poorest four-fifths of the world will necessarily emulate the Western prosperity that it sees on television. If domestic obstacles to reform remain entrenched, as appears likely in many developing societies, one response could be a vast migration to the richer parts of the globe, while others retreat into fundamentalism and reject Western values (especially its conspicuous consumerism). There could also be growing bafflement and resentment in developing countries at the structural obstacles to achieving the standards of living enjoyed by industrial democracies. Instead of creating masses of discriminating consumers of Vuitton suitcases, the coming of a telecommunications revolution to developing countries could well cause billions of "have-nots" to feel ever more angry at the "haves"—including the engineers and managers of multinational companies in their midst.

Globalized communications, moreover, work in many ways. The Islamic fundamentalist revolution against the shah of Iran was orchestrated from Paris by the Ayatollah Khomeini through audiotaped sermons that were widely distributed in his native country. Television also has complex consequences. While viewers in the developing world gape at the riches displayed in programs like *Dallas* and *Brideshead Revisited,* the peoples of the industrial democracies are exposed to frequent coverage of the dreadful poverty, malnutrition, and other effects of wars and natural disasters that continue to afflict Africa, the Middle East, and elsewhere. In the case of a terrible disaster, like the Ethiopian famine of 1985, this sometimes produces a broad public response from horrified viewers in the North. Again, the graphic footage of Kurdish families fleeing the wrath of Saddam Hussein in early 1991—and the reactions of European governments and American public opinion—forced the White House to help create enclaves for the Kurdish refugees.

But television is constantly in search of newer and more dramatic topics, and coverage of such events swiftly fades. Moreover, as mentioned above, individuals who have suffered economically because of competition from developing countries or who believe that the domestic ills of their own society require attention first may be less eager to support moves to assist poorer nations—especially if a significant redistribution of resources is involved. Disaster relief is one thing, structural adjustments are another. Nevertheless, given that 95 percent of future population growth will occur in developing countries, the basic issue remains: how will the peoples of this planet relate to each other at the dawn of the twenty-first century as increasing billions of poverty-stricken peasants view (but do not share) the North's wealth, while millions of prosperous families in the industrial democracies are exposed to the demographic and environmental disasters that their fellow human beings are suffering? Will it produce reforms—or apathy and resentment?

A further consequence of globalization, which will be discussed in detail in the following chapters on biotechnology and robotics, is that companies in the developed world are investing in new technologies which could greatly harm poorer societies, by providing substitutes for millions of jobs in agriculture and industry. Such investment is driven by the same profit-seeking motives that have propelled technological innovation since the Industrial Revolution at least; but just as the intentional creation of the power-driven textile factory, the steel mill, and the railway had profound, *unintended* results for domestic and foreign populations, so also are some of today's emerging technologies likely to have profound consequences for contemporary societies, especially in the developing world. As the twenty-first century approaches, therefore, the peoples of the earth seem to be discovering that their lives are ever more affected by forces which are, in the full meaning of the word, irresponsible.

4

WORLD AGRICULTURE AND THE BIOTECHNOLOGY REVOLUTION

AS "GLOBALIZED" BUSINESS EMERGES IN richer countries while population pressures increase in poorer ones, is there any way that human ingenuity can reverse this ominous mismatch? At the least, could not the problem of widespread malnutrition be tackled by new inventions? The second reason that Malthus's dire predictions about England's future were proved wrong, it will be remembered, was a so-called Agricultural Revolution which enhanced "the power in the earth." What are the prospects of another such escape, this time for the vastly larger populations of the developing world? During the 1980s alone, an additional 842 million people were added to the earth's population,[1] while croplands were eliminated to make way for roads and buildings, soil erosion and degradation caused millions of acres of farmland to be abandoned, and careless irrigation led to widespread salinization of the soil. This makes a significant increase in productivity of the remaining farmland all the more urgent, for otherwise malnutrition and starvation will increase.

Until recently, it appeared that global agricultural output was expanding nicely. From 1950 to 1984, food production rose faster than ever before in human history. World grain harvests rose 2.6 times in those years, which was more than the increase in global population.

Production of root crops, meat, milk, fish, fruits, and vegetables also expanded, in response to worldwide demand for food caused by population growth and enhanced standards of living. Millions of additional acres were cultivated, and newer machines, more fertilizer, better irrigation, and crop rotation were introduced to farming across the world.

The best example of this change was what came to be known as the "green revolution" in Asia, where, in addition to improved mechanization and fertilization, great advances occurred because of biotechnological breeding of newer strains of plants. New hybrid rice strains turned out to be more durable—more resistant to diseases and pests—and produced higher yields. Some new rices yielded two to three times more than traditional varieties. Moreover, because the new strains were readily made available to developing countries by International Agricultural Research Centers, there took place a superb example of international research and applied agricultural science. In consequence, world rice production rose from 257 million tonnes in 1965 to 468 million tonnes twenty years later. "Miracle rice" was said to have averted famines, weaned poor countries off dependence on imported food, and provided political stability.[2] Being swifter and more widespread, the green revolution had a far greater impact than Britain's eighteenth-century agricultural revolution.

Since 1984, however, the pace of increase in global agricultural production has slowed considerably, partly because of intense droughts in the United States and elsewhere that occurred in 1988. Instead of the roughly 3 percent annual increases in grain output of the 1950–84 years, overall production rose by only 1 percent annually between 1984 and 1989. Global production of root crops peaked in 1984 and has declined since then, because of overuse of fertilizers (which seem to expand crop growth for a while, before it levels off), attacks by new diseases, the deterioration of soil quality, and the fact that there was less suitable land available for further planting.[3] Moreover, recent figures indicate that the yields of some crops, especially rice, have now also leveled, suggesting that the miracle increases have run their course.[4] Scientific breakthroughs could reverse this trend; on the other hand, if the reduction of forests and other habitats causes further loss of plant species and reduced biological diversity, that could cut hopes of producing improved strains.*

Overall, global food production continues to increase, but more slowly than before. Production of cereal, the most important food crop, has not kept up with population growth. The period 1984–89 may be too short to show a long-term trend—there was also a similar worry in the early 1970s—but if cereal production continues to rise at about 1 percent a year on average and global population at 1.7 percent a year, the predictable results will soon be felt. This is particularly true in Africa, where the seemingly impressive 23 percent rise in total food production from 1976–78 to 1986–88 has been outpaced by higher population growth, so that per capita food production actually declined 8 percent over that decade.[5] In the Middle East and Latin America, rises in food production have been matched by population increases, a situation which could worsen. Political convulsions in Eastern and Central Europe and the backwardness of agriculture there and in the former USSR make matters worse.

Because global food consumption has exceeded production for a number of years, reserves of carryover stocks have been falling, as Chart 3 indicates for cereals.

1988 may have been a freakishly hot and dry summer, but if the United States experiences further droughts, the reserve stocks upon which more than a hundred food-importing countries rely will fall still further. Thus, we may be at the beginning of an ominous long-term trend in which population grows faster than food production. According to the Worldwatch Institute, increases of 28 million tons of grain are needed each year merely to keep pace with population growth, yet recently the annual net gain has been closer to 15 million tons. This means that the number of seriously undernourished people in the world has been rising, decade upon decade, so that it is now well over 500 million.[6]

In industrialized nations, where massive protectionist subsidies have led to "butter mountains," "wine lakes," silos and even aircraft hangars

*In general, a strain of crop such as wheat and rice will lose its resistance to disease and pests about 5 to 15 years after introduction and need to be replaced by new strains.

Chart 3. World Cereal Carryover Stocks

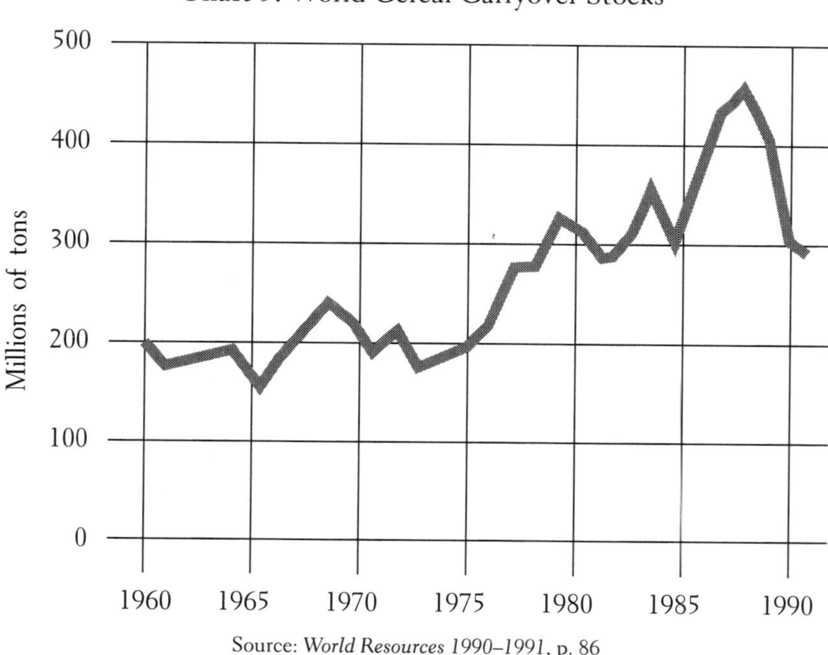

Source: *World Resources 1990–1991*, p. 86

bursting with surplus grain, it may be hard to imagine that there is an impending shortage as farmers idle millions of hectares of cropland. Yet while such additional capacity exists, the use of that land might still not solve the key problem, which is how poorer nations will *pay* for the food they have to import. Because of reduced stocks, world wheat and rice prices have risen considerably since 1986–87, while developing world currencies have fallen in value. Since northern-hemisphere farmers won't grow crops without compensation, an international mechanism would be required to transfer the crops to those nations in a sustained way. While a lot of food aid is donated at present, much more is needed to meet the doubling and trebling of African and Asian populations. But this does not solve the larger problem: an increase in food aid merely increases the dependency of poorer peoples upon their richer cousins, whereas a failure to supply such aid could intensify migration out of food-deficit countries.

Another way to help poorer nations feed their people would be to augment the amount of cropland. While there are now 2,800 square meters of arable land for each person on earth, world population growth will reduce this average to 1,700 square meters a person by 2025, while in Asia there will be a mere 900 square meters per person unless new cropland is created.[7] But where will additional land come from at the rate needed to feed at least two or three *billion* new mouths in the next few decades? In Asia, an estimated 82 percent of potential cropland is already under production. There are large reserves of potential cropland in Latin America, but much of this is marginal soil, unsuitable for major crops, or is Amazonian rain forest, which deserves protection, not denudation; in other regions, too, additional cropland could only come at the expense of forests, accelerating global warming and putting further pressure upon world agriculture in the longer term. In Africa, where food needs are greatest, widespread overgrazing and soil damage have resulted in a net loss of land suitable for agriculture, and few areas receive enough rainfall to support grain crops. Thus spare agricultural capacity lies chiefly in the developed world, especially North America and Europe, not in the countries where the food is most needed; and "cornucopian" writings about this general reserve capacity rarely consider the problem of *global* supply and demand. Moreover, if the forecasts about land degradation and the drawing-down of the water tables are correct,* the Great Plains of the American Midwest may not long provide grain surpluses to feed a world of eight or ten billion people.

Another possibility is to increase the efficiency of farmers in poorer countries. In some East Asian rice fields, up to 40 percent of fertilizers are wasted because of inefficient application, while poor crop management, storage, and handling wastes up to 20 percent of rice grown.[8] The average African farmer produces only 600 kilograms of cereals a year, compared to 80,000 kilograms, or 130 times as much, per agricultural worker in North America. Clearly, there *are* many ways to increase agricultural efficiency in the poorer areas of the world, including better training and instruction, improved access to markets, more skillful handling of seeds, better crops, fertilizers, and farm machinery, and ecologically sound agroforestry. Even so, such piecemeal and local

*See below, pp. 99, 319–20.

improvements must overcome stubborn geographical, economic, and social obstacles; after all, the American farmer is 130-fold more productive than his African counterpart because he owns far larger tracts of land, enjoys a more favorable growing climate and better infrastructure, is much more highly capitalized, uses modern machinery and quality fertilizers and seeds, has access to much more information, and so on. If the conditions of the African farmer were similar, Africa would not be a "developing" continent. The final cruel point is that if African farmers *were* as productive as their American counterparts, there would be a massive displacement of labor, with little prospect of employment by industry or services. In sum, rural poverty in Africa, Asia, and elsewhere will not be solved by technical fixes, if structural and cultural aspects of the problem remain unattended.

Because none of these more traditional solutions seems adequate, attention in recent years has focused upon biotechnology as a possible answer. Biotechnology means "any technique that uses living organisms or processes to make or modify products, to improve plants or animals, or to develop microorganisms for specific uses."[9] It has developed from the remarkable breakthroughs made by scientists since the 1950s in understanding the genetic code. Genes exist in all life processes and contribute to the inheritance of specific characteristics, whether a human being's tendency to overweight or a plant's susceptibility to a certain pest. Scientists can isolate, clone, and study the structure of the gene and seek to understand its relationship to the processes of living things. Genetic engineers are now able to insert into the DNA of a living cell a new gene to improve the organism's strength, or size, or resistance.[10]

Although medical biotechnology has attracted twenty times more capital investment than agricultural biotechnology, it is the latter's potential to improve and possibly even transform agriculture that is important here. This use of biotechnology can be seen as an entirely new stage in humankind's attempts to produce more crops and plants. For thousands of years, farmers have sought to improve their plants and livestock by selective breeding, guessing that some sort of internal element improves desirable characteristics or suppresses unwanted ones. According to one estimate, 70 percent of the increased corn yields in the United States from 1930 to 1980 derived from selective breeding. Today genetic engineers believe that in months or years they can achieve by genetic manipulation improvements in yields that would take decades using conventional plant-breeding techniques.[11]

Given all the publicity about the biotech revolution in agriculture, those achievements need not be described in detail here. They range from inserting a bovine growth hormone into cattle to increase their milk output to genetic alterations of the reproductive cells of fish, poultry, sheep, and pigs; from creating plants that are resistant to viruses or insects to engineering crops that are impervious to certain weedkillers, allowing farmers to spray indiscriminately; from creating faster-growing tropical crops like bamboo to experiments to produce plants that would fix their own nitrogen, thereby reducing the need for chemical-based nitrogen.[12]* Such breakthroughs, when presented by the popular media, all too often suggest that we have reached another watershed in technology and productivity, with beneficial results to all.

As will be argued in the rest of this chapter, such a conclusion is naive. Biotechnology is by no means a menace, but it will produce winners and losers, as all earlier technology-driven revolutions have done.

Some of the concerns about this new technology have less to do with its economic impacts than with health and environmental issues. Hogs into which growth hormones have been inserted are subject to gastric ulcers, arthritis, dermatitis, and other diseases, which makes them not only unappealing but possibly dangerous for human consumption.[13] Herbicide-resistant crops could increase the indiscriminate spraying of "designer" herbicides, which will then be carried away in the atmosphere or water drainage system. Moreover, if weeds and pests develop a resistance to these new biological enemies—as they have done to many chemical agents—the biotech companies will have to invent improved variants, thereby producing a "treadmill" in their effort to subdue nature.

*As will be evident from the rest of this chapter, the time horizon for the commercial applications of these inventions varies enormously. Some are in use now. Others are merely prototypes, and it will be years before they are fully ready *and* receive governmental approval.

There is also danger, scientists warn, in the increasing genetic uniformity of key plants. Traditional farmers cultivated hundreds, even thousands, of types of grass seeds, potatoes, and the like. Modern farmers purchase plants redesigned by genetic engineers who blend the best attributes from various seeds into a new one to increase productivity and meet consumer taste. If, however, billions of rows of essentially identical corn are planted each year, the entire crop becomes vulnerable to a single pest or disease. In 1970, an unexpected epidemic of corn leaf blight destroyed half the crop from Florida to Texas; and as recently as 1984 a new bacterial disease forced the destruction of millions of Florida citrus trees and seedlings. The biotech revolution will enhance yields, therefore, but may also increase the risk of costly crop failures.

Another environmental concern is that biotech agriculture will encourage the *evasion* of fundamental ecological reforms. To put it bluntly, if crop species can be developed that thrive in salty soil or in hot, dry climates, will farmers ignore the sources of environmental damage and simply wait for scientists to engineer new seeds for new conditions? Would genetically modified fish, able to flourish in acidified lakes, undercut the determination to clean up air and water? Instead of dealing with global warming, or the salinization of the soil through excessive irrigation, or the too-swift reduction of the bamboo forests, scientists are inventing plants that attempt to "collaborate" with the environmental changes that human activities are causing. Rather than encouraging farmers to work *with* nature, environmentalists protest, high-yield agriculture has now incorporated biotechnology into its arsenal of weapons, without confronting the larger question of ecological damage.[14] Ironically, a counterargument has been put that because natural habitats for wild plants are disappearing so fast, it is becoming more necessary to develop alternative sources in the laboratory[15]—suggesting that as population pressures erode rain forests and other plant habitats, the greater will be humankind's reliance upon laboratory-based rather than natural produce.

. . .

The potential economic impacts of biotechnology are critically important, both for farming in general and for North-South relations. The new technology is occurring at a time when global agriculture is facing two very different—indeed, contradictory—structural crises. The rich countries suffer from overproduction; the poorest suffer from too little production. This imbalance is nothing new, and the differences between food-surplus and food-deficit peoples were historically one of the earliest and greatest stimuli to international trade. What *is* new is the sheer size of the imbalances, and of the populations affected by them.

Also new—and very different from the gentleman farmers who were responsible for the Agricultural Revolution in Malthus's time—is the existence of large agrichemical and biotech corporations, racing to offer new products. Like multinational companies in other fields, they see their task as bringing new goods to a world market, without worrying about the regional impacts—and social consequences—of this further stage in the product cycle.[16] Because they compete with one another, these companies prefer to shroud their research in secrecy and restrict its use by patents, which is a major difference from the green revolution of the 1960s, in which the technological breakthroughs were created in the public sector—like the UN-funded International Potato Center in Peru—and access to them was relatively unproblematic.[17] In denying their knowledge to rivals in the developed world—or requiring them to pay a fee for its use—the biotech industry is making it more difficult for the developing world to acquire those research techniques.

For large companies engaged in biotech research, the future looks extraordinarily attractive; a totally new industry is emerging as the lines begin to blur between farmers, seed growers, fertilizer companies, food-processing plants, and the other distinct parts of the process of getting cereals and livestock from the farm to the kitchen table. This vertical integration among biotech corporations is qualitatively different from previous types of integration. Chemical companies are now able not only to grow their own feedstocks from patented microbes or seeds, but also to use biotech for food processing. DNA has been described as a new corporate resource that can be patented and owned, designed in the laboratory, and used to replace raw materials; it also can reduce labor costs, circumvent erratic variables like weather, and produce large numbers of scarce materials cheaply. It possesses a language common to chemistry, pharmacology, energy, food, and agriculture, and can be used broadly and efficiently by corporations involved in many fields of high-value-added biological and chemical research.[18]

Precisely because the range of biotech applications is so vast, it is difficult to think through its larger consequences. What needs to be kept in mind, however, is the distinction between biotechnology which enhances food output *in the field,* and the newer science which is creating synthetic products *in vitro,* in the laboratory. Both have profound implications, but it is the latter—obviously, still very experimental and regarded by many scientists as being a long way off—which could bring the more serious consequences.

Like the steam engine and electricity, biotechnology seems likely to introduce a new historical era and greatly change the way people live. It offers new products and improved ways of creating existing ones. It opens new markets, reduces the costs of many manufactures and services, and might alter the pattern of international trade. It could change the way national economies are structured, how investment capital is allocated, and the spectrum of scientific knowledge. It will create many new jobs and eliminate many traditional ones.

And the latter effect is, of course, a major problem for global society and employment. Land, natural resources, and labor have been regarded for millennia as the chief "factors" of economic production, but this is becoming less true as mankind depends increasingly upon service industries, laboratories, and automated factories. Given the need to increase food production *and* the existence of powerful forces embracing the new technology, the biotech movement is unlikely to be halted. But we need to think through the consequent "trivialization" of agriculture, and the possibility that crops will no longer be grown naturally outdoors, anxiously cared for by millions of independent peasants and farmers: that instead they will be the biomass feedstocks for downstream processing by the same companies that designed the seeds and embryos to begin with.[19] To the consumer, biogenetically manufactured food may taste the same; indeed, it will be genetically instructed to taste that way. To the farmers of the world, however, such a revolution in food production will be viewed differently. Like the handloom weavers or coach builders of the nineteenth century, they are threatened with redundancy.

In the developed world, biotech farming is likely to exacerbate commercial relations among the big three trading blocs. While Japan is a food importer, the United States and the European Community have large agricultural surpluses. All three blocs provide subsidies to their farming sectors and quarrel among themselves over protectionism. Although farming is an inherently economic issue, that is not the whole story. Self-sufficiency in agriculture is frequently justified by reasons of national security (e.g., in France), or by a cultural attachment to a particular home-grown crop (e.g., rice in Japan). In all cases, there is a belief—by no means confined to residents of the countryside—that family and village farming represent continuity, stability, and closeness to nature that ought to be protected in a world of bewildering change.

But economic interests also influence the politics of farming in the developed world. Although the percentage of the population engaged in agriculture is not large in developed countries—3 percent in the United States, 4.8 percent in (West) Germany, 2.1 percent in Britain, 6.7 percent in France, 8 percent in Japan, 9.1 percent in Italy—farming lobbies remain enormously influential. From Wisconsin to Normandy, from Upper Bavaria to Kyushu, politicians fear they have little prospect of reelection if they are not seen to be protecting local farmers. Income and price supports given to growers in the industrial countries amount to about $250 billion each year.

Because farmers form such a differentiated industry, their attitudes to the biotech revolution are mixed. Some, chiefly larger operations, have embraced the package of products offered by biotech companies, whereas small farmers have fought against the trend or have only selectively adopted the new technology. National differences also count. Because of the United States' more relaxed policy toward biotech inventions, isoglucose took over one third of the American sugar market within ten years. By contrast, the European Community, traditionally more protectionist in agriculture, erected strict quotas for isoglucose in 1979; had it been allowed to penetrate the market in Europe to the extent it did in America, it is calculated that a substitution of

2.8 million tons of sugar would have resulted, equal to the entire sugar-beet acreage of West Germany.[20]

A second example concerns the introduction of the bovine growth hormone, which pits four of the largest companies in this field—Monsanto, Upjohn, Eli Lilly, and American Cyanamid—against American dairy farmers, or rather against *some* dairy farmers. Should the drug be widely adopted, the number of cows needed to meet America's milk requirements would likely drop from 10.8 million to 7.5 million by the year 2000 and the number of commercial dairy farms would be halved.[21] But while Wisconsin and Minnesota have banned the use of bovine growth hormone, Vermont has approved its use, which raises the issue of a differentiated response to new technology, something not, of course, confined to agriculture.[22] What if certain states or countries encourage new methods while others oppose them? One consequence, in the age of multinational corporations, will be that companies transfer their R&D efforts—and the attendant flow of young scientific talent—to hospitable countries; already, for example, major German pharmaceutical firms have chosen to locate their DNA research in the United States because of restrictions in Germany itself.[23]

Among farming communities in the developed world there exists—understandably—a deep anxiety about the possibility of *in vitro* laboratory production of basic items of food. It is one thing to have a genetically engineered tomato that is pest-resistant or doesn't go soft quickly; it is another to learn that some biotech firms may be creating *in vitro* tomato pulp, orange juice, apple sauce, and tobacco that don't have to be farmed at all. Even if this research is merely experimental at present and faces the obstacle of large production costs, the implications of replacing the traditional citrus or tobacco industry with synthetic products are so enormous—affecting growers, truckers, perhaps even the large foodstore companies themselves*—that this development, when it eventually occurs, might be heavily resisted.[24]

Nevertheless, it could be that richer nations with food deficits will embrace the biotech revolution to save foreign exchange on imported agricultural goods, whereas food-surplus countries will restrict the

*The argument here being that some of the *in vitro* produce could come from a relatively small biotech company, thus threatening the existing operations of large food-processing and foodstore firms.

technology out of deference to their farming constituencies. Here, of course, the contrast between Japan's position and that of the United States and Europe could not be more marked; Japan's difficult geography is exactly the sort of terrain that crop biotechnology is designed to enhance, while animal growth hormones would benefit Japan's consumers—now moving more toward a meat diet—and contribute to national self-sufficiency in food. This could be why Japanese ministries are seeking to eliminate the millions of inefficient, part-time farmers on the one hand yet encouraging massive investments in biotechnology (including buy-outs of or joint ventures with American companies) on the other.[25]

Such a differentiated response could lead to further tensions over agricultural trade, as food exporting countries like Australia and the United States find that their produce, while needed by developing countries unable to pay for it, is not required by rich nations increasingly able to create their own biotech substitutes at home. Japanese-American relations, already soured by other commercial quarrels, would only worsen if Japan were no longer a major market for American farm exports.

It could also lead to the emergence of two biotechnological "regimes" in the world, in one of which genetic engineering was encouraged and in the other restricted. As suggested above, industry and investment would move to those areas where the opportunity for making new products was not prevented. Thus, while inhabitants of the first regime struggled to deal with the dislocating effects of technological change, those in the second would anxiously debate whether they were going to be left behind as the rest of the world embraced a new technological paradigm.[26]

In addition, the widespread acceptance of biotech farming even of the nonlaboratory-based sort may exacerbate North-South relations. Were innovative techniques to enhance production of agricultural goods made by developing countries, which then attempted to increase food exports to consumers in the industrial democracies, farmers in the developed world would feel even more threatened than they do now. The labor costs of raising beef or growing fruit in Brazil are surely lower than in Kansas or Bavaria; but if depressed world food prices made many farmers redundant in richer countries, they would regard developing world competitors with as much hostility as industrial workers who discover that the local factory is being relocated to a cheap-labor country. Here again, the familiar pattern of winners and losers is in sight.

To the developing world itself, biotech agriculture offers the greatest mix of advantages and disadvantages. The gap between population increases and overall food output which has recently developed would be narrowed again if the biotech revolution works. Such a revolution could improve the caloric intake and the living standards of the poorer three-quarters of the world's population and would permit growing in areas of the developing world where the soil is too dry, too shallow, or too high in chemical residues like salt to allow traditional farming. For example, the invention of a hybrid banana that resists black sigatoka disease could have a swift local effect in parts of Africa, where bananas are a staple crop. Biotechnology could also offset environmental damage, if plentiful food supplies reduced today's pressures upon marginal land. Above all, it could remove the "Malthusian trap" confronting poorer societies.

Furthermore, developing countries and their scientists can make substantial contributions in biotechnology, something that is much less likely in robotics or global finance. Many biotech projects are much more research-intensive than capital-intensive, as in the case of Vietnamese farmers who profitably adapted French tissue-culture technology by propagating potato plants from tissue ordered from the International Potato Center.[27]

Even in expensive biotech fields, developing countries have committed funds and personnel. China and India have undertaken the most advanced use of biogas energy sources. There are also joint ventures with companies in the developed world, such as a project between China and International Embryos to boost dairy cattle using embryo transfers, or a French–Costa Rican initiative to turn some 140,000 tons of waste bananas each year into animal feed. Joint ventures and collaborations are also taking place among developing countries, independently of Western assistance.[28] All this is piecemeal and incremental, but the results can add up.

Yet biotechnology also challenges the developing world's chances of improving its relative economic position. DNA-related research—genetic engineering—offers the best prospect of raising overall food output, but it is very costly and is undertaken almost exclusively by agrichemical and biotech companies in the developed world. The promises of enhanced milk yields from the bovine growth hormone are not practical for most livestock owners in poor countries, because the treatment requires skilled technicians and costs as much per year as many people spend on food. In addition, treated animals require large, high-quality, consistent rations of feed and must be given frequent injections, which is unlikely in societies where vaccination of human beings against disease is still far from routine.[29] Herbicides make economic sense in high-capital agriculture and when labor costs are steep, but would be too expensive in lands where labor is abundant and cheap.

Yet even if farmers in developing countries *were* able to afford the newer methods of biotech farming, they would become dependent—like many of their equivalents in the developed world—upon Western corporations for the necessary hormones, seeds, fertilizers, and herbicides. In the words of one critic, the "gene revolution" in the developing world, should it occur, will probably involve extracting genetic resources from less developed countries, incorporating those resources into commercial plant and animal varieties in company laboratories, and later reselling the improved varieties to the less developed countries for a considerable profit.[30] Already there are heated charges that the developing world's genetic resources are being ransacked by the "biological imperialism" of large corporations.[31]

Finally, the possibility of an *in vitro* revolution increasingly permits such companies to produce in their laboratories crops traditionally grown in developing countries. Efforts are now under way not merely to improve the genetic quality of tropical foodstuffs for Western consumers—cocoa, palm oil, vanillin, and sugar—but also to find laboratory substitutes. Such substitutes would drastically reduce major sources of export income for the developing world, and threaten employment just as more and more fifteen-to-twenty-year-olds are looking for work. For example, sugarcane has been replaced by isoglucose or other super-sweeteners, yet the natural product provides a livelihood for millions of inhabitants of the developing world. Vanilla, a major export of Madagascar (per capita GNP $280), can be made by chemists. Barbasco, a plant which produces steroids, was once grown extensively in Mexico but is now manufactured by a chemical process. The export of coconut oil, upon which one-quarter of the Philippine population is at least partially dependent, is threatened with replacement by genetically engineered soybean or rapeseed. It is bad enough for a developing country to be dependent upon a monocultural export like cocoa or sugar, the prices of which fluctuate sharply, but it will be far worse if such produce is no longer needed by foreign consumers who can obtain it from domestic laboratories. The *in vitro* production of rubber, were it to become a reality, could throw an estimated 16 million people out of work in Malaysia, Indonesia, and other rubber-growing countries—with obvious implications for their political stability.[32]

Over the longer term, then, the biotech revolution potentially implies a significant relocation of agricultural production (or its substitutes) out of the developing world, worsening its trading position, indebtedness, and general dependence upon richer countries. Moreover, even if developing countries overcame all the obstacles (lack of laboratories, scientists, supply systems, patented information) and were able to develop their own *in vitro* production, millions of agricultural jobs would be at risk, with mass redundancies provoking a peasant backlash.[33]

With the experts divided in their forecasts, there is clearly great uncertainty about the outcome of the leapfrog race between population growth and agricultural production. The global imbalances in diet and health, bad as they are now, may, as many expect, get much worse. It is also possible that because of new technologies, agriculture stands on the verge of another great advance in productivity which will contradict the prophecies of the doomsters.[34] But even if that is true, the cornucopia will not necessarily reach all who need feeding, while millions of traditional farmers—in developed as well as developing countries—will be hurt as new techniques replace old ways. Whatever the consequences of an expanding world population, farming as we know it seems on its way out.

Paradoxically, then, biotech offers the prospect of both easing *and* complicating the global dilemma. There is no doubt that the world needs continued increases in agricultural productivity. Just as the world could not feed itself today with the farming methods of the 1940s, so farmers can hardly expect to meet the increased global demand in thirty or forty years' time with their present techniques of producing food. Without another agricultural revolution, the fate of the peoples of the developing world especially looks grim. This is why biotechnology, despite all the reservations discussed above, seems such an attractive solution and is clearly poised for further advances; the genie is now out of the bottle and affecting human life in all sorts of ways. What seems much less clear is whether global society can handle the economic and social consequences of a large-scale switch to biotech farming and food processing. On present evidence, that doesn't look likely.

5

ROBOTICS, AUTOMATION, AND A NEW INDUSTRIAL REVOLUTION

STEAM-DRIVEN MANUFACTURE, WHICH began to spread across northern and central England in the late eighteenth and early nineteenth centuries, naturally attracted the attention of many foreigners. Displaying fascination, enthusiasm, and sometimes apprehension, European and American visitors observed the brave new world of industrial production in which steam engines converted heat into work through machines. What impressed people about these machines was that they were "rapid, regular, precise, tireless."[1] Provided the supply of coal was maintained and the machines kept in order, they never flagged in the way that human beings, oxen, and horses did when their "animate" energy was exhausted. Machines could work all day, and through the night; they could work nonstop for weeks, if necessary.

But the real significance of the Industrial Revolution—and the reason observers were so awed by it—was that it placed these steam-driven machines and their human attendants within a *factory system.* Hitherto, most forms of manufacture were decentralized, house-based activities, involving everything from urban candlestick makers to rural handloom weavers, usually paid by piecework. Specialist crafts, from potters to haberdashers, were similarly arranged. Even the largest projects—building a warship, or a palace—were in a way idiosyncratic, irregular enterprises, subject to various interruptions. In a factory system, however, workers were assembled together and required to labor in a standardized fashion to a rhythm *set by the machines*; they worked in fixed "shifts" of ten or twelve or more hours, and were paid an hourly rate. Because the machines' requirements were supreme, the laborers had to live nearby, in employer-provided row houses. The factory system thus begat an urban proletariat, the succeeding generations of which knew less and less of their forebears' preindustrial way of life.

It is easy to understand why foreign observers viewed the new manufacturing with apprehension as well as fascination. The Industrial Revolution clearly enhanced the power of Great Britain, especially during the Revolutionary and Napoleonic wars, when booming exports sustained the coalition forces in their epic struggle against France.[2] A country capable of imitating the British system would also enjoy a relative rise in productivity and national power, whereas states unable to industrialize would be hurt. Industrialization thus gave a fresh twist to the age-old competition among the Great Powers.

A second and larger reason for apprehension was concern about the effects of industrialization upon one's own society. The clanking, steaming new machines might be marvels to watch, but it was clear that working in a factory was hell—not just because of unhealthy conditions, but because of the strict regimen of work. Could the preindustrial inhabitants of the Rhineland or Silesia be turned into a city-dwelling proletariat without inviting social convulsions? Worse still, how would one deal with the mass of craftsmen, handloom weavers, and the like who lost their jobs to the factory system, or influential guilds fighting hard against their redundancy?[3] To fail to match English practices was problem enough; to imitate them would mean profound changes in the way one lived, worked, and earned one's keep.

This dilemma is worth recalling because, two centuries later, we may be on the brink of another revolutionary change in how industrial goods are made—a change led this time not by England but by Japan, involving the replacement of human beings in the factory by robots and other automated equipment. For two hundred years, manufacture and assembly have been amended in all sorts of ways; but whatever the innovations of Taylor and Ford, or "just-in-time" production, the key element was human beings coming together in a place of work. Now we are witnessing a technology-driven revolution which breaks from that process; by replacing factory workers with robots to increase productivity, automation takes more and more human beings *out* of the factory until perhaps only a few supervising engineers remain. If that aim is achieved, the wheel will have come full circle. The industrial "serfs" of the factory system, whose working conditions appalled foreign observers in the England of the 1820s, will finally have been replaced by robots, whose linguistic root is the Czech word for serf, *robotnik.*[4]

Like steam power itself, robotics has many applications, of varying complexity. Apart from simple devices not controlled by a computer and considering only *programmable* machines, there are immense differences of sophistication among industrial robots, field robots, and intelligent robots. The first are fixed machines with manipulators primed to do various tasks automatically, such as spot welding or spray painting. Field robots, by contrast, are designed to operate in an unstructured environment and possess sensors to allow them to move around, respond to an obstacle, and so on; they are often used in operations too difficult or hazardous for human beings, such as mining, fire fighting, treating a contaminated plant, and undersea work; some are steered by teleoperated remote control. Finally, there is the new, exciting field of third-generation intelligent robots, experimental computerized machines designed to use artificial intelligence (the so-called knowledge-based systems) to solve problems as human beings do.[5]

Obviously, the more complex and expensive the task, the further robots are from actual replacement of human beings. The majority of industrial robots are employed in automobile plants—cutting pieces of metal, spot welding, painting—since that industry is the classic example of a factory-line production and assembly system requiring its workers to perform uniform, repetitive movements, like automata.[6] The same is true for the assembly of the components of a radio or CD player. Jobs needing independent actions, like schoolteaching or police work, are not going to be accomplished by machines. Lawyers, doctors, and professors will ensure that automatic emulation will not happen in their fields.

Although most of this chapter discusses the potential impact of industrial robots, it is worth noting that the use of field robots and intelligent robots is also influenced by economic consideration. In the United States, where the costs of long-term medical care are spiraling upward, hospitals are examining the purchase of robots able to move specimens in a laboratory, decontaminate surgical instruments, deliver medications from the pharmacy, and so on.[7] Again, because it will take hundreds of billions of dollars to clean hazardous waste across America, robots are now being recruited; field robots were developed to inspect, take samples from, and clean up the contaminated Three Mile Island plant after its 1979 accident. Other machines have been created for space exploration, for deep-sea mining, and even to act as "sentry robots" equipped with remote-imaging and intruder-detection sensors as well as alarm/communications systems.[8]

In the United States and Europe, most attention has focused upon exotic robotics: machines that can traverse the moon's surface, or play chess. While that research is very important, the fascination for robots in the Jules Verne tradition distracts from the automation of the *manufacturing* industry, to achieve improvements in efficiency and productivity. Industrial robots for assembly or metal-cutting may seem less interesting than robots that play chess, but their long-term effects—economic, demographic, and upon shares of world output—promise to be more significant.

Before considering those effects, however, we should understand why some industrial societies have embraced the new machines while others have not. Why, especially, has Japan become the world leader in robotics whereas the United States—which created much of the original technology and whose scientists still provide new ideas for the future of robotics—has allowed its share of this industry to be eroded? At first sight, Japan's superiority over America in robotics is a further example of what has occurred in related industries such as microprocessors, computers, and electrical goods. Japan possesses many strengths: a highly educated work force, a long-term commitment to develop key industries, easily available capital at low interest rates, high levels of R&D investment, masses of engineers, and a dedication to top-quality design and efficient production. Cutthroat competition among firms in Japan's automobile and electrical-goods industries drove them to invest in new machines to increase productivity; a government-encouraged leasing company (JAROL) offered advice and machines at low cost; and the robots were carefully integrated into a factory culture already practicing "just-in-time" production techniques.[9]

In the United States, conditions were far less favorable, despite the early breakthroughs achieved by companies such as Unimation and Cincinnati Milacron. The government's hands-off policy toward business meant that no help came from that source. No equivalent body existed to do JAROL's work of leasing, publicizing, and advising upon the use of robots. The costs of raising capital in America were greater than in Japan or Germany, and American companies were under pressure from Wall Street to keep profits high (even if this meant investing less). After initial enthusiasm in automated assembly by the major automobile companies, new investment in manufacturing as a whole fell sharply in the mid to late 1980s.[10] The result was a drastic shakeout of the robotics industry; more than half the fifty or so companies making robots in 1985 disappeared by 1990.[11] Those left were acquired by or forced to merge with foreign companies. By 1991 no independent American robotics manufacturers were left.

While a similar tale can be told of other American industries, the different response of Japan and America to robotics was heavily influenced by a special factor: demography. The chief reason for Japan's commitment to automation has been a serious labor shortage, which existed as long ago as the mid-1960s and threatened to reduce Japan's export-led boom. Demographic changes since then—not to mention those to come—are significantly altering the number of Japanese available for manufacturing work. The economic advantages of employing industrial robots are now overwhelming, as the cost of a robot has decreased sharply and the time needed for a return on investment has shrunk accordingly. "If a robot replaces one worker for one shift per day, the payout is roughly four years. If a robot is used for two shifts, it will pay for itself in two years, and if used round the clock, in just over one year."[12]

Yet automated production could not have occurred so easily without the special structure of Japanese industry and the state of management-labor relations. Most large companies in Japan have a policy of lifetime employment, so that a worker whose job has been taken over by a robot will not be fired, but retrained and relocated inside the firm or in related companies within these industrial conglomerates. Moreover, robots were initially deployed in repetitive and/or dangerous jobs, such as cutting metal, spot welding, painting, and transporting spare parts, which relieved workers of unpleasant tasks *and* promised enhanced productivity to be reflected in annual bonuses. Finally, Japanese trade unions traditionally work with management to enhance quality control and ensure that their company does better than its rivals. If robots helped Toyota or Kawasaki Heavy Industries to crush the competition, they would be warmly welcomed.

Not only did Japanese industry ease its labor shortages without destroying the social peace, it also avoided the path followed by German firms—or, for that matter, companies in New York and California—of importing large numbers of guest workers. Japan's commitment to its racial homogeneity was thus preserved, since mechanical "serfs" could do the work instead, while Japanese workers were retrained for other tasks. Whatever migration occurs from South to North in the future, therefore, Japan plans to be much less affected than the United States and Europe while still ensuring its industrial competitiveness.

The contrast with the American experience could not be more marked. Although rising labor costs led U.S. automobile companies to invest in robots during the early 1980s, America has no overall labor shortage; in addition, average wages now are considerably less than those in Japan. Moreover, robots often proved disappointing. To make them work effectively requires significant changes in factory layout and in redesigning products so that robots can handle them more easily. The more sophisticated the robot, the more redesign is required, so that many American firms eventually chose to retain the older methods—and the workers—and to sell off their new machines. In other words, there was no compelling demographic reason for companies to embrace robotics, even if the result was smaller productivity increases in the United States than in Japan.

Finally, American unions see robots as a threat to employment, suspicions well justified, for American industry does not usually retrain workers whose jobs have been made redundant. Following the 1981–82 recession, for example, as many as 2 million Americans with outdated skills lost their jobs. In cities like Pittsburgh, where one might imagine that robots would be welcomed to improve productivity, hundreds of thousands of skilled workers were fired as the 1980s unfolded.[13] While machines that replaced such arduous work as welding were tolerated, in general American labor has opposed robots—and the companies know it.

Therefore, the dominant place in robotics is now firmly occupied by Japan, as shown in Table 2.

Table 2. World Industrial Robot Population, End of 1988[14]

Japan	176,000
Western Europe	48,000
USA	33,000
Eastern Europe, Southeast Asia, rest of world	23,000
Total	280,000

Because Japan has spent much more than any other country on automation since 1988, its lead has grown further. With only 0.3 percent of the world's land and 2.5 percent of its population, it possessed around 65 or 70 percent of the world's industrial robots,[15] recalling that other island country, mid-Victorian Britain, which produced five-sevenths of the world's steel and half its iron.

How significant are the productivity increases coming from automation? A few years ago Nissan upgraded its automobile plants in the Tokyo area with a highly sophisticated method of assembly, using robots. Formerly it took eleven months and cost Nissan 4 billion yen to retool its body assembly for a new car model; now it takes a quarter the time and costs about a third as much[16]—which is the chief reason that Japanese auto productivity continues to rise. Perhaps the famous FANUC manufacturing plant near Mount Fuji comes closest to representing the "factory of the future." Before 1982, a work force of 108 people and thirty-two robots produced about six thousand spindle motors and servo motors each month. After a radical redesign and further automation of the factory, it now employs only sixty people and has 101 robots to produce ten thousand servo motors a month—a *threefold* improvement in productivity which handsomely repays the initial investment. Yet even that is regarded merely as an interim step toward full automation by FANUC's management.[17]

Although the increases in productivity are incremental, they become significant over time, producing not only a steady flow of orders for the Japanese robotics industry, but also a cumulative increase in the quality and efficiency of Japanese manufacturing. Robots do not require heating or air-conditioning; they can work in the dark, and save electricity; they do not become sloppy or tired. They contribute to a greater flexibility in manufacturing, since they can be reprogrammed for different tasks or to assemble different models. Because their movements are perfectly controlled, they do not waste materials—robot spray painters, for example, use up to 30 percent less paint than human workers.

All this suggests that we may be witnessing the beginnings of a new industrial revolution, involving the automation of the manufacturing process. In many ways, the similarities between the steam engine and the robot are striking. Both are a new way of making things that simultaneously reduces the physical efforts of workers *and* enhances overall productivity; a process that creates new jobs and eliminates many others; and a stimulus to social change as well as to new definitions of work.[18] Like the steam engine, robotics affect international competitiveness, raising the per capita output of nations that invest heavily in the newer technology and weakening the long-term relative position of those unable to do the same.

Another similarity seems to be the strong impression made upon visitors who witness the new technology for the first time. Like aghast observers at Britain's early steam-driven factories, foreign visitors* to the FANUC automated factory appear awed by the sight of robots moving around inside the building, clicking and whirring as they solder circuit boards, examining their work with camera eyes, passing items from one robot to another, work which continues after dark, when the lights are dimmed.[19] Both steam engine and robot, people could sense, brought promise and peril to manufacturing.

Since robotics is still in its early stages and heavily concentrated in one country, less attention has been paid to its implications for developed and developing nations in (say) thirty years' time than has been devoted

*About two thousand people a month visit the FANUC factories, which must make it one of the most popular industrial sights in the world.

to biotech or demographic change. Despite the publicity given to FANUC's wonder robots, the use of robotics in Japanese manufacturing is undramatic and incremental as factory after factory installs additional machines. It is also much less headline-catching than breakthroughs in aerospace or supercomputing. Interestingly, although American industry is increasingly dependent upon Japanese robots, few politicians denounce this imbalance as they bemoan America's dependence on foreign-made chips or laptop computers. Even the term "robotics revolution" may be questioned by American businessmen who have had problems using them or see little advantage in the new machines when labor is relatively cheap.

Within developed nations, robotics is likely to progress most where there exists a strong "engineering culture," high per capita average living standards (and therefore high labor costs), and a shrinking pool of skilled workers because of demographic slowdown; after Japan, the leading contenders are Germany and Sweden, each with traditional strengths in machine tools, electrical engineering, and high-quality automobiles. Robotics is less likely to progress in countries where investment in manufacturing remains low, or where trade unions fear robots as job-replacers. Robotics is also unlikely to flourish in the states of the former Soviet Union, for, although the USSR claimed to possess tens of thousands of industrial robots, a top-notch robotics industry cannot function efficiently in an economy backward in computers and microprocessors. In any case, with millions of citizens of the erstwhile Soviet Union looking for work, robots are the last thing that is needed. The economics of investing in automation and a country's demographic and social structures always seem to provide the key.

Since automation increases manufacturing productivity, it adds to the relative power of companies and nations which can automate *and* handle the social consequences. In the global scramble for market shares in the three great economic zones of North America, Europe, and East Asia, robotics threatens to widen the already significant productivity gap between the Nissans and Toyotas on the one hand and the Peugeots, Fiats, and Chryslers on the other. As European bureaucrats and American car manufacturers scramble to meet East Asia's challenge in manufacturing and high technology by imposing import restrictions to give themselves a breathing space of five or ten years in which to catch up, robotics makes their task harder, perhaps impossible, so long as Japan's companies invest more than everyone else in the future. A further consequence of robotics, then, could be to shift the global economic balances away from Britain, France, Italy, and the United States and toward Japan and Germany.

If Europe's and America's responses to robotics are sporadic and hesitant, they are much better prepared to compete—at least in terms of physical and intellectual assets—than societies in the developing world. As with global finance, biotechnology, and multinationals, we are once again looking at a technology-driven revolution that could keep poorer countries at the bottom of the heap, or weaken them further.

Since a few developing countries appear to be detaching themselves from the Third World and catching up with the First,* the following discussion focuses on the fate of the really poor, overpopulated societies of South Asia, Africa, and Central America, not the NIEs of East Asia, which are in a different category. Except for Taiwan,† figures are not available on robotics in the NIEs, but they will probably reflect a more general technology indicator, such as semiconductor production. In that field, South Korea, Taiwan, Singapore, and Hong Kong are making very swift progress, since their governments have targeted electronics and computers as key industries for export-led growth. Because Japanese competitors have invested heavily in robotics—to beat the low-labor-cost products of the NIEs—that may encourage the latter to go heavily into automation. Obviously, it is not yet worthwhile in countries where wages remain low; but the explosion of workers' earnings in recent years in (say) South Korea and the steady decline in fertility rates bring automation closer.

To create its own robotics revolution, a developing country needs surplus capital, a large supply of engineers and scientists, and a labor shortage. Alas, countries in the developing world have few capital resources, and interest payments on international debts result in a net

*See Chapter 10, "Winners and Losers in the Developing World."

†In 1988, Taiwan possessed 682 industrial robots, which was more than European states such as Switzerland, Austria, and Norway.

outflow of capital each year. They also have relatively few engineers and scientists.[20] Finally, since their major problem is a massive surplus of labor, there is no economic or social rationale—from the viewpoint of their troubled governments, at least—in encouraging *labor-saving* systems of manufacture.

If there is little prospect that an indigenous robotics industry will arise in the developing world, might multinational companies establish automated manufacturing in those countries to obtain low-cost production? After all, some of the less developed and most populous countries of Asia—Indonesia, Thailand, Malaysia, China itself—have experienced rapid industrialization, faster than everywhere else in the world, and now export many manufactured goods. This economic growth is due to the relocation of manufacturing to those countries by firms like Fujitsu and Motorola, to take advantage of lower labor costs. Components of, say, a radio or record player are sent to a company's plant in Southeast Asia, where it is assembled and packaged for re-export. Such work improves the developing country's balance of payments, although it also creates unusual employment patterns, since these electronics companies employ almost entirely unskilled and semiskilled female workers.[21] The problem of young, frustrated men without work remains, and may be compounded. Moreover, such an employment structure creates little incentive for the training of native scientists and engineers.

Nevertheless, industrialization does bring *overall* benefits to Southeast Asia—export-led growth, a higher standard of living, a rising number of consumers of manufactures—especially when compared with Africa or the Middle East, where investment by multinational companies is negligible. Even if these developing countries have been "relegated to assembling pieces of high-tech equipment largely for consumption in industrial countries,"[22] that is better than no industrial employment at all.

But what prospect is there of a move by multinationals to *automated* assembly, instead of low-labor-cost assembly, in their developing world plants? Given the structure of the robotics industry, that seems unlikely at present, since it would require a skilled work force (systems engineers, trained maintenance crew), which most developing countries do not have; it would also require adequate infrastructure, power supplies, telecommunications, water, roads, and ports, which many poorer countries desperately lack. In any case, why invest in automated assembly in (say) Indonesia if it retains its cheap labor advantage? Moreover, even if automation did occur—despite all the problems noted above—it would then pose the same threat to local factory employment as it does in other parts of the world.

The final irony—and an awful future possibility—is that low-labor assembly plants established by foreign companies in Southeast Asia may one day be undermined by an intensification of the robotics revolution in Japan. This might seem farfetched at the moment, although at least one writer on "high technology and international labor markets" has argued that labor-saving technology, intensively used, could make the manufacturing of steel, heavy equipment, machines, and even textiles competitive again in industrial countries.[23]

As one indicator of how robotics might permit manufacturing to return to a developed country—or, in this case, not abandon it—consider the remarkable turnaround achieved by a single radio-cassette-recorder factory in Sendai, Japan, in 1985. Suffering from the rise in the value of the yen, acute labor shortages at home, and fierce competition from low-labor competitors in Southeast Asia, the company was in deep trouble. Rejecting the idea of relocating production to cheaper countries, the management embarked upon massive automation—the installation of no fewer than 850 industrial robots. Within a short while, the assembly line required only sixteen workers to reach full production compared with 340 (!) before automation, restoring the company's competitiveness even against Southeast Asian rivals whose wages were a fraction of those in Japan.[24] The "serfs" in the low-labor assembly plants abroad were outbid by automated "serfs" at home. If that was already possible in the mid-1980s, what degree of manufacturing efficiency might the robotics revolution achieve by 2020?

Whether or not the members of the Association of Southeast Asian Nations that are the home of foreign-owned assembly plants will escape from this challenge is impossible to judge at present; probably the more adept of them will. The main point is that multinational corporations in certain industries, already switching production from one country to another according to differentiated labor costs, will gain the further advantage of assessing whether developing-world wages are greater or less than the robot's "costs" in the automated factory back home. After all, the theory of the borderless world encourages managers to be constantly weighing the relative advantage of production in one part of the globe as opposed to others.[25] With the robotics revolution, Fujitsu assembly plants abroad might one day return to Japan and Motorola factories to America. In any event, such decisions will not be made by developing countries or their governments.

The mass replacement of factory workers will not happen overnight. Just as it took decades for the early steam engines to advance from mere curiosities and "wonder machines" to the center of the manufacturing process, so it may take a generation or more before the robotics revolution makes its full impact; and there is always the increase in cheap labor supplies to slow the pace of automation in many societies. Nevertheless, the longer-term implications are disturbing and threaten to exacerbate the global dilemma. If the biotech revolution can make redundant certain forms of farming, the robotics revolution could eliminate many types of factory-assembly and manufacturing jobs. In both cases, multinational companies become the beneficiaries of the reduced value of land and labor. Marvelous though the technologies behind the new agricultural and industrial revolutions may be, they neither offer solutions to the global demographic crisis nor bridge the gap between North and South. For all the difficulties it faced, Malthus's England perhaps had an easier time of it.

6

THE DANGERS TO OUR NATURAL ENVIRONMENT

WHY SHOULD AFFLUENT SOCIETIES IN the northern hemisphere care about the population explosion in the developing world and the spread of mass poverty there? Of what practical concern is it to the farmers of Kansas or the housewives of Tokyo—who have their own problems—that Ethiopians starve and Bangladeshis are overwhelmed by floods? After all, enormous gaps have existed between rich and poor since at least the time of the pharaohs, and famines and natural disasters are common to all centuries. If the sight of human distress on television causes individuals to donate to relief agencies, that is a nice thing; but why should more be done, if that implies changes in one's own prosperity and life-style?

Since poverty has always existed yet never persuaded the rich to curb their life-styles in favor of the poor, it would (alas) be unrealistic to reply that the North's affluent societies should do more because global malnutrition is an affront to human dignity; it was ever so. More practical reasons are needed to show why existing aid and relief are insufficient. One was already given in Chapter 2, that the demographic imbalance between poor and rich societies is producing a migratory flood from the former to the latter, and today's disturbing social and racial reactions to that may be small compared with what happens in a world of 8 to 10 billion people.

During the past decade or so, a second practical answer has emerged to the question "Why should rich societies care about the fate of far-off poor peoples?" It is that economic activities in the developing world, whether the work of billions of peasant farmers or of emerging factory enterprises, are adding to the damage to the world's ecosystem. Because the earth's thin film of life is entire and interconnected, damage inflicted upon the atmosphere by activity in the tropics could have serious effects not just locally but everywhere. The environmental issue, like the threat of mass migration, means that—perhaps for the first time—what the South does can hurt the North.

There is, of course, nothing new in the damage human beings inflict upon their environment and the suffering that follows. In the crowded cities of early-modern Europe—and in the even more crowded cities of Asia—garbage was thrown into the streets, rivers were polluted, and deaths by disease multiplied. Entire forests were cut down to provide fuel, housing, ships, so that the ecology of a whole region, and people's livelihoods in it, steadily altered. The burning of coal and brown coal (lignite), especially by early industry, dirtied the atmosphere and worsened people's health; in one week of December 1873, a great London "smog" killed an estimated seven hundred people with respiratory problems. Human beings have built dams, drained wetlands, diverted rivers, cleared bush and scrublands, and permitted overgrazing of grasslands since ancient times.

But the environmental crisis we now confront is quantitatively and qualitatively different from anything before, simply because so many people have been inflicting damage on the world's ecosystem during the present century that the system as a whole—not simply its various parts—may be in danger. Around 1900, the world was home to about 1.6 billion people. In some regions in the northern hemisphere, where coal was burned as the chief source of energy, pollution and environmental damage were common. Sprawling industrial conurbations in northern England and the Midlands, the Ruhr region, New York, Pittsburgh, and elsewhere emitted a pall of smoke, soot, and ash; salmon and trout had long abandoned the local rivers; buildings bore a coat of grimy soot while their inhabitants spluttered and choked in the foul air around them. Nevertheless, these problems appeared to be local. The well-to-do could escape to their country houses or seaside resorts, where the air was fresh and the waters clean. The more energetic could take strenuous walking holidays in the Swiss Alps or the upper Hudson Valley. If they were really adventurous, they could "explore" Africa, inner Asia, the Brazilian jungle, or the East Indies and observe huge regions virtually untouched by human activity.

By the middle of this century, the world's population had risen to 2.5 billion. What was more, industrialization had increased faster, almost threefold, reaching out to many more areas: Eastern Europe, the Soviet Union, Australia, Japan, India, and other parts of Asia. Alongside the vastly increased use of coal, there occurred an even more spectacular expansion in the use of fuel oils. Thousands of aircraft and ships and millions of motor vehicles poured their emissions into the atmosphere as they drew the different parts of the world together and transported more and more people into hitherto undamaged regions. As soot and ash began to pollute the air around Indian or Brazilian ironworks, the forests in their hinterlands wilted under the human onslaught of building roads, constructing airstrips, and felling woodlands for timber and grazing. In many developing countries, mixed (and reasonably balanced) ecologies were replaced by vast swaths of monocultural production.

As we enter the 1990s, the trends have intensified; world population has more than doubled since the 1950s, yet world economic activity has more than quadrupled. The population surge in developing countries has encroached upon jungles, wetlands, and broad grazing regions, as more and more people exploit surrounding natural resources. That pressure is intensified by further industrialization in Asia and elsewhere: new factories, assembly plants, road systems, airports, and housing complexes not only reduce the amount of natural land but contribute to the demand for more energy (especially electricity) and more automobiles and trucks, infrastructure, foodstuffs, paper and packaging, cement, steel, ores, and so on. All of this increases the ecological damage: more polluted rivers and dead lakes, smog-covered cities, industrial waste, soil erosion, and devastated forests litter the earth. Since midcentury alone, it is estimated that the world has lost nearly one-fifth of the topsoil from its cropland, one-fifth of its tropical rain forests, and some tens of thousands of its plant and animal species. And each new investigation of "The Earth as Transformed by Human Action" reveals the mounting pressures.[1]

Yet while the consequences of this onslaught produce growing concern, it is difficult to see how it can be halted at the local level. Consider, for example, the efforts of a pastoralist farmer in East Africa to maintain himself and his family. Everything depends upon his livestock—*the* measure of wealth in that society—and thus upon his ability to feed his animals. Few grains or other cattle fodder are grown in the region, and in any case it would be too expensive to purchase them. Instead, these herdsmen rely upon grazing and browsing on the grasslands, which at first sight seems natural enough; however, *numbers* now make all the difference. According to the Worldwatch Institute, 238 million Africans relied on 272 million livestock in 1950, but by 1987 the human population had increased to 604 million and the livestock to 543 million. "In a continent where grain is scarce, 183 million cattle, 197 million sheep, and 163 million goats are supported almost entirely by grazing and browsing. . . . As grasslands deteriorate, soil erosion accelerates, further reducing the carrying capacity and setting in motion a self-reinforcing cycle of ecological degradation and deepening human poverty."[2] But how is this cycle to be broken? By taking away the livestock? By inviting the herdsman and his family to move to more temperate climates such as Bavaria or Maryland? Either option is, for political reasons, impossible.

Again, how does one prevent the world's tropical forests from coming under assault, not just by peasant loggers, but also by large-scale indigenous enterprises wanting to clear these woodlands for grazing and crop-growing? Some of this is done illegally, but the greater part is open. In Brazil, much recent deforestation followed government decisions to subsidize forest clearing in the Amazon region.[3] The Indonesian government, in public advertisements, explains that "because its 170 million people have the same aspirations as anyone in the United States, 20 percent of its forests must be converted to plantations to produce teak, rubber, rice, coffee, and other agricultural crops."[4] Whether the deforestation is centrally organized or the result of the individual endeavors of millions of peasants, the results are ominous. In the Himalayas, the doubling of the population in recent decades led to greatly increased demands for fuel wood, fodder, and agricultural land—which in turn caused a massive deforestation (half of the forest reserves were lost between 1950 and 1980), and then to a tremendous increase in soil erosion. It is further alleged, by indignant Indians, that this contributes to siltation and flooding among the densely populated regions down the Ganges and Brahmaputra rivers, hundreds of miles from the cause.[5]

It is also worth noting that the lands now coming under pressure are almost invariably of marginal or temporary utility—unlike the rich Midwest prairies opened in the nineteenth century. The gains are therefore problematic and short-term because of soil erosion and the limited rainfall, whereas the damage threatens to be permanent.

What does this mean globally? About one-third of the land area of the earth (deserts, paved cities) supports little biological activity, one-third is forests and savannahs, and one-third is cropland and pasture.[6] The pasture areas of the world have been shrinking since the mid-1970s as overgrazing converts them to desert; even the share of cropland is falling because of degradation and conversion to nonfarm uses (roads, towns, airstrips, etc.). Most important of all, the rain forests are being cut back at a faster pace than ever. In 1980, it was estimated that the annual rate of deforestation in the tropics was approximately 11.4 million hectares; and one much more alarming (and perhaps unreasonably large) estimate raised that total to 20.4 million hectares of tropical forest annually—equal to the size of Panama.[7]

The disappearance of tropical forests (especially in Latin America, which contains almost 60 percent of them) is of concern to environmentalists for several reasons. The first is the destruction of the way of life of many innocent tribes. It is also the case that these forests have the world's greatest store of plant and animal species by far—Panama itself has as many plant species as the whole of Europe—and the destruction of this fantastic array of biodiversity would deal a heavy blow to humankind's constant need to keep renewing (and improving) pest-resistant and productive crops.[8] Population pressure leading to deforestation would thus curb global agriculture's ability to renew itself—and to provide for the additional billions of consumers. It would also be a blow to the fecundity and fascination of life itself. And all this is happening *so quickly.* According to an alarmed appeal sent to Latin American presidents in July 1991 by Gabriel García Márquez and other distinguished signatories, "by the year 2000 three-quarters of America's tropical forests may have been felled, and 50 percent of their species lost forever. What Nature created in the course of millions of years will be destroyed by us in little more than forty years."[9]

The increasing pollution of the earth's atmosphere is a further result of population growth and a desire to increase living standards. In the planned economies of the Soviet Union and Eastern Europe, for example, the post-1945 political leadership was determined to catch up industrially with the West; hence, utmost priority was given to heavy industry—iron, steel, cement, machinery—regardless of the ecological consequences. After systematic concealment by Communist regimes, the full extent of the damage has only recently become clear. Whole areas of Poland, Czechoslovakia, and the East German provinces were enveloped for decades in a heavy blue haze from industrial emissions, streams and lakes were fishless, the Danube became a deadly sump, and the buildings of many historic towns and cities were blackened by pollution. The forests in particular suffered, as millions of trees were killed or damaged. Even if the collapse of the Communist regimes and the closing of many of the antiquated factories and steel mills will slow environmental deterioration, the resources of the new regimes are at present inadequate to clean up the mess.[10]

Similar damage occurs in parts of the developing world that are also striving to catch up. Again, there are few controls over pollution and the emphasis is upon growth rather than public health and safety. China increased its coal output more than twenty times between 1949 and 1982, while in India emissions of sulfur dioxide from coal and oil have nearly tripled since the early 1960s.[11] According to the World Health Organization, leading cities with excessive amounts of sulfur dioxide and other pollutants include New Delhi, Beijing, Teheran, and Shenyang. In Mexico City, seven out of ten newborns have excessively high lead levels in their blood. Famous monuments, like the Taj Mahal and the temples, murals, and megaliths of the Mayans, are suffering from atmospheric pollution.[12]

Agricultural and industrial development have also affected the quantity and quality of the earth's water supplies. The larger cause, once again, is the increase in global population this century from 1.6 billion to more than 5 billion, with the consequent rise in demand for water. In virtually every city in the developing world, a combination of overpopulation, the reckless pace of industrialization, and an almost complete lack of sewerage and purification plants has destroyed what were once pure waters. The rise in world population has also encouraged massive investments in irrigation. Land under irrigation doubled between 1900 and 1950 and has increased more than two-and-a-half-fold since then, to reach a global total of some 250 million hectares, much of this in developing countries where the population increase is greatest and where often great seasonal or regional variations occur in the supply of water. Nations such as China, Egypt, India, Indonesia, and Peru now rely upon irrigated land for more than half their domestic food production.[13]

Irrigation has proved a boon to millions of the world's peasants and their families, but, like the use of pesticides, the new technology also brings disadvantages. Each year, a vast amount of water—estimated at six times the annual flow of the Mississippi—is removed from the earth's rivers, streams, and underground aquifers to water crops. Over time, this has led to waterlogged and salted lands, declining and contaminated aquifers, shrinking lakes and inland seas, and the destruction of wildlife and fish habitats.[14]

Because all water contains concentrations of salt, a field heavily irrigated throughout the year will receive considerable salt additions per hectare. In India, some 20 million hectares (36 percent of all irrigated land) are estimated to have had their yields reduced due to salinization, and an additional 7 million hectares have been abandoned as salty wasteland. What was originally conceived as a method of increasing crop yields has produced a very different result.[15]

Gigantic schemes to divert the natural flow of water have also created problems. One of the most spectacular was the Soviet effort to boost agricultural output in the Central Asian republics by diverting water from the two great rivers (the Amu Darya and Syr Darya) flowing into the Aral Sea. The rewards from this action seemed clear enough; most of the Soviet cotton crop, as well as rice, fruit, and vegetables, is grown here—but the dry climate requires irrigation. After thirty years of reduced inflow, however, the Aral Sea has dropped fourteen meters and has shrunk from 67,000 to 40,000 square kilometers, losing 40 percent of its area and 60 percent (!) of its volume. Mineral concentrations, especially of salt, have tripled, killing all marine life. The exposed land is now a salty desert, in the midst of which lie the sad former coastal towns of Aralsk and Muinak.[16]

Another example is the ambitious scheme of the Saudi Arabian government to make the desert glisten with water, in order to diversify its economy and invest its oil revenues. Following hefty farm subsidies and the massive extraction of underground water, *twenty times* as much land was under cultivation in 1988 as in 1975, and wheat output had increased about *a thousandfold.* Amazingly, Saudi Arabia is now a surplus producer of wheat, eggs, and dairy products. But the water is nonrenewable from aquifers that accumulated over thousands of years. In less than a decade, this water reserve has dropped by a fifth, and according to one estimate it may be totally exhausted by the year 2007.[17]

Despite very different ideologies, then, Soviet and Saudi leaders favored modernization policies which devastated a natural resource, and called upon technology to implement their grandiose projects. This has also been true across the developing world, from India to Nigeria, where the evidence accumulates of damage inflicted upon land, air, and water by human actions. In some cases, the governments in question have begun to amend affairs: proposals have been made to try to increase water levels in the Aral Sea, despite the engineering costs and the fact that valuable farmland may lose its irrigation; and the Saudi government is rushing ahead with ever more expensive desalination programs. But few other countries in the developing world have the political power or money to alter their earlier modernization plans—unless, perhaps, as will be discussed below, as part of a larger, global bargain.

• • •

All this environmental damage in the developing world was long preceded, of course, by equally unwise measures in developed countries. The smoke hanging over today's Chinese cities and the poor health of the work force are similar to conditions in mid-nineteenth-century Manchester. As recently as 1952 a notorious London smog claimed four thousand lives and left tens of thousands ill—finally provoking the British "Clean Air Act" two years later; efforts by developed countries to control auto emissions are more recent than that. Even today, as many as 150 million people in the United States breathe air considered unhealthful by the Environmental Protection Agency. Public buildings, from U.S. Civil War memorials to the Acropolis, are being steadily eaten away. Pollutants like "acid rain" are carried by the winds from Britain and Germany into Scandinavia, or from the Midwest of the United States into Canada, where tens of thousands of lakes have become strongly acidified. And the depletion of the Arabian aquifers bears comparison with what is happening to the massive Ogallala Aquifer that stretches from Texas to South Dakota and supports one-fifth of the irrigated cropland of the United States. Its depletion has caused many farmers to take land out of irrigation, and parts of the countryside are reverting to the condition they were in before pumping began—raising serious questions about the future of this substantial regional farming economy.[18]

Despite such problems, the rise of environmentally conscious "green" movements in the developed world—whether as a distinct political party in Germany, or at least in the emergence of public pressures upon authorities by Friends of the Earth and Greenpeace—has challenged the old policies of neglect. Respected bodies like the World Resources Institute, popular annuals such as *State of the World*, countless scientific investigations into environmental change, congressional and parliamentary hearings, and reports by governmental environmental agencies have had a significant impact upon politics and legislation in this field. Rivers and buildings are being cleaned up, factory emissions are being controlled, reforestation programs are under way, overfishing is increasingly banned, chemical and nuclear wastes are being treated, and recycling of used material is much more commonplace. As a result, many towns and regions in Europe and North America are, environmentally, a lot more pleasant to inhabit than they were a quarter century ago.

May it not be possible, then, for developing countries to imitate the developed world's recent efforts to repair environmental damage? And if not, why should that bother the inhabitants of Wisconsin or Jutland? Surely, one might think, the damage inflicted on African savannahs or Chinese rivers will be felt only by the local inhabitants, not by peoples five thousand miles away who have at last decided to tidy up their own backyards. If the peoples of the developing world opt to hurt their local environments, shouldn't they be left to do so?

Clearly, the chief reasons that developing societies cannot suddenly institute "green" policies are economic and demographic. It is relatively easy for concerned Scandinavians to divert some of their high per capita income into nonnuclear electricity or cleaning up the rivers. But it is much more difficult for societies whose average incomes are a mere one-hundredth that of Sweden to find the capital and skilled personnel to implement environmentally sound policies. Since the damage is caused either by the population explosion or by industrial emissions, the only way the former could be stopped would be by halting population growth, which simply isn't going to happen in South Asia, Africa, and Central America in the near future; and the only way to check industrial emissions would be to *reverse* industrialization, which many developing societies see as their only chance to escape from their demographically driven poverty trap. If Malthus's England had to endure the early unpleasant side effects of an industrial revolution in order to become prosperous, who can ask Mexico and India to refrain from attempting the same? And who can stop them from doing it? The answer is no one, least of all an inhabitant of the developed world.

While the local and national damage inflicted by acid rain, overgrazing, and water depletion is serious enough, concerned environmentalists nowadays point to what may be the most profound threat of all over the long term: the prospect that human economic activities are creating a dangerous "greenhouse effect" of global warming, with consequences for the earth's entire ecosystem and for the way of life of rich and poor societies alike.[19] If true, then precisely because *that* sort of damage is no longer local, it would inevitably concern Wisconsin and Jutland as well as Bombay and Amazonia.

The scientific theory behind global warming is relatively straightforward and relates to that thin "film of matter" which clothes our planet. In thermodynamic terms, the earth is a closed system, meaning that no material enters or leaves it except for the sun's radiant energy; and the only processes that can occur are those in which material is changed from one form to another. For example, burning autumn's fall of leaves or using up a tank full of gasoline on a lengthy car journey does not *eliminate* that material, it merely transfers it elsewhere in a different form. If this closed system is to run indefinitely, therefore, the transformation process must ultimately constitute a closed cycle, in which material returns to its original form: new resource becomes useful matter which becomes waste which is then absorbed back into the ecosystem to become future raw material. When functioning properly, it is a beautiful and wonderful self-sustaining cycle of life.[20]

It doesn't function properly when one or more of the sequential steps in the cycle is out of balance, thus producing a bottleneck. In earlier centuries, bottlenecks usually occurred in the conversion of raw material to useful matter: population and demand for fresh resources were growing, but the inhabitants of the system were unable to meet that demand (which then led to Malthusian "checks" upon population). Later, technological breakthroughs in consequence of the scientific and industrial revolutions produced new forms of conversion—the steam engine, internal combustion, electricity—and solved that bottleneck to a large degree. It also contributed to the gathering pace of global population growth after 1750, which in turn produced our present dilemma. For the more people you need to support on earth and the better you want them to live, the faster you have to drive the transforming system: hence the enormous growth of world economic activity in recent decades, and the corresponding increase in changing raw resources into useful matter. The problem is that as we have run the ecosystem faster and faster, driven by need and helped by technology, the bottleneck appears to have shifted to the waste-disposal step. Run the system harder and the waste—CO_2 emissions, CFCs (chlorofluorocarbons), acidified forests, polluted rivers—gets worse. Moreover, for various reasons, using technology to remove that bottleneck is likely to be altogether harder than applying human knowledge to capture useful energy and "make" things. Feeding coal to steam engines is easier than absorbing CO_2 emissions into the ecosystem.

How does global warming relate to this basic understanding of the earth as a closed system? Essentially, it concerns the interactions between the sun's heat and certain "greenhouse gases" in our atmosphere. The sun's energy comes to us through radiation, but almost all of that radiant energy is either reflected or reradiated back to space; if it were not, the earth would just keep heating up forever. When it is functioning properly, therefore, a uniquely balanced system exists. But if—as scientists now believe is happening—the composition of the trace gases in our atmosphere is altered by human activity, then more reradiated heat is being "trapped" (as within the glass of a greenhouse), which not only warms up the atmospheric gases but everything else as well. At the same time, scientists are also concerned that the ozone layer, which protects the earth and its inhabitants from harmful solar radiation, is being significantly depleted by chemical emissions like CFCs. The wider the "ozone hole," whether it be over Antarctica or New England, the more vulnerable human beings are, say, to skin cancer.

It is important to understand that global warming per se has always been with us, and is vital to life. Without our atmosphere, the earth's temperature would be about −18° C, not the comfortable average temperature of 15° C that it is. Those 33 degrees of Celsius temperature are why the earth isn't cold and dead like Mars, which, if it ever had an atmosphere, lost it long ago and is lifeless and frozen. On the other hand, Venus, whose atmosphere is overwhelmingly made up of carbon dioxide, is hotter than a baker's oven (450° C), making life impossible. While Mars is a deep freeze and Venus is a furnace, the earth is wrapped in that thin film of matter—including its vital atmospheric gases—that permits life. Should the content of those gases alter dramatically, we would either return to an ice age *or* find our temperatures rising to uncomfortable, or perhaps disastrous, levels.[21]

This latter possibility is the focus of today's earnest debate upon the greenhouse effect. In the last ice age, the earth's temperature averaged about 9° C colder than today, and the CO_2 level was only 190 to 200 parts per million. By the early nineteenth century, the CO_2 level had gradually increased to about 280 parts per million. It was then, however, that humankind began to use great amounts of coal, oil, and natural gas for heat and energy, pouring far larger amounts of carbons into the atmosphere. The clearing and burning of forests—for habitation, grazing, cultivation, and fuel—also added greatly to the process: burning a forest not only increases CO_2 levels, it also reduces the amount of plant life available for photosynthesis.

Atmospheric CO_2 concentrations have risen by about 70 parts per million during the past century and now total around 350 ppm. More than half of that increase has occurred during the past thirty years, which suggests that sheer population numbers are affecting the size of the increases. If the present growth rate of 0.3 or 0.4 percent per year continues, some scientists predict, carbon dioxide levels will be as high as 550 or even 600 ppm by the middle of the twenty-first century, leading to significant rises in the earth's average temperature.[22]

Given the complexity of our biosphere and of the countless interactions between the earth's air, sea, and land, considerable scientific uncertainty still exists about what may be happening to the environment. The computerized models and simulations of the atmosphere, which are extraordinarily complex, are usually simulations for the globe as a whole and much less helpful in allowing scholars to draw conclusions about a particular region. Measurement itself is also a problem: many recording stations may have been affected by "urban heat" as cities and suburbs expanded. Furthermore, individual features of the process of global warming are not very well understood. Would an increase in clouds, for example, warm the globe or cool it? Couldn't an increase in sunspot activity have caused the increase in temperatures? Might not some pollutants (sulfate aerosols) actually reflect the sun's radiation and *counter* global warming? How will ocean currents be affected by global warming? Won't the eruptions of volcanoes like Mount Pinatubo, which in 1991 spewed tons of dirt into the atmosphere, slow the forecast rise in the earth's temperatures? Would twice the level of carbon dioxide in the atmosphere actually increase the size and fertility of plant life—as has already occurred in controlled experiments in laboratories, and may also be taking place in northern Europe's forests—or will there be dangerous side effects? In any case, would that growth in vegetation be merely short-term, falling away as the enhanced CO_2 levels brought rises in the earth's temperature that would ultimately curtail agricultural production?

These uncertainties have encouraged a wide range of opinions on the subject of global warming. Concerned environmentalists believe that we are significantly changing the atmospheric gases, that a rise in global temperatures is inevitable, and that—to reduce the damage to our ecosystem—drastic changes should occur in our way of life in order to cut atmospheric emissions. That stance is vigorously contested by more skeptical scientists and laissez-faire economists, who are opposed to limiting growth and to governmental interference in how businesses operate and individuals live. Like the debate between neo-Malthusians and "cornucopians" over global agricultural prospects, much of the literature upon the greenhouse effect has therefore become very ideological, as each side denounces the other's "special agenda."[23]

Despite these varied responses, the scientific consensus is that average global temperatures are between 0.3° C and 0.7° C warmer than they were a century ago. This is a modest rise, but the real concern is the rising pace of temperature increase in the *next* century, especially as world population and industrial activity grow. It is estimated that double the CO_2 levels will produce average temperature increases of between 1.5° C and 4.5° C by the middle of the twenty-first century. The difference between the "low" and the "high" figures is considerable, but even at a compromise figure of 2.5° C or 3.0° C, most scientists in this field hold that there would be serious consequences. Even at the lower figure of 1.5° C, the Intergovernmental Panel on Climate Change warns, "the rate of change is likely to be greater than that which has occurred on earth any time since the end of the last ice age. . . ."[24]

For example, if substantial global warming occurs, the earth's sea levels could rise, simply because a warmer liquid has more volume than an equivalent mass of cold liquid. If the ocean warms up, then, it cannot help but "overflow" its basin and advance upon the shore. A warmer earth would also mean a net loss in the ice mass of the glaciers of the world, as more ice melts than is replaced by snow each year. In the warming after the last ice age, sea levels rose at the stupendous rate of about fourteen feet per century and covered vast areas of hitherto exposed land.[25]

Although scholars still debate what is happening to the all-important Antarctic ice fields (which contain 90 percent of the world's ice), most scientific studies believe that the sea level will rise as temperatures do—although estimates of the *extent* of that rise differ enormously.[26] Because of the configuration of the earth's landmass, however, even a relatively small rise (say, of up to a meter) would be significant; the geometry of beaches and offshore areas and the dynamics of waves mean that a one-meter rise in sea level can be expected to produce a shoreline retreat of about one hundred meters. Storms would push large amounts of water inland, flooding hitherto safe areas, and seawater would penetrate farther inland and upriver, contaminating freshwater aquifers.

Global warming could affect agriculture and land use, too, although the scientific evidence here also is complicated, incomplete, and at times bewilderingly contradictory. If, for example, global warming means that plants fade in the hotter temperatures but flourish in latitudes which formerly had been too chilly, does that imply a geographical relocation rather than a net reduction? And if this transformation is gradual, will farmers survive by planting crops that are more heat-resistant than those planted a decade earlier? Will agricultural pests become more rampant if global warming allows certain species to expand from the tropics, or would they be inhibited by the higher CO_2 environment?[27] Will the greenhouse effect mean that certain crops, stimulated by the increased levels of CO_2, experience greater agricultural output—and would those gains be sufficient to cancel out the losses in vegetation and foodstuffs elsewhere because of a temperature increase? Little of this is clear at present, although once again most scientists guess that the effects of global warming will be deleterious rather than beneficial.

• • •

This conclusion is particularly worrying for countries in the developing world. If significant sea-level rises occur in the next century, many developing nations are going to be badly hurt. For example, the 177,000 inhabitants of the Maldive Islands would find themselves entirely inundated should there be a two-meter rise in sea level; the same would be true of many atolls in the Pacific Ocean. Even more important for our purposes—for thinking through the political implications of these broad forces for global change—is the plight of countries such as Egypt, Bangladesh, and parts of China, where large populations reside on low-lying deltas. Egypt is already damaged environmentally from saltwater penetration because of the reduced flow of Nile water from the Aswan High Dam, and only 3.5 percent of its land is arable. A one-meter rise in sea level would take between 12 and 15 percent of that territory and turn almost 8 million people into refugees, while the loss of farmland would add to food shortages. With a one-meter rise in sea level, Bangladesh would lose 11.5 percent of its land, where 8.5 million people now live.[28] This does not include areas exposed to devastating storm floods, the likelihood of which would be increased because of both higher sea level and the possible greater intensity of the monsoons.*

As is usually the case, poverty compounds the problem. Egypt's per capita GNP is about $700 and Bangladesh's is a mere $170, one-hundredth that of wealthy European and North American countries.[29] Both Egypt and Bangladesh are on the United Nations list of the ten countries most threatened by sea-level rise, the other eight being Gambia, Indonesia, the Maldives, Mozambique, Pakistan, Senegal, Suriname, and Thailand. That does not mean that the developed countries are safely high and dry, for the water creeps up on both the rich and poor, and is as much a threat to the expensive housing and industry around Tokyo Bay and the Lower Rhine as it is to the Bangladesh deltas. The UN list includes those countries that will suffer

*The hypothesis here is that if global warming further heated up the hot air over the Tibetan plateau, the subsequent movements of the air masses could strengthen the intensity of the monsoon, causing more flooding. More generally, scientists suspect that while the increase in global temperatures will be a relatively gradual process, changes in the atmosphere could well produce increased storm activity, more "freak" weather, and so on, in line with "chaos theory." When critical thresholds—not known in advance—are crossed, instability is likely.

because of *their inability to pay* for either protective measures or a planned relocation to higher ground. Richer countries will pour funds into the defense of their own coastlines—one estimate is that to protect only developed land and the barrier islands of the United States from a one-meter rise in sea level could cost more than $100 billion[30]—though much of this expense may ultimately be in vain and the funds might be better allocated for different environmental purposes.

As we saw earlier, the populations of Egypt and Bangladesh are projected to increase greatly over the next few decades, in Egypt from 54 million (1990) to 94 million (2025), in Bangladesh from 115 million to 235 million during the same period.[31] Thus, the population growth and economic activity that trigger the greenhouse effect may also eventually cause a shrinkage of land area in places struggling with a demographic explosion of their own. The impending tragedies are unlikely to remain local in their impacts. If Egypt collapses under a growing population and a shrinking land base, the repercussions—political and military, as well as social—could greatly affect its neighbors in Israel and Europe. If Bangladesh is devastated by storm surges and inundations, millions upon millions of refugees may pour across the border into the already most heavily populated provinces of India, adding immensely to the latter's problems. The world is already used to the flood of refugees from civil war. There may soon be an even larger flood of environmental refugees as societies break down or experience civil war in the face of natural catastrophes. Already, numerous scholars are pointing to the significance of "environmental changes as causes of acute conflict."[32]

The possible effect of global warming upon agriculture in the developing world is a further cause of worry. Higher temperatures will exacerbate water use, and may interact with atmospheric pollution, overgrazing, and forest depletion; it is also likely to reduce the biodiversity of plant species. Moreover, increases in CO_2 will affect different crops in different ways, favoring temperate-region plants such as wheat and potatoes, but bringing much less benefit to corn and millet, which are critically important staples in Africa. The largest concern is about rice, whose fertility swiftly declines if daytime temperatures go over 35° C (95° F). In many rice-growing Asian countries, the average temperatures in the growing seasons are already close to the limit. A significant rise in global temperatures, say a 4.5° C increase at the "top end" of most estimates, would make current strains of rice unviable and might result in widespread starvation. This is potentially a dilemma for China, which has to consider the effect of increased CO_2 from its industrialization on its agricultural output over the longer term. Higher temperatures, reduced soil moisture, and a decline in rice fertility levels are disturbing to leaders seeking to industrialize, but also feed, a country of well over a billion people.

On the other hand, our earlier analysis of the impacts of biotechnology upon agriculture noted that recombinant DNA technology has opened up many more possibilities in adapting species to new environmental conditions; and there are also ingenious ways, developed by Israeli scientists, to produce good yields with low water inputs. These are not trivial developments, and some of the potentially most useful agricultural research is being done in this area. But the fact remains that they are expensive approaches, more easily available to biotech companies and agribusinesses in developed countries than to peasants in the developing world. For the latter, global warming, if it is coming, seems to threaten yet more trouble.

While the potential damage that global warming might inflict upon richer countries may be less severe, it is certainly worth taking seriously. Switzerland and Montana would not suffer from a rise in the sea level, but the low-lying regions of Louisiana, New Jersey, the Netherlands, and other parts of the developed world would be affected. A rise of one meter in the sea level would cause the United States alone to lose up to eight thousand square miles of wetlands and ten thousand square miles of dry land—a larger area than Vermont or Massachusetts—if no protective measures were instituted.[33] The fight to preserve Venice would be made more complicated, and other valuable cities and towns near the water's edge would be threatened. In many cases, higher seawalls could be built, costing enormous sums and, of course, doing nothing to address the causes of global warming.

The effect on agriculture could also be serious. The estimated increase of 1.5–4.5° C in temperature is an average for the earth as a whole, but the temperature rises are expected to be higher in the middle latitudes where most prosperous countries are located. A number of studies expect that increased temperature will reduce soil moisture in such regions as the North American Great Plains, Siberia, Western Europe, and Canada, where earlier snowmelt will be followed by a more intense evaporation as temperatures rise in the summer; there might also be less spring rain, at least in the Great Plains area.[34] This has global implications, because the United States, Canada, and France produce almost 75 percent of the world's grain exports, filling the needs of food-deficient countries across the world and providing an emergency reserve in times of famine. Should there be a reduction in overall agricultural output, the surplus nations would not be hurt—except in their balance of payments—as much as countries that require imports. While a rich country like Japan could easily pay the higher cost of scarce grain and soybeans, poverty-stricken developing countries could not.[35]

Can regions in which higher temperatures increase agricultural yields make up the deficits elsewhere? Probably, yes; Ontario and Alberta, for example, are expected to experience increased yields of corn, barley, soybeans, and hay if temperatures rise, although food output in their southern parts would suffer as moisture declines;[36] there may also be enhanced crop yields in Northern and Western Europe. None of this will provide satisfaction to the farmers of Oklahoma or southern Italy, who face the prospect of increasingly arid lands. Yet even if there is some compensation in a *global* sense as a poleward shift in the growing zones brings new lands under cultivation, this is unlikely to be enough. Unfortunately, in Siberia and northern Canada much of the soil is thin and highly acidified by centuries of decomposing evergreen needles—so that even if temperatures did rise, it is unlikely that crops would grow as well in those regions as they do in the rich soils of Iowa and the Ukraine. Global warming may also thaw vast tracts of frozen soil and permafrost, causing immense subsidence and swamping and releasing huge amounts of ancient, ice-locked methane and CO_2 into the atmosphere—accelerating the greenhouse effect and creating an ever-worsening cycle of ecological damage.[37]

• • •

All of this suggests the need for reform and, even before that, for better understanding of the *interconnectedness* of the global changes now affecting our planet. Just as we have to realize that the earth is a closed system thermodynamically, so also ought we to comprehend the linkages which our varied human actions—demographic, economic, social—have created. Because of the population explosion and humankind's striving for higher living standards, we may now be subjecting our ecosystem to more pressure than it can take; but as it shows increasing signs of stress it in turn *threatens* us, rich and poor alike, with the consequences of having tampered too much with the earth's thin film of matter.

Those consequences—rises in sea level, depleted agriculture, reduced water flows, increased health hazards (skin cancer, city smogs), more turbulent weather, social strains—all suggest that both developed and developing nations have good reason to worry about global warming. Governments, farmers, and scientists currently have tended to prefer a policy of *adaptation,* turning to new heat and drought-resistant crops and installing ambitious new irrigation systems. But little of that appears to be adequate, given the sheer dislocation involved, even for those who potentially gain. Schemes such as the diversion of Rocky Mountain rivers to make up for the decline in the level of the Ogallala Aquifer would be horrendously expensive, with unpredictable environmental consequences elsewhere; and poorer countries simply can't pay for large irrigation schemes. Newer, genetically altered crops are simply too expensive for most farmers of the world, and in any case the basic problem—of environmental stress—would continue to be evaded by their use.

The alternative way of dealing with global warming is by *prevention,* that is, by changing how we live. Some changes are already under way, or are at least agreed upon. Energy intensity—the ratio of energy demand to real GDP—has been falling in advanced economies because of greater efficiency. Many nations, meeting in Montreal in 1987, agreed to end the production of CFCs by the year 2000, and rich countries have agreed in principle to finance the cost to poorer countries of this transition to newer technologies.[38] Local efforts are being made to reduce methane emissions, from capturing the gas from landfills by piping, to developing new rice breeds that produce less methane, to building enclosed feed lots for cattle. In the same way, many countries—and even townships—have imposed measures to reduce industrial emissions, cut automobile exhaust, and so on. Much of this is being done to address local atmospheric problems, but some reforms also help improve the global warming situation.

Yet such efforts are probably not enough. The CFC replacements (HCFCs) bring technical problems of their own. Moreover, the rate of carbon emissions has been growing at about 3 percent annually, which, if it continues, will double its atmospheric concentration by 2025. An atmospheric concentration of CO_2 double or more the preindustrial level is well beyond the gloomiest "ranges" and scenarios developed by climate modelers. In consequence, one concerned researcher has pointed out, "[a] frighteningly large gap looms between projected growth rates in carbon emissions and the level that atmospheric scientists believe is necessary to maintain a climate that can meet human needs."[39]

If this is to be reversed, or even slowed, full-scale cooperation between rich and poor countries is required, simply because virtually every nation contributes to the collective worsening of our atmosphere. In developed countries, the emissions from millions of automobiles and trucks, power stations, aircraft, and industry pour carbons into the air. In developing countries such as China and India, a heavy reliance upon coal does the same. Throughout the tropics, deforestation and burnings add to the toll. Moreover, it is not only carbon dioxide that is being released in such historically high proportions into the atmosphere. Methane (CH_4), which has twenty to thirty times the capacity to absorb heat as CO_2, comes from such varied sources as landfills, flooded rice fields, and cows' stomachs. Man-made CFCs, used since the 1930s in refrigeration, air-conditioning, and insulation, are up to sixteen thousand times more effective than CO_2 in absorbing heat and (until they are eliminated) contribute some 20 percent of man-made additions to the atmosphere.*

As will be seen in Table 3, each country's contribution to global

*As compared with 50 percent from carbon dioxide, and around 16 percent from methane. Another two sources are tropospheric ozone (8 percent) and nitrous oxide (6 percent).

warming is different. India and China burn lots of coal (generating carbon dioxide) and possess large numbers of cattle or pigs (generating methane), but use relatively few CFCs, especially in relation to the size of their population. Brazil, where so much forestland is cleared by burning each year, has recently been putting huge amounts of carbon dioxide into the atmosphere, but its contributions of methane and CFCs are much more modest—although one purpose of clearing tropical forests is to ranch more cattle (methane). Japan has lots of automobiles, but few cattle. And the United States is profligate in every category.

Many studies have shown what can be done.[40] A worldwide program to create and restore forests would lead to the absorption of large amounts of carbon—a forest of new trees sequesters about 5.5 tons of carbon per hectare as it grows—which would help offset the amounts emitted by deforestation.* Alternative energy sources (wind, photovoltaic, geothermal, biomass-sourced) could be much more extensively developed; photovoltaic power in particular looks enormously attractive as an inexhaustible and nonpolluting fuel if the conversion costs can be further reduced. Above all, however, it is of critical importance to reduce the 6 billion tons of carbon being poured into the atmosphere each year; this implies far greater energy-efficient technologies, from light bulbs to automobile engines to manufacturing plants. Developing countries have to be assisted, through the transfer of modern techniques, in adopting a "noncarbon" path toward industrialization. And the industrial nations have to make substantial reductions in the amount of greenhouse gases produced by their factories, houses, power stations, and automobiles.

But is such an effort possible? Since rich and poor nations alike contribute to atmospheric pollution, it is politically inconceivable—as well as environmentally ineffective—that only some reduce greenhouse-gas emissions while others ignore their responsibilities. Local measures are fine, but, globally, there is little point in Canada's adopting "clean" policies if the United States remains "dirty," or if the rain forests of Colombia are protected while those in Brazil are destroyed,

*At the moment, however, about ten tropical trees are being cut down for every one planted; in Africa, the ratio is twenty-nine to one.

Table 3. Top Twenty-five Countries with the Highest Greenhouse Gas Net Emissions, 1987

(Carbon Dioxide Heating Equivalents, 000 metric tonnes of carbon)

		Greenhouse Gases				
Country	*Greenhouse Index Rank*	*Carbon Dioxide*	*Methane*	*CFCs(a)*	*Total*	*Percent of Total*
United States	1	540,000	130,000	350,000	1,000,000	17.6
USSR	2	450,000	60,000	180,000	690,000	12.0
Brazil	3	560,000	28,000	16,000	610,000	10.5
China	4	260,000	90,000	32,000	380,000	6.6
India	5	130,000	98,000	700	230,000	3.9
Japan	6	110,000	12,000	100,000	220,000	3.9
Germany, Fed. Rep.	7	79,000	8,000	75,000	160,000	2.8
United Kingdom	8	69,000	14,000	71,000	150,000	2.7
Indonesia	9	110,000	19,000	9,500	140,000	2.4
France	10	41,000	13,000	69,000	120,000	2.1
Italy	11	45,000	5,800	71,000	120,000	2.1
Canada	12	48,000	33,000	36,000	120,000	2.0
Mexico	13	49,000	20,000	9,100	78,000	1.4
Myanmar	14	68,000	9,000	0	77,000	1.3
Poland	15	56,000	7,400	13,000	76,000	1.3
Spain	16	21,000	4,200	48,000	73,000	1.3
Colombia	17	60,000	4,100	5,200	69,000	1.2
Thailand	18	48,000	16,000	3,500	67,000	1.2
Australia	19	28,000	14,000	21,000	63,000	1.1
German Dem. Rep.	20	39,000	2,100	20,000	62,000	1.1
Nigeria	21	32,000	3,100	18,000	53,000	0.9
South Africa	22	34,000	7,800	5,800	47,000	0.8
Côte d'Ivoire	23	44,000	550	2,000	47,000	0.8
Netherlands	24	16,000	8,800	18,000	43,000	0.7
Saudi Arabia	25	20,000	15,000	6,600	42,000	0.7

Source: *World Resources 1990–91,* p. 15

or if India agrees to control carbon dioxide emissions while China's continue to rise. The sacrifices have to be global; more than that, they must be as *equitable* as possible, allowing for differing standards of income. Poor woodcroppers in India or African peasants whose animals are overgrazing the savannahs are unlikely to be tempted to change their ways unless societies one hundred times richer make a proportionate sacrifice and offer adequate subsidies to replace lost income. Why, indeed, should developing countries worry about the greenhouse effect when they face—in their view—more immediate local issues like land erosion, desertification, limited access to clean water, colossal international debts, rising protectionism against their exports, inadequate technology transfer, etc.? How many desperate Ethiopians and Kashmiris have time to *care* about the opening of an "ozone hole" over North America?

All this returns us once again to politics, culture, and North-South relations. Global warming involves issues of wealth creation and distribution, of immediate gratification versus long-term gain, of traditional assumptions and modes of living versus newer realities, of international cooperation in place of independent isolationist policies. Like all the related matters discussed in this book, global warming forces us to confront the problem of a world divided into rich and poor.

Three instances illustrate just how sensitive the politics of global warming will be. The first, already mentioned, is the determination of China and India to have their own industrial revolution. Given their huge populations and the economic growth that they have to sustain, they may become the two largest contributors of greenhouse-gas emissions early next century. It is, therefore, desperately important to slow—better, to reverse—the level of emissions. Yet since the per capita GNP of both countries is so low, since their governments are wrestling with a population explosion and a rise in social and economic expectations, and since industrialization is regarded as the chief way to improve national product, how can either society be expected to adopt a "noncarbon" path to growth without enormous assistance from other countries? Even if that assistance should be forthcoming—and many developed countries are delinquent in their contributions to the Montreal Protocol Fund—would New Delhi and Beijing accept such restraint upon their economic sovereignty? Would they agree that they had to be more environmentally responsible than Europe and America were when they first industrialized?

This brings us to a second touchy issue, the destruction of the Latin

American rain forests. Today most people are aware of the implications of that process: the decline in biological diversity, the rise in carbon dioxide emissions from the burning of the trees, the reduction in the amount of plant and animal life. Yet the destruction is such that by the year 2000 three-quarters of America's tropical forests may have been felled. When, in 1988, satellite photos showed the extent of the burning, followed closely thereafter by news of the murder of union organizer Francisco Mendez (who had tried to prevent ranchers from destroying the forest), U.S. congressmen supported the idea of putting pressure upon Brazil—for example, by opposing international funds for a highway through the forests. This transformed the issue into one of North-South politics; Brazilian officials angrily pointed out that North Americans had not halted the destruction of their own forests over the past three centuries, that Brazil intended to develop its economy as any temperate economy would, and that, in any case, U.S. citizens use fifteen times more energy than Brazilians. Before preaching to others, America ought to set a better example.[41] In fact, Brazil now no longer subsidizes forest clearing, but it and its neighbors are still asking for a comprehensive North-South "deal" on this issue.

The third issue is the North's disproportionate contribution to greenhouse-gas emissions, especially carbon dioxide. According to the U.S. Environmental Protection Agency, to stabilize atmospheric concentrations of CO_2 at the present level, carbon emissions must be reduced by 50 to 80 percent, back to the level of the 1950s.[42] Otherwise there is little prospect of avoiding global warming, no matter what happens in Brazil and China. The obstacle here is not so much industrial emissions. Eliminating CFC and CO_2 emissions from factories and supermarkets is costly, and often opposed on that ground by American companies and Republican administrations, yet a great deal can and is being done. The real issue is the need to cut the emissions by vehicle engine combustion. Here the United States is particularly profligate, with 4 percent of world population devouring one-quarter or more of the world's fuel and being number one in greenhouse-gas emissions. Because they waste so much of the world's energy supplies, Americans would have to cut back far more than (say) Norwegians, by measures including stiff rises in gasoline prices, heavy investment in fuel-economy combustion, severe penalties on "gas-guzzling" automobiles, and the development of comprehensive public transportation systems. Yet however logical such a policy is on environmental grounds, it will be much easier to enact in the Netherlands or even Japan than in the United States. Never having had to conserve energy before—apart from during the few temporary "oil shocks" of the 1970s—many Americans would react angrily to strict restrictions on their right to drive, and emit engine exhaust, as they pleased.

Given the nature of American politics, it is difficult at present to imagine much leadership in Washington on global-warming issues.[43] Instead, there is a tendency to point to the differing scientific opinions in this matter, to suggest that fears about the greenhouse effect have been exaggerated, and to indicate that it would be unwise to devote funds and alter life-styles to meet circumstances that might not actually occur;[44] and, as noted above, those arguments are supported by skeptical scientists and economists.[45] All this has the *international* effect of making the United States appear indifferent to cooperation with other industrial democracies concerned with global warming, as occurred during the June 1992 Rio "summit" on environmental issues.

In theory, then, a number of measures could be instituted in both rich and poor countries to slow the rise in greenhouse-gas emissions. The UN Conference on Trade and Development is working on proposals for a forestry convention, a biodiversity convention, and a climate-change convention. Ingenious articles in Worldwatch Institute publications point to the merits of switching from automobiles to bicycles and invite readers to "cycle into the future."[46] Much of this writing might appear eccentric or quixotic on first reading, and the international agreements will be only as strong as the signatories permit, but behind it there lies a concern that there really is a long-term threat to our atmosphere, driven by overpopulation and industrialization. If global warming is as serious as some of the forecasts suggest, it will present our children and, more likely, our grandchildren with severe environmental problems.

And that, ironically, is the main obstacle to reform. Environmentalists are asking today's societies, in rich and poor countries, to make drastic changes—in their economic expectations, way of life, social behavior—in order to avoid deleterious effects a generation or two *in the future*; they are asking them to alter their own assumptions and life-styles now for the sake of their descendants' in thirty or fifty years' time. Since political leaders in many countries find it hard to call on their constituents for sacrifices even for immediate purposes (e.g., reducing the national debt, abolishing farm supports), few outside Northern Europe are likely to implement dramatic measures in response to global warming. One recent estimate, by UN environment authorities, that developing countries would need $125 billion a year to pay for new environmental programs—$70 billion more than *all* the financial assistance they now receive—was swiftly trimmed to a request for an additional $5 to $10 billion a year, in recognition of today's political and economic realities.[47] What is much more likely, therefore, is a number of piecemeal international agreements on environmental matters, especially if further droughts and other evidence of a rise in temperatures occur. That such measures will halt the destruction of the rain forests, the draining of aquifers, the profligate use of petroleum, and all our other dangerous habits seems unlikely—which cannot be good news for the future of the earth's thin film of life.

7

THE FUTURE OF THE NATION-STATE

THE PRECEDING CHAPTERS DISCUSSED demographic, environmental, and technological changes, all transnational in nature, which are bearing down upon human society. Chapters following this will discuss the likely impacts of those forces upon specific regions and nations in light of their ability to respond to such challenges. Not only are countries variably endowed geographically with respect to size, location, and natural resources, their respective inhabitants also differ greatly in their histories, cultural attitudes, social structures, and economic prowess. Some of them are therefore better prepared than others to deal with rising sea levels, or the biotech revolution, or even demographic change. Inequality among nations remains.

But before considering the prospects of different continents as the twenty-first century approaches, we must address one further general issue: what do these transnational developments mean for the future of the nation-state itself, which is the organizing unit that people normally turn to when challenged by something new? After all, to plunge immediately into chapters upon the relative capacities of (say) the German and Ethiopian states to grapple with global changes would miss the point that most of those trends are so far-reaching that perhaps no government agency is well equipped to handle them. Are not the important "actors" in world affairs nowadays the global corporations? Isn't technology creating winners and losers—in employment, and career paths—regardless of where one lives? In an age of twenty-four-hour-a-day currency trading or, for that matter, global warming, have national bodies such as cabinets or commerce departments much relevance? And if they don't, how is it possible to think that countries as a whole can organize to face the century ahead?

For most citizens, the idea that not simply specific industries or activities but nation-states themselves are becoming anachronistic would be profoundly disturbing. It is true that nation-states as we know them are relatively recent creations, first appearing in the "new monarchies" of early-modern Europe such as Spain, France, and England.[1] In view of today's argument that people may be increasingly turning from national governments either to transnational or subnational agencies to achieve their goals,* it is ironic to note that the early-modern monarchies emerged from, and then subdued, a patchwork quilt of dukedoms, principalities, free cities, and other localized authorities such as Burgundy, Aragon, and Navarre; and that as they consolidated power internally, the nation-states also asserted themselves against transnational institutions like the papacy, monastic and knightly orders, and the Hanseatic League—the last being, in many ways, a sort of early multinational corporation.[2] Neither authority from above nor independence below could be tolerated in such egoistical states as Henry VIII's England or Louis XIV's France. Even where authority was shared internally—as between the English crown and parliament—the fact remained that both were national institutions.

As the modern nation evolved, it steadily acquired its basic characteristics, familiar to us now but often novel at the time and opposed by groups marginalized or overtaken by this process of state formation. The "ideal" type of state—for there were exceptions such as the multiethnic, multiterritorial Habsburg Empire—occupied a coherent geographical area, like France or Sweden. It therefore possessed recog-

*See below, pp. 131–33.

nizable national boundaries which, over time, were increasingly supervised by state employees such as customs officers, border police, and immigration authorities. It, along with its fellow nation-states, was recognized in international law and diplomacy as "sovereign"—there was nothing above it—which was hardly surprising, since that law consisted of norms which, at least in principle, countries had agreed to observe. Each state evolved symbols (flag, anthem, historical figures and events, special holidays) to reinforce consciousness of national identity. While its schoolchildren studied universal subjects such as mathematics, science, geography, other elements in the curriculum (especially history) had a national focus, just as teaching itself followed a national pattern. The national language steadily encroached upon such regional tongues as Breton, Welsh, and Catalan, though the resistance was often deep and determined.[3]

Institutionally and economically, too, the nation-state was at the center of things. Adult males were conscripted or induced into the armed services, which steadily changed from private feudal levies into standing national institutions. As state spending rose to meet internal and external needs, financial bodies like a national bank and a treasury department evolved, national assemblies arose to vote on annual budgets, a national taxation system emerged, and national currency units replaced older measures. The mercantilist economic system, intended to boost a country's stock of capital, was also deliberately aimed at making the nation strong and self-sufficient.[4] Reliance upon foreign supplies of textiles, iron, grain, and other goods was reduced by making them domestically, creating jobs, and lessening the outflow of specie. Navigation acts strove to ensure that all seaborne trade was carried in domestically owned vessels, crewed by one's own nationals. Knowledge about how to manufacture, say, porcelain, or new types of textile machinery, was kept from foreigners. All these actions, in the view of people like Pitt, Colbert, and Frederick the Great, would enhance national power and consciousness.

Apart from internal revolution, then, the only real threat to the nation-state could come from another state seeking to enhance *its* relative power, or from a coalition of hostile states. To ensure national security, governments relied upon a mixture of military and diplomatic measures—keeping a standing army, building a fleet, forming alliances or ententes against a common rival. Wars, when they occurred, could be expensive, but they also served to boost patriotic fervor; denouncing the "overwhelming ambition" of France or the guile of "perfidious" Albion was always a good way to increase national solidarity.[5] By the beginning of the present century, nationalistic feelings were being reinforced by renewed naval and arms races, colonial rivalries, the agitations of the yellow press and chauvinistic pressure groups, and the social-Darwinistic notions of an international "struggle for survival." It was little wonder, therefore, that many of the citizens of the European powers marched willingly to war when those antagonisms exploded in 1914.[6]

This steady enhancement of the power and authority of the nation-state was not without certain counterforces. Despite governmental claims of national unity, in Ulster, Alsace, Catalonia, the Alto Adige, Silesia, Bosnia, and myriad other places, ancient ethnic rivalries and local patriotisms simmered beneath the surface. From Adam Smith's *The Wealth of Nations* (1776) onward, increasing numbers of economists, bankers, and businessmen argued that people everywhere would be better off if the hand of the mercantilist, protectionist state were removed from economic affairs and commerce and investment operated according to market criteria rather than governmental desires. The cosmopolitan ideology of liberalism was joined (and challenged), later in the nineteenth century, by a transnational workers' movement called Marxism. Each of these viewpoints opposed the claimed autonomy of the nation-state; yet whenever a grave international crisis occurred—as in 1914, and again in 1939—they were thrust aside. Diplomatic treaties (Versailles, Locarno, the Washington and London naval accords) and institutions (the League of Nations, the Permanent Court of Arbitration at the Hague) were similarly powerless to prevent egoistic sovereign states from going to war.

With the two great "total wars"[7] of this century fought by developed economies and organized by modern bureaucracies, the triumph of the nation-state seemed complete. Even liberal, democratic systems insisted on conscription. Citizens' loyalties were claimed totally; dealing with the enemy was treason, and all prewar trade was frozen. Controls were imposed upon industry and investment, currency dealing, even labor strikes, as the state-at-war sought to extract the maximum production possible from its people. World War I produced the passport—a proof of an individual's nationality but, interestingly, owned by the government, which could recall it when deemed necessary. World War II produced the "gross national product," an economist's device to allow the state full scrutiny of productive activity. In both conflicts, governments steadily augmented controls over information. Even great works of art reflected national need and resolve, as in Olivier's patriotic interpretation of *Henry V* or Shostakovitch's Eighth Symphony.

After 1945 these trends ebbed somewhat in the economic sphere but continued strong in political life. International financial and trading arrangements such as the International Monetary Fund, the World Bank, and the General Agreement on Tariffs and Trade sought to check a recurrence of the damage caused by interwar protectionism and autarky; foreign trade and investment flows boomed. But the rising tensions produced by the Cold War badly affected the climate of international relations and pointed to the continued importance of "national" security. The United Nations, devised as an improved version of the League, suffered accordingly as the superpowers squabbled over, and vetoed, one another's motions. External threats were studied by national security councils or similarly named bodies; wherever an American president went—even on vacation—his "national security adviser" was at his side. National security was used to justify almost everything, from building a highway system to providing science and technology scholarships. It was also used negatively, to withhold certain information, ban specified immigrants, forbid trade and travel with particular countries, suspend technology transfers. At the height of the Cold War, as both the USSR and the United States poured hundreds of billions of dollars each year into defense spending, observers wondered whether each had not become a "national security state"; others, concerned by the massive diversion of capital, R&D, scientists, engineers, and technicians into the arms race, feared for the effect upon long-term national competitiveness.[8]

Such ways of thinking still have a powerful hold today. During Cold War tensions, it was of course easy to argue that threats to one's people were primarily military in nature, and that the nation-state remained the central actor in world affairs. Even with that conflict removed, national security experts and Pentagon officials can still find many potential threats to international stability—and grounds for maintaining large defense forces. The existence of tens of thousands of nuclear warheads in the successor states of the Soviet Union, and the fact that their ownership is uncertain; the possibility of another breakdown in Arab-Israeli relations; ethnic conflict in the Balkans and elsewhere; volatile regimes in Libya, Iraq, and North Korea; the emergence of regional great powers like India and China; the proliferation of sophisticated weaponry to "trouble spots" around the globe—all these imply the continued need for military power, controlled by the nation-state and its instruments (Pentagon, National Security Council, Joint Chiefs of Staff), working in conjunction with international security structures (NATO, U.S.-Japan Defense Treaty, etc.).

These traditional assumptions are coming under increasing pressure, however, simply because of the way our world is changing. With the Cold War over, many writers now argue that military rivalries and arms races are being replaced by economic rivalries, technology races, and various forms of commercial warfare. In consequence, the language used to describe international trade and investment today has become increasingly military in nature; industries are described as coming "under siege," markets are "captured" or "surrendered," and comparative rates of R&D expenditures or of shares of high-technology goods are scrutinized as anxiously as the relative sizes of battlefleets before 1914.[9] Even national security experts now admit the importance of the economic dimensions of power and concede that traditional instruments such as armies and navies cannot be deployed against economic challenges. Yet although that shift seems novel, in fact the older way of thinking remains: the nation-state is still at the center of things, engaged in a ceaseless jostling for advantage against other nation-states. A neomercantilist world order remains, even if recourse to war is no longer regarded as an option.*

• • •

*Except in the extremist literature: see G. Friedman and M. Lebard, *The Coming War with Japan* (New York, 1991).

Yet, as we have seen in the preceding chapters, other experts on international trends are pointing to different causes for concern and to fresh threats to security. Overpopulation in the poorer countries of the world could produce resource wars, exacerbate ethnic tensions, contribute to social instabilities, and fuel external expansionism. A migratory flood from the poorer and more troubled parts of the globe to the richer and more peaceful will bring not only social costs, but also rising racial antagonisms. Differentiated population growth rates of ethnic groups within the same national borders are likely to heighten already existing tensions. The effects of the population explosion on the ecosystem might threaten national interests. In addition to increasing the risk of resource wars over diminishing stocks of water, grazing land, timber, and the like, environmental damage threatens economic prosperity and public health. Moreover, such damage cuts into global food production as world population increases by almost a billion per decade, which could cause massive global hunger and lead to further social and political instabilities, resource wars, and deteriorating relations between the richer and poorer peoples of the earth.[10]

The nation-state and its security are also potentially threatened by the new international division of production and labor. The logic of the global marketplace pays no attention to *where* a product is made, but defense planners—in keeping with traditional national security thinking—are more concerned. Is it not vital, they argue, for a country to maintain its own electronics and computer industry, to preserve shipping and aerospace, to be able to produce its own software for both military and nonmilitary purposes?[11] Unwelcome economic trends may affect national power indirectly as well. A country could be badly damaged if its dairy or beef industry—perhaps a source of large export earnings—were devastated by the advent of biotech methods of food production elsewhere; or if its automobile industry—another major source of national earnings and wealth—were wiped out by the invasion of the home market by more efficient foreign rivals; or if high-tech designs and production moved to other countries, and the national industrial base eroded.

The international financial revolution brings its own challenges to the assumed sovereignty of the nation-state. The borderless world implies a certain surrender of a nation's control over both its own currency and its fiscal policies. That surrender might bring prosperity, but if the international financial system is unstable, there is little or no authority to control potential massive currency flows. With the volume of daily currency exchanges well in excess of the GNPs of many countries, individual governments and finance ministries have much less command over the system than they had a quarter century ago. Simply the awareness of the market's disapproval of certain measures (like raising taxes) can deter so-called sovereign governments from implementing them.

Although very different in form, these various trends from global warming to twenty-four-hour-a-day trading are *transnational* by nature, crossing borders all over the globe, affecting distant societies, and reminding us that the earth, for all its divisions, is a single unit. They are largely out of the control of the authorities of the traditional nation-state, both in the direct sense that countries cannot prevent incoming atmospheric drift and in the indirect sense that if they banned such activities as biotech farming, robotics, and foreign-exchange dealing, that would not stop them operating elsewhere. Finally, these challenges cannot be met by military force, which is the normal way states have handled threats to their security. Carrier task forces and armored divisions have their uses, but they are unable to prevent the global demographic explosion, stop the greenhouse effect, halt foreign-exchange dealings, ban automated factories and biotech farming in foreign countries, and so on.

These developments, together with such secondary challenges as international terrorism and drugs, have suggested to some writers that "new" threats to national and international security are taking the place of the "old" threats of nuclear warfare and large-scale conventional war, and that governments should therefore cease their obsession with military dangers and concentrate instead upon measures to deal with very different challenges to the national well-being.[12]

Such a suggestion probably exaggerates the extent of the recent changes in world affairs. It makes much more sense to think of these newer threats to our way of life as *coming alongside* the older and more traditional threats to security, rather than replacing them. Even if the Soviet-American arms race loses its significance, there will still be many nuclear weapons on this planet; the nuclear powers themselves will also remain, and if attempts to halt proliferation are not successful, they will be joined in the future by other nations, perhaps less scrupulous and almost certainly located in more turbulent regions of the globe than Western Europe and North America. Regional conflicts, driven by their own socioeconomic, cultural, or ethnic dynamic, are unlikely to fade away and in many parts of the world may well increase in number and scope as the struggle for resources intensifies. After all, the continued relevance of nation-states and military power was amply demonstrated in the 1990–91 Gulf War.

Armed forces will remain, therefore, and on occasions will be used. But this traditional military dimension to "security" will increasingly coexist with the nonmilitary dimensions described above, compelling politicians and their publics to redefine their terminology and rethink their policies. On some occasions, indeed, we might also expect the "new" and the "old" security issues to combine; social instabilities caused by population pressure and resource depletion could take place in regions (Southwest Asia, for example) where arms proliferation, ethnic tensions, and territorial disputes have long been a threat to peace.[13] Meanwhile the winding-down of the nuclear arms race may, ironically, produce two distinct types of threat: the more traditional problem of how to prevent hundreds or thousands of former Soviet warheads and missiles from falling into the "wrong" hands, and the newer, perhaps equally difficult task of dealing with masses of nuclear waste, which are a profound ecological hazard. In both cases, one suspects, statesmen and their advisers are hastily scrambling to think through the implications of these new threats, and only the most sanguine observer can assume that they will get it right on every occasion. But what would "getting it wrong" mean?

In this larger and more integrated sense, "national" security becomes increasingly inseparable from "international" security, and both assume a much broader definition; in place of the narrower military concept there is emerging a larger definition which can encompass a whole spectrum of challenges, old and new. Indeed, we may eventually come to agree that a threat to national security means anything on the globe which challenges a people's health, economic well-being, social stability, and political peace.[14]

The problem with such an all-encompassing definition is, however, that it lacks the drama, the clarity, and the immediacy of a military threat to national security. When an enemy army is ravaging an ally or one's homeland is targeted by thousands of missiles, public opinion is relatively easily mobilized. But many people still distinguish between "high politics" (that is, clear threats to the nation) and "low politics" (economic quarrels, environmental reform proposals, trade negotiations); and while the issues of low politics are now attracting lots of attention, it still may be more difficult to convince publics and politicians to make the necessary sacrifices to meet new threats than it was in the period of bipolar antagonism.[15]

These global changes also call into question the usefulness of the nation-state itself. The key autonomous actor in political and international affairs for the past few centuries appears not just to be losing its control and integrity, but to be the *wrong sort* of unit to handle the newer circumstances. For some problems, it is too large to operate effectively; for others, it is too small. In consequence, there are pressures for a "relocation of authority" both upward and downward, creating structures that might respond better to today's and tomorrow's forces for change.[16]

The relocation of authority upward and outward from the nation-state has attracted the greater attention. This refers not only to the *re*emergence of transnational players such as the large corporations and banks, or to the rise of a global communications system largely outside the control of individual governments. It also refers to the increased role of international institutions and agreements, the reasoning being that if the new challenges are global, they can be met successfully only on a global scale, through transnational agencies and commonly agreed policies, ranging from greater cooperation and consultation among the leading industrial democracies (the G-7 summits), to treaties banning the use of CFCs, to the enhancement of the roles and resources of such international agencies as the United Nations, UNESCO, the World Bank, and the IMF. Insofar as the latter can contribute to peace and stability—for example, in the increasing use of United Nations peace-keeping forces in so many regional trouble spots—this is a welcome development; and if they do turn out to be generally successful (a big if in the case of places like Bosnia), that could further enhance the status of international bodies *vis-à-vis* purely national instruments and policies.

Also emerging are supranational organizations of a regional sort, especially for commercial purposes. While forecasts of the impending division of the developed world into three trading blocs and their satellites may be premature, the creation of something such as a North American Free Trade zone (Mexico, United States, Canada) does involve agreements to reduce national economic integrity; within the borders of the zone itself, national differences will begin to blur. This process is even more advanced in the European Community, whose home governments and parliaments have agreed to cede large areas of traditional national sovereignty in order to gain greater economic and political unity; and it is precisely because they have already gone so far that there exists deep political controversy between integrationists and those opposed to the further erosion of national powers.*

The relocation of authority from the nation-state to smaller units is also chiefly driven by economic and technological developments. The breakdown of borders across Europe, for example, permits the emergence (in many cases, the *re*emergence) of regional economic zones, which had been barred by national customs and tariff systems. As new trading relationships develop, the former ones fade; Slovenia trades increasingly with Austria and less with Serbia, Alsace-Lorraine becomes more integrated with Baden-Württemberg than with Paris, northern Italy develops closer links with Alpine states than with Calabria or Sicily. Individual American states, often frustrated by the lack of interest shown by the federal government, open their own "missions" in Tokyo and Brussels in order to conduct investment and trade diplomacy. Russian cities like St. Petersburg declare themselves free-trade zones in order to attract foreign investment.

Many of these developments are innocent enough, and welcomed by free-market economists on the grounds that unrestricted trade follows its own natural (and more beneficial) course. But this relocation of

*See Chapter 12, "Europe and the Future."

authority downward also carries with it the risk of national disintegration—at least in societies where ethnic rivalries and disputed boundaries fuel regional differences. While the most spectacular examples of this decay of national cohesion have recently been witnessed in the Soviet Union and Yugoslavia, there are many examples elsewhere in the world. In much of Africa, the European-style state system is breaking down, borders are permeated, regional and ethnic rivalries are on the rise. This issue of center versus provinces, or unity versus diversity, also drives observer nations into different political positions; a culturally homogeneous Germany might incline to sympathize with the autonomist claims of Slovenes and Croats in Yugoslavia, whereas governments with their own regional/ethnic problems (e.g., Spain) are understandably nervous about encouraging separatist movements anywhere. In all of the tense debates over international intervention—for example, to assist the Kurds—there runs this larger issue of the legality and integrity of the nation-state.

In the light of the broad global trends discussed in the preceding chapters, we should not be surprised if further internal and regional conflicts break out. With population pressures building up in various parts of the globe, the struggle for resources intensifying, and the communications revolution often fueling ethnic animosities rather than producing world citizens, the challenges to national authority—especially in the poorer parts of the world—may well intensify. Two centuries ago, Immanuel Kant observed that nature employed two means to separate peoples: "differences of language and of religion," both tending to produce "mutual hatred and pretexts for war." Within time, Kant hoped, the "progress of civilization" would finally lead to peaceful agreement among all.[17] Perhaps it will one day; but the evidence at present suggests that we have a long way to go, and that the progress of "civilization" is not keeping pace with those trends which are transforming our planet and challenging our traditional political arrangements. On the contrary, fundamentalist forces, partly in reaction to globalization, gather strength to lash back, while even in democracies, nationalist and antiforeign political movements gain ground—all of which hurts their long-term chances of "preparing" for the future.

• • •

This leaves humankind with a conundrum. For all the discussion about the relocation of authority and group loyalties, the older structures exist—and, indeed, in some places are increasingly clung to. There may have been a certain erosion of the powers of the nation-state in recent decades, but the nation-state remains the primary locus of identity of most people; regardless of who their employer is and what they do for a living, individuals pay taxes to the state, are subject to its laws, serve (if need be) in its armed forces, and can travel only by having its passport.* Moreover, as new challenges emerge—be it illegal migration or biotech farming—peoples turn instinctively (at least in the democracies) to their own governments to find "solutions." The global demographic explosion, atmospheric pollution, and technology-driven change each have their own transnational momentum; but it is national governments and assemblies which decide whether to abolish currency controls, permit biotechnology, cut factory emissions, or support a population policy. This does not mean that they will always be successful; in fact, a major argument of this book is that the nature of the new challenges makes it much more difficult than previously for governments to control events. But they still provide the chief institution through which societies will try to respond to change. Finally, if there is to be coordinated action by the peoples of this world, for example, to halt the destruction of the tropical rain forests or reduce methane emissions, then inter*national* agreements, negotiated by the participating governments, are clearly required.

In sum, even if the autonomy and functions of the state have been eroded by transnational trends, no adequate substitute has emerged to replace it as the key unit in responding to global change. How the political leadership of the nation prepares its people for the twenty-first century remains of vital importance even when the traditional instruments of state are weakening—which is why it is now necessary to consider the prospects of individual countries and regions as they respond, or fail to respond, to the challenges of the coming century.

*Or, in the case of Europeans, by having an EC passport.

PART 2

REGIONAL IMPACTS

8

THE JAPANESE "PLAN" FOR A POST-2000 WORLD

ASSUMING THE DIMENSIONS OF OUR GLOBAL predicament outlined above to be roughly correct—that there will be a continuing population explosion in the poorer parts of the world leading to increased environmental damage and social stress, while globalization and newer technologies arising in rich countries may undermine traditional methods (and locations) of agriculture, manufacturing, and business in general—how can any people hope to remain unscathed? Even if the global economy is creating three immensely powerful and privileged trading blocs, in Europe, North America, and Japan, can they—regardless of how well they "prepare" internally for the future—isolate themselves from the turbulences caused by worldwide change? Can they exist as islands of prosperity in a sea of discontents?

As we consider the prospects of the various countries and regions of the earth—in this chapter, specifically Japan—we shall see that complete isolation from the "fallout" from global trends is impossible, although the Japanese will undoubtedly strive to be more successful than other advanced economies in meeting new challenges. Already, Japan is viewed by many commentators as the country best prepared for tomorrow's technologically driven global changes,[1] although the very notion of "Japan as number one" has also drawn criticism from authors more impressed by Japanese weaknesses than strengths.[2] Both strong and weak points are discussed here—as they will be in later chapters, which consider the prospects of other countries. While each region and nation is examined separately in order to provide a reasonably detailed assessment, their position relative to other societies—and, of course, to the general, transnational forces described in Part One—needs to be kept constantly in mind.

The overall conclusion of this chapter is that because of the way their society and economy are organized, the Japanese are probably the people least likely to be hurt by gross and direct damage from global overpopulation, mass migration, and environmental disasters on the one hand or from the globalization of production on the other; but even such a successful nation as Japan will find it hard to escape the larger repercussions of demographic and technological change.

Japan's achievement in creating wealth, decade after decade since 1945 and at a pace unequaled by any other large power (and very few smaller ones), rests upon strong foundations. These include the social and racial coherence of the Japanese people themselves, who have seldom intermarried with other ethnic groups and have enjoyed a lengthy period of relative isolation from international affairs. This cohesion manifests itself not only in a powerful sense of national identity and cultural uniqueness, but also—and, to Western eyes, more impressively—in an emphasis upon social harmony, the need for consensus, generational deference, and the subordination of individual desires to the good of the collectivity. As a result of such social norms, so the argument goes, the Japanese suffer far fewer murders, crimes of violence, and strikes, a greater degree of family and intergenerational bonding, and a higher average life expectancy than people in most Occidental societies. Having suppressed individualist impulses to a large degree, the Japanese function more effectively as a team or, rather, as members of many teams—the family, the school, the company, and the nation.[3]

Education is a critical element in Japan, as it is in other Confucian-influenced societies of East Asia. But while the Japanese emphasize the acquisition of knowledge, they lay even greater stress upon learning as a group activity; rather than encouraging individual excellence, the Japanese seek to ensure that all members of the class attain the required standard levels of literacy and numeracy. Teachers are a highly valued asset in Japan, deference to them is strong, and every year there are many more highly qualified applicants for schoolteaching jobs than places available. Learning in schools is reinforced by further study, at home or in "crammer" *(juku)* institutes, with the emphasis upon factual acquisition rather than the free flow of debate and ideas. Competition to get into prestigious universities is intense, harrowing for the student and eagerly supported by the family. Measured by standards of comparative economic advantage and wealth creation, the results are impressive.[4] Fresh cadres of school leavers, possessing high competency and encouraged to "fit in" to the company which recruits them, become members of a disciplined and skilled work force dedicated to improving the firm's productivity. The more talented will be steered toward careers which underpin a flourishing manufacturing and high-technology base: engineers of all types, scientists, computer specialists, R&D personnel; in other words, people who help to *make* things. By contrast, there are far fewer lawyers and management consultants, who provide services rather than produce goods.

Official statistics confirm this impression of a purposeful, utilitarian education system. The entire Japanese school structure, which consists of around 1.3 million teachers educating 27 million pupils in some 66,000 schools,[5] is tightly controlled and regulated by a powerful Ministry of Education; course offerings, textbooks, teachers' salaries, and even a school's physical plant are under its supervision. While this creates a rigidity and conformity that many other societies would find oppressive, the important fact is that high general standards are set, which everyone strives to reach. Almost all Japanese children (92 percent) attend kindergarten, where the early socializing process begins. Everyone in Japan then receives at least nine years of compulsory education, with the vast majority continuing into high school; and a full 90 percent or more of the population graduate from high school, a rate well above those in the United States, Britain, and most other countries. One result of this is that Japan currently has an illiteracy rate of a minuscule 0.7 percent. Moreover, because Japanese children go to school for many more days each year—about 220 (including Saturday half-days) compared with about 180 in the United States—and because they study longer during each school day, a fourteen-year-old Japanese child has been exposed to as much teaching as an American student of seventeen or eighteen. Japanese children score very highly in international standardized tests measuring mathematical or scientific ability (especially since so much of what they learn is in those fields); yet even on standard intelligence tests, the *average* Japanese student scores 117, compared to 100 for Americans and Europeans.[6]

In higher education the pressures are much less intense, even in the better universities, and the Japanese record is mixed. Receiving a lesser share of total education funding than in other industrialized nations, and with small graduate programs, Japanese universities and colleges have hitherto not done well in creative research; as of 1987, Japanese had won only four Nobel Prizes in science compared with 142 for the United States. This may change as the Japanese allocate much larger sums to pure research than in the past, but it is likely that the greatest amount of scientific investigation in Japan will continue to be carried out in laboratories and institutes of giant corporations, with "pure" knowledge purchased or copied from elsewhere. It is an indication of its preference for the practical that Japan leads the world in the proportion of qualified scientists and engineers (about 60,000 per million people); almost 800,000 Japanese are engaged in research and development, more than in Britain, France, and Germany combined.[7]

Japan's financial and fiscal structures also contribute to the national purpose of wealth creation. Not only does the tax system encourage private savings, but the high cost of housing and the need to save for old age ensure a high level of personal savings. This traditionally has provided banks and insurance companies with masses of capital, then lent at low rates to Japanese manufacturers, giving them a cost advantage over foreign rivals. In addition, banks and companies possess an intricate web of crossholdings of each other's stock, allowing the managers of a firm to plan a long-term strategy—often involving heavy capital investment, and without much regard for quarterly profit returns—to bring new products to the consumer and enhance market shares. These advantages were reinforced, at least until recently, by the government's policy of discouraging imports and of keeping the yen's value low, and by manufacturing companies' intimate links with domestic suppliers for components and ancillary services.[8]

This combination made it difficult for many foreign companies to compete with their Japanese rivals; American firms, for example, had to contend with a less highly skilled and less docile work force, the higher cost of capital, dependency upon the immediate profit-seeking tendencies of Wall Street investors, *and* the built-in difficulties of penetrating the Japanese home market. In addition to these extraneous advantages, Japanese companies also benefited from the quality of so many of their products and of the production system itself. The fanatical attention given to consumer tastes, to efficient and pleasing designs, to "lean production" on the factory floor, to quality control, and to after-sales service is noted in study after study.[9] Much of this passion, it seems, is driven by the strong competitiveness between rival Japanese firms; as Honda challenges Toyota and Nissan, as Olympus Optical battles with Pentax and Ricoh, the planners and personnel in each company devote great efforts to ensuring that their products will be the best. That is, of course, the ideal of competitive capitalist enterprise everywhere, but in Japan it is taken close to its limits.[10]

The result of this economic expansion—and in many ways the driving force behind it—has been the emergence of a number of giant Japanese corporations that possess vast amounts of capital and a world strategy for making and selling their goods. Most of them have used their large bank balances to install ever more sophisticated equipment in order to export competitively as the yen strengthens further; capital spending in Japan recently has exceeded that of the United States in absolute terms, an eye-opening fact when one considers that the American population is twice as large.[11] Ambitious corporations with "industrial intelligence" staffs to scour the world for new products and ideas have bought out foreign companies, established laboratories and research centers in Europe and North America, and funded the research of academics and scientists in different parts of the globe. When foreign experts declare Japan to be deficient in a certain field (luxury cars, computer software, supercomputers), intense efforts are made to eliminate that deficiency.[12] In much the same way, forecasts of increasing European protectionism swiftly stimulated Japanese companies to make heavy European investments, in order to manufacture *within* the EC's boundaries before the further integration of 1992.[13]

The results of Japan's manufacturing miracle have benefited not simply bosses and bankers, but the country itself. Its GNP, one-third of Britain's and a mere one-twentieth that of the United States in 1951, is now about three times Britain's GNP and close to two-thirds of the American total at current exchange rates; moreover, forecasters expect the Japanese economy to grow faster than America's, and probably faster than Europe's, for the rest of the century.[14] Individual Japanese possess a much higher standard of living than they did thirty years ago, a rise reflected not only in their heightened consumer spending, but even more spectacularly in Japanese purchases and travel abroad. As its economy has strengthened, so also has the purchasing power of its currency; whereas visitors to Japan wilt at the cost of everyday goods and services, the Japanese have found foreign countries and their assets (from farmland to Impressionist paintings) relatively cheap. Like Switzerland and several other Northern European countries, therefore, Japan has become a high-per-capita-income society, which is the ultimate economic fruit of enhancing overall productivity.

While enterprising firms have driven the Japanese economy forward, this expansion was clearly assisted by the macroeconomic and structural features mentioned earlier, such as the education system and low interest rates. In addition, many companies enjoyed the support of the Ministry for International Trade and Industry (MITI) in identifying new product areas, collecting information, and funding and sharing scientific research.[15] A further advantage was Japan's virtually demilitarized status after 1945; sheltered under the American strategic umbrella, Japan has spent only 1 percent of its GNP upon defense annually (as compared with American totals that have ranged from 5 to 10 percent and beyond).[16] "Savings" in that sphere have released funds for the continued modernization of its industry. While Japan does not have much in the way of *hard* power (tanks, aircraft), it possesses a growing amount of *soft* power, or nonmilitary influence,[17] as can be seen in its enhanced position within the IMF and World Bank, its acquisition of Hollywood studios and European computer firms, the size of the Tokyo stock market, and the fact that Japan is now the world's largest donor of foreign aid, so that many developing countries now look to Tokyo for assistance, loans, and investments. As politicians from developing countries hasten to Japan, a rising flood of Japanese businessmen, tourists, manufacturers, and capital penetrates most parts of the globe, in a manner reminiscent of Britain's mid-to-late-Victorian expansionism.[18] In the fastest-growing region of all, the western Pacific and East Asia, more and more economies are drawn into a Japan-dominated trading and investment bloc, raising fears that Japan is achieving a "Greater East Asia Co-Prosperity Sphere" by peaceful commercial means with greater success than it ever managed by its warlike expansion of the 1930s.[19] If it has come so far in the space of two generations, how much further will it have grown in wealth, influence, and power in forty years' time?

All this will be familiar to students of international economic affairs. Yet while the achievements are undoubted, they appear to have been gained at high cost to Japanese society itself. Japan's vaunted social harmony, some observers feel, has been secured by insisting upon conformism and deference to the point of repression. Instead of encouraging creativity, the entire educational experience is based upon memorization of facts and "group think"—features which reappear in factory and business organizations, where an unquestioned harmony is supposed to prevail. The system is rigid and hierarchical (the more important the boss, the deeper one's bow to him), and it accords enormous privileges to a select group of *males* who own the large corporations, run the bureaucracies, and manage the ruling Liberal Party. By contrast, the great majority of the Japanese population has to content itself with cramped accommodations, excessive work hours, group calisthenics, and the consolations of national pride. Women are meant to take care of the home, manage the savings, and ensure the children's after-school education.[20]

Furthermore, the emphasis upon uniqueness and "Japanness" reflects not simply a sense of cultural identity but, more disturbingly, a deep streak of racism, which is particularly manifested in Japanese views of Koreans, Chinese, American blacks, and many other ethnic groups abroad, as well as the *burakumin* ("outcasts") at home. Cultural exclusivity makes it difficult for Japan to offer transcendental values to other peoples in the way (it is avowed) that Athens, Renaissance Italy, and the modern United States have contributed to world civilization.[21]

"Japan Inc." has also systematically avoided the rules of international free trade. For decades, foreign goods that rivaled Japanese products were kept out of the home market, either by discriminatory tariffs or (when that led to protests by other nations) by a variety of less obvious obstacles—the distribution system, for example, or the fixing of bids and contracts in private. Unlike that other enormously successful exporting nation Germany, Japan until recently did not import very much, apart from raw materials or goods which it did not manufacture itself (Boeing aircraft, luxury automobiles), which led to its enormous trade surpluses. In industry after industry, American and European critics complain, Japan has targeted a product made elsewhere, bought the foreign expertise required to understand the technology (whether in the form of MIT professors or software engineers), given its manufacturers all manner of support to permit them to catch up, and only then favored free trade in that sector; in other cases, it is claimed, it has hurt foreign rivals by "dumping" goods at below-market prices abroad while keeping them highly priced in the protected home market.[22]

The greatest foreign "victim" of these Japanese business practices, at least measured by the decibels of complaints, is the United States, which in recent years has experienced annual merchandise trade deficits with Japan of as much as $40 to $50 billion, has seen some of its key industries eclipsed by Japanese competition, and has reacted with growing concern as Japan has bought up ever more American assets. This is not only a massive historic irony, in that the American post-1945 occupation encouraged Japan to abandon "militarism" in favor of peaceful commercial pursuits, but a contemporary political irony, since the United States provides strategic security to an ally that contributes much less to the common defense while eroding America's own industrial base. In consequence, U.S. congressmen regularly complain about Japan's status as a "free rider" and press for a greater contribution to international security, a field in which Japan has appeared indecisive and unimpressive as compared with middle-sized European powers like Britain or France—confirming, to those critical of Tokyo policies, that the Japanese are interested only in making money.*

Furthermore, the popular image of all-conquering Japanese corporations ignores many less impressive aspects of its society and economy. The thousands of small family firms and mom-and-pop stores are inefficient, the distribution network is clogged by special interests, and Japanese farming is uncompetitive, having survived only because of special protection which keeps food prices much higher than in North America. The average per capita income of the Japanese people therefore conceals the fact that their real purchasing power is reduced by the high costs of food, consumer goods, land, and housing. Japan also lags behind many other nations in public facilities, sewage disposal, and places of recreation. The global triumph of Japanese capitalism is not yet reflected in *overall* productivity—which is still less than America's—or in the people's quality of life compared with that in certain other advanced industrial societies like Denmark and Canada.[23] In any case, much of the *measure* of Japanese wealth in recent years has rested upon extraordinarily high property prices and almost equally inflated stock prices—that is, on paper assets which can fall deeply in value yet have been used by banks to "leverage" Japan's aggressive spending on acquisitions across the globe, some of which have yet to prove profitable. By the early 1990s, much of the nominal rise in values of the preceding decade had been lost, particularly affecting bank shares, raising the issue of whether Japan's large overseas investments might have to be sold off to increase bank liquidity at home. Should this all end in a crash, not only would Japan's wealth decline, but that collapse might also damage international money and credit networks.

Finally, many of the factors accounting for Japan's post-1950 economic success are themselves beginning to change, which could reduce Japanese growth rates. By far the most important of these is the demo-

*On the other hand, there has always been confusion about whether a large-scale enhancement of Japanese *military power,* together with a reduction in the American strategic presence in the Pacific, really would be wise. Critics who point to Japan's "one-dimensional" strength (i.e., economic power), and to the way it has exploited that position, are among the first to caution against building up the Japanese armed forces—which leaves Tokyo both accused of not spending enough on national security and simultaneously warned not to contemplate large defense increases. Even when Japan paid large amounts of money to finance the 1991 war against Iraq, many foreign critics were unimpressed.

graphic transformation, the consequences of which are discussed in more detail below. Japan will have far more elderly people in the early twenty-first century than now, and the country's traditionally high savings ratios may decline significantly as a result; and, with available capital reduced, Japanese firms may no longer be able to count upon low-interest loans as an advantage over foreign rivals. In addition, any further rise in the value of the yen could force Japanese corporations to move manufacturing offshore, to lower-cost countries. As that happens, the Japanese—like the British and the Americans before them—may increasingly lose their "manufacturing culture," a development already evident in the numbers of talented youths nowadays heading into merchant banking rather than engineering. Caught in the traditional "scissor" of higher costs at home and increasing competition from newly industrializing countries overseas, Japan Inc. could sooner or later find that its special advantages have disappeared.[24]

Throughout the commentaries upon Japan's prospects, there runs an underlying question: is it "special" or "not normal" compared with other advanced industrial societies?[25] Of course, the question itself raises the issue of whether there really is a "normal" Western or American capitalist system from which the Japanese are deviating. This literature suggests that the Japanese way of life has posed a challenge especially to Americans, who worry at being eclipsed economically but are even more worried that they might have to alter their own habits—concerning education, individualism, the role of women—in order to match the Japanese challenge.[26] (Far better, perhaps, to press the Japanese themselves to change *their* habits). The issue of Japan's uniqueness is complicated not merely by untestable claims of superiority by Japanese nationalists, but also by the differing approaches of foreign "experts." Whereas foreigners resident in Japan for many years have generally concluded that the Japanese do have special cultural assumptions which affect economic performance, classical Western economists believe that sooner or later, all countries function according to universal principles. Rational economic man has always found culture difficult to quantify.[27]

Behind this debate lies a larger historical issue: is Japan a normal country which will lose its present advantages one day, or has it found a way of defying laws concerning comparative national advantage and can it thus avoid what might be termed a late-Victorian fate? The phrase refers to the dilemma that faced the British a century ago when they began to lose their early industrial lead as other countries imitated them. In theory, at least, Britain could have avoided being overtaken if its economy had repeatedly switched into ever-higher-added-value production, abandoning the older sectors to foreign competitors. But that in turn would have needed some form of national planning and a long-term economic strategy, and also a constant upgrading of Britain's educational system, its output of scientists, technologists, and engineers, and its levels of investment in research and development, all of which were necessary to keep ahead of the field. Because British society did *not* choose to reorganize itself in that way, its late-Victorian economy was steadily overtaken by others and Britain lost its place as workshop of the world.[28]

According to some economists, the evidence of Japan's own long-term relative decline already exists in the aging of the population; the consumer spending, tourist outflows, and reduction in overall savings rates; the rise in imported manufactures, the shift of production to other parts of the world, and the reduction in its current-accounts surpluses; the steady structural move out of industrial production and into services; the emergence of Tokyo as a global financial center, a latter-day version of the City of London in Victorian times, but one resting upon less secure (because more speculative) foundations; the volatility of its stock market, no longer immune from steep declines; and the changes in cultural attitudes, career choices, and the role of women and other indications of a deep national metamorphosis. The Japanese sun may still be shining brightly, but it is now past the noon hour and beginning to set.[29]

On the other hand, there is also evidence that, while making certain ostensible changes to please internal and external critics (increasing domestic consumption, reducing trade surpluses), Japan is engaged in the most enormous industrial "retooling" for growth that the world has ever seen. It has identified new areas of very high added value (see Table 4) and is moving into them as swiftly as possible. It is constantly improving its own production methods and standards of quality control. Moreover, a great deal of the much-vaunted rise in imports comes from *Japanese* components factories overseas; and although they make global acquisitions to ensure that they are not excluded from critical world markets, its companies remain very Japanese in nature and opposed to a "hollowing out" of the home industrial base. Unlike Victorian Britain, Japan neither rests upon its laurels nor spends on Empire; and its steady increases in productivity, not only in manufacturing but also in services, means that its economic power is still expanding.[30]

In sum, this debate suggests that Japan and its people confront two very plain choices. The first is to make fundamental alterations in a system committed to the steady pursuit of economic growth over the past four decades. Succumbing to external pressures and domestic demand, the Japanese will spend more and save less, they will as a whole be richer and enjoy life's luxuries more, and society will be more cosmopolitan, less deferential and hierarchical, and to that extent less "Japanese." In James Fallows's phrase, Japan will be "more like us," that is, more like Americans.[31] On the other hand, its economy will have matured, its saving rates will be lower, its propensity to import manufactures will increase, its industrial base will give way to services,

Table 4. The Relative Added Value of Manufactures

Product	*Added Value ($/lb)*
Satellite	20,000
Jet fighter	2,500
Supercomputer	1,700
Aero-engine	900
Jumbo jet	350
Videocamera	280
Mainframe computer	160
Semiconductor	100
Submarine	45
Color television	16
NC machine tool	11
Luxury motor car	10
Standard motor car	5
Cargo ship	1

Source: *The Economist,* "Japanese Technology," 2 December 1989, p. 4

and its manufacturing culture will be somewhat eroded, with market shares reduced by Korea, Taiwan, and other late-developing nations. It will be an immensely wealthy people, perhaps the richest in the world; but, like the generations of successful Romans, Britons, or Americans before it, it will tend more and more to the consumption rather than the creation of wealth.

The alternative would see a relatively unchanged Japanese nation, committed to innovative wealth creation and to an expanding global market share in ever more profitable products. With certain modifications, the existing system would remain in place, emphasizing educational discipline, high savings, quality production, massive investments in research and development, and long-term planning orchestrated by company leaders (in conjunction with the bureaucracies), all attended by a retained high self-consciousness of "Japanness." While its corporations accumulated further wealth, much of it would be plowed back into investment rather than released for general consumption; and while some of that growth would be the consequence of enhanced living standards at home, it would also be boosted by a relentless penetration of foreign markets, from East Asia to Southern Europe. Japan would thus remain essentially "one-dimensional," very different from America and other societies, with the exception of its Asian emulators. Moreover, simply because it appeared "less like us," its economic and technological eminence would produce international resentments that it would take enormous Japanese ingenuity to pacify. Even more than today, it would require the assistance of foreign lobbyists, partners, scholars, and publicists[32]—together with generous contributions to philanthropic endeavors, large amounts of foreign aid, and so on—to help mitigate international suspicions that its long-term intentions posed a threat.

It is with the latter meaning in mind that this chapter is entitled "The Japanese 'Plan' for a Post-2000 World." Because Japanese economic expansionism has been so purposeful and systematic, critics feel that there *must* exist a coherent strategy formulated—and regularly updated—by businessmen and bureaucrats in Tokyo, one which takes advantage of the Japanese corporation's capacity for long-term planning and, even more, of the fact that many other economies (especially the American) do not have an industrial or technology policy and still naively rely upon laissez-faire.[33] While Japan experts caution that foreigners ought *not* to view MITI as a sort of economic equivalent to the Prussian general staff,[34] the habit of various ministries and the Nomura Research Institute of issuing "projections" and "visions" about the future suggests that intense scheming is going on to ensure that whatever the next new trend, Japan will take advantage of it. An alternative view, that Japan's long-term economic expansionism is not so much orchestrated by officials in Tokyo as it is driven by the intense competitiveness of its major corporations, is not yet widely understood but seems at least as plausible an explanation.[35] In that sense, references to a "plan" have less to do with national strategy than with the long-term ambitions of individual Japanese companies as they struggle for global market shares.

The chief weakness in this debate upon Japan's future economic and technological place in the world is that it has not paid much attention to international politics or, indeed, to the sorts of global changes discussed earlier in this book. Presenting Japan either as a "rational actor" which can always respond intelligently to new economic opportunities or as a country about to undergo the same process of internal slowdown as previous societies, the literature upon the future of Japan Inc. devotes little attention to how the island state might be affected by broad global transformations. What is generally assumed is a basic continuity in present arrangements and tendencies: a reasonably open trading system, allowing global capitalism to function normally; the total disappearance of the Cold War; sporadic regional conflicts but not ones in which Japan would be directly involved (although the United States might well be); no resurgence of Russian imperialism; touchy but not impossible relations between Tokyo and the European Community; delicate relations with China, the mutual distrust to some extent being ameliorated by Japanese credit; the intensification of Japan's economic influence throughout Southeast Asia; and the preservation of the Japanese-American relationship despite occasional trade and security differences, if only because the Japanese understand that it is necessary to avoid an open break with Washington and, indeed, to "prop up" American power in the Pacific over the next decade or so, until the outlines of the post–Cold War international order become much clearer.[36]

Should this relatively stable international order fail, however, things could look entirely different. Civil war in the former Soviet Union, the withdrawal of America's military deployments overseas, growing Chinese assertiveness, the emergence of India as a regional superpower, and greater rivalry between the world's "haves" and "have-nots" are all possibilities. In such circumstances, with new threats to security emerging just as the American strategic shield was becoming less reliable, a new generation of Japanese leaders might feel it necessary to increase defense capabilities. Whether the Japanese people would agree to that is difficult to say, but the country would be far more capable *economically* of creating modern armed forces than it was in the 1930s, when its total GNP was only one-tenth that of the United States. By around the year 2000, with a GNP perhaps close to that of the American total and with a formidable technological base, things would be different.[37]

Moreover, as will be discussed below, *non*military threats might be as great as if not greater than military dangers in an age of far-reaching demographic and technological change. Instead of the ever-increasing economic integration forecast by proponents of the "borderless world," there could be financial crashes, intensified commercial rivalries in agriculture, manufacturing, software, and services, and rising protectionism—all of which would clearly hurt Japan, so heavily dependent upon overseas markets and prosperity for its own well-being. In noneconomic spheres, from the global population explosion to the greenhouse effect, transnational impacts could also be serious, and perhaps even more difficult for the Japanese to control. Undeniably, Japan possesses considerable strengths when it comes to dealing with the global forces for change outlined in Part One above; to repeat an earlier point, it probably is better "prepared" for the twenty-first century than any other advanced industrial society.[38] But its many strengths, chiefly in the familiar fields of technology, production, and finance, may not be enough to keep it free of trouble.

Such strengths are evident, for example, in Japan's ability to handle the financial and communications revolution, the rise of multinational corporations, and, more generally, the challenge of remaining responsive to new technologies. Although globalization was chiefly American in origin, Japan has been remarkably quick to benefit from the new economic order. Despite declining share prices on the Tokyo stock market, seven out of ten of the world's largest banks in a September 1991 *Wall Street Journal* ranking were Japanese. "Overall, twenty-nine of the world's hundred largest banks are Japanese. Germany has twelve, France has ten, and the U.S. and Italy each have nine banks on the list." Much the same is true of the world's insurance companies (four out of the top five are Japanese) and securities firms (the top four are Japanese).[39] If the free flow of capital—for industrial investment, takeovers, purchases of property, bonds, and stock—is the driving force behind the emerging global economic order, then this society possesses great strength, at least for as long as it maintains high capital resources.

Japan has also distinguished itself by becoming the base for many of the world's largest public companies, the multinationals that now occupy such an important place in the global economy: in 1991 Toyota, Hitachi, Toshiba, and another thirty-four of the world's hundred largest companies were Japanese.[40] Richer in capital assets than most of their American and European counterparts,* and less under shareholder pressure for short-term profits, most of Japan's companies are able to keep investing in the technologies of the future. Moreover, in what may be one of the most significant pointers to the technological "new world order" of the future, how many *influential* patents a country owns, Japanese companies appear to be overtaking or eclipsing their rivals in field after field.[41]

If Japan's technological and manufacturing successes of the past decade are any guide to the years to come, then its breakthroughs into newer fields—aerospace, software, biotech—may come faster than its rivals are prepared for. Between 1980 and 1989 alone, for example, Japan's shares of global exports in certain high-technology products rose dramatically, in some cases literally from nowhere, as shown in Table 5.

Since many of these technologies (microelectronics, telecommunications equipment) provide the physical means for the global financial

*In mid-1991, for example, Toyota Motor had a market value of $44.5 billion on profits (1990) of $3.2 billion, compared with General Motors' market value of $25 billion and a loss of $2 billion.

Table 5. Shares of Global Exports of High-Technology Products, 1980 and 1989[42]

Microelectronics		*Computers*	
1980	*1989*	*1980*	*1989*
1 U.S. (18.3%)	1 Japan (22.1%)	1 U.S. (38.6%)	1 U.S. (24%)
2 Japan (13.2%)	2 U.S. (21.9%)	2 W. Germany (11.5%)	2 Japan (17.5%)
3 Singapore (10.1%)	3 Malaysia (8.9%)	3 U.K. (10.4%)	3 U.K. (9%)
4 Malaysia (8.9%)	4 S. Korea (7.4%)	4 France (8.6%)	4 W. Germany (6.9%)
5 W. Germany (8.4%)	5 W. Germany (5.8%)	5 Italy (6.6%)	5 Taiwan (5.8%)

Aerospace		*Telecommunications Equipment*	
1980	*1989*	*1980*	*1989*
1 U.S. (47.6%)	1 U.S. (45.8%)	1 W. Germany (16.7%)	1 Japan (24.7%)
2 U.K. (19.7%)	2 W. Germany (12.5%)	2 Sweden (15.3%)	2 W. Germany (9.5%)
3 W. Germany (9.1%)	3 U.K. (10.9%)	3 U.S. (10.9%)	3 U.S. (8.8%)
4 France (6.0%)	4 France (10.2%)	4 Japan (10.3%)	4 Sweden (8.1%)
5 Canada (4.4%)	5 Canada (4.4%)	5 Netherlands (9.3%)	5 Hong Kong (6.3%)

Machine Tools & Robotics		*Scientific/Precision Equipment*	
1980	*1989*	*1980*	*1989*
1 W. Germany (25.8%)	1 Japan (23.3%)	1 U.S. (28.3%)	1 U.S. (25.2%)
2 U.S. (14.1%)	2 W. Germany (20.8%)	2 W. Germany (18.1%)	2 W. Germany (18.5%)
3 Japan (11.3%)	3 U.S. (12.1%)	3 U.K. (9.4%)	3 Japan (12.9%)
4 Sweden (9.1%)	4 Italy (10%)	4 France (8.0%)	4 U.K. (9.6%)
5 Italy (8.7%)	5 Switzerland (8.4%)	5 Japan (7.1%)	5 France (5.6%)

Medicine & Biologicals		*Organic Chemicals*	
1980	*1989*	*1980*	*1989*
1 W. Germany (16.7%)	1 W. Germany (15.6%)	1 W. Germany (19.1%)	1 W. Germany (17%)
2 Switzerland (12.5%)	2 Switzerland (12.2%)	2 U.S. (13.9%)	2 U.S. (15.5%)
3 U.K. (12.0%)	3 U.S. (12.2%)	3 Netherlands (10.9%)	3 France (8.7%)
4 France (11.9%)	4 U.K. (11.8%)	4 France (10.7%)	4 Netherlands (8.1%)
5 U.S. (11.4%)	5 France (10.3%)	5 U.K. (8.4%)	5 U.K. (8.4%)

and communications revolution, further advances of the latter provided another boost—a "feedback loop"—to Japanese industry.

While Japan looks to be in strong shape to handle today's technology explosion, it is less well placed with regard to its own demographic future, and still less with regard to global population trends. As many studies have noted, "Japan began its demographic transition from high to low fertility and mortality much later than the United States and other developed countries, but finished it with record speed."[43] In 1925, life expectancy at birth in Japan was about forty-five years and women had an average of 5.1 children. Nowadays, Japanese life expectancy is the highest in the world—seventy-six years for males and eighty-two years for females (1987)—but the total fertility rate has tumbled to well below the average 2.1 children per woman needed to maintain the overall population. In 1989, it fell to a record low of only 1.57 children per woman. Clearly, enhanced prosperity has contributed to this trend, as it has in every other industrialized society, but there seems to be something more at work in the Japanese case: in particular, Japanese women, educated to high levels, are reacting against the traditional expectations that after college they should concentrate upon rearing children—usually in cramped apartments—as their chief aim in life.

Few observers of Japanese society expect that this trend will be reversed. One prominent politician, rash enough in 1990 to moot the possibility that Japanese women should be discouraged from entering higher education, quickly disclaimed the idea after the ensuing uproar.[44] But if there is no demographic reversal, between now and 2025 Japan "will switch from having the lowest ratio of over-sixty-fives to its total population (one in eleven) to the highest (one in four) among the leading industrial countries."[45] This has caused economists to make gloomy predictions about Japan's long-term future: that with increasingly fewer workers supporting every retired person, payroll taxes and social security contributions will have to go up, so that Japan, which had been the most lightly taxed OECD country, will be one of the most heavily taxed; and that the 30 million or more over-sixty-fives in 2025 will draw upon their resources, cutting into the country's critically important savings rate, reducing the amount available for business investment, and weakening long-term economic growth. While lots of relatively prosperous Japanese pensioners are an attractive market in some areas (tourism, medical services), they will not help the country remain technologically competitive.[46] Once again, the specter of an end to the "Japanese miracle" is raised.

There is, of course, an obvious solution to the changing balance between the size of the Japanese work force and the numbers of elderly dependents: permit the immigration of the tens of thousands of Koreans, Filipinos, Pakistanis, Bangladeshis, and other peoples eager to gain employment there. Given Japan's exclusivist policies as well as its cramped geographical circumstances, this seems highly unlikely. While Japan's Immigration Bureau still welcomes foreign scientists, engineers, and other professionals, it has been cracking down on the 300,000 or so illegal immigrants, threatening them with deportation and their employers with fines or jail. Despite the pleas of the Japanese Food Service Association to secure more labor, or even the Tokyo Chamber of Commerce's proposed scheme for admitting up to 600,000 guest workers on two-year contracts, there seems little prospect that the Japanese will welcome this sort of "solution" to their growing labor shortages.[47] Tactless remarks by its politicians about the social weaknesses of America's multicultural, multiracial population reveal that concerns about preserving "Japanness" are always likely to outweigh merely utilitarian arguments in favor of increased immigration.

Still, while the change in Japan's demographic structure is important, it is by no means clear that it heralds economic stagnation. As many domestic critics have pointed out, the declining birth rate reflects the fact that the government's policies have so far failed to provide young Japanese couples with better amenities in life, like bigger and more affordable housing. Prevailing Japanese career norms underutilize women—female participation in the work force is much lower than in Britain and the United States, for example—and more positive policies in this realm could change things. Finally, since many fit over-sixty-fives are still capable of work and want to work, there is a case for rethinking retirement regulations.[48] By a combination of changes in these areas, both an increase in family size *and* a maintenance of the labor force are feasible.

In addition, Japan's larger companies are dealing with the labor shortage—and the high cost of Japanese labor—by going multinational. What was a limited number of overseas ventures a quarter century ago (chiefly assembly plants in Korea) has become a globally organized network of manufacturing plants, automobile factories, components producers, distribution centers, even research institutes, contributing to the parent company's plan. The benefits of this are both obvious and manifold. Not only have many companies found it cheaper to employ female labor in Thailand or Mexico to assemble electrical goods than to produce them in Japan itself, but the "out-sourcing" of components production helps to reduce the imbalance of merchandise trade with Japan's East Asian neighbors; indeed, Japanese ministers can point to these imported manufactures as evidence that the country is trying to reduce its overall trade surplus. Most important, the location of assembly and manufacturing plants abroad ensures access to key markets at a time of open or veiled protectionism: Mexican factories give Japan free access to the American and Canadian markets (and, again, disguise the U.S.-Japan trade gap), while automobile factories in England and Wales provide a European base for the EC market. At the end of the day, the profits go into the coffers of Toyota and Mitsubishi, boosting overall Japanese wealth.

Is this the way forward for Japan, for it to become ever more a *rentier* economy, its aging population reliant upon earnings from overseas investment and production to maintain its standard of living and allow it to purchase goods that can no longer be produced at home? Is this why the Japanese earnestly study the relative economic decline of late-Victorian Britain, and are fascinated by some similar possibilities in present-day America? Unquestionably, Japanese officials and businessmen worry that the unfavorable demographic trend, together with economic and social changes, could lead to Japan's own long-term economic decline. A people which once embraced Ezra Vogel's *Japan as Number One* is, twenty years later, now anxiously studying Bill Emmott's *The Sun Also Sets.*

In theory, of course, Japan *may* go the way of Holland and Britain, if it elects to abandon its manufacturing culture; but, as noted above, the indications from its own businessmen point in the opposite direction. The gloomier forecasts of the economic impact of an aging population all miss, *The Economist* has noted, "the effect of technological progress on productivity growth."[49] This refers not only to increased investments in new plant, machine tools, and high-tech steel mills and shipyards, but also to the fascination with automation and robotics noted earlier.* It is no coincidence that Japan now possesses close to three-quarters of the world's robots and more automated workplaces than anywhere else on earth. For, if their promise holds true, robots offer a wonderful escape from Japan's dilemma; they will keep the country at the forefront of manufacturing *and* compensate for any growing labor shortages, eliminating the need to import millions of foreign workers and their families. Technology thus provides a counter to demography. By initiating this further stage in the Industrial Revolution, Japanese industry thereby prepares itself for the twenty-first century.

By comparison, the challenges posed to Japan by the new agricultural revolution—biotech farming—appear less profound, although they are taken seriously.[50] A mountainous archipelago desperately short of flat, fertile land, yet with millions of full-time and part-time farmers traditionally working plots of one or two hectares, Japan is the least self-sufficient of the OECD nations in food supplies. Because of the enormous gap between industrial and agricultural productivity levels (and incomes), farm production is protected by large-scale subsidies and bureaucratic barriers—to the wrath of American agricultural export lobbies, and to the detriment of the Japanese consumer—yet Japan must still import more food than any other advanced economy. (Were it not for those imports, its current trade surplus would be much larger!) Finally, Japan has not traditionally possessed mighty chemical and agricultural corporations capable of moving into newer forms of food production like biotechnology. For many reasons, therefore, one might assume that the biotech revolution would be marginal to Japan's concerns.

Yet the signs are that this is altering fast. Japanese authorities are now seeking to reduce the number of inefficient farmers and are grudgingly making concessions to American demands to open the domestic food market. As millions of farmers retire or are bought out, Japan might seem even more likely to depend on foreign agricultural supplies.

* See Chapter 5.

In fact, a hard core of around 500,000 professional farmers is emerging, operating larger plots (their dairy farms are as big as those in the EC) and adopting mechanization, crop rotation, and other methods of enhancing productivity. Not only are improved types of cattle being bred at home, but Japanese agribusinesses are reaching out to purchase and manage beef farms in the United States. As Japanese agriculture modernizes itself, the authorities are also encouraging investments in biotechnology to make good Japan's inadequacies in this field. As has happened in other industries, the "catch-up" process frequently involves joint ventures with, or the purchase of, American companies that have the know-how.[51]

Although the biotech revolution in Japan is still in its infancy, the implications are clear enough. It would give the country a share in yet another leading industry of the twenty-first century, while reducing dependence upon foreign suppliers of agricultural goods and related raw materials. All this would play to Japan's existing strengths: easy access to Western technical literature, ample capital to purchase researchers, laboratories, and patents, support from large Japanese companies that want to broaden their product base, and assistance from the Japanese ministries. Perhaps the only objector would be the Foreign Ministry itself, as it tried to imagine explaining to U.S. farmers and congressmen why it needed to import ever less food from abroad.

This suggests that Japan has cleverly positioned itself both to take advantage of new technological trends and to reduce to a minimum the deleterious impacts of demographic change; and that, at least at first sight, the Japanese need feel less concern about global transformations than their competitors. Such a conclusion is probably accurate, *insofar as Japan can reconstruct itself internally to prepare for the future.* The real problems lie in the external realm, which is of course far less under Japanese control. The demographic challenge of preserving an adequate work force (through robots) is one thing; how to handle a China of 1.5 billion people—either increasingly prosperous and powerful *or* ridden with social and economic discontents—is quite another. How, indeed, is Japan to fare in an Asia forecast to surge in population from 3.0 to 4.9 billion over the next few decades (to 2025) while its own population is stagnant and aging? Can it really isolate itself from the impact of major global demographic shifts?

Similarly, how is it possible for a country so dependent upon exports to be assured of continued access to important global markets, especially if its own successes in industry, science, and technology threaten to make redundant the need for foreign produce? Automated assembly plants able to compete with cheap-labor factories in Southeast Asia appear on first encounter like a wonderful technological "fix," as does genetically engineered fruit, meat, and fish. But in practice would not their adoption provoke further resentments by other countries already convinced that Japan takes but rarely gives, and that "managed trade" is always managed in Tokyo's favor? Can the Japanese afford to give a further boost to protectionist sentiments in Europe and North America, especially if those markets become increasingly saturated and the global economy grows only moderately in the coming decades? Even if Asian markets become more important than Western ones, is not the problem—of Japan's unbalanced trade, and the ever-present threat of reprisals—simply transferred? In sum, global economic vulnerability has always been the price Japan has had to pay in achieving global commercial preeminence; and that vulnerability is, if anything, increasing.

The same paradox can be observed in relation to rising environmental challenges. Global warming, for example, presents Japan with a dilemma, although not an insuperable one. Because of its limited area and relatively small agricultural sector, Japan does not confront dire forecasts about a shift of grain-growing areas that faces (for example) Kansas. If, as some scientists predict, global warming leads to greater unpredictability and turbulence in the weather, then Japan may expect fiercer storms, flash floods, tornados; but that hardly seems a major or systemic threat to its well-being, and it could afford preventive and reactive measures. In the same way, while a rise in the sea level would affect low-lying areas, Japan is rich enough to strengthen its sea defenses. Perhaps it can even relocate its coastal settlements. For example, it has already allocated hundreds of millions of dollars to shore up and protect the tiny outlying island of Okinotorishima; if it should be permanently submerged under the rising seas, Japan could lose fishery and seabed rights.[52] Finally, if international agreements are made to reduce carbon emissions or improve energy efficiency, then Japan's record over the past two decades—the World Bank recently cited

Japan as "an environmental paragon" in those respects[53]—suggests it will have fewer problems in meeting new targets than most other countries. Global warming might be a nuisance, but an efficient and rich Japan can cope.

Still, if the next century were to see widespread environmentally induced disasters—interacting, as they probably would, with the global population explosion and massive social distress—one is bound to wonder whether Japan could remain an island unto itself. Could it preserve a technologically created "green" atmosphere adjacent to a continent where the uncontrolled industrialization of billions of people threatens the ecosystem? It is impossible to say at present, but it would surely be imprudent for the Japanese to conclude that deforestation and atmospheric pollution will only be *other* peoples' problems.

What the above suggests is that Japan can approach the twenty-first century with no more than guarded optimism. The best-selling writers predicting Japan's glorious future base their claims upon much valid evidence: the beneficial forces for change (capital, communications, robotics, biotech) are being exploited, the threatening ones (demographic chaos, global warming, financial collapse) either are distant or can probably be contained. Few other nations can feel as secure, especially in regard to technological change.

Nevertheless, there may be considerable dangers ahead for Japan as it prepares for the next century. We have noted the possibility of threatening external events, which are difficult to forecast in advance but—especially in the light of the many political revolutions of the past decade alone—cannot be dismissed. Nuclear proliferation in Asia, foreign-policy adventurism by regimes suffering from internal strains, a surge in Chinese power, confrontations on the Korean peninsula or in the South China sea . . . any of those would confirm Japan's strategic vulnerability. There could also be serious instabilities in its financial sector, which is much less securely founded than its manufacturing base.

Yet the greatest challenges may come, ironically, as a result of

Japan's own successes. If its economy continues to flourish as others stagnate, if it increases its demolition (say) of the American automobile industry and the European electronics industry, if it appears secure and comfortable, benefiting greatly from the international system but contributing little to its preservation, if it seems aloof and unhelpful in a world in which human disasters, regional conflicts, mass poverty, migratory waves, and the gap between "haves" and "have-nots" worsens, then foreign resentments might lead other nations to punish Japan economically—through tariffs, or other instruments—for what they believe to be its selfish policies.

To avoid such a prospect and contribute to the global order, Japan needs enlightened and courageous leadership to help it meet its internal transformations and make greater international contributions than it does at present. But it is in the quality of its political leadership that Japan suffers its greatest deficiency. Unlike its deficiencies in raw materials, this deficiency has not been countered; indeed, if studies of the "enigma" of Japanese power are correct, the political system virtually ensures that enlightened leaders will *not* emerge.[54] Instead, an "old boys' network" (graduates of Tokyo Law School, etc.) in the bureaucracies, big business, banks, and Liberal Party will continue to *share* power, with no one body or person permitted to assume the role of an American president or British prime minister. Thus there can be no "leadership" as Western societies understand it; and foreign observers should cease searching for a rising figure who could be the Japanese political equivalent of Helmut Schmidt or Margaret Thatcher.

This is ironic. Unlike most other societies, in which political leadership is regarded as a key element, if not *the* key element, in the nation's success, Japan appears to have constructed a machine that can go by itself. Rigorous, uniform educational standards, firm social codes regarding obedience, hierarchy, and deference, elite bureaucratic guidance, a commitment to savings and investment, fanatical attention to design and service, a team-spirit ethos determined to succeed against domestic and foreign rivals . . . all these have carried Japan from its 1945 nadir to where it stands now. They also are impressive elements of strength for the future. But as our increasingly complex world heads into the twenty-first century, they may not be enough to handle the nonmaterial political and moral tests which lie ahead, nor to deal with challenges outside Japan's borders. Sophisticated robots can overcome lots of problems. What they cannot do is provide vision, and political leadership, that will allow the Japanese people to operate successfully in the global society of today and tomorrow.[55]

9

INDIA AND CHINA

IN ANY DISCUSSION OF HOW JAPAN, THE United States, or European countries might best prepare for the twenty-first century, population size (although very important) is merely one of several trends to be taken into account. In the case of India and China, however, the demographic factor overshadows every other, with critical implications not only for those two societies but also for the world community. China and India are the two most populous countries on earth. Their respective populations of 1.135 billion and 853 million people are now over 37 percent of the world total. If the middle-range demographic projections are correct, each nation will contain around 1.5 billion people by the year 2025, approximately 35 percent of the whole. The activities of this sheer mass of people will affect global foodstuff demand, energy use, and the environment. For example, China and India already are the world's fourth and fifth largest contributors to the annual increase in the greenhouse effect,[1] and the expected growth in their populations and rate of industrialization are likely to have even larger impacts upon the environment. On the other hand, a marked expansion of their economies, raising standards of living, could greatly stimulate global trade, perhaps providing large new markets for Japan and the NIEs as demand in the developed world slowed. China and India are also important in foreign and military affairs; what they may do in the future could affect regional security in East Asia and South Asia, as well as nuclear proliferation and global disarmament in general.

While already significant in world affairs, both Asian giants are limited by their relative poverty, with China's per capita GNP estimated at a mere $294 in 1987, and India's only $311. This means that India's total GNP is less than half of Italy's, and China's between one-sixth and one-seventh of Japan's.[2] Put another way, if both of them had managed to achieve South Korea's current per capita GNP of roughly $5,000, China would possess the world's largest economy and India's would be almost as big as America's.[3] Such an enormous increase in living standards—difficult to imagine, but theoretically possible—would bring not only much more purchasing power for China and India's citizens but also far greater resources for research and development, science and technology, and infrastructure and education, as well as for military power.

What, then, are the chances that these two nations can escape present low levels of average income and continue to enjoy the high rates of economic growth which, unlike Africa and Latin America, they achieved throughout the 1980s?

If average annual growth rates over the next few decades could be maintained at a reasonably high pace—say, 5 percent in real terms—progress would be assured. It might not fully compare with the much faster growth rates of the East Asian NIEs in recent years; but to the Chinese and Indian peoples the consequences would be positive. After all, although China is poor at present, it was far poorer a decade ago. An average annual GNP growth of 9 percent during the 1980s doubled real incomes, especially among the 800 million rural population, reduced poverty, cut infant and child mortality, and improved consumption levels.[4] Even if the average growth rates for the next twenty years

Table 6. Growth in the GDP of China and India, 1980–1989[5]

	1980–88 (average)	*1988*	*1989*
China	9.5	11.2	3.9
India	5.0	9.8	4.8

were less swift, a steady increase would be welcome—and might, in fact, be preferable to over-speedy growth, which often produces bottlenecks, inflation, and social turbulence.

But this escape from Malthus's trap is threatened by China's and India's twin population explosions, adding millions of new mouths each year. Indeed, were that eighteenth-century sage to return to our planet, he would witness in China and India conditions similar to those he described in his first *Essay.* Advances in medical care (especially vaccinations) and initial rises in food supplies in the past few decades reduced infant mortality, and the populations surged, outstripping available resources and threatening a deterioration in conditions instead of hoped-for improvements.

This problem is so deep that regardless of their different political regimes—democratic and multiparty in India, a Communist Party monopoly of power in China—the respective leaderships have been struggling to persuade couples to limit family size. As in Africa, Central America, and other parts of the developing world, however, that campaign faces formidable obstacles: the belief, deep-rooted in peasant societies, that extra children add to the labor force and thus produce extra wealth; ancestor worship, fear of being unsupported in old age, preference for the extended family, and cultural assumptions about the role of women; and ignorance of and prejudice against contraceptive techniques, together with a resentment of government interference in family matters. Still, fearing demographic increases will outstrip resources and eat into the increases in output, Beijing and New Delhi have striven—often by clumsy and draconian means—to combat the population explosion.

Of the two, China has had the greater recent success, because of its more authoritarian and centralized structures of government. Mao himself had opposed population control, decrying fears that people would outstrip resources and arguing that a socialist economy could handle ever-larger numbers. Since the first decade or so of Communism saw a rise in living standards and the coming of near-universal (if basic) health care, these favorable trends interacted with the existing high levels of fertility to produce a surge in China's population. It was followed, however, by the eccentricities of the "Great Leap Forward" of 1957–61—dividing the population into groups of five thousand households on average, each group with its own land, communal kitchens, even backyard steel mills—which disrupted the economy, reduced food production and distribution, and caused widespread famine, exacerbated by poor harvests. The result was a disaster, with excess deaths estimated at about 30 million people in four years, "probably the largest number of famine deaths in modern times."[6] In reaction to such losses, Chinese families in the 1960s and 1970s were eager to have lots of babies, so that the birth rates leaped to pre-revolution levels of 33–43 births per thousand. The resultant population boom finally forced the government to institute some of the strictest family-planning rules in the world: couples had to marry late (i.e., in their mid-twenties) and were limited to one child, and all this was supervised and enforced by employers, officials, and health workers; those who flouted the single-child target were punished with fines, loss of job, and the withdrawal of social and educational privileges, while the wife was often browbeaten into an abortion.[7] The aim was that China's population should "level off" at 1.2 billion in 2000, and then fall to 700 million by 2050.

The sharp decrease in the number of births per family during the 1970s and 1980s, as well as the earlier dramatic fluctuations, can be seen in Chart 4.

While this plan was rigorously enforced in its early phase—almost 21 million people were reported to have been sterilized in accordance with the one-child policy in 1983 alone—the populace was increasingly resentful; another grisly consequence was a sharp rise in the number of baby girls murdered or abandoned by peasants desperate to ensure that if they could have only one child, it would be a son to look after them in old age.[8] By the mid-1980s, the authorities adopted a rather more conciliatory stance and exchanged their future population targets for less ambitious ones. At the same time, however, the "baby boom" children of the mid to late 1960s were reaching marriageable age. Not only were there more babies per family (especially in the countryside, where it was easier to avoid controls), but there were many more twenty-five-year-olds to have children. In consequence, China's swift

Chart 4. Total Fertility Rates, China, 1945–87[9]

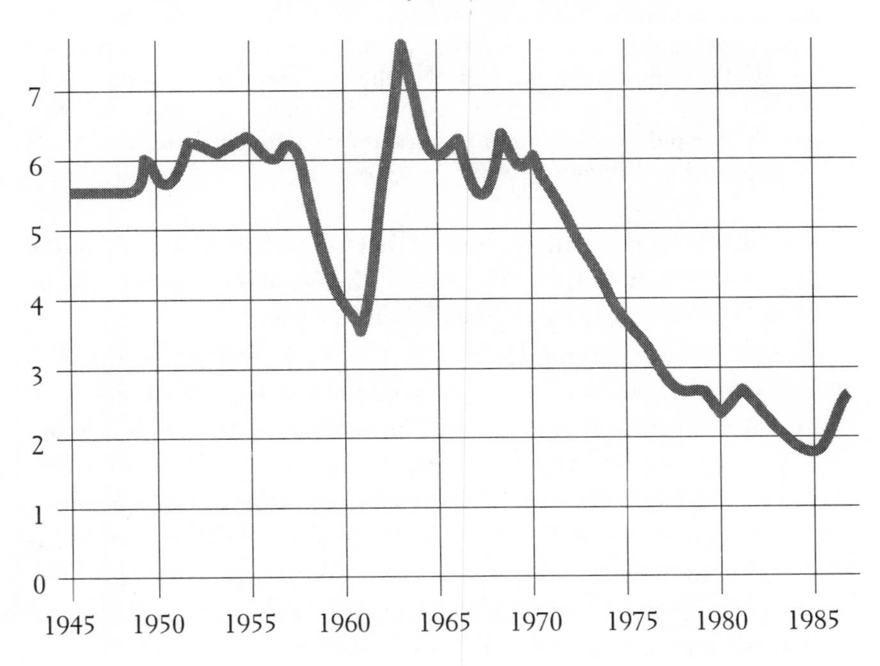

population growth has resumed. The birth rate has increased from 17.8 per thousand in 1985 to 21.1 per thousand in 1987. In fact, 22 million Chinese babies were born in 1987, whereas only 7 million people died—a net increase almost as great as the entire population of Australia.[10] Yet had it not been for population control, officials estimate, 240 million *more* Chinese would have been born over the last two decades.[11]

All this confronts the Chinese government with an appalling dilemma, in the form of a growing mismatch between population and resources. Depending upon the estimates, China's land can sustain between 750 and 950 million people—figures surpassed some two to three decades ago. China contains one-fifth of the earth's population, with only 7 percent of its farmland, much of it of poor quality. Its population density is three times the world average, without a corresponding share of world resources. A Chinese scholar has observed of his country that

> the territory per capita is only one-third of the world average, farmland one-third, pasture land one-quarter, forest one-ninth, and water one-fourth. Compared with those of the United States, they are even lower. Per capita farmland in China is only one-eighth of the U.S. and forest only one-tenth. With China's present level of productivity and technology, excessive growth of population will surely increase the overstretched pressure on the environment and resources.[12]

For politicians and planners hoping that China will participate in the Pacific Rim "boom" then, the threat that economic gains will be swallowed up by population growth is a real one.

On the other hand, the leadership has to take into account that a strictly enforced policy of one child per family is very unpopular. Like the emperors before them—or the Russian czars—they would find a real "peasants' revolt" the most serious domestic challenge of all. In addition, China's demographic policy contradicts its aim of encouraging individual responsibility in agricultural and small-business enterprises. If an individual family is now responsible for developing its own parcel of land or operating a small firm, it will have an enormous incentive—and economic rationale—to produce a number of children, so that the business can expand. Limitations of births to one or two children per couple would inhibit enterprises of that sort.[13]

Finally, there are serious implications for the future demographic structure of China, which is likely to become *more unbalanced* than most. At present, many more children are being born than China's overstretched resources can sustain; but even if the government achieved zero population growth by the turn of the century—an unlikely prospect, admittedly—it would then confront an age profile distorted by the 1960s surge in births, *and* perhaps also by their hoped-for one-child-per-family policy in the 1990s. Zero growth by 2000, one demographer has pointed out, suggests that China's population in 2035 will contain "twice as many persons in their sixties as in their twenties, an age composition that even the most enthusiastic supporter of the virtues of the elderly could scarcely favor."[14]

Although India also has a rapidly growing elderly population,[15] its key problem remains the demographic explosion, simply because population growth rates are swifter. At independence, average life expectancy was 32.5 years for a male and 31.7 years for a female; by the late 1980s, it was about 58 years for both (and still rising), a result of improved health care, diet, sanitation, and general standards of living.[16] However, the fall in mortality rates has not been attended by a similar reduction in fertility rates as it was in China. The Indian government has considerably less power to reach into the villages and cajole peasant families to limit their size; and, with far greater localized poverty and much higher rates of illiteracy and child mortality than in China, the desire to bear children to enhance family income remains strong. It has been reinforced, negatively, by the powerful public reaction against Sanjay Gandhi's forced sterilization program in the late 1970s and by a general mistrust of officialdom, birth-control centers, and inefficient or dangerous contraceptive devices.[17] In any case, there is much greater cultural, religious, and regional diversity in India than in China, so that even if adequate birth-control facilities were available to all, there would probably be a different response from middle-class families in Gujarat than from the hill tribes of Manipur.

Whereas the total fertility rate in China had dropped to 2.4 by 1985–90, one of the lowest in Asia, in India it remained at a stubbornly high 4.3. While China's population increases by about 15 million each year, India's averaged 16.8 million each year in the 1985–90 period.[18] Even the forecast AIDS epidemic may hardly dent that sort of growth. Since India's infant mortality rate is twice China's, improvements in that domain would actually exacerbate the problem. In this respect, India's age structure, with almost 40 percent of the population under fifteen, is closer to that of countries in Africa and the Middle East. Moreover, because India's economy grew more slowly than China's and family income is less equitably distributed, its population surge has led to increases in the poverty level, both in rural and urban areas. At present, it is estimated that approximately half of India's 850 million people live in poverty.[19] Should these trends continue, India may have as large a population as China's by the year 2025, but its 1.5 billion inhabitants will contain a far higher number of the landless, underemployed, undernourished, functionally uneducated, and ill-sheltered already so evident across India today.[20]

. . .

If long-term growth is to continue and famine to be avoided, then—just as in eighteenth-century Britain—agriculture will play a key role. Farming alone contributes almost 30 percent of India's GNP, down from the 40 percent share of 1965 but significantly more than Korea's 11 percent or Japan's 2.8 percent.[21] Moreover, agriculture accounts for 60 percent of India's employment. The agricultural sector of China's economy is even more important; perhaps 80 percent of the population is engaged in farming or related activities. The implication is obvious: if agricultural productivity stagnates, it will be a drag upon the entire economy (as it was in the USSR); if it surges, as happened in China after the 1978 reforms, the enhanced purchasing power of hundreds of millions of small farmers will provide a tremendous boost to the economy, with "multiplier effects" upon the output of tractors, tools, fertilizers, consumer goods, utility supplies, banking services, and so on.

India's rise in agricultural output since independence has also been marked, although some observers believe it could have been more impressive.[22] The most important gains were the result of the "green revolution" from the 1960s onward, which greatly enhanced crop yields. These improvements affected many crops, maize and millet for example, but especially rice and wheat. By using "miracle rice" varieties, Indian farmers gained much greater yields in the irrigated semiarid areas of the northwest. Even more important was the introduction of dwarf wheats, which flourished in north-central and northwest India, producing large increases in output. Overall, India's food supplies have risen sharply over the past few decades, and it normally has sufficient stocks in hand to meet drought and famine conditions; indeed, rice and certain other foodstuffs have sometimes joined traditional crops such as cotton, tea, and jute in the list of India's exports.

Although the increased output is welcome, the signs are that the green revolution has largely spent itself. In any case, the successes of Indian agriculture have not been uniform and the increases are significantly less than in China. The chief reason is that improved strains of wheat and rice also need other important inputs such as fertilizers and irrigation. In states with a hot-wet monsoon climate such as Bengal and

Orissa, traditional methods of rain-fed, intensive-labor rice cultivation continue, since there is no real incentive to adopt the newer seeds. In the drier states, much depends upon the availability of water supplies, which are affected by government irrigation schemes, political influence, and so on. Moreover, high-yielding varieties of wheat seeds require the systematic application of fertilizers and the use of tractors—so that poorer farmers find it hard to adopt the new methods.[23] Both central and state governments in India have been less concerned with countering the massive inequalities among the rural population—which would raise thorny issues of property rights, caste, privilege—than with encouraging agricultural output to rise as a whole.[24] In the same way, increases in milk production have tended to come from, and to benefit, powerful cooperatives with good connections to foreign aid donors, rather than the poorer farmers.[25] While agricultural development and national income rise, the *uneven* gains are probably insufficient to match the population increase.

In China, the rise in agricultural output has been greater, chiefly because the pre-1978 system of communal farming was abandoned. Admitting that the collectivized system had caused twenty years of stagnation in food output, the Deng regime introduced reforms that gave the peasant incentives; land itself remained in collective ownership, but individual families were permitted to farm it as they wished; after delivering a certain portion of their produce to the community, they could sell the rest on the open market; restrictions on hiring farm labor were lifted; and the prices paid for agricultural goods were raised, to provide a further incentive.[26] The result was a remarkable surge in Chinese agricultural output, especially grain, contrasting sharply with the stagnation in the Soviet Union, as shown in Chart 5.

On the other hand, by subsidizing basic food costs for consumers, the government ensured that the urban masses would not face large price increases. As a result, China's hundreds of millions of peasant farmers were better off than ever before,[27] stimulating the economy and more than doubling per capita income within a decade.

For a while, therefore, it looked as if China had achieved agricultural self-sufficiency, and might in fact become a major food exporter. By the end of the 1980s, however, optimism began to fade. While output of cash crops and vegetables continued to expand—peasants could make

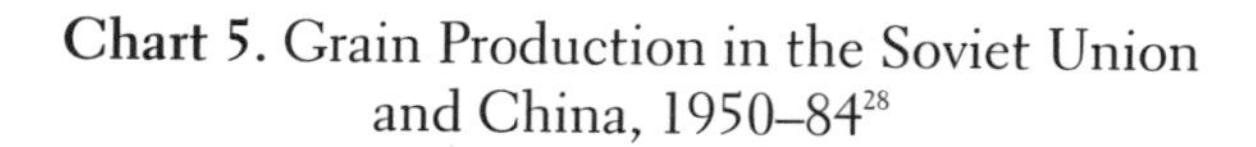

Chart 5. Grain Production in the Soviet Union and China, 1950–84[28]

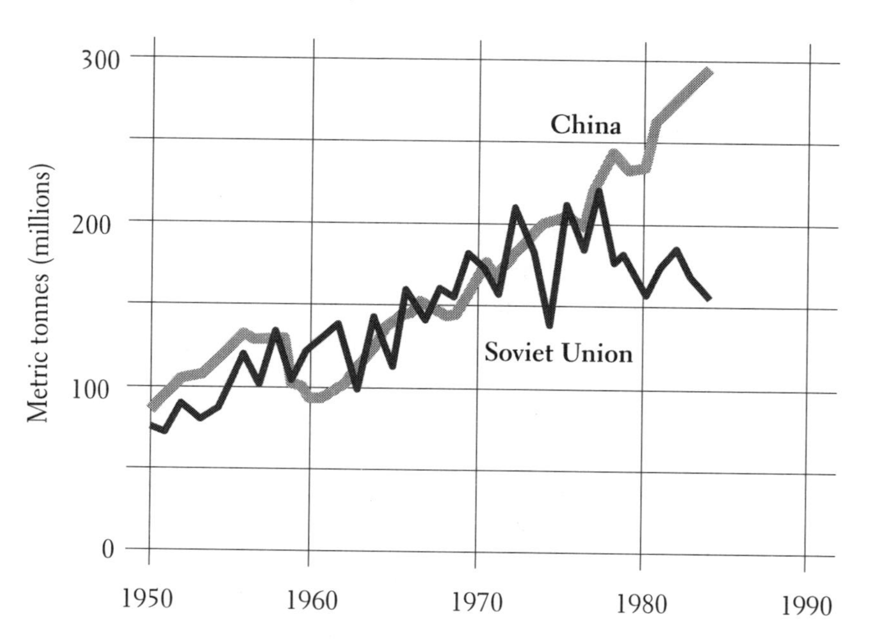

a higher profit on those—the critically important grain harvest did not always meet official targets, leading to large-scale imports of grain, which reduced China's hard-currency reserves. Governmental policy is to increase annual grain output from 400 million tons (the current level) to 500 million tons by the end of the century, to avoid dependence upon foreign supplies.[29] Yet many agricultural economists doubt that this can be achieved, at least not without considerable difficulties. There is little additional land suitable for crops, and as living standards rise, the people are consuming foods of a higher caliber (vegetables, poultry), further increasing demand. Meanwhile, the population steadily grows. For the regime to avoid the political and foreign-currency costs of depending on foreign imports, it will need to spend large sums on irrigation, fertilizers, farm equipment, better seeds, and improved processing, *and* to raise the prices paid to farmers even further.[30] This would favor grain producers over consumers—unless there were enhanced food subsidies, which would exacerbate the government deficit.

It would also take investment capital from other sectors and might hurt economic growth, the key to China's future.

This is not to say that Chinese agricultural policy has entered a cul-de-sac, but it is difficult to see how it can keep increasing crop output to match population growth—unless technology provides another form of agricultural revolution. As things now stand, however, the structural obstacles to such a revolution appear daunting.

While struggling to control population and increase food output, the Chinese and Indian governments must also move their economies into manufactures and services, to obtain higher per capita income and to absorb the tens of millions of new entrants into the work force each year. Industrialization is attractive, not just because it increases national wealth but also because it reduces population growth as the people become urbanized and undergo a demographic transition. This involves another race against time, for the drift of millions from rural areas like Sichuan is already creating enormous shanty cities of the São Paulo type.* Roughly speaking, only 200 million people are needed on China's farms, whereas the rural work force at present totals 400 million, leaving vast masses of peasants either to drift around the countryside—to the alarm of the authorities—or to exacerbate the pressures upon the cities. If economic growth falters or if industrialization fails to create enough jobs for the new urban masses, the future could be grim.

Creating their own industrial revolution, therefore, has always been central to India's and China's plans to prepare for the twenty-first century. Thus, despite a certain deference to Gandhi's notion of a peasant economy, India's leaders encouraged industrialization to strengthen the country's defense base, reduce dependence upon foreign manufacturers, and enhance national income. The route chosen was neither Japan's export-led growth nor the socialist model of the

*Because of this problem, the Chinese government forbids immigration into the larger cities, although families can move to designated medium-size towns.

USSR, but something in between—befitting, no doubt, the Fabian beliefs of many Indian politicians. Like Latin American nations, India chose to replace imports with its own heavy industrial products; iron and steel, cement, locomotives, automobiles, shipbuilding, defense-related production, engineering, and machine tools were all supported by the state. Transport, mining, and utilities were taken into the public sector. Others were given subsidies, very high tariff protection, and government orders. The result was the emergence of a number of publicly owned corporate giants in steel, aeronautics, engineering, and petrochemicals.[31] Where industrialization was not possible by internal means, foreign aid was encouraged—as, for example, Soviet help in building steel plants. By such devices, India planned to become an industrial giant.

Yet while the economy did grow between the 1950s and the 1980s, it hardly kept ahead of its own population increases. *Real income* per person rose by only 1.7 percent a year in the period 1950–65, and by 1 percent a year in the decade after that, causing some observers to joke at "the Hindu rate of growth."[32] In consequence, government economists kept scaling back their growth projections, from one Four-Year Plan to the next.[33] The most disappointing feature has been the pace of industrialization. In 1950, manufacturing accounted for 10.3 percent of the Gross Domestic Product, and crept up to 15.8 percent by 1978–79; it scarcely increased by 1989, when it totaled 16.1 percent (compared with 31.6 percent in Korea).[34] With industry as a whole (including manufacturing) employing only a small proportion of India's population,[35] the country slipped backward economically; in 1955, it was the world's tenth-biggest industrial power, but two decades later it ranked twentieth.[36] As late as 1965, the value of India's manufactured exports was eight times that of Korea's, yet by 1986 Korea's exports were 4.5 times the value of India's.

The reasons for this industrial stagnation are many, ranging from the lack of stimulus from the sluggish agricultural sector to pork-barrel politics which places steelworks or utility plants in inappropriate locations and blocks proposed economic reforms. The greatest cause, however, was probably India's decision to turn away from world markets and protect domestic industries. Without foreign markets and the stimulus of worldwide competition, India's public companies grew to rely upon state spending, saddling the economy with a large and overmanned public sector, while private industry had to contend with some of the most complex bureaucratic regulations in the world.[37] One might assume, theoretically, that such a large domestic economy could generate sustained growth without competing on world markets, but the evidence elsewhere (USSR, Argentina) suggests the contrary. Under prodding from the World Bank and IMF, and from many of their own frustrated entrepreneurs, recent Indian governments have acknowledged the need for trade liberalization and export-led growth, not least because of the large government deficit and external debt. As India turns to such policies, however, it will notice just how far it has fallen behind some of its Asian neighbors.

China's industrialization in the 1950s copied the Soviet emphasis upon central planning and heavy industry, and then was thrown into confusion during Mao's "Great Leap Forward" experiments. This changed, dramatically, with Deng Xiaoping's economic liberalization policies inaugurated in 1978–79. Although the largest transformations occurred in agriculture, progress was also made in manufacturing, commerce, consumer goods, and foreign trade. State industries were encouraged to respond to the commercial realities of quality, price, and market demand; privately run, small-scale enterprises were allowed; joint ventures with foreign firms were permitted, special enterprise zones were set up along the Chinese coastline, and an export-led drive was proclaimed. After ignoring East Asia's economic boom for decades, China relaxed its Marxist dogmas and appeared to be climbing on the free-market bandwagon. "To get rich is glorious," Mr. Deng urged his people, many of whom needed no convincing on that score.[38]

Statistically, the results were as impressive as the visual evidence of bustle and growth. Small-scale businesses sprang up—according to one source, by 1989 there were 225,000 privately run companies in the coastal provinces alone, employing many millions of people.[39] Provincial governments, eager to assert independence from Beijing and to earn additional income, negotiated joint ventures with the foreign entrepreneurs who swarmed into China during the 1980s. New enterprises rushed to fulfill the pent-up consumer demand for televisions, washing machines, and refrigerators; yet because that demand was only partly satisfied, there were still enormous private savings available for investment. While keeping a tight control upon what could be imported, China encouraged the export of textiles, household goods, toys, basic electrical equipment, and other low-tech products. Manufactured exports, worth a mere $9 billion in 1980, leaped to $37 billion by 1989, which was more than double the value of India's exports. In fact, since 1978 China's foreign trade has risen by an average of 13.5 percent a year and equals almost one-third of national income. It is now about the world's fourteenth-biggest trading nation.[40] All this caused optimistic observers to speculate that China might quadruple its GNP by early next century, boosting its already considerable power.[41]

Nevertheless, China's industrial drive has not been easy. To begin with, the helter-skelter growth exacerbated the gap in living standards between the well-placed coastal regions and the less developed inland provinces, where there is little foreign investment, traditional suspicions of capitalism abound, and the bureaucracy is still strong. While Guangdong, next to Hong Kong, saw industrial output soar 70 percent in 1987 and a further 30 percent in 1988 in response to foreign demand, inland neighbors like Hunan complained of the resultant inflation, diversion of foodstuffs and resources, blatant corruption and consumerism, and general unfairness of the new system.[42] Such complaints strengthened the hands of conservatives suspicious of a market economy and confirmed the resentments of groups whose fixed incomes were hurt by the high inflation accompanying modernization.[43]

The problem in China is not simply that of regional economic differentiation—as between northern and southern Italy—but the emergence of two entirely different systems of political economy, one based upon inward-oriented state enterprises and centralized controls, the other modeled upon the bustling, outward-oriented capitalism of Hong Kong and Korea.[44] In fact, much of China's industry still consists of state-owned companies, stagnating because they lack incentive to improve themselves and crippled by their inability to fix prices, dismiss inefficient workers, plan marketing and investment strategies, and acquire hard currencies. Because the government does not want to throw disgruntled workers out of a job, it has poured billions of dollars into state enterprises and permitted them to borrow large sums from state banks to cover their deficits. Despite the resources lavished upon those industries, their performance remains poor; in the partial economic recovery following the Tiananmen Square clamp-down, the state sector grew a mere 3 percent, collectives 9.4 percent, and private companies and joint ventures a remarkable 57.7 percent.[45]

With one part of the Chinese economy resembling Bulgaria and the other increasingly looking like Taiwan, it is not surprising that foreign companies are bewildered and reluctant to invest further. Clearly, this schizophrenic economic condition is related to the intense political struggle between Chinese conservatives and liberals in recent years. The Deng reforms were intended to encourage economic liberalization without conceding political liberalization. While that strategy may have worked for agriculture, it could not hold among businessmen, students, intellectuals, and officials in the coastal regions, who embraced economic freedoms, joint ventures, travel to (and study in) foreign democratic countries, and an increasing amount of Western media. Hence the rising protests in 1989—and the regime's heavy response. If the gap between the inland and coastal regions continues to widen, however, it is difficult to see how national unity can be preserved.

Even more than in India, therefore, leadership in China has sought to enjoy the benefits of trading in the global economy yet remains apprehensive of the larger consequences. There are, in addition, great technical difficulties in the way of abandoning older habits. For example, both countries require foreign technology, expertise, goods, and services to continue modernization, yet that worsens their current-account deficits—in India's case, to an alarming extent. Moreover, even as they seek to create an export-led boom, it is not at all clear that the developed world will permit the surge in imported manufactures that it allowed, in easier global circumstances, to Japan and the East Asian NIEs. Yet the greatest problem is social and political: how to transform ancient societies sufficiently to meet the challenges of the high-tech revolution of "the borderless world" *without* social strains, resentments, political unrest, and regional chaos—and that in countries already finding it hard to handle their population explosion.

Apart from sheer size, India and China differ from neighboring "trading states" in another critical respect: their ambition to be the regional superpower, in South Asia and East Asia respectively. There is little conviction in New Delhi and Beijing of the coming of a new international order; rather, both powers anticipate a "world of the future . . . very much like the world of the past, [where] those with real strength have the final say."[46] India remains in angry confrontation with Pakistan over Kashmir, worries about long-term Chinese policies along their shared border, and believes the "Indian" Ocean is not simply a geographical term but an expression of future strategical realities. The "Middle Kingdom" of China has quarreled with and fought against most of its neighbors (border disputes with Vietnam, India, and the former USSR), remains profoundly suspicious of Japan, dislikes the "hegemonism" and cultural influence of the United States, and still lays claim to Taiwan, not to mention more southerly territories like the Paracel Islands and Spratly Island.[47]

As a consequence, while China and India may appear relatively "less developed" in terms of per capita average income, literacy rates, and public health, they rank considerably higher in global military power. Each has numerous ground forces (China has 2.3 million regular soldiers, India 1.1 million), together with a large number of aircraft; in India's case, there is also a sizable surface fleet. China possesses land-based intercontinental ballistic missiles and continues to test nuclear devices and their delivery systems, and while India is not a full member of the nuclear club, it has the technological capacity to become one. Both are striving to keep defense costs under control, but, as rising powers conscious of regional challenges, neither is swayed by the argument that military force is anachronistic.

As in many countries in Africa and the Middle East, efforts to prepare Indian or Chinese society for the nonmilitary challenges of the early twenty-first century may therefore be stalled, diverted, or overwhelmed by the outbreak of border clashes, and perhaps further regional wars. Moreover, the concern with military strength and the belief that the country ought not to depend upon foreign suppliers have led India and China to allocate large resources—not just funds, but scientists, engineers, R&D institutions, industrial plants—to military-related production rather than to commercial export-led growth. How great a proportion of Chinese resources has been so allocated is impossible to say, but it could not have become the world's third-biggest nuclear power within a decade and a half* without a massive concentration of its limited scientific and technological talent.

In India's case, a powerful and technologically sophisticated military-industrial complex (with more than seventeen hundred research establishments) has been built up since independence. Supporters of this "indigenization" of defense production point to the stimulus given to Indian science and engineering, as well as to local subcontractors. Critics, of which there are an increasing number, retort that the system is not only expensive but also extremely inefficient; protected from external and internal competition, solely or heavily reliant upon state contracts, disinclined (and under no pressure) to sell abroad, its industry exists almost in isolation from the workings of the rest of the economy.[48]

Like the large powers in the developed world—or, for that matter, traditional Great Powers over centuries[49]—China and India today seek to enhance their prosperity within the economic order *and* to defend their interests in an anarchic international system. Whether one regards their pursuit of greater military security as anachronistic or realistic, the consequence is that neither Beijing nor New Delhi feels able to concentrate all national energies upon becoming rich; capital, material, and labor must also go to defense, implying a shift to "nonproductive" investment just when both need to invest as much as possible in long-term growth to catch up with their neighbors.

Despite such drawbacks, China and India possess a resource in which they are potentially very rich: human capital. But the existence of masses of people becomes more useful economically when a society provides quality education, encourages experimentation and entrepreneurship, and contains numerous skilled workers, engineers, scientists, technologists, and designers. As we have seen, a swift-growing population can hinder prosperity if the crush of numbers strains a

*China's first atomic bomb was exploded in 1964; by the late 1970s, it had overtaken France and Britain as nuclear powers.

nation's material resources and the people's talents are not developed. The equation is two-sided. One side, limiting demographic expansion, has already been discussed. It is the other side, the quality of the country's human capital, that requires consideration here.

In both societies, the educational deficits are large, in danger of getting worse, and probably more serious for their long-term prospects than problems like current-accounts deficits. Valiant attempts are being made by India and China to cater to education-hungry pupils. There have been improvements in recent years in public education, and certain scientific and scholarly achievements have won international recognition. Yet despite those positive signs, the educational system in both China and India is marred by sporadic and uneven levels of access, at virtually all levels, and by the very low ratio of skilled to unskilled people compared with those in the developed world.

Literacy—the basic educational statistic—shows the extent of the problem. China has a claimed adult literacy rate of 69 percent; still, that means that some 220 million are illiterate, almost three-quarters of them women—*the* key educational deficit throughout the developing world.[50] In India, the situation is worse. The adult literacy rate is a mere 43 percent of the population, but that again conceals a significant gender gap. More than half of the males are literate compared with only one-quarter of adult Indian females.[51] There are, therefore, over 200 million adult human beings in the country who cannot read or write. These figures will alter over time, since the number of children attending school is rising fast; in China, for example, about 90 percent of school-age children are taking lessons. But it remains an open question whether the schools, existing on threadbare resources, can cope with larger numbers or provide anything more than the most rudimentary coverage.[52] This is even more of a challenge in rural India, where the traditions of education are not strong—in 1981 less than half of the population aged fifteen to nineteen had been to school at all[53]—and the socioeconomic obstacles are enormous.

The statistics also show how the proportion of pupils continuing their education drops off swiftly after secondary school. In China, for example, there were 128 million pupils in primary school and a further 54 million in secondary school (1987 data), but—perhaps because graduates are so poorly paid—less than 2 million remained in higher education, a mere fraction of those in their twenties.[54] In India, although the proportion with *any* education at all is so much lower, there are more students in higher education—over 5 million by one account[55]—a discrepancy reflecting the country's large middle class and less egalitarian social structure.

Just what do these figures imply? Some development economists argue that India pours too large a share of its limited resources into higher education, with its British-imitative preferences (law, economics, humanities), and that those funds would be better employed in increasing primary and secondary education, and encouraging craft and technical subjects more in line with the country's basic needs.[56] On the other hand, planners wanting their country to catch up with Japan may feel that changes in the village are less important than developing manufacturing, design, science, and technology, by which criterion neither China nor India possesses enough skilled workers to compete. India, for example, with a population some seven times larger than Japan's, has fewer than one-quarter the number of scientific and technical personnel engaged in research and development.[57] Unless that gap—a thirty-to-one disparity in Japan's favor—is closed, how can they catch up?

In both China and India, education and science confront further obstacles. One is that, as in most developing countries, it is difficult for the state adequately to finance education. Whereas the United States, Japan, and European countries devote around 6 percent of their GNP to education, in China and India it is a strain to allocate 3 to 4 percent of their much smaller GNPs.[58] Secondly, neither state has used its existing funds very well. For national security reasons, India and China have allocated a large proportion of available capital, scientists, and industrial plant to support their military power. By contrast, the opportunities for commercial science and technology are still relatively small, with the ironic result that although only a minuscule share of the population experiences higher education, too many talented individuals are chasing too few suitable jobs. "In India more than half of the 3.3 million seeking work in 1972 had educational qualifications beyond matriculation level";[59] in consequence, large numbers of economists, engineers, and scientists emigrate to the developed world. In China, according to another report, "more than a third of scientific personnel are estimated to be idle for lack of suitable work."[60] Until a sufficiently large manufacturing sector emerges, much of this human talent will remain underused.

On the other hand, because of the absolute size of their economies and populations, the scientific endeavors of China and India are considerable in many fields. Even if too many science and technology personnel are concentrated in defense-related production, there exists a broad array of manufacturing activities which not only gives technological self-reliance, but permits the export of their products to different market niches.[61] In India's case, those markets are chiefly located in developing countries which require less sophisticated wares than (say) Germany, but it is also possible to find customers in the developed world. China, for its part, has developed a manufacturing base for intermediate-level technology, together with a small number of (chiefly defense-related) advanced products such as communications satellites, medium-ranged missiles, and the like. Most important of all, both countries have shown a keen interest in research and development—followed by production—in biotechnology, crop and earth sciences, forestry, and animal breeding and fisheries; that is, in fields where their indigenous resources can be preserved and expanded.

Because China and India have a technological edge over many developing societies, one might be sanguine about their future prospects—but for two major doubts. The first, the heart of the problem, is whether the potential for enhanced per capita standards of living will not be overwhelmed by the millions of newborn children each year. The second, related issue involves a cruel conundrum: is it actually wise for countries possessing half a billion to a billion peasants to attempt nowadays to follow "the stages of industrial growth" first established in the medium-sized nations of Western Europe 150 years ago, or to try to mimic the high-tech revolution emerging from the very different socioeconomic structures of California and Japan? And does that question imply that China and India should *not* attempt to catch up, a notion likely to be repudiated by politicians and planners for condemning their countries to remain forever behind the West?

Rejecting that notion in favor of technological-industrial growth does not settle the issue. Given their social structures, can India or China take the strain of creating world-competitive, high-tech enclaves (presumably enjoying the material benefits that would flow from their global successes) in the midst of hundreds of millions of their impoverished countrymen? Enhanced technology is supposed to have a "trickle-down effect," but does that work when the ratio of highly skilled to unskilled in the population is so disproportionately low? Might not the resources allocated to catching up with the developed world's computer, aerospace, and communications technology and the rest be more usefully diverted into appropriate technologies to expand productivity in the villages,[62] or into the "soft" investment of education, particularly among women?[63] No doubt the best solution would be to push forward at all levels, advanced, intermediate, in the schools and on the farm; but there is insufficient capital for that, which implies that the prospect of catching up remains limited.

This question of political choice raises yet another question concerning the futures of China and India: do they possess the national unity and purpose to meet the challenges thrown up by the fast-changing global scene, or will they be hindered by internal factionalism, regional tensions, and a general failure to carry the bulk of the population along with the leadership's aims? In China, this problem is fundamental; how can the government join the international economy while retaining a political and ideological monopoly at home? Tiananmen Square indicated that the leadership believes it can have one without the other; but far from settling the problem, Beijing's policies of force and censorship simply evade it. All subsequent reports about "the people's malaise" suggest that widely held feelings of betrayal, mistrust, and fear—especially in the urban population, the educated classes, perhaps also in the armed forces—may hamper economic recovery, and make it more difficult to strengthen China's fragile links with the world outside.[64]

The internal condition of India is altogether more complex, and every bit as serious. A country of 850 million people possessing twenty-five distinct ethnic identities, a stratified caste system, enormous income gaps between elites and poor, a bustling middle class of over 100 million people on the one hand and entrenched trade unions and

Marxist political parties on the other, and Muslim (75 million) and Sikh (13 million) minorities alongside the Hindu majority would be difficult to govern at the best of times. This has not been helped by the fact that India's relatively slow increases in real growth have benefited only some of the people. More important still, the excessive factionalism of Indian politics—hastily formed coalition governments, quarrels between the central government and the states, systematic corruption and favoritism, the subversion of bureaucratic decisions, demagogic appeals on issues of caste, race, and class—has raised in some observer's minds the spectacle of political anarchy.[65] But authoritarian rule by the Indian government—the "administration without politics" syndrome of the Emergency of 1975–77—would spell the end of the country's delicate if messy democracy. The present tendency toward weak central government and excessive political maneuvering has its own regrettable consequences. It plays into the hands of extremists, who, in setting caste against caste and Hindu against Muslim, have provoked bloody violence, worsening the political atmosphere in New Delhi and causing ethnic groups to defend their interests by force.[66] Secondly, it diverts attention from critical reforms of the Indian economy that could improve overall standards of living.[67] As with China, therefore, India's future prospects will be very heavily affected by the quality of the political leadership which will emerge as this decade unfolds—and that in turn depends on the Chinese and Indian peoples themselves.

Given the balance of strengths and weaknesses which these two countries possess, it is evident that their preparedness for twenty-first-century transformations is mixed, at best. With regard to the long-term shifts in the global military and economic power balances—the traditional way of measuring the relative "rise and fall of the Great Powers"—both nations are emerging as considerable regional leaders. However, the extent to which the transnational, *non*military challenges to China and India will affect their hope of becoming rich and strong is much less clear.

Take, for example, the implications of the robotics revolution. As

India modernizes, there could well emerge entrepreneurs, electronics firms, and other businesses possessing the technical know-how, financial capacity, and official support to adopt automated production. India has, after all, an existing machine-tool industry, which is the natural foundation for any serious move into robotics; it has many trained mathematicians and engineers; and it is now eager to emulate East Asia's venture into higher technologies. Provided that better infrastructure is in place and quality control assured, the automation of the workplace in India obviously looks much more feasible than in, say, Ethiopia. This is not to suggest that India would be a serious challenge to Japan's dominance in robotics, but that it can potentially be a medium-sized player like, for example, Italy or Britain.

On the other hand, it must be one of the chief aims of India's planners to create many *more* jobs in assembly and manufacturing as the rural population steadily moves into the cities, whereas FANUC-style production would mean the replacement of workers by machines. If robotic production spreads in other countries, or in India itself, the effect on supply and demand could lower wages and hurt standards of living. Having missed out on the original Industrial Revolution that brought workers into factories, perhaps the last thing Indian society needs over the next few decades is the spread of a technology which takes workers *out* of the factories—or becomes a disincentive for multinationals to establish such plants in the first place.

The rationale against fully automated production is, if anything, even greater in China's case. Its manufacturing boom of the 1980s was, as noted earlier, chiefly due to Beijing's liberalization of the coastal provinces, with "open cities" and "special economic zones" to tempt foreign investment and produce goods for export. The results have been spectacular, with Guangdong Province having enjoyed a *real* growth rate of 12 ½ percent a year since 1979—probably the highest in the world—and the single town of Shenzhen (next to Hong Kong) growing from less than 100,000 people to more than 2 million today. The key here, apart from the liberalization itself, is the low-cost, eager, hardworking labor. Because of its boom, Shenzhen's labor costs are ten times higher than elsewhere in Guangdong, but still only one-fifth of those in Hong Kong. In neighboring Fujian Province, the average factory wage in 1991 ($65 a month) was one-tenth the rate in Taiwan;* presumably, it was a mere one-thirtieth or one-fortieth of the average Japanese factory wage.[68]

Given such disparity in labor costs, the argument here is not that the robotics revolution in Japan (and, later, in Korea and Taiwan) poses an *immediate* threat to manufacturing employment in South China. Over the medium to longer term, however, China's situation will be affected by two developments. The first will be further breakthroughs in automated assembly and manufacturing, reducing the overall costs of employing robotic "serfs"; the second will be the rise in incomes, and thus in labor costs, in those provinces currently enjoying the boom—already Shenzhen has a per capita GDP close to $2,000 a year, while Hong Kong and Taiwan are becoming far too expensive for basic manufacturing.[69] In theory, this rise in labor costs along China's coastline could have a beneficial "ripple effect," spreading into the poorer country and inland provinces (always provided Beijing and the conservative regional authorities agree to extend the economic liberalization measures). Even so, one wonders if there would be enough foreign demand, and willingness to import, to turn hundreds of millions of Chinese peasants into assembly workers. The alternative is that, deterred by physical and political obstacles from investing in the cheap-labor inland provinces, Japanese and Taiwanese multinationals turn to robots to maintain their manufacturing competitiveness. If so, that would reduce China's chance of a steady, stage-by-stage transition toward a modern, high-per-capita-income economy.

On the face of it, the biotech revolution in agriculture appears to offer promise for both countries. With the productivity increases of the "green revolution" beginning to peter out, little suitable additional land available, and the threat of population growth eclipsing food output, the governments of China and India need to encourage all possible ways to improve agricultural yields. If biotechnology, including DNA-type genetic engineering, will permit "the power of the land" to stay ahead of population growth, then many of the feared outcomes—malnutrition, famine, increased mortality rates, social discontents—

*As a further contrast, it was reported in the *New York Times* (27 January 1992, p. A6) that per capita income in impoverished Anhui Province averaged "$74 a year in normal times." Is it any wonder that tens of millions of peasants are drifting into the towns and cities?

could be avoided, or at least mitigated. Creating crops that can grow in semiarid conditions, that are more resistant to disease, or simply that have a greater calorific yield is obviously beneficial. Thus, both countries are committing large resources to biotechnology research and application, from crop breeding, to animal embryo transfers, to producing biogas energy sources. The greater part of this activity plays to both countries' strengths: each possesses many scientists in these fields (unlike most sub-Saharan African nations), and this experimentation is not as capital-intensive as other high-tech ventures.

The dangers to China and India from the biotech revolution in agriculture do not, in the near term, outweigh these potential benefits—but they need to be taken seriously. The first might emerge, ironically, if there actually were to occur year-on-year increases in agricultural yields significantly higher than population growth. Because poor farmers cannot afford the new biotech applications, this may at present seem a remote possibility; but since scientific breakthroughs often occur at surprising speed, it cannot be discounted. In its early years such a productivity expansion would be welcome; over time, however, it could lead to a crisis of agricultural *over*productivity, such as has affected American farming on a number of occasions over the past century. Everything would depend upon the speed of the change: it took one hundred years of productivity increases, coupled with the lure of jobs elsewhere, to reduce American agriculture's share of the work force from a clear majority to the mere 3 percent that it constitutes today. Will India and China, whose agricultural sectors respectively employ nearly two-thirds and four-fifths of their work forces, have enough time to manage the transformation, especially given our present heightened pace of technological change? If not, then the rural discontents could be far more violent than those occurring among French or Korean farmers today.

The other danger might come not from biotech applications enhancing the power of the land but from the massive growth of *in vitro* experimentation and food output from the laboratories of Western agrochemical and pharmaceutical companies—that challenge to every sort of traditional farming discussed earlier.* Exactly how this might

*See Chapter 4.

affect China and India is difficult to estimate. Neither resembles those economies of Central America, the Caribbean, and sub-Saharan Africa that have traditionally earned foreign currency through the export of staples (cane sugar, vanilla, rubber) and now find those natural products rivaled by laboratory equivalents. For China and India, farming is vital to satisfy *domestic* needs, but it is industry and services that focus upon external markets. Still, both countries will want to avoid undue dependence upon Western biotech firms with their tendency toward high-profit, proprietary knowledge, for that would simply add to the current outflow of capital to pay for patents, technical fees, royalties, and the like. Finally, should major breakthroughs occur in laboratory-based food production at the same time as farm-based yields were creating huge surpluses, then the problem of sensibly reducing the agricultural sector would be exacerbated.

Similarity between China and India is far less evident when one considers the likely impact of the global financial and communications revolution. From the viewpoint of China's leadership, fanciful visions of the "borderless world" can only be regarded with suspicion, and not simply because of age-old cultural attitudes toward foreigners. Economically, a system of twenty-four-hour-a-day trading of capital and currencies benefits those companies and societies rich in funds, banks, and other financial services, together with service industries and professionals who "add value" to such transactions. Given the present state of China's political economy, little of this would appear attractive or, for that matter, relevant. To be sure, foreign bankers are needed to arrange funds for a joint venture with a major Western construction company or to handle the exchanges that flow from China's export boom—just as it is hoped that, with their low labor costs, the coastal provinces and enterprise zones will continue to offer an attractive location for the assembly plants of foreign multinationals. But that is not the same as if China itself—or, rather, its state-run banks and industries—were planning to be a major *independent* player on an international field where governments have become largely invisible, and where only shareholders and symbolic analysts count.

The other reason that China's leadership looks askance at the world of interactive electronic mail, satellite transmissions, the unhampered activities of free-market media giants, and the like is that such developments clearly threaten their authoritarian political system. Fax machines connecting students with their renegade brethren abroad, satellites transmitting American or Japanese programs onto Chinese television screens, newspapers and books investigating dangerous themes and questioning the Party's political monopoly, are all suspect—especially after the role they played in the convulsions of 1989. Economic modernization is worth supporting, if cautiously; the free play of ideas, with their tendency to challenge existing authority and traditional social norms, holds no attraction in Beijing.

In these respects, India offers different and intriguing possibilities. It contains, as mentioned, a large and burgeoning middle class. It possesses a considerable number of small to medium-sized businesses (in addition to the large public-sector companies), many of which are engaging in joint ventures. And its population is renowned for producing mathematicians, engineers, and economists. There is also the advantage of familiarity with English as the language of world finance, computers, communications, and international business. Already, high-tech "Silicon Valley" enterprises are clustering around cities like Bangalore in the south. Provided there can be further relaxation of the bureaucratic and legal obstacles that clog India's commercial system, a class of entrepreneurs, designers, software engineers, consultants, lawyers, and middlemen could emerge to play in the global marketplace and reap benefits from the borderless world.

But if that happens, the larger problem remains; as noted earlier, the emergence in developed economies of a class of "symbolic analysts" is already opening up a worrying gap between the minority who can take advantage of the new transnational trends and a great majority increasingly marginalized in the process. If that is going to hurt the social fabric of (say) the United States, how much greater would be the impacts in India, most of which has not yet undergone an industrial revolution, let alone prepared for the transnational provision of high-added-value professional services? Given the even greater gap in incomes and life-styles that would occur in India, how comfortable would it be to have islands of prosperity in a sea of poverty? Would such individuals, resented by the masses and with increasingly fewer local ties, be tempted to escape to overseas locations?

• • •

Ideally the best thing to happen would be for all China and India—entrepreneurs and peasants, technicians and laundry girls—to enjoy a steady rise in real standards of living. This would not bring per capita income up to Western levels, for the gap is simply too great; but it would surely be an immense improvement if the present, dreadfully low average annual income of $300–350 could be raised to that of Mexico (GNP per capita: $1,825) or possibly even Hungary ($2,237).[70]

Unfortunately, unless fresh technological breakthroughs occur in environmental controls and that technology is transferred wholesale to China and India, such rises in living standards would have appalling consequences for their environments. Already there is mounting evidence of the damage caused by population growth and modernization. China's headlong rush into industrialization after 1950 was undertaken without regard for the atmosphere, water supplies, or the countryside in general. As a result there now exist industrial regions whose air is so polluted that they cannot be seen (even in cloudless weather) by satellite reconnaissance for months at a time. Around 5 billion tons of topsoil are lost each year, about 1.1 million acres of farmland disappear annually as the cities and towns spread outward, thousands of miles of river are contaminated by industrial toxins, one-third of the coastal fishing grounds are ruined by pollution, and the air in Beijing is "sixteen times dirtier than it is in New York and an astonishing thirty-five times more contaminated than in London."[71] When great floods occur, as they do from time to time, the loss of topsoil is greater because of deforestation.* Despite a belated recognition of these problems by the Chinese authorities—the creation of natural conservation regions, pollution-control measures, tree-planting schemes—the overall situation continues to worsen.[72]

In India, the story is the same. Because of population growth, the area around New Delhi has lost a staggering 60 percent of its forest cover in the last decade alone, chiefly to firewood cutting. One recent

*And the damage caused by flooding is proportionately greater in recent times because, ironically, peasants now liberated to work on their own plots are more reluctant to be mobilized and sent away to join flood-control gangs.

analysis pointed out that because of poverty, continuing forest devastation, the negative impact of economic development, and sheer greed, environmental pollution had assumed "threatening proportions":

> Of the country's 304 million hectares 50 percent are subject to ecological degradation. About 80 percent of the population lives under substandard conditions. The fourteen major rivers, including the Ganga, which provides nearly 85 percent of the country's drinking water, are all polluted. . . . Human diseases caused by contaminated or substandard food have doubled during the last thirty years. Over 80 percent of all [!] hospital patients are the victims of environmental pollution.[73]

Admittedly, there is increasing awareness of this damage, especially by the middle classes in India, and plans exist to clean the rivers, halt deforestation, preserve wildlife, check unregulated mining, and control air pollution. Yet if, as former Prime Minister Rajiv Gandhi claimed, "mass poverty was forcing the poor to degrade the environment on which they depended for sheer survival," that process of erosion will not be halted until poverty and population growth are themselves checked.[74] The dilemma is acute, for if the only way to reduce poverty is to increase industrialization on a large scale, the Indian environment will suffer still more.

This environmental damage has, of course, profound implications for the health of the Indian and Chinese peoples, as well as for the world's atmosphere. As *The Economist* has noted, Deng Xiaoping's "deceptively simple goal" of raising China's GDP to $1,000 per head by the year 2000 means that the economy has to triple in size:

> Of course that will not happen. But to try to make it happen the easy way—which is the one the Chinese will adopt—will be to build more power stations and factories. These will depend mainly on China's own coal, with its average ash content of 27 percent and sulfur content of up to 5 percent. Millions more Chinese will suffer from respiratory disorders, and a few more cities will disappear from satellite photographs.[75]

The greenhouse effect is also likely to increase if, for example, the Chinese government carries through its well-meaning intention that every home will boast a refrigerator by the year 2000.[76] Should hundreds of millions of refrigerators all release CFCs into the atmosphere, the depletion of the earth's protective ozone layer would be immense. In one journalist's words, "China's industrial ambitions . . . pose a threat to the planet."[77] Presumably, the same is as true for India's industrial ambitions.

This leaves a mighty conundrum for China and India, and for the rest of the world. Both those nations are engaged in a race against time, for if their population explosion continues it will erode gains in agricultural and manufacturing output, reduce expectations of increases in real income, worsen regional imbalances, and damage the social peace. In sum, if they fail to escape from their Malthusian trap, a large proportion of the earth's inhabitants in the early twenty-first century will witness continued poverty and malnutrition. On the other hand, if China and India with their three *billion* people do happily manage to triple their average standard of living (to levels which the West would still find intolerably low), that would not only damage their local environment and public health, but also threaten the earth's overall atmosphere. Although this potential danger is beginning to ring alarm bells in the developed world, it would be inconceivable—and ridiculous—for the West to press China and India to abandon their plans for economic growth; it would also be hypocritical, since advanced societies (especially the United States) inflict much more damage per capita upon the earth's atmosphere.

The only logical solution remaining, therefore, is for the developed world to try to apply its capital, technology, and brainpower to help these two giant populations escape from poverty without harm to themselves and the planet, while at the same time embracing technological solutions, including alterations in energy use and life-style, to reduce its own, even larger damage to the global environment.

How likely this is needs to be discussed further; it is certainly not an issue that American and European politicians, campaigning for office on domestic, short-term issues, seem willing to confront. Yet it is already clear that unless rich and poor nations recognize that they inhabit the same biospace, the dilemmas facing China and India will intensify—and the results will not be merely local.

10

WINNERS AND LOSERS IN THE DEVELOPING WORLD

NOTHING BETTER ILLUSTRATES THE growing differences among developing countries than the fact that in the 1960s, South Korea had a per capita GNP exactly the same as Ghana's ($230) whereas today it is ten to twelve times more prosperous.[1] Both possessed a predominantly agrarian economy and had endured a half century or more of colonial rule. Upon independence, each faced innumerable handicaps in trying to "catch up" with the West, and although Korea possessed a greater historico-cultural coherence, its chances may have seemed less promising, since it had few natural resources (apart from tungsten) and suffered heavily during the 1950–53 fighting. Decades later, however, West African states remain among the most poverty-stricken countries in the world—the per capita GNPs of Niger, Sierra Leone, and Chad today, for example, are less than $500[2]—while Korea is entering the ranks of the high-income economies. Already the world's thirteenth-largest trading nation, Korea is planning to become one of the richest countries of all in the twenty-first century,[3] whereas the nations of West Africa face a future, at least in the near term, of chronic poverty, malnutrition, poor health, and underdevelopment. Finally, while Korea's rising prosperity is attended by a decrease in population growth, most African countries still face a demographic explosion that erodes any gains in national output.

This divergence is not new, for there have always been richer and poorer societies; the prosperity gap in the seventeenth century between, say, Amsterdam and the west coast of Ireland or between such bustling Indian ports as Surat and Calcutta[4] and the inhabitants of New Guinean hill villages must have been marked, although it probably did not equal the gulf between rich and poor nations today. The difference is that the twentieth-century global communications revolution has made such disparities widely known. This can breed resentments by poorer peoples against prosperous societies, but it can also provide a desire to emulate (as Korea emulated Japan). The key issue here is: what does it take to turn a "have-not" nation into a "have" nation? Does it simply require imitating economic techniques, or does it involve such intangibles as culture, social structure, and attitudes toward foreign practices?

This discrepancy in performance between East Asia and sub-Saharan Africa clearly makes redundant the term "Third World." However useful the expression might have been in the 1950s, when poor, nonaligned, and recently decolonized states were attempting to remain independent of the two superpower blocs,[5] the rise of super-rich oil-producing countries a decade later already made it questionable. Now that prosperous East Asian societies possess higher per capita GNPs than Russia, Eastern Europe, and even Western European states like Portugal, the word seems less suitable than ever. With Taiwanese and Korean corporations establishing assembly plants in the Philippines and creating distribution networks within the European Community, we need to recognize the differences that exist among non-Western economies. Some scholars now categorize *five* separate types of "developing" countries* to help assess the varied potential of societies in Asia, Africa, and Latin America.[6]

Relative national growth in the 1980s confirms these differences. Whereas East Asian economies grew on average at an impressive an-

*Ravenhill's divisions (see note 6 to this chapter) are high-income oil-exporting countries; industrializing economies with strong states and relatively low levels of indebtedness (Taiwan, etc.); industrializing economies with state apparatus under challenge and/or with debt problems (Argentina, Poland); potential newly industrializing countries (Malaysia, Thailand); and primary-commodity producers (in sub-Saharan Africa, Central America).

nual rate of 7.4 percent, those in Africa and Latin America gained only 1.8 and 1.7 percent respectively[7]—and since their populations grew faster, the net result was that they slipped backward, absolutely and relatively. Differences of economic structure also grew in this decade, with African and other primary-commodity-producing countries eager for higher raw-material prices whereas the export-oriented manufacturing nations of East Asia sought to keep commodity prices low. The most dramatic difference occurred in the shares of world trade in manufactures, a key indicator of economic competitiveness (see Chart 6).

Thus, while some scholars still refer to a *dual* world economy[8] of rich and poor countries, what is emerging is increasing differentiation. The rest of this chapter examines why that is so.

Chart 6. Shares of World Trade in Manufactures[9]

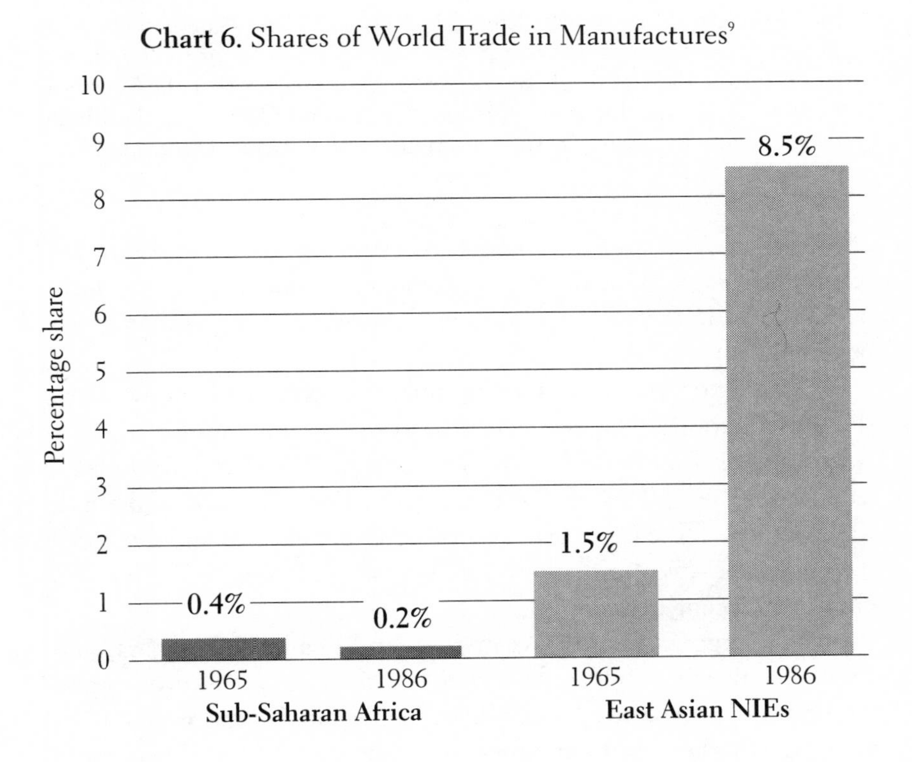

• • •

The developing countries most successfully catching up with the West are the trading states of the Pacific and East Asia. Except for Communist-controlled countries in the area, the Pacific Rim countries (including the western areas of Canada and the United States, and in part Australia) have enjoyed a lengthy boom in manufacturing, trade, and investment; but the center of that boom is on the *Asian* side of the Pacific, chiefly fueled by Japan's own spectacular growth and the stimulus given to neighboring economies and transpacific trade. According to one source:

> In 1962 the Western Pacific (notably East Asia) accounted for around 9 percent of world GNP, North America for 30 percent, and Western Europe for 31 percent. Twenty years later, the Western Pacific share had climbed to more than 15 percent, while North America's had fallen to 28 percent and Europe's to 27 percent. By the year 2000 it is likely that the Western Pacific will account for around one-quarter of world GNP, with the whole Pacific region increasing its share from just over 43 percent to around half of world GNP.[10]

East Asia's present boom is not, of course, uniform, and scholars distinguish between the different stages of economic and technological development in this vast region. Roughly speaking, the divisions would be as follows:

(a) Japan, now the world's largest financial center and, increasingly, the most innovative high-tech nation in the nonmilitary field;

(b) the four East Asian "tigers" or "dragons," the Newly Industrialized Economies (NIEs) of Singapore, Hong Kong, Taiwan, and South Korea, of which the latter two possess bigger populations and territorial size than the two port-city states, but all have enjoyed export-led growth in recent decades;

(c) the larger Southeast Asian states of Thailand, Malaysia, and Indonesia, which, stimulated by foreign (chiefly Japanese) investment, are becoming involved in manufacturing, assembly, and export (it is doubtful whether the Philippines should be included in this group);

(d) finally, the stunted and impoverished Communist societies of

Vietnam, Cambodia, and North Korea, as well as isolationist Myanmar pursuing its "Burmese Way to Socialism."

Because of this staggered level of development, economists in East Asia invoke the image of the "flying geese," with Japan the lead bird, followed by the East Asian NIEs, the larger Southeast Asian states, and so on. What Japan produced in one decade—relatively low-priced toys, kitchenware, electrical goods—will be imitated by the next wave of "geese" in the decade following, and by the third wave in the decade after that. However accurate the metaphor individually, the overall picture is clear: these birds are flying, purposefully and onward, to an attractive destination.

Of those states, it is the East Asian NIEs that have provided the clearest example of successful transformation. Although distant observers may regard them as similar, there are notable differences in size, population,* history, and political system. Even the economic structures are distinct; for example, Korea, which began its expansion at least a decade later than Taiwan (and democratized itself even more slowly) is heavily dependent upon a few enormous industrial conglomerates, or *chaebol,* of which the top four alone (Samsung, Hyundai, Lucky-Goldstar, and Daewoo) have sales equal to half the GNP. By contrast, Taiwan possesses many small companies, specializing in one or two product areas. While Taiwanese are concerned that their firms may lose out to foreign giants, Koreans worry that the *chaebol* will find it increasingly difficult to compete in large-scale industries like petrochemicals and semiconductors and shipbuilding at the same time.[11]

Despite such structural differences, these societies each contain certain basic characteristics, which, *taken together,* help to explain their decade-upon-decade growth. The first, and perhaps the most important, is the emphasis upon education. This derives from Confucian traditions of competitive examinations and respect for learning, reinforced daily by the mother of the family, who complements what is taught at school. To Western eyes, this process—like Japan's—appears to concentrate on rote learning, acquiring technical skills, and emphasizing harmony, rather than encouraging individual talent and the

*While Korea has a population of around 43 million and Taiwan about 20 million, Hong Kong possesses 5.7 million and Singapore only 2.7 million.

habit of questioning authority. Even if some East Asian educators would nowadays admit that criticism, most believe that their own educational mores create social harmony and a well-trained work force. Moreover, the uniformity of the system does not exclude an intense individual competitiveness; in Taiwan (where, incidentally, twelve members of the fourteen-member cabinet of 1989 had acquired Ph.D.s abroad), only the top third of each year's 110,000 students taking the national university entrance examinations are selected, to emphasize the importance of college education.[12] Perhaps nothing better illustrates this stress upon learning than the fact that Korea (43 million population) has around 1.4 million students in higher education, compared with 145,000 in Iran (54 million), 15,000 in Ethiopia (46 million), and 159,000 in Vietnam (64 million); or the further fact that already by 1980 "as many engineering students were graduating from Korean institutions as in the United Kingdom, West Germany, and Sweden combined."[13]

The second common factor is a high level of national savings. By employing fiscal measures, taxes, and import controls to encourage personal savings, large amounts of low-interest capital were made available for investment in manufacture and commerce. During the first few decades of growth, personal consumption and living standards were controlled—by restrictions upon moving capital abroad and importing foreign luxury goods—in order to funnel resources into industrial growth. While average prosperity rose, most of the fruits of economic success were plowed back into further expansion. Only when economic "takeoff" was well under way has the system begun to alter; increased consumption, foreign purchases, and capital investment in new homes all allow internal demand to play a larger role in the country's growth. In such circumstances, one would expect to see overall savings ratios decline. Even in the late 1980s, however, the East Asian NIEs still had high national savings rates, as shown in Table 7.

The third feature has been a strong political framework within which economic growth is fostered. While entrepreneurship and private property are encouraged, the "tigers" never followed a laissez-faire model. Industries targeted for growth were given a variety of supports—export subsidies, training grants, tariff protection from foreign competitors. As noted above, the fiscal system was arranged to produce high savings

Table 7. Comparative Savings Ratios, 1987[14]

Taiwan	38.8 %
Malaysia	37.8 %
Korea	37.0 %
Japan	32.3 %
Indonesia	29.1 %
U.S.	12.7 %

ratios. Taxes assisted the business sector, as did energy policy. Trade unions operated under restrictions. Democracy was constrained, by the governor of Hong Kong, *dirigiste* administrations in Singapore, and the military regimes in Taiwan and Korea. Only lately have free elections and party politics been permitted. Defenders of this system argued that it was necessary to restrain libertarian impulses while concentrating on economic growth, and that democratic reforms are a "reward" for the people's patience. The point is that domestic politics were unlike those in the West, yet did not hurt commercial expansion.

The fourth feature was the commitment to exports, in contrast to the import-substitution policies of India and the consumer-driven policies of the United States. This was traditional for a small, bustling trading state like Hong Kong, but it involved substantial restructuring in Taiwan and Korea, where managers and work force had to be trained to produce what foreign customers wanted. In all cases, the value of the currency was kept low, to increase exports and decrease imports. Moreover, the East Asian NIEs took advantage of favorable global circumstances; labor costs were much lower than in North America and Europe, and they benefited from an open international trading order, created and protected by the United States, while shielding their own industries from foreign competition. Over time, this led to large trade surpluses, and to threats of retaliation from European and American governments, which is a reminder of the NIEs' heavy dependence upon the current international economic system. The important thing, however, is that they targeted export-led growth in manufactures whereas other developing nations continued to rely upon commodity exports and made little effort to cater to foreign consumers' tastes.[15] Given this focus upon trade, it is not surprising to learn that Asia now contains seven of the world's twelve largest ports.

Finally, the East Asian NIEs possess a local model, namely, Japan, which Yemen, Guatemala, and Burkina Faso simply do not have. For four decades East Asian peoples have observed the dramatic success of a non-Western neighbor, based upon its educational and technical skills, high savings ratios, long-term state-guided targeting of industries and markets, and determination to compete on world markets, though this admiration of Japan is nowadays mixed with a certain alarm at becoming members of a yen bloc dominated by Tokyo. While the Japanese domestic market is extremely important for the East Asian NIEs, and they benefit from Japanese investments, assembly plants, engineers, and expertise, they have little enthusiasm for a new Greater East Asia Co-Prosperity Sphere.[16]

The benefits of economic success are not merely seen in East Asia's steadily rising standards of living. Children are on average four or five inches taller than they were in the 1940s, and grow up in countries that are among the world's healthiest:

> A Taiwanese child born in 1988 could expect to live seventy-four years, only a year less than an American or a West German, and fifteen years longer than a Taiwanese born in 1952; a South Korean born in 1988 could expect seventy years on earth, up from fifty-eight in 1965. In 1988 the Taiwanese took in 50 percent more calories each day than they had done thirty-five years earlier. They had two hundred times as many televisions, telephones and cars per household; in Korea the rise in the possession of these goods was even higher.[17]

In addition, the East Asian NIEs enjoy high literacy rates, once again confirming that they are altogether closer to "First" World nations than to poor, developing countries.

Will this progress last into the twenty-first century? Politically, Hong Kong's future is completely uncertain, and many companies are relocating their headquarters elsewhere; Taiwan remains a diplomatic pariah state, because of Beijing's traditional claims; and South Korea still feels threatened by the unpredictable militarized regime in the north. The future of China—and of Siberia—is uncertain, and causes concern. The 1980s rise in Asian stock-market prices (driven by vast increases in the money supply) was excessive and speculative, and destined to tumble. Protectionist tendencies in the developed world threaten the

Table 8. Comparative Living Standards[18]

	Life Expectancy at Birth, 1987 (years)	*Adult Literacy Rate, 1985 (%)*	*GNP per capita, 1988 (U.S.$)*
Niger	45	14	300
Togo	54	41	310
India	59	43	340
SINGAPORE	73	86	9,070
SOUTH KOREA	70	95	5,000
Spain	77	95	7,740
New Zealand	75	99	10,000

trading states even more than external pressures to abandon price supports for local farmers. A rise in the value of the Korean and Taiwanese currencies has cut export earnings and reduced overall rate of growth. Some Japanese competitors have moved production to neighboring low-cost countries such as Thailand and southern China. Sharp rises in oil prices increase the import bills. Higher wages (in Korea they increased by an average 14 percent in 1988, and by 17 percent in 1989) affect labor costs and competitiveness. The social peace, precarious in these recent democracies, is damaged by bouts of student and industrial unrest.[19]

On the other hand, these may simply be growing pains. Savings ratios are still extremely high. Large numbers of new engineers and technicians pour out of college each year. The workers' enhanced purchasing power has created a booming domestic market, and governments are investing more in housing, infrastructure, and public facilities. The labor force will not grow as swiftly as before, because of the demographic slowdown, but it will be better educated and spend more.[20] A surge in overseas investments is assisting the long-term balance of payments. As the populous markets of Indonesia, Thailand, and Malaysia grow at double-digit rates, there is plenty of work for the trading states. A hardening of the currency can be met by greater commitment to quality exports, high rates of industrial investment, and a move into newer, high-technology manufacture—in imitation of the 1980s retooling of Japanese industry when its currency hardened swiftly. Nowhere else in the world would growth rates of "only" 5 or

6 percent be considered as worrying, or a harbinger of decline. Barring a war in East Asia or a massive global slump, the signs are that the four "tigers" are better structured than most to grow in wealth and health.

For confirmation of that remark, one need only consider the present difficult condition of Latin America, which lost ground in the 1980s just as East Asia was gaining it. Here again, distinctions have to be made between various countries within the continent, with its more than 400 million people in an area of almost 7 million square miles stretching from the Rio Grande to Antarctica, and with a range of political cultures and socioeconomic structures. Argentina, which around 1900 had a standard of living suggesting it was a "developed" economy, is very different from Honduras and Guyana. Similarly, population change in Latin America occurs in *three* distinct forms: such nations as Bolivia, the Dominican Republic, and Haiti have high fertility rates and lower life expectancies; a middle group—Brazil, Colombia, Mexico, Venezuela, Costa Rica, and Panama—are beginning to experience declines in fertility and longer life expectancy; and the temperate-zone countries of Argentina, Chile, and Uruguay have the demographic characteristics of developed countries.[21]

Despite this diversity, there are reasons for considering Latin America's prospects as a whole: the economic challenges confronting the region are similar, as are its countries' domestic politics—in particular, the fragility of its recently emerged democracies—and all its countries are affected by their relationship with the developed world, especially the United States.

Several decades ago, Latin America's future appeared encouraging. Sharing in the post-1950 global boom, benefiting from demand for its coffee, timber, beef, oil, and minerals, and enjoying foreign investments in its agriculture, industry, and infrastructure, the region was moving upward. In the thirty years after 1945, its production of steel multiplied twenty times and its output of electric energy, metals, and machinery more than tenfold.[22] Real GDP per person rose at an annual average of 2.8 percent during the 1960s and spurted to an annual average increase of 3.4 percent in the 1970s. Unfortunately, the growth then reversed itself, and between 1980 and 1988 Latin America's real GDP per person steadily fell by an annual average of 0.9 percent.[23] In some states, such as Peru and Argentina, real income dropped by as much as one-quarter during the 1980s. With very few exceptions (Chile, Colombia, Dominican Republic, Barbados, Bahamas), most countries now have per capita GDPs lower than those a decade earlier, or even two decades earlier:

The reasons for this reversal offer a striking contrast to the East Asian NIEs. Instead of encouraging industrialists to target foreign markets and stimulate the economy through export-led growth, many Latin American governments pursued a policy of import substitution, creating their own steel, cement, paper, automobiles, and electronics-goods industries, which were given protective tariffs, government subsi-

Table 9. Per Capita GDP of Latin American Countries[24]
(U.S. $)

Country	*1960*	*1970*	*1980*	*1988*
Chile	1,845	2,236	2,448	2,518
Argentina	2,384	3,075	3,359	2,862
Uruguay	2,352	2,478	3,221	2,989
Brazil	1,013	1,372	2,481	2,449
Paraguay	779	931	1,612	1,557
Bolivia	634	818	983	724
Peru	1,233	1,554	1,716	1,503
Ecuador	771	904	1,581	1,477
Colombia	927	1,157	1,595	1,739
Venezuela	3,879	4,941	5,225	4,544
Guyana	1,008	1,111	1,215	995
Surinam	887	2,337	3,722	3,420
Mexico	1,425	2,022	2,872	2,588
Guatemala	1,100	1,420	1,866	1,502
Honduras	619	782	954	851
El Salvador	832	1,032	1,125	995
Nicaragua	1,055	1,495	1,147	819
Costa Rica	1,435	1,825	2,394	2,235
Panama	1,264	2,017	2,622	2,229
Dominican Republic	823	987	1,497	1,509
Haiti	331	292	386	319
Jamaica	1,610	2,364	1,880	1,843
Trinidad & Tobago	3,848	4,927	8,116	5,510
Barbados	2,000	3,530	3,994	4,233
Bahamas	8,448	10,737	10,631	11,317

dies, and tax breaks to insulate them from international competition. As a result, their products became less attractive abroad.* Moreover, while it was relatively easy to create a basic iron and steel industry, it proved harder to establish high-tech industries like computers, aerospace, machine tools, and pharmaceuticals—so most of these states depend on imported manufactured goods, whereas exports still chiefly consist of raw materials like oil, coffee, and soybeans.[25]

Secondly, economic growth was accompanied by lax financial policies and an increasing reliance upon foreign borrowings. Governments poured money not only into infrastructure and schools but also into state-owned enterprises, large bureaucracies, and oversized armed forces, paying for them by printing money and raising loans from Western (chiefly U.S.) banks and international agencies. The result was that public spending's share of GDP soared, and price inflation accelerated and was further increased by index-linked rises in salaries and wages. Inflation became so large that it was difficult to comprehend, let alone to combat. "In 1989, for example, annual inflation in Nicaragua was more than 3,400 percent; in Argentina inflation reached 3,700 percent, in Brazil almost 1,500 percent, and in Peru nearly 3,000 percent. Ecuador, with only 60 percent inflation, did comparatively well."[26] In such circumstances the currency becomes worthless, as does the idea of seeking to raise national savings rates for long-term capital investment.

Another result was that some Latin American countries found themselves among the most indebted in the world, as shown in Table 10.

In consequence, total Latin American indebtedness now equals about $1,000 for every man, woman, and child. But instead of being directed into productive investment, that money was wasted domestically or disappeared as "capital flight" to private accounts in U.S. and European banks. This left most countries incapable of repaying even the interest on their loans. Defaults on loans (or suspension of interest payments) then produced a drying-up of capital from indignant Western banks and a net capital *outflow* from Latin America just when it

*As mentioned earlier, Japan and its East Asian emulators also sought to protect fledgling domestic industries, but that was in order to create a strong base from which to mount an export offensive—*not* to establish an economic bastion within which their industries would be content to remain.

Table 10. Growth of Latin American Indebtedness, Selected Countries[27]

Country	*Total External Debt (billion U.S.$)*			*Long-Term Public Debt As A Percentage of GNP*		
	1977	*1982*	*1987*	*1977*	*1982*	*1987*
Argentina	8.1	32.4	53.9	10	31	62
Brazil	28.3	68.7	109.4	13	20	29
Chile	4.9	8.5	18.7	28	23	89
Guyana	0.4	0.9	1.2	100	158	353
Honduras	0.6	1.6	3.1	29	53	71
Jamaica	1.1	2.7	4.3	31	69	139
Mexico	26.6	78.0	93.7	25	32	59
Venezuela	9.8	27.0	29.0	10	16	52

needed capital to aid economic growth.* Starved of foreign funds and with currencies made worthless by hyperinflation, many countries are in a far worse position than could have been imagined twenty-five years ago.[28] For a while, it was even feared that the region's financial problems might undermine parts of the international banking system. It now appears that the chief damage will be in the continent itself, where 180 million people (40 percent) are living in poverty—a rise of 50 million alone in the 1980s.

Given such profligacy, and the conservative, "anti-big-government" incumbents in the White House during the 1980s, it was predictable that Latin America would come under pressure—from the World Bank, the IMF, private bankers, Washington itself—to slash public spending, control inflation, and repay debts. Such recipes were easier said than done in the existing circumstances. Islands of democracy (e.g., Costa Rica) did exist, but many states were ruled by right-wing military dictatorships or social revolutionaries; internal guerrilla wars, military coups d'état, and labor unrest were common. Even as democracy began to reassert itself in the 1980s, the new leaders found themselves in a near-impossible situation: inheritors of the massive external debts contracted by the outgoing regimes, legatees in many cases of inflationary index-linked wage systems, targets of landowner resentment and/or of guerrilla attacks, frustrated by elaborate and often corrupt bureaucracies, and deficient in trained personnel. While grap-

*In 1989, the net transfer of capital leaving Latin America was around $25 billion.

pling with these weaknesses, they discovered that the Western world which applauded the return to democracy was unsympathetic to fresh lending, increasingly inclined to protectionism, and insistent on unilateral measures (e.g. in the Amazon rain forests) to stop global warming.

Two other weaknesses also slow any hoped-for recovery. One is the unimpressive accomplishments of the educational systems. This is not due to an absence of schools and universities, as in parts of Africa. Many Latin American countries have extensive public education, dozens of universities, and high adult literacy rates; Brazil, for example, has sixty-eight universities, Argentina forty-one.[29] The real problem is neglect and underinvestment. One citizen recently bemoaned the collapse in Argentina as follows:

> Education, which kept illiteracy at bay for more than a century, lies in ruins. The universities are unheated and many public schools lack panes for their window frames. Last summer [1990] an elementary school teacher with ten years' experience earned less than $110 a month. An associate professor at the Universidad de Buenos Aires, teaching ten hours a week, was paid $37 a month. A doctor's salary at a municipal hospital was $120 a month. . . . At times, teachers took turns teaching, or cut their class hours, because they and their students could not afford transportation.[30]

Presumably, if resources were available, those decaying educational and health-care structures could be resuscitated, helping national recovery; but where the capital can be raised in present circumstances is difficult to see. Moreover, in the strife-torn countries of Central America there is little education to begin with; in Guatemala, the latest census estimated that 63 percent of those ten years of age and older were illiterate, while in Honduras the illiteracy rate was 40 percent.[31] Unfortunately, it is in the most educationally deprived Latin American countries that resources are being eroded by swift population increases.

Despite these disadvantages, recent reports on Latin America have suggested that the "lost decade" of the 1980s will be followed by a period of recovery. The coming of democratic regimes, the compromises emerging from protracted debt-recycling talks, the stiff economic reforms (cutting public spending, abandoning indexation) to reduce inflation rates, the replacement of "state protectionism with import liberalization and privatization,"[32] the conversion of budget deficits into surpluses . . . all these have caused the Inter-American Development Bank to argue that "a decisive and genuine takeoff" is at hand, provided the new policies are sustained.[33] Growth began to resume in Argentina, Mexico, and Venezuela. Even investment bankers are reported to be returning to the continent. Whether these changes are going to be enough remains uncertain, especially since the newly elected governments face widespread resentment at the proposed reforms. As one commentator put it, "Much of Latin America is entering the 1990s in a race between economic deterioration and political progress."[34] Whereas Spain, Portugal, and Greece moved to democracy while enjoying reasonable prosperity, Latin America (like Eastern Europe) has to make that change as its economies flounder—which places immense responsibilities upon the political leadership.

Although it can be argued that the region's future is in its own hands, it will also be heavily influenced by the United States. In many ways, the U.S.–Latin America relationship is similar to that between Japan and the East Asian NIEs, which are heavily dependent upon Japan as their major market and source of capital.[35] Yet there is more to this relationship than Latin America's economic dependence upon the United States, whose banking system has also suffered because of Latin American indebtedness. U.S. exports, which are fifty times larger to this region than to Eastern Europe, were badly hurt by Latin America's economic difficulties and would benefit greatly from a resumption of growth. The United States' own environment may now be threatened by the diminution of the Amazon and Central American rain forests. Its awful drug problem, driven by domestic demand, is fueled by Latin American supplies—more than 80 percent of the cocaine and 90 percent of the marijuana entering the United States are produced or move through this region. Finally, the population of the United States is being altered by migration from Mexico, the Caribbean, and Central America; if there should be a widespread socioeconomic collapse south of the Rio Grande, the "spillover" effects will be felt across the United States. Instead of being marginalized by the end of the Cold War, Latin America may present Washington with a set of awesome challenges—social, environmental, financial, and ultimately political.[36]

Thus, while the region's own politicians and publics have to bear the major responsibility for recovery, richer nations—especially the United States—may find it in their own best interest to lend a hand.

If these remarks disappoint readers in Brazil or Peru, they may care to glance, in grim consolation, at the world of Islam. It is one thing to face population pressures, shortage of resources, educational/technological deficiencies, and regional conflicts which would challenge the wisest governments. But it is another when the regimes themselves stand in angry resentment of global forces for change instead of (as in East Asia) selectively responding to such trends. Far from preparing for the twenty-first century, much of the Arab and Muslim world appears to have difficulty in coming to terms with the nineteenth century, with its composite legacy of secularization, democracy, laissez-faire economics, transnational industrial and commercial linkages, social change, and intellectual questioning. If one needed an example of the importance of cultural attitudes in explaining a society's response to change, contemporary Islam provides it.

Before analyzing the distinctive role of Islamic culture, one should note the danger of generalizing about an area that contains such variety. After all, it is not even clear what *name* should be used to describe this part of the earth. To term it "the Middle East"[37] is, apart from revealing an Atlantic-centered bias, to leave out such North African states as Libya, Tunisia, Algeria, and Morocco. To term it "the Arab World"[38] is to exclude Iran (and, of course, Israel), the Kurds, and the non-Muslim tribes of southern Sudan and Mauretania. Even the nomenclature "Islam," or "the Muslim world," disguises the fact that many millions in the region are Christian, Copts, and Jews, and that Islamic societies extend from West Africa to Indonesia.[39]

In addition, the uneven location of oil in the Middle East has created a dichotomy between super-rich and dreadfully poor societies that has no equivalent in Central America or sub-Saharan Africa.* Countries

*The few oil-producing countries in Africa, such as Gabon and Nigeria, still have low per capita GNPs compared with the Arab Gulf states.

like Kuwait (2 million), the United Arab Emirates (1.3 million), and Saudi Arabia (11.5 million) enjoy some of the world's highest incomes, but exist alongside populous neighbors one-third (Jordan, Iran, Iraq) or even one-tenth as rich (Egypt, Yemen). The gap is accentuated by different political systems: conservative, antidemocratic, traditionalist in the Gulf sheikhdoms; demagogic, populist, militarized in countries such as Libya, Syria, Iraq, and Iran. The 1990 Iraqi attack upon Kuwait and the different responses of the Saudi elites on the one hand and the street masses in Amman or Rabat on the other illustrated this divide between "haves" and "have-nots" in the Muslim world. The presence of millions of Egyptian, Yemeni, Jordanian, and Palestinian guest workers in the oil-rich states simply increased the mutual resentments, while the Saudi and Emirate habit of giving massive aid to Iraq during its war against Iran or to Egypt to assist its economic needs reinforces the impression of wealthy but precarious regimes seeking to achieve security by bribing their larger, jealous neighbors.[40] Is it any wonder that the unemployed, badly housed urban masses, despairing of their own secular advancement, are attracted to religious leaders or "strongmen" appealing to Islamic pride, a sense of identity, and resistance to foreign powers and their local lackeys?

More than in any other developing region, then, the future of the Middle East and North Africa is affected by issues of war and conflict. The area probably contains more soldiers, aircraft, missiles, and other weaponry than anywhere else in the world, with billions of dollars of armaments having been supplied by Western, Soviet, and Chinese producers during the past few decades. Given the range and destructiveness of these weapons, another Arab-Israeli war would be a nightmare, yet many Muslim states still regard Israel with acute hostility. Even if the Arab-Israeli antagonism did not exist, the region is full of other rivalries, between Syria and Iraq, Libya and Egypt, Iran and Iraq, and so on. Vicious one-man dictatorships glare threateningly at arch-conservative, antidemocratic, feudal sheikhdoms. Fundamentalist regimes exist from Iran to the Sudan. Terrorist groups in exile threaten to eliminate their foes. Unrest among the masses puts a question over the future of Egypt, Algeria, Morocco, Jordan.[41] The recent fate of Lebanon, instead of serving as a warning against sectarian fanaticism, is more often viewed as a lesson in power politics, that the strong will devour the weak.

To the Western observer brought up in Enlightenment traditions—or, for that matter, to economic rationalists preaching the virtues of the borderless world—the answer to the Muslim nations' problems would appear to be a massive program of *education,* not simply in the technical, skills-acquiring sense but also to advance parliamentary discourse, pluralism, and a secular civic culture. Is that not the reason, after all, for the political stability and economic success of Scandinavia or Japan today?

If that argument is correct, then such an observer would find few of those features in contemporary Islam. In countries where fundamentalism is strong, there is little or no prospect of education or advancement for the female half of the population.* Where engineers and technicians exist, their expertise has all too often been mobilized for war purposes, as in Iraq. Tragically, Egypt possesses a large and bustling university system but a totally inadequate number of jobs for graduates and skilled workers, so that millions of both are underemployed. In Yemen, the overall state of education is dismal. By contrast, the oil-rich states have poured massive resources into schools, technical institutes, and universities, but that alone is insufficient to create an "enterprise culture" that would produce export-led manufacturing along East Asian lines. Ironically, possession of vast oil reserves could be a *disadvantage,* since it reduces the incentive to rely upon the skills and quality of the people, as occurs in countries (Japan, Switzerland) with few natural resources. Such discouraging circumstances may also explain why many educated and entrepreneurial Arabs, who passionately wanted their societies to borrow from the West, have emigrated.

It is difficult to know whether the reason for the Muslim world's troubled condition is cultural or historical. Western critics who point to the region's religious intolerance, technological backwardness, and a feudal cast of mind often forget that centuries before the Reformation, Islam led the world in mathematics, cartography, medicine, and

*In 1985, adult female literacy in the Yemen Arab Republic was a mere 3 percent, in Saudi Arabia 12 percent, in Iran 39 percent. On the other hand, many women from the middle and upper middle classes in Muslim countries are educated, which suggests that poverty, as much as culture, plays a role.

many other aspects of science and industry, and contained libraries, universities, and observatories when Japan and America possessed none and Europe only a few. These assets were later sacrificed to a revival of traditionalist thought and the sectarian split between Shi'ite and Sunni Muslims, but Islam's retreat into itself—its being "out of step with History," as one author termed it[42]—was probably also a response to the rise of a successful, expansionist Europe. Sailing along the Arab littoral, assisting in the demise of the Mughal Empire, penetrating strategic points with railways, canals, and ports, steadily moving into North Africa, the Nile Valley, the Persian Gulf, the Levant, and then Arabia itself, dividing the Middle East along unnatural boundaries as part of a post–World War I diplomatic bargain, developing American power to buttress and then replace European influences, inserting an Israeli state in the midst of Arab peoples, instigating coups against local popular leaders, and usually indicating that this part of the globe was important only for its oil, the West may have played more of a role in turning the Muslim world into what it is today than outside commentators are willing to recognize.[43] Clearly, Islam suffers many self-inflicted problems. But if much of its angry, confrontational stance toward the international order today *is* due to a long-held fear of being swallowed up by the West, not much in the way of change can be expected until that fear is dissipated.

The condition of sub-Saharan Africa—"the Third World's Third World," as it has been described—is even more desperate.[44] When one considers recent developments such as *perestroika* in the former Soviet Union, the coming integration of Europe, and the economic miracle of Japan and the East Asian NIEs, remarked a former president of Nigeria, General Olusegun Obasanjo, "contrasting all this with what is taking place in Africa, it is difficult to believe that we inhabit the same historical time."[45] Recent reports upon the continent's plight are extraordinarily gloomy, describing Africa as "a human and environmental disaster area," as "moribund," "marginalized," and "peripheral to the rest of the world," and as having so many intractable problems that some foreign development experts are abandoning it to work elsewhere. In the view of the World Bank, virtually everywhere else in the world is likely to experience a decline in poverty by the year 2000 *except* Africa, where things will only get worse.[46] "Sub-Saharan Africa," concludes one economist, "suffers from a combination of economic, social, political, institutional, and environmental handicaps which have so far largely defied development efforts by the African countries and their donors."[47] How, an empathetic study asks, can Africa survive?[48]

The unanimity of views is remarkable, given the enormous variety among the forty-five states that compose sub-Saharan Africa.* Nine of them have less than 1 million people each, whereas Nigeria contains about 110 million. Some lie in the desert, some in tropical rain forests. Many are rich in mineral deposits, others have only scrubland. While a number (Botswana, Cameroon, Congo, Gabon, Kenya) have seen significant increases in living standards since independence, they are the exception—suggesting that the obstacles to growth on East Asian lines are so deep-rooted and resistant to the "development strategies" of foreign experts and/or their own leaders that it may require profound attitudinal changes to achieve recovery.

This was not the mood thirty years ago, when the peoples of Africa were gaining their independence. True, there was economic backwardness, but this was assumed to have been caused by decades of foreign rule, leading to dependency upon a single metropolitan market, monoculture, lack of access to capital, and so on. Now that Africans had control of their destinies, they could build industries, develop cities, airports, and infrastructure, and attract foreign investment and aid from either Western powers or the USSR and its partners. The 1950s–1960s boom in world trade and demand for commodities strengthened this optimism. Although there were individual areas of need, Africa as a whole was self-sufficient in food and, in fact, a net food exporter. Externally, African states were of increasing importance at the United Nations and other world bodies.

What went wrong? The unhappy answer is "lots of things." The first, and perhaps most serious, was that over the following three decades the population mushroomed as imported medical techniques

*As will be clear from the text, this discussion excludes the Republic of South Africa.

and a reduction in malaria-borne mosquitoes drastically curtailed infant mortality. Africa's population was already increasing at an average annual rate of 2.6 percent in the 1960s, jumped to 2.9 percent during the 1970s, and increased to over 3.0 percent by the late 1980s, implying a doubling in size every twenty-two years; this was, therefore, the highest rate for any region in the world.[49] In certain countries, the increases were staggering. Between 1960 and 1990, Kenya's population quadrupled, from 6.3 million to 25.1 million, and Côte d'Ivoire's jumped from 3.8 million to 12.6 million. Altogether, Africa's population—including the North African states—leaped from 281 to 647 million in three decades.[50] Moreover, while the majority of Africans inhabit rural settlements, the continent has been urbanizing at dizzying speed. Vast shanty cities have already emerged on the edges of national capitals (Accra, Monrovia, Lilongwe). By 2025, urban dwellers are forecast to make up 55 percent of Africa's total population.

The worst news is that the increase is unlikely to diminish in the near future. Although most African countries spend less than 1 percent of GNP on health care and consequently have the highest infant mortality rates in the world—in Mali, for example, there are 169 infant deaths for every thousand live births—those rates are substantially less than they were a quarter century ago and will tumble further in the future, which is why demographers forecast that Africa's population in 2025 could be nearly three times that of today.[51] Another reason that this demographic boom will not be halted swiftly is traditional African belief systems concerning fecundity, children, ancestors, and the role of women. Acutely aware of the invisible but pervasive presence of their ancestors, determined to expand their lineage, regarding childlessness or small families as the work of evil spirits, most Africans seek to have as many children as possible; a woman's virtue and usefulness are measured by the number of offspring she can bear. "Desired family size," according to polls of African women, ranges from five to nine children. The social attitudes that lead women in North America, Europe, and Japan to delay childbearing—education, career ambitions, desire for independence—scarcely exist in African societies; where such emerge, they are swiftly suppressed by familial pressures.[52]

This population growth has not been accompanied by equal or larger increases in Africa's productivity, which would of course transform the picture. During the 1960s, farm output was rising by around 3 percent each year, keeping pace with the population, but since 1970, agricultural production has grown at only half that rate. Part of this decline was due to the drought, hitting most countries south of the Sahara. Furthermore, existing agricultural resources have been badly eroded by overgrazing—caused by the sharp rise in the number of cattle and goats—as well as by deforestation—to provide fuel and shelter for the growing population. When rain falls, the water runs off the denuded fields, taking the topsoil with it. None of this was helped by changes in agricultural production, with farmers encouraged to grow tea, coffee, cocoa, palm oil, and rubber for export rather than food for domestic consumption. After benefiting from high commodity prices in the early stages, producers suffered a number of blows; heavy taxation on cash crops, plus mandatory governmental marketing, reduced the incentives to increase output; competition grew from Asian and Latin American producers; many African currencies were overvalued, which hurt exports; and in the mid-1970s world commodity prices tumbled. Yet the cost of imported manufactures and foodstuffs remained high, and sub-Saharan Africa was badly hurt by the quadrupling of oil prices.[53]

These blows increased Africa's indebtedness, in a qualitatively different way. Early, postcolonial borrowings were driven by the desire for modernity, as money was poured into cement works, steel plants, airports, harbors, national airlines, electrification schemes, and telephone networks. Much of it suffered from bureaucratic interference, a lack of skilled personnel, unrealistic planning, and inadequate basic facilities, and now lies half finished or (where completed) suffers from lack of upkeep. But borrowing to pay for imported oil, or to feed half the nation's population, means that indebtedness rises without any possible return upon funds. In consequence, Africa's total debt expanded from $14 billion in 1973 to $125 billion in 1987, when its capacity to repay was dropping fast; by the mid-1980s, payments on loans consumed about half of Africa's export earnings, a proportion even greater than for Latin American debtor nations. Following repeated debt reschedulings, Western bankers—never enthusiastic to begin with—virtually abandoned private loans to Africa.[54]

As a result, Africa's economy is in a far worse condition now than at Independence, apart from a few countries like Botswana and

Mauritius. Perhaps the most startling illustration of its plight is the fact that "excluding South Africa, the nations of sub-Saharan Africa with their 450 million people have a total GDP less than that of Belgium's 11 million people"; in fact, the entire continent generates roughly 1 percent of world GDP.[55] Its share of world markets has shriveled just as East Asia's share has risen fast. Plans for modernization lie unrealized. Manufacturing still represents only 11 percent of Africa's economic activity—scarcely up from the 9 percent share in 1965; and only 12 percent of the continent's exports is composed of manufactures (compared with Korea's 90 percent). There is a marked increase in the signs of decay: crumbling infrastructure, power failures, broken-down communications, abandoned projects, and everywhere the pressure of providing for increasing populations. Already Africa needs to import 15 million tonnes of maize a year to achieve minimal levels of food consumption, but with population increasing faster than agricultural output, that total could multiply over the next decade—implying an even greater diversion of funds from investment and infrastructure.[56]

Two further characteristics worsen Africa's condition. The first is the prevalence of wars, coups d'état, and political instability. This is partly the legacy of the European "carve-up" of Africa, when colonial boundaries were drawn without regard for the differing tribes and ethnic groups,* or even of earlier conquests by successful tribes of neighboring lands and peoples; Ethiopia, for example, is said to contain seventy-six ethnic groups and 286 languages.[57] While it is generally accepted that those boundaries cannot be unscrambled, most of them are clearly artificial. Governments are not a focus of loyalty (except perhaps to kinsmen of the group in power), and ethnic tensions have produced innumerable civil wars—from Biafra's attempt to secede from Nigeria, to the conflict between Arab north and African south in the Sudan, to Eritrean struggles to escape from Ethiopia, to the Tutsi-Hutu struggle in Burundi, to clashes and suppressions and guerrilla campaigns from Uganda to the western Sahara, from Angola to Mozambique.[58]

These antagonisms have often been worsened by struggles over ideology and government authority. The rulers of many new African states

*In this regard, East Asian nations like Taiwan and Korea, possessing coherent indigenous populations, are once again more favorably situated.

rapidly switched to either a personal dictatorship or single-party rule. They also embraced a Soviet or Maoist political economy, instituting price controls, production targets, forced industrialization, the takeover of private enterprises, and other features of "scientific socialism" that—unbeknownst to them—were destroying the Soviet economy. Agriculture was neglected, while bureaucracy flourished. The result was the disappearance of agricultural surpluses, inattention to manufacturing for the world market, and the expansion of party and government bureaucracies, exacerbating the region's problems.

The second weakness was the totally inadequate investment in human resources and in developing a culture of entrepreneurship, scientific inquiry, and technical prowess. According to one survey, Africa has been spending less than $1 each year on research and development per head of population, whereas the United States was spending $200 per head. Consequently, Africa's scientific population has always trailed the rest of the world.

In many African countries—Malawi, Zambia, Lesotho, Somalia—government spending on education has fallen, so that after some decades of advance, a smaller share of children are now in school. While there is a hunger for learning, it cannot be satisfied beyond the secondary level except for a small minority. Angola, for example, had 2.4 million pupils in primary schools in 1982–83, but only 153,000 in secondary schools and a mere 4,700 in higher education.[59] By contrast, Sweden, with a slightly smaller total population, had 570,000 in secondary education and 179,000 in higher education.[60] Among the 5 million inhabitants of Burundi in 1984, only 218 were scientists and engineers. While African scientists urgently call for leadership that "personally

Table 11. Numbers of Scientists and Engineers per Million of Population[61]

Japan	3,548
U.S.	2,685
Europe	1,632
Latin America	209
Arab states	202
Asia (minus Japan)	99
Africa	53

takes science and technology as the key element for the transformation of society,"[62] the circumstances by which so many African leaders rose to power (e.g., military coups d'état) and the struggle to hold their countries together make a science-led strategy highly unlikely.

Despite these relative weaknesses, some observers claim to have detected signs of a turnaround. With the exception of dyed-in-the-wool African socialists,[63] many leaders are now attempting to institute reforms. In return for "structural adjustments," that is, measures to encourage free enterprise, certain African societies have secured additional loans from Western nations and the World Bank. The latter organization has identified past errors (many of them urged upon African governments and funded by itself) and encouraged economic reforms. Mozambique, Ghana, and Zambia have all claimed recent successes in reversing negative growth, albeit at considerable social cost. Democratic principles are also returning to the continent: the dismantling of apartheid in South Africa, the cease-fire in Angola, the independence of Namibia, the success of Botswana's record of democracy and prosperity, the cries for reforms in Gabon, Kenya, and Zaire, the rising awareness among African intellectuals of the transformations in East Asia, may all help—so the argument goes—to change attitudes, which is the prerequisite for recovery.[64] Moreover, at the grass-roots level, there are examples of economic self-improvement, cooperative ventures to halt erosion and improve yields, and village-based schemes of improvement.[65] This is, after all, a continent of enormous agricultural and mineral resources, provided they can be sensibly exploited.

Despite such signs of promise, conditions are likely to stay bad. Population increases, the diminution of grazing lands and food supplies, the burdens of indebtedness, the decay of infrastructures, the reduction of spending upon health care and education, the residual strength of animist religions and traditional belief systems, the powerful hold of corrupt bureaucracies and ethnic loyalties . . . all those tilt against the relatively few African political leaders, educators, scientists, and economists who perceive the need for changes. As Africa struggles to stay connected with the rest of the world, the indications—declining amounts of aid, shrinking trade and investment flows, reduction in media coverage, diminished superpower involvement—are that it is becoming more peripheral. Some experts argue that disengagement by developed countries might have the positive effect of compelling Africans to begin a *self-driven* recovery, as well as ending the misuse of aid monies.[66] Others feel that Africa cannot live without the West, although its leaders and publics will have to abandon existing habits, and development aid must be more intelligently applied.[67] Whichever view is correct, the coming decade will be critical for Africa. Even a partial recovery would give grounds for hope; on the other hand, a second decade of decline, together with a further surge in population, would result in catastrophe.

The developing countries' response to the broad forces for global change is, clearly, going to be uneven. While some are in distress, others are booming—but what else ought one to expect when analyzing nations ranging from Singapore to Burkina Faso? Furthermore, the signs are that the gap will widen; one group enjoys interacting beneficial trends, while others suffer from linked weaknesses and deficiencies.[68]

This is most clearly the case in respect to demography. As noted earlier, the commitment of East Asian trading states to education, manufacturing, *and* export-led growth produced a steady rise in living standards and allowed those societies to make the demographic transition to smaller family sizes. This was in marked contrast to sub-Saharan Africa, where different cultural attitudes and social structures, improved health care, and rising incomes led not to a drop in population growth but to the opposite. Just before independence in 1960, for example, the average Kenyan woman had 6.2 children, whereas by 1980 she had 8.2[69]—and that in a period when Africa's economic prospects were fading.

In Africa's case the "global trend" which influences all others is the demographic explosion. It spills into every domain—overgrazing, local conflicts over water and wood supplies, massive unplanned urbanization, strains upon the educational and social structures, reliance upon imported food supplies (at the cost of increasing indebtedness), ethnic tensions, domestic unrest, border wars. Only belatedly are some African governments working to persuade families to limit their size as people become aware that access to family planning and improved educational opportunities for women produce significant declines in birth rates. Against such promising indications stand the many cultural, gender-related, and economic forces described above that encourage large families. This resistance to change is aided by Africa's general lack of resources. Raising Somalia's female literacy rate (6 percent) to South Korea's (88 percent) to produce a demographic transition sounds fine until one considers how that massive reform could be implemented and paid for. Unfortunately, the projections suggest that as Africa's population almost trebles over the next few decades, the only development curtailing it could be the rapid growth of AIDS.*[70]

In many parts of Latin America, the demographic explosion will also affect the capacity to handle globally driven forces for change. While wide differences in total fertility rates exist between the moderate-climate countries and those in the tropics, the overall picture is that Latin America's population, which was roughly equal to the United States and Canada's in 1960, is increasing so swiftly that it will be more than double the latter in 2025.†[71] Even if birth rates are now declining in the larger countries, there will still be enormous increases; Mexico's population will leap to 150 million by 2025 and Brazil's to 245 million.[72] This implies a massive incidence of child poverty and malnutrition, further strain upon already inadequate health-care and educational services, the crowding of millions of human beings into a dozen or more "megacities," pollution, and the degradation of grazing land, forests, and other natural resources. In Mexico, for example, 44 million are without sewers and 21 million without potable water, which means that when disease (e.g., cholera) strikes, it spreads swiftly.[73] These are not strong foundations upon which to improve the region's relative standing in an increasingly competitive international economic order.

In this regard, many Muslim states are in a similar or worse position; in no Arab country is the population increasing by less than 2 percent a year,[74] and in most the rate is considerably higher. The region's total population of more than 200 million will double in less than twenty-five years, and city populations are growing twice as fast as national aver-

*Discussed above on pp. 27–29.

†The U.S./Canada total in 1960 was 217 million, to Latin America's 210 million; by 2025, it is estimated, the figures will be 332 million and 762 million.

ages. This puts enormous pressures upon scarce food, water, and land resources and produces unbalanced populations. Already, in most Arab countries at least four out of every ten people are under the age of fifteen—the classic recipe for subsequent social unrest and political revolution. "Walk along Avenue Habib Bourgiuba, the main street of Tunis, on any working day and you will see cafés brimming with bored young men; up to 40 percent of Tunisians are unemployed. Sleepy Casablanca has become a city of 3 million souls, with a swelling penumbra of slums. Food riots broke out in Morocco's northern cities in 1984. Greater Cairo is home to 13 million people, hundreds of thousands of whom make their homes in cemeteries, cardboard shanties, alleys, and doorways. . . ." One in five Egyptian workers is jobless, as is one in four Algerian workers.[75] In what is widely regarded as the most turbulent part of the world, therefore, demography is contributing to the prospects of future unrest year by year. Even the Israeli-Palestine quarrel has become an issue of demography, with the influx of Soviet Jews intended to counter the greater fertility of the Palestinians.

There is, moreover, little likelihood that population growth will fall in the near future, since infant mortality rates in many Muslim countries are still high, which means that further improvements in prenatal and postnatal care will produce rises in the birth rate, as is happening in the Gulf states and Saudi Arabia.

As elsewhere, politics intrudes; many regimes are deliberately encouraging women to have large families, arguing that this adds to the

Table 12. Comparative Infant Mortality Rates[76]
(infant deaths per 1,000 live births)

	1965–70	*1985–90*
Algeria	150	74
Egypt	170	85
Sudan	156	108
Yemen Arab Republic	186	116
Saudi Arabia	140	71
Kuwait	55	19
Iraq	111	69
Japan	16	5
U.S.	22	10
Sweden	13	6

country's military strength. "Bear a child," posters in Iraq proclaim, "and you pierce an arrow in the enemy's eye."[77] Countries such as Iraq and Libya offer many incentives for larger families, as do the Gulf states and Saudi Arabia, anxious to fill their oil-rich lands with native-born rather than foreign workers. Only in Egypt are propaganda campaigns launched to curb family size, but even if that is successful—despite resistance from the Muslim Brotherhood—present numbers are disturbing. With a current population of over 55 million Egyptians, six out of ten of whom are under twenty, and with an additional million being born every eight months, the country is in danger of bursting at the seams during the next few decades.

For much the same reasons, we ought to expect a differentiated success rate among developing countries in handling environmental challenges, with the East Asian NIEs way ahead of the others. This is not to ignore significant local schemes to improve the ecology that are springing up in Africa and the interesting proposals for "sustainable development" elsewhere in the developing world,[78] or to forget that industrialization has caused environmental damage in East Asia, from choked roads to diminished forests. Yet the fact is that nations with lots of resources (capital, scientists, engineers, technology, a per capita GNP of over $4,000) are better able to deal with environmental threats than those without monies, tools, and personnel. There is also a "feedback loop" between high educational levels, enhanced ecological consciousness, and a willingness to prevent environmental damage, which suggests that East Asia will be more responsive in this field. By contrast, it is the poorer societies (Egypt, Bangladesh, Ethiopia) which, lacking financial and personnel resources, find it difficult to respond to cyclones, floods, drought, and other natural disasters—with their devastated populations augmenting the millions of refugees and migrants. Should global warming produce sea-level rises and heightened storm surges, teeming island populations from the Caribbean to the Pacific are in danger of being washed away.[79]

Finally, it is Latin America's, South Asia's, and Africa's population explosion that is the major cause for the overgrazing, soil erosion, salinization, and clearing of the tropical rain forests, which, while contributing to global warming, also hurt the local populations and exacerbate regional struggles for power. Elsewhere, in the Middle East for example, supplies of water are the greatest concern, especially in view of growing demographic pressures. Already, the average Jordanian uses only one-third the amount of domestic water consumed in Israel and has little hope of increasing the supply, yet Jordan's population is expected to double during the next twenty years.[80] With all governments in the area striving to boost agricultural output, and highly sensitive to famine and unrest among their peasant farmers, the search for secure water influences domestic politics, international relations, and spending priorities. Egypt worries that either the Sudan or Ethiopia might dam the Nile in order to increase irrigation. Syria and Iraq have taken alarm at Turkey's new Ataturk Dam, which can interrupt the flow of the Euphrates. Jordan, Syria, and Israel quarrel over water rights in the Litani, Yarmuk, and Jordan river valleys, as do Arabs and Jews over well supplies in the occupied West Bank. Saudi Arabia's ambition to grow wheat is draining its aquifers, and the same will occur with Libya's gigantic scheme to tap water from under the Sahara.[81] As more and more people struggle for the same—or diminishing—amounts of water, grand ideas about preparing for the twenty-first century look increasingly irrelevant; surviving *this* century becomes the issue.

On the other hand, the revolution in biotech farming is of great relevance to developing countries, even if the consequences will be mixed. Improved strains of plants and more sophisticated pesticides and fertilizers could, potentially, enhance yields in the developing world, reduce pressures upon marginal lands, restore agricultural self-sufficiency, improve the balance of payments, and raise standards of living. Since much biotech does not involve expensive enterprise, we could witness farmers' groups experimenting with new seeds, improved breeding techniques, cultivation of gene tissue, regional gene banks, and other developments. On the other hand, it is also possible that giant pharmaceutical and agrochemical firms in the "First" World may monopolize much of the knowledge—and the profit—that this transformation implies. Global foodstuff surpluses caused by the biotech revolution could be used to counter malnutrition. They could also undermine commodity prices and hurt societies in which most inhabitants are employed in agriculture. Dematerializing food production would undercut agrarian societies, which is why some biotech experts in the development field call for serious planning in "agricultural conversion," that is, conversion into other economic activities.[82]

As noted earlier,* all this depends on whether the new technology is employed chiefly to enhance traditional ways of growing food and made accessible (through international agencies, technology transfer, etc.) to farmers in the developing world, or is directed toward *in vitro* food production and processing in the laboratories of proprietary multinationals, rendering traditional agriculture obsolete. Should the latter trend prevail, a high-tech manufacturing country with a diminishing agricultural sector (e.g., Korea) will find it easier to adjust than a society reliant upon commodity exports (e.g., Gambia, Ivory Coast, Costa Rica).

While the uses of biotechnology are relatively diverse, that is not the case with robotics and automated manufacture. The requirements for an indigenous robotics industry—capital, an advanced electronics sector, design engineers, a dearth of skilled labor—suggest that countries like Taiwan and Korea may follow Japan's example out of concern that its automation will make their own products uncompetitive. On the other hand, automated factories assembling goods more swiftly, regularly, and economically than human beings poses a challenge to *middle-income* economies (Malaysia, Mexico) whose comparative advantage would be undercut. As for countries without a manufacturing base, it is difficult to see how the robotics revolution would have any meaning—except to further devalue the resource which they possess in abundance, masses of impoverished and undereducated human beings.

Finally, the global financial and communications revolution and the emergence of multinational corporations threaten to increase the gap between richer and poorer countries, even in the developing world. The industrial conglomerates of Korea are now positioning themselves to become multinational, and the East Asian NIEs in general are able to exploit the world economy (as can be seen in their trade balances, stock markets, electronics industries, strategic marketing alliances, and so on). Furthermore, if the borderless world rewards entrepreneurs, designers, brokers, patent owners, lawyers, and dealers in high-value-added services, then East Asia's commitment to education, science,

*See Chapter 4.

and technology can only increase its lead over other developing economies. By contrast, their relative lack of capital, high technology, scientists and skilled workers, and export-oriented industry makes it difficult for poorer countries to partake in the communications and financial revolution, although several states (Brazil, India) clearly hope to do so. Some grimmer forecasts suggest the developing world may become more marginalized, partly because of the dematerialization of labor, raw materials, and foodstuffs, partly because the advanced economies may concentrate upon greater knowledge-based commerce among themselves.

Is there any way of turning this around? Obviously, a society strongly influenced by fundamentalist mullahs with a dislike of "modernization" is unlikely to join the international economy; and it does not *have* to enter the borderless world if its people believe that it would be healthier, spiritually if not economically, to remain outside. Nor ought we to expect that countries dominated by selfish, authoritarian elites bent upon enhancing their military power—developing world countries spent almost $150 billion on weapons and armies in 1988 alone—will rush to imitate Japan and Singapore.

But what about those societies that wish to improve themselves yet find that they are hampered by circumstances? There are, after all, *so* many developing countries, the vast majority of which depend upon exporting food and raw materials. With dozens of poor countries seeking desperately to sell their cane sugar or bananas or timber or coffee in the global market, prices fall, and they are made more desperate.[83] Moreover, although much international aid goes to the developing world, in fact far more money flows *out of* impoverished countries of Africa, Asia, and Latin America and *into* the richer economies of Europe, North America, and Japan—to the tune of at least $43 billion each year.[84] This outward flow of interest repayments, repatriated profits, capital flight, royalties, and fees for patents and information services makes it difficult for poorer countries to get to their feet; and even if they were able to increase their industrial output, the result might be a massive rise in "the costs of technological dependence."[85] Like their increasing reliance upon Northern suppliers for food and medical aid, this has created another dependency relationship for poorer nations.

This structural underdevelopment also extends to communications. Many developing countries have accused richer nations of cultural domination by control of the major news-collecting resources, by the unstinted flow of their cultural products, by the power of advertising agencies, international newspaper chains, and newsprint companies, and by their hold over broadcasting, navigation, and much else.[86] While it is true that *no* government nowadays can control the communications revolution, it remains important politically whose viewpoints (on free enterprise, North-South relations, cultural and religious issues) the new global media will favor. How, it is asked, can poorer countries be expected to benefit from the communications and financial revolution when they suffer from "the swamping effect of this vast machinery" which represses traditional cultures and gives them no voice on the world stage?[87]

In sum, as we move into the next century the developed economies appear to have all the trump cards in their hands—capital, technology, control of communications, surplus foodstuffs, powerful multinational companies[88]—and, if anything, their advantages are *growing* because technology is eroding the value of labor and materials, the chief assets of developing countries. Although nominally independent since decolonization, these countries are probably more dependent upon Europe and the United States than a century ago. Ironically, three or four decades of efforts by developing countries to gain control of their own destinies—by nationalizing Western companies, setting up commodity-exporting cartels, subsidizing indigenous manufacturing to achieve import substitution, campaigning for a new world order based upon redistribution of the existing imbalances of wealth—have all failed. The "market," backed by governments of the developed economies, has proved too strong, and the struggle against it has weakened developing economies still further—except those (like Korea and Taiwan) which decided to join.

While the gap between rich and poor in today's world is disturbing, those arguing this structuralist viewpoint have all too often supported heavy-handed state interventionism and a retreat from open competition, which preserved indigenous production in the short term but rendered it less efficient against those stimulated by market forces. "Scientific socialism for Africa" may still appeal to some intellectuals,[89] but by encouraging societies to look inward it made them less well equipped to move to ever-higher-value-added manufacturing. And a new "world communications order," as proposed a few years ago by UNESCO to balance the West's dominance, sounds superficially attractive but would in all likelihood become the pawn of bureaucratic and ideological interests rather than function as an objective source of news reporting. On the other hand, the advocates of free-market forces often ignore the massive political difficulties which governments in developing countries would encounter in abolishing price controls, selling off national industries, and reducing food subsidies. They also forget that the spectacular commercial expansion of Japan and the East Asian NIEs was carried out by strong states which eschewed laissez-faire. Instead of copying either socialist or free-market systems, therefore, the developing countries might imitate East Asia's "mixed strategies" which combine official controls and private enterprise.[90]

Although the idea of a mixed strategy is intriguing, how can West or Central African countries imitate East Asia without a "strong state" apparatus, and with a weak tradition of cooperation between government and firms, far lower educational achievements, and a different set of cultural attitudes toward family size and international economics? With the global scene less welcoming to industrializing newcomers, how likely are they to achieve the same degree of success as the East Asian NIEs did, when they took off a quarter century ago?[91] Even if, by an economic miracle, the world's poorest fifty nations *did* adopt the Korean style of export-led growth in manufactures, would they not create the same crisis of industrial overproduction as exists in the commodity markets today?

How many developing nations will be able to follow East Asia's growth is impossible to tell. The 1991 *World Development Report* optimistically forecast significant progress across the globe, provided poorer nations adopt "market friendly" policies and richer nations eschew protectionism.[92] Were Taiwan and Korea to be followed by the larger states of Southeast Asia, then by South Asia and a number of Latin American countries, that would blur the North-South divide and make international economic alignments altogether more variegated. Moreover, sustained manufacturing success among developing countries *outside* East Asia might stimulate imitation elsewhere. At the moment, however, the usual cluster of factors influencing relative economic performance—cultural attitudes, education, political stability, capacity to carry out long-term plans—suggests that while a small but growing number of countries is moving from a "have-not" to a "have" status, many more remain behind. The story of winners and losers will continue, therefore, only this time modern communications will remind us all of the growing disparity.

11

THE ERSTWHILE USSR AND ITS CRUMBLED EMPIRE

WHEN WRITING ABOUT THE PROSPECTS for the states of the former Soviet Union, observers confront the same problem that baffled them in 1918: not only is it hard to guess where the region is headed, it is also unclear how far the disintegration from unified empire to splintered subparts will go. So severe and complex is the crisis that the only certain fact is the existence of innumerable uncertainties. This makes it inordinately difficult to estimate the region's ability to prepare for the twenty-first century, since its leadership is primarily concerned with surviving the present chaos and its people are overwhelmed by the daily need to make ends meet. In such circumstances little energy is left to consider global trends, let alone adjust to newer challenges.

Despite its current sociopolitical crisis, the successors to the USSR possess a multitude of material resources. The Soviet Union consisted of 22.4 million square kilometers or 8.6 million square miles, one-sixth of the land surface of the globe. Strategically, that made it remarkably invulnerable to external attack, as foreign warlords from Charles XII of Sweden to Hitler discovered to their cost. Economically, it provided a large internal market and a below-average dependency upon foreign trade, advantages shared by such other extensive countries as China and the United States. It also has, potentially, an enormous agricultural base, with an arable area equal to that of the United States and Canada combined. Its 6,500-mile-wide landmass contains the world's largest array of raw materials; before its collapse, it was the biggest producer of iron, nickel, lead, oil, and natural gas, and the third-biggest producer of coal. It was the world's second-largest source of gold and chromium, and a leading producer of silver, copper, and zinc. Soviet scientists proudly claimed that the country contained "58 percent of the world's coal deposits, 58.7 percent of its oil, 41 percent of its iron ore, 76.7 percent of its apatite, 25 percent of all timberland, 88 percent of its manganese, 54 percent of its potassium salts, and nearly one-third of its phosphates."[1] While such statistical precision seems dubious, these lands are extraordinarily gifted in natural resources.

The exploitation of such resources from the late 1920s onward produced a massive industrial and manufacturing base. By the middle of World War II, and despite huge territorial losses, its economy became the second largest in the world, after America's. A few years ago Moscow boasted that it was first in the production of steel, pig iron, coke, oil, machine tools, diesel and electric trains, cement, mineral fertilizers, tractors, textiles, shoes, and prefabricated concrete structures.[2] In addition to its extensive rail and airline networks, it had a very considerable mercantile marine and the world's largest long-range fishing fleet.

This enormous territory is occupied by 288 million people (1989), with what was claimed to be one of the most comprehensive educational systems in the world. Education was free from seven to seventeen, but millions of children were in kindergarten and many part-time, correspondence, and vocational courses existed for those not in full-time higher education. According to the official statistics, about 100 million people were studying at schools, colleges, and training and correspondence courses in the early 1980s, including over 44 million pupils in 145,000 primary and secondary schools, 4.6 million students in the 4,380 technical colleges, and 5.2 million students in the nation's 883 universities and institutes.[3] The educational system was geared toward economic utility rather than the pursuit of knowledge for its own sake; this was reflected in the huge number of engineers in the Soviet Union—about 40 percent of higher-education graduates—and in the many technological and scientific institutions. Overall, the country claimed to possess about 14.9 million "economically active scientists and engineers" in 1985, supported by a further 17.4 million "economically active technicians."[4] The USSR also possessed 70,000 medical research staff, along with 960,000 doctors and dentists—more active physicians, in other words, than any other country in the world.[5] Given the numbers in science, technology, and engineering, and its achievements in mathematics and science, it is not surprising that the Soviet Union claimed great strengths in many fields, from low-temperature physics to plant research.[6]

In the view of its own leaders, at least until recently, the Soviet Union's greatest achievement was to become one of the world's two military superpowers, equaled only by the far wealthier United States. While the social and economic costs were great, Stalin and his successors never doubted the importance of massive armed forces, both to deter capitalist countries from aggression and, in the second stage, to exert influence upon world affairs.[7] Consequently, the Soviet Union possessed a staggering array of weapons, nuclear and conventional, and a vast force of personnel to use them, if necessary.[8] Even when the Gorbachev initiatives led to considerable reductions in weapons and manpower, the USSR still had the world's largest rocket forces, the second-largest army (after China), the second-largest navy (after the United States), and the largest air force and armored forces. If military power *does* count in the early twenty-first century, a federated successor state to the USSR—or even subparts such as Russia and the Ukraine—will possess plenty of it.

Given such material advantages, the region ought in theory to be better prepared than many less well endowed nations to meet the challenges of the coming century. Yet all this potential is weakened by profound and interconnected flaws that threaten the prospects for survival. As with large empires in the past, territorial size and resources alone will not prevent collapse if the system becomes inoperable.

At the heart of the Soviet problem there lay a triple crisis, each part feeding upon the other and accelerating the collapse. A crisis in the *political legitimacy* of the Soviet system interacted with a crisis in *economic production and social provision,* and both were exacerbated by a crisis in *ethnic and cultural relationships.* The result was an unsurmountable mix of challenges.

The sheer extent of the economic collapse was not realized until recently, partly because of the Kremlin's secrecy, partly because the West overestimated the efficiency of the Soviet economy. It is now evident that there was a long-term slowdown in growth even before the present crisis, as shown in Chart 7.

In all probability, these figures understate the real decline;[9] but the chief point is that while the Soviet economy was expanding throughout the middle third of the twentieth century, it has been stagnating in the final third. The earlier growth was due to massive "inputs" such as

Chart 7. The Decline in the Rate of Growth of Soviet GNP[10]

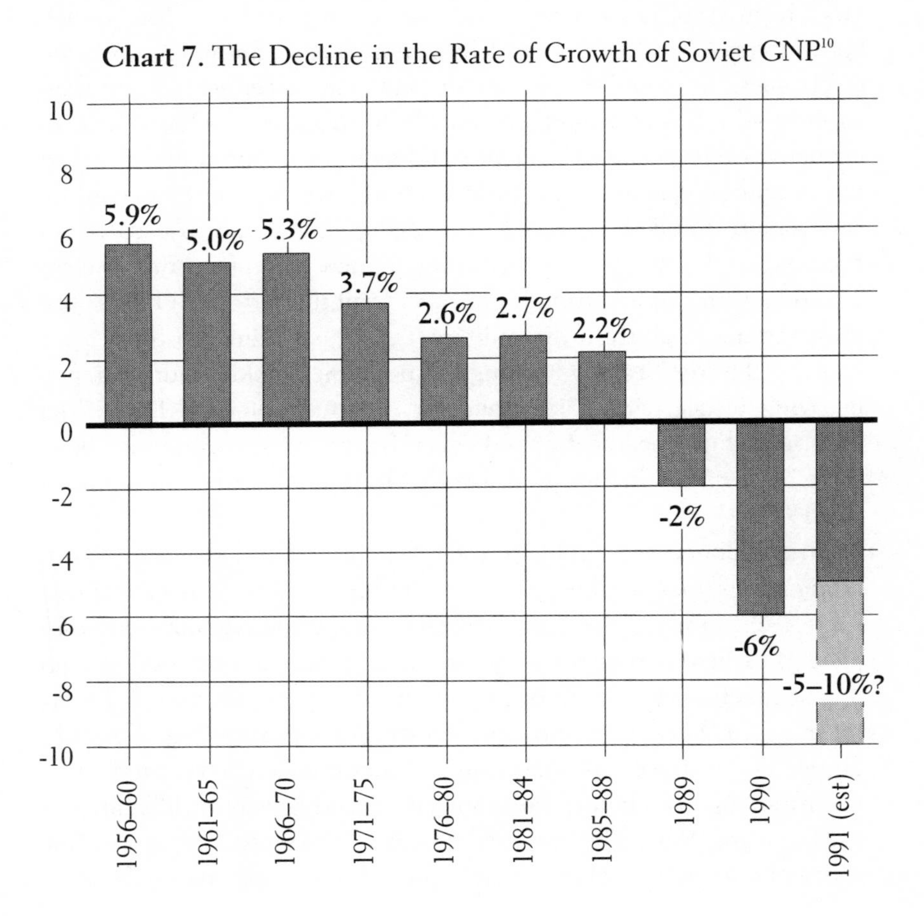

labor, cheap energy, and plentiful raw materials, ideal for building a heavy-industry economy of the 1930s and the postwar construction of the late 1940s and 1950s. Thus, iron and steel, cement, locomotives, machine tools, tractors, textiles, and prefabricated buildings were produced in large numbers according to a central plan. So long as targets were met, this tight socialist planning paid little attention to cost, sheltered management from competition and workers from unemployment, and was unconcerned about the consumer. Indeed, the only "consumers" to get what they wanted were the Soviet armed services, which enjoyed a preferential allocation of factories, machine tools, and skilled workers for military production.

When, from the 1960s onward, world manufacturing began to shift away from traditional heavy goods toward high-value-added, knowledge-intensive, and consumer-driven industries—computers, software electronics, automobiles, civilian aircraft, pharmaceuticals, communications—the Soviet Union was unable to follow suit. Developing an economy driven by consumer demand as in the United States would have required dismantling central planning, while a knowledge-intensive society implied an end to censorship, tight controls, party orthodoxy, and monopoly.[11] Investing in new manufacturing sectors would have meant diverting funds from farm support, from food subsidies, and above all from the military; in fact, spending on those areas continued to rise, leaving nothing for modernizing older industries and decaying infrastructure, let alone for new technologies. The Soviet economy thus became trapped, deep-frozen in an economic "long cycle," shown in Chart 8, that was tied to the industries and inputs of the 1930s.[12]

To compound this problem, the classic inputs of land, energy, raw materials, and labor all became less plentiful, and costs began to rise. Earlier, cheap stocks of oil and natural gas made industrialization possible and earned hard currency; yet while large supplies remain, most of it is at much deeper levels or in permafrost regions. According to one estimate, in the decade prior to 1985 the cost of extracting oil rose by 70 percent and was still increasing.[13] In consequence, oil production was dropping even before the labor unrest and transport difficulties of the following years. This was exacerbated by the systematic misuse and waste of energy throughout Soviet industry, by managerial inefficiency

Chart 8. The Soviet Economy's Long Cycle[14]

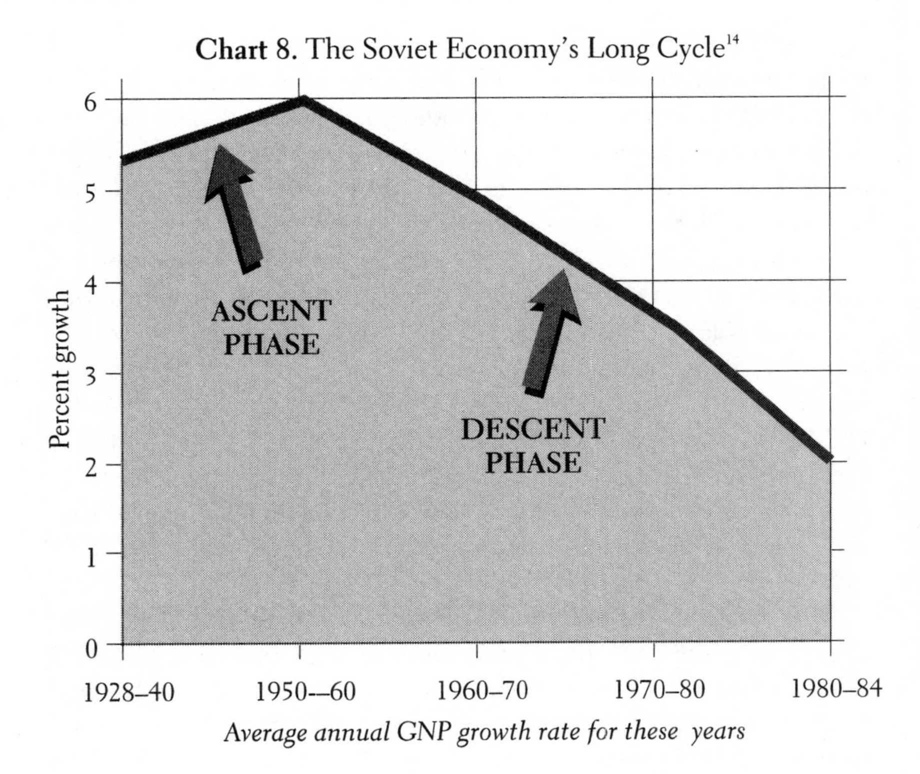

and worker carelessness. Soviet planners had hoped to ease this situation by building nuclear power plants, but the Chernobyl disaster and the public mistrust of nuclear power dashed those hopes. Enormous amounts of capital are needed for the energy sector—to modernize existing plants, to decontaminate the nuclear stations, and to build new natural-gas pipelines—but there are insufficient resources to do this.[15] At the same time, as we shall see below, this drying-up of cheap sources of additional energy is paralleled by a similar trend in the supply of labor.

Since the former USSR can no longer rely upon cheap raw materials and an increasing work force, it logically needs to improve the use of available materials and raise the productivity of existing labor. Such an emphasis upon *quality* over *quantity* is contrary to the Russian practice, which, since the time of Peter the Great, has favored *more* of everything (cavalry, tanks, steel, cement). How does a society now shackled by a badly functioning and inefficient industrial system switch to quality production? Seventy years of experience have demonstrated that centralized "scientific socialism" does not work. Responsibility and decision-making gravitated toward enormous bureaucracies under the ultimate control of the Politburo. New ideas and proposals had to pass the constant test of ideological orthodoxy. Obeying the rules of the system was the most prudent thing to do. As public morale plummeted, inefficiencies multiplied. The Soviet economy became riddled with "contradictions," a gigantic irony given Marx's use of that word to predict capitalism's eventual collapse. As another irony, both Japan and Germany—the losers in 1945—came to possess larger GNPs than the USSR, which slipped from second to fourth place in world rankings even before its economic and constitutional disintegration. Indeed, a recent survey estimates per capita annual income in the region at large at a mere $1,780, which would imply a total output of around $500 billion—far less than Italy's or Britain's.[16]

In agriculture, decades of collectivized farming destroyed all incentives among the work force; vast subsidies kept food prices low but distorted the laws of supply and demand; and bureaucrats, rather than farmers or peasants themselves, decided what was to be grown and when. Admittedly, other difficulties faced Soviet agriculture, from the severe climate to a public infrastructure so bad that much of the harvest never moved or rotted on the way to market. Yet while most farming was collectivized, bureaucratized, and constantly interfered with, private plots (occupying 4 percent of Russia's arable land) produced the remarkable total of around 25 percent of total crop output. Before the Bolshevik Revolution, the country had been one of the greatest food exporters in the world; at present, it is the world's greatest importer of foodstuffs, at enormous cost in hard currency and gold.[17] Finally, the fewer food supplies that reach the shops, the greater the hoarding and the tensions between town and countryside, producing a further turn toward paralysis. This may be mitigated in the future by granting long land leases to peasants, but it is likely that they will grow profitable items such as fruit and vegetables, *not* the critically important grains which are the responsibility of the collective farms.[18]

Much the same is true of the present dilapidated state of industry. Suffering from energy and labor shortages, handicapped by bureaucratic planning and an overheavy concentration upon traditional industries, unresponsive to consumer choice, and protected from international and internal competition, it has steadily ossified. Producing more steel or cement than any other nation was no help when a great proportion rusted or crumbled away in railway sidings. Possessing more engineers than any other country was a dubious distinction when their talents were chiefly wasted. Management itself was a contradiction in a Soviet factory, where production targets were prescribed elsewhere and no deviation from the plan was permitted.

It is easy to list the other problems that brought about the present crisis. *Infrastructure* was poor, reducing the prospect of getting food to market, cement to building sites, felled logs to timber factories, and so on. The *currency* was in an even worse condition; with few consumer goods to be purchased, there were "forced savings" of billions of near-worthless rubles, a massive black market, and a steady return to a barter system—leaving the people unready for any future convertibility of the ruble, without which they will remain on the margins of international commerce, investment, and production. The state of *public health* was deteriorating, because of poor standards of sanitation and public hygiene, the erosion in hospital care, crammed housing, and high levels of alcoholism. In contrast to health trends in other industrialized economies, infant mortality has been rising and average male life expectancy falling in recent years.[19] In this situation, the large numbers of doctors claimed by Soviet statistics became meaningless. Overall, the economy and society were showing ever more signs of joining the so-called Third World than of catching up with the First.

This economic distress would have been bad enough without the other two elements that made the Soviet triple crisis, the lack of political legitimacy and the reemergence of the nationalities problem. Clearly, these elements exacerbated each other; had the economy been working properly, for example, there would have been far less criticism of the Soviet leadership. As it was, the daily evidence of shoddy consumer goods, terrible housing, and mediocre health care stood in contrast to the regime's claims that its system was superior. The emptiness of such claims produced a widespread alienation, not only from the daily drudgery but also from the Marxist rhetoric of the mind-stultifying official media. Given rigorous KGB actions against dissidents, this alienation did not assume a revolutionary form as the 1970s and 1980s unfolded; but it produced cynicism about politics, withdrawal into one's own thoughts, lack of motivation in the factory and office, disregard for getting things right, and lack of pride in what one was producing or farming or manufacturing. A shabby economy and an equally shabby political ideology thus helped to create their own self-destruct mechanism, an ever-shabbier social and economic product, and a general malaise which each year reduced the Soviet Union's relative position in the world.[20]

Perestroika was the recognition that this decay had to be reversed, in both its economic and its political dimensions. Given the present chaos, there is no guarantee that a recovery will in fact occur. Satirists in Russia have joked that while it is relatively easy to turn a fish into a fish stew (that is, to convert a free-market economy into a socialist economy), no one really knows how to reverse the process. There is also the difficulty of converting an authoritarian system into a liberal democracy abiding by the rule of law. It was done earlier when the Allied victors reformed the Axis states after 1945; but whether that transformation can be carried out successfully by the national leadership and general public, and in the midst of economic chaos, is altogether uncertain. Other examples of such returns have taken place in countries very different from the collapsed Soviet Union.* It is not enough to allow free parliamentary elections and independent parties; steps also have to be taken to dismantle the instruments of centralized control, from the state's running of the media to a judiciary trained to observe socialist law. All of that is easier said than done, even if the failure of the August 1991 right-wing coup further discredited the old system.

The danger is, of course, that the former political, constitutional, and governmental structures will disintegrate before newer ones, able to command public loyalties, take their place. With radicals protesting

*In Poland, Czechoslovakia, and Hungary, for example, recent democratization was a return to their interwar condition, and the Communist dictatorship could be described as an "unnatural" imposition from outside. The democratization of Portugal, Spain, and Greece, by contrast, occurred in societies without a Communist economy.

that the reforms are too slow and conservatives that they are too hasty, with constitutional and political changes entangled in debates over controversial economic proposals (e.g., price reform), even the most intelligent reform leadership can become beleaguered. The idea of creating a prosperous, democratic, free-market (or social-market) economy may exist, but it is not possible to achieve it in one short leap. The certainties of the old system (guaranteed employment, food subsidies) have to be surrendered before the arrival of the material benefits of the new (the promised higher standard of living). Lost between the disintegration of what was familiar and the uncertainty of what is to come, people grow fearful. Although intellectuals and speculators thrive in such circumstances, housewives, factory workers, peasants, and ex-servicemen are more likely to become disaffected.[21]

The third, interlinked dimension of the Soviet triple crisis, perhaps the most serious and intractable of all, is the strength of ethnic differences and nationalisms. The Russian and Soviet state formed one of the world's most heterogenous multinational empires. Constitutionally, this was recognized in a federation of fifteen nominally independent republics, each the homeland of a major national group; but within those republics there were many ethnic subgroups, often with their own lower-level administrations. Officially, there were fifty-three ethnically defined political-administrative units in the Soviet Union, but since there are about one hundred separate ethnic groups in the country, half of the nationalities lacked their own unit.[22] Many of these groups are small, known outside their area only to linguistic specialists—Udmerts, Ossetians, Buryats, Karakalpaks, Ingush, Laks, and so on;[23] others, like the Belorussians, Uzbeks, and Kazakhs, have sizable populations, while the Ukraine has over 50 million inhabitants—more than Spain or Poland. Every republic contains ethnic minorities, including Russia itself with its Tartars, Bashkirs, and thirty other different nationalities; as the Russian expert Edward Keenan recently put it, "Only a few of the fifteen Soviet republics are nearly as homogenous as Northern Ireland or Yugoslavia. . . ."[24]

The critical fact was not the rich tapestry of languages and cultures, but that so many were in tension with their neighbors and the metropole. Hundreds of years of rivalry between different groups of nomads, hillfolks, and plainsmen and successive waves of migration and conquest proved stronger than scientific socialism. Differences of race and language were often joined by those of religion, as in Nagorno-Karabakh.[25] In certain areas, the rivalry was caused by population transfers (Volga Germans, Tartars, Don Cossacks) and border adjustments (Moldava) under Stalin.[26] For decades, inter-ethnic tensions were held in check by the Soviet police state. The official propaganda that the Soviet peoples had to stand united against the Fascist and capitalist foe also helped to paper over ethnic divisions. But with the German threat gone, the Cold War evaporating, socialist ideology discredited, and Moscow talking of *glasnost* and *perestroika* at home as well as actually restoring the liberties of the Eastern European peoples, the "cement" holding together the different races of the Soviet Union crumbled.

The tension between center and periphery is also easy to comprehend as the natural result of four hundred years of Russian expansion from the Muscovite heartland. Although many million Russians were moved elsewhere, to the Baltic states, the southern republics, and the Pacific provinces, the basic dichotomy remained; the periphery of the Soviet Union was ethnically non-Russian territory, often far from the Russian heartland:

> Non-Russian lands extend in a vast arc from the shores of the Baltic Sea in the northwest (Estonia, Latvia, and Lithuania); south along the western border (Belorussia, Ukraine, and Moldavia); east across the Caucasus (Armenia, Georgia, and Azerbaidzhan); on to Central Asia (the areas inhabited by Turkmen, Uzbeks, Tadzhiks, and Kirgiz) and the Kazakh steppe; and, finally, across Asia to the Pacific Ocean (homelands of the Buryats, Tuvinians, Altays, Khakas, and other peoples).[27]

These ethnic minorities straining to be independent now clash with the 25 to 28 million relocated Russian settlers who—like the French *colons* in Algeria in the 1950s—desperately want to keep a relationship with the center. To their dismay, *glasnost* and *perestroika* have raised, for the first time since 1917–20, the prospect that they will be submerged by their more populous non-Russian neighbors intent upon changing the official language, public education, and the rest. According to some experts, we ought not to be surprised if these minority-majority tensions produce the sort of conflicts which our present century has seen all too often, when populations, resettled under an imperial regime, were left behind after decolonization.[28]

Inevitably, the rise of such centrifugal forces produced a reaction in the "center." Conservative voices in the military, the KGB, and the rump of the Communist Party called for the reestablishment of law and order, and accused the reformers of bringing the USSR to a state of collapse. There were, for example, warnings to the Ukraine not to discriminate against its 12 million Russian minority. There was also some old-Russian nationalism, fed by decades of resentments of subsidizing the republics, as well as by cultural dislike. According to this viewpoint, the non-Russian areas are encumbrances and should be decolonized, possibly with some border adjustments; since Russia itself possesses so much natural wealth (oil, natural gas, minerals, timber, diamonds), it is the ungrateful Balts and Muslims who would be the losers. A modified version of this attitude would be that all the republics should form a loose association, negotiate commercial relationships on a bilateral basis, and have much more control over their own budgets (including contributions to the confederation).[29] After the failure of the conservatives' 1991 coup, some republics moved in this direction, while others looked on, hoarding their newfound sovereignty. Yet complete independence itself brings its own difficulties, especially economic, since Stalinist planning deliberately ensured that no republic was self-sufficient. (Radios manufactured in the Baltics, for example, rely on parts made in Nagorno-Karabakh, the Armenian enclave in Azerbaijan).[30] Each republic thus has the power to damage others, albeit by hurting itself in the process.

Where these pressures will carry the republics is impossible to forecast. Independence for the Baltic states and some Muslim republics in the south might not mean much, for those border regions would still need to negotiate a workable commercial relationship with Moscow. However, total independence for the larger, resource-rich republics like Kazakhstan—not to mention the Ukraine, the USSR's former breadbasket and a major source of coal and industrial products—would be a heavy and probably fatal blow to any hopes of a reformed union.

Because of the existence of ethnic minorities, independence might also produce convulsions like those which occurred across the Indian subcontinent in 1947. Indeed, in Kazahkstan and Kirgizia, indigenous ethnic groups are only a bare majority, while in the Ukraine millions of Russians are likely to lose their jobs if "modernization" takes place in the mines and factories—which is probably what the IMF and other world economic bodies will demand as the Ukraine's price of membership. As the British discovered earlier this century, once agreement is reached to transform a multinational empire into a commonwealth, it is increasingly difficult to control the process, with results more dramatic and far-reaching than originally planned.[31]

As evidence of Soviet weakness grew during the 1980s, it was often pointed out by conservatives in the West that the USSR still possessed an enormous amount of military force, which would ultimately count in the world of power politics.[32] Yet even these vaunted military capacities were affected—deleteriously—by the nonmilitary developments discussed above. The failure to match the West and Japan in advanced technologies diminished Soviet military power, making it less capable of dealing with sophisticated weapons produced elsewhere. To pour more resources into the military would have been economically counterproductive, however, as well as unpopular with most of the people. Demographic trends also impacted upon the Soviet armed forces, since an increasing proportion of army recruits had to be gathered from ethnic groups who were mistrustful of Russia and did not even speak its language. Well before the dissolution of the USSR, there were widespread refusals in the Baltic and southern republics to enlist, and the Ukraine was insisting that "its" troops not be used to suppress nationalist movements. Even the Red Army, it appeared, could not withstand the fissiparous tendencies.[33] Finally, whatever military power exists after current arms-control agreements and voluntary cutbacks, it is unclear how useful the military will be in dealing with threats that are essentially economic, social, and environmental.

On the other hand, the fate of the armed forces and the weapons of the former USSR is of great importance, not only to the successor states themselves but also to their neighbors, Europe, and the United States. With Russia and the Ukraine spasmodically quarreling over the disposal of the Soviet navy; the Ukraine and Kazakhstan declining to demobilize their strategic nuclear weapons systems; military commanders, republics, and even cities selling off tanks, aircraft, and missiles—the latter being acquired by smaller republic armies and related paramilitary groups (the army of the Dnestr republic, for example); and millions of unpaid and dissatisfied ex-servicemen losing their housing, pay, career, there is good reason for the West to be concerned lest the implosion of Soviet power and the existence of all this military hardware lead to catastrophe.

While all agree that the present crisis cannot go on forever, these structural problems are so deep-rooted that any proposed solution, whether liberal or conservative, provokes counterarguments. Liberalizing the links with the non-Russian republics may ease that aspect of the crisis but could also lead to wars of ethnic succession. Loosening central controls on the ailing economy could stimulate production and food supplies and encourage entrepreneurship; it could also lead to violent public outrage at higher costs, large-scale unemployment, regional differences, and the breakdown of inter-republican trade. Yet to return to a command economy and the principles of scientific socialism would be to worsen the region's relative economic position in the world. A suppression of *glasnost* in any of the republics could cause a collapse in public morale, a decline in creativity, and internal ferment, especially between nationalists and resident Russians. A *Putsch* against the leadership of any republic would probably split it in half, as occurred in Georgia in 1991.

Because of these uncertainties, Western planners have now begun to anticipate a whole spectrum of possible outcomes.[34] Few nowadays expect that there would be a "good" solution to the triple crisis, with the economy reviving smartly, political legitimacy flourishing, and ethnic rivalries subsiding. In a moderately optimistic view, the "Commonwealth" would stay together, and Moscow's controls over the republics would loosen. Economic reforms to encourage free-market activities would lead to mixed results but avoid a total collapse, while political and party ferment would continue but without great violence. This would hardly allow the region to catch up with East Asia, but it would still remain afloat. One can also think of less optimistic outcomes, from a collapse into civil war and internal disintegration to further conservative attempts at a coup d'état. Some scholars use the term "Weimar Russia," suggesting that a bitter and divided populace will increasingly favor extreme policies against internal foes and different ethnic groups.[35]

However the successor states to the Soviet Union fare, they clearly are unprepared for the newer forces for global change. On the contrary, every development discussed in Part One of this study is likely to bring fresh challenges to already troubled societies.

For example, the earth's lopsided demographic future, with all its potential social and political consequences, is mirrored here simply because the USSR's territorial extent made it both "North" and "South." Even by the early 1980s the country's demographic future contained such a compound of problems that experts were increasingly describing it in terms of unrelieved gloom. As one put it:

> On any basis, short-term or long-term, the prospects for the development of Soviet population and manpower resources until the end of the century are quite dismal. From the reduction in the country's birth rate to the incredible increase in the death rates beyond all reasonable past projections; from the decrease in the supply of new entrants to the labor force, compounded by its unequal regional distribution, to the relative aging of the population, not much hope lies before the Soviet government in these trends.[36]

The biggest impact upon the economy was that net additions to the labor force—a key "input" to the earlier expansion—drastically fell as increased numbers retired (or died before retirement age) and the overall birth rate declined. During the 1970s, for example, 22 million people were added to the labor force. In the 1980s, that figure plunged to 7.7 million; and in the 1990s it is forecast to drop further, to 5.7 million.[37] Should social and economic conditions worsen—thus increasing the disincentives to have children—or mass emigration be tolerated, the decline could intensify.

This demographic slowdown is by no means uniform, but disproportionately affects the Slavic peoples in the North. What is happening at present and is projected to continue into the future is a sort of "demographic revenge" by the colonized peoples, especially in the southern Muslim republics, whose birth rates are similar to those in the Middle East. The average annual population growth rates of those republics range from 2.5 to 3.5 percent, which is *three to five times larger* than the 0.7 percent average annual increases in the Russian population.[38] Already, according to one calculation,* Russians represent less than half of the total population, for the first time since the establishment of Bolshevik rule. The same calculation estimates that the Russian share will be 46.4 percent in the year 2000, and then fall relentlessly throughout the twenty-first century, as shown in Chart 9, as the population share of the nonwhite peoples of the Asian republics increases.

These are, the author warns, "only projections"; but the overall pattern was clear some time ago: "already in the early twenty-first century the country will be transformed from a one majority/many minorities structure to a many minorities structure."[39] Even before Gorbachev, Moscow's rule was being demographically undermined from one decade to the next. This may seem less important now that the republics are independent, but constitutional changes alone will not obviate the likely consequences of these demographic trends: population drift from the crowded republics of the South into southern Russia and the Ukraine, minority ethnic groups growing faster than the resident majority, resource disputes, heightened religious feuds, and the rest.

Given the geography of this region, it would naturally be affected in all manner of ways by changes in the environment. For example, global warming, were it to be significant, could make growing crops in semiarid regions even more difficult and shift the zone of cultivation northward—serious enough in itself without the new complication that such a movement might be from one independent republic's border (say, the

*In the 1979 census, the Russians constituted 52.4 percent of the total USSR population, but according to Bernstam, "Trends in the Soviet Population," p. 209, that included members of ethnic minorities living in the Russian republic, and the real figure was 50.9 percent. By 1984, the Russian share had shrunk to 49.9 percent.

Chart 9. Population of the USSR by Major Ethnic Groups, 1917–2100[40] *(in millions)*

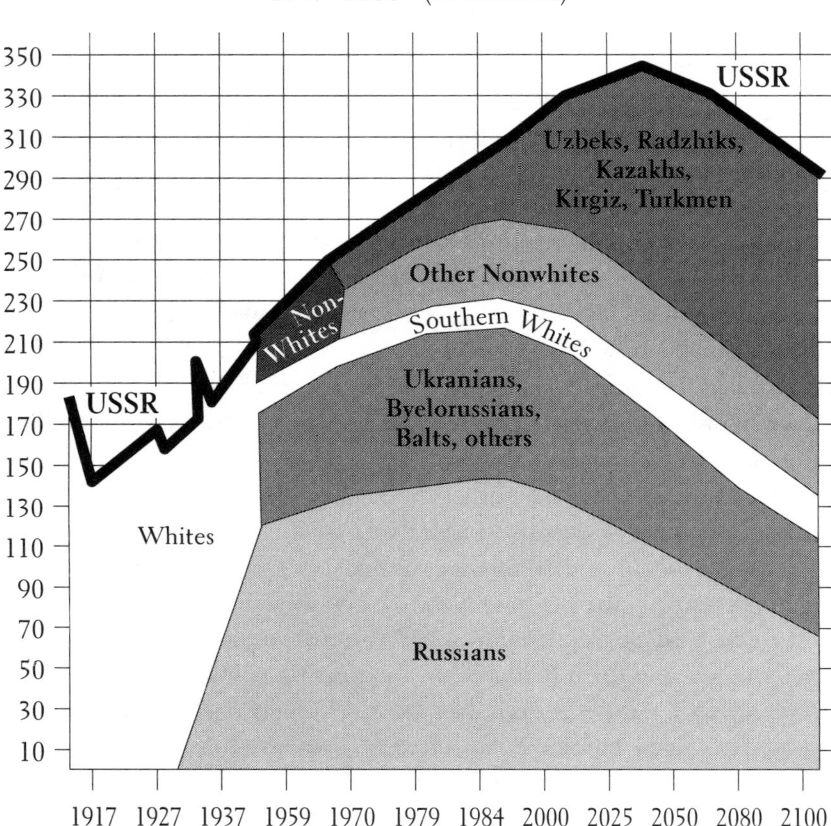

Ukraine) into another's (Russia). Low-lying regions, of which there are many, would be hit by any rise in sea levels. Yet the most serious consequence of higher temperatures could well be the unfreezing of the permafrost zone, releasing methane and increasing flooding. Moreover, such transformations would occur in regions ill equipped financially to provide adequate responses.

At present, with the full extent and consequences of the greenhouse effect still being disputed by scientists, these dangers may appear theoretical—and far less urgent than the immediate environmental problems currently facing politicians and publics. These were caused by the inept and high-handed decisions of state planners since Stalin's time, committed to large-scale industrialization regardless of consequences. As in Eastern and Central Europe, carbon and other emissions polluted the atmosphere, severely damaged the woods and forests, and increased health hazards among local inhabitants powerless to stop official policies. Rivers and lakes have been affected by industrial and chemical wastes, the dumping of oil, and leaching from overfertilized fields. Grandiose schemes to dam or divert water supplies for hydroelectricity have led to erosion or (as near St. Petersburg) dangerous silting. Such problems exist across the erstwhile Soviet Union, and many of them have only recently been made public. By contrast, most of the world knows of the dreadful effects of the Chernobyl disaster: the deaths through radiation of hundreds of adults and children, the pollution of the rivers and lakes, the blow dealt to local agriculture—all damaging a society already bowed low by nonenvironmental disasters.[41]

These newer challenges also exacerbate the demographic, ethnic, political, and economic elements of the Soviet triple crisis. For a good example of this, one need look no further than the drying up of the Aral Sea discussed earlier.* The environmental point is that because the rivers feeding into the sea have been tapped so heavily for irrigation, the decline in the water level has caused massive salinization, left harbor towns high and dry, and increased desertification; and the only way to reverse this would be to cease all water usage throughout the vast watershed area *for the next three decades.* But Central Asia's 33 million people (excluding Kazakhstan) depend upon tapping that river water for their livelihood; Uzbekistan's cotton production, its main cash crop, is grown on irrigated land that is already becoming salinated, but to cease irrigation would be a deathblow. The scarcity of water is already the chief natural reason that the region is so poor—the standard of living in Central Asia is half the national average and many babies starve to death—yet ironically this is where the population is growing the fastest. About 40 percent of the people are under eighteen, and within the next two decades the population will have nearly doubled

*See pp. 101–2 above.

to around 60 million, chiefly Muslim. As in North Africa and the Middle East, therefore, it is easy to foresee future conflicts as water supplies and agricultural output shrink while population booms.

Until recently, a Ministry of Water in Moscow allocated shares of available water to each Central Asian republic and also required each to ensure that a certain amount (clearly not enough) reached the Aral Sea. With the collapse of the Soviet state and the abolition of the Ministry of Water, these agreements have broken down. Desperate to preserve their way of life, farmers in the upstream valleys are taking more water, which means less for those downstream, in Uzbekistan. And all the time the Aral Sea continues to shrink.[42]

Could the biotech revolution in agriculture come to the rescue here? At first sight, this appears an attractive option; genetically altered crops capable of withstanding arid conditions, *in vitro* production and processing of food to relieve the pressures upon the land, enhanced biomass yields to meet energy demand, and a general expansion in agricultural output sound like answers to a prayer. Nor is there a lack of Russian scientists and technicians in plant breeding and related disciplines. However, it would be difficult for poverty-stricken southern republics to pay for the patents and other fees, not to mention the establishment of modern laboratories, factories, and processing plants for large-scale production. Who would fund these enterprises, and the associated investment in education and infrastructure? Certainly not an impoverished government in Moscow, grappling with its own problems and possessing increasingly fewer ties with the Asian republics. Even if a brave Western company undertook to develop biotech agriculture in, say, Uzbekistan and overcame all the other obstacles, that still would not solve the crisis over water supplies.

More generally, while it is conceivable that some parts of agriculture could be improved by the adoption of biotech,* the sorry condition of Soviet farming suggests that its real need is for structural reforms (decollectivization, realistic food prices, improved infrastructure). Yet if these reforms occurred, with farm output increasing at the pace it did in China and standards of living improving smartly, there would

*For example, using bovine growth-hormone techniques to increase milk yields in the Baltic states.

still remain a major disincentive to turn to genetically altered beef and milk; and the global adoption of technologies which "dematerialized" agriculture could have tremendous economic and social consequences in areas where so large a percentage of the labor force is engaged in farming and few alternative jobs beckon.

Much the same may be said about the readiness of the states of the former USSR to confront the automation revolution coming out of East Asia. Despite its innumerable engineers and technicians and the use of simpler robots in certain state-owned industries, it is hard to see how Russia would gain the economic advantages which Japan enjoys from robotics. Whereas the latter moved into automation because of labor shortages and its companies willingly retrain or redeploy workers made redundant by new machines, Russia and the other republics at present possess a chronic system of *under*employment, which widespread automation would only exacerbate.

Furthermore, transforming the republics' economies to embrace the brave new world of robotics, biotechnology, lasers, optics, telecommunications, and the like heavily depends upon the possession of a flourishing computer industry. In fact, that industry is so undeveloped and the number of machines so few—in 1987 there were only 100,000 personal computers in the USSR, compared with the *annual* U.S. production of more than 5 million[43]—that enormous amounts of capital would be needed to create an information society. Such a change involves reliance upon foreign machines and technological expertise which would have to be paid for, and it requires the extensive retraining of the work force, *plus* the appropriate software information, *plus* an efficient servicing network in order to use the machines properly in the first place. Even as Russian planners and foreign advisers grapple with the problem of how and where to commence this process, on either side of the Pacific a flood of new inventions widens the gap between high-tech societies and the rest, making it ever more difficult to catch up.

Finally, any move toward a high-tech economy has to confront the cluster of problems that brought about the USSR's collapse in the first place. The Russian academician Andrei Ershev, who enthusiastically proposes turning his country into an information society by the early twenty-first century, also admits the "apparent absurdity" of such a scheme at present:

> The mediocre living conditions produced by primitive wage-leveling, the difficulties of providing food and shelter, the overloading and alarming degradation of our energy and transportation structures, and the exorbitantly high share of low-skill and manual labor in our economy—all of these things are "real life" and they demand urgent action as well as the immediate concentration of all available resources.[44]

In such circumstances, he concludes, talk of a long-term program to produce a Russian equivalent of (say) California appears to be mere philosophizing, remote from the existing turmoil and backwardness.[45]

Until their economies are restructured, the republics can also play little part in the financial and communications revolution, or in the concomitant rise of the multinational corporation—except perhaps as providers of cheap factory labor, like Mexico and Thailand. It was the Soviet regime's inability to handle—or prevent—the spread of ideas and images via the newer forms of communication which, in part at least, contributed to its collapse. Authoritarian successor regimes set up in certain republics (e.g., Georgia) may also find it difficult to control information, however hard they try. But even where *glasnost* prevails, it is difficult to envisage the emergence of a Kazakhstani equivalent to CNN or the BBC, or a Ukrainian rival to McKinsey. Since the republics lack a convertible currency, international banks, stockholders, and electronic trading institutions, the borderless world of twenty-four-hour-a-day financial flows must appear irrelevant to current concerns.

Some years ago, *The Economist* tartly observed that in 1913 "Imperial Russia had a real product per man-hour three times greater than Japan's [but it] has spent its nigh seventy socialist years slipping relatively backwards, to maybe a quarter of Japan's rate now."[46] In so many ways, the collapsing Soviet Union became the antithesis of Japan: vast in size and rich in resources, compared with the cramped, resource-weak island state; a medley of peoples, compared with one of the world's most self-consciously homogeneous races; socially disintegrating, compared with the coherent, deferential, and group-conscious

Japanese citizenry; disadvantaged by high technology and the "dematerialization" of production, just as Japan is advantaged by the very same; unable, ironically, despite the socialist emphasis on planning, to prepare for the future, compared with Tokyo's apparently purposeful march toward the twenty-first century. As many observers have noted, the untidy, industrially backward, heterogeneous Russian Empire was one of the least suitable places in which to create a Marxist society, assuming such a society was possible *anywhere*.[47] For the very same reasons, its successors do not seem well prepared to deal with contemporary global forces for change—which suggests that in whatever form the republics enter the twenty-first century, they will continue to grapple with their relative backwardness.

These conclusions could, of course, turn out to be too pessimistic. At present, all we see is chaos, struggle, economic collapse, ethnic disintegration—just as the observers of 1918 did. How could they have foreseen then that a decade or so later the USSR would have begun to produce chemicals, aircraft, trucks, tanks, and machine tools and be growing faster than any other industrialized society?[48] By extension, how could Western admirers of Stalin's centralized economy in the 1930s know that the very system contained the seeds of its own collapse? Like any other society on earth, the former Soviet republics could theoretically make harmonious progress instead of suffering serious decline and convulsions. Nevertheless, in view of their existing stricken condition and of the newer challenges that are emerging, it is hard to believe that the future is a rosy one. And since the region's troubles could very easily have consequences elsewhere—from the illegal disposal of nuclear weapons to an enormous increase in opium exports from the southern republics (to gain hard currency)—the Western democracies might be unwise to assume that the collapse of the "evil empire" is going to be an unqualified advantage to themselves.

EASTERN AND CENTRAL EUROPE

Whatever happens to the successor states of the USSR, the policies of *glasnost* and *perestroika* have had enormous consequences for the former Soviet satellites in Eastern and Central Europe. Free elections, the demise of most Communist parties (or, at the very least, their loss of monopoly), the move toward free-market economic policies, the dismantling of the Iron Curtain, the collapse of the Warsaw Pact, the incorporation of the German Democratic Republic into its larger West German neighbor, the beginnings of talks about Hungarian or Czech membership in the European Community—all of these extraordinary developments, scarcely imaginable a few years ago, were possible only because the Gorbachev regime in Moscow was willing to loosen its grip.[49] Whatever the original motives for that liberalization, the political and strategic geography of Europe from the Thuringian Forest to the mouth of the Danube has been transformed as a result—leaving a half-dozen successor governments and their publics to grapple with the new conditions.

Of the populations affected by this change, those in the former East German state enjoy a different status from the rest. Although they face problems of unemployment in adjusting to the capitalist way of life and their infrastructure, environment, and industrial base are so decayed that enormous amounts of capital are needed to bring them up to "west" German levels, these are difficulties of a medium-term nature. Fortunately for the people themselves, they were merged into a state with the world's largest merchandise-trade and current-account balances.[50] Moreover, reconstruction provides a massive Keynesian-type "boost" to utilities companies, road-construction firms, and manufacturing in general. The German budget deficit may soar, but much of this is because of enhanced *capital* spending which is economically beneficial.

While the "east" Germans have been given a free ticket into the prosperous Western community, their neighbors will have to struggle to pay the fare.* Obviously, some have better prospects than others; there is a world of difference between Hungary, which for years experimented cautiously with Westernization, and Romania, which suffered from the economic distortions of the totalitarian Ceausescu regime.

*"It is not fair," a Polish journalist told a Western visitor in early 1991. "Why can't there be a West Poland to come to the rescue of poor East Poland? Why is there no West Poland to take away the bad zlotys, the bad cars, the bad passports, and give us the good ones?" Cited in W. R. Mead, "Dark Continent," *Harper's Magazine* (April 1991), p. 52.

Yet whatever the dissimilarities, each has to move its economy and society from one system to another without collapsing in the effort.

The establishment of secure and politically legitimate democratic governments will be more easily achieved in some of these nations than in others. Because of its cultural and religious unity and its deep sense of self-identity, Poland is the most favorably placed in this respect. The same strengths also assist Hungary. Yet even where democracy flourishes, it could be messy and painful, with coalitions forming and breaking up, angry debates over church policy or economic policy, latent authoritarianism, social radicals being denounced by farmers' parties or leagues of former Communists—in other words, the messy and painful politics of, say, France and Italy in the late 1940s and 1950s as they emerged from their wartime regimes and struggled to modernize. Nevertheless, the Central European states have better prospects of achieving political legitimacy than Romania and Bulgaria, where democratic traditions are much weaker, large numbers of "ex- and not-so-ex-Communists"[51] retain influence, and economic conditions are grim.

Securing political legitimacy will be more difficult if, as in the collapsed USSR, ethnic divisions reemerge. Here again Poland is favorably placed, because of the homogeneity of its population and Germany's renunciation of claims to Polish-held territory. The same is true of Hungary, which is 93 percent Magyar; the problem, from Budapest's viewpoint, is the many Hungarian minorities *outside* the border—600,000 in southern Slovakia, over 400,000 in Yugoslavia, and as many as 2 million in Romania, the last locked in angry confrontation with the Romanian majority.[52] By contrast, the country suffering from the most severe ethnic divisions is undoubtedly the former Yugoslavia, which has never overcome its sixty-year-long history as a confederation of rival cultures, languages, and religions. Apart from the central struggle between Serbs and non-Serbs over Belgrade's "hegemonism,"[53] which has already led to extensive civil war, there also exist enormous problems over the future of Macedonia and Kosovo which could explode at any time.

Although tensions elsewhere are not as severe, most neighboring countries have inherited deep-rooted "majority vs. minority" problems. Since independence the government in Prague has negotiated with the

Slovaks over issues ranging from the country's name to demands for greater Slovak autonomy, but without stemming the move to independence.[54] Romanians resent the agitations of the Hungarian minority, while the latter chafe at Romanian dominance.[55] Turkey complains of harsh Bulgarian treatment of its Turkish-speaking minority, while Greece cannot forgive Turkey's occupation of northern Cyprus. All are carefully watching Macedonia. In the first decades of this century, observers worried whether rivalries in the Balkans would lead to instability and war, dragging in other nations. It would be a sad comment upon how little human beings learn if in the final decade the fears returned—and were justified.

These tensions could be ameliorated by prosperity, but the productivity and living standards of the region are well behind those of the West. According to one calculation, Czechoslovakia's per capita income was 10 percent above Austria's in 1939, but now is about 35 percent *below*;[56] the latter calculation is probably too optimistic, yet Czech living standards are far ahead of those further east, from Ruthenia to Macedonia. Given their industrial decay, inefficient infrastructure, lack of technical and marketing expertise, nontransferable (and increasingly worthless) currencies, and massive ecological damage, some of these societies will find it hard to move to a free-market economy, especially in a decade of increasing capital shortages worldwide. In removing price subsidies, cutting support for state-run enterprises, and reducing bureaucracies as recommended by the IMF and World Bank, even such potentially fast adjusters as Hungary and Poland will endure high unemployment, bankruptcies, and popular agitation against price increases and foreign interference. Many may see their already declining GNPs plunge by another 10 percent before the reforms work and the hoped-for recovery takes place (see Chart 10).

This recovery is made more problematic by the chaos within the former Soviet Union itself. For decades, these countries relied on Soviet oil purchased at below-world-market prices, and on barter. Eastern and Central Europe now confront massive shortfalls in fuel, and have to pay for oil imports in dollars. Shortages in hard currency could be helped by increased exports to Russia—but that presumes that Russia can pay for such goods, and complicates the task of orienting these economies to *Western* markets.[57] Moreover, the worsening con-

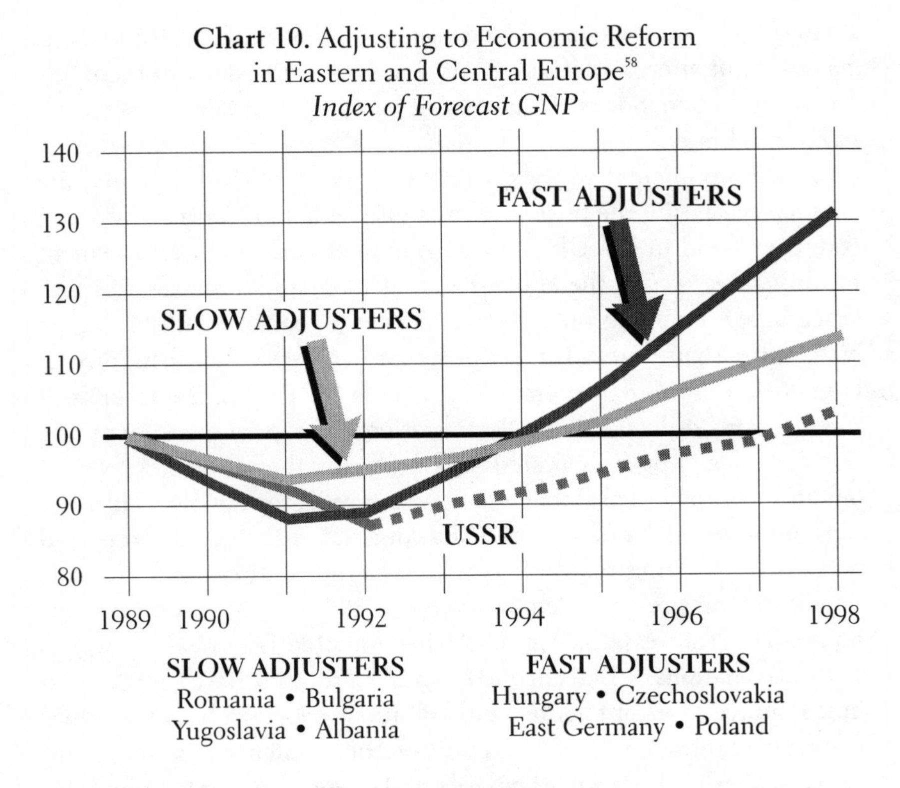

Chart 10. Adjusting to Economic Reform in Eastern and Central Europe[58]
Index of Forecast GNP

ditions in the erstwhile USSR and Romania, together with the Yugoslav civil war, raise fears of a mass exodus westward, placing further strains upon already creaking social services. Already the fighting in Bosnia has displaced millions of people, perhaps permanently. Hence the erection of barriers along the eastern and southern borders of Central European states, creating a new iron curtain to separate the former Soviet satellites from their strife-torn neighbors.[59] Of all the ironies in this region, that could be the greatest.

In sum, the societies of Eastern and Central Europe already have enough to do without having to worry about global changes driven by technology, environmental trends, and demographic change.[60] As they are already aware, ecological damage has badly affected their health and standards of living, and it will take immense sums to repair that damage *and* to adopt alternative fuels, life-styles, and so on. Many of them rely for energy upon Soviet-designed nuclear power stations, which are hazardous but could be shut down only at the cost of immense disruptions. Environmental worries, along with economic uncertainty, are apparently causing the birth rates in all Eastern and Central European countries—and in the Ukraine—to plummet well below replacement fertility rates.[61] On the other hand, demographic change can also exacerbate ethnic tensions within countries (Albanians with far higher birth rates than Serbs, for example) and increase the possibility of large-scale transborder migrations. Again, as in Russia, the farmers of these regions really need decollectivization and capital investment, *not* the challenge of biotech-altered beef and grain; they also need prosperous and accessible export markets, in Western Europe, which will cause tensions with the EC's farmers.[62] Lacking national stock markets, and with their industries requiring basic restructuring, they also have little opportunity at present to enjoy the purported benefits of twenty-four-hour-a-day "futures" trading or of all-automated factories.

But the nations of Eastern and Central Europe *do* have some important resources: lots of talented and ambitious people, a basically sound educational infrastructure, long traditions of excellence in manufacturing (Czechoslovakia) or mathematics and science (Hungary), plus—for the first time in half a century—access to new ideas, ventures, stimuli. Given the tasks ahead of them, particularly in the short to medium term, such native talents may be insufficient to allow the societies of the region to catch up, let alone prepare them for the twenty-first century. But at least they are out of jail, and are free to decide in what direction they wish to travel.

12

EUROPE AND THE FUTURE

COMPARED WITH THE PROBLEMS THAT confront the countries of Central Asia and North Africa, the European Community (EC) nations must appear relatively comfortable as they seek to respond to global trends. Rich in such resources as capital, infrastructure, and (especially) scientific and skilled personnel, and enjoying standards of living among the highest in the world, Europeans have innumerable advantages over the struggling peoples to the east and the south. With Japan and North America, the EC has emerged as one of the three great centers of economic, technological, and political power in an otherwise fractured world. Undoubtedly, it faces problems in redefining its foreign and defense policies in a post–Cold War world and more especially in finding ways to further its unity; but while difficult they are probably not insuperable.

What is much less certain, however, is whether Europeans will be able to enjoy their comfortable way of life *unaffected* by today's global developments. Can Europe's relatively rich societies insulate themselves from the demographic pressures building up elsewhere, or from profound climate changes? Can the EC handle globalization, even as it seeks further to integrate itself? Can it deal with fissiparous political tendencies, the growing resentments against ethnic neighbors and recent immigrants, the new tribalisms? In some parts of the world, the journalist Thomas Friedman has recently observed, robots are assembling luxury sedans. In other parts (Sarajevo), children are being killed by tank fire because they are of another culture and religion.[1] The effects of both technological changes and historical antagonisms "spill over" national boundaries, to be felt some distance away; and the same is true of other transnational forces. If it is unlikely that even Japan will remain a privileged enclave amid the rest of the world's problems, how could Europe—much more closely linked to the regions of turbulence, and more fissured within—expect to go unscathed? And will the continent's political leaders be capable of settling the "old" agenda (future of NATO, the Common Agricultural Policy) while having to respond to newer, less familiar issues as well?

All this is the more difficult to answer because, unlike unified countries such as Japan or the United States or Australia, Europe is at present trying to hammer out its own constitutional form, a process that consumes most of its political energies. To that extent at least, EC politicians and those of the nations of the erstwhile USSR have something in common. While one region struggles toward integration, the other strives to manage disintegration; and neither leadership has much time to spare for what must surely appear to them less urgent issues. In the minds of the Brussels planners, and perhaps also of the twelve member-states that now compose the EC,* the debate over future European unity takes precedence over such matters as global population change, robotics, and the greenhouse effect.

Yet, while the politics of European integration overshadow those broader global trends, the latter cannot simply be ignored. As it is, the governments and peoples of Europe confront the *twin* challenges of hammering out the continent's future shape at the same time as they respond (or fail to respond) to the forces for global change. Because of that, the title of this chapter, "Europe and the Future," implies a double meaning, namely:

(a) what organizational *form* Europe will assume as it moves into the twenty-first century; and

*Germany, France, Italy, the Netherlands, Belgium, Luxembourg, Britain, Denmark, Ireland, Spain, Portugal, Greece.

(b) whatever its shape, how the region will *fare* as it grapples with the transnational changes described in Part One of this book.

While these two questions about Europe's future are distinct, each affects the other. If the Europeans unite, they have a better chance of producing common policies on global warming, immigration, North-South relations, and security; they can also collectively fund technological projects (e.g., the Airbus) beyond the resources of a single European state. Indeed, the fact that the world is altering—shifting strategical balances, differentiated economic growth patterns, the rise of East Asia, and the altered position of the post-1945 superpowers—has always fueled the argument for greater European unification. From the early ideas of Jean Monnet and Robert Schuman to today's proponents of a more tightly knit EC, the motive is plain: if Europe is to recover the relative importance in the world it possessed around 1900, it must avoid wars among its member states, harmonize economic practices, and evolve common policies, including foreign and defense policies. Much as they have tried, individual European nations have not been able to recover their former international position. Only by coming together can they create a bloc of European peoples, more prosperous and perhaps even more powerful than any other state in the world.[2]

At present Europe is a long way from such a vision, although it has come far from its fractured condition of 1945. Since the late 1940s its defense has rested in the North Atlantic Treaty Organization (NATO), with U.S. contributions providing both nuclear-strategic and conventional-force support to deter attacks. In the economic sphere, there exists the loosely structured European Free Trade Association (EFTA), chiefly of smaller neutral states engaged in free trade in industrial products. Altogether more important, however, is the European Community itself, which is usually what is meant when commentators use the term "Europe." Established by the Treaty of Rome in 1957 to create a common customs union as the foundation upon which greater European unity (including political unity) might be developed, the EC possesses a European Commission to act as a central planning executive, a European Parliament, and even a European Court of Justice. As such, it contains the constitutional "skeleton" for a federal state.

However, none of these organizations integrates all European countries. NATO contains the non-European countries Canada and the United States, but not (obviously) European neutrals. EFTA was devised as an EC alternative by states opposed to the harmonization of agricultural, social, and fiscal policies, not to mention political-constitutional integration. As the EC has grown in importance, EFTA's position is in doubt; with the Warsaw Pact dissolved and NATO's future uncertain, some EFTA nations (Austria, Sweden, Switzerland) are reconsidering their assumption that EC membership would conflict with their neutrality. One possibility is to extend the EC's frontier-free single market to all EFTA nations*—such a provisional arrangement was concluded in October 1991—but that is disliked by centralists who fear the bad example of "less-than-full" membership. At present, there is a confusion of memberships: Turkey is in NATO but not the EC (though it has applied to the latter body); Eire is in the EC but not NATO; Norway is in NATO and still wonders about its 1972 decision, by referendum, to decline membership in the EC. The changes in Central Europe and the former USSR have led some of those countries, including Russia, to proclaim a wish to join the EC, and even NATO!

Despite such complications, Europe could become much more important in world affairs. A few years ago, Professor Samuel Huntington suggested that "the baton of world leadership" next century may pass from America not to Japan, or China, or Russia, but to a European federation:

> The European Community, if it were to become politically cohesive, would have the population, resources, economic wealth, technology, and actual and potential military strength to be the preeminent power of the twenty-first century. Japan, the United States, and the Soviet Union have specialized respectively in investment, consumption, and arms. Europe balances all three. It invests less of its GNP than Japan but more than the United States and possibly more than the Soviet Union. It consumes less of its GNP than the United States but more than Japan and the Soviet Union. It arms less than the United States and the Soviet Union but more than Japan.
>
> It is also possible to conceive of a European ideological appeal comparable to the American one. Throughout the world, people line up at the doors

*This would establish a market of 380 million consumers, accounting for over 40 percent of world trade.

> of American consulates seeking immigration visas. In Brussels, countries line up at the door of the Community seeking admission. A federation of democratic, wealthy, socially diverse, mixed-economy societies would be a powerful force on the world scene. If the next century is not the American century it is most likely to be the European century.[3]

This may strike the reader as heady stuff, ignoring Europe's past quarrels and present difficulties. Even a quarter century after the Treaty of Rome the EC remained, in one critic's words, "a maze of border controls, government subsidies to national industries, closed national systems of procurement in military and other key public sectors, and national regulation of industrial standards, copyrights, transportation, banking, insurance and health requirements for the entry of goods."[4] How will it fare, therefore, in the trickier and more critical realms of common immigration rules, a common currency and central bank, integrated (or at least federated) armed forces, and unified foreign and defense policies? Is it not utopian to imagine twelve or fifteen nations, each with a tradition of acting as a sovereign unit, ever becoming a United States of Europe as the early federalists once hoped? Is it not more practicable to undertake modest reform measures (e.g., harmonizing of patents and weights and measures) and be content with a loose federation of peoples possessing close cultural ties and more consistent industrial practices, without wasting energies pursuing the chimera of turning Europe into an integrated world-political player? After all, won't Europe find it hard enough simply to avoid being hurt by *existing* difficulties?

Those desiring a "strong" Europe would probably concede that full unity is impossible at present, but argue that there is a compelling need for economic harmony, as well as encouraging the habit of thinking and acting politically as one. By contrast, those preferring a "weak" institutional center support an enlarged common market for goods and services but abhor bureaucratic controls over business, the distortions of the Common Agricultural Policy (CAP), the costs of harmonizing social-welfare policies, the loss of fiscal sovereignty implied in a common currency and a European central bank, and the transfer of parliamentary and governmental powers to pan-European bodies. Between these poles is a variety of middle positions, depending upon the member state in question: some want to boost the powers of the European Parliament, others to enhance the influence of the Council of Ministers; some want defense integration, others fear it will undermine NATO, and yet others wish to remain neutral.[5] Even voices favoring integration have very different motivations, from Italian automobile bosses wanting a single continental market to German intellectuals eager to "embed" their newly united country within European structures.[6]

Any investigation of the possibilities of an integrated Europe will need to focus not only on the agreed-upon removal of all internal barriers for the exchange of goods and services, but also on more controversial measures like a common currency, enhanced powers for the European Parliament, and coordinated defense policies. It is in those realms that there lie both the greatest potential for transforming "Europe" into something very different from today's geographical expression *and* the greatest cluster of obstacles to changing the existing structure of a continent of nation-states. If these obstacles are overcome, the EC might well develop the place in global affairs which federationists envision for it; if they are not, it could remain what one disgusted Belgian minister called it during the 1991 Gulf War—"an economic giant, a political dwarf, and a military worm."[7]

Although organizations to promote regional cooperation exist elsewhere in the world, none possesses the commercial importance or attracts the intellectual and political interest of the EC. It conducts one-third of world trade. Collectively, its financial resources are enormous, since it possesses many of the world's largest banks, insurance companies, and finance houses. Of the globe's top ten trading nations, seven are European.[8] In industries such as automobiles, pharmaceuticals, machine tools, and engineering goods generally, the EC countries together produce more than any other country in the world.[9] Until the North American free-trade bloc of Mexico, the United States, and Canada is fully in place, it is the largest market in the world. Galvanized by Japanese and American competition, it is pouring large amounts of money into high-tech industries such as aerospace, supercomputers, maglev trains, and the like. All this industrial and commercial activity is aided by, and in turn helps to aid, an enormous array of cultural institutions, research libraries, scientific centers, hundreds of universities, and millions of college-level students and highly skilled workers.*

Europe's resources are divided, however, into twenty-six sovereign nation-states, ranging from Greece to Norway and from Finland to Portugal. The economic rationale for a harmonization of the tariffs, commercial practice, taxes, traffic legislation, and associated activities of these countries is simply overwhelming. A truck that could travel 750 miles from the north to the south of the United Kingdom in thirty-six hours would, upon crossing the English Channel, need fifty-eight hours to cover the same distance from Calais to Milan—because of all the border stops. A citizen of "Europe," touring from one country to the next and changing his money at each resting place into and out of the local currency, would find that about *half* of his original sum was swallowed up in exchange transactions.[10] Add to this the sheer variety of different national standards—from the type of electrical plugs to entire telecommunications systems—and it is easy to understand why businessmen have been pressing for a genuinely common market in goods and services. Such standardization would, it is claimed, give an additional "one-time boost" to Europe's growth as well as ensuring that it possessed more flexible and efficient economic structures to compete in the early twenty-first century.[11] According to the recent Cecchini Report, "the cost of non-Europe," that is, the burden upon the EC economies if they do *not* unify, is horrendous; on the other hand, implementing a common market could result in savings of $200–300 billion and add 4 to 7 percent to the EC's overall product.[12] Europe can either seize this opportunity, the report argued, or fall behind Japan and America.

Following those and other arguments of the European Commission, the free movement of goods, services, capital, and people throughout the Community was agreed upon, that measure taking effect after 31 December 1992. Since that was the original intent of the Treaty of Rome, it was not so controversial as, for example, a scheme for a European central bank or a common defense policy. But it said much for the gap between theory and reality that when, in 1985, the EC commissioner for the internal market (Lord Cockfield) offered his

*Admittedly, there are major resource differences between countries such as Germany and Portugal—in 1984, the former had seven times the number of R&D scientists and engineers per million inhabitants as the latter—but the remarks here are about the EC as a whole.

White Paper on the measures required to achieve a single common market, over three hundred areas for action were identified, ranging from banking licenses to capital controls, civil aviation to tax laws, environmental issues to consumer safety.[13]

With many of these measures implemented and others to come, the prospect of a Common Market galvanized a surge in business mergers, cross-border investments, takeovers, and marketing agreements, as European manufacturers, financial houses, service industries, and media giants prepared themselves for the more open but also much more competitive circumstances of the 1990s. Deutsche Bank and Morgan Grenfell, Siemens and Plessey, Hennessy and Guinness, Volvo and Renault . . . by the late 1980s, reports of such alliances gave the impression that virtually every company was restructuring itself to survive within this colossal market. This burst of acquisitions—together with journalistic talk of a "Fortress Europe"—in turn stimulated American and Japanese multinational corporations into expanding *their* presence within the EC. Once again, household names were involved—Ford and Jaguar, Philip Morris and Suchard, IBM and Siemens, Fujitsu and ICL, Honda and Rover, Mitsubishi and Daimler-Benz; no one, it appeared, wanted to be left out.[14]

Despite this, a completely free EC market is still not at hand, chiefly because of the rearguard action of vested interests that would be damaged by unfettered laissez-faire. Allowing the same accountancy firm to operate in London, Frankfurt, and Milan is one thing; but open competition among, say, airlines is much harder to achieve, because individual European governments want to protect their "national" carriers. Similarly, influential automobile producers like Peugeot and Fiat, which had been able to persuade their governments to restrict Japanese automobile imports, are now concerned at the establishment of Japanese car factories within the EC (chiefly in Britain) and are fighting hard for a period of continued import quotas. At first sight this is a blatant denial of the single-market principle in favor of less efficient producers. To French and Italian manufacturers, things look different; European economic unity was supposed to benefit *European* companies and their workers, not multinationals from a country that has maintained the most sophisticated import controls for the past forty years.

In addition, this frenzy of mergers and acquisitions across Europe struck many critics as socially unbalanced, benefiting the chairmen, stockholders, lawyers, and others in those businesses, but offering little to people as a whole. Given the deep-rooted European cultural conviction that it does *not* want to become like the United States, there is a strong social-policy element to the plans concerning Europe's future. As everyone can see, the previous structure of national boundaries, tariffs, and commercial/legal systems encouraged country-specific industries—airlines, telephone companies, automobile producers, computer manufacturers, banks, armaments works—in each member state. Compared with the roughly similar market size of the United States, Europe will clearly have *too many* airlines, electrical companies, and automakers when the barriers come down; and the less efficient ones will either collapse or (more likely) be taken over—unless home governments, rejecting the spirit of integration, continue to protect them. The "harmonization" of Europe's economies is likely, therefore, to create pockets of local high unemployment, even within the overall stimulus given to growth.

Moreover, this economic unification is happening in a continent with very different levels of income and social welfare: the per capita GNP in Germany, for example, is three to four times that in Portugal and Greece,[15] and the gap in welfare provisions probably even greater. Since a true common market would permit a manufacturer to produce goods anywhere within the Community's boundaries, there is a temptation to direct new investment—or relocate existing production—to the poorer regions with their lower wages and other costs; which, after all, is why a U.S. company moves from Connecticut to Mississippi, or a Japanese firm establishes a factory in Thailand. Here again, because of Europe's different political culture, with its emphasis upon social welfare and the power of trade unions (especially in Germany), such laissez-faire policies are being resisted. Instead, political pressure is mounting to ensure that wages in poorer regions are brought closer to those in prosperous countries, and that there be a uniformity of welfare provisions, in line with those in richer societies. Despite protests from businessmen (and the British government) at the costs involved, the EC seems intent upon enlarging its "social charter." In sum, the European "common market" idea involves not just a free-trade zone (as in a Mexican-U.S.-Canadian trading bloc), but the harmonization of much else besides; and it is precisely in these *non*business spheres of unification that the greater political problems will lie.

In the same way, the Common Agricultural Policy (CAP) does not accord with the logic of the global marketplace and seems, indeed, to be a substantial drag upon overall world trade and growth. By establishing a common tariff to give Community farmers protection against lower-cost non-EC producers, by fixing minimum support prices in key foodstuffs and guaranteeing to purchase farm produce if prices fall to those levels, and by providing generous export subsidies so that surpluses can be sold abroad, the CAP has distorted world agricultural supply and demand.* It also drives food prices higher. Over 70 percent of the EC's spending is taken by agriculture and fisheries, leaving little for social and regional development that could benefit far larger numbers;[16] and the monies go disproportionately to the larger farmers of northern France or East Anglia, instead of the peasants and smallholders of the Apennines. Externally, it has turned the EC into a major exporter of foodstuffs, taking third markets from other farm-exporting nations, producing an upward spiral in world agricultural subsidies, and straining relations with the United States, Canada, Argentina, and Australia. In 1990, support for farmers cost EC governments and consumers $133.4 billion, compared with $74.1 billion in the United States and $59 billion in Japan.[17]

To the supporters of European unity, the CAP nonetheless remains necessary. In their view, a European common market is not just for the benefit of industry. It also has to compensate for the growing gap in living standards between industry-heavy economies on the one hand (Germany) and agriculture-heavy economies on the other (Greece, Portugal), as well as for the differences in income *within* one nation's regions and sectors. If agriculture does consume most of the EC budget, this is a way of transferring resources from the richer nations to Community members containing large numbers of peasant families with low per capita income. To expose farming to unrestricted free

*The industrial equivalent might be for the U.S. government to guarantee to purchase all *unsold* American-made cars and trucks at a fixed price, and then to subsidize the sale of those vehicles abroad. This would no doubt benefit the U.S. automobile companies and workers, but one can imagine the distortions it would create in the global automobile market.

trade would be to create—or exacerbate—regional social problems everywhere from Sicily to Galway; besides, too many powerful parties (such as the CDU in Germany) feel heavily dependent upon the farmers' vote. Finally, there is the aesthetic, emotional, and cultural point: far too many regions and towns, of stunning beauty and outstanding historical importance, have already suffered from population drift.[18] Some form of support for agriculture will be needed as long as it is wished to preserve thriving communities in such areas as the Auvergne, Calabria, and Castile.

Equally tricky is the intention, announced at the 1991 Maastricht meeting of EC leaders, to create a common European currency,* with a European federal bank to control the money supply. After all, a customs union within which twelve or more currencies operate is something of a contradiction. Except for currency dealers themselves, it is claimed that every business—and traveler—would benefit from a common currency, which would also stimulate further cross-border investment. Moreover, given the volatility of the U.S. dollar in recent decades, the international financial system as a whole might gain from a much more broadly based world currency. Since the EC countries have already agreed to coordinate currency fluctuations within a relatively narrow range established by the Exchange Rate Mechanism (ERM), why not take the next step and merge the currencies into one?

The answer is, of course, that currency union would involve a far more substantial assault upon sovereignty—that is, upon the freedom of governments and parliaments to alter interest rates, print money, and run deficits—than schemes for harmonizing professional standards or protecting agricultural incomes. If every national bank were free to print ECUs and if every government (including fiscally lax administrations in Athens and Rome) could run massive budgetary deficits in this new currency and expand their national debts at the rate they did during the 1980s, the result would be a fiasco—which is why, of course, the fiscally conservative Bundesbank is insisting that the only issuer of the new currency be a European Federal Bank, one as independent of

*A European Currency Unit (ECU) already exists. This is simply an accounting device by which EC revenues and expenditures are calculated, with its rates being occasionally adjusted to reflect the relative strength of the member economies. As a notional currency, it cannot be used for everyday exchanges.

political controls as the Bundesbank itself. In fact, because of the strong German economy and the degree to which its neighbors have tied their exchange and interest rates to Germany's, the Bundesbank has already become a sort of European central bank, and these existing tacit arrangements could be formalized in the future, with a Eurofed Bank issuing ECUs in the way that the Bundesbank now issues DMs.

It was for this reason that Mrs. Thatcher told the House of Commons in late 1990, "If you hand over your sterling, you hand over the powers of this parliament to Europe."[19] With monetary unification, it becomes impossible for a single country to "steer" its economy by altering interest rates. What could it possibly mean, for example, for the Bank of France to increase the discount rate by 2 percent if banks and businesses could obtain the same currency at the old rate outside France? In September 1992, unable to bear the costs of keeping their currencies within the narrow exchange-rate bonds of the existing European monetary system, Britain and Italy left that system, dealing a heavy blow to earlier hopes of fiscal union by 1995. But would they even have had the independence to do such a thing had the EC states possessed a common currency? Since a European Federal Bank acting in the same way as the Bundesbank would be an extremely conservative body in its anti-inflationary policies, may not continued membership of the European monetary union eventually produce greater difficulties for France (where the Bank of France has little independence of the Treasury) or other countries which run large deficits?

In its noneconomic aspects also, the trend toward European unity is eroding national sovereignty, despite attempts by various political groups to prevent it. In the European Commission's view, economic integration is occurring so swiftly that it would be "very dangerous for the coherence of the Community" if the political relationships remained backward and immature.[20] This does not mean that agreement over political union will be smooth and steady. The way in which the Kuwait-Iraq crisis exposed Europe's fragmented stance on foreign-policy issues and Denmark and France's 1992 referenda on the Maastricht agreements revealed the strength of public unease at the further loss of national sovereignty were reminders of the difficulties in the way of an advance to a more federated Europe.

If further harmonization is to come, however, changes may be necessary in the functions and powers of existing EC institutions. At present the driving force toward integration is the European Commission, whose seventeen members are required to act independently of national concerns and consider the interests of the Community as a whole. While each commissioner has a department and portfolio—agriculture, competition policy, internal market and industry, regional policy, etc.—they all work toward implementing the various EC treaties on the harmonization of national procedures.

Nevertheless, the European Commission is not the *political* decision-making center of the EC, for that resides in the Council of Ministers—the ministers, that is, of the national states themselves. To several EC countries, in particular France, this is exactly where political power should lie, since those leaders have been democratically elected (whereas the commissioners have not) and Europe will progress only if its member states agree on the agenda together. Perhaps there could be a further watering-down of the unanimity principle—to prevent one or two members from blocking what the others want to do—but the French conception of enhanced political harmonization for Europe consists essentially of the heads of state (and other ministers) meeting more often and making the big decisions.

Such ideas reflect Paris's desire to turn Europe into a factor in world affairs *without* surrendering France's cherished national identity; but this emphasis upon policymaking by doing deals within the Council of Ministers causes concern among the genuine European federalists, who want instead to enhance the powers of the European Parliament, a deliberating assembly of 518 members directly elected for five-year terms with numbers apportioned by population size.[21] Federalists believe this body may become the equivalent of the U.S. House of Representatives, with the power of the purse, ability to vote on policies proposed by the executive, etc. At present, however, it is held in check by more powerful and jealous authorities: the European Commission, fearing that its own pan-European agenda might be blocked by a parliamentary coalition of local interests; the heads of state/Council of Ministers, many of whom dislike the idea of conceding powers to a parliament in which their nationals would be in a distinct minority;* and, finally, the national parliaments and assemblies themselves, most of whom oppose the transfer abroad of their powers. Only slowly have the European Parliament's rights been extended, therefore, and the Strasbourg assembly still possesses "only feeble powers of amendment."[22] It can dismiss the European Commission and reject the budget, but those are dramatic and in a way emergency powers; in practice, many of its decisions bind neither the council nor the commission.

As the EC approaches the twenty-first century, then, fresh proposals for greater integration keep cropping up. Ideas are afoot to establish a second chamber or a "senate" at Strasbourg, or a committee of *national* MPs to scrutinize EC legislation; and, as noted earlier, rival schemes are under way to strengthen either the Council of Ministers (the French preference) or the European Parliament (the German preference), while other countries (Britain and Denmark especially) appear suspicious of all such ideas. Despite the early media excitement about "Europe 1992," the public mood is much more uncertain, suggesting that political unity will not be achieved easily.

Yet, for all the unevenness and messiness, there actually has been a sort of dialectical advance, so that the "Europe" of 1992 is different from that of 1980, just as the Europe of 1973 was different from that of 1957. Whether driven by business pressures for a full common market or by such external trends as the rise of Japan, the movement toward integration rarely slows down for long. Disagreement in one area (agriculture, or currency reform) has not prevented agreement elsewhere (regional policy, or overseas aid), for there are simply too many forces at work for everything to come to a halt. Slowly but surely, it is argued, "the Community is becoming rather less a collection of nation-states and rather more a coherent entity which the rest of the world recognizes as a power in itself."[23]

*Even the larger EC countries can send only eighty-one members to the 518-strong European Parliament.

But if this is true, then Europe must also become a "coherent entity" in the difficult areas of foreign and defense policy. For many reasons, Europe could not develop an independent stance on diplomatic and strategic issues after World War II. Traditions of national rivalry, the shattered state of its economy, the uncertainty about how to deal with Germany, and the mounting pressures on its eastern borders from the USSR all meant that Western Europe's security could be preserved only within a "North Atlantic" foreign- and defense-policy structure dominated by Washington. Several decades later, however, things began to change. Europe not only approached the United States in overall wealth but was also becoming much stronger economically than the languishing Soviet Union. America's productivity and growth rates were slowing, and its increasingly large federal deficits were troubling bankers and congressmen alike. On both sides of the Atlantic, therefore, voices began to call for change, and in particular for Europe to assume an ever-increasing share of its own defense, perhaps even to develop its own defense policies.[24]

In theory, of course, there was a lot to be said for the creation of a common European defense. Europe was rich enough to allocate 4 to 5 percent of its total GNP to defense, sufficient to provide an array of strategic and conventional forces similar to those possessed by the post-1945 superpowers. The scientific and manufacturing structures—and the military-industrial complex—were in place; and if the ground forces of Germany, France, Britain, and Italy alone were merged, there would exist one of the largest and best-equipped armies in the world, albeit one with communications problems. Since this solution was and is feasible, why shouldn't Europe "grow up" and rely increasingly less on the United States for its defense? After all, the transatlantic relationship could remain—because of economic, cultural, and other ties—even after the gradual dissolution of NATO.

With the collapse of the Soviet Union, the debate upon Europe's future defense has entered upon an entirely new course. To be sure, the Cold War's end produced immense relief at the fading of the threat of nuclear obliteration and at the transformation of the political and strategical landscape; amazingly, there had taken place "a deep, multidimensional shift in power to the West,"[25] and a redrawing of the map of Europe, yet without major war. But if that eased the pressures upon Western defense forces—and led to considerable cuts in defense spending—it also threw the planners into confusion as they considered the uncertainties which the vastly altered international conditions might produce. Naturally, the first concern was to demilitarize the great arsenals of the European continent as swiftly as possible, through a series of linked East-West negotiations: the Conference on Security and Cooperation in Europe (CSCE), an outgrowth of the 1975 Helsinki Accords, which brought together all thirty-five states in Europe and North America to work upon further "confidence and security building measures"; the Vienna negotiations on Conventional Forces in Europe (CFE) to establish conventional-force reductions and impose operational constraints on armed forces across the entire continent; and other talks on mutual aerial surveillance (the "Open Skies Agreement"), on the reduction and eventual elimination of chemical weapons, and on crisis prevention.[26]

Assuming that this complex process is not disrupted, policymakers in the West will have to address the longer-term issue of whether NATO itself should continue. Created to meet the extraordinary circumstances of the late 1940s, the alliance served its task admirably, but with the Cold War "over"—indeed, with Russian and Ukrainian leaders occasionally declaring that they hope their states can join—it is not surprising that calls have arisen to replace NATO by something else, more general, more political, less American. In such a period of flux, an entire *à la carte* menu of options could be considered. The nineteenth-century Concert of Europe, that is, a big-powers "club" to keep the others in order, has been proposed as one possible model. The Conference on Security and Cooperation in Europe is another favored forum, partly because no one in Europe is excluded (San Marino, the Holy See, and Liechtenstein are all members) and it possesses a broad political agenda as well as dealing with disarmament and peacekeeping issues.[27]

This search for newer structures to provide for Europe's future security has been further complicated by the reemergence of the "German question," that is, how to achieve a harmonious relationship between the most populous, economically productive, technologically advanced, and (in past experience) militarily efficient nation in Europe and its smaller, less powerful neighbors. This question has deep historical overtones, going back to before Bismarck's time;[28] and while the German question appeared to be "answered" by the post-1945 division of Europe, it proved only a temporary solution. Anti-German circles in Europe and the United States remain suspicious that this large nation, enhanced in size and population, will be tempted to throw its weight around politically, even perhaps militarily.[29] Given the thoroughness of the "denazification" process and Berlin's embarrassment at being drawn into armed conflicts, it is difficult to see how apprehensions about German aggressiveness have any current validity, although so many changes have occurred in European politics recently that it is not surprising such fears exist.

What is more plausible is that Germany's economic importance will give it increasing weight within the EC and toward Central and Eastern Europe; and that the Franco-German "duopoly," which set the pace for EC policies over previous decades, might no longer operate as before. If there is to be a European currency union and a European federal bank, few doubt who will have the largest say in how the new system operates. Diplomatically, if Germany is bent upon an action (e.g., the recognition of an independent Croatia), its neighbors find they can do little but follow suit. It is also possible to imagine German dominance of a future European defense organization, especially in the procurement of tanks, fighters, and the like. Meanwhile, a German commercial and financial *pénétration pacifique* into Central and Eastern Europe is probably inevitable, for geographical reasons and the complementarity of trade relations with countries like Hungary and Romania; indeed, once the Iron Curtain was lifted, a resumption of those links was virtually certain to follow. Although anxious Poles might hint that it is "bad" if foreign investment in Poland is "majority German,"[30] that ratio will change only if other Western countries direct large funds there; if they do not, then German investments are surely better than none.

Whether this unease about Germany's future is anachronistic or not, it exists in some quarters and has caused the German leadership to call for Germany to be more firmly embedded in pan-European structures and for the EC to move as swiftly as possible toward the "strong," integrated European solution. Far from disengaging from its western neighbors, Germany stressed its wish for closer relationships to ensure, in Thomas Mann's words, "not a German Europe, but a European Germany."[31] No doubt this was meant genuinely, but does it address the problem of uneven national sizes (and thus uneven influences) in a united Europe? Before 1989 the EC had enough difficulty in reaching accords when it consisted of four medium-sized nations and another eight medium-to-very-small nations. Will it be more coherent in the future, if it consists of one large nation (Germany), three or four medium-sized ones (France, Britain, Italy, Spain), and, say, ten to fifteen countries of varying smaller sizes? Admittedly, such territorial disproportions exist between California and Delaware and Rhode Island; but this is the "old" world, not the "new," and it remains to be seen whether centuries of European nationalism can be subsumed without rancor into the proposed new structures.

In sum, whether one considers currency issues or defense issues, the EC's dilemma is the same. The "strong" and integrated European solution is extremely attractive in theory, at least to the committed federalists, but it contains innumerable problems in practice. If, however, Europe retains the "weak" and loosely organized solution, it also faces problems. It will remain marginal in world affairs except in economic terms, and even there its massive potential may be hampered by continuing disunity. Far from having settled things by preferring merely a limited amount of commercial harmonization, the EC could find itself facing a contradiction between increasingly integrated, pan-European economic practices on the one hand and increasingly inadequate political structures on the other. For this reason some Community members eager to deepen their unity (the Benelux countries, Germany, Italy) occasionally suggest a "twin-speed" solution, in which they go on ahead, leaving less enthusiastic members (Britain, Greece, and others) to follow suit when they will. Yet that itself, others suspect, brings a fresh batch of problems once the practical consequences are examined.[32]

Will these now-familiar questions—currency harmonization, modifying the CAP, giving more powers to the European Parliament, improving defense coordination, negotiating the admission into the EC of such well-qualified candidates as Austria and Switzerland, hand-wringing over the Community's inability to achieve a unified foreign policy toward (say) the Middle East—also be the sole or main agenda items for European politicians as they and their publics move into the next century? In particular, will Europe be allowed the luxury of concentrating on its own special debate—how far to unify—aloof from the global trends, and possible global turbulences, discussed in Part One of this book? The answer must surely be no. In fact, as will be discussed below, member states of the EC and their citizens are already being affected by demographic trends, migration, environmental issues, the globalization of industry, and the coming of new technologies—and are likely to be further affected in the next few decades. Although undoubtedly prosperous and well equipped compared with much of the rest of the world—and in that sense "winners" rather than "losers"—Europeans would be foolish to assume that they can remain untouched by the broader impacts of demography and technology upon our planet.

This, then, is the "double agenda" for European policymakers: to hammer out the future shape of the EC *at the same time* as they face the broad trends affecting all societies on this planet. Whether the internal controversies will hinder preparations for transnational changes or these changes will stimulate European unity so that an integrated Community will better be able to deal with global forces is the key question.

Demographic trends will clearly be an increasingly important issue for Europe's leaders and their planners. Until recently, the focus was upon "the graying of Europe"; for example, the 10 million out of France's 55 million people aged over sixty will have risen to 15 million by 2020.[33] Because of the plunge in European population replacement rates—especially in Germany and Italy but also in most other countries of Europe—most populations appear indeed headed for absolute decline. In fact, only Ireland had a fertility rate over 2.1 children per mother, the natural replacement level. West Germany, whose population was forecast (in early 1989) to fall from 61 million to 45 million by 2030, was said to be "committing suicide"; if present trends persisted, the same forecast reported, "Europe's vaunted market of 320 million people will peak in 2000—and fall to less than 300 million by 2100."[34] Economists, demographers, and other planners pointed to the economic and social implications of this decline—the closing of schools in rural and inner-city areas, shortages of skilled labor, the need to increase job mobility throughout the EC and to invest much more in training, and the pressures upon social and health-care services as a larger proportion of the population becomes over sixty-five.[35] Perhaps this demographic pattern will reverse itself, as it has done in Sweden and certain other Northern European states in recent years;* but the general tendency is toward a smaller population.

In the special case of West Germany, this declining population trend altered in the late 1980s because the political thaw in the Soviet Union and Eastern Europe allowed an increasing migration of ethnic Germans, from 50,000 (1986) to 200,000 (1987) and an enormous 380,000 as the DDR disintegrated (1989); most of these immigrants were younger people who could be trained.[36] German unification altered the situation again, by incorporating lots of elderly "East" Germans, so the Berlin government now confronts its former long-term demographic challenge—this time with a population of 78 million, not 61 million.

Still, if this were the extent of the EC's demographic problems, they would probably be capable of solution, through better support for young married couples (to increase the birth rate) and—in Germany's case—measures to retrain newly arrived ethnic Germans from Hungary and elsewhere so that they could enter the work force. But the entire situation could be altered by circumstances *outside* the EC's borders and, to some extent, outside its control. The disintegration of both the USSR and of its enforced order over former Warsaw Pact countries opens up the possibility of ethnic tensions, border wars, social turbulence, and the mass migration of refugees.† The horrible example of "ethnic cleansing" in Bosnia and large parts of Croatia in the summer of 1992 drove millions of homeless, desperate people onto the roads, heading north and west. Moreover, economic dislocations across Eastern Europe and the former Soviet Union are adding to the flood of those seeking jobs, shelter, and security. If a full-scale economic collapse occurs—or, on the other hand, a significant reconstruction of industry and agriculture is pushed through, causing the loss of millions

*For further discussion of this reversal, see below, p. 343.
†See the discussion in Chapter 11.

of jobs from inefficient factories and collective farms in the former USSR and Eastern Europe—the temptation for millions to migrate to the EC will be increased. Already, Germany, Austria, and Hungary feel besieged by refugee families.[37]

For France, Spain, and Italy, by contrast, the larger demographic problem lies to the south, in the fast-growing populations of the states of North Africa. Already France contains several million immigrants, chiefly from its former African colonies, and about a million are working in Italy (given illegal immigration, the number could be considerably higher).[38] These newcomers carry out the tasks—fruit-picking, factory work, transport services, cleaning—that Europeans are not eager to do themselves; but their presence has provoked a rise in native resentments, leading to occasional riots, a surge in right-wing political parties calling for repatriation, and worried official discussions about how to handle the problem. The greatest apprehension is that this is only the beginning, and that population and economic trends in Africa will produce a mass future migration unless it is forcibly prevented. As Algeria's population doubles from 25 to 50 million between now and 2025 and Egypt's soars from 55 to 95 million, how else will so many of these new entrants to the global work force find jobs *except* by joining their cousins already on the other side of the Mediterranean? Simply because of numbers and geography, the former Italian minister Gianni De Michelis recently predicted "terrible demographic pressure in the next ten to fifteen years."[39]

Inevitably, these fears make it more difficult for European federalists to push for unimpeded movement of people within the EC borders (and help to explain why the European Commission has been lukewarm to Turkey's membership application and worries about admitting Austria, Hungary, and their neighbors). If some EC governments are opposed to relaxing immigration and customs procedures at airports and ports—pleading the need to check terrorists, drug dealers, and illegal immigrants—how much more worried will they be if an enlarged Community becomes the destination of millions and millions of Eastern European, Russian, Middle Eastern, and African refugees? Unlike the continent-wide United States, European states do not see themselves as melting-pot societies, so the argument that Europe *needs* immigrants to forestall future labor shortages—again, because of the "graying" of its indigenous population—is not a popular one. Even those supporting the liberal Schengen Accord, by which Belgium, France, the Netherlands, Luxembourg, and West Germany agreed to abolish all formalities at their shared frontiers, found their plans suspended, for a while, because of the DDR's economic collapse and concern about a flood of East German immigrants; if nothing else, it was a warning that abolishing frontiers within the EC could produce major difficulties.[40]

In other words, far from being something that Europe can safely ignore, global demographic trends can affect the social order, delay (or reverse) the opening of the EC's internal barriers, and even influence its foreign policy. Over the next few decades, migration may become the single most important aspect of relations between the EC and the Muslim world; and if certain European states eventually contain large numbers of Arabs, will that not affect Europe's stance on Near Eastern conflicts, should any occur in the future? If the nations of Europe have difficulty in forging a common foreign policy toward the neighboring civil war in Bosnia, how likely are they to adopt a united stance over future convulsions in the Ukraine or North Africa? How can European politicians control the surge in nativist reactions against immigrants from Africa and Asia when fresh incidents of unrest in, say, Algiers cause increasing numbers of secular, middle-class Algerians to consider moving to France—while the same reports provoke a surge in popularity of right-wing nationalist leaders like Le Pen? How will European cities retain their character and appeal if, over the next few decades, large numbers of poor immigrants form mass ghettoes of underprivilege; and will the EC's social funds bear the strain? Finally, if strict "Fortress Europe" policies are adopted—essentially, using the armed forces to prevent illegal migration by land, sea, or air—does that really address the larger problem, that Europe's overall population is stagnating while those of neighboring continents are forecast to double and treble by early next century?

The same conclusion—about Europe's vulnerability to events *elsewhere*—may also be true with regard to other transnational trends. In dealing with environmental issues, for example, Europe has encountered the same experiences as other developed areas. Growing population and industrialization during this century led to atmospheric pollution, contaminated rivers and seas, and a damaged countryside; but it also produced environmental pressure groups and efforts to undo the damage, at first nationally and then by international agreement. Predictably, persuading Germans to accept reduced speed limits on their autobahns or Britons to enforce stricter controls on emissions being carried to Norway still causes disagreements. But in Northern and Western Europe the rivers and air are less polluted than a quarter century ago, and even in Mediterranean lands there is growing environmental consciousness. After all, northwestern Europe and Scandinavia are rich enough to pay for an environmentally friendly economy, possess an articulate middle class concerned about such issues, and have a tradition of state intervention for the common good; thus, enacting measures to protect the environment is like legislating worker safety or child welfare. Already the European Commission is pressing for much higher "clean energy" taxes, pointedly noting that Europe is more willing to pay the cost of reducing carbon dioxide emissions than America.[41]

The effects of global warming upon EC and EFTA countries are probably also containable, at least locally. Some studies suggest that Western Europe's climate might become drier, with decreased soil moisture affecting grain output[42]—although that might well be balanced by the enhanced yields from biotech farming discussed below. As in the United States, hotter temperatures could cause crops to migrate northward, hurting some European farmers while benefiting others. Rising sea levels could harm certain low-lying areas like the Netherlands and the Fenlands of Britain, but most of these societies have the engineering and financial resources to protect their coasts, if they choose to do so; competent hydraulic engineering could probably also prevent Venice from meeting its oft-forecast death by drowning. In fact, the biggest impact of global warming on Europe might be to reduce water supplies, as saltwater intrusion expands upriver and into lower-lying regions.

Europe's most serious environmental concerns, therefore, will once again arise from developments elsewhere, in Eastern Europe and the developing world. As noted earlier, heavy-handed industrialization by COMECON countries has left a legacy of poisoned lakes and streams, soil full of chemicals and metals, unsafe power plants, ravaged woodlands, and industrial pollution drifting across the Baltic to Scandinavia. With the collapse of Communism, this can now be arrested and recovery begun. However, given the scale of the damage and the task of upgrading the industrial structures of Eastern Europe, it is doubtful that even the wealthy EC and EFTA will be able to do all they want during the next decade, especially if there are shortages in global liquidity.

Equally worrying environmentally is the massive growth in the populations surrounding the Mediterranean (especially in Turkey, Syria, and North African states), and the even swifter migration from inland villages to water-short, polluted coastal settlements. In Algeria, for example, 53 percent of the fast-growing population squeezes into 3 percent of the land area, and the sewage is untreated—as it is, for that matter, in Athens, Sicily, and other parts of the Mediterranean's northern coastline. Add to this pollution a myriad of small oil spills and the draining of wetlands, the fact that Mediterranean waters (being virtually enclosed) do not renew themselves very swiftly, and the boom in tourism all along its crowded coasts, and the resultant environmental pressures are appalling. While a "Blue Plan" exists to arrest this damage, it is not clear from where the tens of billions of dollars required will come—and all reform measures run a desperate race against population growth. By contrast, being both far less populous and much richer, the Baltic and North Sea states clearly have an easier "clean-up" task ahead of them than Mediterranean countries.[43]

Most societies in northwest Europe and Scandinavia demonstrate a concern, *relatively speaking,* for the developing world as well as for global warming, presumably because they possess well-educated populations with a liberal, humanistic culture and an interest in world affairs. Some of this concern—as in France's case—may also reflect a desire to preserve influence over former colonial territories. Nevertheless, because some European states have recognized that the developing world requires attention, technical assistance, and financial aid, they contribute more than the targeted average (0.7 percent of GNP annually) that OECD nations agree to give (see Chart 11).

In absolute amounts, of course, 1 percent of Norway's or Sweden's GNP may not amount to much; but it offers an example which, if ever copied by larger economies like those of Britain, Germany, Japan, and

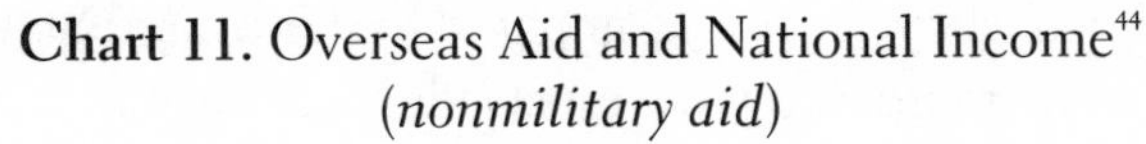

Chart 11. Overseas Aid and National Income[44]
(nonmilitary aid)

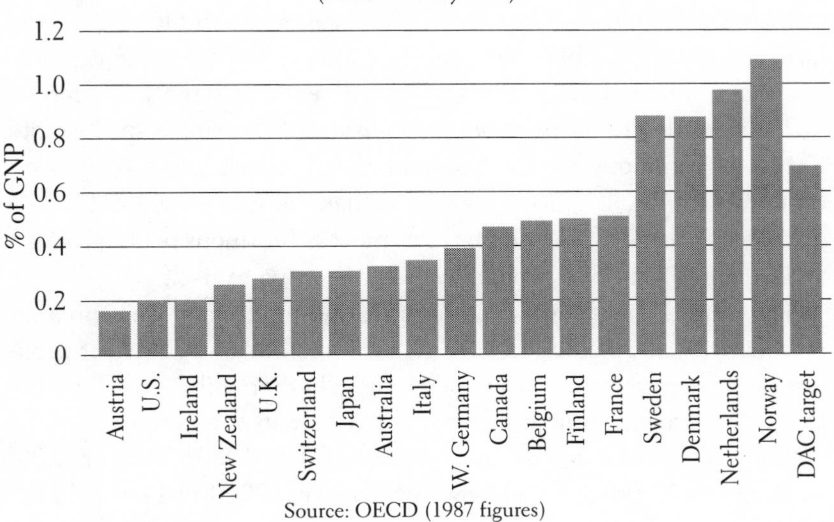

Source: OECD (1987 figures)

(especially) the United States, could massively boost the flow of resources from rich to poor nations. On the other hand, compared with the *needs* of developing countries—and the fact that someday their burgeoning populations and exhausted ecologies may drive families en masse toward the wealthier regions of the globe—even the allocation of 1 percent of GNP to overseas aid may in retrospect appear a totally inadequate premium for achieving global stability.

A much more mixed picture emerges regarding Europe's preparedness to deal with technologically driven global changes. For example, the biotech revolution in agriculture and food processing may at first seem to benefit Europe: the region contains the world's largest chemical companies, which produce one-third of the world's chemical output; it has hundreds of institutes, university departments, and private companies engaged in food research, agricultural studies, biotechnology, marine biology, and so on; and it possesses national governments, and the European Commission itself, working to improve the region's competitiveness. Yet biotech is turning into a political minefield, because of the social structure of European agriculture and the workings of the CAP described above.* Compared to the United States, the EC possesses many more farmers, especially peasant farmers with extremely small plots; in Greece and Portugal, for example, the average farm size is only 4.3 hectares, and the Community's average is just 13 hectares.† Then there is the special way in which the EC supports agriculture, described by *The Economist* as "the single most idiotic system of economic mismanagement that the rich western countries have ever devised."[45] Still, the fact is that the system will not readily disappear, because 10 million farmers possess enormous political weight and enhance Europe's tendency to try to insulate itself.

The biotech revolution in agriculture and food processing threatens these already strained arrangements in numerous ways. First, it promises large increases in output per unit, whether milk, beef, or grain crops; the average annual milk yield per cow in the Netherlands, for example, is forecast to rise from its mid to late 1980s figure of 5,000 kilograms to 8,000–8,500 kilograms by the year 2000.[46] This will place enormous, perhaps impossible strains upon the existing structure of price supports; since the European Commission is trying to *reduce* overall output, a surge in yields would lead to more items (milk powder, butter) put into storage, more cattle stock taken out of production, more farmers leaving agriculture. While one might imagine that countries with large dairy herds (the U.K. average is fifty-seven cows per farm, the Netherlands average forty) would benefit more than those with small herds (Greece's average is three cows per farm, Italy's seven), the 1984 quota system assigns a maximum output for each country, so that productivity rises "will force producers out of the market where the increases are *highest.*"[47] Given the nature of CAP financing and the social and political implications of declining agriculture in many parts of the EC, spending on this sector may have to rise, not fall, as biotech advances over the next decade.

Studies of the biotech revolution suggest that most farmers will become increasingly dependent upon giant agrochemical conglomerates. This may occur fairly swiftly in a laissez-faire economy like that of the United States, but the European record indicates that there will

*See above, pp. 264–65.

†1 hectare equals 2.47 acres.

be a much greater degree of official protection of traditional agriculture. The British government's 1988 decision not to approve the bovine growth hormone BST, ostensibly on public-health grounds, but also for economic reasons; the EC's opposition to isoglucose (seen as a rival to sugar beets), its banning of genetically altered tomatoes, and other regulatory controls upon biotech research are slowing the spread of new products in Europe relative to elsewhere in the developed world. This will not stop further intensive research by biotech companies, but most of that will be done in North American rather than European laboratories.[48]

Still, prohibitions are not going to stop the advance of biotechnology in agriculture and foodstuffs. Banning the bovine growth hormone is one thing; but a whole gamut of improvements such as new seed varieties, advances in animal stockbreeding, increased protein content in plants, and extracting more from by-products is already approved of, steadily pushing up average yields in every area. Moreover, as each sector grapples with its surplus, biotechnology offers ingenious ways (through fermentation, fragmentation, recomposition, protein enhancement) to turn that product into something else, and then to invade *another* sector's traditional market. Starch, for example, previously drawn from maize (imported, and French) and domestically grown potatoes, is increasingly derived from surplus wheat; dairy proteins are being replaced by vegetable proteins, so that condensed milk loses ground to coffee creamers. In consequence, Europe's agricultural "lobby" may dissolve into warring factions, each struggling for market share in an age of increasingly interchangeable materials.[49]

One escape from this crisis might be greater agricultural exports, as well as the near-complete substitution of imports. Some calculations show that it is technically feasible to replace all the EC's animal feed imports (over 20 million tons per year), as well as oil and vegetable fat (over 4 million tons per year), *and* cut imports of forestry products (over 120 million cubic meters per year).[50] Whether or not that would mop up all of Europe's future agricultural surpluses is unclear; but a policy of enhanced exports and diminished imports would certainly produce enormous rows with the United States and other major food-exporting nations and would hurt producers in the developing world.[51] Perhaps the only bright spot is the potential of Europe's farmland to produce energy biomass—to perhaps 100 million tons of coal equivalent a year, according to one estimate.[52] As at present, however, the surpluses remain and the demands for CAP funds grow.

Given the travails of the existing EC agricultural system, one can understand the European Commission's alarm at the idea of membership by the nations of Central and Eastern Europe. Already the absorption of the DDR has cost billions of dollars and increased overall agricultural output, as farmers in Germany's eastern provinces responded to the high CAP prices. The same may be expected elsewhere in Eastern Europe, where farming can be very productive when not hampered by collectivization and Eastern European farmers imitate the more efficient techniques of the West. Such surpluses would put further pressure on CAP's troubled finances and, as agriculture in Eastern and Central Europe modernized and shed workers, on the Community's regional and social funds.* Here, then, is yet another example of how Europe's existing problems are complicated by transnational developments and new technologies.[53]

While the robotics revolution also challenges European societies, it probably will not become as politically controversial and entangled in the debate on the EC's future as advances in biotech. Automating production is a long-standing and incremental process and tends to occur in decentralized fashion, from factory to factory. Also, it has affected only a few European industries (automobile assembly, painting, etc.); and the robots used have engaged chiefly in dirty and dangerous work, so that although Europe's trade unions remain suspicious of automation, they have offered less opposition than might have been expected. Finally, the robotics industry itself, along with the computerized machine-tool industry, has created employment for a considerable number of skilled and highly paid workers.

The likelihood is, therefore, that there will be a steady but undramatic increase in robots employed by European industry, particularly in Germany; but investment in them will follow the usual business criteria—labor-saving potential, expected improvement in quality production, increased output—and will be on a plant-by-plant basis. The

*In the late 1980s, agriculture's share of Eastern Europe's labor force averaged 13 percent—in Romania, 24 percent—which can be compared with 2.6 percent in the EC and 0.8 percent in the United States.

rate of installation might increase more swiftly if Japanese factories *inside* Europe automate at significantly higher rates (say, close to the levels of automation in Japanese home plants), because that would put pressure upon European firms in the same industry. In health care, the use of intelligent mobile robots might also expand steadily, because of shortages of skilled nursing staff for a rapidly aging population. Finally, it is conceivable that automation could become part of the debate over immigration from developing countries. Will some nationalist politicians, observing what is happening in Japan, press for similar levels of automation to obviate the need to import guest workers as the work force shrinks? And will those businesses and service industries which are labor-intensive, not capital-intensive, press instead for continued immigration? Will "white" trade unions prefer robots to working alongside Arabs?

On the whole, Europe is unlikely to follow Japan's systemic move into automation simply because it is not at present facing a general labor shortage. Admittedly, shortages of skilled workers exist in specific EC industries and regions; but officials, businessmen and unions generally believe that the correct response is to increase the skill levels of the work force and to encourage job mobility within the EC.[54] Given the structural unemployment in many EC nations—which would be augmented by the inclusion of the Eastern European states—there would be widespread concern if automation threw lots of industrial workers out of their jobs. Robots may increasingly be used in the wealthier EC countries, but operating alongside human beings rather than replacing them en masse. Whether this will permit European industry to remain competitive with hyperefficient, fully automated Japanese rivals, instead of relying on protection and experiencing relative decline, is much less clear.

More challenging to European societies are the financial and communications revolution and the emergence of the truly multinational corporation. Those transnational developments are, in many fields, partly Europe's own achievements. Its bankers have learned to globalize themselves and to engage in twenty-four-hour-a-day trading. Its giant companies, like their American and Japanese counterparts, have set up assembly plants, research laboratories, and distribution centers in the major world markets. Its consultants, engineers, and merchant bankers offer their services in every continent. Its deep-pocketed media conglomerates buy out foreign newspapers and book publishers. Its airlines (British Airways, Lufthansa, SAS) span the globe. While it receives significant amounts of foreign investment—American and Japanese companies getting into the EC before 1992—it also exports enormous sums of capital to purchase land, companies, equities, and bonds overseas, as well as to finance joint ventures. Theoretically, therefore, Europe is well positioned to become a major beneficiary of the globalization of finance, industry, and commerce, provided, of course, that worldwide financial instabilities do not occur.

However, two serious problems remain. First, the move toward unrestricted globalization might create the social gulf that Robert Reich notes in the United States; that is, the emergence of an upper stratum of lawyers, engineers, consultants, and other "symbolic analysts" catering to transnational demand for their services, while the lower four-fifths of society is increasingly at the mercy of multinational companies moving production *in and out* of regions for the sake of comparative advantage. Yet, while there has been a great expansion of symbolic analysts in Europe in recent years and European countries have shifted some production to countries like the United States to ensure continued access to those countries' markets, the social consequences Reich discusses may not perhaps be so severe in Europe.[55] A deeper sense of company roots and more interventionist state traditions could deter the full-scale transfer of production from one country to another. In any case, relocation of plants to other parts of the EC would make less economic sense if there is "harmonization" of social welfare, minimum wages, and general living standards; whereas if production is moved *outside* the EC the goods may be unable to enter Europe's protected markets. Finally, the EC's higher social security "net" for the unemployed would ease the impact of business closures upon workers.

Secondly, to what extent does the emergence of a "borderless world" contradict the EC's aim of deepening its economic and political unity? As noted already, there has always been tension between those favoring a strong Europe and those wanting a less centralized body. To the former, the EC should steadily eliminate discriminations among its member states (tariffs, capital controls, national subsidies, immigration barriers) and move toward integration *while maintaining and in some ways enhancing the barriers between Europeans and non-Europeans;* after all, there was no sense in creating a unified "Europe" if virtually everyone else could enjoy its privileges. The latter, by contrast, prefer a less exclusive Europe because they do not like walls between it and non-European bodies (the Commonwealth, the United States) and the latter's goods and services.

On the whole, and despite such setbacks as the Danish referendum against Maastricht, the integrationists have been gaining ground, with important consequences for Europe's future and the international economy. The theory of the borderless world implies that a "sovereign" European customer ought to be free to purchase U.S. beef rather than French beef, or a car made in Japan rather than a car made in Italy, if the price is right.[56] By contrast, the CAP's purpose is that the customer should consume European (if not solely French) beef, while many politicians and businessmen clearly intend Europe's industrial tariffs and quotas to deter the customer from buying a Japanese car rather than a native European (if not solely Italian) one. The larger implication here is that far from national borders being dismantled, they are simply being folded into a bigger entity—the EC, a North American free-trade zone, a yen-dominated area—with the world economy increasingly dominated by three enormous regional trading blocs. This would leave the countries outside desperately begging for market access, which they would be unlikely to get if European protectionist lobbies have their way. It would also presumably reduce employment prospects in those countries, and therefore *increase* the pressures to migrate to Europe in search of jobs.

Isn't there, then, an underlying contradiction between what the EC is striving to become and where the global economy is headed? As we have seen, this dialectic between national purposes and transnational changes exists in all countries; but perhaps the contradiction is greater in this case because European nations are moving toward integration into a new "superstate" just when trends in technology and communications loosen state controls, erode all borders, and question our traditional concern with national or regional identities as opposed to membership in the entire human race. In effect, trends in technology—like those in demography—threaten to make redundant the traditional agenda items which have been the focus of EC politics for the past four decades.

European integrationists often deny that they wish to distance their countries from the rest of the world; but they may have to consider more carefully than hitherto what the various policies for deepening Europe's unity mean *in practice* for others. Much of the world worries that access to markets in the advanced economies will be restricted. There is also considerable mistrust among political and business circles in Japan and (especially) the United States concerning European protectionism.[57] In sum, a broad international feeling exists that the EC, in pursuit of its own destiny, is less interested in boosting global commerce by opening markets and more willing to protect its own farmers and industrial workers, even at the cost of worsening trade relations with the developed world and hurting the prospects of the developing world. This concern may be unjustified, and the forecasts (especially prominent in the American press) that a "trade war" will replace the Cold War could also turn out to be exaggerated. Still, as the rest of the world watches Europe's integration, it clearly is concerned by its meaning for others.

It is not simply for economic reasons that great attention ought to be paid to Europe's future. It is engaged in a political experiment of the highest importance concerning how human societies think about themselves and relationships with others. As many experts on world affairs have pointed out, we seem to be witnessing a decline in the traditional loyalties, structures, and associations which have made *nations* the focal point of political and economic identity; instead, there is a growing "relocation of authority" discussed earlier, a relocation which concerns both larger (transnational) and smaller (regional, ethnic) units as politicians and peoples strive to discover what size state will work best in our present and future world. This sounds fine in theory, but one wonders what it means in practice. If a civilized and sophisticated people like the Danes vote against further measures of European integration, will there ever come a time when an organization like the EC will appear legitimate in the eyes of its peoples as national governments were? And how will such an organization relate in a meaningful way to the needs of regional units like Wallonia, Tuscany, the Upper Rhine, and South Wales? Are, in fact, the upward and downward relocations of authority contradictory—or complementary? As we know, the world of the late twentieth century is being moved by two currents. One, driven by technology and communications and trade, tends toward ever greater economic integration. The second is the revived tendency toward ethnic separatism, currently exacerbated by the collapse of a transcendent creed (Communism), the rise of religious fundamentalism, and increasing internal questioning (from Croatia to Somalia) of national borders that were superimposed, often from outside, upon very different ethnic groups; it is also exacerbated at times by economic fears.

In both respects, Europe's role has been critical historically. In the first half of this century, Europe offered dreadful examples of how excessive nationalism, ethnic prejudices, and desire for gain could plunge so-called civilized societies into war. After 1950, however, Europeans have been seeking to learn from past mistakes, creating a structure which would produce economic integration and sink national differences. Considering the fractured relationships elsewhere (East Asia, the Middle East, Central Africa, South Asia), Europe's march towards unity has been remarkable despite its flaws and offers an example to all strife-torn regions. If the leaders of states like Germany and France now wish to be at lasting peace with their neighbors after centuries of conflict and to embed themselves in larger, transnational units, might that not also happen at some time in the future to clusters of countries elsewhere, from South Asia to Latin America? And if it did, would that not be an advance upon today's regional fractures?

Of course, Europe still has a long way to travel and there are innumerable obstacles in the way, not least those thrown up by the new global forces that challenge all societies and—as argued above—pose perhaps special problems for the EC at this stage in its development. Yet it is precisely because of those global forces for change that the integrationists' argument *ought* to prevail over those who merely desire to erect a large trading consortium. In the light of all that is happening in world affairs—the disappearance of the USSR and the possibility of regional conflicts in the successor territories, the rise of East Asian economic power, the emergence of nuclear-armed local Great Powers (India, China), the protracted social and economic difficulties of the United States, the chances of demographically driven struggles, resource wars, and mass migration, the looming population imbalances between North and South, the long-term dangers of environmental damage—Europe surely has no real alternative to *moving forward,* seeking to create an influential and responsible entity capable of meeting these challenges collectively in a way that twelve or twenty separate nation-states simply cannot do. No one will deny that the task is enormous, especially given the tension between "deepening" the Community and "widening" its membership. Yet the profundity of international change, demanding new thinking and new structures, strengthens the position of those who argue that Europe simply cannot stay still.

While the larger logic of historical change favors the integrationists, they in turn need to respond imaginatively to the challenge and opportunity offered. At present, far too much of the rhetoric about Europe's destiny is accompanied by self-serving political maneuvers, bureaucratic infighting, blatant efforts to protect economic inefficiencies, national interests seeking to control and divert pan-European purposes, and protectionist, inward-looking tendencies—all confirming the worst suspicions of the anti-integrationists as well as those of other countries. Furthermore, the typical agenda of EC politics—how to reduce the "butter mountains," for example, or regulate accountancy standards—appears as excessively nitpicking and inward-focused in the light of the enormous demographic and technological forces that are changing the world. Whether any country or group of countries *can* respond effectively to the new transnational developments—some of which may manifest themselves swiftly and unpredictably—is unclear. But if European leaders spend so much time arguing over integration that little or none remains to consider coherent responses to demographic trends, migration, global warming, and the impact of new technologies, then their countries may be completely unprepared to handle the challenges ahead. Even in the early 1990s, it is clear that Europe cannot stand apart from the rest of the world's problems. How much clearer will that be in 2010 or 2030?

In sum, the burden is upon European federalists to outline how they can create a thriving unified body which will assume a responsible world role *without* hiding behind walls, adopting selfish policies, and running against the trends toward globalization; how they can further the EC's internal development at the same time as they seek to cope—and help poorer nations to cope—with global changes. Should it actually manage to reconcile those aims, Europe might find that the next century will be kinder to it than the present century has been. As things now stand, however, resolving such a cluster of major challenges seems unlikely—in which case, both Europe and the rest of the world will suffer the consequences.

13

THE AMERICAN DILEMMA

ALTHOUGH DEBATES ABOUT THE FUTURE of this and that country occur from France to Japan, perhaps nowhere are they more widespread than in the United States. In this large, decentralized, media-rich society, all sorts of controversies from abortion to "the end of History," from race to education, are vigorously debated, in books and newspapers and on radio and television, by pundits, pressure groups, op-ed writers, and lecture-circuit regulars. The controversy over America's future is also fueled by ideological differences: most (but certainly not all) conservatives emphasize American achievements—"winning" the Cold War, the success of capitalism—whereas liberal critics point to a growing legacy of problems—debt, social and educational decay, decline of middle-class standards of living, erosion of the country's economic leadership, and an overly large military presence abroad.[1] Because the debate over American "decline or renewal" has become politicized, the contenders prefer alternative measures of comparison and point to different aspects of the economy or society to support their positions,[2] which makes the matter more complicated.

This debate over the future of the United States is also intense because it occurs among a people who had believed—even before Henry Luce first used the term in 1941—that this is the "American century."[3] However accurate that expression will appear to future historians, it possessed an immense psychological and cultural power, providing emotional reinforcement to the American people. It gave them a sense of being "special," even superior; and once such feelings are acquired, it is difficult to let them go. It was predictable, therefore, that the appearance of books entitled *The End of the American Century, Beyond American Hegemony,* and *America as an Ordinary Power*[4] would provoke responses such as *The Myth of America's Decline, America's Economic Resurgence, Bound to Lead,* and *The Third Century: America's Resurgence in the Asian Era.*[5] Each new study is welcomed as reinforcement by a particular school—"a timely and forceful response to the doomsayers,"[6] etc., etc.—and the debate continues. Whether this outpouring will fade from natural exhaustion is impossible to forecast. What it suggests is a national mood very changed from that of Truman's time or even the experience of the Sputnik shock.[7] The United States is clearly more concerned about its future now than it was a generation or two ago.

What are America's strengths and weaknesses, and how well is it prepared to meet the global challenges outlined earlier in this study? In the traditional domain of "hard" or military-based power, the United States is unequaled by any other nation, including Russia and China. Both possess larger land forces, but there must be serious doubt about their overall quality. In any case, numbers are not as important as morale and training, sophistication of equipment, and capacity to project force to distant theaters; in all those aspects, the United States has devoted large resources during the 1980s to ensure the required standards. Strategically, it retains a panoply of air-, land-, and sea-based missile systems to intimidate another power from attacking it or its allies. Technologically, its armed services are equipped to fight "smart" wars, using everything from Stealth bombers and fighters to AEGIS cruisers and sophisticated night-fighting battlefield weapons. Through satellites, early-warning aircraft, and an extensive oceanic acoustical detection system, its forces usually have the means to spot what potential rivals are up to.[8]

Finally, it is the only country with a truly global "reach," with fleets and air bases and ground forces in every strategically important part of the world, plus the capacity to reinforce those positions in an emergency. Its response to the 1990 invasion of Kuwait by Iraq demonstrated the flexibility and extent of those abilities; in dispatching over 1,500 aircraft and 500,000 men (including heavy armored units) to Saudi Arabia in a matter of months, and in filling the Mediterranean, Persian Gulf, and Indian Ocean with carrier task forces, the United States displayed military power unequaled in recent times. Perhaps the only modern historical equivalent was Britain's "force projection" of over 300,000 soldiers, safely protected by the Royal Navy's command of the seas, to fight in the South African war at the beginning of this century.

As the Cold War fades away, the size and extent of U.S. deployments are being cut significantly; but it would be remarkable if the United States returned to its pre-1941 policy, under which no American military units were based outside the United States and its insular dependencies. As it is, the existence of regimes like those in Iraq and Libya aids the Pentagon in arguing the need to retain considerable and flexible armed forces.[9] Whatever reduction in American military power occurs, it is likely to possess far greater capacity than medium-sized countries like France and Britain and to retain a technological edge over Chinese and Russian forces.

Yet while this military power boosts the United States' place in world affairs, that may not necessarily be a blessing for the nation as a whole. Defense costs have caused some economic damage, and America's ability to handle nonmilitary threats is low. The Cold War provided the political "cement" to bind a majority of Americans, Republicans and Democrats alike, to large defense budgets and entangling alliances. With the Soviet threat removed, this consensus may disintegrate; at the least, it may be difficult for American leaders to justify a worldwide military presence to its own public. While some strategic thinkers debate whether forces should be withdrawn from Europe and concentrated against "out-of-area" threats in the developing world, others wonder about the *utility* of military force in general, since the threats to America may now come not from nuclear weapons but from environmental hazards, drugs, and the loss of economic competitiveness.[10]

As a consequence, the relief that the Soviet Union is no longer an "enemy" is overshadowed by uncertainties about the United States' proper world role.[11] To the traditionalists, it is important that America is present, in Europe, the Pacific, and elsewhere, in order to prevent any return to the anarchic conditions of the 1930s;[12] to the critics, the argument that the United States is "bound to lead" places burdens upon the American people, diverts resources from domestic needs, and takes American democracy further away from its original foreign-policy principles.[13] Such a debate is easily recognizable to historians. In general, the leading power favors international stability, to preserve the system in which it enjoys great influence and wealth; usually it has inherited a vast legacy of obligations and treaties, promissory notes to distant allies, and undertakings to keep open the world's seaways. But executing a special leadership role includes the danger of becoming the world's policeman, combating threats to "law and order" wherever they arise, and finding ever more "frontiers of insecurity" across the globe that require protection.[14] This suggests, therefore, that the debate over the future of American external policy will go on.

Such a debate cannot be separated from domestic concerns, simply because of the cost of maintaining such a global position; $300 billion a year bought military security for the United States, but it also diverted resources—capital, armed forces personnel, materials, skilled labor, engineers, and scientists—from nonmilitary production. In 1988, for example, over 65 percent of federal R&D monies were allocated to defense, compared with 0.5 percent to environmental protection and 0.2 percent to industrial development. Moreover, while engaging Moscow in an expensive arms race, America has had to compete for world market shares against allies like Japan and Germany which have allocated smaller percentages of their national resources to the military, thus freeing capital, personnel, and R&D for commercial manufacture that has undermined parts of the American industrial base. Not surprisingly, this has provoked American demands that allies contribute more to the common defense, or that major retrenchments occur in American defense spending in favor of domestic needs.[15]

Although this controversy usually focuses on the question of whether high defense spending causes economic slowdown, the issue is not as simple as that.* Much more important is the structure of an economy that bears large defense expenditures. If that economy is growing briskly, possesses a flourishing manufacturing base, is at the forefront of new technologies, enjoys a strong flow of skilled labor, scientists and technologists, invests heavily in R&D, is in balance (or surplus) on its current accounts, and is not an international debtor, then it is far better *structured* to allocate 3 or 6 or even 9 percent of its GNP to defense than if it lacks those advantages.[16]

In fact, given the size and complexity of the American economy, it is impossible to categorize it as either hopelessly weak or immensely strong; it is a mixture of strengths and weaknesses.

The single most important fact is that rates of growth have slowed considerably in the final third of this century compared with the middle third, as shown in Chart 12.

Whatever the explanation for this slowdown, the consequences are serious for the United States, with its internal and external obligations. With a high, fairly evenly distributed standard of living, a favorable current-accounts balance, and no foreign commitments, a country like Switzerland, perhaps, or Luxembourg, might suffer a long period of sluggish economic growth and the results, although depressing, might not be serious. But the United States is the world's foremost military power, with commitments all over the globe; its wealth, while considerable, is unevenly distributed, resulting in immense social problems at home; it has a large current-accounts deficit and needs to borrow from foreigners. Given those circumstances, a prolonged period of slow growth compounds its existing problems, making it unlikely that the United States can continue to fund the same level of military security *and* attend to its social needs *and* repay its debts. A country where *real* weekly incomes have fallen steadily since 1973—as in this case—is ever less inclined to fund even the worthiest needs.

Such a dilemma is intensified if other nations are growing faster, leading to changes in economic relationships. The leading Great Power

*In some cases, defense spending can boost economic growth, as the United States discovered in World War II. Again, a reduction in defense expenditures may do little or nothing to assist a country's economic growth if the amount "saved" is then returned into a society which spends it upon imported automobiles, wines, and VCRs; whereas if the same amount were channeled toward productive investment, the economic results could be very different.

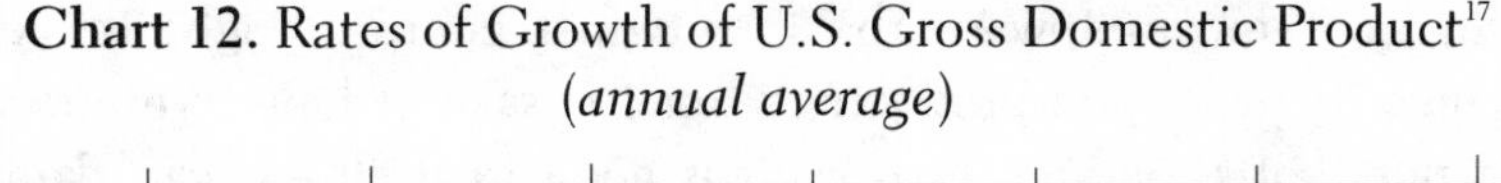

Chart 12. Rates of Growth of U.S. Gross Domestic Product[17]
(annual average)

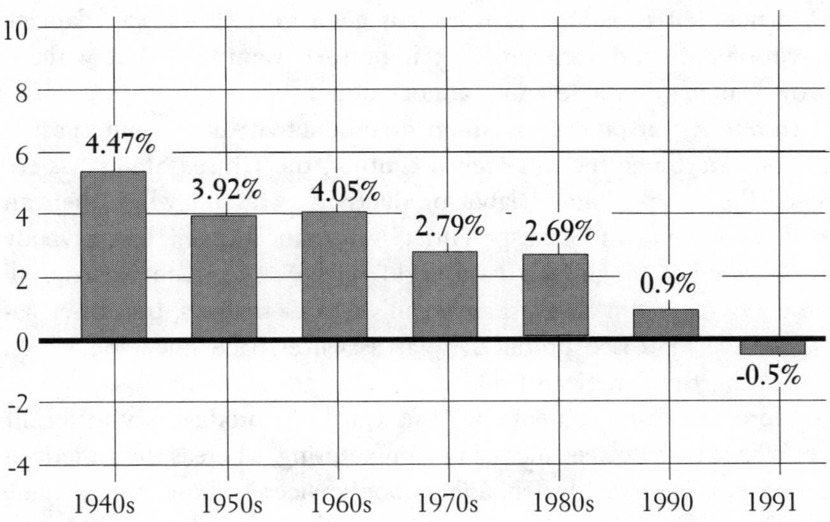

simply cannot maintain its status indefinitely if its economy is in relative decline.[18] Moreover, because this decline is relative and gradual, it is insidious, not dramatic; as one economic historian has noted, "a country whose productivity growth lags 1 percent behind other countries over one century can turn, as England did, from the world's undisputed industrial leader into the mediocre economy it is today."[19] It also turned from a first-class to a second-class power. Presumably, that reasoning was behind Mrs. Thatcher's recent declaration that it would be a "disaster" if the American economy were to grow—as some forecast—more slowly than Japan's in the 1990s.[20] From a realist viewpoint, that would erode America's world position, causing a further shift in the balance from Washington to Tokyo.*

This suggests that the fundamental strategic objective of the United

*Statistically, this is relatively easy to calculate. Suppose the American economy of $4.8 trillion (1988) grew at an average annual pace of 2 percent for the rest of the century: its size would reach $6.1 trillion by 2000, adjusted for inflation. If the Japanese economy of $2.8 trillion (1988) grew at an average annual pace of 4 percent, its size would then be $4.56 trillion. This simple projection makes no allowance for a possible strengthening of the yen—in consequence of greater growth—which would close the gap even more.

States as it moves toward the twenty-first century ought to be to enhance its per capita productivity for the sake of long-term growth. It is not that economic expansion is good in itself—it can damage environments and societies, if it is pursued wantonly—but without growth many desirable aims cannot be met.

In recent years, however, American productivity has become a cause of concern. Since the nineteenth century, the United States has enjoyed the world's highest labor productivity, which is why American national income and "war potential" were much larger than anybody else's when it fought the two world wars.[21] At present, its overall productivity is still larger than Japan's and Germany's, but other nations have increased productivity at a swifter pace since the 1960s, narrowing the American lead.

Moreover, improvements in American labor productivity in recent years have taken place chiefly in manufacturing, whereas the American economy is increasingly dependent upon services,* whose average value of output per employee is low compared with manufacturing or agriculture. Thus an annual increase in manufacturing productivity of 3 percent probably translates into a national rate of growth of 1 percent. Furthermore, much of the enhanced productivity of American industry in the 1980s came not—as in Japan—from higher output per *existing* worker, but from closing factories and cutting the work force, for productivity can increase faster during a recession when lots of jobs are lost than in a period of growth when cost-cutting is less urgent; and productivity increases often accompany actual reductions in overall output.[22]

America's growing indebtedness, the frailty of its financial system, and its persistent deficits in trade and current accounts would also be relieved by increased productivity. Indebtedness occurs at various levels. Nationally, it results from the U.S. government and Congress declining to pay the increasing cost of defense and social programs by additional taxes, a trend already evident in the 1960s, and perpetuated by both Democratic and Republican administrations; it was greatly accelerated by the Reagan government's decision to decrease taxation and increase defense spending during the 1980s. In 1960 the federal

*A few years ago, services accounted for roughly 68 percent of GNP and 71 percent of jobs.

deficit totaled $59.6 billion and the national debt $914.3 billion.[23] In 1991, despite pledges by White House and Congress to get spending "under control," additional expenditures—cleaning up nuclear facilities, bank bailouts—pushed the deficit well over $300 billion, while the national debt itself approached $4 *trillion,* which does *not* include the federal government's other obligations of around $6 trillion under various programs (crop guarantees, loans to farmers and students, insurance programs). Interest payments on the national debt are around $300 billion annually and represent 15 percent of government spending. As the economics editor of the *Wall Street Journal* has noted, interest payments now exceed "the combined amounts that government spends on health, science, space, agriculture, housing, the protection of the environment, and the administration of justice." Not only are these charges likely to increase,* at the expense of other government outlays, but a rising amount of those interest payments are to *foreign* owners of U.S. Treasury bonds, further reducing America's wealth. Finally, if slow economic growth persists throughout the 1990s, the deficit may rise further, since federal receipts will not grow as fast as expenditures.[24]

It was not only the national debt which soared during the 1980s, but every other form of debt. State and local governments began to experience deficits from 1986 onward—a trend exacerbated by cuts in federal grants. Consumer debt, fueled by "easy money" incentives, reached $4 trillion, while repayments diminished personal income. Corporate debt was even worse: "as the 1990s began, about 90 percent of the total after-tax income of U.S. corporations went to pay interest on their debt." Although beginning to slow due to rising economic worries, public and private debt equaled roughly 180 per cent of GNP, a level not seen since the 1930s.[25]

Deficits in the balance of payments and current accounts represented a further change from the 1950s and 1960s, when America had large surpluses in merchandise trade and current accounts.[26] Since 1971—when the United States recorded its first merchandise-trade deficit in over a century—it has consistently bought more than it has

*These totals will also be exacerbated by the coming of Social Security deficits, discussed on pp. 311–12 below.

sold. By 1987 the trade deficit reached a staggering $171 billion, and although the decline in the value of the dollar brought the total down by the later 1980s, deficits of over $100 billion were still being recorded. If the American economy was able to cover its "visible" trade deficit through earnings in "invisibles" such as services, investment income, and tourism, as Britain did before 1914, the position would be less serious; but American invisible earnings are insufficient to close the gap. As a result, the United States now pays its way by borrowing from foreigners roughly $100 billion each year. Once the world's largest creditor, the United States has by some measures become the world's largest debtor nation within less than a decade.[27] The longer this continues, the more American assets—equities, land, industrial companies, Treasury bonds, media conglomerates, laboratories—are acquired by foreign investors.

The heart of the trade deficit problem lies in the long-term erosion of America's relative manufacturing position, which may seem a curious fact when so much of the economy is in services. Yet, by their nature, many service activities (landscape gardening, catering, public transport) cannot be exported, and even where earnings from services are considerable (consultancy, legal work, patents, banking fees), the total doesn't pay for the goods and services imported each year.* Manufacturing is vital for other reasons: it accounts for virtually all of the research and development done by American industry, and a flourishing and competitive manufacturing base is still "fundamentally important to national security."[28]

Any attempt to summarize the present condition and future prospects of American manufacturing, however, is confronted by its extraordinary diversity. Some of its largest companies are world leaders, and many smaller firms (in computer software, for example) are unequaled in what they do. Others, however, are reeling from foreign competition, and their plight is the subject of innumerable commissions, studies, working parties, and congressional hearings. An entire industry (alas, not very distinguished either in manufacturing productivity or in its contribution to the balance of payments) has now

*For example, the total value of goods and services imported into the United States in 1987 was $550 billion, whereas the gross export of services was about $57 billion.

emerged devoted to studying American "competitiveness."[29] The overall picture that emerges is of an industrial structure which, though it has many strengths, no longer occupies the unchallenged position it did in the first two postwar decades.

While this is not a picture of unrelieved gloom, the rise of foreign competition in industry after industry has obviously increased the American merchandise-trade deficit. As Chart 13 reveals, out of eight key manufacturing sectors only chemicals and commercial aircraft were producing an export surplus by the late 1980s.

These deficits occur across a range of industries, from low-per-capita-value-added products like textiles to high-technology goods such as computer-controlled machine tools and luxury automobiles. This does not suggest an economy deliberately moving out of low-level production into more sophisticated sectors, as some have suggested, but one battling at all levels.

Unsurprisingly, the debate over "competitiveness" has not produced unanimity. Appeals for protection from hard-hit industries are opposed by those who fear retaliation in export markets, and by laissez-faire economists. Attacks upon foreigners' buying into America are countered by the argument that Japanese and European companies bring expertise, job opportunities, and much-needed capital. "Buy American" campaigns are resisted by those who feel that consumers should be free to purchase goods regardless of their nationality of origin. Calls for an industrial policy are denounced by groups who feel that government-led actions would be inefficient and contrary to American traditions. Some claim that the relative economic decline is due to a single cause, whereas others offer many reasons, from poor management to low levels of investment, from insufficient technical skills to excessive government regulations. The debate echoes one which took place a century ago in Britain, when a "national efficiency" movement emerged in response to the growing evidence that Britain's lead in manufacturing was being lost.[30]

The present concern about the condition of the U.S. economy is also fueled by a broader unease regarding the implications for national security, for American *power,* and for its position in world affairs. What if foreigners acquire a monopoly in industries that make strategic products for the Pentagon, or if an important military-related item is made

Chart 13. Trade Balances in Eight U.S. Industries[31]

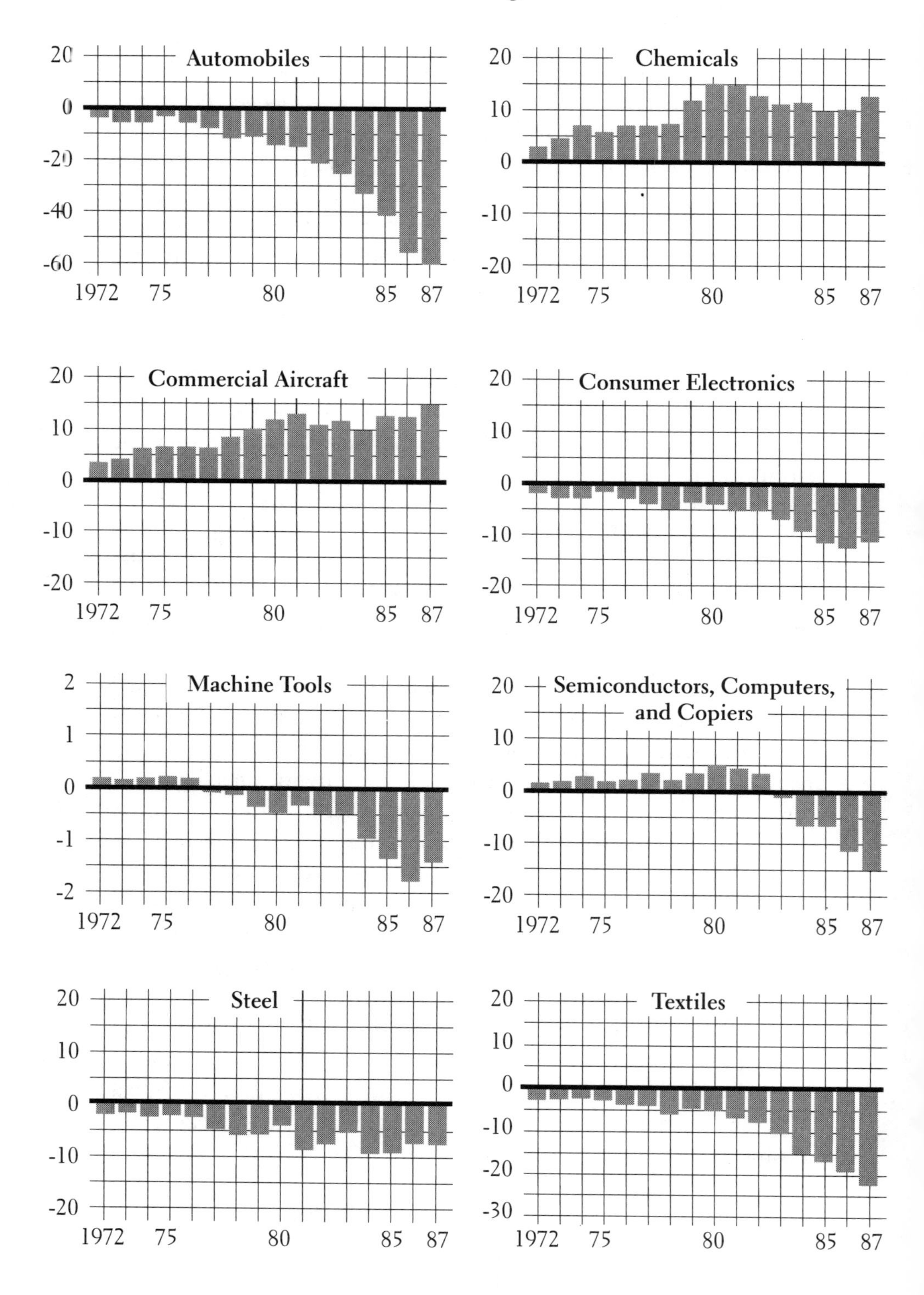

only abroad? What if the country becomes ever more reliant upon foreign capital—will it one day pay a political price as well as a financial one for that dependency? What if its industrial base is further eroded, while it continues with defense expenditures six or ten times higher than those of other countries—will it, instead of "running the risk" of imperial overstretch, finally have reached that condition?[32] What if the economy grows only half as swiftly as Japan's, or the European Community's, for the next decade or two—will not the productive power balances continue to shift,* so that the United States will no longer be Number One? These apprehensions may appear old-fashioned to certain economists—in their view, a sign of "residual thinking" in an age where the nation-state is no longer central and the key issues are about the quality of life rather than rank in the global pecking order[33]—but one suspects that they will remain deeply felt, for all that.

What is one to make of this controversy? To the optimists, what has been happening is perfectly understandable. In the postwar decades the United States occupied an artificially high position in world affairs, because other powers had been damaged by the conflict; as they recovered, the American share of world product, manufacturing, high technologies, financial assets, and even military capacity was bound to fall. Yet the United States remains the most important nation in the world, in economic and military power, diplomatic influence, and political

*J. Zysman, "U.S. Power, Trade and Technology," *International Affairs,* vol. 67, no. 1 (January 1991), p. 90, records the following shifts:

U.S. Output as Percentage of Output in:

	1970	*1975*	*1980*	*1986*	*1987*
Japan	495	317	254	214	188
Germany	547	371	330	469	401
France	706	462	409	576	507
U.K.	820	673	502	764	649
Japan and France	291	188	156	167	137
Japan and Germany	260	173	144	147	128
EEC	158	113	93	131	104
EEC and Japan	113	77	64	77	67

Although the short-lived rise in the value of the dollar (see 1986 column) caused a certain recovery for a while, the overall trend is unmistakable—and would be more marked were the statistics updated to 1991.

culture, though certain domestic reforms are needed.[34] American industry was unprepared for the intensity of foreign competition—and paid a price for that—but since the 1980s it has become leaner and fitter, its productivity has shot up, and it is moving into new technologies and products with unequaled strengths, especially research personnel. The advantages of such competitors as Japan will not last for long. With the dollar's reduced exchange rate and continuous upgrading of American manufacturing, the economy will rebound into prolonged growth, turn the deficits into surpluses, and respond vigorously to what were merely temporary difficulties.[35]

To the pessimists, such reasoning is a sign that many Americans have failed to understand the seriousness of the problem. It is not the country's relative economic decline in the two decades following 1945 that concerns them, since that clearly was the "natural" result of the rebuilding of other economies; it is the evidence that the American position relative to other nations has continued to erode *since* the 1960s in new technologies and patents, key manufacturing industries, financial assets and current-account balances, and international purchasing power. Most pessimists would, no doubt, be delighted to be proved wrong and dislike being called "defeatists" or "declinists." But they remain skeptical of the vague argument that America's "specialness" or "genius" or "capacity to respond to challenge" will somehow restore its position, seeing in such rhetoric the same ethnocentric pride which prevented earlier societies from admitting and responding to decline. While writing about the future, therefore, the pessimists are affected by a sense of the past, and worry that the leadership's indifference to the processes of global historical change may damage America's long-term prospects.[36]

While much of the controversy over American "decline and renewal" naturally focuses upon the economy, failures in the educational system, the social fabric, the people's well-being, even their political culture, are also much debated—presumably for fear that the causes of noncompetitiveness may be more profound than, for example, an inadequate savings rate. Characteristic of this thinking is the assumption that somehow the American people have taken a wrong path. As the popular television commentator John Chancellor expresses it:

> The strength is there, but it is being sapped by a combination of weaknesses—a thousand wounds we find difficult to heal. We have weakened ourselves in the way we practice our politics, manage our businesses, teach our children, succor our poor, care for our elders, save our money, protect our environment, and run our government.[37]

His conclusion is, therefore, that all sorts of changes are required before the United States can return to its earlier state of well-being.[38] Yet how likely such a recovery would be—even if there were a broad public response to his call—is entirely unclear.

To the daily readers of American newspapers, the list of ailments will be drearily familiar: for example, a health-care industry which doubled the number of its employees in the 1980s—thus *worsening* overall labor productivity—and which consumes around 12 percent of GNP, more than twice the share for defense, yet does not provide decent health care for many citizens. In fact, some 37 million Americans lack health insurance, and suffer accordingly. By the end of the 1980s, the number of poor people with health problems—such as babies born with syphilis or AIDS—was steadily rising; in the black community, where half the children under six live below the poverty line, health problems are severe and compounded by poverty. Lacking a national health system, "the U.S. occupies last place among the major industrialized countries . . . in child mortality, life expectancy, and visits to the doctor," although it probably leads the world in politicians who talk about "family values."[39] While life expectancy for older white men and women has increased (much of the rise in health-care spending has gone to those over seventy-five), that for black women and especially black men has fallen.*[40] Because of this widespread poverty, Oxfam America—famous for its aid to developing countries—announced in 1991 that it would also focus, for the first time ever, upon the United States itself.

*The only other example of this decline in life expectancy in a developed society, as noted above (p. 235), was among Russian males. Is it simply coincidence that this took place among the world's two military superpowers?

This uneven health care reflects the structure of wealth and income in contemporary America, where on average managers earn over ninety times as much as industrial workers (up from forty times as much in 1980), but where 30 percent of African-Americans and 20 percent of Hispanics earn less than the official poverty line and live in slums. It is exacerbated by the amount of drugs Americans consume; according to one estimate, the United States—with 4 to 5 percent of the world's population—consumes 50 percent of the world's cocaine. Such addictions strain health-care services, and not simply in the treatment of adults; in 1989 alone, approximately 375,000 Americans were *born* addicted to drugs, mainly cocaine and heroin.[41]

Drugs in turn feed crime, which is significantly higher in the United States than anywhere else in the developed world. Thanks to the political power of the National Rifle Association, Americans have access to deadly weapons—and use them—to a degree that astounds observers abroad. Americans possess an estimated 60 million handguns and 120 million long guns, and kill one another at a rate of around 19,000 each year, chiefly with handguns. Homicide rates per capita are four to five times higher than in Western Europe (while rape rates are seven times higher, and forcible robbery rates some four to ten times higher).[42] Experts suggest that this violence has cultural roots, and cannot simply be linked to poverty; New York's homicide rate is far larger than that in the slums of Calcutta, for example, and in prosperous Seattle—recently rated number one city in the United States for "livability"—the murder rate is seven times that of Birmingham, England.[43] Nor is violence due to lack of police efforts and deterrents; at the last count, American prisons were holding over a million convicted prisoners, a proportion of the population larger even than in South Africa or the former USSR.* Three thousand out of every 100,000 black American males are in prison, whereas South Africa managed to preserve apartheid by imprisoning 729 black males per 100,000.[44]

Doubling the number of people behind bars during the 1980s has not been very effective, therefore, in dealing with the erosion of America's social fabric, partly because of the difficulty of attempting major

*The United States imprisons criminals at a rate of 426 per 100,000 of its population. The rate in Australia is 72, in the Netherlands only 40. The Soviet rate was 268 per 100,000. Blacks, who form 12 percent of America's population, supply nearly half of its prisoners.

social reforms in a politically decentralized, libertarian society.[45] Any attempt to alleviate homelessness and poverty in the inner cities—and the rural South—might cost a great deal of money, and a transfer of resources from the better off (who vote) to the poor (who don't). Since the Boston Tea Party, middle-class Americans have had a deep aversion to paying taxes—with some justification, since unlike Europeans they do not enjoy in return such middle-class benefits as free college tuition, health care, subsidized cultural events, efficient public-transport systems, and so on.[46] Because politicians who favor tax rises are punished at the polls, the temptation is ever present to meet unavoidable fresh demands such as the S&L bailout and rising interest charges on the national debt by borrowing rather than by increasing revenues; and it is almost as tempting to suggest that money is unavailable for social and health-care reforms, however desirable. Perhaps funds could be made available if productivity and real growth were bounding upward; when they are not, changes in spending priorities become part of a "zero-sum game," blocked by groups who would lose out.[47]

But Americans have been willing to invest heavily in education. In 1989 over $350 billion was spent on public and private education, to support 45 million pupils enrolled in primary and secondary schools, as well as nearly 13 million college and university students. In absolute terms, only Switzerland allocates more money per pupil; relatively, the United States devotes 6.8 percent of GNP to education, which is equal to that of Canada and the Netherlands and ahead of education's share in Japan, France, or Germany.[48]

In return the United States could claim, with some justification, to have one of the finest systems of higher education in the world. Apart from many superb liberal-arts colleges, it boasts state university systems that educate an impressive number of students. Above all, it possesses the world's greatest array of research universities and scientific institutes, with faculty recruited from around the globe, achieving disproportionately high international recognition (e.g., Nobel Prizes) and attracting students from many lands. The resources of intellectual powerhouses like Harvard, Yale, and Stanford—with endowments of billions of dollars—are equaled by their high performance and their global reputation. From them emerge annual cohorts of scientific and creative personnel upon which the American economy depends.

Apart from higher education, however, the picture is less favorable. Many Americans are worried by the growing evidence that *general* levels of pre-eighteen public education are relatively mediocre. Since the early 1960s, the scores achieved on Scholastic Aptitude Tests—for what they are worth—have fallen considerably. Despite the opportunities offered by the free mass public education system, pupils are abandoning it in record numbers; between 600,000 and 700,000 drop out of high school each year, which is one-fifth of all high school pupils (and closer to one-half of those at inner-city high schools).[49] Moreover, although the 1980 U.S. census ambitiously and perhaps misleadingly reported a literacy level of almost 100 percent, various studies claim that millions of Americans—the figures range from 23 to 84 (!) million—are functionally illiterate; according to one, 25 million adults cannot read well enough to understand a warning label on a medicine bottle, and 22 percent of adults are unable to address a letter correctly.[50]

How does this compare *internationally*? In a recent standardized science test administered to ninth-graders in seventeen countries, American students finished behind those of Japan, South Korea, and every Western European country, and ahead only of those in Hong Kong and the Philippines. In a test of mathematical proficiency (1988), American eighth-graders were close to the bottom. Other tests reveal that the American ranking *worsens* as children get older—although, ironically, over two-thirds of the high school pupils felt that they were "good" at mathematics whereas less than one-quarter of the South Koreans (who actually scored much higher) felt that way.[51] Only 15 percent of high school students study *any* foreign language, and a minuscule 2 percent pursue one for more than two years.[52] Surveys of the average high school pupil's knowledge of basic history have also revealed great ignorance (for example, of what the Reformation meant), eclipsed only by their geographical illiteracy; one in seven adult Americans tested recently could not locate his or her own country on a world map, and 75 percent could not place the Persian Gulf—even though in the late 1980s many of them favored dispatching U.S. forces to that region.[53] The National Commission on Excellence in Education noted in its landmark 1983 report *A Nation at Risk,* "If an unfriendly foreign power had attempted to impose on America the mediocre educational performance that exists today, we might well have viewed it as an act of war."[54]

Despite the many studies devoted to the problem, the root cause is still not clear. Certain experts caution against drawing too severe conclusions from the declining SAT scores and international tests, recalling that the United States is educating a far larger proportion for its population for much longer than it was forty years ago; by the same token, it may be erroneous to compare the knowledge of the average American high school pupil with that of children in more selective systems overseas.[55] It may also be misleading to compare educational standards of a melting-pot society with demographically stable and ethnically homogeneous countries like Sweden and Japan.

More prosaically, one might note that although America spends large amounts on education as a whole, a disproportionate 40 percent goes to higher education (which may explain why American universities rate high internationally), whereas the share going to other education is less than in other countries.*[56] Again, American pupils attend school for considerably *fewer* days each year (175 to 180 is normal) than their equivalents in Western Europe (200+) and Japan (220+). If by the age of eighteen the average Japanese or South Korean has had the equivalent of three or four years more school than the average American, is it surprising that they know much more algebra and physics?[57] Finally, while the United States is one of the few developed societies lacking nationally mandated education standards which are assessed by uniform national exams—the chief reason a National Research Council investigation on mathematics education felt that "the top-down systems have beaten us hands down"[58]—any suggestion of copying the other democracies is resisted by school boards, education authorities, teachers' unions, and all who celebrate the country's decentralized traditions.

To other experts, technical alterations are less significant than the social culture within which American education has to operate. Displaying nostalgia for what seemed better days—when high school pupils supposedly worked harder and achieved higher scores—some

*The United States spends 4.1 percent of GNP upon primary and secondary education, lagging behind Switzerland (5.8 percent), Japan (4.8 percent), Germany (4.6 percent), and most other industrial nations.

critics suggest, "The crisis is not in the schools but in us. The society we have constructed has given us the education we deserve."[59] The "trivialization" of American culture, meaning the emphasis upon consumer gratification, pop culture, cartoons, noise, color, and entertainment over serious reflection, is portrayed as a self-inflicted wound. Apparently, the average American child has watched five thousand hours of television even before entering school, and by graduation that total will be nearly twenty thousand hours. This anti-intellectual youth culture—continued later by the fascination with sports or "soap" shows—is not helped by the disintegration of the family, especially among African-Americans, which requires so many mothers to cope on their own; or by the great rise in female employment, so that (as is not the case in East Asian societies) the "first educator," the mother, is absent from the home for most of the day. Apart from certain groups who place strong emphasis on the value of education (Jews, Asian-Americans), the average American child is said to be picking up the value system of a shallow entertainment industry rather than the moral standards, discipline, and intellectual curiosity that equip a person to learn. To ask the schools, especially in the inner cities, to remedy this social-cum-cultural crisis is simply to demand too much.[60]

While a fair-minded reader of this gloomy literature may think it too cataclysmic—are the education systems in *other* countries free of problems?—the chief fact is that the literature exists, affecting the national debate about the future. If the average American is poorly educated, does that not also contribute to a trivialization of electoral campaigns, with slogans like "Read my lips," "Make my day," and "Morning in America"? Does an inadequate school system lead to an erosion of proper democratic debate to meet television's demands for quick answers? Is this why fewer and fewer citizens vote?[61] If the average American has little interest in foreign cultures and cannot locate the Persian Gulf on a map, how is he or she to comprehend issues of intervention abroad, or to understand the need for increases in development aid, or to learn about globally driven changes? Is that sort of knowledge to be left to a minority (say, 15 percent of the population, as at the time of the Founding Fathers) consisting of professional-class families whose members *did* go to the right schools and colleges, and whose standards of living, frequency of foreign travel, and access to the international economy have increased nicely throughout the 1980s?[62]

Despite these worrying tendencies, many commentators stress the positive features of their bustling, variegated society. The United States is still the largest economy in the world (unless one counts the European Community as a whole). It is attractive to millions of immigrants each year, and many more who can't get in. Its popular culture is visible around the world, and its language is dominant in business, science, and entertainment. Its commitment to liberty and democracy has inspired oppressed peoples everywhere from China to Czechoslovakia. It is the exemplar of the capitalist system, which its ideological foes challenged and lost. Because of its great military power and diplomatic influence, all eyes usually turn to Washington when an international crisis occurs. Americans, according to the unabashed optimists, should be celebrating their triumphs, their culture, their ideology, their way of life, their "noble national experience . . . the most universally attractive of our era."[63] Even the more cautious "revivalists" may admit that domestic reforms are needed, but argue that the chief danger is that the American people *think* the country is poor and impotent when it is in fact rich and powerful. If it can simply shake off its present mood and make certain adjustments, it will be the world's leading nation in the twenty-first century, just as it has been for the past fifty years.[64]

Despite such optimism, a widespread *Angst* remains. When a conservative columnist such as George Will objects to the levels of poverty and crime across the nation and notes "a gnawing, growing sense that savagery and second-ratedness are increasing in America,"[65] it is clear that the debate about the country's future is no longer one between right and left as in the Vietnam War years, but cuts across traditional party and ideological lines.[66] Discussions over an "industrial policy" or school reform or protectionism reveal new internal groupings and alliances, in its way a sort of domestic counterpart to the changing, uncertain shape of international politics. The very fact that by the late 1980s more Americans thought the Japanese economic challenge to be a greater danger than the Soviet military challenge inevitably provoked a debate over spending and policy priorities different from that of the Nixon years.

All this presents the United States with a dilemma. Apart from a few unreconstructed optimists like George Gilder or Ben Wattenberg who hold that the country is moving effortlessly upward, opinion polls show that most citizens feel things have worsened—in the social fabric, race relations, public education, economic performance, the conditions of the average American family—and will be worse for their children and grandchildren. This has led to a demand for changes: some want the tax system altered, others want the schools overhauled, or a transformation in health-care provision, or changes in industrial policy, or an all-out assault on poverty, or on crime; many Americans would like all of the above. But since most reforms would require a transfer of resources, and since some of them would imply a change in life-styles (a longer school year, for example, or much higher energy taxes), each individual reform provokes opposition.

Reforms that challenge existing arrangements are never easy in a democracy; but the American political structure in particular offers the most marvelous opportunities to *obstruct* changes. The constitutional division of powers means that the president lacks the authority of, say, the British prime minister and cabinet to get legislation swiftly enacted. The relative absence of party discipline makes each member of Congress more independent, but the unrestrained costs of electoral campaigning also make that member reliant upon funding from supporters and interest groups (Political Action Committees) and highly sensitive to the threat that a powerful lobby—the pro-Israel coalition, the National Rifle Association, pro- and anti-abortion movements, the groups representing retired Americans—will campaign against a congressman if it is offended by his or her policies. Consequently, efforts to slash the budget deficit, or trim Medicaid costs, or restrict gun sales usually founder in the "gridlock" of Washington politics.[67] A fragmented political system, coexisting in a social culture which asserts, "Let everyone do his or her own thing," is not the ideal location in which to push through reforms. The very notion of reforming or retooling American society to *make* it more competitive is itself a contradiction of the laissez-faire ethos.

Because of this gridlock, many frustrated citizens seem ready for drastic change, as could be seen in the surge of support for Ross Perot's populist policies in the summer of 1992. Other critics call for some form of national shock therapy. In John Chancellor's words, "What the country needs is a peacetime Pearl Harbor to shake it up, to make Americans aware of the trouble they're in, to tap their energy and their willingness to work."[68] Yet, although it is often claimed that the United States is in a commercial "war" with rival countries, the military analogy is unconvincing, for individual Americans benefit from selling things to Japan, buying that country's products, and receiving its capital. In any case, whatever one believes has "gone wrong" with America, the decline has been a steady and insidious process, quite different from the dramatic aerial assault on Pearl Harbor. One is also bound to wonder whether the circumstances surrounding a major national crisis—one of the favorite scenarios is a banking or stock market collapse—will really lead to bold structural reforms in public education, inner-city poverty, and the level of R&D investment.

How will American society in its present condition interact with the broad forces for global change described in Part One of this book? How well prepared is the United States for the twenty-first century?

Clearly, the United States is going to be affected in many ways by demographic trends. While its population is forecast to grow steadily over the next few decades,* significant changes will occur *within* that population. There will, for example, be many more elderly people by the early twenty-first century. Whereas there were only 16.6 million Americans aged sixty-five and over in 1960, the figure had virtually doubled to approximately 31 million by 1990; after slow rises over the next decade or two, it is then forecast to leap to 52 million in 2020 and 65.5 million in 2030—by which time there will be more elderly people than children.[69] The numbers of people over seventy-five and even over eighty-five—an age group for which the health-care costs per person are disproportionately high—will grow the fastest of all. This means not only that the political power of retirees' organizations will be greater, but also that there could be a further diversion of resources toward

*According to *World Resources 1990–91,* p. 254, America's population will rise from 249 million (1990) to 301 million by 2025. Much depends, of course, upon the annual inflow of legal and illegal immigrants over the next thirty years.

elderly care*—resources that, economically at least, would be better employed in preventing child poverty or improving infrastructure.[70] Over the longer term, however, the most serious consequence will be that the Social Security funds—at present still in surplus, and helping to disguise the true size of the federal deficit—will simply run out, causing a crisis not only in health provisions for the average elderly American, but also in the fiscal system. The politicians then in charge, facing a federal deficit worsened by Social Security losses, will have to make unpleasant choices: slash Social Security provisions *or* other forms of federal spending, or vastly increase taxes upon the relatively smaller proportion of "productive" Americans to pay for the swollen costs of caring for the fast-growing numbers of over-sixty-five-year-olds. The only other alternative would be to risk enormous federal deficits and consequent financial instability.

Meanwhile, the ethnic composition of the United States is also changing. Although the forecasts are subject to amendment—many earlier predictions of the future population of the United States have tended to be notoriously inaccurate—demographers are reasonably confident that the white, Caucasian segment will continue to shrink. This is partly due to the expectation of further large-scale immigration, both legal and illegal, chiefly from Latin America and Asia; as "have-not" families stream to "have" societies, America is seen as the most desirable *and* accessible destination to many migrants. The second reason is the differentiated birth rate between white and most non-white ethnic groups, which has socioeconomic causes but is also affected by different gender roles, women's expectations, and access to higher education. In consequence, some demographers refer to the "browning" of America by 2050, as Caucasians become a minority.[71]

Other experts forecast that this transformation will be less swift because over time immigrants and minorities will conform to white reproductive patterns.[72] Nevertheless, these trends toward the simultaneous "graying" and "browning" of America are going to have lasting consequences. Some writers worry that an aging United States will stagnate economically and call for increased immigration, reminding

*Already (i.e., in 1987), Congress "spent $10,010 per capita on the elderly and only $854 per child." R. D. Lamm, "Again, Age Beats Youth," *New York Times,* 2 December 1990, p. E19.

readers that successive waves of migrants have fueled the country's rise in the past; this argument is often accompanied by gloomy prognoses about Europe's and Japan's long-term prospects as they grapple with demographic decline, yet seek to prevent an inflow of newcomers. Others point uneasily to the fact that most recent immigrants to America have relatively low educational and skill levels, congregate in the inner cities—few of them help to compensate for the declining populations of Great Plains townships—and impose additional demands upon the social and educational services of the poorest parts of the American administrative structure. Demographers predict that perhaps as many as 15 million immigrants will arrive each decade for the next thirty years, and calls are now being made to "bar the door."[73]

Demographic change can also exacerbate ethnic tensions, as between African-Americans and Hispanic-Americans (over jobs), or Asian-Americans and African-Americans (over educational access), as well as stimulate the racial worries of poor whites. Over the longer term, the graying/browning tendency may be setting up a massive contest over welfare and entitlement priorities between predominantly Caucasian retirees and predominantly nonwhite children, mothers, and unemployed, each with its vocal advocacy organizations.* Perhaps predictably, some authors now call for a debate about the implications of "bright, well-educated American women" giving birth to fewer and fewer children.[74]

These outcomes are, at the moment, hypothetical, whereas the political and economic consequences of America's demographic transformation are easier to estimate. Simply because the regional electoral balances (e.g., share of seats in the House of Representatives) do, over time, reflect population change, there is likely to be a further shift in voting power from the North and East to the South and West, from Caucasian to non-Caucasian districts, from Europe/Israel-centered issues to Hispanic/Pacific concerns. The executive, judiciary, and legislative branches, at present with a mere sprinkling of nonmale, nonwhite members, will find it difficult to halt their metamorphosis into bodies

*California, whose population rose by 30 percent in the 1980s alone, is still the favored destination of millions south of the border. In consequence of higher birth rates and continued immigration, half of all children in the state are forecast to be Hispanic by 2030, when whites will compose 60 percent of the elderly population—a troublesome mismatch.

containing many more women and minorities. Schools and colleges, already grappling with the demands to teach both "multiculturalism" and "Western civilization," may come under further social and cultural pressures as the demographic tide advances.[75]

Demographic change will also affect the American economy, both in the composition of its work force and in the larger issue of American competitiveness in a future which, forecasters assert, will be dominated by knowledge-based societies. According to a common economic theory, the United States rose to world preeminence because of its vast, easily accessible raw materials (oil, iron, coal) and foodstuffs, giving it an advantage over resource-poor Japan and Europe. Now that ample supplies of raw materials and food are produced all over the globe, that advantage is shrinking; and it will shrink further with the "dematerialization" of production and the many other changes in the way things are manufactured. Moreover, the continued explosion of scientific knowledge will be best exploited by societies that are steadily raising *overall* educational standards, technical training, and work-force skills, which America is not.[76]

Since the 1970s, the composition of the work force has changed significantly. While manufacturing cut many skilled and relatively high-paying blue-collar jobs, the boom in services created ever more low-paid, low-skill jobs (cleaners, restaurant personnel, drivers, health-care assistants, and the like), most of which paid less than $15,000 a year.[77] The other trend was the growth in white-collar, technical jobs, especially in information and research sectors of the economy, requiring advanced training and higher education. According to the Hudson Institute survey *Workforce 2000,* by the end of this century as many as 52 percent of *new* jobs may require at least some college education.[78]

Yet the supply of so many educated individuals is in doubt. For years the number of American Ph.D.s in mathematics and engineering (and faculty instructing them) has been inadequate, but while that may be another sign of a declining manufacturing culture, the shortfall can be made up by recruiting foreign doctoral students and professors. On the other hand, American industry has found it difficult to recruit workers to fill jobs not requiring a college education. The chairman of Xerox Corporation has declared that the skill levels of American society have "the makings of a natural disaster," while New York Telephone reports that it had to test a staggering 57,000 applicants to find 2,100 people qualified to fill entry-level jobs. As business spends ever more on training (the total may now be over $50 billion annually), there is increasing concern over the extent to which America's educational deficits will reduce economic competitiveness.[79]

Demographic trends suggest the worst is yet to come. Part of America's economic growth since World War II was simply the result of increases in both the overall population and the percentage entering the work force. However, during the 1990s the number of entrants into the work force will grow more slowly than in past decades,[80] unless boosted by a great influx of immigrants. The point here is not race per se, but educational access. Of the new entrants into the work force, white males—currently the best-educated sector of the population, especially in science, technology, and engineering—will constitute only 15 percent, and the rest will be women, minorities, and immigrants.[81] Since the latter two categories have generally gone into low-paid, unskilled jobs, there exists a potentially enormous mismatch between educational levels and the forecast demand for jobs requiring advanced technical or higher education. Unlike Germany, Sweden, or Japan, however, the United States does not possess a systematic approach to remedial training or, the experts say, to vocational education as a whole, preferring instead to retain haphazard, laissez-faire methods.[82]

It appears unlikely that in the near future deliberate federal policies will address this problem by giving additional funds to cities and states in the Southwest to help absorb the tide of immigrants, subsidizing Midwestern and Appalachian states to prevent further rural drift, or above all by a national scheme to finance training, remedial education, apprenticeships and the rest for the millions of poorly educated immigrants and minority schoolchildren who will become a steadily larger share of the work force. The states themselves, and local businesses, will bear the chief responsibility, and most of the costs—if anything is done at all.

Demographic trends also influence the long-term American response to robotics and automated manufacture. While intelligent robots are being designed for specialized circumstances (space exploration, undersea mining, hazardous-waste disposal) and the spiraling costs of U.S. health care may also compel the increasing use of field robots,* manufacturing as a whole has less incentive to automate production than in Japan. Although one might imagine that the "graying" of the Caucasian males among the American population would stimulate automation, the simultaneous "browning" trend provides a cheap labor pool in many repetitive jobs. Just as the relative cost of manual versus automated production hurt America's early lead in robotics, so is it likely that demography and work-force composition will slow any overall move to automated manufacturing.

This generality may not apply to certain sectors of industry—for example, to American factories owned by a Japanese multinational, or companies under pressure from East Asian competition *and* able to raise the capital to make large-scale investments in automation, or firms preferring robots to poorly trained workers. However, with the collapse of America's indigenous robotics industry, around 75 to 80 percent of robots sold to U.S. firms each year are imported, worsening the trade gap. Moreover, if the investment in robots is not accompanied by retraining the redundant workers by either the company itself (as in Japan) or the state (as in Sweden), then the decline in well-paid blue-collar employment would intensify, just as if the surviving workers are not trained to work with robots, the increases in output will be much less than expected.

American agriculture will also be challenged by the newer global forces for change, certainly by biotechnology and possibly by global warming. As argued earlier, the biotech revolution in farming and food processing appears to offer enticing prospects to the large pharmaceutical and agrochemical firms that have invested heavily in both research and production in this field and are constructing large factory complexes or "refineries" which, in essence, replace the traditional farm. As they also increasingly link up with giant food distribution and chain stores, conglomerates are emerging that will control every part of the process of providing food, from the seeds and fertilizer (or the *in vitro* hormones and genes) to the tinned and packaged goods in the supermarket.

*See pp. 84–85 above.

For American farmers themselves—and their communities—these trends are disturbing. Abundant agricultural output made the United States the reserve breadbasket of the world for the past century, earning large amounts of foreign currency. Because of improved technology, American farming is becoming *more* efficient each year; in fact, according to the U.S. Office of Technology Assessment, the United States has the capacity "not only to meet domestic demand, but also to contribute significantly to meeting world demand in the next twenty years," enough indeed to meet the expected 1.8 percent annual growth in world population.[83] While that forecast would be contested by environmental groups that believe that U.S. agriculture's long-term prospects are being damaged by overgrazing, loss of topsoil, decline in water supplies, excessive use of fertilizers, and other unwise methods which aided the original expansion of output,[84] there is no disputing that present productivity per hectare is impressive. But that itself is now a problem.

The challenges facing American farming are large-scale and structural. Even if only 3 percent of the total population is nowadays involved in farming, far more is produced than can be consumed at home. To avoid a crisis of agricultural overproduction—there have been several such crises since the late nineteenth century—farmers have pressed U.S. administrations to discover and open markets overseas. At present, however, such a solution is clouded by chronic imbalances in global supply and demand for farm products. Dozens of poor countries would welcome the continued flow of American food supplies, but have no funds to pay for them. Similarly, the erstwhile USSR and certain of its former Eastern European satellites require food to make up for their own farming deficiencies, but there is no way that those societies can themselves provide the hard currency required; they will need international aid. (In any case, if they do eventually manage to restructure agriculture, all or most of them could well become surplus food producers.) Efforts to lower or remove tariff barriers to American food imports into, say, Japan or Korea provoke violent reactions from local farmers.

Meanwhile the EC's common agricultural policy, which subsidizes and protects millions of farmers, has eroded American farm export shares in both European and third markets—compelling the U.S. government to subsidize its own farmers in expensive ways. Even if agreement were reached to phase out all such subsidies and price supports—which is highly unlikely—the greatest beneficiaries would probably be countries like Australia, New Zealand, and Argentina, whose farmers are efficient enough to oppose agricultural tariffs. While consumers might rejoice at the drop in food prices, many American farming communities would wither away.

With access to foreign markets limited and agricultural prices generally low—though boosted occasionally by drought or reports of fresh credits for Soviet purchases—American farmers struggle against the rising costs of energy and equipment, interest payments and depressed land prices, and the ultimate threat of foreclosure—all this in addition to the scourges of nature and the fact that much farmland is marginal and depends on tapping desert aquifers, the massive use of fertilizers, and so on. Meanwhile farmers are continually being offered improved seeds, newer strains of fruit and vegetables, more efficient fertilizers, all intended to increase local output—but with the macroeconomic effect of exacerbating the national food surplus.

It is upon this already troubled agricultural sector that biotechnology's innovations will make their impact. With artificial sweeteners having cut heavily into the American sugar market over the past decade, and with forecasts that the use of the bovine growth hormone to increase milk production could lead to a 50 percent reduction in the number of dairy farms by 2000, it is not surprising that some groups of farmers are campaigning against the new technologies. However, unless these innovations can be proved positively harmful to health or the environment—and are therefore banned by federal agencies—the response is likely to be mixed. Many better-capitalized farms could be attracted by the promise of greatly enhanced yields from "designer" herbicide-resistant seeds and the accompanying herbicides, or the greater productivity that will flow from new information-technology equipment, reckoning that they will survive the "shakeout" that this increased competition—and decreased prices—will bring.

What might this mean in overall numbers? One study by the U.S. Office of Technology Assessment calculated that the new biotechnology and information technologies would be adopted by more than 70 percent of the largest farms in the United States, but by only 40 percent of the moderate-sized farms and about 10 percent of small farms. Many of the nation's 2 million small farms are run by people with other income, so the impact there might be less. For the moderate-size full-time farms, traditionally the backbone of American agriculture, the results would be very serious as they struggled to compete. By 2000, the number of such farms might have shrunk to 75,000, compared with 180,000 in 1982. By contrast, the largest farms are expected to grow in size and efficiency, and by the end of the century a mere 50,000 of them could be producing around three-quarters of all agricultural output.[85] Whether they will still be regarded as farms or simply as the upstream production facilities of food-processing companies, with wage laborers supervised by corporate-style managers, is an open question.[86] In any case, the traditional style of farming, in middle America no less than rural France, is little prepared for the next century.

Given these prospects, it is to be hoped that the "greenhouse effect" does not result in the temperature rises forecast in the gloomier studies on global warming, for that would increase the pressures upon farmers whose livelihoods are already endangered by the biotech revolution. Consider, for example, the challenges which farms growing feed grains in the southern Great Plains will face over the next few decades. Not only do they have to confront the emergence of agribusinesses, they also face the depletion of water supplies from the Ogallala Aquifer and the possible effects of global warming—a swifter snowmelt in the mountains and less available river-fed water, higher evaporation rates and drier soils, and a northward movement of the growing regions. Although different in form, both the depletion of the aquifers and the rise in CO_2 result from the excessive use of a "shared resource" and contribute to a drying-out of the Great Plains.[87]

It is not simply the water resources and growing areas of the Plains states that would be affected by a significant rise in temperatures. Marine geologists, engineers, and hydrologists estimate that coastal shoreline retreat, which for various reasons is already taking place, will be accelerated by rising sea levels. According to one local study, Massachusetts may lose between three thousand and ten thousand acres of coastal upland by 2025. Since the higher figure assumes a sea-level rise of 1.57 feet over the next few decades, and the same study estimates that by 2100 Massachusetts will have experienced a sea-level rise between 5.5 and 8 feet (!), a considerable further retreat of the shoreline is implied.[88] In other, lower-lying coastal regions, from South Carolina to New Jersey, the retreat would be proportionately greater. Moreover, as coastal bluffs are eroded by higher waves and storm surges, salt water will move farther upstream and into coastal aquifers, contaminating water supplies at the same time that higher average temperatures create greater demand.[89] Some environmentalists suggest that it is a waste of time and resources to seek to check coastal erosion (by building seawalls, reinforcing the foundations of coastal properties, etc.), but local communities and property owners will obviously press for costly protection and restoration measures.

It is not just food crops that might migrate northward in response to global warming. Were carbon dioxide levels to double over the next century, some scientists predict that certain trees (beech, birch, hemlock, and sugar maple) would move five hundred kilometers north to find a more suitable habitat, so that beech forests would disappear from the southeastern United States. There is even more concern among biologists for the impact of such changes upon wildlife, particularly rare birds and animals attached to specialized and limited habitats. While human beings can at least plan to shift locations, plants and wildlife cannot; and although it is known that migration of trees has taken place (e.g., during post-ice-age warming), it occurred over thousands of years, not in the century or half century assumed in the global warming models.*[90]

Clearly, while some rural areas would lose from these migrations, others—in the northern states—would benefit from the rise in temperatures and longer growing seasons. Increased levels of CO_2 can stimulate plant yields. It is also likely that farmers would adjust by changing crop types and using plants with greater drought resistance. Since the global warming process is gradual—though it may be attended, some researchers claim, by increasing volatility and ferocity in the weather—American agriculture *as a whole* can adjust almost as well as American industry;[91] but for some regions and many traditional farmers adjust-

*At the end of the Pleistocene era ten to twelve thousand years ago, as the glaciers retreated and temperatures rose 3°–5°C, beech forests moved about twenty kilometers per century, far less than the five hundred kilometers forecast in the models for the next century.

ment may simply not be possible—for financial as much as ecological reasons.

Environmental changes *outside* the national boundaries are also affecting American society. For example, the recent flood of Haitian refugees to the United States was prompted by political turbulence, but a more important cause is that peasant landowners have eliminated the forests (only 2 percent of the land is still forested) and the subsequent exploitation and loss of topsoil have worn some areas down to the bedrock. With farmable land (only 11 percent of the whole) continuing to shrink, total fertility rates still very high, and population control negligible, more and more people—among a population already the poorest in the western hemisphere—are left with fewer and fewer resources. Given the mass unemployment rates of 30 percent, is it any surprise that many of them struggle to get to the United States and regard repatriation as close to a death sentence? And once they arrive in Florida or New York, is it a further surprise that—through no fault of their own—these immigrants are additional burdens upon the sorely pressed educational and social systems of the inner cities? Here, in microcosm, is an example of how entwined demographic growth, environmental damage, social and economic catastrophe, and mass migration have become.

It is while they confront these challenges that citizens of the United States are being urged to adjust to the borderless world of twenty-four-hour-a-day financial flows, electronic trading, and the globalization of business and communications. Since American society is regarded as the trailblazer in all these developments and their socioeconomic implications have been widely discussed,* there is no need to repeat the conclusions in detail here. The general sense is that America enjoys massive advantages in the form of giant multinationals and banks, traders, consultants and service industries, the dominance of the English language and (though declining) the U.S. dollar, an entrepreneurial culture, and numerous highly educated scientists, engineers, designers, lawyers, and other "symbolic analysts" whose skills are in global demand. On the other hand, the relocation of industries abroad, the increasing redundancy of various occupations, and the inadequate

*See above, pp. 58–60.

educational levels of many workers for high-tech employment suggest that the lower four-fifths (or more) of Americans may not enjoy the oft-proclaimed benefits of globalization. If demographic trends lead to a relative decline in the number of Americans with high scientific skills, if U.S. multinationals find themselves increasingly pitted against foreign rivals with larger capital resources and better-trained labor and conclude that they can only compete by moving production to (say) Mexico, and if American banks, media conglomerates, software companies, and R&D establishments continue to sell out to overseas firms, those benefits may appear ever less obvious.

If the above analysis is generally accurate, the United States may not be a "loser" in the face of global changes, as many desperate societies in the developing world will be; but because of its social and economic structure—its altering demographic pattern, its environmental problems, its educational and social deficits, its political-constitutional gridlock, its fiscal problems—it could be less than a clear "winner." What emerges instead is a mixed picture: some industries rising as others fall, traditional farms losing as agribusinesses gain, consultants flourishing as blue-collar workers face fewer opportunities, the slow growth in overall per capita GNP barely concealing the widening gap between those whose skills are in demand and those whose are not.

Despite expressions of concern by various reform movements at the implications of global and internal trends for the United States, and despite the possibility of some corrective measures implemented here and there as the 1990s advance, the nature of American society and politics makes it unlikely that a national "plan" for the twenty-first century will emerge such as may be formulated in France or Japan. Instead, there will be differentiated responses and local initiatives, in the traditional American way: states and school districts will push ahead with their individual schemes; communities will grapple with local environmental problems; towns and cities will attack urban poverty in various ways; some regions will benefit from fresh foreign investment, others will suffer as American companies transfer production overseas; in the business world especially, "preparing for the twenty-first century" will be seen as a matter of individual company strategy, not the result of a plan conceived by Washington.

There is a lot to be said for this sort of differentiated, decentralized, individualistic response to change: it is in the tradition of American free enterprise and its libertarian culture; and it is what the nation is used to. The United States is, after all, a demi-continent, not a small country like Japan, which finds it necessary to stress social harmony and organization in order for everyone to exist on its mountainous, crowded island chain. America, by contrast, is the home of those fleeing from constraints elsewhere; it offered an open frontier to dissatisfied people; and its sheer size, "escapist" culture, and lack of serious external threat combined to foster dislike of organized, central government. This cultural heritage means that as the United States turns to meet the broad forces for global change, its response is also likely to be differentiated, decentralized, and individualistic, a "muddling through" rather than a coordinated, centralized attack upon the problems. After all, a country like Great Britain "muddled through" for a very long time.

But that returns us to historical analogy as well as to the core of the American dilemma. One hundred years ago, Britain, which was widely regarded then as Number One, was engaged in a similar debate about its future prospects. It was, of course, a very different society from America today, and occupied a different geographical position as the island center of a worldwide empire rather than a resource-rich continental landmass. Nevertheless, the dilemma Britain faced was like the one facing the United States now. Both were preeminent world powers whose economic competitiveness and general international position seemed less assured at the century's end than five decades earlier. In both, alarmed citizens called for changes to improve national competitiveness and "prepare" for the next century. The difficulty was, however, that the proposed reforms would threaten many vested interests. Britain's spending priorities, its public educational system, the efficiency of its industry, its treatment of poverty, its levels of investment, and even its pattern of career choice (not enough engineers, too many lawyers and bankers) might all have to be altered to match the new global competition.

While reformers in turn-of-the-century Britain urged the need for tough solutions and cultural pessimists bemoaned the evidence of "decline" and "decay," many disliked the idea of change. It would mean the loss of institutions and work habits that were familiar, cozy, and reassuring. It implied that national traditions had to be amended in imitation of foreign ones. It upset powerful vested interests and made for uncertainty. It involved costs, or a redistribution of national resources, when economic growth was moderate. Besides, there were many other academic "experts," journalists, and economists who said that things were still fine, that the declinists were too alarmist, and that Britain still had the energies and resourcefulness to remain ahead. All this made sense to a people taught that it occupied a unique historical place, and was an example to others. In sum, there was an understandable and deep-rooted antipathy, both psychological and cultural, to the idea that great changes were needed, especially if they involved pain or money. Rejecting the calls for change, the British people thought it was better to "muddle through."[92] Why, then, cannot America today do the same?

In fact, the evidence above suggests that the United States *will* continue to muddle through, as the debate about "decline or renewal" continues. But the long-term implication of muddling through is slow, steady, relative *decline*—in comparative living standards, educational levels, technical skills, social provisions, industrial leadership, and, ultimately, *national power,* just as in Britain. The British may have avoided hard choices by "muddling through" policies, but that evasion ultimately caused the loss of their place in the world.

While an impressive array of American individuals, companies, banks, investors, and think tanks are scrambling to prepare for the twenty-first century, the United States as a whole is not and indeed *cannot,* without becoming a different kind of country. Perhaps a serious program of reforms might be undertaken following a sufficient shock to complacency, like a financial crash or a broadly perceived external threat; but just how likely that is to happen is impossible to say. Even if there should be such a catalyst, there surely could be no coherent response by the United States unless the political leadership—especially the president—recognized the larger challenges facing the country and had the courage and the ability to mobilize opinion to accept changes which many would find uncomfortable. That, in turn, would require leadership very different from the sort demonstrated by recent incumbents of the White House, whether it concerned domestic deficits or global population and environmental issues. It remains to be seen, therefore, whether traditional approaches will carry the American people successfully into the twenty-first century—or whether they will pay a high price in assuming that things can stay the same at home while the world outside changes more swiftly than ever before.

PART 3

CONCLUSION

14

PREPARING FOR THE TWENTY-FIRST CENTURY

THE PROBLEM RESTATED

THIS BOOK BEGAN WITH A HISTORICAL example from two hundred years ago—Malthus's concern with England's eighteenth-century population explosion—to introduce the reader to themes that would run throughout the rest of the study. This final chapter begins with a more recent example that may illuminate both the continuities and the changes in our modern world condition. In October 1930, a year after the Wall Street Crash but before the Manchurian crisis and the Nazi seizure of power, the London *Economist* somberly surveyed contemporary global problems, and concluded:

> The supreme difficulty of our generation . . . is that our achievements on the economic plane of life have outstripped our progress on the political plane to such an extent that our economics and our politics are perpetually falling out of gear with one another. On the economic plane, the world has been organized into a single, all-embracing unit of activity. On the political plane, it has not only remained partitioned into sixty or seventy sovereign national States, but the national units have been growing smaller and more numerous and the national consciousnesses more acute. The tension between these two antithetical tendencies has been producing a series of jolts and jars and smashes in the social life of humanity. . . .[1]

As it turned out, World War II, with its heightened nationalism and demands upon citizenry everywhere, was soon to resolve that tension between the "two antithetical tendencies" in favor of the nation-state, at least temporarily. The following half century of Cold War, plus numerous regional conflicts, also emphasized political nationalism at the cost of economic cosmopolitanism. At the same time, the collapse of Western colonial empires, and more recently the disintegration of the USSR, meant that national units did indeed become "smaller and more numerous," so that almost three times as many states existed by the early 1990s as there had been sixty years earlier. Without exception, whether a former Soviet republic or French West African colony, the new state established all the usual attributes of sovereignty—national government, armed forces, border/customs posts, budgets, currency, and so on.

Yet this revival of nationalism as old empires dissolved could not alter the fact that the lengthy Great Power peace after 1945, with an American-led coalition protecting a relatively open trading order across much of the globe, was once again pushing trade, finance, and technology toward "a single all-embracing unit of activity," as the pace of economic integration increased from year to year. As a result, today's global society, even more than its predecessor sixty years ago, confronts the task of reconciling technological change and economic integration with traditional political structures, national consciousness, social needs, institutional arrangements, and habitual ways of doing things.

Moreover, efforts to harmonize economic and political structures will be complicated by trends which were scarcely evident three generations ago but now threaten to exacerbate social relations in all manner of ways, and may even threaten the long-term existence of humankind itself.[2]

The first and most important of these is the surge in the earth's population and the rising demographic imbalances between rich and poor countries. When *The Economist* was making its 1930 survey of the world scene, overall population was around 2 billion people. Europe, North America, and such Caucasian offshoots as Australia contained a considerable share of world population (perhaps about one-third), and their fertility rates were well above replacement level.* The populations of Asia, Africa, and Latin America were also growing, but their higher fertility rates were held in check by extremely high mortality rates. All that has now changed: world population has surged to well past 5 billion and may be heading toward 10 billion or more by the middle of next century, and most of that growth occurs in the poorest regions of the world, whereas developed societies have slow-growing or declining populations containing a rising share of older people. The result is a growing mismatch between where the world's riches, technology, good health, and other benefits are to be found and where the world's fast-growing new generations, possessing few if any of those benefits, live. A population explosion on one part of the globe and a technology explosion on the other is not a good recipe for a stable international order.

Meanwhile, the population explosion also produces environmental challenges qualitatively different from those of sixty years ago. Of course, there was dreadful pollution then in the industrial cities of Europe and North America, carbon dioxide levels were rising, and prolonged droughts occasionally turned farmland into dust bowls. But over the past half century there has been exponential growth in industrial emissions, especially in newly developed countries intent upon flat-out growth; the draining of wetlands and aquifers, the onslaught on tropical forests, and the overgrazing of plains and savannahs are nowadays far more extensive; and evidence is at hand of a "greenhouse effect" that could change ecologies in all sorts of ways. As climate changes and sea levels rise, even the most environmentally responsible societies will be affected. It is inconceivable that the earth can sustain a population of 10 billion people devouring resources at the rate enjoyed by richer societies today—or at even half that rate. Well before total world population reaches that level, irreparable damage to forests, water supplies, and animal and plant species will have occurred, and many environmental thresholds may have been breached.

Another trend more in evidence today than in our grandparents' time is technology's way of making redundant traditional jobs, replac-

*France, with its notoriously slow population increase in the nineteenth and early twentieth centuries, might be the exception here.

ing them with entirely new systems of production. This is not unwelcome, of itself; the economic history of the world, and of humankind's growing overall prosperity, flows from the invention of newer, improved ways of making things, from steam-driven textile production to computerized automobile design. But some changes are more sweeping than others; and over the coming decades it is possible that the biotech revolution will make traditional agriculture redundant while the robotics revolution changes a way of manufacturing and a structure of industrial employment that have existed for the past two centuries.

The transformation of agriculture and manufacturing as we know them, should that occur, will not take place in a vacuum, for this process will coincide with a demographic explosion, in which hundreds of millions of people will be seeking jobs that biotech farming and automated manufacturing may make redundant. It will also occur just as multinational corporations, freeing themselves from their local roots, increasingly compete for global market shares and employ every device—relocating production, installing automation, adopting new laboratory-created technologies—to achieve that aim. Such companies are simply acting according to the "rules" of laissez-faire capitalism; the point is that local communities in the developed world, and entire societies in the developing world, will have difficulty in accepting the logic of the global marketplace if it works to their disadvantage. Rather than economic and technological trends leading to that all-embracing unit of activity, the borderless world, they could provoke the commercial clashes and social instability which *The Economist* was noting in 1930. They could also provoke immense bouts of violence, as tens of millions crowd into cities in the developing world and find no work available.

Today's global financial and communications revolution is also more intense than in that earlier era, although even then there were severe currency crises and mass withdrawals of capital (as when U.S. dollars were recalled from Europe in the late 1920s), which made for instability and exacerbated interstate relations. It is unclear nowadays whether our more sophisticated official controls have kept pace with the risk of financial turbulence built into twenty-four-hour-a-day electronic/computerized trading in sums far in excess of most countries' GNP. The greater change, however, is in the realm of global communications.

Fifty or sixty years ago, radio and television were beginning to make their impact, but only among a relatively few rich societies; as our century closes, they are affecting peoples—especially younger generations—across the globe. Moreover, while it once appeared that the new media would enhance the power of governments (as, for example, Orwell argued in *1984*), their effect recently has been the opposite: breaking state monopolies of information, permeating national boundaries, allowing peoples to hear and see how others do things differently. It has also made richer and poorer countries more aware of the gap between them than was possible a half century ago, and stimulated legal and illegal migration.

As a result of these changes, communities and even entire countries appear to have less and less control of their own destinies. Traditional power structures are baffled by below-replacement fertility rates, illegal immigration, and massive currency flows; they have unsatisfactory answers—or no answers at all—to the threat of large-scale redundancy in farming and manufacturing; they find it hard to prevent companies from relocating to other regions, or to muffle information from transnational television and radio; they pause, and worry, at the implications of global warming. And because the established structures are fumbling with these challenges, people are responding with resignation (witnessed in the decreased percentages of voters in many elections), searching for new structures (from the EC experiment to the dismantling of the USSR and Yugoslavia), demanding protection from the global forces for change (as seen in the pressures from French farmers and American textile workers), and turning angrily against recent immigrants. In sum, we are facing again that "series of jolts and jars and smashes in the social life of humanity" noted by *The Economist*; and there seems every likelihood that such shocks will continue in the future.

In view of the speed and complexity of these changes, is *any* social group really "prepared" for the twenty-first century? Clearly, there exist companies (engaged in everything from pharmaceuticals to aerospace) and individuals (chiefly professionals providing high-added-value services) who benefit from current socioeconomic developments and are keenly positioning themselves to gain further advantages. Their prospects are the basis for the many optimistic works by Kenichi

Ohmae, George Gilder, Ben Wattenberg, and others that forecast humankind's ever-increasing prosperity. On the other hand, there are billions of impoverished, uneducated individuals in the developing world, and tens of millions of unskilled, nonprofessional workers in the developed world, whose prospects are poor, and in many cases getting worse. Their plight is the concern of the pessimistic writings about the demographic explosion and environmental catastrophes by the Ehrlichs, the Worldwatch Institute, and others, and it also inspires studies on future career trends and their social implications, like the work of Robert Reich. Initially, it might seem that only one school of thought must be right, but it could be that each has examined different aspects of a single phenomenon, so that the optimists are excited about the world's "winners" whereas the pessimists worry at the fate of the "losers." But if both *are* correct, the gap between rich and poor will steadily widen as we enter the twenty-first century, leading not only to social unrest within developed countries but also to growing North-South tensions, mass migration, and environmental damage from which even the "winners" might not emerge unscathed.

Whereas many individuals and firms seem well positioned for the twenty-first century, relatively few nations appear to be. Of those covered in this survey, the most likely at the moment appear to be Japan, Korea, and certain other East Asian trading states, Germany, Switzerland, some of the Scandinavian states, and *perhaps* the EC as a whole. What they have in common, more or less, are high savings rates, impressive levels of investment in new plant and equipment, excellent educational systems (especially for those *not* going to college), a skilled work force and good retraining systems, a manufacturing culture with many more engineers than lawyers, a commitment to producing well-designed, high-added-value manufactures for the global market, and fairly consistent trade surpluses in "visible" goods. They also enjoy cultural homogeneity and ethnic coherence; but that may not be as important a factor, since cultural and linguistic homogeneity also exist in societies which are much less successful economically.*

However, even technologically better-prepared countries face diffi-

*And Switzerland, arguably one of the "best-prepared" countries, contains three linguistic divisions.

culties in dealing with certain forces for global change: the decline in fertility rates; population imbalances; global warming; financial volatility; the need to cushion farming communities from increasing obsolescence. The fact that they have ample funds to pay for retraining workers or environmental protection is a great benefit, but it is unlikely that money will solve every difficulty. Nevertheless, it is obvious that societies which possess technical and educational resources, ample funds, and cultural solidarity are better positioned for the next century than those lacking all those strengths.

THE DIFFICULTIES OF REFORM

What can be done? How could nations better prepare themselves for the century ahead? Before attempting to answer, we should note the two greatest difficulties facing any program of systematic reforms. The first is the apparent inevitability of overall demographic and environmental trends. With around a billion new mouths being born each decade, does it matter much if there are 100 million more or less; or whether there will be 9 billion human beings on this planet in 2050 instead of 10 billion? In either case the consequences will be enormous, yet, simply because of the number of females who will reach child-bearing age over the next twenty years, large increases are probably unavoidable. Similarly, because atmospheric emissions are rising from year to year, and will expand further because of growing industrialization and global population, CO_2 levels seem bound to increase over time; for this reason, most reforms can merely hope to slow down the rise in greenhouse emissions, not halt them, which is widely regarded as impossible. Again, if India's population growth has already led to the loss of over two-thirds of its forests during this century, shouldn't we expect the current demographic surge to wipe out the remainder, as has happened in Ethiopia and Haiti?* In other words, far from a stimulus to preventive actions, global trends are so large as to induce despair. Since it is unlikely that these trends can be altered much, should we

*Only 14 percent of India is covered by forest today, compared with over 50 percent last century. Forty years ago, Ethiopia had a 30 percent forest cover, which has now shriveled to a mere 1 percent.

not try policies of reaction and adaptation—including, in the case of richer, developed societies, the cruel if necessary policy of blocking the rising migratory floods from overpopulated, impoverished lands?

The second difficulty lies both in the timing and the instrumentality of proposed reforms, from the viewpoint of practical politics. Even if it is worth trying to curb global warming—by banning gas-guzzling cars, curbing factory emissions, halting forest clearing, etc.—the problem is that these actions have to be implemented now for the sake of consequences twenty-five or forty years ahead. Apart from saving for old age (which directly benefits the savers), human beings are usually unwilling to make short-term sacrifices to achieve a distant (and uncertain) improvement in the general good—and most politicians' perspectives are shorter still. Unlike traditional threats to national security, these dangers are less obvious and therefore less likely to induce a unified, determined response. In addition, the usual mechanisms by which nation-states respond to threats seem inappropriate to some of the challenges posed here. To halt global warming requires international cooperation, while the introduction of robots is properly the task of individual manufacturers; in each case, the nation-state is either too small or too large.

Yet even if these newer forces for global change make many national instruments irrelevant, we know that states still remain the chief locus of authority and loyalty. They raise, and dispense, a large share of a society's product. They possess a deliberative system to discuss policies, and a command system to implement them. They establish policy priorities. Only states have the authority to enter international agreements to reduce CO_2 emissions and regulate biotech farming. Furthermore, if a society desires to improve its general preparedness for the next century—by encouraging a skilled work force, or the lowering (or raising) of fertility rates—no other structures possess the *potential* effectiveness of the state itself.* Actively preparing a people for the future as Korea and Singapore have done, or preferring laissez-faire methods to do that job as in the United States, is the decision of national governments and their publics—which is why we should not

**Potential* effectiveness, of course, because of the actual differences between strong states (Korea) and weaker ones (Ethiopia). The discussion above assumes reasonably strong and capable societies which can decide for or against changes.

expect to see uniform responses to these transnational challenges, but a mixture of responses instead; as some states feverishly seek to improve themselves, others will be either unwilling or unable to do much.

Given the difficulties of reform, humankind's instinctive avoidance of uncomfortable changes and its preference to make only minor ones is likely to prevail. Still, for societies willing to prepare for the twenty-first century, a range of measures can be considered. Most of them are specific to the type of country—Botswana obviously has different needs from Britain—but others require international cooperation to be effective. Such reforms will cost money, and thus involve a debate upon spending priorities, but the sums involved are unlikely to equal those devoted to the Cold War arms race.

Since this book is intended as a guide to understanding global changes, *not* as a technical primer for responses to them, it will not recount the many studies which outline in detail actual programs of change. For example, organizations like the Worldwatch Institute have recommended an array of reforms to halt the growing damage to the environment: cutting factory emissions by more efficient use of energy, filter systems, and extraction devices; investing in public transport, developing alternative fuels for automobiles, and taking other measures to reduce dependence upon petroleum; husbanding water resources and cutting reliance upon aquifers; boosting international technology transfers and training to countries in the developing world; and negotiating a pact between rich and poor countries, whereby the latter would protect their forests in return for increased aid, assistance in creating alternative employment, and guaranteed access to markets.[3] Some of the proposals from the environmentalist lobby may be impractical,[4] but others appear perfectly feasible, and cheap; with the "appropriate technology" of a simple solar oven, for example, families in the developing world can cook most meals without the daily scavenging of fuel wood which causes so much deforestation.[5]

There is also no need to repeat here the findings of innumerable works upon how to make one's society more competitive technologically and industrially in an age of globalized production. Every study of "competitiveness" in the United States, where the issue is keenly studied, concludes with virtually the same agenda: increase national savings rates and slash budgetary deficits which drain funds from productive investment; enhance the levels of *commercial* R&D; avoid the diversion of too many resources to the military; escape (but how?) from a business culture that has become too dependent upon Wall Street's expectation of short-term profits; focus upon making well-designed, reliable products for the world's most demanding markets; vastly improve the levels of skill and training among the work force at large and provide opportunities for thorough retraining; and raise educational standards, especially for those not going to college.[6] Either implicitly or explicitly, unfavorable comparisons are made in these studies to Japan and Germany, which are regarded as leading examples of highly skilled, technology-based societies possessing good prospects as the decade unfolds.

Finally, a detailed proposal for dealing with the demographic explosion in developing countries would simply repeat what numerous studies by international agencies have pointed out: that the only practical* way to ensure a decrease in fertility rates, and thus in population growth, is to introduce cheap and reliable forms of birth control—as has happened, for example, in Brazil, where the fertility rate fell from 4.7 children per woman in the 1970–75 period to 3.5 children per woman by the 1983–86 period.[7] This is also true of other developing countries where active family-planning programs have been established. Such a solution obviously faces difficulties—local cultural mores, the disapproval of the Vatican, the opposition of conservative U.S. governments which have not distinguished contraception from abortion—but that does not change the fact that population growth is dangerously high in societies where little family planning is practiced, yet is ebbing in countries where birth control occurs. To be sure, elements like urbanization and the changing role of women also contribute to a demographic transition, but the swiftest way to stabilize family size—and head off the threat posed by a doubling of the world's population in the next few decades—is measures to reduce conception in the first place.

In short, it is not that solutions to such transnational challenges are lacking, but that publics and politicians are equally reluctant to imple-

*In theory, of course, there are other ways, such as abstinence from intercourse and marrying later (which was what Malthus meant when urging "moral restraint"). How that is possible for fifteen-year-old brides in male-dominated societies in Africa or India is difficult to see.

ment changes which cause short-term personal costs to secure long-term general benefits. In many cases such reluctance is perfectly understandable. It is all very well for, say, ecologically conscious and well-educated Swedes to press for drastically reduced CO_2 emissions, higher fuel taxes, abolition of nuclear power stations, and large-scale increases in development aid; given their country's relative advantages, the costs would probably not be crushing. But it would be quite different politically to require farmers in the southern Great Plains, already threatened by biotech and global warming, to cease drawing water from aquifers, switch from automobiles to cycles, invest in energy-saving devices, and so on; it would also be politically unwise to expect support from such farmers for increased foreign aid to enable poorer countries to boost agricultural output. Similarly, while Western liberals agree that improving the role of women in Muslim and sub-Saharan African countries is long overdue, such a transformation poses a great challenge to traditional male-dominated cultures and is likely to be strongly resisted. Since it would be counterproductive for richer nations to try to impose such social changes, the issue will have to be decided within developing societies themselves—and the signs point to a looming clash between secularists and fundamentalists in these sensitive areas.[8] Whether reforms are accepted or rejected will depend upon context, not upon abstract logic.

Yet while this book is not a primer of technical solutions to global developments, it is important to emphasize three key elements in any *general* effort to prepare global society for the twenty-first century: the role of education, the place of women, and the need for political leadership.

THE ROLE OF EDUCATION AND THE POSITION OF WOMEN

If my analysis is roughly correct, the forces for change facing the world could be so far-reaching, complex, and interactive that they call for nothing less than the reeducation of humankind. This is not a new conclusion. Social thinkers from Wells to Toynbee have repeatedly argued that global society is in a race between education and catastrophe; and those stakes are higher at the century's end, simply because population pressures, environmental damage, and humankind's capacity to inflict mass destruction are all far greater.

An enhanced role for education implies many things, both philosophical and practical. For example, since technological innovation creates new jobs as it destroys old ones, developed countries which do not possess a national system for training *and* retraining—on the lines of Germany's apprenticeship scheme or of Sweden's methods of preparing discharged workers to learn a new skill—will probably find themselves more disadvantaged than they are now. Moreover, not only economic productivity but also the social fabric suffers from, say, Britain's inadequate job-training program, or the even less organized American efforts. But the systems that work rely upon planning and cooperation among schools, business, and government, which laissez-faire political cultures dislike and poorer countries lack the resources to sustain.

Still, the challenges facing nations like Britain or Italy in restructuring their educational systems are nothing like those facing the developing countries. In Somalia, where the adult male literacy rate is only 18 percent and the female literacy rate a mere 6 percent, only 37,000 pupils are in secondary education (1986 figures); of the very few professionally trained personnel, several hundred were doctors and, presumably, hardly any were engineers, computer-software designers, and others needed to bring Somalia into the modern world.[9] In South Korea, by contrast, where the male and female literacy rates are 96 and 88 percent respectively, and where 5 million are in secondary and 1.3 million in higher education, large numbers of professionals enter productive employment each year.*[10] Clearly, those developing countries which manage to follow Korea's path can look forward to a bright economic future; but, as we have seen earlier, very few poorer societies are in such a favorable position. Backwardness has many causes, but a leading one is that education is regarded as less important in many cultures than it is in East Asia.

Yet education in the larger sense means more than technically "re-

*Korea's population is about five times larger than Somalia's, but even proportionately, the differences are immense.

tooling" the work force, or the emergence of professional classes, or even the encouragement of a manufacturing culture in the schools and colleges in order to preserve a productive base. It also implies a deep understanding of why our world is changing, of how other people and cultures feel about those changes, of what we all have in common—as well as of what divides cultures, classes, and nations. Moreover, while this process of inquiry ought if possible to be tolerant and empathetic, it cannot be value-free. In the end, it is not enough merely to understand what we are doing to our planet, as if we were observing the changes through a giant telescope on Mars. Because we are all members of a world citizenry, we also need to equip ourselves with a system of ethics, a sense of fairness, *and* a sense of proportion as we consider the various ways in which, collectively or individually, we can better prepare for the twenty-first century.[11] In societies where fundamentalist forces block open inquiry and debate, where politicians, to attract the support of special interests, inveigh against foreign peoples or ethnic minorities, and where a commercialized mass media and popular culture drive serious issues to the margins, the possibility that education will introduce deeper understanding of global trends is severely limited.

Enhancing the role of education is inextricably linked to an even greater issue, namely, the position of women in both developing and developed countries. In the former case, the evidence linking the depressed status of women to population explosion, acute poverty, and economic retardation seems clear.* As the United Nations Population Division's statistics show, in country after country there is a strong inverse correlation between the adult female literacy rate and the total fertility rate (see Table 13).

There are a few interesting exceptions to this rule—Mongolia claims both an adult female literacy rate of 88 percent and a total fertility rate of 5.4—but the evidence overwhelmingly suggests that when education is widely available to women, average family size drops sharply and the demographic transition sets in. The obvious explanation for this—marrying older, postponing the birth of children, choosing a career—is confirmed by an even more thought-provoking set of statistics, shown

*The only exceptions, one suspects, are certain oil-rich Arab states where the woman's status is low, but per capita GNP is high—the latter because of geological accident rather than indigenous creative energies.

Table 13. Adult Female Literacy Rate and Total Fertility Rate, Selected Countries[12]

Country	*Adult Female Literacy Rate*	*Total Fertility Rate*
Afghanistan	8%	6.9
Oman	12%	7.2
Yemen Arab Republic	3%	7.0
Honduras	58%	5.6
Burkina Faso	6%	6.5
Sudan	14%	6.4
Singapore	79%	1.7
Canada	93%	1.7
Chile	96%	2.7
Hungary	98%	1.8
Thailand	88%	2.6

in Table 14, on the relationship between a mother's education and the number of children born in developing countries.

In general, women in developing countries with seven or more years of education (and presumably from the better-off classes?) marry approximately four years later than those without education, have higher rates of contraceptive use, *and* enjoy lower maternal and child mortality rates[13]—so both they and their offspring have better chances in life. This clearly implies that a change in the status of women would significantly reduce population growth in the developing world. But how likely is that in those parts of South Asia, Africa, and the Muslim world where gender restrictions are so pronounced?

In the developed world, where elderly males bemoan the below-replacement fertility rates and ask why "bright, well-educated women"

Table 14. Average Number of Children by Mother's Years of Education, Selected Countries[14]

Country	*No Education*	*Seven+ Years of Education*
Benin	7.4	4.3
Sudan	6.5	3.4
Haiti	6.0	2.8
Ecuador	7.8	2.7
Jordan	9.3	4.9
Pakistan	6.5	3.1
Portugal	3.5	1.8

are having fewer children (or none at all),* the challenge is different—but still involves the position of women in society. Assuming that it is *not* good for a society to fail to renew its numbers—if only because of the strains of the burgeoning "elderly dependency" ratio—then politicians who worry about such trends may need to reassess their own cultural and social norms. In Japan, for example, the evidence suggests that a rising generation of educated women resent the traditional expectation that they become full-time housewives after college, bringing up children in cramped accommodations while their husbands are absent from early morning to late evening.[15] A similar resentment probably exists in Italy and Spain, where total fertility rates have plunged in recent years. No doubt the consequent labor shortages can be partially handled, in Japan's case at least, by the growing use of robots; but if Japan wants to return to replacement fertility rates, more than technical fixes will be needed. In this connection, Japanese and Italian politicians may care to study the case of Sweden, where, after decades of demographic slowdown, the fertility rate has steadily risen from 1.6 (1983) to 2.1 (1990).[16] Initial researches of this development—which also appears in several other Northern European countries—suggest that the reason could be a mixture of excellent social provisions (paid maternity *and* paternity leave, child care, kindergarten, comfortable housing) together with a significant degree of overall gender equality, measured, for example, in the numbers of female politicians and cabinet ministers.

Ironically, then, if the world is to move toward a better demographic balance—lowering fertility rates in poorer societies and raising them in richer ones—the lesson seems to be that while African and Middle Eastern nations need to educate women to Korean levels, countries like Japan, Portugal, Spain, and Italy need to imitate Scandinavian practices. Each involves a change in gender roles and a different set of challenges.

*See above, pp. 154–55, 313–14.

THE ISSUE OF POLITICAL LEADERSHIP

It may seem curious to conclude this work with a discussion of political leadership, since demographic trends and new technologies often appear so irresistible that nothing can be done to affect them. In fact, the thrust of this chapter is not about their inevitability, but about the difficulty of changing entrenched structures and ideas and the danger of remaining culturally blind, given the transformation of global society. After all, there clearly is a broad and lively concern in many countries about where the world in general and one's own nation in particular are headed. Technological challenges, gender issues, migration, the future of agriculture, environmental damage, the implication of globalization, and the impact of all this upon policies, spending priorities, even values and culture, are the subject of intense interest, from France to Japan, from Kansas to Cairo. They explain, at least in part, the search for newer transnational and subnational political structures, the innumerable committees investigating national educational systems, the calls for joint action over global warming or development aid, the anxious debates about commercial open-ness or protection. The man and woman in the street *know* that their world is changing and worry about it. Above all, unease about present or impending changes is behind the widespread disenchantment with political leaderships, whether in advanced industrial nations like America, France, and Japan, in existing or recently dissolved Marxist regimes, in large parts of Latin America and Africa, in the Asian giants of India and China, or, for that matter, in the Muslim world, where discontented youths turn to fundamentalist prescriptions. Much of this is suppressed in authoritarian states, but in both the older and the newer democracies the demand for political *responses* to the new challenges is immense.

Such responses can often be reactionary. Protectionism, anti-immigrant policies, blocking new technologies, and finding new enemies to replace Cold War foes are common reactions at a time of "jolts and jars and smashes in the social life of humanity." Clearly, a society which desires to be better prepared for the twenty-first century will pay a price to achieve that transition; it will need to retool its national skills and infrastructure, challenge vested interests, alter many old habits, and perhaps amend its governmental structures. But this assumes long-term vision at a time when most politicians—in both rich and poor countries—can hardly deal with even short-term problems; and it means political risk, since many of the reforms proposed would be unpopular among vested interests. Alongside voices calling for change there exist large constituencies wanting things to stay as they are, to freeze things rather than respond. Moreover, there is much scholarly disagreement over critical issues. Can we sustain a world of 8 to 10 billion people? Can food supplies keep pace? How fast, if at all, is global warming occurring? Is "managed trade" better than laissez-faire? Should globalization have no checks? And given the differences of view on these questions, why rush ahead with controversial changes?

Since most politicians, especially in such countries as Japan, the United States, France, Italy, and Germany, have risen to the top through a process of compromise, making deals and alliances, and taking care not to annoy powerful interests, they are hardly prepared to endorse controversial policies now for purported benefits twenty years away—especially when experts argue that there is little or no cause for alarm (e.g., over world food supplies), or that further study is needed. As "cornucopians" since Godwin and Condorcet two centuries ago have pointed out, Malthus's forecasts about Britain's future *were wrong,* because of humankind's capacity to develop new resources through technology. If his predictions for the nineteenth century were false, why should any more notice be taken of the alarmist cries of today's "neo-Malthusians" concerning the twenty-first century?[17] It is, moreover, only a couple of decades since the last wave of gloomy predictions (*The Silent Earth,* the "Club of Rome" report, etc.), which provoked widespread concern before it faded away.

Perhaps we should distinguish here between reformers who advocate prudent measures in the near future to control population and limit vehicle emissions, for example, and apocalyptic writers who argue that all will be lost unless a drastic change in human behavior occurs now.[18] In denouncing the latter as both alarmist and erroneous, some conservatives tend to lump all reformers into the same camp. Yet it is proper to note a distinction between the moderate and more radical reform proposals, especially since it is the former that have better prospects of swaying politicians.

Despite divided opinions over where our world is heading, societies ought to take seriously the challenge of preparing for the twenty-first century for three main reasons. The first concerns relative competitiveness. Though economic growth is hardly all that matters, it surely is true that a decent standard of living provides a foundation for much else that groups and individuals deem important—good health, education, leisure, etc. Yet those benefits, deriving from technological innovation and increased growth, do not flow equally to all; they come instead as rewards to successful societies. An economy increasingly unable to keep up with new technologies, experiencing slow (or negative) rates of growth, with per capita income levels static or falling just as demographic changes impose fresh social demands, is less happily placed than one which remains competitive and adaptable. A failure to rethink, retrain, and retool for the future will thus produce yet another crop of History's economic losers.

The second is the need to respond to demographic and environmental challenges, instead of simply hoping that a solution will turn up on its own.[19] Today's consumption of the earth's resources is far greater than in Malthus's day—or even in the 1960s—because of the size of the population, the sheer amounts of material it consumes, and the complexity of economic activities. Consequently, the *speed* of the human assault upon nature has greatly increased: "Whole countries may be deforested in a few decades; most of a region's topsoil can disappear in a generation; and critical ozone depletion may occur in as little as twenty years."[20] In other words, it might be that while the pessimists of several decades ago were wrong in their timing, their overall arguments about the damage increasingly inflicted upon the planet are becoming more valid—and ought not to be ignored. Finally, there is the point that societies best able to adapt are those (like Malthus's England or Japan today) with capital, scientific knowledge, technical expertise, and skilled and inventive personnel, whereas the countries facing the most serious problems in today's world are much less well equipped to respond.

This concern about environmental damage does not, of course, imply that *all* economic growth should be halted, for this would hurt poorer societies most and, in any case, contradicts the argument for enhanced competitiveness. Instead, politicians and publics ought to take far more seriously the proposals for "sustainable growth" which development experts have formulated.[21]

The third and final reason for reforming our existing global condition is a very traditional one: to reduce the chances of political instability, with concomitant threats of violence and war. Admittedly, many such convulsions are impossible to anticipate beforehand; if five years ago we would not have expected the degree of bloodshed and violence that has torn Yugoslavia to pieces, how can we hope to know what wars and tumults will be taking place in a decade's time? Still, many social explosions, such as the outbreak of the French or Russian revolutions, are preceded by a steady buildup of pressures, akin to the increased tensions along the edges of tectonic plates before an earthquake occurs, or, for that matter, the outbreak of an environmental disaster once incremental damage passes a certain threshold. While it is usually impossible to know exactly where or when the irruption will take place, scientists can make a plausible forecast that an explosion *will* someday occur, given the general buildup of pressures. By analogy, it is not unreasonable to suggest that as pressures increase within human societies—rapid population growth, diminishing resources, unemployment, migration to shanty cities, lack of education—social and political explosions are likely to occur, especially if the environmental causes of acute conflicts interact with traditional quarrels over boundaries, water and grazing rights, and so on.[22]

Civil or external wars—with their heavy casualties—were, like famine and disease, among the Malthusian antidotes to a population explosion, and perhaps the most effective of all because they killed people in the prime of life. Such turbulence is not only of local importance. Instabilities could nowadays take place in regions where the possession of advanced weaponry such as medium-range missiles with chemical, biological, or even nuclear warheads by ambitious and threatened regimes makes a potentially lethal combination, with implications that would be far from local.

In sum, we need to be concerned about the condition of our planet as a whole not simply because we face a new agenda of security risks such as global warming and mass migration, but also because these phenomena could interact with and exacerbate older threats to international stability such as regional wars, hostage-taking, and closure of sealanes. While the newer transnational forces for global change appear to be on a different plane from the traditional concerns of the nation-states—as analyzed, for example, in my work *The Rise and Fall of the Great Powers*—they constitute additional causes for social conflict.

Given this array of problems, it may seem that our merely human political leadership has no chance of doing much; that instead we ought to brace ourselves for a continuation of jolts and jars and smashes in the social life of humanity—and on an increasingly global and intense scale. If so, it would be foolish for any country—or social class—to assume that it can isolate itself from future changes, some of which may be unexpected and perhaps dramatic, in the worlds of politics, economics, and the environment. Moreover, in the unlikely event that governments and societies do decide to transform themselves, we ought to recognize that our endeavors might have only a marginal effect on the profound driving forces of today's world. We also ought to be aware that interventions (like enhancing female education in developing countries) could produce their own unforeseen and unintended changes. Nothing is certain except that we face innumerable uncertainties; but simply recognizing that fact provides a vital starting point, and is, of course, far better than being blindly unaware of how our world is changing.

Thus, despite the size and complexity of the global challenges facing us, it is too simple and too soon to conclude gloomily that nothing can be done. Even Malthus was careful enough to end his *Essay on Population* by suggesting that despite the ominous demographic trends, the astounding technical advances of his day could have a positive influence upon the moral and political dimensions of society. Far from overwhelming human beings with a sense of despair, he pointed out that science might actually stimulate constructive responses and alter social habits.[23] While he may have regarded that possibility as unlikely, he was at least willing to admit that *theoretically* humankind could change its ways and avoid the fate predicted for it. The same is as true today.

Many earlier attempts to peer into the future concluded either in a tone of unrestrained optimism, or in gloomy forebodings, or (as in Toynbee's case) in appeals for spiritual renewal. Perhaps this work should also finish on such a note. Yet the fact remains that simply because we do not know the future, it is impossible to say with certainty whether global trends will lead to terrible disasters or be diverted by astonishing advances in human adaption. What is clear is that as the Cold War fades away, we face not a "new world order" but a troubled and fractured planet, whose problems deserve the serious attention of politicians and publics alike. As the above chapters suggest, the pace and complexity of the forces for change are enormous and daunting; yet it may still be possible for intelligent men and women to lead their societies through the complex task of preparing for the century ahead. If these challenges are not met, however, humankind will have only itself to blame for the troubles, and the disasters, that could be lying ahead.

APPENDIX
HUMAN DEVELOPMENT INDEX

THE FOLLOWING TABLE, ASSEMBLED BY the United Nations Development Program, measures three elements—life expectancy at birth, adult literacy rate, and GNP per capita—to produce a composite "human development" ranking of 130 countries. The ranking is in ascending order, so that Niger actually rates lowest and Japan highest. These are based on mid-to-late-1980s statistics, and the position of individual peoples—in South Korea on the one hand, or in the erstwhile Soviet Union on the other—will have changed significantly since then.

	Life expectancy at birth (years) '87	Adult literacy rate (%) '85	Real GDP per head (PPP-adj'd) '87, $	HDI	Rank by GNP per head	Rank by HDI
Niger	45	14	452	0.116	20	1
Mali	45	17	543	0.143	15	2
Burkina Faso	48	14	500	0.150	13	3
Sierra Leone	42	30	480	0.150	27	4
Chad	48	26	400	0.157	4	5
Guinea	43	29	500	0.162	31	6
Somalia	46	12	1,000	0.200	23	7
Mauritania	47	17	840	0.208	40	8
Afghanistan	42	24	1,000	0.212	17	9
Benin	47	27	665	0.224	28	10
Burundi	50	35	450	0.235	18	11
Bhutan	49	25	700	0.236	3	12
China	70	69	2,124	0.716	22	66
Libya	62	66	7,250	0.719	103	67
South Africa	61	70	4,981	0.731	82	68
Lebanon	68	78	2,250	0.735	78	69
Mongolia	64	90	2,000	0.737	57	70
Nicaragua	64	88	2,209	0.743	54	71
Turkey	65	74	3,781	0.751	71	72
Jordan	67	75	3,161	0.752	76	73
Peru	63	85	3,129	0.753	74	74
Ecuador	66	83	2,687	0.758	68	75
Iraq	65	89	2,400	0.759	96	76
United Arab Emirates	71	60	12,191	0.782	127	77

	Life expectancy at birth (years) '87	Adult literacy rate (%) '85	Real GDP per head (PPP-adj'd) '87, $	HDI	Rank by GNP per head	Rank by HDI
Mozambique	47	39	500	0.239	10	13
Malawi	48	42	476	0.250	7	14
Sudan	51	23	750	0.255	32	15
Central African Republic	46	41	591	0.258	29	16
Nepal	52	26	722	0.273	8	17
Senegal	47	28	1,068	0.274	43	18
Ethiopia	42	66	454	0.282	1	19
Zaire	53	62	220	0.294	5	20
Rwanda	49	47	571	0.304	26	21
Angola	45	41	1,000	0.304	58	22
Bangladesh	52	33	883	0.318	6	23
Nigeria	51	43	668	0.322	36	24
Yemen Arab Rep.	52	25	1,250	0.328	47	25
Liberia	55	35	696	0.333	42	26
Togo	64	41	670	0.337	24	27
Uganda	52	58	511	0.354	21	28
Haiti	55	38	775	0.356	34	29
Ghana	55	54	481	0.360	37	30
Yemen, PDR	52	42	1,000	0.369	39	31
Côte d'Ivoire	53	42	1,123	0.393	52	32
Congo	49	63	756	0.395	59	33
Namibia	56	30	1,500	0.404	60	34
Tanzania	54	75	405	0.413	12	35
Pakistan	58	30	1,585	0.423	33	36
India	59	43	1,053	0.439	25	37
Madagascar	54	68	634	0.440	14	38
Papua New Guinea	55	45	1,843	0.471	50	39
Kampuchea, Dem.	49	75	1,000	0.471	2	40
Cameroon	52	61	1,381	0.474	64	41
Kenya	59	60	794	0.481	30	42
Zambia	54	76	717	0.481	19	43
Morocco	62	34	1,761	0.489	48	44
Egypt	62	45	1,357	0.501	49	45
Laos	49	84	1,000	0.506	9	46
Gabon	52	62	2,068	0.525	93	47
Oman	57	30	7,750	0.535	104	48
Bolivia	54	75	1,380	0.548	44	49
Burma	61	79	752	0.561	11	50
Honduras	65	59	1,119	0.563	53	51
Zimbabwe	59	74	1,184	0.576	45	52
Lesotho	57	73	1,585	0.580	35	53
Indonesia	57	74	1,660	0.591	41	54
Guatemala	63	55	1,957	0.592	63	55
Vietnam	62	80	1,000	0.608	16	56
Algeria	63	50	2,633	0.609	91	57
Botswana	59	71	2,496	0.646	69	58
El Salvador	64	72	1,733	0.651	56	59
Tunisia	66	55	2,741	0.657	70	60
Iran	66	51	3,300	0.660	97	61
Syria	66	60	3,250	0.691	79	62
Dominican Rep.	67	78	1,750	0.699	51	63
Saudi Arabia	64	55	8,320	0.702	107	64
Philippines	64	86	1,878	0.714	46	65
Thailand	66	91	2,576	0.783	55	78
Paraguay	67	88	2,603	0.784	65	79
Brazil	65	78	4,307	0.784	85	80
Mauritius	69	83	2,617	0.788	75	81
North Korea	70	90	2,000	0.789	67	82
Sri Lanka	71	87	2,053	0.789	38	83
Albania	72	85	2,000	0.790	61	84
Malaysia	70	74	3,849	0.800	80	85
Colombia	65	88	3,524	0.801	72	86
Jamaica	74	82	2,506	0.824	62	87
Kuwait	73	70	13,843	0.839	122	88
Venezuela	70	87	4,306	0.861	95	89
Romania	71	96	3,000	0.863	84	90
Mexico	69	90	4,624	0.876	81	91
Cuba	74	96	2,500	0.877	66	92
Panama	72	89	4,009	0.883	88	93
Trinidad and Tobago	71	96	3,664	0.885	100	94
Portugal	74	85	5,597	0.899	94	95
Singapore	73	86	12,790	0.899	110	96
South Korea	70	95	4,832	0.903	92	97
Poland	72	98	4,000	0.910	83	98
Argentina	71	96	4,647	0.910	89	99
Yugoslavia	72	92	5,000	0.913	90	100
Hungary	71	98	4,500	0.915	87	101
Uruguay	71	95	5,063	0.916	86	102
Costa Rica	75	93	3,760	0.916	77	103
Bulgaria	72	93	4,750	0.918	99	104
USSR	70	99	6,000	0.920	101	105
Czechoslovakia	72	98	7,750	0.931	102	106
Chile	72	98	4,862	0.931	73	107
Hong Kong	76	88	13,906	0.936	111	108
Greece	76	93	5,500	0.949	98	109
East Germany	74	99	8,000	0.953	115	110
Israel	76	95	9,182	0.957	108	111
USA	76	96	17,615	0.961	129	112
Austria	74	99	12,386	0.961	118	113
Ireland	74	99	8,566	0.961	106	114
Spain	77	95	8,989	0.965	105	115
Belgium	75	99	13,140	0.966	116	116
Italy	76	97	10,682	0.966	112	117
New Zealand	75	99	10,541	0.966	109	118
West Germany	75	99	14,730	0.967	120	119
Finland	75	99	12,795	0.967	121	120
Britain	76	99	12,270	0.970	113	121
Denmark	76	99	15,119	0.971	123	122
France	76	99	13,961	0.974	119	123
Australia	76	99	11,782	0.978	114	124
Norway	77	99	15,940	0.983	128	125
Canada	77	99	16,375	0.983	124	126
Holland	77	99	12,661	0.984	117	127
Switzerland	77	99	15,403	0.986	130	128
Sweden	77	99	13,780	0.987	125	129
Japan	78	99	13,135	0.996	126	130

NOTES

CHAPTER 1
PROLOGUE: OLD CHALLENGES AND NEW CHALLENGES

1. See the broad estimates in G. T. Trewartha, *A Geography of Population: World Patterns* (New York, 1969), p. 30.
2. N. Tranter, *Population Since the Industrial Revolution: The Case of England and Wales* (New York, 1973), pp. 41–42.
3. See the discussion in W. H. McNeill, *Plagues and Peoples* (New York, 1976), ch. 6; and in P. E. Razzell, "Population Growth and Economic Change in Eighteenth- and Early Nineteenth-Century England and Ireland," in E. L. Jones and G. E. Mingay (eds.), *Land, Labour and Population in the Industrial Revolution* (London, 1967), pp. 260–81.
4. T. R. Malthus, *An Essay on the Principle of Population as It Affects the Future Improvement of Society* (London, 1798); reprinted with notes by J. Bonar, New York, 1965, p. 13.
5. Ibid., p. 22.
6. R. L. Heilbroner, *The Worldly Philosophers* (New York, 1986 edn.), pp. 77–78.
7. P. Mathias, *The First Industrial Nation* (London, 1969), p. 452; W. D. McIntyre, *Colonies into Commonwealth* (London, 1966), p. 345.
8. There is a good brief description in Mathias, *First Industrial Nation,* pp. 64–80; see also J. D. Chambers and G. E. Mingay, *The Agricultural Revolution 1750–1880* (New York, 1966).
9. D. S. Landes, *The Unbound Prometheus: Technological Change and Industrial Development in Western Europe from 1750 to the Present* (Cambridge, 1969), p. 1.
10. P. Kennedy, *The Rise and Fall of the Great Powers* (New York, 1987), pp. 146–47; and see the more general discourse in C. M. Cipolla, *The Economic History of*

World Population, 7th edn. (Harmondsworth, Mddsx., 1978), pp. 70ff., 115; W. H. McNeill, *Population and Politics Since 1750* (Charlottesville, Va., 1990).
11. Mathias, *First Industrial Nation*, Table 15, p. 466.
12. Quoted in R. Hyam, *Britain's Imperial Century 1815–1914* (London, 1975), p. 47.
13. This is the theme of Landes, *Unbound Prometheus*.
14. T. S. Ashton, *The Industrial Revolution, 1760–1830* (Oxford, 1968 edn.), p. 129.
15. This figure comes from P. Bairoch, "International Industrialization Levels from 1750 to 1980," *Journal of European Economic History* 11 (1982), p. 294.
16. Ashton, *Industrial Revolution*, p. 129.
17. For this argument, see W. H. McNeill, *The Pursuit of Power* (Chicago, 1983), ch. 6.
18. See in particular E. L. Jones, *The European Miracle: Environments, Economies and Geopolitics in the History of Europe and Asia* (Cambridge, 1981); and C. M. Cipolla (ed.), *The Economic Decline of Empires* (London, 1970).
19. As argued in K. Mendelssohn, *Science and Western Domination* (London, 1976).
20. For a flavor of that concern, see J. Fallows, *More Like Us* (New York, 1989); D. Burstein, *Yen!* (New York, 1988); R. Rosecrance, *America's Economic Resurgence* (New York, 1990); S. Schlosstein, *The End of the American Century* (New York, 1989).

CHAPTER 2
THE DEMOGRAPHIC EXPLOSION

1. Cipolla, *Economic History of World Population*, quoting H. Brown, *The Challenge of Man's Future* (New York, 1954), p. 3.
2. These commonly accepted figures are reproduced in H. Thomas, *A History of the World* (New York, 1979), pp. 49–50. See also W. W. Rostow, *The World Economy—History and Prospects* (Austin, Texas, 1978), pp. 3–7. The 1990 figure comes from *World Population Prospects 1988* (United Nations Population Division, New York, 1989), p. 28.
3. *World Population Prospects 1988*, p. 28; and see also N. Sadik, *The State of the World Population* (U.N. Population Fund, New York, 1990).
4. *Population Today*, vol. 16, no. 1 (January 1988), p. 3; "World Population Pace Quickens," *Wall Street Journal*, 14 May 1991, p. A18.
5. *World Population Prospects 1988*, pp. 27–32. The population totals of the countries referred to were taken from *World Resources 1990–91* (New York/Oxford, 1990), pp. 254–55.
6. *World Population Prospects 1988*, p. 37, Table 2.5.
7. Ibid.; M. Southeimer, "Die Erde ist voll," *Die Zeit*, 28 December 1990, *Dossier*, p. 13.
8. Cipolla, *Economic History of World Population*, pp. 89–90; and see also the discussion in McNeill, *Plagues and Peoples*, passim.
9. *World Resources 1990–91*, pp. 254, 258.
10. Ibid., p. 254.
11. Ibid., pp. 254–55.
12. J. Axelbank, "The Crisis of the Cities," *Populi*, vol. 15, no. 4 (1988), pp. 28–35; Sadik, *State of the World Population*, p. 9. For the "centers of wealth . . . centers of poverty" argument, see R. Wright and D. MacManus, *Flashpoints* (New York, 1991), p. 168.
13. Sadik, *State of the World Population*, p. 8.

14. T. J. Goliber, "Africa's Expanding Population: Old Problems, New Policies," *Population Bulletin,* vol. 44, no. 3 (November 1989), p. 18.
15. T. C. Quinn et al., "AIDS in Africa: An Epidemiological Paradigm," *Science* 234 (November 1986), pp. 955–58; K. Hunt, "Scenes from a Nightmare," *New York Times Magazine,* 12 August 1990, pp. 24–26, 50–51.
16. L. K. Altman, "W. H. O. Says 40 Million Will Be Infected with AIDS Virus by 2000," *New York Times,* 18 June 1991, p. C3.
17. "AIDS in Africa," *Economist,* 25 November 1989, p. 16.
18. Goliber, "Africa's Expanding Population," p. 22, referring to a 1988 unpublished AAAS conference paper by J. Bougaarts, "Modeling the Demographic Impact of AIDS in Africa."
19. See the comparative statistics in *World Resources 1990–91,* pp. 244–65. For analyses of the East Asian "boom," see S. B. Linder, *The Pacific Century* (Stanford, Cal., 1986); J. W. Morley (ed.), *The Pacific Basin* (New York, 1986); M. Smith et al., *Asia's New Industrial World* (London, 1985).
20. R. Rosecrance, *The Rise of the Trading States* (New York, 1985), covers this aspect of history *and* current trends.
21. See A. J. Coale and E. M. Hoover, *Population Growth and Economic Development in Low Income Countries* (Princeton, N.J., 1958), as well as the arguments in D. H. Meadows et al., *The Limits to Growth* (New York, 1972); P. R. Ehrlich, *The Population Bomb* (New York, 1968); and H. E. Daly, *Steady State Economics* (San Francisco, 1977).
22. J. Simon, *The Ultimate Resource* (Princeton, N.J., 1981), p. 6, and passim. See also the more technical comments by D. A. Ahlburg, "The Impact of Population Growth on Economic Growth in Developing Nations: The Evidence From Macroeconomic-Demographic Models," in D. G. Johnson and R. D. Lee, *Population Growth and Economic Development: Issues and Evidence* (Madison, Wis., 1987), pp. 479–522.
23. P. R. Ehrlich and A. E. Ehrlich, *The Population Explosion* (New York, 1990), p. 134. The oil consumption figures come from M. L. Wald, "America Is Still Demanding a Full Tank," *New York Times,* 12 August 1990, p. E3.
24. Apart from the Ehrlichs' *Population Explosion* and P. R. Ehrlich, *The Population Bomb* (New York, 1968), see also L. R. Brown et al., *State of the World 1990,* passim; *World Resources 1990–91;* and *Our Common Future* (World Commission on Environment and Development, Oxford, 1987).
25. Simon, *Ultimate Resource,* passim.
26. See M. S. Teitelbaum and J. M. Winter, *The Fear of Population Decline* (Orlando, Fla./London, 1976), ch. 2.
27. G. D. Foster, "Global Demographic Trends to the Year 2010: Implications for U.S. Security," *Washington Quarterly* 12 (Spring 1989), p. 10.
28. See, for example, K. R. Andrews, *Elizabethan Privateering* (Cambridge, 1974), passim; W. H. McNeill, *The Pursuit of Power* (Chicago, 1983), pp. 185ff.
29. B. J. Wattenberg, *The Birth Dearth* (New York, 1987), passim.
30. *Wall Street Journal,* 5 June 1991, p. A10.
31. *World Resources 1990–91,* p. 257.
32. Ibid., pp. 256–57.
33. "Ten Billion Mouths," *Economist,* 20 January 1990.
34. Teitelbaum and Winter, *Fear of Population Decline,* passim.
35. For one good example, see G. R. Searle, *Eugenics and Politics in Britain, 1900–1914* (Leyden, 1976), passim, but many more are offered in Teitelbaum and Winter, *Fear of Population Decline.*

36. Teitelbaum and Winter, *Fear of Population Decline,* esp. chs. 5–7. See also K. Davis et al. (eds.), *Below-Replacement Fertility in Industrial Societies,* Supplement to *Population and Development Review* 12 (1986).
37. Foster, "Global Demographic Trends to the Year 2010," passim, and N. Eberstadt, "Population Change and National Security," *Foreign Affairs,* vol. 70, no. 3 (Summer 1991), pp. 115–31, are best here.
38. G. V. Scammell, *The World Encompassed: The First European Maritime Empires, c. 800–1650* (Berkeley, Cal., 1981); J. H. Parry, *The Age of Reconnaissance,* 2nd edn. (London, 1966).
39. Cipolla, *Economic History of World Population,* p. 120.
40. T. H. Von Laue, *The World Revolution of Westernization* (New York/Oxford, 1987), passim.
41. "The Would-Be European," *Economist,* 4 August 1990, pp. 14–15.
42. These comments are based on McNeill, *Population and Politics Since 1750,* pp. 60–71; Teitelbaum and Winter, *Fear of Population Decline,* passim; many of the essays in W. Alonso (ed.), *Population in an Interacting World* (Cambridge, Mass., 1987); and S. Castles et al., *Here for Good: Western Europe's New Ethnic Minorities* (London, 1984). See also T. Horwitz and C. Forman, "Immigrants to Europe from the Third World Face Racial Animosity," *Wall Street Journal,* 14 August 1990, pp. A1, A8.
43. *World Resources 1990–91,* pp. 254–55. The Australian projection here already looks conservative, given that country's high rate of population growth: see C. Young, "Australia's Population: A Long-Term View," *Current Affairs Bulletin* (Sydney) 65 (May 1989), pp. 4–11.
44. Eberstadt, "Population Change and National Security," p. 125.
45. D. Johnston, "Rise in Crossings Spurs New Actions to Seal U.S. Border," *New York Times,* 9 February 1992, pp. 1, 30; A. Riding, "France Unveils Strict New Rules on Immigration," *New York Times,* 11 July 1991, p. A5.
46. "One Sign of Our Times: World's Refugee Flood," *New York Times,* 12 August 1990, p. 16 (main section).
47. McNeill, *Population and Politics,* p. 69.
48. Eberstadt, "Population Change and National Security," p. 128.
49. Ibid., p. 129.

CHAPTER 3
THE COMMUNICATIONS AND FINANCIAL REVOLUTION AND THE RISE OF THE MULTINATIONAL CORPORATION

1. Both the statistics in the text and this table come from Bairoch, "International Industrialization Levels from 1750 to 1980," p. 273.
2. M. Moynihan, *Global Consumer Demographics* (New York, 1991), p. 28.
3. *World Resources 1990–91,* pp. 244–45.
4. *World Development Report 1990* (Washington, D.C., 1990), p. iii.
5. R. Aggarwal, "The Strategic Challenge of the Evolving Global Economy," *Business Horizons,* July–August 1987, pp. 38–44; W. B. Wriston, "Technology and Sovereignty," *Foreign Affairs,* vol. 67, no. 2 (Winter 1988–89), p. 71. For other comments about these transformations, see B. C. Resnick, "The Globalization of World Financial Markets," *Business Horizons* 32 (November–December 1989), pp. 34–41; "The Stateless Corporation," *Business Week,* 14 May 1990, pp. 98–105; H. B. Malmgren, "Technology and the Economy," in W. E. Brock and

R. D. Hormats (eds.), *The Global Economy: America's Role in the Decade Ahead* (New York/London, 1990), pp. 92–119. More generally, see the important article by P. Drucker, "The Changed World Economy," *Foreign Affairs* 64 (Spring 1984), pp. 768–91.

6. See again Resnick, "Globalization of World Currency Markets," passim; "International Banking," *Economist* (Survey), 25 March 1989; K. Pierog, "How Technology Is Tackling 24-Hour Global Markets," *Futures,* vol. 17, no. 6 (June 1989), pp. 68–74; G. A. Keyworth II, "Goodbye, Central: Telecommunications and Computing in the 1990s," Vital Speeches of the Day, vol. 56, no. 12 (1 April 1990), pp. 358–61.
7. C. F. Bergsten, *America in the World Economy: A Strategy for the 1990s* (Washington, D.C., 1988), pp. 59–60.
8. K. Ohmae, *The Borderless World: Management Lessons in the New Logic of the Global Marketplace* (New York/London, 1990), passim. See also Wriston, "Technology and Sovereignty"; Keyworth, "Goodbye Central," passism.
9. James N. Rosenau, "The Relocation of Authority in a Shrinking World," unpublished paper, 1990.
10. A. W. Pessin, "Communications and Revolution: 1989, the Year Communications Got a Good Name," *Vital Speeches of the Day,* vol. 56, no. 14 (1 May 1990), p. 425.
11. Ohmae, *Borderless World,* p. 3.
12. Ibid.
13. R. B. Reich, *The Work of Nations* (New York, 1990), pp. 3–4, 8–9.
14. Ibid., pp. 115–16, 126.
15. Ohmae, *Borderless World,* p. 170.
16. S. Strange, "Finance, Information, and Power," *Review of International Studies,* vol. 16, no. 3 (July 1990), p. 274. For a more cautionary viewpoint, see E. Helleiner, "States and the Future of Global Finance," *Review of International Studies,* vol. 18, no. 1 (January 1992), pp. 31–49.
17. For the increasing precariousness of the pre-1914 system, for example, see M. de Cecco, *Money and Empire: The International Gold Standard, 1890–1914* (Oxford, 1974). See also the interesting comments of R. P. Gilpin, *The Political Economy of International Relations* (Princeton, 1987), chs. 4 and 9.
18. I have borrowed this sentence from a commentary by my editor Jason Epstein on the first draft of the manuscript of this book.
19. The executive was from Colgate-Palmolive: see Reich, *Work of Nations,* p. 141, quoting from Louis Uchitelle's important article "U.S. Businesses Loosen Link to Mother Country," *New York Times,* 28 May 1984.
20. The Danville/Portland example is provided by Reich, *Work of Nations,* pp. 295–96. The Arlington/Ypsilanti example comes from C. Harlan and J. Mitchell, "Rage, Relief and Warning to UAW Mark GM Decision on Closing Plant," *Wall Street Journal,* 25 February 1992, p. A8; and G. A. Patterson, "How GM's Car Plant in Arlington, Texas, Hustled to Avoid Ax," *Wall Street Journal,* 6 March 1992, pp. A1, A4.
21. Reich, *Work of Nations,* pp. 295–98, gives many examples of this competitive bidding.
22. Ibid., p. 213. Reich's book offers a very clear analysis of these social and occupational trends.
23. Ohmae, *Borderless World.*
24. Ibid., p. xii.
25. Rosenau, "Relocation of Authority," passim.

CHAPTER 4
WORLD AGRICULTURE AND THE BIOTECHNOLOGY REVOLUTION

1. L. R. Brown et al., *State of the World 1990,* p. 5.
2. B. Johnstone, "Fading of the Miracle," and "Sowing for the Future," *Far East Economic Review,* 1 December 1988, pp. 72–75.
3. These causes are discussed in L. R. Brown and J. E. Young, "Feeding the World in the Nineties," ch. 4 of *State of the World 1990;* and in Ehrlich and Ehrlich, *Population Explosion,* chs. 4–5. For a critique of this "alarmism," see D. T. Avery, "Mother Earth Can Feed Billions More," *Wall Street Journal,* 19 September 1991 (op-ed), and J. L. Simon, *Population Matters* (New Brunswick, N.J., 1990), pt. 2.
4. Johnstone, "Fading of the Miracle," passim.
5. Figures from *World Resources 1990–91,* p. 86.
6. These figures can be found in L. R. Brown et al., *State of the World 1990,* p. 65, and *World Resources 1990–91,* p. 87, respectively.
7. *World Resources 1990–91,* p. 87; and N. Calder, *The Green Machines* (New York, 1986), pp. 109–18.
8. Johnstone, "Sowing for the Future," p. 72.
9. *Technology, Public Policy, and the Changing Structure of American Agriculture* (U.S. Congress, Office of Technology Assessment, Washington, D.C., 1986), p. 4.
10. For descriptions of these techniques, see "Biotechnology Survey," *Economist,* 30 April 1988. See also J. L. Marx (ed.), *A Revolution in Biotechnology* (Cambridge, 1989); S. Prentis, *Biotechnology: A New Industrial Revolution* (New York, 1984); R. Teitelman, *Gene Dreams* (New York, 1989); B. D. Davis (ed.), *The Genetic Revolution: Scientific Prospects and Public Perceptions* (Baltimore/London, 1991).
11. "Biotechnology Survey," *Economist,* 30 April 1988, p. 6; *Agricultural Biotechnology: The Next Green Revolution?*, World Bank Technical Paper no. 133 (Washington, D.C., 1991).
12. For the above, see S. Browlee, "The Best Banana Bred," *Atlantic* 264 (September 1989), pp. 22, 24, 28; K. Schneider, "Betting the Farm on Biotech," *New York Times Magazine,* 10 June 1990, "Business World," pp. 26–28, 36, 38–39; J. M. Nash, "A Bumper Crop of Biotech," *Time,* 1 October 1990, pp. 92–94; "The Tomatoes of the Tree of Knowledge," *Economist,* 14 July 1990, p. 83; D. E. Hanke, "Seeding the Bamboo Revolution," *Nature,* 22 (1990).
13. *Science,* 16 June 1989, p. 1281.
14. J. Doyle, "Sustainable Agriculture and the Other Kind of Biotechnology," p. 173; testimony to *Reform and Innovation of Science and Education: Planning for the 1990 Farm Bill* (U.S. Senate, Committee on Agriculture, Nutrition, and Forestry, Washington, D.C., 1989); M. Mellon, "An Environmentalist Perspective," in Davis (ed.), *Genetic Revolution,* pp. 60–76. For the issue of biodiversity vs. genetic uniformity, see R. E. Rhoades, "The World's Food Supply at Risk," *National Geographic* (April 1991), pp. 74–105.
15. L. Busch et al., *Plants, Power, and Profit: Social, Economic and Ethical Consequences of the New Biotechnologies* (Cambridge, Mass./Oxford, 1991), p. 186 (quoting Balandrin et al).
16. See again Schneider, "Betting the Farm on Biotech," passim.
17. Busch et al., *Plants, Power, and Profit,* p. 184.
18. This is a paraphrase of J. Doyle, "DNA—It's Changing the Whole Economy," *Christian Science Monitor,* 30 September 1987, and "Who Will Gain from

Biotechnology?" in S. M. Gendel et al., *Agricultural Bioethics* (Ames, Iowa, 1990), p. 185—a remarkable article. See also M. Kenney, *Biotechnology: The University-Industrial Complex* (New Haven/London, 1986), ch. 10.

19. D. Goodman et al., *From Farming to Biotechnology: A Theory of Agro-Industrial Development* (Oxford, 1987), p. 138 and passim; E. Yoxen, *The Gene Business* (New York, 1983), esp. pp. 140–48.
20. The calculation is by G. Junne and J. Birman, "The Impact of Biotechnology on European Agriculture," in E. Yoxen and V. Di Martino, *Biotechnology in Future Society* (Aldershot, 1989), p. 79.
21. "Biotechnology Survey," *Economist*, 30 April 1988, p. 17.
22. See K. Schneider, "Biotechnology Enters Political Race," *New York Times*, 21 April 1990; G. Gugliotta, "Bovine Growth Hormone Stirs a Debate in Wisconsin," *Washington Post*, National Weekly Edition, July 2–8, 1990, p. 39; and the letters in the *New York Times* of 19 May and 12 June 1990.
23. D. Dickson, "German Biotech Firms Flee Regulatory Controls," *Science*, 16 June 1990, pp. 1251–52.
24. As suggested in Busch et al., *Plants, Power, and Profit*, pp. 175, 178.
25. "Yesterday's Farming," *Economist*, 20 August 1988, passim; M. L. LaGanga, "U.S. Agriculture, Biotech Firms Cut Good Deals with Japanese," *Los Angeles Times*, 9 April 1990, p. D3; H. Yamaguchi, "Biotechnology: New Hope for Japan's Farmers," *Business Japan*, April 1987, pp. 36–40.
26. See again Dickson, "German Biotech Firms Flee Regulatory Controls," passim.
27. A. Gibbons, "Biotechnology Takes Root in the Third World," *Science*, 25 May 1990, p. 962.
28. C. Juma, *The Gene Hunters: Biotechnology and the Scramble for Seeds* (London/Princeton, N.J., 1989), pp. 117–24—an excellent account.
29. L. R. Brown et al., *State of the World 1990*, p. 71.
30. Ibid.
31. J. R. Kloppenburg, "The Social Impacts of Biogenetic Technology in Agriculture: Past and Future," in G. M. Berardi and C. C. Geisler (eds.), *The Social Consequences and Challenges of New Agricultural Technologies* (Boulder, Colo., 1984), p. 318.
32. Busch et al., *Plants, Power, and Profit*, pp. 172, 175, 181–82, provides these examples and statistics in its fine analysis of the problem.
33. Ibid., pp. 183–85. See also the running commentary in J. R. Kloppenburg, *First the Seed: The Political Economy of Plant Biotechnology 1492–2000* (Cambridge, 1988).
34. Contrast, for example, L. R. Brown's "Reexamining the World Food Prospect," *State of the World 1989*, pp. 41–58, with D. T. Avery, "The Green Revolution Is Our Real Food Security," Hudson Institute, Briefing Paper 112, 18 October 1989. See also the various articles in Davis (ed.), *Genetic Revolution*.

CHAPTER 5
ROBOTICS, AUTOMATION, AND A NEW INDUSTRIAL REVOLUTION

1. Landes, *Unbound Prometheus*, p. 41.
2. Kennedy, *Rise and Fall of the Great Powers*, pp. 126–39.
3. This is nicely discussed in T. S. Harmerow, *Restoration, Revolution, Reaction: Economics and Politics in Germany, 1815–1871* (Princeton, N.J., 1958), chs. 2, 5, and 8.

4. According to P. B. Scott, *The Robotics Revolution* (Oxford/New York, 1982), p. 10.
5. Ibid.; and especially W. B. Gevarter, *Intelligent Machines* (Englewood Cliffs, N.J., 1985), p. 161.
6. See the breakdown of the industries using robots in *Annual Review of Engineering Industries and Automation, 1988,* vol. 1 (UN Economic Commission for Europe, N.Y., 1989), p. 53.
7. *Robotics Technology and Its Varied Uses,* Hearing Before the Subcommittee on Science, Research and Technology, U.S. Congress, 25 September 1989 (Washington, D.C., 1989), testimony of Mr. K. G. Engelhardt; see also K. G. Engelhardt, "Innovations in Health Care: Roles for Advanced Intelligent Technologies," *Pittsburgh High Technology Journal,* vol. 2, no. 5, pp. 69–72.
8. *Robotics Technology and Its Varied Uses,* pp. 15, 19, 24.
9. J. Baranson, *Robots in Manufacturing* (Mt. Airy, Md., 1983), p. 67.
10. Ibid., pp. 39–41, 111–27; *Robotics Technology and Its Varied Uses,* p. 76; P. T. Kilborn, "Brave New World Seen for Robots Appears Stalled by Quirks and Costs," *New York Times,* 1 July 1990, p. 16.
11. Kilborn, "Brave New World Seen."
12. Baranson, *Robots in Manufacturing,* p. 86.
13. *Robotics Technology and Its Varied Uses,* p. 172.
14. *Annual Review of Engineering Industries and Automation,* p. 53.
15. "Japan's New Idea: Technology for the 21st Century," *Industry Week* Special Report, 5 September 1990, p. 42.
16. "Bodybuilding Without Tears," *Economist,* 21 April 1990, p. 138.
17. FANUC's operations have been described in innumerable articles, for example, F. L. Schodt, "In the Land of Robots," *Business Month* 132 (November 1988), pp. 67–75; F. Hiatt, "Japanese Robots Reproducing Like Rabbits: High-Tech Capital Investment Helps Fuel Economic Miracle," *Washington Post*, 2 January 1990, pp. A1, A13.; and more technically, D. F. Urbanials, "The Unattended Factory," *13th International Symposium on Industrial Robots, and Robots 7: Conference Proceedings,* vol. 1 (Dearborn, Mich., 1983), pp. I-18 to I-24.
18. See the extremely stimulating article by M. J. E. Cooley, "Robotics—Some Wider Implications," *The World Yearbook of Robotics Research and Development* (1985), pp. 95–104.
19. See again the articles by Schodt and Hiatt (note 17 above).
20. See Table 11 below.
21. M. Carnoy, "High Technology and International Labour Markets," *International Labour Review,* vol. 124, no. 6 (1985), p. 649.
22. Ibid., p. 650.
23. Ibid., p. 653.
24. "Japan's New Idea," *Industry Week,* p. 69.
25. See the argument in Chapter 3.

CHAPTER 6
THE DANGERS TO OUR NATURAL ENVIRONMENT

1. This early narrative is based upon the following key works: B. L. Turner et al., *The Earth As Transformed by Human Action: Global and Regional Changes in the Biosphere over the Past 300 Years* (Cambridge, Mass., 1990); *World Resources 1990–91,* pp. 1–10; L. R. Brown et al., *State of the World 1990,* esp. ch. 1, "The

Illusion of Progress," pp. 3–16; M. Oppenheimer and R. H. Boyle, *Dead Heat: The Race Against the Greenhouse Effect* (New York, 1990), ch. 2; and Rostow, *World Economy: History and Prospects,* esp. pts. 1 and 6.

2. L. R. Brown et al., *State of the World 1990,* p. 6.
3. S. Hecht and A. Cockburn, *The Fate of the Forest: Developers, Destroyers and Defenders of the Amazon* (London/New York, 1989), passim; K. Maxwell, "The Tragedy of the Amazon," *New York Review of Books* 38 (7 March 1991), pp. 24–29.
4. *World Resources 1990–91,* p. 106.
5. See the discussion in J. D. Ives and B. Messerli, *The Himalayan Dilemma: Reconciling Development and Conservation* (London/New York, 1989), ch. 1. (It ought to be noted that while admitting the impact of deforestation, Ives and Messerli argue that there are also profound geophysical reasons for the siltation and floodings.)
6. L. R. Brown et al., *State of the World 1990,* p. 5.
7. *World Resources 1990–91,* pp. 101–2. The 20.4 million hectares figure is based upon a very uncertain extrapolation to *all* tropical forests from the deforestation rate in the Amazon.
8. Well explained in W. V. Reid and K. R. Miller, *Keeping Options Open: The Scientific Basis for Conserving Biodiversity* (Washington, D.C., 1989), passim.
9. "A Latin American Ecological Alliance" (paid advertisement), *New York Times,* 22 July 1991, p. A11.
10. F. Painton, "Where the Sky Stays Dark," *Time,* 28 May 1990, pp. 40–41.
11. L. R. Brown et al., *State of the World 1990,* p. 100.
12. Ibid., p. 109.
13. For a summary of the various studies of this topic, see *World Resources 1990–91,* ch. 10, "Freshwater."
14. L. R. Brown et al., *State of the World 1990,* p. 43, from the chapter "Saving Water for Agriculture," an excellent introduction to this problem.
15. Ibid., pp. 44–45.
16. *World Resources 1990–91,* p. 171, "The Dying Aral Sea."
17. Ibid., pp. 176–77.
18. S. Postel, *Water: Rethinking Management in an Age of Scarcity,* Worldwatch Paper 62 (December 1984), esp. pp. 20–22; and the witty analysis in M. Reisner, *Cadillac Desert* (New York, 1986), passim.
19. The reason global warming has to be seen as *the* environmental problem of our time is articulated in *World Resources 1990–91,* ch. 2, "Climate Change: A Global Concern," pp. 11–31; P. H. Gleick, "Climate Change and International Politics: Problems Facing Developing Countries," *Ambio* 18 (1989), pp. 333–39; P. H. Gleick, "The Implications of Global Changes for International Security," *Climatic Change* 15 (1989), pp. 309–25.
20. This paragraph and the following rely heavily upon a letter to the author by Kenneth Keller, Senior Fellow for Science and Technology, Council on Foreign Relations, 30 January 1992.
21. S. H. Schneider, *Global Warming* (San Francisco, 1989), esp. pp. 18–19. See also "Under the Sun—Is Our World Warming?" *National Geographic,* vol. 178, no. 4 (October 1990), p. 73—an excellent introductory article.
22. *World Resources 1990–91,* p. 14.
23. S. Shulman, "Hot Air—or What?," *Nature* 345 (14 June 1990), p. 4562; D. L. Wheeler, "Scientists Studying 'The Greenhouse Effect' Challenge Fears of Global Warming," *Journal of Forestry,* vol. 88, no. 7 (1989), pp. 34–36; W. K. Stevens,

"Carbon Dioxide Rise May Alter Plant Life, Researchers Say," *New York Times*, 18 September 1990, pp. C1, C9. For critical comments upon this viewpoint, see the entire issue of the journal *Climatic Change* 6 (1985). Note also Avery, "The Green Revolution Is Our Real Food Security," a sustained attack on Lester Brown's Worldwatch Institute; Simon, *Population Matters*, passim; and W. Tucker, *Progress and Privilege* (New York, 1982).

24. For this "consensus," see the U. S. National Research Council's report *Changing Climate* (Washington, D.C., 1983); J. Hansen et al., "Global Climate Changes as Forecast by the Goddard Institute for Space Studies Three-Dimensional Model," *Journal of Geophysical Research* 93 (1988), pp. 9341–64, a very technical piece; and R. A. Kerr, "New Greenhouse Report Puts Down Dissenters," *Science* 249 (3 August 1990), pp. 481–82, an advance summary of the October 1990 report of the International Panel on Climate Change.
25. D. Goleman, "Antarctica Sheds Ice and Scientists Wonder Why," *New York Times*, 14 August 1990, pp. C1, C8.
26. The Intergovernmental Panel on Climate Change apparently believes that "barring strict controls on greenhouse gas emissions, sea level will rise between 8 and 29 centimeters by 2030," which is a rather modest increase (Kerr, "New Greenhouse Report," p. 481). By contrast, a National Academy of Sciences study, which takes "into account the possibility of further polar ice melting, forecast the rise of roughly 1.5 to 3.5 feet in the next century," which is a very different matter (Goleman, "Antarctica Sheds Ice," p. C8). See also the table in S. Hoffman, "Estimates of Future Sea Level Rise," in M. C. Barth and J. G. Titus (eds.), *Greenhouse Effect and Sea Level Rise* (New York, 1984).
27. See E. D. Fajer et al., "The Effects of Enriched Carbon Dioxide Atmospheres on Plant–Insect Herbivores Interactions," *Science* 243 (1989), pp. 1198–1200. This concerns, however, a single plant-insect interaction.
28. J. Broadus et al., "Rising Sea Level and Damming of Rivers: Possible Effects in Egypt and Bangladesh," in J. G. Titus (ed.), *Effects of Changes in Stratospheric Ozone and Global Climate*, vol. 4, *Sea Level Rise* (Washington, D.C., 1986).
29. Figures from *World Resources 1990–91*, pp. 244–45.
30. J. Hoffman et al., *Projecting Future Sea Level Rise: Methodology, Estimate to the Year 2000, and Research Needs* (Washington, D.C., 1983), passim.
31. *World Resources 1990–91*, pp. 254–55.
32. T. F. Homer-Dixon, "On the Threshold: Environmental Changes as Causes of Acute Conflict," *International Security*, vol. 16, no. 2 (Fall 1991), pp. 76–116; Gleick, "Implications of Global Change for International Security," passim.
33. Hoffman et al., *Projecting Future Sea Level Rise.*
34. See, for example, S. Manabe and R. T. Wetherald, "Large-Scale Changes of Soil Wetness Induced by an Increase in Atmospheric Carbon Dioxide," *Journal of Atmospheric Sciences* 44 (1987), pp. 1211–35.
35. Gleick, "Implications of Global Climate Changes for International Security," passim.
36. D. V. Williams, "Estimated Bioresource Sensitivity to Climate Change in Alberta, Canada," *Climatic Change* 7 (1985), pp. 55–69; B. Smit et al., "Sensitivity of Crop Yields and Land Resource Potential to Climate Change in Ontario, Canada," *Climatic Change* 14 (1989), pp. 153–74.
37. See the illustrations and text on pp. 86–87 of "Under the Sun—Is Our World Warming?"
38. "Energy and the Environment," *Economist* Survey, August 1991; M. W. Browne,

"93 Nations Agree to Ban Chemicals That Harm Ozone," *New York Times,* 30 June 1990, p. A1.

39. C. Flavin, "Slowing Global Warming," in L. R. Brown et al., *State of the World 1990,* p. 21.
40. What follows is based upon J. MacNeill et al., *Beyond Interdependence* (New York/Oxford, 1991), chs. 4–5; Flavin, "Slowing Global Warming," pp. 17–38: *World Resources 1990–91,* pp. 24–30; Oppenheimer and Boyle, *Dead Heat,* passim; Schneider, *Global Warming,* pp. 260ff. For the potentialities of photovoltaic energy, see Y. Hamakawa, "Photovoltaic Power," *Scientific American* 256 (April 1987), pp. 87–92.
41. *World Resources 1990–91,* p. 105.
42. L. R. Brown et al., *State of the World 1990,* p. 20.
43. An important exception here: Senator Albert Gore, *Earth in the Balance: Ecology and the Human Spirit* (New York, 1992)—an excellent overview of the environmental crisis. Will he now, as vice president, be able to translate his ideas into policies?
44. See the articles referred to in note 23 above; and "How to Find an Ozone Hole," *Wall Street Journal,* 28 February 1992, p. A14.
45. W. D. Nordhaus, "Global Warming: Slowing the Greenhouse Express," Cowes Foundation Paper no. 758 (Yale University, New Haven, 1990), passim.
46. M. D. Lowe, "Cycling into the Future," in L. R. Brown et al., *State of the World 1990,* ch. 7.
47. P. Lewis, "Balancing Industry with the Ecology," *New York Times,* 2 March 1992, p. A3.

CHAPTER 7
THE FUTURE OF THE NATION-STATE

1. C. Tilly (ed.), *The Formation of National States in Western Europe* (Princeton, N.J., 1975); J. H. Shennan, *The Origins of the Modern European State 1450–1725* (London, 1974); H. Lubasz (ed.), *The Development of the Modern State* (New York, 1964).
2. For details, see P. Dollinger, *La Hanse* (Paris, 1964), and the shorter analysis in Scammell, *World Encompassed,* ch. 2.
3. See V. G. Kiernan, "State and Nation in Western Europe," *Past and Present* 31 (1965), pp. 20–38; and esp. D. Kaiser, *Politics and War: European Conflict from Philip II to Hitler* (Cambridge, Mass., 1990), ch. 2.
4. For a good example, see C. Wilson, *Profit and Power: A Study of England and the Dutch Wars* (London, 1957); and, more generally, Kennedy, *Rise and Fall of the Great Powers,* chs. 2 and 3.
5. O. Ranum (ed.), *National Consciousness, History and Political Culture in Early-Modern Europe* (Baltimore/London, 1975); C. Jones (ed.), *Britain and Revolutionary France: Conflict, Subversion and Propaganda,* Exeter Studies in History, no. 5 (Exeter, 1983); L. Colley, "The Apotheosis of George III: Loyalty, Royalty and the British Nation 1760–1820," *Past and Present* 102 (February 1984), pp. 94–129; idem., *Britons* (New Haven/London, 1992).
6. M. Howard, *The Lessons of History* (New Haven, Conn., 1991), chs. 4–7; J. Joll, *The Origins of the First World War* (London/New York, 1984), chs. 4–5 and 7–8.

7. Well covered in A. Marwick, *War and Social Change in the Twentieth Century* (London, 1974); and A. Calder, *The People's War* (London, 1969).
8. G. Adama, *The Iron Triangle* (New York, 1981); R. W. DeGrasse, *Military Expansion, Economic Decline* (Armonk, N.Y., 1985 edn.); L. Thurow, "How to Wreck the Economy," *New York Review of Books,* 14 May 1981, pp. 3–8; M. Kaldor, *The Baroque Arsenal* (London, 1982); R. Cohen and P. A. Wilson, *Superpowers in Economic Decline* (New York, 1990).
9. J. Joffe, "Germany After NATO," *Harper's Magazine,* September 1990, p. 31; E. N. Luttwak, "From Geopolitics to Geo-Economics," *National Interest* 20 (Summer 1990), p. 19; N. Munro, "Atwood: New Power Found in Economies," *Defense News,* 4 December 1989, p. 18 (reporting on a speech by U.S. Deputy Secretary of Defense Donald Atwood); C. V. Prestowitz et al., (eds.), *Powernomics: Economics and Strategy After the Cold War* (Lanham, Md., 1991).
10. See the articles in A. H. Westing, *Global Resources and International Conflict* (Oxford/New York, 1986), as well as the specific case study by J. R. Starr and D. C. Stoll, *The Politics of Scarcity: Water in the Middle East* (Boulder, Colo., 1988).
11. T. H. Moran, "International Economics and National Security," *Foreign Affairs,* vol. 69, no. 5 (Winter 1990–91), pp. 80–82; T. H. Moran, "The Globalization of America's Defense Industries: Managing the Threat of Foreign Dependence," *International Security* 15 (Summer 1990), pp. 57–100.
12. See the references in note 9 above, as well as T. C. Sorensen, "Rethinking National Security," *Foreign Affairs,* vol. 69, no. 3 (Summer 1990), pp. 1–18; W. Greene, "An Idea Whose Time Is Fading," *Time,* 28 May 1990, p. 90 (on the changing concept of national security).
13. See S. Hassan, "Environmental Issues and Security in South Asia," *Adelphi Papers* 262 (Autumn 1991), passim; and, more generally, the essays in Westing (ed.), *Global Resources and International Conflict.*
14. See the more extensive discussion in J. T. Mathews, "Redefining Security," *Foreign Affairs,* vol. 68, no. 2 (Spring 1989), pp. 174–77; and the articles in L. Brown et al., *State of the World 1990,* passim.
15. Moran, "International Economics and National Security," p. 90.
16. These paragraphs borrow from Rosenau's discussion of "the relocation of authority" (referred to in Chapter 3, note 9, above).
17. Immanuel Kant, *Zum Ewigen Frieden* (1795); (Stuttgart, 1954 edn.), p. 49. This quotation was brought to my attention by H. W. Smith, "Nationalism and Religious Conflict in Imperial Germany 1887–1914," Ph.D. dissertation, Yale University, 1991), pp. 1–2.

CHAPTER 8
THE JAPANESE "PLAN" FOR A POST–2000 WORLD

1. See H. Kahn, *The Emerging Japanese Superstate* (London, 1971); E. F. Vogel, *Japan as Number One; Lessons for America* (New York, 1980 edn.); E. F. Vogel, "Pax Nipponica," *Foreign Affairs,* vol. 64, no. 4 (Spring 1986), pp. 752–67; Burstein, *Yen!* T. R. Zengage and C. T. Ratcliffe, *The Japanese Century* (Hong Kong, 1988). There is also a good analysis in R. M. Morse, "Japan's Drive to Pre-eminence," *Foreign Policy* 69 (Winter 1987–88), pp. 3–21.
2. J. S. Nye, Jr., *Bound to Lead* (New York, 1990), pp. 154–70; K. E. House, "Though Rich, Japan Is Poor in Many Elements of Global Leadership," *Wall Street Journal,* 30 January 1989, pp. 1, 9; R. Taggert Murphy, "Power Without

Purpose," *Harvard Business Review* 66 (March–April 1988), pp. 71–83; Fallows, *More Like Us;* K. van Wolferen, *The Enigma of Japanese Power* (London/New York, 1989); B. Emmott, *The Sun Also Sets: The Limits to Japan's Economic Power* (New York, 1989).

3. See Vogel, *Japan as Number One,* chs. 3–9.
4. For what follows, see Ibid., ch. 7; T. P. Rohlen, *Japan's High Schools* (Berkeley, Cal., 1983), passim; R. P. Dore and M. Sako, *How the Japanese Learn to Work* (London, 1989); M. White, *The Japanese Educational Challenge* (New York, 1989). See also the interesting article by M. and J. Sayle, "Why We Send Our Children to a Japanese School," *Tokyo Journal,* August 1990, pp. 78–83, for an empathetic description of the system; and "Why Can't Little Taro Think?" *Economist,* 21 April 1990, pp. 21–24, which is much more critical.
5. 1987 statistics: see *Education in Japan,* Foreign Press Center (Tokyo, 1988), p. 17.
6. For these figures, see Dore and Sako, *How the Japanese Learn to Work,* p. 1 (percentage in school); *Education in Japan,* pp. 18–19 (number of school days); *Fortune,* 6 November 1989, p. 88 (science scores); "Why Can't Little Taro Think?" p. 23 (intelligence scores).
7. For these figures, see *UNESCO Statistical Yearbook 1989,* tables 5.15 and 5.17; and Kennedy, *Rise and Fall of the Great Powers,* p. 464. For signs of the Japanese turn toward scientific innovation, see G. Bylinsky, "Trying to Transcend Copycat Science," *Fortune,* 30 March 1987, pp. 42–46; and "Who Are the Copycats Now?" *Economist,* 20 May 1989, pp. 91–94. Also very important is "Japanese Technology," *Economist* Survey, 2 December 1989, with many additional statistics.
8. There is good coverage of this in Burstein, *Yen!;* Emmott, *Sun Also Sets;* and van Wolferen, *Enigma.* See also "The New Global Top Banker: Tokyo and Its Mighty Money," *New York Times,* 27 April 1986, pp. 1, 16.
9. See, for example, J. Womack et al., *The Machine That Changed the World* (London, 1990), passim; "Japan's New Idea," Special Report to *Industry Week,* 3 September 1990, pp. 34–69; B. Bowonder and T. Miyake, "Technology Development and Japanese Industrial Competitiveness," *Futures,* vol. 22, no. 1 (January–February 1990, pp. 21–45.
10. This "ideal" is well argued in M. Porter, *The Competitive Advantage of Nations* (New York, 1990), esp. ch. 5.
11. According to the U.S. Council on Competitiveness, in 1989 Japanese investment in plant and equipment totaled $549 billion, compared with the American total of $513 billion: *New Haven Register,* Associated Press report, 24 June 1990, p. A9. For the yen-to-dollar exchange rate, see "The Joy of High Costs," *Economist,* 4 March 1989, p. 66.
12. See in particular the coverage in Zengage and Ratcliffe, *Japanese Century,* ch. 2; and "Japanese Technology," *Economist* Survey, 2 December 1989.
13. P. Revzin, "Japanese Systematically Invest in Europe Prior to 1992 Changes," *Wall Street Journal,* 10 December 1990, p. A7A.
14. See the table in Linder, *Pacific Century,* p. 12, quoting from a *Japan in the Year 2000* study; C. F. Bergsten, "The World Economy After the Cold War," *Foreign Affairs,* vol. 69, no. 3 (Summer 1990), p. 96.
15. The classic study remains Chalmers Johnson, *MITI and the Japanese Miracle* (Stanford, Cal., 1982); but see also van Wolferen's negative comments upon MITI in *Enigma,* ch. 5, "The Administrators."
16. This is covered in E. A. Olsen, *U.S.–Japanese Strategic Reciprocity: A Neo-*

Nationalist View (Stanford, Cal., 1985), passim; G. Segal, *Rethinking the Pacific* (Oxford, 1990), pp. 242–45.

17. This is also the argument in H. W. Maull, "Germany and Japan: The New Civilian Powers," *Foreign Affairs,* vol. 69, no. 5 (Winter 1990–91), p. 92.
18. See R. Robinson and J. Gallagher, *Africa and the Victorians* (London, 1961), ch. 1, "The Spirit of Victorian Expansion."
19. J. Steingold, "Japan Builds East Asia Links, Gaining Labor and Markets," *New York Times,* 8 May 1990, pp. A1, D18; Segal, *Rethinking the Pacific,* p. 365; the articles in *Far East Economic Review,* 3 May 1990, pp. 46–55; "The Yen Block," *Economist* Survey, 15 July 1989; "Japan Builds a New Power Base," *Business Week,* 20 March 1989, pp. 18–23. I also benefited from Richard P. Cronin, "Japan's Expanding Role and Influence in the Asia-Pacific Region: Implications for U.S. Interests and Policy," Congressional Research Service paper, Washington, D.C., September 1990.
20. See again van Wolferen, *Enigma,* passim; Fallows, *More Like Us,* passim; J. Taylor, *Shadows of the Rising Sun: A Critical View of the "Japanese Miracle"* (New York, 1984); S. Kamata, *Japan in the Passing Lane* (New York, 1984).
21. D. Moisi, "If Japan Is So Successful, Where Are Its Imitators?" *International Herald Tribune,* 24 October 1990, p. 7; Nye, *Bound to Lead,* pp. 166–69. For comments upon racism, see van Wolferen, *Enigma,* passim; and I. Buruma, *Behind the Mask* (New York, 1984).
22. This is most systematically covered in C. Prestowitz, *Trading Places: How We Allowed Japan to Take the Lead* (New York, 1988); but see also the coverage in van Wolferen, *Enigma,* pp. 393ff.
23. "Pity Those Poor Japanese," *Economist,* 24 December 1988; "Japan's Silent Majority Starts to Mumble," *Business Week,* 23 April 1990, pp. 52–54.
24. This is particularly well developed in Emmott, *Sun Also Sets;* but see also "Tokyo Sings the Blues," *Economist,* 24 November 1990, p. 31; and "Can Japan Cope?" *Business Week,* 23 April 1990, pp. 46–51. The demographic changes are covered in L. G. Martin, "The Graying of Japan," *Population Bulletin,* vol. 44, no. 2 (July 1989). The most pessimistic of all accounts is B. Reading, *Japan: The Coming Collapse* (London, 1992).
25. Which is the thrust of van Wolferen's argument in *Enigma,* and in "The Japan Problem," *Foreign Affairs,* vol. 62, no. 2 (Winter 1986–87), pp. 288–303.
26. See D. Halberstam, "Can We Rise to the Japanese Challenge?" *Parade,* 9 October 1983; and Fallows, *More Like Us.*
27. Morse, "Japan's Drive to Pre-eminence," has some interesting comments upon the misunderstandings of non-Japanese-speaking experts. See also van Wolferen, "The Japan Problem Revisited," *Foreign Affairs,* vol. 69, no. 4 (Fall 1990), pp. 42–55.
28. For a discussion of this problem, see M. L. Balfour, *Britain and Joseph Chamberlain* (London/Boston, 1985), pp. 17–19, 207–210, 298–300; and P. Kennedy, *The Realities Behind Diplomacy* (London, 1980), pp. 22–24.
29. See again Emmott, *Sun Also Sets.* For Japan's financial troubles, see "Japanese Finance: Falling Apples," *Economist* Special Survey, 8 December 1990.
30. "Japan's New Idea," *Business Week,* 3 September 1990; Vogel, "Pax Nipponica," passim; Zengage and Ratcliffe, *Japanese Century;* Morse, "Japan's Drive to Pre-eminence," passim; "Japanese Technology," *Economist* Survey, 2 December 1989; "Japan, At Your Service," *Economist,* 20 October 1990, pp. 83–84.
31. See again Fallows, *More Like Us* (although note that his argument is chiefly about *America's* need to change).

32. For examples of this in the United States, see P. Choate, *Agents of Influence* (New York, 1990).
33. Van Wolferen, *Enigma,* pp. 403–5, offers the interesting observation "Although there is no convincing reason to suspect that the [Japanese] administrators have worked out a grand master-plan for industrial domination of the world, what they are doing has the same effect as if there were such a plan." Zengage and Ratcliffe, *Japanese Century,* refers frequently to the Japanese "game plan"; see pp. 192–93. See also T. H. White's alarmist piece "The Danger from Japan," *New York Times Magazine,* 28 July 1985.
34. "Reconsider Japan," *Economist,* 26 April 1986, pp. 19–22.
35. See again Porter, *Competitive Advantage of Nations.*
36. This is suggested in Morse, "Japan's Drive to Pre-eminence." I also benefited from Okazaki Hisahiko's paper "The Restructuring of the U.S.-Japan Alliance," 29 July 1989, an English-language translation of his July 1988 *Bungei Shinju* article on the same topic.
37. See Burstein, *Yen!* ch. 11; D. S. Zakheim, "Japan's Emerging Military-Industrial Machine," *New York Times,* 27 June 1990, p. A23; and G. R. Packard, "The Coming U.S.–Japan Crisis," *Foreign Affairs* 66 (Winter 1987–88), pp. 356–57. Also useful is F. C. Iklé and T. Nakanishi, "Japan's Grand Strategy," *Foreign Affairs,* vol. 69, no. 3 (Summer 1990), pp. 81–95.
38. See again Morse, "Japan's Drive to Pre-eminence," passim; and "From Superrich to Superpower," *Time,* 4 July 1988, pp. 28–31. There is also a very useful analysis of Japan's future options in K. B. Pyle, "Japan, the World, and the Twenty-first Century," in *The Political Economy of Japan,* vol. 2, *The Changing International Context,* eds. T. Inoguchi and D. I. Okimoto (Stanford, Cal., 1988), pp. 446–86.
39. "Rankings," *Wall Street Journal,* World Business Report, 20 September 1991, pp. R8–R9.
40. Ibid.
41. W. J. Broad, "In the Realm of Technology, Japan Looms Ever Larger," *New York Times,* 28 May 1991, pp. C1, C8. (*Influential* patents refers to those cited frequently in subsequent papers and patents, as opposed to eccentric and unimportant patents.)
42. *CIA Handbook of Economic Statistics, 1990* (Washington, D.C., 1990), p. 162.
43. Martin, "Graying of Japan," p. 7.
44. D. E. Sanger, "Tokyo Official Ties Birth Decline to Education," *New York Times,* 14 June 1990; D. E. Sanger, "Minister Denies He Opposed College for Japanese Women," *New York Times,* 19 June 1990.
45. "The Silvering of Japan," *Economist,* 7 October 1989, p. 81.
46. Ibid.; "The Dwindling Japanese," *Economist,* 26 January 1991, p. 36; Martin, "Graying of Japan"; and R. S. Jones, "The Economic Implications of Japan's Aging Population," *Asian Survey,* vol. 28, no. 9 (September 1988), pp. 958–69—an excellent summary.
47. "No Way to Treat a Guest," *Economist,* 2 June 1990, p. 36; "Revised Immigration Law Is Criticized as Foreign Workers Wait to Be Deported," *Japan Times,* Weekly International Edition, 11–17 June 1990, p. 3.
48. Sanger, "Minister Denies . . . ," passim (quoting Professor Kuniko Inoguchi); Jones, "Economic Implications," p. 969; "The Dwindling Japanese."
49. "The Dwindling Japanese."
50. For the following, see M. Maruyama, "Japan's Agricultural Policy Failure," *Food Policy* (May 1987), pp. 123–26; "Yesterday's Farming," *Economist,* 20 August

1988, pp. 58–59; "Here Comes Farmer Giles-san," *Economist,* 8 June 1991, pp. 35–36.

51. M. L. LaGanga, "U.S. Agriculture, Biotech Firms Cut Good Deals with Japanese," *Los Angeles Times,* 9 April 1990, p. D3; Yamaguchi, "Biotechnology: New Hope for Japan's Farmers," pp. 36–40.
52. F. J. Galde and D. G. Aubrey, "Changing Climate and the Pacific," *Oceanus,* vol. 32, no. 4 (Winter 1989–90), pp. 72–73.
53. M. Prowse, "Japan Deserves a Little Respect," *Financial Times,* 7 May 1991, p. 38.
54. Van Wolferen, *Enigma,* passim; House, "Though Rich, Japan Is Poor in Many Elements of Global Leadership," passim.
55. C. Johnson, "Japan in Search of a 'Normal' Role," Institute on Global Conflict and Cooperation (U.C., San Diego), Policy Paper no. 3, July 1992, provides a very useful summary of Japan's dilemmas.

CHAPTER 9
INDIA AND CHINA

1. *World Resources 1990–91,* p. 345.
2. Ibid., pp. 244–45. Since these are national averages, the implication is that many millions survive on less than $100 a year.
3. *Trends in Developing Economies 1990,* p. 244, gives Korea's 1989 per capita GNP as $4,400, which presumably means that the past two years of growth will have brought it close to $5,000 at current prices. Using the *World Resources 1990–91* table of China and India's population (see note 1 above), a per capita GNP of $5,000 for each would produce totals of $5.6 trillion for China and $4.2 trillion for India.
4. *Trends in Developing Countries 1990,* pp. 113–269.
5. Ibid., p. 108.
6. A. Coale, "Fertility and Mortality in Different Populations with Special Attention to China," *Proceedings of the American Philosophical Society,* vol. 132, no. 2 (1988), p. 186. H. Angang and Z. Ping, *China's Population Development* (Beijing, 1991), gives the total as "more than 15 million," p. 13.
7. "China: The Mewling That They'll Miss," *Economist,* 13 August 1988, p. 31; Z. Yi, "Population Policies in China: New Challenge and Strategies," in J. M. Eekelaar and D. Pearl (eds.), *An Aging World: Dilemmas and Challenges for Law and Social Policy* (Oxford, 1989), pp. 61–62.
8. "Peasants' Revolt," *Economist,* 30 January 1988, p. 27.
9. "China: The Mewling That They'll Miss," p. 63.
10. "China: The Mewling That They'll Miss."
11. S. WuDunn, "China, with Even More to Feed, Pushes Anew for Small Families," *New York Times,* 16 June 1991, p. 12.
12. Yi, "Population Policies in China," p. 65.
13. Coale, "Fertility and Mortality in . . . China," p. 189.
14. Ibid., p. 188; and see esp. N. Ogawa, "Aging in China: Demographic Alternatives," *Asia-Pacific Population Journal,* vol. 3, no. 3 (September 1988), pp. 21–64. The above section also benefited from Angang and Ping, *China's Population Development.*
15. M. Tain and R. Menon, "The Greying of India," *India Today,* 30 September 1991, pp. 24–33.

16. The figures for life expectancy at independence come from B. L. C. Johnson, *Development in South Asia* (Harmondsworth, Mddsx., 1983), p. 169; for the late 1980s, from *World Resources 1990–91,* p. 257.
17. B. Crossette, "Why India Is Still Failing to Stop Its Population Surge," *New York Times,* 9 July 1989, Week in Review, p. 3.
18. Statistics from *World Resources 1990–91,* pp. 255, 257.
19. B. J. McCormick, *The World Economy: Patterns of Growth and Change* (Oxford, 1988), p. 251.
20. These are the categories examined in B. L. C. Johnson, *Development in South Asia,* ch. 12, "Levels of Living and the Plight of the Poor."
21. *World Resources 1990–91,* p. 245 (1987 figures).
22. For what follows, see Johnson, *Development in South Asia,* chs. 5–8; McCormick, *World Economy,* pp. 246–48; B. H. Farmer, "Perspectives on the Green Revolution in South Asia," *Modern Asian Studies* 20 (1986), pp. 175–99.
23. See in particular the detailed analysis by P. S. Mann, "Green Revolution Revisited: The Adoption of High Yielding Variety Wheat Seeds in India," *Journal of Development Studies,* vol. 26, no. 1 (October 1989), pp. 131–44.
24. Johnson, *Development in South Asia,* chs. 6–7.
25. L. Kaye, "The White Revolution," *Far Eastern Economic Review,* 24 March 1988, p. 112.
26. J. McMillan et al., "The Impact of China's Economic Reforms on Agricultural Productivity Growth," *Journal of Political Economy,* vol. 97, no. 4 (1989), pp. 781–85; N. R. Lardy, "Agricultural Reforms in China," *Journal of International Affairs* 39 (Winter 1986), pp. 91–104.
27. *The Economist World Atlas and Almanac 1989,* p. 222.
28. This figure, originally taken from U.S. Department of Agriculture, was also reproduced in Kennedy, *Rise and Fall of the Great Powers,* p. 442.
29. Y. Yang and R. Tyers, "The Economic Costs of Self-Sufficiency in China," *World Development,* vol. 17, no. 2 (1989), p. 234.
30. This is the argument in ibid.
31. For this list, see Johnson, *Development in South Asia,* p. 141; and K. Marton, *Multinationals, Technology, and Industrialization* (Lexington, Mass., 1982), ch. 10, "India."
32. "Asia," *Economist,* 23 June 1990, p. 27.
33. A. Vaidyanathan, "Indian Economic Performance and Prospects," in P. K. Ghosh (ed.), *Developing South Asia* (Westport, Conn., 1984), pp. 10–11.
34. The 1950 and 1978–79 figures are from Johnson, *Development in South Asia,* p. 136; the 1989 figure from *Trends in Developing Economies 1990,* p. 264.
35. *Trends in Developing Economies 1990,* p. 269, gives industry's share of the labor force as 13.2 percent in 1980, which suggests that manufacturing's share might be less than 10 percent. See also *The Statesman's Yearbook 1990–91* J. Paxton (ed.), (New York/London, 1990), p. 644, which states that in 1984 only 7.4 million were employed in manufacturing out of a labor force of 222.5 million workers.
36. "Asia," *Economist,* 23 June 1990, p. 27.
37. I. J. Ahluwalia, "Industrial Growth in India: Performance and Prospects," *Journal of Development Economics* 28 (1986), p. 8; "Asia," *Economist,* 23 June 1990, p. 27.
38. For a lively account of this transformation, see O. Schell, *To Get Rich Is Glorious: China in the '80s* (New York, 1985).
39. J. P. Sterba, "Long March," *Wall Street Journal,* 16 June 1989, p. A4.

40. "China," *Economist,* 20 October 1990, p. 40; *Trends in Developing Economies 1990,* pp. 114, 270.
41. For some of those rosy projections, see Kennedy, *Rise and Fall of the Great Powers,* pp. 454–58.
42. "Rich China, Poor China: The Gap Keeps Growing," *Business Week,* 5 June 1989, pp. 40–41; "Amid the Sourness, a Portion of China That Is Still Sweet," *Economist,* 19 August 1989, pp. 21–22. For more details, see also E. F. Vogel, *One Step Ahead in China: Guangdong Under Reform* (Cambridge, Mass., 1990); and D. Goodman, *China's Regional Development* (London, 1989).
43. "When the Reforming Spirit Flags," *Economist,* 1 April 1989, pp. 29–30; J. P. Sterba, "How the Twisting Path of China's Reform Led to Guns of Tiananmen," *Wall Street Journal,* 16 June 1989, pp. A1, A4.
44. "China Begins a New Long March," *Business Week,* 5 June 1989, pp. 38–46.
45. "China's Economy: Joyless Christmas Tidings," *Economist,* 24 November 1990, pp. 32–33; and N. D. Kristof, "At the Businesses Owned by Beijing: The Ink Is Red," *New York Times,* 18 November 1990, Week in Review, p. 2.
46. P. H. B. Goodwin, "Soldiers and Statesmen: Chinese Defense and Foreign Policies in the 1990s," in S. S. Kim (ed.), *China and the World* (Boulder, Colo., 1989), p. 192.
47. For more details, see G. Segal, *Defending China* (Oxford, 1985); Segal, *Rethinking the Pacific,* chs. 12–13; J. Keegan and A. Wheatcroft, *Zones of Conflict* (New York, 1978), ch. 15, "China: The Zones of Vulnerability"; G. Chaliand and J. P. Rageau, *A Strategic Atlas* (New York, 1985), pp. 67, 143–50; R. Delfs, "A Two-Front Threat: China Sees Danger from Japan, Soviet Union," *Far Eastern Economic Review,* 13 December 1990, pp. 28–30.
48. For these criticisms, see the series of related articles by J. Clad, "Power Amid Poverty: India Puts National Pride Before Defence Efficiency," *Far Eastern Economic Review,* 7 June 1990, pp. 47–51; and A. Gupta, "The Indian Arms Industry: A Lumbering Giant," *Asian Survey,* vol. 30, no. 9 (September 1990), pp. 847–61.
49. See the argument in Kennedy, *Rise and Fall of the Great Powers,* esp. pp. 536ff. A good example of this traditional thinking can be seen in A. Prakosh, "A Carrier Force for the Indian Navy," *Naval War College Review,* vol. 43, no. 4 (Autumn 1990), pp. 58–71.
50. Statistics from "Development Brief," *Economist,* 26 May 1990, p. 81; Paxton (ed.), *Statesman's Yearbook 1990–91,* p. 364.
51. "Development Brief"; Paxton (ed.), *Statesman's Yearbook 1990–91,* p. 650, gives the literacy rate (1981 census) as being 47 percent male and 25 percent female, both of which probably increased somewhat during the 1980s.
52. See the details in N. Kristof, "In Rural China, Road to School Is All Uphill," *New York Times,* 3 December 1990, pp. A1, A15.
53. *UNESCO Statistical Yearbook 1989* (Paris, 1989), Table 1, "Educational Attainment."
54. Ibid.; see also Paxton (ed.), *Statesman's Yearbook 1990–91,* p. 364.
55. *UNESCO Statistical Yearbook 1989,* Table 3.11, "Third level: teachers and institutions by type of institution."
56. Johnson, *Development in South Asia,* pp. 213–15.
57. *UNESCO Statistical Yearbook 1989,* Table 5.3, "Scientific and technical personnel in R&D."
58. *UNESCO Statistical Digest 1987* (Paris, 1987), p. 188 (China) and p. 196 (India).
59. Johnson, *Development in South Asia,* p. 214.

60. D. Ernst and D. O'Conner, *Technology and Global Competition* (OECD; Paris, 1989), p. 53.
61. Marton, *Multinationals, Technology, and Industrialization,* p. 236. See also S. Lall, *Developing Countries as Exporters of Technology: A First Look at the Indian Experience* (London, 1982), p. 19 (Table 3.1), which gives details of the geographical destination of engineering goods exports; and *World Link,* vol. 3, nos. 9/10 (September–October 1990), which includes a special "Area Profile" on India, full of declarations about liberalization and competitiveness.
62. See again Johnson, *Development in South Asia,* for consideration of what technologies might be appropriate for India's stage of development.
63. See the comments by Sam Pitroda (Rajiv Gandhi's science adviser) on investing in the "software" of female education rather than the hardware of steel mills, as reported in Crossette, "Why India Is Still Failing to Stop Its Population Surge."
64. See esp. J. Polumbaum, "Dateline China: The People's Malaise," *Foreign Policy* 20 (Winter 1990–91), pp. 163–81; L. W. Pye, "China: Erratic State, Frustrated Society," *Foreign Affairs,* vol. 69, no. 4 (Fall 1990), pp. 56–74.
65. M. P. Singh, "The Crisis of the Indian State," *Asian Survey,* vol. 30, no. 8 (August 1990), p. 815; B. Weinraub, "India Peers at Its Future with a Sense of Gloom," *New York Times,* 14 July 1991, p. E2.
66. B. Crossette, "As Violent Year Ends, India Pleads for Peace," *New York Times,* 1 January 1991, p. A5; A. S. Abraham, "The Failure of India's Fling with V. P. Singh," *Wall Street Journal,* 14 November 1990, p. A16 (op-ed).
67. "India's Upheavals," *Wall Street Journal,* 14 November 1990, p. A16 (lead article).
68. "The South China Miracle," *Economist,* 5 October 1991, pp. 19–44.
69. Ibid.
70. 1987 figures: from *World Resources 1990–91,* pp. 244–45.
71. C. Nickerson, "China Copies Worst Polluters," *Boston Globe,* 20 December 1989, pp. 1, 16. See also "Pollution in Asia," *Economist,* 6 October 1990, pp. 21–26.
72. These measures are described in W. Yuging, "Natural Conservation Regions in China," *Ambio,* vol. 16, no. 6 (1987), pp. 326–31; H. Yuanjun and Z. Zhongzing, "Environmental Pollution and Control Measures in China," *Ambio,* vol. 16, no. 5 (1987), pp. 257–61. Nickerson, "China Copies Worst Polluters," gives details of the tree-planting schemes and the disappointing results.
73. H. Govind, "Recent Developments in Environmental Protection in India: Pollution Control," *Ambio,* vol. 18, no. 8 (1989), p. 429. The exclamation mark is mine; presumably a very broad definition of "victims of environmental pollution" is being used here, and not merely people with respiratory problems. The loss of forest cover in the New Delhi area is reported in T. Wicker, "Battered and Abused," *New York Times,* 25 November 1988, p. A31.
74. Govind, "Recent Developments in Environmental Protection in India," p. 430.
75. "Pollution in Asia," p. 22.
76. Nickerson, "China Copies Worst Polluters," p. 16.
77. Ibid.

CHAPTER 10
WINNERS AND LOSERS IN THE DEVELOPING WORLD

1. *World Tables 1991* (World Bank, Washington, D.C., 1991), pp. 268–69, 352–53.
2. Ibid.

3. See the World Bank publication *Trends in Developing Economies 1990,* pp. 299–303, for Korea.
4. For descriptions, see F. Braudel, *Civilization and Capitalism,* vol. 3, *The Perspective of the World* (New York, 1986), pp. 506–11.
5. See P. Lyon, "Emergence of the Third World," in H. Bull and A. Watson (eds.), *The Expansion of International Society* (Oxford, 1983), pp. 229ff.; G. Barraclough, *An Introduction to Contemporary History* (Harmondsworth, Mddsx., 1967 edn.), ch. 6, "The Revolt Against the West."
6. J. Ravenhill, "The North-South Balance of Power," *International Affairs,* vol. 66, no. 4 (1990), pp. 745–46. See also J. Cruickshank," The Rise and Fall of the Third World: A Concept Whose Time Has Passed," *World Press Review* 38 (February 1991), pp. 28–29.
7. Ravenhill, "North-South Balance of Power," p. 732.
8. W. L. M. Adriaansen and J. G. Waardensburg (eds.), *A Dual World Economy* (Rotterdam, 1989).
9. S. Fardoust and A. Dhareshwan, *Long-Term Outlook for the World Economy: Issues and Projections for the 1990s* (World Bank, Washington, D.C., February 1990), p. 9, Table 3.
10. P. Drysdale, "The Pacific Basin and Its Economic Vitality," in Morley (ed.), *Pacific Basin,* p. 11.
11. See esp., "Taiwan and Korea: Two Paths to Prosperity," *Economist,* 14 July 1990, pp. 19–21; also "South Korea," *Economist* Survey, 18 August 1990. There is a useful comparative survey in L. A. Veit, "Time of the New Asian Tigers," *Challenge* 30 (July–August 1987), pp. 49–55.
12. N. D. Kristof, "In Taiwan, Only the Strong Get U. S. Degrees," *New York Times,* 26 March 1989, p. 11.
13. Figures taken, respectively, from J. Paxton (ed.), *Statesman's Yearbook 1990–91;* and from R. N. Gwynne, *New Horizons? Third World Industrialization in an International Framework* (New York/London, 1990), p. 199.
14. Lest this 1987 figure appear too distant, note that Korea's sixth Five-Year Plan calls for a national savings rate of 33.5 percent in the early 1990s: see *Trends in Developing Economies,* p. 300. Table 7 is taken from T. Fukuchi and M. Kagami (eds.), *Perspectives on the Pacific Basin Economy: A Comparison of Asia and Latin America* (Tokyo, 1990), p. 31 (Table 10).
15. Fukuchi and Kagami (eds.), *Perspectives on the Pacific Basin Economies,* p. 4 (Table 1), shows the different rates of growth, and of export's share of total GDP, of the Asian Pacific nations compared with those of Latin America. See also H. Hughes, "Catching Up: The Asian Newly Industrializing Economies in the 1990s," *Asian Development Review,* vol. 7, no. 2 (1989), p. 132 (and Table 3).
16. "The Yen Block," *Economist* Survey, 15 July 1989; "Japan Builds a New Power Base," *Business Week,* 20 March 1989, pp. 18–25.
17. "Taiwan and Korea: Two Paths to Prosperity," p. 19; "South Korea: A New Society," *Economist,* 15 April 1989, pp. 23–25.
18. "Development Brief," *Economist,* 26 May 1990, p. 81, for the first two columns; the GNP per capita comes from *World Development Report 1990,* pp. 178–79.
19. "When a Miracle Stalls," *Economist,* 6 October 1990, pp. 33–34 (on Taiwan); *Trends in Developing Economies 1990,* pp. 299–300 (Korea); R. A. Scalapino, "Asia and the United States: The Challenges Ahead," *Foreign Affairs,* vol. 69, no. 1 (1989–1990), esp. pp. 107–12; "Hong Kong, in China's Sweaty Palm," *Economist,* 5 November 1988, pp. 19–22.
20. See the detailed forecasts in "Asia 2010: The Power of People," *Far Eastern*

Economist Review, 17 May 1990, pp. 27–58. On industrial retooling, see "South Korea," *Economist* Survey, 18 August 1990, pp. 8–9.

21. *Population: The UNFPA Experience,* (New York, 1984), ch. 4, "Latin America and the Caribbean," pp. 51–52.
22. A. F. Lowenthal, "Rediscovering Latin America," *Foreign Affairs,* vol. 69, no. 4 (Fall 1990), p. 34.
23. Figure from "Latin America's Hope," *Economist,* 9 December 1989, p. 14.
24. Taken from G. W. Landau et al., *Latin America at a Crossroads* (Trilateral Commission, New York/Paris/Tokyo, 1990), p. 5, which reports the source as *Economic and Social Progress in Latin America: 1989 Report* (Inter-America Development Bank, Washington, D.C., 1989), Table B-1, p. 463.
25. For details, see the various national entries in Paxton (ed.), *Statesman's Yearbook 1990–91;* and *Economist World Atlas and Almanac,* pp. 131–157. Gwynne, *New Horizons,* has useful comments on Latin America's "inward-oriented industrialization" (ch. 11), which it then contrasts with East Asia's "outward orientation" (ch. 12).
26. *World Resources 1990–91,* p. 39.
27. Ibid., p. 246.
28. For the above, see *World Resources 1990–91,* pp. 33–48, "Latin America at a Crossroads," passim; McCormick, *World Economy,* ch. 13; "Latin American Debt: The Banks' Great Escape," *Economist,* 11 February 1989, pp. 73–74.
29. For educational details, see Paxton (ed.), *Statesman's Yearbook 1990–91,* pp. 95, 236; for literacy rates, see especially those of Uruguay, Costa Rica, Argentina, and Venezuela in the table "Development Brief," *Economist,* 26 May 1990, p. 81.
30. T. E. Martinez, "Argentina: Living with Hyperinflation," *Atlantic Monthly* 266 (December 1990), p. 36.
31. Paxton (ed.), *Statesman's Yearbook 1990–91,* pp. 584, 605.
32. T. Kamm, "Latin America Edges Toward Free Trade," *Wall Street Journal,* 30 November 1990, p. A10.
33. C. Farnsworth, "Latin American Economies Given Brighter Assessments," *New York Times,* 30 October 1990; "Latin America's New Start," *Economist,* 9 June 1990, p. 11; N. C. Nash, "A Breath of Fresh Economic Air Brings Change to Latin America," *New York Times,* 13 November 1991, pp. A1, D5.
34. "Latin America's Hope," *Economist,* 9 December 1989, p. 15; Nash, "Breath of Fresh Economic Air Brings Change to Latin America," passim.
35. J. Brooke, "Debt and Democracy," *New York Times,* 5 December 1990, p. A16; P. Truell, "As the U.S. Slumps, Latin America Suffers," *Wall Street Journal,* 19 November 1990, p. 1.
36. For these arguments, see especially Lowenthal's fine summary, "Rediscovering Latin America," passim; also G. A. Fauriol, "The Shadow of Latin American Affairs," *Foreign Affairs,* vol. 69, no. 1 (1989–90), pp. 116–34; and M. D. Hayes, "The U.S. and Latin America: A Lost Decade?" *Foreign Affairs,* vol. 68, no. 1 (1988–89), pp. 180–98.
37. This is the subdivision preferred by *Economist World Atlas and Almanac,* pp. 256–71, which discusses the North African states (except Egypt) in a later section, under "Africa."
38. "The Arab World," *Economist* Survey, 12 May 1990.
39. See "Major Religions of the World," Hammond *Comparative World Atlas* (Maplewood, N.J., 1986 edn.), p. 41.
40. G. Brooks and T. Horwitz, "Shaken Sheiks," *Wall Street Journal,* 28 December 1990, pp. A1, A4.

41. "Arab World," p. 12.
42. M. A. Heller, "The Middle East: Out of Step with History," *Foreign Affairs*, vol. 69, no. 1 (1989–90), pp. 153–71.
43. See also the remarks by S. F. Wells and M. A. Bruzonsky (eds.), *Security in the Middle East* (Boulder, Colo./London, 1987), pp. 1–3.
44. D. E. Duncan, "Africa: The Long Goodbye," *Atlantic Monthly*, July 1990, p. 20.
45. J. A. Marcum, "Africa: A Continent Adrift," *Foreign Affairs*, vol. 68, no. 1 (1988–89), p. 177. See also the penetrating article by K. R. Richburg, "Why Is Black Africa Overwhelmed While East Asia Overcomes?" *International Herald Tribune*, 14 July 1992, pp. 1, 6.
46. C. H. Farnsworth, "Report by World Bank Sees Poverty Lessening by 2000 Except in Africa," *New York Times*, 16 July 1990, p. A3; Marcum, "Africa: A Continent Adrift," passim; Duncan, "Africa: The Long Goodbye," passim; "The Bleak Continent," *Economist*, 9 December 1989, pp. 80–81.
47. B. Fischer, "Developing Countries in the Process of Economic Globalization," *Intereconomics* (March–April 1990), p. 55.
48. J. S. Whitaker, *How Can Africa Survive?* (New York, 1988).
49. Goliber, "Africa's Expanding Population: Old Problems, New Policies," pp. 4–49. This is an outstandingly good article.
50. *World Resources 1990–91*, p. 254.
51. Ibid., p. 254 (overall population growth to 2025) and p. 258 (infant mortality). L. K. Altman, "WHO Says 40 Million Will Be Infected with Aids by 2000," *New York Times*, 18 June 1991, p. C3 (for percentage of GNP devoted to health care).
52. See Whitaker, *How Can Africa Survive?* esp. ch. 4, "The Blessings of Children," for a fuller analysis; and J. C. Caldwell and P. Caldwell, "High Fertility in Sub-Saharan Africa," *Scientific American* (May 1990), pp. 118–25.
53. "The Bleak Continent," passim; Whitaker, *How Can Africa Survive?* chs. 1 and 2; Goliber, "Africa's Expanding Population," pp. 12–13.
54. Whitaker, *How Can Africa Survive?*; Duncan, "Africa: The Long Goodbye," passim.
55. "Fruits of Containment," *Wall Street Journal*, 18 December 1990 (op-ed), p. A14, for the Africa-Belgium comparison; H. McRae, "Visions of Tomorrow's World," *Independent* (London), 26 November 1991, for Africa's share of world GDP.
56. "Aid to Africa," *Economist*, 8 December 1990, p. 48.
57. *Economist World Atlas and Almanac* (1989), p. 293.
58. Apart from the country-by-country comments in *Economist World Atlas and Almanac*, see also K. Ingham, *Politics in Modern Africa: The Uneven Tribal Dimension* (London/New York, 1990), passim; K. Ingham, "Africa's Internal Wars of the 1980s—Contours and Prospects," United States Institute of Peace, *In Brief* 18 (May 1990).
59. Paxton (ed.), *Statesman's Yearbook 1989*, p. 84; Goliber, "Africa's Expanding Population," p. 15.
60. Paxton (ed.), *Statesman's Yearbook 1989*, pp. 1159–60 (certain smaller groups of students are excluded from these totals).
61. T. R. Odhiambo, "Human Resources Development: Problems and Prospects in Developing Countries," *Impact of Science on Society* 155 (1989), p. 214.
62. Odhiambo, "Human Resources Development," p. 215.
63. P. Lewis, "Nyere and Tanzania: No Regrets at Socialism," *New York Times*, 24 October 1990.
64. "Wind of Change, but a Different One," *Economist*, 14 July 1990, p. 44. See also the encouraging noises made—on a country-by-country basis—in the World

Bank's own *Trends in Developing Economies 1990,* as well as in its 1989 publication *Sub-Saharan Africa: From Crisis to Substainable Growth,* summarized in "The Bleak Continent," *Economist,* 9 December 1989, pp. 80–81.

65. See esp. P. Pradervand, *Listening to Africa: Developing Africa from the Grassroots* (New York, 1989); B. Schneider, *The Barefoot Revolution* (London, 1988); K. McAfee, "Why the Third World Goes Hungry," *Commonweal* 117 (15 June 1990), pp. 384–85.
66. Duncan, "Africa: The Long Goodbye," p. 24; G. Hancock, *Lords of Poverty: The Power, Prestige, and Corruption of the International Aid* (Boston, 1990); G. B. N. Ayittey, "No More Aid for Africa," *Wall Street Journal,* 18 October 1991 (op-ed), p. A14.
67. Whitaker, *How Can Africa Survive?* p. 231.
68. See, for example, the conclusions in Fischer, "Developing Countries in the Process of Economic Globalization," pp. 55–63.
69. Caldwell and Caldwell, "High Fertility in Sub-Saharan Africa," p. 88.
70. "AIDs in Africa," *Economist,* 24 November 1989, p. 1b; E. Eckholm and J. Tierney, "AIDs in Africa: A Killer Rages On," *New York Times,* 16 September 1990, pp. 1, 4; C. M. Becker, "The Demo-Economic Impact of the AIDs Pandemic in Sub-Saharan Africa," *World Development* 18 (1990), pp. 1599–1619.
71. *World Resources 1990–91,* p. 254.
72. Ibid.
73. Apart from Chapters 2 and 4 above, see again *World Resources 1990–91,* pp. 33–48; T. Wicker, "Bush Ventures South," *New York Times,* 9 December 1990, p. E17; T. Golden, "Mexico Fights Cholera but Hates to Say Its Name," *New York Times,* 14 September 1991, p. 2.
74. "Arab World," p. 4.
75. Ibid., p. 6; Y. F. Ibrahim, "In Algeria, Hope for Democracy but Not Economy," *New York Times,* 26 July 1991, pp. A1, A6.
76. *World Resources 1990–91,* pp. 258–59.
77. As quoted in "Arab World," p. 5.
78. See again Pradervand, *Listening to Africa,* passim. Also important is D. Pearce et al., *Sustainable Development: Economics and Environment in the Third World* (Aldershot, Hants, 1990).
79. F. Gable, "Changing Climate and Caribbean Coastlines," *Oceanus,* vol. 30, no. 4 (Winter 1987–88), pp. 53–56; G. Gable and D. G. Aubrey, "Changing Climate and the Pacific," *Oceanus,* vol. 32, no. 4 (Winter 1989–90), pp. 71–73.
80. "Arab World," p. 12.
81. *World Resources 1990–91,* pp. 176–77; L. R. Brown et al., *State of the World 1990,* pp. 48–49.
82. Juma, *Gene Hunters,* pp. 226–28.
83. D. Pirages, *Global Technopolitics* (Belmont, Cal., 1989), p. 152.
84. McAfee, "Why the Third World Goes Hungry," p. 380.
85. See P. K. Ghosh (ed.), *Technology Policy and Development* (Westport, Conn., 1984), p. 109.
86. A. Smith, *The Geopolitics of Information: How Western Culture Dominates the World* (Oxford/New York, 1980), p. 13.
87. Ibid.
88. C. J. Dixon et al. (eds.), *Multinational Corporations and the Third World* (London/Sydney, 1986), passim.
89. For a good example, B. Onimode, *A Political Economy of the African Crisis* (London/New Jersey, 1988), esp. pp. 310ff.

90. M. Clash, "Development Policy, Technology Assessment, and the New Technologies," *Futures* 22 (November 1990), p. 916.
91. L. Cuyvers and D. Van den Bulcke, "Some Reflections on the 'Outward-oriented' Development Strategy of the Far Eastern Newly Industrialising Countries," esp. pp. 196–97, in Adriaansen and Waardenburg (eds.), *Dual World Economy.*
92. *World Development Report 1991: The Challenge of Development* (World Bank/ Oxford University Press, Washington, D.C., 1991). See also the World Bank's *Global Economic Prospects and the Developing Countries* (Washington, D.C., 1991).

CHAPTER 11
THE ERSTWHILE USSR AND ITS CRUMBLED EMPIRE

1. J. Paxton (ed.), *The Statesman's Yearbook, 1982–83,* p. 1228. For current shares of energy and mineral production see *Economist World Atlas and Almanac 1989,* pp. 96–97.
2. Quoted in P. Dibb, *The Soviet Union: The Incomplete Superpower* (London, 1986), p. 67.
3. Basic statistics from *Statesman's Yearbook 1982–83,* p. 1240. For a different breakdown of rather similar overall figures, see *UNESCO Statistical Digest 1987,* pp. 330–31.
4. Calculated from *UNESCO Statistical Digest 1987,* p. 331, where the figures are presented as "scientists and engineers per million inhabitants." One suspects that the definition of the word "scientist" employed here is a wide one, and not restricted to people possessing Ph.D.s and engaged in laboratory work.
5. J. Paxton (ed.), *Statesman's Yearbook 1982–83,* p. 1240, which can be compared with the U.S. totals on p. 1424. The number of physicians attending the needs of China's 1.1 billion people may be larger again, if one includes those who did not receive a "Western-style" medical education (ibid., p. 355).
6. There are some useful remarks on the achievements—as well as the problems—of Soviet science in V. Z. Kresin, "Soviet Science in Practice: An Inside View," in J. Cracraft (ed.), *The Soviet Union Today: An Interpretive Guide,* 2nd edn. (Chicago/London, 1988), ch. 24.
7. These long-term aims are nicely traced in C. Rice, "The Evolution of Soviet Grand Strategy," in P. Kennedy (ed.), *Grand Strategies in War and Peace* (New Haven/ London, 1991), ch. 9.
8. See *Soviet Military Power* (U.S. Department of Defense, Washington, D.C., annual) or *The Military Balance* (International Institute of Strategic Studies, London, annual), as well as the reports by the Stockholm International Peace Research Institute. For analyses pointing to Soviet military strength, see the various essays in H. S. Rowen and C. Wolf, Jr. (eds.), *The Future of the Soviet Empire* (New York, 1987); for an analysis of its weaknesses, see Dibb, *Soviet Union.*
9. See H. S. Rowen and C. Wolf, Jr. (eds.), *The Impoverished Superpower* (San Francisco, 1990); A. Aganbegyan, *The Economic Challenge of Perestroika,* ed. M. Barratt Brown (Bloomington, Ind., 1988), p. 2; the discussion in Cohen and Wilson, *Superpowers in Economic Decline,* pp. 10ff.; and Meyerson, "Soviet Economic Morass," p. 5.
10. This is a composite table, based upon the following sources: Cracraft (ed.), *Soviet Union Today,* p. 179 (for 1956–84); P. Passell, "Where Communist Economics

Fell Short," *New York Times,* 17 December 1989, p. E3 (for 1985–88); A. R. Myerson, "The Soviet Economic Morass," *New York Times,* 16 September 1990, p. F5 (for 1989); C. H. Farnsworth, "Soviet Economic Output Off Sharply," *New York Times,* 22 December 1990, p. 8 (for 1990, and the forecast for 1991). Because of the intensifying economic crisis, later estimates of 1991 GNP are suggesting declines of 13 percent, 18 percent, or even 25 percent: see "The Soviet Economy: Still Bust," *Economist,* 24 August 1991, p. 21; J. Sterngold, "Coup Is Linked to Debt Crisis by Soviet Aide" (reporting on Grigory Yalinsky's economic statement), *New York Times,* 16 October 1991, pp. A1, A10.

11. See the very good discussion in R. W. Judy and V. L. Clough, *The Information Age and Soviet Society* (Indianapolis, 1989), esp. ch. 1.
12. This is discussed in Cohen and Wilson, *Superpowers in Decline,* pp. 9ff. See also the acute remarks by "Z," "To the Stalin Mausoleum," *Daedalus,* vol. 119, no. 1 (Winter 1990), pp. 311–12, 317–18.
13. "Russia Drills Less Oil, OPEC Keeps It Cheap," *Economist,* 8 June 1985, p. 65.
14. P. R. Gregory and R. C. Stuart, *Soviet Economic Structure and Performance,* 3rd edn. (New York, 1986), p. 325.
15. For the above, see R. W. Campbell, "Energy," in A. Bergson and H. S. Levine (eds.), *The Soviet Economy: Towards the Year 2000* (London, 1983); L. Dienes, "An Energy Crunch Ahead in the Soviet Union?" in M. Bornstein (ed.), *The Soviet Union: Continuity and Change* (Boulder, Colo., 1981); M. I. Goldman, *The Enigma of Soviet Petroleum* (London, 1980).
16. P. Truell, "Western Study Says Soviet Aid May Be Futile," *Wall Street Journal,* 24 December 1990, p. 2.
17. See especially Bergson and Levine (eds.), *Soviet Economy,* chs. 4 and 5; M. I. Goldman, *Gorbachev's Challenge: Economic Reform in the Age of High Technology* (New York, 1987), pp. 32ff.; D. G. Johnson, "Agriculture," in Cracraft (ed.), *Soviet Union Today,* pp. 198–209; B. Keller, "Soviet System Dooms a Bumper Crop," *New York Times,* 20 August 1990.
18. P. Torday, "Chaos Looms for Soviet Economy," *Independent* (London), 29 August 1991, p. 6.
19. See Eberstadt, "Health of an Empire," in Rowen and Wolf (eds.), *The Future of the Soviet Empire,* pp. 221–45; "Sick Men of Europe," *Economist,* 22 March 1986, p. 53; J. Lloyd, "Soviet Citizens' Plight Exposed," *Financial Times,* 18 August 1988.
20. V. Bukovsky, "The Political Condition of the Soviet Empire," in Rowen and Wolf (eds.) *The Future of the Soviet Empire,* pp. 11–39; D. E. Powell, "A Troubled Society," in Cracraft (ed.), *Soviet Union Today,* ch. 30; "Z," "To the Stalin Mausoleum," passim.
21. For impressions of this growing public disarray, see P. Gumbel, "Gorbachev Urges Soviet Congress to Expand Powers," *Wall Street Journal,* 17 December 1990; N. Gardels: "Helping to Diminish the Perils of Perestroika," *Wall Street Journal,* 30 January 1989 (op-ed.); B. Keller, "Soviet Economy: A Shattered Dream," *New York Times,* 13 May 1990, pp. A1, A12.
22. R. S. Clem, "Ethnicity," in Cracraft (ed.), *Soviet Union Today,* p. 306.
23. Ibid., pp. 304–5, provides a full list.
24. E. Keenan, "Rethinking the USSR, Now That It's Over," *New York Times,* 8 September 1991, p. E3.
25. "Gorbachev's Turbulent South," *Economist,* 13 January 1990, p. 45; F. X. Clines, "In Soviet Union, Dizzying Disunion," *New York Times,* 26 October 1990, p. A6.
26. P. Gumbel, "Soviets Are at a Loss About Ethnic Unrest," *Wall Street Journal,*

21 July 1989, p. A12; "The Battle Lines of the Republics," *Economist,* 23 September 1989, p. 58.

27. Clem, "Ethnicity," p. 306. See also M. Hauner, *What Is Asia to Us?* (Boston/London, 1990), esp. pp. 9, 233–34, 247–52; and D. Lieven, "Gorbachev and the Nationalities," *Conflict Studies* 216 (November 1988).
28. See the important discussion of these issues in D. Lieven, "The Soviet Crisis," *Conflict Studies* 241 (May 1991), esp. pp. 20ff.
29. V. Kvint, "Russia as Cinderella," *Forbes,* 19 February 1990, pp. 103–8; B. Keller, "Selling Soviet Unity," *New York Times,* 19 December 1990, pp. A1, A11; B. Keller, "Russia Cuts Share of Soviet Budget," *New York Times,* 28 December 1990, pp. A1, A10.
30. Torday, "Chaos Looms for Soviet Economy."
31. For details, see N. Mansergh, *The Commonwealth Experience* (London, 1969); and B. Porter, *The Lion's Share: A Short History of British Imperialism 1850–1970* (London, 1976). For the Ukraine, see S. Greenhouse, "To Ukrainians, Separation Follows Laws of Nature," *New York Times,* 20 December 1990, p. A10; and Lieven, "Soviet Crisis," passim.
32. See B. D. Porter and J. G. Roche, "The Expanding Military Power of the Soviet Union," in Rowen and Wolf (eds.), *The Future of the Soviet Empire,* pp. 143–61; F. J. Gaffney, "Is Moscow Cutting Its Military? No, It's Building Up," *New York Times,* 17 November 1989 (op-ed.); J. Churba, *Soviet Breakout* (Washington/London, 1988)—a particularly egregious example.
33. A. Karatnycky, "The Many Armies of the Soviet Union," *Wall Street Journal,* 28 August 1990 (op-ed.); J. Fialka, "Soviets Begin Moving Nuclear Warheads out of Volatile Republics," *Wall Street Journal,* 22 June 1990, pp. A1, A4.
34. See D. Ross, "Where Is the Soviet Union Heading?" and H. S. Rowen and C. Wolf, "The Future of the Soviet Empire," in Rowen and Wolf (eds.), *Future of the Soviet Empire,* pp. 259–79, 279–324; T. J. Colton, *The Dilemma of Reform in the Soviet Union,* 2nd edn. (New York, 1986), ch. 4, "Reform and the Soviet Future." See also Cohen and Wilson, *Superpowers in Economic Decline,* pp. 90ff.
35. C. H. Fairbanks, "Russian Roulette: The Danger of a Collapsing Empire," *Policy Review* 57 (Summer 1991), pp. 7–8.
36. M. Feshbach, "Population and Labor Force," in Bergson and Levine (eds.), *Soviet Economy: Towards the Year 2000,* p. 79. See also M. S. Bernstam, "Trends in the Soviet Population," in Rowen and Wolf (eds.), *Future of the Soviet Empire,* pp. 185–214.
37. Colton, *Dilemma of Reform in the Soviet Union,* p. 42.
38. Clem, "Ethnicity," pp. 304–5.
39. M. S. Bernstam, "Trends in the Soviet Population," p. 209.
40. Ibid., p. 208.
41. See M. Feshbach and A. Friendly, *Ecocide in the USSR* (New York, 1992), for harrowing details.
42. "A Way of Life Evaporates," *Economist,* 21 September 1991, p. 59.
43. Judy and Clough, *Information Age and Soviet Society,* p. 29.
44. Quoted in ibid., p. 15.
45. Ibid.
46. "If Gorbachev Dares," *Economist,* 6 July 1985.
47. *Economist World Atlas and Almanac 1989,* p. 209.
48. For details, see Kennedy, *Rise and Fall of the Great Powers,* pp. 320–23.
49. For background analysis, see W. E. Griffith (ed.), *Central and Eastern Europe: The Opening Curtain* (Boulder, Colo., 1984); C. Gati, *The BLOC That Failed*

(Bloomington, IN, 1990); and the essay collections by T. Garton Ash, *The Uses of Adversity* (New York, 1989) and *The Magic Lantern* (New York, 1990).

50. As of December 1990: see "Trade, Exchange Rates and Reserves," *Economist,* 15 December 1990, p. 100.
51. "Democracy in Eastern Europe," *Economist,* 15 December 1990, p. 5 (referring in particular to the National Salvation Front in Romania). For the political debates, see "Eastern Europe Moves Right," *Economist,* 24 March 1990, pp. 21–23.
52. C. Bohlen, "Ethnic Rivalries Revive in Eastern Europe," *New York Times,* 12 November 1990, pp. A1, A12; C. Bohlen, "3 East Europe States Grope for Union," *New York Times,* 16 December 1990, p. 16.
53. V. Meier, "Yugoslavia: Worsening Economic and Nationalist Crisis," in Griffith (ed.), *Central and Eastern Europe,* p. 276. See also I. Banac, "Political Change and National Diversity," *Daedalus,* vol. 119, no. 1 (Winter 1990), pp. 141–59.
54. C. R. Whitney, "Burst of Freedom in Czechoslovakia May Split Czechs from Slovaks," *New York Times,* 3 June 1990, p. 14. See also "Slovakia Pressing Czechs for an Equal Partnership," *New York Times,* 18 May 1990.
55. See again Bohlen, "Ethnic Rivalries Revive in Eastern Europe," passim; and the useful survey "Perestroika: And Now for the Hard Part," *Economist,* 28 April 1990.
56. S. Greenhouse, "Long, Painful Road Ahead to Free Markets for East," *New York Times,* 10 November 1990, pp. 1, 4.
57. J. Dempsey, "Lights Going Dim in Eastern Europe," *Financial Times,* 13 September 1990, p. 27.
58. *Financial Times,* 17 July 1990, p. 2.
59. R. D. Hormats, "Don't Let the West Erect a New Iron Curtain," *Wall Street Journal,* 27 December 1990, p. A8.
60. This is well discussed in the various articles in *Daedalus,* vol. 121, no. 2 (Spring 1992), entitled "The Exit from Communism."
61. F. Barringer, "Birth Rates Plummeting in Some Ex-Communist Regions of Eastern Europe," *New York Times,* 31 December 1990, p. A3.
62. "Europe in Turmoil," *Agricultural Outlook* (July 1990), pp. 28–32.

CHAPTER 12
EUROPE AND THE FUTURE

1. T. L. Friedman, "Old Feuds and the New Order," *International Herald Tribune,* 13 July 1992, p. 1.
2. See, for example, the quote in D. Burstein, *Euroquake: Europe's Explosive Challenge Will Change the World* (New York, 1991), p. 11.
3. S. P. Huntington, "The U.S.—Decline or Renewal?" *Foreign Affairs,* vol. 67, no. 2 (Winter 1988–89), pp. 93–94.
4. S. Hoffmann, "The European Community and 1992," *Foreign Affairs,* vol. 68, no. 4 (Fall 1989), p. 27.
5. There is a useful summary of these mixed positions in "Who Wants What in the Brave New Europe," *Economist,* 1 December 1990, pp. 46–47.
6. G. Agnelli, "The Europe of 1992," *Foreign Affairs,* vol. 68, no. 4 (Fall 1989), pp. 61–70; J. Joffe, "Reunification II: This Time, No Hobnail Boots," *New York Times,* 30 September 1990, p. E3.
7. C. R. Whitney, "Gulf Fighting Shatters Europeans' Fragile Unity," *New York Times,* 25 January 1991, p. A11.

8. The tenth is, admittedly, Switzerland and not a member of the EC: see *Economist World Atlas and Almanac 1989,* p. 87. The greater part of this trade is, of course, with other EC members. For the banking statistics, see ibid., p. 90, "Top International Banks."
9. See the various tables in *Annual Review of Engineering Industries and Automation 1988,* vol. 1.
10. Hoffmann, "European Community and 1992," p. 28.
11. See again Agnelli's arguments in "Europe of 1992," passim.
12. Burstein, *Euroquake,* pp. 129–30.
13. Hoffmann, "European Community and 1992," pp. 27–28.
14. Burstein, *Euroquake,* pp. 25–28.
15. *World Resources 1990–91,* p. 245.
16. *Economist World Atlas and Almanac 1989,* p. 159.
17. G. Bolte, "How Stubborn Can You Get?" *Time,* 8 October 1990, p. 65. The statistics come from T. Roth, "Europe's Small Farmers See Bleak Future," *Wall Street Journal,* 24 April 1992, p. A11A.
18. See, for example, the population figures for virtually every one of the villages included in D. Reperant, *The Most Beautiful Villages of France* (New York, 1990), passim.
19. Quoted in Burstein, *Euroquake,* p. 150, which has a fine analysis of both personalities and issues involved.
20. Ibid., pp. 40ff, 155ff.
21. See "European Community," *Economist* Survey, 7 July 1990, especially pp. 29–30, for a discussion of those constitutional difficulties.
22. Ibid., p. 24.
23. Ibid., p. 5.
24. For coverage of these debates, see G. F. Treverton, *Making the Alliance Work: The United States and Western Europe* (Ithaca, N.Y., 1985); J. Joffe, *The Limited Partnership: Europe, the United States, and the Burdens of Alliance* (Cambridge, 1987); C. McInnes, *NATO's Changing Strategic Agenda* (London/Boston, 1990); J. J. Mearsheimer, *Conventional Deterrence* (Ithaca, N.Y., 1983); R. W. Tucker and L. Wrigley (eds.), *The Atlantic Alliance and Its Critics* (New York, 1983).
25. K. Gottfried and P. Bracken (eds.), *Reforging European Security* (Boulder, Colo., 1990), pp. 3–4—part of the editors' excellent analysis.
26. Ibid., pp. 23ff, as well as the section by J. Dean and S. R. Resor, "Constructing European Security System," in the same volume.
27. For the Concert of Europe idea, see C. A. Kupchan and C. A. Kupchan, "After NATO: Concert of Europe," *New York Times,* 6 July 1990, p. A25 (op-ed). For the above remarks generally, see the analyses in C. R. Whitney, "NATO, Victim of Success, Searches for New Strategy," *New York Times,* 26 October 1991, pp. 1, 5; S. Hoffmann, "Today's NATO—and Tomorrow's," *New York Times,* 27 May 1990, p. E13 (op-ed); A. Riding, "The New Europe," *New York Times,* 20 November 1990, p. A14.
28. See D. Calleo, *The German Question Reconsidered* (New York, 1978); W. Gruner, *Die deutsche Frage* (Munich, 1985).
29. "Saying the Unsayable About the Germans" (interview with British minister Nicholas Ridley), *Spectator,* 14 July 1990, pp. 8–10; W. Safire, "Defending Germany," *New York Times,* 22 June 1990, p. A27.
30. B. Geremek, "The Realities of Eastern and Central Europe," in *Change in Europe* (Washington, D.C.: Plenary of the Trilateral Commission, April 1990), p. 10.

31. Quoted in F. Lewis, "The Bane of Nations," *New York Times,* 28 November 1990 (op-ed); and see Burstein, *Euroquake,* ch. 5.
32. "The Unpopularity of Two-Speed Europe," *Economist,* 14 September 1991, pp. 89–90.
33. "The Graying of Europe," *Business Week,* 6 February 1989, pp. 12–16; A. Riding, "Western Europe, Its Births Falling, Wonders Who'll Do All the Work," *New York Times,* 22 July 1990, pp. 1, 12; H. de Jouvenel, "Europe at the Dawn of the Third Millennium: A Synthesis of the Main Trends," *Futures,* vol. 20, no. 5 (October 1988), p. 515.
34. Quotations from "Graying of Europe"; and Riding, "Western Europe, Its Births Falling. . . ."
35. "The Missing Children," *Economist,* 3 August 1991, pp. 43–44; D. J. van de Kaa, "Europe's Second Demographic Transition," *Population Bulletin,* vol. 42, no. 1 (March 1987), pp. 3–57; J. Gapper, "Skills Shortage Stalls the Workers' March," *Financial Times,* 5 September 1990; Riding, "Western Europe, Its Births Falling . . . ," passim.
36. "West Germany's Unexpected Boost from the East," *Commerzbank* Viewpoint, reproduced in *Economist,* 13 January 1990, p. 62.
37. T. Carrington, "Central Europe Borders Tighten as Emigrés Flood In from East," *Wall Street Journal,* 8 February 1991, p. A8.
38. "Italy: The Numbers Game," *Economist,* 26 May 1990, p. 25.
39. "Graying of Europe," p. 15.
40. Burstein, *Euroquake,* p. 137. See also F. Heisbourg, "Population Movements in Post–Cold War Europe," *Survival,* vol. 33, no. 1 (January–February 1991), pp. 31–43.
41. P. L. Montgomery, "European Community Asks Heavy Energy Tax to Curb Emissions," *New York Times,* 26 September 1991, p. D3.
42. See two technical pieces, C. A. Wilson and J. F. B. Mitchell, "Simulated Climate and CO_2-Induced Climate Change over Western Europe," *Climatic Change* 8 (1986), pp. 11–42; F. Bultot et al., "Estimated Annual Regime of Energy-Balance Components, Evapotranspiration and Soil Moisture for a Drainage Basin in the Case of a CO_2 Doubling," *Climatic Change* 12 (1988), pp. 39–56 (a Belgian study).
43. "Cleaning Up the Mediterranean," *Economist,* 21 December 1991, pp. 19–24.
44. *Economist World Atlas and Almanac 1989,* p. 105.
45. "Europe's Farm Farce," *Economist,* 29 September 1990, p. 17.
46. P. Bye, "Biotechnology and Food/Agricultural Complexes," in Yoxen and Di Martino (eds.), *Biotechnology in Future Society,* p. 77. This volume contains many fine essays.
47. Ibid.
48. Ibid.; *Economist,* 20 October 1990, p. 15; "German Regulatory Firms Flee Regulatory Climate," *Science,* 16 June 1989, pp. 1251–52; K. Green and E. Yoxen, "The Greening of European Industry: What role for biotechnology?" *Futures* (June 1990), pp. 475–95.
49. See G. Junne and J. Bijman, "The Impact of Biotechnology on European Agriculture," in Yoxen and Di Martino (eds.), *Biotechnology in Future Society,* esp. p. 83.
50. Bye, "Biotechnology and Food/Agricultural Complexes," p. 69.
51. "Europe's Farm Farce," passim; Bolte, "How Stubborn Can You Get?" p. 65.
52. Junne and Bijman, "Impact of Biotechnology on European Agriculture," p. 84.

53. See the excellent article "Europe in Turmoil" in *Agricultural Outlook,* July 1990, pp. 28ff, for an analysis of the recovery of Eastern Europe's agriculture.
54. Gapper, "Skills Shortage Stalls the Workers' March," passim.
55. This Reich himself suggests in *Work of Nations,* passim.
56. See again the argument throughout Ohmae, *Borderless World.*
57. For a good example, see P. Brimelow, "The Darker Side of 1992," *Forbes,* 22 January 1990, pp. 85–89.

CHAPTER 13
THE AMERICAN DILEMMA

1. This debate can be followed, virtually on a weekly basis, by comparing the criticisms of liberal *New York Times* op-ed writers such as Anthony Lewis and Tom Wicker with the assertions of *Wall Street Journal* lead articles.
2. See the thoughtful comments by S. Huntington, "The U.S.—Decline or Renewal?" pp. 76–96.
3. See the discussion on this theme by H. Grunwald, "The Second American Century," *Time,* 8 October 1990, pp. 70–75.
4. Schlosstein, *End of the American Century;* D. Calleo, *Beyond American Hegemony* (New York, 1987); R. Rosecrance (ed.), *America as an Ordinary Power* (Ithaca, N.Y., 1976).
5. H. R. Nau, *The Myth of America's Decline* (New York, 1990); Rosecrance, *America's Economic Resurgence;* Nye, *Bound to Lead;* and J. Kotkin and Y. Kishimoto, *The Third Century: America's Resurgence in the Asian Era* (New York, 1988). It will be noted that one of these "responses" is by the editor of *America as an Ordinary Power,* Professor Richard Rosecrance. For his further commentary upon the American position in world affairs, see Rosecrance, *Rise of the Trading States.*
6. Z. Brzezinski's quoted extract on the dust jacket of Nye, *Bound to Lead.*
7. For lengthier analyses of the United States' prospects, see Nye, *Bound to Lead;* Rosecrance, *America's Economic Resurgence;* A. Anderson and D. L. Bork (eds.), *Thinking About America: The United States in the 1990s* (Stanford, Cal., 1988); E. K. Hamilton (ed.), *America's Global Interests: A New Agenda* (New York, 1989); M. Green and M. Pinsky (ed.), *America's Transition: Blueprints for the 1990s* (Lanham, Md., 1990). These are, of course, only a sampling of a now enormous body of literature.
8. Details and analyses of U.S. armed forces can be found in the standard sources: *Report of the Secretary of Defense . . . to the Congress* (annual, Washington, D.C.); *The Military Balance* (International Institute of Strategic Studies, London, annual); *RUSI and Brassey's Defence Yearbook* (annual); *American Defense Annual,* and so on.
9. P. E. Tyler, "Pentagon Imagines New Enemies to Fight in Post-Cold-War Era," *New York Times,* 17 February 1992, pp. A1, A8. See also F. C. Iklé and A. Wohlstetler (eds.), *Discriminate Deterrence: Report of the Commission on Integrated Long-Term Strategy,* (Washington, D.C., 1988), pp. 13–22, for an earlier recommendation along those lines; and M. T. Klare, "The U.S. Military Faces South," *Nation,* 18 June 1990, pp. 841, 858–62.
10. See the references to this literature in Chapter 7 above, especially the articles by Mathews, "Redefining Security," and Sorensen, "Rethinking National Security," as well as R. J. Barnett's thoughtful piece "After the Cold War," *New Yorker,* 1

January 1990, pp. 65–76. For the strategic debate, see the excellent analysis and bibliography in S. Van Evera, "Why Europe Matters, Why the Third World Doesn't; American Grand Strategy After the Cold War," *Journal of Strategic Studies,* vol. 13, no. 2 (June 1990), pp. 1–51.

11. As one of Gorbachev's early foreign-policy advisers, Giorgi Arbatov, put it in 1988, the USSR was going to deprive the United States of its "enemy," thereby confusing American conservative circles in particular.
12. Nye, *Bound to Lead,* p. 239 and passim; P. A. Gigot, "After Communism, World Still Needs U.S. Troops," *Wall Street Journal,* 11 February 1990 (op-ed).
13. For samples of these criticisms, see A. Lewis, "When Decline Hurts," *New York Times,* 26 September 1990 (op-ed); D. Boren, "New Decade, New World, New Strategy," *New York Times,* 2 January 1990; T. Wicker, "The 'Super' Concept," *New York Times,* 25 November 1990, p. E11.
14. For the classic analysis of this tendency, see Robinson and Gallagher, *Africa and the Victorian,* esp. the concluding chapter, with its remarks about the "frontiers of insecurity." For a critique of the current U.S. tendency in that direction, see again Van Evera, "Why Europe Matters, Why the Third World Doesn't," pp. 15ff.
15. See, for example, E. Mortimer, "Sharing the Bill for Peace," *Financial Times,* 14 September 1990, p. 17; A. Ireland, "A Hawk Says: Pull Our Troops Out," *New York Times,* 7 March 1989 (op-ed); W. L. Schlosser, "Let's Cut the Subsidies for Allies Defense," *New York Times,* 27 November 1988 (letters); "Time to Share the Burden," *Economist,* 7 May 1988, pp. 23–24. The 1988 R&D figures come from M. Prowse, "Scales Out of Balance," *Financial Times,* 13 August 1991, p. 10.
16. There is a wealth of literature upon this theme. For samples, see Cohen and Wilson, *Superpowers in Economic Decline,* passim; L. J. Dumas, *The Overburdened Economy* (Berkeley/Los Angeles, 1986), esp. pp. 57–63, 297ff.; B. Russett, "Defense Expenditures and National Well-Being," *American Political Science Review,* vol. 76, no. 4 (December 1982), pp. 767–77; DeGrasse, *Military Expansion, Economic Decline* (Armonk, N.Y., 1985), passim.
17. The decade-by-decade averages can be calculated from *Economic Report of the President* (Washington, D.C., 1990) and, for 1989, *Survey of Current Business* (Bureau of Economic Analysis, July 1990), Table 1.2. I am grateful to Professor Charles L. Ballard for advice here; see also his letter in *Wall Street Journal,* 12 December 1990, p. A17. The 1991 figure is a provisional OECD one, as reported in *Wall Street Journal,* 13 December 1991, p. A10, although a slightly later *Journal* report (10 March 1992, p. A2) gives a 1990–91 figure of 0.4 percent growth in GDP.
18. See Kennedy, *Rise and Fall of the Great Powers,* esp. Introduction and Epilogue, for the full argument.
19. "The Elusive Boom in Productivity," *New York Times,* 8 April 1984, business section, pp. 1, 26. See also "Richer Than You," *Economist,* 25 October 1986, pp. 13–14.
20. D. Gergen, "Can America Stay on Top?" *U. S. News & World Report,* 16 July 1990, p. 68. See also L. Silk, "Who Is No. 1? It's Hard to Say," *New York Times,* 27 July 1990, p. D2; A. Murray, "U.S. Economy Leads Japan's—But For How Long?" *Wall Street Journal,* 13 June 1990.
21. For the comparative statistics, see Kennedy, *Rise and Fall of the Great Powers,* Tables 21, 31, 32.
22. L. H. Clark and A. L. Malabré, "Productivity Indicates Sluggish Economy," *Wall*

Street Journal, 6 July 1989, p. A2; and the table "Output per Employee" (covering 1960 to 1986) in the excellent MIT analysis M. L. Dertouzos et al., *Made in America: Regaining the Productive Edge* (Cambridge, Mass., 1989), p. 29. Note that the latter, p. 31, estimates that 36 percent of the recorded improvement in labor productivity between 1979 and 1986 came from loss of jobs.

23. Kennedy, *Rise and Fall of the Great Powers,* p. 527.
24. For these figures, see A. L. Malabré, *Within Our Means* (New York, 1991), pp. xix–xx; and D. P. Calleo, *The Bankrupting of America* (New York, 1992).
25. The quotations and statistics are from Malabré, *Within Our Means,* pp. 3–5, 11–12. See also B. Friedman, *Day of Reckoning* (New York, 1988); but note "Defining the Debt Bomb," *Economist,* 3 November 1990, p. 75, for a more reassuring picture of corporate indebtedness.
26. See the breakdown in M. S. Feldstein (ed.), *The United States in the World Economy* (Cambridge, Mass., 1987), pp. 562–63, together with the analysis by J. A. Frankel, pp. 560ff.
27. H. Stout, "U.S. Foreign Debt Widened Last Year," *Wall Street Journal,* 2 July 1990, p. 42. The status of being the "world's largest debtor" may be a nominal one at the moment, since American purchases of overseas assets several decades ago ought to yield a far higher value than the actual purchasing price—although it is the latter which is recorded in the totals.
28. Dertouzos et al. (eds.), *Made in America,* pp. 40–41. For the longer argument, see also S. S. Cohen and J. Zysman, *Manufacturing Matters* (New York, 1987); and R. Dornbusch et al., *The Case for Manufacturing in America's Future* (Rochester, N.Y., 1987).
29. For samples, see the many releases and publications of the Office of Technology Assessment (U.S. Congress) and the Council on Competitiveness; Dertouzos et al. (eds.), *Made in America;* M. G. Barons, *Competing for Control* (Cambridge, Mass., 1988); J. S. Yudken and M. Black, "Targeting National Needs: A New Direction for Science and Technology Policy," *World Policy Journal* 7 (Spring 1990), pp. 251–88; G. N. Hatsopoulos et al., "U.S. Competitiveness: Beyond the Trade Deficit," *Science* 241 (15 July 1988), pp. 299–307; and P. Krugman, *The Age of Diminished Expectations* (Cambridge, Mass., 1990), passim.
30. See G. R. Searle, *The Quest for National Efficiency, 1899–1914,* 2nd edn. (Atlantic Highlands, N.J., 1990), passim; F. Crouzet, *The Victorian Economy* (London, 1982), pp. 371ff; E. J. Hobsbawm, *Industry and Empire* (Harmondsworth, Mddsx., 1969), pp. 136–53, 172–85.
31. Taken from Dertouzos et al., *Made in America,* p. 7.
32. Kennedy, *Rise and Fall of the Great Powers,* p. 515.
33. See H. Stein, "Who's Number One? Who Cares?" *Wall Street Journal,* 1 March 1990 (op-ed); Ohmae, *Borderless World,* passim; and Reich, *Work of Nations,* ch. 13 and passim.
34. See esp. Nye, *Bound to Lead,* passim.
35. For examples, W. Hummer, "A Contrarian View: A Short, Mild Recession," *Wall Street Journal,* 7 January 1990; the important series of articles by K. House in *Wall Street Journal* in early 1989, esp. 27 January 1989; C. R. Morris, "The Coming Global Boom," *Atlantic,* October 1989, pp. 51–64.
36. P. Kennedy, "Fin-de-Siecle America," *New York Review of Books,* 28 June 1990, pp. 31–40; Lewis, "When Decline Hurts," passim; H. Allen, "Red, White, and Truly Blue," *Washington Post,* 26 November 1990, pp. B1, B4; R. Bernstein, "Euphoria Gives Way to Fractured Feelings of Gloom," *New York Times,* 23

December 1990, p. E3; H. Carter, "U.S. Could Well Snatch Defeat from the Jaws of Victory," *Wall Street Journal,* 29 March 1990, p. A13.

37. J. Chancellor, *Peril and Promise: A Commentary upon America* (New York, 1990), p. 23.
38. Ibid.
39. W. Meyer-Larsen, "America's Century Will End with a Whimper," *World Press Review,* January 1991, p. 27. (I've amended the sentence order here.) See also R. Pear, "Study Says U.S. Needs to Battle Infant Mortality," *New York Times,* 6 August 1990, pp. A1, B9; W. B. Maher, "Reform Medicine: The Rest Will Follow," *New York Times,* 9 July 1989, business section, p. 3.
40. C. C. Douglas, "In Black America, Life Grows Shorter," *New York Times,* 2 December 1989, p. 84.
41. D. R. Gergen, "Remember the Drug War?" *U.S. News & World Report,* 18 December 1989, p. 84.
42. "Crime in America," *Economist,* 22 December 1990, pp. 29–32.
43. Ibid.; and K. E. Meyer, "A Good Word for Calcutta," *New York Times,* 6 January 1991, p. 18.
44. T. Wicker, "The Iron Medal," *New York Times,* 9 January 1991, p. A21; "U.S. Incarceration Rate Highest in World," *Wall Street Journal,* 7 January 1991, p. B5.
45. L. Uchitelle, "Not Getting Ahead? Better Get Used to It," *New York Times,* 16 December 1990, Week in Review, pp. 1, 6; A. Murray, "Losing Faith: Many Americans Fear U.S. Living Standards Have Stopped Rising," *Wall Street Journal,* 1 May 1989, pp. 1, 10.
46. See the important arguments in Calleo, *Beyond American Hegemony,* pp. 109–113.
47. See L. Thurow's classic, *The Zero-Sum Society* (New York, 1980), passim.
48. "U.S. Is Said to Lag in School Spending," *New York Times,* 16 January 1990, p. A23; J. Hood, "Education: Money Isn't Everything," *Wall Street Journal,* 2 February 1990.
49. "The Stupidification of America," *New Perspectives Quarterly,* vol. 7, no. 4 (Fall 1990), p. 47.
50. J. Kozol, *Illiterate America* (New York, 1985), pp. 4, 8–9.
51. B. O'Reilly, "America's Place in World Competition," *Fortune,* 6 November 1989, p. 88; C. O. Baker (ed.), *The Condition of Education 1989,* vol. 1, *Elementary and Secondary Education* (Washington, D.C., 1989), p. 78; A. Shanker, "U.S. Rock Bottom," *New York Times,* 5 February 1989, p. E7 (advertisement).
52. Kozol, *Illiterate America,* p. 212.
53. C. D. Baker (ed.), *The Condition of Education 1989,* vol. 1, p. 84; G. M. Grosvenor, "Those Panamanian Pandas," *New York Times,* 31 July 1988, p. 25.
54. *A Nation at Risk* (National Commission on Excellence in Education, Washington, D.C., 1983), p. 5.
55. R. Hoffmann, "Ignorance, Ignorantly Judged," *New York Times,* 14 September 1989 (op-ed); *A Nation at Risk,* p. 11. On the other hand, the U.S. twelfth-graders who scored low in mathematics in international tests were themselves a select group.
56. See again "U.S. Is Said to Lag in School Spending," *New York Times,* 16 January 1990.
57. See M. J. Barnett, "The Case for More School Days," *Atlantic,* November 1990, pp. 78–106—an excellent general survey; "Japan–243, United States–180," *Washington Post,* 15 October 1990, p. A14 (editorial).

58. *Everybody Counts: A Report to the Nation of the Future of Mathematics Education* (National Research Council, Washington, D.C., 1989), p. 90. See also D. P. Doyle, "Time for America to Set National Education Norms," *Hudson Opinion,* October 1989, p. 1.
59. N. Gardels, "The Education We Deserve," *New Perspectives Quarterly,* vol. 7, no. 4 (Fall 1990), pp. 2–3.
60. The quotations and statistics are from ibid., pp. 52–55, 18–19. That same issue of *New Perspectives Quarterly* offers an excellent sampling of seventeen articles about the education/social/cultural crisis. See also Senator Daniel Moynihan's op-ed piece "Half the Nation's Children Born Without a Fair Chance," *New York Times,* 25 September 1988, p. E25; and the remarks in E. D. Hirsch, *Cultural Literacy: What Every American Needs to Know* (Boston, 1987).
61. In that latter connection, see the interesting discussion by S. Knack, "Why We Don't Vote—Or Say Thank You," *Wall Street Journal,* 31 December 1990, p. 6; and H. Carter, "We Have Seen the Enemy, and It Is Ignorance," *Wall Street Journal,* 17 November 1988, p. A23.
62. This is well traced in K. Phillips, *The Politics of Rich and Poor* (New York, 1990), passim; and Reich, *Work of Nations,* chs. 14, 17–18, 23–24.
63. M. Novak, "What Became of the Ugly American?" *Forbes,* 30 April 1990, p. 120. See also B. Wattenberg, *The First Universal Nation* (New York, 1990); G. Gilder, "You Ain't Seen Nothing Yet," *Forbes,* 4 April 1988, pp. 89–93; A. Balk, "America Is No. 1. It'll Stay No. 1," *New York Times,* 31 July 1990 (op-ed); and many of the triumphalist pieces (Gilder's especially) in *Commentary,* September 1990, entitled "The American 80s: Disaster or Triumph?"
64. Nye, *Bound to Lead,* passim; Grunwald, "Second American Century," passim; "Yes, You Are the Superpower," *Economist,* 24 February 1990, p. 11.
65. G. F. Will, "Who Will Stoke the Fires?" *Newsweek,* 9 April 1990, p. 78.
66. See M. Lind, "America as an Ordinary Country," *American Enterprise* (September–October 1990), pp. 19–23; and J. B. Judis, "The Conservative Crackup," *American Prospect,* Fall 1990, pp. 30–42.
67. See Chancellor's readable (and angry) description in *Peril and Promise,* passim.
68. Ibid., p. 23.
69. These are the "middle series" estimates: see the table on p. 7 of "Projection of the Population of the United States, by Age, Sex, and Race: 1988 to 2080," *Current Population Reports,* Series P-25, no. 1018 (U.S. Bureau of the Census, Washington, D.C., 1989).
70. J. M. Guralnik et al., "Projecting the Older Population of the United States," *Milbank Quarterly,* vol. 66, no. 2 (1988), pp. 283–308; "On the Economic Implications of Demographic Change in the United States," *Population and Development Review,* vol. 15, no. 2 (June 1989), pp. 379–89.
71. W. A. Henry, "Beyond the Melting Pot," *Time,* 9 April 1990, pp. 28–35.
72. S. Thornstrom, "The Minority Majority Will Never Come," *Wall Street Journal,* 26 July 1990 (op-ed).
73. D. James, "Bar the Door," *New York Times,* 25 July 1992, p. 21.
74. P. Francese, "Aging America Needs Foreign Blood," *Wall Street Journal,* 27 March 1990 (op-ed); F. Barringer, "A Land of Immigrants Gets Uneasy About Immigration," *New York Times,* 14 October 1990, p. E4; R. J. Herrnstein, "IQ And Falling Birth Rates," *Atlantic,* May 1989, pp. 73 et see.; D. E. Bloom and N. G. Bennett, "Future Shock," *New Republic,* 19 June 1989, pp. 18–22.
75. Henry, "Beyond the Melting Pot," passim.

76. G. Wright, "Where America's Industrial Monopoly Went," *Wall Street Journal*, 20 December 1990, p. A16.
77. See again Reich, *Work of Nations*.
78. *Workforce 2000: Work and Workers for the 21st Century*, Hudson Institute (Indianapolis, 1987), p. 98; see also *New Perspectives Quarterly*, Fall 1990, p. 37.
79. The quotation and statistic are from the Report of the Comparison of the Skills of the Average Work Force, *America's Choice: High Skills or Low Wages!* (Rochester, N.Y., 1990), p. 23. See also N. J. Perry, "How to Help America's Schools," *Fortune*, 4 December 1989, pp. 137–42. For the shortages at the higher levels, see R. Atkinson, "Supply and Demand for Scientists and Engineers: A National Crisis in the Making," *Science*, 27 April 1990, pp. 425–32; and "Needed: Home-Grown Talent," *New York Times*, 26 December 1990, p. A30 (editorial).
80. *America's Choice: High Skills or Low Wages!* pp. 19–21.
81. Ibid., p. 21; *Workforce 2000*, p. 25; "On the Economic Implication of Demographic Change in the United States," passim.
82. *America's Choice: High Skills or Low Wages!* has frequent comparisons with what occurs in the European and Japanese educational and worker-training programs. See also J. Jacobs, "Training the Workforce of the Future," *Technology Review* 93 (August–September 1990), pp. 66–72, pointing to the potential in community colleges.
83. *Technology, Public Policy, and the Changing Structure of American Agriculture*, pp. 3, 11. (The 1.8 percent annual increase referred to in this report concerns "world agricultural demand by the year 2000," but that figure is clearly related to expected population growth.)
84. See L. R. Brown et al., *State of the World 1990*, chs. 1 and 4.
85. *Technology, Public Policy, and the Changing Structure of American Agriculture*, p. 20.
86. See the description of agricultural "refineries" in F. Rexen and L. Munck, *Cereal Crops for Industrial Use in Europe* (Copenhagen, 1984).
87. M. H. Glantz and J. E. Ausubel, "The Ogallala Aquifer and Carbon Dioxide: Comparison and Convergence," *Environmental Conservation*, vol. 11, no. 2 (Summer 1984), pp. 123–130.
88. G. S. Giese and D. G. Aubrey, "Losing Coastal Upland to Relative Sea-Level Rise: 3 Scenarios for Massachusetts," *Oceanus*, vol. 30, no. 3 (Fall 1987), pp. 16–22.
89. H. E. Schwarz and L. A. Dillard, "The Impact on Water Supplies," *Oceanus*, vol. 32, no. 2 (Summer 1989), pp. 44–45.
90. J. P. Cohn, "Gauging the Biological Impacts of the Greenhouse Effect," *BioScience*, vol. 39, no. 3 (March 1989), pp. 142–46.
91. W. D. Nordhaus, "Greenhouse Economics: Count Before You Leap," *Economist*, 7 July 1990, pp. 21–24, esp. p. 22.
92. See the account in C. Barnett, *The Collapse of British Power* (New York/London, 1972).

CHAPTER 14
PREPARING FOR THE TWENTY-FIRST CENTURY

1. *Economist*, 11 October 1930, p. 652. (I am obliged to Dr. Maarten Pereboom for this reference.)

2. For a further discussion of these trends, see J. L. Gaddis, "Toward the Post–Cold War World," *Foreign Affairs,* vol. 70, no. 2 (Spring 1991), pp. 102–22; Wright and McManus, *Flashpoints.*
3. L. R. Brown et al., *State of the World 1989,* ch. 10, "Outlining a Global Action Plan."
4. Ibid., *1990,* ch. 7, "Cycling into the Future."
5. D. M. Kamimen, "Technology for Development: Sustaining, not Obliterating, the Environment," *Research & Exploration,* Winter 1991, pp. 3–5.
6. For recent examples, see W. S. Dietrich, *In the Shadow of the Rising Sun* (University Park, Pa., 1991), passim; *Competing Economies: America, Europe, and the Pacific Rim* (Office of Technology Assessment, Congress of the United States, Washington, D.C., October 1991), esp. pp. 13–14; Malabré, *Within Our Means,* ch. 6.
7. *World Resources 1990–91,* pp. 61–62, 256. For a more critical view of Brazilian conditions, see L. R. Brown et al., *State of the World 1992,* p. 96.
8. P. Waldman, "Conflict in Algeria over Islamic Military Pits Father Against Son," *Wall Street Journal,* 23 January 1992, pp. A1, A8.
9. *World Resources 1990–91,* p. 262; Paxton (ed.), *Statesman's Yearbook 1990–91,* p. 1087.
10. Paxton (ed.), *Statesman's Yearbook 1990–91,* p. 785; *World Resources 1990–91,* p. 263.
11. Nicely argued in H. Küng, *Global Responsibility: In Search of a New World Ethic* (New York, 1991).
12. *World Resources 1990–91,* pp. 256–57, 262–63.
13. Ibid., p. 266 (notes to Table 16.5).
14. Ibid.
15. D. E. Sanger, "Minister Denies He Opposed College for Japanese Women," *New York Times,* 19 June 1990; "The Dwindling Japanese," *Economist,* 26 January 1991, p. 36.
16. "The Missing Children," *Economist,* 3 August 1991, pp. 43–44.
17. For use of the terms "cornucopians" and "neo-Malthusians," see the excellent survey by T. F. Homer-Dixon, "On the Threshold," pp. 76–116.
18. See, for example, J. Bellini, *High Tech Holocaust* (San Francisco, Cal., 1986), p. 251; Ehrlich and Ehrlich, *Population Explosion,* chs. 1 and 12. In many ways, the tone of this literature replicates that of the antinuclear lobby: see, for example, J. Cox, *Overkill* (Harmondsworth, Mddsx., 1981 edn.).
19. This closely follows Homer-Dixon, "On the Threshold," pp. 100–101.
20. Ibid.
21. As is repeatedly argued in the annual issues of L. R. Brown et al., *State of the World:* see the 1992 edition, chs. 3, 9, 11.
22. Homer-Dixon, "On the Threshold," passim; Eberstadt, "Population Change and National Security," passim; Foster, "Global Demographic Trends to the Year 2010," passim.
23. T. R. Malthus, *An Essay on Population,* 2 vols. (London, 1914 edn.), pp. 261–62. Malthus continued to produce newer versions of his first *Essay* for another few decades, and was therefore able to amend certain of his arguments.

BIBLIOGRAPHY

Note: Articles in daily newspapers and weekly magazines like *The Economist*—much used for this study—and unsigned articles in other periodicals are not included here but are fully cited in the endnotes.

INSTITUTIONAL WORKS, GOVERNMENT PUBLICATIONS, ETC.

Agricultural Biotechnology: The Next Green Revolution? World Bank, Technical Paper no. 133. Washington, D.C., 1991.

American Defense Annual. Lexington, Mass.

America's Choice: High Skills or Low Wages! The Report of the Comparison of the Skills of the Average Work Force. Rochester, N.Y., 1990.

Annual Review of Engineering Industries and Automation 1988, vol. 1. U.N. Economic Commission for Europe. New York, 1989.

Changing Climate. U.S. National Research Council. Washington, D.C., 1983.

CIA Handbook of Economic Statistics, 1990. Central Intelligence Agency. Washington, D.C., 1990.

Competing Economies: America, Europe, and the Pacific Rim. U.S. Congress, Office of Technology Assessment. Washington, D.C., 1991.

Current Population Reports, Series P-25, no. 1018. U.S. Bureau of the Census. Washington, D.C., 1989.

The Diffusion of Power: An Era of Realignment. Report of the National Security Group. Chicago, Ill., 1988.

Draft Report on Military Dependency on Foreign Technologies. National Security Council. Washington, D.C., April 1987.

Economic and Social Progress in Latin America: 1989 Report. Inter-America Development Bank. Washington, D.C., 1989.

Economic Report of the President. Washington, D.C., 1990.

The Economist World Atlas and Almanac 1989. London, 1989.
Education in Japan. Foreign Press Center. Tokyo, 1988.
Everybody Counts: A Report to the Nation of the Future of Mathematics Education. National Research Council. Washington, D.C., 1989.
Global Economic Prospects and the Developing Countries. World Bank. Washington, D.C., 1991.
The Military Balance 1990–91. International Institute of Strategic Studies. London, 1990.
A Nation at Risk. The National Commission of Excellence in Education. Washington, D.C., 1983.
Our Common Future. World Commission on Environment and Development. Oxford, 1987.
Population: The UNFPA Experience. United Nations Fund for Population Activities. New York, 1984.
Reform and Innovation of Science and Education: Planning for the 1990 Farm Bill. U.S. Senate, Committee on Agriculture, Nutrition, and Forestry. Washington, D.C., 1989.
Report of the Secretary of Defense. U.S. Congress. Washington, D.C., Annual.
Robotics Technology and Its Varied Uses. U.S. Congress, Hearing Before the Subcommittee on Science, Research, and Technology, 25 September 1989. Washington, D.C., 1989.
RUSI and Brassey's Defence Yearbook. Royal United Services Institute for Defence Studies. New York. Annual.
Soviet Military Power. U.S. Department of Defense. Washington, D.C. Annual.
State of the Environment: A View Towards the Nineties. Conservation Foundation. Washington, D.C., 1987.
The Statesman's Yearbook, 1990–91. J. Paxton, ed. New York and London, 1990.
Statistical Abstract of the United States 1990. U.S. Bureau of the Census. Washington, D.C., 1990.
Survey of Current Business. Bureau of Economic Analysis. Washington, D.C., July 1990.
Technology, Public Policy, and the Changing Structure of American Agriculture. U.S. Congress, Office of Technology Assessment. Washington, D.C., 1986.
Trends in Developing Economies 1990. World Bank. Washington, D.C., 1990.
UNESCO Statistical Digest 1987. Paris, 1987.
UNESCO Statistical Yearbook 1989. Paris, 1989.
Workforce 2000: Work and Workers for the 21st Century. Hudson Institute. Indianapolis, Ind., 1987.
World Development Report 1990. World Bank. Washington, D.C., 1990.
World Development Report 1991. World Bank. Washington, D.C., 1991.
World Population Prospects 1988. United Nations Population Division. New York, 1989.
World Resources 1990–91. World Resources Institute and International Institute for Environment and Development. New York/Oxford, 1990.
World Tables 1991. World Bank. Washington, D.C., 1991.
Year Book of Labor Statistics 1988. International Labor Office. Geneva, 1988.

AUTHORED WORKS

Adama, G. *The Iron Triangle.* New York, 1981.
Adriaansen, W. L. M., and J. G. Waardensburg, eds. *A Dual World Economy: Forty Years of Development Experience.* Rotterdam, 1989.
Aganbegyan, A. *The Economic Challenge of Perestroika.* M. Barratt Brown, ed. Bloomington, Ind., 1988.
Aggarwal, R. "The Strategic Challenge of the Evolving Global Economy." *Business Horizons,* July–August 1987.
Agnelli, G. "The Europe of 1992." *Foreign Affairs* 68 (Fall 1989).
Ahluwalia, I. J. "Industrial Growth in India: Performance and Prospects." *Journal of Development Economics* 28 (1986).
Alexander, I., and P. Burnett. *Reinventing Man: The Robot Becomes Reality.* New York, 1983.
Alonso, W., ed. *Population in an Interacting World.* Cambridge, Mass., 1987.
Anderson, A., and D. L. Bork, eds. *Thinking About America: The United States in the 1990s.* Stanford, Cal., 1988.
Andrews, K. R. *Elizabethan Privateering: English Privateering During the Spanish War, 1585–1603.* Cambridge, 1964.
Angang, H., and Z. Ping, *China's Population Development.* Beijing, 1991.
Ashton, T. S. *The Industrial Revolution, 1760–1830.* Oxford, 1968.
Atkinson, R. "Supply and Demand for Scientists and Engineers: A National Crisis in the Making." *Science* 248 (27 April 1990).
Attali, J., "Lines on the Horizon: A New Order in the Making." *New Perspectives Quarterly,* Spring 1990.
Avery, D. "The Green Revolution Is Our Real Food Security." Hudson Institute Briefing Paper no. 112. Indianapolis, 1989.
Axelbank, J. "The Crisis of the Cities." *Populi,* 15 (1988).
Baark, E., and A. Jamison. *Technical Development in China, India and Japan.* London, 1986.
Bairoch, P. "International Industrialization Levels from 1750 to 1980." *Journal of European Economic History* 11 (1982).
Baker, C. O., ed. *The Condition of Education 1989. vol. 1, Elementary and Secondary Education.* Washington, D.C., 1989.
Balfour, M. L. G. *Britain and Joseph Chamberlain.* London/Boston, 1985.
Banac, I. "Political Change and National Diversity." *Daedalus* 119 (1990).
Baranson, J. *Robots in Manufacturing: Key to International Competitiveness.* Mt. Airy, Md., 1983.
Barnett, C. *The Collapse of British Power.* New York/London, 1972.
Barnett, M. J. "The Case for More School Days." *Atlantic* 266 (November 1990).
Barraclough, G. *An Introduction to Contemporary History.* Harmondsworth, Mddsx., 1967 edn.
Barth, M. C., and J. G. Titus, eds. *Greenhouse Effect and Sea Level Rise: A Challenge for This Generation.* New York, 1984.
Becker, C. M. "The Demo-Economic Impact of the AIDs Pandemic in Sub-Saharan Africa." *World Development* 18 (1990).
Bellini, J. *High Tech Holocaust.* San Francisco, Cal., 1986.
Berardi, G. M., and C. C. Geisler, eds. *The Social Consequences and Challenges of New Agricultural Technologies.* Boulder, Colo., 1984.

Bergson, A., and H. S. Levine, eds. *The Soviet Economy: Towards the Year 2000.* London, 1983.
Bergsten, C. F. *America in the World Economy: A Strategy for the 1990s.* Washington, D.C., 1988.
———. "The World Economy After the Cold War." *Foreign Affairs* 69 (Summer 1990).
Bloom, D. E., and N. G. Bennett. "Future Shock." *New Republic,* 19 June 1989.
Bornstein, M., ed. *The Soviet Economy: Continuity and Change.* Boulder, Colo., 1981.
Borrus, M. G. *Competing for Control: America's Stake in Microelectronics.* Cambridge, Mass., 1988.
Bowonder, B., and T. Miyake. "Technology Development and Japanese Industrial Competitiveness." *Futures* 22 (January–February 1990).
Braisted, W. R. *The United States Navy in the Pacific, 1909–1922.* Austin, Tex., 1971.
Braudel, F. *Civilization and Capitalism.* vol. 3, *The Perspective of the World.* New York, 1986.
Briggs, A. *Victorian Cities.* London, 1963.
Brock, W. E., and R. D. Homats, eds. *The Global Economy: America's Role in the Decade Ahead.* New York/London, 1990.
Browlee, S. "The Best Banana Bred." *Atlantic* 264 (September 1989).
Brown, H. *The Challenge of Man's Future: An Inquiry Concerning the Condition of Man During the Years That Lie Ahead.* New York, 1954.
Brown, L. R., et al. *State of the World.* New York. Annual.
Bull, H., and A. Watson, eds. *The Expansion of International Society.* Oxford, 1983.
Bultot, F., et al. "Estimated Annual Regime of Energy-Balance Components, Evapotranspiration and Soil Moisture for a Drainage Basin in the Case of a CO_2 Doubling." *Climatic Change* 12 (1988).
Burstein, D. *Euroquake: Europe's Explosive Economic Challenge Will Change the World.* New York, 1991.
———. *Yen! Japan's New Financial Empire and Its Threat to America.* New York, 1988.
Buruma, I. *Behind the Mask: On Sexual Demons, Sacred Mothers, Transvestites, Gangsters, Drifters, and Other Japanese Cultural Heroes.* New York, 1984.
Busch, L., et al. *Plants, Power, and Profit: Social, Economic, and Ethical Consequences of the New Biotechnologies.* Oxford, 1991.
Bylinsky, G. "Trying to Transcend Copycat Science." *Fortune* 115 (30 March 1987).
Calder, A. *The People's War: Britain, 1939–1945.* London, 1969.
Calder, N. *The Green Machines.* New York, 1986.
Caldwell, J. C., and P. Caldwell. "High Fertility in Sub-Saharan Africa." *Scientific American* 262 (May 1990).
Calleo, D. P. *The Bankrupting of America: How the Federal Budget is Impoverishing the Nation.* New York, 1992.
———. *Beyond American Hegemony: The Future of the Western Alliance.* New York, 1987.
———. *The German Question Reconsidered: Germany and the World Order, 1870 to the Present.* New York, 1978.
Carnoy, M. "High Technology and International Labour Markets." *International Labour Review* 124 (1985).
Castles, S., et al. *Here for Good: Western Europe's New Ethnic Minorities.* London, 1984.
Chaliand, G., and J. P. Rageau. *A Strategic Atlas: Comparative Geopolitics of the World's Powers.* New York, 1985.

Chambers, J. D., and G. E. Mingay. *The Agricultural Revolution 1750–1880.* New York, 1966.
Chancellor, J. *Peril or Promise: A Commentary upon America.* New York, 1990.
Choate, P. *Agents of Influence.* New York, 1990.
Chu, L., "The Chimera of the China Market." *Atlantic* 266 (October 1990).
Churba, J. *Soviet Breakout: Strategies to Meet It.* Washington, D.C./London, 1988.
Cipolla, C. M. *Before the Industrial Revolution.* 2nd edn. London, 1981.
———, ed. *The Economic Decline of Empires.* London, 1970.
———. *The Economic History of World Population.* 7th edn. Harmondsworth, Mddsx., 1978.
Clash, M. "Development Policy, Technology Assessment, and the New Technologies." *Futures* 22 (November 1990).
Coale, A. J. "Fertility and Mortality in Different Populations with Special Attention to China." *Proceedings of the American Philosophical Society* 132 (1988).
———, and E. M. Hoover. *Population Growth and Economic Development in Low-Income Countries.* Princeton, N.J., 1958.
Cohen, E. A. "When Policy Outstrips Power—American Strategy and Statecraft," *Public Interest* 75 (1984).
Cohen, R., and P. A. Wilson. *Superpowers in Economic Decline: U.S. Strategy for the Transcentury Era.* New York/London 1990.
Cohen, S. S., and J. Zysman. *Manufacturing Matters: The Myth of the Post-Industrial Economy.* New York, 1987.
Cohn, J. P., "Gauging the Biological Impacts of the Greenhouse Effect," *BioScience* 39 (March 1989).
Colley, L. "The Apotheosis of George III: Loyalty, Royalty, and the British Nation, 1760–1820." *Past and Present* 102 (February 1984).
———. *Britons.* (New Haven/London, 1992).
Colton, T. J. *The Dilemma of Reform in the Soviet Union.* 2nd edn. New York, 1986.
Cooley, M. J. E. "Robotics—Some Wider Implications." *The World Yearbook of Research and Development.* 1985.
Cox, J. *Overkill.* Harmondsworth, Mddsx., 1981 edn.
Cracraft, J., ed. *The Soviet Union Today: An Interpretive Guide.* 2nd edn. Chicago/London, 1988.
Crouzet, F. *The Victorian Economy.* London, 1982.
Cruickshank, J. "The Rise and Fall of the Third World: A Concept Whose Time Has Passed." *World Press Review* 38 (February 1991).
Daly, H. E. *Steady State Economics: The Economics of Biophysical Equilibrium and Moral Growth.* San Francisco, 1977.
———, and J. B. Cobb. *For the Common Good: Redirecting the Economy Toward Community, the Environment and a Sustainable Future.* Boston, Mass., 1989.
Davis, B. D., ed. *The Genetic Revolution: Scientific Prospects and Public Perceptions.* Baltimore/London, 1991.
Davis, K., et al., eds. *Below-Replacement Fertility in Industrial Societies.* New York, 1987.
de Cecco, M. *Money and Empire: The International Gold Standard 1890–1914.* Oxford, 1974.
Decker, W. L., et al. *The Impact of Climate Change from Increased Atmospheric Carbon Dioxide on American Agriculture.* Washington, D.C., 1986.
DeGrasse, R. W. *Military Expansion, Economic Decline: The Impact of Military Spending on U.S. Economic Performance.* Armonk, N.Y., 1985 edn.

Dehio, L. *The Precarious Balance: Four Centuries of the European Power Struggle.* London, 1963.

de Jouvenel, H. "Europe at the Dawn of the Third Millennium: A Synthesis of the Main Trends." *Futures* 20 (October 1988).

Dertouzos, M. L., et al., eds. *Made in America: Regaining the Productive Edge.* Cambridge, Mass., 1989.

Dibb, P. *The Soviet Union: The Incomplete Superpower.* London, 1986.

Dickson, D. "German Biotech Firms Flee Regulatory Controls." *Science* 248 (16 June 1990).

Dietrich, W. S. *In the Shadow of the Rising Sun: The Political Roots of American Economic Decline.* University Park, Pa., 1991.

Dixon, C. J., et al., eds. *Multinational Corporations and the Third World.* London/Sydney, 1986.

Dollinger, P. *La Hanse.* Paris, 1964.

Dore, R. P., and M. Sako. *How the Japanese Learn to Work.* London, 1989.

Dornbusch, R., et al. *The Case for Manufacturing in America's Future.* Rochester, N.Y., 1987.

Doyle, D. P. "Time for America to Set National Education Norms." *Hudson Opinion,* October 1989.

Drucker, P. "The Changed World Economy." *Foreign Affairs* 64 (Spring 1986).

Dumas, L. J. *The Overburdened Economy: Uncovering the Cause of Chronic Unemployment, Inflation, and National Decline.* Berkeley/Los Angeles, 1986.

Duncan, D. E. "Africa: The Long Goodbye," *New Republic* 203 (July 1990).

Eberstadt, N. "Population Change and National Security." *Foreign Affairs* 70 (Summer 1991).

Eekelaar, J. M., and D. Pearl, eds. *An Aging World: Dilemmas and Challenges for Law and Social Policy.* Oxford, 1989.

Ehrlich, P. R. *The Population Bomb.* New York, 1968.

———, and A. E. Ehrlich. *The Population Explosion.* New York, 1990.

Emmott, B. *The Sun Also Sets: The Limits to Japan's Economic Power.* New York, 1989.

Engelhardt, K. G., "Innovations in Health Care: Roles for Advanced Intelligent Technologies." *Pittsburgh High Technology Journal* 2 (1987).

Ernst, D., and D. O'Conner. *Technology and Global Competition: The Challenge for Newly Industrializing Economies.* OECD. Paris, 1989.

Fairbanks, C. H. "Russian Roulette: The Danger of a Collapsing Empire." *Policy Review* 57 (Summer 1991).

Fajer, E. D., et al., "The Effects of Enriched Carbon Dioxide Atmospheres on Plant-Insect Herbivores Interactions." *Science* 243 (1989).

Fallows, J. *More Like Us: Making America Great Again.* New York, 1989.

Fardoust, S., and A. Dhareshwan. *Long-Term Outlook for the World Economy: Issues and Projections for the 1990s.* World Bank. Washington, D.C., 1990.

Farmer, B. H. "Perspectives on the Green Revolution in South Asia." *Modern Asian Studies* 20 (1986).

Fauriol, G. A. "The Shadow of Latin American Affairs." *Foreign Affairs* 69 (1989–90).

Feldstein, M. S., ed. *The United States in the World Economy.* Cambridge, Mass., 1987.

Feshbach, M., and A. Friendly. *Ecocide in the U.S.S.R.* New York, 1992.

Fieldhouse, D. K. *Unilever Overseas: The Anatomy of a Multinational.* Stanford, Cal., 1978.

Fischer, B. "Developing Countries in the Process of Economic Globalization." *Intereconomics* 25 (March–April 1990).
Fjermedal, G. *The Tomorrow Makers: A Brave New World of Living-Brain Machines.* New York, 1986.
Foster, G. D. "Global Demographic Trends to the Year 2010: Implications for U.S. Security." *Washington Quarterly* 12 (Spring 1989).
Friedman, B. M. *Day of Reckoning: The Consequences of American Economic Policy Under Reagan and After.* New York, 1988.
Friedman, G., and M. Lebard. *The Coming War with Japan.* New York, 1991.
Fukuchi, T., and M. Kamagi, eds. *Perspectives on the Pacific Basin Economy: A Comparison of Asia and Latin America.* Tokyo, 1990.
Gable, F. "Changing Climate and Caribbean Coastlines." *Oceanus* 30 (Winter 1987–88).
———, and D. G. Aubrey. "Changing Climate and the Pacific." *Oceanus* 32 (Winter 1989–90).
Gaddis, J. L. "Toward the Post–Cold War World." *Foreign Affairs* 70 (Spring 1991).
Gardels, N. "The Education We Deserve." *New Perspectives Quarterly* 7 (1990).
Garton Ash, T. *The Magic Lantern: The Revolution of '89 Witnessed in Warsaw, Budapest, Berlin and Prague.* New York, 1990.
———. *The Uses of Adversity: Essays on the Fate of Central Europe.* New York, 1989.
Gati, C. *The BLOC That Failed: Soviet-East European Relations in Transition.* Boulder, Colo., 1984.
Gellner, E. *Nations and Nationalism.* Oxford, 1983.
Gendel, S. M., et al. *Agricultural Bioethics: Implications of Agricultural Biotechnology.* Ames, Iowa, 1990.
Geremek, B. "The Realities of Eastern and Central Europe," in *Change in Europe.* Washington, D.C.: Plenary of the Trilateral Commission, April 1990.
Gevarter, W. B. *Intelligent Machines: An Introductory Perspective of Artificial Intelligence and Robotics.* Englewood Cliffs, N.J., 1985.
Ghosh, P. K., ed. *Developing South Asia: A Modernization Perspective.* Westport, Conn., 1984.
———, ed. *Technology Policy and Development: A Third-World Perspective.* Westport, Conn., 1984.
Gibbons, A. "Biotechnology Takes Root in the Third World." *Science* 248 (25 May 1990).
Giese, G. S., and D. G. Aubrey. "Losing Coastal Upland to Relative Sea-Level Rise: 3 Scenarios for Massachusetts." *Oceanus* 30 (Fall 1987).
Gilder, G. "You Ain't Seen Nothing Yet." *Forbes* 141 (4 April 1988).
Gill, S., and D. Law. *The Global Political Economy: Perspectives, Problems and Policies.* Baltimore, Md., 1988.
Gilpin, R. *The Political Economy of International Relations.* Princeton, N.J., 1987.
———. *War and Change in World Politics.* Cambridge, Mass., 1981.
Glantz, M. H., and J. E. Ausubel. "The Ogallala Aquifer and Carbon Dioxide: Comparison and Convergence." *Environmental Conservation* 11 (Summer 1984).
Gleick, P. H. "Climate Change and International Politics: Problems Facing Developing Countries." *Ambio* 18 (1989).
———. "The Implications of Global Changes for International Security." *Climatic Change* 15 (1989).
Goldman, C. S., ed. *The Empire and the Century: A Series of Essays on Imperial Problems and Possibilities, by Various Writers.* London, 1905.

Goldman, M. I. *Gorbachev's Challenge: Economic Reform in the Age of High Technology.* New York, 1987.
———. *The Enigma of Soviet Petroleum: Half-Full or Half-Empty?* London, 1980.
———. *U.S.S.R. In Crisis: The Failure of an Economic System.* New York, 1983.
Goliber, T. J. "Africa's Expanding Population: Old Problems, New Policies." *Population Bulletin* 44 (1989).
Goodman, D. S. G. *China's Regional Development.* London, 1989.
———, et al. *From Farming to Biotechnology: A Theory of Agro-Industrial Development.* Oxford, 1987.
Gore, Albert. *Earth in the Balance: Ecology and the Human Spirit.* New York, 1992.
Gottfried, K., and P. Bracken, eds. *Reforging European Security: From Confrontation to Cooperation.* Boulder, Colo., 1990.
Govind, H. "Recent Developments in Environmental Protection in India: Pollution Control." *Ambio* 18 (1989).
Green, K., and E. Yoxen. "The Greening of European Industry: What Role for Biotechnology?" *Futures* 22 (June 1990).
Green, M., and M. Pinsky, eds. *America's Transition: Blueprints for the 1990s.* Lanham, Md., 1990.
Gregory, P. R., and R. C. Stuart. *Soviet Economic Structure and Performance.* 3rd edn. New York, 1986.
Griffith, W. E., ed. *Central and Eastern Europe: The Opening Curtain.* Boulder, Colo., 1989.
Gruner, W. *Die deutsche Frage: Ein Problem der Europaischen Geschichte seit 1800.* Munich, 1985.
Gupta, A. "The Indian Arms Industry: A Lumbering Giant." *Asian Survey* 30 (1990).
Guralnik, J. M., et al. "Projecting the Older Population of the United States." *Milbank Quarterly* 66 (1988).
Gwynne, R. N. *New Horizons? Third World Industrialization in an International Framework.* New York/London, 1990.
Hamakawa, Y. "Photovoltaic Power." *Scientific American* 256 (April 1987).
Hamerow, T. S. *Restoration, Revolution, Reaction: Economics and Politics in Germany, 1815–1871.* Princeton, N.J., 1958.
Hamilton, E. K., ed. *America's Global Interests: A New Agenda.* New York, 1989.
Hancock, G. *Lords of Poverty: The Power, Prestige, and Corruption of the International Aid Business.* Boston, Mass., 1990.
Hanke, D. E. "Seeding the Bamboo Revolution." *Nature* 22 (1990).
Hansen, J., et al. "Global Climate Changes as Forecast by the Goddard Institute for Space Studies Three-Dimensional Model." *Journal of Geophysical Research* 93 (1988).
Hartley, J. "Are There Really So Many Robots in Japan?" *Decade of Robotics.* Special 10th Anniversary Issue of *Industrial Robot Machine.* Berlin, 1983.
Hassan, S. "Environmental Issues and Security in South Asia." *Adelphi Papers* 262 (Autumn 1991).
Hatsopoulos, N., et al. "U.S. Competitiveness: Beyond the Trade Deficit." *Science* 241 (1988).
Hauner, M. *What Is Asia to Us? Russia's Asian Heartland Yesterday and Today.* Boston/London, 1990.
Hayes, M. D. "The U.S. and Latin America: The Lost Decade?" *Foreign Affairs* 68 (1988–89).
Hecht, S., and A. Cockburn. *The Fate of the Forest: Developers, Destroyers, and Defenders of the Amazon.* London/New York, 1989.

Heilbroner, R. L. *The Worldly Philosophers: The Lives, Times, and Ideas of the Great Economic Thinkers.* New York, 1986 edn.
Heisbourg, F. "Population Movements in Post–Cold War Europe." *Survival* 33 (January–February 1991).
Helleiner, E. "States and the Future of Global Finance." *Review of International Studies* 18 (January 1992).
Heller, M. A. "The Middle East: Out of Step with History." *Foreign Affairs* 69 (1989–90).
Herrnstein, R. J. "IQ and Falling Birthrates." *Atlantic* 263 (May 1989).
Hirsch, E. D. *Cultural Literacy: What Every American Needs to Know.* Boston, 1987.
Hoagland, J. "Europe's Destiny." *Foreign Affairs* 69 (1989–90).
Hobsbawm, E. J. *Industry and Empire: The Making of Modern English Society.* Harmondsworth, Mddsx., 1969.
Hobson, J. A. *Imperialism: A Study.* London, 1902.
Hoffman, J., et al. *Projecting Future Sea Level Rise: Methodology, Estimate to the Year 2000, and Research Needs.* Washington, D.C., 1983.
Hoffmann, S. "The European Community and 1992." *Foreign Affairs* 68 (Fall 1989).
Holzman, F. D. "Soviet Military Spending: Assessing the Numbers Game." *International Security* 6 (1982).
———. *Financial Checks on Soviet Defense Expenditures.* Lexington, Mass., 1975.
Homer-Dixon, T. F. "On the Threshold: Environmental Changes as Causes of Acute Conflict." *International Security* 16 (Fall 1991).
Houghton, R. A., and Woodwell, G. M. "Global Climatic Change." *Scientific American* 260 (1989).
Howard, M. *The Lessons of History.* New Haven, Conn., 1991.
Hughes, H. "Catching Up: The Asian Newly Industrializing Economies in the 1990s." *Asian Development Review* 7 (1989).
Hunt, H. A., and T. L. Hunt. *Human Resource Implications of Robotics.* Kalamazoo, Mich., 1983.
Huntington, S. P. "The U.S.—Decline or Renewal?" *Foreign Affairs* 67 (Winter 1988–89).
Iklé, F. C., and T. Nakanishi. "Japan's Grand Strategy." *Foreign Affairs* 69 (Summer 1990).
———, and A. Wohlstetter, eds. *Discriminate Deterrence: Report of the Commission on Integrated Long-Term Strategy.* Washington, D.C., 1988.
Ingham, K. "Africa's Internal Wars of the 1980s: Contours and Prospects." United States Institute of Peace. *In Brief* 18 (1990).
———. *Politics in Modern Africa: The Uneven Tribal Dimensions.* London/New York, 1990.
Inoguchi, T., and D. I. Okimoto, eds. *The Political Economy of Japan.* Vol. 2, *The Changing International Context.* Stanford, Cal., 1988.
Ishihara, Shintaro. *The Japan That Can Say No.* New York, 1991.
Ives, J. D., and B. Messerli. *The Himalayan Dilemma: Reconciling Development and Conservation.* London/New York, 1989.
Jacobs, J. "Training the Workforce of the Future." *Technology Review* 93 (August–September 1990).
Joffe, J. *The Limited Partnership: Europe, the United States, and the Burdens of Alliance.* Cambridge, 1987.
———. "Germany After NATO." *Harper's* 281 (September 1990).
Johnson, B. L. C. *Development in South Asia.* Harmondsworth, Mddsx., 1983.

Johnson, C. "Japan in Search of a 'Normal' Role." *Institute on Global Conflict and Cooperation* 3 (July 1992), U.C. San Diego.

———. *MITI and the Japanese Miracle: The Growth of Industrial Policy, 1925–1975.* Stanford, Cal., 1982.

Johnson, D. G., and R. D. Lee. *Population Growth and Economic Development: Issues and Evidence.* Madison, Wis., 1987.

Joll, J. *The Origins of the First World War.* London/New York, 1984.

Jones, C., ed. *Britain and Revolutionary France: Conflict, Subversion, and Propaganda.* Exeter Studies in History, no. 5. Exeter, 1983.

Jones, E. L. *The European Miracle: Environments, Economies and Geopolitics in the History of Europe and Asia.* Cambridge, Mass., 1981.

———, and G. E. Mingay, eds. *Land, Labour and Population in the Industrial Revolution.* London, 1967.

Jones, R. S. "The Economic Implications of Japan's Aging Population." *Asian Survey* 28 (September 1988).

Judy, R. W., and V. L. Clough. *The Information Age and Soviet Society.* Indianapolis, 1989.

Juma, C. *The Gene Hunters: Biotechnology and the Scramble for Seeds.* London/Princeton, N.J., 1989.

Kahn, H. *The Emerging Japanese Superstate: Challenge and Response.* London, 1971.

Kaiser, D. *Politics and War: European Conflict from Philip II to Hitler.* Cambridge, Mass., 1990.

Kaldor, M. *The Baroque Arsenal.* London, 1982.

Kamata, S. *Japan in the Passing Lane: An Insider's Account of Life in a Japanese Auto Factory.* New York, 1984.

Kamimen, D. M. "Technology for Development: Sustaining, Not Obliterating, the Environment." *Research & Exploration,* Winter 1991.

Kant, Immanuel. *Zum Ewigen Frieden.* Stuttgart, 1954 edn.

Keegan, J., and A. Wheatcroft. *Zones of Conflict: An Atlas of Future Wars.* New York, 1978.

Kenney, M. *Biotechnology: The University-Industrial Complex.* New Haven, Conn., 1986.

Kennedy, P. M. "Fin-de-Siecle America." *New York Review of Books* 37 (28 June 1990).

———, ed. *Grand Strategies in War and Peace.* New Haven/London, 1991.

———. *The Realities Behind Diplomacy: Background Influences on British External Policies.* London, 1980.

———. *The Rise and Fall of the Great Powers: Economic Change and Military Conflict from 1500 to 2000.* New York, 1987.

———. *The Rise of the Anglo-German Antagonism 1860–1914.* London/Boston, 1980.

Kerr, R. A. "New Greenhouse Report Puts Down Dissenters." *Science* 249 (1990).

Kiernan, V. G. "State and Nation in Western Europe." *Past and Present* 31 (1965).

Kim, S. S., ed. *China and the World: Chinese Foreign Policy in the Post-Mao Era.* Boulder, Colo., 1989.

Kindleberger, C. *The World in Depression, 1929–1939.* Berkeley, Cal., 1973.

Kloppenburg, J. R. *First the Seed: The Political Economy of Plant Biotechnology, 1492–2000.* Cambridge, 1988.

Kotkin, J., and Y. Kishimoto. *The Third Century: America's Resurgence in the Asian Era.* New York, 1988.

Kozol, J. *Illiterate America.* New York, 1985.

Krauthammer, C. "The Unipolar Moment." *Foreign Affairs* 70 (1990–91).
Krugman, P. *The Age of Diminished Expectations: U.S. Economic Policy in the 1990s.* Cambridge, Mass., 1990.
Küng, H. *Global Responsibility: In Search of a New World Ethic.* New York, 1991.
Kvint, V. "Russia as Cinderella." *Forbes* 145 (19 February 1990).
Lall, S. *Developing Countries as Exporters of Technology: A First Look at the Indian Experience.* London, 1982.
Landau, G. W., et al. *Latin America at a Crossroads: The Challenge to the Trilateral Countries.* Trilateral Commission, New York/Paris/Tokyo, 1990.
Landes, D. S. *The Unbound Prometheus: Technological Change and Industrial Development in Western Europe from 1750 to the Present.* Cambridge, 1969.
Lardy, N. R. "Agricultural Reforms in China." *Journal of International Affairs* 39 (1986).
Larson, T. B. *Soviet-American Rivalry.* New York, 1978.
Lieven, D. "Gorbachev and the Nationalities." *Conflict Studies* 216 (1988).
———. "The Soviet Crisis." *Conflict Studies* 241 (1991).
Lind, M. "America as an Ordinary Country." *American Enterprise* 1 (September–October 1990).
Linder, S. B. *The Pacific Century: Economic and Political Consequences of Asian-Pacific Dynamism.* Stanford, Cal., 1986.
Liverman, D. M., et al. "Climatic Change and Grain Corn Yields in the North American Great Plains." *Climatic Change* 9 (1986).
Lowenthal, A. F. "Rediscovering Latin America." *Foreign Affairs* 69 (Fall 1990).
Lubasz, H., ed. *The Development of the Modern State.* New York, 1964.
Luttwak, E. N. "From Geopolitics to Geo-Economics." *National Interest* 20 (Summer 1990).
MacNeill, J., et al. *Beyond Interdependence: The Meshing of the World's Economy and the Earth's Ecology.* New York/Oxford, 1991.
Malabré, A. L. *Within Our Means: The Struggle for Economic Recovery After a Reckless Decade.* New York, 1991.
Malthus, T. R. *An Essay on the Principle of Population As It Affects the Future Improvement of Society.* London, 1798; reprinted, with notes by J. Bonar, New York, 1965.
———. *An Essay on Population,* 2 vols. London, 1914.
Manabe, S., and R. T. Wetherald. "Large-Scale Changes of Soil Wetness Induced by an Increase in Atmospheric Carbon Dioxide." *Journal of Atmospheric Sciences* 44 (1987).
Mann, P.S. "Green Revolution Revisited: The Adoption of High Yielding Variety Wheat Seeds in India." *Journal of Development Studies* 26 (1989).
Mansergh, N. *The Commonwealth Experience.* London, 1969.
Marcum, J. A. "Africa: A Continent Adrift." *Foreign Affairs* 68 (1988–89).
Marien, M. "Driving Forces and Barriers to a Sustainable Global Economy." *Futures* 22 (December 1989).
Markin, J. H. "Japan's Investment in America: Is It a Threat?" *Challenge* (November–December 1988).
Martin, L. G. "The Graying of Japan." *Population Bulletin* 44 (1989).
Martinez, T. E. "Argentina: Living with Hyperinflation." *Atlantic* 266 (December 1990).
Marton, K. *Multinationals, Technology, and Industrialization: Implications and Impact in Third World Countries.* Lexington, Mass., 1986.
Maruyama, M. "Japan's Agricultural Policy Failure." *Food Policy* 12 (May 1987).

Marwick, A. *War and Social Change in the Twentieth Century.* London, 1974.
Marx, J. L., ed. *A Revolution in Biotechnology.* Cambridge, 1989.
Mathews, J. T. "Redefining Security." *Foreign Affairs* 68 (Spring 1989).
Mathias, P. *The First Industrial Nation: An Economic History of Britain, 1700–1914.* London, 1969.
Maull, H. W. "Germany and Japan: The New Civilian Powers." *Foreign Affairs* 69 (Winter 1991–92).
Maxwell, K. "The Tragedy of the Amazon." *New York Review of Books* 38 (7 March 1991).
McAfee, K. "Why the Third World Goes Hungry." *Commonweal* 117 (15 June 1990).
McCormick, B. J. *The World Economy: Patterns of Growth and Change.* Oxford, 1988.
McCormick, G. H., and R. E. Bissell, eds. *Strategic Dimensions of Economic Behavior.* New York, 1984.
McInnes, C. *NATO's Changing Strategic Agenda: The Conventional Defense of Central Europe.* London/Boston, 1990.
McIntyre, W. D. *Colonies into Commonwealth.* London, 1966.
McMillan, J., et al. "The Impact of China's Economic Reforms on Agricultural Productivity Growth," *Journal of Political Economy* 97 (1989).
McNeill, W. H. *Plagues and Peoples.* New York, 1976.
———. *Population and Politics Since 1750.* Charlottesville, Va., 1990.
———. *The Pursuit of Power: Technology, Armed Forces and Society Since 1000 A.D.* Chicago, 1983.
———. *The Rise of the West: A History of the Human Community.* Chicago, Ill., 1967.
Meadows, D. H., et al. *The Limits to Growth: A Report for the Club of Rome's Project on the Predicament of Mankind.* New York, 1972.
Mearsheimer, J. J. *Conventional Deterrence.* Ithaca, N.Y., 1983.
Mendelssohn, K. *Science and Western Domination.* London, 1976.
Meyer-Larsen, W. "America's Century Will End with a Whimper." *World Press Review* 38 (January 1991).
Moran, T. H., "International Economics and National Security," *Foreign Affairs* 69 (Winter 1990–91).
———. "The Globalization of America's Defense Industries: Managing the Threat of Foreign Dependence." *International Security* 15 (Summer 1990).
Morley, J. W., ed. *The Pacific Basin: New Challenges for the United States.* New York, 1986.
Morris, C. R. "The Coming Global Boom." *Atlantic* 264 (October 1989).
Morse, E. L. "The Coming Oil Revolution." *Foreign Affairs* 69 (Winter 1990–91).
Morse, R. M. "Japan's Drive to Pre-eminence." *Foreign Policy* 69 (1987–88).
Moynihan, M. *Global Consumer Demographics.* New York, 1991.
Mukerjie, D. "Economic Realities Forbid Sweeping Changes in Policy." *Asian Finance* 16 (15 April 1990).
Murphy, R. T. "Power Without Purpose." *Harvard Business Review* 66 (March–April 1988).
Nau, H. R. *The Myth of America's Decline: Leading the World Economy into the 1990s.* New York, 1990.
Nordhaus, W. D. "Global Warming: Slowing the Greenhouse Express." Cowes Foundation Paper no. 758. Yale University, New Haven, 1990.
Novak, M. "What Became of the Ugly American?" *Forbes* 145 (30 April 1990).

Nye, J. S. *Bound to Lead: The Changing Nature of American Power.* New York, 1990.

Odhiambo, T. R. "Human Resources Development: Problems and Prospects in Developing Countries." *Impact of Science on Society* 155 (1989).

Ogawa, N. "Aging in China: Demographic Alternatives." *Asia-Pacific Population Journal* 3 (1988).

Ohmae, K. *The Borderless World: Management Lessons in the New Logic of the Global Marketplace.* New York/London, 1990.

Olsen, E. A. *U.S.-Japan Strategic Reciprocity: A Neo-Nationalist View.* Stanford, Cal., 1985.

Onimode, B. *A Political Economy of the African Crisis.* London/New Jersey, 1988.

Oppenheimer, M., and R. H. Boyle. *Dead Heat: The Race Against the Greenhouse Effect.* New York, 1990.

O'Reilly, B. "America's Place in the World Competition." *Fortune* 120 (6 November 1989).

Packard, G. R. "The Coming U.S.–Japan Crisis." *Foreign Affairs* 66 (Winter 1987–88).

Parry, J. H. *The Age of Reconnaissance.* 2nd edn. London, 1966.

Pearce, D. W., et al. *Sustainable Development: Economics and Environment in the Third World.* Aldershot, Hants, 1990.

Perry, N. J. "How to Help America's Schools." *Fortune* 120 (4 December 1989).

Peterson, P. G., and N. Howe. *On Borrowed Time.* San Francisco, 1989.

Phillips, K. *The Politics of Rich and Poor: Wealth and the American Electorate in the Reagan Aftermath.* New York, 1990.

Pierog, K., "How Technology Is Tackling 24-Hour Global Markets." *Futures* 17 (1989).

Pirages, D. *Global Technopolitics: The International Politics of Technology and Resources.* Belmont, Cal., 1989.

Pollard, S. *Peaceful Conquest: The Industrialization of Europe, 1760–1970.* Oxford, 1971.

Polumbaum, J. "Dateline China: The People's Malaise." *Foreign Policy* 20 (1990–91).

Porter, B. *The Lion's Share: A Short History of British Imperialism 1850–1970.* London, 1976.

Porter, M. *The Competitive Advantage of Nations.* New York, 1990.

Postel, S. "Water: Rethinking Management in an Age of Scarcity." *Worldwatch Paper* 62 (December 1984).

Pradervand, P. *Listening to Africa: Developing Africa from the Grassroots.* New York, 1989.

Prakosh, A. "A Carrier Force for the Indian Navy." *Naval War College Review* 43 (Autumn 1990).

Prentis, S. *Biotechnology: A New Industrial Revolution.* New York, 1984.

Prestowitz, C. V. *Trading Places: How We Allowed Japan to Take the Lead.* New York, 1988.

Prestowitz, C. V., et al., eds. *Powernomics: Economics and Strategy After the Cold War.* Lanham, Md., 1991.

Pye, L. W. "China: Erratic State, Frustrated Society." *Foreign Affairs* 69 (Fall 1990).

Quester, G., ed. *Nuclear Proliferation.* Madison, Wis., 1981.

Quinn, T. C., et al. "AIDS in Africa: An Epidemiological Paradigm." *Science* 234 (November 1986).

Radharaman, R., ed. *Robotics and Factories of the Future '87.* Berlin/Heidelberg/New York, 1988.

Ranum, O., ed. *National Consciousness, History, and Political Culture in Early-Modern Europe.* Baltimore/London, 1975.
Ravenhill, J. "The North-South Balance of Power." *International Affairs* 66 (1990).
Reading, B. *Japan: The Coming Collapse.* London, 1992.
Reich, R. B. *The Work of Nations: Preparing Ourselves for the 21st-century Capitalism.* New York, 1990.
Reid, W. V., and K. R. Miller. *Keeping Options Open: The Scientific Basis for Conserving Biodiversity.* Washington, D.C., 1989.
Reisner, M. *Cadillac Desert: The American West and Its Disappearing Water.* New York, 1986.
Reperant, D. *The Most Beautiful Villages in France.* New York, 1990.
Resnick, B. C. "The Globalization of World Financial Markets." *Business Horizons* 32 (November–December 1989).
Rexen, F., and L. Munck. *Cereal Crops for Industrial Use in Europe.* Copenhagen, 1984.
Rhoades, R. E. "The World's Food Supply at Risk." *National Geographic* 179 (April 1991).
Roberts, J. *The Pelican History of the World.* Harmondsworth, Mddsx., 1980.
Robinson, R., and J. Gallagher. *Africa and the Victorians: The Official Mind of Imperialism.* London, 1961.
Rohlen, T. P. *Japan's High Schools.* Berkeley, Cal., 1983.
Rosecrance, R., ed. *America as an Ordinary Power.* Ithaca, N.Y., 1976.
———. *America's Economic Resurgence: A Bold New Strategy.* New York, 1990.
———. *The Rise of the Trading States: Commerce and Conquest in the Modern World.* New York, 1985.
Rosenau, J. N. "The Relocation of Authority in a Shrinking World." Unpublished paper. 1980.
Roskill, S. W. *Naval Policy Between the Wars.* Vol. 1. London, 1968.
Rostow, W. W. *The World Economy: History and Prospects.* Austin, Tex., 1978.
Rowen, H. S., and C. Wolf, Jr., eds. *The Future of the Soviet Empire.* New York, 1987.
———, eds. *The Impoverished Superpower: Perestroika and the Soviet Military Burden.* San Francisco, 1990.
Rudney, R. S. "Mitterand's New Atlanticism: Evolving French Attitudes Toward NATO." *Orbis* 28 (1984).
Russett, B. "Defense Expenditures and National Well-Being." *American Political Science Review* 76 (1982).
Sadik, N. *The State of the World Population.* U.N. Population Fund. New York, 1990.
Sayle, M., and J. Sayle. "Why We Send Our Children to a Japanese School." *Tokyo Journal,* August 1990.
Scalapino, R. A. "Asia and the United States: The Challenges Ahead." *Foreign Affairs* 69 (1989–90).
Scammell, G. V. *The World Encompassed: The First European Maritime Empires, c. 800–1650.* Berkeley, Cal., 1981.
Schell, O. *To Get Rich Is Glorious: China in the '80s.* New York, 1985.
Schlosstein, S. *The End of the American Century.* New York, 1989.
Schneider, B. *The Barefoot Revolution.* London, 1988.
Schneider, S. H. *Global Warming.* San Francisco, Cal., 1989.
Schodt, F. L. "In the Land of Robots." *Business Month* 132 (November 1988).
Schoenfeld, G. "The Soviet Union: Rad Storm Rising." *Atlantic* 266 (December 1990).

Schwarz, H. E., and L. A. Dillard. "The Impact on Water Supplies." *Oceanus* 32 (Summer 1989).
Scott, P. B. *The Robotics Revolution: The Complete Guide for Managers and Engineers.* Oxford/New York, 1984.
Searle, G. R. *Eugenics and Politics in Britain, 1900–1914.* Leyden, 1976.
———. *The Quest for National Efficiency, 1899–1914.* 2nd edn. Atlantic Highlands, N.J., 1990.
Segal, G. "As China Grows Strong." *International Affairs* 64 (1988).
———. *Defending China.* Oxford, 1985.
———. *Rethinking the Pacific.* Oxford, 1990.
Shennan, J. H. *The Origins of the Modern European State, 1450–1725.* London, 1974.
Sheridan, T. "Merging Mind and Machine." *Technology Review* 87 (October 1984).
Shulman, S. "Hot Air—or What?" *Nature* 345 (14 June 1990).
Simon, J. L. *Population Matters: People, Resources, Environment and Immigration.* New Brunswick, N.J., 1990.
———. *The Ultimate Resource.* Princeton, N.J., 1981.
Singer, H. W. "The African Food Crisis and the Role of Food Aid." *Food Policy* 14 (1989).
Singh, M. P. "The Crisis of the Indian State." *Asian Survey* 30 (1990).
Smit, B., et al. "Sensitivity of Crop Yields and Land Resource Potential to Climate Change in Ontario, Canada." *Climatic Change* 14 (1989).
Smith, A. *The Geopolitics of Information: How Western Culture Dominates the World.* Oxford/New York, 1980.
Smith, H. W. "Nationalism and Religious Conflict in Imperial Germany, 1887–1914." Ph.D. dissertation, Yale University, 1991.
Smith, M., et al. *Asia's New Industrial World.* London, 1985.
Snyder, J. C., and S. F. Wells, eds. *Limiting Nuclear Proliferation.* Cambridge, Mass., 1985.
Sorensen, T. C. "Rethinking National Security." *Foreign Affairs* 69 (Summer 1990).
Spence, J. *To Change China: Western Advisors in China, 1620–1969.* New York, 1969 edn.
Starr, J. R., and D. C. Stoll. *The Politics of Scarcity: Water in the Middle East.* Boulder, Colo., 1988.
Steinberg, J. *Why Switzerland?* Cambridge, 1976.
Strange, S. "Finance, Information, and Power." *Review of International Studies* 16 (1990).
Taylor, A. J. P. *The Struggle for Mastery in Europe 1848–1918.* Oxford, 1954.
———. *The Trouble Makers: Dissent Over Foreign Policy, 1789–1939.* London, 1969 edn.
Taylor, J. *Shadows of the Rising Sun: A Critical View of the "Japanese Miracle."* New York, 1984.
Taylor, P. A. M., ed. *The Industrial Revolution in Britain: Triumph or Disaster?* Lexington, Mass., 1970.
Teitelbaum, M. S., and J. M. Winter. *The Fear of Population Decline.* Orlando, Fla./London, 1976.
Teitelman, R. *Gene Dreams: Wall Street, Academia, and the Rise of Biotechnology.* New York, 1989.
Thomas, H. *A History of the World.* New York, 1979.
Thomas, R. G. C. *Indian Security Policy.* Princeton, N.J., 1986.
Thucydides. *The Peloponnesian War.* Harmondsworth, Mddsx., 1954 edn.

Thurow, L. "How to Wreck the Economy." *New York Review of Books* 28 (14 May 1981).

———. *The Zero-Sum Society: Distribution and the Possibilities for Economic Change.* New York, 1980.

Tilly, C., ed. *The Formation of National States in Western Europe.* Princeton, N.J., 1975.

Titus, J. G., ed. *Effects of Changes in Stratospheric Ozone and Global Climate.* Vol. 4, *Sea Level Rise.* Washington, D.C., 1986.

Tolchin, M., and S. Tolchin. *Buying into America: How Foreign Money is Changing the Face of Our Nation.* New York, 1988.

Tranter, N. *Population Since the Industrial Revolution: The Case of England and Wales.* New York, 1973.

Treverton, G. F. *Making the Alliance Work: The United States and Western Europe.* Ithaca, N.Y., 1985.

Trewartha, G. T. *A Geography of Population: World Patterns.* New York, 1969.

Tucker, R. W., and L. Wrigley, eds. *The Atlantic Alliance and Its Critics.* New York, 1983.

Tucker, W. *Progress and Privilege: America in the Age of Environmentalism.* New York, 1982.

B. L. Turner et al. *The Earth As Transformed by Human Action: Global and Regional Changes in the Biosphere over the Past 300 Years* (Cambridge, 1990).

Urbanials, D. F. "The Unattended Factory: FANUC's New Flexibility Automated Manufacturing Plant Using Industrial Robots," *13th International Symposium on Industrial Robots and Robots 7: Conference Proceedings.* Vol. 1. Dearborn, Mich., 1983.

van de Kaa, D. J. "Europe's Second Demographic Transition." *Population Bulletin* 42 (1987).

Van Evera, S. "Why Europe Matters, Why the Third World Doesn't: American Grand Strategy After the Cold War." *Journal of Strategic Studies* 13 (1990).

Veit, L. A. "Time of the New Asian Tigers." *Challenge* 30 (July–August 1987).

Vogel, E. F. "Pax Nipponica." *Foreign Affairs* 64 (Spring 1986).

———. *Japan as Number One: Lessons for America.* New York, 1980 edn.

———. *One Step Ahead in China: Guangdong Under Reform.* Cambridge, Mass., 1990.

Von Laue, T. H. *The World Revolution of Westernization.* New York/Oxford, 1987.

Wattenberg, B. *The First Universal Nation: Leading Indicators and Ideas about the Surge of America in the 1990s.* New York, 1990.

———. *The Birth Dearth.* New York, 1987.

Wells, S. F., and M. A. Bruzonsky, eds. *Security in the Middle East: Regional Change and Great Power Strategies.* Boulder, Colo./London, 1987.

Westing, A. H. *Global Resources and International Conflict: Environmental Factors in Strategic Policy and Action.* Oxford/New York, 1986.

Wheeler, D. L. "Scientists Studying 'The Greenhouse Effect' Challenge Fears of Global Warming." *Journal of Forestry* 88 (1989).

Whitaker, J. S. *How Can Africa Survive?* New York, 1988.

White, M. *The Japanese Educational Challenge: A Commitment to Children.* New York, 1989.

Williams, D. V. "Estimated Bioresource Sensitivity to Climate Change in Alberta, Canada." *Climatic Change* 7 (1985).

Wilson, C. *Profit and Power: A Study of England and the Dutch Wars.* London, 1957.

Wilson, C. A., and J. F. B. Mitchell. "Simulated Climate and CO_2-Induced Climate Change Over Western Europe." *Climatic Change* 8 (1986).
Wolferen, K. van. "The Japan Problem." *Foreign Affairs* 65 (Winter 1986–87).
———. "The Japan Problem Revisited." *Foreign Affairs* 69 (Fall 1990).
———. *The Enigma of Japanese Power: People and Politics in a Stateless Nation.* New York, 1989.
Womack, J., et al. *The Machine That Changed the World: Based on the Massachusetts Institute of Technology 5-Million-Dollar 5-Year Study on the Future of the Automobile.* London, 1990.
Woodruff, W. *The Impact of Western Man: A Study of Europe's Role in the World Economy.* New York, 1967.
Wright, R., and D. MacManus. *Flashpoints: Promise and Peril in a New World.* New York, 1991.
Wriston, W. B. "Technology and Sovereignty." *Foreign Affairs* 67 (Winter 1988–89).
Yamaguchi, H. "Biotechnology: New Hope for Japan's Farmers." *Business Japan* (April 1987).
Yang, Y., and R. Tyers. "The Economic Costs of Self-Sufficiency in China." *World Development* 17 (1989).
Young, C. "Australia's Population: A Long-Term view." *Current Affairs Bulletin* (Sydney) 65 (May 1989).
Yoxen, E. *The Gene Business: Who Should Control Biotechnology?* New York, 1983.
———, and V. Di Martino. *Biotechnology in Future Society: Scenarios and Options for Europe.* Luxembourg, 1989.
Yuanjun, H., and Z. Zhongzing. "Environmental Pollution and Control Measures in China." *Ambio* 16 (1987).
Yudken, J. S., and M. Black. "Targeting National Needs: A New Direction for Science and Technology Policy." *World Policy Journal* 7 (Spring 1990).
Yuging, W. "Natural Conservation Regions in China." *Ambio* 16 (1987).
"Z." "To the Stalin Mausoleum." *Daedalus* 119 (Winter 1990).
Zengage, T. R., and C. T. Ratcliffe. *The Japanese Century: Challenge and Response.* Hong Kong, 1988.
Zysman, J. "U.S. Power, Trade, and Technology." *International Affairs* 67 (1991).

INDEX

ABOUT THE AUTHOR

PAUL KENNEDY was born in the north of England, at Wallsend-on-Tyne, in 1945. He attended the University of Newcastle, where he graduated with first class honors in history, and received his doctorate from Oxford. After teaching in England, Kennedy moved to the United States in 1983 to become Yale University's J. Richardson Dilworth Professor of History, with a focus on modern strategic and international affairs.

Professor Kennedy has researched and lectured at a variety of places in Europe and North America. He is a Fellow of the Royal Historical Society, and a former Visiting Fellow of the Institute for Advanced Study at Princeton and of the Alexander von Humboldt Foundation in Germany. He is the author of eleven books, including the 1988 international bestseller *The Rise and Fall of the Great Powers*. A frequent reviewer for and contributor to *The New York Times, The New York Review of Books, The New Republic, The Washington Post, The Atlantic* and *The Economist,* Paul Kennedy lives in Hamden, Connecticut, with his wife, Catherine, and their three sons. He also coaches soccer.

ABOUT THE TYPE

This book was set in Electra, a typeface designed for Linotype by W. A. Dwiggins, the renowned type designer (1880–1956). Electra is a fluid typeface, avoiding the contrasts of thick and thin strokes that are prevalent in most modern typefaces.

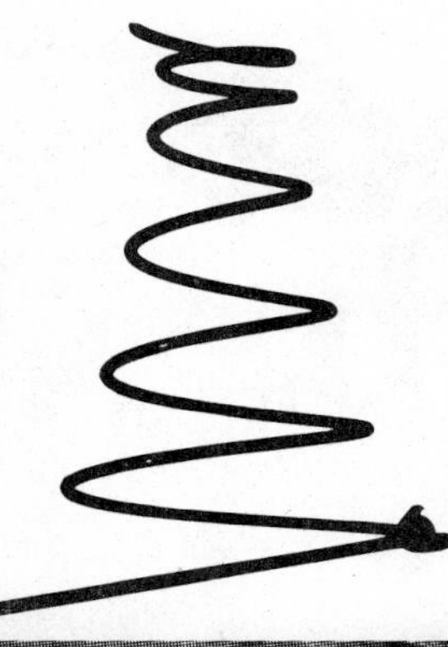

At the left, a spring photographed by the author to demonstrate the stark drama of a product shown without benefit of background or appealing model. Only a few products can be shown this starkly.

Below, the tongue-in-cheek illustration chosen by Holo-Krome Company to call attention to its policy of shipping 90 percent of all orders on the same day they are received. *See page 645.*

Called our man in your area lately?

Your local authorized Holo-Krome distributor is the lead man on our famous Same Day Service relay team, and he's just helped drive us to our all-time high for sales and service: For the entire year 1966, 98.18% of orders placed with us for standard Thermo-Forged® Socket Screw Products have been shipped the same day they were received! We're lapping the field while our competitors lick our heels and their wounds. Call the Holo-Krome distributor in your area. You're really fortunate to have him there and so are we. (If he doesn't tool up in this Oldfield, don't be mad; it may be his day for the 'copter.) Holo-Krome Company, West Hartford, Conn. 06110.

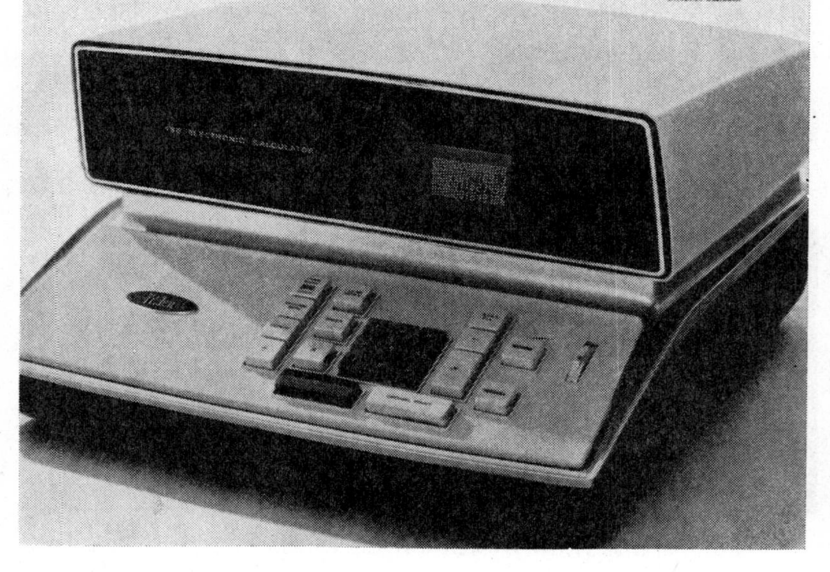

Does not disturb.
Ever try to talk over the din of a mechanical calculator? Or think? Or work?
It's hard. And irritating.
You can soften the noise with acoustical tile. Or you can eliminate it with a 130 Electronic Calculator by Friden.
The 130 has no moving parts, so it can't possibly interrupt your conversation. Instead of levers and gears, it works problems with solid-state electronic circuits. Instead of rotating dials and a shifting carriage, it shows answers on a cathode ray display tube.
Solving a problem on the 130 is a quiet (and simple) joy. You enter everything in a logical 1-2-3 order. As each new factor is indexed, the old ones move up a line in the stack of four registers. To store a constant, simply touch the storage key (this eliminates worksheets—the most common source of operator error).
Your final answer appears in milliseconds. Faster than you could write the entire problem down on a sheet of paper.
Tests prove the 130 can more than double the output of its operator. Which shows what solid-state electronics plus a little peace and quiet might do for your company. Call your nearest Friden office. Or write Friden, Inc., San Leandro, California 94577. Sales and service throughout the world.
Friden
DIVISION OF SINGER

Friden, Inc., Division of Singer, points this up very nicely in its attractive bleed ad illustrated above. The tightly-cropped four-color illustration of Friden's well-designed electronic calculator is without frills or pretense. It makes no bones about its function, which is to acquaint the reader with what the product looks like. This it does well.

Secondary function of this illustration is to show one of the important features of the product—that there are no rotating dials or shifting carriages; the solution to the problem fed into the clean little machine appears on a cathode ray display tube. Figures appear in green against the purple background of the tube. They're nice and legible and easy on the eyes.

This illustration does a bang-up job of presenting the product, which is exactly what it's supposed to do.

Product in Use

Readership studies have quietly laid to rest the old dogma that products *must* be shown in use if the ad is to be read.

However, just because it's not obligatory to show the product in use, there's no need to have the pendulum swing to the opposite extreme and have every illustration look like an imitation of a Volkswagen ad.

Frequently you'll find the best way of conveying a sense of immediacy, a feeling of reality, of causing the reader to project himself into the illustration and identify with the product is to show it being used.

When you're going to use a product-in-use illustration, probably a photograph, take pains to make sure it's authentic. Nothing repels a reader as fast as an illustration that's obviously phony. Do a poor job of staging a photograph and you've lost a lot of prospects.

Many fine product-in-use photographs are set up in the photographer's studio—most of them, in fact, when the product is small enough to be transported, or would logically be used indoors. However, if your product is a dragline or a trencher or a tank trailer, you won't disassemble it and put it back together in a studio just for the sake of staging a picture. It's easier to move a photographer over to a 40-story building in which your super-deluxe dual-glass windows are installed than it is to bring the skyscraper to the photographer. And the cost is usually lower.

A dramatic illustration of the product in use—or even a carefully staged photograph that looks authentic—instantly shows the reader what the product will do for him. An illustration is quick to explain itself, quick to tell the reader there's something in it for him if he'll read the copy.

A good example is the striking four-color spread run by Trojan Division, Eaton Yale & Towne, in *Construction Methods and Equipment* magazine. The ad is shown on the following page.

This illustration has great impact. You can almost hear the engine as the mechanical monster scoops up a giant-sized bite of dirt and rock. How much more effective this illustration of the loader is than it would be if the equipment was just sitting idle, motionless, and not working.

Users of construction equipment of this type can easily visualize their own operators in the driver's seat, they can see in the illustration that this is a huge unit that's capable of handling big jobs fast. The illustration is so credible and just plain interesting that the reader feels compelled to read at least the headline. Once that step is taken, a sizable percentage will proceed into the body copy.

Show Heavy Equipment in Use

This color photograph has stopping power in spades. No amount of photos of construction equipment taken out behind the manufacturer's factory can begin to convey the "feel" that an on-the-job shot can. Equipment of this type is the exception to the "rule" that it's not necessary to show the product in use. On the contrary, heavy equipment should *always* be shown being operated. Construction men and contractors expect it. Fail to give them something they've been conditioned to look for and to get, either consciously or subconsciously, and you've made a negative impression.

Product Features

One of the most widely used illustrations in industrial advertising is that showing features of the product. This type of illustration accomplishes a number of the nine purposes of an illustration that have been discussed.

Strength of the product features illustration lies in its ability to clarify copy claims. It proves again the truth of the old Chinese cliché that "one picture is worth ten thousand words."

When the reader turns to an illustration of product features he sees immediately just what the feature is that the manufacturer feels is so important, and he's able to relate this to himself and his job even before the copy explains it in many instances.

An illustration of a feature of the product, or of several features, permits focusing of attention on specifics the advertiser believes will have the most influence on desirability of the product, hence on sales.

Some products by their very nature are strictly utilitarian—so much so that despite a coat of paint, or a little chrome plate here and there, or some brightly colored plastic knobs—there isn't much the product's maker can do to cause the heart of the beholder to do ecstatic flip-flops.

Few garbage cans for the plant cafeteria, sold to industry through the maintenance superintendent who's in charge of janitorial services, among other things, are particularly lovely. However, the manufacturer of a garbage can that's constructed better than others on the market doesn't have to be a nonadvertising shrinking violet who won't tell industry his product is superior.

Perhaps he spot-welds a reinforcing gusset under the side handles of his product.

This would naturally make the can last longer and prevent handles from tearing or bending the metal when a heavy load is lifted by the mechanical arms of a hydraulic device used to hoist the can and dump the contents into a truck. This would make an excellent feature illustration, of course.

And the top of his can could have a roll-over edge that's larger and heavier than those of the competition. The handle on the lid could be double thickness with an extra spot weld. Or a cross-section of the metal could show corrugations that are deeper than other cans, stiffening and strengthening the can. An extreme closeup might show the galvanized finish is thicker than normally applied to prevent rust and corrosion.

The illustration for this brand of garbage can might well show the can as a whole, then closeups of the various features, perhaps with key numbers or letters to which the copy could refer.

Despite the fact we're all out after the competition tooth and toenail, we must realize most products offered for sale are good. They're good or the companies producing them wouldn't remain in business. You can sell a poor product once through hard-sell advertising and high-pressure salesmanship, but you can't do it twice. Once burned, forever warned.

Even if all products are good, none is perfect. Some are better than others in almost every respect—sometimes, but not often, significantly so—but every product has a weakness or two that's not discussed outside the company. Furthermore, some products that might not rate right up there with the very best in the marketplace still excel in certain features, or for specific applications. Even those acknowledged as resting on the pinnacle of near perfection have features that are better than the product as a whole. These are the ones you'll want to show and talk about.

Spotlight these features, select those that are unique with your product, those the competition can't match, then talk about them in your advertising. Show them in the illustrations. You'll find that you can exploit just a few features—even one that's really significant—enough to carry the product story. Readers usually assume that a product is superior in most respects if it is in one and you can convince them of this. It's up to your ad to do this.

Winchester Electronics, Division of Litton Industries, uses a product-feature illustration in the attractive ad the film ran in *Electronics* magazine. The ad is shown nearby.

Headline works well with the illustration; it reads:

The hole advantage of our wire-wrap connector.

An arrow points to the hole, which is actually a tooling hole to simplify production lineup, eliminate tolerance buildup and reduce machine downtime by aligning the connector quickly and perfectly, according to the copy.

Very properly, though, Winchester Electronics didn't rely on the reader to read the copy. He might not have. The illustration of its product quickly explains the feature the company wants to emphasize, and does so much faster than words could.

Here the illustration really carries the ball.

Ideally, when this type of illustration is used the features should be relatively simple so they can be understood at a glance. You're ahead of the game right at the start if the feature is one that can't

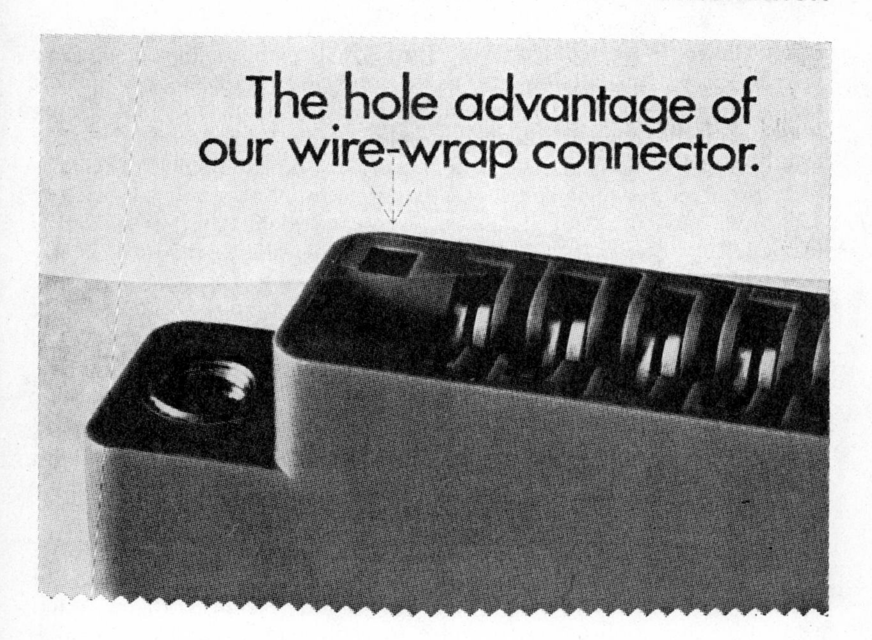
The hole advantage of
our wire-wrap connector.

be equalled by a competitive product, or if it's a new feature on an existing product, or an important feature of a new product.

If the feature is on mechanical equipment, chances are it will result in better quality of output, increased production, or lower costs. All of these are near and dear to the heart of the reader. Show him in an illustration how he can handle his job, or even a small part of it, easier and faster and you have a reader who'll devour every word of the headline and body copy.

Showing the reader what the product will do for him by explaining features in the illustration makes it remarkably easy for him to visualize the product in use on his job. You can write or talk until you're blue in the face about a water cooler that's also a refrigerator without making too much of an impression. But in a recent ad one manufacturer illustrated this feature of its water cooler with a photograph of the unit, door open, showing cold cuts, cheese, bread, and beverages nicely tucked away inside. This illustration explained that feature of the product instantaneously.

The job was done equally well by The Prime Mover Company in an ad that appeared in *Construction Methods and Equipment.* It is illustrated on the following page.

Everybody is familiar with the sight of a man struggling to push a wheelbarrow load of concrete through deep mud, or on slippery boards, in a construction site. The job's a brutally tough one. It takes too much time. It wastes manpower and runs up costs. Doing it the same old way it's been done since man began mixing mortar hundreds of years ago is an anachronism. Technological advances have occurred, even if some construction companies and contractors are unwilling to admit it. Even they can't deny the wheelbarrow propelled by one manpower is an inefficient, slow, wasteful, costly way to transport a load of concrete from mixer to forms. Frequently this bottleneck results in other employees standing around gazing off into outer space while they wait for another load to be delivered; and this costs money, too.

The Prime-Mover Company manufactures a high grade line of equipment used to take the manual labor out of construction jobs, thus cutting costs. In its ad are two dominant illustrations. Both show self-propelled wheelbarrows—called "buggies"—hauling heavy loads of wet concrete in a typical construction area.

Incidentally, never hesitate to show equipment used in ugly surroundings if that's where it's normally found. Any attempt to "pretty up" the scene will result in an illustration with as much credibility as a politician's promise to reduce taxes.

Immediately obvious in the left-hand photograph is that this isn't an ordinary wheelbarrow. The housing under the latch-on bucket is foreign to the run-of-the-mill wheelbarrow from the corner hardware store. It telegraphs to the reader that it contains a power source, and this impression is reinforced by a glance at the arms of the workman handling the unit; they're bent, not straight and strained as they would be if he was pushing a heavy load.

The right-hand photograph explains the powered feature even faster, for this lucky worker using this piece of Prime-Mover equipment really has it made: He sits down and moves 12 cubic feet—2,000 pounds—of concrete! Next thing you know, they'll mechanize hod-carrying and the country's Irish will be destitute.

Making work easier for people is something every management wants to do if possible. This is an appeal, but the illustration also makes it very obvious that this Prime-Mover equipment handles bigger loads than a man could push around, and it's easy to assume it does so with much greater dispatch and efficiency.

This is a good example of illustrations that explain the features of the product merely by showing them; even without a word of copy, readers would grasp the general idea quickly. Not every advertiser is so fortunate.

"We pour concrete faster and cheaper with Prime-Mover..."

MODEL M-15B — Latest model of the original walk-behind powered buggy. Places 12 to 17 cu. yds. of concrete per hour. 10 cu. ft./1500 lbs. capacity. Latch-on bucket quickly interchangeable with flatbed without tools. 31½" wide, 65½" long.

MODEL M-20 — New riding type powered buggy. Provides larger capacity, faster traveling speeds for longer hauls. 12 cu. ft./2000 lbs capacity. Automotive type steering, hydraulic brakes, torque converter transmission.

One man and a Prime-Mover...a real cost cutting combination!

"The new Prime-Movers purchased for our high school project paid for themselves quickly, since our records have shown we placed concrete at about one-third the cost of other methods we have used," reports Connecticut contractor of Prime-Mover fleet.

"We are completely sold on using these power buggies for many kinds of construction material handling, and our men get more work done with them."

For over 15 years Prime-Movers have proven their cost-cutting ability on all kinds of jobs from coast to coast. Modern Prime-Movers deliver even lower cost concrete placement on most jobs because their initial cost and maintenance requirements are lower than other methods. They require less job preparation and no equipment assembly. There is less clean-up time and no disassembly when job is completed. They provide more versatility from job to job and are operated by your laborers — not operating engineers.

Prime-Movers are the most rugged powered buggies available and can climb up to 20% ramps fully loaded. Safest units to use anywhere — especially on upper floor work.

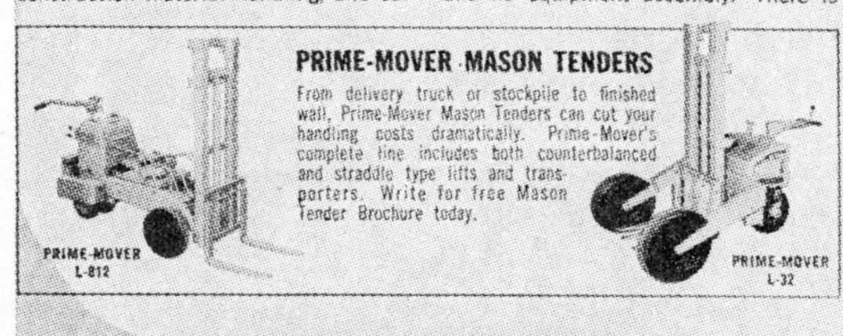

PRIME-MOVER MASON TENDERS
From delivery truck or stockpile to finished wall, Prime-Mover Mason Tenders can cut your handling costs dramatically. Prime-Mover's complete line includes both counterbalanced and straddle type lifts and transporters. Write for free Mason Tender Brochure today.
PRIME-MOVER L-812
PRIME-MOVER L-32

ALL ENCLOSED DRIVE

Phantom view shows the rugged Prime-Mover transmission-differential-axle assembly — all enclosed and sealed in one housing. One oil reservoir lubricates the entire drive for a minimum of maintenance. No moving parts are exposed giving all-weather protection. Clutches are heavy duty. Prime-Movers provide maximum traction because drive wheels are under the load.

THE PRIME-MOVER CO., MUSCATINE, IOWA 52761

No attempt was made by the Prime-Mover Company to "pretty up" this effective advertisement. The audience is a group of knowledgeable contractors, and the illustrations become credible to them in natural surroundings.

User Benefit

The benefit his company derives from the product is infinitely more important to the industrial buyer than is the product itself, of course. After all, he doesn't personally consume the product; it isn't used to gratify any of his personal tastes or desires or ambitions.

For this reason the user-benefit illustration is an excellent one for industrial advertising. This type of illustration immediately answers the reader's question, What's in it for me?—meaning, of course, his company. Nobody is remotely interested in a turret lathe *per se*. No turret lathe is a thing of beauty, none stirs men's souls, nor did any ever inspire a poem or a revolution. It's what the turret lathe produces and how fast it produces that's of interest.

It follows, then, that if you can develop a creative illustrative idea that sells the squeal instead of the pig, you're well on your way to a highly effective advertisement. Frequently you'll find it easier to illustrate a user benefit than a feature, explanation, comparison, or what have you.

This all boils down to a basic tenet of industrial advertising: The reader is looking for a *reason why* he should buy the product that's advertised. Show him in the illustration the reason why he should, tell him why in the headline and in the body copy, and you have a presold prospect whose sales resistance is significantly lower than before he read the ad. The ad has made a partial believer out of him. Your salesman will find completing the process easier because of the advertising.

Many manufacturers of products such as rowboats, yachts, travel trailers, trucks, jet airplanes and overhead doors are vitally concerned with the weight of the finished product. Lightness in weight is synonomous with extra quality and extra earning ability in many instances. Yet these same manufacturers are faced with opposing demands of building to a minimum weight and, at the same time, producing a product that will stand the stress of exceptionally severe service.

This is where aluminum comes in. Although aluminum has many other desirable characteristics—it won't rust, it requires little maintenance, it doesn't have to be painted—its lightness is probably the attribute that's most salable. Nobody except one former defense chief ever deliberately selected a heavy fighter-bomber for the armed forces, for example. But, then, he's not there any longer.

Accordingly, when a new campaign to extoll the virtues of the lightweight metal was being created for The Aluminum Association,

Are kids stronger today? No. Boats are aluminum.

You don't have to be a weight-lifter to carry an aluminum boat.

An 11-year-old can hold up his end with ease.

Aluminum is so light (one-third the weight of steel) and so strong (some aluminum alloys are stronger than structural steel), the role it plays in all forms of transportation keeps getting bigger.

Today's jetliners are 75% to 85% aluminum. There are 2,000 *tons* of aluminum on the S. S. *United States*, world's fastest ocean liner.

The most modern railroad cars are aluminum. So are the newest buses, trucks, mobile homes, travel trailers.

Aluminum makes automobiles look better, perform better, wear better.

Aluminum is a wonderful homebody, too. Aluminum siding is rustfree, practically maintenance-free, and hardly ever needs painting.

A great deal of the frozen food you buy comes packaged in aluminum. And every woman knows how good aluminum foil is.

Aluminum is big today. And it's going places. Come on along.

May your future be as bright as aluminum's.

The Aluminum Association

The mark of aluminum, symbol of the world's most versatile metal.

it was only logical to consider the user benefits that are most important. Lightness was selected as the major one.

The ad from *Modern Metals* magazine, illustrated above, is a little gem. There's sunlight and warmth and a lighthearted feeling about this wonderful illustration, and a pure joy in being alive. Lightness of the boat is strikingly apparent, as is the smallness of the two happy boys. Also apparent is that they're not struggling with something beyond their capacity; otherwise they'd look strained and tense, boys being boys.

But they're just as pleased as punch about getting the boat out on the water for a trip, and this comes through in this fine photograph. Having the oars in the boat is proper, of course. They belong there. But having the dog in the boat is an inspired touch! It's the clincher that ends all arguments. The dog rules out any possible question in the reader's mind about the weight of the boat.

This illustration is such a happy thing the reader *can't* pass it by without looking at it and smiling. Only an unfeeling individual could then refrain from reading the headline. And the headline alone puts the name of the product (aluminum) in the reader's mind, even if the body copy isn't read in its entirety. But the body copy is so well written, so loaded with information that's honestly interesting, that it enjoyed high readership.

Come up with an illustrative idea this good for your user-benefit ad and you'll have a sure winner.

Comparison of Products

Carefully done, a photographic illustration comparing your product with a competitive one is a potent piece of salesmanship.

Note especially that *photographic* illustration is specified for this purpose—not artwork of any kind. Photography is realistic, art is impressionistic and subject to interpretation, or even to distortion.

The reader knows this. Everybody's a photographer these days. Everybody accepts a photograph as being an impartial, unbiased representation of an object exactly as the eye sees it. When you show your product and another one side by side in an illustration, making mighty sure they're unretouched, the reader believes without question. Make the mistake of retouching the photo, though, and more likely than not it'll look as phony as a three-dollar bill. Then you'll have a reader you'll have a tough time *ever* convincing.

Another thing: If your product's superiority is plainly evident in the photograph, copy claims are automatically changed in the reader's mind from mere claims to statements of fact. Some advertising managers are blessed with products that *look* so superior there's no great need to belabor the point in copy. When the photograph makes this obvious it speaks for the manufacturer and the reader tends to accept this almost as he would a testimonial or endorsement given by a third party. We should all be so lucky!

There's a danger inherent in using the products-comparison illustrative technique, though. This is that you might end up looking as if you're slamming the other guy's product. This is poor practice, as any good salesman will admit. Take a slap at another product in a negative way and you actually accomplish just the opposite of what you intended to do. You call attention to your competitor and his product, and you make yours just a little bit distasteful because your ad engages in name-calling.

This is no argument against the highly competitive ad. Far from it. Avis did itself nothing but good by mentioning Hertz; Braniff's determined attack on the plain plane acknowledged the unspeakable, that other airlines existed and that they have planes in the air. Yet Braniff's traffic climbed enormously, and is still going up. You can use brass knuckles and name names if the tone of your ad—illustration *and* copy—are positive and if it leaves a good taste in the reader's mouth rather than alienating him and possibly turning him to your competition. Some ads do just this.

An ad with a very convincing product comparison illustration was run in *Successful Farming* magazine by Autolite, Division of Ford Motor Company. It is shown on the following page.

The illustration shows two examples of a prosaic product—spark plugs. The one on the left is an Autolite, while the one on the right isn't identified. Interesting is that the Autolite plug, because it's glass-sealed, doesn't leak. The other plug, Brand X maybe, apparently without too many miles on it, has failed. Powder is leaking out. This is a very convincing illustration.

It is strengthened with subordinate illustrations of a racing driver, an Army officer, a jet pilot, and a photo of a typical prospect to whom the ad really is slanted—a farmer.

Copy brings out that the military and the CAA both specify zero leakage in spark plugs—meaning a glass seal—for best possible performance. And Autolite assures the farm reader the spark plugs made for farm tractors measure up to the same high standards because Autolite uses a glass seal.

This type of illustration inspires belief.

How to Use the Product

Readers read business publications to educate themselves. When you use an illustration that shows how to use your product, you're helping them along. You're educating them.

What Kind of Man Would Ever Believe There's a Real Difference Between Glass-Sealed and Powder-Sealed Spark Plugs?

This kind.

It is no accident that most spark plugs in American civil and military aircraft are glass-sealed! Or that you couldn't find a powder-sealed spark plug under the hood of any army vehicle destined for combat service if you tried. Or that the winningest race drivers in America classify the powder-sealed spark plug right along with the riding mechanic and the clincher rim.

Zero leakage is important enough to be required by CAA (Civil Aeronautics Authority) law for aircraft, and it is specified in writing for army combat vehicles.

If both of these highly respected governing bodies answer this requirement with a glass seal—don't you think it is the best method for all spark plugs? So does Autolite. They heat-seal every single spark plug they make, including the ones for your tractors. Some manufacturers don't, you know.

YOU'RE ALWAYS RIGHT WITH

There are two main classes of illustrations that show how to use a product. The first is a highly detailed thing which generally is similar to photos found in an instruction manual—perhaps complete with diagrams. It's designed to teach the reader how to do something; drive a bulldozer, fly a jet airplane, handle a punch press, operate a tape recorder. Frequently the illustration will show a hand moving various levers, punching buttons, and moving other controls. This is primarily a how-to-do-it type of illustration and it is directed to personnel farther down the pecking order than the buying influences most industrial ads are prepared for.

Many manufacturers use this type of illustration to instruct the actual operator of his equipment how to get the most out of it, as well as to show the executive how easy it is for his people to familiarize themselves with it. This implies there is no need for a lengthy and costly training program for shop employees if the advertiser's widget is purchased and installed on the assembly line.

The other class of how-to-use-the-product illustration is educational also, but it is concerned with showing how the product can be used to achieve a desired objective. For the most part, advertisers taking this tack concentrate on processes, how to produce products using their process, raw material, or equipment. They're not concerned with illustrating how the product operates, in the case of mechanical equipment, for example.

A good example of this latter class of illustration—and they're far more rare than a photograph showing how to perform a simple, repetitive task—is in the unusually striking four-color insert ad run by Alcan Sales Inc. in *Metal Progress* magazine. It's on page 662.

Alcan's illustration establishes a mood by showing a very old and much used blacksmith's anvil; a horseshoe being made; tongs, hammer, and leather bucket. The setting is perfect right down to the tiniest detail, such as the dirt floor and roughhewn board wall. Alcan then injected a note that's as up-to-date as next year's calendar.

Contrasting with this colorful old-fashioned setting, both in shape and material, as well as by having the extruded shape in a "cold" tone as opposed to the "warm" tone of the setting, is an intricate aluminum extrusion. Of course, Alcan markets aluminum, and this ad is part of a campaign designed to stimulate basic demand.

Copy points up the versatility aluminum makes possible, the "impossible" shapes extruders routinely produce, and that the industry finds aluminum saves money in many uses.

The illustration has great impact and did more than its share toward the ad's success.

Storytelling Illustrations

Ever since his childhood the reader has been conditioned to read, enjoy, and accept the picture story.

Readership studies show that ads with more than one illustration

"Impossible" design shapes are possible with aluminum extrusions

Shapes considered too complicated for other metals may be extruded in aluminum. That's why a look at aluminum extrusions may reveal new ways to save time, cost and weight in your production assembly.

The man to see is your Independent Extruder. He is prepared to help solve your extrusion requirements. And if he uses Alcan aluminum he is backed by a world of experience in research, technology and fabrication.

Call your Independent Aluminum extruder or nearby Alcan sales representative.

You may find yesterday's "impossible" problems have a solution today.

ALCAN SALES INC.
111 West 50th Street • New York, N. Y. 10020
ATLANTA • CHICAGO • DETROIT • LOS ANGELES • ST. LOUIS

ALCAN

The Alcan "use of product" ad discussed on page 661.

are, on the average, read by around 15 percent more people than are those with just one illustration.

Arrange your pictures so there's a logical sequence, so they tell the reader a story either by themselves or with the help of the copy, and readership climbs rapidly. Two kinds of reading matter that *must* communicate quickly to wide masses of people with various levels of education and basic intelligence—comic strips and instruction manuals—both rely on the picture story. Both use captions, "balloons" with dialogue in comic strips, to augment the pictures. But the pictures nonetheless carry most of the load.

A Picture Story Ad

Plan a picture-story ad and you're on firm ground. This is especially true when the message to be conveyed is complex and not easily illustrated with just one or two illustrations. Some subjects won't compress into an arbitrary one-picture illustration; they require the greater latitude that can be achieved with a number of illustrations.

Take Sperry Rand, for instance. A major communications objective for the company in its campaign directed to the business community is to create awareness of the fact that the company is synergistic. Webster defines synergism as: "Cooperative action of discrete agencies (as drugs or muscles) such that the total effect is greater than the sum of the two or more effects taken independently—opposed to antagonism." Synergistic is merely serving as a synergist—cooperating, that is.

The three-dollar word is a "hook" to pull the reader into the ad by arousing his curiosity, and to permit the company to be reasonably modest while patting itself on the back by telling the business community how great it is. Copy tone is light and factual. Reading is highly interesting.

The picture story in the powerful four-color spread ad from *Business Week* is an example of the impact this type of illustrative technique produces. This is reproduced on the following page.

Each of the illustrations "carries" well; none is small or insignificant. The box of blueberries—you can almost *taste* them, the color is so superb—is almost 7 inches across; the giant thumb measures just about the same.

This is an excellent concept for this ad. Each illustration cooperates with the others to strengthen the impact of the whole. The illustrative idea itself is synergistic, as it was intended to be.

Caption of the thumb illustration is: *We shrink. At Sperry, we've developed complex electronic circuits smaller than a match-head.* And between thumb and forefinger is a tiny integrated circuit, that miniature marvel of this age of electronics.

The farm illustration is captioned: *Chop. This piece of New*

Holland farm machinery cuts and chops silage crops in one fell swoop.

From the computer's caption the reader learns that: *Seat. Airlines use our Univac computers to reserve your seat, schedule your crew and even see that your steak is aboard.* (This is reassuring; the author has always had a secret horror, never mentioned until now, that someday on a trip to the West Coast the airline might forget the food.)

Plot. Sperry gyrocompasses and autopilots work beautifully together to hold your ocean liner on course. No matter what. That's the caption beside the ship.

And by the luscious looking blueberries we read: *Pick. Today, blueberries are picked by machine—one of thousands powered and controlled by our Vickers hydraulic systems.*

Body copy ties in beautifully with the headline-picture-story format. It starts out: *We do a lot of different things at Sperry Rand. And we do each one better because we do all the rest. That makes us synergistic. Like 2 and 2 adding up to 5.*

And the kissoff says: *At Sperry Rand, everything hangs together. That's why we're synergistic.*

All of which adds up to an unusually persuasive, convincing story, as well as to an exceptionally hard-working marriage of illustration, headline, and body copy.

New Coleman UV-VIS-NIR spectrophotometer. So good, we'll let its charts do the talking.

New Coleman Model EPS-3T Hitachi Spectrophotometer is the first all-solid-state instrument of its kind. It's a double-beam, ratio-recording instrument that yields sophisticated data throughout the 170 to 2600 mμ range. It has 12 features not found on any other spectrophotometer under $10,000.

Here are some examples of its work:

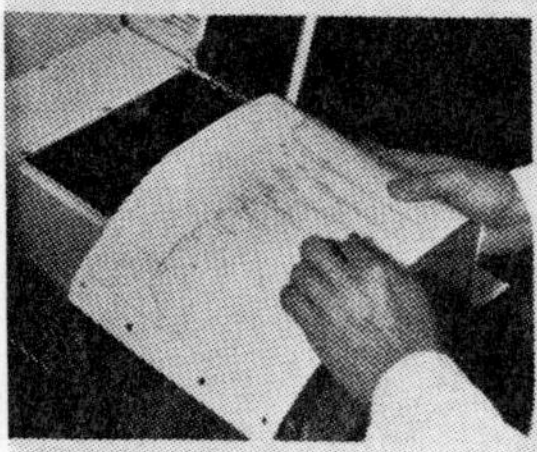

The chart above shows the remarkable resolution of Coleman Model EPS-3T. Critical adjacent peaks on the complex benzene vapor profile are clearly delineated.

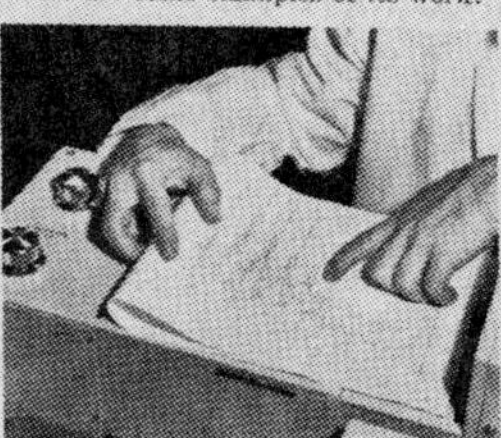

To demonstrate repeatability, the instrument overprints the same chart from the same sample. Note that chart presentations are all linear, not logarithmic.

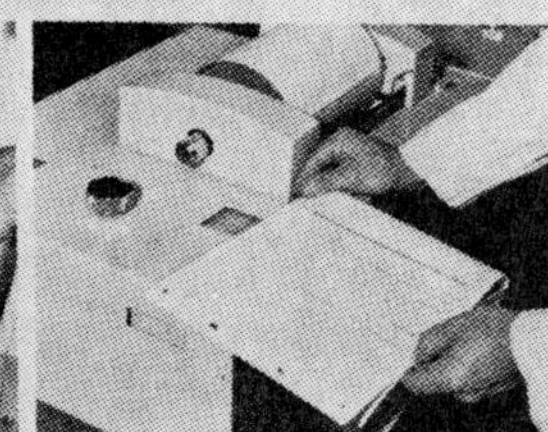

A significant mercury spike, perfectly centered at 253.7 mμ. Wavelength accuracy is not affected by changes in ambient temperature. Photometric accuracy is 0.3%T.

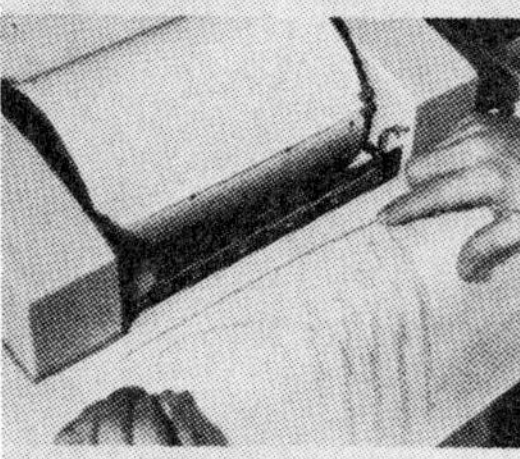

Above, the 100% T line of the Coleman Model EPS-3T at maximum sensitivity. The line is demonstrably flatter than that of any similar spectrophotometer.

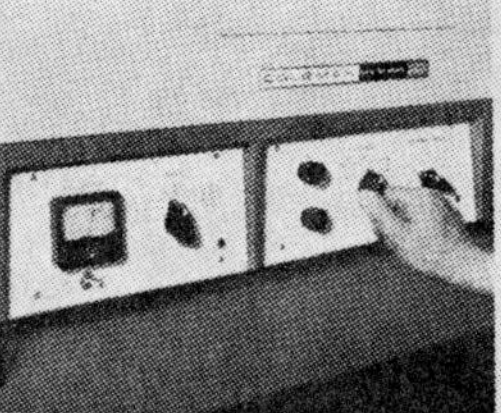

Model EPS-3T offers a wide choice of operating parameters. Nine scale modes. Six scanning rates, from 1.5 to 60 minutes. Any member of your staff can easily operate it.

You open the sample compartment and insert cells without touching any of the controls. With this safety shuttering feature, you leave operating parameters set, while you run test, after test, after test.

Sorry, there's no room left for a picture of Model EPS-3T. But we've saved this, and a number of other pleasant surprises for you. Call Coleman for the name of the nearest dealer and a demonstration.

Send for brochure B-306

COLEMAN INSTRUMENTS CORPORATION • MAYWOOD, ILLINOIS 60153

Budgets don't have to be gigantic to enable an advertiser to use the picture-story type of illustration. Coleman Instruments, a division of The Perkin-Elmer Corporation, relies on one-page black-and-white ad in *Research/Development* magazine to tell its story. The ad is shown above.

The illustration follows the traditional pattern of a half-dozen good sized halftones—2¼ by 2⅝ inches—with captions beneath each. Features and benefits of the Coleman UV-VIS-NIR spectrophotometer are presented one right after the other, quickly and convincingly. The reader believes what he sees in a photographic illustration. And readership of the captioned picture story usually runs 16 or 17 percent above that for an ad with one dominant illustration.

Sometimes you're faced with the problem of showing elapsed time, a variety of locations, a sequence of events which are closely related to each other and must be shown, a radical change in equipment used in a specific place, or a progressive alteration in the appearance of something in process—a skyscraper under construction, for example.

The picture-story illustration is made to order for these and similar situations. You can take a leaf from the ad manager of a major airline who frequently illustrates happy tourists boarding one of his airplanes, sightseeing all over the globe, then returning home—tired, sated with exotic sights, and impoverished. This last is understood, but not illustrated, of course.

Implication

Ofttimes you'll encounter a situation where you can *tell* the reader how great your product is, how adaptable it is to a variety of applications, how much more it will do for him than a competitive item—but you find yourself right up against it as to how to illustrate this to him.

Maybe you're not slipping. Maybe you've not run out of ideas. Perhaps the primary idea you want the illustration to put across is one that cannot be illustrated. Possibly the idea is too complex, or too abstract to permit a good visual presentation.

In this case you'll frequently find you're better off to come up with an illustrative idea that *implies* the benefit the reader will realize from use of your product, rather than settling for an illustration that does less than a creditable job of showing him. After all, the reader does have imagination. He's able to make the mental transition from the implied benefit he sees illustrated and adapt it to his own circumstances—if it's a logical implication, and if the illustration hews close and hard to the benefit without getting way out in left field.

When you illustrate an implied benefit a whole new area of illustrative subject matter is opened up. And techniques that are regularly used to excellent advantage in consumer advertising but are seldom seen in the industrial field may be used with outstanding effectiveness. Despite what we, who feel a deep fondness for industrial advertising, claim we prefer to think, the fact remains that the level of sophistication in consumer advertising is much higher, particularly in illustrative and layout techniques.

With the implied benefit illustration we can legitimately borrow some of the flair and style and feeling of the best that consumer advertising has to offer. We can adapt and mold to suit ourselves and to mesh new and improved techniques into what we now do.

The approach used by Pittsburgh Plate Glass Company, Chemical Division, in the impressive four-color spread ad illustrated below is from the consumer world of fashion, from all appearances. Distinctly stylish, the illustration could well be used for high-fashion clothing, perfume, or cosmetics, and might have appeared in *Vogue*. Presumably this route was chosen in order to attract as large a qualified audience as possible in both vertical and horizontal business publications.

There's no disputing the illustration's stopping power. Imagine for an instant how the average reader of a business publication reacts when he turns the page and comes upon this illustration after going through a book full of pictures of drums of chemicals, barrels of floor-sweeping compound and dramatic close-ups of replacement V-belts! Breathes there a male buying influence who wouldn't stop, look, and read?

Incidentally, though, research shows that men actually prefer pictures of men, and women prefer those of women. It's much easier to identify with an illustration that depicts one's own sex.

Pittsburgh Plate Glass Company's copy sells hard the company's caustic soda and carbon bisulfide, basic raw materials for rayon. Naturally, the lovely subject of the illustration happens to be dressed in a costume made of rayon. Copy points out that versatility is rayon's forte, whether it's the latest velvet for a discotheque gown from Paris, or material for a splashy $6.95 blouse, and that an infinite variety of colors, textures, and other characteristics may be imparted to rayon.

The advertiser also talks about its pioneering in improved tank car linings to improve the purity of basic chemicals used for rayon fabric manufacture, as well as other specialty chemicals used to make and bleach pure white chemical cellulose, rayon's starting point.

And the copy does all of this with a deftness and persuasiveness that makes the reader believe, which is the name of the game. But he's playing the game because the illustration brought him into it.

Humor

Humor is one of the most controversial subjects in industrial advertising.

Advertising agencies, some of the large, successful ones, have as a firm agency policy that humor is never used. Never. Official policy is that it's unsuited for an industrial advertisement. Others, just as large and just as successful, believe implicitly in humor as a highly effective device for attracting reader attention—favorable attention, of course—to the advertisement.

Industrial advertisers themselves are divided on the subject. Many who have run highly effective campaigns based on humor (Republic Steel, for example, whose outstanding campaign was discussed in Chapter 9) are unalterably of the opinion that humor sells, and sells hard. They have facts, figures, and a wealth of accumulated information to back up their arguments, making them almost impossible to refute. It's always hard to argue with success.

On the other hand, there is an even larger number of industrial advertising managers who are vociferously opposed to humor in any shape or form in their ads. They don't hesitate for a minute to hold forth at length, usually for as long as anybody will listen, on the "fact" that "humor isn't for industrial advertising; fun and games are fine in their place, but it's someplace else."

These industrial ad managers who cast aspersions on humor at the drop of a hat are actually calumniators who are making an unwarranted attack on a form of communication that really carries the mail. For the most part, ad managers who launch into bitter diatribes against humor start out by citing chapter and verse of arguments against humor; they cull up from the depths of their memories every antihumor statistic they've ever heard or read, some going back a couple of decades.

They don't hesitate to quote McGraw-Hill's highly respected Laboratory of Advertising Performance analysis of the effect of humor on readership. It documents the results of a study of 5,502 industrial advertisements whose readership was determined by the publisher's Reader Feedback system. The ads appeared in *American Machinist, Engineering News-Record, Factory,* and in *Textile World*. According to the study, ads without humor scored 22 percent higher readership than did ads with humor.

Interesting, though, is that of all these 5,502 ads only 176 used humor as an attention-grabbing device. And there's no indication whatsoever as to whether the ads that did use humor did so in an effective way—or whether it was pure cornball.

Analyzing what these antihumor advertising managers *really* mean when they're holding forth against it points up that they're invariably talking about competitors' ads—ads that in their heart of hearts they instinctively feel are performing ably. Fact is, most industrial advertising managers haven't had any past experience with using humor in their ads. It's human nature to be wary about the unknown and to hesitate to leap aboard a bandwagon whose horsepower isn't known. But the mark of a professional advertising man is that he maintains an open mind. To do otherwise irrevocably closes many avenues of communication. The ad man suffers, as does his company or agency.

One thing about using humor, though: It must be funny—*really funny*. Humor that's not genuinely funny, humor that falls flat because instead of being funny it's corny or precious or contrived will fail faster than you can say The Dartnell Advertising Handbook.

And, because the ad manager's usually too close to the trees to see the forest, he's often unable to evaluate whether a humorous illustration is humorous or not; too often he conceived the idea himself and finds it next to impossible to judge it objectively. It's odd, too, because an advertising manager whose judgment and ability to analyze any other type of illustration is beyond reproach encounters difficulty here. Probably this is because humor is a subjective thing that appeals to the emotions. And it's highly personal. What's uproariously funny to one person leaves another as cold as a loan-shark's heart. Each of us regard most things differently and our senses of humor are as different as day and night. Best to get other viewpoints if there's any doubt in your mind about the humorous illustration.

Another word of caution about the use of humor: Be sure, absolutely sure, that it's pertinent. In some way or other the humorous illustration must be involved with the product or the benefit the ad is to promote. If the illustration is totally unrelated to the product or its use, the reader is left in the lurch; he has no idea of the message the illustration was supposed to convey to him. And because he has no idea, his impression of the product—if he retains one after looking at an irrelevant humorous illustration—is nebulous and vague and can just as easily be negative as positive.

Humor at Millers Falls

The two main types of humorous illustrations are photographs and cartoons. Millers Falls Company, a leading manufacturer of metal cutting saws—hand and power hacksaw blades, handsaw blades and hole saws—decided to use a cartoon illustration for its promotion of an industry-leadership image.

Millers Falls was concerned at this time about a research study among industrial distributors, a key outlet for its products. The study revealed the company's reputation and strength in these key factors in the marketing of metal cutting saws was not on the rise as it should be.

Many vigorous steps were taken to correct this situation. A number of new sales tools were produced and new, more extensive advertising was planned for the business press.

However, as a communications problem, metal cutting saws have always been difficult. A prime communications objective was to create and maintain a leadership image by telling about new Millers Falls products and improvements, superior performance the user gets with Millers Falls saws, breadth of the company's line, and high level of user acceptance.

Toughest thing of all, however, is getting people to read about metal cutting saws. This is akin to a grocer running a large display ad in the Saturday shopper's edition of the local paper featuring salt. If anybody read it, he must have wandered into the ad with nothing better to do with his time.

Metal cutting saws are regarded as staple items that are purchased routinely, particularly compared to glamour products such as numerical controls that are advertised in the same publications Millers Falls must use. Too, product improvements in metal saws are hidden and much less dramatic than radical innovations in the machine tool field. *Legitimate* product claims are likely to seem dull after many manufacturers have made flamboyant and extravagant claims for years about product performance—with little or no supporting evidence.

Therefore, advertising had to be created to gain attention and get the highest possible readership on a product that's of low inherent interest.

Millers Falls research showed unmistakably that the end-user audience was the key one for its products. Buying influences get well down into the shop level in metalworking establishments. Top management isn't concerned with the purchase of metal saw blades, nor, for the most part, is middle management. Men on the floor who have day-to-day contact with the product are the ones who determine what brand is bought.

For this reason Millers Falls concentrates its schedule in books like *Machine, Tool Blue Book*, and *Modern Machine Shop*, as well as in *American Machinist* and in *Machinery*. No management publications such as *Iron Age* are used for the metalworking field.

"Bull O' the Woods" Was Choice

With this in mind, the company and its agency looked for a technique with high reader appeal and high attention-getting ability for readers with in-the-shop backgrounds.

For many years the "Bull O' the Woods" cartoon by the late J. R. Williams (of "Out Our Way" fame) appeared as an editorial feature in one of the metalworking industry magazines, and it enjoyed tremendous popularity. When Millers Falls' agency's copy chief suggested an adaptation of these cartoons for the new advertising campaign, the idea was recognized as a natural by both agency people and the company's advertising manager.

The agency located a talented artist, Ellis Potter, who could capture the same flavor and style as the late Mr. Williams imparted to the "Bull O' the Woods," and the campaign was firmed up.

A recent ad in this lively campaign is shown on page 672.

Its effectiveness was immediately apparent from readership studies. A total of 77 advertisements were checked by Starch in one

issue of *Machinery*. On a cost-ratio basis, the Millers Falls cartoon ad turned in the phenomenal performance given below:

First among 77 ads for Noted.

First among 77 ads for Seen/Associated.

Third among 77 ads for Read Most.

Raw scores were: Noted, 36; Seen/Associated, 31; Read Most, 14.

Since then, the campaign has consistently scored spectacularly well whenever it was studied by readership research—Reader Feedback and Mills Shepard in *American Machinist,* Fosdick and Ad-Gage in *The Tool and Manufacturing Engineer,* Read/Ad in *Machine* and in *Tool Blue Book,* Ad-Ed Audit in *Metalworking,* Adscor in *Tooling and Production,* and Starch in *Machinery. Purchasing,* and *Production.*

IARI Group Letter Grades on a recent ad were:

All ads: A+

Same size ads: A+

Same product ads: A+

Not only was the campaign an instant success, but it has maintained its high attention-getting and readership performance, an analysis of eight ads appearing in recent Starched issues of *Machinery* shows:

Five ranked first for Noted on a Cost Ratio basis among all ads studied.

One ranked second.

Two ranked fourth.

Average Cost Ratios for the eight ads were:

Noted: 224

Seen Associated: 215

Read Most: 201

This campaign has been viewed with some serious reservations by a few editors of business publications. They apparently subscribe to the philosophy that the world of business paper advertising is strictly a stern and earnest one.

They're overlooking one thing, though. People *like* humor.

A wonderfully happy, light-hearted ad that does a tremendously effective job is illustrated nearby. This four-color illustration in General American Transportation Corporation's ad from *Business Week* magazine uses humor just exactly as it should be.

It doesn't pay off.

What does pay off is leasing railroad cars and storage services from GATX.

When you lease from us, the only business you're in is your own. You don't have to worry about selling the equipment when you're through with it.

That's our problem.

You don't have to worry about service and maintenance.

That's our problem, too. (After all, shouldn't the guys who make 'em know more about fixing 'em.)

But, most important, we're ready to work with you today on tomorrow's problems.

The fact is, as you develop new products, we'll work along with you, developing new ways to carry and store them.

So the next time you've got a job to do, remember GATX.

And you won't find yourself tied up with a lot of troubles.

YOU DON'T HAVE TO BUY A TRAIN EVERY TIME YOU'VE GOT A JOB TO DO.

The fabulous photographic illustration is right—right in every tiny little detail. The "Perils of Pauline" approach is tongue-in-cheek, eyecatching, and loaded with inherent interest. There's a real treasure-trove in happenings of the past 30 years or so, as evidenced by books about early movies, a new generation of fans for early jazz, and reissuance of many of the fine jazz records of the 1920's and 1930's. Models are perfect in their roles in the photo. Blonde Pauline is not merely tied, she's *overtied* with rope strong enough to haul a stuck Patton tank out of a six-foot-deep bog, burlesqueing the original "happening." The caped and top-hatted villain is properly villainous; the mustache, gloves, cane, and facial expression couldn't be improved upon. And, to wrap everything up, there's smoke behind the trailing end of the villain's black cape, obviously from the approaching train that's to do the dastardly deed. The satire couldn't be bettered.

General American Transportation Corporation—GATX, as it's called—didn't make the mistake of using a humorous illustration only for the sake of spreading a little good cheer. Jack Sheehan, manager of advertising and public relations of the railroad car leasing firm, explains that the campaign was carefully thought out and that humor was used functionally, with a purpose. The humorous illustration is pertinent and related to the message GATX wants to convey because it's tied in closely with the company's product—rather, with the service it sells.

What does the illustration show, in the broad sense? Somebody—the villain—with a job to do. So, the headline picks up from there and says: *You don't have to buy a train every time you've got a job to do.*

A nice, neat, logical tie-in, particularly when the body copy then takes over and explains that GATX saves you all of this bother of buying a train—because it leases railroad cars and storage services at lower cost than the reader could do it for himself. He's saved the bother and expense of buying and maintaining cars and storage facilities, freeing him to concentrate on the line of business he's really in, not the business somebody else—GATX—is in. The selling proposition is interesting and it's sound.

Give the reader something to chuckle about and you've put him in a pleasant frame of mind. And that happens to mean he's in a receptive frame of mind when it comes to your message, introduced by a humorous illustration.

Use humor wisely and it will do well for you.

Borrowed Interest

Some advertising men don't consider the borrowed interest illustration a separate and distinct breed of cat.

Their argument, and admittedly it has merit that's hard to put down, is that *any* illustration other than one showing the product alone is of the borrowed interest variety. Otherwise, they ask, what is anything other than the product doing in the illustration if it isn't to borrow interest from something the advertiser isn't selling—that is totally unrelated to what he's really interested in?

However, since one of the primary functions of the illustration is to attract the attention of the reader, something must obviously be done other than merely showing the product, especially if that product is lacking in strong inherent interest. Many products are of that type. They lack interest. They're not particularly pleasing esthetically, or they're simply so prosaic that to show an illustration evokes a ho-hum attitude, boring the reader so much he promptly turns the page. No amount of devotion to company or *esprit de corps* or gung-ho attitude on your part is going to change that one little bit, even if your livelihood does depend on increasing sales of the good old widget.

Some Products Not Photogenic

Suppose, for instance, your product is a nail, saw blade, file, wet mop, lubricating grease, putty, paper towels or something similar. You can't honestly think for a minute that a disinterested reader is going to be anything other than disinterested if you pop a picture of a lump of putty in front of him, can you? Even if it *is* your product?

It follows, then, that you have to borrow interest from something else if your illustration is to stop the reader and entice him into your ad even as far as the headline. As noted, there are 21 basic types of illustration, 11 of which have been discussed. Any of these, under the right circumstances, will do the job. Now, however, let's see just how we go about borrowing some interest from something not directly connected with the product, but related to it. (Bohemian advertising managers will please forgive the use of the word "borrowed." There's no way around it).

Let's say your company manufactures bearings. You could feature an illustration showing a product that incorporates bearings, maybe lots of them. SKF Industries, Inc., did this very successfully with a dramatic full-color spread ad in *Business Week.* The illustration, a color photograph, was taken from high in the air; the nose of a naval jet fighter plane was in the immediate foreground and far below and about the relative size of a bar of soap in a bathtub was an aircraft carrier upon which it was going to land. The illustration was colorful, action-packed, exciting. It served the purpose of stopping the reader admirably well.

And the product was there, even if it wasn't visible; a caption on a subordinate illustration on the copy page told the reader that SKF bearings were on the U.S.S. Enterprise's rudderposts. This is excellent placement, incidentally, for this information. Captions invariably receive far more readership than any other element of the ad except the headline.

Or you could do as Electro-Mechanical Products Division, Stackpole Carbon Company, did in a one-page, four-color ad. The product is a miniature rotary switch; it's hardly enough to cause the reader to get into a lather just from seeing it. But Electro-Mechanical Products showed the switch partially buried in sand on a deserted beach at sunset, partially awash, and with an ancient rusty ship's fitting beside it for atmosphere. This illustration borrows interest from a circumstance, a locale, and a prop. All are contrived, but all are interesting and pictorially appealing.

Then, if you happen to produce space-age materials, you could use what's fast becoming an illustrative cliché, an illustration of some space hardware screaming through the frigid night of outer space. Overworked, of course, but much more interesting than an illustration of a space-age bolt all by itself.

Son-of-a-Pup Tent

American Viscose Division, FMC Corporation, produces a blend of cotton and a special Avisco rayon fiber. Not very interesting, unfortunately, but some of the applications for the material are. They can be borrowed. The company proved this with a really fine four-color bleed ad on the third cover of *Business week;* the illustration was of a pup tent in a jungle setting. Headline, *Son-of-a-pup tent,* is reversed out of the side of the pup tent and the dark "doorway," while body copy goes on to explain the superior properties that make this material a wise choice for everything from a shelter half to a truck tarp. (Two shelter halves buttoned together make a pup tent. Theoretically it sleeps two soldiers, each of whom owns—and carries—half of the portable abode. In practice this works reasonably well if it doesn't rain, which it always does, and if neither is as tall as the author; if either is, something sticks out into the elements. You have a choice of head or feet).

Also, you can borrow interest very effectively by putting something in your illustration that obviously doesn't belong there. When an object is conspicuously foreign, completely out of place in its surroundings, the reader feels compelled to look at the illustration just to see what's going on there. Imagine for a moment you're at a wedding reception, balancing a plate of cake and ice cream on your knee, a cup of punch in one hand and silverware in the other. Just then a rhinoceros walks in. It's fair to assume that the best man could fall into the punch bowl and nobody would notice him at the moment. And if you saw that illustration in an ad, the compulsion to look would be almost as strong.

The cat is the attention-attracting foreign element in International Equipment Company's ad illustrated (partially) above. Without the sleepy looking cat, the ad is merely another ad for a well-designed piece of equipment that some advertiser is willing to sell if you ask him nicely.

Ads of this type are practically popping out of the woodwork.

Addition of the cat, however, transforms this ad into something distinctive as far as the reader is concerned. He wants to know *why* a contented fat cat is loafing on top of the refrigerated centrifuge. (The top of a refrigerated centrifuge *is* an odd place to loaf). The reader wants to know why he's there, what he's doing, what this has to do with what the advertiser is selling. International Equipment Company ties the cat in with the illustration in the copy with the explanation that the motor purrs quietly at low speeds so there's less stress and strain on working parts. The centrifuge *does* do more work longer because it, like the cat, loafs instead of working itself to death.

All advertising, consumer and industrial, is cat-happy of the last few years, with felines ranging in size from full-grown tigers all the way down to pedigreed house cats—and a few from alleys, too. Personal prejudice, but as a cat-hater the author devoutly hopes the pendulum will swing and advertisers everywhere will start putting on the dog.

Argus Chemical Corporation, subsidiary of Witco Chemical Company, Inc., is considerably more imaginative than most cat-using advertisers, so reaps readership rewards as a result. Three of its ads for polyvinyl chloride stabilization (the PVC in the headlines) are illustrated on the following page. These illustrations are attention grabbers and it's an odd reader indeed who can pass by one without a reaction ranging from considerable interest to a double-take to a "there's another #$%&*)(cat!". Actually, if it weren't for the fact that a *cat* is shown, these illustrations would have considerable charm and appeal. Argus Chemical's cat's changes in hats, and the language and vernacular difference in headline and copy add additional interest and emphasize the worldwide scope of the company's sales and service. Now, if Argus wanted to change, it could start the campaign with an English springer spaniel to symbolize its English operation.

If you don't have interest, borrow some. But make sure it's relevant and *interesting.* Interest that isn't interesting is a horrible prospect.

Contrast

Sharp contrast is always an eye-catcher.

Contrast stops the reader because it's interesting by its very nature. The device arouses curiosity. The reader instinctively wants to find out *why* the contrast between two objects is shown in the illustration. He wants to know *why* one item appears as it does, why it differs so radically from one that's apparently very similar. He wants to know what this difference means to him and to his company.

For example, suppose you're in the valve business. Your company installed some very large and expensive valves in the boiler room of a major utility company long before you came on the scene, approximately 40 years ago. These valves have given yeoman service all of these years, with no corrosion, no leakage, no maintenance problems.

However, 20 years ago one of your competitors managed to get his foot in the door at this utility (obviously by bribing the purchasing agent) and installed the same number of valves in the same kind of service. Fortuitously, the valves are side by side. Your company's valves are of much higher quality, however, and appear

Clever cat illustrations carry the message of Argus Chemical Corporation: That the company's worldwide sales and service organization speaks the language of customers everywhere.

Nous parlons le PVC partout.

We speak PVC from Acapulco to Zanzibar. And in any city in between where an SOS on polyvinyl chloride stabilization is sounded. Argus, with its Mark Stabilizers and Drapex Plasticizers has been involved in scores of new vinyl products, processes and problems. Whether your company is here or there, you'll find Argus ready to talk your language. We have affiliates in: Guelph, Canada; Manchester, England; Sao Paulo, Brazil; Mexico City; Brussels; Tokyo; Madrid and Milan.

ARGUS CHEMICAL CORPORATION
SUBSIDIARY OF WITCO CHEMICAL COMPANY, INC.

to be in as good condition today as when they were installed four decades ago. Competition's valves are of vastly inferior quality, however, and have almost had it. They have required all sorts of maintenance over the years; they leak, the metal was too soft and become badly chewed and worn, and they *look* bad.

Here's a natural illustration showing the contrast between your high quality valves and competitive ones that failed. The appearance alone will stop the reader; he'll wonder about the difference, what happened to the competitive valves, why some look good and some don't. It will be obvious in the illustration that the valves have had the same general use and were exposed to exactly the same conditions because they're alongside each other. Headline and copy can hammer hard at the benefits the user will receive from using your valves, and it will do so believably. The illustration has set the stage for this.

Drill Presses, Electrodes, What Have You?

Or the illustration could show two drill presses next to each other, both at work. One could be using a new type of hardened drill with a special carbide tip comparable to a diamond in hardness. Both are drilling into identical pieces of steel, but the carbide-tipped drill has produced more hole by about 50 percent than the old fashioned drill, and in exactly the same time, too. The contrast in the amount of work done, very evident in the illustration, interests readers enough to pull them into the headline. It could be a testimonial from the general foreman, production superintendent, or other first-line manufacturing executive to the effect that his company saved X-number of dollars and X-number of machine hours in a specified period of time due to use of the new carbide-tipped drill.

There's no end of good illustrative situations like this. Smart advertisers take full advantage of the comparison technique to boost readership of their ads and stress user benefits of their products.

The illustration is Ex-Cell-O Corporation's striking two-color ad from *Production* magazine is an excellent example. It is shown on the following page.

Graphics are unusually powerful. Eye-catching white space initially attracts the reader's eye. Then the short, punchy one-two headline and the vivid contrast of two identical parts—one perfect, the other obviously at the ragged end of its tether—pulls the reader into the copy with a force that is almost irresistible. He simply *has* to find out why one electrode, shorted 16 times, shows no ill effects

Shorted 16 times **Shorted once**

You can spark out an ECM electrode without getting burned. The difference between left and right is our ECM machine's new electronic control system. It spots shorting conditions well in advance, then stops the machine. Even if the electrode touches the work, you're still safe. Because the current breaks in 5 milliseconds. The system would pay for the machine if all it did was prevent spark-outs. But it goes even further and allows you to safely use the maximum feed rate. And the more you feed, the fatter you get. For more details, write Ex-Cell-O Corp., Lectra-Form Dept., Detroit, Mich. 48232. A short note will do.

while another electrode that's identical was shorted just once and is ready for the ash can.

This is realism that cannot be questioned. The photograph is unretouched and the reader accepts it at face value. The mood has been set, he's been pulled into the copy and he's eager to learn more about an electrode that can save him money. Ex-Cell-O goes on to explain in the body copy just why its new ECM machine doesn't wreck electrodes when they're sparked, making possible savings from prevention of spark-outs that can pay for the machine.

Although the ad as a whole is well done, the excellent illustration with the contrast between two identical parts can claim most of the credit for stopping the reader.

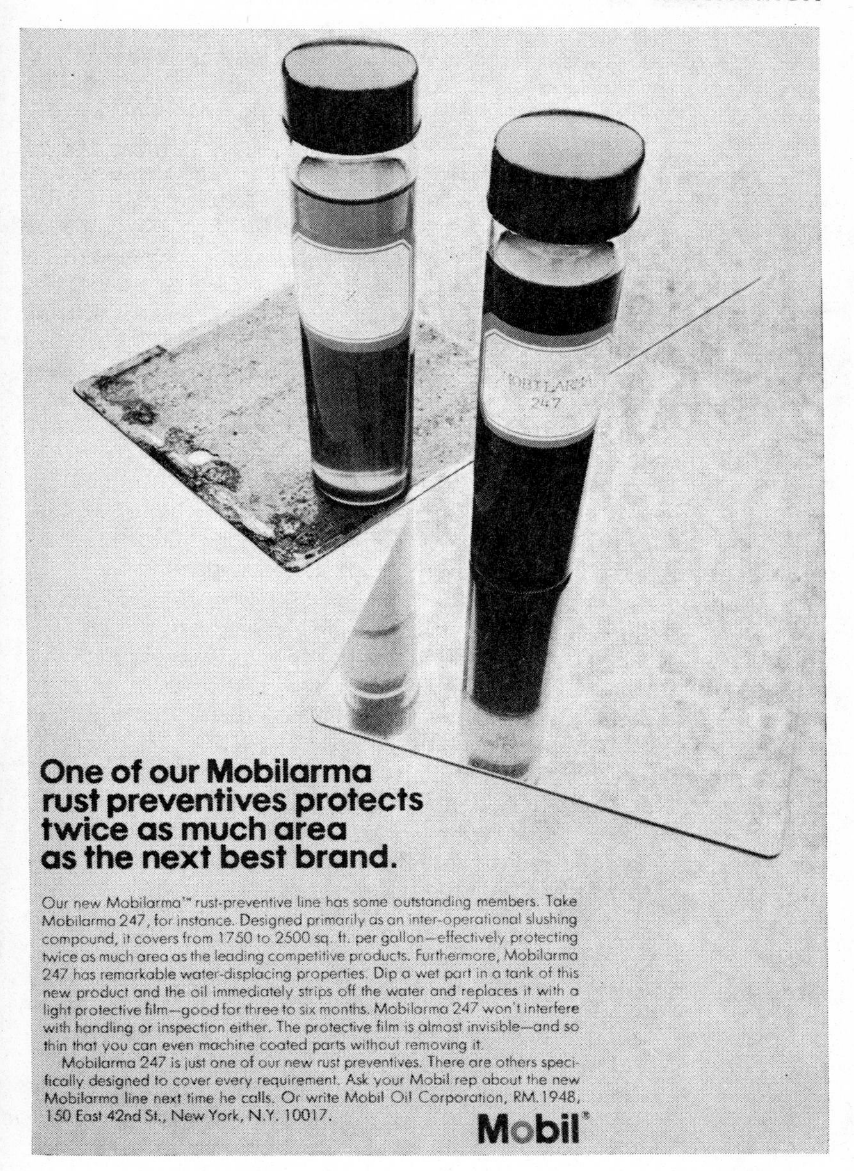

MOBILARMA
247
One of our Mobilarma rust preventives protects twice as much area as the next best brand.
Our new Mobilarma™ rust-preventive line has some outstanding members. Take Mobilarma 247, for instance. Designed primarily as an inter-operational slushing compound, it covers from 1750 to 2500 sq. ft. per gallon—effectively protecting twice as much area as the leading competitive products. Furthermore, Mobilarma 247 has remarkable water-displacing properties. Dip a wet part in a tank of this new product and the oil immediately strips off the water and replaces it with a light protective film—good for three to six months. Mobilarma 247 won't interfere with handling or inspection either. The protective film is almost invisible—and so thin that you can even machine coated parts without removing it.
Mobilarma 247 is just one of our new rust preventives. There are others specifically designed to cover every requirement. Ask your Mobil rep about the new Mobilarma line next time he calls. Or write Mobil Oil Corporation, RM. 1948, 150 East 42nd St., New York, N.Y. 10017.
Mobil

The contrast illustration is an easy way to emphasize the difference in what two competitive products will do for the reader if they're used for the same purpose. In copy you can tell the reader what your product will do, you can laud it interminably, tell the reader again and again how much more it will do for him until you're out of space. This won't make nearly the impression that a good illustration will.

Mobil Oil Corporation proves this point by using the contrast technique unusually well in its attractive four-color ad for Mobilarma.

When discussing Mobilarma rust preventive, the primary user benefit the advertiser wants to stress is economy for the user. This means, for this product, that a given amount of Mobilarma will go twice as far as the same amount of a competitive product. This must be illustrated to the reader, of course, and the most effective way to do this is to contrast the coverage a given amount of Mobilarma will give with what the ubiquitous Brand X will produce.

So Mobil illustrated two vials of rust preventives, carefully labeled "X" and Mobilarma 247, on two steel plates of identical size. It is apparent immediately that the plate protected with Mobilarma 247 has protection over its entire surface, while Brand X protected only half of the plate on which it was applied.

Graphically and simply and quickly the point was made by using contrast in the illustration. Mobil telegraphed its point to the reader, then repeated the user benefits in the headline and explained the reasons why in the body copy.

This is industrial advertising as it should be—direct, hard-hitting and right to the point.

When using the contrast technique in your illustrations, be *sure* to contrast like items. The reader would be quick to receive the impression you're trying to trick him or (horrors) even tell an outright untruth if you compare unlike objects; they couldn't logically be expected to provide the contrast you need to put the message across.

Arousing Curiosity

The word "curious" implies a desire to learn. In the case of the reader of business publications it is particularly apt, for, as we've seen, this reader is educating himself to improve performance on his job.

And "curiosity," of course, means that which is curious—or designed to excite the attention. It isn't some kind of stuff used to kill cats.

A curiosity-arousing illustration in an industrial advertisement has one prime purpose: To excite the reader, to make him desire so strongly to find out what the purpose of the illustration is that he finds it almost impossible to refrain from reading the headline.

Whether curiosity actually killed the cat is a moot point. One thing is certain, though: Curiosity is a very strong emotion, one that most people cannot shrug off lightly. Given a reasonable opportunity, people gratify their desire to assuage this feeling for, unless it is appeased, they know full well from past experience they harbor a sense of frustration. Even Alice during her trip to the never-never land of New York City—or was it Wonderland?—was in an emotional tizzy when she became "curioser and curioser" and lacked the opportunity to gratify her yearning for learning about the strange sensation which possessed her.

Use a provocative, curiosity-arousing illustration in your advertisement and the reader responds immediately. He wonders why you show it to him. Or if the object illustrated doesn't explain itself, he'll wonder why you used it. Then, if the headline provides an explanation that satisfies his innate sense of logic by bridging the gap between the unexplained illustration and the body copy, your ad has every chance of being well read.

The young lady as used by Bostitch, Inc., a Textron Company, well-known fastening methods manufacturer, *is* enough to arouse the reader's curiosity. The ads are shown together nearby. First question that comes to mind is, "What is she doing there, taking a bath in an ad?" Second question which follows hard on the heels of the first is, "And just what kind of bathtub is *that?*"

HOW TO PACKAGE HOT WATER AT A HEARTWARMING PROFIT

A West Coast manufacturer of water heaters found himself in hot water. And his customers without it. He knew his trouble. Crating methods in his shipping department acted as a bottleneck on production.

So he called in his BOSTITCH man.

A new corrugated shipping carton with wooden inserts was designed. That cut his packaging materials cost 50% immediately.

But more important, he could then switch to BOSTITCH Staplers for carton assembly. Packaging speed jumped 500%. So water heater production could be stepped up 133% to meet the demand.

Unusual?

Yes. But not surprising because BOSTITCH fastening methods can package or assemble so many products better and faster.

Put the speed and security of BOSTITCH stapling to work for you. Call us. We have 479 phones in 123 cities listed under "BOSTITCH" in most phone books. Or write direct. BOSTITCH, Inc., 546 Briggs Drive, East Greenwich, R. I. 02818.

Fasten it better and faster with

BOSTITCH

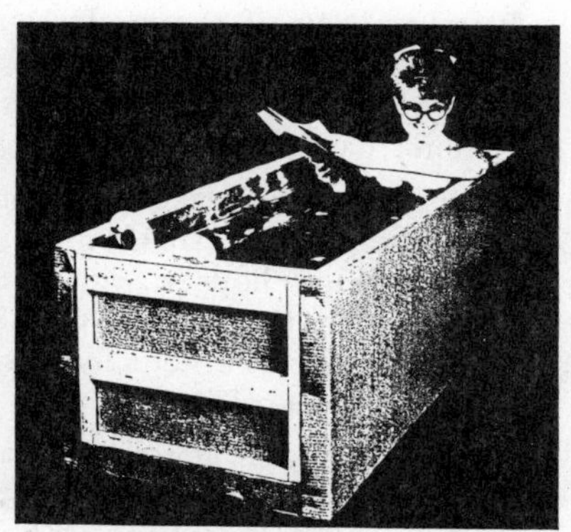

BOSTITCH HELPS PACKAGE HOT WATER AT A HEARTWARMING PROFIT

A West Coast manufacturer of water heaters found himself in hot water. And his customers without it. He knew his trouble. Crating methods in his shipping department acted as a bottleneck on production.

So he called in his BOSTITCH man.

A new corrugated shipping carton with wooden inserts was designed. That cut his packaging materials cost 50% immediately.

But more important, he could then switch to BOSTITCH Staplers for carton assembly. Packaging speed jumped 500%. So water heater production could be stepped up 133% to meet the demand.

Unusual?

Yes. But not surprising because BOSTITCH fastening methods can package or assemble so many products better and faster.

Put the speed and security of BOSTITCH stapling to work for you. Call us. We have 479 phones in 123 cities listec under "BOSTITCH" in most phone books. Or write direct. BOSTITCH, 204 Briggs Drive, East Greenwich, R. I. 02818.

Fasten it better and faster with

BOSTITCH A textron COMPANY

Both headlines—Bostitch used two, to test which one produced the better response—continue to whet the curiosity, talking as they do about "packaging hot water at a heartwarming profit." Only when the reader has been enticed into the body copy, and the illustration and headline work well together to assure that this happens, is the mystery unfolded.

Body copy tells the story of a manufacturer of water heaters who found himself in hot water due to a bottleneck in his crating department. A Bostitch man solved his problem pronto by designing a new shipping carton; it reduced packaging materials cost by 50 percent, desirable in itself. Better yet, the Bostitch man solved *his* problem by switching the manufacturer to Bostitch staplers to assemble the cartons and thus boosted packaging speed 500 percent, ending the bottleneck. This enabled water heater production to be stepped up 133 percent to keep up with sales.

One version or the other of the two ads ran in *U.S. News & World Report, Newsweek, Purchasing Week, Factory, Mill & Factory, Handling & Shipping, Modern Materials Handling, Materials Handling · Engineering, Package Engineering,* and in *Modern Packaging.*

Flying Tiger Line uses a strong combination of a curiosity arousing illustration of a pair of luscious legs and a two-part headline to stop the reader right in his tracks. The compelling black-and-white ad appeared in *Business Week* magazine.

First reaction of the reader is, "My, what luscious legs!" Next, he settles down a bit and thinks, "You mean the skirt's going to be shorter yet?" Then, "What's this bit with the Flying Tiger Line—they don't have stewardesses?"

By this time the reader's thoroughly hooked, so he proceeds on to the body copy to learn that Flying Tiger Line is the stand-by of famous fashion houses which depend on speedy, economical air freight to keep the pipeline to the marketplace filled with the latest numbers—which are actually perishables when you equate demand with feminine capriciousness.

Naturally enough, it follows that if the Tigers can perform so ably for fashion, they can come to the rescue of any troubled manufacturer who finds that time is a critically important factor in his distribution process.

This ad is unusually persuasive and convincing, and it got the chance to persuade and convince because the illustration delivered the readers. Sic 'em, Tiger!

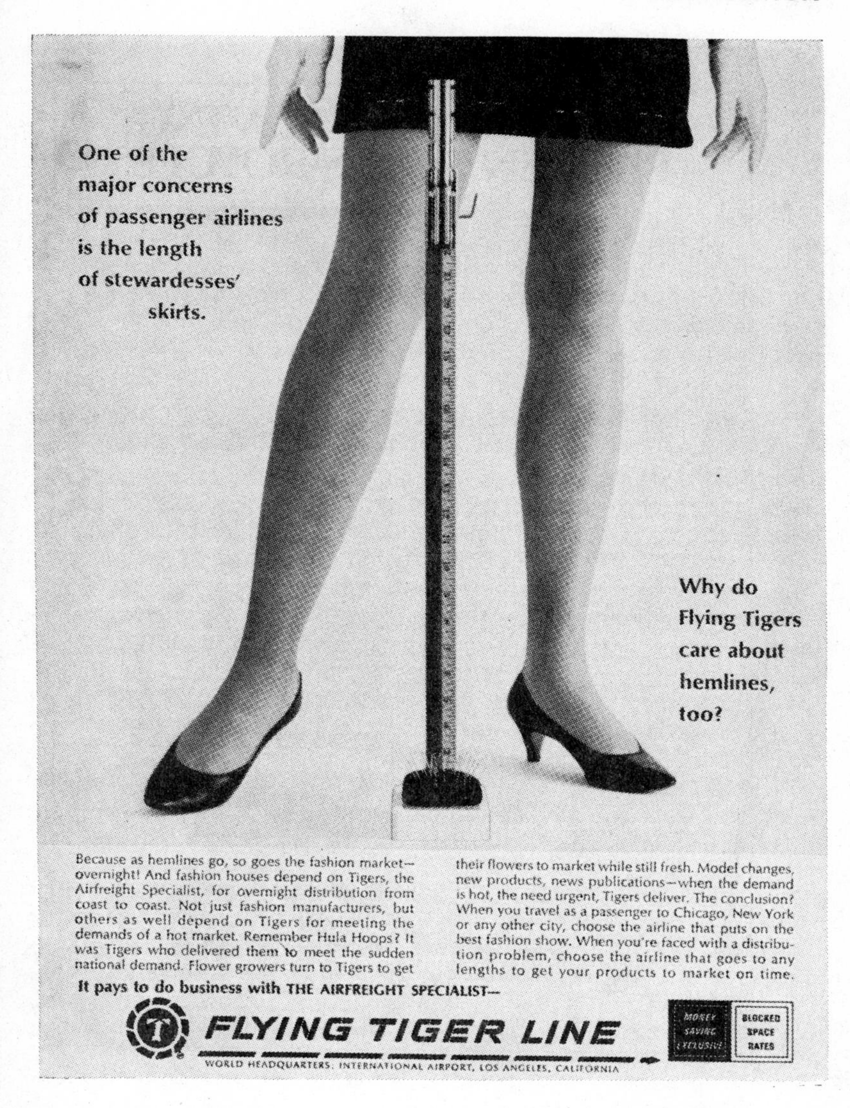

Charts and Graphs

With an appropriate chart or graph you can summarize a complex mass of numerical data so the reader can grasp it at a glance.

Engineers and others accustomed to analyzing complicated performance figures for components being incorporated into a finished assembly are vitally interested in these data. They find them greatly simplified and much easier to grasp when presented in the form of a chart or graph. The advertiser's message is presented succinctly and in much less space than copy could explain such detailed information.

McGraw-Hill's Laboratory of Advertising Performance ranks charts and graphs third from the top in readership. This isn't because charts and graphs have high interest for the average reader, but because they satisfy one of the reader's most important objectives in reading business publications. Charts and graphs present useful information, stripped of all except essentials so the reader can evaluate without fuss or fanfare.

The technical reader has a gut-feeling about this. He believes that the advertiser who presents charts and graphs is taking an approach toward his product that is open, frank, and unbiased. He's not trying to con the reader. Believability of charts and graphs is exceptionally high. Technically-oriented readers have a basic distrust of much advertising because it relies heavily on *words* to disseminate the message. Words are something the technical man would just about as soon do without, unless they're spoken ones. Show him something in a way that he's accustomed to working with when he's doodling with his product or its development and you immediately have a man who's prepared to believe what you have to say. Obviously you can't step out of the pages of the book with a slide rule clutched firmly in your hand, nor can you wave a blueprint in the reader's face. But you can do what he considers the next best thing: Show him what you have to tell him visually with a chart or graph, or both.

It's not advisable to rely completely on charts and graphs, however. Research shows that most industrial advertisements using charts and graphs are strengthened when the illustration also contains a photograph or artwork *in addition to* the chart and graph. This permits the advertiser to show the product, show how it's used, illustrate important features, or do whatever else is called for to arouse reader interest in the ad.

Effectiveness of this combination is exploited with considerable skill in the LKB Instruments, Inc. ad illustrated nearby. This black-and-white ad discusses the first commercial instrument to integrate a gas chromatograph, a molecule separator, and a mass spectrometer. It's little short of amazing this hasn't been done before, come to think of it.

The mass spectrum of PLASTOQUINONE A which occurs widely in plant material.

Even greater versatility by using the New Direct Inlet Probe.

LKB 9000 Produces the Right Answer

The ANSWER–provided by the first commercial instrument to integrate a gas chromatograph, a molecule separator and a mass spectrometer–to analytical problems in chemistry dealing with amino acids, sterols, steroids and bile acid esters, biological toxins and narcotics, barbiturates, tranquilizers, pesticides, carbohydrate derivatives and many others.

The ANSWER to the demand for Speed, Accuracy and Flexibility of operation.

The ANSWER to temperature sensitive or unstable samples as well as to samples with low vapour pressure–The Direct Inlet System.

The ANSWER to effluent containing unresolved compounds–The Accelerating Voltage Alternator.

The ANSWER in fact to everything a scientist could ask for in performance, convenience and dependable, trouble-free operation–a new dimension in GC-MS.

We have given only a few ANSWERS.

If you have some QUESTIONS why not write today to the address below for All the ANSWERS on the LKB 9000 Gas Chromatograph-Mass Spectrometer.

LKB INSTRUMENTS INC. • 12221 PARKLAWN DRIVE • ROCKVILLE Md. 20852

OTHER HEADQUARTERS FOR SALES AND SERVICE

SWEDEN
LKB-Produkter AB
Box 76
Stockholm–Bromma 1

UK
LKB Instruments Ltd
232 Addington Rd.
S. Croydon, Surrey CR2 8YD

NETHERLANDS
LKB-Produkten N.V
Zeekant 35,
The Hague

DENMARK
LKB Instrument A/S
Amagerbrogade 34
Copenhagen S

The ad has an attention-getting photograph in which the two men are so interested in the information coming from the instrument that you almost wish you could look over their shoulders.

Then, in reverse (white on black) is information portrayed graphically—far too much to explain in copy; it is crystal clear here, though. On the right is a diagram illustrating the operation of the equipment's direct inlet system, also easily understood by the technical audience to whom the ad is directed.

Copy does a good job of suggesting applications and performance characteristics of the instrument, and it makes a strong bid for action.

Technical people dig charts, graphs, diagrams, schematics, and so on. Give them what communicates with them.

Cutaway or Cross Section

An average reader of a trade publication is not blessed with either X-ray vision or extrasensory perception. More's the pity. However, if he were, he'd not be reading trade publications where your ads run—he'd be hanging onto a table at Harold's Club in Reno.

When you're faced with presenting a complicated mechanical product that's all neatly housed in a very solid metal case that's impossible to see through, yet you want to explain all of the intricacies and wonderful workings of the contraption, you could write a learned dissertation only a whisker shorter than the one Tolstoy titled *War and Peace*. Even then, chances are you'd fall short of something that satisfied either you or the reader.

Yet you can't merely photograph the thing because all you'd end up showing is its shape, with the exterior nice and smooth and painted and mighty unmechanical looking. This wouldn't do any good, or very little anyway. Nor would merely showing what the contrivance *does* be an acceptable solution.

There's a way out, though, so don't despair. One thing you can do is to show a cutaway view of the device. This is simple to do in either one of two ways.

You can have a product actually physically cut—have the outer wall sliced away with a grinder or power saw to expose the workings of the mechanical marvel. Then all that remains to be done is to have the working parts photographed when they're exposed. This usually works out very satisfactorily. Many well-done industrial advertisements use this type of illustration. Old though the technique is, it results in excellent illustrations of engines, transmissions, and similar items.

An example of the cutaway illustration is the Bendix starter drive in the black-and-white ad run by Bendix Automotive, division of The Bendix Corporation, in *Automotive Industries* magazine; it's shown nearby.

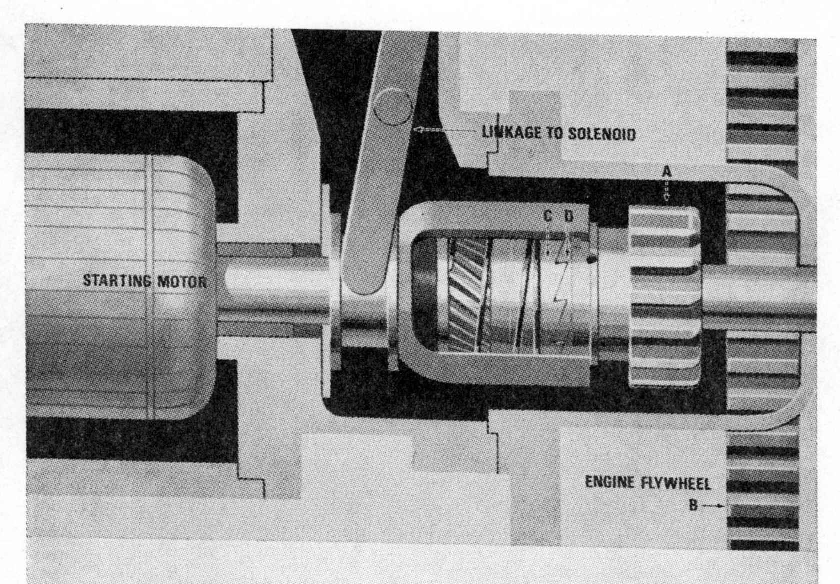

A Bendix starter drive won't kick your flywheel in the teeth.

This is the Bendix* Positork* starter drive. It offers performance that's far superior to sprag-type designs, that's for sure. Positork's unique indexing ability automatically aligns its pinion teeth (A) with flywheel teeth (B). Only then does cranking action begin. After the engine fires, a unique separator mechanism automatically disengages dentile clutch teeth (C) and dentile pinion teeth (D). There's no chance of damage caused by prolonged high-speed pinion overrun.

What about grease seals? Spline covers? Positork doesn't need them. Price? Less than competitive models. Positork is for all your heavy-duty construction equipment, large industrial engines and large over-the-highway trucks, gasoline or diesel. For complete details, write: The Bendix Corporation, Motor Components Division, Elmira, New York 14903.

This artwork depicts the relatively complicated mechanical assembly just as if the housing of the Bendix Positork starter drive unit had been carefully cut in half just as you'd cut a ripe canteloupe to get at the good eating. Then, by keying the different elements, A, B,

C, and D, copywriting and explaining how the unit operates is greatly simplified.

Studies show that cutaway illustrations consistently rank at the top as far as readership is concerned. Using a cutaway illustration almost guarantees readership, if such a thing is possible.

Another technique that's highly self-explanatory is the cross section. This is particularly effective when the advertiser wants to discuss the composition of his product. For example, the manufacturer of bar steel might want to tell the reader that the molecular structure is consistent from the exterior surface of the bar all the way to the center. To illustrate this, a bar could be sawed, then photographed to show the manufacturer's claim is based on more than fond hopes and desires.

Yet another excellent method of illustrating that which cannot be readily seen is the X-ray view, or the so-called phantom view. They're very similar but not quite the same. In the case of the actual X-ray, the illustration is photographic, of course. Phantom views are usually artwork.

Either is highly effective when the advertiser knows it's necessary to show the reader the internal parts of the product. This may be done to show either how it operates, or how it's constructed. Many advertisers take this tack in order to show how their products—usually small in comparison to the completed assembly—are used by manufacturers of the end products.

An excellent example of the phantom-view technique is an unusually interesting black-and-white ad run by Shell Oil Company. It shows the Chaparral 2F sports car in carefully delineated line art. Shown clearly are mechanical details of more than passing interest to the reader of a number of business magazines in which the ad appeared. Details are emphasized and brought to the reader's attention by lines leading from the feature to an explanatory caption. Shell products used in the automobile are also shown in this manner.

Copy is short, to the point, and very convincing. It stresses that Chaparral as well as Ferrari and Ford's sports prototype teams race only with Shell motor oil. And it's not a special racing oil they use, but a branded Shell product—the same high-quality oil the average motorist puts in the family station wagon at his corner Shell station.

Copy then points out that fleet operation is just as tough on an engine oil as racing is, hence fleet operators using either gasoline or diesel power plants benefit from using Shell oil just as much as racing teams do.

With men's proven high interest in automobiles and in phantom

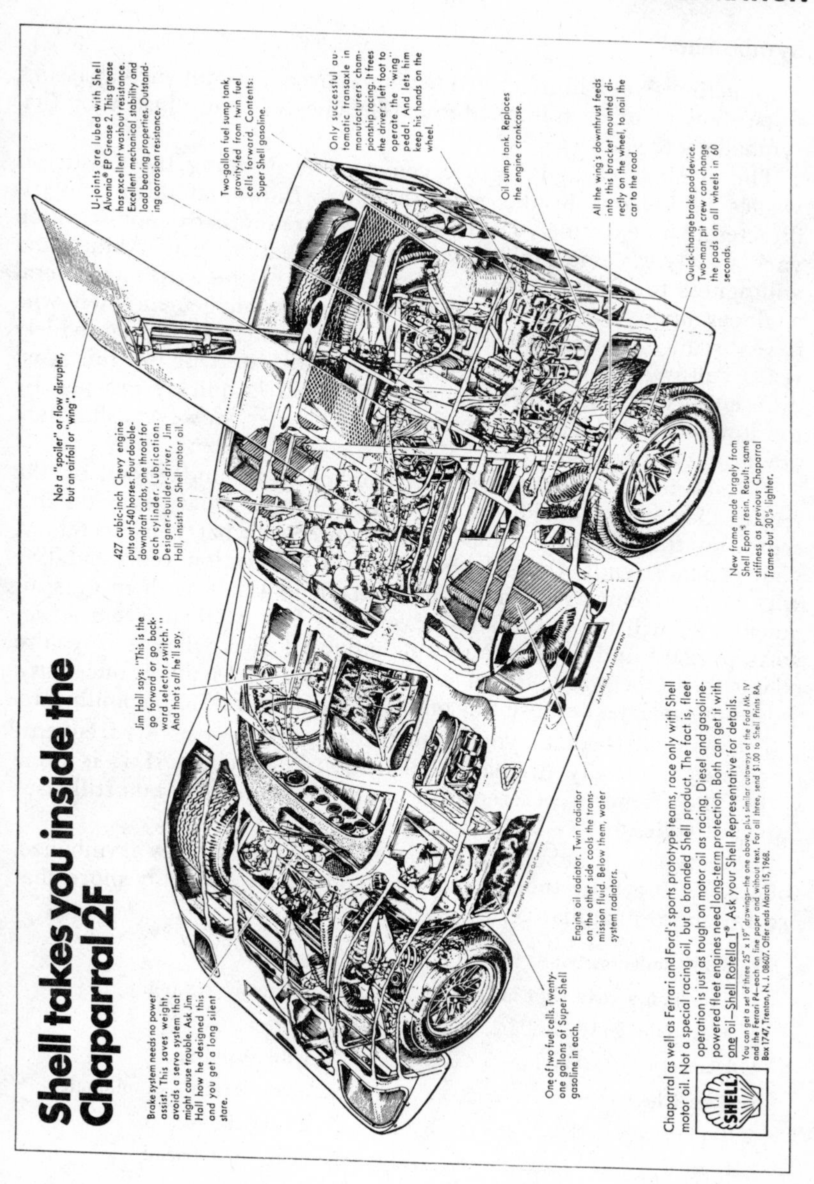

views of mechanical products, this illustration has every chance in the world of delivering outstanding readership to Shell.

Shell takes you inside the Chaparral 2F
Brake system needs no power assist. This saves weight, avoids a servo system that might cause trouble. Ask Jim Hall how he designed this and you get a long silent stare.
Jim Hall says: "This is the go forward or go backward selector switch." And that's all he'll say.
427 cubic-inch Chevy engine puts out 540 horses. Four double-downdraft carbs, one throat for each cylinder. Lubrication: Designer-builder-driver, Jim Hall, insists on Shell motor oil.
Not a "spoiler" or flow disrupter, but an airfoil or "wing".
U-joints are lubed with Shell Alvania® EP Grease 2. This grease has excellent washout resistance. Excellent mechanical stability and load bearing properties. Outstanding corrosion resistance.
Two-gallon fuel sump tank, gravity-fed from twin fuel cells forward. Contents: Super Shell gasoline.
Only successful automatic transaxle in manufacturers' championship racing. It frees the driver's left foot to operate the "wing" pedal. And lets him keep his hands on the wheel.
Oil sump tank. Replaces the engine crankcase.
All the wing's downthrust feeds into this bracket mounted directly on the wheel, to nail the car to the road.
Quick-change brake pad device. Two-man pit crew can change the pads on all wheels in 60 seconds.
New frame made largely from Shell Epon® resin. Result: same stiffness as previous Chaparral frames but 30% lighter.
Engine oil radiator. Twin radiator on the other side cools the transmission fluid. Below them, water system radiators.
One of two fuel cells. Twenty-one gallons of Super Shell gasoline in each.
SHELL
Chaparral as well as Ferrari and Ford's sports prototype teams, race only with Shell motor oil. Not a special racing oil, but a branded Shell product. The fact is, fleet operation is just as tough on motor oil as racing. Diesel and gasoline-powered fleet engines need long-term protection. Both can get it with one oil—Shell Rotella T®. Ask your Shell Representative for details.
You can get a set of three 25" x 19" drawings—the one above, plus similar cutaways of the Ford Mk. IV and the Ferrari P4—each on fine paper and without text. For all three, send $1.00 to Shell Prints RA, Box 1747, Trenton, N. J. 08607. Offer ends March 15, 1968.

Symbolism

Sometimes your illustrative idea is too broad, too all encompassing, to be shown—or even implied. Such ideas call for an illustration that symbolizes them.

The symbol selected for use conveys the meaning the advertiser wishes to implant in the reader's mind. Industrial advertising is directed to an extremely large universe where levels of sophistication vary widely, as does ability to interpret what is seen. Ability and willingness to interpret ranges from the low of the extremely literal engineer up to the high represented by top management men who have broad educational backgrounds; these men are often widely read, cultured, and possess vivid imaginations. Due to this vast difference, the symbol used must be one that is quickly grasped by the lowest of the common denominators. Never, however, illustrate down; never condescend.

It's absolutely essential that the symbolism be understood by the reader, however. Should you have any question whatsoever on this score, try the illustrative idea on for size. See what your secretary, your lunch friends, the sales manager, a publication representative who calls, a company engineer, think about it. If all of them grasp it quickly, so will the reader. However, if a few of them seem somewhat puzzled and require an explanation of just what it is you're trying to do, be wary. Better search for another symbol, one that's more appropriate, because this one is destined to fail to communicate.

The symbolist—that's you when you're using a symbol—frequently creates unusually dramatic illustrations, especially if it is done within the frame of reference of the average reader, but still uses flair and style.

Some typical symbolic illustrations, and what they symbolize, follow. With a little thought you can come up with many more that are far more imaginative, of course.

1. Skull and crossbones .... poison.
2. Cross, on a road sign .... railroad crossing.
3. Mars (the god) .... war.
4. Democratic donkey .... wild spending.
5. Eros (the god) .... love, usually not platonic.
6. Trojan horse .... deception.
7. Dog .... man's best friend.
8. Boatman at River Styx .... death.
9. Bearded gentleman in bed sheet with scythe .... the passing year.

10. Red-clad horseman with scabbarded rifle in snow-covered mountains .... rugged he-man.

The connection between the symbol and the idea should be readily apparent so the reader will cross-reference the two immediately.

It's when the illustrative idea symbolizes a concept, rather than a tangible object, that you have to tread lightly and be mighty sure you're not too far out in left field to be understood.

An unusually sensitive and touching symbolic illustration created by a gifted visualizer appears in Wallace Pharmaceuticals' tasteful spread ad shown below in full and sectionally enlarged.

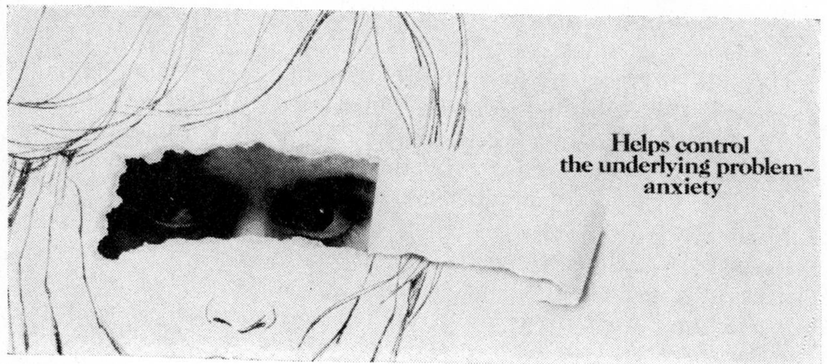

Unfortunately, the copy cannot be reproduced so that it is legible; the ad appeared in a publication edited for the medical profession. The advertiser does not want lay people to read about Miltown, a tranquilizer well known to apprehensive advertising men, which is available only by prescription. The ad as a whole is shown, though, because the spread is so well balanced with fine legibility in the copy page and with the spread tied together by having a small, subtle portion of the art carried over onto the right-hand page (see top photo, page 695).

A close-up of the artwork also is shown. It is an exceptionally creative combination of pencil drawing and four-color process photography, reproduced offset. The woman's eyes were either photographed in color through the torn pencil rendition, or more likely, were combined by paste-up of the two different illustrations during makeready when it was being prepared for the camera for offset lithography reproduction.

Symbolism in Wallace Pharmaceuticals' impressive spread is perfect, letter perfect. Total effect of the unusual technique is to portray vividly an apprehensive patient who suffers the anguish of anxiety. Doctors being human, there's every reason to feel this illustration communicates with them as professional men, as well as on an emotional basis. When you develop an illustrative technique that communicates objectively and subjectively, guard and cherish it and use it time after time after time. Such illustrations are few and far between.

Symbolism is a touchy area. Good symbolic illustrations are outstanding. Poor ones flop resoundingly.

Negative Appeal

The negative appeal frequently involves use of the scare technique —the look-what-can-happen-to-you-approach.

Because the reader finds what the advertiser shows him is distasteful, it's possible for the illustration's negative appeal to backfire with disastrous results. The reader may retain only the negative impression produced by the illustration and from then on take a dim view of the product that was advertised.

Used properly, however, the negative appeal shows a situation the reader is anxious to avoid. It's one that will cause him personal distress. It can hit him in that tenderest of spots, the pocketbook. It can affect his career adversely. If the product being advertised promises the reader he won't encounter such unpleasant situations, and if the ad convinces him of the truth of the claims being made, the advertisement that uses the negative appeal is frequently extremely effective.

An illustration for safety shoes in an ad, for instance, may show a worker grimacing in pain, standing on one foot holding the other in both hands; nearby is a heavy object on the floor. This is certainly negative. It conjures up all sorts of dire happenings—employee compensation claim, lost production by a key worker, trouble with the union about a temporary replacement worker, increased insurance costs and so on. None of them are very appealing.

Or the illustration could show the interior of an office, charred papers strewn about, files gaping open with contents burned and water-soaked, a safe sprung open and scorched by intense heat. This

It's 14 to 1
you too are
inviting this tragedy

EVERY FIFTY-SIX MINUTES, 14 more firms are victimized by fire. And 13 of these victims are seriously handicapped because they lose current records . . .

Fire destroys the contents of steel files in a few minutes—Even in "fireproof" buildings*. And insurance money can't replace records.

Because of the current, widespread interest in the value of business records burned (estimated by NFPA to be *triple the property loss*), Shaw-Walker has published a 4-page folder of basic fire facts: "Only the Victims Know".

This revealing folder pictures a few typical losses in "fireproof" buildings.—Also the happier results for the 1 in 14 who took advantage of the modern technology that produced Shaw-Walker Fire-Files*.

Fire-Files provide the most practical "point-of-use" fire protection obtainable for records. In each Fire-File, you get the protection of a Safe and the convenient drawer operation of the finest Filing Cabinet.

If you have any current records in steel files or desk drawers, our fire-facts folder "Only the Victims Know" is *must* reading. Phone your Shaw-Walkerman for it. Or write for the name of our nearest representative.

*The office pictured is in a "fireproof" building. The fire wasn't hot enough, long enough, to destroy the wooden chair in the background—but every record in steel files was turned to ashes.

SHAW-WALKER
Largest Exclusive Makers of Office Equipment
32 Division St. Muskegon, Michigan 49443

is exactly the type of illustration Shaw-Walker, largest exclusive makers of office equipment, used in its striking two-color, one-page ad from *U.S. News & World Report*. The ad is shown on page 697. This sickening scene is realistic, believable, and downright frightening. Everybody is familiar with statistics that prove that very few businesses reopen after a major fire—at least, in medium to small companies.

Shaw-Walker's illustration is exceptionally lifelike because of restrained and effective use of the second color—brown. There's just enough brown to make things look charred and scorched; you can almost smell the wet, smoky odor such a fire causes.

When businessmen see an illustration like Shaw-Walker's, they imagine the results of lost accounts receivable; or of having to duplicate thousands of man hours that have already been expended in doing work that's now lost forever.

The Threat of Fire

E. F. Houghton & Company ran an ad in *Iron Age, Factory, Purchasing Week,* and *Precision Metal Molding* magazines with an illustration that's just about enough to scare the pants off a businessman reader if he thinks of it in connection with his own firm. The ad shows silhouetted firemen pouring the water on what looks like a three-alarm blaze destroying a commercial establishment. It sets the stage for Houghton's persuasive story about its fire-resistant hydraulic fluids, enabling the advertiser to make a point with much impact and great believability.

A negative illustration can launch an extremely positive product story with user benefits every reader wants—if you use it with caution and are sure the total effect is positive.

How fire resistant is a synthetic "fire-resistant" fluid that's diluted with petroleum?

Not very. And we suggest you get the facts on any that your company is considering, rather than find out later, the costly way.

A ruptured coupling on a high pressure hydraulic line sprays oil on a red hot forge oven... poof... you've got a fire that might have been prevented. The same thing can happen with a diecasting machine, a press, or any other source of high heat. The potential is almost unlimited. Though the chances are mathematically low, this only has to happen once because... when you're out of plant, you're usually out of business.

It may be time for prudent management to ask if the gain using such a fluid is worth the risk of having it on the premises. Ask your machine operator. Ask your safety director. Ask yourself.

Then ask your supplier . . . what are the alternatives? There are far less hazardous hydraulic-fluids. Water-glycols. Phosphate esters. There has been no known large loss where these two fluids have been used. And . . . there was a time when almost *nothing else* was acceptable. That was shortly after the "big fires," caused by oil-base hydraulic fluids, some 15 years ago. You may recall . . . you may have forgotten. But it's time to remember. Because in recent years, when hydraulic fires have been virtually wiped out through the use of fire-resistant fluids, some people have become careless about this yellow fever of industry. Today, the dangers and the potential losses are greater. To the profit-and-loss minded: three-shift production, more expensive production tools, long lead-time on replacement, tighter delivery schedules, higher plant investment, higher insurance rates, incalculable tragedy of loss of life.

Houghton has long been the leading supplier of the major types of fire-resistant fluids, with over 15 years of experience in their development, application and use. All the Houghto-Safe® water-glycols and phosphate esters meet the "less hazardous" fluids standards and are approved by Factory Mutual Engineering Corporation.

Isn't it time to ask your Houghton man in? Ask him . . . and any other supplier . . . to show you, prove to you, the results of *all* significant flammability tests. After all, isn't fire about the worst thing that can happen to *your* plant . . . and to *your* business? E. F. Houghton & Co., Dept. F, 303 W. Lehigh Avenue, Philadelphia, Pa. 19133.

INDUSTRY'S PARTNER IN PRODUCTION

The scare device is legitimate, but there's a precaution you should be sure to take. Be *sure* that the positive result of using the product you're advertising is stressed in the ad—not just mentioned, but stressed. And not just once, but repeated. Repetition drives a point home. Stated once it can be forgotten. Actually, the product being advertised solves a problem before it occurs; present it this way and you're on firm ground.

A typical four-color insert for Anaconda Aluminum (not shown) speaks softly and eloquently of the advantages of using aluminum, rather than that other metal, for air conditioner housings. This is scare technique pure and simple, and it's so logical and believable it's accepted without question by the reader. Just show the ad to him, don't even let him read the modest, unassuming headline, and he'll nod in complete agreement with the premise that's advanced—aluminum is better than steel for many purposes. Such ads were in *Iron Age, Purchasing,* and *Modern Metals.*

Make-Believe Figures

Fantasy is fascinating. Fantasy has universal appeal. In each of us there's at least a little dash of Walter Mitty, a touch of the romantic, a bit of the escapist. Unexpressed, but nonetheless there, is a twinge of desire to get away momentarily from the humdrum and indulge in an occasional flight of fancy.

Few indeed are those of us who no longer delight in the sight gag. The sight gag was ancient and hoary and securely established long before Mack Sennett's time, long before the Keystone Kops took a single pratfall. Comedians from Bob Hope back to the court jester knew it as a sure-fire formula to earn an appreciative laugh—and to establish a rapport with the audience.

Perhaps the world changes, but people don't. In industrial advertising the time-proven sight gag, refined and polished and going under a variety of names, is used with telling effectiveness. Use it and you appeal to the desire of the average reader for something that will briefly lift him up and take him out of his familiar surroundings and let him give free rein to his imagination.

When you do so, you entertain. But this is not the purpose of industrial advertising, even though some misguided members of the smart-aleck school seem to think so.

By entertaining in the illustration you capture the full attention of the reader. You not only have his undivided attention, but you have it when he's in a receptive frame of mind, assuming your illustration is fresh and appealing.

Make-believe figures in advertising have real appeal. You remember the insurance company whose campaign featured the little man with the key protruding from his back so he could be wound up; the Volkswagen ad with the key to wind the bug up, proving it doesn't *really* have to be pedaled; the delightful little puppet, Speedy Alka Seltzer; the Jolly Green Giant; Rockwell's brawny T-shirted mechanic; Hastings piston rings' soft-hearted tough guy; and many others of similar persuasion.

These make-believe people assumed real identities and personalities. Used time after time in campaigns, they identified the product in the reader's mind and invested it with attributes attributed to the imaginary character. In one-shot uses, for the illustration of a single ad, the odd, grotesque and far-fetched can capture much interest and produce very high readership.

The weird and wonderful little bearded Viking in Standard Pressed Steel Company's skillfully executed black-and-white ad from *Iron Age* is an example of delightful whimsicalness and a fine flair for illustration.

Layout of this fine ad is clean and orderly, typography is good and readable, and the advertiser's logo and products are shown to excellent advantage. All in all, this is a good ad, better than the average you'll find in any representative trade book. But there's nothing outstanding about the ad except the illustration. It is superb.

Not a cliché ad showing the typical "tired businessman" worrying about deliveries—instead Standard Pressed Steel Company used this fey little figure representing a Viking. Eye-catching is a guarantee of such creative use of illustrations.

It lifts the ad up out of the ordinary. It does a great job of doing just what the illustration is supposed to do—stopping the reader.

Visualize the ad if Standard Pressed Steel Company had done what undoubtedly came to mind. The company could have used a tired cliché—the inevitable close-up of the worried businessman, forehead creased by concern over a problem the advertiser's product can solve. This has been done to death for so many decades the reader has developed a conditioned reflex which causes his fingers to grasp, his hand to move, and the page to turn.

Instead, SPS used a fresh approach that probably required a little more mental effort, but it paid off with much higher readership.

Johns-Manville's ad in *Chemical & Engineering News* is a stopper. Immediately it's apparent that whatever's being cooked up is even more potent than witches' brew. Even a self-respecting witch would be more than a little bit impressed by the little monster peering from the bubbling beaker. The monster illustration works hand-in-glove with the headline—*Whatever you're cooking up, Colorceran table-tops can take it!*

No product, no process, no production line in this illustration—just an utterly out-of-this-world monster over a steaming cauldron. Yet this illustration ties in perfectly with the headline of the advertisement.

Of course, the reader realizes the illustration is a spoof, yet it makes its point forcefully with no possibility of the reader's mistaking it. And it does so with no hint of boasting or exaggeration. This is a strong ad.

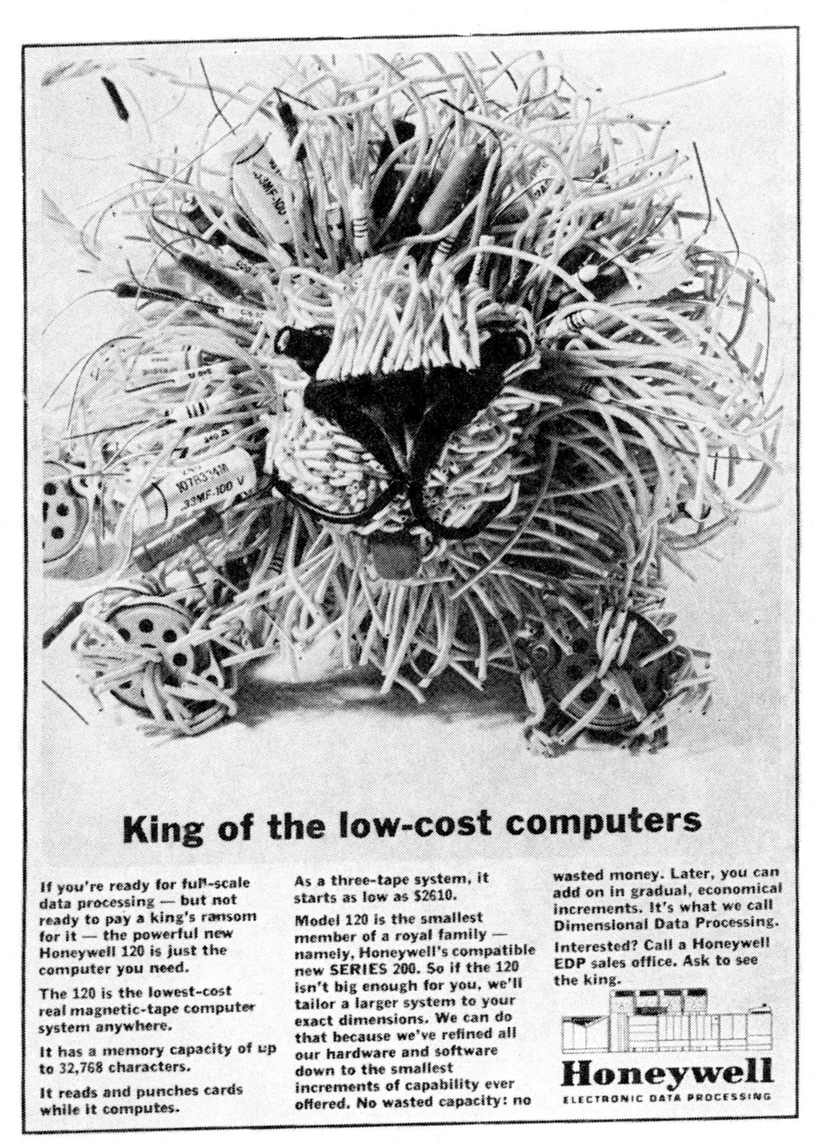

Make-believe figures—actually created figures is more descriptive —in the outstanding four-color ads run by Honeywell, Inc. are nothing short of brilliant. These ingenious little critters are beautifully designed and painstakingly built out of integrated circuits, transistors, and other electronic gadgetry used in Honeywell computers. The logic is faultless.

Evolution of the campaign is apparent from the first four-color ad used. This is the lion, king of beasts, working in full partnership with the headline—*King of the low-cost computers.* Both illustration and headline lead naturally and inevitably into the body copy. This highly creative campaign got off to a great start and has picked up steam ever since.

There's a little bit of chicken in all of us, reads the headline of a succeeding Honeywell ad. In color, the startlingly lifelike electronic chicken has a red comb, brown transistor feathers, a dark tail and yellow legs. Feet are white. Form and dimension and sculpture are tremendously realistic.

Although this chapter is on illustration, it's fitting to quote the copy in this fine ad; only if illustration, headline, and copy work closely together, only if they *belong* together, can the ad achieve its full potential. This one does. Copy reads:

There's a little bit of chicken in all of us.

One big trouble with being chicken is that you can wind up with nothing much to crow about.

Consider, for example, the job of picking a computer.

If you back off from the computer you honestly think is best and pick another one just because it's "safe," you're not doing yourself (or us) any good.

So get plenty of facts, then base your decision on them.

Find out which new-generation computers have been selling and why . . . and if you now have an older computer, which new models make conversion easiest.

Find out who has the best record for delivering both software and hardware on time.

Find out who has the widest choice of rental and purchase plans, and how this can save you money.

Find out who is best equipped to provide computer speed and capacity for both today's needs . . . and tomorrow's.

Get all the facts, then be hard-nosed about your decision.

Don't be chicken . . .
be right.

Competitive, hard-hitting—but such obviously good advice the reader can't possibly fault Honeywell for wanting the business.

Honeywell's make-believe animals are so lifelike. The eyes of the springer spaniel seem as limpid and soft and loving, as those of a flesh-and-blood springer. Again, headline and copy are married to the illustration. They read:

Would we bite the hand that feeds us?

Not us. Not Honeywell.

We kept the user in mind when we engineered our third-generation computers. Purposely kept them less complex, easier to handle. We wanted the power you pay for to be the power you can use.

We made all eight of our Series 200 computers modular, so they're easy to expand. And compatible, so you can move to a larger model without starting over.

We took a practical, sensible approach with our software, too. Made it modular, easy to learn, easy to use.

For a very good reason: The quicker your computer pays off for you, the happier you'll be doing business with us.

We want to be known as the businessman's best friend.

Give us a whistle.

Honeywell didn't merely cast about for an illustrative idea, hit upon the sculptured components animals, despite the fact that you can almost hear the raven croak, "Nevermore."

Communications objectives of this highly creative campaign are based upon well-defined marketing objectives. Primary one is to increase Honeywell's share of the computer market. The company plans to do this by increasing its customer base, and by assisting customers to expand their use of computers by using Honeywell

Few could miss this page with this multicolored chicken and intriguing headline.

Would we bite the hand that feeds us?

Not us. Not Honeywell.

We kept the user in mind when we engineered our third-generation computers. Purposely kept them less complex, easier to handle. We wanted the power you pay for to be power you can use.

We made all eight of our Series 200 computers modular, so they're easy to expand. And compatible, so you can move to a larger model without starting over.

We took a practical, sensible approach with our software too. Made it modular, easy to learn, easy to use.

For a very good reason: The quicker your computer pays off for you, the happier you'll be doing business with us.

We want to be known as the businessman's best friend.

Give us a whistle.

Honeywell

ELECTRONIC DATA PROCESSING

Would we bite the hand that feeds us? Honeywell's answer is quite convincing.

applications packages (systems and programs) and people who can make them work.

Major communications objective is to make business management aware of the fact that Honeywell is in the computer business. More specifically, the company is now the Number 1 challenger and wants to be recognized as such.

Each ad in the campaign has a specific copy objective, as will be noted in the two pieces of copy which were quoted. The competitive situation was stressed in the "chicken" copy, for instance, and very effectively so.

All objectives are defined through research such as awareness studies and by analysis of reports and studies of the industry by publications, consultants, Honeywell marketing management, and by its agency.

Management media used for this fine campaign are selected by a computer analysis of publications according to a profile of desired management audiences, plus various surveys of management personnel to determine reading habits and preferences. Honeywell's schedule includes the following books:

U.S. News & World Report

Newsweek (Eastern and East Central regional editions)

Business Week

Fortune

Business Management

Dun's Review

Financial Executive

Armed Forces Management

In addition, technical media are used as follows:

Data Processing

Data Management

Datamation & Business Automation

Honeywell's budget is arrived at by the task method, with additional considerations being previous budgets, as well as anticipated sales.

Effectiveness of this outstanding campaign is shown by a continuing series of awareness studies begun with the first ad. Then Honeywell rated fifth, but since this campaign was kicked off has shown a dramatic rise to a strong second place in three main areas: (1) Awareness of Honeywell as a computer supplier, (2) confidence in Honeywell as a supplier, and (3) awareness of Honeywell com-

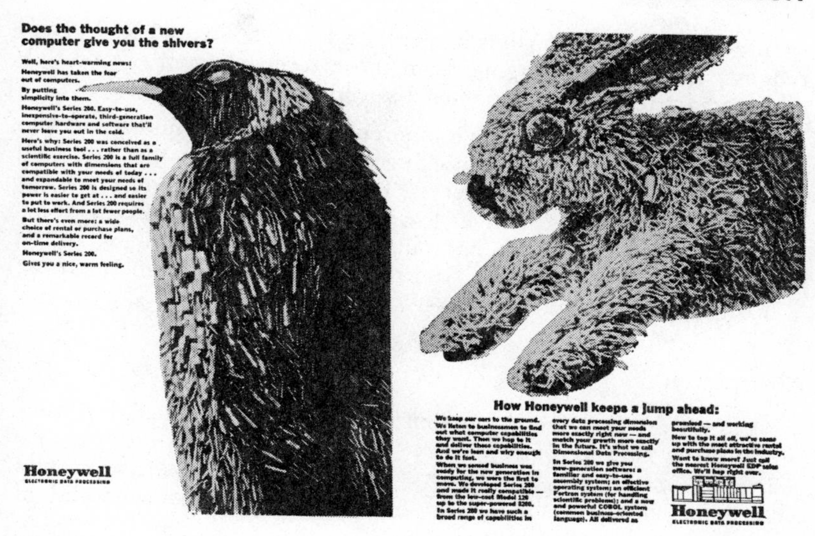

puter advertising. This has been accomplished even in the face of heavier advertising investment by at least two of the eight major computer manufacturers who compete with Honeywell.

Starch, Mills Shepard, Ad-Chart, and other readership studies show the campaign received exceptional readership. A number of the "sculpture" ads received No. 1 Noted scores in Starch reports on readership of advertisements in *Business Week*.

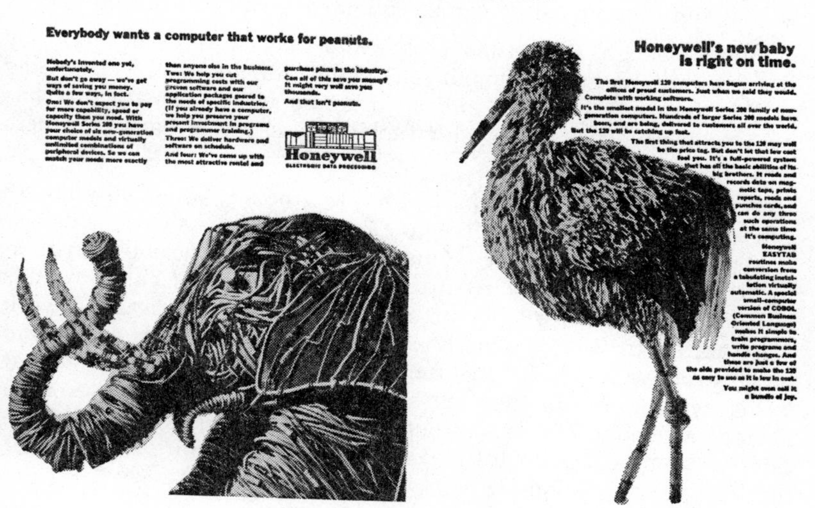

In addition, the campaign has received unprecedented kudos and requests for reprints ranging from those received from school children and art teachers to top executives in major corporations.

These illustrations have high inherent interest—the intangible that every advertising manager is seeking and too seldom finds. The land of make-believe is usually reserved for the special enjoyment of the very young, who have not yet learned to deprive themselves of its pleasures. Honeywell's ads have universal appeal to all ages, in the business world and out of it. And this campaign is still going strong in 1976, many years after it first saw print.

Abstraction

Abstract art in advertising illustration is not complex, but very simple. It is nothing more nor less than a device the advertiser has embraced to capture the reader's attention. The abstraction was created for an agreed-upon price by a commercial artist who had an assignment with a deadline.

There are those who won't take kindly to this. They prefer to regard an abstraction in different terms. They believe, or profess to believe, one of two things: (1) That the advertiser has, for altruistic and humanitarian reasons known only to himself, included in the abstraction a hidden message of tremendous significance, or (2) unknown to the advertiser, a struggling genius, unrecognized and unknown, has incorporated a profound meaning into the abstraction so that suffering humanity can be enlightened and enthralled.

Oddly, though, this visual Holy Grail may be discerned only by the truly discerning. Although remarkably few of us are discerning to this degree, the ability to read meaning into an abstraction has nothing whatsoever to do with snobbishness. Some have it, others don't. It's that simple.

To digress for a moment, some people—the author actually knows a few—even claim to be perceptive enough and sensitive enough to read something (they don't say just *what*) into the Picasso monstrosity that clutters up the courtyard of Chicago's Civic Center. At this writing it is unknown whether or not the welds of Picasso's work were tested by the Magnaflux process or some other recognized nondestructive testing procedure. Good industrial practice is to test welds; whether or not Picasso's standards are as high as those on an average assembly line turning out hot water heaters is open to question. It would seem doubtful. You do have to admire a put-on of that magnitude, though!

chemical attraction

Attracting people with vigorous imagination is the powerful force in our continuing successful growth as a chemical company.

So we search for exceptional people. Provide a climate in which ideas are nurtured. Shared. Rewarded. We charge them with responsibility for their professional growth. And ours.

They've made us the foremost producer of acetic acid and formaldehyde. A world-wide supplier of basic bulk chemicals. Plus some very specialized ones.

We combine their technical contributions with constantly expanding physical resources. New equipment, machines, technologies. This combination makes it possible to improve market service in existing product lines and to explore new areas of chemistry. So we can serve the markets of the future.

Our search has produced sound, practical results. Exceptional people. Products. Profits. Which means exceptionally fine service to all of our customers. Celanese Chemical Company, 522 Fifth Avenue, New York, 10036.

Celanese®

An abstraction can have grace and charm and it can have force and vigor. Feeling in the headline and copy can be reflected by movement of lines of force and mobile representational masses that capture the dynamics of the message.

Celanese Chemical Company has a well-known and well-read campaign running in management publications based on highly impressionistic abstract art. An example of this four-color bleed campaign that appeared in *Business Week* is shown nearby.

Objectives of this campaign are:

1. To project the image of Celanese as a modern, progressive, well-run company whose future growth is inevitable.
2. Increase favorable awareness of Celanese as one of the major bulk chemical producers, with strong production technology, modern manufacturing facilities, and a highly skilled, experienced sales force.
3. Portray Celanese as a good place to work, in terms of its dynamic growth and forward-looking personnel policies.
4. Increase awareness of specific products, and their advantages.
5. Continue to stress the broad line of bulk chemicals not available from Celanese.
6. Strengthen Celanese's reputation for R&D capabilities.

These are all legitimate communications objectives, of course, and well within the ability of advertising to deliver.

That Celanese uses abstractions and impressionistic art effectively is beyond question. Celanese ads have consistently been in the top sixth in Starch readership surveys. Bench-mark studies and followup surveys have shown that the company's audience has increased by about 10 percent in its recognition of Celanese as an entity of the sort defined by the company's objectives.

What's more, the company has experienced a large and unforeseen demand for reprints of the abstract illustrations. Requests came in in such quantity that Celanese couldn't supply ad reprints to each inquirer; also, an ad was hardly the right thing to send to an inquirer. He'd already seen it.

So Celanese had a black-and-white merchandiser printed; it served to recap the advertisements and illustrations, with legible copy. Also, an explanation of the rationale behind use of the abstractions was given on the inside fold. It explained:

The art of managing and integrating the scientific disciplines of marketing and technology is the core of our operation at Celanese. It has continuously generated our progress. It still does. It always will.

In seeking appropriate graphics to communicate the essentials of our philosophy no ordinary form would do. The search by-passed the commonplace and moved toward the experimental . . . the bold.

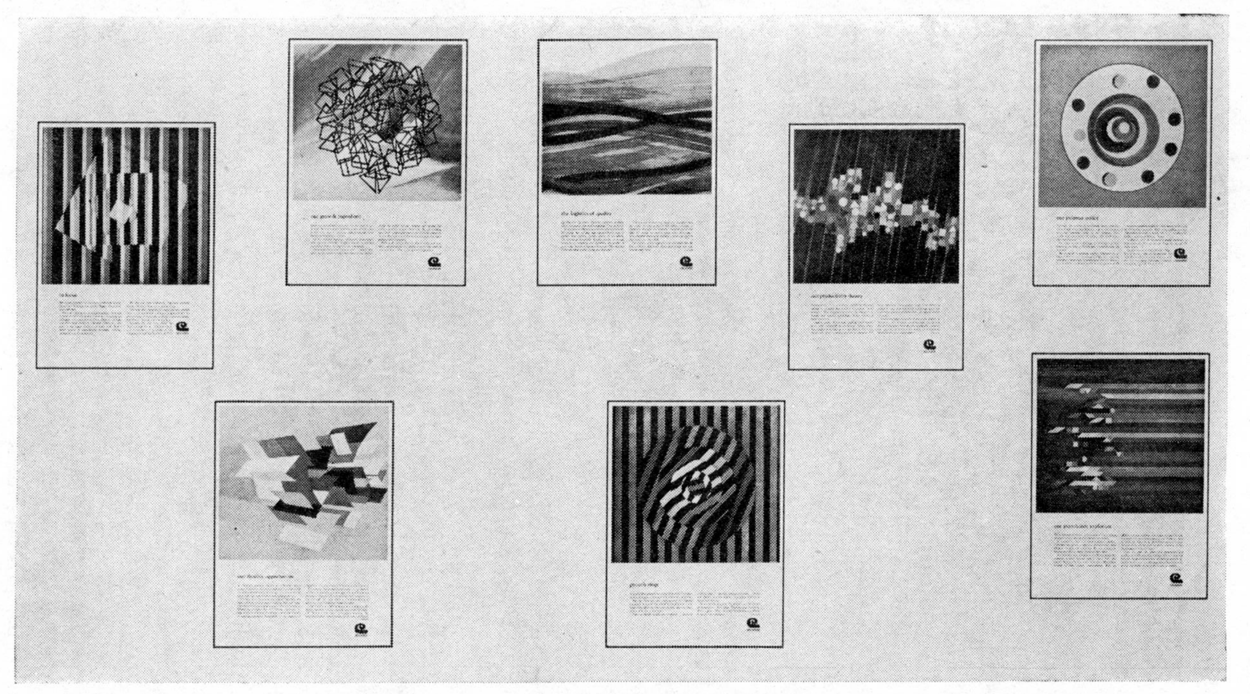

This is the merchandiser Celanese Chemical used to display and offer reprints of its abstract ad art.

> *Abstractions were developed to symbolize dramatically, the interdependence of our creativity and science. The result: Variations within a geometric theme that consistently states our belief in disciplined freedom.*
>
> *Gallery prints of these abstractions are herewith presented along with reproductions of the advertisements in which they were used. We hope they will be of aesthetic as well as practical interest to you.*

The merchandiser and eight four-color reproductions of the abstract art, on heavy paper and suitable for framing, were mailed to the inquirer in a neat double-pocket folder.

If you have precise objectives, abstract illustrations will deliver a well-defined audience. And if you don't have precise objectives, why don't you?

Rebus

The rebus ad is an advertisement using a particular illustrative technique, but it's also using a particular layout technique. Many seasoned ad men don't or can't differentiate between the two and tend to use the name "rebus" interchangeably; actually, there's no reason why they shouldn't.

A rebus ad is an ad that usually has fairly long copy. Instead of the type's being set solid, however, or set solid and broken up with subheads, the rebus ad has the copy opened up with small line drawings, or, less often, with half-tones. It makes for a highly effective advertisement, one that has much to recommend it.

Readership studies show the average rebus ad, if it's well written and thoughtfully illustrated, frequently gets as much as 40 percent more readership than a conventional ad with one or more illustrations. Explanation for this attractiveness of the rebus ad to the reader is just that—it is attractive to him.

The small illustrations open the ad up. It is inviting to the eye. There's a fresh feeling, as if something nice were about to happen. The copy looks shorter than it actually is, and it looks easy to read. The small illustrations make it look as if they were carefully chosen. Small illustrations—often anywhere from six to 12 or even more in a one-page advertisement—add a sense of drama to the ad. They provide continuity and act as an incentive to the reader to continue reading all the way to the end of the copy. The reader tends to think of the rebus advertisement as a related series of events in type,

The beginning of a Sherwin-Williams finish.

When you ask us for a finish, the finish we come up with is THE finish.

And here's how we reach the finish.

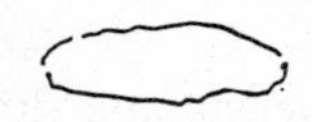

You call us in and ask us about an acrylic or vinyl or alkyd finish for your aluminum or steel product.

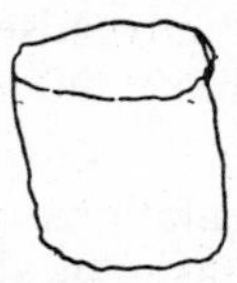

Nothing specific yet. (Some of our competitors recommend one or two finishes before they know all of your requirements.)

You tell us what characteristics you'd be willing to give up in order to gain others.

You tell us how important you think it is in your case to get exceptional formability, hardness, flexibility, pressure-marking resistance, economy of cost, etc.

For example, you might want a finish with excellent color retention more than you want a finish with excellent chemical resistance. (Common sense tells you that you can't always have everything.)

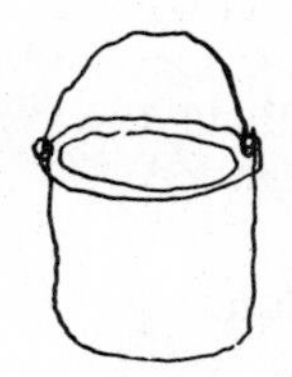

Then we recommend a vinyl plastisol or an alkyd amine or a solution vinyl or a vinyl organisol or a thermosetting acrylic or a fluorocarbon or a silicone-polyester finish.

We engineer them in any combination to satisfy any of your specific requirements.

What it comes down to is this: While we don't recommend a finish in the beginning, we do at the finish.

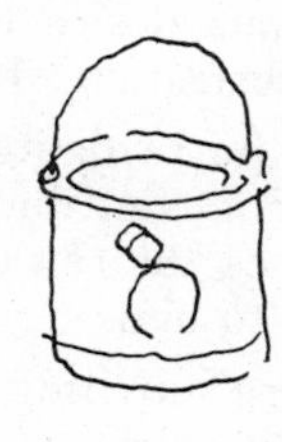

By then, we know it's the *one* finish for your product.

Now, begin. Write Chemical Coatings Division, The Sherwin-Williams Co., 101 Prospect Avenue, Cleveland, Ohio 44101.

We'll start from there.

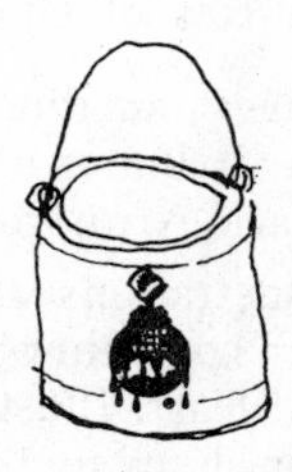

something like a picture story or a comic strip that builds toward a climax at the end. To him, stopping reading before he's completed the ad would be to deprive him of the sense of suspense the ad generates; it would be similar to turning off the television while Matt Dillon is pinned down by a fusilade of fire from a band of desperados —unthinkable.

Sherwin-Williams uses the rebus technique with a fine sense of the dramatic and with admirable restraint. Its fine ad that appeared in a metalworking magazine is shown nearby.

Copy is pithy and punchy and is supported throughout by the rebus illustrations. The illustrations themselves are deceptively simple little spot drawings, pen and ink, which heighten the feeling of action and contribute to an overall impression of something pleasurable happening.

Note that as the story unfolds, the final, complete illustration takes form. This subtle technique acts as a gentle hint to the reader that he's expected to read all of the copy, and that if he fails to do so he won't benefit from having read what he did. Everybody has a subconscious desire to see a project completed, and so it is with the line illustration of the can of paint.

As the reader gets deeper into the copy he subconsciously feels that he is contributing toward making the illustration complete. This is one of the rewards he receives here, that and information that is useful to him.

There's inviting white space aplenty, the layout is clean and simple, and the only spot of color is in Sherwin-Williams' red logo on the paint can in the lower right hand corner. The *completed illustration* shows the advertiser's logo. This is a very delicate psychological boost for the Sherwin-Williams logo and company name. It leaves a definite, positive impression about the company and its products in the reader's mind—as was intended.

Qualities of Good Illustrations

Invest an illustration that's exactly right for your advertisement with attributes of people and you should have a graphic combination of Jack Armstrong and Mr. Clean.

Illustrations are supposed to be nice-guy representations. They never bore, they never repel. They're always in good taste, or should be, at least. Illustrations are never blatant, cheap, or tawdry and they never show anything likely to offend even the most sensitive member of any ethnic or religious group—or even a stern-faced, flinty-eyed stuffed-shirt who's opposed to almost everything. To commit any of these cardinal errors is to risk alienating the reader, perhaps forever.

To be really cogent and to exert the greatest possible influence on the reader, the illustration should possess in generous measure four major qualities: Stopping power, believability, balance, and good composition.

Let's look at each one, one at a time, and see just what's involved in achieving these qualities.

Stopping Power

Some have it, some don't. Different types of illustrations have the ability, the power, to stop readers with varying interests and pull them all into the headline and body copy. Engineers, for instance, are inordinately fond of cutaways and cross sections; they also dote on charts and graphs with figures and lines substituting for words. Run an ad like that and they'll eat it up.

Whatever illustration is used in the industrial advertisement must excel in ability to cause the reader to stop, look—and then look again. It must interest him enough to cause him to read the headline. It must telegraph to him that something of more than passing interest follows, and it is in his self-interest to find out what it is. The examples we've already seen have this ability for the most part.

In industrial advertising the audience for your ads is almost exclusively male. Granted, an occasional woman may be involved in buying decisions in industry, especially if style and color are highly important. Women also exert some small bit of influence if they happen to be the wife or partner or owner of a business. Mostly, though, it's safe to ignore this tiny fraction of your universe when considering the illustration. This is not to say that you should deliberately use illustrative matter that would offend women, just that you should not choose subjects that cater to their special interests.

To stop an audience that's overwhelmingly male, you use subjects that appeal to men in the illustration, of course. Following is a list of subjects of high inherent interest to men, as a number of research studies over the years have shown. They are not necessarily listed in order of importance.

Other men
Business
Home
Sports
Outdoor life
Automobiles
Animals
Clothing (men's)
Science
Hobbies
Entertainment
Adventure
Travel
Machinery
Tools
News
Humor
Do-it-yourself
Sex

Here are a few illustrative facts of life that aren't widely recognized, judging by industrial advertisements currently running in the business press.

Crowds repel people, as far as an illustration in an ad is concerned. Your illustration has far greater appeal if you concentrate attention on one person, or a small group.

Do not, however, use an extreme closeup of one person; enlarged pores, blackheads, wrinkles and other evidences of mortality that we all have are repulsive to most people. Readers flee in droves from such illustrations.

Avoid graphic clichés—a jumble of type faces; scissors cutting a dollar bill in half to illustrate cutting costs; a piggy bank to indicate savings; illustrating the earth to denote a world of ways to do something; the model with the fatuous grin pointing to the product; a policeman scowling threateningly to indicate the reader should stop doing whatever it is he's doing that doesn't involve the advertiser's product—such as using a competitive product; and *never* show a picture of The Factory unless you're trying to sell it.

There's no disputing that the four basic necessities of man are: Shelter, food, self-preservation, and sex. Every person on earth possesses these four drives, but in varying degrees and order of importance.

Research shows that people prefer pictures of people with whom they can identify. In movies and television shows, men prefer to watch actors and women would rather watch actresses because each can identify with his own sex. Watch *Gunsmoke* some night and you'll sympathize with Kitty when she's having trouble. You'll be attracted to her as a lovely woman, but you can't identify with her for that very reason. You can identify with Matt Dillon, however, for you can project yourself into his place and share his feelings, frustrations, and aspirations.

Exactly the same thing holds true for illustrations in advertisements. In consumer advertising women exhibit an overwhelming preference for illustrations of other women. Next, they prefer illustrations of babies. Men are far down the list. Just the opposite is true for men, as would be expected. Studies show that the illustration that attracts the greatest interest is one showing another man, or a small group of men.

An illustration of a product with people in it will always out-pull one without people. Show a male audience an illustration of the product with a believable looking man in it and it is far and away the most effective technique. Most research shows approximately

Here's an engineer's magazine even your wife will love
It's the portable chart paper magazine from our new Mark 250 Strip Chart Recorder. Now you can take the record home with you, or any place for that matter! Manual turning knobs let you roll the chart forward and back. Later, you can re-record on the same chart for side-by-side comparison. Chart take-up is automatic. And you can reload the magazine in seconds. (Many users get an extra magazine . . . study one while the other is in the recorder.)
But the world's slickest chart magazine is just one of the Mark 250's great new features. Step response over the full 4½-inch span (10% to 90%) is 40 milliseconds . . . records up to 100 cps . . . flat to 10 cps full scale! Choice of 21 interchangeable preamps. Pushbutton selection of 12 chart speeds. Crisp, clear, rectilinear presentation. Patented, pressurized inking system. Owners say there's no other strip chart recorder in the same league.
Words just don't do it. You have to see a Mark 250 to understand why it's called "the first strip chart recorder for the perfectionists of the world." A call to your local Brush Sales Engineer brings a Mark 250 right to your office or lab. Go ahead. Even our wives will love you for that. Clevite Corporation, Brush Instruments Division, 37th & Perkins, Cleveland, Ohio 44114.
CLEVITE
brush INSTRUMENTS DIVISION

10 percent higher readership of an industrial ad with this type of illustration than one with the product alone.

At last we come to sex. Now, the fact is that sex appeal is definitely *not* a figment of a disordered imagination. Sex appeal is for real. Sex exists. And it *is* appealing. Furthermore, it's highly unlikely that sex will disappear, despite the blue-nosed attitude of some Puritans who oppose it as they oppose most of life's other little blessings. It's quite safe to assume that sex is here to stay, and when you use sex in an illustration you can do so secure in the knowledge you're not using something that will soon be passé.

Use sex with a deft touch—in the illustration of your industrial advertisement, that is—and you'll have an illustration with all of the tremendous impact and stopping power of "The Nailer" which Modesty Blaise uses with such devastating effectiveness.

Every red-blooded man is attracted to the movies' sex kittens; Bridgitte Bardot isn't really much of an actress, but who cares? Marilyn Monroe didn't win Oscars on the strength of her Thespian ability alone; nor did male TV addicts delight in the *Beverly Hillbillies* solely because Elly Mae endorsed blue denim by wearing jeans all of the time; and *The Great Race* is truly a hysterically funny movie, but Natalie Wood fetchingly clad only in unmentionables failed to detract one whit from it. Only the pixilated or the peculiar would want to delete *those* scenes.

Shown with taste, sex in the illustration can arouse such intense interest that it cannot fail to stop the reader and deliver him, fully charged with anticipatory interest, into the headline and body copy.

Brush Instruments Division, Clevite Corporation, used sex with impressive results in its ad from *Research/Development* magazine illustrated nearby. Think for a minute: Name three men you know under the age of 85 who can pass by that illustration without taking a second look, without reading the headline, and without proceeding into the copy. Never mind—name just *one*. This is quite obviously a situation into which the reader relishes projecting himself.

But Brush didn't just throw a little sex into the illustration promiscuously (you'll forgive use of the word). To have done so might possibly have alienated a Puritan. No, Brush did it right—note that reference in the headline to an engineer's *wife*. This takes any possible curse away from the enticing scene because the faceless gentleman is greeting his wife—not a warm-hearted secretary, friendly receptionist, or lonesome neighbor.

According to James W. Graham, marketing services manager at Brush, the rationale for the ad is that just because a man is an engineer does not mean he is isolated from human emotions and appeals. The advertiser is aware that technical journals should provide the serious editorial diet that will aid in growth and discipline of the engineer.

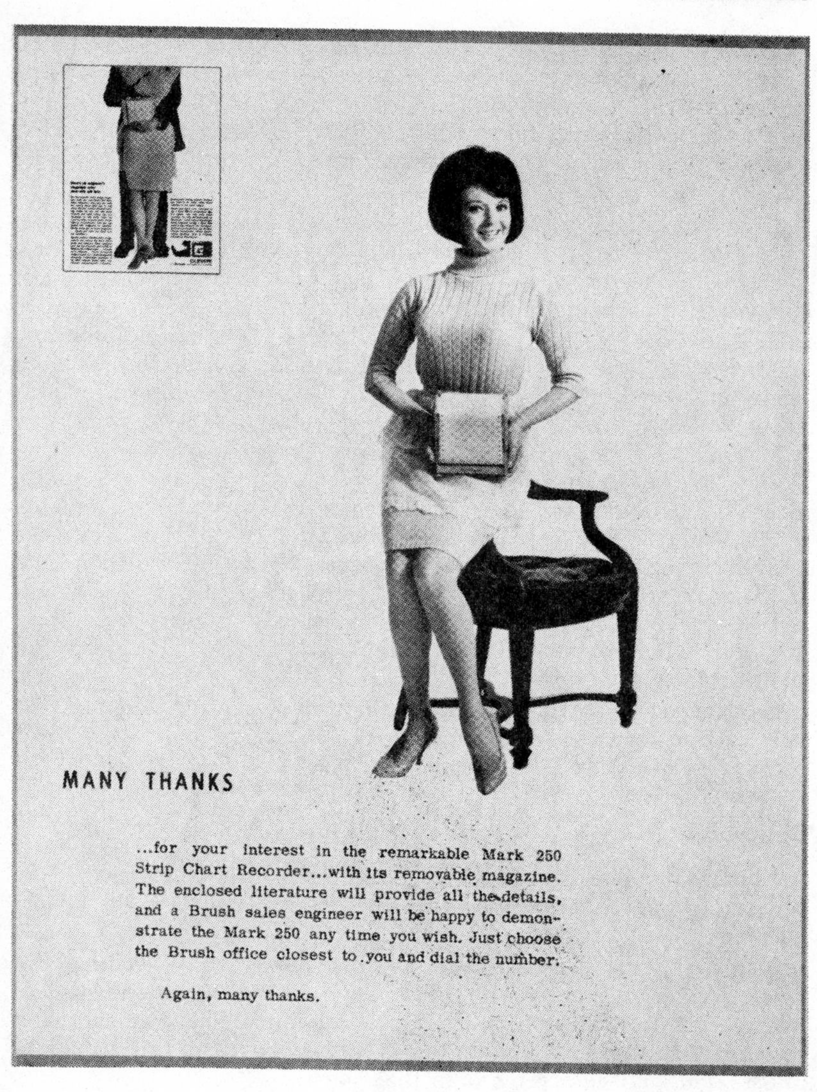

MANY THANKS
...for your interest in the remarkable Mark 250 Strip Chart Recorder...with its removable magazine. The enclosed literature will provide all the details, and a Brush sales engineer will be happy to demonstrate the Mark 250 any time you wish. Just choose the Brush office closest to you and dial the number.
Again, many thanks.

Inquiries are answered with appropriate technical material and covered with the "front view" reply piece. Brush produced this because so many letterhead inquirers asked to see the "other side" of the model. And aren't they happy they did! This is smart promotion, and the company gets the last inch of mileage out of the advertisement.

However, Brush's purpose in marketing communications is first of all to attract the reader, then educate him about Brush products, and ultimately to sell him on the idea of requesting a demonstration. The advertiser wants him and his company to know about Brush so that the doors will open a bit easier when a Brush sales engineer calls.

Communications objective is to draw attention to the company's new Mark 250 Strip Chart Recorder, and since one of the hottest features of the recorder is the highly portable chart magazine, this method of illustrating it was conceived.

The ad *did* stop readers. Its first appearance pulled several hundred inquiries. And customers came into Brush's booth at the I.E.E.E. Show in New York City *talking about the ad.* The impression this ad made lasted.

A young fighting man in the Marine Corps who "reads everything he can get his hands on" wrote from Vietnam to praise Brush's illustration and to thank the company for making his nights a little shorter. He'd gotten hold of a friend's copy of *Scientific American* in which the ad ran. Of course, he wasn't too interested in the copy, and he wasn't buying any recorders right at that moment, but his reaction proved the illustration appeals to every man from engineer to fighting man in a dark and bloody jungle halfway around the world.

Sex can do a job for you that nothing else can. It's unique in its appeal. Use restraint in illustrating it, however. Don't overplay it because a heavy hand spells ruin.

Believability

Illustration, like copy, must be believable if it is to succeed in convincing the reader of the truth of the claims made in the advertisement.

Naturally, this doesn't apply to illustrations with make-believe figures, cartoons, humorous situations, or other legitimate devices which exploit the built-in appeal of fantasy. The reader easily recognizes this type of illustration as a device used to inject interest into the ad, and he accepts it in that spirit.

But an illustration that looks phony for some reason or other will alienate the reader—and it won't waste any time in doing so. The product may be used ineptly, for example, by a professional model who has no idea what it actually is, what it's supposed to do, or how it's supposed to be used.

This situation should never exist. Part of the advertising manager's responsibility is to supervise photography or to pass on the validity of illustrative art from pencil sketch to finished art. He must weed out jarring notes. Otherwise, the illustration is stamped as staged and unrealistic. Not only does this fail to convince the reader of the truth of statements made, but it insults his intelligence. Never forget the reader may be even more familiar with the product than you are!

Or the model may be the wrong type, again grating on the reader's sensibilities. The Arrow-collar model, handsome and well groomed, would be exactly wrong seated in a heavy-duty truck cab or working with greasy hands at a machine tool. Little things—a model in improper clothing, clean fingernails on a mechanic's hands, failure to wear safety glasses or safety shoes—any one of a hundred minor details can ruin the illustration as far as believability is concerned.

So, too, can retouching if it's carried too far. Almost every photograph used as an illustration for an industrial advertisement must be retouched to some extent. Slight imperfections in the product—a ripple in the sheet metal, a rough spot on a cast housing, a dust ball in the paint, an unwanted reflection—any of these may necessitate retouching. How much retouching is done and how it's done are of great importance. A heavy-handed retouching job can make the illustration look like "boiler plate"—stark whites and jet blacks, lines so straight and well defined they're simply out of this world, surfaces so inhumanly smooth and perfect the mind immediately rejects them as impossible, tiny details overemphasized. This is retouching that shrieks "phony" in a loud, strident voice.

Some retouching is almost always called for, however, and good retouching actually improves the picture. It does so without being obvious, though. The reader never notices skillful retouching because it blends in with the picture; it's so unobtrusive and self-effacing and soft-spoken that it contributes without intruding. You always make a mistake when trying to save a dollar by buying retouching that's anything short of first class. Retouching done by a first-rate craftsman can run from $25 to $150 or more per black-and-white photograph. That's a lot of money, but compared to the $600-700 cost of producing a 7x10 black-and-white ad and the thousands of dollars in space cost to run that advertisement, retouching is insignificant. Don't try to economize there.

Believability suffers also when the general impression the illustration creates is one of doubt or skepticism. Many things can contribute to the uncomfortable feeling that something's not quite right. Props—the objects used to impart atmosphere to a picture—must be well chosen and must be exactly right, not almost right. One wrong note

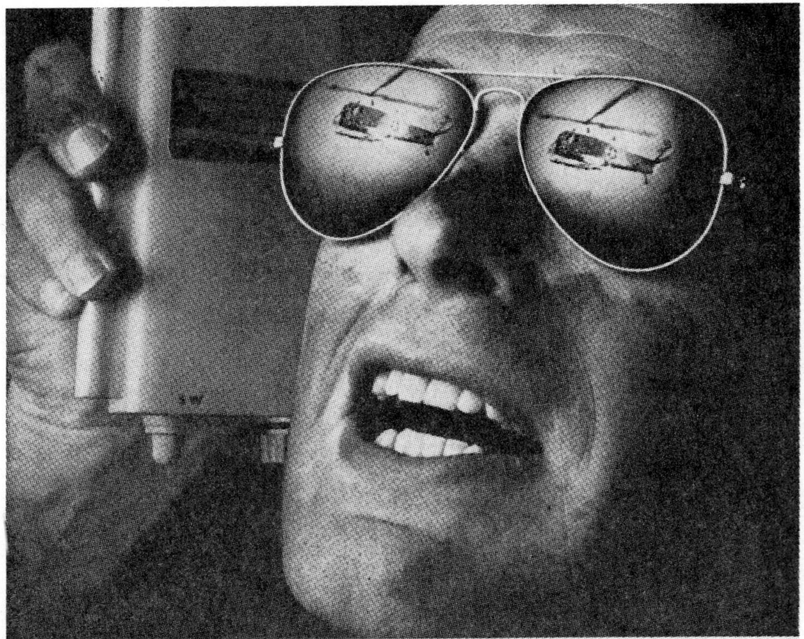

ACR Electronics needed a battery that could beam an S.O.S. signal at least 100 miles.

Mallory made it.

What can we do for you?

ACR Electronics needed a battery. A battery to power their Personnel Survival Transmitter and Light Beacon. A battery that could push a distress signal 100 miles and keep it radiating for at least 8 hours. A battery that at the same time could flash a high-intensity strobe light. Yet a battery resistant to extremes of temperature, and capable of holding its power for years.

Mallory made it. The battery—a Mallory mercury battery. It packs long-lasting power into a tiny space, keeps its voltage high even during continuous transmission. It can take temperatures from below zero to +160°F. And it has a shelf life of over 2 years.

Mallory leads the way in miniature power sources for every need. Mallory mercury batteries such as the one in the ACR rescue unit give you a maximum of energy in a minimum volume. Ounce for ounce, size for size, these batteries have more long-lasting energy than any other primary battery in their price range.

If you're considering a battery system for one of your new products, think of what Mallory can do for you. Mallory's long-lasting batteries may cost a bit more in some cases, but they pay off with reliability and built-in long life.

For more information, please write the Technical Sales Department, Mallory Battery Company, a division of P. R. Mallory & Co. Inc., South Broadway, Tarrytown, N.Y. 10591. Phone: 914-591-7000. (In Canada: Mallory Battery Company of Canada Limited, Sheridan Park, Ont.)

It's good business to do business with Mallory

there and the entire illustration collapses and is branded false by the reader. Backgrounds must be in character and contribute to the illustration as a whole. Great care must be taken to achieve 100 percent believability; 99 percent isn't close enough.

Mallory Battery Company, a division of P. R. Mallory & Co., Inc., achieved excellent believability in its dramatic photographic illustration shown nearby.

The product is a highly sophisticated miniature battery used to power the radio that beams Mayday messages from downed pilots and other members of our armed forces. Product performance must be perfect; there's no margin of error permitted because men's lives depend on this mighty little battery.

And Mallory had to achieve 100 percent believability in its illustration if the ad was to put across the product benefits to readers so they'd accept them as solid fact. The powerful close-up of the pilot speaking into his rescue transmitter, and the Army helicopter reflected in the Bausch & Lomb Ray Ban sun glasses (that prop's exactly right!) are unquestionably authentic despite having been set up in a studio 10,000 miles from Vietnam. Darkness around the pilot is natural in the jungle, just as it's natural for the chopper to be well illuminated because it's in the sunlight above the dank, dense foliage. Careful attention to details, in addition to the interesting, topical illustrative idea, resulted in an illustration with excellent believability and great stopping power.

Always strive for believability. Don't settle for less than perfection. Partial believability is as useless as none at all, something like a woman's being partially virtuous. There's little demand for half measures in a number of commodities.

Balance

This isn't a discussion of layout; that subject will be discussed in the next chapter. However, the illustration must be planned to achieve an attractive balance in order for the ad as a whole to be aesthetically pleasing.

Achieving precisely the right balance between illustration, headline, copy, logo, spot illustrations, product listings, slug lines containing names of other divisions of the company, and all of the other many sacred cows included in much industrial advertising is a delicate and fragile task.

There's much room for personal opinion, preference, prejudice, and plain old-fashioned whim. This is especially so because there's not necessarily a right or wrong, there are no hard-and-fast rules. The matter is subjective and the instances are many in which circumstances alter cases.

The fact remains, though, that most of the time the illustration should be of ample size in comparison with the rest of the advertisement so that it's quickly seen and easily interpreted. Properly it should be the dominant element in the ad—although there are any number of excellent examples in any major trade publication where this requirement has gone by the wayside. Unquestionably it is desirable that the illustration should attract the reader's eye through sheer size alone—although this is not an inflexible rule.

Most products fit well within conventional formats, so that the complete illustration in the advertisement is a square, or a horizontal or vertical rectangle. Most of the examples reproduced thus far in this book fall within one of those categories, although there is no hidebound dictum that this *must* be. Sometimes a product is of such a shape that it literally defies attempts to confine it within so-called standard formats. If such is the case, there's every reason to outline it or to have it photographed in highkey so the product "floats" with neither background nor floor visible. It can then be dropped into the available space in the ad in such a way that it is shown to best advantage.

Such a product is the micropipet advertised by Eppendorf Division, Brinkmann Instruments, Inc. in the attractive black-and-white ad from *Science* magazine shown nearby.

The micropipet is long and slender and an attempt to show it in a conventionally shaped halftone would result in an illustration that runs across the entire page but is only about an inch and one-half deep. Hardly a prepossessing format. However, Eppendorf solved the problem very nicely by having the instrument held by a hand and putting it at the side of the page in the upright position in which it is normally used. Setting the type ragged right (uneven, or unjustified, on the right) so that it follows the outline of the micropipet contributes to a feeling of action and heightens interest.

Good Composition

Getting the proper spatial relationships, showing the product so there's a good balance and the right "feel" to the ad is primarily a function of the art director at the agency, or an art studio with which the ad manager works. However, many smaller industrial advertisers use neither an agency nor a studio and it's up to the advertising manager to do all of this. Best guideline is good taste and a questioning attitude. Constantly ask yourself whether the ad looks right, whether it's appealing and attractive enough to ensure visual effectiveness.

The illustration is specified by the man who writes the ad—advertising manager, account executive, or copywriter. The writer

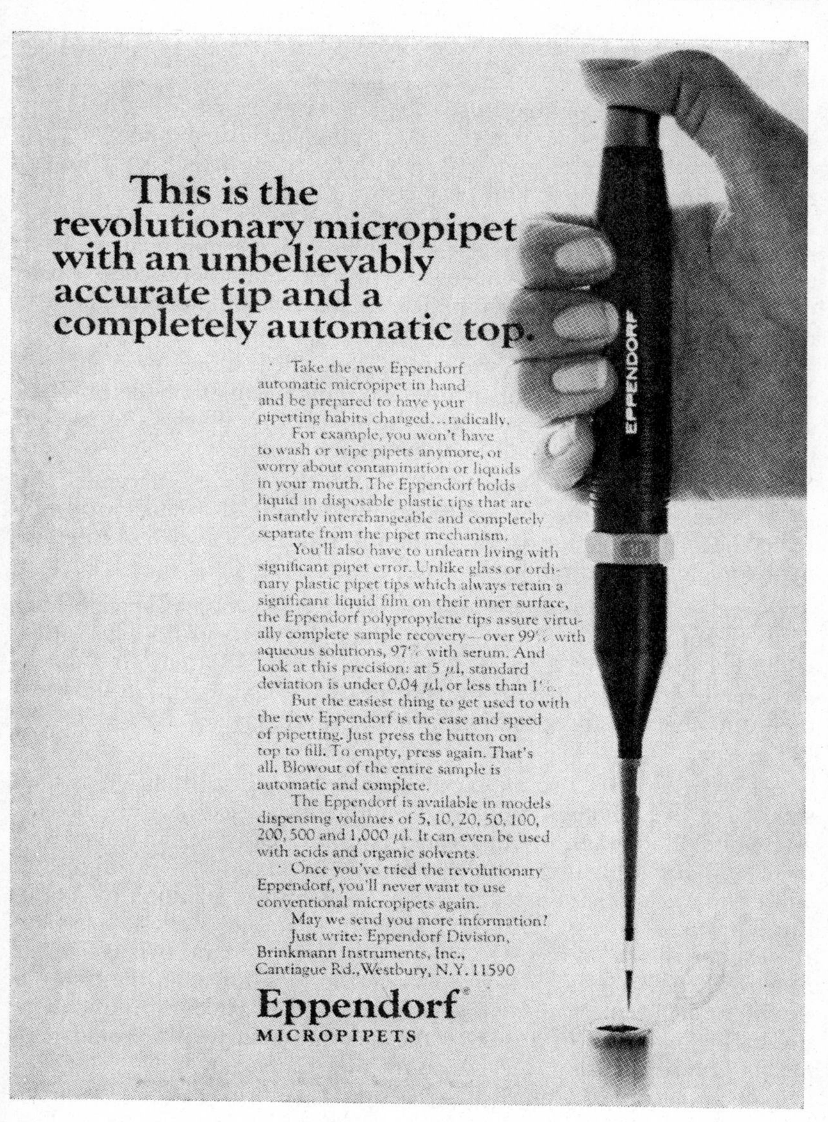

is able to visualize the complete advertisement; he can conjure up in his mind's eye the ad with the illustration properly in place, type set, and the advertiser's logo dropped neatly where it's supposed to be. The ad may not spring full-blown into mental imagery in glowing color, but assisted by a copywriter's rough or thumbnail sketch, it's there nonetheless.

Just because you're able to see the ad before it has actually taken shape doesn't necessarily mean you automatically assume an art director's title and ability, nor do you acquire an artist's or photographer's knowledge of how a picture should be composed. You should, however, be familiar with general rules of good composition so you'll be able to judge work shown to you for approval. Easiest thing to do is to select competent artists and photographers. Then part of your job will be simplified because you'll have no poorly composed work submitted for review.

Whether it's art or photography, the illustration for your ad should have a strong center of interest. This means that the product should dominate all other elements in the picture, or else the person using or operating it should be the center of interest.

A center of interest becomes dominant through its placement in the picture area. If the subject of the illustration is, for instance, far from the reader's point of view, the inference is it's of less interest than some object nearer to the reader.

An artist or photographer also punches up an object by lighting. The eye automatically is attracted to the lightest area of a black-and-white picture, particularly if it is immediately adjacent to a dark area for vivid contrast. Careful control of the lighting in an illustration can concentrate attention where the advertiser wants it—on the product.

Selective focus is also an excellent way to confine attention to one small area of a photograph. This technique was used in a fine black-and-white photograph used by Lindberg Hevi-Duty for an advertisement and for sales literature. Note that the product is razor-sharp, while the model in the background is deliberately subdued by being thrown out of focus. This and another example of how selective focus pulls the eye directly to where the advertiser wants it is shown nearby. Los Angeles photographer Jason Hailey took the second example, deliberately throwing both the immediate foreground and the background out of focus so the heart of the picture would pop out and make a strong impression on the reader.

The subject of the illustration should never be centered. If it is centered, it's perfectly symmetrical. In perfect symmetry lies boredom.

Illustrations should be composed by what photographers and artists call "the principle of thirds." This is an effective guide to good composition. The principle of thirds states that the object

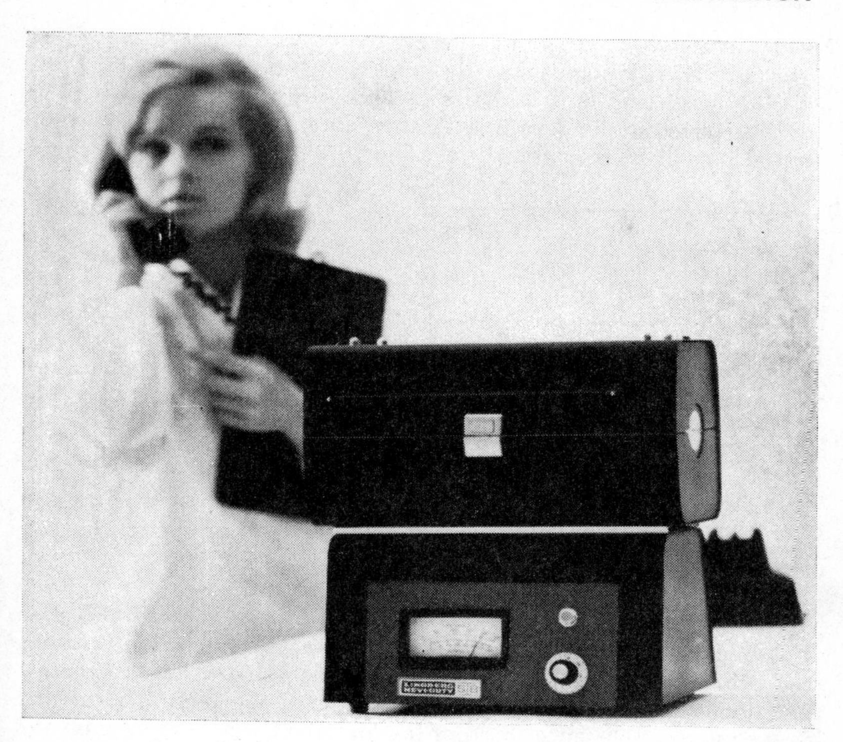

Two photographs illustrating selective focus and the use of this technique in industrial advertising. Above, the photographer focused sharply on the Lindberg Hevi-Duty instruments. This put the model in the background slightly out of focus, thus keeping her from distracting the eye from the product. At the right, the tubing and connections in the foreground were important to the ad story, therefore the background was not focused upon sharply.

which is to be the center of interest should be located in the picture area so that it is approximately on one of the interesting lines that divide the picture into thirds, both vertically and horizontally. This is illustrated in the sketch with the centers of interest shown by round dots at intersections of the lines.

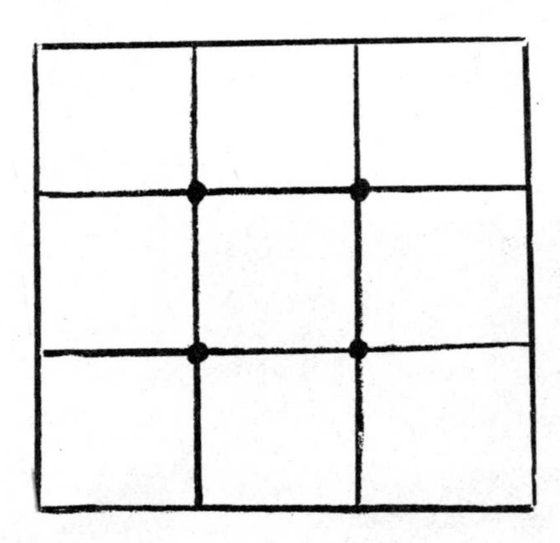

The sketch illustrates the "principle of thirds" which is found within the composition of every good illustration. A photograph on the following page also demonstrates this principle.

On the opposite page is a photo taken by the author in British Columbia, along the Athabasca River, some years ago. It illustrates the principle of thirds, for the rustic little cabin is approximately one-third of the way up from the bottom of the picture area, and about the same distance in from the left hand side. The tree on the left frames the picture, while trees on the right lead the eye to the center of interest, the cabin. The same principle applies whether the subject is a turret lathe, a putty knife, or a bulldozer.

It is *not* needless to say that an effective illustration should be free from clutter, extraneous objects, unexplained items, and other elements that do nothing except detract from the illustration. It is necessary to say this because illustrations found in a vast mass of the industrial advertisements produced today *are* cluttered—so much so they distract the eye and prevent the illustration from doing its job. Eliminate an element and you invariably strengthen the illustration. Simplicity is the keynote. If in doubt about whether or not to include something—don't. There's no need to illustrate this; look through the trade publications for your industry and see for yourself how unappealing many illustrations are simply because of this failing. And it's so useless.

There should be good contrast in the illustration. Contrast in size, distance from the reader, color if color is used, good tonal gradation in black-and-white photographs—the range of tones from

pure white to jet black—to separate the planes and the objects from each other. If, for example, a photograph was taken in black-and-white of a mechanic wearing a typical light blue work shirt, operating a milling machine that's painted a light grey, and with the control panels, the bins holding the work, and other elements painted medium green or buff, this photograph would be a confusing mass—a confusing *mess*—of middle tones. Everything would be the same dreary light gray, nothing would stand out, nothing would contrast with anything else. The picture would be devoid of inherent interest, drama, and appeal.

Although you're not expected to be either a great artist, magnificent photographer, or highly qualified art critic, use judgment—select pictures that have impact. If they have impact to you, if they're clean and free from distracting elements, if you've hired a good man to produce them for you, chances are they're more than adequate for the job.

Art or Photography?

Upwards of three-quarters of all illustrations used in industrial advertising today are photographs. Various types of art make up the balance.

The photograph excels in believability. Readers are familiar with photography, they accept it as representing the product as it actually appears, and they realize that a photograph represents reality. A photograph of an object can't be taken unless the object exists. There's no question of whether a product is under consideration, is being developed, or whether it actually has been produced. If a photograph of it is shown, that product is here and here right now. No two ways about it.

When art is used, regardless of how well done it is, how beautiful the technique, the reader is always aware that art is interpretive. The art illustration of the product or situation is the result of a man's interpretation of it, of his idea of how it should be shown to produce the effect the advertiser desires. This makes the reader *dependent* on the artist to some extent and he realizes this—and resents it subconsciously. He recognizes that he is unable to make a decision by himself about a product as it's shown because an unseen artist has injected himself into the situation. This puts the reader at a psychological disadvantage. He is aware of this disadvantage and he doesn't like it.

Despite photography's credibility and widespread acceptance, some campaigns call for art; photos would be inappropriate and they couldn't possibly produce the impact that art does. Examples will follow.

Types of Art

In the meantime, let's look at different types of art and the advantages of each.

If you've decided to use art for illustrations in your advertisements, it's necessary to be specific about the type you'll use. This includes whether the art will be interpretive, or realistic, just as there are a number of different techniques—each called a "medium." Sometimes a medium is particularly well suited for doing a specific job or type of job, as will be seen from the brief discussion of each which follows.

Oil and Acrylic Paintings

The oil painting is a heavy medium and is the old stand-by when something solid and dignified and distinguished is desired. Acrylic is very similar to oil and has the same character; however, it is somewhat more translucent than oil, enabling the artist to paint over some colors with others and still see the original color through the overlay. This is highly desirable. Acrylic paint dries very fast and doesn't stay tacky as oil does. This is a desirable quality also in an advertising illustration, which is frequently finished, then put directly into production. Because acrylic drawings dry fast, they're less likely to incur accidental damage.

In the four-color spread advertisement illustrated nearby is a striking example of a combination medium. The Great Northern locomotive was drawn by the tremendously talented Tom Fawell, West Chicago, Illinois, artist, for Electro-Motive Division, General Motors Corporation. These impressive ads run in a number of railroad publications, and in *Fortune*.

Fawell's first step is to make a pencil sketch for approval by the Marsteller Inc. agency art director; when it has been approved, reflecting any changes that are desired, a comprehensive chalk sketch in color is prepared for submission to the client and to the railroad.

Then the work begins—from 60 to 90 hours per illustration. The artist first paints the illustration in acrylic, finishing it completely in this medium, and waits for it to dry. He then paints over the acrylic paint with either tempera or casein to incorporate fine detail impossible to achieve with the heavier medium.

The original drawing is made in 20″ by 30″ size. Colors used are those of the individual railroad which is the subject of the illustration, although the artist has some leeway to change them slightly in the interest of creating a more attractive illustration if he deems it necessary.

The diesel-electric locomotive is accused by many railroad buffs of destroying the glamor and romance of railroading. They remember with fond nostalgia the day of the steam locomotive when people had time to be friendly and engineers waved at small boys alongside the tracks as they passed through sleepy little towns.

One purpose of this campaign is to restore some of that glamour and air of excitement through a colorful advertising program. Each advertisement in the campaign features a different railroad, and all are, of course, customers of General Motors' Electro-Motive Division. The original art is mounted, framed and presented to the president of the railroad. These executives are always delighted and flattered to receive the art and they hang the paintings with pride in their offices. The program has brought Electro-Motive much goodwill.

This is important because Electro-Motive has approximately 85 percent of the locomotive market. A great deal of additional penetration into the market would be difficult to achieve, but it is vitally important to the company that it retain customer goodwill and thus help retain the dominant share of the market it enjoys.

Oil and acrylic paintings are expensive, make no mistake about that, especially when they're done by top talent. However, they reflect enormous prestige and project an aura of quality that is inherent in the medium.

Tempera Painting

Tempera is a heavy, solid medium with paint of great opacity much like oil. Primary difference is that the color is mixed with water rather than oil, although it has the same body and thickness and exhibits the same characteristic brush marks and strokes as oil. Some artists dilute it so that it appears much like water color, however, when the occasion calls for it.

The average individual cannot tell the difference between thick tempera and oil. Most artists prefer tempera to oil for advertising illustrations because it dries very rapidly, speeding their work. A high percentage of advertising illustrations that the public thinks are oil paintings are actually tempera, for tempera imparts the same dignified, desirable impression of a quality illustration of a quality product that has long been associated with oil.

Tempera looks exactly like oil and will reproduce just as well, but will probably cost somewhat less because the artist can work faster.

Watercolor

Watercolor isn't seen too much any more. It has just about disappeared from the industrial advertising scene.

Watercolor has various tones when reproduced in black-and-white, of course, just as oil, acrylic, and tempera paintings do. However, the color is not laid on as thickly as with the heavier mediums and the color is weaker to start with. Fine detail is not possible with watercolor. What's more, the reader does not receive an impression of stark realism from a watercolor illustration because it is quite obviously an interpretation by an artist.

There's a place for watercolor in advertising illustration, though, because it has considerable charm and grace and appeal. To illustrate a consumer advertisement, particular for an item sold to a feminine audience, watercolor is frequently effective.

Even in industrial advertising, watercolor can be employed with telling effect if it's used by a sensitive and highly talented artist. The medium is most useful when no attempt is made at a literal rendition of a product or an object, but a stylized, individualistic approach is taken. Such is the case with the outstanding illustration used by The St. Paul Insurance Companies in its forceful one-page black-and-white ad shown nearby.

This rib-tickling illustration of an ailing computer is a delightful thing. Art is wonderfully light hearted and appealing and cannot fail to stop the reader. This outstanding illustration was painted in watercolor by the late Boris Artzybasheff. Mr. Artzybasheff will be remembered for numerous covers of *Time* magazine, all of which had a remarkably sure touch and an inspired sense of humor.

Crowning touch is the comical little angel with a bouquet of dollar signs flying to console the computer.

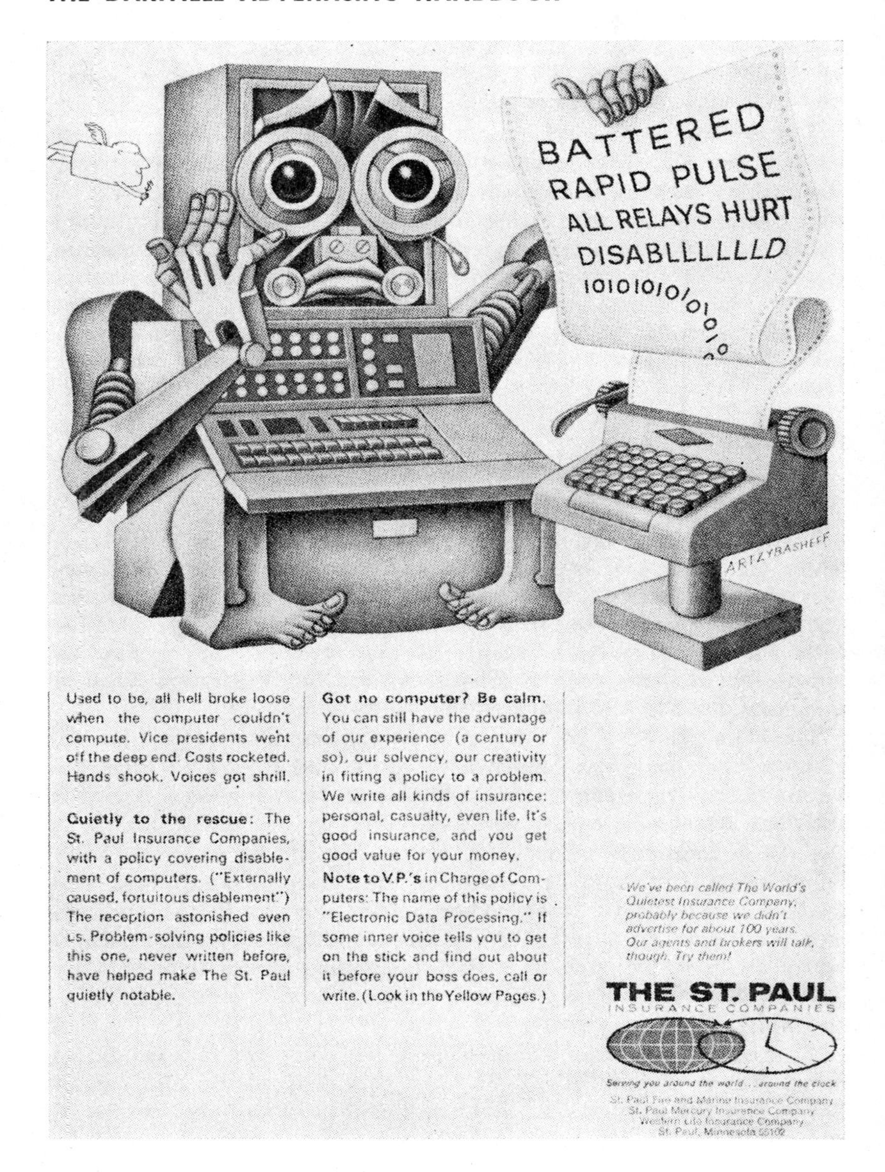

This art was produced by a master and is very close to perfection. It is brilliant in concept and in execution and performs its job in a highly workmanlike manner.

Watercolor is not especially suited for hard mechanical products as a rule, nor for scenes which show heavy masculine objects such as factory assembly lines, machinery, construction sites, or metallic parts.

Wash Drawing

Wash drawings approach quite closely the realism that distinguishes the photograph illustration, although they lack the ability to delineate fine detail.

Basically, a wash drawing is merely a painting done in one color—usually black or brown in various shades, although the color is invariably reproduced as a black-and-white illustration. Wash permits the artist to control shadings and contrast quite precisely, providing high-quality half-tone reproductions.

When an advertising manager is faced with the task of illustrating an "impossible" scene or product, often his first thought is to turn to a wash drawing. As far as the product is concerned, it might be a battery of equipment installed in a customer's plant, each piece either painted differently or marred by use so it wouldn't be at all attractive in a photograph. For a photographic illustration to be made, the equipment would have to be cleaned with a solvent to remove all of the accumulated oil, grease, and other film, then repainted so that it puts its best foot forward. All of this preparation is expensive in time and actual labor. Furthermore, it's quite possible it would result in lost production for the customer, making his approval of the project a pretty difficult thing to come by.

There's a way out, though. A good wash drawing of the product in use would be almost as realistic as a photographic illustration and the reader would accept it as depicting things as they actually are. This would solve the ad manager's problem. Even if a campaign relies on photographs for the illustrations, the wash drawing wouldn't appear too much out of place if there was no way around using it.

Dodge Trucks, a division of Chrysler Motors Corporation, uses wash drawings in its entire campaign. A typical spread ad with a wash illustration is shown on page 736.

Basic technique in this case is a posterized-graphic one to produce strong, flat shapes in wash. It is felt this style enhances the Dodge Truck "Toughness" campaign. Imparting as it does a feeling of brute strength and power, the medium is well suited for the product.

While no attempt has been made to show fine detail, the truck cab in the tilted position nonetheless shows accessibility of the

engine-transmission-radiator area so the reader is able to visualize how easy the truck is to service. The illustration projects a feeling of massiveness and strength. The "at work" illustration on the opposite page has a fine flair and feeling to it, almost photographic in quality.

Line Drawings

If you're looking for sharpness and clarity of detail, line drawings excel.

The line drawing is always done with pen and ink in stark, contrasty black and white with no shadings of grey. Line is direct and uncompromising. Each little detail is shown faithfully and literally. Emphasizing a particular part of a product or a specific feature is easily done by having the artist use broader pen strokes or by having less white space—or more white space, depending upon the object involved—between the strokes.

Drawing in line usually costs less than drawings with middle tones. Line reproduces with exquisite fidelity and line drawings are favorites of printers because of the ease with which they are handled.

Line drawings have additional appeal because of their flexibility. The line technique may be used for a relatively complicated illustration, or it may be used for a number of small spot illustrations

"One Man Gang" Materials Handling System DOES A HUNDRED JOBS
SCRAP AND SALVAGE
HOT MATERIAL AND DUST
ONE OF THE
DEMPSTER DUMPSTER
SYSTEMS
LIQUIDS
BULK REFUSE & WASTE
RAW MATERIALS
One-Man, One-Truck, DEMPSTER-DUMPSTER System STORES . . . COLLECTS . . . TRANSPORTS Material
For storage and transport of materials . . . in-plant or over the road . . . check the Dumpster containerized system. A low-investment hoisting unit mounted on a truck serves any number of a wide variety of standard or special-purpose containers.
While materials accumulate at many points in your plant, the "busy-beaver" Dempster-Dumpster works continuously picking up containers, hauling, dumping and returning "empties" . . . all without waiting for time-consuming loading or unloading. Small wonder one Dumpster outworks five conventional trucks!
Write today for a no-obligation survey by your nearby Dempster Materials Handling Consultant, or we will be happy to send a free, informative brochure.
DEMPSTER BROTHERS, Inc., Knoxville, Tenn.
Dempster Brothers, Inc. Dept. FM-11
Knoxville, Tennessee
Please send: Consultant
Brochure
Name
Title
Company
Address
City
State

A "clutch" of line illustrations.

used to show individual product features. Line illustrations may be greatly reduced in size with absolute assurance they will reproduce well and retain all of the detail the artist included.

The one-page black-and-white ad illustrated nearby was run by Dempster Brothers, Inc. in *Factory* magazine. It is a good example of effective use of simple line drawings. Illustrative material consists of a very realistic wash drawing of a truck equipped to handle the Dempster-Dumpster materials handling system, combined with line-drawing spot illustrations to point up individual features of Dempster Brothers' system and its various applications.

Line is also used for the exploded view that's used occasionally in advertisements and very frequently in instruction manuals and parts manuals. The exploded view illustrated just below is typical, and is very well done. It is the work of Russ Eales, of Eales-Attaway Art Associates, specialists in highly technical illustrations for complex mechanical and electronic equipment.

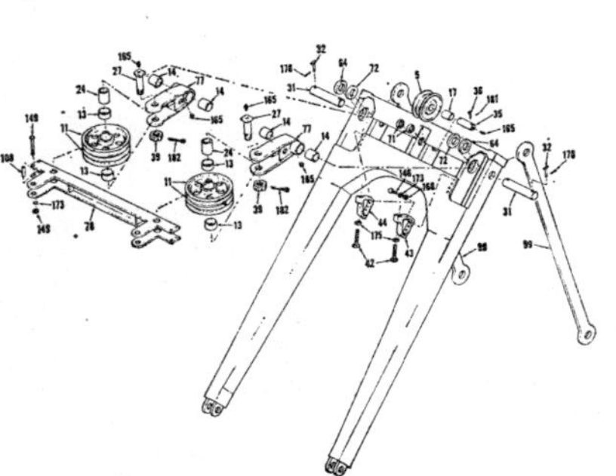

To the layman, the exploded line drawing at right is a bewildering jumble. But to the engineer it is a beautiful picture—one which he can assemble in his mind's eye.

Cost of art for an ad like Dempster Brothers' is well within the budget for the average industrial advertiser. He realizes other benefits from the art besides its use in the ad, of course, for it is equally applicable for sales literature, instruction manuals and similar uses. Too, line art doesn't date itself, so has a long life.

Pencil, Crayon, and Charcoal

Neither fish nor fowl are pencil, crayon, and charcoal. They are part way between line art with its complete absence of middle tones and the full range of tones of oil painting or photography.

Good detail may be captured with these processes, although they are chosen primarily for the freedom of expression they give the artist, and for the special impressionistic feel a skilled artist can produce.

When used in its simplest form, pencil comes very close to giving the same effect as line art in ink. The excellent humorous sketch in American Air Filter's black-and-white ad illustrated nearby shows how expressive this medium can be. This illustration combines the

Relax. You've only got two kinds of air pollution problems.

Inside and outside

AAF will help you put an end to both of them. Air pollution problems are many things to many people. A small machining operation throws oil mist and filings into the air. A battery of furnaces covers a community with smoke and fumes. The list is almost endless. But AAF's *complete* line of dust and fume control equipment assures you the best solution to any specific problem. Never any danger of trying to fit your problem to a limited product line or vice versa.

In fact, there's a good chance we've already solved many problems similar to yours. When a new puzzler pops up, AAF's unequalled experience in all types of air decontamination pays off big. Make us prove it.

First of all, get AAF's ***Dust Collector Selection Guide.*** Ask your AAF representative for a copy, or write: Robert Moore, American Air Filter Company, Incorporated, 266 Central Ave., Louisville, Kentucky 40208.

hardness of line art with the softness of pencil with appealing results. There's almost the feeling of an editorial cartoon about the clever illustration of the hard-working little sales engineer atop the tall chimney; subconsciously the reader notices this, although he doesn't stop and hang a name on the feeling he gets from the illustration. He does, however, react favorably to this type of illustration. It strikes a responsive chord because of the pleasant emotional reaction it produces.

Pencil Is a Flexible Medium

Pencil is an unusually flexible medium. Artists using it can give free rein to their imaginations and make full use of their creative ability. Using pencil, an artist can recreate history and capture the feeling and mood and air of excitement that's always present when great events are being shaped.

The illustration in the black-and-white ad run by Basic, Incorporated for its line of refractories is a case in point.

This striking series of illustrations was used in a corporate advertising campaign and for product advertising as well. *Fortune* magazine is used for the former, metalworking books for the latter.

Illustrations were done by artist Paul Calle, one of the country's leading illustrators. To produce this fine pencil illustration, the artist gave the smooth side of a piece of masonite a random thick-and-thin coating of casein. He then drew the illustration on this surface, using various hardlead pencils.

That most people are intrigued by high quality illustrations has been proven to Basic, Incorporated by this campaign, according to Arthur P. Clark, director of communications. He noted that the company doesn't have a single customer who doesn't know as much about the products as the company itself. As a consequence, Basic's advertising is largely institutional, and is designed to sell company image rather than products *per se.*

A primary objective of the corporate campaign—and the product campaign as well—is to place reminders of Basic's goodwill in the offices of customers and prospects.

Secret ingredient used to do this important job is a handsome portfolio titled "The History of Steel." The portfolios that bring such a large volume of requests are offered in a one-line picture caption in very small type below the illustrations.

Clark reported over a thousand inquiries in response to the company's first ad in *Fortune,* with subsequent ads producing a similar response. Letterhead inquiries are regularly received from top executives in companies to whom Basic wants to sell; the art prints are framed and exhibited in countless walnut-paneled offices throughout heavy industry.

If you would like a large fine art print of this illustration, please write.

First Man-made Iron

Four thousand years ago, the Egyptians produced iron in a blast furnace that was a mound of earth filled with iron ore and charcoal. Only within the last hundred years has iron, refined into steel, become the universal metal. Over half of this time, Basic has provided refractories essential to steelmaking.

BASIC
REFRACTORIES
845 HANNA BUILDING
CLEVELAND, OHIO 44115

Requests for reprints from the first ad—from *Fortune* and from the trade publications in which it appeared—totaled more than 4,000. This phenomenal response is due to three things: A striking, compelling illustrative technique; subject matter of inherent interest to the public as a whole, and to Basic's universe in particular; and a well-known company with an established position making an offer of an item of real value at no cost to the inquirer. This formula cannot be topped.

Fine art prints in the portfolio Basic offers are richly printed on a heavy, attractively textured stock, already matted with a well-proportioned border, ready to be framed.

One illustration shows an ancient artisan checking the quality of a famed Damascus blade. Steel was first produced in Hyderabad about 400 B.C., where skilled artisans combined black magnetite sand, bamboo charcoal, and the leaves of aceous plants. This charge was then sealed in a clay crucible and smelted to yield buttons of metal which were alternately melted and cooled to form two- to five-pound pieces known as wootz cakes.

This high grade steel was discovered in India by Persian merchants and carried to Damascus where armorers heated and hammered the cakes into the legendary Damascus blades. After annealing, these blades were quenched in a live slave, according to legend; the red-hot blade was thrust to its full length into the bound body of the slave so the body temperature would quickly bring the blade to the proper temperature to impart the desired metallurgical qualities. The system worked to perfection, but the rate of attrition of slaves was rather high—one blade, one slave.

Blades were then drawn to the desired hardness. Polishing and etching them then served to bring the distinctive "damask" pattern to the surface. When finished, these blades were so supple they could be bent from hilt to tip and still take a cutting edge that has never been surpassed.

Almost all of Basic's customers and prospects are aware of this fascinating bit of steel-making history, yet until now none of them has ever had access to a fine piece of art depicting it.

Crayon is frequently combined with other mediums, wash, for example. When this is done crayon still retains the vigor to enable it to reproduce with almost line-drawing strength and character. These combination drawings are often made dry, without water, with the water-soluble crayon producing an effect similar to wash when water is brushed over the completed work.

Charcoal is at its best when used for work calling for broad, full-toned illustrations in which fine detail is not desired. The medium is bold and vigorous and has a fine flair with great appeal to the masculine audience.

Neither crayon nor charcoal are used to any great extent in industrial advertising.

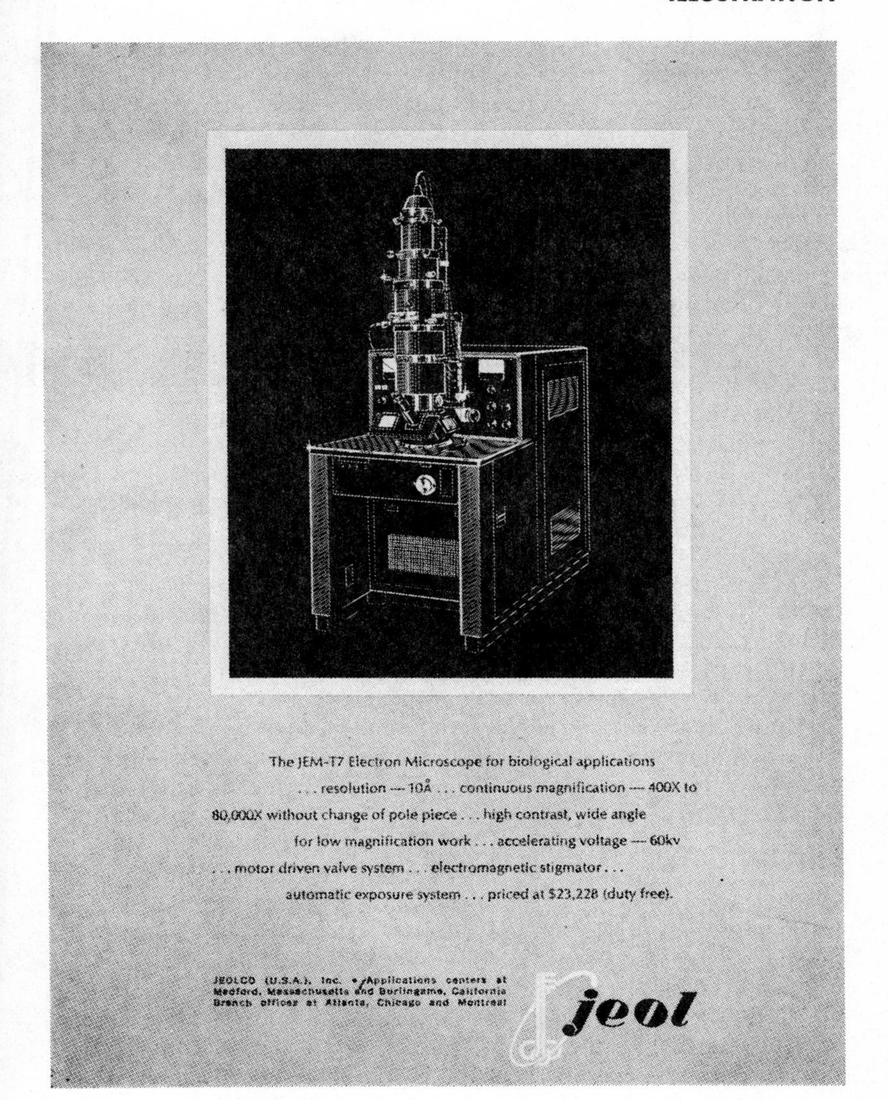

Scratchboard

This medium is a breed apart, almost unrelated to other art mediums. It is actually a modern imitation of an old white-line wood-cut. Although an artist can create a scratchboard illustration much more quickly than a wood-cut can be made, great care is required nonetheless. It is a demanding medium.

A scratchboard illustration is done with black ink on a special paper with a surface specifically made for this art form. Black ink is applied very liberally to almost the entire picture area, except for any well-defined broad masses that are to appear white in the finished illustration. The artist then uses X-acto knives, paper clips, pieces of barbed-wire fence, and an amazing assortment of scraping and etching tools to pick, scrape, gouge, and chew away the black ink. Where the ink is removed a white line or area remains—just as if the artist were making a wood engraving.

The scratchboard illustration imparts a feeling of quality to the product in the advertisement. It is so distinctive and different that readers are greatly attracted to it. Readership of ads with scratchboard illustrations is usually quite high despite the fact that the large mass of black causes some readers to regard the technique as funereal and overpowering. The fact remains that the product looks solid, substantial, and desirable.

On page 743 is an interesting one-page, black-and-white ad run by Jeolco. It has a scratchboard illustration that imparts an air of dignity and great precision to the JEM-T7 Electron Microscope the company manufactures for biological applications. The tiny, many-sided "stars" are typical of the scratchboard technique and most artists include one or more in every illustration.

A good scratchboard illustration usually runs from around $800 to $1,500, depending upon the amount of detail involved, the location, and just how busy the artist happens to be at the time he receives the commission.

Clip Art

Every once in a while you'll encounter the need for a spot illustration, possibly of an offbeat subject or one with a definite feel, possibly an old-fashioned technique. More often than not the budget is limited and doesn't contain the wherewithal to hire an artist to do the job, especially since the illustrative idea itself frequently is an afterthought dreamed up to "put more punch in the job."

Despair not. There's a solution to your problem. You *can* afford first-class professional art of excellent quality for a few cents.

The way out of your dilemma is found in books of original art produced for sale to advertisers and agencies by a number of reputable art studios around the country.

Clip art is reproduced in book form—usually loose-leaf for ease of use—on high quality enamel paper. Most advertising men actually clip it from the book with scissors and give the piece of art to the engraver, hence the name, "clip." Of course, the entire book could be sent with other material, layout, type, photos and so on, but this would entail needless extra handling of the book with possible damage or loss, and also would tie it up and make it unavailable just when you might need it again without delay.

Books of clip art, usually grouped by subject matter, are available from a studio the author can recommend as producing excellent work at a price you can't turn down. This is:

Dick Sutphen Studio
Scottsdale, Arizona 85251

This studio offers the following volumes at this time and at the following prices, although it constantly produces new art to reflect topical happenings, changing styles, and so on.

Antiques, Filigree, and Rococo	$ 8.00
The Mad Old Ads	4.95
The Wildest Old Engravings and Illustrations	10.00
Uncensored Situations	10.00
Old Engravings and Illustrations. Volume One: *People*	10.00
Old Engravings and Illustrations. Volume Two: *Things*	10.00
The Cartoon Clip Book	20.00

Dick Sutphen Studio prefers check with order, or a company purchase order; orders with payment enclosed are shipped prepaid within *four hours* of receipt of order, well packed, via Special 4th Class Book Rate unless otherwise specified. Any other form of shipping will be charged to the buyer; average weight of one book is 2½ pounds.

Let's take a more detailed look at some of Sutphen's books to see what's in them.

In *Antiques, Filigree, and Rococo,* there are hundreds of beautifully executed steel engravings. The subjects are almost limitless, and include antiques of all kinds, frames, tapestries, mosaics, lacework, borders, plaques, trophies, ornamental ironwork, and so on. Pages of the book are printed on 80-pound matte-finished enamel to assure the very finest reproduction possible. The book comes to you in a vinyl-covered ring-bound notebook. Pages are easily removed or clipped.

Volume One: People contains, in part, the following:

People in routine situations from colonial times to 1907, in period dress.

People in wild situations.

Artists.

Cowboys and Indians.

Military, Revolutionary War through the Civil War.

Foreign military.

Farming.

Sculpture, including the world's most famous sculpture.

Ancient times, people and situations.

Medieval times, knights and heraldry, costumes and situations.

Religion, from Christ's birth through the crucifixion.

Famous people.

Anatomy.

Volume Two: Things contains the following:

Architecture from ancient times to 1907, incuding world-famous architecture, old castles, street scenes, and interiors from prison cells and opera houses.

Furniture and room settings.

Mechanical things.

Nature, including landscapes, storms, flowers, and plants.

Transportation, balloons, boats, trains, and so on.

Horse-drawn vehicles.

Military weapons large and small, including naval battle scenes.

Animals including birds, fish, and insects.

Miscellaneous including money, commercial props, household items, and so on.

THE CARTOON CLIP BOOK	46

These two volumes from Sutphen add to rather than "me too" the existing books of this kind. There's no need to request permission to reproduce any of the illustrations. All of them are yours to use as you see fit without permission or payment to anybody.

Since Sutphen has grouped art by subjects and titles, you can purchase only what you need at the time; there's no need to make a major investment in art that's inapplicable to your product or needs. And considering that you get hundreds of pieces of art all ready for the camera and that each can be reproduced as often as you wish, the art is the best buy you're likely to encounter in years.

Incidentally, the author has never met any of the Sutphens, has no interest in the studio and no ax to grind; this isn't a "plug" but is recognition of good art at a price that's really right.

Typical art is shown nearby. While representative, so you can see the fine touch and good quality, subject matter of the book is tremendously varied and even includes some clip letters to enable you to produce distinctive display-type messages right at your desk.

But it's in *Uncensored Situations* you will find everything from hysterically funny old engravings and illustrations to some that are downright morbid. A few are shown that are typical of the 191-page book.

Shown is a duke's mixture to give an indication of the fantastic material you'll find in this unique book. There's no copyright on any of the illustrations; you can use them as you see fit. The volume is a worthwhile addition to the advertising department's library and will pay for itself many times over.

Typical scenes from Uncensored Situations.

More gems from
Uncensored Situations.

Photography

There's probably no product or process in existence that has been perfected to the point where there's absolutely no room for improvement. Everything changes and usually for the better. Technology is in a constant state of flux. New products, new developments, and better ways of doing things are introduced so often in so many highly specialized fields that even the technical man in industry has a difficult task confronting him if he's to keep current about advances in his own discipline.

Photography is no exception. Comparing J. M. Daguerre's tintypes to today's fantastically fast films—both black-and-white and color—is much like discussing the Wright Brothers' venture at Kitty Hawk in the same breath with a moon probe, complete with soft landing and thousands of pictures flashed back to earth across a quarter-million miles of cold, black, empty space.

Photography has not been perfected in the sense that it is static. Just the opposite is true, for the art—and it *is* an art just as much, if not more, than it is a craft—is constantly updated and improved with a flow of radical new tools, materials, and techniques from the laboratories of Kodak, Du Pont, and General Analine & Film to broaden photography's scope.

Today, photographers routinely take outstanding pictures of what were, just a few years ago, "unphotographable" subjects. They do so under conditions that previously would have caused them to throw up their hands in abject despair. Film speeds make possible high speed action shots, even in color, under existing light conditions that would have tried photographers' souls a decade ago. And extremely fast stop-action stroboscopic photographs of bullets in midair, blades of a turbine spinning at 10,000 rpm, and laboratory experiments that cannot even be seen with the naked eye are now commonplace.

Only photography can capture and show minute detail so crisply and sharply and clearly that the reader needs no explanation of what he's seeing—such as this picture of an exquisite, graceful old flintlock, bullet pouch and powder horn hanging on square nails on a wall of an old log cabin. This photograph was taken by the author in color for a magazine cover, and was also shot in black-and-white at the same time. Notice the texture of the logs and clay "chinking"; only photography can show this. And only photography can faithfully reproduce thousands of individual items in one picture, each of which stands out separately and distinctly, whether it's a photomicrograph of the molecular structure of a cell or the structure of a basic metal enlarged 600 times.

At right, an ordinary camera catches every detail of the flintlock musket and fittings on the grained walls of a log cabin. Below, a photomicrograph reveals the molecular structure of a basic metal—image enlarged 600 times.

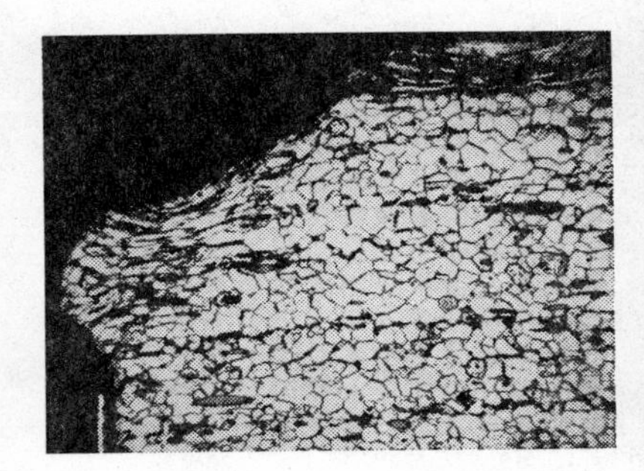

What's more, photography stands alone when it comes to carrying conviction. Readers, most of whom are snapshot artists, know from their own personal experience that a photograph shows something just as it appears to the eye.

Only photography can record faithfully the serene beauty and the clean sparkle of fresh snow under a brilliant blue sky at 11,000 feet, as in the photo on the next page. Here, photography captured every tiny detail of this magnificent panorama high atop the Beartooth Plateau, right down to each tiny tree far below on the shores of this lost lake. Photography reveals the texture and the subtle shades of different strata of the rock; the vivid realism of photography projects you right into the scene. The author took this photograph one cold day in mid-July.

Illustrations such as this are reader stoppers because everybody is interested in beautiful scenery; borrowing interest from nature herself can lead to an effective illustration for an industrial advertisement.

Photographs have the capability of imparting credibility, believability, to the illustration. There's a sense of reality and immediacy about a photograph that is lacking in other mediums. The photo is factual and literal and it instills confidence in the reader. He accepts the product that's shown photographically and automatically transfers some of this belief and trust to its manufacturer. It's difficult to attach a price tag to this.

The camera is a tremendously flexible tool. A really good photog-

rapher is more artist than craftsman, more illustrator than technician. He's incredibly versatile. From his camera comes everything from an extremely literal picture of the product alone, stark in its simplicity, to highly imaginative interpretive scenes from history, recreated and staged to perfection. Thus the camera which uses tiny fractions of seconds as *its* tool can also ignore time—even hundreds or thousands of years of it, at will.

Range and scope of the camera almost stagger the mind, for it can be dramatically incisive and cut right to the heart of the matter by excluding all extraneous detail, or it can generalize and capture breathtaking panoramas that encompass an entire mountain range, or, in the case of a camera carried into orbit, tens of thousands of square miles of the earth's surface—or even an entire galaxy in the heavens.

In the right hands the camera has no limitations.

A Better Selling Job

Furthermore, photography excels in the one most important function of an advertising illustration: *It outpulls and outsells art, any type of art.*

Photography delivers more readers to an advertisement than art does. Each reader tends to examine the photographic illustration at greater length and with greater interest than he would if it were art. This has been proven in study after study, as well as by hundreds of individual advertisers who used two illustrative techniques for the same ad—a photograph, and the same scene exactly but shown with art. Then, by split-running the ads in the same publication, they were able to determine *exactly* how much readership each received, and how many inquiries each technique produced.

This takes all of the guesswork out of the subject and makes it easy to arrive at an objective evaluation of the two mediums. Split runs, which will be discussed at greater length in the media chapter, are merely regional editions of publications; advertisers are permitted to use different plates (different ads, that is) in various editions for a very modest extra charge. This enables them to run two ads simultaneously over the same quality circulation list for test purposes, and to present different messages to different segments of the total market.

Greatest difference in readership of ads with photographs as compared with ads with artwork illustrations is reported by McGraw-Hill's Laboratory of Advertising Performance. According to LAP, "less realistic illustrations" produced an average Reader Feedback Score of 8 percent, whereas ads for the same product, manufactured by the same company, scored 16 percent when the illustration was a photograph of the product. Exactly double. That's quite a difference.

Over the years, advertisements that the author has produced for clients and companies have consistently scored higher readership ratings when photographs were used for illustrations. There have been exceptions, but these were rare. In instances when artwork produced higher readership it was due primarily to greater inherent appeal of the product, as well as to an almost unlimited art budget which made it possible to buy the work of top-flight illustrators.

Black-and-White Photography

Photography divides itself neatly and simply into two classes—black-and-white and color. Each will be discussed separately, black-and-white first because it's used more often.

When you have black-and-white photography taken of a product, the product you receive from the photographer is the familiar black-and-white print, usually an 8- by 10-inch glossy. And it *is* called a print, not a picture. A picture is what is shown in the print—a product, scene, building, or person.

The print is merely a piece of paper, coated on one side with an emulsion which contains light-sensitive particles of silver. In the single-weight glossy you'll encounter most frequently, the sheet of photographic paper costs the photographer approximately 10 cents, depending upon the quantity in which he buys. Yet he may well charge you anywhere from $10 to a thousand dollars or more for extremely complicated pictures; more on this later.

Naturally, the difference between the cost of the piece of paper and the finished product which will be used to illustrate your advertisement represents the photographer's cost of doing business—his equipment, transportation, rented or purchased props, model fees, his know-how, and his salary. Some photographers have been known to consider this last item one of the most important, but there are crass, commercial types wherever one goes these days.

This glossy black-and-white print didn't spring full-blown from the photographer's mind, nor did it come directly from his camera. As a rule a great deal of hard, exacting, and highly technical work precedes this last step in the photographic process. The photographer, with anything from one to a small army of assistants, makes a setup—that is, he stages the photograph to be taken. A fantastic amount of care and attention to minute detail is called for. Nothing is overlooked. Nothing *can* be overlooked, for the camera lens is all-seeing and reveals any mistakes that have been made with pitiless exactness. The lens is ruthless. Setups may involve anything from a room setting to a grand ballroom full of people dressed in formal attire, or 50,000 flashbulbs strung on wires around a mile-long curve in a railroad track in the mountains to be fired just before a train comes. Or it may be a relatively simple arrangement of lights used to photograph small objects in a studio.

The product itself is combed, curried, brushed, polished, washed, painted, touched up, coated with dulling spray or what have you; highlights are either reinforced artificially, or are knocked down depending upon the circumstances. Unwanted reflections or shadows are killed. If the photograph is taken in the studio, rather than out of doors, giant floodlights and spotlights are arranged with incredible precision to light the product to best effect. This in itself may require hours or even days of a photographer's time and that of assistants. And even before the set is lighted it may have to be built specifically for this one photograph.

Then, once the entire scene is lighted to perfection and there are no stray highlights or unwanted shadows, no flare or glare, the photographer at last puts film in his camera and shoots the picture.

He exposes the black-and-white film to light through the lens for a carefully determined length of time, usually a fraction of a second, timed with great precision by the camera's shutter.

Film is then processed in a darkroom through developer, shortstop, and fixer before it becomes a negative. Following an hour's washing in vigorously running water, the negative reveals the picture in various tones of gray ranging from a pure black to a clear white, exactly opposite the way the tones appear in brightness to the eye.

Final step in the process is the easiest—that of making the print from the negative. This negative is printed either by direct contact with the paper if it's a large negative, or by projection—enlargement of the image through a lens—if the negative is small.

Glossy Prints Preferred

You'll find it's usually best to get a glossy print from which to reproduce. This is a print that has been dried, after the fixer is washed out, with the face of the print in contact with either a ferrotype tin or a highly polished drum of a gas-heated or electric print dryer. This leaves a coat of gloss on the dried photographic print.

Photoengravers who make the plates from which printing presses produce magazines prefer the glossy print for illustrations, although this is probably due mostly to habit of long standing. If much retouching is to be done on the print an engraving of equally good quality may be made from Kodak Illustrators' papers—Illustrators' Azo for contact prints, or Illustrators' Special for enlargements. These papers are identical except for the difference in emulsion speed (sensitivity to light) necessary to make them suitable for the two different printing methods. Illustrators' paper has a fine-grained luster surface that is ideal for retouching or other art work; it is preferred by retouchers for its superior tooth. They can, however, work equally well with glossy paper simply by rubbing it with lava stone or other mild abrasive to give it tooth so the retouching colors will adhere.

Contrast in black-and-white photography may easily be varied considerably by the film that's used, for the slower films with fine grain are inherently contrastier than high speed films. In addition, use of specific emulsions on photographic paper permit the photographer to control contrast further.

Paper contrast is determined by the grade number of paper used. It ranges from very soft, Number 1, to extremely contrasty, Number 5. By matching the paper contrast grade to the tonal gradations of the negative, the photographer can produce a print of normal contrast despite any minor shortcomings in the negative.

Even greater control is provided by Du Pont Varigam paper, and by Kodak Polycontrast. Both are very similar in that contrast is controlled by various filters which change the color temperature of the light source, allowing only the desired color of light to reach the emulsion. A skilled craftsman can even use two or three different contrasts on the same piece of paper, in the same print. Possibilities for control and for producing special effects are endless.

Occasionally the "wrong" contrast paper is deliberately used to produce a desired special effect; in posterization, for example, the photographer may be instructed to produce extreme contrast in the negative by using a "hard" developer on a hard or contrasty film. Overdevelopment builds up what is normally considered excessive contrast very quickly. Then when the negative is printed on a hard, contrasty paper, a picture is produced with almost no middle tones between a stark white and a jet black. This procedure frequently results in highly daring, dramatic illustrations, although it's largely impressionistic and designed to attract attention rather than depicting the product or scene faithfully. No fine detail is shown, of course.

Black-and-white photography has much going for it. To start with, black-and-white film is fast, fiendishly so, some of it. Speed of b/w film—as it's frequently abbreviated—ranges from around 25 to as high as 1,000 on a scale established by the American Standards Association. This matters little to you as an advertising man, except that availability of film to your photographer that's so fast it can do a workmanlike job under extremely adverse lighting conditions is something to keep in the back of your mind.

Resolution, the ability of a film to record extremely fine detail, decreases as film speed increases. There's no getting something for nothing, even in photographic processes. As a rule, you'll probably want to discuss resolution with your photographer; highest possible resolution, consistent with sufficient film speed to do your work, is always desirable. Along with high resolution goes fine grain, which means the silver particles in the film emulsion do not clump together in large grains, thus impinging on peak resolution and sharpness. When you get the best resolution, fine grain automatically accompanies it.

Instruct your photographer about permanence. Most commercial and illustrative photographers worth their salt "fix" photographic prints so they're as permanent as the paper they're printed on, and this is measured in generations. However, some volume workers cut corners and make prints designed to last a few months, or a few years at best. Talk this over with him and give instructions that your prints are to be made for posterity. Cost is the same to you, a few extra minutes in the hypo bath and wash water is all that's required of the photographer.

Getting the "Feeling" You Want

Black-and-white photography is a rich and versatile medium.

The range of middle tones between white on the one hand and black on the other is long and varied and interesting. Tonal gradation reveals and enhances every subtle nuance of difference in color, shape, form, and texture of your product. A b/w photograph taken by a sensitive photographer is mellow and deep and expressive and it can interpret a mood or a feeling, or it can be brutally frank and as literal as an engineering drawing or a bill of materials.

You can get *exactly* the feeling you want in a photograph if you make it crystal clear to the photographer *exactly* what it is you're looking for. Most photographs that are unsatisfactory for their intended purpose aren't suitable because the advertising man did something less than a satisfactory job of issuing instructions. When working through an agency art director this hazard is avoided because art directors and photographers speak each other's special language.

The black-and-white photograph is easily retouched, which helps you hold production costs down. Usual method is for a retouch artist to use an airbrush, smoothing out rough spots, "repainting" the product where paint has been scraped or gouged, removing extra highlights, lightening shadows, removing an unwanted background, "sweeping" the floor or asphalt parking lot or removing a skid from under the product, or picking up trash from an outdoor scene. In this way telephone poles, unwanted people, cars, or whatever else that's unsightly can be deleted.

There's almost no end to the cleanup work a good retoucher can do. A good rule of thumb, though, is that you're better off with the least possible retouching; an over-retouched photograph is said to have a "boiler-plate" appearance, meaning it looks painted and artificial.

Cost of retouching can run from $25 or $35 on up to $400 or $500, depending upon the complexity of the job, how fast you push the artist to get it done, and what he thinks the traffic will bear. The law of supply and demand applies here, too.

Photographic negatives remain the property of the photographer unless this matter has been discussed and agreed upon to the contrary. Although negatives remain in his possession, you're naturally at liberty to order additional prints at any time. Price is usually nominal. When a photographer surrenders negatives to you, it is customary for him to add on a modest extra charge for each negative, called a surrender fee; often, though, when the customer is from another city a photographer automatically gives him the negatives along with the first prints at no extra charge.

Negatives should be handled with extreme care. They are easily damaged on both the fragile emulsion (dull) side, as well as on the backing (shiny) side. Best practice is to file them in heavy kraft negative envelopes made for this purpose; they're special and have a special glue that doesn't bleed through the paper and damage negatives in this way. Write the date, subject, photographer's name, name of customer who owns the equipment shown, his address, and other data on the envelope.

Facts like this can easily slip your mind, and a year or two later you can find it embarrassing. File by a negative number, cross-indexing with a permanent photograph book of the three-ring binder type with glassine pages containing a print, or file by model number of product, date, or some other system. Whatever system you use, stick with it. Don't jump from one system to another. And write down the system you use in the book of photographs so that when you're on vacation other people looking for a photo won't be at loose ends.

An excellent system is to have photographers make "file card prints"—contact prints or small enlargements—and put these in a small file in an established sequence. Give the file card prints and the negative envelope the same number, of course.

A system that has worked well for a number of advertising managers is to number the negatives like this: First digit is the month, second digit(s) the day of the month, then the year, then a letter for the individual exposure taken on that date, and another digit or alphabet letter to show to what series of pictures the foregoing refers.

For example, take the following negative and photograph number: 11178C3. This tells us immediately that the photograph was taken on November 17, 1968, the "C" shows that this negative is the third (A-B-C) one taken of the subject, and that this was the third subject photographed that day. Every subject fits into this system, and the file card prints can then be filed either according to this number, or by subject.

Black-and-white photography is relatively inexpensive and can do yeoman service for you. Buy well, and use it liberally. It sells hard.

Color Photography

Unless instructed otherwise, when you hire a photographer to photograph your wonderful new Widget in color, you won't receive a print.

Instead, you'll be presented with a positive transparency, in full color, with each tone and value just as the eye sees it. This transparency is not a reproduction of any kind, but is the actual film that was exposed in the camera—after it has been processed, of course.

You'll receive it in a transparent plastic jacket to prevent its being scratched or fingerprinted. Fingerprints are the mortal enemies of *both* black-and-white and color photographs, negatives, and transparencies. Grease in the skin etches into sensitive emulsions, leaving a big, fat fingerprint the FBI can use to identify you with—right smack in the middle of the print.

Depending upon the size of the camera the photographer used, the transparency will range in size from 35mm. to 8 by 10 inches, or even larger. You'll be ahead of the game if you specify 4- by 5-inch negatives; this is the preferred size because it's large enough for high quality reproduction, yet small enough so that cost is held to a minimum because the photographer does not have to waste time manhandling bulky, expensive equipment on the job when it's not really needed.

Four-color separations are made directly from the transparency for four-color printing. This offers savings in time and cost of production. No intermediate print is required unless, for some reason or other, extensive color retouching is required. If such retouching is done, you may be better off to have the photograph retaken rather than invest in expensive art—which is what retouching actually is—than to run the risk of having an unnatural-looking end product.

To retouch the color transparency itself, the retoucher need have the soul of an exceptionally gifted artist and the eye of a pronghorn antelope. Dye transfer prints in full color can be made, however, and these can be retouched more easily. They're frightfully expensive, though, and can play hob with a budget.

Modern film, such as Kodak Ektachrome, is beautifully lifelike and has marvelous color fidelity. Color film has been improved so much so fast that it's truly one of today's technological marvels. As recently as just before World War II, color photography and color printing in magazines was the exception and was seldom seen in industrial advertising; it was reserved for those with massive budgets with which to advertise cake mixes and cosmetics and toothpaste to hordes of more or less eager consumers. Today, though, color photography and four-color reproduction are commonplace in industrial advertising.

If you have a specific reason for wanting a color print you can have your photographer shoot the product in Ektacolor film and then have a color print delivered to you along with a color negative. This negative will have the colors reversed—that is, primary colors will appear in their complementary colors. Red will be green, green will be red, and so on through the scale. In addition, a typical Ektacolor negative has an odd brownish-buff-gray cast. It's a distinct breed of cat all by itself, but yields results that are very fine indeed. Photographers like to use Ektacolor because the film has much greater latitude—that is, the exposure need not be quite so precise and there's more room for error without resulting in inferior quality in the print.

A color print is relatively easy to retouch, much more so than retouching an Ektachrome transparency, primarily because it's so much larger and because the retouching is done on paper rather than film.

Separations for four-color printing can be made from color prints made from Ektacolor negative film, or from dye-transfer color prints made from Ektachrome transparencies. Dye transfer is much the better of the two. A print made from either process is an additional reproduction step, however, and with each process there's a slight but inevitable loss of quality. Best four-color printing results from separations made directly from the transparency.

Almost every good commercial and illustrative photographer shoots both black-and-white and color today as a matter of course. There's nothing esoteric about having color photography done, although most photographers charge more for color on a per-picture basis because their costs are higher—and also because they know they can get it.

The photographer's thinking is that if an advertiser has a budget that permits advertising in color, he should have one that will let him purchase photography that costs more than mine-run black-and-white. And you can't really blame him for thinking that way.

Then there's the fact that the photographer works harder when he's shooting color. For example, lighting is more critical in both intensity and in balance between highlight and shadow, and color temperature—degrees Kelvin, after the British Lord of the same name who first discovered how to measure color temperature—must be precisely controlled and balanced for the particular emulsion number of the color film that's being used. This requires tests beforehand to ascertain if filtering the film is required to alter the color balance for most pleasing rendition. This costs the photographer in time and money.

When you're having color photography done, *always* have black-and-white pictures taken at the same time whether you see an immediate need for it or not. Of course, it's possible to have a color-corrected black-and-white negative made from either the color transparency or from the Ektacolor negative and then have black-and-white prints made in the usual fashion. But the prints are never quite as good. They always seem to lack a little something. A slight loss occurs when the additional step is taken because the print is one more process removed from the original picture. Nothing comes free in the graphic arts.

Colors used in color photography should be warm, that is, toward the red end of the spectrum. Warm colors attract, cool colors can be passed by by the reader without causing him to tear his heart out in anguish. Red is an exciter color; this explains the old-time advertising man's cherished slogan, "I don't care what color it is, just so it's red."

Choice of Colors Critical

Although people are attracted to vivid colors, it's terribly easy to go overboard. Use taste and judgment. Avoid the muted, the cool, and the overly subtle. Naturally, the subject matter will to some extent dictate the colors and whether they'll be warm or cool, as will the product itself. A hard-and-fast rule hasn't been laid down, but a good guideline has.

Color film is not nearly as fast as black-and-white film, which means you'll either have to have more of your color photography done out of doors, or in a studio under high-intensity lights. Speed of color film ranges from around 32 to 100 ASA, much less than black-and-white and much more critical as far as the correct exposure is concerned. The photographer doesn't have much margin for error when he's working with color. Furthermore, color film will not handle as great a range of contrast—the difference between the darkest part of the picture and the lightest—as will black-and-white film.

Resolution of color film is exceptionally good, and the grain is very fine. There's never a problem on either score. Color film will show with great fidelity and high resolution the tiniest little detail just as it appears to the eye.

Kodak and other manufacturers of color film make a point of

printing a disclaimer on the box containing the film. It's to the effect that the manufacturer does *not* warrant the colors in the film against deterioration or change. The fact is, colors used in the manufacture of color film are inherently unstable over a prolonged period of time, although the author's good friend Ed Wiegand, an unusually sensitive and expert photographer, has any number of color transparencies taken during World War II that are apparently in as good condition today as when they were taken more than a quarter-century ago.

Just how well the colors stand up and for how long depends to a great extent on the storage conditions; high humidity and high temperatures are the mortal enemies of color film. That's why you'll find color film of knowledgeable amateurs and professionals alike stored in the refrigerator.

If you're having photography taken for "the record" and it's important that it last indefinitely, have it done in black-and-white.

The Cost of Color

Let's assume you've had original color photography taken of a product and now want prints for framing in the conference room, for salesmen's portfolios, and for reproduction in a four-color ad. What will prints cost?

Color Technique, Inc., leading professional processing laboratory in Chicago, lists the following prices that were effective when this was written in 1975:

High Quality Ektacolor Prints

These Ektacolor prints are first-rate in every respect. With the virtual disappearance of dye transfer prints, first and deepest love of advertising people, photographers and engravers, the quality color labs of the country were forced to embrace Ektacolor prints. To their credit, they've done a bang-up job. Ektacolor prints will never quite measure up to dye transfer, but economic facts are economic facts and dye transfer prints have been priced out of the market. Fortunately, high quality Ektacolor prints are perfectly suitable for any use, especially when color retouching is to be done and separations are to be made from reflective art. Color Technique's prices for these top quality prints are:

	Sizes					
Quantity	4x5 & 5x7	8x10	11x14	16x20	20x24	30x40
First print	$11.00	$12.00	$24.00	$35.00	$60.00	$115.00
2-10	2.45	3.00	6.00	12.00	30.00	40.00
11-25	2.00	2.40	4.80	9.75	24.00	35.00
26-49	1.60	2.00	4.50	8.50	20.00	30.00

Quantity Color Prints

These prints are designed for display or portfolio uses, and Color Technique offers rapid delivery schedules to meet the needs of those planning sales meetings or exhibits.

Quantity prices are based on a minimum of 50 prints or more, from any one negative or other original. The original must be clean and its exposure must be very nearly correct, for at this low price it is not possible to provide extensive color correction or dye retouching.

As Color Technique has this service set up, it is a package program. No approvals are submitted. Prints leave the laboratory as brilliant, neutral prints, balanced for cool white fluorescent. Prices are:

Quantity per each original	Unit Cost per Print				
	4x5 & 5x7	8x10	8½x11	11x14	16x20
50 each	$1.00*	$1.25*	$2.00*	$3.50*	$8.50*
100 each	.85	.89	1.50	3.00	8.00
150 each	.80	.85	1.45	2.80	7.00
200 plus each	.75	.80	1.40	2.60	6.00

*Indicates no first-print cost.

Duplicate Color Transparencies

Duplicate color transparencies are made in two different grades by Color Technique—Reproduction Type and Display Type. They are discussed below.

Reproduction Type

These transparencies are true reproduction quality and are produced to be complete in all respects for direct use in electronic scanners, or any other conventional system through which color separation negatives are prepared for photomechanical reproduction.

No further retouching or other corrections are necessary. Sizing can be followed for the closest scale reduction or enlargement required.

These reproduction duplicate transparencies can be prepared from originals as small as 35mm and up to 8x10.

	Size of Duplicate			
Quantity	4x5	5x7	8x10	11x14
First duplicate	$18.00	$24.00	$34.00	$50.00
Second duplicate	10.00	12.00	16.00	25.00

Display Type

These duplicate color transparencies for display purposes are made with the highest quality possible within the limitations of the duplicating film available. User should inform Color Technique of the type of lighting being used in display units. Prices are:

	Size of Duplicate						
Quantity	4x5	5x7	8x10	11x14	16x20	20x24	30x40
First duplicate	$14.00	$16.00	$22.00	$32.00	$48.00	$65.00	$140.00
2-12	7.50	9.00	12.00	20.00	30.00	45.00	75.00

Copies of Full Color Art

Color Technique makes excellent copies of color art, either a color negative or a color transparency; price is the same for either one.

Internegatives

All internegatives are made only from positive color transparencies. Maximum size of originals is 8x10, minimum size is 35mm. All sheet film originals are made contact (same) size.

Color Film Processing

Color Technique has chemistry lines to service Ektachrome, Ektacolor, Kodacolor, Fujicolor, GAF print film, 6120 Dupe film, Vericolor-1 and C.P.S. Prices are rock-bottom competitive and service is superb.

Color Technique's Rush Service

Three classes of service are offered by this well-known Chicago processor; 6-hour regular service; 4-hour special rush service; and 2½-hour service for a limited volume. This last is probably referred to—internally, at least—as the frantic service.

And for those who are really in a bind, Color Technique will process on weekends, as well as on overtime during the week. Naturally, this results in higher costs. But if a deadline is at hand and you've just plain run out of time, the modest extra costs are inconsequential.

Color costs, no matter how you look at it. Color photography, color prints, and color printing all cost more than black-and-white, but they sell harder as we'll see in the chapter to come.

So You Can't Use Photography?

Sometimes you're trapped into artwork. A situation exists about which you can do nothing. Photography is out of the question, so there's no use sitting around moaning about your fate. The thing to do is call in an artist, or have your agency contact one to render something you'd actually rather illustrate photographically.

Maybe, for example, you want to illustrate a famous event that's already transpired. Granted, you can't very well send a photographer back into history to take pictures of George Washington crossing the Delaware or of the Pilgrims landing on Plymouth Rock. And mighty few photographs of Custer's Last Stand are floating around; Sitting Bull must have forgotten to ask his public relations counsel to arrange for photographic coverage of the event. If your heart is set on this type of illustration, art it will have to be.

But just because you can't hire a photographer and send him someplace doesn't mean that perfectly good, usable photography doesn't exist, and that you can't benefit from it. Many times stock photos that are available from a number of sources will do your job

Collins' first environmental test lab

The time is 1934.

The place is near the South Pole.

The tent houses Admiral Richard Byrd's Communication Center — equipped with Collins' Radios.

The temperature is −82 F.

Communication with the outside world is reliable and consistent.

Today, of course, the environmental testing facilities are much more sophisticated.

But the results are just the same.

COMMUNICATION / COMPUTATION / CONTROL

COLLINS RADIO COMPANY / DALLAS, TEXAS • CEDAR RAPIDS, IOWA • NEWPORT BEACH, CALIFORNIA • TORONTO, ONTARIO
Bangkok • Beirut • Frankfurt • Hong Kong • Kuala Lumpur • Los Angeles • London • Melbourne • Mexico City • New York • Paris • Rome • Washington • Wellington

just exactly right. Later we'll go into this subject more thoroughly.

Collins Radio Company went more than 30 years into the past for the arresting illustration nearby. This illustration shows the communications center used by Admiral Richard Byrd on his Antarctic expedition in 1934. At the time the picture was taken, the temperature near this desolate spot by the South Pole was a slightly chilly 82 degrees below zero.

Copy in Collins' ad points out that this was actually an environmental test laboratory for the company's radios that were used by the Byrd expedition, and that they functioned perfectly and reliably and consistently.

Naturally, Collins' advertising manager wasn't along on the expedition; he didn't snap the picture with his trusty Brownie. But he did go to a source such as a stock photo house or the Bettmann Archives to get a photograph that works hand in glove with the intriguing headline.

Or perhaps you'll encounter a set of circumstances like this:

1. The equipment cannot be shown due to military security.
2. The technical operation of the equipment could not be described in the copy, nor could features of the product be described—for the same reason, of course.
3. End results of use of the product couldn't be shown, also for reasons of military security.
4. Use of the equipment couldn't be mentioned in connection with the war in Vietnam, site of the product's primary application.

This was the knotty situation facing Texas Instruments and which led to the striking illustration in the ad from *Space/Aeronautics* magazine shown nearby.

A liberal dose of ingenuity solved the problem without fuss or fanfare. A plastic model of a McDonnell Phantom II jet fighter plane was used to cast a shadow on a small section of an aerial photograph of a Vietnamese rice paddie; the shadow on the photograph was then photographed and a print was made. Lo and behold, finished art, ready to use in the ad!

Nothing violates security and no secrets were given away, but the illustration has all of the impact and stopping power of the real McCoy.

There's no intent to deceive the reader, no deliberate attempt to infer anything that isn't true. Texas Instruments built both the infrared mapping and low-altitude radar for this reconnaissance plane, this electronic equipment is in service in Vietnam, it's doing an outstanding job just as the copy says.

Day or Night...

No Cover for Charlie

Outfitted with both infrared mapping and low-altitude radar built by Texas Instruments Incorporated, the McDonnell RF-4C is equipped to do one of the toughest jobs of all — find the enemy.

TI's AN/APQ-99 Forward-Looking Radar helps guide the Phantom II to and from target areas at extremely low altitudes, with outstanding reliability.

The advanced AN/AAS-18 Infrared Mapping System provides high-resolution, photographic-quality reconnaissance information — also day or night.

The combination of TI's two sensors adds substantially to the mission capability of the RF-4C. Other TI radar systems are operational aboard the A-7A, F-111A and C-130.

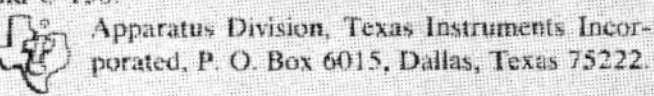

Apparatus Division, Texas Instruments Incorporated, P. O. Box 6015, Dallas, Texas 75222.

TEXAS INSTRUMENTS
INCORPORATED

This just goes to prove that some things can't be photographed, yet a photograph of them can be used to illustrate an advertisement.

Despite customer restrictions or obstacles of other kinds, advertisers must capitalize on the timeliness of illustrative material. Look long and hard and you'll find a way to get photographs of the unphotographable.

How to Buy Art and Photography

When the time comes to purchase art or photography, you've undoubtedly already made up your mind which it is to be.

Your decision will have been made after considering media—whether the advertisement is for a trade publication, a chamber of commerce annual extolling the virtues of your city, or whether you're producing a direct mail piece. Also considered is the question of realism; just how realistic is it necessary or desirable to be? And is it possible to use photography if that's the way you're inclined? Most important consideration, though, is to continue using the same illustrative technique that's been used thus far in your campaign. This maintains campaign identity and aids in reader recognition of your ads as being yours.

Let's take art first, and assume you're buying it yourself rather than having your agency or a studio handle this task for you. (You *do* save the commission or markup, of course).

If you've decided on art, you've also undoubtedly made at least an initial selection of what medium you feel is most suitable—oil or acrylic, tempera, line, pencil, and so on.

Now the thing to do is to choose the artist who can produce the kind of art you need at a price you want to pay in the length of time you can allot to the job. You can feel perfectly free to call your agency about this; it's a fact of life that many advertising managers buy some services direct without funneling the job through the agency. This is done to save money, naturally. Ask your account executive, who will ask your art director, or phone him yourself if you're well acquainted.

Explain what specific type of art you have in mind and ask for the names and phone numbers of three or four artists who are well qualified to handle your commission. Chances are the art director will have a number of names on the tip of his tongue.

However, if you prefer to handle this without involving your agency even to this extent, and if you don't know any artists personally, a fine source of reference is the telephone directory. The Chicago directory, for example, lists the following in the white pages under art:

Art Appraisers Association of America

Art, Arthur Studio

Art-by-Mail

Art Composition Company

Art Counselors, Inc.

Art Directions

Art Directors Club of Chicago

Art Directors Service, Inc.

Art for Advertising, Inc.

Art Forum Studios, Inc.

Art Institute of Chicago

Art Kraft Studio

Art Line Associates, Inc.

Art Photo Associates, Inc.

Art Unlimited

This is quite a list, particularly so since it doesn't include a large number of other listings, such as Art Barber Shop, which wasn't given because we're not particularly interested in haircuts at the moment; also skipped was Art & Judy's 62 Club, because we're talking business, not fun and games.

Let's assume you've decided you want a scratchboard illustration. So you pick up the phone and start at the most likely place to find an artist—the Art Directors Club of Chicago. During the day art directors are directing art, not lounging in the club. But artists are known and listed there for the benefit of art director-members. And you'll find the young lady who answers the phone most helpful if you explain what you're looking for; she'll put you in touch with several artists who work in scratchboard. If she can't, chances are she'll refer you to an artist who *can.* The advertising-art-photography-printing field is close-knit, and even in major cities widely overlapping acquaintances make people or their work well known to a large part of the advertising fraternity. And everybody customarily helps everybody else, so you'll encounter no problem in that respect.

Now you've found, let's say, two artists who are available—that is, they're not booked so solidly they have no open time—who work in scratchboard. You may prefer to visit their studios, or you may want to ask them to come to your office. Either procedure is proper enough.

When you talk with the artist, ask first of all to see samples of work in scratchboard that he's done for other clients. He won't have the original art, of course, because he sold that. But he will have reproductions, such as ads, direct mail pieces, brochures, annual reports and so on, showing the type of work he's accustomed to doing.

An artist's samples, for the most part, not only reflect what he has done but what he *can* do. Technique, thought processes, past experience, hopes and aspirations, and even personality are reflected in the output of an artist. This applies to photographers also, although to a somewhat lesser extent.

If the artist you're talking to seems to have a feeling for your type of product, or the type of illustration you have in mind, you'll know it at once from his samples. If he doesn't, this will also be readily apparent and you can break off discussion before wasting either your or the artist's time.

The Sticky Matter of Price

Assuming the artist is right for you, that you find his samples have flair and feeling, and there's every reason to believe you'll receive a satisfactory job from him, then discuss price.

Always discuss price *before* commissioning the work.

This will avoid any unpleasant surprises and equally unpleasant discussions when the invoice arrives. Make sure that both you and the artist have reached a complete understanding on what the art is to depict, the final use to which it is to be put, the medium, approximate size of the original art, approximate amount of fine detail to be shown, when the job is to be completed, and the amount you are to be billed.

Then, to be businesslike and not just because you're short of your share of trust in your fellow man, either write a confirming letter to the artist summarizing your conversation and agreement, or have your company issue a formal purchase order for his work. Either is acceptable, although the purchase order is probably more binding in the event of misunderstanding.

All of this may sound grim and forbidding. There's little reason to approach the project with a negative attitude, however. Seldom does an artist—who's also a businessman—and a client have a serious disagreement that can't be settled over a cup of coffee. It can happen, though, and you can accidentally fall in with a thoroughgoing scallawag who's out to bilk your company. Play it safe, wrap the deal up in a businesslike way, and there's no risk involved for either party.

When it comes to price, that's a vast wilderness that's either completely unexplored, or else it keeps changing so constantly that any maps that have been issued are obsolete before the ink dries. Odd as it may seem, neither you—the buyer—nor the artist—the seller—really has any concrete idea of what the art is worth. The only guideline you have is that you're forced by an inflexible budget to stay within a certain sum. This makes the art worth this figure to you and no more.

As far as the artist is concerned, he'll be giving you a piece of coated board that he bought for a few cents, some black ink that cost even less than that, and as much of his time and effort as is required to produce a piece of work that measures up to standards he has set for himself.

Naturally, his standard of living and the salary level he has established for his talent will be reflected in the price he sets. So, too, will how busy he happens to be at the moment. When demand is brisk, the price of art rises; when business is slow, the price is reduced in an attempt to make it perk up, much like any other commodity or service in the marketplace.

Use to which the art will be put also affects the price. If a piece of art is to be used in four-color spreads in *Reader's Digest, TV Guide, Ladies' Home Journal, U.S. News* and *World Report, McCall's* and other big consumer books, the price will be several times what it would be if the art were to be used for an ad to be placed in *Refuse Removal Journal,* the magazine that serves the garbage collection industry.

A good scratchboard illustration will cost, in Chicago, from $800 to $1,500 or even more. Average is probably around $1,000.

Self-defeating is any attempt to buy art at the rock-bottom minimum price you can find by scouring a city. There are always second- or third-rate artists who are perfectly willing to sell poor quality art for whatever price it commands. Buy poor art and you'll end up with a poor illustration; a poor illustration will weaken the entire ad, thus costing far more in the long run than does first rate art to start with.

Another thing: a practice that will make your name anathema in the graphic arts community is that of attempting to chisel every artist with whom you do business. Granted, there may be times when the artist's price seems a bit high and you have an absolutely firm budget for a given piece of art. In such instances most artists will "work with you," meeting you halfway in the interest of prospective future commissions by shaving their price. To request this every time, though, and to make it standard operating procedure to beat artists down to the lowest possible dollar they'll accept, will cause every commercial artist except those starving in garrets to be so disinterested when your name is mentioned, or uninterested and "busy" when you call, that you'll find it next to impossible to buy art.

And commercial artists starving in garrets have remarkably little to offer. If they had great talent they'd be in demand. No top-flight professional lacks work for long.

Shown nearby is the American Association of Advertising Agencies' "Standards of Practice in Handling Artwork." Everything said, except point number eleven, applies just as much to an industrial advertising manager in his dealings with artists as it does to agencies. What the standards of practice actually boil down to, if you'll read them closely, is fair, honest, businesslike dealings between art buyer and artist. This is what everybody wants, of course.

You'll find that artists—and photographers—are some of the finest people you'll meet in your business life. Chances are some of them will become personal friends over the course of years. Do right by them and they'll more than reciprocate by giving you more and better work than you have a right to expect for the price.

Photographers Also Specialists

Photographers also have sample books, usually duplicate prints or color transparencies of work they've done for other customers. When you're thinking of assigning a job to a photographer with whom you haven't worked before, always ask to see his sample book. This will enable you to evaluate the man's ability and judge whether or not his work is of the type you can use.

Just as artists tend to specialize in either a certain medium or a specific type of subject matter, so do photographers. The major breakdowns in photographic specialties are portrait, commercial, and illustrative. The last two usually overlap, of course.

An industrial advertising manager is usually pretty certain of getting something less than top quality commercial or illustrative work if he goes to a portrait photographer. This isn't to denigrate portrait photographers as a class of highly skilled photographers; they are, but in their own field. You're much better off to hire the type of photographer who specializes in your requirements rather than hoping a specialist in another field can adapt himself to something he has deliberately chosen to avoid.

In small towns and out in the hinterlands this is particularly true when the nearest major city is a considerable distance away; here you'll find the local photographer is almost always primarily a portrait man because that's where the necessary volume comes from if

STANDARDS *of* PRACTICE *in* HANDLING ART WORK

American Association of Advertising Agencies

THESE STANDARDS are predicated upon the belief that adherence to a code of fair practice, agreed upon in advance, will contribute to the welfare of the Advertiser, the Creative Craftsman and the Agency and will reduce the opportunities for misunderstanding and inefficiency in handling Art Work.

1. An artist or photographer should not be asked to speculate with or for an advertising agency, or asked to do work on any basis which entails the possibility of loss to him through factors beyond his control.

2. An artist or photographer should not be expected to suffer any loss that is due to poor judgment on the part of the advertising agency.

3. Dealings with an artist or photographer should be conducted only through an Art Director or art buyer who is the authorized representative of the advertising agency.

4. Orders to an artist or photographer should be in writing and should include all details for which the supplier will be held responsible. The price, whenever possible, and delivery date should be set at this time and included in the written order.

5. Changes or alterations in drawings or photographs that are demonstrably made necessary by mistakes on the part of the artist or photographer should not be paid for by the advertising agency, but the supplier should be compensated for major revisions resulting from a change in agency plans or instructions.

6. If the purchase price of a drawing or photograph is based upon limited use, and later this material is used more extensively than originally planned, the artist or photographer should receive additional remuneration.

7. If comprehensive layouts or other preliminary art work or photographs are published as finished work, the price should be adjusted to include additional compensation.

8. If preliminary drawings, photographs or comprehensives are bought from an artist or photographer with the intention or possibility that someone else will be assigned to do the finished work, this should be made clear at the time of placing the order for preliminary work.

9. Work stopped by the advertising agency for reasons beyond the control of the artist or photographer after it has been started should be paid for on the basis of the time and effort expended.

10. Should an artist or photographer fail to keep his contract with the advertising agency through unreasonable delay in delivery, or non-conformance with agreed specifications, it should be considered a breach of contract by the artist or photographer and should release the advertising agency from responsibility.

11. There should be no concealed charges in art work as billed by the advertising agency.

12. No personal commission or rebate should be asked or accepted by the art buyer from an artist or art service.

he's to make a living. Often the local portrait photographer can do a creditable job on a commercial assignment, especially if it's fairly routine. Almost all of these dual-purpose operators have their studio cameras, big and bulky to impress the local citizenry, as well as the famous Speed Graphic for use on location. Note especially, however, that these jacks-of-all-photographic-trades can handle portrait and commercial work—*not* illustrative photography of the caliber required for advertising use, especially if the subject matter is complex or will be greatly enhanced by an interpretive treatment.

Photographers, the good ones, are just as much artists as are those who work with oil or pencil or charcoal. The day of the technician clicking a shutter and proudly proclaiming a picture is long past. A good commercial or illustrative photographer is a sensitive visualizer who puts the stamp of his personality on his work, who imparts a definite flair to the finished print or transparency.

Usually you can find a photographer who's right for you by using the same process used in finding an artist. Ask your agency, ask the studio you've dealt with, ask your printer, or just start phoning.

When you're faced with having your product photographed out of your city, however, perhaps in a far distant location, the problem is a bit different. Just finding any commercial photographer can be a chore—and then there's the fact that if you do your photographer-selecting on a hit-or-miss basis you stand about one chance in three of getting exactly the kind of photograph you want.

Often you'll find it's well worth the price of an airplane ticket, a night in a motel, and a few meals for you to go to the scene and supervise the photography yourself. When you compare these relatively minor expenses with the photographer's invoice, cost of producing an advertisement, and the space it will occupy—not to mention the result it is expected to produce—this is inconsequential.

There's an easy way to choose a photographer in a distant city, though, and that's to use the *Directory of Professional Photography*. The Directory is published primarily as a service to the members of the Professional Photographers of America, Inc.—the PPofA, it's called. However, the ultimate service is provided to three specific groups: Buyers of photography; suppliers of photographic goods and services; and the professional photographers listed in the 218-page directory.

The directory is essentially a buyer's guide—a where-to-find-it in the sense that buyers of photography can search for and find photographers in almost any geographical area, or in virtually any photographic specialty.

Of special interest is the *Qualified Listing*. To earn this classification, photographers must have submitted samples of their work to a PPofA Board of Review. It isn't just handed out hither and yon. Those studios and individual photographers who are Qualified are listed alphabetically within cities and states, making it convenient to locate a really good photographer near the job. It's a great little time- and telephone-bill saver.

The author has used the PPofA Directory with great success for a number of years. In almost every instance, even before the advent of the Qualified Listing in 1958, the resulting photographs were of acceptable quality—or better.

Choosing a Qualified photographer has boosted even that excellent batting average. Every single Qualified photographer the author has hired—and this has been in every section of the country, in major cities and out in the boondocks—has delivered work of superior quality without exception. There are no plumbers in the Qualified section.

Establishment of the Qualified Listing has eliminated the bugaboo of hiring blind, of not having any assurance except that from a disembodied voice on the other end of the telephone, and of worrying about the quality of the photographs which will arrive in the mail. Advertising managers can rely on the Qualified photographers found in the directory to do a bang-up job every single time. Naturally, they'll need instructions from you, what to be sure to do, what to be sure not to do, camera angles, preferred backgrounds, whether or not people are to appear in the pictures, and so on.

Classified By Code

The PPofA directory is highly useful in another way. It enables you to choose a photographer who specializes or who has had considerable successful experience in the area in which you're most interested. There's a classification code for this purpose, simplifying use of the book. Various classifications are:

Ae........Aerial photography, obliques and verticals.

AM........Aerial mapping with specialized aerial cameras and facilities for scale production and mosaics.

An........Animal photography; specialists in livestock and pets.

Ar........Architectural photography; fine quality work for architects, builders and suppliers for national architectural magazines—not ordinary exteriors and interiors.

AS........Art studio; layouts to finished art.

Ba........Banquets or large groups; specialists in this field.

Bi........Biological photography; specialized work for the medical profession.

CAPS........Advertiser in the Directory.

CB........Commercial photography, general; black and white only, normal exteriors, general publicity, small groups, meetings, copies, products in use, studio set-up products, catalogs.

CC........Commercial photography, general; color and black and white, normal exteriors, general publicity, small groups, meetings, copies, products in use, studio setup products, catalogs.

Color........Studio operating exclusively in color. Does not solicit black-and-white work.

Cr..............Criminal; photography, photomicrography, and radiography, as practiced in criminal investigation.

Cx..............Commercial photography, occasional; the average picture that any photographer can be expected to make with ordinary equipment. Most studios in smaller cities, unless exclusively portrait, are so listed.

DP.............Direct color and processing.

DT.............Direct color for trade; prints and film processing for other studios.

En..............Enlargements and blowups; made for other studios.

Fu..............Furniture; experienced in photographs of furniture for sales use of furniture manufacturers with studio facilities for same.

HS.............High speed motion pictures and stills; specialists with proper equipment.

I..................Industrial illustration; large industrial installation, interiors, exteriors, with or without models, machines in operation, large machinery on location, creative work for advertising and publicity.

IA..............Illustrative and advertising photography; creative work with or without models, in studio or on location, making sets, furnishing props, etc.

IM.............Industrial motion pictures; complete production, including editing, titling, sound, etc.

La..............Lantern slides; only for exclusive slide studios or quantity producers.

Le..............General legal; experienced in photographs for use in court.

L-F............Legal-forensic; specialists in having knowledge of evidential photography used in casualty, liability and negligence trials with competency to testify on technical considerations involved in making, processing and properly presenting evidence photographs.

Ma.............Marine photography; specialists only in photographing boats, races, and so on.

Mi..............Microfilming; only if microfilm equipment is owned by the studio.

MP............Motion pictures; taking only, but can furnish finished product.

P.................Portraiture; including studio, home, passport, school, groups, children.

PE.............Photoengraving; only when plant is conducted in connection with studio.

PF.............Photofinishing; when performed as a sideline to the studio's major types of work.

Ph.............Photostats; rectigraph and similar photography, not ordinary copying.

PJ.............Photoreporting; photojournalism in telling a complete story with a series of photographs.

PM............Photomurals; equipped to handle complete job at listed studio, including mounting, also on location installations.

PP.............Print production, quantity; prints and postcards.

PR............Public relations and publicity; experienced in posing and handling people, knowledge of publication media requirements.

PW............Photofinishing, wholesale, including mail order and fine grain work.

q............Qualified; see yellow pages (in PPofA Directory).

SE............Conventions and special events; expositions, meetings, and conventions.

SF............Slidefilms; the complete production of sequences.

SP............Stock photographs; studio maintaining cataloged stock prints for sales.

SR............Sound recording studio; for slides and motion pictures.

ST............Scientific and technical; specialists in such techniques as photomicrography, and metallography, persons and organizations equipped and offering these services.

Th............Theatrical photography; specialists in "show business."

The *Directory of Professional Photography* is available without charge to legitimate buyers of photography. Write:

Professional Photographers of America, Inc.
1090 Executive Way
Oak Leaf Commons
Des Plaines, Illinois 60018

The News Services Available

Another way to get fine photographs in out-of-the-way locations is to call on a service that specializes in serving advertisers and agencies regardless of how remote.

For example, Wide World Photos, Inc., 50 Rockefeller Plaza, New York, New York 10020, maintains staffers—competent photographers and frequently skilled reporters to work with on case histories—all over the United States and throughout most of the free world.

Let's say you want to have one of your automated widgets shot in North Africa. You'd arrange with Wide World to have a local man shoot it, carefully following your directions about camera angle, direction of light, special care to be taken about showing or not showing certain features; this photographer would also be guided by a rough layout you would supply, as well as any other instructions you feel desirable. Wide World handles all details and gets sharp, clean, well-composed photos by airmail a few days later and forwards them to you, along with an invoice.

And the invoice isn't the rub. Rates for foreign photography are usually very modest; the minimum charge for up to five negatives is $75—although you can usually depend on paying about double the minimum, plus mileage, model fees, prop rental, and other extras that are found even in your home city. Extra negatives are $15.00 each.

This is a far cry from the tab you'd expect to pick up if you sent your local photographer to Casablanca, considering the time and expenses involved! Even the airplane ticket would play hob with the budget for months to come.

In addition to this service, Wide World has on file a number of stock photos available to you at low prices.

An unusually efficient photographic service is provided by Compix—the commercial photography division of United Press International. Headquarters is at 220 East 42nd Street, New York, New York 10017.

Compix, or UPI, as it's frequently called, also has branch offices in Boston, Chicago, Cincinnati, Dallas, Detroit, Philadelphia, Pittsburgh, Minneapolis, New Orleans, San Francisco, and Washington, D.C. Foreign offices are in London, Paris, Rome, Milan, Frankfurt, Tokyo, and Montreal.

On-location assignments are handled economically by strategically located photographers; they're in many other cities and countries besides those listed, of course, although work is assigned from the nearest office. These photographers are capable individuals who can photograph almost anything to your exact specifications, and to your layout if you supply one. Their work is usually somewhat better than average.

Compix also has a very efficient field photo and reporter service which involves a team effort by a photographer and a reporter. These teams are available in almost every city of any size throughout the world; they make it remarkably easy for you to get good coverage of your product's performance regardless of where it's installed.

These knowledgeable teams practically put the reader at the scene of the application of your product. Standard service supplies you with six to eight photographs, a 1,500-word written application story gathered by a skilled industrial reporter and rewritten by experienced editors, as well as an interview questionnaire report on the key men located on the site.

LogEtronics Photoprint Service—which is a coined name that doesn't communicate, even if the service does do good work—is also offered by Compix.

This is simply giving the advertiser bulk prints from the original negative (no copy negative!) with excellent quality, usually as good as that of hand-processed prints, and at a price that's competitive with bulk-process rates. In addition, Compix has a new "Pushbutton" rush distribution service which provides same-day distribution of captioned LogEtronics prints to the nation's top 100 newspapers. This can get tremendous coverage in the press for your news releases if something really hot warrants it.

Besides offering the services of photographers who are skilled journeymen, Compix has what it calls the "Signature Group of Photographic Illustrators"—a network of 14 of the country's most talented illustrators—who are on call to Compix when something truly outstanding is needed.

And if you're stuck for a photographer and need one fast, Compix will send a man in to do your product shots for catalogs and advertisements. UPI photographers are experienced in both consumer products and industrial equipment and can work with a minimum of supervision, in case you're going to be out of the office for some reason. This can be a real boon when a vacation is coming up at the same time a new product is scheduled to be born, and your regular photographer is on vacation, out of the city on assignment, or sick. Compix also offers stock photographs from decades back; almost everything imaginable is in its files.

One thing: When dealing with any of these services, be sure to stress the fact that you require model releases. North Africa is too far away to be worrying about getting the signature of some Arab for one dollar.

Price Range Suggested

When you've found the photographer whom you want to do your photography, discuss the price and come to an agreement with him. In many cases it won't be an absolutely firm price and it's to your advantage that a specific figure isn't set. Most photographic jobs involve some intangibles that can't be foreseen by either you or the photographer.

Ask a photographer for a firm price and he will of necessity quote you the maximum price based on anticipated labor involved and assuming the worst about unforeseen circumstances. Instead of establishing an exact figure, agree on a price *range* with minimum and maximum figures. Photographers are just as hungry for a dollar as any of the rest of us, but they're a very decent and likable group of businessmen as a whole.

After you've worked with a local photographer for a while it won't be necessary to get a quote and an agreed-upon price range before assigning every job to him. This need be done only when the project is unusually complex, when extensive time and travel are involved, if expensive props must be rented or built or purchased, or if the assignment is so different and demanding that the photographer must rent or buy specialized equipment to handle it. This latter situation occasionally crops up and is not one in which the photographer should be penalized by expecting him to absorb unusual costs, even if he were willing to do so for the sake of good business relations.

Prices of photography vary widely, as much as 300- to 400- percent according to different geographical regions. In the Northeast, Midwest, and California they're highest, with the South the lowest, followed by the Southwest and the Pacific Northwest. In general they reflect the cost of living of various sections of the country and the prevailing wage and salary structure.

The Professional Photographers of America does not set any price guidelines for member photographers, feeling that this is strictly up to the individual or to the studio owner. Photography, like any other goods or service, is priced according to the law of supply and demand. If it's overpriced, advertisers will switch to artwork until the price becomes what they consider is right.

Some regional associations, however, have prepared suggested price ranges or published estimating manuals to help advertisers—and agencies, too, for that matter—arrive at an informed guesstimate of what it will cost to have the widget's picture taken.

Price and Service Manual

The professional photographers' association of a large state has prepared a manual for this purpose and has quoted typical prices which follow. The association hastens to point out that the manual should not be construed as an attempt to fix prices; however, it is a guide to fair value for services the buyer of photography receives.

A fair price to both the photographer and client should, of course, cover the following:

1. The photographer's time, overhead and material.
2. Provide a reasonable return on his capital investment.
3. Recognize the photographer's technical ability, ability to create, and his experience.

Minimum prices which the photographers of this association consider fair for various classifications of work are:

AERIALS, DAY RATE:

B/W		Color	
½ day	$200	½ day	$400
1 day	$350	1 day	$600

Developing and proofs, full day: $125. This is a cost-plus day, which allows the photographer to take as many pictures as the client desires. Additional expenses include helicopter rental at $100 to $200 per hour. When shooting color, also allow for cost of film, processing, proofs, and printing if prints are desired.

COMMERCIAL

Standard size for black-and-white prints is 8 by 10 inches.

Studio	B/W	Color	
		4 x 5	8 x 10
Minimum, one setup	$45	$60	$100
Additional setups, each	$35	$45	$65

Allow 30 minutes for each setup. When a setup takes longer than 30 minutes, add $25 hourly time charge to the above minimums.

Quantity Discounts: Large numbers of similar objects that can be photographed without changing focus, lights, or background may be billed at 10 percent reduction from these prices.

Location	B/W	Color		
		4 x 5	5 x 7	8 x 10
Minimum, one setup	$50	$75	$85	$175
Additional setups, each	$35	$50	$75	$125

Allow 30 minutes for each setup. When setup takes longer than 30 minutes, add the time charge to the above minimums.

	B/W		Color	
Day Rates	½ day $200	1 day $350	½ day $350	1 day $600

This is a cost-plus assignment allowing photographer to take as many pictures as the client desires. Expenses to be included: film, developing, processing, proofing, prints, travel, and mileage expenses.

COPY CAMERA

Studio	B/W	Color		
		4 x 5	5 x 7	8 x 10
Flatwork which fits a standard 24 x 30 copy-board:	$10	$45	$50	$75

Additional negatives made without changing the camera may earn a 15 percent discount. Above prices are for making the negatives, only, which become the property of the client.

LOCATION	B/W	COLOR		
		4 x 5	5 x 7	8 x 10
Minimum, one setup	$50	$75	$85	$175
Additional setups, each	$35	$50	$75	$125

When a setup takes more than 30 minutes, add $25 time charge to above minimums.

EDITORIAL

DAY RATES	B/W		COLOR	
On assignment, the minimums are:	½ day	1 day	½ day	1 day
Photographer	$200	$350	$250	$400
Assistant	$75 and up			

Expenses are in addition to above minimums· include film, developing, proofs, and prints.

FASHION

STUDIO OR LOCATION, DAY RATE	B/W	COLOR
Photographer	$500	$1,250

Add to the above minimum, all expenses, including film, processing and developing, proofs and prints; also those expenses singular to the setup, such as wardrobe people, stylist, models, props, home economist, hair dressers, make-up artists, and assistants.

ILLUSTRATIVE/ADVERTISING PHOTOGRAPHY

Illustrative photographers are of high individual performance . . . possessing special skill, talent, and ability. These photographers have well-equipped studios, maintain good equipment, and are well trained. They are the highest paid in the profession. Realistic prices for illustrative work is a balance between advertising budget and the photographers performance. An important consideration is *usage* . . . based on the value received from the original investment. If the illustration is very successful and used for major magazine space, the returns will be greater than if used in a limited way, such as a brochure.

	Local	Regional	National
Brochures/ Reports	150-500	200-600	300-1000
Newspaper	150-500	200-600	500-1500
Billboards/ Posters	150-500	200-600	450-1500
Trade Publications	150-500	200-600	500-1500
Magazines	200-600	300-800	750-3000

MOTION PICTURES

Pricing of industrial films ranges according to ultimate use of the film, and includes a finished sound color answer print. The price indicated covers average situations, interior and exterior shooting. Additional charges would be made for special lighting, special equipment, and where optical effects are needed; also where Screen Actors Guild members are involved, their scale varies for different uses of the film. Location, travel and model fees are also additional.

Basic Prices 16mm	One Minute	25 Minutes
16mm color film	$1,200	$25,000

A news story in black and white, 16mm, silent, includes coverage of the event, processing editing scripting for station announcer's off-camera voice, and delivery of prints to local stations, plus one extra print for the client. Out of town delivery should be sent air mail and special delivery. This is a complete service. You keep the negative and a print, which might be used in the client's annual report, for instance, at some future date.

	B/W	Color
16mm, one minute	$400	$400 plus $25/print

NEWS AND PUBLICITY

Studio and Location	B/W	Color		
		2¼ x 2¼	4 x 5	8 x 10
Minimum assignment	$50	$40	$75	$150
First photograph	$10			$ 60
Each subsequent photo	$ 9			$ 30

In working out color charges add cost of film, processing, proofing, and prints. Figure travel time and mileage charges at $10 per hour and 15 cents per mile.

SLIDES

From Furnished Negatives	B/W		Color	
	First slide	$10	First slide	$20
	2 through 11	$ 6	2 through 4	$ 4
	12 upward	$ 4	5 upward	$ 2

From Prints or Flat Art, 24 x 30 Maximum	B/W		Color	
	First slide	$12	Minimum	$40
	2 through 11	$ 8	First slide	$10
	12 upward	$ 6	Additional	$ 6

There will be minor variations in price from studio to studio, involving differences in sizes of negatives, prints, and slides rendered. For the original-photography costs for slides, use rates applicable to the particular type of photography required.

Until we look at a specific example, this is largely theoretical, so let's see just what some actual photographs cost and determine whether the charges were justified.

Meet a man who fires alumina ceramic pieces within a ± .003 inch tolerance...
LINDBERG HEVI-DUTY

The two pictures in the ad at right, shown larger in a previous section of this book devoted to testimonials, cost $75. One is a photo of a ceramic kiln, the other is of the owner and the plant superintendent. In contrast, the photo on the opposite page cost $1,000. But this photo was also used on the cover of an annual report, a piece of sales literature, and two industrial ads.

First case in point is Lindberg Hevi-Duty's testimonial ad already shown; for ready reference it's reproduced in small size nearby. The photograph of this kiln, and the one of the owner of the ceramics manufacturing company and his plant superintendent were billed at $75. This was fair to both the photographer—Sammy Gold, Gold's Studio, who is rated as Qualified—and to the advertiser. The photographer didn't put in more than 45 minutes on location and no artificial lights were used. Furthermore, location of the equipment is in Corpus Christi, Texas, where prevailing prices of most services are on the low side. The photograph was taken for one use only—a trade advertisement which appeared in just two publications: *Ceramic Industry* and *Ceramic Age.* Circulation of both books is in the general neighborhood of 20,000.

Next, we see a photograph that for all practical purposes cost $1,000. This photograph is one of a large number taken by Los Angeles illustrative photographer Jason Hailey, a top man in the field, for an agreed-upon day rate of $1,000. This figure was to cover all expenses except model fee; model Barbro Holmgren received approximately $200 for eight hours before the camera.

Is this a high-priced photo? It is out of line? The answer has to be a good, strong "no" if you consider the mileage the company received and the superb quality of the photograph, here seen unretouched. To start with, two of the machines shown—die and wire bonders used in manufacturing electronic devices—were trucked to the photographer's studio early in the morning. Several hours

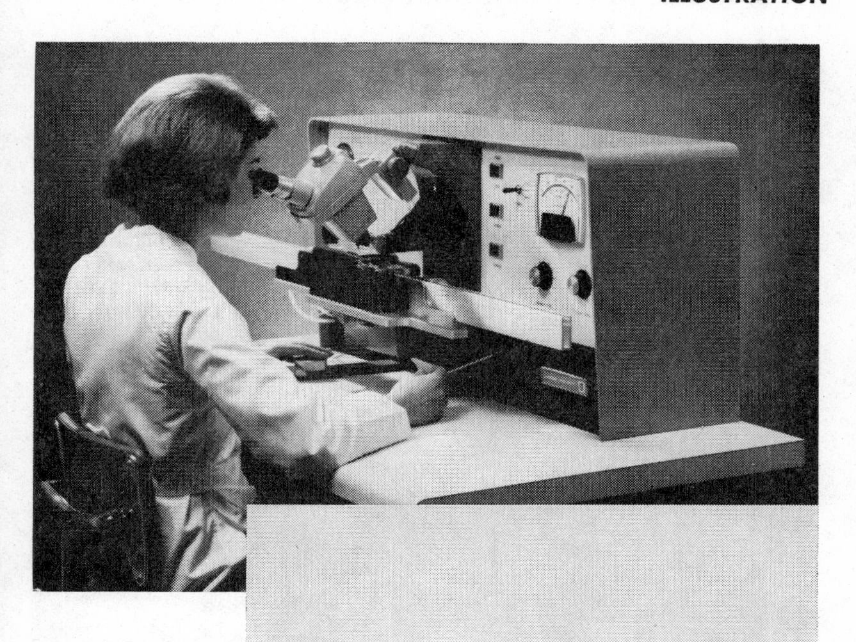

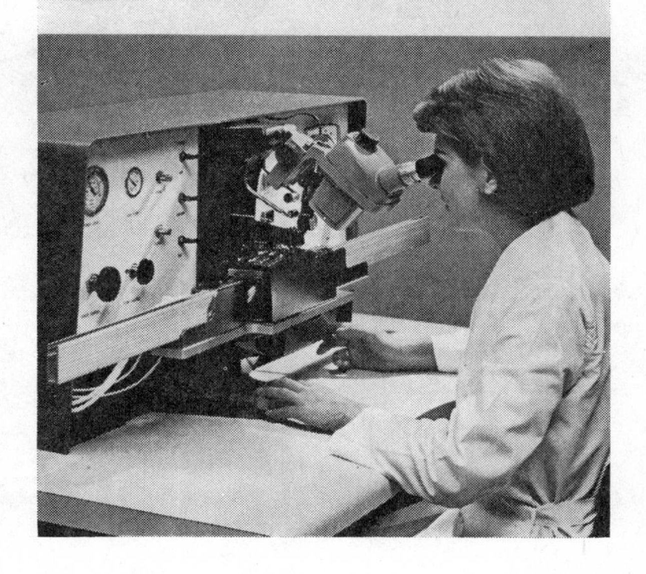

Two shots from each side of the machine yielded photos for an annual report, a product brochure, and publicity prints.

Two industrial ads were among the other uses found for the photos from setup that cost $1,000 in photo, model fees.

were spent by the photographer and his assistant in making a setup, perfecting the lighting, and achieving a satisfactory pose of model with machine.

Both pieces of equipment were photographed from either side. Shooting from both sides meant the setup had to be reversed, of course. The lighting had to be reversed and the camera had to be shifted. This meant as far as the photographer was concerned that he was taking a completely different picture.

Furthermore, backgrounds were changed to complement different colors for the different machines, thus creating what amounted to completely new pictures as far as those who saw them were able to tell.

This excellent photograph was used in a four-color insert advertisement, in the two-color piece of product literature, and in four-color in the parent corporation's annual report. In addition, the picture was used extensively for publicity in announcing the new product. And to top all this off, some months later a similar picture of a look-alike machine which was photographed at the same time was also announced to the electronics industry. This photograph also received excellent mileage. One more use also occurred several months later when a new trade show booth was built and this color photo was reproduced as a huge four-color translite.

Insert ad, sales literature, annual report, publicity twice, trade show—that's six major uses for the photographs taken that one "expensive" day. This was a day, incidentally, which lasted until 11 o'clock that night. The photographer and his assistant worked hard and steadily, produced excellent photographs, and certainly were not overpaid.

Layout Is Helpful

So that both artists and photographers will have some firm direction, you should always give them a layout to work from to show the final use to which their work is to be put. The artist, of course, will use it to make a rough pencil sketch for approval before proceeding with his work. The photographer, though, does both his preliminary and finished work at one sitting, so it's even more necessary in his case.

Even a "copywriter's rough"—doodled by the advertising manager, account executive, or art director, will be of great assistance. Show the photographer past advertisements from the same campaign, give him reprints of them so he can see the shape and format into which he must confine "live matter" in the photograph.

Then, perhaps while he's in the office with you, sketch out what you're looking for in the photograph, discussing it with the photographer at the same time. If you're working by mail or long-distance telephone, you'll have to be a lot more explicit the first time around because you won't have the verbal give-and-take you enjoy with a local man with whom you're familiar.

Another thing you should do is familiarize yourself with the working tools of the photographer.

You don't have to delve into this so deeply you become an accomplished photographer yourself, of course, nor are you expected to know all of the technical ins and outs of complicated and delicate equipment the commercial or illustrative photographer uses on your jobs.

If you have a reasonable idea of the limitations of each major type of equipment, however, you'll be able to give the photographer instructions which he'll understand much more quickly than if cameras were a complete mystery to you. Also, when you're on the phone you'll be able to describe a proposed photographic job in terms of the equipment the photographer will most likely need, thus discussing a technical matter in the language that communicates best.

Let's look at the basic types of cameras most photographers use. Almost every well-equipped photographer has one or more of almost every type. To simplify things, cameras will be grouped by size, with the smallest discussed first.

35mm Cameras

This camera, typified by the Leica which was developed in Germany in the 1930s, is small, highly portable, light in weight, and holds a large supply of film without reloading—36 exposures. With a supplementary magazine arrangement, film capacity is greatly increased and a motor-driven mechanism advances the film and cocks the shutter very rapidly, making possible "bursts" of pictures taken a split-second apart.

The typical 35mm camera has an extremely fast lens, usually around f/1.4, enabling it to take pictures under very adverse light conditions without resorting to flood, flash, or stroboscopic lights.

Pictures produced by the best 35mm cameras are of high quality, although the small negative size—roughly 1 by 1½ inches—makes it necessary to enlarge them several times. That is, they must be blown up several diameters before they are large enough to evaluate or to use. This can be done without difficulty, however.

Results from the small negatives are never the equal of photographs taken on large-format negatives. The larger the enlargement—the blow-up—the more loss of print quality there inevitably is.

35mm Single-Lens Reflex

This type of camera has taken the photographic world by storm, starting shortly after World War II when the now-obsolete Exacta paved the way for all similar cameras to follow. The trend shows no sign of tapering off.

The 35mm single lens reflex, often called simply the SLR, is typified by the Nikon, Pentax, and Konica cameras, all made in Japan, and by the newer Leicaflex, which is German. Although Japan turns out low-priced cameras, including SLRs, that are scarcely out of the junk class, the higher priced Japanese cameras and lenses are of superb quality, equal to the best German items in every respect.

35mm SLRs use the same 35mm film in cartridges that the familiar Leica does.

Only the body of the SLR is different. Still small, portable, and very easily handled, the SLR is heavier, thicker and infinitely more complicated mechanically than the Leica.

Viewing is done through the lens with a complex mirror-and-prism arrangement, through a viewfinder as with non-SLR 35mm cameras. This means the photographer sees *exactly* what will be captured on film before he trips the shutter. Absence of parallax, the difference between what is seen through the viewfinder and what the lens sees, can be critical, especially when working up close to the object being photographed.

Another important advantage of the 35mm SLR is ease of interchanging lenses. Since the photographer looks through the lens, he always sees exactly what the camera does; when lenses of different focal lengths—wide angle, or telephoto, for instance—are substituted for the normal lens there is no need for an auxiliary viewfinder to show what is included in the picture area that will be captured on film.

Like the Leica-type 35mm camera, the 35mm SLR is ideal for fast action shots, picture stories involving a sequence of pictures of the candid variety, "fish-eye" extreme wide-angle pictures, and numerous other photos where mobility for the photographer is important.

Best quality 35mm SLRs are exceedingly fine instruments which are capable of producing superior work. Their only limitation is the small film size.

Twin-Lens Reflex

The twin-lens reflex, best known of which is the superb German-made Rolleiflex, has been one of the main work horses of the professional photographer for almost 30 years.

Negatives produced by the Rollei, "rolly" as it's affectionately called, are 2¼ by 2¼ inches and are taken on 120 roll film. Professionals use professional film, usually Plus-X or Tri-X panchromatic black-and-white films, depending upon the speed and resolution desired, or Ektachrome or Ektacolor roll films for positive transparencies or color negatives respectively.

The Rollei gets a full dozen pictures on a roll, thus permitting considerable shooting without reloading. Viewing is on a ground glass, equipped with a magnifier for fine focusing, although the image cast on the ground glass is thrown by an extra lens, not the lens used to take the picture. It is from this that the Rolleiflex received its name, the twin-lens reflex.

Everybody considers the Rollei a superb precision tool of almost unequalled quality with either the Schneider or Zeiss lenses. It takes photographs of almost incredible sharpness. Most knowledgeable advertising men have a tough time telling photos taken with a Rollei from those made using cameras with larger film sizes.

A primary advantage of the Rolleiflex is the crank-operated film advance and shutter-cocking mechanism; it performs both functions with a flick of a crank on the right hand side of the camera in a split second, making it remarkably easy for the photographer to shoot picture after picture with incredible speed, especially when he's viewing the scene through the sports finder incorporated into the reflex hood.

Almost all types of photographs *except those requiring wide-angle or long-focal-length lenses* may safely be assigned to the versatile Rolleiflex, with uniformly fine results.

2¼-Inch-Square Single-Lens Reflex

This is an awfully unhandy "handle" for a remarkably handy little camera. Just in the past few years the 2¼ SLR square—the inch part of the name is generally dropped when talking about the camera—has come into its own, paced by the remarkable Hasselblad which is made in Sweden.

This tremendously flexible but frightfully expensive SLR has all of the attributes of the 35mm single-lens reflex—lenses that are quickly interchangeable, a wide range of wide-angle and telephoto lenses, a tremendous battery of accessories and through-the-lens fousing.

In addition, the Hasselblad has an interchangeable back, enabling the photographer to switch from black-and-white to color and back again easily and quickly, thus taking identical pictures in each medium.

Only drawback to the Hasselblad is that it's a delicate thing and can't stand the relatively rough treatment that doesn't faze the rugged Rolleiflex.

Photos taken with the Hasselblad are needle sharp and of superb quality.

Large Format Single-Lens Reflex

Cameras of this type are seldom encountered any more; in fact, few advertising men who came on the scene in the last 10 or 15 years have seen one.

The old Graflex, although obsolete, is still a precision instrument capable of turning out top quality work. It handles film up to 5-by-7 inches in size.

Lenses are quickly interchangeable, and the back may be turned from horizontal to vertical easily and quickly. Drawbacks are that the camera is large, heavy, and difficult to handle; the shutter requires a minimum of a Philadelphia lawyer *and* an M.I.T. engineer to set it unless pondered over for a day or two, more or less. Too, the tall, collapsible focusing hood into which one peers can get a photographer killed when he's near fast-moving traffic or any natural hazards.

Hand-and-Stand Cameras

Best known and unquestionably the best camera of this type is the massive, indestructible Speed Graphic.

Best all-around film size, and it's made in 2¼-by-3¼ inches, 3¼-by-4¼ inches, and 4 by 5 inches, is the 4x5. Primarily this is because from a 4x5 negative comes the standard 8x10 print with no cropping, nothing lost, no waste time or motion. Required is only a two-diameter enlargement, so there's no loss of print quality, no loss of sharpness.

All other formats require the photographer to make a decision when making an enlargement: He must decide just what is to be cropped off of the finished print—that is, what is not to appear in the picture.

This is because the 35mm format, for instance, is too long in proportion to its width to make a "perfect" 8x10 print. And the 2¼-inch-square negative is just that—square. To make it into an 8x10, which isn't square, means that something has to give. That something is something left off of the finished print.

But the 4x5 negative size is ideal. The 4x5 Speed Graphic is a bulky, heavy old warhorse that's taken more classic news pictures than any other camera ever marketed—ever.

For decades it was the standard camera of all press photographers and indeed became their symbol. It is still widely used, although press photographers are like most of the rest of us—they're getting lazy and want something light to carry.

The Speed Graphic has two shutters—a between-the-lens shutter for speeds up to 1/400 second, and a focal-plane shutter for speeds up to 1/1,000 second; the focal-plane shutter is far behind the "front" or between-the-lens shutter. One shutter or the other must be open when the other one is being used, of course, or no picture will be taken because light does not reach the film.

The Speed Graphic uses cut film or film pack so the photographer can shoot and develop one picture if he wishes with no waste, no waiting to finish a roll.

There's a choice of two viewfinders, as well as ground glass focusing when the camera is put on a "stand"—a tripod.

The Speed Graphic has limited lensboard movements, similar to but not as many as those found on the view camera. It is an excellent all-around camera, and with quickly changeable lenses is suitable for the vast majority of all commercial or illustrative assignments.

View Cameras

The view camera is the most flexible camera of all, although even it has its limitations.

Some things that the little 35mm cameras do with great ease are outside the scope of the big view camera. View camera lenses slip onto the camera, one after another, so that whichever one is needed at the moment can be mounted with ease.

View cameras use large format film—from 4x5 to 11x14 or even larger. The 8x10 film is widely used in view cameras, although the camera of necessity is large and heavy and unwieldy. The view camera must be used mounted on a tripod; it cannot be hand-held because the only method of viewing the subject and of focusing is on the ground glass, and the image is cast upon it through the open lens.

Movements of the lens board, up, down, on a vertical or horizontal axis, combined with swings and tilts of the back and a long bellows, make for extreme versatility. Lines can be straightened, lines can be kept from converging, buildings can be straightened up and kept from falling over backwards, perspective may be corrected, foreshortening can be avoided, all with movements of the lensboard and back. No other camera has this built-in versatility and ability to handle almost every assignment that comes along.

The view camera will handle more different types of photography than any other one camera. For commercial and illustrative use it is the one essential tool the photographer must possess and the last one that most photographers would be willing to part with.

When you're hiring a photographer to shoot a job for you, he'll want to know approximately how many photographs are involved so he'll know how much film to bring. Have the job planned so you'll be able to tell him this.

Also, knowing something about cameras and how you want the finished illustrative photograph to look, you'll be able to give good general instructions on whether you feel artificial light sources are desirable; the photographer will make the final decision on this, of course, since he's responsible for making the photograph.

You can tell him, however, that you think it's a "Rolleiflex type of job," or that he's going to have to make corrections to make sure vertical lines are vertical and horizontal ones are horizontal in the picture. Only the view camera can do this correcting of perspective to the ultimate degree, although the Speed Graphic can to a lesser extent.

Being able to direct the photographer saves time for him and money for you. What's more, you make both of your jobs that much easier. Your photographer will be happy to go over the various types of cameras with which he's equipped, brief you on each, show you how each one works, and how things look to him through them. Ask him.

He'll be flattered that you're interested and will take great delight in showing you his expertise and his array of exquisitely delicate and complicated equipment. He's proud of it. And he has a large investment in it. You'll find the experience interesting and informative and you'll pave the way to getting better photographs at less expense.

And, who knows, you might very well make a friend in the bargain. That could be best of all.

Stock Photos

Yes, Virginia, there *is* a pot of gold at the foot of the rainbow for advertising men looking for a top quality photograph when they have neither time nor much extra money in the department budget.

This pot of photographic gold is called "stock photos."

Stock photos are instant photos. They already exist, there's no waiting to get them, no hiring of models or photographers, no praying for sunlight, no frantic search for exactly the right scene to photograph, no worry about the season of the year.

All you have to do is pick up your phone, or write an airmail letter to have a good selection of high grade photographs on your desk a day or two later.

Probably the best source in the country for quality stock photographs is this one:

The Photography of H. Armstrong Roberts
4203 Locust Street
Philadelphia, Pennsylvania 19104

This company has been in business since 1920 and is thoroughly reliable and reputable.

Roberts' rates are realistic and a price quotation accompanies each approval selection. Rates are based upon the reproduction rights needed, of course. In most cases, Roberts issues an invoice-license to reproduce the picture for specified media, with the transparency to be returned after separations are made. Transparencies are also available on an exclusive basis, either in a certain field, or for a specified period of time, or for outright purchase of all rights. A quotation on any basis you prefer will be made upon request.

Roberts' camera covers almost every conceivable subject. People, of course, account for the bulk of the pictures because people are interested in people. The butcher, the baker—where's that other tradesman?—or members of their families from the moment of rising in the morning, brushing teeth, having breakfast, off to school, shopping, at work, going to bed. All are there.

All such daily activities on every day of the week, all through the year, every age group, in all seasons, at work and at play; Roberts shows people in every activity from babyhood through the retirement years. Photographs are dramatic and realistic, well-lighted and well-posed. And the pictures, *with model releases on file,* are available to you immediately.

Almost as varied are the photographs Roberts has of places. With coast-to-coast coverage of points of interest in the nation, including typical scenes of each state, you can choose industry, farmland, forests, waters, or mountains. Similar substantial coverage of foreign countries is also available.

Nearly every everyday situation involving people—and many without people—can be found in Roberts' extensive file of stock photographs. The file contains close to a half-million individual pictures. A partial list of the categories from which you may select includes:

Accidents and ailments
Aerial
Airplanes
Animals
Astronomy
Automobiles
Autumn
Babies
Banking
Basketball
Beach
Boating
Brides
Buildings
Business
Children
Children with adults
Christmas
Cities
Crowds
Dining
Dogs
Easter
Fall scenes
Families
Farming
Fires
Fireworks
Fishing
Flowers
Food
Football
Foreign
Gardening
Girls
Golf
Graduation
Gunning
Halloween
Hands
Historic
Horses and racing
Houses
Housework
Industrial
Interiors
Laboratories
Landscapes
Medical
Men
Money
Negro
New Year
Nurses
Office scenes
Patriotic
Picnics
Portraits
  Babies
  Children
  Men
  Women
Pools
Religious
Rockets
Scenic
School
Shipping
Shopping
Sleep
Sports
Spring
Story situations, men
Story situations, women
Summer scenes
Symbolic and still life
Teenagers
Telephone
Television and radio
Thanksgiving
Transportation
Travel
Winter
Women
Workmen

In addition to offering excellent black-and-white prints, Roberts has a large and growing library of color transparencies, mostly 4 by 5 in size, mounted for viewing ease and protection of the transparencies; each is numbered for positive identification and orderly presentation.

Selections, based upon your specifications, will be sent for 10 days on approval. The only obligation you incur is to handle the transparencies carefully and return any you do not accept promptly,

A selection of "people photos" from H. Armstrong Roberts.

well protected and by insured mail or registered with an appropriate valuation declared.

So you'll obtain the most useful selection, it's advisable to supply to Roberts as much information as possible about your requirements. For example, most transparencies will crop either vertically or horizontally, although some, because of subject matter, will not.

More people, here "doing things," from H. Armstrong Roberts.

Photographs of things could be almost unlimited, of course. Except for product shots, the choice of things photographed by Roberts is almost enough to stagger the imagination. The obvious and typical are well represented in Roberts' files, of course, ranging from ant eaters to zebras, or buildings, bridges, or you name it. Chances are

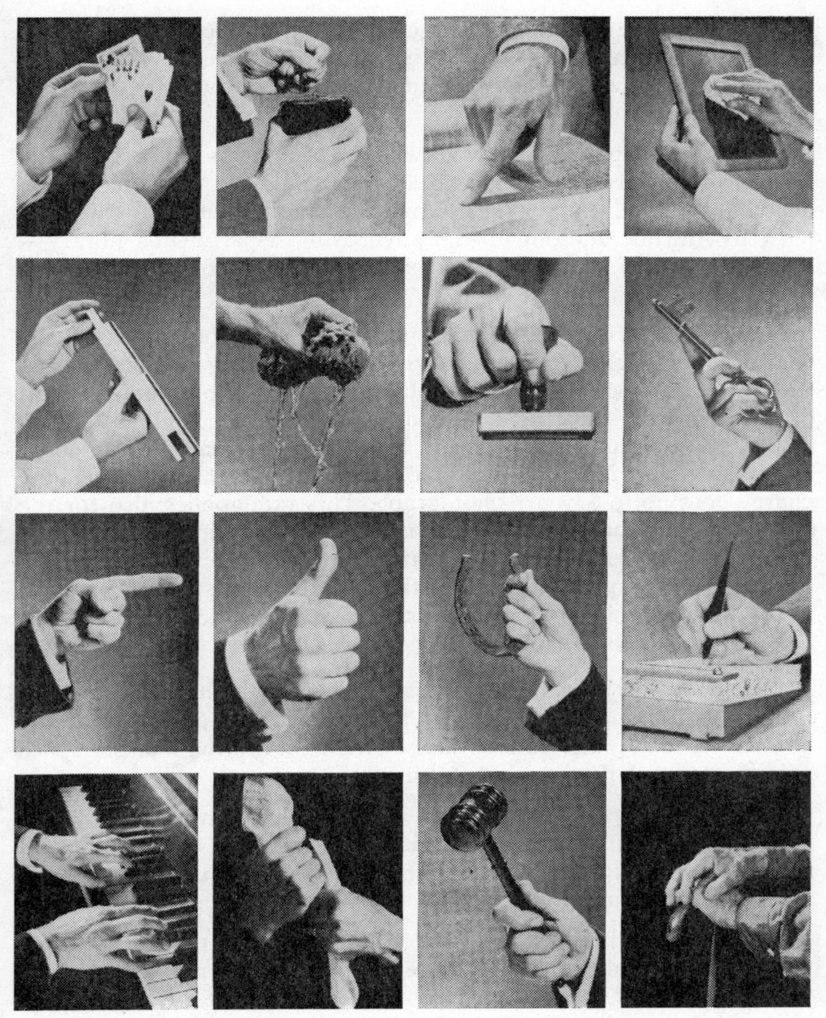

There's ad material in this collection of hands by H. Armstrong Roberts.

when you need a quality photographic illustration, Roberts will have it on hand.

The one weak area in this vast file of illustrative material is spot news pictures. Compix has those, so that's no problem, although you must take care about showing identifiable people without model releases.

Representative selections of all categories of Roberts' pictures are shown in catalogs of 76 pages issued several times a year. They contain miniature reproductions of almost every subject under the sun.

Any photography buyer who writes to Roberts on a company letterhead will receive one of these comprehensive catalogs and be kept on Roberts' mailing list to receive future editions. This is a most worthwhile addition to the advertising department's library—and one that can save the day when the chips are down and a deadline is starring you in the face.

Charges for the stock photographs vary with the extent of the use, as is only right. The base charge for advertising or promotion is $20, modest indeed. This is for local use of the photograph in local or minor media—such as a local newspaper, direct mail, TV, store display, or for an advertisement in a trade journal. For regional advertising (or for four cities) or for multiple minor media, the charge goes up to $35 per photograph. This rate applies also for the non-newsstand magazine that has national distribution. The average price for an advertisement in a national magazine is $125 per photo. This rate is also quoted for use of the picture in newspapers nationally. Those are basic charges—prices for other specific media, such as *U.S. News* and *World Report*.

Larger business firms are generally charged higher prices, however. This is not because of their ability to pay, but because of the greater value they derive from use of the photo through larger space ads, greater distribution, and so on.

All photographs reproduced in the catalog have an index number; it's necessary only to mention this when ordering. All orders and requests for photos on approval are shipped the same day, and you may specify airmail or special delivery to speed things up.

It's obviously impossible to reproduce hundreds of thousands of photos economically, although more than likely Roberts has the exact picture you need, even if it is not shown. In that case, phone or write and describe exactly what it is that you're interested in; chances are good that you'll receive a selection of pictures on approval the next day—and in it there will be the one that is exactly right for your use.

Stock photos can be a real time- and money-saver, and a budget stretcher as well. There's almost no chance the reader will remember ever having seen the photograph before, so you needn't worry on that score.

Illustrative Faux Pas

It's remarkably easy to contract an acute case of hoof-in-mouth disease, illustratively speaking.

Not a shred of evidence exists that this ailment is contagious. However, there are strong indications that it accompanies a widespread mental aberration which breaks down the body's defense mechanisms, making resistance to the shallow-thinking syndrome virtually ineffective.

One of the early symptoms of this dread ailment is selecting a nondescript word, apparently at random, for a product characteristic (usually not a benefit) that's very obviously considered nothing short of ineffable. As a rule, the word is of such a generalized nature there's not one thing in this world that would prevent the advertiser's most bitter competitor from switching names and logos and using the same illustrative idea—and often the same copy, as far as that's concerned.

For instance, there's the one-page, black-and-white advertisement run by Sinclair Refining Company in *Factory* magazine. The illustration is the buffalo side of an Indian-head nickel, the long-gone coin that will now buy a penny postal card. Headline, predictably enough, is:

Low profits got you buffaloed?

The subhead, though, is even worse if that's possible. Once the reader has stopped flinching at the headline, he then sees, also in display type:

Start cutting costs . . . everything starts with Sinclair

That literally boggles the imagination; having the imagination stretched is bad enough, but to have it boggled is too much. It's enough to give one the vapors.

Then there's the one-page, *three*-color (yellow, red, black) advertisement run by The Mechanex Corporation in *Commercial Car Journal.* Because Mechanex grease or oil seals top every other brand, Mechanex used an illustration of a grinning giraffe, which everybody knows is the tallest of the ruminant mammals, hence tops all other four-legged critters—and two-legged ones, too, for that matter.

Just what relationship the giraffe has to oil and grease seals is open to question, however. So, too, is the advisability of using an illustration that any competitor of The Mechanex Corporation could use with just a slightly different headline.

Low profits got you buffaloed?

Start cutting costs...everything starts with Sinclair

If you're having trouble keeping your costs under control, if you've got lubrication problems that have defied solution, or if your present supplier of lubricants has been taking you for granted, it's time to take action.

Call the friendly people at Sinclair. You'll get top treatment and attention. To reduce costs, step up production, and minimize downtime, Sinclair offers you hundreds of specialized lubricants and fuels. The more we help you, the more it helps us. Call, write or wire us at Sinclair, and find out why..."Everything starts with Sinclair." DRIVE WITH CARE AND BUY SINCLAIR.

Sinclair Refining Company
Technical Service Division
600 Fifth Ave., New York, N.Y. 10020 • Phone: 212-246-3600

Sinclair

This is the ad discussed in detail on the previous page. The illustration of the buffalo nickel is eye-catching enough, but author Stansfield points out that the play on words in the headline and subhead are too obvious. Main objection, though, is that the idea could be used by any advertiser for any product.

TOPS 'EM ALL
in performance
and savings*

mechanex

NO. 1 SEALS ON ANY WHEELS
(OIL OR GREASE)

AND NOW...the revolutionary
NEW DRIVE AXLE SEAL

SERIES 4000

★ Simplicity of design makes installation fool-proof ...and NO TOOLS are needed

★ Runs cooler than any other seal

★ Usual Mechanex double seal...keeps dust out... keeps lubricant in

★ Assembles as ONE-PIECE unit

★ Replaces ANY SEAL...AND...at lowest cost! AND...like any Mechanex seals it is made of a special compound to resist heat and additives... performs equally well on worn spindles and hubs... requires no sealant

all to lower your maintenance costs.

FREE LITERATURE available on this 4000 series

Write for 20 ADVANTAGES OF MECHANEX SEALS

THE
mechanex
CORPORATION
3773 South Jason • Englewood, Colorado 80110

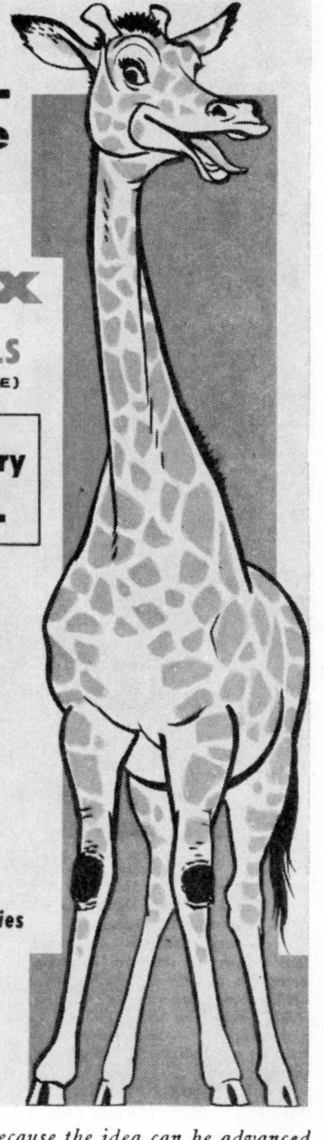

Another ad cited by the author as lacking force because the idea can be advanced for any product by any advertiser. The giraffe "tops" all animals; therefore "Brand X" tops them all, whatever the product. More sophistication is needed today.

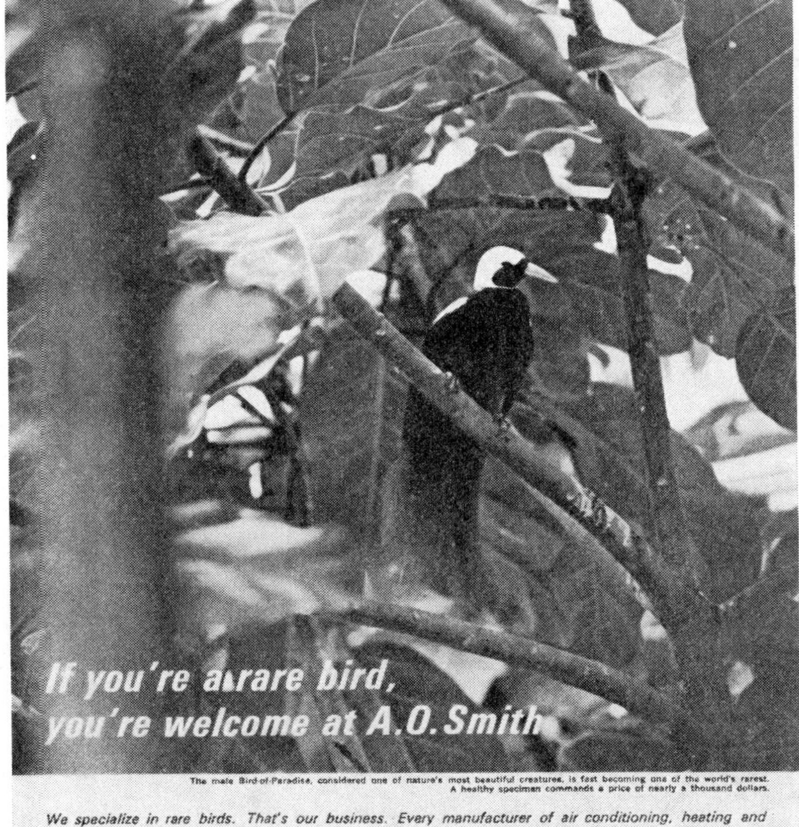
If you're a rare bird,
you're welcome at A.O.Smith

The male Bird-of-Paradise, considered one of nature's most beautiful creatures, is fast becoming one of the world's rarest. A healthy specimen commands a price of nearly a thousand dollars.

We specialize in rare birds. That's our business. Every manufacturer of air conditioning, heating and refrigeration equipment has his own special, unique requirements . . . and with problems to match. But because we specialize in custom-engineering electric motors, we've been solving these rare problems for years. We believe we can solve yours. For example, one A. O. Smith innovation that could solve your blower noise, draft and air distribution problems is the "rara avis" at the right — our automatic blower control motor. A solid state control regulates speed automatically to provide continuous air circulation. For facts on this new ABC motor, call or write A. O. Smith Corporation, Electric Motor Division, Tipp City, Ohio.

AOSmith

Automatic Blower Control Motor

A. O. Smith Corporation, Electric Motor Division, uses a beautiful four-color insert in a metalworking magazine to tell an exceptionally strong capability story.

The advertiser's story is convincing and persuasive and the company obviously has much to offer. The ad is a strong one and it received excellent readership, as did the other ads in this fine campaign. A. O. Smith shows the product—an automatic-blower-control motor—in a spot illustration in the lower right hand corner; this is all to the good.

The dominant illustration of a fantastically colorful Bird-of-Paradise meshes well with the headline:

If you're a rare bird,
you're welcome at A. O. Smith

Nonetheless, the question remains whether A. O. Smith wouldn't have been better off to use some other device to attract the reader, rather than taking a word from the headline and illustrating it.

Equally sorry is the trite situation, although, praise be, it's becoming more scarce with each passing year. It used to be you couldn't pick up a trade book in any industry without finding either a white-smocked druggist happily whipping up a tasty little prescription to cure whatever ailment the reader had—fortuitously with the advertiser's product, of course. And sure as shootin', up there in the headline as prominent as could be was a big ℞.

Some advertisers simplified things a bit and saved a buck at the same time by not bothering to hire a model; they merely showed a close-up of the advertising manager's hands mixing with mortar and pestle. The ℞ was still there, though, big as life.

Then there's the ubiquitous, luscious blonde with the fatuous grin, not a hair out of place, in an office that never saw a day's work in its life, showing her boss that the file cabinet drawers *really* open. Or she might be gleefully adding something on an adding machine to prove it *really* adds, still with that same self-satisfied smirk. Illustrations like this fall flatter than Twiggy's chest. Triteness and clichés, hoary with age and encrusted with moss, have no place in the advertising illustration. Use them and you're throwing money away.

The Medicine-Man Fetish

And there's the medicine-man approach, which makes a fetish of illustrating something equally applicable to any product. This type of illustration is a direct descendant of a consumer advertising campaign. In this class is the half-page, black-and-white ad run in *Production* magazine by Omark-Winslow Aerospace Tool Company, a subsidiary of Omark Industries, Inc. The illustration of a bottle of headache pills—presumably Anacin—is a takeoff on the TV

FAST, FAST, FAST RELIEF
for splitting headaches!
Here's a quick cure for drill splitting and web thinning problems: our Model 400 WINSLOMATIC Splitter that handles up to 500 drills an hour. It's highly accurate, fully automatic with 180° indexing. The 400 splits drills in the full range from 1/16" to 1/2" and web thins drills from 1/16" to 1 5/8." Works both sides of the drill in a single cycle and indexes automatically. This compact, rugged machine is so simple to set up and use an operator can master it within an hour and attain maximum production within less than a day. For proof of its capabilities, write for our new WINSLOMATIC 400 catalog. And for further information on the Winslow line of drill pointers, send for literature and price list. (Or send us some of your dull drills for pointing—free. We'll return them shortly, sharply!)
OMARK-WINSLOW
AEROSPACE TOOL COMPANY
A Subsidiary of OMARK INDUSTRIES, INC.
47 St. Joseph Street • Arcadia, Calif. 91006 • (213) 446-8221 • 681-7134

commercials for Anacin and promises a fast, FAST, *FAST* relief for splitting headaches. But there's nothing in it to give the reader even a vague hint of what the ad's about. This means it doesn't qualify readers, it doesn't help the individual reader decide whether or not it will benefit him to read the advertisement.

Copy is well-conceived, however, and it's a shame the illustration and headline are so trite. Omark-Winslow has a good story to tell and the copy doesn't beat around the bush with long-winded introductions; it gets right into user benefits that go with the Model 400 Winslomatic Splitter.

The copy is believable, persuasive, and does a fine job of convincing the reader that this is a product he should know more about. After the strong bid for action, the company offers to repoint the reader's drills free, just to show what kind of work its machine turns out. Kind of hard to overlook an offer like that—and a hard-selling one it is, too.

Put thought and plenty of it into the illustration for your ad. After all, it can make or break you.

How to Get Greater Impact Into Illustrations

There is no magic formula that will assure a constant flow of fresh ideas that results in powerful, effective illustrations that excel in stopping power. Developing really good illustrative ideas is much like writing copy—it seldom comes easy.

One thing is obvious, though: The reader must find the illustration interesting. This means that more likely than not he'll skip over one that's been done to death in one variation or another. And he'll ignore one that doesn't offer some incentive to read the ad or reward him for his time. You can't serve up a bland illustrative diet when your competitors are offering seven-course visual offerings.

Numerous studies have proven that you *can* deliberately set out to produce an illustration specifically to garner more than your share of readership—and pull it off. A few ideas that will work follow. Mull them over and they should trigger plenty more.

First, you should be *different* in your illustration. Different, but with a reason—not merely kooky. The kooks and smart alecks have enjoyed great popularity in consumer advertising, but their influence is waning. We in industrial advertising should offer up heartfelt thanks that the malady didn't strike in our field. Much of the insanity foisted on consumer advertisers who should have known better would have gotten an industrial advertising manager, account executive, or copywriter an invitation to depart the scene.

Stop-motion stroboscopic photographs of something that's obviously moving at spectacularly high speed always attract attention. The clubhead flattening the golf ball; a bullet in midair; an egg being splattered by the blades of an electric fan, each drop of yolk momentarily halted; a drop of water striking a highly polished surface; these are examples. You've seen many, but you don't pass them by. This type of illustration, when used for good reason, invariably attracts the reader. He's intrigued by the sight of something he can't see with the naked eye.

Does TRW build steering linkages that fail?

We make sure they fail.

At TRW we spend a fortune to break them.

We built a test track for that purpose. And we spend thousands of dollars to buy the machines to do the breaking.

Obviously our job is not only building completely safe steering linkages, but also knowing when they'll fail and why. And the reason is, if we know where all the weaknesses are, then we know precisely the strength. What kind of strength requirements do we have?

We test the entire steering assembly by at least 3 times the vehicle requirements. (It can range much higher for heavy-duty truck equipment.)

If, as a prospective customer, you would like to see the range and the methods of TRW's test facilities, call us. We feel they are important enough for you to see.

After all, there's a lot riding on them.

TRW Michigan Division, TRW INC., Warren, Michigan 48093.

TRW

Close kin to the stop-motion photograph is the multiple exposure, usually also made with the ultra high-speed stroboscopic light. Multiple exposure with partially formed, ghost-like images almost shouts "motion" to the reader. The technique is dramatic and the resulting photographs are always interesting. The reader feels a sense of excitement, of looking at something that's actually happening. Multiple exposure photographs pull him into the headline approximately 31 percent more often than would a staid, stodgy photograph of the product alone, or even with a self-conscious model casting an admiring smile in its direction.

TRW Michigan Division, TRW, Inc., proves this quite nicely in its arresting one-page, black-and-white advertisement in *Automotive Industries* magazine. Illustration is a tremendously impressive multiple exposure of steering linkages, close up and framed by a tire and brake drum. The feeling of action is unusually strong. The reader can easily visualize this mammoth vehicle going at great speed, bouncing over chuck holes and rough pavement. Illustration teams up with a fine teaser headline to pull the reader into the body copy, where TRW Michigan Division tells a powerful quality story. This ad carries great conviction.

For a switch, try to stump Amphenol

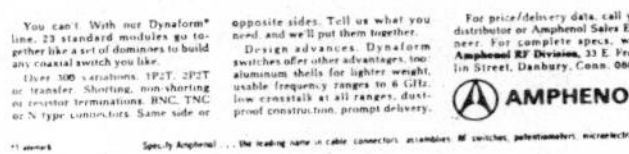

Another eye-catcher that rates high in interest value is the extreme close-up. It's inherently interesting and the reader feels a sense of involvement with the illustration because he's *right there.* He finds it difficult to pass by an extreme close-up without stopping and

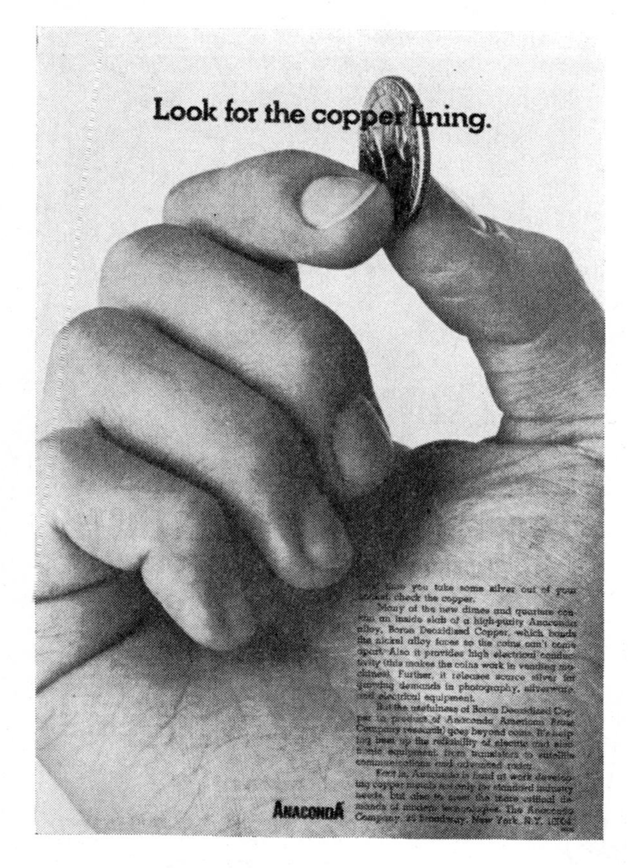

Anaconda knows how to use the close-up to good advantage in ad illustration. Few readers can ignore this photo.

taking another look—and, before he knows it, he's into the headline. The Amphenol RF Division, Amphenol Corporation, uses the close-up technique with telling effectiveness in its fine spread ad illustrated nearby. Illustration and headline are tied together with both logic and charm, for there's both a play on words and a play on a situation. This gives Amphenol and its agency, Marsteller Inc., the perfect opportunity to get the product in there without being "product-y" about it.

What's more, the dominoes are perfect to show the size of the product, and they're not as out-of-date as you'd think. In the South, adults play dominoes often.

The Anaconda Company's fine four-color advertisement from *Iron Age* is an excellent example of the attraction the extreme close-up has. Few and far between are readers who can ignore this interesting close-up of a man's hand holding a piece of minimoney (the new silverless quarter which is of little intrinsic value).

Illustration and headline work well together and with the copy in what must have been an incredibly difficult communications job—calling attention to the fact the country's coinage is composed of a sandwich of two metals that are worthless, monetarily, in order to tell about the capability of The Anaconda Company. There's no denying, however, that the illustration is effective.

Anaconda used an extreme close-up, but The Aluminum Company of America uses ultraclose-up microphotography for one illustration in its powerful four-color spread in *Modern Casting* magazine.

The illustration nearby shows a photomicrograph of Alcoa IFG Ingot, alloy 142. The photograph makes it easy for the reader to see there is no oxide and no porosity in this high quality casting. Caption calls attention to the fine dispersion of the alloying elements. Magnification of this photomicrograph is approximately 450 times. The rest of the ad is crisp and clean, but not of paramount importance here.

Alcoa *really* shows a close-up. The reader likes extreme magnification of well-known objects because he sees things he's never seen before, and probably wouldn't have the opportunity to see anyplace

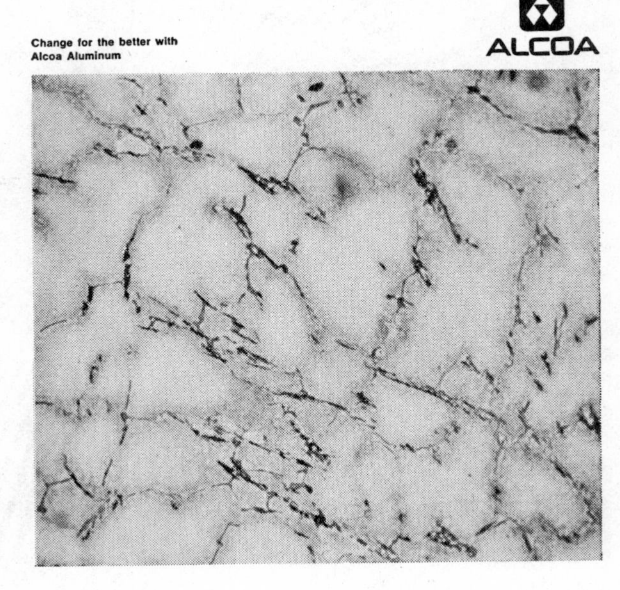
Change for the better with
Alcoa Aluminum
ALCOA

Alcoa used this photomicrograph to prove there is no oxide and no porosity in a high quality casting.

except in the advertisement. This type of illustration is great for technical men; it attracts them in droves. And Alcoa wisely got some sell into the caption of the ultraclose-up, for if a reader reads only one thing in an ad, it's the caption of the illustration. He can skip headline and body copy, but he seldom skips captions. Captions receive almost unbelievable readership.

The screened illustration, if it's well done, is also an attention-grabber. Sloan Instrument Corporation's ad has an illustration that practically jumps off the page at you. This fine ad ran in *Electronic Packaging and Production, Journal of Applied Optics,* and in the magazine that unlocks the most inaccessible door in industry, *Research/Development.* Personnel in research and development are almost impossible for a salesman to see; advertising must carry most of the burden.

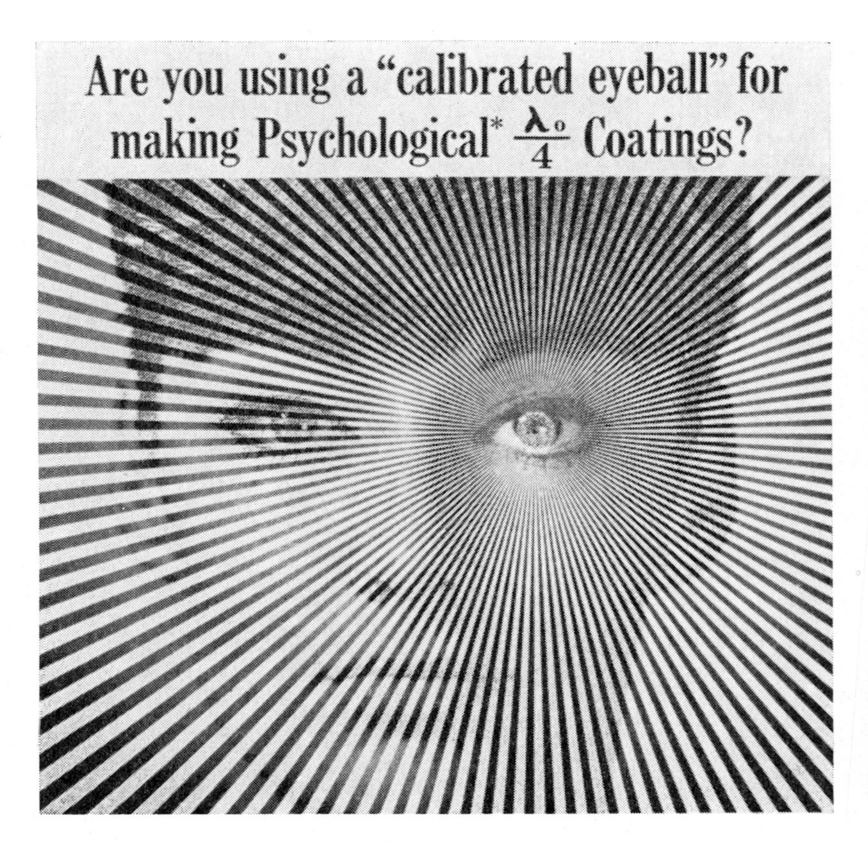

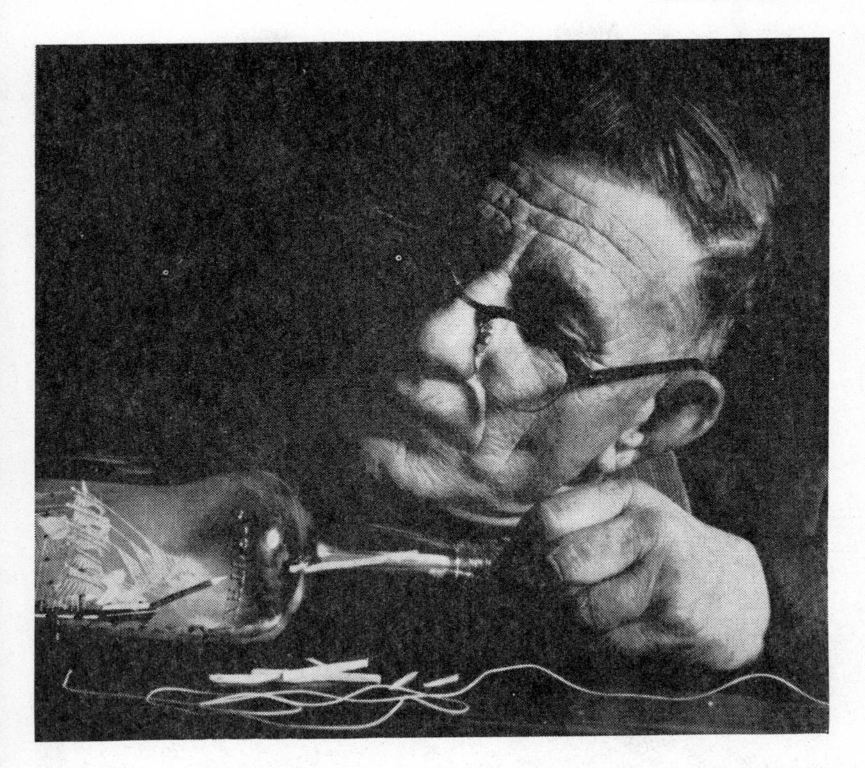

This is a far cry from picturing the product in a static pose and then proudly proclaiming how great it is. This deadly practice is seen in far too many industrial advertisements. Here, however, there's a natural tie-in between illustration, headline, and body copy —as there should be. It's a sort of a progression; a baiting of the trap. The illustration, because it's different, stops the reader, the headline arouses his curiosity, and the body copy holds him in a warm, affectionate grip to satisfy his yearn to learn until Sloan makes its point.

Low-key photography—or artwork, for that matter—is also a device that the reader finds appealing because it's far removed from the mine-run illustrations he's accustomed to seeing. Low key is simply having most of the area in the illustration very dark, or even black, in tone and separating the subject by having it lighter than the surrounding mass. For this reason it attracts the eye.

The Standard Register Company's excellent ad, illustrated above, has a highly dramatic low-key photograph. It packs great reader appeal because it is, first of all, a close-up of a man doing something interesting. It's not static. Secondly, it's low key and this, too, rivets the gaze. The heavy area of black serves as a frame and concentrates the reader's attention on the boat-building pickpocket. Ordinarily an ad gets better readership if the illustration is at the top of the page; in this instance, however, due to the weight of the illustration, it seems to belong at the bottom.

Another example of low-key photography is the one taken by the author underneath the Michigan Avenue bridge across the Chicago River. The somber masses of heavy, dark girders create a mood, cause the eye to go immediately to the lightest area of the picture—the figure of the man in the trench coat.

Note that the principle of thirds was used for this composition; the man is approximately one-third of the way from the bottom of the picture, and about one-third of the way from the right hand side. Low-key pictures are extraordinarily dramatic and intensely interesting, although they're not entirely suitable for all subjects.

A high-key illustration is just the opposite of low key, of course. In the typical high-key illustration—particularly the photographic one—the vast majority of the tones are in the middle to the upper end of the gray scale. Backgrounds are either white or very close to it.

There's always at least one spot of pitch black, of course, for photographic quality demands that it be there—but it's invariably small and is certainly not the most important element in the picture.

Subjects which are naturally light in color or tone are ideal for high-key photography—blonde women, blonde cocker spaniels, fair-

This high-key photo is in sharp contrast to the dark bridge picture opposite. The blonde model sets a tone here.

skinned children, and so on. You're familiar with the famous photographic exercise of photographing a white egg against a white background on a white dinner plate. It's a bit difficult, but it can be done and done attractively. A word of caution is in order, however, about high key. High key is basically a feminine medium, well-suited for high fashion shots of cadaverous models who appear to be refugees from a tubercular sanatorium. Seldom does an industrial product appear at its best in high key.

The Bristol Brass Corporation's attractive ad from *Business Week* is an excellent example of the impact the high-key photographic illustration can achieve. Bristol made the most of a lovely blonde model by using this technique.

Because it's the exact opposite of a low-key picture, the eye is attracted to the darkest area in the high-key picture. In the case of Bristol's photograph, this is the model's eyes; from there, the reader's eye naturally goes to the next darkest element in the illustration—which, here, is the headline. Good composition and well-planned layout helped attract a large number of readers.

Camera Angles and Other "Angles"

Unusual camera angles, sometimes deliberately exaggerated by lenses of very short focal length to create distortion, just cannot be ignored. The reader's curiosity is aroused and he's drawn into the ad. For the most part, such photographs—artwork is seldom used for the weird perspective—are called "worm's-eye views," just the opposite of the "bird's-eye view." The extremely low angle can be applied to almost any photographic subject, whereas the extremely high camera angle frequently involves either an aerial shot from an airplane or helicopter, although some such shots are sometimes made from a tall building if it happens to be in the right spot. It's kind of hard to move a skyscraper just to use it for a camera platform, though.

What *has* to be the world's longest-legged model was created with a combination worm's-eye view and an extremely short lens for Ametek, Inc.'s powerful four-color ad from *Fortune.*

The model, verging on the grotesque, teams up with the headline set on a slant and the diagonal cropping of the photograph to repeat the strong lines and arouse reader interest.

Beside this glamour photo we see how Los Angeles photographer Jason Hailey did a typical industrial scene with a worm's-eye view. Photographer Hailey achieved much added impact through use of the low camera angle. It adds that additional bit of interest to a

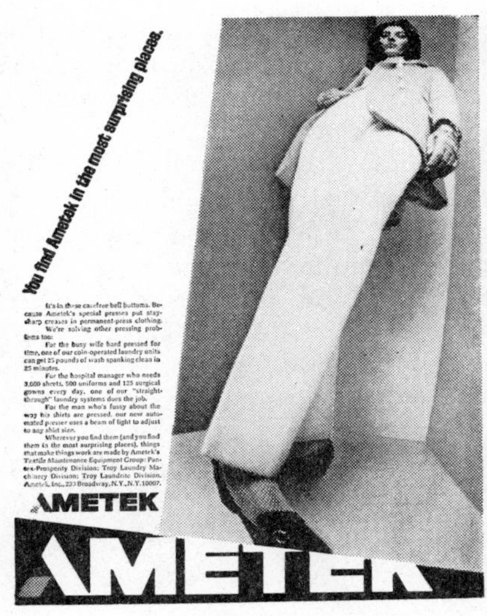

Unusual camera angles, used judiciously, can provide impact to the advertising illustration. Here are two "worm's-eye" views. At left, Ametek's ad is given strength not only by the camera angle, but also the type arrangement. At right, Jason Hailey added interest to a commonplace industrial scene with a low angle.

commonplace scene by showing it to the reader in a way he's not accustomed to seeing. As far as the reader is concerned, this makes the photograph one that's completely new and fresh and different, rather than merely a picture of a hard-hatted workman reading some gauges and dials.

Quite possibly your product is one that you can *literally put in the ad,* gaining an entirely new dimension and creating an exciting advertisement that's a departure from the ordinary. This is possible with some products.

For example, you can obviously put ink in an ad if that's your product; or you can tip on (glue on) chips of paint or enamel; small swatches of vinyl or fabric can be tipped onto an insert ad; perfume has been mixed with printer's ink many times in consumer ads to create "smellies"; everything from a new kind of bottle cap on up to things so bulky you'd find it hard to believe have been tipped onto insert ads, then the insert itself tipped into a trade publication.

For obvious reasons a halt had to be called to the practice before somebody tipped on a six-wheel dump truck capable of hauling a gross load of 72,000 pounds, thus making the magazine both too heavy for the post office to deliver and for the reader to handle.

Accordingly, the post office instituted some more rules and regulations that almost nobody can read and comprehend until they're carefully typed out in English after translation from the original Bureaucratese.

One advertiser who used this technique with outstanding effectiveness is Norton Company, leading manufacturer of abrasives. Its excellent insert ad is a veritable product in print—as P. A. Binney of Norton Company said—aluminum oxide abrasive was baked onto the wheel, giving it an extra dimension. The grinding wheel looks like a grinding wheel and it *feels* like one, too. The texture's there visually and when you touch it you know you have hold of a real, honest-to-gosh grinding wheel. The realism is terrific. When the reader touches, Norton has him, even before he looks or starts to read. He simply cannot resist reading the headline (The original is at the other end of your phone), then turning the page to get the message on the flip side (So are several thousand others).

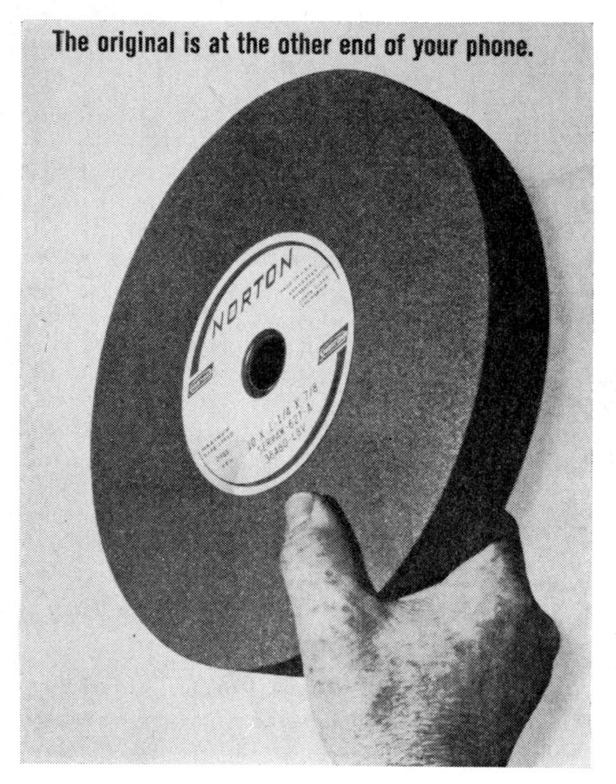

A thin coating of an abrasive was put on the surface of the photo of a grinding wheel, so customers could feel product.

Second page (the other side) of the insert is printed in two colors, blue and black. A well-composed and well-lighted photographic illustration shows the texture and the range of sizes of typical Norton grinding wheels. Copy sells hard on product quality and availability from industrial distributors across the nation; the reader learns that it is unnecessary for his company to tie up lots of money and space stocking a large supply of grinding wheels. Norton inventories them instead, and they're there when needed.

This is an unusually powerful advertisement. It has consistently drawn top readership ratings in the publications in which it has appeared, and it holds the *all-time* top readership rating in several major trade publications including *Mill & Factory* and *Machinery*. An all-time best readership rating is a tough mark for any ad to shoot at, much less to top. It may be years before any advertisement beats this great one!

Then, there's the use of type itself as an "illustration." When this is done the type is actually a design element, as well as the medium that conveys the message. Two ads from an unusually bold campaign run by Fairchild Semiconductor, Division of Fairchild Camera and Instrument Corporation, a leader in its industry, are illustrated nearby.

Ads are two-color, red and black, with the large firm name printed in black, and partially cut off.

Few industrial advertisers have either the inclination or the intestinal fortitude to chop up the company name this way. And few should, unless they're in the happy position that Fairchild is in—unquestioned industry leadership. Occupying this position makes it possible to be bold and brash without looking presumptuous.

Even when it's shown only partially, and with the firm name in the tiny little type tucked away in an inconspicuous corner, there's no doubt that the name of Fairchild comes through loud and clear. And that it makes a vivid impression on the reader's mind. This is particularly so because Fairchild had enough self-confidence to run the ad. Few indeed are the advertisers who would have had the courage to do so.

Short copy in one ad asks this simple question:

How many semiconductor manufacturers delivered more than one million integrated circuits last month?

One.

Then the name, Fairchild, minus only the "d" and a small part of the "l," literally leaps up off of the page at the reader. He simply cannot ignore it, nor can he overlook it.

The other treatment asks the reader a provocative question:

How many integrated circuit manufacturers shipped more units last December than all others combined?

One.

Again the name "Fairchild," abruptly chopped off after one leg of the "h" is shown, dominates the spread and immediately tele-

graphs the message. Nobody in the electronics industry—customer, prospect, or competitor—could possibly harbor any doubt about what company was doing the talking in this ad.

Primary objective of this striking campaign was to emphasize Fairchild's leadership and dominance of the industry in the manufacture of integrated circuits. The campaign exploited a positive asset that Fairchild's competitors would give an eyetooth to have, of course.

This illustrative technique rests on a strong foundation borrowed from tactics used by consumer advertisers. If your company's position is as well-established in your industry as Fairchild's, it's a ploy you might want to consider. However, if your company doesn't actually dominate the industry *in the mind of the reader,* this is the road to disaster.

Sure way to get an extra helping of attention from the reader is to take the offbeat path. Be different in your illustration. Don't settle for the tried and proven, the stodgy, the static picture of Our Product shown before a nice, clean, even-toned background.

Use Whimsy—With Care

Whimsy, for instance, always attracts. Most people like the far out, the very different, the fresh and humorous, and the incongruous. Imagination used imaginatively in an advertisement reaches out and grapples with readers and yanks them right into the ad. The reader finds he's unable to pass by without giving your ad a minimum of a second glance—a maximum contribution on his part of reading your entire ad.

Although it's not the most wildly creative idea that ever came down the pike, The Mutual Life Insurance Company of New York's one-page, black-and-white ad in *Dun's Review* has an illustration that's hard to resist. It's shown on the following page.

Apparently neither copywriters nor art directors can forget the title of Budd Schulberg's tremendous book, *What Makes Sammy Run?,* nor can they refrain from pinching the basic idea for headlines and illustrations. However, a new generation has grown up and entered the business world since the book was written and if it's new to them, it's new, period.

MONY's chopped-up man has a fine feeling of motion, excitement, of something interesting and exciting and compelling just on the verge of happening. And the copy, carefully split up into bite-size blocks with clever lead-ins in each instance, is a delight to read. The

What makes a MONY pension specialist run?

A get-ahead head. It's crammed full of facts that can help your pension program move ahead fast. We make sure he gets the latest investment news from a staff of alert specialists. This staff hunts down unusual sound investment opportunities to get more work out of every dollar.

A flexible portfolio. Every company has particular investment goals and problems. The MONY man's portfolio is flexible to help you meet those goals and solve those problems. He can offer you a general portfolio. Or a separate equity investment account. Or variable annuities. He can tailor a pension plan to your company's exact needs. Or show you ways to improve your profit-sharing plan without increasing its cost.

A tight fist. He tightfistedly guards every penny of your investment. And for good reason. An improvement of ½% in yield can produce as much as 12% savings in costs for you over the long run.

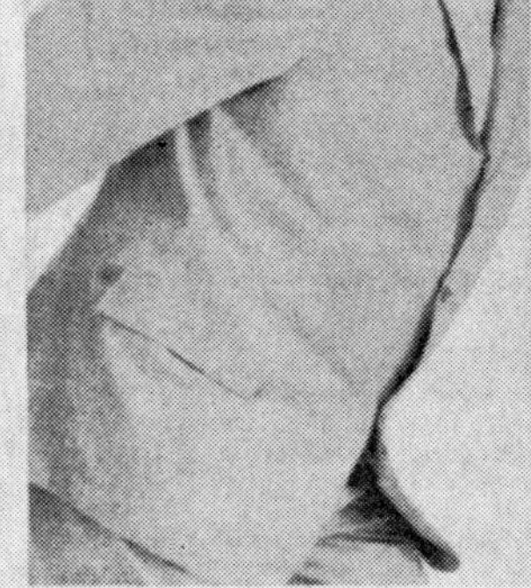

A strong suit. His strong suit is this: MONY looks for good investment possibilities in every investment area. That includes stocks. And bonds. And mortgages. We consider any sound investment possibility worth attention.

Lots of legwork. He stays on his toes for his clients. He'll help you dig up whatever information you need—and he'll do it fast. Want proof? Ask us to run a MONY pension specialist over to your office. Phone or write: Donald L. Coe, JU 6-4000, Ext. 752, Room 5-15, 1740 Broadway, New York, New York.

THE MUTUAL LIFE INSURANCE COMPANY OF NEW YORK, NEW YORK, N.Y.

entire ad is unusually well done and does an unusually effective job of selling MONY's pension service to the business community.

The incongruity of a businesslike salesman sitting knitting halts

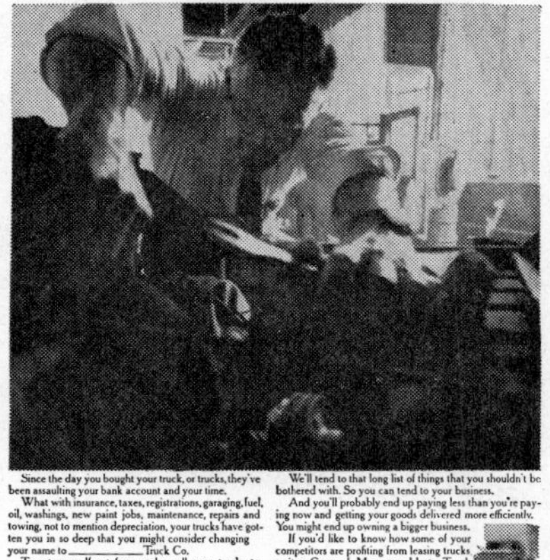

the reader right now and makes AT&T's illustration a hard worker. There's no doubt in anybody's mind that American Telephone & Telegraph Company's selling proposition is a sound one. Short copy, good proposition, incongruous illustration, and lots of eye-catching white space make this ad from *Dun's Review* a potent one.

Hertz Truck Leasing, part of the Hertz System, Inc., uses an offbeat illustration to good advantage in its black-and-white ad run in *Dun's Review*.

Merely showing one of the company executives in white shirt and necktie, leaning into a greasy engine, sleeves rolled up and grimacing in distaste, is enough to make the reader stop, look, and read—especially when the illustration appears beneath a headline that's almost overpowering.

The Posterization Technique

Posterization of a photograph is an effective way to impart a sense of the dramatic to what would otherwise merely be a picture of a grimy industrial subject. Photographer Jason Hailey's two prints, one conventional, the other posterized, illustrate the effect that may be obtained this way. Posterization is usually done either with a texture screen placed in contact with the printing paper, or is done by over-developing a negative to get coarse grain, then printing on

Top photo is conventional; print below has been "posterized."

a paper that is several grades too hard, thus achieving high contrast.

In addition, you can use Xograph color prints in three dimensions as a method of stopping the reader. This relatively new process won't let you step into the picture, of course, but the illustration gives the impression that you almost can.

To achieve roundness so that the viewer could see around the object, Xograph, Visual Panographics, Inc., 488 Madison Avenue, New York 10022, developed a completely new process; this was done in collaboration with Eastman Chemical Products, Inc., a subsidiary of Eastman Kodak Company. Harris-Intertype Corporation built the special printing press that was required.

The printing process is done letterpress, and is limited to a range of about a 120-line screen; if dots are refined further there's trouble with ink flow and clogging, causing inferior printing.

When a 3D picture is taken for reproduction by this process, a screen is put in front of the film as the photo is taken. This screen divides the picture into hundreds of tiny, vertical, parallel strips. The photo is then developed, and press plates are made in the conventional manner. In the process a viewing screen is applied by coating the printed surface with a special plastic. This screen focuses on the tiny strips in the picture and provides the viewer with the illusion of depth.

Then, when viewed by the reader, his eye has the opportunity to pick up literally thousands of tiny pairs—stereo pairs, if you want to compare it to stereo photography. In this way Xograph is able to project and the reader is enabled actually to look around an object.

A typical Xograph, this one of a building under construction, is shown nearby. Reproduction in flat black-and-white doesn't do justice to the amazing sense of depth and roundness the original reproduction imparts.

Xograph illustrations either have to be tipped onto the printed page, or tipped onto furnished inserts supplied to the publications. Cost is substantial, although the process does do a fantastic job of doing what an illustration is supposed to do: stopping the reader, attracting his attention, pulling him into the advertisement.

For example, Eastman Kodak Company used a three-dimensional Xograph on the cover of its annual report in 1965; subject was a young man and woman leaning on a rustic fence. Bucolic charm abounded.

Each year the Eastman Kodak Company offers its shareholders reprint copies of the four-color photographs which appear in the report. Within two months of the distribution of this annual report, Kodak received requests for reprints which were 300 percent greater than the preceding year—its previous all-time high. Of interest, too is that in previous years most requests came in on post cards. In this case, though, requests for the report were typewritten on quality stationary and hand-signed. Assumption is that Xograph enhanced the quality image of the report, as well as the reaction from the stockholders.

They may have been merely curious, however.

Also in 1965, Rust-Oleum ran an Xograph insert in *Business Week* magazine and it received one of the highest Starch ratings ever recorded for the magazine, and by far the highest for the issue. Scores were:

Noted 77%   Seen-Associated 70%   Read Most 22%

This past year Rust-Oleum repeated the ad with a new Xograph insert. Result: By far the highest Starch Noted score in *Business Week* history. The scores were:

Noted 84%   Seen-Associated 78%   Read Most 18%

This illustrative medium unquestionably has great stopping power. It is quite possible that due to their novelty Xograph illustrations are succeeding with both good and bad ads. Time alone will tell whether the process can continue to produce such amazing results.

Authenticity is always a desirable quality in an illustration, but frequently a difficult one to achieve. When you have a pressing need for a picture on a bright sunny day in a sunny clime, there's always a blizzard howling outside and the temperature is 10 below. Or, if you need a winter scene for an ad for a manufacturer of tire chains, it'll invariably be a balmy day in June just to drive *you* balmy.

Changing seasons and transporting the product at will through time and space is the forte of the projected background technique used so effectively by Pohlman Studios, Inc., 527 North 27th Street, Milwaukee, Wisconsin 53208. This studio is the leading illustrative and commercial photographer in this part of Wisconsin, and it pioneered in perfecting the projected background.

Even when it isn't used to create a special scene or setting, the projected background technique is an excellent device to dramatize a photograph of a product that's pretty run-of-the-mill, when appearance is concerned.

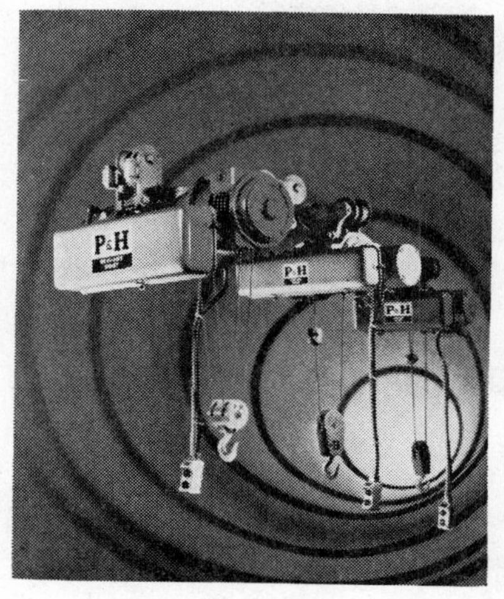

Futuristic background gave emphasis to this photograph of P&H hoists. A piece of art work first was photographed—then that image was projected behind the hoists for the final print.

For example, the P&H hoists illustrated nearby were photographed by Pohlman for the Harnischfeger Company, under the direction of its agency, Baker, Johnson & Dickinson. Although the hoists are of exceptionally high quality, they lack inherent interest. Good lighting, exceptional print quality, and unusually sharp photography do much for them. *Piece de resistance,* though, is imparted by the dramatic background—here a piece of artwork that was photographed, then projected behind the product. This photograph sings!

The striking photograph of the two little boys looking plaintively through a chain-mesh fence at a beach—with an ominous sign warning that the beach is closed due to water pollution—was also taken by Pohlman Studios. Pohlman took this fine photo for Buchen Advertising, Inc., and its client, Rex Chainbelt, Inc.

This is a front-screen projection with the background made in the studio. No weather worries when working with a setup like this.

An excellent one-page, four-color ad was produced using this

POLLUTION PROBLEM

How do you end the pollution and contamination of waterways and beaches caused by municipal or industrial wastes? Effective answer: waste treatment systems built by REX Engineers. Examples: Steel mills employ REX treatment systems to remove cooling oils, mill scale and other contaminants from process water before discharging it into sewer lines. Paper mills clean up rivers by modernizing existing treatment plants with REX equipment. Refineries stop waterway pollution with REX automated waste treatment plants. Whatever your industry, if you have a water pollution problem, let us tell you in detail how

REX CAN SOLVE IT.

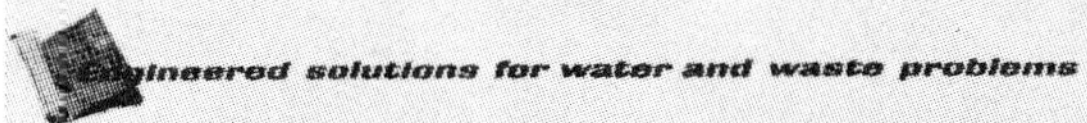

For informative data, write REX CHAINBELT INC., Conveyor & Process Equipment Division, 4606 W. Greenfield Ave., Milwaukee, Wis. 53201

INDUSTRY'S HELPING HAND

illustration. The ad is timely and topical and arouses intense interest because of the critical problem it discusses. The illustration does a fine job of stopping the reader, the headline is short, succinct and to the point—and also is a grabber in itself. Copy is tight and well written; it gets to the heart of the matter without wasting time or beating around the bushes.

Rex engineers have the know-how to put a halt to the pollution problem, and the copy gives specific examples—waste treatment systems built by Rex are used by steel mills to remove cooling oils, mill scale, and other contaminants from process water before discharging it into sewer lines; paper mills clean up rivers by modernizing existing treatment plants with Rex equipment, and so on.

This is an advertising campaign that not only does an effective job for the advertiser, but in the long run benefits everyone.

This man is in a studio, not a shop. The shop atmosphere is provided by a projected background. Lighting is made simple in such a setup, and shop production is not interrupted.

The shop-coated man holding a husky piece of a product was photographed the same way. Pohlman literally put the man in the shop by projecting a photograph background of a Kearney and Trecker Corporation milling machine and associated controls. The picture was made for Hartmann Hydraulic Division of the Koehring Company, and directed by its advertising agency, Fensholt Advertising, Inc.

Solarization is another offbeat technique to produce unique results. In this instance, the print, not the negative, was partially solarized and deliberately stained by turning on the white light when the print was partially developed. The streaked areas of solid tone

are characteristic of the process. This striking photograph is the work of Willard D. Pease, head of Images West, 24 East Burlington, Riverside, Illinois 60546. Bill Pease is one of the Chicago area's better commercial photographers. Although this photo's subject matter is not commercial or industrial, the technique can be very effective on everything from nuts and bolts to bulldozers.

Innumerable tricks are up the photographer's sleeve if you really want to go wild. He can, for instance, deliberately reticulate a negative; this produces a granular, striated picture with jagged lines going unpredictably in every which direction. There's little control over the process and each reticulated negative is unique, as is the resulting print. Have your photographer make a reticulation for you so you can evaluate it yourself.

Or a bas relief can be made; this consists of a picture which is predominantly a solid middle-tone of gray with pure white and jet black lines hinting at the subject matter of the photo. It's done by making a contact print of the negative on a piece of film, developing and fixing it, thus ending up with a positive print on film. The two pieces of film—one a negative and the other a positive—are then sandwiched together, fastened with Scotch tape slightly off register with each other, and a print is made, usually by enlargement. The bas relief is always an amazing thing and a real attention grabber, although it doesn't actually illustrate very much. It *does* arouse the reader's curiosity and pull him into the ad, though.

The same fine photographer took the dramatic close-up of a power tool about to tap a hole that's been drilled in a die (Photo A). The photograph is an excellent shot that shows imaginative use of selective focus and superb skill in handling lights to show the subject to best advantage.

Another of Bill Pease's fine photos is shown in Photo B. Setting a bearing on a flat surface and then blasting away with a camera to achieve a good clear close-up would have been easy, although the resulting photo would have fallen a bit short in the interest depart-

PHOTO A

PHOTO B

PHOTO C

ment. And the photographer could have lined up a number of bearings like a row of wooden soldiers (Photo C). Instead, Pease used his ability to visualize the finished advertisement to make something dramatic out of one of the most prosaic subjects the commercial photographer is likely to encounter.

Incidentally, when he was asked for some pictures for this book, Pease was also asked to select subject matter that lacked inherent interest. After all, it's relatively easy to take a dramatic subject and produce a dramatic photograph.

Handling of typical nuts and bolts of industry is a horse of a different color, however. When an *illustration* is produced, instead of just a picture that's technically acceptable, the man behind the camera is more than another photographer. He's an illustrator.

Lighting of highly polished metal, with surfaces ranging from irregular curves to circles to flat, with each of the surfaces composed of different metals so that reflectance or absorption of light varies radically, always poses a difficult problem for the photographer. Photo D is the result of such an exercise. Here photographer Pease manipulated his lights so skillfully that there's texture in the wood base of the display element of a vacuum furnace, as well as a glistening metallic feeling in ferrous and nonferrous metals, and in the high-alloy center itself.

Final example of this excellent product photography is a close-up of three products shown in Photo E. Both glass and metal are tests of the skill of the photographer, and when combined as they are here, unwanted highlights are extremely difficult to avoid.

The photographer can ignore highlights and shoot away and let the advertiser have retouching solve the problem, of course, but that's the expensive way to do it. And any photographer worth his salt intensely dislikes putting out work like that under his name.

PHOTO D

PHOTO E

In this instance delicate control of the light sources eliminated unwanted reflections and highlights. The photograph is very effective as it is, although it may well be even better with the background blown back by retouching to about a 20 percent gray when the reproduction is made.

Compelling closeups literally *demand* the reader's attention and never fail to stop him momentarily—if they're well done.

Jason Hailey's striking high-key portrait of a crankshaft (Photo F) is an excellent example; it is razor sharp, every tiny detail is shown crisply and clearly and reflections are unusually well-con-

PHOTO F

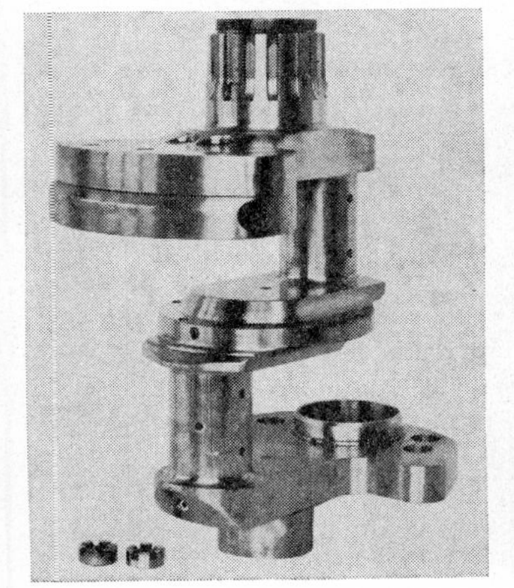

PHOTO G

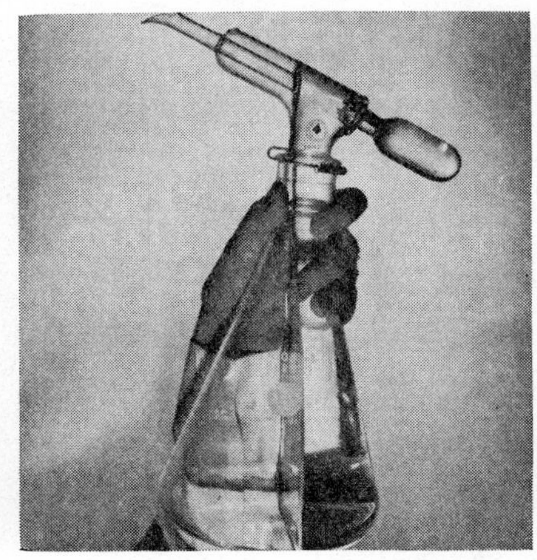

PHOTO H

PHOTO I

trolled. Knocking down stray highlights and preventing unwanted reflections in shiny metallic surfaces is not the easiest photographic exercise the photographer can engage in.

Another fine product close-up is shown in Photo G. Here the new product is of Pyrex, which presented photographer Bill Pease with reflection problems, as well as necessitating lighting that looks equally good when it's reflected, as it does when it's seen *through.* A baby spot thrown on the seamless-paper background lends a touch of vignetting to the illustration by darkening the corners to concentrate interest where it belongs—on the product. This fine photo is used courtesy of Packard Instrument company; ad manager Wes Curry kindly granted permission to reproduce it here.

Photos H-I-J-K show an exceptionally fine series of photos taken

PHOTO J — All photos this page: Shooting Equipment, Inc., Chicago — PHOTO K

PHOTO L

PHOTO M

by Pease for Shooting Equipment, Inc., Chicago; they are reproduced courtesy of the company and Richard D. Wentworth, product manager for the firm's extensive line of commercial and police shooting-range equipment.

Shooting Equipment, Inc. manufactures everything for ranges—backstops, bullet traps, times, target carriers, baffles and so on, as well as planning the range for the customer. These superb photographs show an extreme depth of field, that is, objects are sharp and in focus from a point immediately in front of the camera to infinity. Lighting for subjects such as these calls for all of the skill a top-flight professional photographer can muster if it's to be well controlled and even so as to show the entire scene to best advantage.

Two fine photos by Jason Hailey, in Figures L and M point up how pictures that would—or *could*—be static and uninteresting if they lacked a feeling of action gain dramatic qualities by skillful handling of both the camera and people in the picture. You can almost hear the man in the airplane saying, "Easy, now, lower it slowly," And the two men in the weather observation bubble make the picture. Incidentally, considering how intense the sunlight is on the white exterior, Hailey did an outstanding job of holding shadow detail; the photo exhibits an excellent range of tones, all the way from pure white to jet black and with a long middle-tone scale—the way it should in first class work.

Chances are you've seen product photography where straight lines converge and are distorted by use of a lens with too short a focal length, failure to use the view camera's swings and tilts, or lack of ability on the part of the photographer. Such photos make a poor impression for the product, and fail to show it as the eye is accustomed to seeing it.

Photographer Bill Pease photographed a Liquid Scintillation Spectrometer manufactured by Packard Instruments (Photo N), and held every line as straight and true as it is in the actual product. Even lighting, razor sharpness, and a fine range of tones makes this an excellent photo. Layout calls for the product to be blocked out, so its merging partially into the background shown means nothing.

PHOTO N

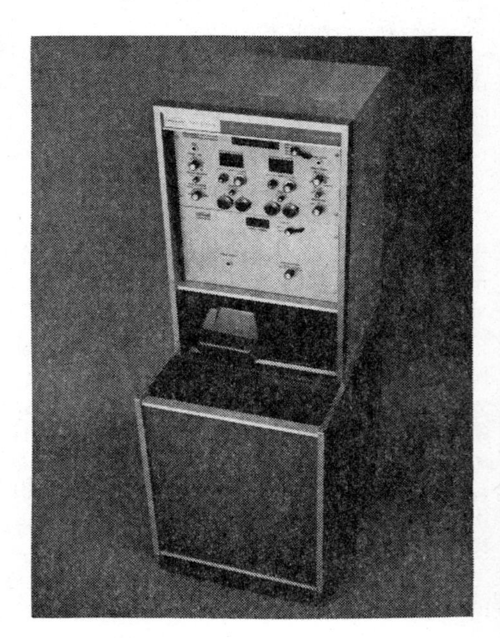

Chapter 11

LAYOUT

THERE's nothing complicated about layout, nor is there any form of voodoo or black magic or anything else mysterious. Yet it's in this stage of its evolution from idea to completed selling tool that an advertisement most frequently hears the mournful tolling of the death knell to its effectiveness.

Layout must present the advertising message forcefully and attractively, and it must have an orderly structure.

A layout is merely a guideline, a blueprint, a road map, an architect's drawing. A layout is an idea drawn on paper. It performs the same functions for people in the advertising business that these other forms of layouts do for those engaged in other crafts. Just as the civil engineer uses his working drawings to determine the path and grade of a new interstate highway, the advertising manager uses a layout to spell out in detail the precise placement of every element in his advertisement.

An element, incidentally, is a complete entity in itself, and is almost always one of several in the ad. The illustration, for example, is an element. So is the headline, each column or block of body copy, each spot illustration, the logo, and so on. We'll go into this more later on.

To be effective, a layout must be tasteful. *There is no substitute for good taste.*

Immediately obvious is that this is getting into a highly subjective area. What is one man's meat is another man's poison. Nobody can fault you for preferring blondes, while the author happens to prefer brunettes—and neither of us is right or wrong. The man in the next office may have bought a shocking-pink car at one time (a few actually were sold, you know, back in '56) ; to him, it was the most beautiful, inspiring, delightful set of wheels that ever left Detroit. Most people were in complete agreement in their reaction to the color—*urrrrp!* But that still doesn't make them right and the buyer wrong.

There's plenty of room in advertising, just as there is any other field, for different viewpoints. And there's more than one way of performing creative chores such as writing, making layouts, and what have you. Many are just as persuasive and forceful, perhaps equally so, as if they were done in any of several other ways; and many are in such impeccably good taste that no justifiable criticism can be made on that score despite the vast difference in approaches.

Given a forceful, tasteful layout, the climate is established in which the selling message can be presented with peak effectiveness.

However, if the layout is plodding and unimaginative, the ad will lack force and vigor and vitality. It cannot do as good a job.

But if the layout is tasteless and crude and vulgar, if it offends the sensitive and shocks the perceptive, the ad is doomed to be unsuccessful.

Happily, though, what is tasteful and what is tasteless isn't entirely a subjective thing. There are many ground rules that help you hew to the tasteful, effective side of the layout street and keep you from wandering off into a morass of wasted time and effort and money.

Now that we know what a layout is, we'll go into some of them.

Why a Layout Is Needed

The copywriter is the first person to face up to the fact that a layout is needed, and he's the first to do something about it.

Usual procedure when writing an ad, a piece of sales literature, a brochure, or what have you, is to make a "copywriter's rough." The copywriter's rough is simply a hastily drawn layout in very crude form and often in greatly reduced size. It shows how the copywriter feels the various elements in the ad should be arranged.

In addition to showing a suggested arrangement, the copywriter's rough serves an even more important purpose—that of establishing the relative importance of each element in the ad, and how much space in the advertisement each should occupy. For instance, if several different widgets are to be illustrated, the copywriter's rough would show which widget should be dominant, which ones should be subordinate, and to what degree.

The copywriter is qualified to perform this important task of assigning space in the advertisement according to the importance of the different elements because he has access to far more information than an art director or layout artist. He knows the product, its functions, and its user benefits; he knows the market into which it is to be sold, he knows the buying influences with whom the ad must communicate.

As a rule not too much of this information is readily available to the man who lays out the ad, nor is this individual greatly interested in it. It's outside his province. For the most part, art directors and layout men are a step or two removed from contact with the advertising manager and manufacturer marketing people, although in the really good advertising agencies they become involved in client problems and client thinking because it's mutually beneficial.

The man who writes the ad transmits directions and instructions by making a copywriter's rough, sometimes called a "thumbnail" because it's actually a rough layout in miniature. A typical copywriter's rough of a one-page ad with illustration, headline, three copy blocks, and logotype of the advertiser is shown life-sized beside a matchbook cover.

Small it may be, but a copywriter's rough (left) is invaluable to artist.

It's quite obvious why the term is used; most copywriters are not artists and when they attempt to draw something the result is apt to be little short of ludicrous. Frequently they'll label each element so the layout artist will be able to identify it. What's more, such layouts are called thumbnails because the average writer, when he thinks of making a copywriter's rough, immediately decides to make it in reduced size. Perhaps this is to compensate for his deficiency in the art department, or perhaps it's because it's less work; in any event, most copywriter's roughs of a one-page ad are about half the size of a playing card. And small and rough as they are, they're still a good guide for the art man. He always welcomes them and feels almost lost when he doesn't get one. Many art directors complain bitterly that the copywriter is deliberately making it difficult if they're not supplied with a copywriter's rough. It pays off in better ads to do so, and it also pays off in better-natured art directors; some are on the temperamental side.

One of the most important reasons for making a layout is so the advertiser can visualize his completed advertisement when it's still in process. A drawing or rendering of the completed ad bears such a close resemblance to the finished product that even a poor visualizer can see enough to have an informed opinion of whether or not this ad will express the thought he wants to convey. If it doesn't, or if by making a change here and there the idea can be expressed more forcefully, little is lost at this stage of the game.

Working with a copywriter's rough, the artist can "rough out" a layout in just a few minutes for advertiser comment or approval. If changes are to be made they can then be reflected in the next rough. Or, if the layout is close enough to what is wanted in the completed ad, any modifications can be incorporated into the next stage in the layout; it will be discussed later.

When he has a layout to see, the advertiser isn't working in the dark. He's not asked to approve something as nebulous as an idea expressed in words. What he is to evaluate has been put on paper so it can be seen and studied and considered at leisure.

Make any changes you want to make in the advertisement *now*—not later. After the layout stage is past, changes are terribly expensive and wasteful.

The layout serves also as a guide for the photographer or artist who will create the illustration. When he has the layout, this individual can see the exact size and proportions of the finished work he is to produce, and how it will appear on the page. This is of inestimable help because it comes as close as it is possible to ensuring work that will measure up to to expectations and satisfy all concerned. Photographers and artists usually take the layout or a Xerox copy of it with them to use as a reference when making the illustration.

By using the layout as a guide it is also possible for all production people to estimate the cost of producing the advertisement. They can show it to the typographer, for example, and let him see how much space so many words of copy are to occupy, thus enabling him to submit a very close estimate of his charges.

And when getting bids from printers, the layout is also used; printers are accustomed to working with layouts since they are always ready long before the final keyline and finished art are available. If production people had to wait until all camera-ready finished material was on hand, the pace would be impossibly hectic; they couldn't work ahead and save precious days when they are most needed.

Printers, working with the layout, can tell quite closely how much stripping time, how much extra camera time, how much retouching time, and how many extra operations they'll have. Estimates based on good layouts are remarkably close to actual invoiced charges in most instances.

Types of Layouts

Some industrial advertising departments are as fully staffed with artists, production people, and traffic people as an advertising agency; these departments are capable of handling every step of the manufacture of an advertisement from original idea to getting material ready for the engraver.

However, the typical industrial advertising manager usually has either his agency perform the art and production functions, or he hires a studio to handle the mechanics for him. The art studio—in many instances actually a small, specialized advertising agency—concentrates primarily on production of collateral material; sales literature, brochures, booklets, films, and the like. Many have branched out as their business has grown, and offer a complete advertising service including media analysis and purchasing of space in publications. Also offered, of course, are copywriting, layout, and production.

A good, reliable studio that can produce finished art of good quality and do so in a minimum of time is a jewel to be guarded and treasured. Many times you'll have jobs that must be "banged out" fast, and they're really too small to make them profitable for your advertising agency. Yet art is required, and there's type to spec, layout to be made, keyline to be done, and so on; this is probably work that you either cannot do, or simply do not have time to do.

When this situation arises, the studio is the obvious answer. It's good practice to put the bulk of your business through one studio so that your business is valued there, although it's equally good business to get competitive quotations on some jobs just to keep everybody on their toes and to assure yourself your business isn't being taken for granted—and that the price stays right.

Layouts are presented in three forms: Rough, ruled comprehensive, and type comprehensive.

The rough layout is just that—a crudely drawn indication of what the final advertisement will look like. Usually it's done with

either the ubiquitous squeakie (felt pen), or with chalks of differing shades of gray and black. Whatever medium is used, the rough layout reflects the artists' thinking—not his ability to render an illustration. It should be accepted for just what it is, and the rough should be judged on what it shows, rather than how it shows it. You're not paying for an El Greco now, and you shouldn't expect fine art.

A typical rough layout, this one done with a squeakie, is shown. Note that the headline, subhead, and logo are indicated, rather than being lettered in. This is sufficiently indicative of how the advertisement will look, and there's no use in having an artist waste his time lettering on a rough. Frequently this is called "Greeking in" the printed matter—possibly after the Greek alphabet which, to most people who aren't Greeks, looks like Greek. Copy blocks, three of them, are indicated by rough lines.

While it's still inside the agency the rough is usually submitted by the artist to the chief art director, the creative director, or to the account executive handling the account—frequently to all three, and often to the copywriter as well. If it reflects the thinking of all of those inside satisfactorily, the account executive may want to show it to the client. Or he may pass judgment on its merit himself, depending upon how familiar he is with the account, his relationship with the client, and whether or not he believes the rough represents what the advertiser wants—and should have. Sometimes these two aren't the same thing at all.

Next stage is to make a ruled comprehensive layout, commonly called a "comp." A typical comp layout is shown on page 842.

Instead of rough doodling that indicates merely the vague outline of the elements in the illustration, and the other elements in the advertisement, the comp has been drawn with some care.

A photostat of the photograph which will illustrate the ad (called a "stat") has been made to the exact size the engraving will be and carefully pasted into place where the halftone will be in the completed ad. This shows the advertising manager how it looks and will later be given to the engraver for his guidance.

Copy blocks are indicated quite close in size to what they will be in the actual advertisement, and the logo has been roughed in. Note, however, that the headline and subhead, while lettered in in a close approximation of the type face to be used, do not use the exact words which will be set in type. Artists and art directors are notorious for misreading or mislettering headlines and subheads. If it's critical that the exact wording appear, their work should be carefully checked. However, since the type will occupy approximately the same amount of space, the precise words don't really matter.

Interestingly, the matt around the ad is always made *exactly* one-half inch too wide to fit into an account executive's attaché case. This is standard in all agencies and may well be a part of a world-wide plot hatched by artists to bedevil account executives. This is

the one essential that artists never fail to get exactly right. This forces the account executive to go to the mailroom, wrap the layouts and carry an extra item when going to call on the client. Even if it's empty, the account executive cannot leave his attaché case behind; without it he's not really an account executive. He'd be like Linus without his blanket. For the account executive, happiness is having an attaché case to carry.

Switching to powder metals?
we'll help you lower processing costs

At this stage of the game the advertiser can see just what his forthcoming advertisement is going to look like. There isn't so much invested, though, that a change can't be made. If changes must be made, this is the last opportunity to make them without running up production costs and wasting money.

Final stage in layout is to go to the type comprehensive. Such a type comprehensive is shown.

This consists of the ruled comprehensive layout, with stat still in place, but with type set and pasted down. Except for the stat's mediocre quality—stats compress the tonal range of art or photographs, show less middletones and thus appear more contrasty than the original subject matter—the ad appears much as it will when an engraving has been made and proofs have been pulled.

The Touchy Problem of Changes

Here again, the advertiser can still push the panic button and make a change, of course, if it's absolutely essential and there's simply no escaping it. However, type has been set and any changes now will necessitate all new type; patching is not always possible because of a difference in the weight of the impression of type set at various times. Too, agencies like to set type all new when a client has made a last-minute change because this tends to teach the indecisive client a costly lesson. Henceforth, he'll probably remember it and not cause the fuss and furor that inevitably results when changes have to be made and the deadline is near and everybody had considered this job completed.

The habit of looking at type comps is a bad one to get into. It's almost as vicious as smoking cigarettes, although not quite, and equally costly. The type comp represents an extra step that causes your invoices to climb amazingly. It stands to reason, when you stop and think about it, that when a job has to be handled at the agency or the studio that somebody's going to pay for it; and this is an extra handling. Then your account executive has to hop in a cab and drive out and show it to you, or rent a Hertz, or—horrors—mail it to you. This runs up the cost of doing business with you.

Actually, a rough will suffice in most cases for you to pass judgment on an ad. And certainly a ruled comprehensive layout is adequate to enable you to visualize what the completed ad will look like, and it will be sufficiently close to let you explain to the sales manager, marketing manager, or product manager what they're going to get to carry the message to the marketplace. Train your people internally to expect nothing further after they've seen a ruled comp layout. You'll spoil them if you let them know there's an additional step; as soon as they find out, they'll want to take it with you. And as sure as the sun rises in the East, they'll force you to make changes when type's been set.

Properly, however, you should clear retouched photos with product and sales people if there's any doubt in your mind about whether or not they show the product to best advantage, or if a technical question arises. Technical people can also pass on art, but from a technical viewpoint; they shouldn't be encouraged—or even permitted—to render any verdict on either art or photography as far as technique is concerned. This is your province. You're the expert here. Just because all engineers are draftsmen doesn't automatically qualify them to pass judgment on art or photography.

You'll find you're far better off if you don't even intimate you want any kind of opinion. Once you have ad reprints you can then drop any number of gentle little hints about what a fine piece of art it is, or how good the photography is. After all, you didn't give birth to the art or photo, so you can legitimately brag on the work of others—almost, at least.

If you're going to make your own layouts, you'll find you're better off to go the thumbnail route as a method of developing ideas. Thumbnails are excellent time savers for they can be doodled out almost as fast as ideas come to mind.

However, when you decide you've come up with *the* idea, or with one you want to pursue further, by all means make a full-sized layout. Only when it's sized up to the approximate dimensions in which it will appear in the publications can you judge accurately whether or not it measures up to your standards and meets with your approval.

Chances are you'll find that thumbnails are a bit deceptive. What looks just great when it's matchbook size frequently falls apart—fails to "carry" when it's "up."

Cost of Layouts

Layouts don't come free to an industrial advertising manager. Almost every industrial ad manager who's on a commission basis with his agency, rather than an agreed-upon fee basis, pays for layouts. Copy is free if it's written by the agency, but not the layout. Agencies regard copywriters and account executives as necessary personnel, but for some reason or other, artists, layout men, and art directors are considered overhead personnel who must be charged off against what they produce; this work is billed to clients.

Most agencies are very fair about layout charges and turn a legitimate profit for this work, one they're entitled to. Nobody is in business for his health. Some agencies, though, particularly the marginal ones which specialize in mailing lists at inflated prices and similar bits of larceny, make it standard operating procedure to gouge the client with puffed-up layout charges. The art department in these so-called agencies has become a profit center. This shouldn't be.

What you'll be charged for layout naturally depends to a large extent on how much work went into the layout. This includes initial "think time" for the layout man, time actually spent working, and normal agency markup or profit.

The more changes that are made, the higher the price that's paid. Every change involves time spent by the account executive and the layout artist as well as others involved in the account. Changes are costly little items, so try to get your own thinking tidied up before giving instructions to the agency.

If the agency makes an error and goes off onto a tangent, you won't be charged for this. Most agencies are honest and above-board and have no desire to penalize their clients for mistakes which are bound to happen.

Total price for a layout for a one-page, black-and-white ad for a trade publication shouldn't be over $150, and closer to $100 would be about an average charged to an industrial advertiser. This can be broken down, though, so you'll see where you can save some money.

For instance, if you're content to see a rough layout—and if you're a good enough visualizer so that you're able mentally to translate the rough into a finished ad, you can save a substantial sum here. Most agencies will make a good rough, either in squeakie, or chalk, matted so it's presentable as far as showing it to your marketing people are concerned, for somewhere between $50 and $100. Spacial relationships will be very closely approximated, and the illustrative idea will be readily recognizable. Needless to say, though, you won't receive anything like a piece of finished art.

Most agencies flinch at the thought of presenting roughs to clients. One reason is that they feel clients are frequently not qualified to judge whether a layout is good or not by merely looking at a rough.

Many times they're right. But if you have confidence in your agency—and your agency has confidence in you—the rough layout can save both time and money. If you're short on experience, get comps for a while and gradually cut back to roughs; check your impressions and see if they're right. If so, you have no further worry on this score.

Should you desire to be a little more certain of what you're going to see when all of that money has been invested and the work has been done, you can get a ruled comprehensive layout for around $100 to $200. This will include a sized stat of either the photograph or the artwork, and the headline, subhead, captions, copy blocks, and logo indicated so your mental transition will be an effortless one. This is the safest course to take and the proper one if there's a question in your mind.

You can depend upon paying from $150 to $250, depending upon the agency and the section of the country you're in, for a type comprehensive. That's because there's more time and work involved in making the layout neat enough to show to the president of the company, and because type has been set and bought, proofread, then cut and pasted onto the layout in position.

All of this takes time and involves several agency people including the account executive, copywriter, layout artist, production man, keyliner, and finally traffic and accounts payable (for the typographer must be paid).

Unless there's a specific reason for the type comp—such as presentation to management of a new campaign, for instance—avoid the type comp as a dollar-eater. You don't need it.

Definition of Black-and-White

Black-and-white is a term that's been thrown around in this handbook pretty loosely up 'til now without once being defined. It's so elementary, though, that most advertising men never give it another thought.

However, the author has encountered pockets of misconception throughout the country where black-and-white is *not* understood. Let's clear this one up for good and for all.

When an ad is in black-and-white, it's a one-color ad. This means simply that black ink has been printed on white paper. Granted, neither black nor white are actually colors in the true sense of the word, but for practical purposes in advertising they're considered colors.

This page you're reading is in black-and-white—black type on white paper. Because there are two "colors," however, doesn't make this page a two-color page. It's a one-color page because the basic color of the stock—the paper—doesn't count as a color. Only the different colors laid down by the printing process are counted as colors when describing an advertisement.

For an additional charge you can have your advertisements printed in brown ink—or red, purple, chartreuse, blue, green, orange, or whatever silliness occurs to you. But as long as the publication's printer laid down only one color of ink, you still have a one-color ad.

However, you have a two-color advertisement when your ad is

printed in the publication's basic ink color—black—and another color is added. Let's assume you're going to run your ad in two colors, and the second color is that favorite old exciter, red. (As the older generation of industrial advertising men used to say, "Let me have any second color, as long as it's red.") So now you have a red and black ad—the second color is usually given first when discussing a two-color ad—on the basic "color" of paper that publications use, which is white. Although you actually have a red, black and white ad, it nonetheless is still a two-color ad, not a three-color one. Remember, the color of the paper doesn't count.

By the same token, a three-color ad is one in which the basic black ink is used, plus the addition of any other two colors. Used functionally, three colors can do a tremendously effective job. Used decoratively, however, with color splashed around indiscriminately just because the money's in the budget to pay for it, three-color ads are ghastly monstrosities that nauseate and repel.

Shy away from using three colors unless there's a very logical reason for doing so—*a very logical reason.* They don't come along very often, and happily, happily you don't encounter too many of these gruesome three-color monstrosities. They're horrible horrors.

Later on in this chapter the four-color process will be discussed (beginning on page 969). Several case histories follow.

Fundamentals of Good Layout

A layout starts with a blank piece of paper. Whether an advertisement is a rousing success or a dismal failure depends to a large extent on what the layout artist does with this piece of paper.

He can be given an illustration that's so well-conceived and so beautifully executed that it almost brings tears to the eyes and really motivates the reader to want to stop and read every last word of copy; and he can be handed copy that softly sings a siren song of such persuasiveness that the reader is morally convinced the product is even *better* than the advertisement will admit in all of its modesty.

These two elements *are* essentials, of course, but not one bit more so than a layout that's equally good. It's all too easy to arrange a fine illustration and sparkling copy so that the various elements clash and distract and fail miserably to communicate a single salient fact to the universe because the ad is so uninviting.

This is a major sin committed unknowingly by far too many advertising managers of small industrial companies; these ad managers frequently are what amounts to one-man agencies for their companies, they specify and purchase the illustration, write the copy, and make the layout. Frequently these talented individuals do a remarkably competent job, but layout is usually the area in which they're weak.

Most advertising men are word-oriented rather than design- or art-oriented and their work suffers in effectiveness due to inept layout more than any other area. Working with a good agency, a competent art studio, or even with a free-lance artist would avert disastrously poor layouts and do more than anything else to boost the productivity of the advertising program.

A good, clear visual interpretation of the selling concept increases readership tremendously.

To enable the advertisement to succeed, the layout must let the various elements of the ad work together to do the entire job—the illustration, subordinate illustration, if any; headline, subheads, if any; charts or graphs, body copy, logotype, and any other elements or devices the ad includes.

A good layout helps the other elements do an effective job, whereas a poor layout hinders them and makes it difficult—if not impossible—to accomplish the objective of getting readership.

To enhance the effectiveness of the other elements, layout needs to have four "musts." These musts must be present in each and every layout, not just one once in a while. They are:

1. It must be attractive.
2. It must have "feel."
3. It must have balance.
4. It must have individuality.

Attractive Layout

Bill Souder, a gifted art director with whom the author worked for several years (and a longtime friend), once explained over lunch that to him a really good layout can logically be compared to a beautiful woman.

He rationalized it this way: Both are attractive. Both have built-in eye appeal, so much so that one is practically compelled to accord them considerably more than a mere passing glance. And both have elements arranged in an orderly and logical fashion so that one element inevitably leads the eye to the next in unerring and predictable sequence.

What's more, a beautiful woman may be scanned in a split second, but the connoisseur's eye invariably returns to the focal point, the face, then proceeds at a more deliberate pace to inspect and admire eyes, hair, mouth, figure, and legs in that order. A practiced girl-watcher can accomplish the entire process almost instantaneously, of course, before returning for seconds.

An attractive layout catches the eye in much the same way. It lures the reader into the advertisement, it involves him. While eye-paths will be gone into a little later, it's worthwhile to note that the reader examines an advertisement in much the same manner he would a woman. First of all, he starts with the illustration, then his attention goes to the headline, then the body copy, and finally the logotype.

Where a woman has several chances to make an impression—with charm and poise and warm personality—the advertisement has just one opportunity to register with the reader.

Layout alone can give your ad its big chance—if it's good. It must be attractive, and instantly so. It must be appealing to the reader. It must be inviting so that it makes him come to the conclusion that reading the ad will not be a chore, but might well be something that's desirable because it will be in his self-interest.

On the other hand, a poor layout such as some we'll look at later can muff the big chance and your ad will receive little readership and return little on the investment made in it.

Attractive layout actually costs not a penny more than does layout that leaves something to be desired, if you're inclined to be charitable, or layout that's offensive and repulsive if you're willing to face facts and talk frankly.

Getting attractive layout may require stronger direction on your part. Too, it may necessitate your brushing up on what's good and what's bad and just what it is that separates the two. But the effort is well worth while because layout can make or break you.

Often it's just as difficult to point to a layout and declare with great finality and supreme self-confidence that it is attractive—and then give a defense of your position with a well-reasoned rationale—as it is to proclaim that a woman is beautiful, then explain why. There's a certain amount of subjectivity about the specific stimuli needed to turn any one of us on. The list of reasons why a layout is either good or bad is so long that it could comprise a book all by itself. Most of them don't apply to all layouts, but only to the rare ones that happen along occasionally.

Picking specific good points or faulting a layout on the basis of specific bad points is relatively easy. Let's look at a layout that is

too busy to write your Congressman?

He was elected to represent you. To voice your opinions on legislation that affects you and your family — today, tomorrow, ten years from now. To do it, he needs to know first what your opinions are. So write and let him know.

Too busy? Well, next time you're just passing time watching TV, working crossword puzzles, or rehashing last week's ball game, remember: if you don't let your Congressman and other public officials know what you think, you have to let them think for you. So don't put off writing.

And when you do write, we hope you'll choose Hammermill Bond, the world's best-known letterhead paper. This crisp, white paper adds importance to your point of view.

Hammermill Paper Company (headquarters: Erie, Pa.) makes Hammermill Bond and 32 other grades of paper. There's one for each of your printing and communication jobs.

A paper-thin voice is a powerful persuader.

attractive, one that is eye catching and does an excellent job of delivering the reader for the advertiser: Hammermill Paper Company's great black-and-white ad from *Business Week.* It is deceptively simple. The photographic illustration is handled with much finesse; there's a subtlety about it due to the unusually skillful handling of the lighting which appears to be coming from the television set, which is as it should be. The illustration, when looked at as a picture, is interesting. We're all able to identify with the executive-type man shown relaxing in his paneled den.

Set in clean, fresh white space, the illustration is located properly to catch the eye immediately, for the average individual's eye almost always enters an advertisement from the upper left-hand corner. Then, the direction of the gaze of the man in the illustration very neatly draws the reader's eye immediately to the headline—as it was intended to do.

The headline is set in easy-to-read lower-case letters, big enough and bold enough to carry well without overpowering any of the other elements in the ad—or without usurping extra space on the page at the expense of the layout as a whole.

Then, in nice logical progression, the second line of the headline deposits the reader's eye right at the start of the first line in the copy block. Once the eye goes to the end of the second line in the headline, there's no place else for it to go. It's hemmed in by the white space, so there's no reason for it to wander or lose its way and thus avoid the crucially important body copy.

There's so much of intense interest in the copy that it's difficult to see how very many people could possibly pass it up; once in, the eye progresses through and into the bold-face punch line at the bottom of the copy, then on to the advertiser's powerful logo.

Only five elements comprise this ad; all are beautifully and tastefully arranged. Simplicity is the keynote, and it serves to create an unusually attractive and cogent layout.

Incidentally, not only does the clean layout make a very favorable impression on the reader, the copy also leaves a strong and positive impression about the advertiser and his product because it advocates good government through individual participation. Copy is so unusually fine it deserves to be quoted here.

**Too busy to write
your Congressman?**

He was elected to represent you. To voice your opinions on legislation that affects you and your family—today, tomorrow, 10 years from now. To do it, he needs to know first what your opinions are. So write and let him know.

Too busy? Well, next time you're just passing time watching TV, working crossword puzzles, or rehashing last week's ball game, remember: If you don't let your Congressman and other public officials know what you think, you have to let them think for you. So don't put off writing.

And when you do write, we hope you'll choose Hammermill Bond, the world's best-known letterhead paper. This crisp, white paper adds importance to your point of view.

Hammermill Paper Company (headquarters: Erie, Pa.) makes Hammermill Bond and 32 other grades of paper. There's one for each of your printing and communication jobs.

A paper-thin voice is a powerful persuader.

This impressive advertisement sells the product hard, strengthens the finest system of government yet devised, and creates the impression of a company with an excellent line of products—and one with a sincere interest in the welfare of our country. What more can one ad do?

Layout With "Feel"

There's an ineffable something, an intangible called "feel" for want of a better name, that's present in every fine layout. Yet it's next to impossible to put your finger on it, to give it a specific name and describe it precisely so that any layout artist worth his salary can crank it automatically into every layout he produces for you.

Nevertheless, feel—or call it atmosphere, if you like—cannot be overlooked. It is vitally important. The contribution feel makes to the layout and to the success of the advertisement as a whole cannot be denigrated. Feel of a layout wields great influence on readership of the ad.

This feel, or atmosphere, or subconscious impression the layout creates in the reader's mind can often be described as an aura of excitement, or of a happening that's just about to happen, of something that cannot help but affect the reader personally, or of a dramatic accomplishment. None of this is in words, of course, just as none of it is imparted to the layout because the art director said to himself as he sat down, "I'm going to put some real feel into this layout. I'll give 'em such a heavy hunk of atmosphere it'll have 'em rolling on the floor beside their desks."

Sometimes a layout has more than an ample measure of feel in it as much for what it *doesn't* contain as for what it does. This usually results from the copywriter working with such close rapport with the art director that their combined output is synergistic.

An inspired copy concept, for instance, will frequently spark an equally inspired layout idea. When this happens you have an award-winning ad, although awards aren't really important. What is important is that you have a truly memorable ad that creates a strong and lasting positive impression about the product in the mind of the reader. True, the ad becomes something of a classic in the advertising field, but it does what's far more important—a tremendously effective sales job for the advertiser.

Feel is very hard to describe, yet ridiculously easy to see and to experience.

Take the excellent ad run by De Laval Separator Company, for example. This one-page, black-and-white bleed ad has a delightful feel to the layout.

Product illustration is properly located in the upper left-hand corner of the ad. Although it's small and illustrations should *not* ordinarily be small unless there's a valid reason, it's effective because the eye enters the ad right there.

The illustration pulls the reader directly into the headline-copy, which is all in display type in a serif face that's easy to read. Copy is short and to the point; it spells out the primary user benefits of De Laval's plate heat exchangers and makes a bid for action in the form of inquiries.

The great thing about this fine ad is how wonderfully well the illustration, copy, and layout work together to drive home the point the advertiser wants to make; it does so with sledgehammer impact. Since the number one user benefit enjoyed with De Laval's product is a commodity that's always in short supply—extra floor space—the layout deftly emphasizes this by showing the reader the approximate amount of free floor space, in terms of percentage, he'll get when he buys the product. And the headline *Free floor space,* is a jewel.

Copywriter and art director worked together on this ad with marvelous results.

Another example (page 856) of a layout with a fine feel and atmosphere is that of the outstanding black-and-white ad run by Westinghouse Tube Division. Westinghouse's ad is a real stopper. After halting the page-turning reader, it almost compels him to read because the layout is so gripping. It's able to achieve this much impact because it works in very close harmony with the headline, illustration, and body copy. This is one of those rare blendings of

A De Laval plate heat exchanger takes up 1/10th to 1/2 the floor space of a tube and shell type to do the same job. Heats or cools nearly any free-flowing liquid. Cleans by circulation without disassembly. Enlarges or rearranges if your capacity or process changes. Want details?

DE LAVAL
Just contact the De Laval Separator Company,
Poughkeepsie, New York; Chicago, Ill.; Burlingame, California.

Free floor space

The benefit promised in the brief copy for this ad by the De Laval Separator Company is emphasized by the generous space surrounding the bottom line, "Free Floor Space." This is what the ad is talking about, and the dramatic distribution of space makes the point sink in. In order to accomplish this, the product illustration is small, but it is located where the eye starts to travel.

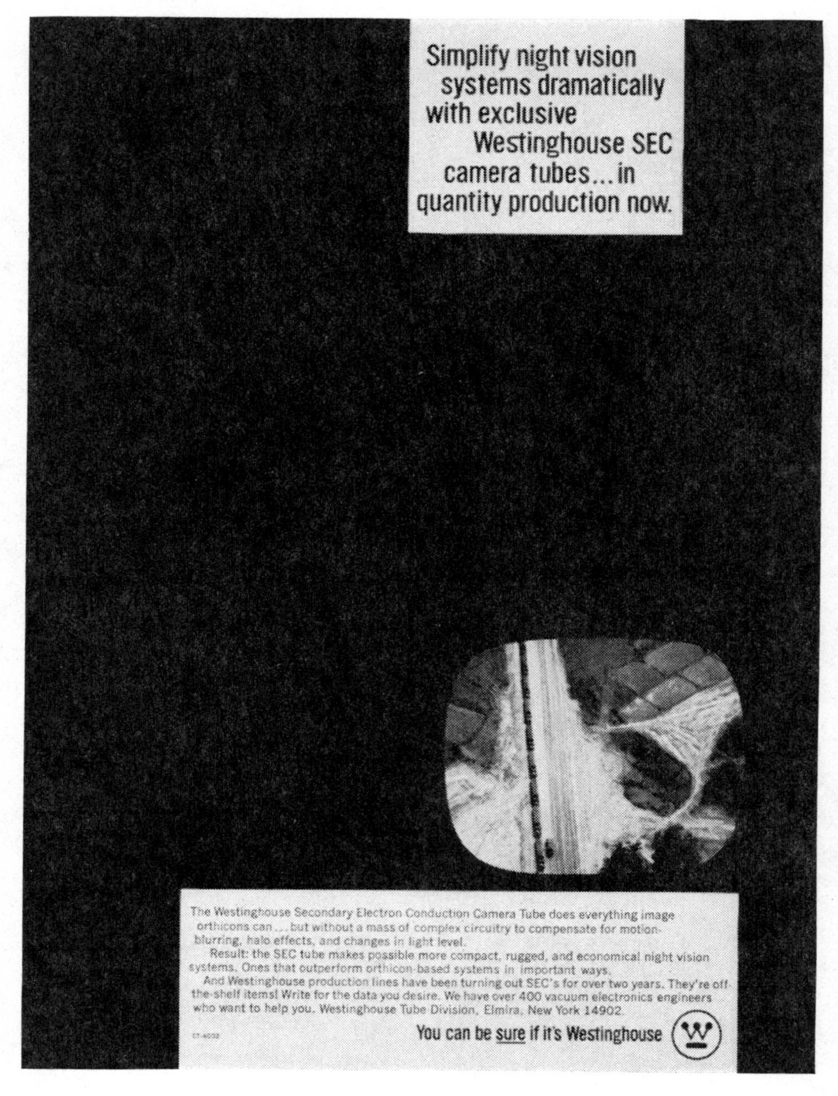

every element of the ad that builds to a high pitch of excitement, carrying the product story right along.

Simplify night vision systems dramatically with exclusive Westinghouse SEC camera tubes... in quantity production now.
The Westinghouse Secondary Electron Conduction Camera Tube does everything image orthicons can ... but without a mass of complex circuitry to compensate for motion-blurring, halo effects, and changes in light level.
Result: the SEC tube makes possible more compact, rugged, and economical night vision systems. Ones that outperform orthicon-based systems in important ways.
And Westinghouse production lines have been turning out SEC's for over two years. They're off-the-shelf items! Write for the data you desire. We have over 400 vacuum electronics engineers who want to help you. Westinghouse Tube Division, Elmira, New York 14902.
You can be sure if it's Westinghouse
W

The illustration of a convoy of trucks on a rural road at night, apparently taken from an altitude of several thousand feet, is timely, topical, and of universal interest.

This headline is powerful, containing as it does "exclusive," "now," and the name of the advertiser, all of which increase readership. In addition, a promise is made that the reader will find something easier and simpler. A good appeal.

What's particularly inspired, though, is the layout—the use of all of that dramatic black to emphasize that the product performs as promised at night, quite obviously on nights as dark as a black cat in a closet at midnight. This impressive layout device is perfect for this ad and for this product and application.

Without deliberate nit-picking, it's impossible to see how this layout—and this ad as a whole, for that matter—could have been improved. Westinghouse has a very good thing going for it here. This advertisement carries great conviction.

Balance

There's nothing complicated about balance, no walking a tightrope blindfolded or anything like that.

Balance is simply giving each element of the ad the proper "weight" or size, so that when they are placed within the confines of the predetermined size and shape of the advertisement their relationship with each other is esthetically pleasing.

And because of the harmonious relationship of elements, the ad as an entity appears orderly, logical, and inviting to the eye. Nothing is oversize in proportion to anything else, nothing is "overweight"—oppressively dark, heavy, or massive in appearance—in comparison with other elements.

Having a well-balanced layout boils down to a question of taste and judgment and of putting both to good use.

Illustrations must be considered in light of length of copy, length of headline, typeface to be used for the advertisement, size, shape, and weight of the logotype, presence or absence of subheads, captions, and any other elements which will appear in the ad.

A well-balanced layout isn't static and sterile, though, with every single element measured down to the last silly millimeter to make certain it will fit a formula or ratio that is preconceived and inflexible. This would inevitably result in an antiseptic dullness. Such a layout would have no balance because it would be overbalanced, lacking in any feeling of motion or movement.

Precisely the right balance was achieved in Sylvania Electronic Systems' attractive and tasteful one-page, black-and-white ad illustrated on page 858. Relationship of illustration to headline-copy area is just right.

If your computer doesn't get the message, draw it a picture.

Computers are useless until you tell them what to do.

But some things just can't be put into words, or easily translated into the digital language that computers understand.

Like topological maps. Or architectural drawings. Or complex equations. Or bridge designs. Or the action of the human heart. Or the sequence of drawings in animated cartoons.

So, we developed the Sylvania Data Tablet DT-1. Now you simply draw a picture. The Tablet converts it into digital data, and the computer takes it from there.

And it's as easy as it looks. You can trace directly on the Tablet. Or you can draw on any nonconductive material—paper or film up to ½ inch thick—placed between the stylus and the surface.

You can use the Tablet at a desk or console, or as a transparent overlay. And you get exceptional accuracy: resolution is one part in 4000; linearity is 1% or better. You also get hard copy.

Here's how it works: as the ball pen stylus moves across the Tablet, it creates an electrical field that the Tablet converts into the numerical language computers understand.

So now you don't have to be a genius to talk to computers. You just have to know how to draw. Give us a call and we'll show you how it works.

Sylvania Electronic Systems, 40 Sylvan Road, Waltham, Mass. 02154.

SYLVANIA

GENERAL TELEPHONE & ELECTRONICS

The headline type is bold and heavy, but it needs to be in order to balance the large black square in the illustrative area. And the body copy is set in a serifed typeface of good weight; had body copy been set in one of the weak, light sans-serif typefaces currently in vogue it would have been pallid and grey—it wouldn't have "carried." As is, though, the body copy weight and "color" stand up well and help unify the entire layout.

Balance also enters into the illustration, for it must reflect the thought and tone of the copy, of the message Sylvania wants to convey. This excellent photographic illustration strikes just the right note, for the product is being used—being tried out, apparently—in a lighthearted yet hardheaded way. This illustration does a good job of flagging the reader's attention and makes it immediately apparent that Sylvania's new Data Tablet DT-1 passes the test it's being put to; it says without actually saying it that the reader can be very sure it will handle problems put to it in terms more closely associated with the everyday business world.

One reason Sylvania achieved such a fine balance in this advertisement is because the layout is so clean and simple. There's not an extra element, no little extra logos, association membership bugs, slogans, or tricky trade names that mean nothing to anybody except the advertiser. And there has been no abortive attempt to include everything except the kitchen sink in one ad.

Strike a pleasing balance like Sylvania did, and your ads will succeed.

Individuality

Lurking where least expected, such as behind the cork of the agency's conference-room walls, is an enemy ready and able to dilute the effectiveness of your sales calls in print.

This is the agency layout.

Agencies have a fondness that's little short of inordinate for the so-called "agency layout"—which is merely a layout that looks like the layout prepared for every other client of the agency. Most agencies are too honest and too conscientious, of course, to pawn off second-hand work on their clients. But all of the layout artists and art directors in many first-rate shops tend to turn out work that bears such a striking family resemblance to everything else that's turned out for every other client that there's no other name for such layouts except "agency layouts."

Granted, the work is usually exceedingly good. This is, of course, exactly the quality of layout work you want and expect to get. However, there is no assurance whatsoever that what is right for one client who happens to sell monstrous draglines to the coal mining market is equally right for your company; you may sell integrated circuits the size of a pin-head to electronics people who scarcely know what coal is.

Agencies produce agency layouts—and cling tenaciously to one beloved typeface—for a very simple reason: It makes the agency's work stand out so that it's readily identifiable as having come from Smith, Jones, Brown & Johnson, Inc.

This practice gives people in the advertising community something to talk about. It gives the agency instant recognition for having created a campaign that may be the greatest thing since sex. In effect, this is a publicity program for the agency. It helps create an image of success so that hiring away key creative people from other shops is made easier—if any agency ever wanted to stoop to such an underhanded practice.

The fact remains, though, that if you get an agency layout you're not getting individualized thinking and individualized layouts to solve your individual communications problems. As advertising manager, it's up to you to watch this, to keep a running check on the output of your agency and to put the kibosh on canned layouts if they're suggested to you at new campaign time.

Individuality is nice. It's just ducky, in fact. It's highly desirable. It separates you from the herd. But the fact remains it's not the easiest thing in the world to come by. You can vary the appearance of your advertisements in any number of ways. You can, for instance, have more white space or less white space; reverses; change typefaces; go from photos to artwork or vice versa; change the proportion of the illustration to copy space; and countless other little tricks that produce mass production individualization. But if you do, you sacrifice campaign identity and company identity to a certain extent, and you may end up scuttling what might have been a highly effective advertising campaign.

Early Decision Needed

The time to decide if you want—or need—a highly individualized layout and visual approach is when you're in the process of planning a new campaign. At that time you, your account executive, copywriter, and art director can get your heads together and kick around a succession of ideas until you achieve unanimity of thought and come up with *the* idea for the forthcoming year.

Any number of routes may be chosen—some good, some better—and hopefully the one that's the very best for your circumstances at the specific time it's selected will get the nod.

Don't make the mistake of being drastically different merely for the sake of difference itself, however. Do so with a solid reason. If your reason is right, your advertisements that bear little resemblance to all of the other advertisements in the books you use can get tremendous readership and do an outstandingly effective job for you.

A layout and visual approach that's a radical departure from any currently being used in industrial advertising, as far as can be determined, is used with good effect by The Rotor Tool Company in its one-page, black-and-white bleed ads that appear in *Electronic Packaging and Production* magazine and a number of other business publications.

Rather than use the conventional illustration-headline-body copy format, Rotor Tool Company used a salesman's call report, attached to a picture of the salesman busily at work solving a customer's problem right in his plant. An engraving was then made from the complete assembly.

An ad typical of those in this imaginative campaign is shown on the next page.

The only bit of type in the entire advertisement is up at the top, quite small, and it's the theme for the campaign: *When we sell you a tool, it's the beginning, not the end.*

This is a reassuring statement and it inspires confidence in Rotor Tool, of course, for when a company purchases any item of capital equipment the question of after-sale service always arises. Availability of after-sale service can exert a profound effect on what brand is purchased; it can make or break a sale in most instances. Buying an orphan with poor parts and service availability just to save a few dollars at the time of the purchase is poor, short-sighted policy and industry is well aware of it. Rotor Tool hits hard at this point, and rightly so. There's lots of pay-dirt to be mined in this area.

Copy in the ad has built-in believability, something on the order of that achieved with testimonial copy.

As far as the layout is concerned, it achieves Rotor Tool's objective—which is making the company's ads stand out from the parade of ads in every trade publication. You cannot afford to overlook the fact that *every* advertiser is a competitor, not just those actual competitors who make products that are sold against yours in the marketplace. When it comes to advertising, every advertiser is competing for the reader's time and attention regardless of the product involved.

Rotor Tool Company has much going for it with this campaign and it will undoubtedly achieve the communications objectives set

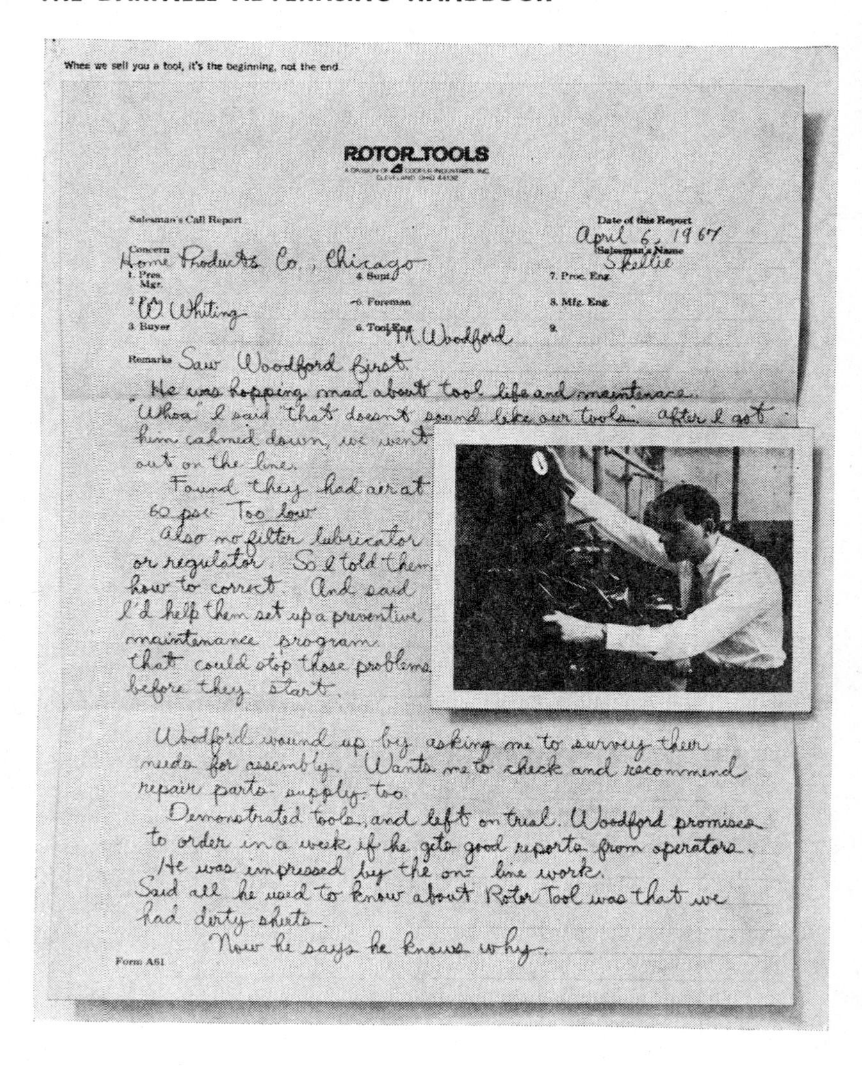

for it. As with any advertising campaign, however, there's a minor flaw. In this instance it's that the ad is difficult to read. The advertiser is aware of this, of course, and took the calculated risk the ad would arouse sufficient interest to overcome this obstacle. Chances are it will.

When we sell you a tool, it's the beginning, not the end.
ROTOR TOOLS
Salesman's Call Report
Date of this Report
April 6, 1967
Salesman's Name
Skellie
Concern
Home Products Co., Chicago
1. Pres. Mgr.
2. P.A. W. Whiting
3. Buyer
4. Supt.
6. Foreman
6. Tool Eng. M. Woodford
7. Proc. Eng.
8. Mfg. Eng.
9.
Remarks Saw Woodford first.
He was hopping mad about tool life and maintenance.
"Whoa" I said "that doesn't sound like our tools." After I got him calmed down, we went out on the line.
Found they had air at 60 psi Too low
also no filter lubricator or regulator. So I told them how to correct. And said I'd help them set up a preventive maintenance program that could stop those problems before they start.
Woodford wound up by asking me to survey their needs for assembly. Wants me to check and recommend repair parts supply, too.
Demonstrated tools, and left on trial. Woodford promises to order in a week if he gets good reports from operators.
He was impressed by the on line work.
Said all he used to know about Rotor Tool was that we had dirty shirts.
Now he says he knows why.
Form A61

Landis Machine Company, the world's largest manufacturer of

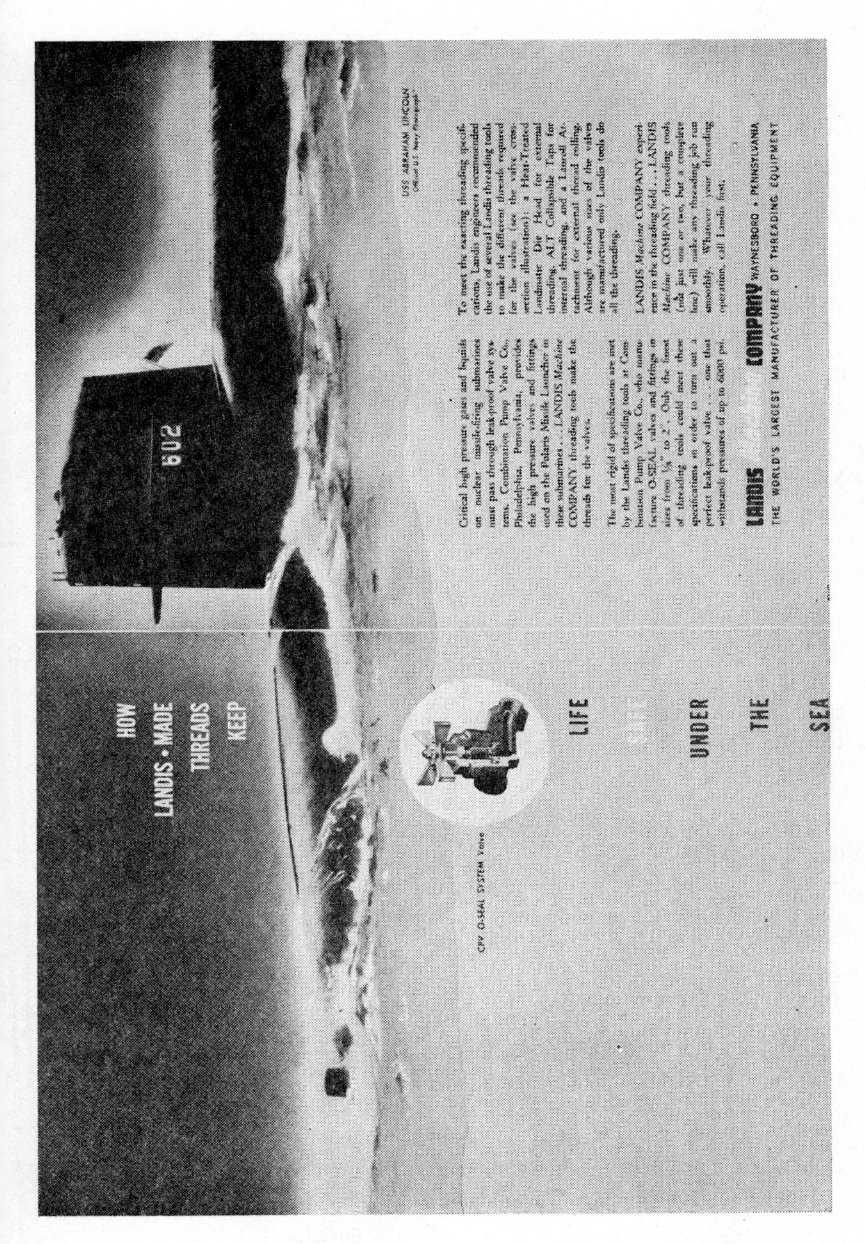

threading equipment, recently ran a two-color spread that is truly arresting; it is illustrated above.

This advertiser benefits from one of those fortunate situations that more of us wish we could exploit, but can't. Landis produces the threading equipment that's used by a contractor who supplies leakproof valve systems for our nuclear submarines that prowl the ocean depths of the world armed with Polaris missiles. There's no question about whether or not the product must perform up to expectations in this application. It *has to* to protect the lives of the brave Navy men who man the sub fleet that helps preserve world peace, such as it is.

Thus the advertiser is presented with a platform from which to speak, and with a testimonial that simply cannot be topped. It is quite obvious that Landis' threading tools are quality built to produce an end product of utmost reliability—as proven by the dramatic U.S. Navy photograph of the submarine USS Abraham Lincoln, our beautiful flag flying proudly and water boiling over the hull as she proceeds on the surface.

Layout takes full advantage of the wide, shallow shape of the photograph. Here's a situation in which the spread advertisement really comes into its own; a one-page ad couldn't possibly have done justice to this exciting photograph.

Additional impact comes from functional use of the second color —blue, what else?—to simulate the sea. A slight screen of black is used for approximately one and one-quarter inches below the sub to give shape to the illustration; below that the blue is laid on solid with no screen.

As dramatic as this ad is, it has one minor fault. Legibility is impaired somewhat by having the copy overprinted on the blue. Copy would have been easier to read if it had been printed on white, in a box, although that would have introduced another element to the layout and might well have distracted the eye from what is now a striking spread and a well-conceived layout.

The "On-Side" Approach

Individuality was achieved by Sharp Electronics Corporation by a layout device that's almost as old as advertising itself; the one-page, two-color ad is turned on its side!

The second color, brown, is used only in the illustration; it gives a pleasantly old-fashioned look to this interesting photograph.

Just what having the ad on its side does for readership is a moot point indeed, because not enough ads are run lying down to develop definitive answers to this question. Most studies on the subject are either inconclusive or else indicate that readership is not affected very much one way or the other. On the whole, though, research

tends to indicate that it is inadvisable to run ads sideways, although none of the readership evaluation services has strong opinions pro or con on the subject.

You don't expect your wife to operate efficiently with obsolete equipment. Why do you expect it of your bookkeeper?
Those cumbersome mechanical calculators date back to the ice box age.
The Sharp is a totally efficient electronic calculator priced like mechanical models.
It is so simple to operate, novices can master it in twenty minutes.
There are four models, all available for immediate delivery. Your old mechanical,
in any condition, will be taken in trade.
For particulars, ask your office equipment dealer
or write Sharp Electronics, Department 86,
178 Commerce Road, Carlstadt, New Jersey 07072.
SHARP

It stands to reason, though, that the rare ad run sideways should stand out, and, by rights, should stand a better than even chance of scoring a higher Noted rating than if run conventionally; this probably would hold true for Read Most, also. After all, it's pretty hard to miss Sharp's ad, isn't it?

Sharp's illustration is excellent and it works in close collaboration with the headline. Both stimulate the reader and arouse his curiosity, making him want to read the body copy to see what Sharp has to say.

The combination of the ad running in a different position than all the other ads in the book and the brown illustration—for all the world like the old gravure sections of Sunday newspapers of 30 years ago—give Sharp Electronics Corporation an individuality that cannot be denied. It's quite a pleasing ad, the selling proposition is interesting and sound, and the possibility of trading in an obsolete piece of equipment that's been written off years ago is nothing short of mouth-watering.

What a Layout Does

Every industrial advertisement in every trade publication published has one thing in common with every other one: Both occupy space. And this space must be divided so that the ad makes a maximum impact on the reader. This means, of course, that each element of the advertisement has to be allotted an amount of space deemed sufficient for it to accomplish its objective.

This apportionment of space would be greatly simplified if hard-and-fast rules for proper division of space existed—or, for that matter, if there even was such a thing as a "proper" division of space.

Guidelines exist; a layout must be attractive, it has to have feel, balance, and individuality. Too, it needs a sense of proportion so that the different elements will have a relationship to each other that is esthetically pleasing. This is, when all's said and done, what separates most successful advertisements from the also-rans. Industrial ads that didn't quite make the grade failed because of poor layout more often than any other reason.

Space in the advertisement is never divided equally so that each element is given exactly the same area. To do this would unfailingly create a static, dull, dreary, uninteresting ad. It would be an ad without a fluid sense of motion. Excessive symmetry is always just that—excessive.

Instead, space is divided so there are dominant and subordinate elements, so the white space that remains plays a key role, so the layout does its job to best effect. The layout must produce an ad that is harmonious and appealing to the eye. This is its critically important job.

First of all, one-page, black-and-white advertisements and some two-color ads will be discussed. These are, of course, the most widely used forms of space advertisements in the business press. Fractional pages will also be gone into, although not to as large an extent.

The Classic Layout

Various names are attached to the so-called classic layout. One that crops up more often than any other, and one that instantly identifies the classic layout to the layout artist, art director, or studio, is "Ayer Number 1."

Advertising legend has it, rightly or wrongly, that the classic layout was originally one of a number of basic layouts, all identified by number, developed by N. W. Ayer & Son, Inc., one of the country's largest and most successful old-line advertising agencies. The classic layout is supposed to have been developed several decades ago. Through long usage in both the consumer and industrial fields, it has proven itself to be what is, without question, the one layout that deserves the name classic.

Readership studies have proven repeatedly over the years that this is the one layout that is fairly certain of success. Use this layout for your advertisement and you have an edge going into the great game of enticing the reader to read your ad in preference to all of the others in the book.

The classic layout has ideal proportions, an innate sense of structure and nearly perfect division of space so that values are precisely as they should be for the ad to have an optimum chance to accomplish its objective. Naturally, if *all* ads were laid out in the Ayer Number 1 format, advertising would be incredibly monotonous. But in the business press where everybody tries to out-scream everybody else, where clatter and clutter abound and there's apparently either a desire for tastelessness—or an inability to produce tastefulness—the classic layout is a sight for eyes grown tired of layout anarchy.

Let's look at a beautifully done industrial advertisement with the classic layout and dissect it to see why it's good and what its strong points are.

As attractive an advertisement from the trade press in quite some time is the deceptively simple one-page, black-and-white ad run by

The 9¢-an-hour inspector
It's the ST-1 closed-circuit television camera from Diamond Power.
It checks conveyor belts for fast, full, economical operation. Inspects products for minute flaws. Or monitors material flow from receiving to shipping.
The ST-1 does all this, and more, with up to 800-line horizontal resolution. Picture clarity more than double that of home television.
This inspector is tough. The ST-1 is all silicon transistorized for long life under almost any conditions. It endures heat up to 140 F. Its thick steel housing is pressurized to keep out dust.
It has solid state sweep failure protection, built-in electronic light compensation, and wide tolerance circuitry for maximum picture stability—features not found in ordinary cameras.
You can get more than a camera from Diamond. With controls and accessories you can add-on, adapt or ruggedize the Diamond camera for close-ups, 360° inspections, or extreme environments.
Nine cents an hour puts the ST-1 on your payroll. That will write-off capital costs in three years, and pay for maintenance and electricity too.
Diamond Power Specialty Corp., Lancaster, Ohio.
Diamond Power

Diamond Power Specialty Corporation, a subsidiary of The Babcock & Wilcox Company.

It's a bleed ad; the illustration goes off the page on the top and on both sides. As the advertisement appeared in the publications, the illustration is 7⅞ inches deep; this leaves a whisker less than 3¼ inches for headline and body copy. These proportions are highly pleasing and there's a serene sense of logic and order and well-being imparted by the ad. Very obviously it is a well-constructed ad, it's laid out for one prime purpose—to communicate. That it does exceedingly well.

The large photographic illustration of the closed-circuit television camera manufactured by Diamond Power is shown at work on an assembly line, checking conveyor belts. The illustration is the dominant element in the ad and rightly so because its function is to stop the reader, to attract his eye, to keep him from continuing on through the book. This layout makes it possible for the illustration to accomplish this crucially important task.

Headline is easily read, of a tasteful size, and is set in lower-case type except for the lead capital letter; this is the easiest to read and attracts highest readership.

Copy is laid out in two blocks. Readership studies prove this arrangement attracts the eye more readily than any other. Type arranged in illogical blocks, or scattered at random (at least to the unanalytical reader) throughout an ad decreases readership very appreciably.

The signature is quite similar in weight and size to the headline, resulting in a neat, businesslike appearance that's absolutely devoid of pretense or ultrafancy logotypes that probably do more to confuse the reader than they ever do to increase advertiser identification.

Picking a Few Nits

Diamond Power Specialty Corporation's advertisement is so close to perfection it's almost a shame to mention that the type is set a few characters too wide according to what it should be as pointed out by numberless readership studies to achieve the absolute maximum number of readers. It's best to confine it to a measure of no more than 40 characters.

This fine, clean layout, then, consists of five elements as shown in the overlay on page 870. Each of five elements is numbered—illustration, headline, two copy blocks, and signature. The fact that there are only five elements means there is not a single superfluous item in the ad. Every element has its job and does it. The minimum number of elements resulted in simplicity and in a quiet and restrained elegance that speaks far louder than a jumble of type faces, screaming headlines, or blaring reverses ever could hope to.

However, if all industrial advertising was of this high caliber, industry would be far better off than it now is. By making its ad

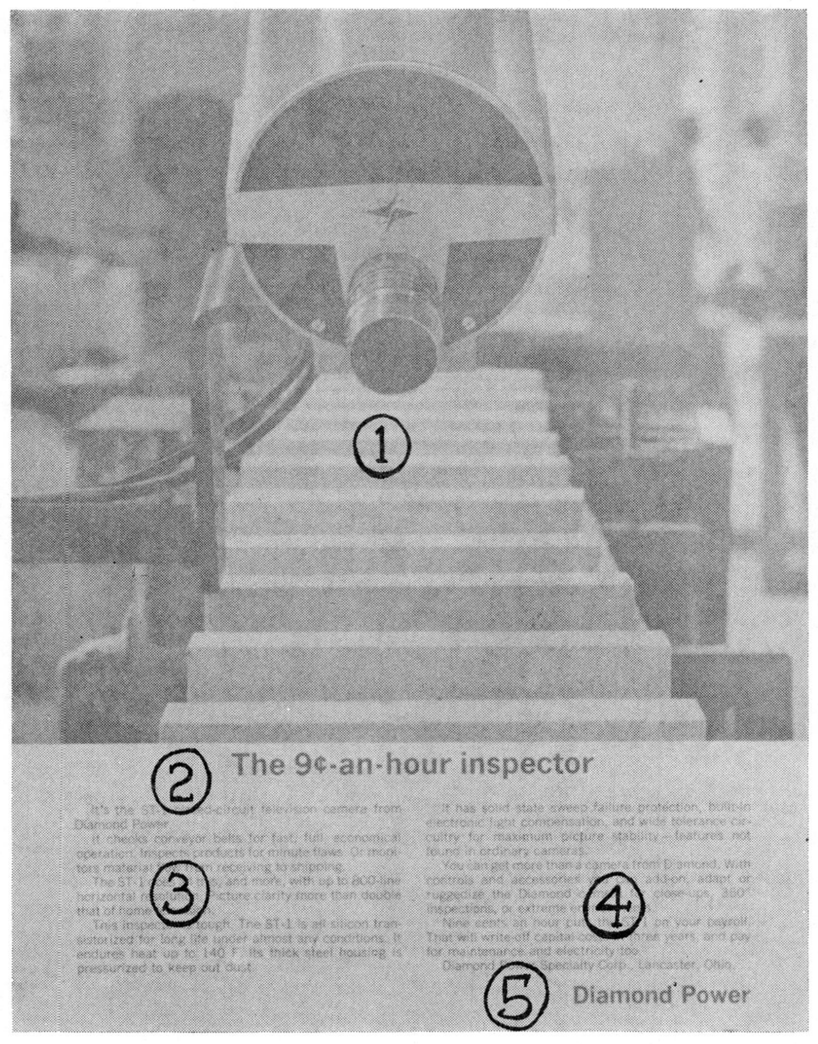

Only five basic elements in the Diamond Power ad: (1) illustration, (2) headline, (3) copy block, (4) copy block, and (5) logotype.

easy to read and inviting to read, Diamond Power *got* people to read. Which is why the ad was run in the first place.

H. B. Fuller Company's well-organized one-page, black-and-white ad from *Business Week* is illustrated nearby. The wild and wooly-

Glue can do WHAT for my hair?
All we said was a little glue could make her hair behave again. But we forgot to explain that the glue is the bonding base for our Tuff-Lite® Epoxy Conductive Terrazzo, a unique floor designed to eliminate the build-up of static electricity in such critical areas as hospital operating rooms, laboratories and other areas where explosive atmospheres could develop.
It is attractive and tough. It will not dent, spall, flake or break. It is sanitary, seamless and nonabsorbent. Can be installed as a new floor or over existing floors . . . even over floors that have lost their conductivity.
Tuff-Lite® is just one of the thousands of products Fuller formulates to solve problems in hundreds of industries. Adhesives to bond oily steel together. To replace concrete as a base material on building exteriors. For making cigarettes, envelopes, bags. To bind books. To package foods.
If any phase of your business involves fastening or bonding, protecting, coating, refurbishing a building, or whatever, Fuller probably has an adhesive that can do the job better than your present method. If not, Fuller Research will develop a product for your specific application. .
That's a strong statement. We can back it up.
LEADER IN ADHESIVE TECHNOLOGY
HB FULLER COMPANY
1150 Eustis St., St. Paul, Minn. 55108 Dept. 28900

Another good example of the "classic" layout—again we see the five basic elements. Coupled with this is an arresting illustration—the fuzzy-haired woman ties in quickly and logically with the static-reducing qualities of the product—an epoxy base glue.

haired woman piques the curiosity and the headline ties right in with it, as it does with the body copy—and with H. B. Fuller Company's selling proposition as well.

The company, a leader in adhesive technology, tells about its epoxy base for Terrazzo floors that prevents build-up of static electricity, which is what caused the fuzzy-wuzzy hair-do of the distraught woman in the illustration. This is critically important in hospital operating rooms, laboratories, or other areas where explosive atmospheres could develop.

This ad is so attractive and so readable, though, because of its classic layout. This is the same layout as used by Diamond Power, except this is the standard 7 x 10 ad (7 inches by 10 inches—the size of "live" matter in a one-page, nonbleed ad in all standard-sized business publications; it's usually referred to as either a one-page ad, or merely a 7x10 ad, with the inches not mentioned. And it's not called a 7 "x" 10, ad, but a "7 *by* 10" advertisement).

The illustration is the dominant element, naturally. In the actual ad it measured 6 5/16 inches in depth. Width is 7 inches. This leaves 3 11/16 inches of depth for headline, body copy, and signature.

H. B. Fuller's ad is well-balanced and the proportions are both pleasing and effective. It invites readership because each element belongs there, each element has an obvious job to do, and the elements are arranged with precision and logic.

Again, there are just five elements in the ad—illustration, headline, two blocks of body copy, and the signature-logo-address. This last is tastefully combined to concentrate reader attention on both name and logo, rather than trying to make two separate impressions on the reader, which is a wise course. This way both logo and signature are impressed upon the reader, whereas if they had been separated he might easily have missed one or the other.

This is what a well-laid-out 7x10 ad should look like—and too few do.

The one-page, black-and-white bleed ad run by Eastman Kodak Company in *Editor & Publisher, Industrial Photography, Infinity, National Press Photographer, Photo Methods for Industry, The Professional Photographer,* and *The Rangefinder* is illustrated below.

Free with Kodak boxtops

Service, that is. Most photographers think of Kodak Technical Service as a kind of insurance. If you are turning out work in really large volume, Kodak Service is insurance against down-time that could wreck production schedules. If the finished print is intended to reflect in high degree your personal creativity, Kodak Service is insurance that the print will give you back what you put into it.

Kodak representatives and dealers who bring this Service to you are the underwriters of this insurance. They see that you get the latest news about the newest methods and materials. The Kodak man, particularly, is a top-flight representative of the world's foremost photographic engineering staff. Through him, on a person-to-person basis, you share in the important findings of the Kodak research and development laboratories.

Add it up. It's all included—when the box you buy is labeled "Kodak." Professionally, you can't afford less.

Kodak

EASTMAN KODAK COMPANY
Rochester, N.Y.

Clean, simple, uncluttered—those are the benchmarks of a classic ad. The Kodak layout at left is another example of what has come to be known as the Ayer Number 1 treatment.

Clean and simple and uncluttered, this layout is a close relative of the Ayer Number 1. Kodak's ad differs only in that the headline is offset to the left and the body copy is laid out in three blocks rather than two. Also, the signature and logo appear at the bottom of the third copy block rather than being centered at the bottom of the page.

Many art directors prefer to block the type in three columns. This enables it to be set approximately 40 characters wide, which is the optimum for ease of reading. Having one additional column of type increases the number of elements in the advertisement from five to six, but that's of little consequence when an ad is as beautifully simple and tasteful as this one of Kodak's.

Merely having type in three copy blocks frees some space between the illustration and the headline, and between headline and body copy. This means there can be some attractive white space up there to make the ad look inviting and easy to read; this space is not available when the type is set in two columns because it must necessarily run deeper, assuming the same measure, of course.

Photography in Kodak's illustration is superb, as is to be expected. Every tiny detail is shown crisp and clear and razor sharp. Gradation of tones is long, the white shirts of the two men are not "burned up," and there's detail in the shadows even in a halftone reproduction. Too, the picture is exceptionally well composed.

The direction the two men are looking automatically guides the reader's eye to the heart of the picture where the negative is being retouched, and from there directly to the headline. This is why the headline is offset to the left, incidentally, to take full advantage of the eye path of the reader.

Much thought and a great degree of knowledge of human nature went into Kodak's fine ad. Note that once the reader's eye follows the path established for it, it goes to the headline where the power-word, "free," immediately lures him into the body copy.

This tasteful and pleasing ad did a highly effective job for Kodak.

Space Divided Horizontally

Divide space exactly in half, or so nearly half that it appears to be equally split, and you have a dull and dreary sameness in the layout.

In nature, for example, nothing is perfectly symmetrical. No two trees are exactly the same height, no two boulders exactly the same size and shape, no two rivers exactly the same width, no two mountains of equal mass. Even people's faces have distinct halves and when compared by means of split photographs flopped and pasted together show that symmetry, perfect symmetry, is nonexistent.

Any attempt to achieve precise uniformity in a layout by allotting an identical amount of space to various elements in an advertisement, or by splitting it equally between illustration and copy-headline-signature-logo will result in a visual Donnybrook, each element striving to achieve dominance, but none succeeding. The ad will not succeed, either.

Following are five ads as examples of how space may be divided horizontally, with brief comments on each. They are illustrated nearby.

Space appears to be almost evenly divided in T. B. Wood's Sons Company's one-page, black-and-white ad from *Factory* magazine.

Space is almost equally divided between illustration and copy in this advertisement. Had the illustration been deeper on the page—or even shallower—the impact of the ad would have been stronger. Even balance is static.

To the eye, space seems to be divided so that the illustration cuts the ad almost exactly in half, although use of a ruler shows that it is dominant by a scant quarter of an inch. Coming as close as it does to achieving a static equality, the advertisement lacks impact and appeal and a feeling of excitement, although the advertiser's product seems to be excellent, the headline promises a user benefit, and the copy comes through with an explanation of the benefit and offers a strong selling proposition. If only the illustration had been deeper—or even shallower—the ad would have been stronger.

An advertisement laid out with an illustration that occupies less than half the depth of the page is also shown. Illustration for the 7x10 black-and-white ad is 4 7/16 inches deep, leaving room for a caption, stacked (two line) headline, a subhead, three blocks of copy, logotype, and slugline listing other divisions of Lindberg Hevi-Duty's parent corporation. Sluglines, incidentally, are dearly beloved by management which is under the impression they are *read.* Frequently a listing of products as long as a dreary winter is offered to the reader in a slugline in hopes he'll rush right out and buy other products of the company.

Sluglines are inelegantly referred to in the advertising business as "garbage." Although it's almost impossible to do, try to dissuade management from cluttering up your ads this way. Little benefit accrues from addition of garbage to an ad—but another element is added to detract from the layout.

Another Lindberg Hevi-Duty ad shown is a four-color insert that ran in *Semiconductor Products & Solid State Technology* magazine—which *has* to be the longest name in the world for a quality trade publication.

This ad is particularly well balanced. Illustration is 7⅛ inches deep, leaving 3¾ inches for the headline, white space, copy, logotype, and slugline. Additional depth comes from using an insert which the advertiser printed. Live matter can extend clear to the bottom of the page if desired.

In this ad the horizontal division of space is not equal and the ad as a whole gains impact as compared to that shown on the opposite page. Note that here the space occupied by the illustration is less than text.

Automated carburizing, carbonitriding and heat treating operation—REX CHAINBELT INC., Milwaukee, Wisc.

We may not be production experts

But we can probably teach you something about heat processing and automation.

Like how automated heat processing increases profit—by improving product quality, speeding production, and relieving labor.

Automated heat processing—developed by us over six years ago—is just one of the new roles heat is playing to cut production costs. The entire heat process is programmed on a simple card. Including atmosphere control. Cycling. Sampling. And quenching. Tray-stacking is about the only manual job.

Rewards are great:

1. Better quality control: Load after load, parts meet tight tolerances. Machining time is often saved.
2. Less labor: You need at least one less man each shift. One manufacturer eliminated his entire third heat treating shift by programming a long carburizing and quenching process for that time. And he left it unattended, except for a simple alarm.
3. Easier work: Hot-job drudgery is eliminated. So you can hire—and keep—good workers.
4. Faster production: Once a process is programmed, you can repeat it time and again. Quickly. Accurately.

Is all this worth the money? Most say yes. For about a 5% added investment, you'll eliminate at least one man a shift. Improved QC and increased production are bonuses. We've found that automation pays its way in 12-18 months.

But all's not rosy. We've heard of automated heat processes that sit idle—because they weren't designed right.

That's where we come in. Heat is our business—has been for over 50 years. We don't claim to be production experts, but we do understand how heat can improve manufacturing processes. And we can recommend solutions from the broadest line of heat processing equipment available.

Want to learn more about heat processing and automation? Give us a ring. Or write to 2450 W. Hubbard St., Chicago, Illinois 60612.

LINDBERG HEVI·DUTY SB
DIVISION OF SOLA BASIC INDUSTRIES

OTHER DIVISIONS: ANCHOR ELECTRIC · ENGINEERED CERAMICS · HEVI-DUTY ELECTRIC · SOLA ELECTRIC

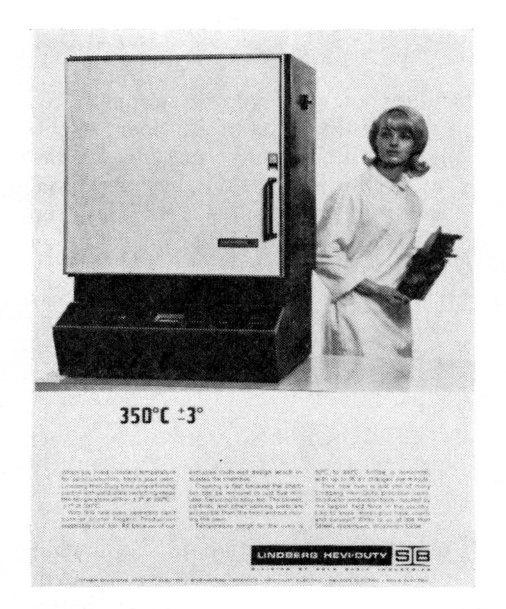
350°C ±3°
LINDBERG HEVI-DUTY

This ad runs deep. The added depth is gained because it was preprinted as a magazine insert. As in the preceding advertisement for Lindberg Hevi-Duty, the "live matter" can go to the very bottom of the page. Illustration takes more than half of the space available, thus avoiding a static look.

An illustration that's still deeper is seen in the excellent one-page, four-color advertisement run by Potlatch Forests, Inc., in *Business Week*. This interesting illustration of the product and tools "floating" before a forest backdrop runs quite deep on the page, a full 8 1/16 inches. There's ample room for a stacked headline, three

We invented a new kind of
building material
Potlatch pfi

At right, an ad that runs quite deep on the page. Nevertheless, layout provides plenty of white space for the copy and a prominent logotype. The stacked headline adds to the airy impression of this advertisement for Potlatch Forests, Inc. Illustration "floats" in front of an improvised forest background.

blocks of copy, the logo and slugline, however, even when sufficient white space is left to create an airy impression. Although it's lower on the page than most illustrations extend, Potlatch Forest's ad is pleasing and pleasant to look at.

Deepest illustration you're likely to encounter, unless it bleeds four sides, is that in Owens-Illinois' impressive four-color advertisement, also from *Business Week* magazine.

An example of the extreme in depth of illustration. Here the copy message was institutional, and could be told in the limited space below the photo. Headline is reversed at the top of the illustration. Running the logo on a slant keeps it from being lost at the bottom of the layout.

Owens-Illinois could use an illustration 9⅜ inches deep because the headline is reversed out of the illustration up at the top of the ad, thus saving space in the copy panel at the bottom. Too, the copy is very short and is almost institutional in tone.

Use of an ad that's almost entirely illustration certainly results in an oversize measure of impact. Few readers could pass by this ad without noticing the illustration, looking at it, reading the headline and—as a minimum—noticing the advertiser's signature. It stands out because it's on a slant.

This is a well-balanced advertisement, but it's not every advertiser's cup of tea. Few can tell the story that has to be told in this small a space. For those who can, well and good. There's absolutely nothing wrong with the extremely deep illustration, and there's much to recommend it.

When every advertisement in the book is fighting fiercely to get the reader's attention, you can weight the odds in your favor by using the unusually deep illustration. It's a stopper.

Space Divided Diagonally

Not too many industrial advertisements use the layout device of dividing space diagonally. This is, perhaps, because it's a bit more difficult for the layout man who's accustomed to thinking primarily in terms of things horizontal or vertical.

Diagonals are dramatic. They express movement. When a diagonal division of space is employed, a flowing feeling and an atmosphere of excitement is imparted to the layout. This signals the reader that something a bit out of the ordinary is occurring in the advertisement. It makes him want to see what's happening.

Whereas the horizontal line represents rest and tranquility, the diagonal is exactly the opposite.

Diagonal lines are especially effective in layouts for advertisements for hard goods with moving parts—machinery of all types, for instance, ranging from machine tools to shoemaking machines to earthmoving equipment. The reader receives the implication from diagonals that the ad concerns a product with power and strength and vigor, one that will produce and accomplish.

Seldom is an ad divided diagonally by the methods customarily used—copy blocks, tint blocks, an illustration cropped to a diagonal, and so on. Many very strong industrial advertisements are *symbolically* laid out to capitalize on the inherent strength of diagonal lines, however. A good example is United Shoe Machinery's fine ad, which ran in *Boot & Shoe Recorder* magazine (on opposite page).

You'll note that this ad, which bleeds on all four sides, definitely is not divided diagonally by an arbitrary device, but nonetheless *is* divided diagonally—as proven by the rough layout for this advertisement that's shown beside the ad. The author doodled this to show masses only to make it apparent that the diagonal division exists.

Type set ragged right (not justified on the right hand side of the column) and the line caused by the shape of the machine divide the ad diagonally just as surely as would a heavy black line.

In this case the reader's eye is attracted first by the headline, then by the illustration; it shifts back to the headline and then proceeds into the body copy. This may not be the ideal layout in terms of eye path, although the ad as a whole is quite effective. Its major weakness lies in lack of legibility caused by the black type's not having sufficient contrast with the dark-gray background on

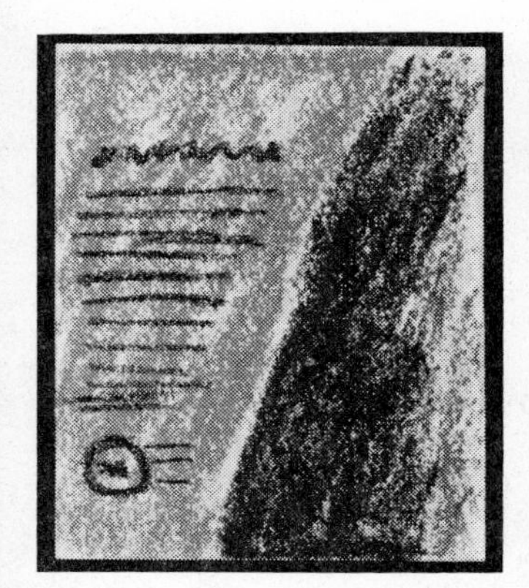

Above, copywriter's rough shows that United Shoe Machinery ad at right really is divided diagonally. So subtly is this division of space accomplished by the layout that it is not easily apparent to the untrained eye. Yet subconscious impact of such division of space is strong.

which it's overprinted; had the type been in a panel against white, it would have been much easier to read.

Another advertisement with a diagonal division of space is the two-color bleed ad run in *Commercial Car Journal* magazine by The Echlin Manufacturing Company. Unlike United Shoe Machinery's advertisement, Echlin doesn't symbolically divide the space diagonally, but does it literally with an orange-and-white lightning flash. This represents electrical energy, of course, and is very appropriate because the advertiser is one of the big names in the automotive aftermarket with ignition parts and other electrical items, as well as fuel system parts, brake system parts, and speedometer cables.

Echlin's ad, while divided diagonally by the lightning flash, is also divided horizontally due to the necessity of allotting space in the layout to both the illustrative area, as well as the space reserved for the copy block and signature, and for the catalog that's offered in the tint block in the lower right corner of the ad. The tint block is AAAA orange, laid on solid.

The tint block itself further divides the layout, this time vertically, so that it is approximately two-thirds for the copy portion and one-third for the catalog-offer portion. See page 880.

Combinations of horizontals, diagonals, verticals, and curves can

Again a subtle division of space diagonally by means of the lightning flash. This ad also is divided horizontally by the relationship of the illustration to the headline and the copy block at the lower left of the layout.

be made esthetically if the number of elements in the layout isn't excessive so that clutter results. If in doubt, count. If the total is more than six or seven elements, discard and simplify until your advertisement is able to communicate rather than confuse.

However, it's all too easy to get too much of a good thing, and if the layout man gets overly enthusiastic he's likely to produce something that confuses the eye so it doesn't know where to go next. Confusing the reader results in losing him. He'll not stick around to figure out a layout that's too busy and complicated and contains far too many elements.

Space Divided Vertically

If you take a 7x10 space and divide it into equal halves, vertically, it's just as dreary and dull and unappealing as if the layout had cut the space in half horizontally.

However, if you offset the copy to one side or another by devoting a major portion of the space to the illustration—or even do just the opposite, for that matter—you neatly avoid bisecting the ad in half. And you automatically create an interesting situation due to the inequality of the segments of space.

In addition, the layout with space divided vertically achieves a certain measure of individuality because the overwhelming majority of all industrial advertisements are laid out so the space is divided horizontally. What's more, vertical lines suggest power and dignity, something like the giant redwoods in Muir Woods, north of San Francisco. A connotation such as this can increase readership. The reader doesn't stop to rationalize why the layout creates this impression, and he isn't consciously aware that it does—even if it does.

Keep in mind, however, that every illustration cannot arbitrarily be drastically cropped so that it becomes an effective vertical with proportions of roughly two and one-half to one, as far as length-to-width is concerned. If you're planning a campaign laid out so that your illustrations will be verticals, with the space divided vertically, be sure the illustrations reflect this and are not adaptations of illustrations that would actually look better if horizontal. This could result in ads that are very weak indeed.

An ad from *Space/Aeronautics* magazine shows how space should be divided vertically so that the illustration dominates the copy space. In this two-color ad run by Sperry Gyroscope Company, Division of

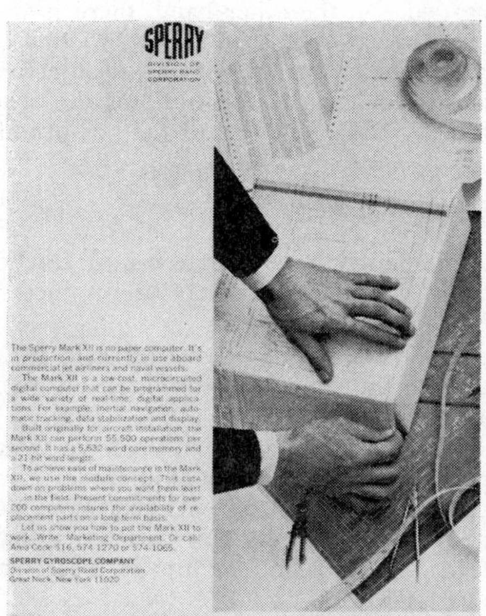

Here is strong vertical division of space. The eye-travel path of the reader begins with the Sperry Gyroscope logotype, then goes into the illustration, and finally moves up the left-hand side of the layout into the body copy. Use vertical division of layouts carefully—they are a definite break with tradition.

Sperry Rand Corporation, the duotone illustration is 3 15/16 inches wide, while the copy space is 3 1/16 inches wide, giving it a pleasing 4-to-3 ratio.

Note that the illustration was *planned* to be a strong vertical; there's no impression of anything missing or left out, despite the tight cropping of the illustration to include only the man's hands. Interest is concentrated on what the hands are doing, what they're holding, rather than on the unseen figure to whom they belong.

In Sperry Gyroscope's advertisement, the reader's eye goes first to the Sperry logo in the upper left corner of the ad. It then proceeds down through the illustration, reads the headline, and then goes up the left side of the page into the body copy. This is the normal clockwise pattern and normal point of eye entry.

Some very effective ads have resulted from dividing the space vertically. For the most part, however, you're bucking tradition, you're up against the lifetime habit of expecting to find material on a printed page arranged so that it's divided horizontally. This can cost as far as readership is concerned. Unless there's a compelling reason—such as product shape, perhaps—to divide the space vertically, you're better off not to.

Both tradition and habits of a lifetime are not to be lightly regarded. On the other hand, there is no rule or regulation that says you have to take them as law, written or unwritten. Produce a well-conceived campaign with solid objectives and strong individual ads and it really matters little how the space is divided. The important thing is the overall effect the ads produce on the reader.

Fractional-Page Ads

Budgetary woes dictate use of fractional pages on occasion, especially for minor markets or products of minor importance in the overall sales picture.

No truer words were ever said in all of advertising than those uttered by some long-forgotten ad man who said, "The bigger the ad, the more it's read."

A one-third page ad will receive more readership than a one-sixth page ad; a two-thirds will likewise be read by more readers than the one-third unit; a page attracts more people than a two-thirds page does; a spread gets more attention than does a one-page ad; gatefolds, popouts and multipage inserts do still better—but more on this later on.

If the money isn't there, though, there's nothing else to do except to be philosophical and practical and run fractionals, as they're called. A consistent program of fractionals with regularly scheduled insertions keeps the advertiser's name and product in front of prospective purchasers.

This is vitally important because the reader has a remarkably short memory. Run a page now and then, disappear for months at a time from key business publications while hoarding the precious dollars in the budget to make another ego-soothing splash of a page or a spread, and you're diluting the impression your advertising has worked so hard to make. When your company isn't in key publications, your competitors *are*. They're making points, building identity, creating brand preference, and preselling their products.

There is no substitute for continuity.

It's better by far to appear regularly in publications you know reach your universe and do it with fractionals than it is to go the in-again, out-again route.

Sporadic advertising actually accomplishes remarkably little except to give the powers that be within the company the feeling that, by golly, our firm is full of vigor and vitality and it's proceeding under a full head of steam. Advertising spasmodically *does* accomplish a negative goal: It lulls management into a false sense of security because it's under the mistaken impression that advertising is working for the company, when it is not. Unless advertising is constant and continuous, it's doing no such thing.

The immediate question here, however, is how should fractionals be laid out in order to attract as many readers as possible?

Research has proven quite conclusively that a vertical division of space is the best choice to make in business publications of standard size, where pages are ordinarily laid out in three columns. Most books do, though, have a part of their editorial pages laid out in both two columns and three. This provides flexibility in accepting advertisements of varying sizes, as well as giving visual relief from a format that could become tiresome.

If you're considering a one-third-page ad, you can buy space for a vertical one-third page—frequently called a one-column ad, although this terminology isn't as specific as referring to what fraction of a page is being used—as shown in "C" of the sketch, page 884. This is a vertical format. However, the same amount of space at the same price—one-third of a page—is also shown in "D," although this is almost a square format. The one-column fractional shown in "C" will receive much more readership, other things being equal.

Then, too, you can buy a half-page. This half-page of space can

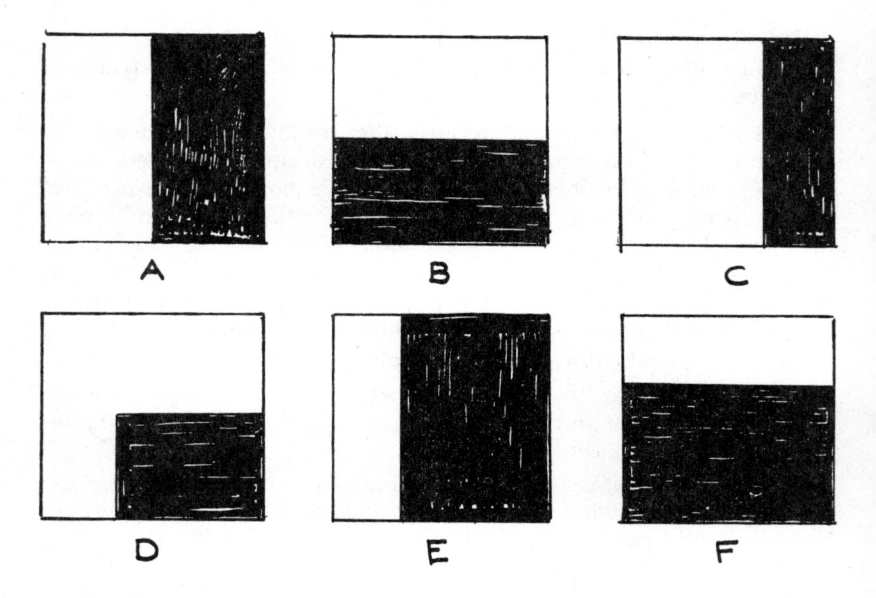

be purchased as either a vertical half as shown in "A," or it can be a horizontal half as in "B." Cost is exactly the same, but there's no problem in making the selection. A vertical half page will receive almost 25 percent more readership than will a horizontal half. Just why there's such a large difference isn't entirely understood, although it's well-known that the reader's eye tends to scan the top half of a page first, then drifts downward, looking for something attractive to pursue further.

Largest fractional page offered in standard size business publications is the two-thirds page. Here again, it can be specified as a vertical segment of the page, as in "E" or as a horizontal two-thirds, as in "F." Use "E" and get much more readership for the same money.

Incidentally, most first-class business books will make a determined effort to make sure that editorial matter occupies the other column of a two-thirds page ad, thus, in effect, giving the advertiser the benefit of having the entire page for his advertisement. This is called dominating the page. Evidence exists to indicate that a good, strong, two-thirds page ad will receive more readership than it can rightly expect due to people reading the editorial matter, than automatically continuing on into the advertisement. This is a fringe benefit you can count on with the two-thirds page fractional.

SURE SHOT

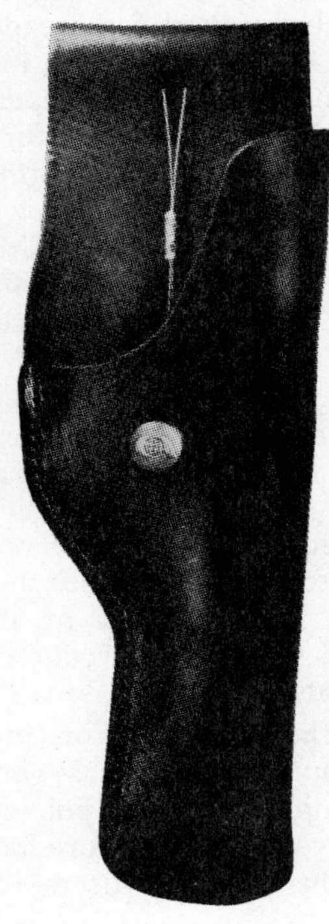

New micro-miniature switch.

Available in single-pole model; multi-pole and sequencing varieties to come. Function time is less than 1 millisecond at 2 amps firing current.

It's one of a wide variety of Atlas explosive-actuated components and systems that offer infinitely greater reliability . . . in smaller space . . . with less weight . . . and with lower power requirements than any other type of electro-mechanical system. Think of this when you work on one-time performance systems.

Send for technical literature giving specifications and characteristics on a variety of Atlas explosive components — switches, actuators and specialty devices and systems.

ATLAS

CHEMICAL INDUSTRIES, INC.
Aerospace Components Division
Valley Forge, Pa. 19481

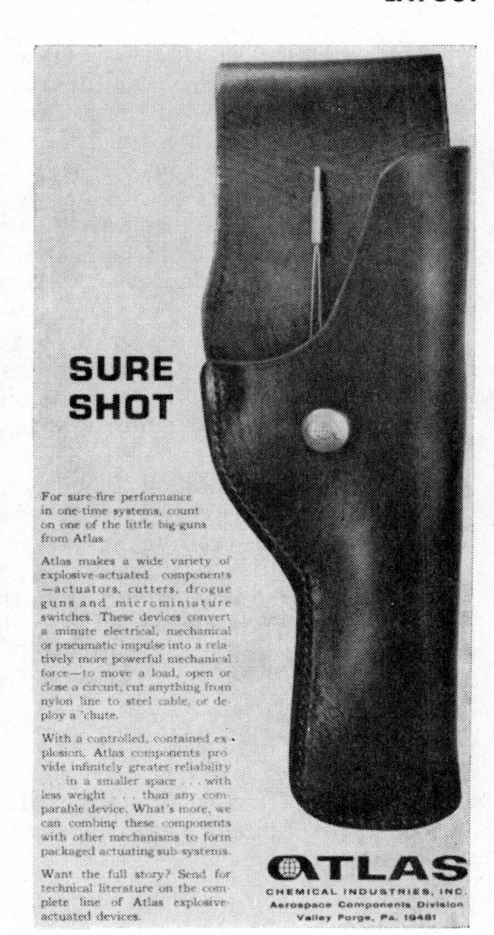

SURE
SHOT
For sure-fire performance in one-time systems, count on one of the little big guns from Atlas.
Atlas makes a wide variety of explosive-actuated components —actuators, cutters, drogue guns and microminiature switches. These devices convert a minute electrical, mechanical or pneumatic impulse into a relatively more powerful mechanical force—to move a load, open or close a circuit, cut anything from nylon line to steel cable, or deploy a 'chute.
With a controlled, contained explosion, Atlas components provide infinitely greater reliability . . . in a smaller space . . . with less weight . . . than any comparable device. What's more, we can combine these components with other mechanisms to form packaged actuating sub-systems.
Want the full story? Send for technical literature on the complete line of Atlas explosive-actuated devices.
ATLAS
CHEMICAL INDUSTRIES, INC.
Aerospace Components Division
Valley Forge, Pa. 19481

Beginning with the excellent two-thirds page layout illustrated above, Atlas Chemical resized and rearranged the elements into the one-third page ad reproduced at the left. Note that while both treatments are fractional pages, there is plenty of white space in them.

In an exceptionally clean and attractive two-thirds page black-and-white ad, Atlas Chemical Industries, Inc. had the good taste and the courage to do what all too few advertisers using fractionals dare to do, even though it's right—it made effective use of white space. Industrial advertising has been severely infected for decades with an obsessive desire to cover every inch of the paper with ink, as if that way and only that way lay assurance the ad would speak in a strong enough voice to be heard. Nothing at all, in the form of white space, is actually a layout element and should be regarded as such.

Atlas wisely selected a vertical two-thirds page and made the most of it with a layout that emphasizes the strong vertical format and the vertical lines of the illustration itself. The ad enjoyed excellent readership and did quite well as far as pulling inquiries is concerned.

Using the same illustration and adapting the copy through shortening and a little rewriting makes it possible to convert a larger ad into a smaller one—resizing the ad, as it's called. Atlas Chemical Industries resized its basic two-thirds-page ad, although a different photographic illustration with a different product was substituted. The smaller ad retains the inviting open, readable look of the original, and the strong vertical lines. It, too, was highly productive in terms of both readership and reader response.

You'll find that if you put a little more thought and effort into your fractionals, and schedule them so your program has good continuity without intervals when you're completely out of publication advertising, fractionals will do right by your program, product, and company. Indeed, many successful industrial advertisers use nothing but fractionals.

Bleed

When an advertisement's live matter extends flush to the edge of the page, rather than stopping short about one half inch, it is said to "bleed" off of the paper. It is then called a bleed ad.

Bleed ads are much bigger ads, and they look like it even if they are on the same sized page in the same publication. For example, we measured ads in an issue of *Production* magazine. Tinnerman Products, Inc. has a one-page, black-and-white ad directly opposite a one-page, black-and-white ad run by Laminated Shim Company, Inc.

Tinnerman's ad is a nonbleed ad, so measures 7 by 10 inches; it's a 7x10 ad, that is. It has 70 square inches of available space for illustration, headline, copy, signature, and logo.

Laminated Shim's ad, however, is a bleed ad and it measures 8 3/16 inches by 11 3/16 inches, which is the trim size of the book. It has 96 square inches of space for the advertisement—37 percent more.

Bleed is no exception to the rule that most things in life worth having have a price tag attached to them. Most publications charge a premium price for bleed, usually 15 percent of the basic page rate. Even at a 15 percent bump in price, though, bleed is a tremendous bargain. Getting 37 percent more of a product—whether it's space or what have you—for 15 percent more money can't help but be a bargain.

However, when you're buying something such as space to use to communicate with a vast audience, value must be based on effectiveness. A massive amount of research has been done on the readership of bleed ads compared to nonbleed ads. McGraw-Hill analyzed 7,548 advertisements that appeared in 135 issues of the company's magazines over a 10-year period. More than 13,000 readers were personally interviewed. Bleed advertisements had better readership than nonbleed ads in 68 percent of the cases.

Readership Up 25-35 Percent

When a bleed ad *doesn't* outperform a nonbleed ad, the reason lies elsewhere, not with the fact that it's a bleed ad. Most readership studies put the increase in readership between 25 and 35 percent—which is certainly a good return on a 15 percent greater investment in space dollars.

That bleed outpulls nonbleed ads so substantially is due in part to the additional space bleed makes available for the illustration. The larger the illustration, the better the chance of attracting the reader's attention, of arousing his curiosity, and enticing him into the ad. When an illustration bleeds, there's an inviting feeling of roominess, of a complete lack of crowding of any elements of the ad. Bleed is the best buy of any of the space "extras"—such as preferred position (excepting second and fourth covers) and so on.

Layout artists and art directors like to work with bleed space. The much larger size of the overall advertisement gives them more latitude, more elbow room. Elements of the ad must still be arranged so they're esthetically pleasing and in such a way they will attract the reader's eye, of course, but more often than not bleed permits a feeling of airiness, or roominess, to be imparted to the ad in measure entirely out of proportion to the 37 percent increase in available space.

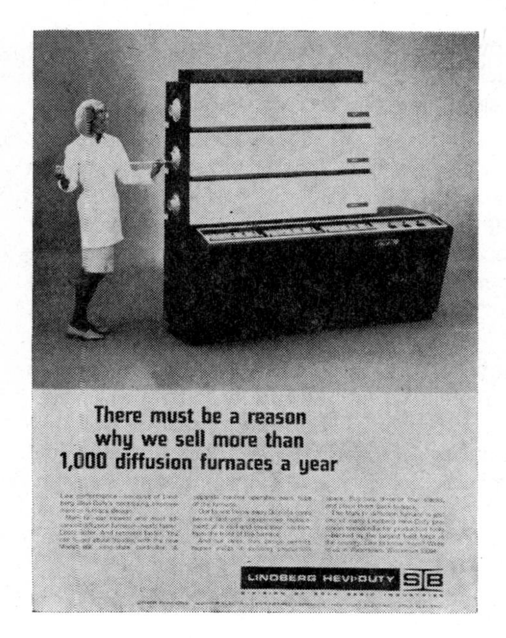

The Lindberg Hevi-Duty ad at left bleeds at the top and both sides, allowing the illustration to come up big and bold. Ad industry research shows that the use of bleed pages increases readership more than the extra cost of such media space.

Full bleed, where the ad goes off the page at top, bottom, and both sides, makes a dramatic impact. Note that the flame in the illustration bleeds off the top of the page and the glass bleeds off the bottom, creating a vertical division of space.

Most bleed ads bleed off of the page in three directions only—top and both sides, as does the Lindberg Hevi-Duty four-color advertisement illustrated nearby. This is a typical bleed layout, with the illustration approximately 8¼ inches wide and 7 inches in depth. Bleed enabled the advertiser to use the extra space to make the illustration bigger and bolder and to boost its stopping power. Copy is printed normally in black type on the white stock.

Another effective method of laying out a bleed ad is to bleed the illustration top and bottom and both sides. This is frequently referred to as a full-bleed ad, and the technique is widely used because the resulting ad has terrific impact. An arresting example of the full-bleed ad is the four-color Mobil Oil Corporation layout nearby.

Mobil's striking illustration has the bottom of the glass bleeding off the bottom of the page, and flame bleeding off the top creates a vertical division of space; the illustration is properly the dominant element in the ad.

Note that the copy is overprinted; with a strong magnifying glass it is very apparent that all of the four colors are represented in the "background" of this fine ad. Color is light enough, though, so that the type reads well.

DeJur-Amsco Corporation's excellent ad also is full bleed. In this instance elements are arranged as they are in a classic layout, with

While DeJur-Amsco's full bleed ad at the right ties all the elements together neatly, the gray background against which the body copy must be read presents some bar to readability. For additional cost, engravers can arrange for a white background.

the difference being the photographic illustration occupies the entire page. Copy is overprinted on a light gray background and is easily read—although not as easily as if it had been printed against the white of the page.

Bleeding the ad on all four sides ties it together in one neat whole, creating a feeling that every element is exactly where it belongs. Having the ad bleed fully serves another purpose, too: Even though it's a one-color ad, DeJur-Amsco separated itself from the advertisement by means of this device, while gaining additional readership at the same time.

The impact of bleed is intensified by the dramatic camera angle used for the illustration in this effective ad for Ford. The dark tones of the low-key photo are overcome by setting the headline in reverse and by putting the body copy against a white background.

Another way to lay out a bleed ad is shown in Ford Motor Company's powerful advertisement. Here the dramatic illustration really dominates the ad, as it was intended to. Combination of an extremely low camera angle, rough, off-highway roadbed and the vehicle on an incline all contribute to a sense of action and excitement. Ford's truck catches the eye immediately, then the gaze drops to the headline which is reversed out—that is, having white type against the dark background. Copy is set in a small panel and it's printed in the customary black against the white background for good legibility.

Bleed buys a lot for you—impact, attention, extra readership. It's a best buy.

Element Placement

Now that you've made a decision as to whether the space will be divided horizontally or vertically—or diagonally—and have determined approximately how much space is to be allotted to each element, the time has come to look at factors which influence placement of the elements.

Each element—and the white space between them—must be placed so that their relationship with each other contributes to a harmonious whole. End result must appeal to the eye. The ad must be inviting. It must appear easy to read. Show the reader an ad that looks as if it would require hard work on his part to wade through it and you've lost yourself a potential prospect without ever having had the opportunity to talk to him in print.

The reader is not viewing the ad from a great distance, like looking at the patterns fields and cities and rivers make when seen from a jet airliner at 39,000 feet. He doesn't have the advantage, if advantage it is, of being able to back off from your advertisement to see if the pattern it makes from a distance is one that's pleasing to him or not.

And he's not omniscient, either. He's unable to judge immediately whether or not an advertisement is of interest to him because he cannot examine the entire ad at one time. He has to scan it, look over the elements, and then make up his mind if this is something in which his time will be well invested.

Location of the elements within the ad will determine to a large degree to what extent your ad is read.

Fortunately, though, you don't have to fly blind and place the illustration, headline, copy, and logotype by guess and by golly. Many studies have been made to determine where the reader's eye spends its time. This has been done on a large scale with concealed motion picture cameras equipped with telephoto lenses to bring the eye of volunteer subjects up close so it could be determined with certainty at all times, by frame numbers on the film, at what portion of a page the subject was looking. By giving these subjects magazines in which all material had previously been cross-referenced with film frames, researchers obtained excellent insight into the reading habits of different classes of individuals.

Educators and the armed forces have also gotten into the act in an effort to devise methods of improving the clarity of instruction material and to develop material that is easier to read and easier to assimilate.

It has been found that the reader's eye is naturally attracted to the top of the page because, ever since kindergarten, we have been trained to regard what is at the top as the beginning. In other cultures, where writing proceeds from bottom to top of page, this would, of course, be just the opposite. The reader has long been accustomed to looking at the top of the page first, because this is where he "starts."

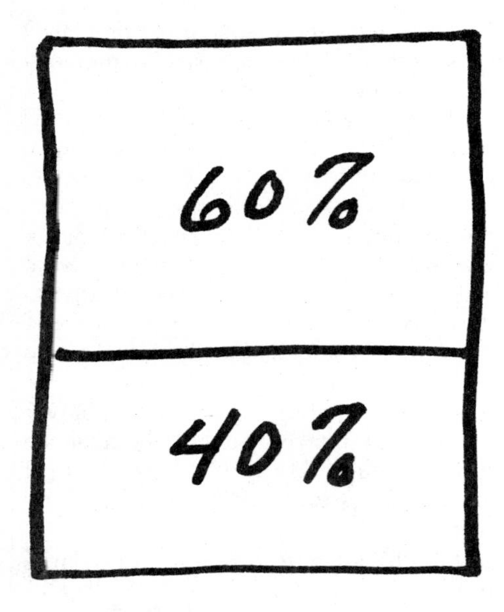

Ad research shows that the dominant element in an ad—almost always the illustration—belongs at the top of the page. This is where 60 percent of the "eye dwell" has been shown to be located in eye-travel studies.

Time spent by the reader's eye has been divided approximately as shown in the 60-40 percent diagram, although no attempt has been made to locate the dividing line with great precision because no definitive study has been made that is accepted by all communicators. For all practical purposes it's enough to know that 60 percent of the reader's eye time is spent in an area that comprises roughly 55 percent of the page—the top portion. Below that line, the eye lingers 40 percent of the time.

This is enough to dictate that the element of strongest inherent interest—almost always the illustration—should be located in the upper portion of the page.

An old campaign of Lindberg Hevi-Duty's was based on a layout that placed the illustration at the bottom of the ad, as illustrated

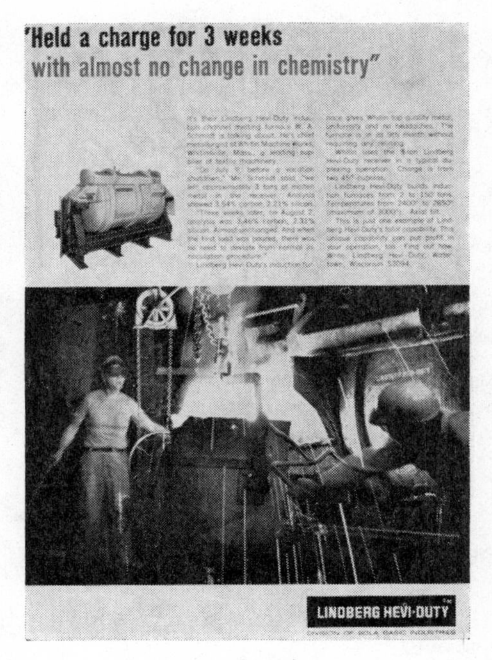

Readership scores on the ad at right were not what they should have been because the illustration was placed at the bottom of the page. The eyes of too many readers went from the headline to the illustration, then went back to the copy only briefly if at all. In some cases eyes were attracted to the photo again.

nearby. Although the layout is clean, typography is fairly good, and there's sufficient white space to prevent giving the impression the ad is soggy and hard to read, it still fell short of receiving as much readership as it should have gotten.

With all of the above going for it, in addition to a dramatic illustration and tightly written, highly informative copy, the ad should have scored stronger. The eye of the reader, instead of going initially to the illustration and then proceeding naturally into the copy, went instead to the illustration at the bottom of the ad—too far to make the jump back up to the copy block.

The all-revealing motion picture cameras also disclosed the percentage of time the reader's eye spends in each quarter of the page. Divided into half, of course, it's 60 percent in the top half of the page; but when the top part is divided in half, vertically, it was found that 40 percent of the eye time was put in on the left half of the page, and only 20 percent on the right.

Time devoted to right and left halves of the bottom portion of the page showed the same tendency. Here, the left half received 25 percent of the total of 40 percent of the time spent below the dividing line, while the right half received only 15 percent.

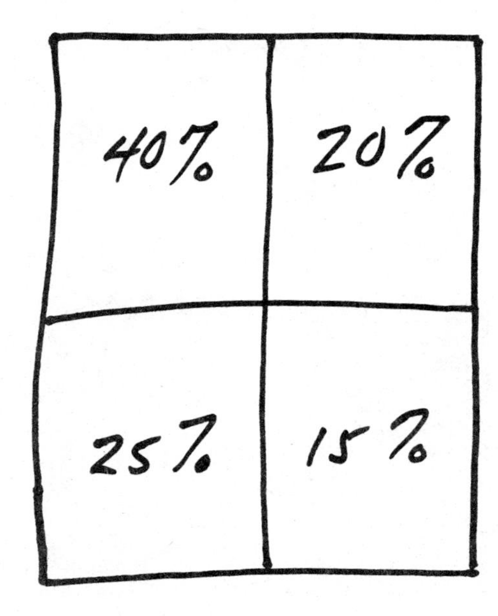

Using motion-picture cameras to follow eye travel, research determined that the average reader's eye spent 40 percent of time on the left side of the top of a page, but only 20 percent on the right side. Again, on the bottom half of the page, the eye spent 25 percent of the time on the left side, and only 15 percent on the right side.

Eye-dwell percentages are shown graphically in the illustration above.

Layout should be greatly influenced by the amount of time the reader's eye dwells in each section of the page. Elements of greater importance should obviously be placed so that the reader is likely to devote more of his time to the area in which they are located. Lesser elements can be positioned so they do not infringe upon the critically important 60-65 percent of the top-left, bottom-left space and thus reduce effectiveness of the entire ad.

A word of caution on this subject, though. It would be a mistake to adhere slavishly to what these research data suggest. Factors which influence layout and element placement are too numerous and vary far too much from one advertisement to another to force an art director to rely entirely on theory at the possible expense of the effectiveness of the layout as he intuitively feels it should be.

With this basic information on the habits of the reader, you're in a better position to place elements logically and objectively rather than resorting to hunch and hope.

Eye Path of the Reader

The reader's eye enters your advertisement in the upper left quarter of its area. His eye stops for the first time approximately

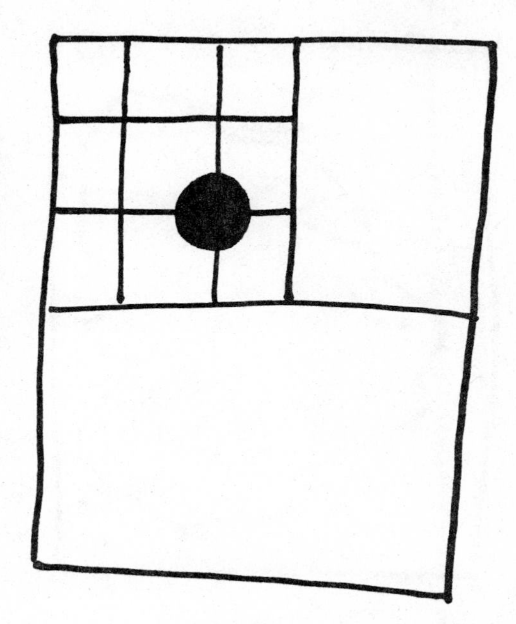

Lines divide the "most looked at" area of this rough chart into thirds. At any one of the four inner intersections is a place for the reader's eye to start making a detailed examination of the ad's contents. In this case, the point where the large dot appears was selected. From this point on the eye scans the ad clockwise.

where the large dot is in the diagram nearby. Note that this is not only in the upper left hand quarter of the page, but it is also at the approximate location of one of the intersections of lines dividing an area into thirds, as discussed in Chapter 10. This is helpful in planning an illustration, of course, as well as in laying out the advertisement.

Depending upon the layout of the ad, the normal movement of the reader's eye is then in a roughly circular pattern, clockwise, until it returns almost to the point where it originally entered the ad.

Most studies indicate that the eye does not describe a nice, neat, round path around the ad, but that it wanders, makes jagged jumps to various elements—or even to white space, which is a total lack of elements—as it pursues its way through the ad. The motion picture camera, set on slow motion, shows these lightning-fast eye movements very clearly, and also emphasizes that the eye path is anything but a smooth and steady one. In general, however, the eye does travel in a clockwise pattern in most instances.

A rough indication of this eye path is illustrated here. The path shown, starting at the point of entry into the ad as indicated by the large dot, is just the *initial* path. After the average reader completes a clockwise visual scanning of the ad, his eye then is approximately where it started. At this time, if the ad interests him, his eye then

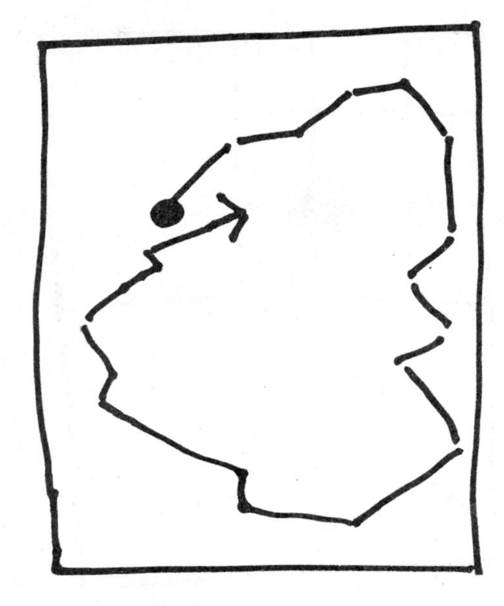

The clockwise scanning of the ad is only the initial path, leaving the reader's eye about where it started. Then, if interested, the eye starts making a detailed examination of the contents of the ad. It darts and roves until it reaches the body copy, then settles into the normal back-and-forth pattern of reading.

starts making a detailed examination of its contents. There's little rhyme or reason to the eye path from then on; at this time the reader's eye wanders. It darts up and down, roves from side to side, then gradually settles into the familiar back-and-forth pattern of reading as it moves into the copy.

Reflecting his lifelong habit, the reader's eye customarily leaves the advertisement after reading is completed at the lower right hand corner, just as if a book were being read. After all, this is where one completes reading a page, an ad, or what have you.

Advertisements should be laid out so they take advantage of the normal eye path. Layout can make the ad both easier to read and more interesting.

Let's see how this works out in actual practice.

George Wickstrom, advertising manager of Sealed Power Corporation, a leading manufacturer of piston rings and engine parts for original equipment use and for the automotive aftermarket, supplied a one-page, two-color ad that Sealed Power Corporation ran in *Commercial Car Journal.* It is aimed at the lucrative fleet market, a market within a market.

Layout takes full advantage of the known eye path of the reader. In this ad, the eye naturally enters a little higher and farther to the left than normally. This is because the first thing that's noticed and

Supreme confidence in the product is required to prepare an ad like this. But the copy is convincing and sells the concept of quality hard. For a sketch of the eye-travel path in reading this ad, see the following page.

read is the picturesque, tattered reward poster—obviously tacked up by somebody who used the butt of a Colt single-action Army revolver for a hammer. The type face carries out the old-fashioned theme.

The poster in itself sells very hard. Sealed Power offers a $50 reward to any mechanic who reports a product failure; in this instance it means a set of Sealed Power DLS-40UW heavy-duty oil rings with plugged vents. This is supreme confidence in the product, considering the millions of sets of rings the company produces, and it speaks highly for quality control in the advertiser's factory, and for the engineering that went into the product.

After reading the poster, or even after merely scanning it, the reader's eye then goes to the headline: *Nobody has ever claimed this reward.* It's just to the right (clockwise) of the poster. The eye then drops to the DLS-40UW heavy-duty oil ring with the subhead inside it; this would count as one element in the layout.

Then the reader's eye drops to the distinctive red Sealed Power box, the logo, and then it goes up to where it started—at the bottom of the reward poster. This is an excellent position for the reader to proceed into the body copy from. When he has read the copy, the eye is then at the bottom of the page; he will then either turn to the next page, or perhaps the logotype and package will make one more impression. If so, so much the better. If not, the ad has already done its job very effectively.

An overlay with the reader's eye path drawn on it illustrates this sequence of events.

Reader's eye starts with the reward notice, then goes to headline. Eye next roves about subhead in oval frame, finally goes back up into layout to read body copy. Final eye stop is at the logo in red.

Chandler Evans Control Systems Division, a part of Colt Industries, ran a striking ad in *Space/Aeronautics* that also illustrates the clockwise eye path and a layout made to exploit it for all it's worth.

The ad's second color is very close to the army's olive drab. The olive color reflects the mood of the illustration and adds impact and authenticity to it.

When an overlay is placed on this ad, we see that the reader's eye wavers between the headline, *When Accuracy Is Essential,* and the back one-third of the guided missile. It then absorbs the headline, moves to the right (clockwise) to the soldier firing the recoilless fieldpiece, then drops down to the spot illustration of Chandler

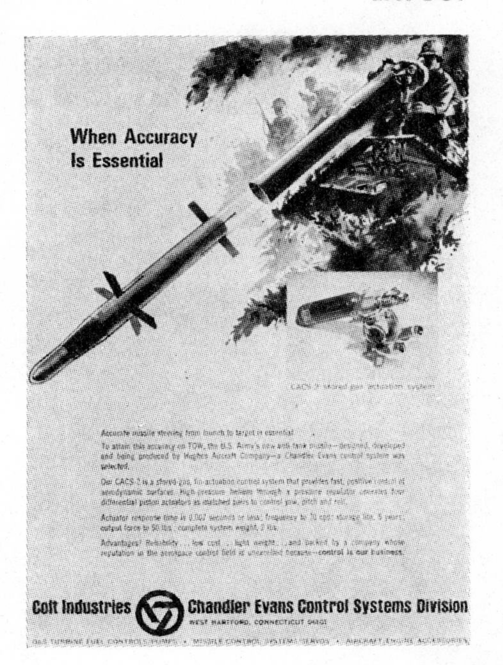

This ad for a division of Colt industries was run in two colors. The second color, an olive drab, added authenticity to a message about Army guided missiles. The eye path of this ad is traced on the following page.

Evans' product that's used to actuate the missile, continues to the bottom of the ad to take in the signature and logo, then moves back up to the missile. Gaze then drops to the copy block, the reader reads it, then his eye leaves the ad at the bottom right hand corner.

One thing that's just about 110 percent fatal is to make the eye path a rocky one that's difficult to follow. This discourages and confuses the reader. He's in doubt about where he's supposed to look next.

The business world is confusing enough without having additional confusion heaped onto one's head by a communications medium that's supposed to be simplicity itself, so the natural tendency when a hard-to-read ad is encountered is not to read it.

Reprinted by permission of Computer Sciences Corporation is that company's dramatic, well-written advertisement from *Space/Aeronautics.* The illustration is interesting because the reader always finds a night photograph eye-arresting. This may be because, as snapshot artists, we still tend to think of a photograph as something that's taken in a brightly lighted studio, or else at high noon on a bright blue day when a picnic is in progress.

Computer Sciences Corporation's headline is provocative and

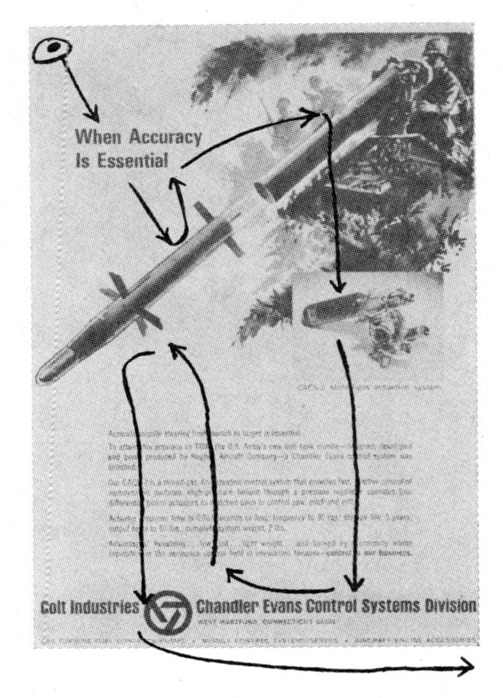

Eye path for the Colt Industries missile ad on the previous page. Eye starts at headline, takes in part of missile illustration, pauses at headline again, moves through illustration of field-piece and missile down to the signature and logo. Then eye takes in missile once again, and finally proceeds to read copy and move out of ad.

advances a concept the reader is very interested in learning more about.

The ad falls short of achieving all it might have, though, due to a deficiency in layout. Too much eye movement is required for the reader to absorb the message. His eye will enter the advertisement in the illustrative area, drop down to the logo, hesitate between proceeding on to the bottom of the ad to the headline—or else go back up to the point of entry.

If he *does* read the headline, the reader's eye is forced to make quite a journey back to the starting point, then drop back down again to the body copy. Too much is asked of the reader in this instance.

It's too bad, because the ad is so well-done otherwise. Computer Sciences Corporation's message is well-written, and the copy is convincing and persuasive. As convincing as it is, there's no reason in the world to think the reader wouldn't instinctively feel that this is a company well worth contacting to see what it can do for him.

Also in *Space/Aeronautics* magazine was the one-page, two-color (blue and black) advertisement run by Wellman Dynamics

Here's a layout that looked good on the drawing board, but failed to set up a good eye path. There are too many places where the eye can enter the illustration, and movements thereafter are erratic, causing many readers to miss the headline or the body copy, both of which are important to message.

Corporation. This ad seems to *try* not to be read. The layout artist seems to have *tried* to make things just as difficult for the reader as he possibly could. The headline, for instance, bleeds off *both* the top and the bottom (sit back for a minute and think that one over!).

Bleeding as it does at the top, there's naturally a bit of confusion as to whether the word is "were" or if it's "we're," and there's certainly a world of difference between the two. Losing half of that apostrophe doesn't do legibility any good at all. It makes interpreting the first word of the headline downright difficult, and when the reader has to work at interpreting a headline, guess what he'll do?

Only the size of the type in which the headline is set tells the reader that he's supposed to read "we're," then proceed to the very bottom of the advertisement to read "looking." Both words are in blue, of course, but so are three of the copy blocks that are scattered through the rest of the ad. This in itself is distracting as all get out.

In the unlikely event that many readers made the jump from top to bottom and back up to the top again, there's still an eye path to travel that's a far cry from a superhighway, or even a game trail wending its way up a boulder-strewn mountain.

Bleeding the headline at top and bottom doesn't do anything except make it hard to read. The ad contains 12 elements, compared to the five in the "classic" layout. And, to read everything, the eye is forced to work hard all the way.

The layout requires the reader's eye to go to what is apparently the main copy block, then zigzag back and forth between spot illustrations and copy blocks and, finally, take in yet another copy block, two symbols that are apparently the company's logotype, and, at long last, the signature.

This advertisement contains a total of 12 elements—*seven more* than the classic layout. And that's giving it the benefit of doubt and calling the square and circle one element under the assumption it's a logotype; if it isn't, there are 13 elements.

Guiding the Reader's Eye

A layout contains lines to guide the reader's eye, even if they're not carefully ruled and printed in ink on the paper. Horizontals, rest; diagonals, movement; verticals, power.

Recall the fine advertisement that Kodak ran for just a moment. The two technicians were looking at a negative, and the direction of their gaze then carried the reader's eye directly to the headline; immediately below the headline was the first block of body copy. The reader's eye was directed straight to it. It wasn't left to wander around alone, unaided. Kodak took no chances; it didn't want him lost, it wanted that advertisement read.

The eye is naturally attracted to the largest mass in a given space. Two drawings nearby show three masses of approximately the same "weight" or darkness, but of different sizes. In each instance the eye immediately is attracted to the largest mass, then to the next largest, and so on. This holds true whether the largest mass is at the top of the ad, on the right, left, or at the bottom. However, in a third arrangement the eye is attracted to the largest mass, of course, but it is *directed* to the next largest mass (here it's supposed to be a spot illustration).

How the eye can be manipulated with layout techniques is shown in these illustrations. The drawings above show how the eye is attracted first to the largest mass, then the next largest, etc. At left, the eye is attracted to the largest mass, but redirected to a smaller mass because that area is stronger and bolder in color.

The headline's first line of type has been screened back so that it's approximately 50 percent, thus it has less weight and carrying power than the lower line which is printed in solid black. This, together with the fact that the subordinate illustration is considerably darker than the main illustration, compels the reader's eye to go there immediately after it skims the illustration and headline.

So, although the reader's eye habitually follows a well-known path, it can be manipulated to focus it on portions of the advertisement that we want to stress. The reader finds it easier and more natural to conform to what is easiest for him due to habit, although he can be made—forced, actually, although there's a nasty connotation about the word—to look where the advertiser wants him to look. This is done through various layout devices.

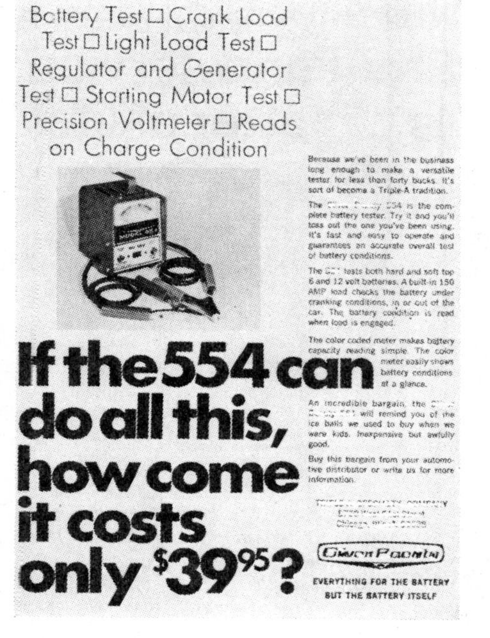

Here the headline at the bottom of the ad has the greatest mass and weight of all the elements in the layout. Thus, it creates confusion, since few readers will know what a "554" is. And readers do not like to work.

A manufacturer of automotive test equipment recently ran a one-page, black-and-white advertisement in *Motor Age*.

This ad is clean as a whistle as far as clutter and an excessive number of elements is concerned. Sum total of elements is only five—subhead, illustration, headline, copy block, and signature-logo.

And there's some white space, nothing seems crowded, and the type face has enough weight to be readily readable.

Only thing, the headline at the bottom of the ad is the element with the greatest mass and most weight. The eye goes to it immediately, even before it lights on the tiny little illustration. For somebody who hasn't the foggiest notion of what a 554 is, this can be disconcerting as all get out. Here the reader is drawn into an ad by a headline talking about a 554 and it could easily be a new jet airliner, a new high-intensity rifle cartridge designed for taking the Big Five in Africa, a stereo tape recorder, or a dehydrated computer that fits into a shirt pocket and does everything one of the massive IBM's does, except twice as fast.

There's no indication whatsoever as to what the ad's about, so it doesn't qualify readers to weed out the good prospects from those who couldn't care less. This is this ad's weakness, and it's a major one indeed.

Eye path is top (point of entry into the advertisement) to bottom in one huge jump, then back to the point of entry again to take in a display-type subhead that's formidably long, then to the illustration, to the copy block, and finally to the signature-logo and slogan. This is all too complicated and complex and unnecessarily involved. And there's no help along the way for the reader who's an eye-weary traveler by now, there's nothing to guide his eye and make reading the ad either easier or more pleasurable.

Eye-Steering Techniques

Among the devices that can be used effectively to guide the reader's eye is one that's as old as advertising itself—the pointing finger. Bourns, Inc. does this to lure the reader into the headline in its black-and-white bleed ad from *Electronics* magazine (page 906).

Usually it's not necessary to use any kind of guidance system, inertial or otherwise, or it shouldn't be, at least. The headline should pop right out, almost jump off of the page it's so readable and attractive and inviting. Bourns must have had a mental reservation about the jumble of type faces in the stacked headline, however, and felt the necessity to do something—maybe just about anything except setting the headline in one face so it could be read easily—to get the reader to read the headline and the advertiser's name.

Then there are ruled lines. They're a layout man's stock in trade when he can't think of anything really creative, and typographers carry them in stock just as they do the letters of the alphabet. Lines can be inserted judiciously to separate various elements and mark

Even though the pointing finger has been overdone in advertising, the device was given a refreshing new twist here. The finger keeps the eye on the headline, which many might try to resist because of the mixture of type faces. The pointing finger here is not the usual "Uncle Sam Wants You" approach.

a trail for the reader's eye to follow, something like hacking a piece out of a tree every hundred yards so you'll be able to find your way back to the game you've downed when you return with the pack horses.

Also, the direction in which people in the illustration are looking causes the reader to look in that same direction. There's the intimation that the model must be looking at something that interests him, so the reader automatically assumes it will be of interest to him, too. Layout should be planned to take advantage of this device, for it works remarkably well. Everybody's usually curious about what somebody else is looking at.

Steaks Eleven Stories Up

Everybody stops to see what's what when somebody starts with the neck-craning bit on the street, you know that. A case in point occurred some years ago when the author was an account executive at a well-known AAAA Chicago advertising agency. The word came down from on high one bright blue day that all salaried personnel in the agency would henceforth have an additional job to do—one over and above the first-line responsibility.

It was very simple: get publicity for the agency.

Do things. Write things. Get the agency talked about. Get its name in the newspapers and in the trade press. Almost anything was acceptable, as long as the agency was mentioned, its name was spelled properly, and the stunt didn't end up getting the agency employee incarcerated or result in *un*favorable publicity for the agency.

A little afterthought by management added that the agency would absorb any reasonable expense in connection with the manufacture of this publicity--if it resulted in ink in reputable publications.

Well, being a doer, the author immediately turned the swivel chair toward the south office window and looked out at the Wrigley Building on North Michigan Avenue.

Lo and behold, right outside the window was that captivating little footwide ledge that had already started all sorts of things stirring thoughtwise—such as inching along it and tapping at the window of a friend's office from the *outside* as he was busy writing copy, thus scaring hell out of him, and similar jolly little happenings.

Now, however, something legitimate could be done with that ledge. The author believes in doing things legitimately if possible.

So a friend was promptly buttonholed and plans were made for the next day, weather permitting.

That evening a sojourn to a suburban supermarket resulted in the accumulation of a pair of prime steaks, rabbit food, and all of the other goodies that a really lavish lunch calls for.

The station wagon was loaded with the food, salad dressing, plates, tablecloth, utensils, and a portable charcoal grill. All of this was lovingly carried up the elevator to the 11th floor and into the author's corner office long before anybody else arrived in the morning, except for the friend who was to participate in the production of agency publicity.

At high noon when everybody else rushed for their favorite restaurants and Michigan Avenue was crowded with girl-watchers enjoying the sights and the beautiful spring weather, the author and his friend crawled out the window and proceeded to charcoal-broil steaks on the foot-wide ledge on the wall of the 11th floor of the building. There was a thigh-high pipe railing as a safety factor of sorts.

Soon a smudge of steak-smelling smoke arose, much to the delight of secretaries on floors above; they peered out of their windows, waved, shrieked approval, and invited themselves to the skyscraper cookout.

Proof that people delight in the unexpected is in this photo of Author Stansfield and friend eating lunch on a skyscraper ledge. Daily newspapers covered the stunt without encouragement, and publicity also was obtained in the advertising trade press.

Passersby on the sidewalk far below stopped, traffic stopped, a voice was heard to say, "It's a bird. No, it's a plane. No, it's Superman!"

Another voice replied, "Superman, my foot. It's two kooks cooking on a little ledge up there. Looks like a couple of steaks!"

A police officer out in the middle of Michigan Avenue was blowing his whistle frantically, urging motorists to proceed, to unjam the traffic jam, while the author and friend casually put jam on biscuits and ate excellent steak.

All in all, this episode proved that people will always look where other people look, that the offbeat is hugged to the heart to cherish and enjoy, and that people delight in the unexpected.

Publicity? Certainly.

A photographer took the picture that's shown nearby through the author's office window. The author is that jovial individual on the right, friend Wim van der Graaf is on the left. The photograph ran four columns wide and a foot deep in one of the major Chicago newspapers, and it received widespread pickup in the advertising trade press. In every case the agency was mentioned, making management as happy as little larks until the expense account was submitted to cover steaks, culinary delights, mileage, and other odds and ends. The reaction then was, "$7.60 for two *raw* steaks?"

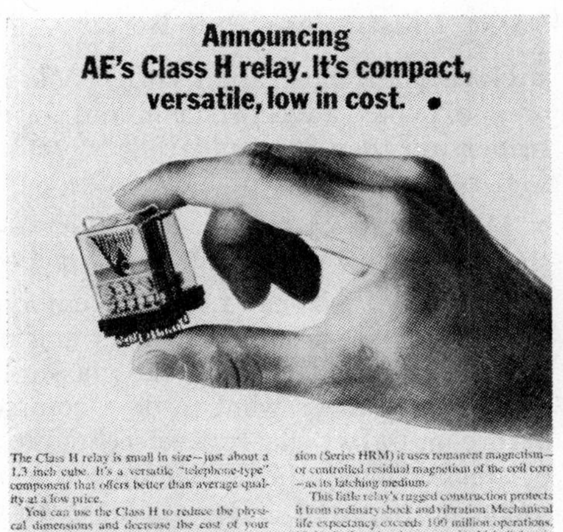

Announcing
AE's Class H relay. It's compact, versatile, low in cost.
The Class H relay is small in size—just about a 1.3 inch cube. It's a versatile "telephone-type" component that offers better than average quality at a low price.
You can use the Class H to reduce the physical dimensions and decrease the cost of your products. It's well suited for business machines, vending machines, communication equipment, computer peripheral equipment, aircraft and missile simulators. These applications take advantage of its small size, versatility of mounting, and large switching capacity (maximum of 6 form C or 4 C and 2 D contacts).
The Class H can be direct-mounted or socket-mounted to a PC card. Or it can be socketed into a panel. It also has a socket that mounts on a rack.
The Class H is made as a regular quick-acting relay (Series HQA). It's also available as a short or long pulse "latching relay." In this version (Series HRM) it uses remanent magnetism—or controlled residual magnetism of the coil core—as its latching medium.
This little relay's rugged construction protects it from ordinary shock and vibration. Mechanical life expectancy exceeds 100 million operations. Molded pileup insulators provide high dielectric strength and dimensional stability. Contact actuation is by a lift-off card method—which eliminates the problem of contact sticking.
A clear heavy-duty plastic cover provides protection from contamination and abuse. Once this cover is snapped into place, it's not readily removed. This discourages tampering.
Want helpful, detailed specification and application data? Send for Circular No. 1100. Just write to the Director, Relay Control Equipment Sales, Automatic Electric, Northlake, Illinois 60164.
AUTOMATIC ELECTRIC
GENERAL TELEPHONE & ELECTRONICS

A layout that makes it almost impossible to miss the product, since it is held between fingers that lie in the most-looked-at area of the ad. From the product, the reader's eye goes quite naturally into the copy.

One surefire way that can't help but lure the reader's eye to whatever you want him to see is to have somebody hold it—or, if it's small, to have a disembodied hand hold it.

Automatic Electric, a subsidiary of General Telephone & Electronics, does a very fine job in its one-page, black-and-white advertisement in *Electronics.*

The new Class H relay that's shown is held at the exact point where the reader's eye normally enters the ad—and this undoubtedly is not by accident. There's simply no missing the product. And the eye then proceeds to the headline, moving in a clockwise and upward direction as it initially does, then drops down to the body copy. This ad is laid out to take full advantage of normal eye movement, and it's guided so that the advertisement can receive the most possible readership.

By arrangement of elements, lines, arrows, pointing fingers, weight of elements, eye direction, etc., you can pull the reader's eye to the exact spot in the ad that you want if you'll give a little thought and planning to the layout.

Large Illustrations Pull Better

Have your illustration large enough to occupy two-thirds of the area of your advertisement and it will receive 18 percent more readership than it would if it were smaller. This was proven in a McGraw-Hill study of 5,398 ads.

This means, of course, that in a standard 7x10 ad the illustration should be 6⅔ inches deep and 7 inches wide.

Naturally, you can't always embrace the classic Ayer Number One layout like a long-lost lover and never deviate one iota from it. Situations arise in which the classic layout won't do the job. You may, for instance, want to do a complete-line advertisement. Or the before-and-after illustrative technique may be called for. A number of smaller illustrations that show various features of a new product might be required. Then again, there might be so much to say that copy length alone precludes having space enough to devote to an illustration that occupies two-thirds of the page.

Some advertising men—and a number of interested critics of contemporary advertising—have dubbed the 1960's as "the decade that type came into its own."

This is because there's a current fad to set things, particularly headlines, in 72-point type that's readily readable from one end of a football field to the other—almost, anyhow. It has spread faster than a plague of smallpox before Dr. Edward Jenner developed vaccine in 1798.

What we now need is an anti-large-type vaccine. All art directors and layout artists should be vaccinated.

Type this large obviously occupies space, much space, and this means there's just that much less space available for other elements of the advertisement. Without fail it's the illustration that takes the drubbing. Little does it matter that the illustration is charged with stopping the reader, interesting him, and delivering him safe and sound into the headline and body copy.

Type lovers nonchalantly ignore this truism and casually disregard all research that proves it. They dismiss the illustration with a flick of the wrist to make it apparent to one and all that illustration is far beneath them.

It's discrimination, that's what it is. The Supreme Court should legislate against it.

When they do this to an industrial advertiser, 99 times out of 100 they're short-changing him at least 18 percent in readership, and possibly even more in some instances.

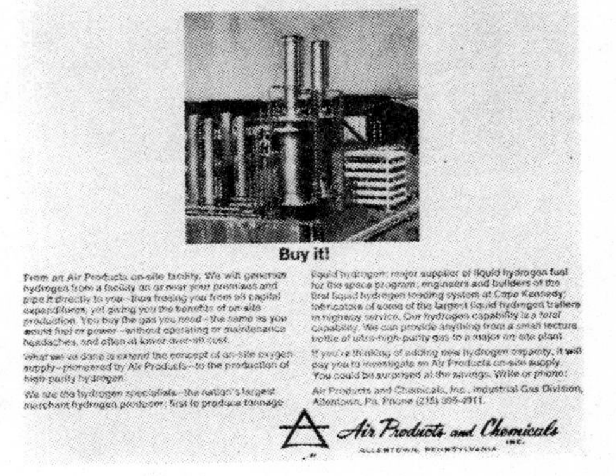

In order to use big type to make this headline arresting (which it is), the layout man had to squeeze a good illustration smaller than it should have been. Following fads like the "big type" craze leads to ads which are imbalanced.

Provocative and interesting though it is, the headline in Air Products and Chemicals' black-and-white, one-page ad from *Electronics* magazine doesn't really carry the mail compared to what an outstanding illustration of adequate size would have done. The ad is shown nearby.

Granted, this advertisement has eye appeal. There's white space. It isn't cluttered with extraneous elements and the type face has sufficient weight—it's easy to read and doesn't look gray.

This is not a weak ad; in fact, it probably did a pretty good job for Air Products and Chemicals. But it could have done a *better* job if the layout artist hadn't decided that he wanted to show everybody how creative he is by reducing what would have been a good photographic illustration down to 2⅞ by 3 inches. This isn't right.

On the other hand, it's very apparent there is heightened interest and extra pulling power in the large, interesting illustration in Parker-Hannifin's splendid one-page four-color ad on page 912.

This unusually strong advertisement's oversize dose of impact is due partially to the excellent closeup color photograph, and also the

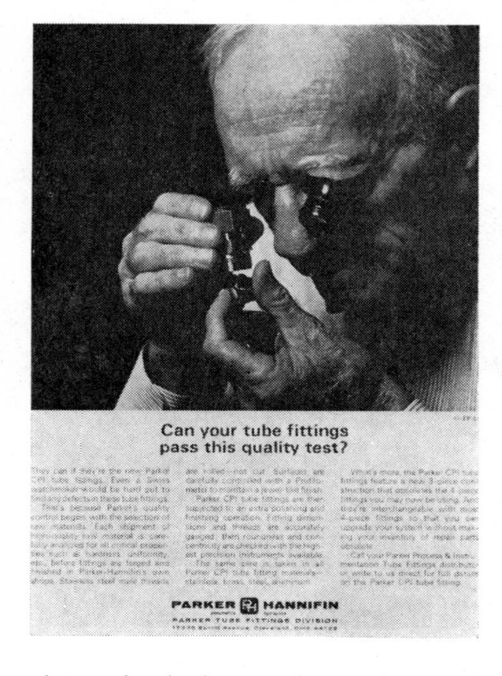
Can your tube fittings
pass this quality test?
PARKER HANNIFIN
PARKER TUBE FITTINGS DIVISION

Here the layout artist was well aware that the big illustration pulls the reader into an ad. A banked headline is large enough to start—not startle—the reader into the body copy. Type is clean and bold but not overpowering.

clean, simple layout that assigns priorities in proper order. The illustration was allotted enough room so that it is big and attractive and can't be missed by a reader who's turning pages quickly.

Note that simplicity is one of the advertisement's virtues; only six elements are in the layout—illustration, headline, three copy blocks, and the logo-signature. This ad was laid out with one thought in mind: getting high readership. The layout artist was well aware that the big illustration pulls the reader into the ad faster than anything else, and he took full advantage of it.

Type and Logotype

Type is far more than a necessary evil, something that has to be in your ad to convey your message. Weight, form, style—all contribute to the impression your advertisement makes.

Choice of typeface and the way it's handled exerts tremendous influence on the layout of the ad, determines whether or not the ad is readable, whether or not it's interesting looking—and whether or not it will be read.

A powerful illustration will overshadow a weak typeface, one that doesn't "carry" well, so the copy appears weak and gray and lost and lacks appeal. When copy has no visual character, no strength, it's pale and pallid so that readers avoid it in vast numbers without realizing why.

On the other hand, it's terribly easy to select a typeface so wrong for the advertisement that it weakens it and detracts from it. A type face that overshadows the illustration, for example, does this because it has too much weight. The dividing line is fine indeed, and both good taste and good judgment are required to refrain from overstepping it in either direction.

A thorough study of type faces (there are almost 6,000 different ones in existence, although only a comparative few are in general use) is interesting and well worth one's time.

Right now, however, it's desirable to mention a few ways in which type can be laid out so that your advertisement will receive maximum readership—and also to discuss briefly some pitfalls to avoid. The author is indebted to International Paper Company for making available much helpful information on this subject, and on paper and printing. Especially useful is the company's "Pocket Pal," a graphic-arts digest for printers and advertising production managers. It is available upon letterhead request from:

International Paper Company
220 East 42nd Street
New York, New York 10017

Usually the advertising manager relies on the experience and judgment of his art director at the agency, upon his art studio—or upon a printing salesman or representative of a typographer. This is good practice. These individuals live with type day in and day out, and they're expert in choosing the right type face for the job at hand. As a rule, there isn't enough time for an advertising manager to become a typeface expert unless he pursues it as a hobby in his leisure time. Some do.

You should, though, be aware that type not only puts words on paper in front of the reader, but it also implies certain qualities and characteristics are possessed by the product with which it's associated. For example, Black Letter or Text is commonly associated with the church, old manuscripts, and wedding invitations; it's frequently called Old English.

Jim Crow, Gold Rush, and P. T. Barnum are faces that are strongly suggestive of the immediate post-Civil War era; they're strong on flavor, but very dated and of little use except in instances when you want to telegraph the impression you're discussing something from that period, or if you're setting the stage for something. This is mood type.

Many advertising men feel the sans serif typefaces, such as Futura and Grotesque, that are used in so much industrial advertising today, somehow connote something mechanical and complex and metallic. These are said to be "nutsy and boltsy" faces.

At the opposite end of the scale are the serif faces. These typefaces suggest elegance and dignity, solidity and integrity. They are at the top of the list when it comes to legibility. Baskerville and Garamond are two excellent faces with much character. They are among the most beautiful.

Actually, however, there are seven main groups of typefaces. They are as follows:

Oldstyle Roman. This group of faces was derived from early Dutch, Venetian, and English typographic designs. It looks better in mass, on the page, than it does when you examine it letter by letter. Legibility is excellent because the letters are open, wide, and round, and have pointed serifs that provide a pleasing contrast between heavy and light strokes. Caslon and Garamond are examples of this face. This book is printed in Oldstyle.

Transitional. This family of typefaces was designed to be a lighter, more refined type than Oldstyle Roman. There is a greater contrast between the hairlines and the main strokes, and the face has long, rounded, curved serifs. Most pleasing characteristics of Oldstyle Roman have been retained. Century and Baskerville are examples.

Modern Roman. The term "modern" doesn't actually refer to a period in time, but to a style of type that was designed almost 200 years ago. Characteristics of the group are greater contrast between thick and thin strokes, square serifs, and rounder, more mechanically perfect curved letters. Bodoni and Scotch Roman are examples.

Sans Serif. This comparatively new face has gained widespread acceptance only in the last 50 years—and in industrial advertising it has swept the country in the past 10 or 15 years. Letters have no serifs and with few exceptions are optically evenly weighted. Because of lack of contrast between the letters, sans serif faces are less legible than either oldstyle or modern. In addition, they are colorless and tiresome and repel the eye after seeing them in ad after ad after ad, on a monkey-see, monkey-do parade of me-tooism. You'll note that editorial matter in well-done trade publications is *not* set in sans serif type—publishers want magazines to be read. News Gothic, Futura, and Grotesque are examples of sans serif type faces. They have their place in some headlines and subheads. The chapter titles of this book are set in Futura Medium.

Square Serif. This contemporary type style became popular in the 1930's. Letters have square, or blocked, serifs and generally are evenly weighted. Many of the square serif types are quite geometric in design. Some, however, have roman characteristics of a transitional type face. Clarendon and Stymie are examples.

Script. This typeface simulates handwriting or hand lettering. It is of limited use and should not be used for body copy. Often you'll find it in invitations, announcements, or other places when a special effect is wanted. Typo Script and Commercial Script are examples.

Black Letter. Sometimes called Text, this group of faces is fashioned after the hand-drawn letters of early scribes whose job it was to copy manuscripts before the advent of printing. There's usually a religious flavor about it. It's used for certificates, diplomas, and wedding invitations. Otherwise, it isn't used very much, primarily because it is old-fashioned and almost impossible to read. Old English and Engravers Text are examples.

With the help of your art director, select a typeface that's right for your campaign, your product, and your company. Then stick with it. Don't deviate from it; don't hop, skip, and jump from a serif face to a sans serif face and back again. This way lies loss of campaign identity and reader confusion. It's as bad as having a radically different layout for every individual advertisement.

A few tips on type handling that will boost readership of your ads follow:

In an industrial advertisement type should not be set in a measure of more than 40 characters—more than 40 characters in width, that is. People read by letting the eyes take "bites" of type; some people absorb entire phrases and clauses at one bite, others who read more slowly look at each individual word. When you have a line of 40 characters in width the average person takes this in with three or four bites, or eye movements. Don't consider this a commandment that can never be violated, but it's a good rule of thumb to go by if you want to have your copy read.

How much you'll get into a line of 40 characters naturally depends upon the size of the type. Type size is measured in "points"—each point being approximately 1/72 of an inch. This means, of course, there are 72 points to the inch. All printers, typographers, and artists think of type in point sizes, whether in foundry or machine composition type. Typefaces are available ranging from 4 to 144 points, but you'll encounter sizes from 6 to 72 points most often. There is little need for tiny type or the monstrously large.

Other things being even relatively equal, the most readership accrues to him who uses nothing smaller than 10-point type—and 12-point is even better. The average reader isn't like the average industrial advertising manager; he doesn't have a magnifying glass in the center drawer of his desk. And even if he did, he wouldn't get it out to read an advertisement with type set so small he needs it.

Line spacing also affects readership. The amount of space between lines of type is called "leading." It's pronounced "ledding," like "bedding." Although there is no hard-and-fast rule to follow, a few things should be borne in mind.

Leading is measured like type—in points. If you have one-point leading, for example, you've allowed an extra 1/72nd of an inch between the lines. Two points leading provides 2/72nds of an inch extra space. Use two-point leading in all advertising body copy and you'll reap a reward of 10 percent *extra* readership. Use of proper leading is one of the easiest ways there is to lure more readers into your body copy because it makes the type so attractive and inviting. It looks easy to read and pleasant to read.

Too much leading can make copy very hard to read, however, so don't overdo it. A point or two is sufficient.

This page has body copy set 10 on 11, as it's expressed. That means that the type is 10-point in size, with an extra point of leading.

The wider the measure of text composition, the more leading is needed between the lines to make it easy to read. If, for some good reason, you're going to have body copy set wider than 40 characters, be sure to have additional leading. Otherwise you'll end up with copy set solid so that it repels the eye.

The first paragraph should be short, as discussed in the chapter on body copy. This pulls the reader's eye into the copy.

And speaking of paragraphs, have them indented. Indented paragraphs attract more readers than do flush paragraphs by some 10 percent. There's no earthly reason to make your advertisement's job more difficult by not indenting, is there?

However, if you can't convince a bull-headed art director that paragraphs should be indented without having a major skirmish that would result in what he'd consider an affront, make sure there's additional leading between paragraphs to separate them. Otherwise the reader will be confused and not follow the transition in thinking as different subjects are discussed in different paragraphs.

Having *no* paragraphs is a sin so horrible it won't even be discussed. *Don't do it. Don't ever do it.* Not if you want your advertisement to be read by anybody except the typographer, the art director, the account executive, the agency proofreader, the agency production manager, your secretary, and yourself. That would make it rather an expensive ad.

The one-page black-and-white ad illustrated below was run by Protective Lining Corporation in *Food Engineering.* The illustration is quite good, the product is shown to excellent advantage, and the illustration is the dominant element because it was allotted sufficient

A good ad with but one serious flaw—the body copy is set in far too wide a measure and is not broken by paragraphs. Typographers say a line should contain at most an "alphabet and a half"—which is 39 characters. The lines in this copy contain an average of 115.

space to produce a real impact on the reader. Furthermore, the company's selling proposition is sound and the copy is well-written, colloquial, direct, and to the point.

This is a good ad—*except.*

It has a major weakness, however, and it's a fatal one. Type is set 6⅛ inches wide—about 115 characters in width. (You count the periods, apostrophes, and spaces as characters, incidentally.) This is far too wide. Type in such measure is uninviting. It repels the eye. The reader automatically says to himself that there's too much copy there, it must be boring because it's set solid like school books of two or three decades ago, and the lines have a tendency to "swim" or waver because they are too wide. This causes the eye to shift momentarily—actually for a fraction of a second—to a line above or below that which is being read. This causes loss of comprehension of the message, confusion to the reader, and a why-bother-with-it attitude.

What's more, there are no paragraphs and there's precious little leading, if any. Protective Lining Corporation has 16 lines of copy there, and the eye is presented with a solid mass of words with no relief whatsoever. It's too much to take in stride—or even out of stride, for that matter.

Learn to Love Widows

As has been discussed, short paragraphs open up copy, make it airy and appealing—and make it read. Widows, left-over words at the end of a paragraph that appear as just one or two words on a line, also open up the copy. Some years back it used to be considered the height of bad taste to have widows, and copywriters labored long and hard "filling out" lines so they would be flush and even on both right and left. However, because widows let in air, they actually result in additional readership.

This is quite true, despite the fact that the late *Life* magazine made heroic efforts to kill every widow, and pretty largely succeeded, especially in captions and short copy blocks of less than 500 words. Love and cherish widows—those in type, that is—and you'll have ads that invite the eye, invite readership rather than merely making it available.

Despite the reader's having been accustomed to thinking of type as being justified on both sides, flush right and left, that is, quite frequently type is set "ragged right." That is, it is unjustified on the right. This adds interest to an advertisement and imparts individuality to the layout. Actually, it acts as a design element in many instances and can lead the reader's eye to the place the advertiser wants it.

The clean looking one-page black-and-white ad illustrated nearby was run by Dennison Manufacturing Company in *Business Week* and in *The Wall Street Journal.* It's an excellent example of type-handling that contributes to the layout and the overall design and appearance of the ad.

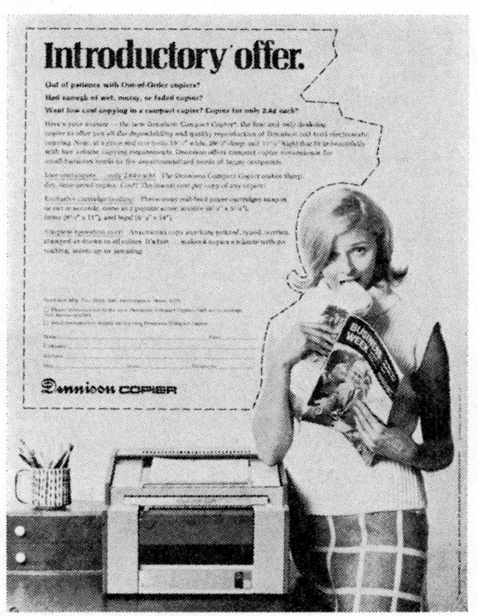

An example of body copy which is set "ragged right"—that is, lines are not justified on the right side. In this case the impact and feeling of action is added to by the dotted line which follows the type outline and leads the eye directly to the coupon which the advertiser hopes to have filled in and mailed.

Headline is properly set in upper- and lower-case, it arouses reader curiosity, the subheads are short, readable, and give a one-two-three punch to reinforce it. Body copy is highly readable, and is in a serifed typeface—which is certainly all to the good.

Serif typefaces are *much* easier to read than sans serif faces and should be used if you want to get the maximum amount of readership your advertisement can deliver. Sans serif faces are dull and monotonous and mechanical, devoid of grace and charm and eye appeal. Dennison chose very wisely for its fine ad.

Note that the ad makes an unusually strong bid for inquiries, since it is actually almost a giant coupon itself, what with the outline around the body copy and the ragged diagonal line leading the eye directly to the coupon. This ad invites response, and it delivered the goods.

by Theodore Levitt, Professor of Business Administration, Harvard Business School

"You can be sure if it's Westinghouski."

Did you know that the practice of using brand names and trademarks on products is under attack in this country?

That certain governmental actions and judicial rulings are moving implacably toward the possible destruction of brand-name marketing?

The great debate that is going on points up the issue of what trademarks and brand names really mean. But, there is, I believe, more instructive value in a look at Soviet experience with branded products than in all the tangled rhetoric expounded by lawyers, economists, professors, businessmen, and politicians in recent years.

A few years ago several Russian factories manufactured identical 17-inch TV sets. On more than one occasion, even though consumers were clamoring for more sets, many simply were not being bought. Inventories piled up. After a good deal of fruitless and wasteful searching for an explanation, the answer came. Because the public could not identify the factory source of any one 17-inch set, and one factory habitually produced "lemons," soon sales of all 17-inch TV sets fell. This refusal to buy was the public's only way to protect itself. But it threw the Soviet central economic plan badly out of kilter. Even worse, it caused a lot of public discontent with Soviet officials.

Factory Marks. It was at this point that Soviet trademarks began to appear. At first, their function was little more than to identify (for the convenience of the authorities) the factory source, but the result was far more than the Russians bargained for. Here is what trademarking did:

(1) It enabled the consumer to choose the output of a plant with a good reputation, and to avoid the plant with a poor one.

(2) Though the sales of the factory with the poor reputation fell, and therefore it failed to meet its economic plan, this caused less economic dislocation than when the entire industry's sales had slumped previously.

(3) It resulted in consumer discontent being shifted from the political (Party) authorities to the trademarked plant with the poor quality.

(4) It created a form of consumer sovereignty—a way of giving the consumer the power to reward quality and punish shoddiness—by enabling him to identify easily the source (trademark) of the output.

In sum, trademarking rewarded quality and efficiency, and punished shoddiness and waste, by making it easy for the quality producer to sell his product because the consumer had developed confidence in his trademark. From experience, the consumer had, in effect, learned that "You can be sure if it's Westinghouski."

Further Developments. The Russians have, since this incident, expanded the practice of trademarking, or branding, the output of different plants. Soviet plant managers now guard the integrity and reputation of their trademarks with the vigor of Cossacks bearing down on revolutionaries. They safeguard the purity of their brands as sedulously as they watch their operating expenses. Their houses depend heavily on what happens to both of these.

The fact that the Russians have adopted brand names and, now, advertising simply reflects the fact that they are more responsive to the dictates of economics, technology, and good sense than to the muddled abstractions of obsolete philosophers. Moreover, the Russians have learned that with brand names, instead of economic planners having to establish arbitrary quality standards and hire engineers to enforce them, the sovereign consumer automatically establishes and enforces the high standards.

The net result has been not only an almost automatic and continuing improvement in Soviet consumer-product quality and design, but also an accelerating tendency to use brand-name advertising as a means of reassuring consumers about the quality and desirability of particular brands and therefore raising their sales and profitabilities.

The Soviet experience clearly demonstrates how the consumer can use the brand as a means of protecting himself and of punishing the producer of trademarked products that do not meet consumer expectations.

From an article by Professor Levitt, "Branding on Trial," in the Harvard Business Review, March-April 1966.

Magazine Publishers Association
An association of 365 leading U.S. magazines

Another sure way to boost readership with type is to use a large lead-in letter at the start of the first copy block. This proven device can make a difference of several percentage points in the amount of readership your ad receives. The large lead-in letter lures extra readers into the ad's body copy—where you do the real selling.

Magazine Publishers Association's one-page black-and-white ad from *Fortune* has an exceptionally strong story to tell, one that's of genuine concern to all of us in advertising—to all in business, for that matter. It concerns the governmental actions and judicial rulings that are moving implacably toward the possible destruction of brand-name marketing. The warning is timely and necessary, for unless the entire business community becomes aroused about the bureaucratic attacks on business by the advocates of Big Government, brand names are in peril. For that matter, so is private enterprise itself.

This all-type advertisement uses the two-line initial to pull the reader's eye from the headline into the body copy. This is an extremely effective device, and is one that's encountered less frequently today than in the past. If the average advertising manager knew how much more readership his ads would get simply from using the two-line lead-in letter, he'd use it regularly.

So that you can see how the large lead-in letter looks in an ad with an illustration, the outstanding one-page four-color ad run in *Fortune* by Friden, Inc., Division of Singer, is shown with an arrow pointing to the initial.

Here the headline is big and bold and unmistakable and unmissable. The eye enters in that one-third of the page and it stays there long enough to read the headline. After that is when the large

Arrow marked on ad at right shows how initial letter helps the eye into the body copy after taking in the large-type headline. To go into the relatively small body type without this aid might discourage some readers. Use of the initial is a sophisticated device which should not be overdone.

lead-in letter "I" goes to work to pull the reader into the body copy. It's an invitation to read.

Notice that type is set ragged-right in the left hand copy block, and set ragged-left in the right hand block. This is done with a reason, not merely to be different, for it follows the outline of Alice and adds interest to the layout.

And the illustration of the radiant mother-to-be is tastefully and beautifully done. Props are just exactly right. There's the orchid the girls in the office gave her when they took her to lunch on her last day, and the daintily wrapped going-away gift. Although a smile isn't usually considered a prop, in this case it works like one; this young woman's smile is full of joy and expectancy. A finer note couldn't have been struck than Friden did here. This is an exceptionally fine ad.

Type set in reverse, which is white type on a black background (or white on any dark color) always receives less readership by far than would the same type set in black on white stock. All of our lives, ever since we were old enough to read, we've been conditioned to think of type as being darker than the stock on which it appears.

Princeton Applied Research Corporation recently ran a striking

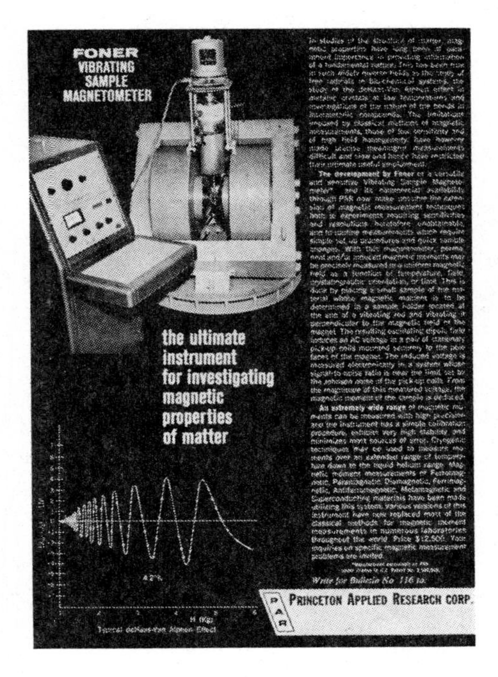

This ad, all in reverse type, is distinctive and easily noted. It is, however, extremely difficult to read because of the body copy reversed out of the black background. Eye studies have shown that vision begins to "swim" after only a few lines of such difficult reading.

advertisement, one page black-and-white in *Analytical Chemistry.* The photographic illustration of Princeton Applied Research's equipment is excellent; fine detail clearly shows. There's a graph to explain quickly how the vibrating sample magnetometer performs and the type of results the user may expect from it.

Headline is in two parts, rather widely separated for maximum ease of reading, for much eye travel is called for. Where the ad falls down, though, is that the body copy is set in reverse. It's almost impossible to read. When the average reader tries to read body copy in reverse, he does so with relative ease for the first line or two; after that there's an inescapable tendency for the type to "swim"—actually to seem to move due to the eyestrain involved.

Display type reversed out of a dark background is readily legible because of its size, of course, and it will be read. Too, it's short and there isn't much reading involved.

Unquestionably Princeton Applied Research Corporation receives an unusually high Noted rating on its ads; they're distinctive and not easily overlooked.

The advertiser's signature is *not* reversed, you'll notice, but is in a white panel in the lower right hand corner of the advertisement. This stands out against all of the black, so it's noticed also. There's no lack of advertiser identification.

Reverse and Readability

But being noticed and achieving a high Noted rating isn't an end in itself. The prospect must read the body copy of the ad if it's to perform to its full potential. Should he fail to do that, a lot of money is going down the drain.

Body copy in reverse against black (or almost any other color, for that matter) quickly scuttles most advertisements very quickly. They are not read.

True-Trace Corporation recently ran a full-bleed, spread, two-color (green and black) advertisement in *Metalworking* magazine. It is shown on page 924. Incidentally, True-Trace is the world leader in machine tool tracing control systems and attachments.

Quite an investment was made in this ad from the production standpoint alone. Art is excellent, as is the photography, and the retouching is very well done. The copy blocks relating to each of the spot illustrations are properly located to explain what they show and how they relate to the equipment that True-Trace produces.

Copy is well written and very convincing. It's particularly believable because True-Trace uses the proved technique of name-dropping, that is, telling who the customer is and what results the customer company had with the equipment it bought from True-Trace. Selling proposition is sound, the equipment intrigues, and the company has an outstanding reputation.

Seemingly the ad has everything in its favor. And it does, except for one thing.

It cannot be read.

The eye-jarring mottled effect caused by reversing the type out of a background tone that is not solid, but varies according to the tone values of the art, makes reading the main copy block on the left page virtually impossible.

Difficult as reading the main copy block is, reading the smaller type on the right hand page is infinitely harder. Actually, it's a task that can be accomplished only by reading a word or two at a time—in some cases a letter at a time to determine what the individual word is. When each letter has to be searched out and formed into a word, then the words have to be formed into thoughts.

The reader of business publications does not have this much time to spend on one advertisement. And there's absolutely no reason to think he'd be interested in doing so even if he had time to while away.

This ad no doubt looked great in layout form. Chances are it was presented as a ruled comprehensive with the background artwork roughly indicated in green and black, and with type ruled in quite strongly. There was no way the advertiser could have known beforehand how illegible the ad would be in final form.

Too bad, because production and space cost exactly the same whether the ad is read or not.

An arresting one-page, bleed, two-color (blue and black) ad run by TRW Electro Insulation, a division of TRW, Inc., is shown nearby.

The art is impressive and does an excellent job of stopping the reader. Lightning bolts are so real looking there's almost an odor of ozone emanating from the advertisement, and a brawny Zeus appears quite capable of hurling them with fantastic force and accuracy.

Without doubt the illustration stopped the reader and the lightning leads the eye into the headline. It's readily legible, but the body copy suffers from being in reverse and in a relatively weak sans serif type face at that. What's even worse, though, is that it's printed over a solid blue background. It's only with considerable difficulty that the copy can be read.

This ad suffered in readability principally because the body copy, in black, was overprinted on a solid dark blue. This is a tremendous handicap for the clearest and most readable type to have to overcome.

When copy is overprinted over solid red, either process or AAAA red, the eye rebels. It refuses to be subjected to the blinding strain of trying to decipher the advertiser's message. Bellows-Valvair, Division of IBEC, has a campaign now running consisting of consecutive right-hand pages in *Factory* magazine. All are overprinted on a solid—either blue, which is bad enough, or process red or 4-A red; the latter two simply defy all efforts to read them. And Bellows-Valvair doesn't build advertiser identity by using every color in the rainbow like this; all it does is make certain its ads won't be read. Noted scores may be satisfactory, but it's beyond the realm of belief that more than a tiny fraction of 1 percent of *Factory's* readers would suffer the eyestrain and the frustration of wading through ads when the advertiser deliberately makes reading a painful task.

Caps and Lowercase

Headlines should be set in lowercase type, with the possible exception of the first letter. Many seasoned art directors who have made a lifelong study of the subject refuse to use *any* capital letters in the headline unless they're used on a proper name or the firm name.

No doubt exists on the question—lowercase letters are much more easily read. Even in a Roman face, the most easily read, having both uppercase and lowercase letters in the headline slows the reader down, prevents the message from telegraphing itself and delays absorption of the meaning. And when a face like News Gothic is used in both uppercase and lowercase, reading is difficult indeed. Worst possible choice for a headline is News Gothic Condensed; the message becomes lost with unbelievable speed. Refrain from making it hard for the reader to read.

This line is set in News Gothic Condensed.

Here's a hypothetical for-instance. No, it's not actually hypothetical, for this very headline really appeared in a 1968 issue of *Production.* Only the advertiser's name and product is not given.

To Maintain Our Record
of "Immediate Shipment"

We Have Built This Plant

Then, the body copy of this advertisement is very short and general and advertiser-oriented. Naturally, it ran under a picture of Our

Factory, highly retouched and looking about as real as an unretouched photograph of the man in the moon.

**Whatever Your Requirements,
We Are Equipped in this Largest
Exclusive Widget Plant to Provide
Stock Shipments of Your Widget,
Feed Finger, Pad, and Yo Yo Needs.**

Always Smith Quality

The Best

You can see how hard copy is to read when excess capital letters are thrown around with gay abandon, for reasons known only to the advertising manager. Perhaps for the same reason some people aim the little finger like a battlewagon's 16-inchers when they're

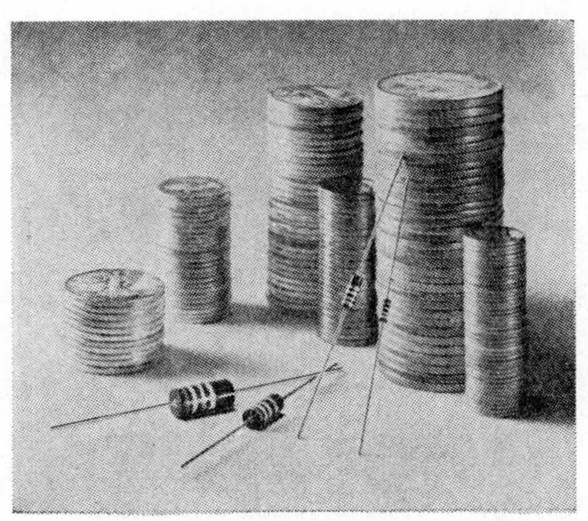

Too many capitals in the headline is all that Author Stansfield can find to fault in this ad. But readership studies have shown that it would require more time and effort to read it than had it all been set in lowercase except for the first letter.

Quality Need Not Be Expensive

Some people would have you believe that to buy the best, you must pay the most. This is not necessarily true. Price is only a measure of value—never a substitute for it.

At Stackpole, the real value of any resistor is determined by a combination of its performance record and its price. Perhaps this is why so many of our customers continue to specify Stackpole resistors year after year to maintain top performance for established products and for their new ones, too. Such confidence and loyalty cannot be based on price alone.

Uniformity has become the accepted characteristic of Stackpole resistors. Unique production methods, coupled with in-depth experience in manufacturing and testing are your assurance that Stackpole resistors will give you absolute performance. The resistors you order today will be identical in every way to your last order.

Most leading manufacturers of electronic equipment have long recognized Stackpole resistors for reliability. Whether it be the rugged demands of portable television or the critical tolerances of space age communication and tracking equipment, Stackpole resistors deliver the performance you expect—the kind of dependability that builds a reputation for your products.

Why continue to pay a premium for quality? Let us prove that you get value from Stackpole. Quality resistors, economically priced, are delivered promptly and backed up by our complete corporate facility. Next time, specify Stackpole. There's a family of fine resistors available in sizes of 2, 1, ½ and ¼ watts. For samples and additional information, write: Stackpole Carbon Company, Electronic Components Division, Kane, Pa. Phone: 814-837-7000 — TWX: 510-695-8404.

holding a cup at a tea in high society. They want to prove they're genteel.

Stackpole Carbon Company, Electronic Components Division, produced a fine one-page black-and-white ad which ran in *Electronics* magazine. It is shown on page 927.

Layout of this ad is excellent. It is simple and clean and attractive. The illustration dominates the page, as it should. There's lots of reader interest in the showing of genuine silver money. Size of the electronic components is shown very nicely by comparison with the silver coins. And the layout includes five neat elements; illustration, headline, two copy blocks, and the logo-signature. This is the way ads should look.

Headline, however, suffers from being set in uppercase and lowercase letters. In this instance it isn't too objectionable because the typeface is quite legible, although there's still that jumpy feeling, and there's no getting around the fact that more time and effort is required to read it than if it had been all lowercase.

Then there's the one-page black-and-white advertisement run in *Motor Age* magazine by Grey-Rock, Division of Raybestos-Manhattan, Inc. Automotive brake shoes and brake linings are not par-

Using brake components to frame the headline and copy was an effective device in this ad for Grey-Rock, Division of Raybestos Manhattan, Inc. It also allowed advertiser to show how parts are installed, an important bit of product information for clients in the service market.

ticularly exciting or attractive of themselves, and few are the mechanics who would rather look at an illustration of such a product instead of a pin-up girl.

Grey-Rock did an excellent job of showing the product to good advantage, however, and used considerable ingenuity to keep the ad from being static and dull. Using brake components to frame the headline and copy is an unusual technique, and an effective one. It enabled the advertiser to show both the primary and secondary lining, each of which is carefully marked by Grey-Rock to prevent an error in installation. This prevents puzzled mechanics and undoubtedly earns their gratitude.

The headline is a real stopper, since it tells the reader the *product* is a real stopper. Since it's a new and greatly improved brake lining, there's no disputing it.

Copy is well written, user benefits are spelled out convincingly, product quality is believable because the advertiser points out that the new copper combination brake linings are the first to master the grueling Pennsylvania state road test based on S.A.E. (Society of Automotive Engineers) procedures.

The layout includes attractive white space, it's not cluttered, and it's inviting to the eye. Despite having the illustration in two halves so that it counts as two separate layout elements, there are still only five elements in the ad—the ideal number.

The ad has one weakness, though, and it's in the stylized type in the headline. This slows down the eye and makes reading a bit difficult; it may have resulted in some readers abandoning the ad as too difficult, rather than proceeding on into the body copy. Furthermore, the body copy would have been easier to read if it had been set in two columns rather than in such wide measure. Since it's well leaded, though, there's little reason to suspect that readership suffered very much from type set approximately 70 characters in width.

Final example in a discussion of type at this time concerns the Burroughs Corporation's ad from *Dun's Review.*

This one-page ad is in two colors, blue and black. The second color is used quite liberally, since the illustration is a duotone—a combination of both the primary and secondary color.

Duotones are usually quite pleasing and this one is no exception. Cool colors—blues and greens—usually result in the most appealing duotones for industrial advertisements; use of reds and browns and oranges tends to result in colors that are something less than appealing.

A standard AAAA second color costs from 10 to 15 percent more

Burroughs Introduces
Series E3000

A new approach to low-cost management reports.

Now it is possible for many more businesses to enjoy the benefits of electronic accounting.

Important benefits, like the timely management reports produced by the E 3000 . . . reports previously available only from much higher priced systems. Reports produced during the *routine* of a highly automated daily accounting operation. Reports produced at a lower cost than previously possible.

Through the E 3000's unique electronic capabilities, you get the reports you need to help manage your business, when you want them, arranged in any format you want. Inventory figures. Sales reports . . . by salesman, product or territory. Comprehensive payroll data.

In fact, any data you put into the E 3000 can be made to come out in report form. And since the E 3000 Systems are modular, you can expand them to meet your growth requirements.

The most powerful system in the E 3000 Series is the E 3500 shown above. It offers the latest electronic logic and computational capabilities . . . plus an expandable electronic core memory and a new data retrieval ability through the use of magnetic striped ledgers.

The E 3000 Series is the newest addition to our family of electronic accounting systems. For details on the system with the productive power just right for you, call our local office or write Burroughs Corporation, Detroit, Michigan 48232.

Burroughs

This Burroughs ad is clean and well laid out. The only strange and quite unnecessary element is the headline in the upper right-hand corner. This says nothing that the headline proper and the body copy below do not impart in better fashion.

than cost of the basic space, but it's not as good a buy as bleed according to almost all readership studies. Second color used properly *does* increase readership in many instances, but usually not sufficiently to warrant the extra cost. Other justification exists, however, for using a second color, as we shall see later on.

Burroughs' ad is clean and well laid out. It contains only five elements—illustration, headline, two copy blocks and signature-logo. This latter is in the second color, hence stands out vigorously. The other element, the one that hasn't been counted, is the additional headline up in the upper right hand corner of the illustration. Research shows that having a headline overprinted in the illustration reduces readership and detracts from the effectiveness of the illustration itself.

Headline of the advertisement is properly set in lowercase type, although it's in a face that isn't especially easy to read due to the short ascenders and descenders (an ascender is the upper stroke of the lowercase "d," while a descender is the lower stroke of the letter "p"). What's more, the face is too heavy. It has too much mass so that it literally overwhelms the illustration, even though the body copy is set in a "dark" strong face that carries well.

This doesn't kill this ad, though, for its total effect is pleasing.

And there's not a shade of doubt that type of this weight makes a strong impression on the reader. He finds it very difficult indeed to overlook Burroughs' ad.

The Logotype—Holy of Holies

Time was when the advertiser's logotype was of considerably greater importance than it is today. Several decades ago, for instance, the percentage of illiterates in the population was many times higher than it now is. The logo at that time identified the company for those who couldn't read, and presumably strengthened the identification and image even for those who could. There's not nearly as much need for logotypes today as there was in the past, but anybody who thinks he will live to see the decline and fall of the sacred logotype is a prime candidate for the funny farm, white suit with the bow in back and all.

Cynics have long recognized that there's a passionate love affair, almost incestuous, between the advertiser and his logo. This cunning little design has been invested with near-human properties. It's regarded as a favored offspring to be cherished and chaperoned and protected from the embraces of any except those who have the honor of *using* it.

Agency men in general and layout artists and art directors in particular harbor a mighty cynical attitude about the logo. Among themselves they always proclaim that if the ad has nothing to say, the selling proposition isn't good, the product is almost impossible to promote for any one of a number of reasons, the copy approach leaves something to be desired, or the illustration isn't everything it should be, there's a magic formula for satisfying the advertiser, the client. Regardless of whether the advertisement is worth three whoops or not.

All that has to be done is to bump up the logo in size. Make it the dominant element in the ad. Show it big, *really BIG*.

This attitude is wrong. But the thought behind it shouldn't arbitrarily be shot down in flames. An advertiser wants identification—he needs identification.

Logotypes are usually shown at the bottom of the advertisement, below the copy block, and most of the time appear in the lower right hand corner, the point of exit for the reader's eye. This is done on the assumption that the last impression the reader will receive from the ad is the identity of the advertiser. He won't be left wondering just who in blue blazes manufactures that wonderful little widget he read about the other day in—what was the name of that magazine?

There's much to be said for this theory. The reader's eye *does* generally depart for other parts from the bottom right hand corner of the ad. A logo there *is* noticed most of the time. The reader may or may not remember it, or—as complicated and far-fetched as many logos are today—he may or may not be able to interpret it and ascribe it to the company that fathered it. Be that as it may, the bottom fraction of the ad is the proper place to put the logo; that way it doesn't do a disservice to the advertiser by cluttering up his ad and adding a distracting element.

Already illustrated have been a number of advertisements with the conventional treatment of the logotype, where it's tucked away neatly in the bottom right hand corner, so there's no need to go into this. Some advertisers use the logotype as a design element in itself, however, and this bears looking into.

M&T Chemicals Inc. had its agency, Marsteller Inc., produce the exceptionally tasteful one-page black-and-white advertisement illustrated nearby to run in a number of the chemical books.

Layout is simple and beautifully proportioned. Illustration, headline, three copy blocks, and the signature add up to six elements.

The problem in this layout was —what to do with the company logo? The artist handled it quite neatly by reversing the company initials in the lower right-hand corner of the ad. Size of the logo was critical—it had to be large enough to be seen, but not so large as to throw the layout out of balance.

Type is nicely laid out so the signature fits in at the bottom of the center column gracefully and logically. But there's no room for the logo without drastically reducing the size of the signature or stealing room that's needed for copy.

Consequently, the art director reasoned quite properly that the logo could be reversed out of the lower right hand corner of the illustration—if it was kept small and relatively unobtrusive, yet large enough to make an impression on the reader. This was done, and although it adds another element and although readership is known to go down when type is placed in the illustration, in this instance the logo was handled so tastefully it's not really possible to fault it.

When a company's initials are used instead of a logotype, or, more properly, are used *for* a logotype, they can become an important design element that strengthens an advertisement and also identifies the company instantly. This is the case with the one-page four-color ad run by The National Cash Register Company on the third cover of *U.S. News & World Report.* Incidentally, there are more than 100 publications on NCR's media schedule.

The initials logo of the National Cash Register Company is quite distinctive. Here, since the ad as a whole is airy, the logo can be used quite large—and still there's space for a four-color spot illustration of the product alongside. In most cases, a logo will not look well this large.

Here the initials-logotype is used very prominently. Because the shape of the typeface used required somewhat less than three-fourths of the width of the page, this neatly left room for a four-color spot illustration of the product.

There's an unusually clean, airy feeling about National Cash Register's ad, created in part by the air between the headline and body copy, as well as by the semihigh-key illustrative technique. The illustration, incidentally, is of a loop of the punched tape that programs the advertiser's model 400 electronic accounting system.

Showing it in the advertisement, rather than the entire machine, enables the company to tell the story of how easily the machine is changed from one program to another, and that it is absurdly easy to operate. These two user benefits, along with solid state circuitry and modular design, are the primary ones that NCR wants to convey to its management audience.

Using the logo this large is, in this instance, still in good taste. There's nothing horsey or objectionable about NCR's large-letters-logo, and there's the plus that it certainly provides instant identification!

Name and Logo Together

Then there's the use of the company name *and* the logo as a design element, often to tie the two pages of a spread advertisement together. This device is frequently used in industries that are frantically competitive, where product differences are relatively insignificant, or are unusually difficult to present convincingly to the reader.

Nothing is inherently wrong with this device, and there's no question that if it does nothing else, it will succeed in identifying the advertiser and making at least a "name" impression on the reader. Naturally, if this is the only impression the ad makes—a Noted for the name—that's a pretty expensive piece of space. Any number of advertisers are apparently unwilling to take even a tiny little chance on having anything more than the name read, however. They want to be sure of that one thing.

Giddings & Lewis Machine Tool Company's attractive four-color spread is an example. Name and logo act as a unifying force to identify the ad instantly as a spread so that no reader can possibly make a mistake and think the illustration is editorial, the other page is an ad, or some similar boo-boo. Despite the massive type at the top of the pages, there's no oppressive feeling, no connotation of things being crowded or hemmed in. This is due, no doubt, to the presence of so much attractive white space.

GIDDINGS & LEWIS

Newbury put four G&L N/C drills to work ... and saved $100,000 in production costs

[illegible]

$25,000 saved in layout

[illegible]

PUT G&L TO WORK FOR YOU

Giddings & Lewis is fully aware of the importance of white space and doesn't feel an unconquerable compulsion to cover every fraction of an inch of space with ink as so many industrial advertisers do. It's refreshing.

If you have a sound, logical reason for bumping up the firm name or logo, by all means have at it. Go right to it. There's no real need to, however, because almost all research on the subject indicates that the reader will identify the advertiser even if his name is set in type the size of that used for the body copy.

Indeed, some research leads one to believe that having the advertiser's identity shown in inordinately large type actually causes some readers to skip over the ad and the name without devoting enough attention to it to hang a mental name tag on the company that's picking up the tab for the space.

Being too large can be self-defeating. You're better off to stick with the conventional, rather than trying to burn up the track and leave all other advertisers in a cloud of dust.

Mostly it won't work.

Clatter and Clutter

Clatter and clutter are two insidious enemies that lurk in ambush waiting for a chance to launch a sneak attack on an unsuspecting layout.

Clatter and clutter generally succeed in completely destroying a layout's effectiveness, and, as a consequence, the advertisement itself.

Let's define clatter: The abrasive noise created by the jangling clash of an impenetrable jumble of typefaces, roman and gothic, italic, boldface, script, hand lettering, and every conceivable variation that one can dredge up from the depths of a desk drawer full of type books, a disordered imagination, lack of taste and lack of experience—or all of them at one horrible time.

A high clatter level stills the voice of the advertisement so the message cannot possibly break through to the reader.

Clutter is simply having a junky-looking advertisement, usually the result of trying to put enough in it to go into three or four ads. For the most part a cluttered advertisement has anywhere from 10 to 20 elements (honestly, this is not a put-on). All of them are fighting each other for the reader's attention, all at the same time. None of them make the slightest bit of headway because the reader has already skipped the ad and gone on to something else.

Clutter is a surefire way to avoid getting readership, or of getting as much as the ad would get if it were clean and simple. Unfortunately, clutter seems to be an objective that a distressingly large number of industrial advertisers strive very hard to achieve.

Both clatter and clutter can be avoided by simplifying the layout. Confine yourself to no more than two typefaces—one for display or captions, the other for body copy. Avoid the fancy and the ostentatious with great determination. Reduce the number of elements in the ad to five or six, and make absolutely certain their relationship with each other is right.

Remember that something has to be the dominant element. Everything can't be dominant. Everything can't be big, despite client desires. All type can't be in display size.

Let's look at several examples of clatter and clutter and see just what it is you should avoid.

First is a one-page, two-color (green and black) advertisement run in *Motor Age* by Chicago Rawhide Manufacturing Company.

Objective of the ad is to promote one of the interminable "deals" offered to the automotive aftermarket by manufacturers much more interested in peddling the wares of premium purveyors than they are in extolling the virtues of their own products.

Headline is hand-lettered in a style that's fairly legible, although not nearly as much so as a good, readable type face. It cost more,

Type, hand lettering, line drawings, halftones, water colors, check marks, a coupon—this ad has everything. Author Stansfield counts a total of 16 elements making up a prime example of clatter and clutter.

so maybe that's why it was used. It's in green, the second color. That's element No. 1, and the fun has just begun.

Dominant illustration is a water-color drawing of a smiling individual, ivy wreath on his head and with emphasis marks floating in the air around him for some reason that's not explained. The ivy is green, naturally. That's element No. 2.

Subhead, "to your family," also in green, is element No. 3.

The line drawing of the applauding woman (apparently applauding her hero) is element No. 4.

And the artwork of the family waving and blowing kisses, either at the hero or at the lady under the hairdrier, is element No. 5.

Because of different tone values, the drawings of the picnic table and thermos jugs have to be considered separately, and become element No. 6.

The two watches are close together, however, and are seen at one glance; they are element No. 7.

"And your customers" is in a slightly different style of hand lettering, and is printed in black, so constitutes element No. 8.

The grease seal (at last, after eight elements we get to the product) is No. 9.

The two-line subhead, "simply try the New C/R SAFETY SERVICE AWARDS PROGRAM!" is in black, and represents yet another element. This makes 10, exactly enough for two advertisements. But we're not through.

Check marks, although in black, belong with the copy block printed in green. They make No. 11 and No. 12.

The official-looking Customer Satisfaction Guarantee Certificate has a green border and the advertiser's logo and lots and lots of tiny type, too small to read. This is element No. 13.

Element 14 is the Chicago Rawhide logotype; it's printed in green.

A reproduction of a plaque given for Safety Service Awards Program—from whom, to whom, or by whom isn't legible to the naked eye, although a magnifying glass shows copy reading: FOR THE LEADER WHO IS WILLING TO TRY A NEW SERVICE HABIT. This is element No. 15.

Final element—for a total of 16—is a coupon. It's remotely possible that some innocent soul with time to kill waiting for quitting time waded through all of the clatter and clutter. Possibly he even wended his way to the bottom right hand corner of the ad and then clipped the coupon and returned it. Remotely possible.

Another Element Count

Thomson Industries, Inc. is a consistent advertiser and is well aware of the value of continuity; its ads are apparently in the right books for its market, and they're there with commendable frequency.

Without knowing Thomson's communications objectives it's not possible to be absolutely sure whether merely being Noted and having the company's name in front of prospective purchasers of its products is sufficient return from the advertising program, or not. It seems a bit unlikely.

Most advertisers want more, otherwise they would have set in nice, easily read type, *Courtesy of Smith Widget Manufacturing Company,* and have this put smack dab in the center of the page in a little box—and leave the rest of it as white as the driven snow.

However, it seems more than likely that Thomson wants its ads read, although there's just too much in them to realize this goal. Take the one shown nearby, for instance.

The clatter level and clutter level are nothing short of amazing. And all of that black, and the huge white type screaming at the reader in serif, sans serif, italic, reverse, nonreverse, uppercase, lowercase, type set on an uneven keel; it's all just too much. The author even gets worn out writing about it.

Here's another ad with a high level of clatter and clutter. Putting everything in reverse ads to the effect. Author Stansfield counts the elements in this advertisement and comes up with an amazing total of 22. The elements are detailed below and on the following page.

Let's list the elements and see what the total tally is:

1. Cutaway drawing.
2. THOMSON INTERCHANGEABLE.
3. die-set BALL BUSHINGS.
4. N E W !
5. GO ANTI-FRICTION.
6. with a simple bushing replacement.
7. and (1) Improve performance of your *present* dies.
8. and (2) Reduce tool room costs.
9. Illustration of the die-set ball bushing.
10. Write for literature and name of our representative in your city.
11. (box) . . . in the PRESS ROOM.
12. Copy block.

13. (box) . . . in the TOOL ROOM.
14. Copy block.
15. Illustration of some kind of a tool or jig.
16. Signature in a panel.
17. Manufacturers of BALL BUSHINGS—The Linear Ball Bearing and ROUNDWAY Bearings—The Linear Roller Bearing.
18. Two illustrations.
19. 60 Case—Hardened & Ground Round WAYS and Steel Shafting, and BRONZE Case—Steel Shafts with Bronze Bearing Surface.
20. Illustration.
21. NYLINED Bearings—Sleeve Bearings of Du Pont Nylon.
22. Illustration.

As Maxwell Smart would say, "I find that hard to believe."

To expect the reader to look at, read, and absorb a total of 22 separate, individual elements in a one-page advertisement is not only unrealistic, it's fantastically naive.

The reader isn't going to do it. He isn't going to look at even *half* that many. Thomson Industries could wrack up a lot more readership if it would cut the clatter and clutter and forget the reverse type.

Then there's the one-page, four-color advertisement from *Foundry* magazine, run by Modern Equipment Company, the Metallurgical Division of Alco Standard Corporation. This ad has:

1. Headline
2. Subhead.
3. *Three* captions.
4. *Four* four-color illustrations.
5. Copy block.
6. Logotype.
7. Signature.
8. Address-slogan.
9. Slugline.

A good share of clutter isn't all that's wrong with this ad. The four halftones in the illustration area are not sharply defined, and the tonal values are too much alike. Type is set too wide and ragged left, which usually reduces readership.

This adds up to 14 individual elements in this advertisement. As high as the clutter level is, that isn't the most serious shortcoming of the ad, however. Although it may not show up in a black-and-white reproduction of the four-color illustrations (all *four* of them), they merge into each other so that it's extremely difficult to tell just what it is you're looking at. Very confusing. And there's a narrow white border about 1/16-inch wide between the illustrations; it isn't nearly wide enough to separate them and prevent the visual merger.

Combine all of this clutter with type set too wide and set ragged *left,* which usually reduces readership, and a signature-address-slogan-slugline that's out of this world, and you have a sadly confusing layout. The reader doesn't know where to start, read, finish, or what have you. This one's far easier skipped.

To show how an advertiser can unwittingly run ads that are dreadfully cluttered, an old advertisement from a discontinued campaign of Lindberg Hevi-Duty is illustrated nearby.

To start with, there's an unexplained element in the upper left corner—some kind of symbol, apparently, that has a meaning only to the advertiser. Considering that this four-color ad ran on the fourth cover of *Research/Development*—and fourth covers in four-

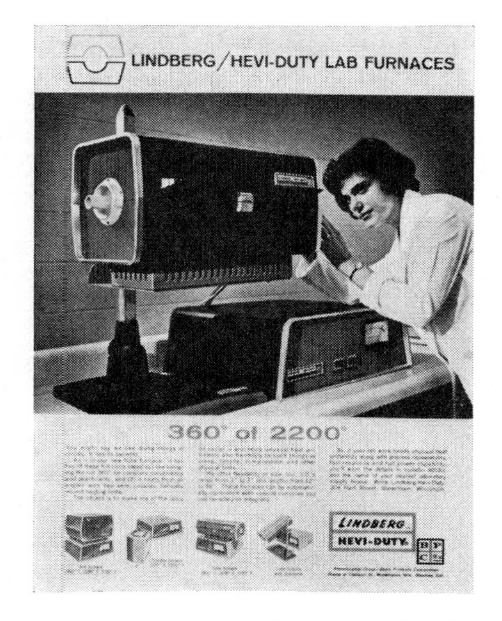

A major criticism of this ad is the fact that the lighting is brightest on the model, thus attracting the reader's eye to her rather than the product. Also, the top line of the ad is institutional and meaningless insofar as the ad's message is concerned.

color aren't exactly given away just because the publisher happens to be a very nice guy—this is paying quite a price to talk to one's self.

Of course, it's possible that employees of the company, and maybe even the field sales force, understood the significance of the cryptic, unexplained symbol. They could have received a mimeographed letter about it, though, and then the ad wouldn't have had to be cluttered up with it.

The advertiser's name and the generic name of the product set in the white space above the illustration is terribly confusing. This white space is going to waste; fourth-cover position automatically includes bleed, so the advertiser is sacrificing a large area that should have been devoted to getting a lot more impact with a larger illustration. This would have pulled in many additional readers, rather than putting a headline up above the illustration that really doesn't say anything at all—to the reader, at least. All it succeeds in doing is raising the clutter level.

The illustration itself is adequate, but that is describing it charitably. The equipment is shown prominently, but not well; it's neat and clean and apparently the model is handling it properly. But the model's face is the warmest (in color) area in the illustration and it's also the most brightly lighted area, hence the reader's eye is attracted to the girl, not to the product. Chances are this is the last thing the advertiser wanted. But when an industrial advertiser uses a portrait photographer for his illustrative work this type of thing frequently results; this may well have happened here.

Headline is printed in red. This is permissible and may have resulted in its being Noted by a large percentage of those who even skimmed the ad. But it really doesn't say anything. It doesn't pull the reader into the ad.

The "Clutter" Continues

However, there are three copy blocks and the type is a very light sans serif that doesn't carry well. And it's so small—apparently about seven-or eight-point—that it is so difficult to read that it discourages the average reader. Make your type too small for the average pair of middle-aged eyes and watch your readership ratings plummet. All of us aren't 22 anymore. And few legitimate buying influences in industry are, either.

Adding more confusion to a layout that is already badly cluttered, there are shown no less than four additional pieces of equipment the advertiser manufactures. Each of these four has a caption. That's a total of *eight* elements cluttering up the bottom of the ad.

Then, there's a large logotype printed in blue and black with a TM and a R beside both of the sections of the company's name and a separate little box with letters, sheaves of grain, and bolts of electricity beside it. For good measure, throw in a stacked two-line slugline and you end up with a sum total of 18 elements—enough for three tasteful advertisements with three elements left over to start another one.

Clutter seen here is undoubtedly the result of an amateurish attempt to make every advertisement in the campaign be all things to all men. Every ad theoretically showed the reader the complete product line. Inexperienced advertising managers frequently make this fatal mistake.

While there's no debating the desirability of informing the reader as to the extent of the product line, there's also no questioning that in this case a fuzzy, poorly conceived objective resulted in an advertisement that blurs the message and fails to emphasize the major point.

An advertisement can do one job only. One job only. To try to "save money" or "get a free ride" and put everything except the kitchen sink into every advertisement accomplishes just one thing:

It assures that none of the ads will perform as well as if the layout had been clean and crisp and uncluttered.

Lindberg Hevi-Duty's later campaign for the same product line is shown for comparison. It is seen in the one-page four-color ad illustrated nearby. This ad also ran on the fourth cover of *Research/Development* magazine, the key to the most inaccessible door in industry.

The difference is both striking and refreshing. The new ad contains the following elements: Illustration, headline, three copy blocks, logo. There's also a slugline without which the ad would have been improved, but it's small and detracts little.

There is no clatter, no clutter, no unexplained symbols, no attempt to make one advertisement do the job of an entire campaign. This ad is thoroughly professional in every respect, in vivid contrast to the advertiser's discarded campaign which was incompetent at worst, amateurish at best.

Also, note the vast improvement in the quality of the photographic illustration. Here the product is quite properly the center of interest due both to skillful lighting and selective focus; the product is correctly lighted more strongly than is the model, and it is razor

Unlike a previous ad which this one replaced, the lighting here favors the product rather than the model. In fact, the model was thrown off focus slightly as another means of guiding the reader's eye to the product. Layout is clean, open.

sharp. The model is just enough out of focus to provide a pleasing contrast. This is the type of photography an *illustrative* photographer produces as a matter of course, while the portrait photographer almost never does. Cost is a bit higher, of course, but the extra return from high-grade work makes the slight additional investment well worth while.

How to Use Second Color

When space is purchased in a business publication, that publication agrees to print the advertisement that's to go in it. But the publication's responsibility is limited to printing the ad in the basic color of ink the book uses—black.

Rather frequently you'll encounter books that have special news sections or editorial sections devoted to current price structures prevailing throughout the industry, or something on that order. And these special sections may be printed on a colored stock; usually it's a very light color, perhaps buff, green, or blue.

Although the book may print on colored stock in black ink, oftentimes a very dark ink of the color of the stock will be used—dark brown on buff, for instance, or dark blue on light blue stock. When this is the case the ads appearing in this special section will be printed with the ink color used for the editorial material as a matter of course. This is attractive to readers and does not increase cost of production for the publisher.

So what is a second color? It is any color that appears in the advertisement in addition to the basic color in which the publication is printed, usually—but not always—black.

Incidentally, when writing informally about a two-color advertisement, such as in an agency media schedule, a note to an agency by an advertising manager, or an internal memo within an agency, two-color is frequently abbreviated and written "2/c." Without the quotation marks, of course.

Happily, advertisers can't pick any color out of the rainbow and specify this as the second color for their ads. If this happened, business publications would be so garish and tasteless as each advertiser clamored stridently for attention that one's stomach might stage an instant revolution at the sight when leafing through pages.

The American Association of Advertising Agencies, in cooperation with American Business Press, has established standards for second (and third) colors. This information is given in a booklet entitled: *Recommended Standard Second Colors for Business Pub-*

lications. You may get a copy of this helpful booklet at no charge by writing to either of the following—letterhead, of course:

American Association of Advertising Agencies
200 Park Avenue
New York, New York 10017

American Business Press
205 East 42nd Street
New York, New York 10017

Prior to 1951, most business publications offered at least one second color which was designated "standard." Inasmuch as each publication determined what its own "standard" would be, there was naturally a considerable difference in hue and shades of the various colors that were offered.

Both advertisers and agencies recognized the problem and urged that business publications attain a greater uniformity in colors. Accordingly, a joint committee was formed which represented the American Association of Advertising Agencies, Associated Business Publications, and National Business Publications.

This committee selected standard colors for industrywide use, and recommended that all business publications adopt them.

A joint committee representing the AAAA, American Business Press (formed as a result of the merger of Associated Business Publications and National Business Publications) and the Magazine Publishers Association met during 1965 to review previous recommendations on color. Not only were improvements in design and illustration made, but several hues were also changed quite significantly.

It should be stressed that this standardization effort in no way was intended to influence a publication as to the number of colors it offers as standard, nor with respect to its policies on special matched colors which some advertisers demand.

Before choosing the standard colors, the joint committee studied samples of second colors submitted by 326 business publications. The most popular colors were red, offered by 312 publications; blue, offered by 293; green, offered by 282; yellow, offered by 277, and orange, offered by 261.

One of the samples of each of these five colors was selected and approved by the joint committee.

These five standard colors can be duplicated by any business publication. Inks that will reproduce them may be obtained from any of the leading ink manufacturers; any printer can get them. Scientific specifications of the standard colors permanently identify them. They are given below for your convenience; frequently advertising managers want to duplicate exactly the ink used in a publication, on material developed within the company and printed by a commercial printer.

AAAA Specifications for Ink Manufacturers

Scientific identification of the Recommended Standard Second Colors has been established by means of the "PPG-IDL Color Eye" process. The following trichromatic coefficients and other color specifications were obtained by taking readings on the "Color Eye" of each of the colors selected, so that consistent quality can be maintained over a period of time, and the original identity of these colors preserved.

"Wet" samples of the Recommended Standard Second Colors may be secured by ink manufacturers from AAAA Headquarters, or ABP Headquarters.

Ink	*Color Eye Filter Values*	*Chromaticity Coordinates*	*Dominant Wave Length*	*Excitation Purity*
AAAA	X—83.7	x— 0.439	573.5	82.0%
YELLOW	Y—75.2	y— 0.492		
	Z— 9.0	Y—65.730		
AAAA	X—62.5	x— 0.542	592.5	83.0%
RED	Y—36.2	y— 0.394		
	Z— 5.0	Y—31.726		
AAAA	X— 7.5	x— 0.169	476.0	69.0%
BLUE	Y—16.1	y— 0.162		
	Z—57.0	Y—14.110		
AAAA	X—79.2	x— 0.500	583.0	85.5%
ORANGE	Y—56.0	y— 0.445		
	Z— 6.0	Y—49.078		
AAAA	X—18.0	x— 0.264	517.0	18.0%
GREEN	Y—27.2	y— 0.407		
	Z—18.8	Y—23.838		

Ink	Inkometer Readings (300 ft./1 min.—75° F 50%—Relative Humidity)	Pigmentation
AAAA YELLOW	9.5—10.0	10.60% Benzidine Yellow 0.40% Benzidine Orange
AAAA RED	9.5—10.0	20.00% Red Lake C 6.00% Barium Lithol
AAAA BLUE	9.5—10.0	5.00% G.S. Phthalocyanine Blue 13.00% Peacock Blue
AAAA ORANGE	9.5—10.0	2.50% Red Lake C 3.50% Benzidine Yellow 8.00% Benzidine Orange
AAAA GREEN	9.5—10.0	5.00% Benzidine Yellow 4.50% G.S. Phthalocyanine Blue

When you use a second color in a publication, don't expect an identical reproduction of the recommended standard color. Instead, look to the book to give you a "commercial match" of the standard colors. Colors are bound to vary somewhat. Primary causes of variation are slight differences in paper, temperature, printing plates, makeready of the press, and ink flow as the press is running. This last is regulated to give best results for all colors in a given color row, of course.

Overprinting of colors of comparable hue and density, such as black on solid red, should be avoided.

Proofing should be wet, color down first.

Illustrated nearby is a proof sheet put out by the American Association of Advertising Agencies and the American Business Press to provide samples of the approved colors. This one happens to be red, although blue, yellow, green and orange are also supplied in the booklet.

Note that the proof sheet shows how a line illustration will reproduce in solid second color, how a halftone will reproduce, as well as duotones and various strengths of screens ranging from 25 percent on up to solid. Each tint block is identified with the percentage strength of both the second color and with the black. This

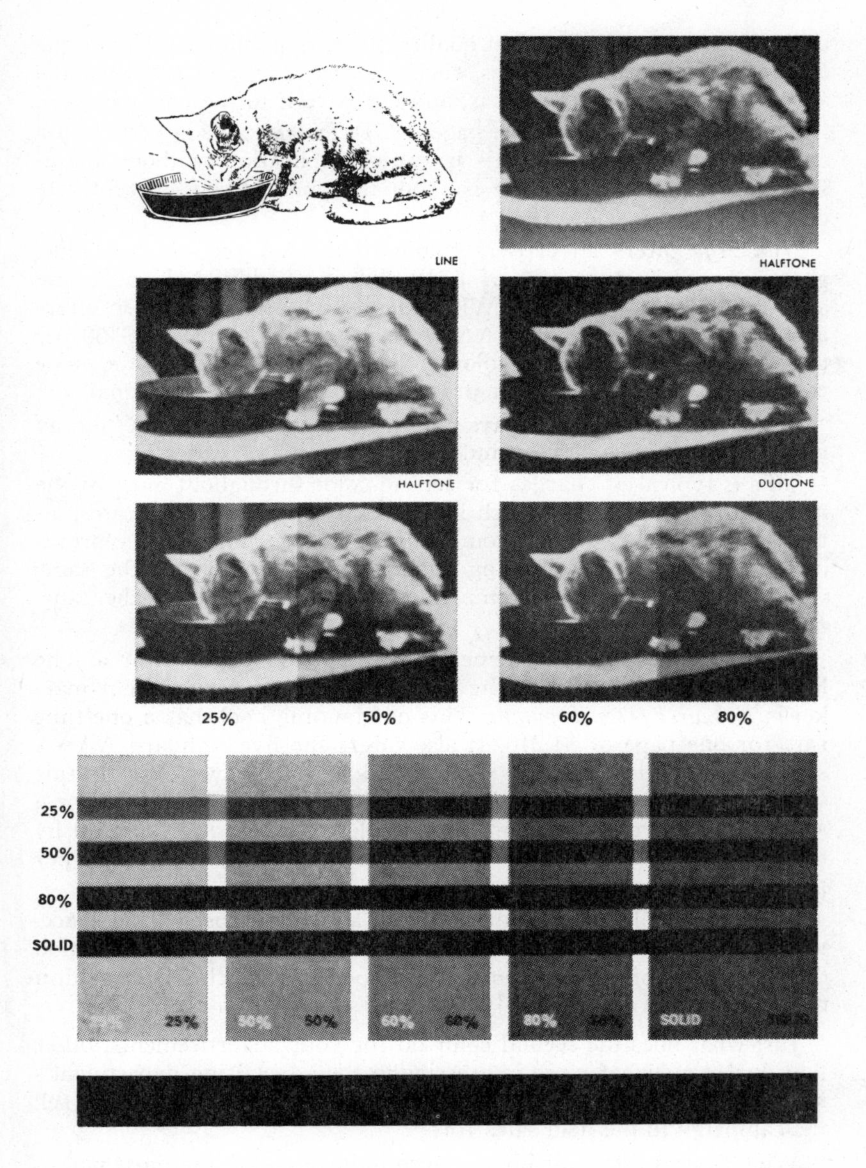

indicates how various percentages will appear when overprinted with varying strengths of black.

There's a catch, of course—a price tag attached to the second color. Let's take a typical first quality business publication that is the leader in the market it serves, such as *Iron Age,* and see what the actual cost of a second color is, and compare it to the cost of space.

Rate per insertion, for one page, ROP, in *Iron Age* is $2,195 on a one-time basis. As noted, this is run-of-publication, without a preferred position. Information is from the publication's current rate card.

Iron Age offers advertisers Standard AAAA red, orange, blue, green or yellow at a cost of $340 per page additional—over and above the cost of the space. What's more, the publication also offers a matched color other than AAAA standards at a cost of $460 per page additional. For three colors (two colors and black), the same rate applies as for four-color process: $675 per page additional.

Color used functionally pays for itself in many instances; the ad manager must balance cost and additional impact/readership.

This is typical of charges for second color throughout most of the business press. However, each individual book has its own rates, although they tend to be very competitive as publications have approximately the same cost of doing business, they need about the same profit margin, and when competing directly, have about the same circulations.

Now, let's look at a magazine from an entirely different area. The leading publication serving the lush research-and-development market is *Research/Development.* This outstanding book has a one-time rate for one page of $1,210. It also offers the five standard AAAA second colors. Its price is somewhat lower, however, for at this writing the cost for a second color is $135 for a one-page ad. For a spread, the extra charge for second color is $195. Also offered by the book is matched color (except metallic) at a cost of $185 per page; $275 for a spread.

So, for roughly 15 percent over and above the cost of the space, you can have a two-color ad. (This doesn't take into consideration the extra cost of production of the two-color ad; this cost seldom runs more than an extra $150 or so.)

Just what does the second color do for your advertisements, other than look somewhat more impressive in the advertising department's sample book and possibly help you to a certain extent when you sell the campaign to the field sales force?

Well, first of all, available research indicates—for the most part—that a second color *might possibly* help corral some extra readership for you. This isn't by any means a foregone conclusion, though, and is certainly a conclusion you shouldn't leap to.

At least one major study on the subject leads inescapably to the conclusion that color used decoratively in an industrial advertisement has no influence whatsoever on readership ratings—either to help or to hinder.

On the other hand, one of the biggest and best industrial advertising agencies in the country doesn't hesitate to say that decorative color *decreases* readership, which is only what a lot of us have suspected through the years but have been unable to prove.

Furthermore, Daniel Starch conducted an analysis of the effects of color variables on advertisement recall based on 3,819 ads. Results showed that black-and-white advertisements rated 100, one-page two-color ads only 97, and two-color spreads 105.

In a two-year study made by a large agency, a comparison of Noted scores showed absolutely no difference between black-and-white ads and two-color ads. However, the Seen-Associated (name registration) was 7 percent *lower* for the two-color ads. Some 5,000 ads were studied.

Color Loses Its Novelty

Color is far less of a novelty to the reader than it used to be, so an ad with color in it doesn't automatically draw the reader's eye like a magnet picks up iron filings. In fact, the trend is so much the other way that if it continues not too many years will pass before the black-and-white ad will be a novelty, one that will pull in readers merely because it represents something seldom seen. Industrial advertising will then have gone full circle.

To show how the use of color has grown by leaps and bounds (it's more than doubled of recent years), a tally of all ads of one page or more (fractionals weren't counted because they would have weighted the results), in a recent issue of *Iron Age* showed the following: 41 black-and-white ads, all either one page or spreads. However, appearing in the same issue were a total of 66 ads of two, three, or four colors; all were full pages or spreads. That's a 3-to-2 ratio of color over the traditional black-and-white.

Whether or not you receive extra readership as a reward for having invested a few more dollars for a second color depends almost entirely on how it's used.

Produce a pastepot ad in which the layout man slaps tintblocks and areas of solid color around as if there won't be any colored ink after this one issue, and you're due for a big disappointment. The same holds true for an "artistic" type of advertisement where color is used purely for design purposes and to show that you don't really give three whoops about what happens to your message. You might accidentally pick up an additional percentage point or two of readership, but don't bet any of *your* money on it. Use the company's.

When color is used functionally and selectively and with restraint to accomplish a specific objective, it can produce excellent results that far outweigh the modest additional investment involved.

Here are some of the things, not necessarily all, though, that the second color should do for your advertisement. If it doesn't do *any* of these, don't use it. Save the money and put it into more space.

1. Call attention to your illustration.
2. Indicate or suggest action.
3. Relate the headline to the illustration.
4. Relate the copy to the headline.
5. Separate the product from the background in the illustration, or separate a special feature of the product from the rest of it.
6. Show the color of the product if it is important in its sale; for instance, in a sporting magazine blaze orange was used in an illustration of a hunting jacket because this is the safest known color.
7. Highlight key words in the headline, and, possibly, though far less likely, in the body copy.
8. Be used for subheads to break up large blocks of copy.
9. Show structure, shape, or design of the product.
10. Dramatize how the product works.
11. Point out what the product produces.
12. Show how the product should be installed.
13. Point up the simplicity of maintenance.
14. Define an eye path the reader is to follow.
15. Separate elements of graphs or charts.
16. Identify the company—Kodak's yellow is an example.

Functional use of a second color unquestionably results in higher readership. In a study that McGraw-Hill made, the average Noted scores of advertisements in *Power* magazine were 19 percent higher than scores of black-and-white ads that were comparable in all other respects.

In Read Most, though, was where the payoff came when second color was used functionally. The 68 ads studied achieved 32 percent more readership than did black-and-white ads.

This is very comparable to the extra readership that accrues to bleed ads. The difficulty is, that far too many industrial advertisers fail to differentiate between mere *use* of second color and its *functional* use. It's entirely possible, too, that they may not know there is a difference, so believe that because they are using a second color this surge in readership is something their ads are bound to get.

Second color, by and large, isn't something the industrial advertising manager should become enamored with. Quite likely he has no real reason to use it. It's more than possible his ad would be stronger without it. One large agency, Marsteller Inc., customarily recommends against using it. When an agency recommends against something that would increase its billings, it has the client's welfare at heart—and it's mighty sure the recommendation is to the client's advantage.

Functional use of second color—you could call it *logical* use with just as much justification—tells all and sundry that color is used properly. It *looks* right. Compared to ads that look for all the world as if they'd been in the path of a derailed freight train whose ruptured tank cars dumped ink promiscuously all over the landscape, the ad with functional use of color is restrained and sensitive and effective. The difference is strikingly apparent.

An exceptionally effective use of second color was made by Sylvania Electric Products, Inc., a subsidiary of General Telephone & Electronics, in its superb one-page two-color ad that appeared in *International Science & Technology* magazine. It is on page 954.

This ad was produced by an advertiser with a well-honed sense of what is exactly right, of what he wanted to say, and how best to say it. Only the airmail stamp is in the second color—red, which is the actual color of the stamp, of course.

This vivid spot of color attracts the reader's eye immediately. Compare this great ad with one that has color splashed tastelessly all through it, with tint blocks here, screaming headlines there, little duotone subordinate illustrations, big shouting reverses and what have you that are inflicted on the defenseless business reader. Do this and Sylvania's ad is like finding a safe haven from a horrible storm.

Super stamp

It's just an ordinary airmail stamp. Until you put it under ultraviolet light. Then it turns into a glowing super stamp that lets the Post Office sort 30,000 letters an hour!

Sylvania phosphors did the trick. After seven years of research. Several thousand were tested before two were selected from Sylvania.

Now, the phosphors are simply added into the stamp ink. A red-orange for airmail, a green for the rest. When the letters come in, they are fed through special electronic equipment that cancels and sorts them automatically.

Sounds simple, but it took some doing. The phosphors not only had to luminesce brightly under ultraviolet, but had to be as fine as confectioner's sugar (normally antagonistic characteristics).

Altogether, we offer hundreds of different phosphors. Some detect counterfeiting, some illuminate safety devices, some coat fluorescent tubes, some trace air currents, some make plastics glow, some brighten your TV picture.

Maybe we can solve your materials problems too. After all, we've been a leading phosphor producer for over 25 years. We're also a leader in tungsten, molybdenum, specialty industrial inorganic chemicals, and semiconductors.

For information, write to Sylvania Electric Products Inc., Chemical & Metallurgical Division, Towanda, Pennsylvania 18848.

SYLVANIA
GENERAL TELEPHONE & ELECTRONICS

Only the stamp in the top center of this layout is in color—a red like that of the airmail stamp it depicts. Restraint like this makes color work. Splashing color all over an ad is a technique that accomplishes nothing.

Rationale for the succinct, curiosity-arousing headline and the simple, provocative illustration that pulls every eye to it at once, is that Sylvania manufactures the phosphors that are added to the ink used to print the airmail stamp. Phosphors transform the airmail stamp into a super stamp that glows vividly under an ultraviolet light, enabling the Post Office to sort 30,000 letters an hour with an automated system.

Copy goes on to say that a red-orange phosphor is used for airmail stamps, a green one for all of the others. Incoming letters are fed through special electronic equipment that cancels and sorts them automatically at a very fast rate. Sylvania describes the incredible complexity of its phosphors, as well as giving additional use for the products.

This is an exciting ad, and it's both convincing and persuasive. What's more, it's in impeccably good taste, which is what we need much more of in industrial advertising.

Gerald Ryan, advertising manager for this product line at Sylvania, reported this great ad received excellent readership. And well it might, for this advertisement did right by Sylvania and by the reader; it sells hard for the advertiser and rewards the reader with information that's presented interestingly and believably. This is a combination that works every time.

Industrial Equipment Group, ESB Incorporated's one-page ad is about as different from Sylvania's as it's possible to be, but it, too, uses the second color functionally.

Another ad illustrating restraint in the use of color. Because it is reproduced here in black and white, we have to tell you where the color is—one-half of the circle around the ESB logo and the letters of the name, "Exide," in one corner are in red.

This advertiser used a small halftone illustration of the battery and one-half, as it's called, but set it in an inky sea of black. All of the type, headline and body copy, is in reverse. Legibility is better than one would expect, however, due to a serifed "reader" type face having been used. The only spot of color is the half of the circle over the ESB logo in the lower right hand corner, and in the Exide name; it appears in red.

Second color serves the same purpose as in Sylvania's ad despite their marked dissimilarity. Here, the small spot of color is also used to attract the eye, although it's used primarily as an additional means of achieving greater advertiser identification. The restraint that was used resulted in an attractive ad. It could easily have been awful, though, for few things are as gruesome as large masses of red combined with equal amounts of reverse out of black.

Here's a "Recipe for Profit" by American Monorail...
AMERICAN MONORAIL
Take...One enterprising Jellies manufacturer
Add...One versatile American Monorail stacker crane
Blend...for PROFIT!
PLEASE SEND FOR COMPLETE INFORMATION ON AMERICAN MONORAIL STACKER SYSTEMS TODAY
AMERICAN MONORAIL, 1111 East 200 St.
Cleveland, Ohio 44117
Phone: 216-486-6000
AMERICAN MONORAIL

The ad at left is an example of a pertinent use of color. To make the product—an overhead crane—stand out, it was reproduced in a stark black and white —while a duotone of black and blue was used for the background halftone. A duotone of the background served to subdue and glorify a fairly unattractive jumble.

Next is an advertisement in which the second color is used very liberally; approximately three-fourths of the ad is printed in blue. However, American Monorail, Division of Fischer Industries, had a very good reason for using the second color, and used it to good effect.

This manufacturer produces engineered materials-handling systems—which is a fancy way of saying overhead conveying systems. Few things in life are as cluttered and junky looking and downright confusing as the ceiling of the average factory that's engaged in mass producing relatively large or complicated metal products.

Hooks dangle, hoists skitter back and forth over the production area, older buildings have holes cut in the floors to lower or raise things to a different assembly area, pipes and plumbing and air lines and electrical conduit crisscross each other without apparent reason. The scene is something less than esthetically scrumptious.

Photographing an overhead conveyor against such a maze-like background would be enough to drive the ordinarily philosophical photographer straight to drink. There's simply no way possible to light such a scene to separate the product from the junk behind it. One solution would be to "blow back" everything in the background with retouching, making the background a ghostly gray, but this would look too unreal; the reader, after all, is accustomed to seeing cluttered looking factory ceilings. Take away the clutter, you take away the realism and the authenticity. You destroy believability.

The other solution, and the one that American Monorail adopted, is to do as was done in this fine advertisement. The background is a duotone, a combination of blue and black, and the product is in the usual black-and-white so that it stands out prominently.

Separated from the background in this way, the product is easily seen, as is the way it's installed. The illustration, through use of the second color, tells the advertiser's story very clearly, and it does so without wasting the reader's time. If a reader has to make an effort to determine where the product is, where it ends, how it's attached and what not, he's not going to spend any time on that ad; he won't make the effort. He'll go on to reading the editorial matter, or go into a competitor's advertisement.

American Monorail stopped him neatly by making it easy for the reader to visualize its product in his plant, doing his work. This is a very effective advertisement, one that works hard and delivers a return on the investment.

Advertiser identification is the most important thing to Servo Corporation of America, whose strong one-page ad from *Electronics* magazine is shown here.

The "v" in Servo is in red on the company's letterheads. The same treatment is given the company name in this advertisement. The red letter (in two places) is the only use of color in the layout.

Message and approach is semi-institutional in character, for the advertiser merely tells about the products the company manufactures without getting into the nuts and bolts of any of them. This may very well satisfy the communications objectives for this campaign.

Layout is relatively simple and the ad is attractive. Second color is red, used in only two places in the ad—both times in the stylized "V" in the company's name-logo. This same V, also in red, appears on the company's letterheads. Because so little of the second color is used, the reader's eye goes immediately to it so the ad makes two distinct impressions of the advertiser's name.

A new-product announcement ad uses the second color very effectively when the headline is set in red, as Johnson Control, division of Johnson Service Company, did in the ad shown next.

This headline in this ad literally jumped off the pages of *Factory* and serves to pull the eye into the illustration as the next step in reading the ad. The second spot of color is in the lower half of the logo in the lower right, making an invisible eye path for the reader to follow—headline to illustration to logotype. This assures absorption of the message that here is a new product, the first of its kind, and that it was developed by Johnson Control. The eye goes next to

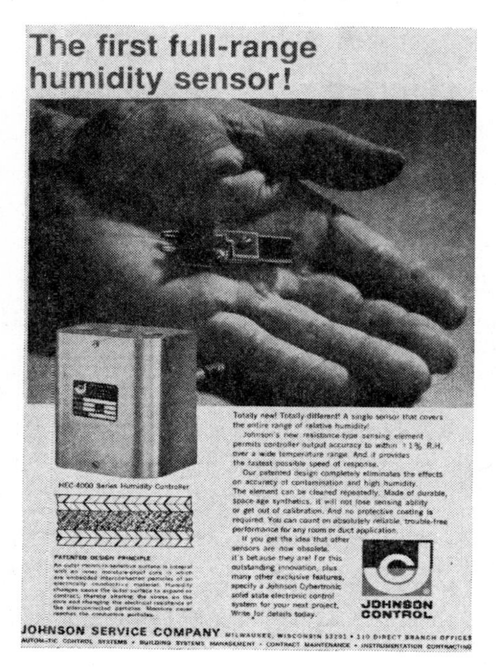

The headline of this advertisement was in brilliant red, announcing a new Johnson Control product. The only other use of color was in the bottom half of the company logo at the lower right of the ad.

the line drawing, then to the complete controller, then into the body copy.

Despite having seven elements, this ad is easy to assimilate and easy to read.

How to Misuse Second Color

High time it is that some perceptive advertising executive formed a new organization—S.P.C.C.

This stands for the Society for the Prevention of Cruelty to Color. Misuse constitutes the cruelest kind of cruelty to advertising as a whole, to advertising effectiveness, to the advertising manager's company, and to long-suffering readers of the business press.

The S.P.C.C. should have a governing body, naturally, composed of advertising men who have proved their mettle and the quality of their output over a period of years; this should probably be judged and evaluated by a panel of recognized experts. The governing body would be empowered to appoint a panel of exceptionally competent, well-known industrial advertising practitioners from both agencies and advertisers. This should be done with all possible dispatch.

Now, this panel would be called the Cruelty Consideration Committee and all suspected cases of cruelty to color would be referred to it for impartial judging, and then recommendation of necessary action, if any.

Advertisements which have been tried and found guilty of being cruel to color would be constructively critiqued and a confidential report sent—marked *Personal and Confidential*—to the offending advertising manager and his account executive. Purpose would *not* be merely to tear down an individual and his work, a company and its products, or an agency and its output. Rather, the objective would be to *help* industrial advertisers by telling them the facts of life as regards color and then showing them what is wrong with the advertisements that misuse color. How to correct the fault would also be discussed in detail, naturally.

Objective in looking at ads which follow is precisely the same as that of the Cruelty Consideration Committee (even though it will never be formed), the enforcement arm of the Society for the Prevention of Cruelty to Color (which also will never materialize).

Ah, well, 'twas a thought.

Let's examine a few of the more common crimes in which color is misused to the advertiser's detriment.

Color used merely as a background wastes money three ways. This is, of course, color that's printed either as a solid or as a tint over the entire page or pages of the advertisement. When it's screened down so its depth is not so great as if it were printed solid, this is nothing more nor less than a tacit admission that some vague stirring of the advertising manager's subconscious has given him fair warning that this is misuse of color.

In any event, when color is used as a background it does three things for the industrial advertiser:

1. It costs approximately $200 for extra production expense for plates.
2. Space cost is boosted around 15 percent.
3. The ad receives approximately 30 percent less readership than it would have if it had been a simple black-and-white advertisement.

An expenditure made to buy something that will pay a return on the investment can never be faulted by anybody, so items (1) and (2) are relatively inconsequential.

But to incur additional expense to buy something that returns less is inexcusable.

The Use of Yellow

The nosedive in readership of an advertisement with copy overprinted on a strong color is due to lack of legibility. The reader finds it so incredibly difficult to read an ad of this type that he simply skips over it without consciously considering just why he does so.

Type printed over a solid yellow or orange can be read reasonably well because the color is light enough in tone and the apparent depth of tone is considerably less than that of the black type if it were regarded monochromatically with appropriate filters. Screen the yellow or the orange back and it's more legible yet, although overprinting nonetheless results in a decided reduction in the number of those who will read the ad.

Soabar Company's one-page, yellow-and-black ad from *Factory* magazine, illustrated nearby, has the second color laid on with a lavish hand. The entire page has what looks like an 80-percent screen of yellow; exception is the circles in which the small drawings and a part of the product appear.

Ten elements make up this layout. Six circular illustrations, the product, headline, copy block, and copy-block-logotype-addresses. Despite having twice as many elements as a clean layout calls for,

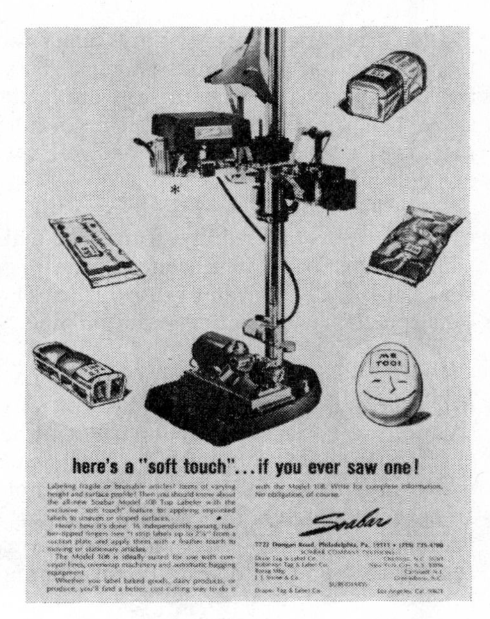

In color, this ad was a case of yellow jaundice. Yellow was splashed over every one of the spot illustrations—in some areas screened to a lighter yellow; in others the color was solid. It was a case of much too much.

the ad is not distressingly cluttered. There's enough open area to keep from repelling the eye.

The price tags in each of the spot illustrations are also printed in yellow, including the "Me too" on the smiling egg. They are a solid yellow, however, with no screen. Color depth and apparent difference is slight, though. Just think how much this advertisement would have been improved if the yellow hadn't been applied with such reckless abandon. Since the price tags on the fragile foodstuffs are obviously very important to the message—because Soabar's Model 108 Top Labeler handles everything with a soft touch—they could still have been printed in yellow. With no other color in the ad they would have popped right out of the page, making the advertiser's point with telegraphic speed and certainty.

As is, however, the labels merely merge into the vast mass of yellow and practically disappear as far as creating any real impact on the reader is concerned.

Overprinting black over a solid blue or green is next worse, perceptibly so because the tone is so similar to black when viewed monochromatically. Black type tends to merge right in with the second color. Reading is just too hard to bother with for the majority of readers.

It's surprising, however, how many industrial advertisers continue to overprint on solid blues and greens, year after year, ad after ad, apparently with a wistful hope that just having the second color there will somehow enable them to catch the elusive brass ring of increased readership. Might as well face up to it, though: You're not going to.

One thing can be said for overprinting on blue or green: Neither of these colors causes eyestrain that makes reading virtually impossible. If you have an unconquerable urge to overprint, if you can't shake it off, if you can't ignore it, can't forget it, if it obsesses you, by all means select either green or blue, yellow or orange. You could do worse.

Walter Kidde & Company, Inc., ran a one-page, blue-and-black ad in *Space/Aeronautics* magazine that's exceptionally simple and well balanced and clean. It is illustrated nearby.

Layout is comprised of only four elements; the abstract black-and-white illustration is so stark and simple that it's almost hypnotic. It does an outstanding job of catching the reader's eye at the approximate point of entry into the advertisement because there is a feeling that you're looking down a tunnel or at a target. Something

Eye-catching—yes, even eye-holding—is the abstract black-and-white illustration in this ad for Walter Kidde & Company. Author Stansfield finds only one fault here—the light sans-serif type is printed over solid blue, making it almost illegible. Here's an ad that would have been better without any color at all.

seems to pull you into that illustration so that even if you wanted to resist it wouldn't be the easiest thing in the world to do. Then, there's the copy block, the logo, and the headline.

Aside from questioning the placement of the headline, the ad has a major weakness that more than offsets its many good qualities. Body copy is in a light sans-serif type face that doesn't carry particularly well even when it's printed on white. But in Kidde's ad it's printed on a solid blue, making it legible—but barely. This is more than enough to discourage even the most interested reader who has a strong hankering for information about the advertiser's Cool Gas Generators. Too much work is required to wade through the copy.

This same identical ad in black-and-white would have delivered far higher readership to Kidde at considerably less cost.

The well-thought-out advertisement that was run by Siliconix Incorporated in *Electronics* magazine has much to commend it. It is illustrated.

Siliconix used a layout device that's seldom seen, but which accomplishes its objective without fuss or furor—the border around the ad ties all layout elements together very effectively; no worry about any straying off to strange range. This border is an attractive

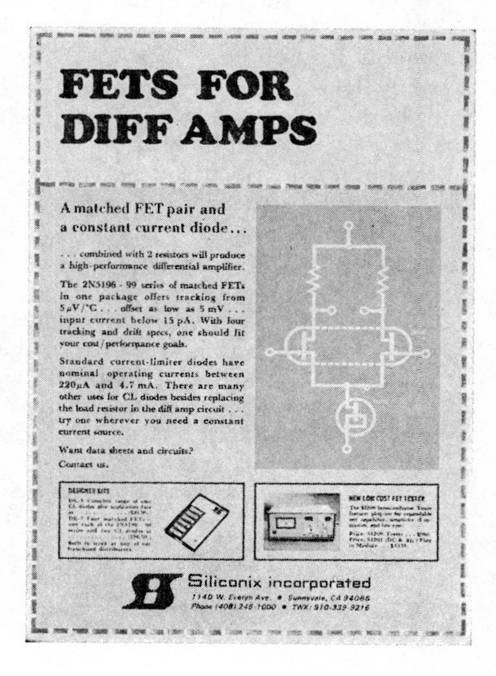

The border around this ad for Siliconix holds all the elements together. It is a pleasing gray, accomplished by screening the black plate back to 60 percent. The solid blue used **on the** *blueprint is fine, but the type should not have been overprinted on blue, even though it was screened back.*

shade of gray achieved by screening the black back to approximately 60 percent.

Nowhere in the ad does an explanation appear as to just what a "FET" might be, but these electronic types speak their own native tongue and it isn't English, so this apparently is permissible. Copy does a good job of selling matched FETS (whatever they might be) and assures the reader that a matched pair and a constant current diode, combined with two resistors will produce a high-performance differential amplifier. Ducky!

The ad contains only six elements and they're arranged simply and logically and without confusion or clutter. The ad's only weakness is that it's in two colors that are used decoratively, not functionally.

The Perils of Overprinting

Fortunately, though, the blue over which the copy is printed has been screened back so that the copy is legible, particularly since it's in a serif typeface that carries well. It's not as legible as if color hadn't been used, however. Only the diagram, which is in reverse, has a panel of solid blue. And here it's called for if color is to be used because vivid contrast is required to show the diagram and the little numbers well.

Infinitely worse is overprinting on either process red—which is actually a hideous, repulsive, purplish-reddish-magenta—or on a standard AAAA red, for that matter.

Lately there's been a sudden rash of overprinting on process red. If ever a color were to be given the assignment deliberately to repel the reader, to cause him to shudder in revulsion, to create doubt in his mind as to whether or not he'll be able to retain his lunch, this one is it. Look no further.

Although it is not repulsive, type overprinted on 4A red is equally hard to read. Nothing is wrong with the color as far as color itself is concerned, for this is an especially vigorous, clean and attractive hot red with nothing of the blue-purple about it. However, it, too, is practically impossible to read when there's black type on it.

Any shade of red, either process or AAAA-recommended red, has a built-in barrier that precludes an advertisement's receiving very much readership if the color is laid on solid and copy is overprinted. This is because the normal eye reacts to these strong, hot primary colors by forming a mental reaction to them; the mind actually suggests that the reader sees the complementary color when normal eye movement occurs from phrase to phrase, line to line.

What this means is that the subconscious automatically reacts to the extremely strong stimulus of the vivid color before the eye and causes an automatic counterreaction which causes the reader to receive an impression that he's "seeing" exactly the opposite color of the spectrum that's before him. Different lighting conditions—which are actually different color temperatures—influence this phenomenon and the degree to which it appears to occur.

Check this for yourself. Take two advertisements, one with a process red (magenta), and one with AAAA red, both of which are printed solid with no screen. Show them to several people in your office—your secretary, your assistant, clerk, mail boy. Don't implant the idea in their minds that they mentally "see" the complementary color, but have them read the entire ad, then look quickly at a neutral-colored wall immediately after looking up from the ad. Then ask them what is the first mental impression they receive. If they don't say "green," repeat the experiment under a stronger light. Make no mistake about it, it will occur and when it's recognized the guinea pig will probably spontaneously volunteer that he "saw" green when ordinary eye movements caused a split-second loss of focus on what he was reading.

This is extremely distracting, hard on the eyes, and something the reader will simply not endure merely for the sake of reading your advertisement. Don't expect him to.

You can get an argument, and a fast one, too, from those who are all hopped up on splashing on color with broad strokes. They'll proclaim to everybody who will listen that using the same color in all of the company's advertisements aids in campaign identification and advertiser identification as readers come to associate the color with the product and the company that makes it.

This is quite true. If all the advertiser wants is to have his advertisement Noted—*and not read*—this is one possible way to go about it. A probability exists that the Noted score might be rather high; after all, who can miss anything as blatant and tasteless and garish and obtrusive as this type of ad?

Regardless of the Noted score, though, it's inconceivable that merely achieving this distinction can possibly satisfy a principle communications objective for the campaign—if any thought and planning preceded running of ads.

Tint Blocks Overpower

Using tint blocks of the second color is almost as discouraging to better-than-average readership as is use of solid second color. This is because ads employing this technique are confusing to the reader. He doesn't know where he should enter the ad. He can't tell what he's supposed to look at first. Even if he figures this out, the confusing use of color doesn't let his eye follow the natural path, clockwise, around the ad that it normally would if the color weren't there to distract him.

Then, for good measure, throw in the fact that type overprinted on *any* color of tint block—and this includes a light screen of black, which is gray, of course—is more difficult to read than that same type printed on white. This gives you a situation that is wide open for improvement. Much improvement.

Clatter level and clutter level of ads using the decorative tint block technique are fantastically high.

Typical is the one-page two-color (red and black) ad run by EIS Automotive Corporation in *Commercial Car Journal* magazine. It is illustrated nearby.

Element count shows a total of 23 (count 'em, 23!) separate, distinct, different, individual elements in this advertisement. That's enough for four and three-fifths ads. Clutter like this you don't see every day in the week, even in books serving the automotive after-

If there's anything this ad with a total of 23 elements doesn't need, it's a tint block. But one is there, nevertheless, serving to increase the level of clutter and clatter.

market where almost every advertiser screams at full lung power as a matter of course.

You can't really lay all of the blame on the hapless layout artist for this jumbled mess, either, for that innocent soul undoubtedly had some account executive say something like: "It's this way, Clyde. The client wants a big picture of the product shown. And he wants a big logo—preferably in red—at the top of the ad. And he wants the headline big and red, at least part of it. Maybe you'd better throw in a tint block or two to get some color in the ad. That'll make him happy. And he wants the copy bulleted so that everybody will be sure to read every last word. Then there are all of these line drawings of the different fittings and adapters that go with the gizmo, and a little line drawing or three. Why don't you reverse them out of an outline . . ."

By that time the dispirited artist slunk away to take a long lunch hour during which he muttered dark and dire imprecations aimed at all account executives and all clients, and bemoaned the fact that he didn't decide to become a forest ranger many years ago. Sometimes the advertising business isn't quite fair to those who give it their very best.

EIS Automotive Corporation's ad shows, down at the very bottom:

ALSO AVAILABLE . . . VARIOUS ADAPTERS FOR IMPORTED CARS

Wonder why they weren't illustrated?

In *Factory* magazine was the one-page two-color (orange and black) ad for the hoists manufactured by Wright Division, American Chain & Cable Company that's shown on page 968.

Illustrations—all four of them—are duotones, a combination of the orange and black. This isn't altogether unpleasant, but it creates exactly 13 separate spots of color, considering that some of the products have separate pieces that are divided by portions of the product that are shown in black-and-white. It's confusing.

Then, there are other spots of color spotted throughout the advertisement. Four of them appear in the four points of the compass in the center of the illustrative area. Four more are inside the circle of the compass to show the points of the compass, although for some reason or other North is not at the top as it normally is if the directions are oriented properly. Then, inside of that is another spot of color—the Wright name, logotype style.

There are 28 spots of color in this ad. The four duotones in orange and black are pleasing, but 24 other dabs of orange at points of the compass and various places in the headline and body copy create color clutter.

Floating around in various places in the headline and body copy are five additional spots of color. These patches of orange underline what apparently are key words, although all of them are just one word, the same one, that is—"way." These underlinings appear to be afterthoughts because with a magnifying glass it appears the underlinings were scored out of the plate with some kind of a sharp instrument; they are not clean and straight as they would be if they'd been set along with the type. But it's very difficult to see that they contribute anything to the ad except more confusion.

Finally, there's yet another spot of color; it's in the logotype-signature in the lower right hand corner of the ad.

Total of the little dabs of color here and there is 28—28. In-cotton-pickin'-credible.

Type is set about 82 characters in width, a little over twice what it should be for maximum reading ease.

And there is a total of 12 elements if each column of copy below the main copy block is tallied up as just one element, rather than two. This is logical because they're broken up with that little dabble of color. Almost two-and-one-half times too many elements.

Here again clean layout and avoidance of using second color

would have resulted in a much stronger ad. It's too bad that Wright Division handicapped itself this way; the ad makes it obvious that the company produces a superior product in an unusually wide range of sizes and capacities. But the reader will not absorb this information from an ad as cluttered as this.

Long gone are the dear days when merely having a second color in an ad caused the natives to jerk upright in sheer astonishment. If the trend continues as it has in the past, two-color ads will be in the majority from now on—despite there being very strong doubt as to whether or not they're as effective as the time-proven black-and-white in the majority of cases.

However, if you're dead set on using two-color, use it *functionally,* or don't use it at all. That's a better idea yet.

Four Color

Four color refers to a process, although it's a term commonly used to describe an advertisement, piece of literature, calendar, envelope stuffer, or what have you that's been printed in full, natural color so that it looks just as the eye sees the object that's shown.

In the chapter on production, this process and how it's accomplished and what it costs will be covered in detail. For the present, however, it's sufficient merely to mention that full color results from four separate impressions made on the paper by the printing press.

Four different colors of ink are laid down—yellow, blue, red, and black. When one is on top of the other, the result is color as the eye sees it, although in some instances when a dramatic effect is desired, as the camera sees and captures it in the color transparency. The transparency may have been deliberately exposed so as to imprint an off-color or ethereal effect, or an impression of something weird or wonderful or exciting.

You can have four-color ads by taking two entirely different routes. What you get, as far as quality is concerned, and how much it costs varies considerably depending upon which way you choose to go.

One route is four-color ROP (run of publication) which will be discussed now, and the other is the four-color insert, which will be gone into shortly.

Undoubtedly you've noticed the tremendous increase in four-color pages in the major business publications, both in editorial pages as well as in advertisements. This is due to the fact that publishers are doing everything possible to produce a more attractive package for advertisers, one that will be more attractive for readers and hence increase advertising effectiveness.

Such prodigious use of color—and it continues to proliferate in most of the better business books—is economically possible because these publications are now printed by web offset, an extremely fast, efficient method of producing quality printing at fantastic speed and lower cost.

Advent of web offset has made it feasible for publishers of business magazines to reduce drastically the price of four-color advertisements. This benefits everybody concerned. Readers prefer and are attracted to four-color material, so they're happy about the whole thing. Publishers must have high readership, readership that can be documented, in order to sell space in their books, so the trend toward more and more four-color printing is all to the good as far as they're concerned. And advertisers benefit greatly from both higher readership of editorial and from higher readership of their ads.

ROP Color Comes of Age

Some years ago the quality of publication-printed color left much to be desired. Most of it was somewhat better than comic pages, but nonetheless was dull and flat and lifeless looking, without the vigor and bite the really good four-color reproduction has. Since web offset, though, ROP color has become better accepted due to lower cost and greatly improved quality. ROP color today is not as good as the individually-printed four-color insert or piece of literature you prepare with tender loving care and admonish a printer to pour his heart and soul into, and it probably never will be. But it *is* good, though, and certainly is no longer to be considered either experimental or risky to use. Quality control of the final printing job of the good business magazines is excellent. When you buy ROP color you can be the next thing to absolutely certain that you'll receive an attractive ad.

As one large advertising agency noted recently, it's indeed an old question that keeps cropping up with relentless regularity—what is the value of color in advertising? More specifically, just what is it that a four-color ad can accomplish that the same ad in black-and-white cannot?

Inherent in the question is the implication that black-and-white advertising may really be more efficient in terms of readers reached per dollar invested.

Researchers have reviewed all available published information on the use of four-color in advertising, but there's remarkably little that can be classified as solid fact when viewed dispassionately. Much of the incremental benefit claimed for four-color is in the area of intangibles, such as "impact," "prestige," and "implied image."

We in advertising recognize the merit of these intangibles, but they are indeed difficult to justify to management when making a budget presentation. In order to do this, they should be measured definitively, although to date this has not been done.

Other accepted benefits of using four-color are equally difficult to pin down. These are:

1. Memorability—greater retention value.
2. Realism—product or situation appeal.
3. Identity—when used as a characteristic of a certain product or company.
4. Psychological implications—warmth, coolness, and other factors that the reader associates with a product or company.
5. Intrinsic appeal—beauty, personal involvement.

Actually, there's no end to such a list. It could go on and on. However, definitive *quantitative* measurements of the effects of using four-color in advertising have been limited pretty largely to two areas: Inquiry production and readership scores.

Daniel Starch & Staff performed a massive analysis of 5,000,000 (that's five *million*) inquiries and found that color produced 53 percent more returns per 100,000 circulation than did black-and-white.

Furthermore, Starch conducted an analysis of the effects of size and color variables on ad recall, based on 3,819 ads in seven different product categories in now defunct *Life* and *Post*. These were consumer ads, to be sure, although there is no reason to feel that results would have been significantly different had it been in the industrial field. Results showed:

	1 page	2 pages
Black-and-white	100	100
Four-color	153	150

It's quite interesting to note that the 53 percent advantage for four-color in the one-page ad is identical with the advantage for color disclosed by the analysis of inquiries.

Similar studies seem, for the most part, to center on a figure of approximately 50 percent as the relative advantage of four-color over black-and-white. This is borne out by analysis of two years' of readership scores in *Time* magazine, as reported in Starch Ad-Norms.

During this two year period Starch studied nearly 5,000 ads of all size and color combinations in *Time,* certainly a large enough number to permit averaging and comparing readership of specific combinations without sacrificing reliability. Among the 5,000 ads studied, 3,305 were one page or larger in size, split as follows by color: Four-color, 1,554; black-and-white, 1,751.

A comparison of Noted scores shows a 43 percent higher average for the four-color advertisements. However, it's when comparing Seen-Associated—which includes whether or not the advertiser's name registered and made an impression on the reader—that the four-color came into its own. Here four-color rated 52 percent higher. Read Most scores showed the least variation, as might be expected because thorough readership is more a function of content and inherent interest than of physical format. Four-color scored 21 percent higher than black-and-white in the Read Most category.

Regardless of the analysis applied, Starch figures lead to the inescapable conclusion that four-color produces at least half again as much response to an advertisement as does black-and-white when it is used in increments of one-page or larger ads.

Interestingly, ads of less than one page seem to utilize four-color even more effectively than do larger space units. Four-color increased recall by as much as 85 percent over black-and-white levels, according to Starch.

However, McGraw-Hill reports that an analysis of *all* run-of-publication advertisements in *Business Week* (except second, third, and fourth covers) for an entire year, involving more than 7,500 personal interviews, advanced a potent argument in favor of four-color. Both bleed and nonbleed ads were studied. Four-color pages had an average Noted score 77 percent higher than black-and-white, while spreads averaged 63 percent higher. In both cases the increase in readership was much greater than the increase in cost.

Cost figures for *Business Week* at the time of the study are those shown in *Standard Rate & Data* for the appropriate period. For both one-page ads and for spreads, the cost for four-color was 60 percent higher than for black-and-white.

When you cost out four-color, it more than pays for itself. *Iron Age,* for instance, has a current page rate on a one-time basis of $2,195 per page. The additional charge for running an ad in four-color is $675, which is just 31 percent higher. This makes it just about a Mexican standoff as far as the return on investment is concerned.

Iron Age space would cost $4,390 for a spread, and here the additional charge for four-color is a bargain indeed. *Iron Age's* four-color charge for the spread is $1,350, on a one-time basis, of course, still figures out to only 31 percent more than the black-and-white rate.

Since four-color spreads receive *at least* 50 percent higher readership, there are 11 percentage points the advertiser can pick up free of charge. This is almost as nice as finding money in the street.

This being the case, the intangible benefits mentioned earlier are the real payoff. Use of color in industrial advertising imparts added impact, prestige, importance, and memorability to the message the advertisement presents—and, by inference at least, to the advertiser and his products. Putting a price tag on these benefits is an impossibility, but they certainly have solid value nonetheless, and shouldn't be overlooked.

Color Case Histories

Let's go into three examples of run-of-publication four-color advertisements; they were, of course, printed by the publications' printers, or in captive print shops owned by the publishers.

First is a one-page four-color ad run in *Electronics* by Centralab Electronics Division, Globe Union, Inc. The ad has a certain feeling about it and there's curiosity value in having the products submerged in water, with one floating downward from the "surface." But this surely isn't enough to overcome two glaring layout deficiencies that quickly put the kibosh on receiving very much readership.

Then the second half of the headline (it isn't a subhead, it's the other half of the headline) is set in wavy fashion to suggest waves. This is extremely disconcerting to the reader and studies show that it cuts readership at least 40 percent—so there goes most of the benefit out of the window from using four-color.

Besides, the headline is advertiser-oriented and so is the copy. Few are the readers who have a burning desire for a clear picture of Centralab, and even fewer are those who will keep an eye on Centralab's ripples. Not over a prolonged period of time, at least. Then the body copy says such things as:

> *In our years of manufacturing miniature and subminiature components, we've made many ripples, and a few splashes, in the electronic industry.*

Here's a lot of copy that the copywriter obviously intended to be read. But it's set in a measure averaging 80 characters per line and overprinted on a dark blue background—two things which cut down readability for an ad.

This is the opening paragraph. Copy then goes on to talk of Centralab's achievements over the last 40 years, which includes designing and producing the world's first carbon-composition potentiometer. Next paragraph says, believe it or not, that:

> *Centralab sales have increased substantially every year and our services have grown proportionately. Our products are, sold, by separate sales groups and from separate warehouses, to original equipment and distributor markets.*

Topping off all this, the copy ends with a promise the advertiser will keep his feet wet. Precious, that.

Type is set approximately 80 characters wide and in a light sans-serif face that isn't the easiest thing in the world to read. Add the fact that it's overprinted on a good strong blue—at least 70 percent—and it's terribly hard to read.

The ad isn't all bad, it's the execution of the idea that caused it to fail. Had the products been illustrated in the same underwater setting, but in a good-sized illustrative area at the top two-thirds of the space, and the headline been below the illustration, then the copy in two columns approximately 40 characters wide, and the logo been below the copy, the ad would have enjoyed several times as much readership. This is a mighty long "if," but it's a mighty unreadable advertisement.

Next exhibit is Pinkerton's, Inc.'s impressive four-color advertisement from *Business Week.* Say "private detective" to a large number of people and the name conjures up either a picture of hard-as-nails Phillip Marlowe, or of Travis McGee doing a bit of philosophizing like Plato, Plutarch, and Peale while doing a lot of crime-solving, or else of a grubby little man peeping into a bedroom window.

Pinkerton's does, of course, have private eyes for all sorts of investigative work, but in its more than 100 years the company has developed an industrial security service second to none; it is used by many of the country's largest corporations to maintain the security of sensitive areas, as well as for general plant protection.

Pinkerton's is building an excellent image of itself with advertising of this caliber. The acrylic illustration is of superb quality and it conveys the feeling of reliability and competence and safety due to quality art and its representation of the neat, well-equipped, intelligent security officer at the gate of the refinery.

As far as type is concerned, it is set in too wide measure, but it is highly legible due to use of a serifed face that encourages readership.

This is a vigorous, forceful, attractive advertisement that received much better than average readership.

This type also is set in too wide a measure, but this is saved by two differences from the ad on the opposite page. The type is large and serifed. Also, it is well-spaced between the lines. All this tends to maintain readability for what is, overall, an excellent ad.

Why 400 of the 500
largest U.S. companies
use Pinkerton's
For over 100 years Pinkerton's Security Service has been built to provide a quality of protection that can't be equalled. This is achieved through carefully investigated guards, modern electronic methods, superior supervision and extensive training. With millions at stake in plant investment, employ the oldest, the largest, the best. Pinkerton's, Inc., 100 Church St., New York, N.Y. 10007
Pinkerton's of Canada, Ltd. Pinkerton Electro-Security Co.
For details call your nearby Pinkerton's office . . . or write

The stacked headline—an unusually strong one, by the way, with an implied endorsement that can't be equaled—and use of a short last line to lead the eye right into the body copy—is highly effective. Because the body copy is short, interesting and persuasive, and because it advances a selling proposition that can't be refuted, the reader is more than likely to read all of it. And he'll believe what he reads.

In its cogent one-page, four-color advertisement from *U.S. News & World Report,* Douglas Aircraft Company, Inc. makes very effective use of color, enhanced as it is by a clean, well-balanced layout. Copy appeal does dual duty.

Let's look first at the layout. It's clutter free, has just six elements, and is highly attractive. The four-color illustration attracts more than half again as many readers as a black-and-white one would, and there's enough white space to create a feeling of openness that extends an invitation to read.

Both the headline and body copy are set in a serif face of the transitional group; both are easy to read and are indeed a welcome relief from the deluge of sans-serif faces that advertising men have clutched to their hearts, even though they should know better.

In this ad Douglas Aircraft has an important message for the businessman—that he can fly short distances in the same comfort that he enjoys on longer flights. The DC-9, a midrange jet plane, is the subject of a fact-filled copy story that has high interest for a special audience.

Body copy is in three columns, set ragged-right. It's personal opinion, of course, but somehow or other ragged-right leaves a feeling of something lacking. The ad may have been stronger if type had been justified, although readership studies on this subject tend to disagree with each other. In any event, this is certainly not a major sin in an ad that's excellent in every other respect.

The headline is great. First half is a teaser with enough interest built in so that nobody with anything approaching a normal share of curiosity can refrain from reading the second half—and that's where the name of the company and the product appear. This is smart advertising. If a reader reads nothing else, at least Douglas has made a name impression on him.

Copy is fact-filled, informative, and reader-oriented. It serves to promote the wonderful twinjet DC-9, as well as the four-engine DC-8 jetliner. It's common knowledge among all of us who fly extensively that the DC-9 has brought the jet age to the boondocks; no longer do you have to fly between New York, Chicago, Los Angeles, and San Francisco to enjoy the smoother, quieter, faster jets. Most feeder airlines are switching to the midrange jets.

Somehow, though, the thought of *not* buzzing a herd of antelope with a DC-3 evokes a feeling of nostalgia.

In this fine ad Douglas points out very persuasively the advantages of flying in Douglas jets; in the case of the DC-9 it's making trips as short as 100 miles at the same speed and with the same roominess and comfort as you get in the four-jet jobs. Multistop flights are quicker; there's far less of that interminable ground time when the ground crew works in slow motion to see just how long they can keep the big bird down on the ground. The DC-9 doesn't depend on ground power supplies for air conditioning, heat, or lights.

This is potent copy for the businessman, who to a large extent comprises the universe of *U.S. News & World Report.* Besides that, businessmen who run airlines also read *U.S. News,* so they are aware of how Douglas is creating a "brand preference" in airplanes, to coin a term for this type of attitude change. This remains in their minds, needless to say.

Obviously there's no way possible to determine whether or not this fringe benefit from Douglas' campaign is of major importance to the advertiser, but it surely can't hurt future business.

Shown on page 978 is another Douglas ad from the same campaign; it's shown merely to illustrate type-handling of the headline. This headline, *Easy going. Douglas DC-9.,* is seven characters shorter than the commuter headline, so the art director felt the size of head-

Author Stansfield feels that the type in this headline is just a trifle too big, robbing the sensational photograph of some of its impact. The dramatic halation of light around the plane resulted from shooting the picture into the rays of the setting sun.

line type should be bumped up as a consequence. Although it is still legible and attractive, the feeling persists that the size of headline type in *Commuter's friend* is a better choice because it's not so overpowering.

Incidentally, the illustration of *Easy going* is tremendously impressive; the halation around the plane resulting from taking the photograph into the setting sun is both realistic and pictorially attractive.

Recently while returning from Los Angeles, the author was taking sunset pictures in color out of the window of a Douglas DC-8 at 39,000 feet. Due to the direction of flight a great deal of neck-craning and stretching had to be done, and not quite enough sunset could be seen for best photographic results.

So a request was made to the cute little stewardess who promptly phoned the Captain, and the DC-8 was turned 90 degrees for approximately two minutes—ample time in which to shoot a sequence of sunset pictures. These included the wing of the plane for reference, of course, and finally the sun itself perched on the very tip of the wing. The slides are nothing short of breath-taking when run through fairly rapidly on a Carousel automatic projector.

The sun sets rapidly when flying partially away from it, so when the stewardess asked a couple of minutes later "if the Captain could get back on course now," permission was granted with a hearty thanks to the girl and to the kind Captain. As a matter of interest, most airline captains will turn a plane for a spectacular sunset or sunrise (if you get up that early) for the benefit of shutterbug passengers if the plane is either ahead of schedule, or on schedule with favorable winds.

And if you happen to be in a commercial jet when, for no apparent reason, it banks sharply right or left and parallels an unusually awesome and colorful display by nature's pytotechnics, it's more than an even bet that the pilot or copilot are shooting color slides. One good friend of the author's who is a captain on one of the largest airlines has infinitely greater opportunity to take color slides than the business traveler—as proven by his collection of magnificent pictures. One of them shows the "pilot's cross"—a circular rainbow, in full color, above the clouds, with the shadow of the plane in the center of the circle.

Inserts in Full Color

One of the first questions that arises when you're planning a four-color advertising campaign is, "R.O.P. color or inserts?"

Inserts are frequently referred to as "furnished inserts" because they usually are supplied to the publication by the advertiser, already printed and ready to put into the book.

Most important consideration of all is readership, of course. As we've already noted, four-color ads as a group receive more than 50 percent higher readership than do black-and-white ads.

Four-color inserts tend to receive higher readership than do R.O.P. color advertisements, although this depends to a large extent on the individual ads involved. Many intangibles occur that make direct comparison more subjective than is desirable.

For instance, ads about products of high inherent interest will always be better read than advertisements for sweeping compound or salt to melt snow on the company's sidewalks and driveways. Numerous R.O.P. four-color ads consistently out-pull four-color inserts for this very reason.

What's more, there is always a difference in the creative approach used by two different advertisers. This is impossible to standardize, even if it were desirable to do so. But the fact remains that this sharp variation in the "quality" of the creative approach and of the advertisement itself is a factor that can produce either unusually high or unusually low readership—either with or without color.

In general, though, and this can be accepted as a rule of thumb, one-page four-color inserts receive the highest readership of any kind of advertisement that you can produce.

One-page four-color inserts have approximately a 5-to-10-percent edge on R.O.P. ads of the same size, other things being relatively equal.

Under your direct control, when you use the furnished insert, are creative approach, quality of the illustration, quality of the copy, and quality of the printing job. Excel in every area and run a truly great four-color one-page insert ad and what can happen to you? Your biggest competitor picks this exact time to kick off a new campaign that produces tremendous impact. Your insert that would have easily shown its heels to every other ad in the book still looks good, by comparison with all ads, but it may have suffered considerably at the hands of the competitive ad. This you cannot control, of course.

Always remember, too, that a dull, uninteresting, poorly conceived four-color ad won't receive even one little bit more readership than will a dull, uninteresting, poorly conceived black-and-white ad.

Granted, the Noted score may be higher with the four-color ad that's a crushing bore, but the Read Most certainly will not.

One thing that's not to be overlooked is the fact that the advertiser who pays the price to furnish four-color inserts can tip the scale in his favor. This is something like going to Las Vegas and rolling a pair of loaded dice into the game.

Heavier Stock Permitted

Inserts automatically attract more attention than publication-printed ads regardless of the number of colors involved. That's because most publications will accept inserts on paper that's much heavier than that used in the magazine. *Iron Age's* rate card, for example, shows that the book accepts inserts with a maximum weight of stock (paper on which the insert is printed), basis 25x38, four-page inserts or less—100 pounds coated, or 80 pounds uncoated. For inserts of more than four pages, or fractional page inserts of more than two thicknesses, the maximum weight is 80 pounds for coated stock, and 60 pounds for uncoated.

Since an insert is usually heavier and thicker than the rest of the pages around it, the book "breaks" to your insert ad—that is, it opens to the insert when the reader casually starts flipping pages.

His fingers automatically turn to your ad, and you know from your own experience how likely you are to read something that's stopped you in such preemptory fashion.

This is giving your advertisement every break—actually, one more than it could rightfully expect unless the insert was used. This holds true even for a single-sheet insert, but even more so for multipage inserts with their increased weight and bulk.

On the following page is a four-page foldout, a color insert ad run by I-T-E Circuit Breaker Company in *Factory* magazine.

Layout and difference in colors divide the ad right down the center; undesirable as this usually is, in this case it is not unattractive because of the vivid contrast in the colors. Left half of the ad has a blue background, and the product is a blue-gray with a red control button; right half of the ad has a warm reddish-brown background, with the product picking up some of the surrounding color.

What really stops the reader instantly, though, is the fact that the magazine breaks open instantly to this advertisement—every time. Open it up one fold and there's a one-and-one-half-page ad, with this background of strong yellow. Upon opening the yet-folded ad completely, there's a full-page four-color product-line ad with a colorful and impressive display of I-T-E's circuit breakers and other controls.

Foldouts Increase Readership

When the reader has read this and refolds the ad and turns the page, there is the windup on I-T-E's product line ad with four small four-color illustrations of typical units. The ad concludes with a bid for action and the company signature. This is in an attractive white area in which there's plenty of room for an imprint by a local distributor or by the manufacturer's district sales office. Much planning went into this layout.

Foldouts and gatefolds usually produce 6 to 8 percent more readership than run-of-the-mill multipage inserts.

This hardworking insert is almost a catalog, and it serves much the same purpose. Since it is easily removed from the magazine, chances are good that many prospects filed it for future reference.

General Electric Company, Metallurgical Products Department, recently ran the one-page four-color insert illustrated nearby in books serving the metalworking market. It's interesting to note that this insert deviates from the layout most commonly seen only because it's sideways; otherwise, proportion of illustration to copy, amount of copy, and so on are almost identical.

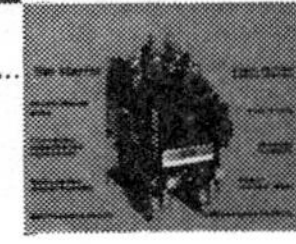

A

D

Go I-T-E all the way . . .

PUSHBUTTON STATIONS

Standard-duty, heavy duty, oil-tight—whatever your need, I-T-E has a pushbutton for the job. Compact and easy-to-wi n, I-T-E pushbuttons come in a variety of enclosures for flush or surface mounting. They also can be custom assembled to meet any special requirement.

MANUAL STARTERS

(FRACTIONAL-HORSEPOWER) Positive, 1-phase protection with interchangeable parts for motors up to one horsepower, and 240-volts are available over-the-counter in 1-pole or 2-pole, key- or toggle-operated construction with optional lights and selector switches.

(INTEGRAL-HORSEPOWER) Up to 10-horsepower, 3-phase, 600-volts . . . designed for non-reversing, reversing and two-speed applications in a variety of enclosures. NEMA 12 units are suitable for loom switch applications.

INDUSTRIAL RELAYS

Available in 300- and 600-volt ratings, electrically or mechanically held, with a total of 12 circuits for any normally open or normally closed combination. Circuits may be converted in the field. Block-type construction for basic magnet and coil with multiple four-circuit contact blocks provide complete flexibility for machine tool and industrial applications.

CUSTOM CONTROL PANELS

I-T-E's simple, compact motor control components—combination starters, relays and other units—are designed for easy installation in a variety of custom control panels. A single panel containing many controls can thus eliminate a clutter of separate units individually housed—and reduce costs substantially.

Contact your local I-T-E distributor or sales office, or write I-T-E Circuit Breaker Company, Philadelphia, Pennsylvania 19130.

Pushbutton Stations

Manual Starters—Fractional-Horsepower

Manual Starters—Integral-Horsepower

Industrial Relays

One design concept—one standard of quality for all your motor control needs

I-T-E CIRCUIT BREAKER COMPANY

Control by I-T-E
. . . featuring
a completely new concept
in motor control design
Starters feature one-design concept for all sizes. They mount in any position in the vertical plane. All connections are up front for easy inspection. Snap off the cover and the contacts are there. No tools required.
Coils are encapsulated, control circuits are built-in, with no leads or terminals . . . no wires to disconnect. Overload relays plug in, for fast, sure installation. There are provisions for a third overload relay and 6 auxiliary circuits.
These and many other exclusive innovations make I-T-E the newest, simplest, most reliable and advanced starters you can buy.
Starters and contactors in NEMA sizes 00 through 8 cover all ratings up through 900-horsepower, 600-volts. They are available in NEMA 1, 12, 4, 7, 9 enclosures.

HEART OF I-T-E MOTOR CONTROL . . .
Simplicity is the key to I-T-E magnetic starters. One basic design, one flexible modular concept, provide identical high-performance and functional characteristics throughout the line. This means you get the same advanced features and dependable operation in all Motor Control by I-T-E.

Now, I-T-E stands ready to serve your total motor control requirements with a complete new line from pushbuttons through custom control panels.

B

This foldout color insert for I-T-I Circuit Breaker Co. begins with the attractive page at upper left. As the page is turned, it folds out to a page and a half (at left), and finally to a two-page spread of product display (below). The foldout concludes with a call for action (above) and the firm signature. There also is, on this page, plenty of room for an imprint by a dealer or distributor.

Control by I-T-E
. . . featuring
a completely new concept
in motor control design
Starters feature one-design concept for all sizes. They mount in any position in the vertical plane. All connections are up front for easy inspection. Snap off the cover and the contacts are there. No tools required.
Coils are encapsulated, control circuits are built-in, with no leads or terminals . . . no wires to disconnect. Overload relays plug in, for fast, sure installation. There are provisions for a third overload relay and 6 auxiliary circuits.
These and many other exclusive innovations make I-T-E the newest, simplest, most reliable and advanced starters you can buy.
Starters and contactors in NEMA sizes 00 through 8 cover all ratings up through 900-horsepower, 600-volts. They are available in NEMA 1, 12, 4, 7, 9 enclosures.

HEART OF I-T-E MOTOR CONTROL . . .
Simplicity is the key to I-T-E magnetic starters. One basic design, one flexible modular concept, provide identical high-performance and functional characteristics throughout the line. This means you get the same advanced features and dependable operation in all Motor Control by I-T-E.

Now, I-T-E stands ready to serve your total motor control requirements with a complete new line from pushbuttons through custom control panels.

C

CARBOLOY
CEMENTED CARBIDES

Another achievement of advanced precision powder metallurgy . . .

POSITIVE RAKE CARB-O-LOCK.

Look closely at these inserts . . . notice the built-in chip control groove . . . the unique hole . . . the 10-degree relief angle . . . and the precise, unground cutting edge. Trapped securely in advanced-design toolholders, they deliver the superior cutting action of Carb-O-Lock in positive rake applications.

An exacting blend of process, equipment, and controlled technologies is required to mold tungsten carbide into inserts with such demanding configurations and extremely close tolerances. Uniform quality, dimensional accuracy and repeatability are essential in the Carboloy Advanced Powder Metallurgy manufacturing process.

Today, the steadily expanding Carb-O-Lock line is setting new standards for machining efficiency in negative and positive rake applications. And, Carboloy is continuing to add new dimensions to its powder metallurgy capabilities . . . dimensions that promise many more contributions to metalworking technology.

Contact your local Carboloy distributor now for Positive Rake Carb-O-Lock and the complete line of Carboloy cutting tools. Metallurgical Products Department, General Electric Company, Detroit, Michigan 48232.

GENERAL ELECTRIC

Interesting is that General Electric then produced another four-color *spread* insert for approximately the same media schedule. This was done with the same set of four-color separations, saving something in the neighborhood of $800-900 or even more; this is an excellent way to stretch budgets and make one production dollar do the work of two. More on this later on.

Also illustrated is still another General Electric ad for the Metal-

THIS IS ADVANCED PRECISION POWDER METALLURGY

This is the precise blend of process, equipment, and controlled technologies that made the Carb-O-Lock® insert possible. During the 1960's you have used Carb-O-Lock toolholder/insert combinations that have set new standards for metalworking efficiency. Advanced powder metal techniques enabled Carboloy to mold tungsten carbide into an insert with a unique cam-pin hole, chip-control groove and cutting edges held to extremely close tolerances . . . *all without grinding*. The inserts produced are uniform in quality and dimensional accuracy. Repeatability is maintained to a degree that qualifies Carb-O-Lock for virtually all machining operations. Yet, Carb-O-Lock inserts cost less than ground inserts and deliver superior cutting action. Precision powder metallurgy didn't just happen . . . it took several years of concentrated research and development. The result was the first Carb-O-Lock tooling. As early as 1961, it was demonstrating cost savings as high as 40%. Since introduction, the Carb-O-Lock line has expanded steadily. And this is just the beginning. Precision powder metallurgy has added new dimensions to Carboloy capabilities . . . dimensions that promise many more significant contributions to industry. Metallurgical Products Department, General Electric Company, Detroit, Michigan 48232.

For further information use Reader Service No. 622.

GENERAL ELECTRIC

lurgical Products Department's Positive Rake Carb-O-Lock tungsten carbide inserts for machine tools. This ad is shown merely to point out that every single ad in a campaign does not necessarily have to have the same exact layout in order to preserve campaign identity. There is little possibility of the reader's not relating this advertisement to others he's seen for the manufacturer's tungsten carbide inserts. The process of manufacturing this ultrahard metal is a fascinating one, and the end product is as space-age oriented as anything you can think of offhand.

Tungsten carbide is almost diamond-hard. The author has a number of tungsten carbide dies used to reload pistol and revolver ammunition. Ordinary dies of hardened steel wear so badly after a few thousand rounds have been run through them that they must be replaced; friction between the soft brass cartridge cases and the die walls causes the wear. Dies with tungsten carbide inserts, however, have so little apparent wear that it's inconceivable that one will have to be replaced in a lifetime of hard use. Cost of the TC die is roughly three times that of one of plain steel, but it is more than justified.

Die-cut insert of coffee cup shown at left was printed on heavy card stock. It scored the highest in readership in one magazine in which it ran, and second in another. The reader's hand went naturally to the handle of the cut-out cup. Because a die-cut ad is different from all others in a book, it is noticed.

The "coffee cup" insert run by Bliss & Laughlin is die cut. It's a real reader stopper. When it ran in *Purchasing* magazine it scored the highest readership of any ad in the issue; run elsewhere, it placed second. It is one ad in a campaign that we'll see more of later.

Die-cutting an insert, either to produce a "peep hole" or to create an insert of offbeat size and shape, is a surefire device to attract the reader's attention and arouse his interest in an ad. The resulting advertisement is decidedly different from all of the rest of the ads in the book, and the reader will devote some time to it for this reason alone.

Hewlett-Packard used a die cut with excellent effect in a striking four-page four-color insert ad illustrated nearby. It has a peek-a-boo die cut.

The ad ran in *Aviation Week, Electronics, Industrial Research,* and *Telemetry Journal.* According to Don Teer, publications advertising coordinator, the die cut is a device that was used strictly to pull the reader into the ad.

During the first month, bingo card response from *Electronics* was 154, from *Industrial Research,* 68, and from *Telemetry Journal,* 28. This is good response although very little more than a good one-page black-and-white ad will produce in the same publications.

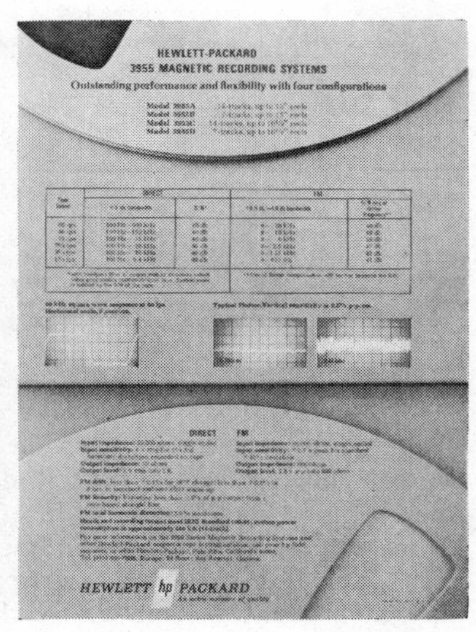

Front page of Hewlett-Packard insert with peek-a-boo die cut is shown at left; back page is at right. Center spread is illustrated on the following page.

There's no doubt the ad was read, however. In *Industrial Research,* the only book in which the advertisement ran in a studied issue, the first page of this insert was rated first when compared to all ads in the issue, and right at the top of the heap in Noted, as determined by Starch. The spread of the insert ranked second of all ads in the book, while the last page slipped to 28th in the book. Raw scored for Noted, Seen Associated, and Read Most are:

Page	Noted	Seen Associated	Read Most	Noted Rank
1	47	38	26	1
Spread	44	43	19	2
4	21	20	11	28

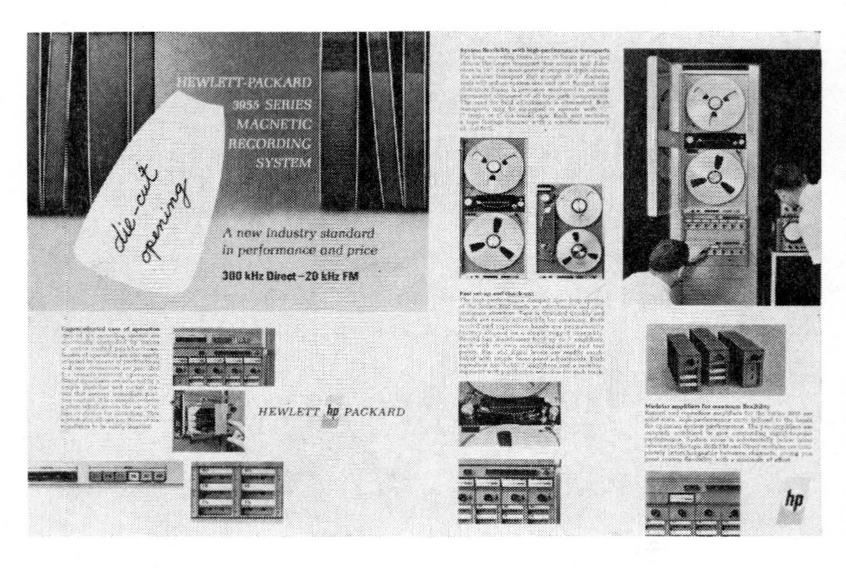

The spread of this information-packed advertisement is shown. Shape of the die cut is seen clearly here. Note the clean, orderly layout, white space, and how readable the excellent serif typeface is. Last page of the four-page insert suffered from low readership—low compared to the outstanding readership of the first page and the spread, that is—not low compared to other ads in the book. This may have resulted from the reader's assumption that he had all of the information he needed about Hewlett-Packard's 3955 Series Magnetic Recording Systems. Or it may have been due to the fact that the type size is relatively small and it is overprinted on rather a deep shade of blue-gray; legibility is much lower than for the spread, and it's also lower than for page one because the type was much larger there.

Hewlett-Packard got a bonus from the ad, for it printed an extra

8,000 inserts; 6,000 were mailed along with a covering letter to the manufacturer's European mailing list, and 2,000 were distributed to the field sales force for discretionary use. This is a fringe benefit that's often realized—and always should be—when inserts are produced.

The Product Tip-On

Consanguineous to the die-cut insert is the advertisement with a tip-on. One utilizes lack of a part of the space, the other makes use of an addition to the space, as it were, by attaching something designed to attract the eye of the reader.

This device is employed with telling effectiveness by AMAX Aluminum, a Division of American Metal Climax, Inc. in its striking advertisement from *Iron Age.*

Here!

Wreck this piece of
pre-finished aluminum.
Bend it double. Bend it back.
Waggle it...break it.
Really wreck it.
Now: check that finish.
COLORPLY®
The world's most workable pre-finished sheet.
Make your torture test as rough as your fabricating method. Colorply® can take it. You can punch it, stamp it, roll it, draw it. No peeling... no separation, now or later.
Every Colorply system is tailored to your fabrication method and product end use. Shouldn't you be using pre-finished aluminum (and get out of the paint business)?
See your local AMAX Aluminum representative, or write to
AMAX Aluminum/Mill Products, Inc.
A DIVISION OF AMERICAN METAL CLIMAX, INC.
1495 Columbia Ave. · Riverside, California 92507 · (714) 683-0140
1400 West Bristol Street · Elkhart, Indiana 46514 · (219) 264-2128
601 West Street · Bloomsburg, Pennsylvania 17815 · (717) 784-7481

The black rectangle in the ad at the right was fire-truck red in the two-color original. The sample of prefinished aluminum, approximately 1½ by 4 inches, was hard for readers of the publication to ignore.

A strip of AMAX Colorply prefinished sheet aluminum, painted fire-truck red, has been tipped onto this black-and-white ad. The small sample, approximately 1½ by 4 inches, is marked, apparently die-struck, with the name and trademark of the advertiser. It's as hard for the reader to ignore the red-painted aluminum standing out from the page like a bull in a china shop as it would be to overlook a bull in a china shop.

The sample of the product isn't attached for no reason, then conveniently ignored. It works hand-in-glove with the headline and illustration. Headline says:

> **Here!**
>
> **Wreck this piece of prefinished aluminum.**
>
> Bend it double. Bend it back. Waggle it . . . break it. Really wreck it.

The illustration shows a sheet of Colorply being painted, it's a complex and highly technical process. It lends credence to the copy which sells hard and with excellent believability. Preceding the bid for action is the snapper—"Shouldn't you be using prefinished aluminum (and get out of the paint business)?" Which is a mighty potent appeal.

The layout is clean and uncluttered, and designed to attract attention to the product and the challenge thrown down by the headline. This is a very hard-working ad and one that did an outstanding job for AMAX Aluminum.

The first time the ad ran it pulled 108 bingo-card inquiries, in addition to 48 letterhead inquiries. Tipping on the product really pulled readers into the ad and procured response!

Three dramatic four-color spreads run by Weyerhaeuser Packaging are taken from the company's "awareness" campaign which was produced by the advertiser's agency, Marsteller Inc. because research had shown that not very many management people in industry associated Weyerhaeuser with the packaging business, or as a source of folding cartons and shipping containers.

In fact, though, the company is a major supplier of such items and it wanted to be recognized as such.

During the year these arresting ads produced approximately 800 inquiries of unusually high quality. Interestingly, more than 90 percent of them were letterhead responses to the ads, according to Donald G. Maize, director of advertising and sales promotion. Such inquiries are usually regarded as of better quality than masses of bingo-card returns, of course.

The ads achieved their objective. Followup studies after the campagn had run for a year showed greatly increased awareness of Weyerhaeuser as a significant supplier of folding cartons and ship-

"In the sporting goods business we've got to deal with a lot of odd shapes. For golf clubs we need a package that protects for shipment and looks good at point of sale. It has to be easy to set up for display and easy for the customer to handle. Carrying it is a problem too. How about a handle and..."

The Weyerhaeuser Way in Packaging tells about our products, services and packaging experience. May we send you a copy? Write on your company letterhead to Weyerhaeuser Company, Packaging Group, 100 South Wacker, Chicago, Illinois 60606.

You've come to the right place

Weyerhaeuser Packaging

"We have plenty of flavors but so have our competitors. It's pretty hard to be different in the ice cream business. Sure, an attractive package helps, but what else can we do? How can we get a better package? You know, better flavor and texture retention, simple opening, easier serving. Maybe we need some research in the market and..."

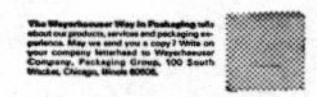

You've come to the right place

Weyerhaeuser Packaging

A trio of dramatic ads from a packaging firm's "awareness" campaign.

"Sure, the albums look great. That's not really the problem. Right now jackets are made up of at least four pieces. After they've been assembled, we have to insert the records by hand. Why not a one-piece jacket and a system to load it automatically. Then give us full-color both sides without added cost and we'll really..."

You've come to the right place

Weyerhaeuser Packaging

The Weyerhaeuser Way in Packaging tells about our products, services and packaging experience. May we send you a copy? Write on your company letterhead to Weyerhaeuser Company, Packaging Group, 100 South Wacker, Chicago, Illinois 60606.

ping containers, and that this awareness level had risen dramatically —and measurably.

Reason for showing three inserts from this one campaign is to emphasize once again that individual advertisements within a campaign *can* be treated as individuals. They do not have to be identical in layout and overall appearance, although they should bear a recognizable family resemblance to each other so that it is immediately obvious they are a part of a unified campaign.

The golf club ad has the illustration bleeding from the top and both sides, while the ice cream ad has its illustration bleeding from the bottom and both sides. The phonograph record ad's illustration bleeds from all four sides, and the copy is on a separate page entirely.

Note that in all three advertisements the type face is identical, the copy block offering a booklet to inquirers is identical, the campaign theme, *You've come to the right place* (logo) *Weyerhaeuser Packaging* is identical. Repetition of these elements also produces a cohesive effect to identify the ads as parts of an overall campaign.

Double-duty was done also by the eight-page four-color insert ad run by Lindberg Hevi-Duty in *Semiconductor Products and Solid State Technology* magazine.

This furnished insert is both an advertisement and a piece of product literature. It is packed with nuts-and-bolts information about the highly sophisticated little packages of complicated electronic gear, yet it is very promotional in tone.

Layout is clean and uncluttered and the illustrations are of a generous size, yet pages are clean and have attractive white space to open them up. Actually, the insert is a bit copy-heavy, so type was selected for easiest readership consistent with having a face that permitted "page stretching" to get more copy in.

Approximately 24,000 copies were shipped to the publisher of *Semiconductor Products and Solid State Technology* to be bound into the book, a couple of thousand were printed to take to a trade show, and a sizable supply was produced for use throughout the year the products were expected to be current in this volatile industry.

Cost of the literature was nominal, consisting as it did only of paper and additional press time; all costs of preparation were amortized in the space advertising budget.

Moreover, Lindberg Hevi-Duty used the same four-color separations to print one-page four-color inserts to be run singly throughout the year in *Semiconductor Products and Solid State Technology,* and in *Semiconductor Packaging & Production.* (Apparently it is

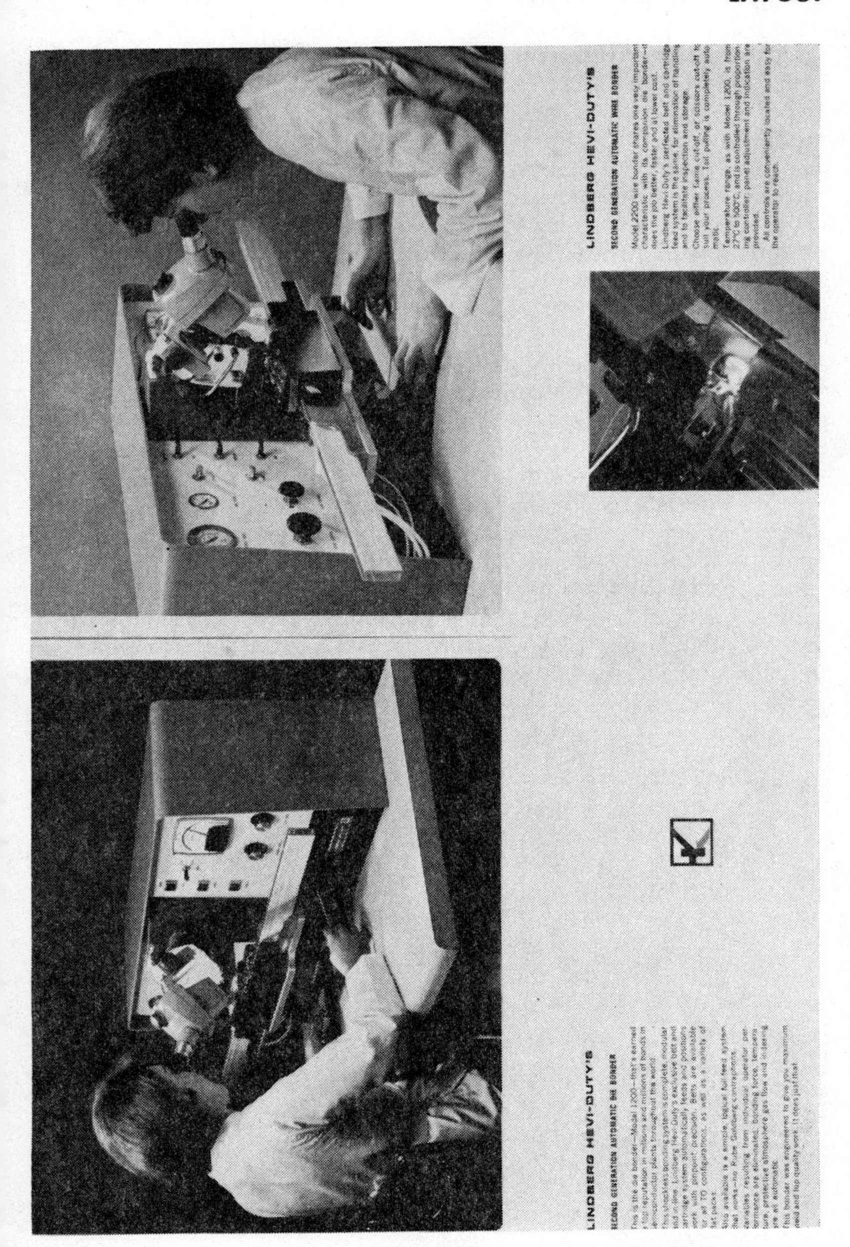

Four-color insert ads also provided inexpensive sales literature.

mandatory that all magazines for this market have names so long you'd almost think they're a put-on.)

These were exceptionally hard working production dollars that Lindberg Hevi-Duty invested; an eight-page four-color insert, six one-page four-color inserts, and product literature were produced for use throughout the year, all from the one set of separations.

Gatefold inserts, so called because of the way they fold, snag the reader's attention fast. The average reader is intrigued by a gatefold insert so that he almost cannot pass by without at least opening it up, perhaps to see if there just happens to be any $20 bills tipped into the inside fold. Just because he hasn't found any yet doesn't necessarily mean that someday he may not.

Pittsburgh Steel Company ran a dramatic eight-page four-color gatefold insert in *Iron Age*. This action-filled advertisement is illustrated nearby.

Note that this gatefold isn't radically undersize as some of this type of inserts are. Pittsburgh Steel Company realizes that its fine insert isn't any likelier to be missed than is a barracuda in the swimming pool, so feels no compulsion to be smaller than necessary to assure the reader's not passing over the insert. The insert measures exactly eight inches wide when it's completely folded; this means it comes within a quarter-inch of the edge of *Iron Age*, just enough to make sure the reader opens the first fold.

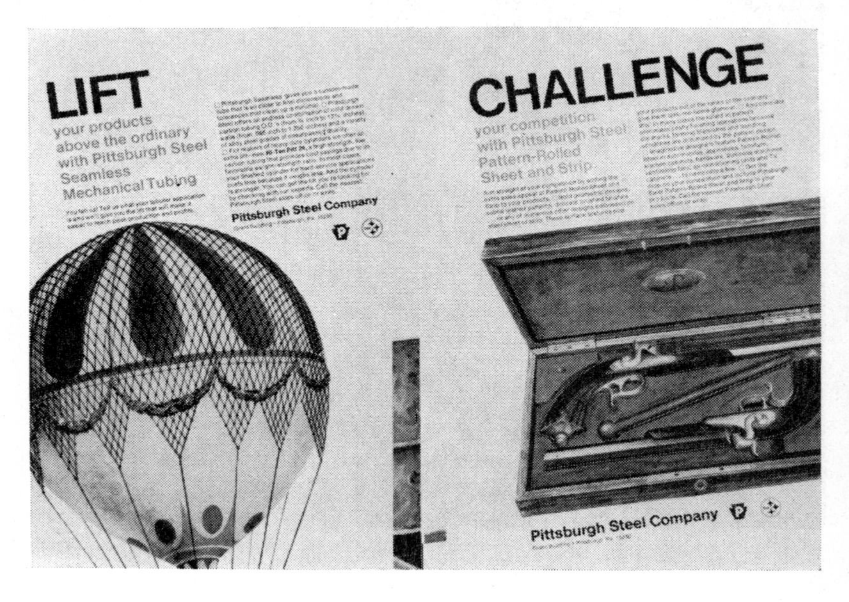

Front page, the first one the reader sees, is a wrap-up of the action-packed elements to come inside. Shown in four-color art—and good art it is, too—are a winning runner in a track meet; a cased pair of old cap-and-ball dueling pistols; a speedy sailboat; a gladiator; an Indian warrior with lance at the ready astride a fiery pony; and a ship's controls.

When the reader opens the insert it measures 16 inches—almost all of the way across the opened book. This shows, on the left hand page, four-color art of a circus-like balloon such as old-time stunt men used for parachute jumping and similar shenanigans at county fairs and carnivals 30 years ago, along with display type that reads:

LIFT

Your products
above the ordinary
with Pittsburgh Steel
Seamless
Mechanical Tubing

A copy block inside the display type subhead explains the user benefits of Pittsburgh Steel's mechanical tubing.

Then, on the facing page, which is a spread in *Iron Age*, appears an illustration of the dueling pistols, complete with a "P" monogram. Display type here is also filled with action.

CHALLENGE

Your competition
with Pittsburgh Steel
Pattern-Rolled
Sheet and Strip

Again, copy ties right in with the subhead and illustration and is benefit copy.

Open both sides of the gate and the powerful spread—four pages wide—is shown. It is impressive, and that is an understatement. Despite the huge size and the excellent four-color artwork and the large size of the display type, there is ample white space to give a feeling of openness and freedom from clatter and clutter.

Key words in the display type are tied in delightfully with the illustrations, showing how headlines and illustrations can work together.

TRIM, for example, is accompanied by an illustration of a sleek sailboat with its sportsman crew trimming the sail.

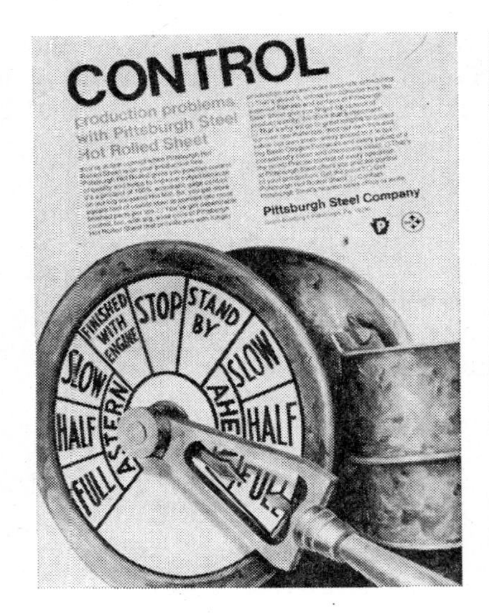

CONTROL is illustrated by a strong closeup of the control of an ocean-going ship.

COMBAT is shown by a gladiator, bloody sword at the ready, shield poised to be thrust into the line of an attacker's weapon.

SPEED has a winning runner breaking the tape at the finish line of the race, arms outstretched, cleats digging in.

ATTACK is symbolized by the expressive artwork illustration of the Indian warrior in war paint, astride a snorting black stallion, braided hair, feathered headdress and all.

The gatefold isn't the pot of gold at the foot of the rainbow, waiting to be snatched up by a bumbler who'll produce a gatefold that's done poorly, or, at best, only reasonably well, in anticipation of having everyone who receives the book read his ad. It doesn't work that way.

The gatefold *does* deliver readers out of proportion to the number of pages involved, but it isn't the panacea every overworked advertising manager has been looking for. Regardless of the built-in advantages of the gatefold—extra room to produce more impact; extra room to show more art to attract more readers; extra room to develop a product story fully; extra room to produce a layout that's clean and simple and attractive; extra room to create an image of the company as a leader—the gatefold still must do one thing.

It must be a good ad.

Pittsburgh Steel Company's ad is excellent in every respect. Visually it is exciting. Graphics are well done. And copy is well-written and persuasive. Pittsburgh Steel has a good formula here; if this is the kick-off ad in a year-long campaign of four-color inserts, it can do the company nothing but good when sales results are tallied up at the end of the year.

Using what little prognosticative prowess is available, the logical thing for Pittsburgh Steel Company to do is to reuse these separations, perhaps as the nucleus of an insert campaign that alternates one-pagers and gatefolds. There's much mileage to be realized from this art and the separations yet—in space advertising, as well as in product literature, direct mail, and what have you.

Insert Costs

Since you've decided to use four-color, the first thing you'll need is artwork in full color, or color photography. Both cost considerably more than black-and-white. Properly, though, this additional cost should be budgeted as a separate item and not arbitrarily tacked onto production costs for space advertising.

Assume for the sake of illustration you've decided to produce a one-page four-color insert ad for *Iron Age,* although you'd also like to consider cost of a spread at the same time before arriving at a decision as to what size space you'll use.

On the following page is an actual quotation from Kistler Graphics, Inc., one of Denver's finest offset printers whose specialty is unusually high-quality four-color work. The quotation covers printing of both a one-page and a spread insert.

Kistler's quotation was prepared by Wayne Jarvis, General Manager, with an assist from Kistler's in-house computer. It was prepared as carefully as if for an actual job. Costs in 1975, in the Rocky Mountain West, are both valid and competitive when you bear in mind that they cover top quality work from a printer with an enviable reputation for excellent work and on-time delivery.

Although circulation of *Iron Age* is only 106,000, when an insert is run the magazine requires a total of 114,000 inserts to take care of spoilage, ruined copies, poor backup, and so on.

The quotation includes printing this quantity on good-quality enamel stock of 100 lb. weight; this will assure good reproduction of the illustration and a paper weight that will make the book "break" to this insert. Incidentally, when planning a four-color insert always make sure to specify that it is to be printed with the *grain long*—direction of the grain of the paper, that is.

Kistler Graphics, Inc.
4000 Dahlia Street • Box 5467 • Denver, Colorado 80217 • (303) 399-2581

PRINTING PROPOSAL

Richard H. Stansfield
123 Any Street
Whatsitsname, Colorado 81001

Date December 27, 1974

JOB NAME	Magazine Insert for Iron Age Magazine
SPECIFICATIONS Quantity	114,000 of one - Item A or Item B as described below.
Trim Size	Item A - 8¼ X 11¼ or Item B -11¼ X 16½
No. of Pages	Item A - Single page printed one side only. Item B - Center spread - 2 pages printed as a run across.
Composition	Camera ready art will be furnished by customer. All copy will be in page position according to layout supplied for preparing this quotation.
Art Work and Illustrations	As above with 1 - 4" X 5" transparency to be color separated, press proofed and stripped to position after customer approval - see remarks.
Paper: Body	25 X 38 - 100# White Wedgewood Coated Offset Enamel Book.
Paper: Cover	None
Process: Body	To be carefully made ready and lithographed in four colors one side of press sheet only.
Process: Cover	None
Ink Color	All colors are high quality process inks and will be printed to match color OK proofs.
Finishing	Untrimmed press sheets are to be skid packed, wrapped with chipboard, steel banded and shipped via truck to Iron Age Magazine.
Remarks	Item A color separation - finished size to be 5" X 7" Item B color separation - finished size to be 8" X 10". Color separation to be a commercial match of transparency.

Quotation

Item A as above		Item B as above	
Paper	$1,382.	Paper	$2,526.
Separation & proofing	350.	Separation & proofing	375.
Plates & printing	1,250.	Plates & printing	1,796.
TOTAL	$2,982	TOTAL	$4,697.

• This proposal is subject to the Printing Trade Customs as reproduced on the reverse side of this page.

Wayne Jarvis
C.W. Jarvis, General Manager

All printing papers have a direction in which the fibers of the paper predominantly align while the sheet is being made. Sometimes insufficient thought is given to grain direction of the paper when it is ordered. A sheet of paper will fold easily along the grain, but will very likely crack when folded against the grain. This can ruin the appearance of spread inserts very easily.

When your printer orders paper for your job, chances are he'll buy grain long; it doesn't hurt to mention this to the printing salesman who handles your account, however.

In sheet-fed offset lithography, paper is usually ordered grain long. This is done routinely because (1) overall dimensional changes are greater *across* the grain or the short dimension of the sheet, and (2) an offset plate cannot be lengthened or shortened sideways to compensate for paper stretch or shrinkage. Slight changes in dimension can be compensated for in the direction of sheet travel by shifting the press packing from plate to blanket and vice versa.

An insert—or a brochure or catalog, for that matter—may not be satisfactory if the grain of the paper used is running in the wrong direction. Pages may belly and be difficult to handle and bind. The printed piece will have a much better feel if the grain is correct. Spread inserts, brochures, or sales literature printed with the grain wrong may have to be scored before folding; this is a separate operation at the printer's or at the bindery and it runs up costs needlessly.

How to Tell Grain Direction

You can use two simple methods of determining the direction of the grain:

1. *The tear test:* Paper torn *with* the grain will tear more easily and uniformly. Against the grain, the tear will likely be ragged and run off at a tangent.
2. *The fold test:* Paper folded *with* the grain gives a more uniformly smooth crease. Against the grain, the fold is rough and the paper tends to crack, giving a poor folding crease.

For this example, Kistler estimated paper at $1,382 for the 114,000 one-page inserts. This is both reasonable and highly competitive. Printers are in business to make money, just as the rest of us are. They customarily mark up paper approximately 17 percent to compensate them for the cost of handling, storing, inventorying, insurance, and so on.

You can save this 17 percent by buying your own paper and having the paper merchant, or the paper mill if quantity is large, ship it directly to your printer. Although this results in a slight loss for the printer, few of them object very strenuously because handling paper is not their business—printing is.

According to International Paper Company, a few tips when ordering paper are to anticipate your needs well in advance. This applies to standard sizes and weights stocked at the mill, as well as making orders in special sheet sizes or rolls.

The average paper merchant represents several mills (different paper manufacturers) and cannot be expected to carry the many thousands of stock items. He does, however, carry a representative stock of popular items. Many paper mills can ship stock sizes overnight to a market within 200-300 miles.

Try to combine items from the same mill so you'll get a lower price. Special sizes and weights will have to be made to order and therefore will usually take longer for delivery, depending on mill schedules and how your luck is running on that particular day.

One thing to remember: Printers have been known to disclaim responsibility for an unsatisfactory job printed on paper the customer bought. It's remarkably easy to fault the paper with all sorts of technical mumbo-jumbo and wayout technical terms the advertising manager will find impossible to cope with. This won't happen if you deal with a quality printing house, however; in printing, as in anything else, you get exactly what you pay for. It pays to buy the best.

The author has purchased many, many carloads of paper from International Paper Company and from Warren Paper Company and never once had anything except uniformly excellent results. Don't fall into the trap of using off-breed paper, and don't buy the cheapest grade of paper from the good houses, either. Your job will suffer. There's an old saying, and one that is indubitably true: Paper is the cheapest part of the job. Get the very best.

In the Kistler quotation we're looking at, separations and proofing are priced out at $350, based on giving the printer one 4x5 color transparency of truly fine quality. This cost is more than reasonable. It is possible, however, that the advertising manager might go to a first class engraving house and buy separations himself and save a few dollars in the process. The printer's price includes his markup, of course, although this is legitimate.

This charge is perfectly legitimate, although this is an area to look to if the budget is unusually tight and the dollars won't quite stretch far enough. The author bought separations directly from Jahn & Ollier, Chicago's finest color engraving house, for many years and never once encountered a problem. Lack of problems may well have been due to dealing with an engraver who has an outstanding reputation for top quality work, not only in the Midwest, but nationally. Avoid separations from the picture postcard houses and other sources of that ilk; you'll have nothing but headaches, one after another. In addition to work you're ashamed to show.

"Separation and proofing" in the Kistler quote, priced at $350, includes proofs (you'll get progressive proofs, "progs," from the engraver if you purchase the four-color separations yourself). Progressive proofs, pulled in the printing sequence of the four colors, will be supplied as well as a proof of the four colors combined.

The complete proof will be given to you at the same time the printer shows you the progs, as a rule; this is the time to make any changes, either in color in local areas, or of the color balance of the entire job. Afterwards it's either well-nigh impossible or else changes come so dear you'll soon discard the thought.

"Plates and printing" includes printing the insert, of course, trimming to size (if the publication so desires), packaging for shipping, and wrapping, banding and skidding if required. Printers usually ship FOB their plant. They will, however, prepay the freight (usually via truck unless you're in a bind for time and you're willing to pay a premium to ship via Flying Tigers or Emery Air Freight, the two most reliable air carriers the author has found). Prepaid shipping costs will be invoiced on the printing invoice.

Total price for printing the four-color insert, according to Kistler's quotation, is $2,982. Over and above this is the shipping cost to get the insert to the publication(s).

Extras—Always a Few Extras

There's the space cost, too, of course, plus a couple of extra ones that don't amount to too much, but nonetheless add up to a tidy little sum in the course of a year.

First is backup—printing somebody else's ad on the back of your insert; this is done either by the publications' printers, or in their captive shops. *Iron Age,* for example, charges $350 to backup a one-page insert. This $350 is *not* charged to the advertiser whose ad is printed on the back of your insert, but to *you.* After all, your insert caused the printer to have to handle this separate production problem, not the other advertiser's wanting to run an ad in the book. It's generally conceded that this is not a money-making operation for the publisher, but is handled on an accommodation basis to those advertisers whose business is valued.

In addition to backup, there's another little problem that arises: The publisher now has a massive stack of inserts with your fine four-color ad on one side, and another advertiser's ad—probably a black-and-white one—on the other side. But the inserts are stacked on skids on the floor of a print shop. They're not spreading your message of good cheer about your product far and wide. There remains the small task of getting the inserts into the magazine.

Some publications demand a flap along the side of the insert; this actually is paper left over from cutting it oversize in one direction. The flap is usually about one inch, or a bit more, to permit stitching or stapling the insert when the book is assembled. Most books, though, trim the inserts to the exact size of the magazine, then tip them in. This is the term applied to a glueing operation that puts a narrow strip of glue along the entire length of the insert, and then putting it in place in the book. This is an operation that has to be done very precisely so that the advertisement on the back of yours won't be interfered with, nor will it interefere with the page to which it is tipped. Most publications charge from $250 to $350 to tip in an insert. Labor cost in that area, and even at that specific time, and the publisher's desire to encourage or discourage inserts, can influence the price you pay.

Let's see what this looks like for total cost of getting a one-page four-color insert into the hands of 106,000 readers of *Iron Age.*

Printing, complete	$2,982
Shipping (estimated)	275
Backup	350
Tip in (estimated)	250
Space	2,195
	$6,052

This is considerably above *Iron Age's* R.O.P. four-color price for one page—$2,195 for space and $675 for four-color, for a total of $2,870. In fact, it's a whopping $3,182 more, which is almost as much as the average industrial advertising manager's monthly salary.

So how do you justify going the insert route in the face of the determined drive that the leading business publications are putting on to get more four-color R.O.P. advertisements?

First of all, you own the four-color separations—or you have access to them through your printer if he purchased them for your job. (Separations are the printer's property if he purchased them, even if they are for your job and your company picked up the tab for them; this is much like the photographer retaining title to all negatives shot for you).

Having separations or having them available means you can use them for other jobs. You can bump them up or down in size at least 15 to 20 percent and produce four-color illustrations for direct mail, other inserts, booklets, the annual report, or what have you—all without having to make the investment of another red cent.

When you have existing separations, almost a third of the price of a four-color printing job won't be incurred; in the case of a small run, say of 5,000 to 10,000 copies of a piece of literature, cost of paper is insignificant, so all you really spend extra money on is the additional press time. There's no way around this, but it's not prohibitive.

There's this little trick to consider, too, which the author has used for many years at a tremendous saving in money and to achieve a much greater impact with miscellaneous printed material.

When you're having inserts printed, have the printer run the color part of your sales literature "in blank." This means you don't have the final black type printing done, just the four-color portion. A two-page, four-page, or six-page (fold out) piece of literature will then be ready for the printer to print the black-and-white text, or two-color text, and drop in black-and-white halftones or duotones. This can be done at any time in the future when you've written and laid out the piece.

This gives you four-color sales literature for just a whisker more than the price of the extra colors you print later on, except for the press time required to run a few thousand extra impressions. You'll find that four-color sales literature, which you've undoubtedly yearned for but couldn't afford, is well within the budget since the expensive preparation (prep) cost doesn't have to be incurred.

This is making one dollar do the work of three.

Three, because there are other residual benefits you always realize from going the four-color insert route.

You can use this same trick with the same savings to produce four-color direct mail pieces that the budget couldn't possibly afford otherwise.

And you can use the fact that you're going to be on the press with a four-color run as leverage to get another manufacturer to use your product's picture in *his* ad. Here's how this works.

The Good Old Tie-In

Many complex mechanical items manufactured today are merely assembled by the end manufacturer. They include, among many others, electric motors, diesel engines, transmissions, axles, oil filters, window glass, cutting blades, gears, controls, potentiometers, and what have you that are manufactured by other companies in entirely different markets and industries than those to which your company sells.

Some years ago when the author was with the old Diamond T

Motor Truck Company, the firm brought out a new Tilt-cab diesel tractor. A four-color insert ad was being prepared to place in the fleet publications. In addition, a four-color direct mail piece and a six-page, four-color piece of sales literature were going to be run while the insert was on the press. These two pieces were thus acquired at a giveaway price.

About this time, though, the thought occurred—why not have somebody else get in on the act, get a bargain for himself, and get Diamond T some additional exposure?

A few phone calls to the advertising managers of manufacturers of components showed that Reynolds Metals, maker of the aluminum used to fabricate the truck's cab, was not only receptive to the idea, but was anxious to tie in with Diamond T's introduction of a revolutionary new model. Accordingly, Reynolds had four-color inserts run also—at nominal cost, and at Reynolds' expense, of course.

So that was sales literature, a mailer, and a tie-in ad that Reynolds paid for, all for the price of one set of separations and a little extra press time. These were indeed hard-working production dollars.

Had Diamond T used publication-printed R.O.P. four-color, these residual benefits wouldn't have been realized.

Incidentally, when you're having your inserts printed, be sure to have the bingo card number (Reader Service Card, that is) printed on the bottom of the insert when it's on the press. This requires only a line of type in the black plate at a cost of just pennies for the type. Do this and you don't have to pay the publication to do it for you.

Make arrangements ahead of time and the publications used regularly will be happy to assign your company a permanent bingo card number that won't vary from issue to issue. This means you can gang-print inserts, saving additional money, without having to worry about changes in bingo card numbers.

Something else to remember is change of addresses. Frequently when all advertising and printing is handled by a central advertising department in company headquarters, the company wants inquiries fed to technical people or marketing people in outlying plants, sometimes in other states. This poses no problems whatsoever.

All that's required is a simple change of address in the black plate of the insert, and instruct the publications to forward bingo-card inquiries to that location. No fuss, no expense.

Some advertisers habitually print and furnish one-color and two-color inserts to the trade press. When printing is done in just one color, it's usually done on colored stock.

This is a terrifically costly way to prepare an advertisement, however, and is certainly not recommended—unless there is an exceptionally good reason, such as putting an abrasive on the insert as Norton did. Few advertisers have this natural a thing going for them, though, and those who don't are pouring money down the drain with one- and two-color inserts. They would be far ahead of the game if they'd take that production money and invest it in either R.O.P. four-color, or else in additional space.

Just about the only exception to this is when the advertiser is printing a piece of literature for a trade show or some such special purpose—usually a "full line" catalog in abbreviated or condensed form. This just happens to be a natural for an insert because it exactly meets a communications objective. Then by all means make the overrun and insert it in proper media.

Among the arguments advanced by the anti-insert bigots is the fact that having to print an insert deprives an advertiser of scheduling flexibility. This is true to a certain extent, at least enough to advance it as an argument with a perfectly straight face. However, the advertising manager who plans ahead farther than the end of his nose doesn't encounter any problems in this area.

Plan for the Unexpected

Plan insertions, schedule them, and then adhere to the schedule unless something entirely unforeseen occurs; plan for the unexpected at that time, not ahead of time. When your schedule is firmed up for the year—or at least for six months ahead of time—you can just as easily as not print several inserts at one time. Ganging them in a press run reduces printing costs very appreciably.

Furthermore, it's more than likely that you'll want to repeat one or all of the advertisements scheduled in a fiscal year, so print the required double dose of each insert at one time, saving additional money. Going back on the press is always an expensive proposition; it's much less costly to keep it running for a few hours in the first place.

Bliss & Laughlin, one of whose inserts was shown, produced a total of five inserts at the same time. Print run was massive for industrial advertising—a total of 2,155,000 four-color inserts were printed on *both* sides. Four of the die-cut inserts are on page 1004.

Gang-run (printed at the same time), the total production cost including art, layout, type, keyline, and printing, came to only $34,000. This figures out to a little less than $7,000 per insert, and there were 431,000 of each printed two sides.

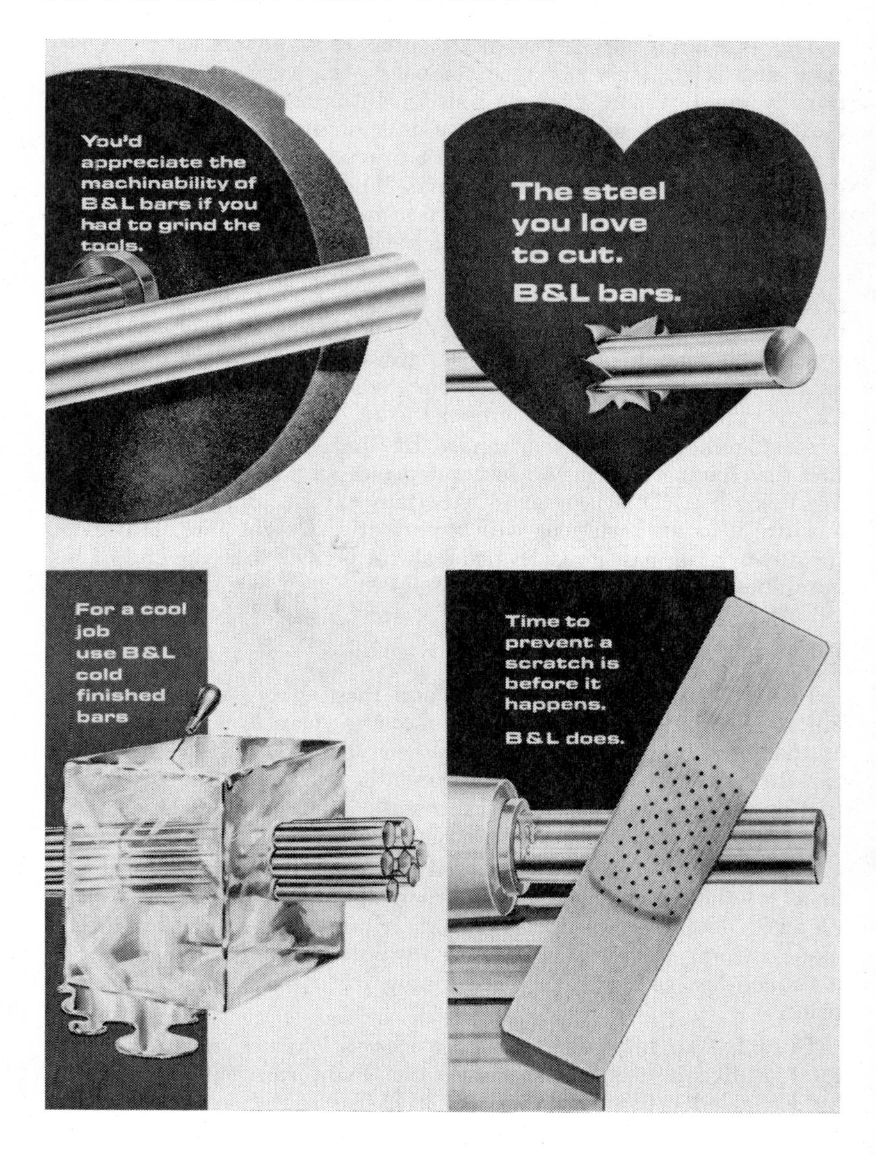

Die-cutting is equivalent to another time through the press as far as cost is concerned. This is reasonable, considering the program was set for months ahead. All that's required is shipping to the books on time and having the agency send out insertion orders. That's where agency income comes from, so there's never a need to worry about insertion orders getting issued.

Lack of flexibility is not really a valid argument if the program has been planned well ahead of time. Crises are invariably expensive and pushing the panic button and crowding a printer just to get a job out under a pressing deadline is no way to run an advertising program unless you have so much extra money in the budget you just can't figure out a way to get rid of it.

Finally, and nobody disputes this, when you produce and furnish four-color inserts to the publications you use, you do so with the absolute certainty that you're putting in the books the finest possible four-color printing that can be bought. This assumes, of course, that you or your agency ride herd on the job, and that you haven't made the mistake of giving it to the low bidder in an effort to save an inconsequential handful of dollars.

Finest possible quality in itself says something about your company and its products. There's simply no getting around the truth of the old adage that when you present a quality product in a quality manner, you've made a quality impression on the reader. It implies that everything about the company and its products are first class, all the way. Top quality four-color printing creates an image of success and prosperity and solidity all out of proportion to its cost.

The Agency Markup

One last thing, and this is controversial to say the least. When your agency produces four-color inserts for you, it naturally marks up the printing, separations, type, keyline and what have you that's involved in the job to the tune of 17.65 percent. This is proper and it compensates the agency for the time and effort and expense involved in supervising your work.

A few agencies habitually gouge their clients in this area and mark up incoming invoices to the agency a full 40 percent—or even more. Some have been known to go the dummy invoice route when padding bills to clients. Two ways to avoid being clipped like this is to have a good idea what things cost, and to deal with an honest agency. Honest ones are in the overwhelming majority.

However, and your agency won't particularly appreciate this, but it will nonetheless purchase space and have inserted in the publications the inserts that you—the client—had printed and produced. You can save 17.65 percent here if your agency relationship is less than it should be and you don't really think it can be ameliorated to any great extent, or if you have made this agreement with the agency beforehand strictly due to budget limitations. Both situations exist, and inserts are advertiser-produced and agency-placed as a common practice, usually for one of the two reasons above.

One place you could run into trouble in printing your own inserts is in the variation of sizes that different publishers require for different magazines. Careful tabulation of the finished sizes and producing to a common-denominator size—after discussing this matter thoroughly with your printer—eliminates this bugaboo. It's mostly clerical detail to start with, although size differential can wreck an insert program unless it's taken into account early in the program. Your printer can trim to proper size, even leaving flaps on some inserts if necessary, and ship the correct sizes to the proper publications. If he goofs, it's his responsibility to get reshipments made. Be sure to have this understanding in writing before undertaking an insert program.

The furnished insert is the one best way to go first class, and the best method ever devised to attract the most possible readership to an advertisement. If you can justify advertising to your management, you can certainly justify use of four-color inserts.

Spreads

The larger the advertisement, the more readers it attracts.

Spreads—ads of two pages, facing each other—invariably attract much more readership than does a one-page ad. They cost a bit more, too. Twice as much, in fact.

Therefore, it's only logical to assume that if you invest twice as much in space, you're entitled to receive twice as much readership—right? But it doesn't work out that way.

Daniel Starch has found that readership for black-and-white ads averaged 19.8 percent in certain publications, whereas the typical spread advertisement received only 31.5 percent; this is a far cry from twice the readership of the one-page ad, since that would be 39.6 percent.

And when it comes to four-color ads, Starch found that typical one-page advertisements in books being studied received 35.2 percent readership, whereas four-color spreads received but 53.2 percent. Doubling of the one-page ad readership would have resulted in a score of 70.4 percent.

What's more, McGraw-Hill has found in 5,400 personal interviews with readers of 14 of this company's publications that the average readership for 2,936 one-page advertisements is 16.7 percent, while the readership for 212 spread ads is 22.9 percent. Doubling the one-page readership rating would have resulted in readership of 33.4 percent. The spreads, however, received only 73 percent higher readership.

There's this to consider, though: McGraw-Hill research also pointed out that both pages of spread advertisements—when considered as individual pages—received more readership than did one-page ads. The left hand page of spreads checked by this study received 24.4 percent readership, while the right hand page received an even 24 percent readership. None of the spreads studied had a layout wherein one full page was given over to the illustration with the copy occupying the other page.

On a readers-per-dollar basis, spreads certainly are not the best buy, although many valid reasons exist to justify running spread advertisements. The first and usually considered the most important is dominance. Dominance impresses the reader, it attracts him, it stops him, it gives you a jump on your competition and enables you to put in a stronger pitch for your advertising program with your management and your sales force.

In almost every major business publication, the *average* ad is a one-page ad. But who wants to be average? Average implies mediocrity. You'd be incensed indeed if somebody said that you are an average advertising manager, or an average account executive, or that you work for an average company, your product is average, or you have average intelligence.

So why tie yourself down to an advertisement that, at best, can be only average?

Visually, the spread is the perfect unit of advertising space because it's the *whole* that the eye sees. When your advertisement occupies the whole, you're not competing for the reader's attention with the fellow across the gutter. You have the reader's entire attention.

As a matter of fact, the idea of the visual whole is so simple that few advertising men think of it in this way. They don't realize that anything less than a spread is actually fractional space. Usually we think of one-thirds, one-halves, two-thirds and so on as fractionals, but not full pages. However, unless we're talking about the back cover position, a single page is only one-half of the whole that the eye sees.

Another thing about spreads: You get the chance to tell your story without crowding. You have room to move around. The layout man has the opportunity to get in those strong heads and large illustrations *plus* a lot of copy. And he does so without jamming things together so tightly that only you and the president of the company are willing to read the ad—if he'll struggle through it.

Furthermore, spreads exert a strong psychological effect on the reader. The spread looks important. It compels attention. It's difficult to pass by. The spread creates a feeling of bigness and progressiveness and it automatically makes the advertiser appear to have more stature. Instinctively the reader feels that this is a company that occupies an unusually strong position in its industry.

Then, too, there's something a lot of advertising men tend to underestimate, and that's the feeling of pride that outstanding advertising generates throughout the entire company, all the way from the board chairman down. Salesmen especially can be motivated to produce more because the company's advertising enthuses them, makes them downright proud of the company for which they work.

Let's look now at how space is usually divided in spreads. Illustrated here are eight spread "layouts" to show the most common divisions of space. The illustration, of course, is the dark area that's been doodled in with artist's chalk. Also obvious is that the author will never become an art director—at least as far as producing finished art or comp layouts is concerned.

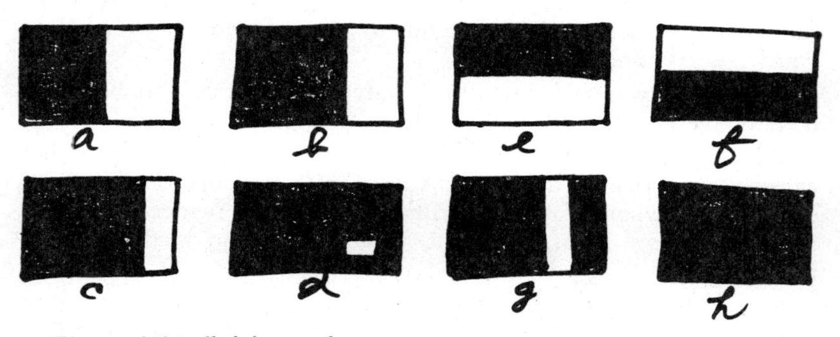

These eight divisions of space are:

a. One page devoted to illustration, the other to copy.

b. One and one-third pages devoted to illustration, the copy in the balance of the space.

c. One and two-thirds pages devoted to illustration, copy in one column.

d. Illustration is full bleed and covers all of the two pages; copy is set in a panel against the page's white background.

e. Illustration occupies the top half of both pages, copy is on the bottom portion.

f. Illustration occupies bottom half of both pages, leaving the top for copy.

g. Illustration is full bleed on both pages except for a panel the depth of the page, usually one column wide, in which copy is printed.

h. Illustration is full bleed on both pages; copy is overprinted, usually in a light area of the illustration.

Before looking at some actual spread advertisements, let's look at an ad that's *almost* a spread, but not quite.

This is the ubiquitous minispread, otherwise known as the one and one-third page format, here illustrated by the fine two-color (red and black) advertisement run by Marbon Chemicals, a division of Borg-Warner Corporation. The ad appeared in *Plastics Design & Processing* magazine.

Many advertisers find this one and one-third page technique particularly useful because it enables them to list a large number of dealers, jobbers, factory branches, district offices, or similar tabular information. This can be done without cluttering up the ad and making it junky looking, and with no sacrifice in space used for

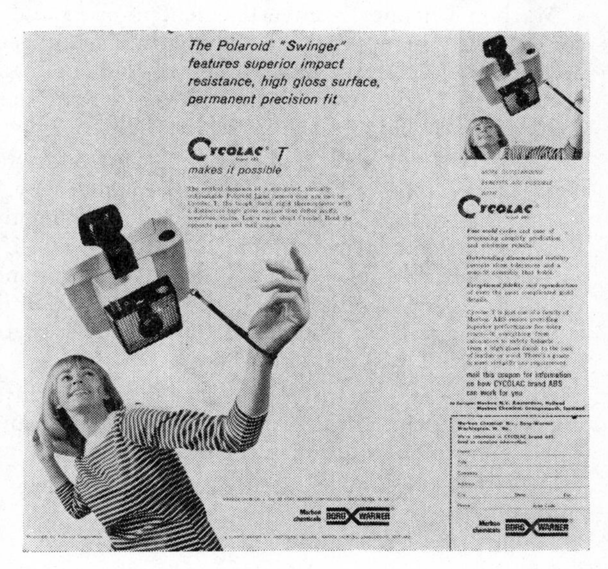

A "minispread," or one and one-third pages. This allows an advertiser to dominate a spread without paying for the space. A list of dealers or a coupon can be used without cluttering a nice clean layout.

illustration or copy. Something like having your cake and eating it, too.

Marbon Chemical's rationale for use of one and one-third pages is quite basic. The company felt this would give it the opportunity of dominating a spread without the expense of purchasing it. This is because most magazines have a policy of running editorial between ads, if possible. Furthermore, having the extra one-third page permits Marbon Chemical to expand and vary its product message, as well as coupon the ad to stimulate inquiries.

Interestingly, when this campaign first started, studies received by the advertiser indicated that the reader thought Marbon Chemical had purchased both pages!

According to the advertiser, it has been a little bit difficult to determine whether or not this page and one-third technique has generated more inquiries than would be received from the customary one-page ad. Marbon Chemical used the same technique the previous year, and has seen a steady increase in the number of inquiries that have been received. It is believed this is an indication of the advantages of continuity for any program, whether it is fractional page, single page, or multipage campaigns.

Incidentally, all of Marbon Chemical's inquiries are followed up immediately by *telephone* in an effort to qualify them for personal calls by the company's salesmen.

Marbon Chemical's advertisement is open and inviting and very consumerish in appearance. The large amount of white space is inviting and attractive and, combined with the swinging "Swinger," produces a feeling of motion and vigor. And the ad is easily read due to use of a highly legible serif typeface. That always helps.

Business Week magazine carried B. F. Goodrich Company's excellent R.O.P. four-color spread illustrated nearby. Space division is five-sixths for the illustration, which is a dramatic photograph of a B. F. Goodrich conveyor atop Oroville Dam (California), the largest earthfill dam in the world; this leaves one column for copy on the far right. It's a wonder this dam was not built in Texas, considering it is the biggest anywhere and overshadows anything anybody else has. You can't win them all, though.

Progress report from B. F. Goodrich overprinted in italics in the upper left corner of the left hand page helps assure high readership. There's an implied promise of something newsy and interesting and informative about it, and this is the first page the reader's eye stops on.

Having the illustration carry over onto the right hand page is

another device to boost readership. The reader's eye automatically looks at the entire illustration, and when it does it's attracted to the white space in the upper right, above the column of copy; it then drops into the copy.

The headline is a delightful light touch, for it reads:

> **We're part of
> the biggest dam
> project California's
> ever seen**

Copy is replete with a case history full of facts and figures and user benefits. It really does right by B. F. Goodrich.

This layout is clean as a whistle and is an excellent example of how simplicity can contribute to an unusually effective spread advertisement and a great campaign.

Combustion Engineering's magnificent four-color R.O.P. spread ad from *Business Week* is a real stopper. The cool green of the trees, the blue of the rushing mountain stream, the blue sky with a puffy white cloud, and, in the distance, the faintly-purple, snow-covered peaks all add up to a scene so restful and tranquil that it's a rare executive indeed who can ignore this beautiful spread.

The headline, *Air, land or water, CE helps keep it clean,* meshes wonderfully with the illustration, for it shows a lovely scene that's

clean and unspoiled by beer cans and candy wrappers strewn all over the landscape by tourists in undershirts and too-tight shorts.

Again, one-third of the right hand page is reserved for a column of copy, but in this instance Combustion Engineering used a device that's almost guaranteed to keep the reader's eye from straying. The panel with the copy is set in from the edge of the page, permitting the arresting illustration to bleed on all four sides of the pages.

Everything's right about this ad: Terrific illustration, fine layout, four-color, headline tied in with the illustration, serif typeface, good copy. This is money invested to produce a return.

Certainly one of the most impressive campaigns to run for some time is that of Ingersoll Milling Machine Company. A typical ad from a metalworking magazine is illustrated.

This is a highly imaginative illustration and a daring layout. Use of this much white space in an industrial advertisement is almost unheard of. This technique is straight from the land of the consumer and his mass circulation books. Illustration and the stacked, two-part headline fit together as if they were made for each other, as the saying has it—and they were.

There's absolutely no question about what the reader did when he turned the page to this great spread, none whatsoever. He stopped, maybe did a double take, then he read.

That he read is fully verified by the independent readership scores; Ingersoll Milling Machine Company's ads have consistently rated

far above average—in the top 10 percent of all ads in the book, issue after issue after issue.

When you buy EDM from us,
you'd better get used to the
Ingersoll Man.
He'll be right on your heels.
INGERSOLL

What's more, they have produced a sizable volume of inquiries, good ones; the company traces more than 200 inquiries to this campaign. This is considered rather remarkable because the ads are not inquiry ads *per se,* and the product they're advertising is strictly a big-ticket item with a price tag of hundreds of thousands of dollars.

In addition, the manufacturer's salesmen are enthusiastic about the campaign because their customers and prospects mention it to them. That's a sure-fire way of telling whether or not the message is getting across.

More important, though, is that Ingersoll's campaign has scared one major competitor enough so that it changed the direction and format of its advertising campaign—apparently to counteract the interest and excitement generated by Ingersoll's advertising. This is a real accomplishment!

Some advertising men might feel this is too expensive a way to advertise—using two pages of space when one actually would have been able to handle the job. True, it could have. But Ingersoll would never have made the impact the way that this ad achieves, and never would have aroused as much excitement and caused as much talk. And probably Ingersoll wouldn't have sold as many milling machines, either, as far as that's concerned.

It isn't just every advertising manager who has enough courage in his convictions to present a campaign like this to his management. The ones who do, though, are advertising managers who influence sales. Which is what advertising is for, no?

Final spread we'll look at is a three-page, R.O.P. four-color spread. No, it's a three-page fold-out. No, a three-page . . .

Well, one thing is sure: Fuller Transmission Division, a division of Eaton Yale & Towne, Inc., ran this fine ad in *Commercial Car Journal.*

The ad occupied the second cover (inside the front cover of the book), plus an extra page that was added to make the cover a fold-out, in addition to the page on the other side of the foldout.

For such extravaganzas as this, arrangements with the publisher must be made well in advance, of course, when the campaign is in the planning stage. Seldom can an advertiser ask for and get a second, third, or fourth cover just because he happens to want it; these preferred positions are sold and there's usually a waiting list of those who want them.

To produce the magazine with extra pages, *Commercial Car Journal* had to cut and print as one unit the (1) front cover, (2) Fuller's ad which occupies an extra page, (3) the name of the book on the spine, and (4) the back cover and inside (third) back cover. This required planning in the production department to coordinate everything and prevent a *STOP THE PRESS* situation.

Fuller received extremely high visibility and it dominates the entire front of the magazine. Almost every reader will notice the inside front cover—which, in this case, is the cute little wooden-shoed Dutch girl in light blue long-Johns with her finger in the crack in the dike.

Fuller's name is given right off because it's what's up front that counts, then a take-off on the illustration, then the name of the customer. In this instance it's a well known common carrier domiciled in Holland, Michigan.

Layout of the spread is clean and uncluttered; left hand page contains just six elements, and there's lots of nice, clean looking white space to attract the reader's eye. The illustration occupies the entire right hand page, and shows a Holland Motor Express Fuller-transmission-equipped rig with a typical Dutch windmill in the background.

Three four-color pages are used here, but the heavy-duty truck transmission business is highly competitive. Clark Equipment Company and Dana Corporation don't exactly remain silent about the merits of the transmissions they manufacture, so Fuller needs to make a splash with its advertising to make a lasting impression on the reader.

This three-page spread ad is exceptionally well done, and the campaign enjoys extremely high readership. It's doing a job.

Try Good Layout (Almost) Above All Else

While the reader's eye goes to the illustration first of all, it's the layout that he actually sees when all is said and done. This is so even though he doesn't realize there is such a thing as a layout.

Try in every single advertisement for cleanliness, simplicity, freedom from clatter and clutter, and for a layout that lets the advertisement achieve the objective established for it. It isn't always the easiest thing in the world, but it can be done if enough effort and thought are invested.

There's no need to launch a lengthy dissertation on things you should do; they've been covered before this. Bear one thing in mind, though, that there is no established formula, no set rules, no hidebound do-it-this-way-or-else dictums laid down by anybody.

Layout exists only to produce an effective ad.

If it does that, there's no reason to criticize it because it happens to have six elements instead of five, or because one person is shown more than once, or what have you.

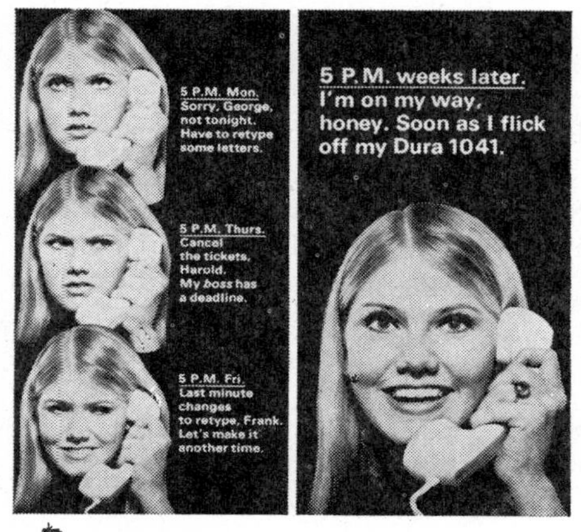

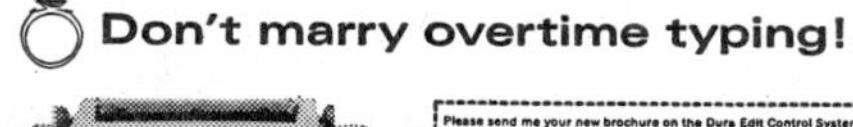

In advertising as in other arts, it's OK to break the rules when you know what the rules are. In this layout containing 16 elements, a chaos of clutter could have resulted. But so effectively was the theme developed that it's a good ad in spite of the rules.

Dura Business Machines, Division of Walter Kidde & Company, Inc., proved this very thoroughly with its strong black-and-white ad from *Business Week*. If you count individual elements, you end up with an amazing 16, 11 more than the classic number.

This should, by rights, produce the most cluttered up mess it's possible to create. But Dura's ad, while it breaks all of the rules of layout, is nonetheless very readable and highly effective.

It benefits from repetition of the overworked blonde secretary whose love life suddently becomes so smooth she receives a huge diamond—all because a Dura 1041 electric typing system with Edit Control made her work life so much smoother.

Don't hesitate to innovate.

Be sure at the same time to temper creativity with taste, an inclination to be flamboyant with discretion, and the desire to be completely different with a large dash of prudence.

Let layout work for you, not against you.

Chapter 12

CREATION

A CHAPTER in this book titled "creativity" had been promised to Dartnell, but at the last minute the author's stomach staged a one-stomach revolt and proved unable to tolerate this particularly vulgar bastardization of the English language—in display type heading a chapter, at least.

To the advertising man who unabashedly loves his chosen field, words are wonderful things, things to be fondled, arranged and re-arranged, admired and treated with tender, loving care. Both written and spoken English is in a constant state of flux, of course, and that's as it should be if the tongue is to reflect sweeping changes in our culture.

Deliberate mongrelization of the tongue is too much to tolerate, though, especially when words are apparently coined in desperation due to an inability to express one's self. When advertising men who are supposed to be articulate stoop this low it is truly deplorable. It is consanguineous to engineers' tagging inoffensive new products with nonword nonsense names, although a major difference exists: Engineers don't know any better, advertising men do.

"Creativity" is a cliché that's much admired and vastly over-worked. It's bandied about hither and yon on the slightest pretext, or, as often as not, with no pretext whatsoever. It is universally regarded as an excellent topic to kick around while wearing an erudite expression and a faintly supercilious air.

"Creativity" is lovingly discussed and examples are held up for all to admire throughout ad-dom, for all the world as if this non-word referred to a very special charisma bestowed from on high upon a fortunate few, thus enabling these favored ones to achieve upon a level we peasants can never even aspire to.

In the frenetic world of consumer advertising where lofty thoughts about cake mixes and hair spray and dog food and under-arm deodorants are regarded as Pronouncements, a premium is placed on the offbeat and the kooky.

Much of the advertising that results from such thinking is superficially intriguing until upon closer examination it becomes painfully apparent that the wild "mod" layouts and jumble of typefaces and psychedelic colors and way-out copy with "high camp" puns and "in" slang have next to nothing to do with the product, they don't *say* anything, and they are totally unrelated to the advertiser's marketing objectives.

Then dawns the realization that such advertising actually is a massive put-on. It is intended to communicate only to bearded, beaded flower-wearers, those who affect bearskin vests and World War I army blouses, and other real cool cats in competitive agencies. This "advertising" was created by spoiled adolescents to achieve *their* primary objective—having fun and games and impressing the absolute living hell out of their contemporaries. And, to a somewhat lesser extent, to build up a sample book to prove to one and all how bright and precocious and terribly, terribly clever they are. They used the client's money to show themselves off, of course.

Strictly from Squaresville, man, is the grim thought of producing advertising designed to exert a positive influence on sales (how crass and commercial can you get?), or stooping to cranking out advertising that talks intelligently in terms of their own self interest to mature adults in Keokuk, Wichita and Pueblo who are neither turned on nor dropped out.

They Forgot the Name of the Game

The creativity cult has forgotten completely, conveniently ignored, or never knew that the name of the game is selling more of the product at a profit and reducing the cost of selling.

Perhaps the preceding has been an exercise in digression. At the present time it's the height of good taste and the in thing to do to follow the thundering herd of industrial advertising men and pan most consumer advertising—and in the very next breath shout from the roof tops that industrial advertising is not phony like *that,* that industrial advertising gives the reader facts and figures and information that he needs about the product.

Industrial advertising doesn't wear a hat to these ostrich-like ad men whose heads are buried in sand up to their armpits—it wears a halo. And industrial advertising men never go swimming—they walk on water like senators who run off of bridges.

Before getting any farther into this, though, let's get onto firm ground with solid rules that don't have to be made up as we go along.

First of all, let's see just what "creativity" is. Until the most recent (and most controversial) edition of Webster, there was no such word as "creativity." There is another word, though, that's both accurate and descriptive when it's applied to the process of producing a campaign or an individual advertisement out of nothing except thoughts and experience and, perhaps, hunches; it applies, too, to the analytical process by which knotty marketing problems are solved and programs developed, The word is "creation."

Webster says that *creation* is: "(1) Act of creating, or fact of being created, specifically the act of causing to exist, or fact of being brought into existence . . . and (2) Act of constituting or investing with a new character, title, or the like (3) The presentation of a new conception in an artistic embodiment (4) Something which is created."

Definitions (1) and (3) obviously apply, except when we're talking about the end product itself, the campaign or advertisement—or, for that matter, a layout, an illustration, a piece of copy, or a marketing plan.

Furthermore, Webster says that one definition of *create* is: "To produce as a work of thought or imagination, as a work of art." And *creative* means: "Having the power or quality of creating." This last, it would seem, is close to the intended meaning of what we still insist is a nonword, "creativity."

Far too many practitioners of industrial advertising are perfectly content to remain in peace and quiet with their heads buried in sand, neither knowing nor questioning whether their output and that of their agencies is good, bad, or indifferent. They are satisfied with drifting aimlessly without a communications plan—and very probably without a written marketing plan, as a rule—and continue to produce, approve, place, and pay for advertising that hasn't a chance in a million of achieving its objective because no objective has been set for it.

Objectiveless advertisements in trade publications probably account for at least 90 percent of the total of all pages sold. Many examples have been discussed and illustrated so far.

This is much like the product manager who is in charge of several other product managers in a small satellite plant of a medium-sized corporation. This gentleman, in a meeting in the vice-president-marketing's office with the advertising manager, the sales manager, and three agency men, said that his marketing objective for the year was *to sell more*. The pathetic thing was that he was serious; he had no marketing objectives; the vice-president of marketing had no marketing objectives, no written marketing plan, hence didn't realize how naive this sounded. The advertising manager and the agency men were aghast. Speechless. Even the Wizard of Oz couldn't have miraculously created a more inane remark if he'd tried.

The really sad thing, though, is that management of these industrial companies doesn't really give three whoops either, because for far too many years too many industrial advertising managers either haven't had the guts to get up on their hind legs and explain advertising to management—to *sell* it—or else they've tried, found they were talking to closed minds as solid as a brick wall, and given it up as a hopeless job.

This is a far cry from being a one-way street, though. While it's quite true that industry's advertising manager hasn't contributed his full potential, it's usually because he hasn't been permitted to. And it's equally true that he is frequently the one lonesome individual in the small-to-medium-sized company who has even the haziest idea of what the marketing concept is and what it can help accomplish if it's embraced enthusiastically.

Surrounded by engineers and other technical men, the advertising manager is often in the unique position of being able to guide the company's marketing activities. He doesn't do it in his name or over his title, of course, but manages to accomplish this through the sales manager or the engineer who has miraculously been transformed into a marketing executive through a change in title. Industry is full of these. Most of them have never even *heard* of a marketing plan.

More often than not, though, management is so archaic and deeply rooted in nuts and bolts and in the dim, dead past, that the advertising manager who persists—for the good of the company—to try to plant ideas and stimulate thinking about updating the company's marketing efforts finds himself a thorn in the side of these throwbacks to the era of selling hardware.

These inept throwbacks invariably come up with a bright idea—such as preferring to sell "standard" or "price book" products to "save engineering cost." This self-defeating policy which passes for thinking in such circles is a fantastically costly one. It completely ignores the wants and needs of the marketplace. Incompetents who pursue such a seller-oriented policy can guide their companies only one way—down.

Babes in the marketing woods that they are, these misfits from some engineering department have yet to learn that the day is long since past when the seller can dictate what will be sold.

Shocking as it may seem to them—if they were to hear somebody say it—the success of a venture rests in the hands of the buyer, the failure in the hands of the seller.

Advertising managers who meekly give up and sit back and accept inadequate budgets because this enables management to "increase profitability" instead of "wasting money on advertising" do their companies a far graver disservice than do those who make a determined effort to bring the throwbacks into the twentieth century, but don't quite make the grade. Abandoning the field to the engineers and nonmarketing technical men has cost industry untold billions in lost sales that can never be recovered.

An Advertiser's View

One top management man who is both knowledgeable and concerned about industrial advertising is William F. May, chairman and chief executive officer of the American Can Company.

In the keynote address he gave at the 44th annual conference of the Association of Industrial Advertisers,* Mr. May said, in part, "We have a strong tendency to seek change and newness. At the same time we have an inclination to sameness and conformity that can clearly be seen in the trends of advertising over the years.

"Look at today's advertising. This is the year of the big, bold headline or half-page color photograph with copy block underneath. These are recent sameness patterns. You can find more if you go back over the years.

"If the agencies and American business can achieve change in advertising, followed by conformity, why is it so difficult to achieve better advertising?

"I'm talking primarily now about the *look* and the *language* of industrial advertising. The style in which the reader receives it. I'm aware that some of today's advertising, particularly industrial, is quite technical and is read for the information it contains. But does the majority of it *have* to be repetitive and dull?

"I believe there is too much sound and fury surrounding today's advertising that doesn't contribute a damn thing. There seems to be a tendency to try to talk the problems of the profession to death.

"If you were to agree with me that advertising is fast approaching the point where it's inundating the prospective customers, that a large percentage of today's advertising is dull and unattractive and that its critics are constantly increasing in numbers, wouldn't you also agree that basic remedial steps are *all* that is necessary?

*Now Business/Professional Advertising Association.

And I don't mean a full-blown debate that explores in depth the economic, the social, and the cultural aspects of advertising.

"What I do mean is a return to the 'ITT' of advertising.

"That's spelled with two T's and, prosaic as it may seem to some, stands for intelligently-conceived, truthfully-written and tastefully-presented.

"Possibly you are as bored as I am with the literally millions of words that are written about what should be done to improve advertising and the infinitesimal amount of attention and ultimate action these words seem to generate.

"This has made me aware, as you assuredly are, of the lexicon of today's advertising world. It has all the earmarks of a foreign language. I believe it was Aldous Huxley who said that 'words are indispensable but also can be fatal.'

"A perusal of a number of publications in the field disclosed the following terms: qualitative values, product differentiation, ethical and social responsibilities, behavioral science concepts, linear programming, societal expectations, factor analysis, and statistical decision theory.

"I have no quarrel with application of scientific judgment to the creative function, nor with the development of copy based on scientific judgment, so long as the finished product isn't as a teenager might put it: 'From Dullsville.'

"I also took a look at some of the letters-to-the editor columns of some of the more prominent advertising publications. If they accurately reflect the interest of a segment of the advertising profession, it is easy to understand the lack of attention given some of the more basic aspects of the profession.

"The corresponding professionals seem to be more interested in expressing views on why the XYZ 'look' is just a flash in the pan; on an abhorrence of colored airplanes; on the sheeplike tendencies of some advertising agencies; on a casual remark made about Texas in an advertisement; on use of the words 'junk mail'; and on the thought that business and industry will never consider you people mature and responsible professionals if some of the advertising columnists didn't stop referring to you as 'Madison Avenue Ad Boys.'

"This interest on the part of advertising professionals may have prompted a responsible writer of an equally responsible advertising magazine recently to make a statement that should be of interest to this group. He said: 'What's mostly wrong with industrial advertising is that *it is monumentally boring.*'

"As head of an industrial organization that spends $23 million a year on advertising and promotion, with a good chunk of it in the industrial area, that statement interests me. And let me hasten to assure you that I do not believe the responsibility for doing something to improve industrial advertising lies exclusively with agencies or the business publishers.

"Business and industrial advertisers must accept their share. Certainly any major advertiser should be capable of looking at a proposed campaign and determining if it is intelligent, truthful, and tasteful. If he can't he shouldn't be advertising—possibly he shouldn't be managing.

"At the American Can Company, advertising plays a prominent role in our marketing approach—one that we anticipate will increase as our organization continues to grow and diversify. We have taken advertising fully into our plans in conjunction with the recent corporate restructuring of the American Can Company that has resulted in our organization being completely market-oriented.

"Approximately two years ago we were completely decentralized as a company, functioning under the divisional concept. Today we operate as one company, completely market-oriented instead of product-oriented. Every aspect of our business, with emphasis on advertising, reflects this fact.

"Let me again emphasize what I said earlier. I believe in advertising. I have great respect for the talents and capabilities of the advertising professional who has played such a major role in creating this mass consumption society.

"If I've conveyed anything in this brief discussion, however, I hope it's that the buck for 'ITT' advertising stops with the advertiser. If the advertiser doesn't insist on high standards for advertising, no amount of regulation, policing, codes, or conversation will bring it about.

"The primary impetus for 'ITT' advertising, however, can come from only one source: The advertiser. It's his money, his product, his reputation, and his business that is on the line every time he advertises. If management of American business must be more knowledgeable about the basics of advertising, it will have to learn. As I said earlier, the major advertiser who can't determine if a campaign is intelligent, truthful, and tasteful shouldn't be advertising."

Now They Sell Systems, Solutions

Industrial advertising *per se is not* monumentally boring, however. Only about 95 percent of it is.

Yet only a decade or two ago the picture was even dimmer. Back then every advertiser had had drummed into him from the Year One that *Everthing Had to Be told. Everything Had to Be Told.*

Industrial ads were replete with dry-as-dust exposition about every tiny little detail of the product, its engineering, its construction, its materials, and so on ad nauseam. And every last nit-pickin', cotton-pickin' iota of information conceivably related to the product was there in five- or six-point type. Engineers in the company advertising the product loved it.

Things have changed, though, and for the better, praise be.

For one thing, industry today no longer sells hardware. That is, the industrial companies that pace the pack, those that outstrip all of the others in their industries, sell systems and solutions to problems and automation.

Either gone or rapidly disappearing is the seller of standard price-book widgets. Whether such companies survive depend upon management's waking up to the fact that it does *not* determine what will be sold. This is the prerogative of the buyer, one he isn't about to abdicate. The 1890's are long gone, and it's doubtful if they return.

Of course, management of these backward little companies can continue to instruct the field sales force to sell standards, to concentrate on price-book equipment. This they'll do despite reduced commissions until a better opportunity arises in a modern company, then no more sales force. Such managements grudgingly accept orders for what the buyer wants, but don't actively seek to sell such products.

In the meantime, guess what the competition back at the ranch is doing? What any alert, up-to-date company should be doing—determining just what it is that's wanted in the marketplace, then advertising exactly that very line of products aggressively, selling in increasing volume, and making nothing but money. It's all so very simple.

Gone, too, is the buyer who formerly said, "I need a drill press to drill holes in this part." Instead, today's buyer says, "How can I put these holes in here the cheapest way? Punch them? Drill them? Die cast a part with the holes already in? An investment casting?"

Cincinnati Milling Machine Company formerly sold milling machines, and did quite well at it, too. Now, though, as the company's great ad in Chapter 8 made quite clear, the company sells solutions to problems—solutions based on use of its machining systems. In this and similar ads the copywriter is writing to the buyer, not to the seller.

A few years ago that was kind of a revolutionary concept in itself.

Only the advertiser is interested in the trivia of detailed descriptions of the nuts and bolts that go into the product.

Just what is selling solutions to problems? Isn't this merely another way of saying it is the marketing concept—of selling what the buyer wants and needs, not what the seller wants him to have?

Isn't it at least 30 years behind the times to talk seriously of selling so-called standard widgets, or price-book widgets, to hold down the engineering costs, thus making more profit? Or maybe 40 years? Doesn't the customer pay the engineering costs—isn't he perfectly willing to do exactly this if the seller solves his problem, thus enabling him to achieve *his* marketing objectives?

And isn't it quite true that companies which have taken the biggest bite of their markets for themselves—IBM, Xerox, Polaroid, General Electric, and so on—haven't those companies stopped thinking of themselves as manufacturers, don't they regard themselves as problem-solvers?

New Directions Set

The marketing concept has given "creativity" in industrial advertising a real shot in the arm. New meaning, new purpose, and new direction are apparent in the advertising of companies that understand it and which have embraced it. Their advertising is vigorous, vital, compelling, persuasive—and quite effective.

Every dollar invested in advertising pays them a handsome return. What's more, it has shown up the vast bulk of industrial advertising for what it actually is—dull, stuffy, pretentious, self-serving and a relic of the dim, dusty, dead past.

If Mr. May is right—and *leading* industrial advertisers and *leading* industrial advertising agency men agree that he is—just why is it that so many industrial companies are perfectly content to plod along with advertising that is dull and pedestrian and pedantic and tiresome; advertising that makes no impact, advertising that produces no strong impression, advertising that is forgotten a moment after it is read, if read it is at all?

Certainly it's not that industrial advertising is placed in the wrong medium. The better business publications unquestionably reach the people who make the decisions about whether or not to buy our products, and these decision-makers read these publications.

The medium is right, the audience is right and the product that we present is one they need. This vast universe needs what advertising does for it, needs information only advertising can present.

And advertisers realize the necessity to motivate the people to whom their advertising talks if they are to broaden the market for their products or make a greater penetration into the one that exists.

If we grant that this hypothesis has any validity whatsoever, there's quite obviously a missing ingredient. Could it possibly be that advertising's approach is wrong? Could it be that both the ridiculous hysteria that characterizes the worst consumer advertising and the monotonous drivel characteristic of *most* industrial advertising are at fault? That it isn't the medium, it's not the universe, it's not advertising *per se?*

The Weak Link

This means, then, that the creative approach to industrial advertising is the weak link in the chain. For want of an approach that is genuinely creative, original, fresh, inspired, imaginative—rather than a tired rehash of all that has happened in the past—industrial advertising finds itself in the untenable position of failing to achieve its objective of informing and stimulating and motivating.

A woefully weak creative approach for most industrial advertising is responsible for the waste of hundreds of millions of dollars that are invested—squandered, actually—every year.

Squandered, not invested, because if the creative approach is a pallid echo of past pallid echos the advertiser is not casting bread upon the waters. With pathetic naivéte he is pouring money down a bottomless hole with a childlike expectation of receiving a return. There's little likelihood he will.

When psychologists and other experts who profess to know what makes the individual think and react and do so predictably discuss the creative process, or "creativity" as they seem to prefer to call it (they're so erudite it almost sounds like a genuine word-word when they use it, rather than a nonword word), the high-flying terms really proliferate.

Conceptual fluency, reality orientation, rationalization of self-motivation, societal expectations, want-need trauma, autonomous action, behavioral science concepts, relativistic, innovative function, linear programming, authoritarianism, heterogeneous, and rushing torrents of similar words flow forth to obscure what may be recognized, but most assuredly isn't said.

This unspeakable thing that's automatically swept under the carpet is that in every discussion of the state of the industrial advertising art, either overlooked or left unsaid is the fact that most industrial advertisers are as pure and innocent as newborn babes. They have no written marketing plan, no formal communications plan, they do not realize that their advertisements are tired and tiring and tiresome, nor do they have an inkling that they are not being read.

This sad situation can be attributed primarily to four things. First, a self-oriented, product-oriented attitude, rather than an awareness that success accrues to the marketing-oriented. Second, a barnacle-encrusted belief that all the reader of the business press wants is facts, and lots of 'em. Third, a reliance on the dicta of the motivation analysts and the dogmas of the market research men. There is no denying the necessity for either, of course, nor is this to advocate plowing blindly ahead, guided purely by hunch, hearsay and hope. An insight into the involved process most individuals use to arrive at decisions, and of the major factors which move them to action, coupled with solid, verified facts about products and product features the marketplace demands, provide vitally necessary background information for the creative man. Fourth is a dismaying lack of quality in the creative approach.

Both the analyzers and researchers attempted to usurp both the advertising function and the creative function in many companies. They attempted to dictate not only the tack to be taken, but *how* it was to be taken.

This resulted in some pretty esoteric formulae for advertising in general, industrial advertising in particular, and rigid rules from which no deviation was permitted in creating communications plans, advertising campaigns, individual advertisements—and even the components in each and every advertisement, layout, illustration, copy, and signature.

Needless to say, the result was invariably a fiasco. Having the creative approach dictated by noncreative people is folly. It can result only in a shambles.

Many industrial companies that should have known better wasted time and money and effort—and lost sales—by producing a spate of technically superb but terribly sterile campaigns for a number of years. A few are still at it, although these campaigns have apparently accomplished little.

The "Hot" Creative Shops

All the while there has been an increasing amount of discussion and analysis of the creative function and of creative thinking. Already the pendulum has swung sharply; the slide-rule-and-formula approach is almost a thing of the past.

This is due not to the fact that industrial marketers very suddenly grew tired of hard facts or developed an aversion for cold statistics, but to the formation and rise to prominence of the "hot creative shops"—advertising agencies that justify their existence by developing fresh, original, daring campaigns for both consumer and industrial clients. These campaigns were a roaring success, by the way. They caused advertisers to think.

There's no scoffing at agencies that started with nothing and a couple of years later billed $50 million a year. And there's no denying that agencies—hot creative shops, all—such as Doyle, Dane, Bernbach; Wells, Rich, Greene; Rink, Wells Associates; Jack Tinker & Partners; Carl Ally and others of that caliber have been fantastically successful in attracting new business.

Their success is due not to scintillating personalities or wearing tire-tread sandals, but to producing highly creative advertising *that sold the product.*

Adult urban males on the managerial and executive level are the recipients of more than 1,600 advertising impressions each and every day. And there is no indication whatsoever that this burden on advertising—or on its targets for that matter—will be smaller in the years ahead. In fact, just the contrary is true. There is every reason to think that it will increase, although it is difficult to see how many more impressions could be registered than now are.

This imposes another burden that also grows larger and heavier with each passing year, that on the creative quality of industrial advertising. For, much as we would like to think otherwise, there comes a time when the business world is bombarded with so much advertising that much of it is pretty largely ignored due to its sheer volume.

As this happens—and it is happening right now—the only way the advertiser can realize a return on his investment, the only way his communications objectives can be achieved, is through a rejection of hidebound thinking and embracing a creative approach that will get his advertisements read.

What is involved in the creative process? Actually, it's deceptively simple, or else it's deceptively simple to oversimplify.

Ideas Come From Facts

Creative ability is essentially the ability to solve problems. When applying it to the advertising man, implied is the ability not only to solve the problem, but to solve it in a unique way, a way that's different from any solution ever before devised for the same or a similar problem.

What this means, of course, is that the advertising man who desires to create advertising that stands out, advertising that is better and more effective than other advertising, has to do his home work and do it well. He must do his research and read the research that's been done for him. He has to know his product intimately and be thoroughly familiar with the markets for it. Furthermore, he has to be aware of changing conditions in the marketplace, he has to know the objectives set forth in the company's marketing plan, and he has to develop a communications plan that's right—then keep it in mind.

The Honeywell Philosophy

As Dean B. Randall, vice-president-merchandising, Honeywell, Inc., said in *Marketing Forum:* "At Honeywell each division of the company performs seven steps that the company is convinced produces exciting advertising. These are: (1) A thorough fact-finding process involving marketing, sales, advertising and the agency is conducted, and a "fact book" on each product or family of products is produced; (2) Define the market in writing. What industry? Who is the key buying influence? Where is the 20 percent that buys the 80 percent?; (3) Define the selling proposition in writing. What are we selling? Why would a buyer select us? What are our pluses? What are the competition negatives?; (4) Write objectives for each ad; (5) Prepare the advertisement; (6) Present a written media plan; (7) Propose methods for measuring results. Propose something. Even if we decide not to measure, we at least have agreed it's measurable."

Except for number 5, "preparing the advertisement," Honeywell's philosophy on the precreative portion of producing a campaign or an ad is that all concerned must ground themselves in facts and more facts so that every iota of information is available to the creative man. This enables him to opt for any idea or any approach with unruffled equanimity, with perfect aplomb, comfortably aware that he's lacking nothing as far as basic background information is concerned.

But that's the crux of the creative process—developing an idea. The truly creative individual and the seasoned advertising professional—all wrapped up in one bundle—has conceptual fluency, as the psychologists are inordinately fond of saying. This means, simply, that copywriters and to a somewhat lesser extent art directors and layout artists are perceptive and sensitive and have the mental makeup that enables them to produce an almost constant flow of ideas. Many of the ideas are unusual and daring and different, some too much so; many are good, many must be discarded. But all are as original as anybody's idea can be; everything is rooted in something, of course.

Optimum conditions favorable for problem solving, which is merely developing ideas, according to the Yerkes-Dodson Law, occur when the individual's motivation is neither extremely high nor extremely low. One tends to stifle the ability to develop creative solutions, the other encourages a don't-care attitude. Both prevent a steady flow of good ideas, while moderate motivation acts to increase the productivity of the creative individual and results in a large number of ideas that are "keepers."

Time and time again it has been proven that far more good ideas are produced than are recognized as being good. Indeed, studies have made it very evident that certain ideas are advanced, either discarded or ignored, only to be brought to light again and then recognized as ideas of exceptional merit. This can be called the Slapped Forehead Syndrome, particularly when accompanied by a cry of, *egad, that's it!*

Actually, the creative process in advertising bears marked similarity to that encountered in the fine arts or in science. All have one thing in common: The act of creation contradicts the rules of logic. The majority of the really significant advances in science, the most magnificent examples of fine art—and the most memorable advertisements, as far as that's concerned—have been due to an idea that occurred as the result of intuition.

Use that word carefully, though.

Engineers, if told this, would immediately raise a great howling hue and cry to the effect that you simply cannot engineer a better widget by relying on intuition. They'll proclaim loudly that it takes a slide rule and formulae and equations and mathematics and trigonometry and calculus and blueprints and protractors and triangles and hundreds of hours in drafting time.

This may well be true.

But who conceived the original idea about the better widget in the first place? Who determined there was a need in the marketplace for the better widget? Who researched the marketplace to ascertain how much demand existed for it? And who specified what form the new widget was to take, what features it should possess to make it more desirable, to make it better?

The engineers?

Unlikely.

The basic idea that this widget was needed to fill an existing gap in the product line and that it was necessary for the company to market it rather than continuing to rely on standard price-book widgets undoubtedly originated with a marketing man—more often than not the sales manager, marketing director, or advertising manager.

A Victory for Intuition

At Bausch & Lomb, leading producer of superior quality optical goods—microscopes, binoculars, precision scientific instruments, and so on—the originator of Bausch & Lomb's famous externally adjusted telescopic sight for big-bore sporting rifles was the company's advertising manager. Undoubtedly, when the concept of external adjustments was advanced, it was viewed with considerable scepticism simply because all other manufacturers produced internally adjustable 'scopes.

This advertising manager, J. F. Brandt, persisted, however, and by sticking to his guns ultimately was responsible for development of the BALvar 8 and other members of the family of the finest 'scope-sighting system (scope, clamp-ring assembly, receiver mount) yet devised for high-power sporting rifles. Bausch & Lomb's 'scopes are more rugged, more fog-free and less prone to accidental damage because of the solid-tube construction that external adjustments make possible. Sturdier elements and construction may be used in their manufacture because there are no holes in the tube for internal-adjustment controls with all of their attendant problems.

One of B&L's company engineers undoubtedly *could* have developed this idea, and it's even possible that it occurred to one or more of them at some time or other. But the fact remains that it was not recognized as a superior idea; and this engineer, if one did indeed conceive of the idea, didn't know how to determine its practicality as far as sales and marketing were concerned.

An unrecognized good idea has less merit than one that is somewhat better than mediocre, but whose potential is grasped immediately for obvious reasons.

Intuition has led to a scientific theory that exerts a profound effect on the fate of the entire world today; Albert Einstein's theory of relativity which made nuclear energy possible. Einstein himself later said, "The really valuable factor is intuition," when discussing his development of that revolutionary concept. He added, "There is no logical way to discovery of these elemental laws. There is only the way of intuition, which is helped by a feeling for order lying behind the appearance."

And Darwin credited an intuitive realization of the fundamentals that led to his theory on survival of the fittest. He explained later, "To my joy, the solution *occurred* to me."

Other brilliant creative thinkers in the sciences. literature, and in the field of advertising also credit intuition with playing a large role in the formulation of some of their most successful ideas.

The late Leo Burnett, who headed the giant Chicago advertising agency that bears his name, said in the old *Printers' Ink* that a "wee voice" guides the creative advertising man. "In the lonesome caverns of his mind, and in his private viscera, he develops a *thing* of some kind—an idea, a technique, a phrase, a graphic design, whatever. It strikes him as appropriate to the problem he's trying to solve—it seems accurate and sound, and hopefully *new* and *fresh* and *desirably different.* He may not quite know where it came from, but here he is with a *creation.*"

Printers' Ink added, "Advertising, as everyone reminds everyone else, is a dollar-and-cents business. Its objective is sales, not the development of scientific theories or the enjoyment of perceivers. The *substance*—what's being said—is more important than how you say it. There's ample evidence that this attitude is dead wrong."

The outstanding creative idea in advertising is different from any other idea ever conceived. Substance may be similar, but how it is expressed and and how it is shown makes it as different as night and day. Being different is what makes it creative, what sets it apart from all of the kissing cousins that look something alike and sound something alike.

Because the really good creative ideas *are* different, they're regarded with deep suspicion by noncreative people in advertising agencies whose burning desire it is not to rock the boat by offending the client—and by the noncreative client himself who may never in his life have produced anything more creative than pages for a parts manual.

These noncreative people are superbly equipped to produce anything you can think of *except an idea.*

When they encounter a good idea, they take a very dim view of this offspring of the creative man, much as you'd regard a small green three-eyed man with antennae sprouting from the top of his head if you opened your garage door some morning and there he stood, all 3 feet, 5 inches of him.

This is because the noncreative types find it exceedingly difficult to identify with the person who has ideas. They simply do not understand that ideas can be the result of anything else except black magic—or of that semiobscene intangible, intuition.

They are unable to rationalize the fact—and barely able to accept it—that the creative individual's intuitive solution to the problem, his better idea for an advertising campaign, a single advertisement, or even an illustrative idea or a piece of copy, is other than a forehead-slapping, "egad" type of inspiration.

The Discipline of Intuition

Noncreative people are constitutionally unable to conceive of the rigid discipline the creative man has subjected himself to all of his working life, as well as the vast amount of research, self-analysis, trial and error, and past experience that makes possible the realization that this particular intuitive idea is, after all is said and done, the one that solves the problem best.

This is because if the creative idea *is* new and different—completely new and different—there is nothing they can subject to objective analysis. It's impossible to poke and pry and pick out an element of the idea here, and one there, and then run them through a computer to determine what the success ratio was in the past when these various elements were present to either a greater or lesser degree.

Indeed, they find the entire process mystifying. They take solace only in the fact that the creative person's intuition did not result in recommendation of something so far-fetched and blue-sky that they are unable to understand its rationale. If presented for approval properly, with patient, humble explanations, accompanied by both the agency's and the advertising manager's blessings, the idea often—but by no means always—finds acceptance, grudging though it may be.

Unfortunately, though, no creative individual bats 1,000. Even the best, the most prolific, and highly respected creative advertising men with a long string of successes come forth with a resounding flop on occasion.

When this happens, the "I-told-you-sos" may not ring from the rafters, but they're there nonetheless. Then it's up to you to mend the fences and rise up on your hind legs and defend advertising.

Nobody comes into this world with any kind of a guarantee, not even of living to the ripe old age of five. Nor does the creative man, the agency, nor the advertising manager offer an ironclad guarantee that an idea will inevitably achieve meaningful results. Such an assurance would be nothing more than pure fraud if one stooped low enough to offer it in a weak moment.

The problem, it seems, is to encourage creative thinking, to refrain from accepting the fact that committees pass on both creative ideas and on finished copy, and to bear the following in mind:

HOW TO STIFLE "CREATIVITY" WITHOUT REALLY TRYING

1. Never rock the boat.

2. Always take the line of least resistance.

3. Don't ever suggest, even in jest, measuring what the advertising program has accomplished.

4. Always submit budget requests based on a heavy media schedule in books you know the president and the vice-president of marketing like.

5. Avoid mentioning objectives; chances are the word is unknown, but don't take a chance.

6. Read the riot act to your agency frequently. Make it toe the line. Let it know *you* give the directions, you make the decisions.

7. Discourage agency people from contacting either management or your field sales force. They might cause somebody to think like a marketing man. That would cause a giant flap throughout the organization.

8. Jump up and shout, *"Yes, sir!"* if your president lays down the law that your company is going to concentrate on selling standard price-book widgets to save engineering costs. Your next year's statement may look good, and maybe you won't be there the following year.

9. Refrain from coddling the agency. Crack the whip. This business about needing two weeks to produce an ad is for the birds. They can do *yours* overnight. After all, you can stop right now and write one immediately. And they can always get an extension from media.

10. Be sure to doodle out a "suggested" layout for your agency. Two-color, small illustration, lots of tint blocks and reverses, long copy, sans-serif type, and get the logo up BIG. The president likes that. Don't let 'em go off on any tangents.

11. Lay down firm guidelines. Make sure the agency knows that you want to see pet expressions that "communicate" in every ad. And let there be no mistakes, technically. All of your competitors have ads that are technically correct, so make sure yours are full of nuts and bolts and dimensions and tolerances and weights, all correct to four decimal places.

12. Resist any and all suggestions of a fee for the agency, or of additional compensation for research, redoing layout, or other extra work. Doesn't the agency get the same as all other agencies—15 percent from media?

13. Dissect every piece of copy word by word.

14. Then submit all copy to a copy committee. Make sure all of the engineers read it, and that engineering is well represented on the committee. It wouldn't do to let anything wrong slip by and get into print.

15. Stand up for your rights. Don't let your agency push you around. Never let them throw a group of ads at you at one time; chances are they're just trying to get out of work by having them all look alike and all having a single theme. This is obviously done to save the agency's time making layouts and writing copy.

16. Always keep the agency guessing. Throw in some veiled threats every time you talk, even on the phone. Let 'em know that other agencies are soliciting your account, and that they've given you some pretty good ideas. This will keep your agency on the ball and prevent your receiving second-rate thinking.

17. Make the agency give you new thinking as often as you can. This business of running a campaign more than one year is from hunger, strictly.

Before looking at some examples of creative thinking and creative problem-solving, it's appropriate to consider what Marsteller Inc. has to say about the advertiser who tires of his advertising. In a mailing piece, this great industrial advertising agency said:

BORED WITH YOUR OWN ADS?

Everyone is usually enthusiastic about a new campaign.

The sales idea seems sound, the approach good, the format powerful, the copy alive. "Best campaign we've ever had," everyone says.

Then succeeding ads in the campaign begin coming through. First in layout. Then art. Then brown prints. Then proofs. Then preprints. And finally in the publications. Did you ever stop to think how many times you see every ad?

At first the only evidence of boredom is a lack of expressed enthusiasm. But then there are murmurs, faint but growing louder. "Wonder if we don't need a fresh approach?" "How about a change of pace?" It builds up into a kind of pressure that too often bursts forth in the form of a decision:

"Let's do something different."

So the campaign is dropped. It is dropped in spite of a fact so well-documented and so often repeated that it has become a cliche: By the time an advertiser is thoroughly fed up with his campaign the buying public is just becoming really conscious of it.

And along with the campaign are dropped all the cumulative values it may have built up: readership, impact, recognition. The new campaign must start from scratch.

This is obviously wasteful, but it happens all the time. How do you prevent it?

We know of one very practical method. It is based on common sense, it is simple, and it works.

First, in advance of a campaign, provide for evaluating the results. *Your yardstick will, of course, vary with your campaign and its objectives—inquiries, readership, direct sales, etc.*

Second, watch *results carefully from ad to ad. Is the trend up or down?*

Third (and this is extremely important), keep everyone concerned in your company informed *about results.*

If results are good, there will be very little agitation for "something new and different." It is very difficult to get bored with success.

If results are bad, the campaign ought *to be dropped.*

Either way, you're making your advertising dollars work harder. You're investing them not on the basis of internal company opinion, but on the demonstrated reactions of potential customers.

And it's only their *votes that can be tabulated on the cash register.*

This is another way the death knell frequently tolls for a creative idea that could have accomplished much for a company—scuttling a campaign long before its useful life had run its course. It happens all too often in industrial advertising, more's the pity. When you have a good campaign running, explain it, defend it, sell it, preserve it.

Thinking creatively leads to a *different* solution to a problem, one that's never been thought of or used before. It will be unique in both concept and approach, as well as because the problem itself is frequently analyzed from an entirely different vantage point, much as if the creative man took a mental walk around it and attacked it from an angle never before considered.

Take railroad cars, for instance. The railroad car definitely isn't a glamor item, yet North American Car Corporation's entire business consists of renting and leasing tank, refrigerator, covered hopper, stock, box, and gondola railroad cars to industry, usually for a long period of time at a time.

Railroads own railroad cars, of course, in which they haul freight belonging to customers. But these shippers with problems peculiar to certain industries or to certain segments of industries frequently have highly specialized requirements as far as cars are concerned; railroads can often provide the special cars such shippers demand, but sometimes only after waiting for the appropriate car to be emptied, or to be returned from another trip. This is time-consuming and costly because the shipper's product piles up in the factory, shipping dates aren't met, promises to customers aren't kept.

As a consequence, many companies own their own railroad cars, while others find it more economical to lease specialized rolling stock from firms such as North American Car Corporation. Cost of rental or lease is a tax-deductible item of business expense, of course, and may well be more advantageous in many circumstances than amortizing the purchase price of a car or number of cars over a period of years.

Even so, it's not exactly the easiest thing in the world to take a product that's inherently less than lovely and transform it into something that, while not beautiful, is desirable.

A Challenge Is Met

This is the problem that account executive-copywriter Wim van der Graaf faced when he landed the assignment to develop a new campaign for North American Car Corporation.

One approach would have been to show an illustration of a railroad car and run a headline saying, *We rent railroad cars,* or something similar. Not very creative, however, and the advertisement immediately would have evoked a so-what, shrugged-shoulder response and next to no readership—unless somebody just happened to be hard up for a railroad car right at that particular moment.

Or a box or refrigerator or covered-hopper car could have been shown sitting on a siding with a headline proclaiming, *You can lease me.* This is a little bit more buyer-oriented, less self-interest on the part of the seller, but something less than a stopper either in the illustration or in the copy approach.

What was obviously needed was to set the product and the service and the company apart from similar products and services offered by competitors, for they, too, lease railroad cars and they're all built by the same car makers, they'll all transport the same number of pounds, gallons, or cubic feet of freight—and they're hauled by the same locomotive with the same horsepower over the same tracks. Cars leased by the competitors didn't haul merchandise any faster, the ride wasn't any smoother, and the cost was undoubtedly remarkably close to a Mexican standoff.

First thing required for a memorable campaign was a unifying theme to weld it into a cohesive entity rather than a series of individual advertisements. This required looking at the problem—actually, looking at North American Car's business—from a different angle. A fresh, creative evaluation of NACC's operations brought to mind, perhaps intuitively, that the company actually operated in a logistical capacity. Logistics was the key to the new campaign.

North American Car promptly defined logistics for its prospects in ads in *Traffic World, Railway Age, Traffic Management, Chemical Week,* and in *Oil, Paint & Drug Reporter.*

A black-and-white spread told readers that many dictionaries disagreed on the proper definition of "logistics," some still stoutly insisting it was the art of supplying military troops in the field with the necessities of life and with material and equipment to enable them to carry on military operations.

The company, however, grabbed *el toro* by the horns and proclaimed that logistics is the carrying out in an orderly manner a massively complicated program; the art of managing materials; the skill of delivering the goods where wanted, when wanted, at maximum profit.

North American Car didn't hesitate to state that it acted as supplier, inventor, designer, and catalyst in the development of new and better ways to improve the logistics of business—and to put more profit in distribution systems. This set the stage and set it promptly and properly.

A highly imaginative campaign followed. One of the first one-page black-and-white ads is shown on the following page.

This advertisement violates almost every rule in the book as far as layout is concerned. Illustrations are small; captions are a headlong flight into frivolity; on first consideration neither illustrations nor captions appear to be relevant as far as the product or service is concerned; there's a jumble of type faces and body copy is set in a simulated typewriter face that's really a bit too light to carry well; and nonexistent characters converse with each other about the product-service being offered, thus sacrificing believability.

All of this is true enough.

The next observation, though, has to be that this is an inspired solution to North American Car's communications problem. Creating a situation as a platform from which to talk and populating it with people who *could* easily exist in the business community personalizes the message and enables the reader to identify with them.

Miss Friday quickly accumulated a following of loyal fans, and well she might for she is as cute as a button and she imparts a tasteful dash of that wonderful ingredient, sex appeal, to the ads.

Unquestionably this is a great campaign and the individual ads are also great. It's highly creative, daring, imaginative, different. It has a fine flair, flavor and a delightful light touch.

Furthermore, the approach is unique in this field. That a unique campaign could be produced is due to the copywriter's taking a fresh look at what the advertiser offers for sale and a fresh look at the problems he is encountering in the marketplace. The gifted copywriter automatically does this; the capable copywriter occasionally does; the also-ran copywriters almost never do.

Initial impression of the advertisement as a whole is that the layout is unusually clean, and that there are almost acres of nice,

MEMO ON LOGISTICS:

Re: Sag Junction Terminal

To: Mr. McCall From: Miss Friday

I was so excited when you asked me to take personal charge of this important research project. I just know you won't regret giving me this wonderful opportunity. After all, a secretary is as distribution minded as anybody!

I did as you said, and got a map from Charlie in Traffic. He's nice. There it was —Sag Junction Terminal near Lemont, Illinois—right in the middle of the Tri-State Tollway, U.S. 66, the Cal-Sag Channel, the Illinois Waterway, and surrounded by railroads. All just a short shopping trip from Chicago's loop.

Thank you for letting me use your expense account. After I called the limousine service in Chicago, I discovered I only had $2.27 cash. The chauffeur remembered you from last year's convention, so I just signed for it. I also figured I'd need an outfit for this safari. Nothing special, you understand, just a few casual things and some boots.

Let me tell you about the darling little hat I got when I arrived at the Sag Junction Terminal. It's a cute little hat with a visor. As you can see from the picture, these are safety minded people.

This research project may take a little longer than I thought, even though I have the limousine to drive me around. Before I give you a complete report on all the facilities, I want to check where all those pipelines go. Whether all those tanks are being used. Just what all that steam from the steam house is for. I wonder how they remember just what is in each of those storage tanks...they all look alike. I'm sure I'll have a lot more to report tomorrow.

Your girl,

Friday

The hat was cute, safe, too.

Nothing special on the expense account... just a few casual things and boots.

If you can't spare your best secretary, send yourself, or write to Terminal Services Division,

NORTH AMERICAN CAR CORPORATION
77 South Wacker Drive, Chicago 6, Illinois

LOGISTICS *is our business*

clean, inviting white space to make the ad attractive to the eye. The smaller top illustration is properly located to take advantage of the reader's known eye path, as is North American Car's campaign theme, as well as the headline.

Copy in this first ad in the campaign is so fine, it sets the stage so skillfully, it deserves to be carried here. It reads:

MEMO ON LOGISTICS

Re: Sag Junction Terminal

To: Mr. McCall *From: Miss Friday*

I was so excited when you asked me to take personal charge of this important research project. I just know you won't regret giving me this wonderful opportunity. After all, a secretary is as distribution-minded as anybody!

I did as you said, and got a map from Charlie in Traffic. He's nice. There it was—Sag Junction Terminal near Lemont, Illinois——right in the middle of the Tri-State Tollway, U.S. 66, the Cal-Sag Channel, the Illinois Waterway, and surrounded by railroads. All just a short shopping trip from Chicago's loop.

Thank you for letting me use your expense account. After I called the limousine service in Chicago, I discovered I only had $2.27 cash. The chauffeur remembered you from last year's convention, so I just signed for it. I also figured I'd need an outfit for this safari. Nothing special, you understand. Just a few casual things and some boots.

Let me tell you about the darling little hat I got when I arrived at the Sag Junction Terminal. It's a cute little hat with a visor. As you can see from the picture, these are safety-minded people.

This research project may take a little longer than I thought, even though I have the limousine to drive me around. Before I give you a complete report on all the facilities, I want to check where all those pipelines go. Whether all those tanks are being used. Just what all that steam from the steam house is for. I wonder how they remember just what is in each of those storage tanks . . . they all look alike. I'm sure I'll have a lot more to report tomorrow.

Your girl,
Friday

If you can't spare your best secretary, send yourself, or write to Terminal Services Division,

NORTH AMERICAN CAR CORPORATION

(address)

LOGISTICS *is our business*

That's as fresh as a morning breeze off a mountain lake. It's sprightly, lively, and appealing. It *sounds* feminine and has just exactly the right amount of flightiness as the captions make clear. The top one says, *The hat was cute, safe, too.* And the lower one reads, *Nothing special on the expense account . . . just a few casual things and boots.*

There was a mighty deft hand on that typewriter.

The second ad in this appealing campaign follows Miss Friday in her adventures and discoveries at Sag Junction as she has a ball unearthing a number of solid-selling propositions about North American Car's giant facility. For some reason or other, barge captains, tank truck drivers, and miscellaneous employees around the place welcome her enthusiastically—almost with open arms, you might say.

Three illustrations instead of two this time, each of which makes it apparent that Miss Friday is a Miss and not Joe Friday in disguise. Again light-hearted captions arouse the reader's interest and curiosity and pull him right into the body copy. It shows an exceedingly sure touch and an understanding of human nature. The copy reads:

MEMO ON LOGISTICS

Re: On the spot at Sag Junction

To: Mr. McCall *From: Miss Friday*

What a spot to be in! I don't mean the spot you are in . . . trying to move all your production into the Mid-America market; I mean the spot Sag Junction Terminal is in to move it for you! I decided to check available transportation to Sag Junction Terminal personally, so I took the barge today. Can you imagine me, like Cleopatra, floating down the Cal-Sag Channel on a barge? I really saved the expense money though, and the captain even served coffee.

When I docked, I got a ride with a real nice truck driver. I know you don't approve of a young lady hitch-hiking, but I just couldn't walk—the place is too big.

MEMO ON LOGISTICS:

Re: On the spot at Sag Junction

To: Mr. McCall From: Miss Friday

What a spot to be in! I don't mean the spot you are in...trying to move all your production into the Mid-America market; I mean the spot Sag Junction Terminal is in to move it for you! I decided to check available transportation to Sag Junction Terminal personally, so I took the barge today. Can you imagine me, like Cleopatra, floating down the Cal-Sag Channel on a barge? I really saved the expense money though, and the captain even served coffee.

The captain even served coffee

When I docked, I got a ride with a real nice truck driver. I know you don't approve of a young lady hitch-hiking, but I just couldn't walk—the place is too big.

The tank cars are North American

Many things here are automatic. The driver even muttered something about how he would like to see them try to automate truck driving. Frankly, I wouldn't tempt them. You never know what these logisticians will do next!

After the truck driver dropped me off at the track, the train track I mean, I found out that North American Car Corporation not only leases automobile rack cars, they lease almost any kind of railroad car including the two North American Car tank cars you can see whizzing by in the background.

The truck driver was nice

The thing I like most about Sag Junction Terminal is that you can get here any way you want—water—rail—highway. You can even fly in by helicopter! There's more space here than I could cover today. More about space in tomorrow's report.

Your girl,
Friday

If you can't spare your best secretary, send yourself, or write to Terminal Services Division,

NORTH AMERICAN CAR CORPORATION
77 South Wacker Drive, Chicago 6, Illinois

LOGISTICS *is our business*

Many things here are automatic. The driver even muttered something about how he would like to see them try to automate truck driving. Frankly, I wouldn't tempt them. You never know what these logisticians will do next!

After the truck driver dropped me off at the track, the train track, I mean, I found out that North American Car Corporation not only leases automobile rack cars, they lease almost any kind of railroad car including the two North American Car tank cars you can see whizzing by in the background.

The thing I like most about Sag Junction Terminal is that you can get here any way you want—water—rail—highway. You can even fly in by helicopter. There's more space here than I could cover today. More about space in tomorrow's report.

Your girl,
Friday

If you can't spare your best secretary, send yourself, or write to Terminal Services Division,

NORTH AMERICAN CAR CORPORATION

LOGISTICS *is our business*

This copy is fresh and believable and typically feminine. The writer was a real professional, so knowledgeable about what he was doing and about his audience and how they would react, that he intuitively knew it was the right thing to do to have the little non sequiturs in the copy.

After the truck driver dropped me off at the track, the train truck I mean, humanizes Miss Friday, breathes the breath of life into her, makes her seem so real that it's actually straining the imagination to believe that she doesn't actually exist as a real flesh-and-blood secretary having fun doing a special job for her boss.

Copy makes it very obvious that North American Car Corporation has the cars, the storage facilities, the mass of equipment and the technical know-how to offer a superior logistical service. It makes the company's statement—made by Miss Friday—that the men she talked with are logisticians one the reader accepts.

Readership of this exceptional campaign was unusually high. The advertiser reaped an oversize return on his investment in terms of prospect interest and in strengthening the company's identity.

And North American Car's final words in every ad in the campaign are nothing less than perfect. The bid for action—*If you can't spare your best secretary, send yourself, or write to Terminal Services Division, North American Car Corporation.*

Superb!

Another Flight of Fancy

Eastern Air Lines' great black-and-white spread advertisement from *Business Week,* shown on page 1046, proves the copywriter took a flight of fancy to develop a highly original advertisement for air freight.

Selling a service in industrial advertising isn't the easiest thing in the world to do. Whether advertisers like it or not, the fact remains that competitors are not all miserable, uncouth ruffians who offer such a terribly inferior product for sale that it should be legislated off the market. In truth, whatever the industry, product or service, any number of competitors are pretty decent guys who market a product that is almost as good as the one the advertiser offers, and in some instances and some ways, sometimes a better one.

Advertising must make the advertiser's product *seem* more desirable.

For instance, any number of excellent airlines offer air freight service; in fact, most airlines delight in hauling freight along with the passengers on every scheduled flight. This is almost like finding money in the gutter because few of today's big jets are loaded near rated capacity when they take off. Hauling freight doesn't consume any additional fuel to speak of, it requires no additional personnel to fly the beast, no extra stewardesses to serve coffee, tea, or milk, or otherwise coddle the freight. And freight never hijacks a plane and takes it to the land of the bearded Red hippie.

Then, too, there are the air freight specialists such as Slick Corporation, Flying Tiger Lines, and numerous smaller operators who prefer freight to people and do a mighty fine job of it. This is very tough competition for the scheduled passenger airlines to buck. The freight carriers are aggressive and make a determined effort to keep those airplanes full, for they have no herd of passengers milling around the terminal waiting to board, thus paying for the fuel, salaries, depreciation, landing fees, maintenance, etc.

Showing a nice, clean 727, 707, or DC-8 in an advertisement, even in living color with a gorgeous sunset, along with a headline proudly proclaiming that Wild Blue Yonder Airlines hauls air freight if you want to ship it, by cracky, lacks a little something. The approach isn't quite as creative as it might be.

And having an illustration of a nice, colorful topographical map with lines drawn neatly on it and little top-views of the airplanes—perhaps as viewed from a satellite in a low orbit—has been done to death, too. This is no solution, unless there's a story to tell that's

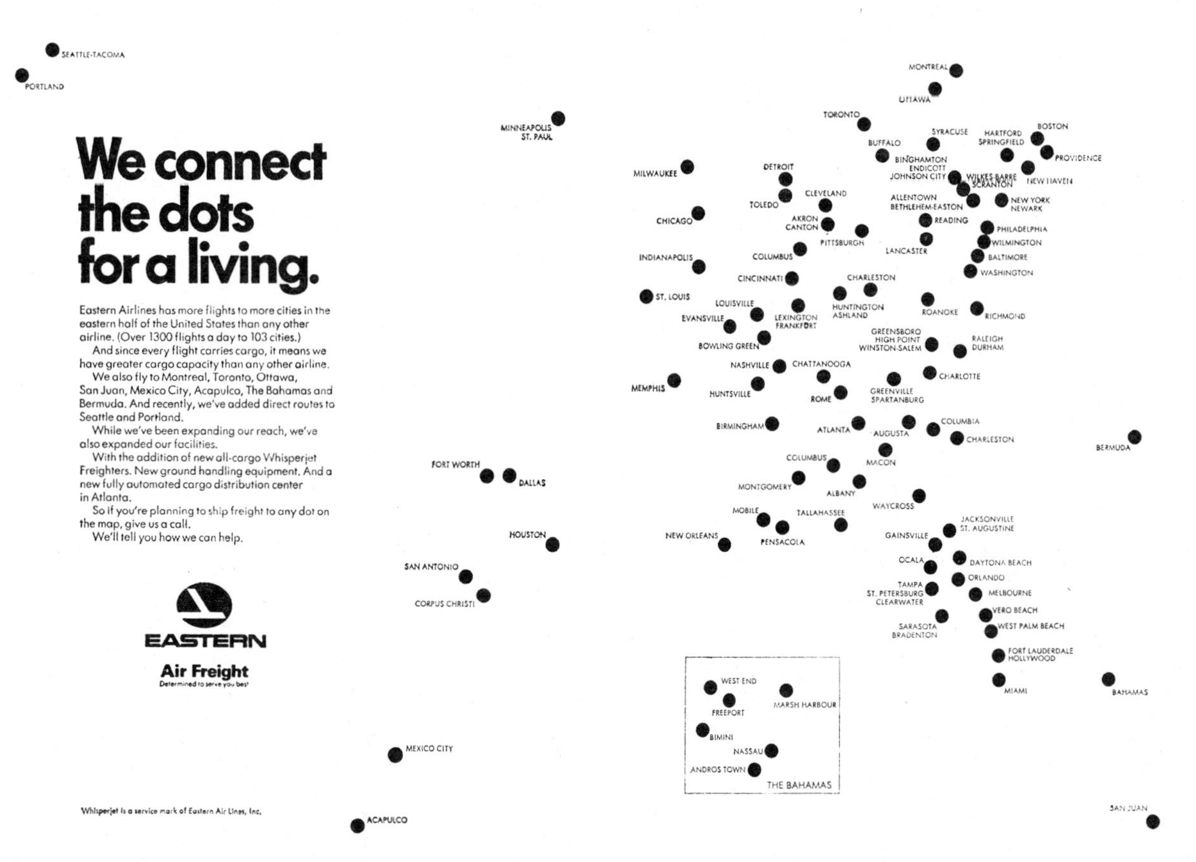

Eastern Airlines chose a most creative way to talk about air freight.

so sensational it would almost make the papers as news, not as an advertisement. Those are few and far between.

Eastern Air Lines, though, came up with a different twist in its ad.

Eastern's illustration showing dots for cities, all identified, with the headline, *We connect the dots for a living,* is just whimsical enough to have lots of reader appeal. This is another case of the advertiser proving the business world isn't all grim and competitive and hard-sell.

The advertiser tells its story in a straightforward manner, selling the fact that Eastern has more flights to more cities in the eastern half of the United States than does any other airline, and that it now flies nonstop to Seattle-Tacoma and to Portland, as well as to other farflung places—and it does so very persuasively.

Copy ends with this bid for action: *So if you're planning to ship freight to any dot on the map, give us a call. We'll tell you how we can help.* Only two words with more than one syllable.

This is a highly creative, effective approach to selling a service that isn't very easy to sell—or to illustrate. Eastern did well by itself.

The Product Is Service

Another service that practically invites a hackneyed approach to advertising is the food-service business. After all, food is food, we're all perfectly familiar with it, we encounter it three times a day and have all of our lives. There's almost nothing we don't know about it, or will admit that we don't know about it, at least. Every man fancies himself a suave, sophisticated gourmet.

The food-service industry is rife with advertisements that are nothing short of works of art. Magnificent meals on fragile china with a small fortune in sterling carefully placed on snowy-white linen are photographed with great skill and reproduced with exquisite fidelity in four-color inserts. And you can't quibble about it—this shows the product as the advertiser visualizes it in his fond imaginings and as he wants prospective buyers to think of it.

Then again, he may have decided to get really wildly creative and *not* show the luscious meal ready for consumption, but show instead the high quality food before it's prepared—raw steaks, fresh vegetables with little droplets of dew still on them; when in the eyes of the potatoes, they're actually dewey-eyed. Such ads are also very old hat.

What all food-service management firms actually offer to their clients and would like to sell to their prospects is not food *per se*, strange as it may seem. The "product" that is up for sale is service—purchasing, accounting, preparing, portioning, training of personnel, supervision, professional dietary planning of meals, and so on and on.

Almost no food-service management firm, with the exception of Szabo Food Service, Inc., one of the leaders in this booming industry, realizes or recognizes this, according to Raymond F. Neuzil, Szabo vice-president and director of corporate communications.

Because Szabo does, the company was able to develop a particularly creative, highly effective advertising campaign for its Hospital Services Division. A typical one-page two-color (red and black) advertisement is illustrated.

This ad is beautifully simple and tasteful. Only a spot of second color is used—in the lipstick imprint on the cup. Because of its subtlety, the illustration achieves tremendous impact and works very closely with the headline.

Although it's 196 words long, the copy is informative, interesting, and very convincing. It reads:

> **Sorry,**
> **this just isn't our cup of tea.**
>
> *Cups like this shouldn't get beyond the dishwasher. And when Szabo operates your dietary department, your personnel are expertly trained to see to it they don't.*
>
> Training your employees . . . is *only one of the important features of Szabo's total dietary management program. In addition, Szabo, through its resident food-service director, handles all the time consuming details connected with staffing, employee relations, purchasing, record keeping, and inventory control. This leaves you more time to devote to your prime responsibilities.*
>
> *These are but a few of the meaningful advantages enjoyed by Szabo's clients throughout the country. Important, too, Szabo provides timely executive supervision of your dietary department by knowledgeable staff supervisors, including ADA dietitians. Also, significant savings in dietary budgets are brought about by Szabo's operating know-how and massive purchasing power.*
>
> *In short, you enjoy all of the advantages of a highly professional dietary management program*—yet you retain complete control.

To learn how Szabo does it, ask for our free 8-page booklet, "Professional Dietary Department Management—A Key To Better Patient Care." There is no obligation, of course.

This excellent creative approach was made possible by a critically objective analysis of what the advertiser's business really consists of, and how it might best be explained and made desirable to this segment of its market.

Szabo's fine campaign has enjoyed outstanding readership, as well as producing a substantial volume of inquiries. Inquiries are of unusually high quality and a number have been converted into sales. This is industrial advertising that is creative—industrial advertising as it should be done.

Teflon—Challenge to Du Pont

E. I. Du Pont de Nemours & Company faced a marketing problem that required creative thinking to solve during its introduction of Teflon, which is Du Pont's registered trademark for its TFE and FEP fluorocarbon resins and nonstick finishes.

The product discussed here, in a generic sense, is cookware treated with Teflon.

When such cookware was first introduced on the consumer market, there was a brief sales flurry followed by an abrupt downward sales trend even before national distribution was achieved. There was every indication that Teflon utensils would join the slag heap of unsuccessful products that are so prevalent on the American market.

The relatively short history of Teflon cookware dramatically reveals the forces of competition at work and the need for adequate market planning and control. Importance of advertising research is also highlighted, as well as benefits attained when a judicious mixture of promotional approaches is applied to a chaotic marketplace. Reflected, too, is the need of constant evaluation of advertising strategies in light of changing conditions brought about by forces at work in a competitive distribution system.

There are many uses for Teflon resin, especially in industrial and military markets which are superficially treated in this case study. No attempt has been made to evaluate the full market potential for the entire range of Teflon products or the promotional programs that have been undertaken outside the cookware field. The degree of success or failure in promoting Teflon-treated kitchenware represents only one aspect of the overall demand for the product. Teflon has achieved success in other markets and offers a rich potential for further development in the years ahead.

Teflon, Du Pont's family of fluorocarbon resins and materials, has an extremely low coefficient of friction which is comparable to rubbing two pieces of ice together. Teflon is almost completely inert to most chemicals, does not enter chemical reactions with food and water, is nonflammable and retains its functional properties in a wide temperature range—from well below the temperature of dry ice to temperatures in excess of 700 degrees Fahrenheit.

Du Pont, as a major chemical firm, is primarily a supplier to industry rather than a producer of end-use goods for the consumer market. Although the company does produce some consumer goods, the bulk of Du Pont sales are made to other manufacturers and fabricators who, in turn, use Du Pont chemicals and derivatives in their production processes.

Du Pont produces and sells Teflon plastics, finishes, fibers, and other derivatives to industry. In this position, as a producer of basic industrial materials, often of an extremely sophisticated nature, it follows that Du Pont has a dual role to play.

Through its basic research program it not only unlocks the door to chemical secrets, but then must develop efficient production processes within the Du Pont organization to turn out these products. However, this is only the first step.

No new product necessarily finds a ready-made market breathlessly awaiting its arrival on the scene. Industry must first be made aware of the existence of the product through a communications program.

In effect, a basic innovator such as Du Pont must undertake an educational program to inform industry that a new item is not only commercially available, but also how the item can be used. It is also necessary to explain what fabrication processes are involved, and how the product might be incorporated in existing or potentially existing technology to bring about improvements in efficiency.

For example, Du Pont developed Teflon and then set about to find a practical means of producing Teflon resins on a commercially feasible scale. Within the Du Pont laboratories there was also much experimentation to develop an efficient process for applying Teflon finishes to various surfaces (steel, glass, aluminum, and others).

Du Pont supplies Teflon in two liquid forms: as a "raw material" of particles of resin suspended in an aqueous solution, and as a completely formulated finish.

This distinction is more than academic, for it must be borne in mind that nothing sticks to Teflon. How, then, could Teflon be made to adhere to a surface? Teflon finishes were the answer to this contradiction. After this process had been largely perfected, Du Pont naturally could have followed one of two basic courses.

It could have invested in plant and equipment and gone into the business of applying Teflon to other materials in response to industry needs; or it could pass along its know-how resulting from research to other companies. They, in turn, would enter the application business. The latter course was followed because it was in line with Du Pont policies and tradition.

Through technical releases, personal visits, and other means, data were circulated to industry. With Du Pont encouragement more than two-dozen firms became custom applicators of Teflon.

After Two Decades—"Nowhere"

However, almost 20 years after Teflon resins were first discovered in its laboratories, this Du Pont trademark was still relatively unknown in the U.S. consumer market. For all practical purposes no Teflon-treated consumer items had yet appeared in domestic retail stores. All Du Pont promotion and advertising had been directed to the industrial market. Teflon, unlike Dacron, Lucite, Mylar and many other Du Pont trademarks that are household words, was virtually unrecognized by the consumer.

On a somewhat modest scale entries had been made into both the industrial and military markets, and experimentation was continuing to broaden usage and to find new applications.

During the early part of the 1950's the unusual "nonstick" properties of Teflon had led to some experimentation to determine whether or not it was feasible to apply it to food processing equipment and cooking utensils. A few manufacturers had shown some interest in the product, and early research generated sufficient interest for Du Pont to consider the safety of cookware treated with Teflon and to determine whether Federal Food and Drug Administration clearance was necessary.

Extensive experiments conducted by Du Pont and independent laboratories showed that Teflon coated utensils were safe for conventional kitchen use. Du Pont took the matter up with FDA, which issued a statement to the effect that pans coated with Teflon are safe for conventional kitchen use.

It was at this time that French and Italian firms achieved quite a good sales success in the European market. The two firms exported to the U.S. market, which led to consumer demand here because Teflon made possible fat-free frying—low cholesterol dieters welcomed this development with open arms.

Importers were unable to meet demand for the coated utensils, Du Pont was selling Teflon finishes domestically to all buyers, and soon a number of U.S. firms were producing similar cookwares. Burgeoning demand led to appearance of "shabby" frying pans coated with Teflon as certain manufacturers (both U.S. and European) cut corners by using metal of too light a gauge, and applying Teflon finishes improperly or by using the raw liquid Teflon. This inevitably led to a deterioration in the Teflon marketing situation as purchasers of inferior utensils coated with Teflon became dissatisfied.

Finally, sales of Teflon to housewares manufacturers fell almost to zero. Du Pont had to reevaluate its position.

One possible approach was to do nothing. Du Pont could have abandoned this particular market because Teflon sales in other markets continued to increase very nicely. However, the manufacturer realized that (1) logically, Teflon had properties which could demonstrably improve most kinds of cookware from the user's viewpoint and (2) technically, there was absolutely no reason why Teflon finishes could not be properly applied to these items.

Du Pont determined to see what, if any, steps could be taken to revitalize the market.

Emphasized Another Benefit

There still existed an uncertainty at this time about two major dimensions of the problem. One involved consumer attitudes and the other related to the efficacy of Du Pont's undertaking a consumer-oriented advertising and promotional program on behalf of Teflon. Unavailability of empirical data as to consumer attitudes and on the degree of risk in launching an advertising program made obvious the fact that field research was needed.

When this was completed the validity of the "no-fat cooking" sales appeal was seriously questioned, and it had been used exclusively up until this time. It was decided to drop this appeal and substitute the more universal appeal of "ease of cleaning" due to Teflon's nonstick surface. This opened up a far larger market than ever had existed in the health-conscious segment which had bought Teflon coated cookware until this time.

A marketing program was developed and explained to key segments of the cookwares trade to enlist their support and cooperation. Du Pont assured its customers that Teflon was here to stay, that it has a universal market, and that problems connected with it were being solved.

The program presented by Du Pont and its advertising agency, N. W. Ayer & Son, was built around six points:

1. Changing the creative strategy behind the promotion from a health appeal to no-stick cooking, no-scour cleanup. This was an appeal that could be directed effectively at all consumers, rather than just those interested in weight reduction or low cholesterol.

2. Offering a certification mark or "quality seal" to the industry. This showed that Du Pont was assuming a completely new role. No longer did the company simply operate as a supplier to the housewares industry. The seal was to go only to those manufacturers who applied Teflon to cookware according to Du Pont specifications.

   Du Pont would set standards and would police quality through frequent spot checks of the product output of those who were awarded the coveted seal.

   Any manufacturer who did not coat according to Du Pont specifications would be denied use of the seal.

3. Development of new colors for Teflon and stressing their availability.

4. Expanding the coated cookware line to include a wider assortment of utensils.

5. Providing useful product information to the trade, especially designed to educate retail sales clerks so they could promote Teflon to the consumer with greater effectiveness.

6. Launching an advertising campaign in a number of test markets. Details of the program follow.

The need to advertise the concept of "easy cleanup" and to promote the Du Pont Quality Seal appeared logical. However, there was a reluctance on the part of Du Pont top management to commit huge sums to support those efforts without facts on which to base judgments. The author has yet to encounter a management that did not exhibit this same idiosyncrasy, incidentally!

No one really knew if advertising Teflon in the national market would be successful either in generating demand from consumers, or in remedying a demoralized trade situation. What's more, this approach represented a drastic departure from the past. Although Du Pont had tentatively decided to play a more active role in marketing Teflon in the consumer market, the company nonetheless was basically a supplier to other manufacturers.

And the cost of Teflon incorporated in finished utensils represented only a small fraction of overall unit production costs or selling prices. For example. a pan made with Teflon that sold at retail for between three to 10 dollars had less than 2 percent of the selling price invested in the Teflon.

This meant that a question remained: What level of Du Pont advertising was necessary to move finished cookware, and would the funds needed to do an adequate promotional job in the consumer market be prohibitive from Du Pont's point of view?

At one time providing cooperative funds to the cookware industry was considered, but Du Pont decided not to make co-op money available. It was felt that a unified Du Pont-controlled program would be far more efficient in redirecting the basic appeal away from "no-fat" and to promoting the "quality seal" approach.

Consumer education was vitally important, and Du Pont was fully aware that Teflon had failed up until now due to lack of control of market development. Du Pont's own advertising, bought and paid for and managed by the company, was the only logical means available to bring about an orderly reintroduction of the product into a shattered market. Once this decision was made, approval was given by Du Pont's top management to move ahead with advertising research to provide a better factual basis on which to proceed.

Why Television Was Chosen

Advertising research that was undertaken was simplified by the decision to use television as the prime medium. This was based upon a number of considerations, chief among them that the merits of Teflon could best be shown by a demonstration. In-store demonstrations conducted earlier had been successful when imported coated products first reached the market. Television was chosen with the full knowledge that print media are more easily merchandised to the trade, for the objective here was to cause consumers to act; if this objective was accomplished, it was believed trade problems would practically solve themselves.

Advertising research involved testing three levels of advertising effort during two 11-week periods. By means of an experimental crossover design, it was possible to test at national levels of

$1,000,000 (10 one-minute commercials in the fall and seven one-minute commercials in the winter), $500,000 (five and three), and $250,000 or a "promotional" campaign (five and none). Thirteen cities were used for test and control cities.

Due to certain retailers refusing to cooperate in the research venture, measurement of sales was based on telephone interviews with 1,000 female heads of households, randomly selected, in each of the test markets and during each of the test periods during both fall and winter.

Research indicated, among other things, that:

1. Sales of cookware finished with Teflon could be increased with a proper level of advertising.
2. Test markets where advertising on TV was carried on at lower levels showed no discernible effect on sales.
3. Promotional effort in test markets at the one-million-dollar level resulted in the doubling of sales as compared with the lower level or of the no-advertising test markets.
4. There was strong evidence of a "carryover" effect of advertising in test cities where promotion was carried on at the million dollar level of expenditures.

One critically important element was omitted in the test design. Normally, the national television effort would be the subject of a trade advertising program to retailers. Without retailer backing, particularly by department stores, neither a test nor the projected national program could be expected to be operational.

Enlisting the cooperation of the retailer was left entirely to the participating cookware manufacturers. Here Du Pont was overly optimistic; word filtered down too slowly from the manufacturers' organizations to the retailers in the test markets.

Accordingly, Du Pont used its own personnel plus a special outside group to contact key outlets on an emergency basis to acquaint retail buyers with the advertising program; this had to be done to get them to stock sufficient coated cookware in their outlets.

These and other research data provided Du Pont with a solid basis for planning a national advertising effort. There had always been a supposition that advertising could work; now there was evidence as to how much of an investment would be needed in the national market to make advertising work profitably.

In the meantime, research was undertaken to determine the consumer attitude toward products finished with Teflon. This was done by mailing 734 Teflon-coated cooking utensils to a consumer test panel—one to a home. A mail questionnaire was used to solicit response at the end of five months; a return of 624 showed that consumers consider nonstick cookware desirable. Ease of cleaning was the most often noted advantage. It appeared obvious that consumers appreciate the merit of the product once exposed to it. This research also indicated that advertising at a realistic level would be able to tap the market potential.

At this time Du Pont management approved a budget of approximately $1,000,000 to promote Teflon to consumers via television, and to the trade in trade publications; in addition, certain specialized vehicles were chosen to carry messages to two additional key groups—doctors and home economists.

Daytime TV was to be used to concentrate coverage on women who were considered the primary target and to take advantage of the economy of daytime television to permit an adequate degree of frequency. The campaign was conceived as follows:

Advertising Objectives	To educate consumers to the benefits of Teflon when used on cookware and bakeware.
Creative Strategy	To demonstrate the ease and convenience of cooking with Teflon, summed up by a "no-stick—no-scour" theme.
Audience	To reach a broad cross-section of women.
	To concentrate efforts on daytime television—television because of its ability to demonstrate the benefits of Teflon, and daytime television in particular because of its economy in reaching women.
Timing	To key the weight of advertising effort to the seasonal ups and downs of cookware sales at retail.

In addition, during the first few weeks participation spots were purchased in new nighttime television shows to provide extra reach at the start of the advertising program, and to create additional merchandising impact on the trade.

Net result was a total of 115 daytime-participation one-minute commercials from mid-September to the end of the calendar year. During an average week seven to eight commercials were aired over network television. In addition to these sustaining commercials, eight one-minute commercials were purchased on nighttime network television during the first part of the program.

The trade was recognized as a very important target for Du Pont advertising. Past experience pointed this up, and it was also reflected in the proposal of N. W. Ayer, Du Pont's agency, to management.

Strategy underlying the trade program was highlighted in the agency presentation:

The retailer is important to Du Pont, for his willingness to stock, display, and promote cookware finished with Teflon is an important influence on sales. And as distribution improves, so does the effectiveness of Du Pont's advertising.

Outlook for Teflon at the retail level now seems encouraging. Reports from the field and a recent trade show indicate the trade is willing to take a second look at Teflon. But some deep-rooted prejudices against Teflon must be dispelled before the outlook can be called exciting. Hopefully, we will begin to move in that direction . . .

. . . as the retailer begins to feel the response *in his own store* to Du Pont's television advertising,

. . . as the retailer is exposed to Du Pont's continuing advertising program in the trade press, and

. . . as he becomes more aware of the Teflon-coated lines and promotion plans being offered by his own cookware resources.

Notwithstanding this limited success, we think consistent trade advertising should play an important role because:

. . . Most of the trade is likely to miss Du Pont's daytime television advertising, so it must be continually merchandised to them through trade advertising;

. . . Many retailers may feel Du Pont's efforts are merely a promotional shot in the arm; through trade advertising Du Pont's long-range commitment to Teflon will be stressed and made crystal-clear.

. . . And finally, trade advertising will enable Du Pont to keep the retailer abreast of Teflon development, such as success stories, new products that become available, new colors. etc.

Copy approach, as envisioned by the advertising agency, was to "present the facts quickly and clearly, with as much detail as needed to get the dealer to apply the Teflon program to his own sales situation." Pocketbook appeal was built into the copy platform, of course. Copy would stress the following facts uncovered during the advertising research project:

1. All cookware sales went up 20 percent in the test markets.

2. Cookware finished with Teflon accounted for almost a third of total sales in these markets.

3. Teflon television commercials would reach some 90 percent of the nation's housewives an average of nine times per month for four months during the kick-off campaign.

4. The Teflon "quality seal" would be available on the products of at least 10 top manufacturers, and these manufacturers would be identified in trade promotions. (It's interesting to note that several months later some 28 manufacturers representing 80 to 90 percent of the total output of metal cookware production were making at least some utensils coated with Teflon and were carrying the Du Pont seal on their qualified merchandise.

As stated by Du Pont's agency, the copy approach to the trade would be essentially "news, presented factually with authoritative-looking layouts in one-page size, with credence lent by the name of Du Pont."

Open With "Pocketbook Appeal"

On page 1061 is the hard-hitting two-color advertisement to the trade that appeared in *Hardware Retailer* and *Housewares Buyer,* both monthly publications, and in *Hardware Age,* a bi-weekly, as well as in *Housewares Review,* also a monthly.

This ad makes very effective use of the pocketbook appeal. The headline, *New Du Pont Teflon Program Increased All Cookware Sales 20 percent in Multi-City Test,* immediately causes dollar signs to flash in front of the reader's eyes, as well as arousing his curiosity to see just *what* this program of Du Pont's is that it can do this for one of his profitable lines of merchandise. Subhead, *This Proven Campaign Goes National September 4,* is timely, topical, and pulls him into the body copy.

Body copy hammers home that cookware finished with Du Pont Teflon snared 35 percent of total cookware sales—sales that were up 20 percent, and that Teflon means quality cookware. Copy also stresses the support Du Pont TV advertising will give to the retailer, and that the entire promotional program isn't something that's being gone into with fingers crossed and dewey-eyed optimism, but that it is a proven program that has already worked in test cities. Selling theme—"No-Stick Cooking with No-Scour Cleanup" is explained and given believability by stating it is the opinion of consumers who tested Teflon finished cookware, not the advertiser's.

Another exciting trade ad is headlined, *How Du Pont Teflon captured 35 percent of total cookware business . . . while boosting ALL cookware sales 20 percent.* This advertisement again lists the manufacturers who earned Du Pont's Quality Seal and presents the central selling theme. Copy then proceeds to describe the consumer TV promotion and an arrow points to the kick-off date for the consumer campaign and makes a bid for action by the retailer.

Quality Seal Always Stressed

This ad is clean and attractive and well laid out; the inviting white space, coupled with the feeling of motion and excitement produced by the large symbols, pulls the reader right into the ad.

Rigid factory control program assures you Du Pont quality in cookware finished with TEFLON is the headline of another good ad (not illustrated). The Quality Seal itself is the illustration, circled with an attention-grabbing circle, rough and crude to impart a sense of immediacy and excitement to the advertisement. This ad does much to remove the curse from Teflon that any dealers might associate with the substandard merchandise that was marketed in the product's early days before Du Pont launched this program. Again, leading manufacturers of cookware who earned the right to display the Quality Seal are listed.

Another trade ad in the campaign has a primitive abstraction for the illustration and the headline: *New selling idea for cookware finished with Du Pont TEFLON attracts over 90 percent of women.* It leads into a very convincing discussion of the selling theme and of how Du Pont can be so sure its appeal is right, the very best one that can be used.

The next Du Pont ad again headlined the pocketbook appeal, as well as merchandised to the hilt its consumer advertising program. Headline reads: *Du Pont TV advertising produces profitable retail results for cookware finished with TEFLON.* Body copy plays up profit first of all, then introduces the facts that back up Du Pont's statement. It is very logical and believable, and accomplished its objective of increasing trade awareness of Du Pont's efforts in the consumer area.

NEW DU PONT TEFLON* PROGRAM INCREASED ALL COOKWARE SALES 20% IN MULTI-CITY TEST

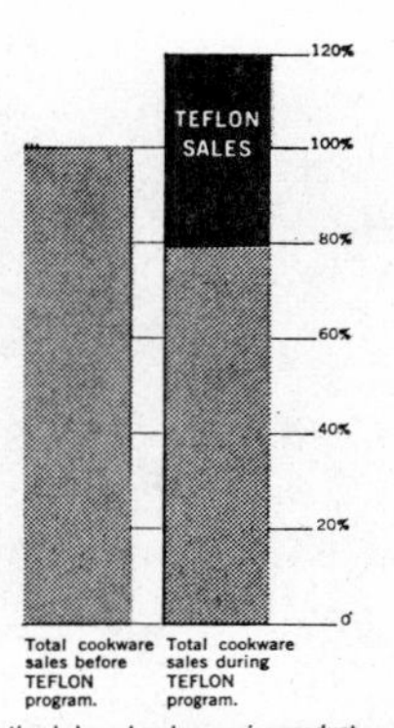

This Proven Campaign Goes National September 4. Sales of all cookware up 20% ... cookware finished with Du Pont TEFLON snaring 35% of total sales ... profits soaring with this new business ... that's what happened when high-profit "Controlled Quality" cookware finished with Du Pont TEFLON was promoted through a new selling approach and shown on TV in a multi-city test.

This tested, proven program goes national on September 4. Just check the TV schedule to see the heavy support planned for your area. And this is only the beginning—Du Pont will be behind TEFLON all the way again in 1964, starting in January. We're going about it in a big way because we know it will work. It already has worked.

The TV promotion is based on impressive product demonstrations, just like the ones that have been so successful in stores throughout the country. The central selling idea is "No-Stick Cooking with No-Scour Cleanup," the feature liked by over 90% of the women who tested cookware finished with TEFLON. Then there's the new Du Pont Quality Seal that assures you and your customers of Du Pont quality in TEFLON finished cookware.

What else is there to say? Except jump aboard and get a share of the new cookware business generated by Du Pont TEFLON.

LOOK FOR THIS SEAL

TEFLON

DU PONT — BETTER THINGS FOR BETTER LIVING ... THROUGH CHEMISTRY

*TEFLON is Du Pont's registered trademark for its TFE-Fluorocarbon finish.

TEFLON TV Schedule. This Fall, 90% of America's housewives will see TEFLON commercials an average of nine times. Daytime and nighttime shows in your city:

- Eleventh Hour
- Jack Paar
- The Dakotas
- Laramie
- Saturday Night at the Movies
- Breaking Point
- The Fugitive
- Mr. Novak
- Danny Thomas
- Wagon Train
- Queen for a Day
- General Hospital
- Who Do You Trust
- Seven Keys
- Say When
- Your First Impression
- Loretta Young

A wide variety of cookware finished with TEFLON is available from these companies, each of which has already earned the Du Pont Quality Seal.

- Anchor Hocking Glass Corp.
- Club Aluminum Products Co.
- Mirro Aluminum Co.
- National Presto Industries, Inc.
- Northland Aluminum Products, Inc.
- Regal Ware, Inc.
- Wagner Manufacturing Co.
- Wayne Manufacturing Co.
- Wear-Ever Aluminum, Inc.
- The West Bend Co.

One of the first Teflon ads aimed at retail dealers by Du Pont.

During this period N. W. Ayer recommended to Du Pont a space advertising program directed to the medical market; it was to be based on the health angle of cooking with utensils finished with Teflon. This selling theme had been used in the early days when Teflon achieved something less than a tremendous sales success.

Six ads were run in *The Journal of the American Medical Association.* Copy stressed the health appeal and contained a coupon offer for product literature and a Teflon-coated fry pan on a reduced price basis. These six advertisements produced some 2,600 requests for booklets and cookware from doctors. Because of this success and the interest the ads generated, it was recommended and approved by management that the program continue.

Additional ads stressed Teflon's role in low-calorie, low-cholesterol diets.

NO FATS,
NO OILS
NEEDED TO FRY FOOD
IN PANS FINISHED
WITH DU PONT TEFLON®

Lets you give patients new diet freedom. Now, thanks to a new development by Du Pont, your dietary patients can be allowed to eat fried foods without worry. TEFLON® TFE fluorocarbon resin, a new finish for frying pans and other cookware, permits frying without fats or oils. With the addition of this frequently forbidden category of foods, diets become less rigid, more easily followed.

Pans finished with TEFLON are so slick, hardly anything sticks to them. Fried eggs, for instance, slide easily from the pan even though not a single drop of butter, fat or oil is used. Housewives are also pleased to learn that these non-stick pans are easy to clean. A quick rinse and wipe is all that's needed. Never any scouring. The special TEFLON finish is available now on cookware produced by a number of manufacturers.

It's easy to prove the value of TEFLON. Du Pont would like to prove to you that cookware finished with TEFLON can perform a significant service for you and your patients. The coupon below offers you any or all of the following: a supply of folders, containing facts about cookware finished with TEFLON, which you can give to your patients; a regular or an electric fry pan with a TEFLON surface (offered at manufacturer's cost) for your personal use and/or experimentation. If you already have a frying pan finished with TEFLON (many doctors do), please feel free to order a supply of descriptive brochures.

®TEFLON is Du Pont's registered trademark for its TFE fluorocarbon finish.

E. I. du Pont de Nemours & Co. (Inc.)
Div. MJ 4-13, Room N-2507
Wilmington 98, Delaware

Please send me:

☐ A supply of folders containing facts for me and my patients about cookware finished with TEFLON.

☐ A 10" fry pan with a TEFLON surface, a $5 retail value, at manufacturer's cost of $3. My check is enclosed.

☐ An 11" electric fry pan with a TEFLON surface, a $20 retail value, at cost of $10. My check is enclosed.

Name______________________

Address______________________

City______________ Zone____ State__________

BETTER THINGS FOR BETTER LIVING . . . THROUGH CHEMISTRY

One of these excellent ads is shown. Copy appeals to the doctors' main "job" interest—welfare of their patients. User benefit of the product, elimination of fats and oils when preparing fried foods, is stressed, as is the power word, "new."

Du Pont's advertising program was so successful that manufacturers producing utensils finished with "Teflon" were over-sold and had such large back-orders that this special-market campaign was delayed and finally canceled before its second year.

The trade media schedule follows:

Publication	Space Unit	Frequency	Unit Cost	Total Cost
Home Furnishings	2 pp. fcg. B&W	4X	$1,845	$18,204
Daily (Tabloid)	7x10 unit B&W	22X	492	
Department Store	2 pp. fcg. B&W	2X	1,350	8,100
Economist	1 p. B&W	8X	675	
Hardware Age	2 pp. fcg. B&W	2X	1,020	6,120
	1 p. B&W	8X	510	
Hardware Retailer	2 pp. fcg. B&W	2X	1,060	6,360
	1 p. B&W	8X	530	
Housewares Buyer	2 pp. fcg. B&W	2X	830	4,980
	1 p. B&W	8X	415	
Housewares Review	2 pp. fcg. B&W	2X	820	4,920
	1 p. B&W	8X	410	
Chain Store Age	2 pp. fcg. B&W	2X	1,530	9,180
(Variety Store Edition)	1 p. B&W	8X	765	
		Total Space		$57,864
		Preparation		15,500
		TOTAL		$73,364

Another special promotion was undertaken, this one directed to home economists. It was designed to acquaint them with the "No-Stick—No-Scour" benefits of cookware finished with Teflon, and also to put into the economists' hands both "Teflon" teaching materials and cookware finished with "Teflon."

Advertisements were produced and run in *What's New in Home Economics* and in *Forecast for Home Economists.* This approach was an initial means of reaching consumers, although indirectly; when the extensive consumer campaign was launched, the promotion to the home economists was discontinued.

The headline, *What's new in Home Economics from Du Pont,* is reversed out of the illustrative area just where the eye normally enters the advertisement. It arouses interest and curiosity, and when

TEFLON® Finishes for NO-STICK, NO-SCOUR COOKWARE

Even burned food won't stick to the super-slick surface of cookware finished with Du Pont TEFLON*. Lets you cook, bake or fry the stickiest of foods . . . then clean the pan with just a quick wash and rinse. No scouring pads. No scouring powder. Calorie counters can fry in pans finished with TEFLON, while using little fat or oil (or none at all), and still get fast, easy cleanup.

Free teaching aids, explaining how to take advantage of the work-saving and dietary benefits of cookware finished with TEFLON, can be ordered by coupon on page 000. You can also order professional discount schedules from several manufacturers with this coupon.

Look for this seal on: Fry Pans, Saucepans, Griddles, Casseroles, Muffin Pans, Roasting Pans, Cookie Sheets, Cake Pans, and many other items.

TEFLON

DU PONT

Better Things for Better Living . . . through Chemistry

*TEFLON is Du Pont's registered trademark for its TFE-fluorocarbon finish

Home economists were the next target for Du Pont's Teflon campaign. This ad stresses the benefits of Teflon cookware to homemakers, and offers a "professional discount."

the illustration makes it plain how remarkably easy it is to clean a greasy pan with only a simple rubber spatula, the ad really has the reader hooked. She can hardly refrain from reading the subhead, *TEFLON Finishes for NO-STICK, NO-SCOUR COOKWARE.* By this time Du Pont has telegraphed its message with an interesting illustration and the provocative subhead. If the reader proceeded no further, she still was made aware of Teflon and of its primary user benefit.

Body copy stresses ease of cleaning, that even burned food won't stick to the superslick surface of cookware finished with Du Pont Teflon. In addition, copy mentions the reduction in calories possible with cooking done with no fats, no oils.

Free teaching aids are offered, as is a discount from several manufacturers—a professional discount, it's pointed out.

Du Pont's "quality seal" is displayed prominently just above the company's logotype. Such close association provides a favorable "rub-off" onto the "quality seal" from the logo.

Four smaller illustrations in the next advertisement highlight the user benefits of the amazing Teflon finish. In the upper left, there's a fresh egg casually being poured from the skillet—no sticking, no

Another ad stressing the user benefits of Teflon cookware. While still directed to home economists, the campaign is now developing a definite consumer orientation.

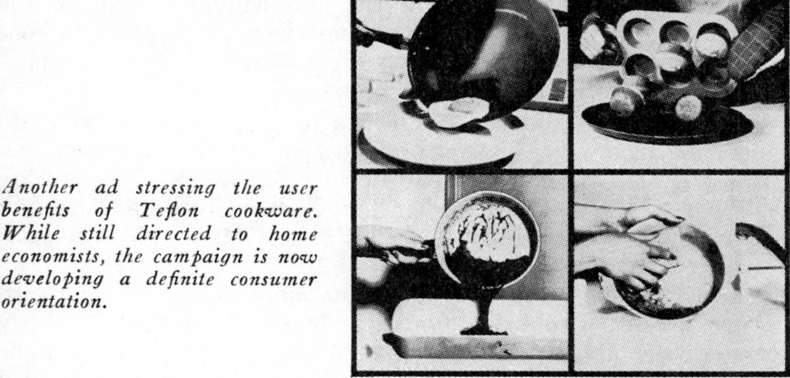

Cooking and baking utensils finished with TEFLON®
give you NO-STICK COOKING with NO-SCOUR CLEANUP!

Even burned food won't stick to the super-slick surface of cooking and baking utensils finished with Du Pont TEFLON*. Lets you cook, bake or fry the stickiest of foods ... then clean with just a quick wash and rinse. No scouring pads. No scouring powder. Calorie counters can fry in pans finished with TEFLON, while using little fat or oil (or none at all), and still get fast, easy cleanup. Full lines of this amazing cookware are available from several manufacturers. More will soon be on the market.

Free teaching aids, explaining how to take advantage of the work-saving and dietary benefits of cookware finished with TEFLON, can be ordered by coupon on Page 000, as well as professional discount schedules from several manufacturers.

Look for this seal on: Fry Pans, Saucepans, Griddles, Casseroles, Muffin Pans, Roasting Pans, Cookie Sheets, Cake Pans, and many other items.

DU PONT

Better Things for Better Living ... *through Chemistry*

*TEFLON is Du Pont's registered trademark for its TFE-fluorocarbon finish.

having to use a spatula to pick it up, and no fats or oils used in frying. Upper right illustration shows a housewife easily pouring muffins out of the pan, no sticking, no paper cups, no having to run a knife around each individual muffin and pry it loose from the pan. And look how clean the pan itself is! The two lower illustrations flash across the message that cookware finished with Du Pont Teflon almost cleans itself so little effort is required.

Now, if we'd had cookware finished with Teflon in the Army in World War II, life would have been much easier! The pots-and-pans detail, always one of the worst for less than eager KP's, would have been one of the easiest, better even than egg-cracking or head-counting.

Headline of this ad is: *Cooking and baking utensils finished with TEFLON give you NO-STICK COOKING with NO-SCOUR CLEANUP!*

Body copy advances the easy-clean, low-calories story quickly and convincingly. Again, the "quality seal" appears just above and to the right of the Du Pont logotype. It's in good company.

As plans were finished and approved, it became possible for

Du Pont advertising management to prepare a budget covering the introduction of Teflon, both for the first half-year, and for the following 12 months. Included was television advertising to consumers, trade advertising, and promotions to special target groups—the medical profession and home economists.

Furthermore, direct mail pieces had to be prepared in order to satisfy the requests of coupon respondents, and for other purposes. Plans were also made to participate in trade shows. The "quality seal" had to be designed, produced, and disseminated to manufacturers whose processing methods met Du Pont's high standards. Literature was needed for sales clerks.

And as Teflon became available in more colors, a color-card became necessary to help purchasers make a selection. Publicity releases were prepared, and the costs of research activities had to be met. The budget included these, plus other related functions needed to produce a unified program.

A condensed version of the budget is shown below:

TEFLON-COATED COOKWARE ADVERTISING AND SALES AIDS BUDGET

	Introduction Year	Second[1] Year
Total Consumer Advertising	$652,100	$1,145,000[2]
Retail Trade	51,300	75,400
Professional Trade	27,100	11,000
Advertising Research	40,800	26,500
Direct Mail and Printed Matter	24,800	14,000
Exhibits	3,000	3,000
Travel and Operations Expense	24,700	20,000
	$823,800	$1,294,900

There is no grand finale to this well-planned product introduction, for it succeeded just as it was supposed to do. As the program got into high gear the volume of sales of Teflon to the cookware industry increased each month during the first two years, and it continues upward. There is every indication it will continue to do so, for as more manufacturers are approved and the number of coated utensils rises, so, naturally, do Teflon sales.

[1]Introduction year figures are based on eight months of actual expenditures and four months forecasted expenditures. Figures for all of second year are forecasted amounts.

[2]Difference in TV budget results from full second year national TV advertising versus only last half of introduction year on national basis and first half with test market costs only.

Teflon became a hot item in the housewares field. The display of confidence in the product by major utensil producers helped to generate interest in other areas. Waffle irons, ice cream scoops, and even a Teflon-coated rolling pin have been introduced onto the market. And one manufacturer produced an electric oven with removable Teflon-coated wall panels to make it easier to clean; other manufacturers are exploring the possibility of using Teflon for such products as range hoods and soleplates for irons. Teflon-coated safety-razor blades also appeared on the market.

New Markets Appear

Use of Teflon isn't confined to products for the kitchen, or for the home, however. At least one manufacturer is exploiting Teflon's slickness to make work easier for the home handyman and for the professional carpenter; this toolmaker is producing a handsaw coated with Teflon. This eliminates binding and a large part of the work, for a reduction in friction naturally means less physical effort is required.

Interestingly, sales predictions made on the basis of Du Pont advertising in test markets largely materialized on the national scene.

Unquestionably the market for coated cookware had been revitalized. Consumers were purchasing Teflon finished merchandise in large quantities; manufacturers had greatly expanded, or were in the process, their offerings featuring Teflon; retailers and jobbers were once again excited over future prospects and acted accordingly; new applications were being found for Teflon; the Du Pont "quality seal" had been instrumental in bringing about high quality standards; added advertising support by the trade reinforced Du Pont's continued national promotional efforts. Teflon was becoming a readily recognized household word.

The continuing research program indicated that 52 percent of all cooks in test markets covered by TV commercials were aware of Teflon. This figure was approximately the same throughout the national market.

Du Pont pulled Teflon out of the doldrums and reestablished it—successfully—with creative thinking. Well-conceived market research, sound planning, and effective advertising. These are the necessary steps in any successful promotional program.

Chapter 13

MEDIA

"MEDIA" is the plural of the word "medium." Media are *not* a group of turban-swathed mystics who claim to be intimately familiar with the supernatural and who, after peering intently into the depths of a crystal ball, pass on messages from those who have passed on.

Rather, media are vehicles that carry messages. Typical media are jungle drums, skywriting, a chit impaled on a forked stick, smoke signals, the heliograph, the semaphore, and pennants fluttering from a ship's mast.

In industrial advertising when we think of the best possible medium to disseminate the message we've put in our advertisements, we ignore the marginal media mentioned above and think instead of a business publication—or a number of business publications.

The business press is the most efficient and economical means yet devised to reach the untold tens of thousands of hidden buying influences throughout industry—and of reaching the largest possible number of primary buying influences.

As industrial marketers have become more sophisticated and increasingly aware of the necessity of an effective, productive communications program, the value of the business press impressed itself on them more and more. Approximately 65 percent more advertising dollars are invested in business publication advertising today than 10 years ago. More than 1,250,000 pages of advertising is run annually in the business press.

Advertising managers and industrial advertising agencies have as a secondary goal the creation and placing of the best advertising they're capable of producing. The goal that's always uppermost is increasing sales and reducing the cost of selling. This is what industrial advertising does if the program is well-planned and well-conceived.

Space advertising in the business press isn't accepted on blind faith. It isn't endorsed, recommended, or purchased just because somebody claimed he thought maybe it was the thing to do. No space program was ever launched by an advertising manager who knew what he was doing merely because his competitors did it.

To achieve its present place in the mixture of media and techniques that comprise the arsenal at the disposal of the well-armed industrial marketer today, space advertising in the business press had to earn its position by proving its worth.

Advertising people are curious by nature. They're questioners. They accept very little without analyzing and evaluating and comparing with the tried and proven from past experience.

For example, American Business Press tells about the direct mail lists that were compiled from salesmen's call reports by American Hard Rubber Company. All 2,937 customers and prospects on the list were asked to supply the names of others in their companies who would be interested in the company and its products.

A total of 402 replied and named 232 new people who, in their opinion, had buying influence and who should be on the mailing list.

American Hard Rubber then surveyed these 232 people to see if they were being reached by the company's business publication advertising; 93 percent of those who replied said they read one or more of the publications in which the company advertised. The conclusion was obvious: even though the company had not known these influences, they had an opportunity to know the company.

Some Research Studies

Time after time research conducted by industrial advertisers—not by their agencies, or by any outsider with an ax to grind—prove beyond a shadow of doubt that people in industry who are contemplating a purchase look first to business publications for product information.

The Du Pont study on the influence of industrial advertising asked this question: "How do you obtain information about industrial supplies and equipment?" 78 percent said from business publications; most of the rest said from direct mail.

The American Screw Company asked industrial buyers how they first heard of the Phillips recessed-head screw. Of all, 71 percent said through business publication advertising; 23 percent named salesmen, direct mail, exhibits and what have you.

In a study covering buying influences in six fields of industry, a manufacturer of heavy equipment asked, "Which of the following has been most helpful in keeping you up to date and providing you with information about products?" Business publication advertising was mentioned first by 71 percent, and 19 percent said by direct mail.

A manufacturer of electrical controls recently reevaluated its entire marketing operation. Everything was questioned. No area where waste or inefficiency might exist was accepted without careful analysis to see if improvements could be made for improved efficiency and lower costs. Among other things, space advertising in the business press was thoroughly examined. A study that required several months was performed and an unusually large sample was asked, "How do you get information which enables you to compare competitive products (in our line) before buying?" Of these, 83 percent specified space advertising in the business press; 14 percent said direct mail; the balance mentioned salesmen, trade shows, catalogs and other random answers.

George C. Kiernan, president, George Kiernan Associates, Inc., successor to the Eastman Research Organization, the 25-year-old firm that specializes in editorial research in the business press, recently wrote a very enlightening article for *Media/scope* magazine.

Among the conclusions reached after a quarter-century's detailed analysis is that business publications are extremely well read, and that they are held in high regard by the business community *if* they are well edited.

If they are well edited—be sure to note that qualifier.

Furthermore, the research expert stated unequivocally that business publication advertisements are read intentionally, not accidentally. And he backed up his conclusion with some meaningful statistics.

For instance, 85 percent of the 9,513 people interviewed in 174 separate Reader Performance Surveys on 45 different business publications had either completed or started their reading of the surveyed issues while the issues were still current. Furthermore, 64 percent of these had completed reading the studied magazines.

A very healthy 51 percent of those interviewed had read both feature articles and the departments of the various magazines.

Of those who had read any part of the surveyed publications, 95 percent read the advertising either "on purpose" (68 percent) or at least "by accident" (27 percent).

In fact, many readers reported having devoted as much time and attention to the magazines' advertising as they did to the editorial matter—31 percent devoted as much, 14 percent more. And a resounding 78 percent of the business publication readers reported finding something in the publications that applied directly and immediately to their work.

The advertising manager and the agency naturally look at each publication analytically—to determine if it has real merit and if it is right for the company and its products, but they don't question the merit of the business press as a whole.

If a member of top management seriously questions readership of the business press in its entirety, this reveals either a personality defect—one that is unbelievably negative—a gaping void in this individual's business education, or a lack of management ability. This person's qualifications to manage are, to say the least, questionable.

The business press is unique. The business publication is the most economical, most influential, most penetrating path to specialized groups. All good selling is specialized, and nothing specializes like the business press.

It is good sense, and good advertising, to cultivate the people who are immediately and directly concerned with the purchase and use of your product in the language, atmosphere, and reading environment of their job interest. Business publications, the working press, provide you with this opportunity.

Each medium of advertising has, or should have, distinctive characteristics—things that make it different and, for certain purposes, better than any other medium. Business publications are unique inasmuch as men read them for the job benefit alone. They are used for profit and not for pleasure. Only in a business publication can you always find your sales prospect with his mind on business—when he is *editorially conditioned* to absorb your business message.

Prime, Low-Cost Audiences

Because business publications serve specialized audiences, their circulations are compact and relatively small. Their rates are modest accordingly. Thus, a campaign of dominance, something strong enough to stir excitement is well within the pocketbook reach of just about every advertiser. This powerful medium is the lowest-cost, least-wasteful of any at your disposal.

Do not, however, let this low cost make a catchall of your business publication advertising program. "Buying across the board" is pretty unsophisticated. The best advertisement you can produce will not achieve maximum effectiveness unless it appears in the *right* business publications to reach your prime prospects.

Shortly evaluation of business publications will be discussed to see just how they're rated and analyzed to determine which is best. First, however, let's take a brief look at just what it is that comprises the business press.

Industrial Marketing magazine, in its most recent issue on the subject, listed more than 2,400 business publications in the United States and Canada. This listing was published as a special supplement to the regular edition of the magazine, and it is both very complete and very helpful. Every industrial advertising man should receive and read this authoritative publication; it is the voice of industrial advertising. Membership in the Association of Industrial Advertisers (AIA) automatically includes a subscription; however, if for some reason you don't belong to AIA, you should by all means subscribe to *Industrial Marketing.* Its articles are timely and helpful and down to earth; there's no blue-sky stuff.

The 2,400 publications listed range from *AAMA Bulletin,* the official publication of the American Association of Medical Assistants, to *Wisconsin Motor Carrier,* official organ of the Badger State's for-hire carriers.

Each of the 2,400 books listed in the guide is under the basic industry which it primarily serves, such as aerospace, construction, transportation, and so on.

Multiple and group publishers with a number of magazines in their "stables," such as McGraw-Hill, Chilton, Cahners, and so forth are listed under the name of the publishing company. Home office address is given, as is the phone number, a complete list of the company's publications, alphabetically; they are, of course, listed fully in the guide in its two sections.

And Standard Rate & Data Service, Inc., 5201 Old Orchard Road, Skokie, Illinois 60078, publishes a massive volume of some 1,400 pages each month. It is titled *Business Publication Rates and Data;* SRDS also publishes *Canadian Advertising Rates and Data.* Companion volumes cover consumer media—magazines, newspapers, TV and radio stations and networks.

This book, usually called merely SRDS from the initials of the publisher, contains not only a listing of business publications, but detailed information that advertisers and agencies require about each medium in order to plan a media program efficiently.

Here's a tip: Most agencies are happy to give this expensive volume to clients at no charge immediately upon receipt of next month's issue. Although some of the information is made obsolete by the newer volume, much of it is not and the industrial advertising manager always finds that a copy of SRDS on business magazines is one of the handiest things he can have around the office. All sorts of questions can be answered without wasting time calling the agency.

The thousands of business publications listed in *Business Publication Rates and Data* are not listed alphabetically, but are divided into classification groupings according to the market served. Some numbers are not yet used. Classifications are:

1. ADVERTISING & MARKETING
2. AIR CONDITIONING, PLUMBING, HEATING
3. AMUSEMENTS

3A. APPLIANCES

4. ARCHITECTURE
5. ARTS

5A. AUTOMATIC DATA SYSTEMS

6. AUTOMOTIVE
7. AVIATION & AEROSPACE
9. BAKING
10. BANKING
11. BARBERS, BEAUTY SHOPS, HAIRDRESSERS, ETC.
14. BOATING
15. BOOKS AND BOOK TRADE

15A. BOTTLING

16. BREWING, DISTILLING, BEVERAGES
17. BRICK, TILE, BUILDING MATERIALS
18. BRUSHES, Brooms & Mops
19. BUILDING

19A. BUILDING Management & Real Estate

20. BUSINESS

21A. CAMPS & CAMPING

22. CANNING
25. CEMETERY & MONUMENTS
26. CERAMICS
27. CHAIN STORES
28. CHEMICAL & Chemical Process Industries
29. CLEANING & DYEING
31. CLOTHING & Furnishing Goods (Men's)
32. CLOTHING & Furnishing Goods (Women's)

32A. COAL MERCHANDISING

32B. COIN-OPERATED and Vending Machines

33. CONFECTIONERY
34. CONTROL & INSTRUMENTATION SYSTEMS

34A. CORSETS, Brassieres & Undergarments

34B. COSMETICS

34C. DAIRY PRODUCTS

35. DENTAL

35A. DEPARTMENT & SPECIALTY STORES

35B. DISCOUNT MARKETING

35C. DISPLAY

35D. DRAPERIES & CURTAINS

36. DRUGS, PHARMACEUTICALS
38. EDUCATIONAL
39. ELECTRICAL
40. ELECTRONIC ENGINEERING
41. ENGINEERING & CONSTRUCTION
44. FARM IMPLEMENTS

44A. FARM SUPPLIES

44B. FASHION ACCESSORIES

44C. FEED, GRAIN & MILLING

45. FERTILIZER, Agricultural Chemicals
46. FINANCIAL

47. FIRE PROTECTION
48. FISHING, COMMERCIAL
48A. FLOOR COVERINGS
49. FLORISTS & FLORICULTURE
50. FOOD—PROCESSING & DISTRIBUTION
52. FUNERAL DIRECTORS
53. FUR TRADE, Fur Farming, Trapping
54. FURNITURE & UPHOLSTERY
55. GAS
56. GENERAL MERCHANDISE
57. GIFTS, Antiques, Art Goods, Greeting Cards
57A. GLASS
59. GOLF
61. GROCERY
62. HARDWARE
63A. HOME ECONOMICS
63B. HOME FURNISHINGS
65. HOSPITAL ADMINISTRATION
66. HOTELS, Motels, Clubs & Resorts
67. HOUSEWARES
68. ICE CREAM
69. INDUSTRIAL
69A. INDUSTRIAL DESIGN
70. INDUSTRIAL DISTRIBUTION
70A. INDUSTRIAL PURCHASING
70B. INFANTS', Children's & Teen Age Goods
71. INSTITUTIONS
72. INSURANCE
73. INTERIOR DESIGN & Decorating
73B. INTERNATIONAL TRADE
74. JEWELRY & Watchmaking
75. JOURNALISM
77. LANDSCAPE, Garden Supplies
78. LAUNDRY
79. LEATHER, Boots & Shoes
80. LEGAL
81. LIGHTING & Lighting Fixtures
82. LINENS & DOMESTICS
82A. LUGGAGE & LEATHER Goods
83. LUMBER & Forest Industries
83A. MAINTENANCE
84. MARITIME, Marine, Shipbuilding, Repair & Operating
85. MATERIALS ENGINEERING
85A. MATERIALS HANDLING & Distribution
86. MEATS & PROVISIONS
87. MEDICAL & SURGICAL
88. METAL, Metalworking & Machinery
89. MICROFILM MEDIA
90. MILITARY & NAVAL
93. MINING
94. MISCELLANEOUS
95. MOTION, Talking, Sound, Commercial Pictures, etc.
96. MOTOR TRUCKS & Accessories
97. MOTORCYCLE & Bicycle
98. MUNICIPAL
99. MUSIC & MUSIC TRADES
101. NOTIONS & Fancy Goods
101A. NUCLEAR SCIENCE & Engineering
102. NURSING & Health
102A. NUT CULTURE, Nut & Popcorn Trade

103. OFFICE Equipment & Stationery
103A. OFFICE METHODS & Management
104. OILS (Vegetable)
104A. OPTICAL & Optometric
105. OSTEOPATHIC
107. PACKAGING (Mfrs.) Paperboard, Wood Boxes & Barrels
107A. PACKAGING (Users)
108. PAINT
109. PAPER
110. PARKS, Public
111. PETROLEUM & OIL
112. PETS
113. PHOTOGRAPHIC
113A. PHYSICAL DISTRIBUTION
114. PLASTICS & Composition Products
115. PLUMBING
115A. POLICE, Detective & Sheriff
115B. PORTS
116. POULTRY & Poultry Products
117. POWER & Power Plants
118. PRINTING & PRINTING PROCESSES
119. PRODUCE
120. PRODUCT DESIGN ENGINEERING
121. PUBLIC TRANSPORTATION
122. RADIO & TELEVISION
124. RAILROAD
125. REFRIGERATION
126. RELIGIOUS
126A. RENTAL AND LEASING EQUIPMENT
127. RESTAURANTS AND FOOD SERVICE
128. ROADS, STREETS
129. ROOFING
130. RUBBER
131. SAFETY
131A. SALES MANAGEMENT
131B. SANITATION
132. SCHOOL ADMINISTRATION
132A. SCIENCE, RESEARCH and DEVELOPMENT
133. SEED & NURSERY TRADE
134. SELLING & SALESMANSHIP
135. SEWAGE DISPOSAL
137. SPORTING GOODS
139. STONE PRODUCTS
140. SUGAR & SUGAR BEETS
140A. SWIMMING POOLS
141. TEA, COFFEE, SPICES
142. TELEPHONE & TELEGRAPH
143. TEXTILES AND KNIT GOODS
145. TOBACCO
147. TOYS, HOBBIES and NOVELTIES
147A. TRAILERS & ACCESSORIES
148. TRANSPORTATION, Traffic, Shipping & Shipping Room Supplies
149. TRAVEL
151. VENETIAN BLINDS
152. VETERINARY
153. WAREHOUSING, Storage
155. WATER SUPPLY
156. WELDING
158. WIRE & WIRE PRODUCTS
159. WOODWORKING

This is a total of 173 different categories of business publications, and in many of the categories are 10, 20, 30 or more individual magazines. In group 87, for example, MEDICAL & SURGICAL, there are a total of 213 separate magazines serving this "industry."

A Typical Analysis

As an example of what the book contains, let's take *Construction Methods & Equipment,* a McGraw-Hill publication, and look at SRDS's information about it.

First of all, the name of the publication is listed. It appears in classification 41, for all publications devoted to engineering and construction.

Then we note that the logos of ABC—Audit Bureau of Circulations; and ABP—American Business Press, Inc., are shown, denoting that the magazine is a member in good standing of these spokesmen for the business publication industry, and its auditing organization.

Following this is the information that *Construction Methods & Equipment* is published monthly by McGraw-Hill, Inc., 1221 Avenue of the Americas, New York, New York 10020.

Editorial concept as set forth by the publisher is that *Construction Methods & Equipment* is edited to provide "risk insurance" for construction contractors. Its purpose is to help contractors function more profitably, more efficiently or more effectively in building the heavy construction projects on which they work. Its purpose is to provide the reader information which will help him do his job better at more profit to his customers and to himself. The book uses the case history approach. Editorial deals with planning, supervision and field execution of construction operations. Actual examples of successful problem-solving and on-site stories are supplemented by detailed specification files of equipment that's available, exclusive cost tables and pricing tables of materials and equipment. Intended audience is then defined.

Mail instructions are then given; this covers space contracts and insertion orders. Additional information is given concerning mailing plates, engravings, electros, and so on to the publication's production department. Also noted is that furnished inserts are to be shipped directly to *CM&E's* printer, properly marked as to quantity of insert in each carton, and with the name of the advertiser, plus the issue in which the inserts are to be inserted.

After this basic information come 18 separate subcategories of necessary information about every publication listed in this vast reference work. These are:

1. PERSONNEL

Publisher
Advertising sales manager
Promotion manager
Production manager
Editor

2. REPRESENTATIVES AND/OR BRANCH OFFICES

All of McGraw-Hill's offices throughout the country are listed, complete with telephone numbers and the names of the local representatives. For example, you'll find for Colorado's Mile High City the listing reads as follows: Denver 80202—Harry B. Doyle, Jr., Advertising Sales, Tower Building, 1700 Broadway, (303) 266-3863. Addresses and names of representatives are given for England, Germany, Italy, France and Japan.

3. COMMISSION AND CASH DISCOUNT

15% to agencies on space, color, bleed and position; 2 percent 10 days from invoice date on net billing for advertisers with agencies, on gross billing for advertisers without agencies.

4. GENERAL RATE POLICY

Copy service: copy ordered from publisher to be charged at cost.
Advertising rates: The rates on this and following pages are approximate—not current. Ad rates are always subject to revision.

5. BLACK/WHITE RATES

	1 Page	2/3 Page	1/2 Page	1/3 Page	1/4 Page	1/6 Page	1/12 Page
1x	$1,795	$1,240	$955	$650	$515	$340	$192
6x	1,765	1,215	940	635	500	330	190
12x	1,740	1,190	930	625	490	325	188
24x	1,715	1,175	920	615	485	320	186
48x	1,690	1,165	910	605	480	315	184

72 pages—$1,665
96 pages—$1,640

6. COLOR RATES

Second colors available in all sizes of display ad units. Standard AAAA 2nd colors (yellow, orange, red, blue and green) used.

Standard 2nd color on single page, space cost plus $225
Standard 2nd color on spreads, space cost plus $450
Matched color 2nd color, space cost plus .... $ 85
(in addition to charge for standard 2nd color)
Metallic inks .... (contact publisher)

Offset coated stock color forms:

4-color process	1 time	6 times	12 times	24 times
Per page	$2,440	$2,385	$2,335	$2,300
	48 times	72 times	96 times	
	$2,265	$2,235	$2,205	

3rd & 4th consecutive pages $85 less on each. Contact publisher for larger units.

7. COVERS

a. Cover Rates: Include 4-color process and bleed. Cover rates are minimum and are not affected by other space used by an advertiser within the contract year; but each cover can be applied in earning frequency rates for other advertising space used.

	Covers II and III	Cover IV
Rates for Covers:	$2,340	$2,540

Rates include 4 process colors and bleed.

b. Cover Schedules: Can be cancelled only on notice of ninety days prior to date of issue, and, if cancelled before cover schedule is completed, are subject to short rate of $105 for each cover used.

8. INSERTS

Check publisher on all insert matters, specifications and quantity needed. The regular black-and-white space rates apply to furnished inserts which meet all specifications, are ready for binding and do not require trimming, back-up, etc.

Inserts that must be backed-up, tipped-in, trimmed, or require special handling will be charged to the advertiser at our prevailing rates—to be furnished on request. All special charges will be in addition to space rates and are not commissionable.

9. BLEED

a. Rates for Bleed or Oversized Pages: No Charge.

b. Specifications for Bleed: See Mechanical Requirements #13. (Bleed is one of the biggest bargains an advertiser can get. The entire page is his, not a 7x10" segment floating in the center, thus giving him the entire "stage," not part of it. Before most publications started printing web-offset, bleed was an extra cost item, although well worth it. In all fairness, it must be admitted that bleed formerly cost publishers more to produce, but they, in turn, passed that charge on. They now don't charge for it. The advertiser benefits.

10. SPECIAL POSITIONS

Special Positions (other than covers) are available and rates are furnished on request. Check with publisher for position restrictions.

11. CLASSIFIED, READING NOTICES, ETC.

"Professional Services," "Searchlight," "Where to Buy," and "Employment Opportunities" section rates on separate card, and in SRDS.

12. Regional Editions or Split Runs

Information on request.

13. Special Issue Rates and Data

Not offered.

14. Contract and Copy Regulations

Specific and detailed references are published monthly in SRDS.

15. Mechanical Requirements

Information required by production men.

16. Issue and Closing Dates

Published monthly; issued first Wednesday of publication month. Definite space reservations due the 5th of the preceding month if proofs are desired. Furnished inserts ready for binding due 10th of preceding month.

Inserts requiring back-up due 5th of month preceding issue date.

Pacific Coast advertisers should ship material 10 days prior to these closing dates. No cancellations accepted after closing date. Contracts may be canceled by advertiser or published on written notice 30 days in advance of closing dates.

17. Special Services

AIA Media data form.

Ad readership studies.

18. Circulation

Established 1919. ABC audited.

Average total number of subscriptions	60,129
Average total paid circulation (6 mos.)	60,129
Unpaid distribution (not included above)	3,928
Advertisers, agencies, checking copies	1,636
Staff copies and miscellaneous	2,292

Total unpaid is 3,928; this is comprised of checking copies, staff copies, copies that go to advertisers and agencies, and miscellaneous copies.

Geographical breakdown of circulation follows, in SRDS. Business analysis of subscriptions follows, in SRDS.

Each one of these thousands of publications must abide by the Contract and Copy Regulations which follow, as set forth in SRDS *Business Publication Rates & Data:*

CONTRACT AND COPY REGULATIONS

1. Insertion instructions shall be supplied for every advertisement and shall clearly state the following information: name of publication, name of advertiser, date to be inserted, size of advertisement, identification of advertisement (proof of ad to be furnished if possible) plus any special instructions such as bleed, color, etc.

2. No conditions, printed or otherwise, appearing on the space order, billing instruction or copy instructions which conflict with the publishers stated policies will be binding on the publisher.

3. All advertising orders are accepted subject to the terms and provisions of the current rate card. Orders are accepted subject to change in rates upon notice from the publisher. However, orders may be canceled at the time the change in rates becomes effective without incurring a short rate adjustment, provided the rate has been earned up to the date of cancellation.

4. Orders acceptable for not more than one year in advance.

5. A contract year, or twelve-month period, starts from the date of the first insertion. Twelve-month periods do not overlap: in other words, space counted in one contract period to determine the rate for that period, cannot be counted again toward determining the rate for the subsequent or past periods.

6. T. F. Contracts will be billed at rate earned through the previous twelve months or billed at rate earned through contract year period without incurring short rate, provided that the same frequency is maintained up to the time of cancellation.

7. Space orders wherever possible should specify a definite schedule of insertions, issues and sizes of space.

8. The forwarding of an order is construed as an acceptance of all the rates and conditions under which advertising is at the time sold.

9. The publisher reserves the right to void any contract unless the first insertion is used within three months from date thereof.

10. Contracts may be discontinued by either party on 30 days' written notice.

11. Verbal agreements are not recognized.

12. If more or less insertions are used within one year than specified in the order, charges will be adjusted in accordance with established rates.

13. Cancellation of space order forfeits the right to position protection.

14. The publisher reserves the right to give better position than specified in the order, at no increase in rate.

15. Advertiser and advertising agency assume liability for all content (including text representation and illustrations) of advertisements printed, and also assume responsibility for any claims arising therefrom made against the publisher. It is the advertiser's or agency's responsibility to obtain appropriate releases on any items or individuals pictured in the advertisement.

16. Acceptance of advertising for any product or service is subject to investigation of the product or service, and of the claims made for it in the advertisement submitted for publication.

17. All advertising is subject to the publisher's approval. The publisher reserves the right to reject advertising which he feels is not in keeping with the publication's standard.

18. The advertisers' index is prepared under the regulations and policies of the publisher as an extra service to the advertiser over and above his space order. The publisher, therefore, does not assume liability for errors in the index notwithstanding all normal precautions.

19. The publisher's liability for any error will not exceed the charge for the advertisement in question.

20. The publisher assumes no liability if for any reason it becomes necessary to omit an advertisement.

21. All agreements are subject to strikes, accidents, fires, acts of God, or other contingencies beyond the publisher's control.

22. Failure to make the order correspond in price or otherwise with the rate schedule is regarded only as a clerical error and publication is made and charged for upon the terms of the schedule in force without further notice.

23. The publisher reserves the right to limit the size of space to be occupied by an advertisement.

24. Two or more advertisers are not permitted to use space under the same contract.

25. Association advertising ordinarily takes the rate earned for space used by the association advertising alone. Individual members of associations cannot bulk their individual company space with the association space to earn a bulk rate for themselves.

26. Supplied inserts shall be charged regular black and white space rates plus additional production costs incurred. A charge lower or higher than actual black and white space rates would be considered price discrimination.

27. Agencies are entitled to only one copy of an issue regardless of the number of advertisements placed by the agency in the publication.

28. When change of copy, covered by an uncancelled insertion order, is not received by the closing date, copy run in previous issue will be inserted.

29. The publisher assumes no liability for errors in key numbers, or its Reader Service Section, or advertisers' index.

30. Any deliberate attempt to simulate a publication's format is not permitted, and the publisher reserves the right to place the word "advertisement" with copy which in the publisher's opinion resembles editorial matter.

31. Advertisements offering prizes, or contests of any nature, are accepted provided prior approval has been obtained from the Post Office at place of publication entry.

32. Requests for specified position at R.O.P. rates are given consideration but no guarantee is made unless the position premium has been provided for in the contract.

33. An advertiser requesting that a standard full page plate be printed without the name and page number appearing on the page shall be charged a premium.

34. No allowance is made to advertisers for furnishing complete plates, text and illustrations for their advertisements.

35. Advertisements ordered set and not used will be charged for composition.

A few additional facts about the business press make it obvious that business publishing is a huge industry that serves other industries that go from tiny to tremendous.

For example, last year the editorial pages in all business publications was in excess of 850,000. More than 14,000 editors work full time to find, evaluate and interpret information that's useful to the specialized businesses they serve.

No other publications or information media render this type of concentrated service to specific types of business, or to people in specific job categories.

Most top managements, the good ones, urge that all of their technical and management people read the business publications in their fields—and many insist upon it.

Most business publication editorial is engineered to give readers important information fast, to let readers discover quickly what they want to study closely, and what they'd just as soon pass over. Business publications are essential tools. Without them the progress of business and industry, science and medicine would be greatly hindered and slowed down.

More than 1,250,000 pages of advertising was carried in the business press last year. Advertising revenue was almost three-quarters of a billion dollars. Circulation of all publications was more than 60 million.

Media Evaluation

Progressive, up-to-date management is fully aware of the value of the business press. It realizes its importance as the one most efficient and most economical medium with which to communicate with the vast audience to whom you must tell your product story.

A question that inevitably arises at this stage is: But there are so *many* business publications! How do you choose between them? How do you select the ones that are right for your company, the ones that will do the most to help you achieve your communications objectives? Since any number of magazines are published to serve your industry, and since they compete with each other, how do you determine which are best?

This is quite a problem and it is not one that can be solved by drawing straws, shooting poker dice, or by a few wise words mumbled over the current copy of *Business Publication Rates & Data.*

Objective evaluation of media is necessary so that you can make an informed choice of publications that will do your program and your company the most good. Such an evaluation, using specific criteria, is possible and is relatively easy to accomplish, as we'll see. Once you've evaluated media for one program—perhaps for one given market, or even for one year—this should lead to a formal media appraisal system which you can establish with all of the guidelines and rules firmed up and written down.

There is no magic formula, though, that will enable you to perform the task effortlessly, and this chapter won't qualify you for an agency media director's position; it will, however, point out most of the better means of evaluating media successfully. It will give you a good working knowledge of media so you won't have to rely on direct mail pieces and contradictory claims in media mailings or from media salesmen.

Even before getting into this, though, it's well to examine a problem that's prevalent throughout industrial companies—the existence of anywhere from one to a dozen or more "media directors" in the company.

Every one of these individuals has strong opinions about any number of publications, particularly those published by technical societies to which they have belonged for most of their working lives. This long familiarity with these media makes each of the media directors supremely self-confident. After all, they know their industry, so it naturally follows that they are well qualified to judge the merits of magazines they've seen around for years. These gifted individuals have strong opinions and they don't want to be confused with facts.

An advertising manager faced with this situation—and it's a common one—must arm himself with facts and more facts which enable him to ascertain that certain publications are desirable and others are not.

Only facts, coupled with an explanation of how media are evaluated, will enable him to scuttle the poor books and use those which should be on the schedule. He has to make his viewpoint prevail. After all, the advertising manager is the company's advertising professional; it's his business to be able to evaluate media. And he's responsible for company money and for a program that influences the degree of success the company achieves in the marketplace. This can't be jeopardized by personal opinion founded on instinct and little else.

However, often the "true facts" fail to dissuade many of those in the company who are staunch proponents of marginal publications just because they've "seen them around for years." Although this situation crops up in all kinds of industrial firms, it is much more prevalent in companies in industries that are somewhat less than progressive as well as in individual companies whose managements are strongly engineering-oriented.

An explanation for the prevalence of this attitude may be found in a provocative article in *Research/Development* magazine. The author, Harold K. Mintz, is an experienced technical editor-writer, as well as a teacher whose specialty is to teach engineers to write.

In his 13 classes—in that many years—Mr. Mintz was able to analyze a total of 275 graduate engineers from virtually all of the major disciplines of modern technology. These engineers work for 85 different organizations, including private industry, the armed forces, the civil service, "think tanks," and public utilities. Included in the companies represented are such giants as General Electric, Westinghouse, and medium-sized companies like Polaroid and Sanders Associates.

These engineers to whom the author taught English held degrees from 57 different colleges and universities scattered all over the country, as well as six overseas institutions. Among them were MIT, Rensselaer, and a number of the Ivy League schools.

Principal objective of the course Mr. Mintz taught was to "sharpen the students' ability to communicate technical information with clarity."

A secondary objective was "to escalate some of the engineers—the more literate minority—beyond that modest level so as to write competently."

Of 197 engineers surveyed, 104 took no English courses beyond freshman English. English literature was taken by 35. And 20 studied public speaking. A total of 13 studied engineering writing. Shakespeare was taken by five. And four engineers studied world literature.

Note the heavy emphasis on literature courses, the glaring lack of a composition course, and the negligible number (13) who took an exposition course.

A questionnaire disclosed that the engineers themselves, in a self-critique, recognized the following weaknesses:

Grammar	2
Getting started	5

Spelling	10
Finding information	18
Using artwork	44
Paragraph structure	97
Lack of clarity	101
Sentence structure	109
Organizing information	115
Wordiness	161

These engineers were responsible for writing the following material in the course of their everyday duties on their jobs—writing that required between seven and nine and one-half hours a week; the average being slightly over eight and a half hours per week:

Brochures and catalogs	6
Magazine articles	14
Product description	47
Process description	65
Specifications	83
Proposals	107
Instructions	111
Letters	170
Reports	198
Memos	225

The article in *Research/Development* concludes that "the dilemma of engineers who can't write" may be overcome only by additional education, and that it can be prevented in future engineers by a more well-rounded curriculum to prevent the graduation of inarticulate engineers who are unable to communicate.

What wasn't mentioned, however, is that *most engineers cannot read,* either. Rather, they do so poorly, and this in itself discourages a desire to read and contributes to their not reading. Engineers are not communications-oriented, they are not word-oriented.

Most of you are familiar with what is jokingly referred to as "copy" produced by engineers for product literature, specifications, proposals—and even the letter from the company president to employees at Christmas.

To classify this rape of the English language as "writing" is not taking poetic license. It is taking an indecent liberty.

The average advertising manager in a company that manufactures technical products spends a large part of his time translating tortured engineerese into English so that it will be intelligible to prospects; if he uses engineerese in product literature, for example, without rewriting it, the end result will be dull, plodding, pedestrian, uninteresting, verbose, trite and semiliterate at best. What's more, the literature will certainly not be promotional in tone—as it should be if it's to accomplish its purpose. More on this in the chapter on literature.

The written horrors that leave a large percentage of the industrial companies doing business today in the form of letters and proposals are nothing short of appalling.

Recently a friend who is an advertising manager wrote a memo to his vice-president of marketing, suggesting that certain key personnel take a course in business writing that was being offered by a well-known university in the city. When no reply was received, this ad manager advanced the suggestion personally, along with several particularly horrible examples to point up the desirability of trying to achieve better writing within the company.

The vice-president of marketing, himself a graduate engineer, *did not understand* the necessity for clearer, less verbose, more forceful writing. So he vetoed the idea.

Remember that the individuals who write those amazingly long-winded, involved letters and memos, the men who start a written description of a product by saying, "The widget is essentially . . ." are the media directors you'll have to contend with. They relish poorly written, poorly edited, crudely laid out and cheaply printed publications that pander to the interests of the advertiser rather than of the reader.

They do so not from any ulterior motives, not from malice, but because they are incapable of making an informed, objective analysis of media; they have never been told that this can be done, nor how it is accomplished.

Recently the president of a company that manufactures highly technical capital equipment, some of it with a six-figure price tag attached to it, wrote the company's advertising manager a memo asking why a certain little publication was not used in the advertising program.

It seems that the publication's editor-publisher-owner had attended an association meeting—as usual—and also as usual had done considerable high-level space selling. This "publisher's" so-called "business publication" is a fantastically profitable venture because it greedily gobbles up advertising budgets and returns nothing to the advertisers. It is the antithesis of a well edited, useful magazine. It is actually a farce and provides no job-help for decision makers. This book will print anything at all that an advertiser sends in as a publicity release, however, including magazine articles—if they can be called that—written by all of the inarticulate engineers in that industry.

This advertising manager then wrote the following memo which ended discussion of the matter, at least for the time being. However, sacred cows in the media pasture are hard to round up and drive to the shipping pens to slaughter.

The memo is genuine, it was actually written to the president of a company that is a major factor in its industry. And the publication, such as it is, still exists. Only the names have been changed.

TO: Mr. Smith Date: 3-29-68

SUBJECT: Media

Dear Ralph:

I'm glad to have your memo of March 28 about *Commercial Cooling* magazine because it gives me a chance to discuss briefly how media are evaluated.

Ralph, all of us in advertising, whether in an agency or with an advertiser, analyze media thoroughly and carefully and systematically to determine their desirability as far as our company is concerned.

Following are 10 of the points which are basic criteria used to make an objective analysis:

1. Editorial policy.
2. Editorial content.
3. Editorial format.
4. Circulation.
5. Publication image.
6. Readership.
7. Market potential.
8. Advertiser acceptance.
9. Services to advertisers.
10. Space cost.

Briefly, I'll take up each of the criteria as they relate to *Commercial Cooling* magazine.

1. EDITORIAL POLICY

Commercial Cooling has no editorial policy. It does not define critical issues in the industry, nor does it take a stand on them even if they are vitally important to individuals and companies. *Commercial Cooling* vacillates because in vacillation lies safety. You irritate nobody if you refuse to take a stand.

2. EDITORIAL CONTENT

Commercial Cooling is what is known in the advertising field as a "pastepot book." That's because its so-called editorial material is largely rewritten after it has appeared originally in legitimate publications, or it is material contributed at no cost to *Commercial Cooling* by manufacturer personnel. The publication has, to the best of my knowledge and that of the agency, *one* editor. No field editors, no Washington editor, no corresponding editors, no other editors period.

In this connection, I might mention that the *one* thing an advertiser buys when he purchases space in a business publication is editorial content. When it's good, the magazine is read, his ad is read and the money is well invested. In the absence of good editorial, money is wasted.

3. EDITORIAL FORMAT

In this respect *Commercial Cooling* is as up-to-date as the Stanley Steamer.

Years ago the offbeat size—digest-sized, square magazines, *Life*-sized magazines and what have you—enjoyed a brief (fortunately) burst of popularity. Some publishers rationalized that their magazine's being off-size made it stand out.

Soon, however, reason prevailed and today almost all of the good business publications are approximately 8¼ by 11¼ inches. This is necessary, Ralph, because many advertisers (including ourselves) print their own four-color insert ads. Without size standardization, business publishing would be a jungle.

Commercial Cooling magazine sells its front cover. Back in the early days of the business press this was considered smart business. It simply isn't done today. Can you imagine *Business Week* or *Iron Age* or *Fortune* or *Factory* with an advertisement on the front cover?

Layout inside *Commercial Cooling* is typical of pastepot books. Deadly dull, no four-color—not even any two-color—in the editorial pages, no white space, no imagination, no vitality, no invitation to read. It repels the eye.

4. CIRCULATION

Next to editorial (policy, content, and format), this is the most important criterion by which value of a book is judged.

Commercial Cooling lags in qualifying recipients of the book, according to its own BPA Statement. The publisher stated that 18.7 percent had not been qualified for three years, and that 81.3 percent not qualified for two years.

This is not good enough in today's industry with its mobility of personnel.

Additionally, under Section 3C of *Commercial Cooling's* BPA Statement, the publisher would not state the "Mailing Address Breakdown of Qualified Circulation." The publisher did not give the following requested information:

a. Individuals by name and title/or function.

b. Individuals by name only.

c. Titles or functions only.

d. Company names only.

e. Bulk copies.

As a publication to consider seriously, no professional in advertising would give a second glance to a publication with a circulation such as this.

5. PUBLICATION IMAGE

In this instance this is a nebulous thing, although with quality publications it is almost a tangible and it can be measured.

Commercial Cooling's image with nonadvertising people in advertiser companies—primarily company presidents and other top executives—is good. The publisher does *not* call on advertising professionals, either in agencies or in advertiser companies. They are familiar with publications of this type and recognize them for what they are.

6. READERSHIP

Commercial Cooling retains no rating service—Starch, Ad-Chart, Readex, Reader Feedback, Ad-Gage, Mills Shepard, or any other service.

This means the publication offers no proof of readership, either quantitatively or qualitatively. It offers no means of measuring advertising effectiveness. Every legitimate publication does, however, with almost no exceptions.

Ralph, this is opinion, but I think a valid one: I feel quite sure that the readers of *Commercial Cooling* are on *neither* a specifying nor a decision-making level. The publication simply does not have reader appeal for personnel of that caliber.

7. MARKET POTENTIAL

The market which *Commercial Cooling* professes to serve is huge.

8. ADVERTISER ACCEPTANCE

Commercial Cooling enjoys good advertiser acceptance because it is sold to nonadvertising professionals. Ralph, here's another opinion: I'd guess that many of our competitors—smaller companies, by and large, you know—do not have professional advertising management.

This function may well be assigned as an "extra" duty to some willing individual who is completely lacking in qualifications. That individual is probably impressed as can be with seeing all of his competitors' ads in *Commercial Cooling*. He is also probably fearful of making a horrible mistake, so readily assumes that the book has merit. I have encountered this situation several times over the years.

It is interesting to note that the company's last three advertising managers all recommended dropping this book, and that our former agency did also. In addition, our present agency states flatly that *Commercial Cooling* is a complete waste of money.

I sincerely hope that all of our competitors continue to pour money into *Commercial Cooling*. This drain on their promotional funds will prevent their investing in publications which would help them achieve their marketing objectives.

9. SERVICES TO ADVERTISERS

Commercial Cooling offers absolutely none, in vivid contrast to every legitimate business publication.

No merchandising. No mailing. No market research. No market analysis.

No marketing information. Nothing.

10. SPACE COST

Space cost is low, but is overpriced for what is offered.

Offhand, I can't think of even one business publication that has to be turned on its side to read a conventional 7 x 10 ad.

Ralph, good trade magazines are read and read thoroughly. They are good and getting better all of the time. And as they do, time is running out for the parasitic publisher that has quietly sucked away promotional dollars to no end but his own.

In my years in the advertising business I've seen many *Commercial Cooling* magazines—by one name or another. All of them had just one goal: to make a fast buck for a fast-buck artist. Advertisers wasted money on them, sometimes for years, but ultimately saw the light.

You asked me, Ralph, what to tell the publisher of this book the next time he buttonholes you and tries to get you to have the book added to our schedule. My suggestion is that you ask him to talk to me, or to our agency. You might say that in your organization advertising management's function is to manage the advertising, and that you have more important things to occupy your mind.

You can do this courteously and then you'll have the problem solved by placing it where it belongs—with me.

I hope this has helped, and I'll be happy to go into any of these criteria with you, either in a memo, or personally if you'd like.

Sincerely,

/s/

J. J. Jones
Advertising Manager

This memo made quite an impression. This company president had always thought heretofore that media are selected on the basis of personal likes and dislikes as far as salesmen are concerned, or on what magazine just happened to appeal to the advertising manager. That media could be measured and evaluated was an entirely new concept. This memo, incidentally, ended discussion of this pastepot book.

These criteria will be covered more thoroughly a little later on, but let's first take a look at how business publications present themselves to prospective purchasers of space.

AIA Business Publication Data Form

Until 1967, when the new Business Publication Data Form was developed by the Association of Industrial Advertisers, business publications presented advertisers and agencies with a statement about themselves in a variety of forms.

Audited publications used either a BPA Form or an ABC Form; unaudited publications used one of hundreds of forms of their own devising, printed to look pretty and official and impressive.

All of these forms made a stab at showing circulations, geographical breakdowns of circulation, recipients of the publications, and similar information deemed necessary either to sell space in the particular book to the advertiser or to make forming an informed opinion about the magazine easier.

Controlled circulation publications—those that are sent without charge to a carefully screened list of qualified recipients—used a form devised by Business Publications Audit of Circulation, Inc. At the present time BPA audits some 640 publications and charges from $360 to $1,500 for an audit, depending on the size of the circulation. BPA audits only business publications; no consumer or general interest magazines.

Business publications with a paid circulation use the ABC form developed by the Audit Bureau of Circulations. ABC currently audits around 260 business publications, and it also audits newspapers and farm magazines.

Both BPA and ABC have governing bodies composed of equal numbers of advertisers, agency personnel, and business publication publishers.

Advertising Age reported a startling development which transpired at the annual meeting of BPA in February, 1968. At this meeting Arthur E. Earley, the new board chairman of Business Publications Audit of Circulation, proposed that a new single auditing organization be formed to make it possible to perform audits and supply *comparable* data on all business publications. Comparability is essential if computers are to be used as a tool in helping evaluate media.

When a vote was taken, 99 percent of the BPA membership favored the proposal, and it had tentative approval, pending ironing out of details, of the chairman and president of ABC; they attended the meeting, marking what is believed to be the first time that representatives of ABC have ever done so.

Objectives of the long-proposed single audit would be:

1. To provide uniform, comprehensive, comparable data about all business publications.

2. The audit form should be expanded to include "other pertinent, auditable information" needed by advertisers and agencies for the comparison and evaluation of business publications, so that this new, improved audit form can become the basic data form and thus eliminate the multiplicity of reports now necessary for media evaluation.

3. Development of a new audit report form.

4. That a tripartite board of directors comprised equally of members of advertisers, agencies, and business publishers manage the new auditing organization.

Reaction of the advertising world is indeed encouraging.

Joseph H. Allen, president of McGraw-Hill Publications, said in a full-page advertisement in *Advertising Age* a week or two later:

"We of McGraw-Hill Publications wish to express our opinion.

"The practical difficulties of implementing this bold proposal are obvious.

"The details of organizing and establishing this new audit are many and, as yet, uncertain. But this is not, we believe, the time to anticipate difficulties and debate about details.

"This is a time to take a stand.

"We, therefore:

"Enthusiastically applaud Mr. Earley's proposal, as a constructive and feasible plan.

"Unequivocally endorse the basic objective of this proposal—to provide the advertiser and his agency with better, more useful, and more comparable audit data.

"Pledge the support and cooperation of McGraw-Hill Publications in furthering this proposal."

Commenting on the proposal, Warren Reynolds, board chairman of the Audit Bureau of Circulations, called it "a breath of fresh air," and expressed his opinion that business publication members of ABC would welcome the principle, provided that the highest standards of validation are maintained.

Phillip Gisser, president of the Association of Industrial Advertisers (now Business/Professional Advertising Association), said that he "completely endorses" Mr. Earley's proposal.

Both BPA and ABC forms are still used because both organizations still audit publications used by industrial advertisers.

Some agencies do everything they can to prevent clients from using them. Marsteller Inc., for instance, always specifically calls it to a client's attention in writing if an unaudited magazine is on the media schedule for some reason or other. And Meldrum & Fewsmith does not recommend unaudited business publications "unless we can't get coverage in certain fields." For years that agency has attached stickers to all media contracts that go out of the agency saying, "Audited circulation is a keystone of confidence. We need your help."

Why aren't all business publications audited? Because many cannot afford to invest the modest sum that would make their products more salable, perhaps. But also because many cannot afford disclosure of information that would reflect derogatorily on them. This is the assumption many veteran advertising men make.

Granted, some publications, and very high quality ones at that, honestly are of the opinion that an audit is unnecessary, therefor why go to the trouble and waste of money that an audit entails? Unless pressure from advertisers is brought to bear, publishers will continue to have this attitude. The *Journal of the American Medical Association,* for example, is unaudited and it may well have the largest income from sale of advertising space of any specialized business or professional publication anywhere.

In the case of this highly respected journal, failure to have an audit does not cast suspicion on it. The fact remains, though, that when reputable, responsible publications achieve such acceptance and operate so successfully without an audit, they tempt lesser publications to do the same. And it is the lesser publications upon whom prospective advertisers look askance due to lack of an audit.

Indeed, Phillip Gisser, AIA president and director of marketing services of U.S. Industrial Chemicals Company, a National Distillers division, has made a proposal to the AIA board of directors—that the board urge its members to drop out, for one month, of all publications that do not offer an audit, according to *Media/scope,* the magazine that serves the buyers of advertising.

Media/scope added that: "Industrial advertisers need a single audit of *all* business publications. Until and unless they get one audit, they will not be able to apply modern methods of media analysis—computerized or otherwise—to the task of selection of publications."

There's better than an even chance that industrial advertisers will have the single audit. This will be a massive step forward. It will benefit good publications, it will force less desirable ones to improve, to measure up to set standards—or go out of business.

There's no doubt about the desirability of the single audit. Among other things it would solve a problem that has become more pressing each passing year—development of a standardized form that would permit comparing competing media. It has become increasingly difficult to do this due to the manner in which information is presented by many publications, as well as the fact that some desirable information is either obscured or not presented at all.

The AIA Model Form

Accordingly, AIA, through its Media Comparability Committee, devoted many months of effort toward the development of a data form that would solve the problem by eliminating the shortcomings of existing forms—BPA, ABC, and the multitude dreamed up by publishers. Result was the AIA Business Publication Data Form. AIA expects publishers to update the form every year so it is always current.

4 RESEARCH AND DEVELOPMENT

12.

CIRCULATION TO FIELD SERVED ANALYZED BY PLACE OF DELIVERY:

	Number of copies
Home	1,896
Business Establishment	68,215
Newsstand sale	0
Other explain below)	0

Source and Date of Above Information: Publisher's circulation count.

Is this information: Audited? ______ (show symbol) Unaudited? ✓

For Items 13 and 14, publishers participating in BPA Comparability Programs should fill in market and date. This publication conforms to the uniform business occupational breakdown, which was developed by the BPA advertiser, agency and publisher committee for the ______ market on ______ (date)

DOES NOT APPLY

13.
14.

CIRCULATION TO FIELD SERVED ANALYZED BY BUSINESS CLASSIFICATION AND OCCUPATION, TITLE AND/OR FUNCTION:

	BUSINESS CLASSIFICATION				
Occupational Title or Function	Industrial Laboratories	Independent Labs. & Consultants	University or Colleges	Government Laboratories	Hospital/Medical Laboratories
Corporate Officers	2,845	1,689	85	122	64
R&D Executives	5,112	791	600	680	216
Project Managers	16,591	1,458	6,133	4,167	1,539
Professional Staff	15,348	1,434	4,952	3,925	746
Technical Personnel	584	75	144	140	43
Librarians	154	16	22	34	2
Other Personnel	339	12	18	29	2
Percent	58.4%	7.9%	17.0%	13.0%	3.7%
Total	40,973	5,475	11,954	9,097	2,612

Source and date of above information: BPA Publisher's Statement, December 1973.

Is this information: Audited? YES (show symbol) BPA Unaudited? ______

15.

GEOGRAPHICAL BREAKDOWN OF CIRCULATION TO FIELD SERVED (REGIONS, STATES, PROVINCES, FOREIGN, ETC.) SHOW UNITS REACHED:

Area	Total Circulation	UNITS REACHED**					Total Units
		Industrial Laboratories	Independent Labs & Consultants	College/University Laboratories	Government Laboratories	Hospital/Medical Laboratories	
039–049 ME	141						57
030–036 NH	236						112
050–059 VT	104						35
010–027 MA	3,697						1,239
028–029 RI	280						108
060–069 CT	1,551						525
New England	6,009 8.6%	1,384	343	176	102	71	2,076
100–149 NY	7,258						2,472
070–089 NJ	5,102						1,518
150–196 PA	5,536						1,586
Middle Atlantic	17,896 25.5%	3,731	820	473	323	229	5,576
430–458 OH	4,090						1,176
468–479 IN	1,290						411
600–629 IL	4,055						1,340
480–499 MI	2,185						705
530–549 WI	1,003						414
East No. Central	12,623 18.0%	2,731	392	433	236	254	4,046

A typical page from an AIA Form. Data are on Research/Development *magazine. Incidentally, the old AIA changed its name to Business/Professional Advertising Association in 1974, but most of us think of it as AIA, new name notwithstanding. BPA initiated an "Audit of Responsibility" on* R/D's *circulation to make sure every recipient of R/D actually works in the area defined in paragraph 1 of the BPA statement. Due to* R/D's *strict qualification form, the book immediately qualified for this special Audit of Responsibility—the only book in its field to so qualify. This means the advertiser's message goes* only *to prime buying influences. No waste circulation to pay for.*

The AIA has this to say about its new Business Publication Data Form:

> "This form is designed to be used in conjunction with *Standard Rate and Data,* publisher's rate card, circulation audit (or statement of circulation) and other available data. It's purpose is to assist advertisers and agencies in their media analysis by helping publishers to present pertinent information in a concise and orderly manner.
>
> "This Business Publication Data Form is sponsored and approved by the Association of Industrial Advertisers, Association of National Advertisers, American Association of Advertising Agencies and American Business Press. It may be used in conformity with the bylaws and rules of the Audit Bureau of Circulation and the Business Publications Audit of Circulations by member publications.
>
> "Registration of this form at AIA Headquarters does not constitute validation of the information contained herein or endorsement of the publication by any sponsoring association. No attempt has been made to value-judge the items herein or place them in any rank order. Responsibility for proper use of this information rests entirely with the media planner."

Research/Development's AIA Form has been expanded, as is permissible, from a basic 8 pages to a full 20 pages to include information the publisher feels it desirable for advertisers and agencies to have.

Incidentally, AIA requires that all publishers fill out the form *completely,* and where a question is not pertinent to enter "Does not apply" or "Not available" in answer to that question.

Reference will be made to this AIA Business Publication Data Form from time to time in this chapter as different topics are discussed. The reader is advised to write for the data form of a publication in which he is particularly interested and spend some time analyzing it.

Editorial Policy

If a business publication is to be of any genuine value to both the readers in the market it serves and to its advertisers, it must have definite, specific objectives.

The publication should define its responsibilities to its readers and describe very clearly and concisely its editorial character.

Doing this is quite similar to an industrial company's development of a written marketing plan and establishment of formal communications objectives. Without a formal plan and objectives, the manufacturing company drifts aimlessly.

Without editorial objectives and goals, as well as a precise definition of its responsibilities and a sound editorial philosophy, the publication lacks viability. Without them its sole apparent reason for being is to make a profit. Making a profit is both desirable and necessary. But pursuit of profit, if stressed above everything else, will prevent a publication's achieving stature and acceptance and respect in full measure from both its universe and its advertisers.

All of us have encountered fast-buck books and thin, marginal magazines whose position is precarious at best. These are the publications whose reason for being is to make a fat profit, if humanly possible, for a money-hungry publisher, or whose reason for being hasn't really been thought through. Such books drift and imitate—they never lead and innovate.

Steer clear of both classes of publications, for to use either is to squander the budget dollars with little hope of realizing a return from the investment.

If you're in doubt about a publication's purpose in life, ask its representative the next time he calls on you. Remarkably few publications have put their objectives into print—although the worthwhile ones have. And these good magazines provide this formal, written rationale of what they strive to be and hope to accomplish to their representatives so they can give it to you. It's something you need, something you have every right in the world to request.

> *Publication X is edited as a relatively independent weekly intending to merit the attention and respect of mature adults in commerce, industry, and public affairs.*

Generalities as weak and wishy-washy, and perhaps wistful in a pathetic sort of way, as in the above, are a reliable tip-off to editorial matter with about as much impact as a ping-pong ball falling out of a basement. Publications that make statements like that, and there are more than you'd believe until you check for yourself, simply do not merit serious consideration for your media schedule.

On the other hand, when a publication can make a simple, relatively short statement that makes sense and denotes a sense of purpose as does this one from *Production* magazine, it obviously knows what it wants to do:

> *It is the purpose of* Production *to recognize and to fulfill*

the special needs of engineers and managers who are concerned with improving manufacturing efficiency, costs, and quality in production metalworking plants.

Research/Development magazine shows it knows its objectives, that it obviously knows what it's doing, where it's going, and how it can best help readers and advertisers. Its statement from its AIA Form is as follows:

> Research/Development *is edited for the scientist, engineer, and manager. Its horizontal coverage includes all fundamental, applied, and developmental research activities. To provide usable information to its readers from the corporate management level to the professional at the laboratory bench, the editors balance content dealing with diverse areas—research management, research techniques, new research tools, and personal professional development. In all these areas, the primary effort is to produce an editorial content that will be of the most concrete help to the reader.* Research/Development *is edited "to" and "for," not "about" its readers.*
>
> *A special editorial section on Vacuum Technology is included each month. High vacuum is a widely used "tool" of today's researcher, having important applications in such areas as aerospace, metallurgy, electronics, and chemical processing. This section of* R/D *represents the first time this important research technique was accorded formal and continuing coverage by a domestic periodical. A Vacuum Technology Directory and Specifications Catalog is published annually in March.*
>
> *The editors of* R/D *rely on two things to insure that their efforts are useful to readers. First is their own professional background, judgment, and experience in science and engineering. Recognizing that any staff cannot encompass all disciplines served by the magazine, the editors reinforce their knowledge by constant referral to an active editorial board. Field trips by* R/D *editors are not only used to initiate new material for the publication; but a continual effort is made to evaluate the usefulness of published material through interviews with working professional scientists and engineers.*

The publisher of *Research/Development* said something in his statement. He spelled out in rapid-fire order whom he's talking to, what they do, where they are, what he's telling them, and how he knows this is what interests them. This information is extremely useful to the advertising manager and to the agency. It shows purpose and scope and direction, as well as the fact that the magazine has a well-thought-out rationale for existing. There's nothing hit-and-miss or hope-and-pray here.

Also to be considered along with editorial policy is the stability of the publication. Publications that drift without purpose tend to fall into a pattern; they change either their names or their owners, or both, for no apparent reason other than that they have yet to find their niche—if, indeed, one exists. These changes come with fantastic frequency with some business publications.

Beware the publication with just one or two full-time editors. As overworked as they are, they can't possibly produce first-rate material, nor can they even rewrite contributed material to meet quality standards they themselves would prefer to see.

Something else to check is duplication of names of editors in publishers' stables of magazines. If, for example, a publisher lists an editor—or several editors—as "full-time editors" for one magazine, then lists one or more of these same people as "full-time editors" of another publication, something is fishier than all of the sardines in Portugal.

This is done on occasion even in publishers' sworn statements. When you encounter it, run, don't walk, to your telephone to call your agency to have any space you might be running in that magazine canceled.

From *Research/Development's* AIA Form we also note that the magazine has four contributing editors; these are not part-time employees, but individuals retained by the publication because of their expertise in their disciplines and for their intimate knowledge of fast-changing technology. In addition, the magazine has an editorial board of distinguished scientists with whom its editors consult regularly. These scientists confirm editorial opinions and provide an invaluable sounding board by considering proposed editorial matter from a scientific viewpoint.

Quality publications, depending upon the field they serve, invariably have contributing editors, correspondents, bureaus in major metropolitan centers identified with a particular industry, a Washington editor, and, frequently, foreign correspondents.

All of this represents a very sizeable investment by the publisher and is a strong indication that he is committed to giving the reader what he wants and needs—and to giving the advertiser a stronger, better-read magazine to carry his advertising message. Leading publications in every industry are perfectly willing to make this investment. They realize it benefits both the advertiser and themselves. However, marginal publications are unable to follow suit and trash magazines that exist solely to siphon off advertising dollars to enrich the publisher have no desire to do so.

Editorial Content

Regardless of how wonderful it may sound, editorial policy is a collection of pallid platitudes unless it's translated into vigorous, timely, interesting editorial material that makes the reader *want* to read it.

The attitude—or philosophy, more accurately—of the publisher is reflected in the content of the magazine. Take the statement made by the publisher of *Iron Age,* for instance, and then compare it with any issue of the book. Philosophy is transformed into words, pages, departments, and features. Philosophy and attitude come alive before your eyes. Let's see just what *Iron Age* has to say on the subject:

EDITORIAL PHILOSOPHY

> *Iron Age* serves metalworking as a primary communications force—pulling this vast industry together and fostering its efficiency and advancement.
>
> The most valuable contribution of the *Iron Age* is its outside view of the metalworking industry, coupled with non-biased, interpretative reporting of the significant events which shape it. *Iron Age* provides:
>
> - News features about management, finance and labor.
> - Technical articles on significant advances in metalworking processes.
> - Timely market and price information.

Also to be considered and tabulated and compared with competitive publications are cold statistics. For example, you'll want to know exactly how many pages were in the average issue of the book for the past year—both in editorial and in advertising. Any publication you use or are considering using should be looked at from this standpoint.

In its AIA Form, *Research/Development* reports a gradually increasing number of editorial pages in the last five years. This can easily be divided by 12 to determine the monthly average.

Besides merely giving the number of editorial pages, though, the magazine also lists the percentage of editorial pages to advertising pages for the past five years, as is required by the Association of Industrial Advertisers.* Rule of thumb in judging publications on this score is that they should hit a 60-40 advertising-editorial ratio, or perhaps a bit better. However, the economics of the publishing business seem to require six pages of advertising to float four pages of editorial, and there's little likelihood of this being changed.

Publications that have a 65-70-75 percent ratio—the wrong way—invariably have too few editors, poorly qualified editors, or else the publisher is trying to milk advertisers for all the traffic will bear without investing in a property that stands a slim chance of becoming a significant voice in its field.

Research/Development magazine uses business English with an R&D accent; there is no gobbledegook in its articles. While technical subjects are covered, of course, they are written so as to be understood by scientists and engineers with varying scientific disciplines. Copy style is informative. Necessary technical data is worked into illustrations and panels—it doesn't clutter up the main stream of thought and slow down the reader.

Guest authors have a message that is timely, significant, and useful to the book's readers *on their jobs.* This material is always presented in accordance with the book's high editorial standards and in its particular style. *Research/Development* does not buy editorial material. Major signed articles are prepared, usually at the publication's suggestion, as "contributions to the literature of the industry of discovery."

All nonsigned material is rewritten by *R/D's* editorial staff in the interest of conciseness and clarity. No publicity handouts are used.

The magazine's reader inquiry key card system is used beyond advertisements and department items, primarily as a means of service to the reader, as well as a method of evaluating interest by the publication's audience.

Through its own reader research, the editorial staff of *Research/Development* constantly measures the timeliness and appropriateness of feature and department material, and reshapes and restyles the editorial content to reflect reader preference.

When you're either analyzing one publication or comparing one with another, it's always helpful to list the titles of feature articles from one issue selected at random. This enables you to assess the relevance of the articles to the publication's editorial objectives and to its audience—and to your products, naturally.

*Now Business/Professional Advertising Association.

What cannot be learned about a publication from any tabulation of facts, a perusal of the table of contents, or a mass of dry statistics, is the *feel* of a leading publication in its field.

This is a very special character imparted to a business magazine by a number of factors, each significant in itself, although none are of overriding importance, unless, perhaps, it is the reflection of the personality of the individual at the helm.

In the case of *Commercial Car Journal,* the magazine of fleet management, this may well be editor Bart Rawson's almost incredible depth of knowledge about the fast-changing trucking industry that the magazine serves.

Commercial Car Journal not only serves its readers by helping them solve day-in and day-out operating, personnel, and maintenance problems, but it also reports and interprets legislative trends and the impact they inevitably will make on trucking operations. This influences the equipment required to take advantage of them, of course, as well as labor contracts, financing, and every facet of the business.

The magazine speaks authoritatively, and it is a respected spokesman for the industry. *Commercial Car Journal* has no official status as an association organ, but it has industry-wide respect that means as much, or even more, perhaps.

That the magazine could achieve such a position and maintain it for decades is due, in part, to Chilton Company's policy of investing in its properties so they become leaders in the industries they serve. Of course, this is self-serving to the extent that space in publications with genuine prestige is easier to sell, but it also benefits the advertiser whose message appears in conjunction with editorial material with built-in believability and acceptance.

CCJ's years of leadership are due also to the editorial staff's understanding of the trucking industry, an industry to which, when all is said and done, they are personally dedicated to helping. Personal involvement, publisher permission to *build* a publication rather than merely harvest the profits, has resulted in a magazine of such stature that when it speaks editorially the trucking industry, the unions, and the government listen to what it has to say.

Exceptionally fine editorial content has helped *Commercial Car Journal* rise to the top of the heap and stay there. An example of the hard-hitting business press journalism for which CCJ is famous is an article in the January, 1968 issue; it was written by Neil R. Regeimbal, the magazine's Washington Feature Editor. Title of the article is: "CARGO THEFT—They Steal by Night." Part of this provocative, stimulating article is reprinted from the January,

1968 issue of *Commercial Car Journal*, copyright 1968 Chilton Company, by permission.

CARGO THEFT

They Steal by Night

The inside story of a billion dollar bleed-off

I can steal one of your tractors.

I can hook it to one of your loaded trailers and steal a complete, loaded rig out of your terminal and get away with it.

It doesn't matter whether you're a common carrier or a private operator. It applies to almost anybody.

The grim truth is that I can steal a rig in any major U.S. city where trailers are loaded and unloaded.

I have "stolen" rigs to demonstrate to my own satisfaction how easy it can be done. And I could have sold the load just as easily as I stole it.

The assignment was not inspired by journalistic sensationalism. The wholesale theft of trucks and their cargoes is a pressing problem that has become more acute each year. *What* was happening was not new. *How* it was happening needed a critical analysis and an objective report to the industry so that remedial action could be taken to ameliorate an intolerable situation.

As the direct result of the article, many segments of the trucking industry have mounted intensive antitheft campaigns. The writer, Editor Neil Regeimbal, was invited to address the Board of Governors of the Regular Common Carrier Conference, the American Trucking Associations Terminal Operations Council, the ATA Industrial Relations Committee, and the New Jersey Motor Truck Association. More than 100,000 reprints have been distributed, or published in other noncompetitive magazines. A followup article reporting progress was scheduled.

This is representative of the caliber of editorial content—and editors—that the best business publications have, and the respect with which top magazines are regarded by leaders of the industries they serve.

A price tag cannot be put on an editorial climate such as this.

Questionable Practices

When you run across a publication that devotes one-fourth to one-third of its editorial space to new product announcements and announcements about the availability of new literature, stop, look, and look again. Unless it's a new-product type of publication, you've come across a book that lives on handouts from manufacturers who scurry hither and yon in search of every last little bit of ink they can get—as free publicity is termed. Such announcements require very little editing—and frequently are given none—little technical knowledge, little industry knowledge, little effort, and little investment in people and research.

This does not apply, of course, to tabloid-type new products publications. They serve a legitimate purpose and have as their reason for being their ability to disseminate this type of material and present it to their readers in an orderly fashion with most of the puffery edited out.

Something else: Many publications are special-issue prone. They'll devote an entire issue of the magazine to a certain subject with what is to most advertisers, dismaying frequency. Often there's a valid reason for having a special issue—intense interest in an esoteric new process, a development that has wrought a radical change in an industry or production method, such as numerical control in the machine-tool field for example, or other legitimate, newsworthy subject.

On the other hand, most advertising men suspect the special issue is a gimmick designed solely to increase sale of space in that particular month. Sometimes the special issue just happens to be published in a month that's normally slow for the publisher. This is lucky for him, of course.

A legitimate topic for a special issue is the one major trade show of the year for a major, specific market, or the annual convention of a society that represents the decision-making element in an important field, or something on that order.

This is something you'll have to judge on the individual merits of the magazine you're analyzing, and of that special issue. Beware, though, of the book that publishes one special issue after another; more often than not this is merely a thinly disguised attempt to entice advertisers into buying more space than they normally would have scheduled.

Another practice that is ethically questionable is publishing a magazine 13 times a year. Some publications attempt to whipsaw advertisers into buying space in a special issue by not giving the customary frequency discount unless that special issue is used. This attempt to blackmail the advertiser into buying something he really may not want and may not need is, happily, fast disappearing. Most legitimate publications and reputable publishers have long since discontinued this shady practice. Those that haven't should be viewed with a jaundiced eye. Even with two jaundiced eyes if you can stand the strain.

The American Association of Advertising Agencies has this to say about business magazines that are published 13 times a year: "Some publishers who have only 7- and 13-time rates make it obligatory to use a directory or special issue in order to earn the lower rate in regular issues. In order to make best use of directory or special issue space, it is often necessary to prepare a special advertisement appropriate only for that particular publication and that particular issue.

"Publishers who quote such extra-time rates are urged to offer the customary 6- and 12-time rates in addition. Even more equitable would be the use of the customary 6- and 12-time rates with the extra space for the directory taking the 6- or 12-time space earned by the regular space program."

It's just about an even bet that when you unearth a publication that publishes 13 times a year, and that bases its frequency discounts on a 7- or 13-times basis, you'll also find by doing a little digging that this book plays footloose and fancy-free with the truth in a number of areas.

Some marginal publications make it a practice to charge the advertiser for editorial cuts—engravings—used for illustrations of products announced in the magazine's new products section. This is not strictly a dishonest practice, although it is one that no worthwhile publication engages in. When you run across this, best thing to do is steer clear of that publication. Remove it from your publicity list and by all means don't even consider it for your media schedule for a minute.

Another practice of some business publications of less than debatable merit is not allowing agency commission. Incredible as it seems, a few actually exist in the face of accepted practice of almost a half-century. Invariably, when you run across one of these, you'll find upon analyzing it that the magazine obviously disallows agency commission because it is afraid to have agencies examine it.

Most such marginal publications never have representatives call upon agencies—if they have representatives, that is—because these knowledgeable advertising people would instantly recognize such a publication as an out-and-out fraud. Most such books publish only pirated material, have no art director, but rely instead on the printer who sets type and drops in halftones; typically it has no four-color editorial section, and sometimes doesn't even have two-color editorial pages. Flee as a bird from any of these.

Yet another shady practice that was devised purely to sell space is that of presenting a so-called "award" to a company—either for one of its products or to one of its better-known executives. This is usually done in hope of receiving additional advertising space, or else the "award" is made when space in a book has been discontinued or greatly reduced. As transparent as the practice is, some managements have been known to be overwhelmed at the honor; often the advertising manager is promptly instructed to waste scarce space dollars on the questionable book. This should be resisted strenuously.

Editorial Format

Don't discount appearance when evaluating media. Readers don't.

A smartly turned out publication invariably is one in which both the publisher and the editors take pride. It's a publication in which an investment has been made and is being made. Attractiveness is expensive.

On the other hand, it is ridiculously easy to grind out a pastepot publication; all that is required is to employ part-time hack writers to filch articles from leading publications, rewrite them using the same hard facts, then rearranging the sequence of thoughts so the legitimate publisher can't file suit for plagiarism. One "editor" can thus assemble the book and make a crude dummy.

Then, with copy in hand, the publisher of the schlock book trots off to a cheap printer, has him set type and print the thing, has a mailing service mail it, and he's in business. He's a business publisher.

Schlock books, such as our hypothetical *Commercial Cooling,* are characterized by deadly-dull, dingy, drab, dreary pages singularly unappealing and unattractive. They march in a monotonous parade of black-and-white, one boring page after another. Type is invariably set in two sterile columns. There is no ROP four-color, not even any editorial second color, as a rule. Everything is done as cheaply as possible to avoid making an investment. The publisher of the pastepot magazine has the philosophy of the slum landlord who won't invest a nickel to improve his property; he just lets it run down while he milks every last red cent out of the operation that he can.

Such magazines have no layout, no attempt at art direction; halftones, almost always squares or rectangles, are dropped in place by the printer. There's no white space to alleviate the monotony because white space is paper on which ink could be laid—either "editorial" or paid space advertising.

What's more, the publisher of the marginal business magazine seldom, if ever, uses artwork; that has to be bought and would eat into the return on his investment—if you can call it that.

Needless to say, such publications are "edited" for the advertiser, not for the reader. Just as water seeks its own level, though, as industrial management becomes more knowledgeable about advertising the worthless publications and the parasitic publishers will slowly disappear.

Let's look at some examples of good editorial format as it should be in first-class publications. There is no need to illustrate the schlock book—you know what it looks like.

First, the cover of the October, 1974 issue of *Research/Development* magazine is shown. Originally, it was four-color, of course, as are covers of almost all leading business publications.

The illustration is a superb example of color photography. It depicts one major subassembly—a printed circuit board loaded

Beautiful photography and excellent printing characterize this cover of Research/Development. *Although highly technical, subject will interest this particular readership.*

with LSI microprocessor chips and other components—to lead the eye to a new instrument. Inside the case, two other major subassemblies—one containing a printer, power supply and an LED display, the other the keyboard—plug together to form a totally digital integrator for chromatography. How this new instrument fills a gap in units available to meet research and development needs is told in an interesting and well-written article within the magazine.

The photographer used a red and a blue light, in addition to the normal ones, to add punch and a feeling of the dramatic to the illustration. He did a bang-up job. The usual colors found in a printed circuit board are there, yellow, green, red and, of course, white. All of this gains added interest due to use of a jet black background to hold the composition together, as well as to provide the ideal tone from which to reverse the name of the magazine.

The second cover we'll look at is that on the September, 1974 issue of *Production*. Proportions are pleasing; approximately two-thirds of the area is given over to the interesting four-color illustration of the start of the new DNC machining system. One of the material-handling transporters is in the center, in position to automatically load and unload a vertical turret lathe. On the

PRODUCTION
the magazine of manufacturing
march 1968
THE HEAVY TRUCK INDUSTRY
The challenge of manufacturing variety
PROGRESS WITH TURBINE ENGINES
Next step, turning prototypes into commercial products
CLEANING-PLATING-FINISHING
Survey of the production metalworking industries' current practices
MOTIVATING FOR COST SAVING
A suggestion plan that really works
A NINE NC-MACHINE SYSTEM EPITOMIZES FLEXIBILITY

This hard-working cover, well laid out and with a powerful illustration, also intrigues the prospective reader with overall indications of the editorial content to be found in this particular issue.

right, the first of three OM3 Omnidril four-axis drilling machines is seen in action. This is a very hard-working cover. It does dual duty in attracting the reader with clean layout and an interesting photographic illustration, and also arouses his interest with some of the topics discussed in the editorial pages. Titles of the articles are given to assure the reader before he cracks a page that the content is timely and will be both interesting and helpful to him.

Production's publisher and editors are fully aware of this and are willing to pay the price for superior quality in this area. *Production* is rich in four-color ROP editorial which increases both the reader's appetite for the book and the readership. Layout is fresh and open and inviting, as will be seen from a previous and equally well-done issue. (See below.)

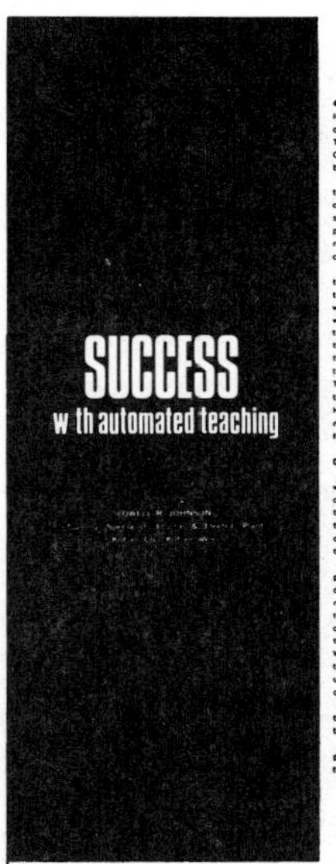

March 1968 PRODUCTION 181

• The Kohler Co. has found that technical job training time can be effectively reduced through the use of programmed instruction. Using an "Automated Teaching Systems" approach, developed by the Ken Cook Co. of Milwaukee, Kohler has been able to do a better job of training in half the time.

In the past, training problems in Kohler's controller assembly department were acute. Due to the complexity of the skills required, a training period of six months to a year was needed to bring new employees to production standards. A high turnover rate, resulting in part from the long training period, also contributed to the problem.

A solution which would drastically reduce training time was needed. After much study of possible solutions, the "Automated Teaching Systems" approach was chosen. This system uses slides in conjunction with recorded programmed four-track tapes. One tape track serves as the electronic control responsible for the automatic changing of slides and the stopping of the tape. The other three tracks are used for narration or questions which require student responses. The hardware employed is a combined slide projector-tape player operated by the student at his own speed. He advances the tape after completing a question. If necessary, he can stop it in order to take more time for his reply.

Development Steps

Development of the new training programs began with a detailed review of the problem by all parties concerned—Kohler supervisors, product and production engineers, training coordinators, and writers from the Ken Cook Co. This was done to familiarize the consultant's writers with the problems for which the training was to be developed.

After several familiarization sessions, the consultant prepared the proposed programs in draft form. These drafts were closely evaluated by Kohler's review committee consisting of product and production engineers, the job foreman and instructors, and the training coordinator. The drafts were evaluated according to the following criteria: Was the information correct? Was enough information given to properly instruct the trainee as to the operation to be performed? Was uniform terminology used? Were the pre-established objectives fulfilled?

After the suggested changes were incorporated, the training programs were produced, and the slides and tapes were assembled as completed programs.

The review committee then re-examined the completed programs and evaluated them as before with two additional considerations. First, the slides and

A trainee is shown receiving both graphic and verbal instruction from the automated system.

Left page of this pair has the title of the article boldly reversed out of a page-deep panel of black, leaving room for one column of type; type in this particular article is sans serif, primarily for the sake of making a change to liven up the appearance. The bulk of the book is set in serif faces.

The left page has ample white space, and enough black space, too, for that matter, to appear interesting to the reader, especially when it's directly opposite page 151. Here the photograph is reproduced in four-color with clean, open white space above and below the illustration. This spread makes the reader *want* to read it.

Feature article in the March, 1968 issue of *Commercial Car Journal* is titled: "Trucking's Stake In Air Freight." It is promoted on the cover of the magazine with excellent and attractive four-color art that shows the back end of a loaded tractor-trailer, with a four-engine jetliner overhead.

air

Note the attractive, open layout of pages 70-71, and the interesting, descriptive art. On page 70 the only spot of color is the word "air," carrying out the visual theme; here it's in bright AAAA red. Page 70 is so open and visually stimulating it doesn't need additional color to add interest for the reader. There's plenty there now.

Page 71 uses a strong, masculine slash of color, seemingly done with a broad, flat chalk, on each of the five trailers near the cargo jet. Here the art is deliberately rough and stylized; it appears to be either pencil or crayon.

Captions on both pages near the illustrations increase readership because they provide a succinct statement as to what the article is about; and since captions are almost always read if nothing else is, they perform the important task of drawing additional readers into the body text.

Although it doesn't hold true 100 percent of the time, you can usually rely on the fact that if a business publication *looks* good, it's worth analysis and consideration. Granted, there are publishers of trade books who put everything into art direction and very little into editorial in an effort to impress the gullible, but there aren't too many of them.

While mere good appearance shouldn't be the only criterion to include a book on your media schedule, poor appearance is reason enough, in most instances, to include the book *off* the schedule.

Circulation

A trade magazine can have the finest imaginable editorial content and be so beautifully put together that it simply takes your breath away, but if its circulation isn't such that it reaches most of the prospects you must talk to, the book is of no value to you.

First thing to consider, of course, is the circulation policy of publications you're considering using. This is found in the AIA form. In the case of *Research/Development,* with its controlled circulation, to receive the magazine regularly the individual must qualify under the following policies:

> *Qualified recipients are research directors, supervisors, project and group leaders, scientists, engineers, standards engineers, and scientists, and technical libraries, associated with nonclinical research-development establishments, pilot plants and field experimentation groups. Recipients must state that they wish to receive* Research/Development *and be engaged in (or responsible for) research and development work at a higher level than that of "technician."*

How a publication gets readers, both for paid and controlled circulation, is an important consideration you'll want to look into. Paid circulation books—the good ones, that is—offer enough to the reader so that subscriptions come in over the transom, or are readily obtained by the publications' circulation staffs.

Good business magazines receive subscriptions without offering an 85-foot, twin-diesel-powered yacht, six months for two with all expenses paid in Acapulco, or a 90-day safari in Africa with a choice of white hunters as inducements to part with a few dollars that will go on the expense account anyhow.

Books that have to offer a bribe to subscribe, including a drastic reduction in price so that it's put at a ridiculous level, are books whose publishers are having a hard time making them appear attractive to readers.

You're perfectly entitled to ask how publications get their circulations, and, indeed, this is a question you *should* ask.

Additional information you'll be interested in because it is a tip-off as to the desirability of the publication *as judged by the reader* is the rate of subscription renewals; percentage of subscriptions sold at full price vs. a cut-rate inducement; percentage sold in quantity to distributors for their customers; percentage sold in quantity to an association or trade group for its membership; percentage of subscriptions in arrears over the last five-year period; and how long a subscriber is "carried" after his subscription expires.

Besides this information, ask the percentage of subscriptions sold to individuals as opposed to those sold to companies; find out if subscriptions are sold for one year, or for shorter or longer periods. One year is customary; less than that assures far too much reader turnover, longer than that would indicate that the magazine is giving something away merely to achieve a large circulation, and the readers may not actually be readers—they may merely be recipients.

When it comes to controlled circulation—unpaid, that is—ask how the circulation list is built, what methods and sources are used to change the circulation. Here again, *Research/Development* is used as an example, and the following is extracted from the magazine's AIA Form:

> *A continuous effort is made to expand and upgrade* R/D's *already effective circulation coverage of research/development leaders. Toward this end news releases, news items, show attendance lists, professional society rosters, directories, reader inquiry cards, and carefully chosen purchased lists are all used to develop circulation coverage and depth. All such prospective names are sent an explanatory letter together with a circulation qualification questionnaire. Returned questionnaires are carefully screened to meet standards set forth above (which have been discussed).*

This is standard practice and the conscientious publisher of a quality magazine such as *Research/Development* is extremely selective about adding names to its circulation lists.

This is, of course, in vivid contrast to the publication that "forces" circulation through ceaseless mass mailings and where "qualification" of new recipients of the book is little short of farcical. Questionable in the extreme, for example, is a publication's claiming to cover its universe thoroughly and in depth and suddenly "discovering" an additional 10,000 or 15,000 "qualified" recipients it had somehow overlooked before.

This happens oftener than you'd think, and if you encounter it look long and hard at that book's circulation list. Ask to see galleys of the list, either of one letter of the alphabet selected at random (you select it), of a specific SIC, or of a half-dozen or so companies with which you're very familiar. This will enable you to spot "padded" circulation rosters quickly.

The Numbers Game

It's an unfortunate fact of life, however, that it's much easier to tell that one publication has a 10 percent advantage in total circulation than it is to analyze the *quality* of the circulation, or the quality of the editorial. The numbers game—forcing circulation up artificially—results in much higher space cost for the advertiser with no higher readership among individuals who can make buying recommendations or decisions. As a rule the second and third ranking publications serving a market are the ones tempted to play the numbers game and force up circulation; after all, they have to have some apparent advantage to tout.

From the AIA Form you'll be able to determine the total number of copies of the publication sent to qualified individuals. Notice, too, this is broken down by copies addressed to individuals *by name* and copies addressed to a title or job function only; the mail boy in most companies usually isn't an M.I.T. graduate, and some things can reasonably be expected to perplex him. Names of individuals within the company, he understands; functions of these same individuals probably mean about as much to him as would a dissertation on the gold drain to an unclothed Ubangi.

According to its AIA Form, *Research/Development* addresses 70,111 copies of the magazine to individuals by name and title. This is high-quality circulation. These people receive *R/D* without having to rely on the mail boy to remember what every person's job in the company is. In addition, the publication mails exactly six copies to titles or job functions only, it distributes 400 other issues to miscellaneous recipients such as authors, and 228 copies to libraries. This latter undoubtedly reaches many future buying influences, as well as desirable scientists and engineers not yet located by the magazine's circulation director.

What is extremely important is that *100 percent of Research/ Development's* circulation is addressed to a specific individual *by name and title.* The ad manager who uses this book *knows* he's buying a medium that puts his message in front of those who can buy his product. *Every* recipient of *R/D* must be engaged in or responsible for research and development *to qualify to get the book.*

Also in the circulation analysis is the five-year average circulation. Seeing the slow, steady progression of the rising circulation makes it immediately apparent that *Research/Development* hasn't had to resort to playing the numbers game due to competitive pressure. Circulation has risen right along with rising business activity, especially in the research-development area, of course. This is as it should be.

The magazine's publisher states a total of 1,896 readers receive the magazine at their homes and 68,215 receive it at their offices. Opinion is divided as to which is better. It's a known fact that a business magazine receives more thorough readership at home, and this applies to both editorial and to advertising.

However, when the magazine is read in the recipient's home that's as far as the advertiser's message gets—just that one reader. But when business publications are read in the office, more than 80 percent of publications are passed on to others within the organization; in fact, most researchers tend to agree on a figure in the neighborhood of 3.5 readers per magazine—each copy of it, that is—as being about right, although most advertising men feel this is a somewhat conservative figure. This gives the advertiser 2.5 "free" readers, although many studies beyond reproach establish the number of pass-on readers as high as 3.5 per copy.

Breakdown of the circulation figures for Research/Development *shows all except one percent are prime buying influences. As a matter of interest,* R/D *is the only magazine whose audit proves that all who get it are bona fide prospects for advertisers' products.*

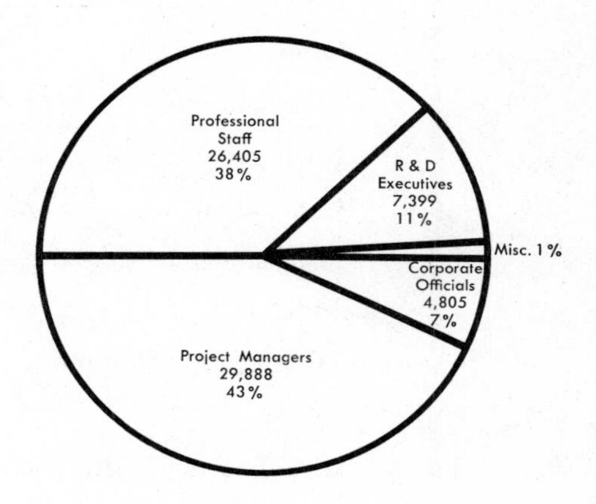

Naturally, you want to be sure your advertising messages will be read in the geographical area of the country most important to your sales efforts, always analyze a magazine's circulation geographically. Oddly enough, some magazines that claim to cover a given market thoroughly have excellent coverage in some sections of the country, but are very spotty in others. If it happens that a certain publication is spotty in an area of critical importance to your company, perhaps because of distributor strength, unusually strong product acceptance, or some other good reason, this could very easily make the publication exactly wrong for your company and exactly right for your most vigorous competitor.

Research/Development breaks out circulation by state in its AIA Form, and in a supplement gives the exact number of establishments that receive the magazine. It is 40,973 research-development laboratories. This enables advertisers to be sure, when they use this publication, they're hunting ducks where the ducks are. And they can be sure the ducks are there because *Research/Development's* circulation is audited by BPA.

A bit of statistic examining shows the following 13 states account for 79.3 percent of all research and development in the United States:

California	19.7%
New York	11.6
Pennsylvania	7.6
Illinois	6.6
New Jersey	7.9
Ohio	6.0
Massachusetts	5.0
Michigan	3.4
Connecticut	3.1
Maryland	2.5
Indiana	1.9
District of Columbia	1.6
Texas	2.4

Turning to California in *Research/Development's* AIA Form, we find 8,216 recipients of the magazine in that state—just a whisker under 11.7 percent of total circulation. Matched up with the 19.7 percent of research and development activity in the country, this shows good market coverage without forcing circulation to unrealistic levels.

And New York, with 11.6 percent of all R&D activity has 7,275 readers of *Research/Development,* well within the ball park.

Universe coverage is a question that should be raised when analyzing any publication's desirability. Only if the magazine covers the overwhelming majority of the establishments that comprise your universe will you want to consider it seriously; marginal publications always fall short here, as do regional publications, of course, although in some instances the regionals have considerable merit if they reach a particularly strong market in their section of the country—and it's of prime importance to you.

The research-development market is an especially difficult one to reach except with a highly specialized publication such as *Research/Development.* The door to the research-development laboratory has been called, and with good reason, "the most inaccessible door in industry." Here are the top secret items, the military and commercial goodies-to-be that can't be discussed or seen—just as the personnel of the laboratories cannot be seen by outsiders.

Universe for *Research/Development* is the total number of scientists and engineers engaged in research and development in the "physical" disciplines (this excludes medical, life, social, and economic) as follows:

Industrial and independent 284,500
(Per Bureau of Labor Statistics,
Bulletin 1418, page 9)

Government 38,733
(Per National Science Foundation Report
65-4, pages 37-40, Table A3)

University and College 22,300
(Per National Science Foundation Report
64-28, page 63, Table III)

Total Universe 345,533

Let's see how this unapproachable army of scientists and engineers are reached by *Research/Development* magazine; the picture looks like this:

Research/Development circulation, July 1, 1974 70,111

Pass-on readership of 3.9 per copy 273,432

Total audience of *Research/Development* 343,543

Coverage of universe 99.4%

This pass-on readership figure is the one the magazine is convinced is right for its circulation as determined by studies on the subject.

Considering how incredibly difficult it is to define the research-development market (it has no SIC), locate the establishments, and hang names and titles onto individual buying influences within them, this is outstanding coverage that probably cannot be equaled.

Coverage of the universe is one thing, and coverage of known buying influences within that universe is a horse of a different color. Leading publications retain independent research organizations to make studies on this, among other subjects, so they can have this information to give to advertisers—and of course to use in helping sell prospective advertisers.

A study was done for *Research/Development* by John T. Fosdick Associates, Inc. to determine whether the publication was actually read by those with authority to specify and to buy.

A key question was: *Are you personally involved in the purchase, specification, or evaluation of materials (being studied)?* A total of 7 percent of those surveyed evaluated materials, 70 percent purchased or specified, 23 percent did neither.

To the question: *Do you specify materials for research, prototype, or production?*, 83 percent specified for research; 56 percent specified for prototype production; 41 percent specified materials for regular production.

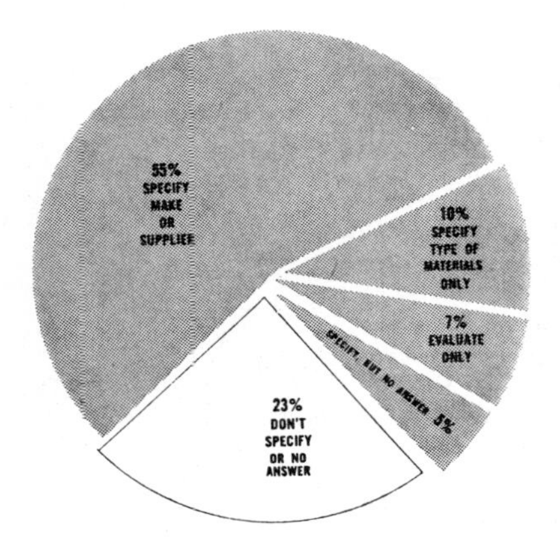

Pie chart of magazine's readership shows that 55 percent specify make or supplier for materials their companies use. Another 10 percent specify the make or type of materials, while 7 percent evaluate only. Latter group is still a buying influence.

This is the type of information the advertiser *must* have if he's to make an informed comparison and decision about media. It is the responsibility of the business publisher to invest enough in his property to make this data available to the advertiser and his agency.

The Company Mailing List

Incidentally, it's the advertising manager's responsibility to see to it the company's key people receive the major magazines in its industry. Subscription expense is always a legitimate expense-account item, and key personnel should subscribe to paid-circulation books; in the case of controlled-circulation magazines, the advertising manager should have the agency ask the publisher to add the names.

Even district sales managers out in the field should receive the most important magazines. That's because, first of all, it's advisable for them to see your advertisements in the magazines—instead of merely as preprints or reprints. Secondly, these are the future sales managers and marketing directors in your company; their familiarity with the business press will make your job easier in future years.

One thing, however, is definitely very undesirable and should be discouraged vigorously. This is for business publications to put every dog and his brother in the company on their promotional mailing list. All this accomplishes is to get the natives all stirred up unnecessarily.

Thing to do is to insist to the media representatives who call on you that he instruct his home office to delete the superfluous names from the magazine's promo list—not from the publication list, but the promo list. Magazines are very familiar with this problem and will accede to your wishes. You can't blame them for trying to make their names familiar with everybody who conceivably could influence a page or two of space for them.

Publication Image

"Image," in the communications field, is a word that means many things to many people. It's one that's pathetically overworked.

Advertising men who have nothing to say can usually be depended upon to launch into lengthy harrangues about image, or even to make formal speeches about it if the occasion arises.

It does all too frequently.

Properly applied to media, or to a specific medium, rather, image simply means the opinion the magazine's universe has of it, how it's regarded, how it's thought of.

Books such as *Fortune, Iron Age, Business Week, Production, U.S. News & World Report, Barron's* are acknowledged leaders in their fields. They're respected; looked up to; quoted; considered authoritative; relied upon; influential; believed. All of these attitudes and more contribute to publication image.

Publication image, according to Marsteller Inc., is the third dimension that must be evaluated correctly in order to increase the effectiveness of business paper selection, and thereby increase the effectiveness of client media dollars. The agency carries on continuous research to develop additional qualitative media yardsticks so that editorial material and publication image may be analyzed more scientifically.

First dimension is circulation, of course, and the second is the editorial job done by a publication.

Some years ago the agency developed useful, workable criteria to measure both the first and second dimensions—prior to working on the third dimension of publication image, how the reader regards the magazines he reads.

Perhaps the most popular method for measuring business publication reader reaction is the magazine readership, or reader preference, study. Thousands have been conducted.

If the questionnaire is well-designed and the mailing list is good, such surveys can be very helpful. More on this a little later, though.

Where readership studies fail is that they don't give all of the necessary information about *why* a reader reads a certain publication, why he prefers it, why he considers it "most useful"—which is a question often asked.

Marsteller's research technique was deliberately designed to be relatively simple so that technique wouldn't obscure results. The way the study was conducted makes it possible for any advertiser or agency grounded in the most basic research techniques to conduct the same type of research.

After going into editorial objectives with publishers, Marsteller then attached the problem of editorial recall and impact. The author is indebted to this fine agency for its assistance and for background material on this subject. The entire Marsteller media department was especially helpful.

The problem was identified as: Could you, as a reader, identify the newspaper you read every morning by its appearance, format, and method of presentation, if its name were not visible? Or could you have identified the format of *Life, Look,* and *Post?* How about the marketing and advertising publications most of us see regularly—

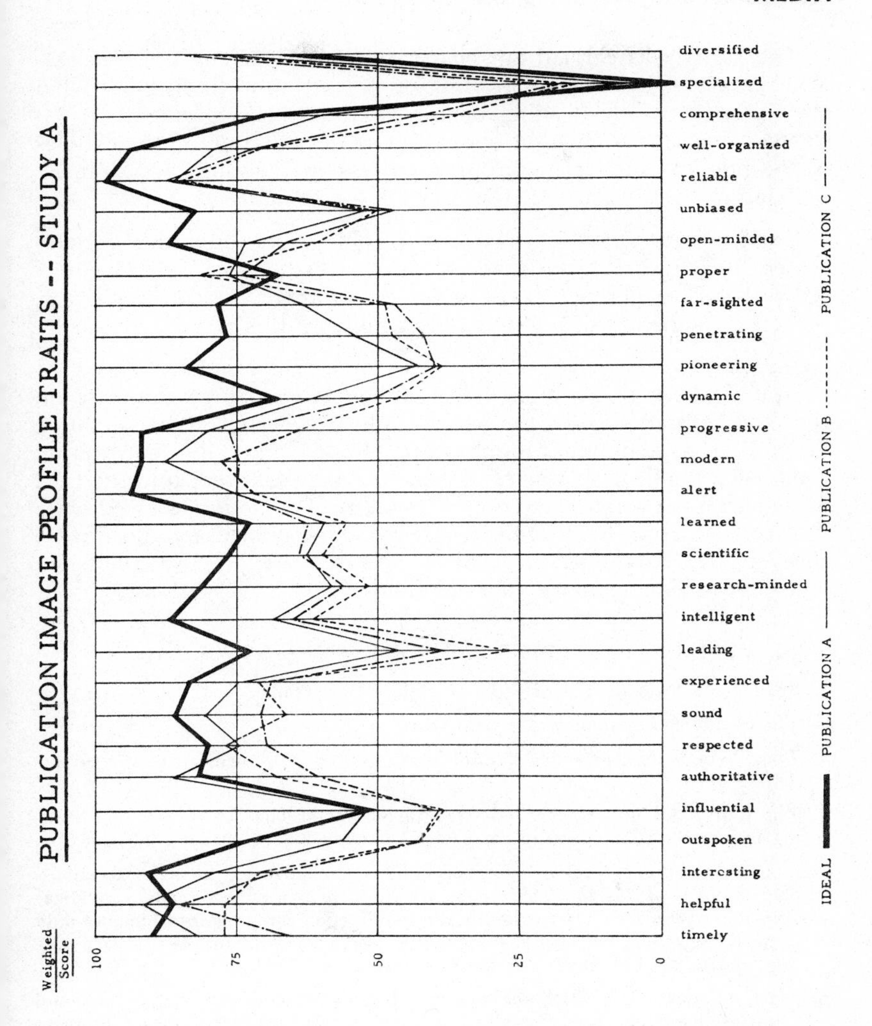

Advertising Age, Sales Management and *Industrial Marketing?*

If you are a *real reader* you probably would not have too much difficulty in doing so.

In order to test this theory, and to get some additional ideas to add to its store of knowledge regarding the measurement of editorial quality, the agency undertook what it calls Editorial Recall and Impact Research.

The study was carried out by personally contacting a representative sample of individuals in a major industry and finding out what they thought of the leading business publications serving their industry—what they thought about the subject matter of the articles in the publications, from the first impression (physical appearance) standpoint.

Good editors strive to turn out a publication containing articles which literally *ask* to be read. Marsteller was trying to find out if it's possible to put one book ahead of another because of success, or lack of success, an editor has in achieving this goal.

Marsteller researchers analyzed a total of one year's issues of the publications to be studied so that the article, format, and so on that was most typical of the books could be selected. Representative articles from the publications were clipped and all identification from each publication was removed. Interviewers went into the field armed with the articles and a questionnaire. People interviewed were individuals in a field with a common job function—those who theoretically would be most likely to read the publications being considered. The agency's analysis follows:

PUBLICATION IMAGE PROFILE STUDY—CONCLUSIONS

1. Readers do form images of the publications they read.
2. These publication images are definable.
3. These images can provide an additional qualitative dimension to the advertising buyer.
4. The individual importance and strength of specific character traits contributing to a publication's overall image tend to vary by the reader's job function.
5. A combination of specific character traits contributes to the general atmosphere, mood, or frame of reference within which a reader reads a publication. An advertiser's knowledge of this publication image assists him not only in media selection, but also enables him to adjust his own product or corporate presentation to that image for the best result.
6. Some publications, which have developed weaknesses in circulation and editorial, have previously established such strong positive images that these present limitations are often overlooked. Consequently, such publications are being carried by the impetus of past reputation.
7. There appears to be a correlation between the strength and sharpness of a publication image and the strength and rating of a publication on readership, reader preference, and editorial studies which this agency has previously conducted.

SUMMARY OF GENERAL CONCLUSIONS

1. There are real differences in editorial character of business papers and they are roughly measurable, so long as conclusions are not based on a single factor.

2. Editorial evaluation measurements, even if they are inadequate but so long as they are not empirical, force the space buyer to examine editorial on an organized basis and are therefore desirable.
3. Measures of editorial objectives, character and performance can very definitely increase the effectiveness of business publication selection.
4. Few advertisers and agencies currently use a qualitative measure on editorial, and few business paper salesmen are really trained to interpret it.
5. Business publications have definable images based on specific character traits. Knowledge of such images helps the advertiser in media selection as well as in his presentation of the advertising message.

The image of a publication affects not only readership of editorial material—which, after all, is what you're *really* buying when you plunk down the dollars for space—but there's also a rub-off as to the credence the reader places in everything he reads in the publication.

This includes the advertising.

Publications with all of the attributes the reader wants and looks for unquestionably are the best vehicles to carry your advertising message. When it's viewed in this way, image isn't such an intangible after all.

Readers

In its circulation statements and in accompanying material, the first rate business paper is able to describe accurately and concisely the *type* of reader it attracts, and to define its readers as a group.

For example, *Research/Development* magazine has a well-thought-out editorial objective and editorial policy. This enables the editors to tailor the magazine so that it appeals to a certain segment of the total business universe. The typical reader of *R/D* is better educated by far than is the average technical man on a similar level in other phases of industry. A breakdown of the book's readers by educational background shows the following degrees have been earned:

PhD	32.8%	17,407
MS	21.8%	11,533
BS or BA	34.1%	18,067
MD	1.3%	702
Other Degree	5.2%	2,776
No College Degree	4.8%	2,527

Any leading business magazine can supply a breakdown of its readers for you, by job title and/or function, areas of specific interest of recipients of the book, whether they have specifying influence, buying influence, or if they are members of professional societies. Much other detailed information is available that enables you to plan your advertising campaign with the readers' interests in mind.

Areas of technical interest among readers of *Research/Development* magazine, for example, are shown in the following tabulation. Following each specialized interest is the number of readers who have indicated they are concerned with this function in their companies. The total is more than the circulation of the magazine, of course, due to overlapping responsibilities and interests of the various individuals.

Applied Disciplines	
Aeronautics	3,045
Analytical Chemistry	24,298
Biochemistry	10,061
Biology	8,760
Biophysics	4,623
Chemistry	30,423
Electrical/Electronic	27,951
Medicine	5,837
Metallurgy/Material Science	17,837
Physics	16,876

Current Work Area	
Aerospace	6,947
Analytical Instruments	28,323
Chromatography	17,267
Control Systems	16,113
Cryogenics	6,862
Electrical/Electronic Research	16,152
Electronic Data Processing	15,901
Lasers	7,847
Metals & Alloys	13,682
Nuclear & Radiation	8,966
Optics	15,753
Pollution	16,745
Polymers	11,293
Solid State	11,037
Spectroscopy	19,222
Systems Engineering	12,103
Vacuum	32,142

Sometimes after you've finished analyzing them, there are two or even three publications in a given field that all have approximately the same "score." Making a selection of just one, if that's all the budget will permit, is exceedingly difficult.

However, it is absolutely essential that you select the best publication(s) to carry your advertising messages to the maximum possible number of interested prospects for your product.

To do this, you need to know one thing: Which publication among those on your list of possibles is preferred by the readers you're trying to reach? Which publication is most read, which one means the most readership for your advertisements?

Going to Your Prospects

If you've reached an impasse as far as making the final decision is concerned, there's only one way open to you that will let you get the information you need to make an objective decision—assuming you've analyzed all prospective publications thoroughly. That's to go to your prospects and ask them what their preferences are.

The advertising manager of Lindberg Hevi-Duty was faced with this situation when planning a campaign directed to buying influences in the metalworking market. The company was planning to advertise to support its marketing objectives for heat-treating furnaces.

This ad manager's dilemma was compounded by the fact that a number of very fine publications serve the metalworking market, and choosing between them was not the easiest task he'd ever attempted.

All prospective publications had been analyzed and a tabulation of the score each received on each specific criterion had been duly entered, weighted as experience dictated, and the sums totaled. Cost was considered last, of course.

At this time it was decided to do a readership survey to determine just what publications the universe actually preferred.

This survey did not fall into the trap that so many do, however. It did *not* fail to seek the attitudes of *prospective purchasers* of the manufacturer's line of heat-treating furnaces and accessories. This is often a weakness that seems to be inherent in most advertiser-conducted readership surveys.

Far too many advertisers make a survey over their own mailing list. Naturally, it consists primarily of customers and hot prospects compiled over a period of time from leads from the sales department, the field sales force, lists of visitors to the company's booth at trade shows, and similar sources.

When this is done the manufacturer making the survey ends up talking to himself because the questionnaire reaches only those who are presently familiar with the company and its products. The sample is not representative of the universe. Absent from the list is the vast army of companies and individual buying influences who have little or no awareness of the manufacturer and his products because they buy from competitor companies.

Overcoming this weakness is simple, though, and is accomplished merely by using a nonweighted mailing list. In Lindberg Hevi-Duty's case it was the Dun & Bradstreet list; very obviously some present customers would be on this list, but so would even more prospects who had never bought anything from Lindberg Hevi-Duty.

Names from the Dun & Bradstreet list were selected at random on an every *nth* name basis; the list was on IBM cards purchased by SIC classifications. A representative mix, as far as company size is concerned, was then selected, and care was also taken to assure a good geographical spread.

Questionnaires were individually addressed to 1,000 top production men in metalworking firms that do on-premises heat treating. Typical titles included vice-president, manufacturing; vice-president, production; director of manufacturing; works manager; plant manager; and others on that management level.

The company's advertising manager wrote the following letter and had it reproduced by multilith with a signature in blue ink on the company's letterhead:

Mr. R. W. Wilberforce
Vice-President, Manufacturing
Smith Widget Manufacturing Company
123 Any Street,
Podunk, Iowa 12345

Dear Mr. Wilberforce:

Will you take two minutes to help us?

We want you to see our advertising, so we need to know if we use magazines that you read.

Simply check the ones you read on the enclosed questionnaire.

Then put it in the enclosed stamped envelope and drop it in your "out" box.

There's no need to sign your name, and no need to identify your company.

Many thanks . . . and have a cup of coffee on us!

Cordially,

/s/

R. Howard Sanderson
Advertising Manager

The letter is short, straight to the point—and only small words are used in short sentences and short paragraphs. It is extremely easy to digest; there's no struggling over involved thoughts.

And the return envelope was *stamped*—not an envelope with the company's postage-paid indicia. Using a stamped return envelope invariably boosts the returns from a mailing. There's something about seeing a stamp on an envelope that triggers action. Maybe it's because people cannot bring themselves to throw away a stamp, nor do they find it easily ignored. This is a point to remember when you're interested in pulling a good return from a mailing—and the cost is little more.

A shiny, new dime was Scotch taped to the covering letter for "coffee money" and as an incentive to reply. This gimmick also always increases the returns on a questionnaire type of mailing. The dime is exactly right, incidentally; you cannot really compensate an individual for his time because it was his company's time he invested. Too, an attempt to do so would run the cost sky high.

Some researchers have tipped on quarters and half-dollars. There is no indication that enclosing more money produces more returns. Buying somebody a cup of coffee is a friendly gesture and is well received. (Now, in 1977, better send at least 25 cents!!.)

The questionnaire is of the aided-recall type to make it easy and fast to check off the publications the recipient read. Included is the now-defunct *Steel.* The questionnaire reads:

PUBLICATION PREFERENCE QUESTIONNAIRE

1. Please check which publications you read regularly (3 out of 4 issues).

American Machinist
Automotive Industries
Factory
Industrial Heating
Iron Age
Light Metal Age
Machinery
Metal Progress
Metal Treating
Modern Metals
Precision Metal Molding
Production
Steel

2. Now, please *circle* the *one* publication you find most useful and helpful in your work.

3. Which *one* activity is most closely related to your work:

Company management
Purchasing
Engineering
Plant operation or Manufacturing
Metallurgy
Other (specify)

....

4. Your title, please ....

5. Total employment at *this* plant: Less than 250 More than 250

THANK YOU . . .

AND ENJOY THE COFFEE!

Out of 1,000 questionnaires mailed, Lindberg Hevi-Duty received a return of 597—just a bare whisker under 60 percent. Anywhere from 15 to 40 percent is considered a worthwhile return and is statistically valid, so Lindberg Hevi-Duty's return was exceptional.

When tabulated the average respondent read 3.6 publications regularly, which were in addition to daily newspapers and consumer magazines, of course. The results showed the following:

RANK BY READ REGULARLY (3 out of 4 issues)

Rank	Publication	Total Mentions
1	*Iron Age*	451
2	*Steel*	388
3	*Factory*	292
4	*American Machinist*	262
5	*Production*	246
6	*Machinery*	219
7	*Modern Metals*	87
8	*Metal Progress*	81
9	*Automotive Industries*	58
10	*Industrial Heating*	47
11	*Metal Treating*	46
12	*Precision Metal Molding*	41
13	*Light Metal Age*	24
14	*Several miscellaneous books*	7

The shift that took place between mentions for Read Regularly and Most Useful are interesting indeed.

Iron Age placed first in both, of course, and by a substantial margin at that.

Fourth-ranking *American Machinist* climbed to second place in the Most Useful category, indicating an exceedingly high quality of editorial content; almost always magazines with outstanding editorial rank up near the top of the ladder when this question is asked.

Industrial Heating magazine, which ranked 10th in Read Regularly, received only three mentions out of a return of 597 when publications were ranked by Most Useful, so it dropped to the last on the list. And *Production* magazine, fifth in Read Regularly, climbed to fourth in Most Useful. *Factory* exactly maintained its status quo, third in both questions.

The Most Useful category looked like this when tabulated:

RANK BY MOST USEFUL

Rank	Publication	Total
1	*Iron Age*	92
2	*American Machinist*	78
3	*Factory*	70
4	*Production*	59
5	*Steel*	54
6	*Machinery*	21
7	*Modern Metals*	18
8	*Metal Progress*	10
9	*Metal Treating*	6
10	*Automotive Industries*	5
11	*Precision Metal Molding*	3
12	*Industrial Heating*	3

JOB FUNCTIONS OF RESPONDENTS

Rank	Function or Area	Total
1	Plant operation or manufacturing	183
2	Company management, not specified	162
3	Purchasing	33
4	Engineering	29
5	Metallurgy	15

SIZE OF COMPANY OF RESPONDENTS

Less than 250 employees	349
More than 250 employees	246

Many advertising managers consider there is a factor present that cannot be controlled, weighted, or otherwise compensated for when making a readership survey—and that is frequency of issue of the publications involved.

On the face of it, it's quite obvious that a weekly publication will make *more* impressions on the reader than will a monthly publication. For this reason a poor weekly may receive more mentions than a good monthly.

Read Regularly is considered a significant question, and it is one that certainly indicates where your advertising will stand the best chance of being seen and read. It cannot be overlooked.

Which publication do you consider most useful is, without doubt, the key question in the survey. It measures attitude, or image. What's more, it tells without equivocation which publication the respondents prefer over all others because he considers this publication to be the most help to him on his job. This is unquestionably the one publication in which he places the most faith—which means that this is the publication with the editorial climate that's ideal for your advertising.

Market Potential

One major factor influencing selection of media is the potential of the market that a given publication serves.

For example, most advertisers intent on marketing to the metalworking market are much better off to use broad horizontal publications such as *Iron Age, American Machinist,* and so on in an effort to reach as many buying influences in the marketplace as possible with their advertising messages.

Within the metalworking market media are any number of vertical publications that concentrate on one narrow segment of this vast industrial complex. A publication can be outstanding in its field, have editorial that's unquestionably first rate, circulation clean and well-directed to reach the people the magazine is edited for, and have a publication image that makes it come off like a printed Western sheriff saving the heroine from villains who were going to do her in and steal her ranch.

Let's take *Ordnance* magazine, for example. It is the official publication of the American Ordnance Association and is both authoritative and highly respected. The publisher's editorial statement says:

> Ordnance *is edited for members of the American Ordnance Association who are officers and scientists within the Army, Navy, and Air Force, and the executives, engineers and scientists of industry responsible for turning military needs into industrial end products. Feature articles discuss major areas of interest to the members. Weapons Technology contains technical papers of importance to the recipients. Departments include: Underwater Ordnance; Missiles and*

Aeronautics; Air Armament; C.B.N. Defense; Nuclear Energy; New Developments; Materials Progress; Book Reviews and Association Affairs.

The author has been familiar with *Ordnance* for a number of years and knows it is a well-edited publication that cannot help but be of intense interest to those for whom it is produced. Articles are factual, accurate, penetrating, and highly interesting. Those on interior and exterior ballistics and on small arms and ammunition are on a par with those in *American Rifleman,* official journal of The National Rifle Association of America, although those in *Ordnance* have more emphasis on military applications than do articles in *American Rifleman,* as a rule.

Then, there is *Wire & Wire Products* magazine, another vertical publication that serves a segment of the vast metalworking market; it has this editorial objective:

A technical monthly edited for those in the wire industry whose interests concern the manufacture of wire rod, bar, wire, fabricated wire products, electric wire, and cable. Subscribers are presidents, vice-presidents, works managers, superintendents, engineers, chemists, and purchasing agents. Contents are of interest to those concerned with manufacturing, and material and equipment procurement. News articles relate to personnel changes, new products, new developments and book reviews. Editorial articles cover new products and equipment, processing techniques, safety, plant management, production controls, material handling, statistics, etc.

And there are hundreds and hundreds of business publications that serve highly specialized portions of various broad markets; they do their job so well for the most part that the advertiser who sells *only* in these narrow, well-defined markets does well to use such books. Their coverage of the specific area they've staked out for themselves is usually excellent. Their editorial is geared to fit the individual with specialized interests in a specialized market and it does so without wasting time on trying to be all things to all men. Price of these vertical publications is almost always less per page than that of horizontal books because total circulation is usually always much smaller.

However, if you're selling a certain type of steel to almost every SIC within the metalworking market, for example, it takes a whopping big budget to use *both* horizontal and vertical publications. Not too many industrial advertisers have sufficient wherewithal to do this. Assuming a shortage of funds hampers your plans for including every medium that's good and that serves all, or a significant portion, of your market, just how do you go about determining the market potential for a given publication in order to analyze its desirability?

Every legitimate publication will supply you with a statement or description of the industries or fields it serves, usually broken down by SIC, and frequently by SRDS Business Publication classifications. This will enable you to determine just where it fits into the scheme of things in reference to your overall picture. Market data in your files and that given to you by the publication makes this easy.

Using this information, you can determine the size of the total market by number of establishments and where these smokestacks are located.

Working with information such as that supplied in *Iron Age's Metalworking Marketguide,* you can spot the total dollar volume of goods and services produced by the entire industry, that of individual states and counties, as well as the number of employees per establishment within the geographical area(s) in which you're most interested.

This enables you to ascertain with good ball-park accuracy the dollar volume output of individual establishments, using number of employees as a basis for making the estimate. All that's required is to determine the dollar volume output per employee, then do a little multiplying—or have your secretary do it, better yet.

Leading business publications usually report—at least annually—the anticipated dollar volume of expenditures for new plants and for equipment of specific types used in the production processes found within each industry. This is yet another way to guesstimate the size of the market these publications serve.

Information leading publications present is remarkably accurate, incidentally, and is usually based on field research and government figures, along with those released by trade associations, state chambers of commerce, and similar sources. You can rely upon it with only slight mental reservations because, after all, nobody knows a market as well as the best business publications that serve it.

What's more, the really good management-oriented business publication such as *Iron Age* always uses its prognosticative prowess to keep readers informed about market trends—industry growth; forecasts, immediate and long-range outlook; week-by-week recapitulations of significant events such as changes in government or military procurement policies; customer buying patterns; changes in weekly output of both ferrous and nonferrous metals; fabricators' workloads; changes in inventory; drastic changes in unit-size purchases and their frequency; labor outlook; various factors which affect distribution.

Carefully analyze this mass of available information in your spare time and you can pinpoint practically to the silverless quarter of a non-goldbacked dollar the size of the market and its potential for your company. And you can do this for all of the markets to which your company sells, then use this information to aid you in selecting the proper media mix to communicate most effectively with your universe.

Advertiser Acceptance

Anybody can make a mistake and purchase the wrong product—whether it's a chrome-laden automotive monster that turns out to be the worst lemon ever to leave Detroit, a television set that requires so many service calls the neighbors think the TV repair man's truck belongs to a close friend who calls often, or a magazine that doesn't deliver the goods for an industrial advertiser.

Chances are, of course, you'll never buy that make of car again, sooner or later you'll trade off the never-ending service calls on a new TV, and you'll cross off your media schedule the book that didn't produce.

Not only is this human nature, it's also sound business judgment.

For this reason, you can form a pretty sound initial impression of a publication merely by judging it by the company that keeps it.

If a magazine paces the pack, if it leads its competitors in total advertising pages year after year, there has to be a reason. The collective judgment of many hundreds of advertising managers and media directors and account executives has said, in effect, that this is the best book in the field in their considered opinion.

In the pages of *Research/Development's* AIA Form is an endorsement that shows quite clearly why it is the leading publication in its field. The magazine lists a total of 335 advertisers who bought space in the magazine the preceding year. Of this number, 168, just over half, have advertised in *Research/Development* for five or more years. Altogether, these 168 industrial advertisers have accumulated a total of 1,786 years of experience in selling to the research-development market through the pages of *Research/Development* magazine. Such long-term advertiser loyalty is a tremendously strong endorsement of the ability of the magazine to produce meaningful advertising results. Common sense indicates that if the magazine had failed to deliver the readership and the end results these advertisers—most of them leaders in *their* respective fields, incidentally—expected, the book would have been dropped from their schedules long ago.

Also in *R/D's* AIA Form is a breakdown of the total pages of paid advertising over the past five years. This naturally reflects the nation's economic climate, but the trend is very healthy indeed. *R/D* advertisers use the book consistently, without violent swings.

This information is essential if the advertising manager is to be able to evaluate the long-range advertiser acceptance.

Incidentally, *Research/Development* customarily runs more than 100 pages per year more total advertising than its closest competitor, and has far more *exclusive* advertisers than that book does. This, too, reflects the collective opinion of all of the people who continually evaluate and compare media and tabulate the results their advertising produces.

When you're considering adding a publication to your schedule, take several recent issues and leaf through them. List the advertisers. Look for your competitors. They're not always right, but if they're there and the other advertisers that use the book are substantial, successful firms, chances are the magazine is worth further evaluation. Frequently it's very revealing to phone the advertising manager of companies that use a publication you're evaluating. Naturally, you won't phone direct competitors because they have no desire to help you. But the advertising manager of a company that's not a competitor, but sells to the same market, more often than not will prove to be a veritable fountain of wisdom.

Notice that telephoning is suggested, not writing. Most people will open up on the telephone and volunteer all sorts of interesting and informative and helpful information they usually wouldn't take the time to give you in a letter. They might not care to put it down in black and white. The phone lets you take advantage of this facet of human nature.

These knowledgeable ad managers will give you their opinion of a book—its editorial, its circulation, its image as far as they've been able to determine it, and most important, what results their advertising has produced. Whether they're after inquiries or a check by return mail, don't question the validity of their objectives; after all, companies are different and communications objectives are all over the lot. And it's not their objectives you're really interested in as much as whether the magazine helps these advertisers achieve them.

One time the author telephoned the advertising manager of Fisher Scientific Company, Lewis McKinstry, about media. Fisher markets instruments, apparatus, furniture, and chemicals for laboratories—it's a laboratory supply house, in other words, and about the biggest in the country.

Fisher's ad manager was interested primarily in inquiries for the company salesmen to follow up on. And the firm for which the author was working was interested in inquiries, also, so there was much to talk about.

From a program that he had run for several years, McKinstry reported that *Research/Development* magazine produced 1249 inquiries, *Science* magazine produced 898, and *Analytical Chemistry* brought in 486. Fisher had used another magazine in the research field, but dropped it because it failed to produce inquiries in volume, and the inquiries it did produce were questionable as far as quality was concerned.

Decent thing to do after such a conversation as this is to write the ad managers a letter thanking them for their time and help. And if your company is one that goes the gimmick route, send them an 8-foot steel tape, Zippo lighter, cuff links with the company emblem engraved on them, tie bar, or something that shows you appreciate the courtesy.

A half-dozen such calls will prove very revealing, particularly if you take pains to select dissimilar firms, yet companies that might well have advertising objectives similar to yours. Be sure to include a good geographical spread, round out the size of the companies and the products to get a representative group of advertisers in the magazine.

This method of determining what others think of a publication has been extremely helpful to the author and a number of friends over the years. Invariably the collective judgment of other advertising managers has shown much merit.

Although inquiries are probably not your primary objective, inquiries nonetheless are important when it comes to comparing two competing publications that appear to be close rivals for your space dollars.

Bingo Cards vs. Letterheads

When comparing inquiry production, ask the publications how many inquiries they produced in each of the last five years. They'll give you this information, and most will break it down, bingo cards versus letterheads, although the vast majority of letterhead inquiries go directly to the advertiser. Some do go to publications, though.

Keep in mind there are ways to produce an artificially high

volume of inquiries. Most publications run the traditional Reader Service Card in the book with key numbers corresponding to advertisements and editorial publicity listed for the reader to circle those he's interested in. This makes it relatively easy for a number-checker to send off for huge quantities of literature and ask for all sorts of information in which he's only remotely interested. This cannot be avoided and is a fact of life that has to be lived with.

Some publications bind in several bingo cards so pass-on readers can also send them in. This raises the book's total number of inquiries by several hundred percent, but it also raises the question of just how valuable such inquiries are.

Still other magazines publish separate bingo cards, sometimes containing capsule descriptions of products and processes, for each item in the magazine. When the publication also binds in a postage-paid envelope, as some do, this usually results in a very large return of the cards, although inquiry quality is open to question.

Inquiries will be covered as a separate subject in the next chapter.

Something else to consider when you're evaluating media is the apparent difficulty, or the lack of it, that a magazine might encounter in selling its premium-priced space—those preferred positions that smart advertisers gobble up and retain in the best books for years at a time.

Almost all leading business publications today have a minimum amount of four-color reproduction that includes the cover (not sold in publications worth running space advertising in), back cover, second cover, and third cover.

As a rule of thumb you can assume that if there's a large turnover in advertisers in these preferred positions, something's amiss. If this space is producing as it should, advertisers wouldn't renounce their right to retain it. Preferred positions in top ranking books have a waiting list of advertisers who are eager to buy.

What's more, if a magazine prints four-color covers and then runs black-and-white advertisements on its fourth cover, that's another tip-off that the publication is short on advertiser acceptance. No industrial advertiser is going to shortchange himself by running black-and-white in premium-priced space when for just a few dollars more he could have quality four-color ads. And quality is consistently good in the best business publications; their production people and web-offset presses combine to produce mouth-watering color quality. This is a showcase for the magazine and no publication will accept less than the very best. He'll get attractive appearance on the covers regardless of cost.

When a book with a four-color cover is running black-and-white ads on the fourth cover—and they may change, one advertiser then another very frequently, or even from month to month—you can suspect with reason that publisher is giving that space away at the same price as he sells an inside page for. He's doing so just to get somebody, anybody on that fourth cover. He can't very well run a "house" ad there.

Also ask to see the results of buying studies that the publication has made—and remember the good ones have several that will be interesting to you. They were made, in almost every instance, by outside research firms and they document action taken by readers of the magazine, frequently those who inquired via bingo cards. They prove, too, that magazine readers have the authority and the jobs that enable them to buy and to specify—vital if your advertising is to be effective.

Proof of readership as determined by readership studies performed by a recognized research firm is also an essential you'll want to review thoroughly. Leading magazines use recognized services—sometimes their own, such as McGraw-Hill's Reader Feedback, or Chilton's Ad-Chart—but always ones that are accepted and respected in the industrial advertising field.

For instance, *Research/Development* uses Fosdick for its readership studies; other books in this field are: *Scientific Research,* which uses Mills Shepard; *Science & Technology,* which uses Starch; *Science,* which also retains Starch; *Analytical Chemistry,* which uses Com/Pact. Several minor publications serving this market do not list any readership measurement studies, hence offer no proof of readership. This makes comparison difficult unless you take lack of studies as proof that the publication itself doubts its readership.

Services to Advertisers

Publications with something to offer—as far as editorial and circulation are concerned—invariably offer a wide range of services to their advertisers. Marginal and less than marginal publications seldom do.

Important among these services are merchandising and direct mail; they will be discussed in subsequent chapters.

Leading publications offer a vast amount of market research, as has been mentioned. Those that do not are usually publications that are marginal at best, worthless at worst.

One mark of a publication with an excellent circulation is it has acquired a truly encyclopedic knowledge of its market in the process of building its circulation. The publication committed to making a genuine contribution to the market it serves always starts by becoming intimately familiar with that market, every aspect of it. It probes and digs and analyzes; its appetite for facts and information is insatiable. And this information is yours either free or for a very modest fee. Avail yourself of it.

Research in the marketplace which would help the advertiser sell his product is extremely important to that advertiser. Few indeed are the industrial companies with market knowledge even approaching that of the leading magazines in their industries. Quite often publication information constitutes the bulk of hard-core data that is available to smaller companies without research departments of their own.

Iron Age, for instance, has gone farther than the government; it has broken down and defined industry finer than the customary four-digit SIC. *Iron Age* has classified all of the metalworking industry by six-digit SIC. This greatly simplifies market identification and location for the advertising manager, as well as for the sales manager who finds it exceptionally helpful in his planning.

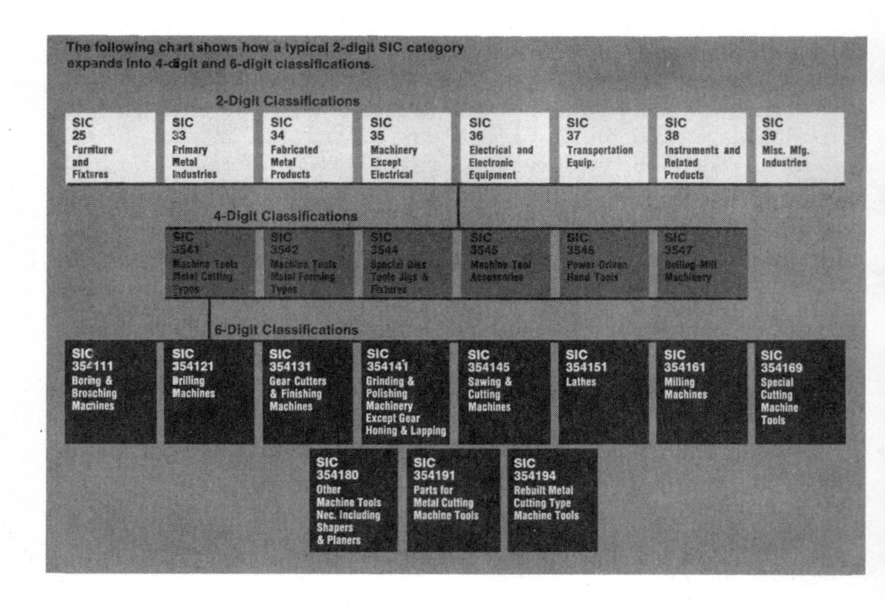

An outstanding reference to the metal trade is the *Iron Age Metalworking Margetguide.* This highly valuable book provides a statistical summary of *Iron Age's* continuing census of the metalworking industry. Included in the *Marketguide* is the following absolutely essential information:

- Description of the metalworking market—detailed information on the size and scope of the market and its relationship to all other manufacturing markets.

- Description and explanation of the SIC system.

- Market tools and how to use them.

- National two-digit SIC analysis.

- National four- and six-digit SIC analysis—showing count of 214 product groups at the four-digit level, and 1,427 different products at the six-digit level.

- State summary of plants and employment.

- Metal Service Center data—state summary and employment information on 1,717 centers.

All of this data, stored by *Iron Age* in a computer *Metalworking Data Bank,* is available in numerous forms at surprisingly low rates considering the value and accuracy of the data. (See pages 121-122.) This kind of information is basic to the success of your market and media plan. How many thousands of man-hours would it take to develop through your company's facilities? Think that one over.

Then, there's the massive study titled *Patterns in Materials Purchasing by R&D Scientists and Engineers* made by John T. Fosdick Associates for *Research/Development* magazine.

As the publisher of *R/D* pointed out, during the past 18 years the research and development sector of our economy has experienced a fantastic growth—from a lowly $3 billion in 1950 to almost $25 billion in 1968. That's more than 800 percent in just 18 years.

During this time the evaluating, specifying, and purchasing power increased just as dramatically. But the secrecy that surrounds research-development work has kept marketing men from obtaining "hard information" on *who,* within the laboratory, buys *what* and *why.*

The technological explosion the country has witnessed has produced a chain reaction of new markets and new materials to fit them—as well as new uses for old materials. Creating new markets, new processes, new uses, falls almost entirely within the realm of research and development. Having created, the scientists or engineers must shoulder a large share of the responsibility for specifying, evaluating, and even purchasing the materials that will go into the new product.

To help define the new marketing factor represented by these R&D men, and to delineate the depth and breadth of their role, *Research/Development* magazine had a comprehensive study conducted by John T. Fosdick Associates to provide information never before available to industrial advertisers and industrial marketing men.

Who specifies materials, what kinds, and for what? How far does the R&D influence reach into production? What are the society affiliations, the industrial and technical areas of work of scientists and engineers who buy, specify and evaluate materials?

The answer to these and many other marketing questions are in the report the magazine had prepared. It is, of course, available to advertisers for their use.

Research/Development's survey was made by mail, using 1,500 readers selected on an every *nth* name basis at random. The mail questionnaires were coded so a followup mailing could be made to nonrespondents.

As still another quality control, 100 names were selected at random in major cities where John T. Fosdick Associates had resident interviewers. These interviewers then telephoned the readers; the organization completed interviews with more than 95 percent of them.

Returns from the two mailings and the telephone interviews were tabulated separately and no significant differences were found. Fosdick concluded, as a result, that the study is statistically reliable and the results are projectable across the entire circulation of the magazine. The results follow:

The Research/Development market for CRYSTALS, OPTICAL MATERIALS, LASER, ETC.

The following market statistics are based upon a 1965 survey of *Research/Development* magazine readers. A sample of 1,600 readers was selected systematically to be representative of total circulation. Mail questionnaires were sent to these men and one followup mailing made to nonrespondents. A total of 757 mail responses was received. In addition, personal telephone calls were completed with 99 men who did not answer the mail questionnaires. Thus a total of 856 responses (54%) was received. The telephone questionnaires did not include the long list of 26 materials so that the questions below dealing with a specific material are based upon the 757 mail responses. We believe the figures reported below are statistically representative of the entire circulation of *Research/Development.*

1. Percentage of *R/D* readers who report that their company now uses crystals, optical materials, laser, etc. (base 283) 37%

2. Percentage of *R/D* readers, who having reported their company now uses crystals, optical materials, laser, etc., and also reported they PERSONALLY SPECIFY or PURCHASE materials (base 283) 75%

3. Percentage of these readers, who while they do not personally specify or buy materials, reported they have the responsibility of evaluating the performance of new materials or materials from potential new suppliers 5%

   TOTAL of those whose companies use crystals, optical materials, laser, etc., who either personally specify, purchase or evaluate new materials 80%

Readers were asked in what WAY they were involved in the specifying of materials. Percentages below are based upon all readers whose companies use crystals, optical materials, laser, etc., rather than the more limited number who specify (base 283)

Specify for research, testing, and evaluating 64%

Specify for prototype production.......... 41%

Specify production quantities.......... 21%

Readers were also asked HOW they specified materials. Percentages below are based upon all readers whose companies use crystals, optical materials, laser, etc., (base 283)

Percent who specify only by name or type of material 18%

Percent who specify make or supplier of material 63%

Relating back to the original base of 757 mail returns, 30% of the total respondents purchase, specify or evaluate crystals, optical materials, laser, etc.

4. Readers whose companies use crystals, optical materials, laser, etc., were asked to report on their PRIMARY professional society. Results are given below. The base for these percentages is the readers who purchase, specify, or evaluate materials. The same base applies for tables 5, 6, 7 and 8 (base 227).

ASME, ASM, ASTM, and AIME 13%

All other professional or engineering societies 63%

Not reported 24%

5. Readers were asked to report how long they had been a member of this society. The table below shows the distribution of these answers by five year periods (base 227) who purchase, specify, or evaluate crystals, optical materials, laser, etc.

Member less than 6 years	16%
Member 6 to 10 years	18%
Member 11 to 15 years	13%
Member 16 to 20 years	12%
Member 21 to 25 years	6%
Member over 25 years	7%
Not reported	28%

Average length of membership 13 years

6. Titles of these readers of *Research/Development* who purchase, specify or evaluate crystals, optical materials, laser, etc. (base 227).

President, corporation officer or director, owner, partner	7%
Manager, superintendent, division head	11%
Supervisors, department heads, group or section leaders	6%
Chief engineer, manager of engineers, senior engineer	10%
Chemical or process engineer	*%
Project engineer, research engineer	10%
All other engineers and scientists	23%
Chemist	5%
Research and development technical specialists	18%
All others, including professors, no answers, etc.	10%

7. Readers were asked to report the disciplines in which they normally work. Results based upon the 227 who purchase, specify, or evaluate crystals, optical materials, laser, etc., are reported below: (This information taken from circulation qualification forms.)

Aeronautics	8%
Biology	2%
Chemical engineering	15%
Chemistry	37%
Electrical/electronic	62%
Mathematics	35%
Mechanics	35%
Metallurgy	33%
Physics	61%
All others and no answers	7%

*Less than .5%

8. Further, readers were asked their areas of technical interest. These figures, also taken from circulation qualification forms, are reported below, based upon the 227 who purchase, specify, or evaluate crystals, optical materials, laser, etc.

Aerospace	32%
Ceramics	20%
Chemical processing	22%
Clean rooms	21%
Communications	20%
Control systems	22%
Cryogenics	19%
Data handling	25%
Electrical/electronic design	40%
Environmental testing	33%
Evaluation engineering	17%
Finishes	15%
Food processing	4%
Human engineering	11%
Hydraulics	10%
Instrumentation	41%
Maser-laser	17%
Mechanical design	29%
Metals and alloys	31%
Nuclear	13%
Optics	36%
Petroleum	5%
Plasma physics	11%
Plastics	22%
Pneumatics	7%
Quality control	15%
Solid-state physics	28%
Standards engineering	6%
Vacuum	43%
Other and no answers	*%

*Less than .5%

9. Standard industrial classification identifications of companies now using crystals, optical materials, laser, etc. (base 283).

Extractive industries, including agriculture, forestry, mining, natural gas, etc.	2%
Manufacturers of lumber and wood products	–%
Manufacturers of stone, clay, and glass products	1%
Primary metal manufacturers	–%
Manufacturers of fabricated metal products	3%
Manufacturers of machinery, electrical	41%
Manufacturers of machinery other than electrical	5%
Manufacturers of transportation equipment	1%
Manufacturers of professional, photographic and scientific equipment	6%
Manufacturers of food and related products	*%
Manufacturers of textile products	–%
Manufacturers of paper and allied products	–%
Manufacturers of chemical and allied products	8%
Manufacturers of petroleum and coal products	–%
Manufacturers of rubber products	–%
Miscellaneous manufactured products not listed above, including tobacco, printing, leather, molded plastic products, etc.	7%
Utilities—transportation, power, etc.	6%
Business services	*%
Professional and related services, independent consultants	20%
Government—federal, state, and municipal, including military	6%
Not reported	–%

No marginal publication supplies such a wealth of necessary marketing information to its advertisers. It can't—it doesn't have the information to give. In fact, many a marginal publication uses marketing information developed by the leaders in its field; this is done by "borrowing" and reprinting the data, disguising it so it won't be readily identifiable, as well as through developing editorial material and circulation with information developed by competing magazines.

Such publications shouldn't be carrying your advertising. The climate is not right for the caliber of reader you want and need, and it's not right for the atmosphere you want your product to be evaluated in.

*Less than .5%

Tiffany never presents an exquisite jewel on the lid of a garbage can.

Most of the better business publications make available to their advertisers a copy service that's used by those advertisers who don't have agencies and who want professionally written copy; there's usually no charge for this service. What's more, most business publishers have translators who will translate English into whatever language the export publication is printed in; as a rule there's no charge for this, either.

A number of business papers maintain files of photographs that may be of help to their advertisers, and they also have bulging files of case histories gathered by their editors when they're on field trips. Advertisers whose equipment is mentioned are generally welcome to this data, and it's almost always accompanied by photographs of good quality. This can save time and expense in gathering case history material for a campaign.

Some publications of editions are broken out geographically; they're called "regional editions." *Iron Age,* however, goes one major step beyond this. It also offers 13 Mini-Zip areas, corresponding to the 13 prime metalworking centers. This allows national advertisers to direct separate selling messages to as many as 13 selected market areas in the same issue. For regional advertisers, usually those with limited distribution or who sell only in a limited geographical area, it thus becomes possible to single out individual zones, or use combinations, to match sales, distribution and expansion potential area by area. In short, *Iron Age's* Mini-Zips add another important element to the flexibility of marketing communications.

Using only one edition enables you to test copy and other components of an ad—as well as the basic selling proposition and the copy appeal that the ad advances, as well as the appeal of the product itself, and it does so inexpensively.

Split runs are also broken out according to SIC, as *Iron Age* does with its Primary Metals Edition. This portion of *Iron Age's* circulation goes only to SIC 33, the basic ferrous and nonferrous metal producing mills and foundries; it provides exceedingly fine coverage of these establishments. Quite often *Iron Age,* although edited for the entire metalworking market, enjoys higher readership in metal producing mills and foundries than will monthly magazines edited specifically for them. This is because *Iron Age* is a weekly and presents timely news of the market, along with significant trends that enable management to plan its activities with greater effectiveness.

When you have a sticky problem and need some help, ask the

best business publication that serves your market—even if the problem doesn't directly involve space advertising.

Chances are the book will be able to come through for you, that it will do so in an incredibly short time, and that the cost to your company will either be nominal, or nothing at all. Business publications are very service-minded—at least, the good ones are.

Space Cost

Many of the better things in life are cheaper by the dozen, and space in business publications is no exception. In fact, space in the business press goes other things one better because it is also cheaper by the *half*-dozen.

Except for a few marginal publications that publish 13 months of the year—attempting to coerce advertisers into using a special issue that may hold little interest for them by giving only one-time, 7-time, and 13-time rates—business publications give what is called a "frequency discount" to their advertisers.

Frequency discount is simply a reduction in the per-page price as more and more space is purchased. Another term for this reduction in price is "earned rate"—which means the advertiser has earned a lower price or rate through the amount of his purchases.

Some publications break down the frequency discount even finer, however. *Factory* magazine, now published by Buttenheim Publishing Corporation, a subsidiary of Morgan-Grampian, Inc., is one of them. *Factory*, in its Rate Card No. 3, effective January 1, 1975, shows a frequency discount in increments of one page, from 1 through 36. Major frequencies in bold face in the Rate Card show these costs:

	1 Time	6 Times	12 Times	18 Times	24 Times	30 Times	36 Times
1 page	$2,400	$2,185	$1,950	$1,880	$1,860	$1,837	$1,815
2/3 page	1,780	1,545	1,380	1,345	1,323	1,305	1,288
½ page*	1,400	1,190	1,065	1,050	Rates upon request		

*(island) Fifteen percent premium for island half.

Charging less for space—the product it has for sale—is not due to an eleemosynary attitude on the publisher's part, however. That would conflict with the worthy gentleman's responsibility to his company, which is to see the property he's in charge of returns a profit to the stockholders. Rather, it is in the nature of an inducement to the advertiser to maintain continuity and frequency and to refrain from diluting the effectiveness of his advertising program by scattering his advertising space dollars through too many publications.

Price of space and additional information agencies and advertisers must have about a book is presented in the publication's "rate

6 COVERS:

a. Cover Rates: Include 4-color process and bleed. Cover rates are minimum and are not affected by other space used by an advertiser within the contract year; but each cover can be applied in earning frequency rates for other advertising space used.

Rates for Covers:	Covers II & III	Cover IV
	$2,340	$2,540

Rates include 4 process colors & bleed.

b. Cover Schedules: Can be cancelled only on notice of ninety days prior to date of issue, and, if cancelled before cover schedule is completed, are subject to short rate of $105 for each cover used.

7 FURNISHED INSERTS:

a. Furnished Insert Specifications & Costs: Check publisher on all insert matters, specifications and quantity needed.

The regular black and white space rates apply to furnished inserts which meet all specifications, are ready for binding and do not require trimming, back-up, etc.

b. Back-up and Handling Charges: Inserts that must be backed-up, tipped-in, trimmed or require special handling will be charged to the advertiser at our prevailing rates – to be furnished on request. All special charges will be in addition to space rates and are not commissionable.

8 SPECIAL POSITIONS:

a. Rates for Special Positions (Other Than Covers): Positions available and rates furnished on request.

b. Position Restrictions: Check with Publisher.

9 COLOR:

a. Rates for Color and Colors Offered (Other Than Black):

Second colors available in all sizes of display ad units. Standard AAAA second colors: yellow, orange, red, blue, green.

Black & 1 standard color:

	1 Page	2/3 Page	1/2 Page	1/3 Page	1/4 Page	1/6 Page
1x	$2,020	$1,460	$1,170	$860	$720	$540
6x	1,985	1,430	1,150	840	700	525
12x	1,955	1,400	1,135	825	685	515
24x	1,925	1,380	1,120	810	675	505
48x	1,895	1,365	1,105	795	665	495

72 pages—$1,865
96 pages—$1,835

b. Rates for Special Inks:

Matched Color: $85 plus the black and 1 standard color rates above.

Metallic inks .... contact publisher.

c. 3 or 4 Process Colors:

	1x	6x	12x	24x
1 page	$2,440	$2,385	$2,335	$2,300
	48x	72x	96x	
1 page	$2,265	$2,235	$2,205	

3rd & 4th consecutive pages $85 less on each.
Contact publisher for larger units.

10 BLEED:

a. Rates for Bleed and Oversized Pages: No Charge.

b. Specifications for Bleed: See Mechanical Requirements #13.

11 CLASSIFIED, READING NOTICES, SPLIT RUNS, ETC.:

a. Classified: "Professional Services," "Searchlight," "Where to Buy," and "Employment Opportunities" section rates on separate card or consult SRDS.

b. Special Mail Order or Book Advertising Rates: None.

c. Regional (including international) and/or Split Run: Information on request.

d. Reading Notices: None.

e. Book Advertising: Regular display rates.

12 CONTRACT AND COPY REGULATIONS:

a. Regulations Not Stated Elsewhere: Specific and detailed references are published monthly in SRDS.

13 MECHANICAL REQUIREMENTS:

Follow AAAA/MPA Standard Specifications for advertising reproduction material for magazine web offset printing.

Publication Trim Size: 8 1/8" x 10 7/8".

Standard Unit Size In Inches: Space can be used only in the following forms:

Space Unit	Vertical Width-Depth	Horizontal Width-Depth
1 page	7" x 10"	....
2/3 page	4 9/16" x 10"	....
1/2 page*	4 9/16" x 7 7/16"	7" x 4 7/8"
1/2 page	3 3/8" x 10"	....
1/3 page	2 3/16" x 10"	4 9/16" x 4 7/8"
1/4 page	3 3/8" x 4 7/8"	....
1/6 page	2 3/16" x 4 7/8"	4 9/16" x 2 5/16"
1/12 page**	2" x 2 1/8"	....

*Two-column one-half page accepted on condition advertising can be placed on top, bottom or side of it.
**Standard rule border (2 3/16" wide x 2 5/16" deep) is placed around each 1/12 page ad by publisher.

Advertisements exceeding size in any dimension are considered bleed or oversized, except for gutter bleed in two (facing) page spreads.

card." A new rate card is published whenever there has been a significant change in data.

In the case of space, a new rate card is usually needed at least every other year. Never in the memory of living man has a business publisher been put to the bother and expense of printing a new rate card because of a *reduction* in space prices. Two pages from the rate card for *Construction Methods and Equipment* are shown above. This is the Standard Form of Rate Card recommended by the American Association of Advertising Agencies. Data is presented in the specified sequence so it is easily compared to that of any other publication that also uses the approved form.

Cost of space hinges on circulation, of course, and the larger the circulation the higher the per-page price you'll pay. Some books force circulation by using massive drives—by direct mail, salesmen, dealer-distributor organizations, and by offering the book at trade shows, industry association meetings, and just about every other conceivable place—all to boost circulation.

These same publications frequently seem to make only a nominal effort to qualify those whom it solicits; net effect of all this promotion is to dilute the value of the circulation, while at the same time charging more for it. They can get by with this because the numbers are larger, that is, the circulation is larger—hence leading to the name of this practice, the "numbers game."

It is inevitable, of course, that circulation of legitimate publications that do *not* force circulation will also rise; this reflects the larger size of the business community, growth of the gross national product, and the population explosion of the country as a whole.

This is all well and good and publications whose growth is gradual and parallels that of the industry they serve cannot be questioned on this score. It is only when the circulation of a publication is swollen by leaps and bounds—say, 10, 15, 20 percent at one swell foop—that a jaundiced eye should be cast upon the book's policies.

Just a little bit hard to swallow is the glib explanation the publisher invariably advances under these circumstances—that "Book X now covers an even *greater* percentage of the market for your widgets" and so on and on.

One question that may logically be asked at this time when you're talking to the magazine's representative is, "And just who the hell needs this additional circulation?"

Doesn't it stand to reason that if the book was giving you as much coverage in the market as it could economically provide without turning over every log in an effort to flush out an additional relatively logical recipient for the magazine, that it's a bit odd that circulation should leap ahead like a missile being launched from its pad? And that this many truly qualified people could be found all at one time is even odder?

Space cost is boosted substantially to pay for both the promotions that "found" the additional "qualified" readers, as well as to pay for this extra circulation. The advertiser pays for both, of course. No altruistic publisher picks up the tab out of goodness of heart. You can be sure of that.

Best way to tell if circulation of a book you're using or considering using has taken any of these numbers-game jumps is to look at its AIA Form and examine the circulation figures for the past five years. Gradual growth is fine, sharp surges of 15 percent or more are highly suspect.

Also in the AIA Form are space costs—rates—for the publication for the last five years. Rates of business publications in general have gone up over the years, just as everything else has gone up. There's a fixed relationship, however, between space cost and circulation; this varies with individual publications, but it's there and can be determined with a little pencil-and-paper work.

The Cost Per Thousand

Something else to consider is the cost per thousand, often abbreviated as "CPM." This is the circulation divided into the cost per page of space. In the case of *Research/Development,* for example, the cost per page of space is shown in the AIA Form as $1,835. Circulation at that time was 70,111. This figures out to a cost per thousand (CPM) of $26.17.

CPM is a tremendously handy unit of measurement in consumer publications where circulation is circulation, all of it just about the same as far as quality is concerned.

However, in the industrial area it's relatively easy to increase circulation beyond the requirements of the market that's being covered by the publication—particularly in smaller, highly specialized, vertical markets.

If undue emphasis is placed on CPM, the obvious thing that will occur to publishers is to boost circulation (and raise rates, of course) so that cost per thousand comes down—even if rates do go up.

Playing the numbers game and indulging in circulation races with competitive books can result in oversaturation of the market for the publication; there is a limit, after all, to the number of readers who are really and truly buying influences in any market or for any product.

Reaching down the ladder on the corporate table of organization—or reaching too far up it, for that matter—to snare some additional recipients of the magazine accomplishes one thing as sure as you sit there reading this: It raises the cost of doing business for a publication.

This added cost is not going to be absorbed out of profit. It's going to be passed on to you know who. And when all is said and done, if a publication's circulation is good, if the editorial is excellent, if the book is useful to you, if it reaches the people you want to talk to, if it does so without straining to reach every single pea-pickin' individual in the universe, that's all you can logically expect.

After all, you don't buy circulation. You buy readers.

Cost per thousand of a given publication should be reasonably well in line with competitive publications, but don't base a buying decision solely on CPM.

In the last dozen and a half years the cost of advertising in business publications has risen sharply. According to *Media/scope,* a random sample of 157 business publications in 76 SRDS classifications was used to determine just how much it has risen. Combined circulation of these publications is over 10 million—or approximately 26 percent of all business publication circulation. Changes are calculated on average one-time, black-and-white page rates, and average circulations.

Using an index of 100, which equals the average ad cost and average cost per thousand for the base year 1956, figures show that in January, 1950 the cost of a business publication ad was 64, while cost per thousand was 88.

In 1968, the cost of a business publication ad was 182, while CPM had risen to 132.

This is an 82 percent increase from 1956 in cost, a 32 percent increase in CPM; lower percentage increase in CPM is due to mushrooming circulations, of course. When we compare 1968's costs with 1950's, though, the percentage of increase in cost is almost 300 percent, and in cost per thousand it's exactly 50 percent.

As a matter of interest, cost of advertising in business publications has risen more than has cost of using consumer magazines, daily newspapers, or spot radio. Only the bright-eyed electronic monster has surpassed business publications in having an insatiable hunger for advertisers' dollars; spot TV has risen to 231 on the cost index.

There's no indication the business press rates will either level off or get out of the upswing they're in. Cost of publishing has risen steadily and continues to do so. Salaries are up and continue to go up as inflationary pressure raises the cost of living. They're up some 36 percent since 1958.

Paper, too, has steadily posted higher prices and this trend appears to be one that will also continue. Printing costs have gone up more than 30 percent in the last 10 years.

And the government itself, through that vast, archaic organization of bureaucratic dinosaurs, the post office, has hit the business press a body blow with dismaying frequency. Second-class postage, used by publications with a paid circulation, is today 74 percent above what it was in 1958. And postage for controlled circulation publications is 23 percent higher. Coupled with larger circulations, this is a tremendous increase in costs the publishers must make up somehow. Furthermore, third-class mail, heavily used by publishers, jumped sharply with the other increases.

In the face of financial facts of life like these for publishers of business papers, only a dewy-eyed optimist would predict stabilization of rates in the business press.

Media Representatives

Chances are, some of the best friends you'll make in the advertising business will probably be media representatives. As a group, they're fine people, knowledgeable, informed, helpful—downright nice guys.

Like attracts like in this field as it does in any other. Almost invariably the leading publications will have better salesmen than will lesser magazines. Water seeks its own level, and there's no changing that.

The typical media representative—the space rep, as he's often called—is actually a fairly outstanding individual. He knows his publication backwards and forwards. There's remarkably little he can't tell you about it off the top of his head. And not only does he know his magazine, his product, but he knows the market it serves inside-out, also backwards and forwards.

A really good space rep is a gold mine of information; he sees so many people that he detects trends while they're still not sharply defined. And on top of everything else, he's usually a pretty good advertising man.

Although it's from the agency point of view, Marsteller Inc. has formalized a procedure and questions that should be asked when a media representative is being interviewed. That agency's how-to-do-it point of view follows:

HOW TO INTERVIEW MEDIA REPRESENTATIVES

1. Could you make available circulation galleys for a particular company?
2. Please relate your publication's audience to my client's products.
3. What is your total market, and what percentage of this total market do you cover?
4. What is your editorial objective?
5. For whom is your publication edited?

6. Can you show me some articles from your publication that would interest my client's prospects? Which of these articles have produced the most reader reaction? Why?

7. A hypothetical question—if you were me, Mr. Space Representative, which of your competitors' books would you add to the schedule after yours? Why? (Or, what's the second best book in the field?)

8. What do you think of my client's campaign in your publication?

9. In your opinion, Mr. Space Representative, what advertisers in your magazine are doing an outstanding job of advertising? Which campaigns are getting particularly good results? Why?

10. Would you please point out the competitive differences between publications in your field?

11. What is your volume of requests for editorial reprints? (Be wary of individual requests versus total number of reprints sent).

12. What kind of merchandising program do you offer advertisers?

13. Does your publication have a policy concerning advertising quality control—truth, taste, etc.?

14. In what way is your publication contributing to the industry? Do your editors take stands on controversial issues?

15. When did you last visit my client?

16. Occasionally request that the representative summarize his arguments in letter form, specifically relating his story to your individual client.

One of the best checklists to rate salesmen is one that the late G. C. Buzby, board chairman of Chilton Company, presented to his own staff. It follows:

The buyer speaks (of salesmen)

How much does he know about my company, product, my marketing posture? Has he ever called on any of my distributors, dealers, or users? Is he *really* interested in my problems or does he expect me to be interested in his?

Does he give me the impression he knows my market and my place in it? Is he selling a marketing service with full understanding of the function of media advertising, or is he just peddling space?

Does he come to me with a standard pitch which he grinds out for everybody, or has he tailored his approach to my situation, my interests, and my objectives?

When he receives a contract from my company, does he consider the case closed until he shows up 11 months later for the renewal? Or does he realize that when he got the order, his responsibility just starts?

Does he tell me the same story over and over and then wonder why I don't want to see him? How often has he written me between calls, passing out information helpful to me or a clipping from his magazine, or even some competitive magazine?

If he were in my position, would he place advertising in his publication? Really? Does he know why? Has he thought it out?

On the occasions I've called on him for information or services, how promptly and effectively has he responded? Has he followed up on these requests?

How well does he know his own publication? Does he read every issue himself? Does he ever call on any of his own subscribers and readers? Does this result in case histories which are of interest to me?

When I make a reasonable request for market information or help, does he go back to his publisher and knock himself out getting the answers or does he arm-wave me?

Does he slug his competitors trying to prove that they are robbers and thieves and that his book is the only good one? Does he realize that some of them are good friends of mine?

Does he waste my time with long-winded anecdotes, painful pleasantries and bum jokes, or with sales calls that have no aim or purpose except to generate a call report to his boss?

> How courteous and pleasant is he to our receptionist, my secretary, and others in my company with whom he comes in contact?
>
> Does he try to be a hero by telling five or six agencies that my account is ready to be plucked—especially when he picked this up as an unfounded rumor?
>
> Does he think he can buy my business with alcohol and outings or does he know that the old gladhanded prince of a good fellow salesman is passe? Mind you, I don't mind a lunch or a cocktail now and then while we talk business.
>
> Does he know that by a strange quirk of nature I like to be sold? I don't really like to give business to people who haven't earned it.

One very good bit of advice is: See media representatives. Don't make the mistake of regarding their calls as useless, time-consuming and nonproductive. Good reps have something to say, and it's a really rare advertising manager (or account executive) who doesn't learn something from them.

Do not, however, encourage calls made merely for the sake of the rep's conscience. This merely wastes your time and that of the representative. Make it known you *want* to see media representatives when they have something significant to tell you. Don't be the unapproachable, unseeable advertising manager whose switchboard or secretary fends of all callers because he is "too busy."

Granted, there will be days when you're writing, when you're working on an especially important report, when you're planning a new campaign, when you honestly cannot spare time to see reps. Have your secretary explain the circumstances and apologize for you.

Quite often you'll find it is helpful to expose other people in the company to the space salesman—at least to those from leading publications serving markets in which you're most interested. These representatives not only help you sell the medium for which they work, but they help sell advertising in general.

Furthermore, the well-informed representative—and all of the good ones are well-informed—can often impart specific market information to your people that they can use. This can be done without being patronizing or making the product manager or the market manager feel that he is being force fed information *you* want him to have.

Also mentioned was "competitive information"—details or clues as to what competitor companies are up to. Reps see many people within an industry and most advertisers are something less than reluctant about picking up competitive information these media men might have.

The Media Plan

For a company to spend money on advertising without having firm, well-defined, written objectives makes about as much sense as failure to adopt the marketing concept.

These two failures usually go hand in hand, however, and the company whose management is determined to sell standard price-book widgets is generally the company whose vice-president of marketing calls the advertising manager in when the new fiscal year rolls around—then innocently says, "Your budget for next year is $000,000. Now, I like Book B, you know, and Book D, and Book F and such-and-such trade shows (they're usually in swinging cities, of course). Why don't you develop a program for me, using these magazines and these shows, plus any others you think belong, and I'll pass it along to our fearless leader for approval."

Such childlike faith that this course of action will accomplish anything positive is, unhappily, much more common in industry than we'd prefer to believe.

Developing a media plan involves some of the world's hardest work—thinking.

Despite the mental agonizing and the effort entailed, having a plan is essential if the advertising dollar is to be invested rather than spent, and invested so it produces the highest possible return.

Marsteller Inc. says its eight-step checklist enables it to develop a media plan that's exactly right for any specific client, and all without fuss and furor. The checklist reads:

THE MEDIA PLAN

Here's a checklist of eight steps important in the analysis and selection of industrial media:

1. *Marketing objectives.* Absolutely necessary to build the industrial media plan. Marketing objectives put us in the right ball park.

2. *Communications objectives.* Must be specifically oriented to the marketing objectives and given priority by their relevance to each marketing objective. Communications objectives define the *boundaries* of the ball park.

3. *Circulation.* Numbers and characteristics of those numbers are always a fundamental factor. Audited figures from ABC and BPA are the media buyer's fact source.

4. *Editorial.* Evaluation of the editorial content and quality is also essential. This analysis yardstick gets the most lip service and least actual application of any media technique.

5. *Readership.* What we buy from a medium is readership. The measurement of this critical factor is dependent partly on the effectiveness of the medium itself and partly on the creative message used. Readership measurement methods are still primitive in many respects.

6. *Publication image.* This relatively new media yardstick often tips the scale to one book when all other factors seem equal. A publication image has a "rub-off" effect on the advertiser. Therefore, the two images had better be compatible.

7. *Media strategy.* This will often in itself dictate or at least narrow the final selection. Strategy concerning frequency, dominance and impact, national versus regional coverage, horizontal versus vertical industry reach, are all important factors. So, too, are such elements as product market share, competitive pressures, and marketing strategy.

8. *Budget.* Budget limitations often dictate the advertiser's ability to employ a balanced communications mix and/or to apply extra impact through any given media.

When all is said and done and the media plan is finally developed, what it really does is to show how publication space can best be used to help achieve the company's marketing objectives—and what additional media such as direct mail, trade shows, merchandising, and so on can do to augment the basic program. In industrial advertising, space advertising is the one basic, fundamental tool we can't dispense with.

A trend today is to have more and more internal media specialists in the industrial companies. These specialists work with agency media people, rather than relying entirely on the agency for media selection as was common several years ago. In smaller advertising departments, the advertising manager is usually the media specialist, as well as the specialist in almost everything else, of course.

When all of the chips are down and the schedule is almost ready to be typed, a decision still has to be made. Will media recommended by either the agency and/or the internal media specialist be used, is there a conflict of opinion, or are more suitable media available and more advisable?

This decision will be made by the man who's responsible for the company's money—the advertising manager, the advertising director, or whatever title the top ad man in the company wears. Specialists recommend, and rightly so, but the advertising manager has the ultimate responsibility. And he usually has a more complete picture of all of the various forces exerted on and in the marketplace, as well as a *feel* for the market that cannot be imparted to media people.

Computerization of media data and greater comparability are worthwhile goals, of course, and it is very possible that the computer will play a bigger and bigger role in media selection in the future than it does right now; its importance has been growing year by year.

That doesn't alter the fact that the man responsible for helping achieve vitally important marketing objectives still is charged with that responsibility, though. Computers have been notably slow to accept responsibility for their actions. Some feel this is an irresponsible attitude.

Computers could, for example, select a whole bevy of fine media. Each and every magazine could measure up to agreed-upon criteria in every respect. Editorial could be outstanding, circulations exactly right, publication images the greatest. And the computers, lacking judgment in this one area, could recommend buying one and all of these media to disseminate the message near and far with great dispatch.

The only thing, there seldom is enough money in the budget to go this route, not and achieve any dominance in the one or two *best* publications in each market, that is. Computers lack judgment—they could easily recommend a program encompassing so *many* media the advertiser wouldn't dominate the most important one or ones. This could make his program look weak and spotty and cause it to fail completely as far as making impact is concerned.

It's always better to dominate the one best book, then build from there if there is additional money available.

Cost of dominating the one or two best books is invariably less than that of scattering advertisements haphazardly throughout many "deserving" publications. And dominance can buy a market for the advertiser—"scatteration" never can.

Monthlies Versus Weeklies

This is one of the moss-covered questions that always arises when making media decisions, and it is certainly one that should have been quietly laid to rest lo, these many years ago.

The Basford agency in New York made some very revealing comments in its assessment of this question that seem to analyze the situation as well as it has been done.

If an advertiser is going to run only six advertisements in a publication during a year, will he be better off using a monthly, or a weekly? Suppose he's able to schedule only three ads, then what?

This question, or one very much like it, was asked of Basford several times a year. The agency checked into it carefully, and the answer appears to be that frequency of issue should *not* be a prime consideration. Media should be selected on the basis of its *circulation, rates, and editorial content*—these three considerations only, according to Basford. (No mention was made of publication image.)

Contrary to what many advertising men think, if a reason cannot be found to choose one publication over another except frequency of issue, it is just as well to select the one that is issued *most* frequently.

Off hand, this might seem contrary to good sense. However, when the problem is considered in this light, it takes on an entirely different aspect:

1. Does an advertisement have a better chance of being seen in a weekly or a monthly?
2. Will a series of advertisements, if they all *are* read, make more of an impression on a reader if they appear, let's say, in every other issue of a monthly, or in every eighth issue of a weekly?

George Kiernan, who is head of George Kiernan Associates, Inc., formerly the old Eastman Editorial Research, and others who do editorial research, says there are wide differences among publications in how many issues a typical reader reads—but the differences stem from how "vital" or interesting the books are, not from frequency of publication. A good weekly will be just as thoroughly read—and just as many issues will be read—as a good monthly.

Readers spend more time per issue, but less time per page, on a good thick issue than on a good thin one. Since good weeklies are usually thinner than good monthlies, there may even be some advantage to the weekly. The fact that a monthly "sits around" for a longer time than a weekly is not valid; the page on which an advertisement appears doesn't get exposed any more often.

Inquiry records show that inquiries come in just as long from a weekly as from a monthly, showing that life of the two kinds of publications is the same. McGraw-Hill's Laboratory of Advertising Performance reports both weeklies and monthlies secure reader action for two or three months. For example, only 63.5 percent of the reader actions had occurred at the end of four weeks for the monthly, and only 75.3 percent for the weekly. By the end of eight weeks, the monthly figure is 95.8 percent and the weekly 94.4 percent, showing weeklies and monthlies have a very similar length of life.

From the standpoint of an ad being seen, then, there are very real differences between publications—but these differences come from how well the publication meets the readers' needs and interests, not from its frequency of issue.

How about the impression a *series* of advertisements makes? Is the impression stronger when ads appear every other month in a monthly magazine, rather than every other month in a bimonthly or a weekly?

No evidence has been found that this makes the slightest bit of difference. When you stop to think about it, this is only logical. The reader you are trying to reach will be exposed to hundreds—thousands, really—of ads between one appearance of your advertisement and the next appearance, whether your ad appears in a weekly magazine or in a monthly one.

Almost certainly, if the reader sees one of your advertisements today, and another one two months from now, he won't even remember *where* he saw today's ad. And he couldn't care less. Only the advertiser, not the reader, worries about things like that.

Is there any evidence to support all of this? Emphatically yes!

Some business publications have been such good advertising buys that they became very fat, in both income and in physical format. They then increased their frequency of issue in order to reduce their thickness. There was no change in editorial content or editorial approach.

In every case where this has happened, so far as is known, advertising readership scores and inquiries per advertisement have gone just one direction—up. This has probably been because the resulting issues were thinner, but it supports the case for giving at least equal consideration to the book with the greater frequency—assuming circulation, rates, and editorial content are equal.

Directories

In addition to trade publications, other print media used widely in industrial advertising are directories.

These massive publications—frequently several heavy, thick volumes one could slip a disc just lifting—contain detailed listings of tens of thousands of individual manufacturers and their product lines, as well as paid space advertisements run by many of these companies.

Directories are the purchasing agent's right arm. The PA knows that almost anything an industrial company could conceivably purchase is listed in one or more of his directories, complete with product description, sometimes prices, and always the names and addresses and phone numbers of the makers of these products.

When the purchasing agent knows who makes the product, it's a very simple matter to look in the local phone book for a local office of the manufacturer, for its rep, or to write, phone or wire asking to have a salesman call.

Untold millions of dollars in sales result each year merely from a listing in the various directories. Especially when the product is one that is used or consumed in manufacture, or is used for plant or equipment maintenance, most purchasing agents buy by directory description and issue purchase orders without ever having seen that particular manufacturer's representative or salesmen; these PO's often say "advise price" instead of giving an existing price because it may not be known.

In the case of capital equipment, however, the purchasing process is very different as we've seen. Even when expensive capital equipment is involved, however, use of directories is advisable. It is insurance that your company will not accidentally be overlooked by a buyer or purchasing agent with an information-gathering assignment which includes compiling a list of prospective vendors.

Actually, the directory publishers do all of industry a favor by publishing. Listings are often given at no charge for the basic product line or lines. Advertisers in the directories usually receive bold-face listings, additional listings, and a much finer breakdown of product lines with listings under a number of different product classifications; this is an incentive to take a space advertisement in the directory, of course.

The average directory has an unbelievably long life span. Most of the major directories are issued annually, but it is not at all unusual for advertisers to receive queries—or even actual orders—from buyers who are referring to a directory that is anywhere from two to 10 years old. This situation is particularly prevalent overseas, especially in countries that are not highly industrialized.

Undoubtedly one of the best known and most widely used of the industrial directories is *Thomas' Register.* Original edition of *Thomas' Register of American Manufacturers* was published for the years 1905-1906; it weighed a pound and a half, contained slightly over 1,200 pages, and "rented" for $10.

In 1975, the 65th edition of *Thomas' Register* was produced. (The directory was published at 18-month intervals during World War I because of a paper shortage.) The 1975 edition occupied 11 huge volumes shown below.

A recent survey indicated that over one-quarter of a *billion* dollars worth of annual business can be directly attributed to use of *Thomas' Register,* and that the massive directory is referred to more than 1,000,000 times a week.

Latest development in the *Thomas' Register* is Thomcat. Thomcat, a catchy name if there ever was, is a well-thought-out and very thoroughly effective way to get your catalog or product sales literature into the hands of those who want to buy from you.

Your catalog or literature is bound into Thomcat. And because Thomcat is between sturdy, stiff covers, the printed sales messages are well protected and instantly available for buyers who want and need immediate information about your product.

Thomcat has been phenomenally successful, even though it was introduced on the eve of an advertising recession. Nonetheless it won instantaneous and continuing support from advertisers for one reason: it sells the products.

Another very fine directory, and one which tens of thousands of buyers and purchasing agents swear by, is MacRae's Blue Book. It is published in five huge volumes; a line conversion illustration of the five volumes is shown here.

MacRae's Blue Book is an industrial directory/catalog service produced and published annually in February. It is directed to purchasing agents, plant engineers and top management, and is distributed to approximately 25,000 of America's leading specifiers of goods and services. Although its circulation covers the gamut of industry, the majority (approximately 80 percent) is in metalworking—S.I.C.'s 33-39.

Listed alphabetically are around 50,000 company names with addresses, telephone numbers, capital asset listings, plus branch and sales office locations and their telephone numbers. Also included is an index of trade names.

Space is relatively inexpensive in directories, and your advertisement lives for at least a year—often for many years. All of this is yours for the price of one insertion, one production cost. Directories are excellent buys, and as many should be used as the budget permits.

Chapter 14

INQUIRIES AND INQUIRY HANDLING

FEELINGS about inquiries, either pro or con, are inclined to be strong among members of the industrial advertising fraternity.

Few shades of gray are recognized or acknowledged. Inquiries are regarded as either black or white. There is virtually no middle ground. And there is remarkably little fence-straddling.

On the one hand, there's a large and highly vocal group that is unalterably of the opinion that inquiries are the most rapturously wonderful thing to come down the pike since the invention of the wheel, and they don't hesitate to say so.

When these advertising men receive their monthly quota of inquiries from one of the publications on their media schedule, they tend to exhibit what has been called the Inquiry Syndrome; they writhe rapidly in their chairs, wiggle their toes in their shoes—and sometimes without shoes—and otherwise make it obvious they are experiencing an ecstatic sensation beyond description. Furthermore, they feel what is apparently a deep moral obligation that approaches religious fervor to rise up on their hind legs and defend inquiries against all attackers—and attackers *do* exist.

Then, on the other hand, there's the opposite camp (the word "camp" is used here not as a measurement of in-ness or out-ness)—those who strongly espouse the opposing philosophy.

They are equally outspoken, of course, and never hesitate to blurt out to one and all that inquiries are nothing more than a major nuisance, that inquiries are actually of very little tangible value (if any, their tone of voice and curl of lip imply), and salesmen never follow up on them. So why bother?

As with most other questions, there is a certain amount of merit to both viewpoints.

And a fact of life that cannot be ignored, regardless of which group you gravitate toward, is that inquiries are like dandruff.

They are not going to just go away.

Despite personal feelings in the matter, irrespective of whether you are passionately fond of inquiries, detest the sight of the things, or are somewhere in the middle of that relatively small gray area where opinions shade off into a neutral tone that's neither black nor white, inquiries are going to be around for a long, long time. Longer than any of us, in fact.

Three perfectly logical explanations exist for the strong feelings about inquiries which pervade industrial advertising:

1. Ad men who cherish inquiries and watch them appear in increasing numbers are those who *know* what inquiries mean to them. They know how to produce inquiries, how to handle them, and how to get the most out of them. These industrial advertising practitioners can predict within a fraction of a percentage point just what incoming inquiries mean to their companies in terms of sales volume.

2. Advertising men who denigrate inquiries simply do not understand them. They do not realize that inquiries enable them to search out a market, determine the specific segments of a market wherein their product has the greatest potential, and, finally, determine the buying influences within that small part of the total market who are willing and eager to buy their products. Furthermore, these advertising men who customarily downgrade inquiries lack basic knowledge in handling them—and this includes establishment of a basic system, screening, tabulating, followup, and other facets of the function.

3. Those with no strong feelings on the subject tend to view inquiries as routine paperwork that gives them something to do—some paper to shuffle. These are the ineffectuals within the advertising community; for the most part they hold down a desk in backward companies that are not marketing oriented and hence place little importance on the advertising function because *it* is not understood. For this third type of advertising manager inquiries are about the only concrete, tangible thing he can produce in the way of hard data to justify either his existence or that of advertising. As a consequence, he is more pro than con, although this is a sad justification for inquiries, his job, or for advertising itself.

However, when all is said and done, inquiries do present conclusive evidence that somebody out there read your advertisement. This is something positive in itself. And even more important, the ad motivated the reader to respond, to take the action you wanted him to take. He contacted your company as your ad urged him to do.

50 Million Inquiries Can't Be Wrong

Each year, *Industrial Marketing* reports, industrial advertisers generate more than 50,000,000 (that's 50 *million*) inquiries via the business press. *IM* said the figure was established by the prestigious Center For Marketing Communications. The Center is the highly competent research arm of industrial advertisers.

A bit more about the Center For Marketing Communications: Industrial advertisers who believe in advertising (they're the *leading* advertisers and the *leading* companies in their industries, for the most part) find they can increase advertising's effectiveness by using research done by CFMC. In one recent year, for example, the Center (formerly Marketing Communications Research Center) scheduled eight major studies:

1. Optimum distribution of the marketing dollar.
2. Characteristics of effective industrial catalogs.
3. How to develop marketing information on limited budgets.
4. Better use of publication reader service information.
5. Measuring effectiveness of industrial direct mail.
6. Merchandising advertising.
7. Standard functional classifications for industry.
8. Role of communications in introduction of new products.

The Center, organized in 1952, performs basic marketing research cooperatively for subscriber members; at the present time there are approximately 200 such members, around 100 industrial advertisers and the rest agencies, publishers, consultants, and associations.

CFMC's address:

Center For Marketing Communications
575 Ewing Street
Princeton, New Jersey 08540

Research made prior to writing this chapter put the author in touch with agencies and advertisers in Chicago, New York, Phila-

Typical Reader Action Audit of inquiries generated.

delphia, Los Angeles, and elsewhere, as well as with major business publishers throughout the country. The figure that recurred time and time again in correspondence and over the telephone is 70 million—sometimes as high as 75 million. It's a figure that is virtually impossible to establish with any assurance of being absolutely right, of course, or of being within plus or minus 10 percent.

One magazine alone, *Product Design & Development,* produced 912,373 inquiries in 1973 with its 12 regular monthly issues; in addition, the *PD&D Product Encyclopedia,* an annual, produced more than 100,000 inquiries that were processed in 1974—and inquiries from the *Encyclopedia* continue to come in for two or three years after it's published.

Shown nearby is a miniature marked copy of *Product Design & Development* showing a typical spread with the number of inquiries generated by both editorial matter and advertisements. This is called a Reader Action Audit.

The new-product tabloid, published by Chilton Company, is strictly a new-product publication; it has a controlled circulation of 108,400 and is sent primarily to executives and engineers responsible for the design and modification of durable goods in 20 SIC groups.

Where Inquiries Come From

A massive survey was recently performed by *Product Design & Development.* In the tabulation of results are listed 250 industrial companies in various industries throughout the United States, complete with the number of inquiries each company receives from all sources. Given is the source of inquiries for each firm, as well as a number of other facts relating to inquiries. This study is, perhaps, the most definitive of its type made to date.

According to *PD&D,* the source of inquiries of these 250 companies, in percentages, breaks down as follows:

Advertising	43.5%
Editorial mentions (publicity)	21.1
Normal operations	19.3
Direct mail	12.6
Other	3.5

Percentages will vary, of course, depending upon the companies surveyed; factors that affect the percentages would include company size, pattern of distribution, size of sales staff, communications objectives, and many others—in addition to a vast difference in products.

The percentage of inquiries also varies tremendously according to the type of advertisements that are run. Ads designed deliberately to pull inquiries usually succeed in producing them in quantity if they're created by knowledgeable advertising men.

For example, you can run a coupon in your ad and increase the amount of response by 300 percent. The coupon waves a flag in the reader's face and practically shouts the fact that the advertiser wants him to respond, that the advertiser will do something for him, if he does—send literature, send a salesman, analyze the reader's plant's requirements for a certain widget, or whatever is offered in the ad.

ITT Semiconductors, Division of International Telephone & Telegraph Corporation, recently ran a three-color ad in *Electronics* magazine that is a real reader stopper. It is illustrated nearby.

Red and blue reproduce the familiar air mail symbol in three languages and immediately impress upon the reader the fact that this is no ordinary advertisement. ITT Semiconductors is obviously talking about an urgent matter.

Copy is anything but heavy-handed, and is certainly straight to the point. It shows an excellent knowledge of problems electronics manufacturers encounter, and an equally fine knowledge of human nature and how people react. Copy is printed in black.

"AIR MAIL" is overlined in red and underlined in blue to carry out the theme and to induce the reader to respond right now, without wasting another minute—even before he finishes reading the article in which he may have been engaged.

ITT Semiconductors used good judgment in having the coupon large enough to write upon; although all coupons inform the reader a response is wanted, he is irked by little coupons on which he cannot write a short name such as Vincent J. Gruzczyznski, and a short title like Assistant Chief Engineer, Electronic Components—and still have room to get his firm, city, address, state and Zip Code in. Make it easy for a prospect to inquire and your inquiry rate will go up.

This advertisement doesn't make a plea for inquiries just for the sake of receiving inquiries, you'll note. It tells the reader he's to attach blueprints so that ITT Semiconductors can demonstrate to him how its products qualify for a place in *his* products. This makes it very obvious this ad is not directed at the literature collectors and the idly curious, but to bona fide prospective customers.

A. W. Cameron, ITT Semiconductors' advertising manager, re-

AIR MAIL PAR AVION CORREO AERO AIR MAIL

Dear ITT: I'm tired of

☐ slipped deliveries

☐ incoming QC rejections

☐ out-of-line prices...

...from my present small signal transistor suppliers. To qualify your PNP/NPN high speed switches, NPN core drivers and general purpose amplifiers per the enclosed prints, rush test data and samples by return AIR MAIL

Please qualify your devices per the attached prints.

NAME

COMPANY

ADDRESS

CITY STATE ZIP

AIR MAIL PAR AVION CORREO AERO AIR MAIL

semiconductors ITT

ITT SEMICONDUCTORS IS A DIVISION OF INTERNATIONAL TELEPHONE AND TELEGRAPH CORPORATION, 3301 ELECTRONICS WAY, WEST PALM BEACH, FLORIDA 33407

FACTORIES IN FLORIDA • CALIFORNIA • MASSACHUSETTS • ENGLAND • FRANCE • GERMANY • PORTUGAL • AUSTRALIA

ported receiving 203 inquiries from the specific issue of *Electronics* from which this ad was clipped. For competitive reasons the conversion rate is not available, but from the slant of the ad and the proposition offered to the reader, chances are more than good that a sizable percentage of those 203 inquirers became new customers of ITT Semiconductors.

This is an excellent example of using advertising and the inquiries it generates to flush out new prospects.

Just the opposite of ITT's fine advertisement, which was designed solely to produce inquiries, is Microdot's long-copy ad from its great "Connector Thing" campaign. Shown is another of these great ads that consistently pull inquiries by the hundred—even by the thousand—month after month after month. Readership of these ads is fantastically high and response, in terms of inquiries, is an ad manager's dream, according to Leon Levitt, manager of advertising and public relations at Microdot.

And the zany replies from nonzany buying influences flooded Microdot with quality inquiries that meant sales. No coupon, a kooky kind of offer, a light touch that entertains as it informs—that's Microdot's formula. It works for Microdot, but it certainly is not for everybody. There's a time and a place for the light touch, just as there's a time and a place for the straightforward, no-nonsense appeal for reader action. Both work.

Companies with an annual sales volume under $1 million and those with sales over $20 million tend to generate a higher percentage of inquiries from space advertising than do companies between these two sales ranges. But when the annual sales climb up around the $100 million volume, many industrial companies put more money and more effort into publicity as a percentage of the total promotional budget than do their smaller competitors.

Top company on the inquiry tally in *Product Design & Development's* study was Aluminum Company of America with an average of 12,000 inquiries per month. Second highest was Indiana General Corporation, manufacturer of magnets and magnetic equipment, with 3,500 inquiries coming in every 30 days.

Low in the survey was Rotary Seal Division, Muskegon Piston Ring Company, maker of mechanical face-type seals for rotating shafts, which receives 35 inquiries per month.

Most industrial companies surveyed by the magazine receive between 250 and 300 inquiries per month as a result of *all* activities, including normal operations.

Of the companies in *PD&D's* study, 9.3 percent received from 0 to 50 inquiries a month, and 2.8 percent tallied up an inflow of more than 2,000 per month. The other 87.9 percent of the companies are somewhere in between these two extremes.

THE connector THING

A periodical periodical designed to further the sales of Microdot Inc. connectors and cables. Published entirely in the interest of profit.

Everybody wins! Play Microdots Historical Spaghetti Grams

In the words of Virginia Woolf, it's time for fun and games.

For this new national pastime, you simply need a smattering of history, mythology and current events. And some information about Microdot's cable products. We'll supply you with the latter. For the rest, go listen to Walter Cronkite.

We got started on this activity while we were sitting around one evening with a bottle of Slivovitz (we ran out of Scotch), trying to think of memorable ways to remind you of the various unique features of Microdot cables. Like—

Like our Mini-Noise cable—reduces noise voltage from shock and vibration by a factor of more than 100 to 1 compared to untreated cable. This makes possible the transmission of extremely faint signals through coax cable without audio frequency noise. Off-the-shelf.

Like our microminiature coax cable—uses a fine silver-plated copper steel-covered wire. You get 50 ohm impedance, and even with the addition of dielectric, outer shield and protective jacket, the nominal O.D. does not exceed .080". And we can get that O.D. down to .025" in a range of hundreds of different cables.

Like our new complete in-house capability to produce precision quality multiconductor cables, which includes twisting, extruding, shielding and jacketing—the whole deal. All under one roof. And we can cable hundreds of conductors into one unit.

Like we're the only one to produce a high temperature, low weight, low capacitance coax cable through the use of a *cellular Teflon* dielectric. Especially suited to the requirements of video tape recorders.

Like Microdot's Twinaxial cable—to be used when you need to send two signals from a single source which must both terminate at the same point. No need to use two coax cables; therefore lower cost and greater flexibility.

Now when you think of cables, you think of cablegrams. And when you drink a lot of Slivovitz, it sort of takes you back through time and you come up with stuff like this:

Low noise Spaghetti-Gram:
"You lose. Signed, Calvin Coolidge."

High temperature Spaghetti-Gram:
"Julius, honey, ain't nobody home tonight but me. Signed, Cleopatra."

Miniature size Spaghetti-Gram:
"Cancel that order for bras. Signed, Twiggy."

Dual shield Spaghetti-Gram:
"I can lick any guy in the joint. Signed, Brunhilde."

Large size multiconductor Spaghetti-Gram:
"Send more elephants. Signed, Hannibal."

Get the idea. You can use any of the features of any of our cable products, such as low noise (Mini-Noise), special requirements (Multiconductors), high temperature, low weight, and, of course, small size. You don't really need the Slivovitz. It works well even with Sanka.

About the fork

No, Melvin, we won't explain the relationship between cable and spaghetti. We call it a cable fork, and if you don't want to use it for eating cables that's your problem. The manufacturer describes this handy gadget as a "revolutionary breakthrough that leaps forward from antiquated hand labor to the modern machine age!" We won't try to top that. We'll just explain that you stick it into the pasta and then turn the little handle to save getting spaghetti all over your celluloid collar.

Want one for your very own? Okay. Just send us a Microdot Spaghetti-Gram scribbled on company stationery and taking off from any of the product features we've discussed. We'll send you a beautiful cable fork along with more literature on our cable products than we care to mention.

But hurry. We've already run out of Slivovitz. It won't be long before we run out of cable forks. (That means offer is limited.)

WIN YOUR OWN CABLE FORK

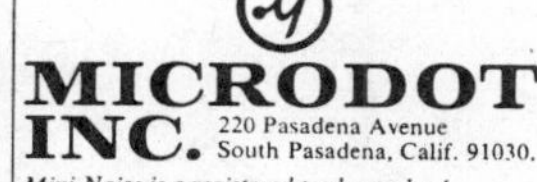

MICRODOT INC.
220 Pasadena Avenue
South Pasadena, Calif. 91030.

Mini-Noise is a registered trade-mark of Microdot Inc. Cable Fork is open to question.

Incidentally, in *PD&D's* survey "other" includes miscellaneous promotional activities such as press conferences, trade shows, 100th anniversary celebrations, and similar cats and dogs.

The overwhelming percentage of incoming inquiries received in the typical industrial advertising department come in as a result of readers' having returned a "bingo card"—otherwise known as a Reader Service Card, Reader Inquiry Card, Business Reply Card, or some other such name. Almost all business publications include one of these postage-paid cards with numbers keyed to advertisements, editorial matter, or publicity.

Shown are bingo cards from *Research/Development, Iron Age, Production,* and *Product Design & Development.* All have certain features in common; numbers referring back to products about

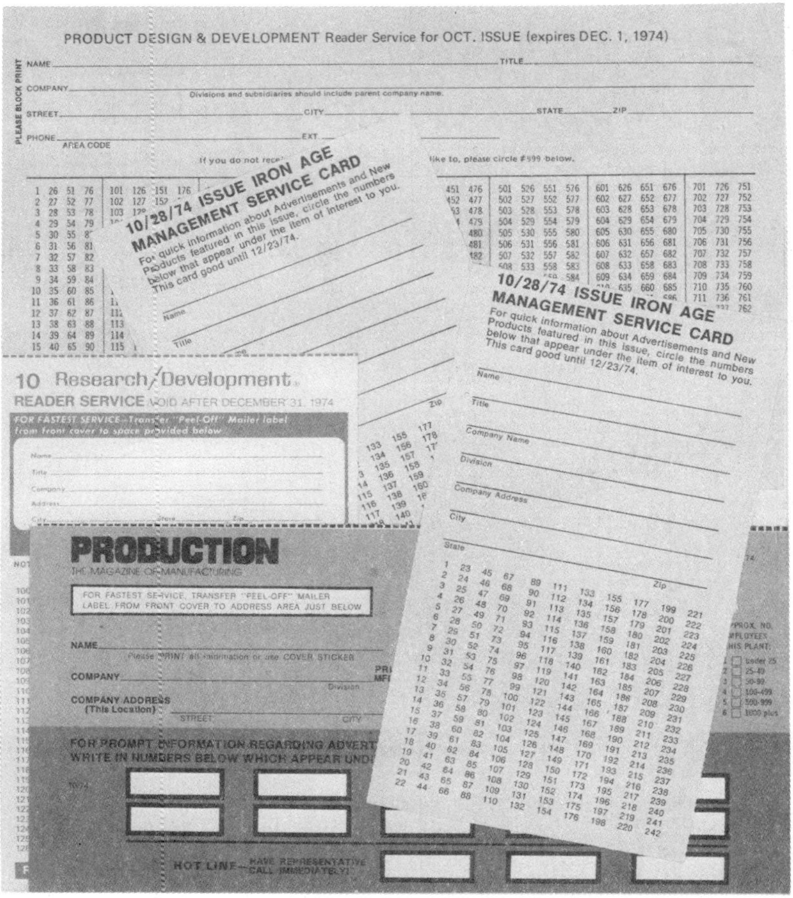

PRODUCT DESIGN & DEVELOPMENT Reader Service for OCT. ISSUE (expires DEC. 1, 1974)
PLEASE BLOCK PRINT
NAME ____ TITLE ____
COMPANY ____
Divisions and subsidiaries should include parent company name.
STREET ____ CITY ____ STATE ____ ZIP ____
PHONE ____ AREA CODE EXT ____
If you do not rece[illegible] like to, please circle #999 below.

1	26	51	76	101	126	151	176	451	476	501	526	551	576	601	626	651	676	701	726	751				
2	27	52	77	102	127	152		452	477	502	527	552	577	602	627	652	677	702	727	752				
3	28	53	78	103					478	503	528	553	578	603	628	653	678	703	728	753				
4	29	54	79						479	504	529	554	579	604	629	654	679	704	729	754				
5	30	55							480	505	530	555	580	605	630	655	680	705	730	755				
6	31	56	81						481	506	531	556	581	606	631	656	681	706	731	756				
7	32	57	82						482	507	532	557	582	607	632	657	682	707	732	757				
8	33	58	83								533	558	583	608	633	658	683	708	733	758				
9	34	59	84										584	609	634	659	684	709	734	759				
10	35	60	85												635	660	685	710	735	760				
11	36	61	86															711	736	761				
12	37	62	87																	762				
13	38	63	88	113																				
14	39	64	89	114																				
15	40	65	90	115																				

10/28/74 ISSUE IRON AGE
MANAGEMENT SERVICE CARD
For quick information about Advertisements and New Products featured in this issue, circle the numbers below that appear under the item of interest to you. This card good until 12/23/74.
Name
Title

10 Research/Development
READER SERVICE VOID AFTER DECEMBER 31, 1974
FOR FASTEST SERVICE—Transfer "Peel-Off" Mailer label from front cover to space provided below
Name
Title
Company
Address
City State Zip

PRODUCTION
THE MAGAZINE OF MANUFACTURING
FOR FASTEST SERVICE, TRANSFER "PEEL-OFF" MAILER LABEL FROM FRONT COVER TO ADDRESS AREA JUST BELOW
NAME ____
Please PRINT all information or use COVER STICKER
COMPANY ____ Division
COMPANY ADDRESS (This Location) ____ STREET CITY
FOR PROMPT INFORMATION REGARDING ADVERT[ISEMENTS] WRITE IN NUMBERS BELOW WHICH APPEAR UND[ER]
HOT LINE—HAVE REPRESENTATIVE CALL IMMEDIATELY!
APPROX. NO. EMPLOYEES THIS PLANT:
1 under 25
2 25-49
3 50-99
4 100-499
5 500-999
6 1000 plus

10/28/74 ISSUE IRON AGE
MANAGEMENT SERVICE CARD
For quick information about Advertisements and New Products featured in this issue, circle the numbers below that appear under the item of interest to you. This card good until 12/23/74.
Name
Title
Company Name
Division
Company Address
City
State Zip

1	23	45	67	89	111	133	155	177	199	221
2	24	46	68	90	112	134	156	178	200	222
3	25	47	69	91	113	135	157	179	201	223
4	26	48	70	92	114	136	158	180	202	224
5	27	49	71	93	115	137	159	181	203	225
6	28	50	72	94	116	138	160	182	204	226
7	29	51	73	95	117	139	161	183	205	227
8	30	52	74	96	118	140	162	184	206	228
9	31	53	75	97	119	141	163	185	207	229
10	32	54	76	98	120	142	164	186	208	230
11	33	55	77	99	121	143	165	187	209	231
12	34	56	78	100	122	144	166	188	210	232
13	35	57	79	101	123	145	167	189	211	233
14	36	58	80	102	124	146	168	190	212	234
15	37	59	81	103	125	147	169	191	213	235
16	38	60	82	104	126	148	170	192	214	236
17	39	61	83	105	127	149	171	193	215	237
18	40	62	84	106	128	150	172	194	216	238
19	41	63	85	107	129	151	173	195	217	239
20	42	64	86	108	130	152	174	196	218	240
21	43	65	87	109	131	153	175	197	219	241
22	44	66	88	110	132	154	176	198	220	242

which the reader has read, blanks to solicit information about inquirers, an offer to send a qualification form to the inquirer so he can receive the magazine—if he qualifies under the requirements of the magazine's circulation policy—and so on.

By checking numbers on his incoming inquiries from the publications the advertiser can easily determine whether the inquiry is the result of the reader's responding to his space advertisement, or to editorial matter or publicity.

For the most part, industrial advertisers receive more than 90 percent of all of their inquiries on bingo cards—the ones that come through business publications, that is. Business publications do generate letterhead inquiries and telephone inquiries with both space advertising and editorial—and publicity, too, for that matter—to make up the balance.

On the surface all such inquiries might seem to be of the same approximate quality, although publications go to some lengths to enable an advertiser to determine to some extent how hot inquiries are—and to give the ad manager some means of measuring how valuable they are to him.

For example, *Product Design & Development* asks for the telephone number and extension number of the inquirer on its bingo card. Now, it certainly stands to reason that if a man is merely a literature collector, or is idly curious about a product he's read about in PD&D, he probably will omit his telephone number because he's smart enough to know that giving it will encourage a salesman to contact him.

Yet, more than 80 percent of all inquirers who return bingo cards to *Product Design & Development do* give phone numbers and extensions. These busy men are also serious men.

Few industrial advertising managers deprecate bingo cards. The cards are truly ubiquitous today, and are used by almost every business publication of merit. Those not willing to make the investment in handling the returned cards and those unwilling to pay the nominal price to index advertisements and key them for bingo card response don't use the cards. Such publications are almost always marginal and don't belong on your schedule anyway.

Another practice held in low esteem throughout the advertising community is that of printing page after page after page of "summaries" or brief product descriptions—even brief descriptions of *advertisements*—and calling this "editorial." Some publications do this and even have blanks inquirers may fill in with their names, firms, and so on; when these are mailed to the publications they are handled much like the conventional bingo cards.

Presenting the casual reader with page after page of such enticements to respond usually succeeds only in triggering response from pass-on readers and others too far down the pecking order to be classified as legitimate buying influences.

Good "Books" Do Generate Quality Inquiries

Nobody wants inquiries to result in sales any more than the publisher of quality business magazines. Many of them go to great lengths to help raise the level of inquiries, both in quality and in quantity. Frequently this involves considerable research and extra effort that is costly, but reputable publications are more than willing to make the effort.

For instance, *Research/Development* magazine makes a determined and highly successful effort to help both the reader and the advertiser. From the time of its first issue some 18 years ago, *Research/Development* used reader service key numbers at the bottom of display advertisements, as do most other magazines. *Research/Development* used them also at the conclusion of editorial material as an additional service to the reader who wanted to dig a bit deeper into the technological details of the subject that had been discussed.

This new concept was carried on very successfully for several years. Then *R/D's* editors developed a new twist and began handling offers of additional information in a way that was unique and unprecedented.

Instead of carrying a bold-faced number at the foot of the item, or at the bottom of the last column of an article, the editors began "burying" key numbers in feature articles, News Notes, Progress Reports—and in just about any department of the magazine.

The Buried Key (copyrighted method of editorial research) was set in the same roman type as the rest of the editorial. Thus it could be acted upon *only* by those who read the article and found the key. The first such Buried Key appeared in the October, 1959, issue and produced 295 requests for more information.

"Frankly," said the editors of *Research/Development*, "we didn't realize the scope and power of our own innovation—this specialized use of an inquiry system. Initially, we had only meant to facilitate the dissemination of information to our readers—certainly an activity consistent with editorial objectives.

"It took only a few issues for us to realize the tremendous value of the Buried Key mechanism.

"Here we had not only a new reader service, but an invaluable tool for the editor. A built-in reader interest study! A way to determine reader interest without any chance of bias, without any of the inherent disadvantages of the questionnaire techniques."

The real eye-opener was the variation of reader interest, the high degree of *selectivity* of reader response. During 1965, for example, 39 different Buried Keys produced an average of 297 inquiries per key. But in this group the low was 9, the high was 999—900 apart!

Analysis of reader response to Buried Keys not only gives the editors of *Research/Development* a good measure of readership, but it provides a feedback on reader interest by subject. It also defines the degree of interest at various functional levels within the R&D community; by scientist or engineer, by group or project leaders, by second echelon administrators, by the executive-level professional man.

Readers of *Research/Development* thus told its editors, by the selectivity of their response, just what they were looking for in a magazine. In fact, they told them what kind of subject matter they did or didn't want, what they didn't get anywhere else.

This dialog has enabled the editors to tailor *R/D* magazine's editorial content directly to the demonstrated interests and needs of its audience. Departments and special sections have been added or discontinued, and feature subjects selected, on the basis of the editorial staff's continuing, long-term analysis of reader response to Buried Keys.

Buried Keys are an exceptionally valuable tool for advertisers, too. When a key is buried in a News Note about a new process, for example, the response generated is an excellent indication of the interest the scientific community has in it. This can help a manufacturer plan on whether or not to develop a product, it can augment the manufacturer's own market research, it makes planning easier for advertising people.

And if a Buried Key appears in a description of a new piece of literature offered by a manufacturer, or in a new product announcement, the Buried Key is an effective cross-check on bingo card response. It is one more bit of intelligence to make it easier for an advertiser to trace down the source of interest in his product—by industry, and by buying influence.

A vast difference exists in the number of inquiries certain classes of products generate, of course. Capital equipment will, if other things are relatively equal, pull fewer inquiries than will component parts for OEM use. Unless it's new equipment and unless it's truly revolutionary—something like numerical control for machine tools when introduced several years ago—capital equipment won't pull as many inquiries for the simple reason fewer pieces of it are sold. And there are relatively fewer buying influences to respond to the ad.

Letterhead inquiries tend to increase in percentage as the volume of inquiries rises. For example, say a certain ad for a product produces 100 inquiries a month on the average. That ad will probably generate three or four letterhead inquiries each month, certainly not more unless it's an unusually strong ad, the selling proposition is outstanding, or the product is nothing less than sensational, fantastic, revolutionary, unbelievable, and terrific. Not too many products are all those.

But if an advertising campaign consistently generates, say, 500 inquiries a month, the volume of letterhead inquiries should be more than five times as high as that produced by a campaign that resulted in only 100 monthly inquiries. The percentage in the 500-per-month program might run from 5 up to 10 percent, or even more.

Letterhead inquiries are generally conceded to represent a greater sales potential and a higher caliber of inquirer because a letter requires more effort than does circling a number and tearing a card out of a magazine—if for no other reason.

Telephone Inquiries Grow

A third way that inquiries come in—and it's one that is growing faster than Topsy ever dreamed of—is the telephone. More and more advertisers are urging the reader to pick up the phone and call them in the advertisement's bid for action. This means of getting inquiries is proving productive beyond the wildest dreams of most industrial advertising managers. This is due, in part, to management's having stopped the old-fashioned "rationing" of long distance telephone calls. Long distance used to be an esoteric means of communicating, something that was used as a last resort and always with a weather eye on the three-minute egg timer. Not so now that business operates at a faster pace and the emphasis is on productivity —of people as well as machines.

Telephone inquiries are usually not from the curious with nothing else to do at the moment, nor are they from minor draftsmen, literature collectors, or mail boys.

When Lindberg Hevi-Duty started listing telephone numbers and the names of the company's product people in its advertisements a couple of years ago, the response was little short of amazing. Since doing this, hundreds of thousands of dollars in sales have resulted from advertisements that asked the reader to phone—because readers responded just that way. They called, gave the listener their problem, and usually had a salesman on the way to their office to discuss the matter further within hours. This method of generating inquiries works, and it delivers high quality sales leads.

One thing that should be done when a telephone inquiry comes in is to make sure—always make sure—to find out where the caller saw the product advertised. Get the name of the publication. This information is vitally important when it comes time to evaluate media and determine the effectiveness of the advertising program as a whole. Most of your product managers and marketing people will keep a simple tally for you if you explain why it is so necessary. Giving them a simple mimeographed form to use helps get the information for you.

Another way of keeping a record is to list a fictitious name, or one that's semifictitious. You can, for instance, make sure that product manager Steve Salisbury gets all incoming inquiries for a new automatic widget he's responsible for. His correct name, Steve Salisbury, can be listed in Magazine A; however, in Magazine B he could be John Salisbury; in Magazine C, Ralph Salisbury, and so on. This always works out very well because all Mr. Salisbury has to do is just what comes naturally for most of us—when answering the phone, say "Salisbury," or "Salisbury speaking."

This shows the inquirer he's talking with the right man, the one the advertisement asked him to call. This puts the burden on Mr. Salisbury only to keep a tally of all the Steves, Johns, Ralphs, Georges and what have you; there's no need for him to cross-reference to a magazine. That job can be done in the advertising department when he reports monthly that Steve Salisbury received 17 phone calls, George got 9, Ralph had 23, and so on. The system is simple to put into effect and easy to keep going. You have only to supply the company's Steve Salisbury's with each of their "names" and a simple form.

The switchboard has to be instructed to ask for him by name, however, or to keep a tally herself. This is done in most companies by asking the caller, "Which Mr. Salisbury did you want, sir?" The inquirer assumes several brothers or several people work for the company with the same surname—a frequent occurrence.

Ways to Increase Inquiry Volume

The following subjects have been touched upon briefly elsewhere, or will be, but it's desirable to summarize them very briefly so these factors that exert such an influence on the volume of inquiries will be at your fingertips.

Four-color ads achieve something better than a 50 percent increase in readership and they consistently produce at least 50 percent more inquiries than do black-and-white.

Make an offer to the reader, use the word "free"—and bump it up in size so it's really prominent—and your ad will produce approximately four times as many inquiries as it would have without the offer and use of the magic word. Naturally, you can't offer free milling machines and stay in business very long, but you *can* offer a free piece of literature on milling machines, or an analysis of how your new machine could up production and cut costs on the reader's production floor.

Use a coupon in your ad, and preferably more than a little token coupon so there's room for the reader to write, and you'll increase your inquiry volume by more than 300 percent.

Increase the size of your advertisements and the amount of inquiries goes up to direct proportion, although not in the same proportion. A one-page ad, for instance, will not produce twice as many inquiries as a one-half-page ad, nor will a spread produce twice as many inquiries as a one-page ad. Rather, when you double the size you can reasonably anticipate receiving about two-thirds more inquiries than the smaller ad has been pulling.

Try to get your advertisement in the front one-third of the publication and you'll have a slight edge and garner a few additional inquiries because of higher readership in the front of the book—although not nearly as much so now as a few years ago.

Run nothing except outstanding advertisements that rate near, or at, the top of the heap in the readership ratings, and that ad will produce more inquiries by far than an advertisement that wasn't as well read.

The trick, of course, is knowing how to produce a winner every time!

Issue Life and Inquiry Life

Daniel Starch has reported in *Media/scope* that roughly half of all inquiries produced by a monthly magazine that was studied were received during the first month after it was distributed, and that approximately the same percentage of inquiries was received from a weekly magazine during the first week of issue.

In McGraw-Hill's Laboratory of Advertising Performance, the Columbia Ribbon and Carbon Manufacturing Company, Inc., reports running a campaign consisting of 14 one-third and two-thirds page advertisements in one calendar year in *Business Week* magazine.

Inquiries came in for an average of 7.6 months after the issue of *Business Week* was mailed to subscribers. All advertisements were couponed and key addressed so the company was able to make a thorough study of each ad and each publication in which it appeared.

Longest life of an issue was 19 months; inquiries were received that long after the magazine was mailed; shortest life span was one and two-thirds months.

Interestingly, a further check on Columbia Ribbon and Carbon's inquiries showed that 69.7 percent were received from top management or purchasing titles. According to the manufacturer, almost half of the sales leads (48.4 percent) were classified as "excellent, good, or fair" in quality.

In the case of annual publications such as *Product Design & Development's Product Encyclopedia, Vacuum Technology Buyer's Guide, Thomas' Register, MacRae's Blue Book,* the Conover-Mast *Purchasing Directory,* and so on, inquiries come in over the transom for *years* after publication. Technical publications of this type are usually filed in the department that uses them, and/or in the purchasing department. Issue life is simply fantastic. Everybody has favorite stories of inquiries from old, old directories.

Tally Incoming Inquiries

The first thing to do when inquiries come to your company from business publications is to make certain the mail room realizes their importance and doesn't delay delivery to the advertising department.

Inform the head mail room man that inquiries are *not* third class mail, that they are *not* to be delivered when the mail boy doesn't have anything else to do, that is if your company customarily divides mail deliveries by class of mail—or by appearance, in some instances.

Then, when the inquiries are received in the advertising department, they should be tallied up immediately. You'll probably find it easiest and most convenient to keep a record of all incoming inquiries by publication; naturally, a master record kept by your secretary will reflect the source of inquiries. You may, however, want to keep a record yourself that contains other information—information to which you refer frequently.

A form that has worked well for clients of O'Grady-Anderson-Gray, Inc., advertising agency in Park Ridge, Illinois, was given to the author by old friend Bill Cason, president of the agency. It's simple enough that it can be produced in the company printing de-

MAGAZINE INQUIRY REPORT

PUBLICATION	PRODUCT	TOTAL INQUIRIES	RUNNING TOTAL

partment, or on the office multilith machine. Have it set up so spaces are correct for the typewriter in case you decide to have your secretary handle it, and also so there is adequate room to contain figures that don't necessitate use of a microscope to decipher.

You'll undoubtedly want to keep a record of product model number and so on that drew the inquiries, although the ad number and key number from the publication would provide that information with cross referencing.

Depending upon your method of distribution, you likely will find it advisable to show on your running record the geographical area or sales territory which produced the inquiry, as well as the territory that is tops in inquiry activity, and to which dealers or distributors the inquiries were referred.

Some advertising managers find this information extremely helpful to have available at a glance when they're planning media schedules, particularly when reviewing regional publications.

A separate tally, similar to the one for your ad inquiries, should be kept for inquiries produced by publicity. Break this tally down by book, month, and key number, also, as well as by product and model.

Incidentally, *Product Design & Development's* study of 250 indus-

MAGAZINE ______ MONTH, YEAR ______ AD NO. ______

AD HEADLINE ______ AD KEY NO. ______ AD SIZE ______

LITERATURE SENT ______ PRODUCT ______

DATE	1	2	3	4	5	6	7	8	9	10	11	12	13	14	15	16	17	18	19	20	21	22	23	24	25	26	27	28	29	30	31	TOTAL	RUNNING TOTAL
JAN.																																	
FEB.																																	
MAR.																																	
APR.																																	
MAY																																	
JUNE																																	
JULY																																	
AUG.																																	
SEPT.																																	
OCT.																																	
NOV.																																	
DEC.																																	

DEALER FEEDBACK	JAN.	FEB.	MAR.	APR.	MAY	JUNE	JULY	AUG.	SEPT.	OCT.	NOV.	DEC.	TOTAL	RUNNING TOTAL
SALES														
DEMONSTRATIONS														
FUTURE PROSPECT														
NIXIES														

Form for yearly tally of ad inquiries by months.

trial advertisers shows these firms keep a record of inquiries by source for the following reasons:

Media evaluation	74.6%
Advertising response	27.2%
Cost analysis	26.2%
Product interest	16.2%
Salesman followup	3.5%

This totals more than 100 percent because many companies give more than one reason for breaking out inquiry sources.

Ideally, when tallying inquiries, the SIC of the inquirer's company should be entered on the tally form in a column provided for this purpose. This is a tremendous help when determining where new, untapped markets exist and identifying markets that offer the most potential. Too many industrial advertising managers neglect to do this. It is one of the most important breakdowns they can supply to management.

About as often as not letterhead inquiries mention the magazine in which the inquirer saw your advertisement. When he does there's no problem in keeping the tally accurately. Roughly half of the time, however, the inquirer will merely say he's seen your widget advertised, would like more information on it, and to please send him a piece of literature posthaste.

Such an inquiry is potentially just as valuable as if he had mentioned the name of the book a dozen times—and you'll want to handle it just as quickly. Simply maintain a record of unidentified inquiries, so headed, and you'll find this presents no problem.

Efficient publishers clip either a tear sheet of the ad, publicity article, or what have you, directly to the inquiries. It's good policy, it makes a favorable impression for the book (which the publisher is trying to sell) and it helps you.

Maintain Your Own Cross Index

In addition, you should have a department clerk go through each publication when the advertising department copy arrives; the clerk should cross-index every reference to your company—in advertisments, editorial, publicity. It's also a good policy to do this for major competitors also, then, when the vice-president of marketing calls you unexpectedly and asks you if you know anything about such and such in some magazine or other, you can pat yourself on the back—you know all about it. And without a lengthy search, either. That really gives the impression of a well-organized department.

You'll want to key all of your advertisements so the name of the magazine, month of publication, and the ad number can be determined by checking the key number that appears on bingo card returns.

And there's the old dodge of using a variation of the firm's street address. Suppose, for instance your company is located at 4401 West Industrial Street. By varying the address—4400, 4402, 4430, 4440, 4460, and so on and on,—it's very easy to determine the publication involved, the subject of a news release, the product discussed in an advertisement, a specific trade show, or even the company from which a questionnaire is being returned. Your local post office will cooperate and have all mail routed directly to your company despite any minor differences in the address; a couple of theater tickets a couple of times a year, or some similar small but welcome gift, will help.

Data you compile about inquiries concerns not only the advertising department, but is an invaluable source of marketing information for the sales department, production, marketing, and others, including top management. It reflects very accurately the amount of interest that exists in various products or product lines; this enables management either to put a push behind products that have either slipped, or haven't caught on, or to make a reasoned, well-informed judgment as to the advisability of withdrawing them from the market.

One last thing on which a record should be kept, and most industrial advertising managers need no urging about this, is known conversions to sales. A compilation of all of the sales traced directly to inquiries, complete with dollar amounts, sales territories, names of district managers, and similar helpful information will make a hero of you when you submit the memo to management. This should be done on a fixed schedule. It shows that all of that money spent on advertising is not wasted, and it shows good management of the advertising department. And it shows that sales are the most important thing to you, just as they are to the sales department.

Handling Inquiries

Handling of inquiries by industrial advertisers ranges from very simple systems to some that are almost incredibly complex.

There's usually a reason for the existence of a system, any system, or at least a rationale of why the system that's used is used; how it evolved from the one that formerly was used. This isn't double talk, for most industrial advertisers have found inquiry handling is a far more complicated subject than it appears to be on the surface, and methods of handling inquiries have undergone a radical metamorphosis.

Let's back up for a minute and see just what we're talking about. *Product Design & Development's* survey of inquiry-handling systems, the definitive one on the subject, lists the following percentages of companies as receiving this quantity of inquiries; quantities given are undoubtedly projectable across industry as a whole, with the possible exception of companies manufacturing capital equipment—and even they probably fall pretty much in line with these findings:

Question: What is the number of inquiries received each month from all sources:

Quantity	*Percent of companies receiving this quantity*
0 to 50	9.3%
51 to 100	15.3
101 to 250	21.4
251 to 500	28.4
501 to 1,000	16.3
1,000 to 2,000	6.5
Over 2,000	2.8

So more companies receive between 251 and 500 inquiries per month than any other quantity, although one company in six receives between 500 and 1,000. Handling this much paperwork poses a problem in itself.

But handled they must be, and the sooner the better. Never for an instant lose sight of the fact that when you receive an inquiry from a prospective customer via the bingo card route—or even a letterhead inquiry—*the chances are your competitors also received an inquiry from the same individual.*

That's right—your competitors also received that selfsame inquiry from that same person.

Too many industrial advertising managers fall into the self-oriented trap and regard inquiries as something uniquely *theirs,* that *their* advertisements and *their* publicity shook those prospects out of the bushes for the sole use of *their* company.

At the risk of sounding iconoclastic, there's comment that has to be made:

'Tisn't so.

More than 64 percent of inquirers who circle your number on a bingo card also circle one or more numbers belonging to your competitors. If not in the same magazine, then in one that competes with it. These inquirers ask your competitors about a product directly competitive with your beloved widget. Horrible, isn't it?

Don't let this dash cold water on your enthusiasm for your advertising program and for advertising *per se,* however. It's very likely that your ad *did* shake the prospects out of the bushes, that it *did* convince them your product would likely solve their problems, and that they honestly *are* interested in more information about it.

What your advertisement also did, though, was to wake up the prospect to the fact that other manufacturers produce competing widgets. And because industry usually does not leap to have purchasing agents write purchase orders without an information-gathering period, followed by one of evaluation of all available products, doesn't necessarily mean your advertisement hasn't accomplished anything except to alert your competitors to the fact that here's a bona fide, live prospect.

In all probability your ad triggered the response from the inquirer —and as a result your company has the inside track when a salesman gets down to brass tacks and asks for the order after his presentation or proposal.

Fine and dandy as this is, it shines a bright light on a situation many industrial advertisers ignore. This is that inquiries are woefully mishandled.

Inquiries *are* woefully mishandled.

But isn't this paradoxical, for isn't advertising created, produced, and placed in the best media to do just two things: (1) Inform prospective customers about your product, and (2) induce them to respond to the advertisement as you want them to?

Isn't it?

Yet industry as a whole fails miserably to take the first step to make contact with a prospective customer after he has taken that first step to contact the seller.

This failure, incredible as it is, can be laid right at the doorstep of either naivé marketing management or an inept advertising manager.

When I was advertising manager of a large truck manufacturer, an unexplained mystery was the fact that no inquiries came in. I found that all inquiries from advertising and publicity were routinely sent to the sales engineering department. The engineers didn't know what to do with the inquiries, so they threw them away. *They threw them away!* To the engineers' pleasure, I took inquiries henceforth —then sent literature and a salesman.

Time Is of the Essence

Promptness is vitally necessary because the inquirer's inquiry has already been in the pipeline for anywhere from a few days to several weeks; most progressive business publications forward all inquiries to advertisers once a month as a rule, although some forward several times a month if the volume warrants it.

You can assume the average length of time that elapses between the reader's filling out and mailing the bingo card and his receipt of literature about the product he's interested in is four weeks. Add to this any delay in the advertising department and you can see how even a hot prospect has plenty of time to cool down—or to be sold by a competitive salesman!

In its survey *Product Design & Development* also asked the average time between receiving and handling inquiries. Results are:

Average time	*Pecentage of companies*
1 day	9.0%
2 to 4 days	32.1
5 to 7 days	39.5
8 to 14 days	16.5
Over 14 days	2.9

Despite the majority of companies' handling inquiries in five to seven days, this is very casual treatment indeed of a potentially large volume of "extra" sales. Unless some kind of emergency exists within the advertising department—illness, an unusually heavy volume of work due to a major trade show, being in the throes of new-campaign planning—every incoming inquiry should be transformed into an outgoing reply, complete with literature, within 48 hours. And this doesn't mean 48 working hours in the office—it means two working days.

If the advertising department cannot handle what is bound to be a normal work load and get the inquiries handled in this length of time, it is under staffed and a request should go in immediately for an extra girl—or two—to bring personnel strength up to an adequate level. Ignore the problem and you'll always find yourself in a bind.

As a rule, if the inquiry level is less than 1,000 a month one clerk can easily handle this load. This would include all internal paperwork in connection with the inquiries except screening; this should be done by either the advertising manager or his assistant. The function is far too important to delegate to subordinate personnel.

Product Design & Development explored this facet of inquiry handling in its survey. Answers to the question, "How many people are required to handle your inquiry system?" showed the following:

People required	*Percentages*
Less than 1	5.6%
1 to 2	43.6
2 to 3	31.6
3 to 4	12.0
4 to 5	5.1
5 or more	2.1

Interesting thing here is that most companies say it takes from one to two people to handle their inquiries, and the biggest percentage of companies surveyed by *PD&D* receive between 251 and 500 inquiries per month. This shows either poor systems or lack of organization.

Incidentally, *Product Design & Development* also asked whether an outside firm was used to handle inquiries. It develops that 13.6 percent of the surveyed companies do use an outside firm, whereas 86.4 percent do the work internally. This reflects the fact that it's the consensus of most advertising men that handling inquiries is a function that belongs inside the company where it can be controlled better and supervised more closely.

Another way a high percentage of industrial firms misuse inquiries is to handle them well and reasonably promptly, then mail the reply by third-class mail. With the postal situation as deplorable as it now is—and with no improvement in sight—answering an inquiry by third-class mail is tantamount to presenting your competition with first crack at an eager group of prospects.

First-class mail and airmail are slow enough; but if the material you send in response to inquiries is sent either of these ways you're fairly sure it will be delivered anywhere in the country in five or six business days.

On the other hand, third-class mail can easily consume 10 days or two weeks once the material leaves your office. Post office policy seems to be to handle third-class mail when there's spare time, when the mood strikes the workers, or when enough mail users complain loudly.

Using first-class mail increases costs, but postage seldom accounts for more than 15 or 20 percent of the total cost of handling inquiries —if that much. Skimping on postage can easily result in loss of an incalculable sum in sales. It isn't worth it. Use first class or airmail.

Physical Method of Handling

Long gone are the days when a business man expected a reply written with a quill pen, or, for that matter, even an individually-typed reply.

With the paperwork load getting heavier in the business community every year, almost everybody in industry is accustomed to forms of one type or another. We've all been taught to cringe in mortal terror at the mere thought of stapling or mutilating an IBM card that accompanies business invoices—and even monthly bills received at home. Labor- and time-saving forms are an integral part of everyday life and are no longer regarded as slighting the person who receives one.

Advertising managers surveyed by *Product Design & Development* reflect this acceptance of the ubiquitous form. When they were asked, "What type of form is used in your inquiry handling system?" the following was disclosed:

Type of form used	*Percentage using it*
"Snap-out" form	31.7%
Personalized typed letter	26.1
Reply card or reply form	12.2
Printed form letter	11.7
Multicopy internal forms	9.1
No forms used	13.9

Amazing is the amount of personalized, typed letters; this requires a tremendous amount of time and the expense of typing a letter over and over again is unbelievable, what with clerical salaries higher today than secretarial salaries were a few short years ago.

Also nothing short of astounding is that a total of 23 percent of these industrial companies used either multicopy internal forms, or no forms at all. When the internal forms are used, the inquirer receives nothing in the mail except a piece of literature—no thank you for your interest, no nothing. Can't help but make a poor impression. The inquirer feels the company isn't interested in him.

However, 9.1 percent of these firms at least bucked the information about the inquirer on to their sales force with a copy of the internal form. But the 13.9 percent of those advertisers who used no forms apparently mailed literature and then dropped the matter right there with a dull thud.

And 3.9 percent of the surveyed firms did not report sending names of inquirers to their salesmen for followup. This is indeed difficult to understand. The reasoning there is too elusive to surmise. One thing it *does* prove is the day of miracles is not past—companies not seeking any additional sales are doing business today. Must be pretty soft.

The "snap-out" form used by more firms than any other surveyed by *PD&D* has come into its own of recent years. Use of this handy little form greatly simplifies handling of inquiries and facilitates prompt mailing of material to the inquiring party.

A typical snap-out form is that used by Lindberg Hevi-Duty; it is illustrated on page 1188.

Let's take a look at this form since it is typical of those used by many companies throughout industry.

On the top sheet is the company logo and address on the left side, with a place for the inquirer's name, title, company, address, city, state and zip code. Left half of this top sheet is detached and becomes a mailing label for the envelope of literature; it is gummed on its reverse side. This saves the clerk much time and additional typing.

The right half of the top sheet is filled in with the name of the publication from which the inquiry was received; it is paper-clipped to the literature mailed to the inquirer. Note that on the bottom there is room for the numbers of the pieces of sales literature so there's a permanent record in the advertising department, and the salesman receiving a copy of the form is also aware of what was sent.

Paper is thin, and a very thin carbon sheet is between each form.

The second sheet, the salesman's copy, is rather a deep yellow. On it is a carbon of the inquirer's name, firm and so on; a record of what magazine produced the inquiry; what literature was sent; plus room for the salesman's evaluation of the lead. Space is also provided for entering the date the individual was contacted, his equipment needs, and whether he is a live one, somebody to see again in the future, or other—"other" is a polite way of saying literature collector.

UARCO BUSINESS FORMS
CHICAGO

FROM:

LINDBERG HEVI·DUTY SB
DIVISION OF SOLA BASIC INDUSTRIES.
2450 WEST HUBBARD STREET • CHICAGO, ILLINOIS 60612

DATE:

Dear Sir: Here is the information you requested concerning

As described in

For further information or to have your name added to our mailing list, please fill in and return the attached card. Our nearest sales office is listed below; they will be pleased to be of service to you.

We appreciate your interest.

LINDBERG HEVI·DUTY SB
DIVISION OF SOLA BASIC INDUSTRIES

TO •

LIT. SENT:

EVALUATION: Individual contacted: ________ Date: ________

Equipment Needs: ☐ Immediate ☐ Future Other: ________

Did contact result in: ☐ Quotation ☐ Sale What type equipment? ________

Is this a potential account? ☐ YES ☐ NO

COMMENTS: ________

ADD TO MAILING LIST – CHECK AREAS OF INTEREST

☐ Heat Treat Furnaces
☐ Vacuum Furnaces
☐ Kilns
☐ Pilot Plant Equipment
☐ Laboratory Equipment
☐ Melting Furnaces
☐ Ovens
☐ Induction Heating Equipment
☐ Gas Process Equipment
☐ Semiconductor Equipment

SALESMAN'S COPY

Next in line is a pink copy with exactly the same information on it, but it's marked "followup copy." This is for the advertising manager's use as a tickler file to make sure salesmen are following the leads sent to them. The tickler file can be set up so that all inquiries not reported on will automatically come up; at this time they can be Xeroxed and the copy mailed to the salesman with a handwritten note in red ink asking for a report. This can be set for every 30 days, 60 days, 90 days, or whatever length of time you feel is desirable.

Final copy, which is yellow, is the file copy; it stays in the advertising department. It, too, contains the same printed information and has space for inquiry evaluation to make tabulation every 90 days an easy matter.

Last form in Lindberg Hevi-Duty's snap-out form is a postage-paid reply card. Carbon on it is placed so that only the individual's name, firm, and address is typed when the departmental clerk handles the inquiry initially.

The inquirer is given a number of options, as you'll notice, including having his name added to the company's mailing list; stating he is interested in a particular type of equipment; asking for additional information about a specific product or product line; a quotation; or, praise be, asking for a representative to call. The card is addressed to the advertising department.

Return of the card from an inquirer automatically qualifies him as an honest-to-goodness live prospect, at least live enough to be called on. The field sales force is notified immediately as cards are received and requested to make an immediate call. These inquiries are treated like money in the bank!

In general, the letter method of handling inquiries is both more costly and less efficient. If your volume of inquiries is very low, perhaps it is adequate; however, when it rises to several hundred a month you'll be far ahead of the game to use snap-out forms.

Most business printers, such as Uarco Business Forms and others, can produce a snap-out form that will be exactly right for your needs. Cost is modest, and you'll be money ahead to purchase an estimated year's supply at one time. Cost per thousand comes down sharply when volume goes up, just as it does in all printed matter.

You can also buy "canned" snap-out forms—one basic design that many advertisers use and like—from Sales Essentials Mfg. Co., 9427 River Street, Schiller Park, Illinois 60176. This form contains carbon paper, of course, and the following:

1. Thank-you page to go to the inquirer.
2. Gummed label.
3. Salesman's copy.
4. Sales department copy.
5. Followup copy.

Handling Inquiries Outside

For most industrial advertisers the physical handling of inquiries is not such a huge project that it constantly taxes the capacity of the advertising department's manpower. Most advertising managers get inquiries in and the appropriate material out to the inquirer without too much trouble. Seldom is more than one pint of blood lost in the daily process.

When inquiry volume consistently runs into the thousands every month, though, it is often considered advisable to have the routine work farmed out to a specialist—an organization that makes a living handling inquiries.

This is true especially when inquiries surge sharply up in volume, from a routine 500 a month to three, four, or even five thousand. As infrequently as this happens, is still occurs with *predictable* frequency—such as when a major push is put on a product, introduction of a new product line, or a major trade show coincides with another major promotion.

A solution that's proved right for many industrial advertisers is to retain a firm such as Sales Development Service, a division of Chilton Company.

Sales Development Service is dedicated to increasing marketing effectiveness through sales leads—and the proper handling of them. The company noted there is a dramatic rise in inquiry activity during the past few years; this obviously indicates that manufacturers place a growing importance on their use.

These sales leads—inquiries—quickly lose their value unless the followup on them is executed properly and promptly. This is where Sales Development Service comes in, for S.D.S. is organized to process all types of inquiries at a very economical rate—and usually in much less time than most manufacturers are now processing them. Sales Development Service has highly automated systems, in addition to data processing equipment for handling statistical information.

Using this efficient system, inquiries can be processed within 48 hours or less. In addition, tabulated reports of all inquiries by name, products, and source of inquiries will be available for the advertising manager each week.

This inquiry handling system is broken down into five main elements:

1. *Personal reply.* A personally addressed and typewritten letter is enclosed with the appropriate literature forwarded to the inquirer.

2. *Complete listing.* A listing of all inquiries received during the current period sorted by your sales territory or territories. Three copies of this report will be submitted to you for sales followup. Carbon copies may be sent to field sales offices, distributors, or representatives if you wish.

3. *Tabulation by source.* A tabulation of inquiries broken down by source is provided. This report can be used as a measure of evaluating the inquiry pulling power of different media.

4. *State breakdown.* A tabulation of inquiries broken down by state is supplied; you can use it in evaluating your sales territory distribution.

5. *Tabulation by product.* A breakdown of inquiries by product category will help indicate your company's sales effectiveness for each different product line or individual product.

For complete information on Sales Development Service, write to:

Manager
Sales Development Service
Chilton Company
Radnor, Pennsylvania 19089
Telephone: (215) 748-2000

A similar inquiry handling service is offered by Hitchcock Publishing Company. Here's the way it works, according to Don Hogan, who's in charge of this phase of the business.

The advertiser receives his inquiries from the magazines in which he advertises as usual, and then he forwards them to Hitchcock. Here they are turned over to specialists in inquiry handling to be keypunched.

Each advertiser using Hitchcock's inquiry handling service has supplied appropriate product literature, catalogs, envelope stuffers and so forth that is to be mailed to the inquirers. This material, along with a custom-printed inquiry form produced by Hitchcock's printer for each different advertiser, is inserted into the envelope and mailed.

The advertising manager receives a monthly tabulation of all inquiries handled, listed by publication that produced the inquiry, by issue of the publication, and a tally of total inquiries handled.

In addition, the advertiser is supplied with a list of names of the inquirers; these can be broken down in any desired manner for ease of handling internally—such as adding to a mailing list, or using in special promotions.

Average handling cost per inquiry at Hitchcock is 59 cents. This includes 22 cents postage, but does not include the cost of the envelope in which the material is mailed; most advertisers prefer to supply their own, although Hitchcock can have them printed for him, of course.

For the whole story, write to:

Mr. Donald R. Hogan
Manager
Inquiry Handling Services
Hitchcock Publishing Company
25W550 Geneva Road
Wheaton, Illinois 60187
Telephone: (312) 665-1000

Publishers themselves find inquiry handling is such a perplexing problem *they* farm the job out! If handling 500 inquiries a month seems like a chore, imagine the job that *Product Design & Development* has in handling 912,373 inquiries a year, plus more than 100,000 additional ones from the *PD&D Product Encyclopedia!*

Of course, Chilton is in the inquiry-handling business and is staffed and equipped and computerized to take this massive load in stride. Many smaller publishing houses, as well as many individual magazines, simply are not set up to cope with such a volume; and many have no desire to do so. After all, magazine publishers are publishers. Inquiry handling is one business, publishing is another.

Nielsen Clearing House, a Division of A. C. Nielsen Company, is the mecca many publishers with well-developed Reader Service systems turn to when they bog down in a sea of inquiries.

Established in 1962, Nielsen Inquiry Service (a part of Nielsen Clearing House) has refined the inquiry handling process down to a scientific system that's perfect to the last dotted "i." Today some 60 publishers and more than 100 leading business magazines have contracted for this efficient and cost-reducing service.

Richard R. Paper, manager of the firm, said:

"We highly recommend evaluation of individual inquiries to prevent nixies and literature collectors from obtaining information.

"First of all, we have a screening process and eliminate the apparent kooks. Since we process a multitude of magazines, we can easily identify many of these kooks.

"Also, we encourage the publisher to print certain qualifying questions on the reader service card which must be answered by the reader in order to obtain the information he is requesting. Many publishers require inquiries to be processed only when they are directed to a company and the individual requesting the information gives us his job title. They also ask such questions as number of employees, type of operation, and so on.

"This not only enables us to eliminate these kooks, but enables the advertiser to evaluate the inquiries since this information is also passed on to him through our service."

How It's Done at Westinghouse

Sales leads: Profits or problems? Let's hear from John L. DeFazio, marketing communications representative, Electronic Components and Specialty Products, Westinghouse Electric Corporation, whose major product is semiconductors.

Mr. DeFazio developed what is widely considered to be the most effective inquiry handling system in use in industry today. The following discussion of how inquiries are regarded and of his system of handling them at Westinghouse is based on a very enlightening phone conversation with Mr. DeFazio, and on remarks he made at the Scientific Apparatus Makers Association meeting in Miami. His help was graciously given and is gratefully acknowledged.

Inquiries developed by advertising, publicity, trade shows, and so forth mean many different things to different people and companies. They can, for instance, be the lifeblood of a selling program, a source of sales leads when the inquiries are properly screened, an aid to product literature distribution, a measure of advertising effectiveness —or merely a bothersome mishmash of slips of paper sent to the mailroom and then promptly forgotten.

There's another way to look at inquiries; they can be regarded as a vitally important pipeline in the flow of ideas, ideas that play an absolutely indispensable part in the sale and distribution of industrial products. From this viewpoint, inquiries form a circle.

The circle starts with readers—or inquirers—seeking information. They're asking for ideas and are using the established inquiry system to get them.

Funneled through publishers, readers' inquiries—requests for information—are distributed to the source of that information, the advertisers.

To complete the circle, the information then goes back to the reader who made the request.

Another significant meaning and interpretation can be made about inquiries. They are very likely the means by which the market is trying to talk to the manufacturer and his dealers. If only the manufacturer and dealer would listen, they would learn much about the changing needs and problems of the market. This would profit both of them.

The role of inquiries from the point of view of the industrial marketer is that communication from the marketplace via inquiries can be valuable in two entirely different ways. One is the provision of immediate or future sales leads. This is well known, though oftentimes neglected.

The other, less known, use of inquiries is as a tool for marketing intelligence. Looked at in this light, each inquirer is someone in the marketplace with a problem.

By accumulating records of these problems over time and judiciously interpreting the records, some advertisers have developed extremely worthwhile information about new markets, new product applications, and to test advertising effectiveness.

Such intelligence has been used successfully to aid sales forecasts, production scheduling and to meet future market demands. Successful new products have been developed from this same information.

As academic as it is, perhaps it's worth stressing again that the keystone of modern marketing is to begin by the manufacturer finding out what the customer—or prospect—needs to solve his problems.

Once this is learned, the other elements of marketing fall naturally into place. A product is developed by the manufacturer to fill these needs. The characteristics of the product are communicated to the customer or prospect by the manufacturer through his advertising, and a distribution system is set up to get the product into the hands of the prospect.

However, the complexities of the industrial marketplace are such that many roadblocks—marketing problems—retard the carrying out of this inherently simple process. Probably the most formidable is in the area of communications.

The worst and most serious marketing problem is communication from the customer to the manufacturer.

Because of this, it is safe to say that many manufacturers—most of them, probably—have a very faulty knowledge of what their potential customers need, or who and where these prospects are.

Developing this information is the responsibility of the manufacturer.

Here lie lost opportunities and the main source of the high cost of selling (and buying) industrial products.

And never forget for an instant that the success of a firm rests in the hands of the buyers of its products, its failure in the hands of the seller.

Anybody can produce standard price-book widgets. Having enough marketing savvy to determine what the marketplace wants, and then producing *that* and selling it at a profit requires a mind that exists in the twentieth century. This is where the Neanderthal managements succeed in looking incredibly inept.

Advertising as an Investment

Westinghouse has developed a system that closes the information gap involving inquiries between the company and its likely interested customer-prospects. The system enables Westinghouse to retrieve vital marketing information from "hidden" data in the inquiries it receives.

According to Mr. DeFazio, *it is essential that industry accept the fact that advertising is an investment, not an overhead.*

Few things are as difficult to accomplish, however, as determining just what you receive in results from the money invested in advertising and communications. Yet it is vital that precise results from the communications program be documented, because advertising has become one of the biggest—if not *the* biggest—of the controllable expenditures in the corporate budget.

Advertising *is* an investment; *apply* advertising and communications as an investment; *prove* it as a return on investment. Live with this principle and you'll find your entire program more meaningful.

Communications may be taken for granted, but a prospect cannot become a customer for a product he does not know exists. By the same token, a prospect cannot become a customer until he has sufficient information about a product to determine how it might solve his problem on his job.

"Sales seek individuals, not companies," Mr. DeFazio is fond of saying. Advertising and marketing managers concern themselves with SIC's and companies, but sales managers and salesmen must know the *people* who specify and buy in the company.

Although this is elementary, it is often overlooked when advertising programs or communications projects of one type or another are being planned.

All of this brings us to the crux of the matter, and Westinghouse's John DeFazio put his finger on one problem that's universal—failure to handle inquiries promptly, and attaching too little importance to them. He said, "Inquiries demand immediate action, undivided attention."

Too often overlooked is that today's sales accrue as the result of yesterday's work. And tomorrow's results depend on what we do today. Convince yourself of this by picking up a handful of old inquiries—*letterhead inquiries*—12 or 18 months old. Review each one. You may be shocked to find many problems and ideas that are today's successful new products discussed in them.

But what was done with those inquiries at the time?

Were they really followed up vigorously, was everything possible done to solve these prospective customers' problems at that time?

It's highly unlikely.

But it's in this area where some research effort could produce vital intelligence for the marketing and sales plan—as it has done at Westinghouse.

"Get objectives in writing that can be measured. Always 'keep the monkey on management's back' by asking for their measurable objectives by priorities, specific markets, the job function to be reached, and appeal to each function," DeFazio said.

And he's unquestionably right because by doing this the advertising manager can *prove* without a shadow of doubt that advertising is an investment with a measurable return.

But he can prove this *only* if objectives are firm, in writing, and measurable.

As pro-advertising as those of us are who *know* what industrial advertising can accomplish, nonetheless when a company drifts without marketing direction the money spent on advertising would probably produce more of a return if it were invested in hiring a marketing vice-president to replace the engineer in that spot right now—or even in adding additional salesmen to the field force.

In no way is this intended to be an anti-advertising diatribe. Rather, it is an indictment of inept management of a fantastically high percentage of industrial companies doing business in this country today.

Managements that are engineering-oriented, production-oriented—and even sales-oriented—but ignore the marketing concept, ignore marketing as an activity vital to their companies, ignore development of a written marketing plan, ignore setting marketing objectives, ignore development of a written communications plan, ignore setting communications objectives, ignore the role marketing communications alone can play, are incapable of managing effectively.

They should be replaced with top people who would *demand* and *get* smart marketing as the *only* way to improve significantly the company's position in its industry.

"Lost Business" Reports

The relationship between inquiries, negotiations, and sales must be established very precisely. Again, "keep the monkey on the back" of sales management by asking for *accurate records of negotiations activity by product.* Insist also on a system of "lost business reports." This will enable you to develop important intelligence about what occurs between the negotiations and sales stages.

What can be done between the inquiry to negotiations stages? Work out a system to determine what transpires during this time and you'll be able to prove a return on advertising investment.

To do this, it is essential that you accept only objectives that advertising can perform—such as securing a greater share of mind, creating interest, motivating distributors, supporting the sales organization. Such objectives will show that *advertising can measurably increase negotiations activity.*

Educate your people, your immediate management group, your sales force, anybody else who'll listen to you, about the role of marketing communications. Advertising is an investment, so let's treat it as such and prove it is just that.

Educate everybody that advertising cannot directly sell the product, even if an occasional order does come in over the transom due to advertising. Don't stress these sales because you'll be stressing a role that industrial advertising isn't supposed to play.

Never forget for an instant that the important role of marketing communications is measurably to increase negotiations activity. Advertising can take full credit for digging up new prospects and putting them in touch with the company—and it should.

If sales do not result, you can still prove you met your communications objectives successfully—and management will have to look elsewhere to determine why. Always tie the advertising and communications program and budget to negotiations activity only. Converting negotiations to sales is the responsibility of the sales force. That is beyond your control.

Westinghouse's Mr. DeFazio says there is a "communications flow" that consists of separate phases. These follow, and here he is quoted.

"There are three communications steps to a sale. The first is the inquiry step where the inquirer (prospect) asks for more information, such as, what is it? What can it do? Give me a price list? Why is it better than a competitor's product? And so on.

"The second step, the negotiations step, is the bartering step with the inquirer seeking more specific information, such as, can you meet this spec? What is my discount? Delivery? And so on and on.

"The third step is placing the order. Steps two and three are talents best cultivated by salesmen. Get the salesmen to concentrate on the negotiations step and processing the order and you have accomplished maximum salesmen's efficiency."

These are the two major ways in which advertising reduces the cost of selling, of course—by bringing prospect and salesman together in the first place, and by enabling the sales force to sell more in the same amount of time.

The inquiry step in the sale is best handled by company or division headquarters, in the advertising department.

Certain inputs are essential for the process, Mr. DeFazio said. "Now for the inputs. You create interest—which are the inputs—four ways. By advertising, publicity, trade shows, and annual catalogs and directories. At this state I'm not talking about a manufacturer's, or distributor's catalog, but rather about annual buying guides such as the one produced by *Research/Development* magazine, or annuals such as *Thomas Register* and *Sweet's Catalogs.*"

Created interest generates raw inquiries. Convert raw inquiries to verified, or qualified, inquiries and in the process a certain percentage of hot leads is the fallout.

At Westinghouse, even qualified inquiries are not sent to the sales force, but are sent to a product expert at the appropriate plant. This is to avoid the back-breaking administrative exercise that ensues because the salesmen cannot answer every question the inquirer asks.

We've all seen far too many instances where the field sales force has had to "get on the horn" to the inside product people when actually in the company of a live prospect. This is disruptive, time consuming, and does not do anything to inspire customer confidence in the salesman.

Westinghouse product experts spend at least a half-day a week telephoning all hot leads; after discussing the matter with the inquirer, the product man determines the next step. If the lead is really hot, a salesman's call is warranted.

Another important reason Westinghouse product experts handle qualified inquiries by phone is that the product man is the one who needs all of this information and intelligence to keep abreast of all new developments. Westinghouse has found it is an effective and economical way to get the most accomplished in the shortest period of time and with personnel used with greatest efficiency. This method is considered *extremely* important at Westinghouse.

Verified prospects make up Westinghouse's Prospect Mailing List. Regular mailings are made to keep the prospects advised of the latest product information, new prices, new applications, and so forth. Technical data sheets, brochures, price sheets, catalogs, and other material is mailed to these verified prospects quite frequently.

It's impossible to overstress the importance of this activity to Westinghouse. These verified prospects are the best and primary return on the investment. Mr. DeFazio advocates making at least 24 mailings a year to them—if the list is kept virgin-pure. When it is, the mailings are rifle shots, as opposed to the shotgun activity of arousing interest.

The customer mailing list at Westinghouse's Semiconductor Division is made up by salesmen who submit names of people on whom they call at each customer establishment. The customer mailing list breaks down as:

60—70% purchasing agents

20—30% design engineers

1— 5% R&D

On the other hand, the prospect mailing list from verified inquiries breaks down just the opposite; it looks like this:

60—70% research and development

20—30% design engineers

1— 5% purchasing agents

For all practical purposes this means that the customer mailing list actually makes up the buyers, and the prospect mailing list makes up the specifiers. Having this information gives Westinghouse marketing people a wonderful understanding of today's business—and an excellent insight into tomorrow's.

"Tap the static that goes on between each step and you are really on your way for real growth in your markets," Mr. DeFazio said. "The marketer of tomorrow will become the one who masters this technique.

"The static between inquiry stage and negotiations reveals new market trends. The static between negotiations and sales steps can determine sales forecasting, lost-business reports, and marketing intelligence by products."

At Westinghouse it is emphasized that there are only two ways to increase sales volume.

One is to increase and improve the conversion rate of negotiations to sales; this can be done either by making sales aids available to the sales force, or conducting sales or product training for the sales force.

The other way to increase sales volume is to increase the negotiations base, and to increase the negotiations base the inquiry base must be increased. It's that simple.

Of course, the manufacturer must develop the need in the marketplace, it must have the right product, at the right time, and at the right price. Furthermore, distributors must know their conversion rate of negotiations activity—that is, quotes, bids entered, proposals, or whatever it's called in each industry. And he has to have his salesmen well-trained by the manufacturer about the product if they're to operate at peak efficiency.

Three-Stage Data Processing

Proof of the pudding at Westinghouse is provided by the data processing inquiry system developed by Mr. DeFazio to be a basic means of establishing the fundamental relationship between marketing communications and sales.

The data processing inquiry system was designed to get product information to a prospect; to get more information on prospect needs; and to follow up with personal selling to produce sales.

Inquiries are handled in three stages. The first stage is called the raw inquiry stage; this division of Westinghouse pulls more than 20,000 inquiries a year. The second stage is the process of verifying, or qualifying; it reduces the raw inquiries to 8,500 in number. The last stage is referred to as the "hot" lead stage; here the total quantity is only 750.

Interestingly, the ratio of raw inquiries to hot sales leads is 40 to 1—2½ percent.

Here's how Westinghouse semiconductor's system works.

First step is to answer *immediately* all raw inquiries generated by advertising, publicity, or trade shows by sending information requested; along with a letter of transmittal and a questionnaire reply card.

The questionnaire reply card is the second stage of the system—the verification or qualification process.

When Westinghouse processes a raw inquiry, a source code is entered in area "A" on the questionnaire card; it identifies where and how the inquiry was generated. Thus the company can specifically identify the specific advertisement and the publication that produced the inquiry, the publicity release, and the publication or the trade show.

This verification procedure is very similar to most systems used by controlled circulation magazines. The card requires information in considerable detail concerning the inquirer's job function, product interest, and data about his company, whether the application is commercial or military—and boxes to check for "have your salesman phone" or "have your salesman visit me." When the inquirer completes and returns the card, he is considered a qualified prospect.

A customer or noncustomer code is assigned in area "B" on the card, and all of the information is punched on data processing cards. The information loop, for all practical purposes, is closed. Westinghouse now has a complete record of an inquiry from the time it originates until—or if, that is—it becomes a sale.

Third stage of inquiry handling comes about when processing the questionnaire reply card. Should the inquirer complete area "C" —asking for a salesman to phone or visit him—this information is immediately reproduced on the Inquiry Follow Form and sent out within 24 hours of its receipt to the salesman handling that particular area or account. This is the hot lead stage, the *only* time a salesman is asked to follow up with a prospect immediately.

"I believe there are basically five important by-products accomplished with this inquiry handling system," said Mr. DeFazio.

The first is a virgin-pure mailing list that is effectively offering economy because of its selectivity—sending out information only to those who are genuinely interested. The system is also easily maintained on a current status, with a known turnover rate of approximately 40 percent a year.

This is remarkably close to what is considered the normal attrition rate of personnel, as far as remaining on one job in one company is concerned; this figure is generally considered to be approximately 35 percent. Which means that 35 percent of your prospects are no longer prospects at the end of a year because they're someplace else, in another position, in another company. They may, however, be prospects there as well.

Second important result of Westinghouse's system is the identifiable sales efficiency. The system has done away with cold calls and replaced them with hot leads. It isn't very difficult to guess which the salesmen prefer. Phone numbers are listed on the form so Westinghouse salesmen are encouraged to make quick contacts.

Over the past five years, it has been shown that three out of four of the hot leads have lead to immediate negotiations or a sample order. *Every* hot lead has been qualified *by Westinghouse salesmen* —not by the advertising people—as a good prospect. In every case, the salesman assigned a full-line catalog to the prospect. This catalog definitely is not handed out to literature collectors.

Every three months, a galley run-off of all verified inquiries is assembled for each salesman by accounts in his area. This galley shows new prospects in the area. Salesmen and their inside back-up salesmen have a tool that helps give them a better "commercial" feel of the area, since the galley also includes job functions of the inquirers.

Again, the salesmen realize the contribution of marketing communications because they can also save valuable time during customer calls by phoning new prospects listed in the organization—all from their reception room phone. This obviates scheduling additional, separate calls and eliminates much back-tracking and duplicated effort by the sales force.

The third important benefit realized from Westinghouse's system is the reports that show market trends by analyzing the information furnished on the questionnaire card.

Also on a quarterly basis, Mr. DeFazio receives an incremental report and a cumulative summary report from the system. The reports are broken down by all field sales areas with a complete listing of customer versus noncustomer potential by product interest, product application, and industry group.

Over five years the reports reveal inquiries from noncustomers—fine prospects to *become* customers—have never been less than 80 percent of the total. Proof to top management that advertising is an investment, or that the communications program has met its objective of creating interest in the product. This is proof that cannot be disputed.

And it is obvious to all that advertising extends the reach of salesmen and flushes out prospects they never knew existed!

What's more, the quarterly incremental report detects new markets or accelerating market trends. The summary report displays gradual market shifts by areas, by products, and by industry.

Fourth important result of the system is the invaluable marketing intelligence feedback found in the salesmen's hot lead reports. This information and intelligence is used to produce new products, learn of new product applications, new customer contacts, and new product lead time for sales.

By having every inquiry customer or noncustomer coded, Westinghouse is able immediately to match all purchase orders entered for the first time by a new customer with any inquiries received from his organization. Not only can it be shown that inquiries definitely lead to sales, but Mr. DeFazio and his staff can accurately measure the time it takes from the inquiry stage to the actual sale—and do it by product line.

As an example, it was found that the minimum time sales could be expected to be made following inquiries was six months. By plotting the negotiation activity curves recorded by sales management and superimposing them over actual sales curves, it was immediately apparent that negotiation preceded sales by three months.

All industrial advertising managers should explain the time lag between advertising and measurable results to their managements. Recognize, though, that the time between inquiry and sale varies tremendously depending upon the product. In the case of major capital equipment used for a manufacturing process it can be months, even a year or more. A management sitting in walnut-paneled offices with bated breath, watching the sales curve and expecting it to surge instantaneously and miraculously just because the company started an intensified advertising campaign, is a management doomed to disappointment. And when this happens, this is a management doubly hard to convince about advertising's effectiveness and advertising's contributions to attaining marketing objectives.

The last important thing in the way of beneficial results produced by the inquiry handling system at Westinghouse is ease of evaluation of the marketing communications program. This analysis matches what was planned and expected from an advertisement in a given publication or trade show with actual readout results.

A media evaluation report provides a total of 12 areas for evaluating the effectiveness of advertising copy, as well as the media themselves; it is very easy with this system to determine both the quantity and the quality of inquiries of all of the publications on Westinghouse's schedule.

Cost of Handling Inquiries

The industrial advertising manager who *knows* for sure exactly what it costs his company to handle the average inquiry received from a trade publication is a member of a minority group so small it couldn't even organize a first-class riot. This group could hold its annual convention in a broom closet, with no crowding, no jostling, nobody cramped, and with no feelings of claustrophobia.

Inquiries can have value. They are used effectively by thousands of companies, including many of our industrial giants such as Westinghouse, as well as by many of the smaller companies most of us have never heard of. They are used as sales, marketing, and promotion tools, and in dozens of other ways.

Also, though, there's no getting away from the fact that inquiries are expensive. If you're advertising manager of a typical industrial company and you're doing a better than average job of followup on your inquiries, that job is costing money—lots of it.

Furthermore, it's a pretty safe bet you're spending at least 50 cents to handle each and every inquiry, and this figure is so low it borders on the absurd. Mighty few companies can handle an inquiry for this sum today; most companies spend something between 50 cents and $2.50 to handle one inquiry, but this figure does *not* include:

1. Cost of generating inquiries—via advertising, direct mail, publicity, trade shows, or what have you.
2. Cost of literature and/or samples sent to inquirers.
3. Postage—and it's going up so often it's difficult to remember what it costs any more.
4. Cost of salesmen's followup calls.

However, for most companies the cost *does* include:

1. Typing the label.
2. Getting the material in the mail.
3. Simple recordkeeping.

If you're doing the job for *under* a half-dollar, you are a financial genius on the order of J. Paul Getty, H. L. Hunt and Hugh Hefner. Your management should cherish you and give you much tender loving care and frequent salary adjustments, always upwards. And on your part, you should cherish the inquiry handling system you've developed and give it plenty of tender loving care. Don't change it in even the tiniest way for the world.

The truth is, though, that many good, large, sophisticated companies that spend hundreds of thousands of dollars to generate inquiries and tens of thousands to handle them haven't the foggiest idea what the whole thing costs. They'd stomp off in high dudgeon if told so except in the pages of a book, though. The truth always hurts.

Although the following chart won't pinpoint to the nearest mill what it costs your company to handle an inquiry, it will nonetheless give you a good, ball-park figure. And it may prove to be a real eye-opener!

Charge or function	*Monthly cost*
1. Your time (only what you spend on inquiries).	$........
2. Your secretary's time (ditto above).	....
3. Other supervisory or executive time—such as your assistant, for instance.	....
4. Their secretaries and/or assistants.	....
5. All clerks, typists, messengers, etc., and this includes the mail boy, the labor used to haul your literature in and out of the supply room, and so forth.	....
6. Warehousing and inventory control.	....
7. Mechanical costs, including collating, stuffing, metering, bagging, labeling, etc.	....
8. Supplies and services, including letterheads, envelopes, inquiry forms, labels, telephone, typewriter ribbons, paperclips, and so on.	....
TOTAL	========

Once you've tallied all of this up if you really want to be accurate, as well as fair about the whole thing, you should by rights add a fair share of fringe benefits to the labor costs you used above. Also standard overhead items—rent, light, heat, taxes, maintenance, watchman, etc. And maybe even a few cents for recruiting and training.

Tally up the total monthly cost, then divide by the average number of inquiries you process in a month. If that figure comes to less than 50 cents per inquiry, you win a gold-plated key to the executive washroom.

There's another little item to be added in before we complete all of the addition—that's whatever it costs you to prepare and print each copy of that brochure, catalog, or booklet you send out to inquirers. Don't forget to add in all labor, overhead, and so on to the cost per piece of literature. This brings it up to what—40 cents, 50 cents, $1.25, $2.00—or more?

Finally, add in that little item of postage. What does it cost to mail one inquirer packet—a quarter? A half-dollar?

You'll find, if you're accurate about all cost items, that handling one inquiry from the time it arrives in the advertising department until the requested material is in the mail, that you've spent approximately $2.15. And that figure isn't on the high side if you produce quality literature, perhaps, in four-color, using good art and/or good photography and first-class printing. Actually, this figure is below what more than half of all industrial companies spend on the function.

Screening Inquiries

Not every industrial advertiser has either the budget or the manpower to set up an elaborate and highly effective inquiry handling system like that used by Westinghouse.

Every industrial company, however, should screen its inquiries and refrain from feeding salesmen a huge mass of raw inquiries. Nothing discourages a salesman faster—and actually turns him against both inquiries and advertising—than sending him on one wild goose chase after another when all he accomplishes is wasting his time, wearing out his car, and handing some literature to a junior draftsman, mail boy, or other literature collector.

Detailed examination of the replies from all of the companies surveyed in *Product Design & Development's* massive study on inquiries reveals that, for the most part, screening of inquiries is remarkably casual. Little importance is attached to it. This may well be because of a chronic shortage of manpower in the typical industrial advertising department, although it may also reflect a near-total lack of understanding of *why* inquiries should be screened.

Let's see how some individual companies do their screening of inquiries.

Indiana General Corporation manufactures magnets, soft ferrites, magnetizing, demagnetizing equipment, memory cores, planes, stacks, precision motors and so forth. When asked by *Product Design & Development* "What screening and sorting is done with inquiries at the home office?" officials said, "First round, none." All inquiries —100 percent—are bucked out to the company's field sales force. The salesman is free to use his own judgment as to whether the inquiry should be followed up, although a return post card is sent to the inquirer. Indiana General Corporation receives approximately 3,500 inquiries per month.

Hunter Spring Division, Ametek, Inc., receives more than 1,000 inquiries each month. This company makes little effort to screen them, and answered *PD&D's* question by saying, "Segregation by product and territory; inquiries from competitors are considered separately; 'casual' foreign inquiries where we cannot sell are discarded." Hunter Spring Division sends 99 percent of all incoming inquiries to its field sales force. Individual salesmen are to use their own judgment about whether or not to follow up. The company added that letterhead inquiries are considered important and well worth followup effort; bingo card inquiries are a good source of names and companies worth pursuing.

Anaconda American Brass Company is the recipient of more than 1,000 inquiries a month; they are sorted as to product, geographical location, manufacturer, or student by "a senior employee familiar with our products." Sixty percent of these inquiries are sent out to the field sales force.

Hamlin, Inc. receives a substantial number of inquiries each month; upon receipt, they are counted and recorded in a log covering each advertisement or publicity release *by magazine.* They are then coded as to the sales representative (territory) who handles them. The original is sent to the mail room and the label is affixed to an envelope containing the proper product literature and a cover letter showing the name, address, and phone number of the appropriate representative. These envelopes are prepacked and coded with the number of the representative, so all that remains for the mailman to do is match code numbers on the labels to those on the envelopes. The duplicate label that comes in from the publication is sent to the rep for his followup activities. Hamlin added that several publications do not send duplicate labels, making extra work; for this reason Hamlin has decided not to advertise in them! No effort is made to screen inquiries.

Barber-Coleman Company, manufacturer of AC motors, DC motors, relays, actuators, valves, impressors, control systems and so on, receives around 1,000 inquiries a month—with 850 the result of advertising, 150 editorial mentions (publicity) and 50 from direct mail. The only screening that is done is to remove competitors, catalog collectors, and some foreign countries. Salesmen get 100 percent for sales followup—and interestingly, the company states that approximately 5 percent are "hot leads;" this is just about *double* the usually accepted percentage of hot leads as determined by both industrial companies and insurance companies who have analyzed their inquiries.

Blue M Electric Company, manufacturer of electric ovens and furnaces, temperature/humidity environmental cabinets and so forth, gets an average of 250 inquiries a month from advertising, 250 from publicity, and another 100 from direct mail. Inquiries are screened to weed out competitors and, when possible, literature collectors. That little qualifier, "when possible" is Midwestern humor at its best. Blue M's sales force receives all inquiries for followup at its discretion. Salesmen are obliged to follow up and submit a report within 30 days of receiving inquiries, however, so their discretion is limited.

Gates Rubber Company, Industrial Division, manufacturer of industrial hose, V-belts, and automotive products, answers all inquiries and encloses a postage-paid reply card with the appropriate literature, along with the inquiry-handling form. Return of the reply card, which contains a questionnaire, qualifies the inquirer as a live one—and Gates averages a 12 percent return of cards. Inquirers who do not use the card are also referred to the field sales force, but to be followed up with discretion. Naturally, all of the hot leads —the qualified inquiries—are followed up immediately.

Most industrial advertisers use mail, via the ubiquitous post-paid reply card, to screen inquiries and to determine who among all that mass of paper work is an honest-to-goodness prospect and who should be contacted by the sales force.

With the cost of an industrial sales call running at $71.27 and climbing every year, it is mandatory that these inquiries be screened some way if the sales force is to operate efficiently and not dissipate its efforts. And since advertising's prime function is to lower the cost of selling by making the salesmen more efficient and productive, it certainly will not do the job by dumping a mass of names on a salesman's desk, muttering darkly, "Go, man, go."

One way to determine just who is a live one and who isn't is to run two boxes in ads that are couponed. One box says, "I'm interested." The other one says, "I'm serious." This automatically qualifies inquiries immediately with no additional steps required. People are honest about checking the boxes and this system has worked beautifully for several industrial advertisers who use it. It sorts out the wheat from the chaff fast.

The Telephone Screen

A faster way than mail to qualify inquiries is by telephone. With WATS lines (Wide Area Telephone Service) being used by more and more companies, the long-distance call is not prohibitively expensive for routine use; WATS line users are charged a fixed amount and allowed unlimited long-distance calls.

Paying $2,000 for unlimited calls anywhere in the continental United States each month is a rare bargain; compare this to about 43 salesmen's calls at the going price and they cost out exactly the same. But the WATS line is the biggest bargain to be had today. When salesmen follow only hot leads their sales shoot up amazingly, and use of the telephone provides plenty of hot leads plus all of the application information salesmen need to close sales with less calls. This method of screening inquiries truly reduces the cost of selling and does it *now*.

John O. Cook, formerly advertising and public relations manager of Marbon Chemical, Division of Borg-Warner Corporation, reports that his company screens 100 percent of its incoming inquiries by telephone in an effort to qualify them for personal sales followup. A phone call and an individual's time together cost a little less than $71.27, which is the salesman's cost to do the same job—not taking into account the lost time for the salesman if the inquiry turns out to be a dud. Marbon Chemical values inquiries and considers them highly important. And effective use is made of them.

Johns-Manville used the WATS line a short time ago to follow up on inquiries that resulted from an 8-page insert advertisement for Dutch Brand electrical tape. The calls made a tremendous impression on startled inquirers who found it a little hard to believe (as Maxwell Smart would say) that a major company like Johns-Manville was calling *them* long distance after they'd inquired about one of the company's products. The inside salesmen who did the calling were able to qualify inquirers with great precision as to product, application, the brand of tape they were currently buying, and much additional marketing information. Distributors received the data unearthed by the telephone calls and made very effective use of it.

The telephone can also be used efficiently to determine the quality of the inquiries that come in. Recently one large advertiser called at random a number of inquirers who had returned bingo cards from *Research/Development* magazine. *The inquiries were over a year old!* After some three days on the telephone talking to industrial firms, educational institutions, government and such defense establishments as NASA, it developed that *more than one-third* had purchased the product about which they inquired more than a year previously. In addition, 22 percent had intentions of buying the product, or a similar one, and 27 percent stated they had gathered information as part of an overall program of equipment procurement that had not as yet taken place. These inquiries were of extremely high quality.

The telephone survey to determine the intent of inquirers is extremely helpful, and it is a great aid in media selection. It pinpoints intent to buy and enables the advertising manager to predict with reasonable accuracy the dollar volume of sales that can be expected from a given number of inquiries. Publications vary widely in the quality of inquiries they produce, as some telephoning will point out.

You needn't let lack of a WATS line or an understaffed advertising department prevent taking advantage of the telephone in screening inquiries. A number of firms throughout the country specialize in this. One reported by *Marketing Forum* is Inquiry Evaluations, Inc., of New York City, which qualifies inquiries by telephone. Among its clients are U.S. Industries, Du Pont, Celanese Corporation, Enjay Chemical, and other giants of industry.

Inquiry Evaluations employs about 100 retired engineers scattered around the country to cover most key points. The advantages claimed for using this service are (1) the detailed information which can be gathered by personal conversation, (2) speed of the telephone, (3) interviewers who can talk on technical subjects, (4) the small percent of "no answers" compared with mail methods.

Howard Hansen, president of Inquiry Evaluations, admits there are sometimes problems with salesmen who don't like the intrusion of an outsider speaking directly to a prospect. "But, we've found this distrust disappears once they get leads," which Inquiry Evaluation clients confirm.

The telephone, Hansen says, usually digs out one good lead out of five calls. Each call runs about $3.50, which means a prospect costs the client between $15 and $20. Since a sales call costs $71.27 on the average, Hansen believes a prospect dug up through conventional selling can cost $150—or more. The figures bear him out.

Another telephone method is Chilton Company's Wide Area Telephone Service (WATS), used for many purposes, only one of which is followups. Chilton uses professional interviewers to find out if inquirers received the information they requested, the type of work they are engaged in, the use they have in mind for the product, and so on. The company charges clients around $2.50 to $3.00 per call (per interview, that is), although it can sometimes range up to $5.00.

Both telephone methods have their advantages. Inquiry Evaluation is favored where an understanding of highly technical information is of critical importance, and Chilton is chosen when questions that are relatively standard are involved—such as in a sample survey to be tabulated.

A number of business publications have been doing inquiry followups for advertisers; sometimes for promotional reasons, sometimes to uncover new applications for products, and sometimes to dig up other data. The fact remains, though, that the company that systematically analyzes this type of followup is in the minority.

The same may be said as far as evaluating raw inquiries in the advertising department is concerned, as we've seen from the typical companies surveyed by *Product Design & Development*.

One problem quite prevalent in smaller companies is that the advertising department, which normally handles this work, must choose between holding up the inquiry for analysis and getting the information to the inquirer and the field salesman in a hurry.

Work is being done by publications to upgrade inquiry handling. At McGraw-Hill, for example, where service bureaus do most of the work, the company's own computers now produce reports and labels for some of the company's magazines. A spokesman for the company said, "We're wondering whether we couldn't turn over punched cards or tape to the advertiser and let him do the rest—send out the material, analyze the inquiries, or whatever. This may be a problem for the small guy who can't handle computerized information, but there may be answers to that, too. Actually, we think we haven't even scratched the surface of processing inquiries."

He may well be right. Who would have dreamed, a few years ago, of a system as sophisticated as that used by Westinghouse?

Conversion Into Sales

This is the bugaboo of most industrial advertising managers. They're all intent on "proving that advertising sold X number of dollars worth of widgets."

Fallacy here is that these advertising managers are going to much trouble and great lengths to prove something that's unprovable—because 'tain't so. Unless the advertisement made a direct plea to send in a check or money order for an item bought by mail (mail order), advertising doesn't sell.

Industrial advertising *presells,* it puts the buyer and the company's salesman in touch with each other. As Westinghouse says, it "increases the negotiations activity." And this includes submitting a proposal, putting in a bid, and so forth—whatever your company calls it.

Advertising can and does put a large number of buyers and salesmen in touch with each other and thus produces a substantial volume of sales; but the sales were made and closed by the salesmen, not by the advertisements.

Of course, it's quite true that occasionally an advertisement will result in an over-the-transom order for a piece of equipment. All of us have had this happen a number of times, although such an occurrence is certainly an exception to the rule. When an ad does produce a sale, or bring in an order without a salesman's having been involved, don't rush frantically hither and yon calling it to everybody's attention.

Those who don't understand the function of industrial advertising —which is to reduce the cost of selling by enabling the sales force to sell more in the same amount of time—will inevitably view such a sale as something advertising should do *more often.*

They may very well ask you, or, at the least wonder to themselves, why you go through all the back-patting routine just because "advertising has done what it's supposed to do—sell." Encouraging this attitude can do you nothing but a disservice in the long run, and it can undermine what little faith exists in advertising among members of management of industrial companies.

New customers shaken out of the bushes by advertising are not merely inquirers, as many industrial advertisers know—they're prospective customers, prospective buyers. When they inquire about a product they want information on which to base a buying decision. Inquiries handled promptly and properly and with proper product information sent to the inquirer are frequently like money pouring in straight out of the blue.

Lindberg Hevi-Duty found this to be the case with two of its products. Illustrated nearby is one of the company's one-third page, black-and-white ads on electrical heating elements.

Such elements are used by a large and broad segment of industry, with no specific SIC's accounting for a dominant share. The elements are put around piping, and otherwise used in various processes in the chemical, petrochemical, and similar fields. For the most part they are needed by those engaged in research work.

Since the advertising budget was extremely limited, the decision was made to use fractional-page advertisements in the one best medium to cut across all of industry in the research area—*Research/Development* magazine.

The ad ran unchanged every month and consistently pulled from 85 to 125 inquiries; performance of the ad, as far as measurable results in terms of inquiries was concerned, was so good the publication presented the company's advertising manager with the plaque shown. This is *Research/Development's* "Top Ten" Award presented to advertisements that are outstanding inquiry producers.

It marked one of the very few times the "Top Ten" Award was won by a fractional-page advertisement.

Interestingly, this ad ran in *Research/Development* for more than two years and inquiry level remained approximately the same from month to month, year to year. This proved it was still being read just as well as it was the first time it made an appearance, and it also proved there was no need to change either the copy, illustration, or layout.

If the heating system you want hasn't been built yet... build it!

At left, the ad which ran unchanged for two years and consistently obtained from 85 to 125 inquiries per month. Below, the "Top Ten Award" presented to Lindberg Hevi-Duty by Research/Development *magazine.*

It's simple—with Lindberg Hevi-Duty building blocks of heat. These flexible, low-cost elements can be assembled in countless ways.

They're perfect to heat piping systems where liquids must be kept at constant temperature. Or for special lab requirements that don't justify a furnace. Or where there isn't a furnace to do the job.

They have excellent capacity. High watt density. 1000° or 1200° C. Control them manually, or automatically.

They're available from leading lab dealers in sizes, shapes, and lengths to fit your projects.

Write for bulletin 50910, Lindberg Hevi-Duty, Watertown, Wis. 53094.

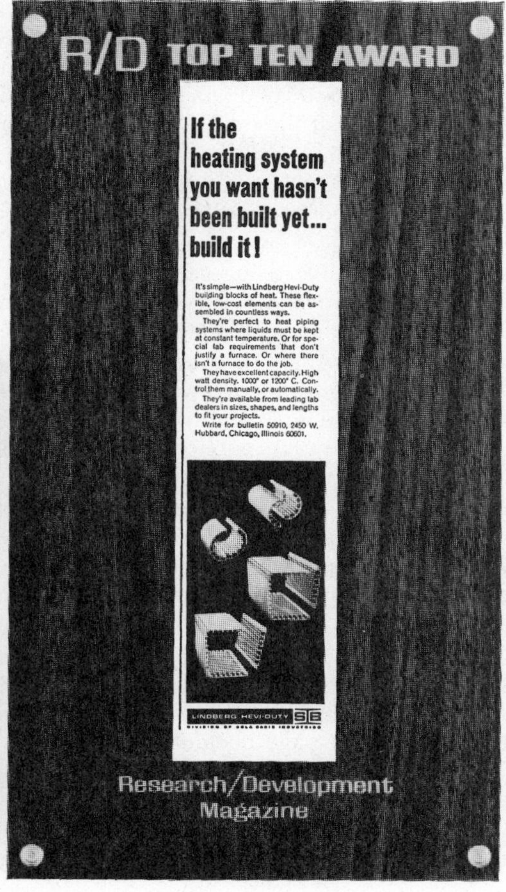

All inquirers were immediately sent a four-page, two-color piece of sales literature on heating elements. The literature retains the "building blocks of heat" concept from the ad, and sells hard on the first page; the other three pages give detailed information about sizes, shapes, wattages, and temperature ranges for the various elements.

Immediately after the literature was mailed to the inquirers, the salesmen's copy of Lindberg Hevi-Duty's snap-out inquiry form was sent to dealers who handle this product line; in this instance they are laboratory supply houses.

Frequently, inquiries are one thing and sales are another and entirely different breed of cat. Here, however, this advertisement was an outstanding performer in producing *both* inquiries and sales.

Conversion rate has never been exactly established down to the last fraction of a cent, although it is exceptionally high. The dealers sell more than $200,000 worth of these heating elements each year—and this has been the only promotional support given to the product.

It would be interesting indeed to see what effect on sales a more aggressive advertising drive would produce. Very possibly sales could be doubled by investment of just a few more dollars.

Another highly productive advertisement that proves the relationship between advertising-generated inquiries and sales is an advertisement for Lindberg Hevi-Duty's ultrasophisticated Multi-Vac, an advanced metallurgical vacuum system.

The advertisement illustrated nearby was prepared and run in only one magazine—*Research/Development;* this medium was selected because of the proven high quality of its inquiries, and because it is the only publication in its field to have a section of the magazine devoted to vacuum technology in every issue.

This ad and a similar one were run a total of five times—all the budget would permit. That's five times between the two ads, not five times each. Inquiry activity was excellent, and the inquiries came from some of the biggest corporations in the country, as well as from research centers in the educational field and in government.

All inquiries were screened by the product manager in charge of Multi-Vac; depending upon the apparent hotness of the lead, this was done either by telephone or letter. This followed mailing of a two-color, eight-page booklet, of course.

Multi-Vac is not an inexpensive plaything that is purchased on an impulse. Price, depending upon accessories ordered with the basic piece of equipment, ranges from $15,000 to $30,000.

These five insertions of the two ads in *Research/Development* pro-

Quick change artist! It's like a roomful of vacuum chambers rolled into one!

Shown below are four Multi-Vac System conversion possibilities:

Talk about getting mileage out of your capital investment! This new Lindberg Hevi-Duty Multi-Vac system converts to handle half a dozen different vacuum and inert-atmosphere metallurgical processes.

Multi-Vac changes quickly from an induction melting furnace to an inert-gas welding chamber . . . or a high temperature vertical furnace . . . a high temperature horizontal furnace . . . an arc melting and casting furnace . . . or an inert-gas manual dry box. Conversion is simple. Anyone can do it on the spot.

Savings are tremendous compared to the alternative: many single-purpose units. And Multi-Vac takes far less floor space . . . with one power supply, one pumping system, one chamber.

There's more to the Multi-Vac story. You'll want to review every bit of it. So see your Lindberg Hevi-Duty sales engineer. Or write direct to Lindberg Hevi-Duty, 2450 West Hubbard, Chicago, Illinois 60612, for catalog 20002.

This ad was a good magnet for inquiries. It was better when a coupon was added, as in the ads on the following page.

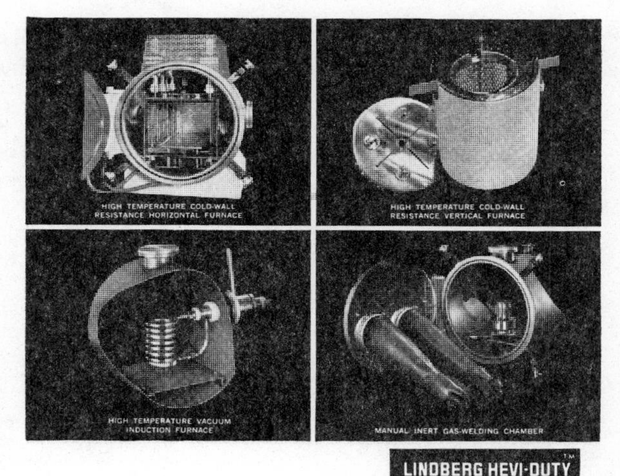

LINDBERG HEVI-DUTY™

DIVISION OF SOLA BASIC INDUSTRIES

duced inquiries that the product manager converted into five sales whose total was approximately $100,000.

But that's not all. In addition to those sales, formal proposals were made to more than a dozen more inquirers who definitely were live ones. These proposals were made after a personal sales call by the product manager and the local field salesman; at least half of them resulted in sales.

The inquiries from *Research/Development* for the Multi-Vac were of such outstanding quality, both as to establishments and the individuals making the inquiries, that Lindberg Hevi-Duty decreased the size of the ad to a two-thirds page ad *with a coupon* to make it immediately obvious to readers that the company wanted a response.

Two new advertisements were produced by Marsteller Inc. to go

From vacuum to quench in 10 seconds

Quench parts quickly—without exposing them to air—with Lindberg Hevi-Duty's Multi-Vac vacuum furnace system. Vacuum-to-liquid quench is a new accessory that enables Multi-Vac to work even harder.

Of course, Multi-Vac already does the work of six furnaces. It's a high-temperature horizontal cold-wall. Or a vertical cold-wall. An induction melting furnace. An arc melting and casting furnace. Or a manual welding chamber and manual dry box. Just by changing chamber accessories.

Buy the system with only the accessories you need. Add others when you need them.

For the full story, return the coupon to Mr. Bill Henneman, 2450 West Hubbard Street, Chicago, Illinois 60612. Or call him at 312/666-3443.

Mr. Henneman, please send me the full story on the Multi-Vac system.

NAME
TITLE
COMPANY
STREET
CITY STATE ZIP

LINDBERG HEVI-DUTY SB
DIVISION OF SOLA BASIC INDUSTRIES

OTHER DIVISIONS: ANCHOR ELECTRIC · ENGINEERED CERAMICS · HEVI-DUTY ELECTRIC · NELSON ELECTRIC · SOLA ELECTRIC

Melt, weld, treat and cast with this one vacuum furnace

This Lindberg Hevi-Duty Multi-Vac system converts to handle half a dozen different vacuum and inert-atmosphere metallurgical processes.

Multi-Vac changes quickly from an induction melting furnace to an inert-gas welding chamber . . . a high-temperature vertical furnace . . . a high-temperature horizontal furnace . . . an arc melting and casting furnace . . . or an inert-gas manual dry box. Conversion is simple. Anyone can do it on the spot.

Savings are tremendous compared to the alternative: many single-purpose units. And Multi-Vac takes far less floor space . . . with one power supply, one pumping system and one chamber.

For the full story, return the coupon to Mr. Bill Henneman, 2450 West Hubbard Street, Chicago, Illinois 60612. Or call him at 312/666-3443.

Mr. Henneman, please send me the full story on the Multi-Vac system.

NAME
TITLE
COMPANY
STREET
CITY STATE ZIP

LINDBERG HEVI-DUTY SB
DIVISION OF SOLA BASIC INDUSTRIES

OTHER DIVISIONS: ANCHOR ELECTRIC · ENGINEERED CERAMICS · HEVI-DUTY ELECTRIC · NELSON ELECTRIC · SOLA ELECTRIC

on the first page of *Research/Development's* Vacuum Technology section; they dominate the page because the other column is the table of contents for this specialized section of the book. This page naturally enjoys high readership.

Response is made easy because of the coupon—and also because Bill Henneman's name (he's the product manager who handles Multi-Vac) is given, as is his phone number. Telephone response has been little short of amazing. Mr. Henneman initially took rather a dim view of having his name in the ads—not because of bashfulness, but because he honestly wasn't convinced it would accomplish anything.

No longer does he doubt the effectiveness of having the name of the man in charge of the product in the ad—not after an unbelievable number of prime buying influences in major research establishments throughout the country called him long distance for additional product information, application information, prices, or to request that he pay a personal call on them. Such requests—and Mr. Henneman has had a number of them—result in a very high ratio of sales. Few people ask a man to fly halfway across the country to call on them merely because of idle curiosity, particularly individuals who occupy the important positions these inquirers hold.

The couponed two-thirds page ads Lindberg Hevi-Duty ran alternately in *Research/Development* produced the following returns in the first six times up at bat:

From vacuum to quench . . .	25
Melt, weld, treat and cast . . .	28
Melt, weld, treat and cast . . .	44
From vacuum to quench . . .	38
Melt, weld, treat and cast . . .	32
From vacuum to quench . . .	*27
Melt, weld, treat and cast . . .	*29

This is an average of 33 inquiries from complete months, although *Research/Development* usually pulls inquiries for several months after issue. The number of returns is by no means sensational, but this is to be expected. The total market for this intricate, specialized product is not large. According to the product manager, telephone inquiries continue to come in at a surprising rate—and they are, of course, in addition to the bingo cards received.

Quality of the inquiries continues to be outstanding, and a number of sales have been made; the potential number of sales runs so high that Mr. Henneman says, "It kind of scares me to think about it."

A recent study for Bausch & Lomb showed that its inquiries were being converted at a rate that is most satisfactory. The manufacturer ran a two-thirds-page, black-and-white ad in *Research/Development* that generated 39 inquiries.

When followed up by mail, 22 questionnaires were returned; this is a response of 56.4 percent.

Of those inquirers who responded, two had already purchased

*Incomplete

a Bausch & Lomb V.O.M.-6 Recorder when an inquiry followup was done; this is 9 percent of the inquirers.

What's more, *nine* other inquirers stated there was a "good likelihood" they will purchase a V.O.M.-6 Recorder; this is 41 percent of the inquirers.

Since the instrument is priced at $700, this one fractional page ad produced $1,400 in sales and developed a potential of an additional $6,300 in sales. And this is only from inquiries; there is no way to determine how many more prospects might be considering purchasing one of Bausch & Lomb's Recorders, but have yet to take the first step toward doing so.

How to Get the Most Out of Inquiries

There's no magic formula, no pie-in-the-sky when it comes to milking the largest possible dollar volume of sales out of the maximum number of clean inquiries your advertising-communications program can generate.

Notice that *clean* inquiries are specified. Clean inquiries come from publications with proven performance when it comes to converting inquiries to sales. Far too many magazines sell circulation—circulation that has been forced past the point where the universe has been saturated. This inevitably results in a larger volume of inquiries, but many of them will be from Indians too low on the corporate totem pole to be honest-Injun buying or specifying influences.

You're much better off with fewer inquiries of higher quality—cleaner ones, that is.

And don't let your enthusiasm run rampant and your hopes fly high due to a large number of created inquiries. These are inquiries that some publications produce by multiple listing of products; first, for example, may be an advertisement you run. Then comes a publicity release about the product which coincidentally appears in that same issue. After this comes a wrap-up of some offshoot of the bingo card, cloaked in sanctimonious pseudo-editorial language, all ready to clip and shoot in for more free literature. Such inquiries don't produce much in the way of sales as a rule.

Instead of concentrating with grim tenacity on producing the most possible inquiries, publishers rather should try to screen inquiries for advertisers.

A ridiculous mistake made by many advertising departments is to forward literature to an inquirer and send a copy of the inquiry-handling form to the appropriate salesman—but neglect to tell him one little thing. Such as what product or model of the product is involved. This leaves the salesman in the dark so he's unable to tailor a presentation for this particular prospect. So simple, yet it happens so often. And it reduces the value of the inquiries.

Other industrial advertising departments generalize too much. On the off-chance of selling somebody something, just anything apparently, a footlocker full of literature on every product the company has manufactured in the last 60 years is sent to any and all inquirers. This leaves *them* out in the cold because nine times out of 10 the literature is not specific; it doesn't present the one product they're interested in, it doesn't discuss the one application they have for it. This cools prospects off fast.

Few industrial advertisers give prices, apparently feeling that charging a fair price for a well-made product is inherently unfair and that the industrial buyer isn't able to judge value received with any great degree of exactitude.

This is a false assumption. Surveys have shown that more than two-thirds of all industrial inquirers have expressed a desire for price information—yet it's almost never supplied.

Don't harbor the impression that a salesman can "soften the blow" of what your product costs. If the quality is there, if your company reputation is up to par, and if delivery is made when it's promised, price comes afterwards; it won't scare off the prospect. More than likely quoting at least a ball-park price will increase the returns on your inquiry qualification cards by approximately 20 percent. Try it and see.

It's a known fact that mention of price increases readership of ads. McGraw-Hill's Laboratory of Advertising Performance reports two instances. In the case of power supplies, price mention increased the Seen rating of ads by 80 percent and the readership *more than two and one half times*. With test and measuring equipment and instruments, Seen was up 19 percent and Read was up 31 percent when price was given in the ad. Inquiries go up as readership goes up, of course.

Generate inquiries, screen them, handle them fast and properly and they'll produce sales. Fumble any one of the steps and you're shuffling paper.

Chapter 15

READERSHIP MEASUREMENT

DETRACTORS of advertising—and industry harbors an overabundance of them—are wont to declare whenever the opportunity arises (they'll even *make* the opportunity) that advertising is an inexact art; it is not a science, it is created by hunch and hope, and it is largely intuitive. That last word is a dirty one, by the way, and is supposed to be a real crusher.

These detractors immediately add, as if this eliminates all questions as to the validity of their antediluvian babblings, that nobody has yet proved the effectiveness of industrial advertising.

Its only staunch upholders are the company's advertising manager and his agency counterparts, and they have, after all, a personal stake in advertising.

Maybe, say the dinosaurs who achieved management status by pure chance and by constantly looking backward, never forward, as well as by always keeping a closed mind, we're actually squandering all of that money to run advertisements nobody reads!

When that remark is made you can see past the horror-stricken look—without benefit of X-ray vision—the slide rules sliding in those engineering minds as they compute the profit the company *could* have shown if only that wasteful advertising had been entirely eliminated.

This is a wonky argument indeed.

Without going into how to justify advertising to management at this time, let's look instead at methods of determining the actual readership your advertisements received, and how you can put this information to good use in your planning and in your creative activities.

Having firm data also enables you to refute the "advertising isn't read" chant from the walnut-paneled offices.

Readership of your advertisements is measured regularly by organizations whose specialty this is. They use a carefully controlled sample, usually a given number of people, from the circulation of the publications whose readership they measure. The information they develop is solid. It's authoritative. It is statistically correct within a negligible margin of error. Readership isn't a dream or a hope or a yearning, it's something definite that has been proven. It simply cannot be questioned.

These measurements, called readership studies, are conducted by both independent research organizations who are paid either by the advertisers and/or the publications, or entirely by the publications.

In addition to telling how well read advertisements are, readership studies tell *why* some ads are well read and others get the back of people's mental hands—if the results are carefully analyzed.

Such reasons why ads perform as they do, why people are attracted to them and read them provide the background information that leads to guidlines the ad manager and agency people can follow. Such guidelines greatly reduce the chances of producing an ad that "bombs out," as the teen-agers are wont to say.

Perhaps the most valuable benefit of all from readership studies, though, is the fact that they make possible an honest, objective evaluation of advertisements you're currently running. Studies enable you to see if your ads are achieving the communications objectives of your program, or coming close to it. Regardless of what the objectives are, your ads must be *read* before they stand a chance of achieving them.

What's more, readership studies make it possible for you to analyze the strengths and weaknesses of *your competitors' advertising.*

Naturally, this is not to suggest that your copy borrow, "improve upon the technique," or otherwise scuttle your own program and adapt a competitor's to your company and your product. If your competitors happen to be running a particularly effective campaign, it behooves you to know about it. Never react to competitive advertising, however. Doing so puts you on the defensive.

The intelligence you garner from close examination of the analysis of your competitors' ads cannot help but be very revealing about their communications objectives, and perhaps it will even enable you to make an informed guesstimate as to their marketing objectives.

And examining the readership ratings your competitors achieve will give you a good clue of how close they're coming to achieving what they set out to do.

Business Magazine Readership Studies

Almost 300 leading business publications offering nearly *five times* that many readership studies to their advertisers are tabulated annually by Tom A. Kallas, vice-president and director of research, Buchen-Reincke, Inc., Chicago.

Some publications offer readership studies by more than one research organization.

One prominent construction book, for example, has studies conducted by Daniel Starch & Staff made in February, March, April, May, August, and November. In addition, the publication is studied by Readex in January, March, April, May, October, and November. This gives advertisers an opportunity to compare the results of studies taken independently of each other. It is a very desirable cross check. Corroboration of an advertisement's performance by a different service results in a high degree of validity.

And *Purchasing* uses Readex for six issues, Starch for another half-dozen.

Using two different firms is expensive for publishers; for that matter, using even one research organization to conduct studies is costly. But it is worthy of note that the *leaders* in business publishing offer this service to their advertisers.

They have nothing to fear in having advertising readership disclosed; marginal publications seldom offer such services, perhaps for this reason. Readership of advertisements is contingent upon readership of editorial, and this is where the marginal publications falter badly.

Averaged out, the grand total of studies reported by Kallas comes to only five per book for the entire year.

This is too few.

It is simply not enough on which to base an informed judgment of how your campaign is doing. In the case of a book offering just four studies, for instance, this means that only four out of a minimum of six ads you'll probably run can be studied. And if one or two ads happen to be repeated during that period, you'll learn much less.

By rights, every issue of a monthly publication should be studied, at least 13 issues of a biweekly should be studied, and the figure should climb to a minimum of 26 times for a weekly magazine.

This is particularly true because publishers understandably put an extra sales push on studied issues, using the study as an inducement to persuade advertisers to buy space in those issues. What this accomplishes is having advertisers tending to concentrate their ads in studied issues to the exclusion of nonstudied ones immediately preceding and following.

As a consequence, studied issues are usually fatter by far than are regular issues. Traditionally, ads have encountered harder going in fat issues than in thin ones due to the intensity of the competition for the reader's time. Using studied issues when there are only a few during the year could thus place the advertising manager in the untenable position of deliberately selecting issues that he knows ahead of time will be less productive for his company.

Upshot of this is that the publisher who is ostensibly doing the advertiser a great big favor by providing the readership service in the first place, actually does his advertisers a disservice by forcing them unwittingly into issues where the competition is much greater.

The *only* way out of this built-in booby trap is for industrial advertisers to clamor long and loud for more studied issues.

How Readership Studies Are Conducted

A discussion of the major services follows, along with a brief description of how the studies are conducted. All of the studies discussed are continuing studies, not occasional ones or one-time-only efforts. Again, the author is indebted to Tom A. Kallas of Buchen Advertising, Inc. for his assistance, and to the research organizations themselves for their help in supplying information and background material.

Measuring readership of industrial advertisements in the business press has approximately a 20-year history. During this period some 25-30 different services have sprung up, encouraged by the intense interest industrial advertisers have exhibited in determining how well-read their ads are.

Statisticians and psychologists continue to probe and experiment for new and better tools with which to measure readership, and to interpret the results once they have them.

An area in which a glaring weakness exists and in which there is a dearth of information is in projectability of the results of the studies. So far few, if any, of the services have proven to the satisfaction of hard-nosed skeptics among us that the results of the surveyed sample of a publication's circulation can be projected across the entire circulation with anything approaching 100 percent accuracy—or even 90 percent, for that matter.

In addition, more information as to *why* readership ratings result as they do is needed; this calls for additional research.

Starch Readership Service

Starch reports will be discussed first because Daniel Starch pioneered in measuring advertisement readership in the business press. Starch reports are available from Daniel Starch & Staff, Boston Post Road & Beach Avenue, Mamaroneck, New York 10544.

The Starch Readership Service measures the reading of advertisements in the business press using a standard technique developed by

Dr. Daniel Starch and his staff in some 28 years of continuous experience in readership studies.

More than 500,000 advertisements have been studied since the beginning of the service. Annually, the Starch program covers 30,000 advertisements in 1,000 issues of consumer and farm magazines, business publications, and newspapers. Over 240,000 personal interviews are made each year in order to carry out this program.

The Starch Readership Service provides a continuous source of readership data that answers the following questions:

1. To what extent is my advertisement seen and read?

2. Are my present advertisements better read than past advertisements?

3. Are my advertisements better read than those of my competitors?

4. Is the reading of my current campaign increasing or decreasing?

5. How can I tell my ad story so that it will be better read?

Starch employs the "recognition" method in its surveys. With the magazine open, the respondent tells to what extent he has read each ad. Three principal degrees of reading are measured for each advertisement:

"Noted"—is the percent of readers who remembered that they had seen the advertisement in the particular issue.

"Seen-Associated"—is the percent of readers who have seen or read any part of the ad which clearly indicates the product or advertiser.

"Read Most"—is the percent of readers who read 50 percent or more of the written material in the ad.

In addition, data are collected on the observation and reading of the component parts of each ad—headline, subheads, pictures, logotype, copy blocks, and so forth.

Starch studies use a national sample of 20 to 30 areas for each study. Each sample parallels circulation by geographic area and urban and suburban areas.

Interviewers must find, within a particular area, an assigned number of readers; it is intended that the results obtained will be representative of the readers of the magazine studied. Most interviews are conducted in the respondent's place of business.

Size of the sample varies by publication. It varies from 100 to 200 interviews, depending on the size and type of the magazine; 100 is the sample size for most business publications.

Each interviewer working for Starch is assigned a specific number of interviews to be obtained on each publication assigned to her. To minimize bias, the quota for each interviewer is small. Thus, a Starch study reflects the work of 30 to 40 interviewers.

Interviewing begins a reasonable length of time after the issue has been mailed, to permit respondents time to obtain and read their copy. Interviewing is conducted on weekly and biweekly publications only after respondents have had sufficient time to read their magazine—usually from 10 days to two weeks. Interviewing periods were established as a result of tests to determine the optimum time period for obtaining typical readers.

Before interviewing, each ad to be studied is "coded" uniformly in the interviewer's copy in accordance with a bulletin prepared in Starch's home office. The bulletin lists code numbers for the component parts of the ad. Thus, the readership of the various parts of all ads is reported uniformly.

The sample is not a panel. No respondent is *asked* to read the issue prior to the interview. The first step is to determine if the respondent has possession of the issue and qualifies as a reader because he had previously opened and read some part of the issue prior to the interview.

Having fulfilled these requirements, the respondent is then questioned on his observation and reading of specific ads. The interviewer goes through the issue with the respondent page by page inquiring about each ad under study. The starting point is randomized in order to equalize the fatigue element in long interviews.

The respondent is asked, "Did you see or read any part of this advertisement?" If yes, he is asked to indicate exactly what was seen or read. These questions determine which component parts of each ad the respondent saw or read. Component part readership is obtained: (1) to assure that the respondent actually had read the advertisement, and (2) to determine what parts were seen and read.

All data resulting from the interviews are recorded on standardized questionnaires. After the interviewing is completed, approximately one week is allowed for all interviewers' sheets to reach the Starch home office where they are tabulated, and printing requires about three weeks.

Readership results are placed on IBM cards and tabulated by IBM machines.

Results are expressed for the three degrees of reading: "Noted," "Seen-Associated" and "Read Most" in terms of percentages, readers per dollar, cost ratios and ranks.

Percentages reflect the actual percentage of readers who indicated they saw or read a given ad. For example, of the 100 readers interviewed on a certain issue of *Production* magazine the readership of a Continental Screw Company ad might be:

Noted	Seen-Associated	Read Most
37%	29%	13%

Readers Per Dollar indicates the number of primary readers attracted by the ad for each dollar invested in space cost.

"Readers per Dollar" = Magazine (Primary) Readers Multiplied by % "Noted" "Seen-Associated" or "Read Most"

Divided by Space Cost.

Cost Ratios express the relationship between Readers per Dollar and the corresponding *median* average Readers per Dollar for all half-page or larger advertisements. A Noted Cost Ratio of 175, for example, would mean that from a standpoint of having stopped the reader, the ad did 75 percent better than par for all ads in the issue.

Ranks show the numerical order of the Readers per Dollar for all ads listed from the highest (Rank 1) to the lowest.

In addition to these figures for each ad-as-a-whole, percentages are computed to show seeing and reading of the various component parts of each advertisement.

The final report consists of a summary sheet showing the overall percentages, readers per dollar, cost ratios, and ranks for all ads, grouped by product categories. The summary sheet is attached to a labeled copy of the issue in which each ad is marketed to show the percentage results for the ad-as-a-whole and for each component part checked for readership. All ads one-half page or larger are included in these studies. Smaller ads may be included on advance notice.

Starch gives some overall findings. Among them are that ads differ enormously in readership. Two ads may be of equal size and color, for the same type product, appear in the same publication, in fact in the same issue, and one may attract two or three times as many readers as the other—and as much as seven or eight times as many thorough readers.

Readership provides data on two factors causing this difference:

1. Product Interest. People are more interested in some products than they are in others.

2. Communicative power of an ad is indicated by the extent to which the readership of a particular ad or campaign rises above or falls below the general interest level or the product group.

How to Use Starch Reports

The readership data contained in Starch reports are actually "working tools" with which an advertiser or agency can build better ads. These working tools must be acccumulated before performance of the campaign can be determined. If the data on a single ad is merely compared to the results of another ad, the data can serve only as a "score sheet." Figures for individual ads should not be used for sharp comparisons, but should be regarded as broad indicators subject to modification with the addition of more data. The Starch Readership Service is designed to provide continuous surveys on a large number of ads.

In order to realize the greatest potential use of the readership data, the following points must be kept in mind: (1) Average figures for several insertions rather than use figures for single ads, (2) look for recurring factors so as to establish trends and principles, and (3) season judgment with common sense.

There are many ways in which readership data can be meaningful. The method to be used depends upon your needs and desires. Outlined below are several ways in which the data can be compared:

1. Comparison of your ads (and your competitors') against previous ads.

2. Comparison of your current campaign (and your competitors') against an old campaign.

3. Comparison of your campaign (and your competitors') against product group averages.

4. Comparison of your campaign averages (and your competitors') against broad averages—Adnorms Reports.

Starch Readership data can be used to determine:

1. Relative effectiveness of size and color, page position, season of the year, and so on.

2. Relative effect of internal characteristics such as headline, illustration, layout, and so forth.

3. Best scoring ads.

Use of Starch Readership Reports in this manner will provide a useful analysis of the performance of your advertising, as well as a practical means of improving its effectiveness in the future.

Reports are purchased directly from the Starch organization. They usually become available about six or eight weeks after issue. Cost of individual reports varies from around $25 to $75, depending upon the quantity purchased and the magazine studied. The publishers whose books are being studied actually pay the major cost of these studies.

Starch stresses that average figures for several insertions are more meaningful and useful than are single ad figures. The studies usually cover 80 to 90 items. This includes the ads, plus the editorial measurements that are delivered to the publisher on a confidential basis. Starch tries to avoid measuring as many as 100 items in an issue and feels that it would probably be more accurate to state that up to 80 ads can be included in the study.

Anaconda's High-Rated Ad

How Starch annotates studied ads is shown by Anaconda American Brass Company's outstanding one-page four-color ad. This ad, which appeared in *Production* magazine, scored an exceptionally high Noted rating of 64, as will be seen from the large sticker at the top of the ad—the one headed "Ad as a whole."

Seen-Associated rating for Anaconda American Brass Company's great ad is an unusually high 47, and Read Most is 14.

This ad topped all other studied advertisements in this issue of *Production* in all three degrees of readership. This ad beat all others in attracting readership, even four-color spreads.

And when it comes to delivering a large number of prospects on a readers-per-dollar basis, Anaconda's advertisement really produces measured against this criterion, also. Cost ratios, according to Starch, are as follows: Noted, 181; Seen-Associated, 171; Read Most, 175. This means the ad worked a bit over three-fourths again as hard as the median for the book.

Because it is a four-color advertisement, the ad would have been expected to produce approximately 50 percent more readership than would a comparable black-and-white ad, of course. But this ad did even better.

THINK COPPE
READ
3
AD AS A WHOLE
64 47 14
SEEN
64
READ
41
You'll net greater durability and fatigue resist
with modern coppermetals
Today's fatigue-resistant coppermetals are design to resist st nd strains either indoors or out . . . stand up
against conditions that often cause other metals t ak away at the point they're most needed.
Think of the durability and fatigue resistan netals. Then think of their other practical
qualities, such as conductivity, machinability, bility, corrosion resistance and the wide
range of colors and finishes available. Then call us.
TEXT READ
SOME MOST
17 14
SIGNATURE
46
For High Performance Alloys Think...
ANACO
AMERICAN BRASS

Not illustrated is the back-up of the four-color ad, this page in two-color, orange and black. This also achieved unusually high readership. This is due in part to a rub-off effect from the preceding four-color ad which really pulled the readers in, as well as to the fact that the advertiser gave the reader product benefits and solid nuts-and-bolts product information. And even with all of the individual elements in the ad, layout is clean and attractive—and the advertiser used a highly readable serif type face that's easy on the eyes.

One-Color Ad Scores Well

Let's look now at the number one black-and-white one-page advertisement in the same issue of *Production*, Kimberly-Clark's fine ad illustrated nearby.

The ad as a whole received a Noted score of 35, Seen-Associated 28, and Read Most 10. Compared to the issue median of 21 percent Noted, this ad lured a full 60 percent more readers than did the ad that ranked right in the middle.

It's apparent from the scores on various elements of the ad that readership was thorough and that interest for the reader was sustained from illustration to signature. Every element held up its end and contributed to the total impact.

Kimberly-Clark Corporation's excellent ad ranked 17th in the issue of studied ads, Starch said. Considering that this compares a one-page black-and-white ad with spreads, two-color spreads, and one-page four-color ads—as well as four-color spreads—this is bragging performance, nothing less.

Even more noteworthy, though, and of greater importance to the advertiser is the teriffic job the ad did of delivering an unusually large number of readers per dollar.

Cost Ratios of Kimberly-Clark's black-and-white ad were extremely high—highest, in fact, of any studied advertisement in this issue of *Production* with the exception of one two-thirds page two-color ad on saw blades and drills. What makes the performance of Kimberly-Clark's ad especially impressive is that it is for a product of low inherent interest. Despite a heart full of love for the homely disposable paper wipers that bring in the salary, even industrial marketing manager T. L. LaPin admits the product lacks inherent appeal—although Kimberly-Clark's *selling proposition* is superb.

Here are the Cost Ratio figures for this ad: Noted, 189; Seen-Associated, 193; Read Most, 238. Hard-working advertising dollars, those!

Starch always includes directions on how to use and interpret the study in every copy that's sent to a client; it's a handy memory refresher. Also available on request from Starch headquarters or one of the many local offices across the country is a variety of literature explaining the Starch system in more detail, and with many

PRODUCTION December 1967

AD AS A WHOLE
Noted Seen-Asso. Read Most
M% 35 28 10
W%

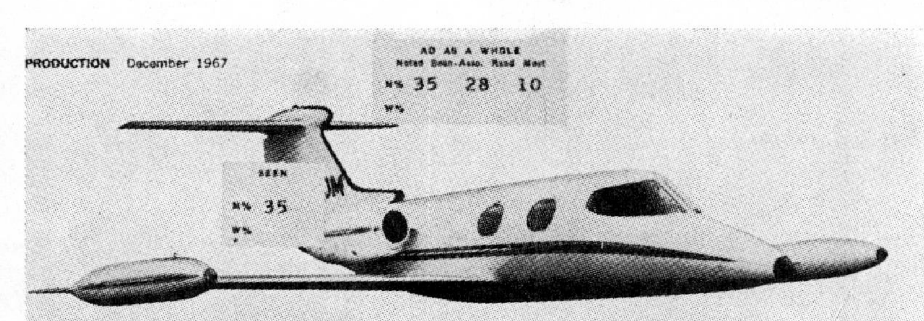

Although this builder
of executive jets

READ
M% 26
W%

ves a small fortune
by using our
disposable paper wipers
instead of cloth,

True, the r... is not to be sneezed at. Savings of over $5,(... shop towels is definitely a ... ore. Our towels are inert, ... ive, clean, and fresh. They ... gs, cuttings, or paint chips—things that can infest even a newly-laundered cloth towel.

TEXT READ
SOME MOST
M% 12 10
W%

So our wipers are perfect for all manufacturing that cannot tolerate contamination of any sort. And this holds for everything from jets to jellybeans.

If you too have a critical wiping operation, why not call your local distributor or write us at Neenah, Wisconsin? We know what counts.

that's not what counts.

KIMBERLY-CLARK FAMILY
NDUSTRIAL WIPERS
WELS® KIMWIPES® KAYDRY® LITHOWIPES® TERI®TOWELS

Write, wire or call Commercial Products Department
KIMBERLY-CLARK CORPORATION
Neenah, Wisconsin 54956 · 722-3811 (414)

This one-page black-and-white ad by Kimberly-Clark Corporation outscored two-color and full-color spreads in the same magazine.

helpful suggestions for making more effective use of the research material once you have it. You'll probably find it interesting.

Ad-Chart Awareness Study

Ad-Chart Awareness Studies are available from Ad-Chart Services, Chilton Company, Chilton Way, Radnor, Pennsylvania 19089.

Reports must be ordered directly from Ad-Chart Services, and they must be reserved in advance of the study. Cost is $50 per report. The reports are mailed from seven to nine weeks after issue date.

Ad-Chart Awareness and Advertising Management studies are an advertising measuring tool which gauges communication in selected business publications by means of:

1. Scientific probability sampling methods.
2. Personal interview of qualified primary readers of the magazine by trained personnel.
3. Carefully designed, pretested questionnaires.
4. Exact coding and tabulating procedures.

The studies reflect "how informative" an advertisement was to issue readers. Also, a highly useful separate section of the report lists both readership and information scores for those readers *who claimed purchasing or specifying influence in individual product or service categories.* These are the individuals to whom your message is primarily directed; these are the individuals who can make or break your company's sales.

Using Ad-Chart Awareness and Advertising Management studies helps the advertising manager answer the following kinds of questions:

- To what degree was my advertisement noticed and read?
- How informative did the readers find my advertisement?
- How well did the readers who claimed purchasing or specifying influence in my product category read my advertisement? How informative did they find it? Is there any difference between the scores of total respondents and those who claimed purchasing or specifying influence?
- What are the job titles, job functions, or job responsibilities of the reading audience?

- What is the effect on readership of a long-term advertising campaign?
- How did my advertisement's readership scores compare with the scores of other advertisements of the same size, and same color, and of the same type? How did it compare with ads in the same product category? (These would be ads run by competitors).

Studies are based on a minimum of 100 personal interviews of primary readers—not pass-on readers. Respondents are scientifically selected by means of a probability sampling procedure unique among reader measurement surveys. The sample represents the major characteristics of the publication's circulation, including geographic location, type of industry or business, and job title or job responsibility of respondents.

All personal interviews are conducted by professional Chilton Research personnel. The reader must first verify the claim that he read the issue. He is then taken through the publication (page starting points are varied to minimize position bias) and asked to indicate the extent to which he saw and read the advertisements under study, and how informative he found them.

Profile data on each respondent are also obtained.

Coding, tabulation and preparation of reports are under the direction of Ad-Chart Services.

What the Report Contains

An Ad-Chart Advertising Management report consists of three sections:

I. ANALYSIS OF RESPONDENTS provides the following basic profile information about the readers interviewed:

1. Respondents' job titles and functions.
2. Respondents' number of years in specific industry.
3. Respondents claiming purchase influence in each product category.

II. READERSHIP AND INFORMATION INDEX OF TOTAL RESPONDENTS provides quantitative information on reader traffic and information scores:

1. Readership scores for advertisements divided into "Noticed," "Started to Read," and "Read Half or More" percentages.

2. Scores ranked by advertisement size and color within each product category.
3. Informative scores for advertisements.

III. READERSHIP AND INFORMATION INDEX OF RESPONDENTS CLAIMING PURCHASE INFLUENCE IN PRODUCT CATEGORIES provides quantitative information on reader traffic and information scores:

1. Purchase influence readership scores for advertisements divided into "Noticed," "Started to Read," and "Read Half or More" percentages.
2. Scores ranked by advertisement size and color within each product category.
3. Informative scores for advertisements.

Definitions of Report Terms

Product Category—Division into which the product or service advertised is placed according to use and function.

Advertiser—Name of manufacturer or company.

Page—Page number in issue where advertisement is found.

Size/Color—Shown by following code: P-page; BW-black-and-white; 2C—two-color; 3C—three-color; 4C—four-color; INS—insert; BLD—bleed; SPRD—spread; ROP—run of press.

Averages for Product Category—Average percentage scores of all advertisements in product category. Advertisements are ranked within each product category according to size and color.

Questions frequently asked about Ad-Chart Awareness and Advertising Management studies are:

How does Ad-Chart differ? Ad-Chart is not just another readership study. Rather, it is a management and marketing tool for advertisers and agencies. Readership information is only one part of an Ad-Chart report.

Some of the ways that Ad-Chart is different include the following.

A. National probability sample of magazine's circulation.

B. Results scientifically projectable to primary reading audience. (This is one of the possible shortcomings of other studies.)

C. Telephone screening determines current issue readers.

D. Valid, time-tested questioning technique.

E. Personal interviewing.

F. Only primary readers interviewed.

G. Readership and informative scores *for purchasing influence respondents,* as well as total respondents.

H. Number of items studied per issue limited to reduce respondent fatigue.

What are the advantages of Ad-Chart probability sampling? Professor George Katona, of the University of Michigan Survey Research Center, says, "for reliable, scientific investigations, aimed at a predetermined substantial degree of precision, there is no substitute for probability sampling." This is from his work, *The Psychological Analysis of Economic Behavior.*

Ad-Chart respondents interviewed are subsampled from a probability sample of a magazine's primary circulation, reflecting in miniature all of the major characteristics of the circulation.

These include geographic distribution, SIC, age, education, job title, job function and purchase influence in the case of business magazines. Appropriate demographic and marketing characteristics are also reflected for circulations of consumer magazines.

The most prominent advantages of an Ad-Chart probability sample are:

A. Projectability of results to total primary reading audience of a specific issue at the time of interviewing.

B. Accurate representation of actual reading patterns and market characteristics, at a fraction of the cost of a census-type survey.

C. Quick determination of changes in the character of the reading audience.

D. Objective evaluation of advertising performance and effectiveness.

E. Consistency in reporting results over time.

Is a sample of 100 really large enough? This question is asked frequently about Ad-Chart, as about other readership studies. In the case of Ad-Chart, the answer is an unequivocal *yes,* considering the normal needs of the user.

As a true probability sample, the Ad-Chart sample accurately reflects the percentage distribution of the major characteristics of a magazine's circulation—including readership—with an average sampling variation of less than four percentage points.

Composed of at least 100 completed personal interviews, an Ad-Chart sample is subsampled from a substantially larger probability sample of recipients of the publication.

Actually, the proportion of total circulation names drawn into an Ad-Chart sample is higher than the proportions used in many widely accepted government surveys.

The Ad-Chart probability sampling technique, based on a high completion rate, has proven to be reliable over hundreds of studies.

Moreover, since separate samples are used for each Ad-Chart study, the major characteristic results attain even more reliability over time.

What does an Ad-Chart Awareness Report include?

A. Full disclosure of methodology and procedures used.

B. Profile and marketing information about respondents interviewed.

C. Readership and information scores for 50 advertisements, presented by product groupings, of total respondents.

D. Readership and information scores for all respondents claiming purchasing influence, by product category.

Why Scores Are Higher

Why are Ad-Chart scores higher? The quality of Ad-Chart research reflects reading of an advertising and editorial message that is much closer to reality.

Quality controls, including a national probability sample, telephone screening for verified readers, and *personal* interviews with primary readers only, partly account for higher scores. Valid readership research, for example, has shown that primary readers read more intensively than do secondary readers.

Another factor is the number of advertisements and editorial items studied. Many readership services study as many as 125 items per issue; Ad-Chart limits items to 60. Thus, respondent fatigue is minimized and a more accurate response is obtained from the studied items.

In every Ad-Chart Awareness and Advertising Management study is a checklist to help the advertising manager make the most of the information the study provides him. This reads:

USE THIS CHECKLIST TO HELP ANALYZE
YOUR AD-CHART SCORES
IN THIS ISSUE OF *IRON AGE*

- ☐ Carefully check profiles of readers (white pages) to determine if publication is delivering the kinds of readers you desire.
- ☐ Compare your ad scores (yellow pages) with those of competitors.
- ☐ Compare your ad scores (yellow pages) with the averages for product categories.
- ☐ Compare your ad scores (yellow pages) with the averages for all ads of the same size and color on the green page.
- ☐ Compare readership scores for total respondents (yellow pages) with purchase influence scores on the blue pages.
- ☐ Compare your purchase influence scores (blue pages) with those of competitors.
- ☐ Compare your purchase influence scores (blue pages) with averages for product category.
- ☐ Pay particular attention to all your "informative" scores and relate them to your ad objectives.
- ☐ Have Ad-Chart complete a special breakout showing readership and nonreadership of your ad by corporate officials, engineers, department heads, etc., or perhaps by number of years in the field.

Mills Shepard Reports

Mills Shepard Reports are available from Mills Shepard, Inc., Hotel Gramatan, Bronxville, New York 10708.

The report is based upon a minimum of 100 completed and validated interviews.

The 100 sample is distributed so that it parallels the circulation of the publication being studied in the following major characteristics:

1. Geographic distribution.
2. Type of industry.
3. Title or responsibility of respondent.

The research technique employed is known as the "recognition method." As applied by Mills Shepard, it is based upon the following principles:

1. Personal face-to-face interviews.
2. Interviews with primary recipients of the book.
3. Careful determination of who had the issue prior to the interview.
4. Where the interviewer had an opportunity to go through the magazine, page by page, with the respondent, determining to the interviewer's satisfaction whether each advertisement had been seen previously and, if so, the extent, in detail, to which it had been read.

Fosdick Ad-Readership Service

Fosdick reports are available from John T. Fosdick Associates, Inc. 135 East 44th Street, New York, New York 10017.

Fosdick Associates has approximately 30 publications in the United States and Great Britain as clients. This independent market research firm has offered advertising readership measurement services since 1955.

Fosdick claims to be the only service that offers both mail and personal interview techniques. Which is used depends on the publisher's preference or discretion—and, perhaps, pocketbook. Most surveys are made by mail.

Sample size, Mr. Fosdick says, "is around 100 responses, as with nearly every other United States service." When personal interviews are used, the sample consists of 100 completed interviews with readers—persons who report they have already read the issue being measured; this takes place in 10 to 12 cities.

In the mail studies, questionnaires, including Product Application affidavits, are mailed to a systematically selected sample of readers. Like most other advertising readership services, Fosdick tabulates and reports results based on the first 100 mail responses.

What is different about the Fosdick service is that it includes a feature—Product Application Based Scores—not usually offered by other independent readership services.

Product Application Based Scores are a measure of the percent of survey respondents who exercise "buying influence" for a specific product or product class—that is, the percent who can be considered to be active prospects for the product at the time the survey was taken.

(Ad-Chart, it will be recalled, also determines how many *prospects,* as opposed to readers in general, read studied ads).

Fosdick computes and reports readership scores for each ad measured, first for all respondents (total sample), then separately for these active prospects.

Survey respondents complete a "buying power affidavit form"—in which each respondent is asked to check those product groups (tailor made for each publication) which have a direct application to his present job, and for which he participates directly or indirectly in the purchasing act.

Manville Ratings

This study is available from Richard Manville Research, Inc., 230 Park Avenue, New York, New York 10017.

The Manville Ratings are based on approximately 100 personal interviews with a cross section of a magazine's readers. These are "randomly drawn from the subscription lists in urban markets." Cities are preselected. A new sample is selected for each issue studied. No sample names are repeated. No home subscriptions are included in the sample.

Measurements are obtained for:

1. Percentage of readers who saw the ad.
2. Percentage of readers who read the ad.
3. Percentage of readers who read one-half or more of the ad.
4. Attitude-Change Score: An index score which attempts to measure the change in the reader's feelings toward the product as a result of exposure to the ad.
5. Manville Effectiveness Ratings: A composite index obtained by multiplying the Seen Score by the Attitude Change Score.

Attitude Change was measured as follows: For each ad read, respondents were asked, "In what way, if any, has your opinion *of this product* changed as a result of seeing this ad?" The scale is a numerical rating ranging from plus 4 to minus 4.

In a recent letter to the author, Mr. Manville observes—and it's very difficult to refute his contention—that "There is no necessary correlation between an ad which scored a high 'noted' score and ads which were effective. By 'effective' we mean an advertisement that increased the favorable attitude *towards the product.* Note that we are not measuring the ad, but the mind of the reader."

And the weight of logic is on Mr. Manville's side when he says, "We have dozens of case histories to show that ads which scored high in 'noted' scores, scored low in persuasiveness."

Noted and Persuasiveness do not necessarily go hand in hand like two lovers in the spring, but the fact remains that *to get the chance to persuade, the advertisement must first be noticed by the reader, it must stop him, interest him and he must read it. All of this precedes the act of persuading him.*

Other Measurement Services

Many highly professional readership measurement services are available to the advertising field. A number of them are listed below, together with their addresses. Information as to the scope and methodology of their services may be obtained from:

Ad-Chek Reports, 444 Madison Avenue, New York, N. Y. 10022

Ad-Reach Reports, 430 Park Avenue, New York, N. Y. 10022

Adscore Reports, P.O. Box 2446, Cleveland, Ohio 44112

Advertising Impact Measurement, 205 East 42nd Street, New York, N. Y. 10017

Cahners Audit, 221 Columbus Avenue, Boston, Mass. 02116

Com/Pact Reports, 2 South Devoe Avenue, Yonkers, N. Y. 10705

Dart Reports, 812 Huron Road, Cleveland, Ohio 44115

Media Echo, 345 East 47th Street, New York, N. Y. 10017

Read/Ad Reports, 2100 Lake View Avenue, St. Joseph, Mich. 49085

Reader Evaluation Reports, 2100 Lake View Avenue, St. Joseph, Mich. 49085

Reader Feedback Reports, 330 West 42nd Street, New York, N. Y. 10036

Reader/Rating Reports, P.O. Box 2608, Houston, Texas 77001

Reader Recall Reports, 850 Third Avenue, New York, N. Y. 10022

Reader Response, 820 Second Avenue, New York, N. Y. 10017

Reader's Choice Reports, P.O. Box 1589, Dallas, Texas 75221

Readerscore Reports, 537 Post Road, Darien, Conn. 06820

Readex Reports, 140 Quail Street, St. Paul, Minn. 55115

Score Reports, P.O. Box 28125, Washington, D. C. 20025

Perhaps in no other area of industrial advertising does as much confusion exist as in making use of the readership ratings that advertisements we've created have received.

Most industrial advertising men need a registered, bonded, well-trained guide to lead them through the bewildering labyrinth the various services have created due to a complete lack of comparability.

As Roger Barton wrote in *Media/scope,* "One of the factors that militates against the use of advertising readership studies on a comparable basis is differences in methods and findings that are found among the more than two dozen rating services.

"For instance, the average noted score for a one-page black-and-white advertisement studied by one service is 18 percent, that produced by another service 55 percent, and that by a third 33 percent."

This wide variation in what is considered "average" is indeed striking when it is seen in tabular form. Below is a list of the averages established by some of the leading services:

Service	What is Measured	Average Rating of a One-Page, Black-and-White Advertisement
Starch	Noted	18%
Mills Shepard	Remembered Having Seen	31
Ad-Chart	Noticed	55
Reader Feedback	Saw	33
Readex	Interest	12
Ad-Gage	Interest	5.9*
Advertising Impact Measurement	Read	34

Comparing the scores an advertisement earned in different publications that were studied by competitive services means nothing if the raw figures are compared because they are obviously apples and oranges, hence are not directly comparable.

Attempting to compare them can be very deceptive and lead to erroneous conclusions—particularly as regards how well-read various advertisements actually are. This is due in part to the methodology of various services, as well as to the fact that some ratings are for *interest* and others are for *readership.* There's a vast difference between them.

The only way in which the ratings become meaningful is if they are both compared to the average score for the particular issue of the publications that were studied. An ad is either average, above average, or below average. No figures can dispute this.

The striking difference that different readership services can show for the same striking advertisement is shown by the four-

*This figure is based on 49 studies conducted for *Foundry* magazine at this writing. The figure varies slightly from one issue to another, although seldom more than .2 percentage points.

What's a little bug
like you doing in
CINCINNATI?
Just making sure that NEW Acramatic IV is the world's most reliable NC contouring system . . .

The best NC
marriages are made in
CINCINNATI
Your new continuous path machine and our Acramatic IV would make a perfect match, because Acramatic IV has all the qualities an eligible contouring control should have: Feedrate control at any angle / Feedrate coded in four digits to 000.1 ipm / Automatic acceleration and deceleration / Continuously variable feedrate override / Feedrate division by 2, 4, and 8 / Tape search / Mirror image / Full range floating zero shift / Manual data input by selector switches.
This new integrated circuit system comes with a dowry of an APT III postprocessor, and full courses of instruction for your programmers and maintenance men. At your option, (for a reasonable price) you can also have our Acramatic IV with 500 lines per second tape reader, parabolic interpolation, circular interpolation, and cutter diameter compensation.
Better get in touch with us today. If you want a copy of our Acramatic IV catalog, ask for publication M-2869. If you want to talk business, ask for Jim Stergiopoulos, Manager of Sales, Cimtrol Division.
CINCINNATI
The Cincinnati Milling Machine Company
Cincinnati, Ohio 45209

Above: Pages 1 and 4 of four-page ad. Below: Inside spread pages.

page, four-color ad run by The Cincinnati Milling Machine Company. All four pages of this ad are shown so that readership ratings can be discussed.

As if being the most reliable NC contouring control system weren't enough, New CINCINNATI Acramatic IV is also the world's smallest and fastest . . .
Come off it, CINCINNATI. Where do you get this "world's most reliable" stuff?
Acramatic IV is the first continuous path NC system to use full integrated circuit logic. Accelerated life tests through millions of device-hours of operation, and more than a year of testing under actual production conditions, have demonstrated that Acramatic IV is ten times more reliable than previous systems. It is actually less subject to stoppage than the machines it controls!
You mean that all of Acramatic IV fits in that box? Where do you hide the rest of the hardware?
There isn't any more. One integrated circuit logic board in the new system replaces as many as ten in the old system. Every bit of Acramatic IV—tape reader, manual controls, readouts, logic, air conditioner are housed in that one box. (Oh yes—there does have to be a flexible cable to link Acramatic IV with whatever it controls.)
Let's get this speed business straight. Just what do you mean, "fastest"?
Is minimum cycle time of 0.00035 seconds fast enough to qualify for the record? The fastest other system we know about is 100 times slower. Such fast cycle time means that the control can use the fastest tape readers available. It can feed out interpolated span points and modulated feed rates faster than raw data can be fed in.
There must be something Acramatic IV doesn't have.
Well, Acramatic IV doesn't have a lot of precedents. It's too new. It's setting the pace. And Acramatic IV doesn't have an inflated price tag; in fact, it can cost less than earlier contouring systems. And you get so much more value—a faster, smaller, more reliable system.
And furthermore . . .

When this advertisement ran in now defunct *Steel* magazine in January it was rated along with the other ads in that issue; Daniel Starch & Staff conducted the study.

During the previous year, products in this category—machine tools—achieved the following average Starch Scores:

			Cost Ratios	
No. Ads	Noted	Read Most	Noted	Read Most
83	22.9	7.3	91.1	100.2

Cincinnati Milling Machine Company's excellent four-page, four-color ad scored as follows, with ratings for first page, the spread, and page four of the ad:

			Cost Ratios		
Page	Noted	Read Most	Noted	Read Most	Noted Rank
1	63	28	213	331	3
Spread	39	6	67	38	12
4	36	11	122	131	15

Noted ranks are based on readership percentages, regardless of size and cost of space. Cost Ratios are based on published rates. Preferred position charges are used for covers or when position charge is over 15 percent. Issue median for one-page ads, exclusive of inserts and/or four-color ads, is 21 percent. Here again, use of color paid off in much higher Noted scores and in higher readership, as well.

The month before Starch rated Cincinnati Milling Machine Company's four-color ad in *Steel,* Mills Shepard, Inc. studied the December issue of *American Machinist.* The ad ran in this issue of this publication, also. And here is one of the frustrating, confusing things about readership ratings—how very different they are from one research service to another, and from magazine to magazine.

In *American Machinist* Cincinnati Milling Machine Company's ad received the following readership, Mills Shepard reported:

Page	Remembered Having Seen	Read Partially	Read Thoroughly
1	80%	62%	45%
Spread	78	59	26
4	66	47	22

Starch's "Noted" and Mills Shepard's "Remembered Having Seen" are directly comparable—the classes of readership, that is, not the scores. So, too, are "Read Most" and "Read Thoroughly."

Yet Starch tallies up *more than three times* as high a Noted score as it does a Read Most, and Mills Shepard comes very close to reflecting this pattern.

On the surface, it would seem possible that *American Machinist* is a better medium for Cincinnati Milling Machine Company—and presumably for other manufacturers of machine tools—than is *Steel.* This is because of the higher readership this advertisement received in *American Machinist* as shown by the two studies.

This is one of the pitfalls of readership studies, however, and usually is not indicative of a valid conclusion. To assume one would be to compare dissimilar items and ignore all ground rules—or salient parameters, as the researchers are fond of saying. (It *is* a resounding way of saying "ground rules" and might look impressive in a memo if you're inclined.)

As we've seen, *the base scores for Mills Shepard ratings on one-page black-and-white advertisements are slightly more than 58 percent higher than the same ratings as determined by Starch—for any given ad.* This same relationship should hold true for four-color pages and for multipage four-color ads, as well.

Only when comparing the performance of the ad against the median for the issue, and for the median in the specific product category, can it be clearly seen just how well or how poorly an individual advertisement performed. Starch gives this information in its reports; none of the Mills Shepard reports at hand make this data available.

Upshot of it all is that figures don't lie, but it certainly pays to keep a weather eye on those who use them—or interpret them.

Because of this wide variation an Advertising Readership Committee was established by the Business/Professional Advertising Association. It set standards so that results of the different services would be more directly comparable without so much figure juggling. Another objective, according to *Media/scope,* was to set standards for the use of such research so it could be employed most profitably —and not misused. Figures can prove *anything.*

Advertising scores, as provided by the various readership services, have just one main purpose for being. By providing a yardstick, they encourage advertisers and agencies to prepare more effective ads.

Until something is measured it is pretty hard to make it better— or to know how to, that is.

So observed the Center For Marketing Communications (formerly MCRC) some years ago when considering the question of readership scores. The extreme difficulty of comparing and interpreting the scores caused the problem to be considered initially.

Too many questions remained unanswered. What, for example, does a score of 15 mean? Is it good, bad, or indifferent? And how good, bad, or indifferent?

The Letter Grade Ad Scoring System

Center For Marketing Communications is quick to point out there is yet another complication. For reasons as yet unknown, the *level* of scores will vary from issue to issue of the same publication as rated by the same service. Usually this variation is only a few points. However, it is not at all uncommon for the average score for one-page ads to vary all the way from 11 to 22 during the course of a year. In one issue of a book the Center analyzed, a score of 22 would be just average; in another issue of the same publication it would be one of the top ads in the book.

Inconsistency was the name of the game.

So CFMC determined just what it was that caused the discrepancies. It quickly found that different practitioners of industrial advertising had developed their own individual ways of interpreting scores. One way is to use issue medians, as discussed. Median scores are calculated for different-sized ads, and then individual ad scores are reported as so many points above or below the median.

However, there are several stumbling blocks in such a solution to the problem. First, it involves much time-consuming work. Second, there may not have been enough advertisements of a given size or product group in the issue to have the medians mean anything. Finally, users of the data are prone to exaggerate the significance of small differences from the median—if an ad is merely one or two points above the median, they are apt to assume immediately that it is an excellent ad, or vice-versa.

CFMC's Project Council for Analysis of Advertising Readership Studies worked assiduously for a year and a half on ways of cutting through this confusion, and in 1961 it introduced the Letter Grade Ad Scoring System.

This system, which is outlined below, surmounts most of the difficulties previously mentioned, and the reports based on it have been found to be easily understandable and meaningful to the users of readership scores.

As a matter of interest, it has been found that more than 80 percent of all industrial advertisers with budgets of more than $100,000 are consistent users of readership studies. Firms with lower budgets are occasional users, although a large number of smaller advertisers never avail themselves of the wealth of information at their fingertips—usually free for the asking. This may well be because of the confusion and lack of comparability of scores.

A total of 78 business publications have announced they will supply Letter Grade scores on ads; this is in addition to the readership ratings they normally make available to advertisers. In addition, a number of other magazines will give you Letter Grade scores *if you make the request.* Ask for them—they cost nothing and are immensely useful.

Essence of the Letter Grade Ad Scoring System is to rank ads as follows:

A—Ads that compare with the top sixth of all ads in the past year.

B—Ads that compare with the next sixth.

C—Ads comparable to the middle third of all ads in the past year.

D—Those in the next to bottom sixth.

E—Those in the bottom sixth.

Besides the basic A, B, C, D and E scores with which we've all been familiar since grammar school days, the very best advertisements are so outstanding they deserve special attention—so a special A+ classification has been established for these ads that are in the top 5 percent of all advertisements.

Readership By Prospects vs. Readership By Total Audience

Most industrial advertising managers, and agency men, too, for that matter, are preoccupied with readership ratings. They are beset with the obsession that their ads *must* achieve outstanding readership ratings; otherwise, they seem to feel, it is a reflection on their honor, their character, and their loyalty to flag and country.

Everybody concerned is hypnotized by sheer numbers, with quantity, with a burning desire to out-achieve all competitors in the great game of readership ratings. They are enamored with high ratings. Entirely overlooked is that the ads may be absolutely terrific, so great that the magazine's audience simply cannot refrain from reading. In fact, *most* of the audience reads the ads even if they have not one whit of interest in the product, don't need it, don't want it, can't use it, can't specify it, can't purchase it.

This is plain silly. It's carrying the matter far too far and attaching far too much importance to the ratings an ad receives.

It's much better to attract the attention of those who are legitimate prospects, those for whom your product solves a problem, those who can specify and purchase it.

This holds true despite the fact that your advertisement itself should qualify the readers so that those who are not prospects can skip over it, and those who are will—hopefully—read it.

If the advertisement is well-conceived and well-constructed and the right people read it, it can be a roaring success if it achieves only a 12 percent Noted, a 6 percent Seen-Associated, and 3 percent Read Most. If those who are your prime prospects are those who are reading your ads, those are very successful advertisements indeed.

You can determine this to some extent by the response to the ads. If your inquiry volume is high, if your negotiations activity is high, if your rate of conversion to sales is high, your ads are working overtime for you.

Now a readership service has related the readership of ads to the application of the product, service, or material to the reader's present job. John T. Fosdick Associates, Inc. customarily do this, relatively new as it is in the industrial field. This has been done for consumer audiences for some time, however.

Readership of the ad by *bona fide* prospects is, after all is done and said, of more critical importance than mere masses of readers who may or may not be prospective live customers. And this is undoubtedly one of the more important elements in measuring advertising effectiveness insofar as a readership service can determine it.

Fosdick's Product Application Test

To accomplish this, Fosdick has each reader report on each advertisement studied, stating whether the product, service, or material has an application in his work. Readership scores are then reported on this base as well as on total circulation.

This report not only tells you how many prime prospects an ad communicated with, but it tells you where they are and what their titles and/or job responsibilities are. This is invaluable information.

The outstanding one-page four-color ad run on the inside front cover of *Research/Development* by Ultek Division of Perkin-Elmer is shown as it appears in the annotated copy of the magazine. The original Fosdick stickers are attached to it. Let's see how this advertisement performed.

First of all, in the Total Reader Based Ratings, Ultek's ad achieved a phenomenal 62 percent in Noted, which is tops for this issue of the magazine. And in Read Some it scored 33 percent, also higher than any other advertisement in the January *R&D*. Not an ad to stop there, this great advertisement then went on to rack up a score of 14 percent in Read Over One-Half—again the highest such rating in the issue. Those high ratings apply to the magazine's entire audience, but this Fosdick study also measured Product Application.

Let's see how Ultek's ad did there.

As mentioned, when Fosdick measures Product Application, this means that readers who read the advertisement stated the product is used by his company. Besides that, though, he also either purchases the product or participates in purchasing it when it is bought by his firm. This is most significant because it measures the direct market potential for the advertised product in this specific magazine's audience. Again, Noted, Read Some, and Read Over One-Half are measured; this time, however, they are measured in relationship to readers who are actual prospects for the product.

Here, too, Ultek's fine ad romped away with the top Noted score in the book—a resounding 70. Second highest was 67 for an excellent Honeywell ad, but no other ad in the issue scored in the 60's or 70's. Ultek's ad garnered more readers who Read Some, with a rating of 50 percent; second highest score in this category was 32. When it comes to Read Over One-Half, Ultek scored a solid 15 percent; this was second in this issue of *Research/Development*. Top score was 23, although most of the other scores were under 10.

Thus it is apparent this fine four-color ad of Ultek's was read by the vast majority of all recipients of the magazine, which is desirable, of course. Even more important, though, it made a definite, measurable impression on most prospective purchasers of the advertised product who receive *Research/Development* magazine.

If Fosdick's measurement of prospects who read the ad prove to be projectable over the entire circulation of publications using this service, this will be a massive step toward providing additional meaningful information advertisers and agencies have long needed.

Readership Scores and Media Selection

Advertising men most familiar with readership studies—and even the various services themselves—strongly urge that readership ratings should not be used in selection of media.

Systems and numerical values used by the services differ too greatly to permit comparing results an advertisement achieved in one publication versus another magazine. An extremely high score in one book does not necessarily mean that medium is better for a given product or a specific advertisement than is a magazine in which the ad received a rating that was something less than sensational.

However, it is interesting to note that the various services have very carefully refrained from accepting as clients magazines that are direct competitors such as *Iron Age* and now defunct *Steel, Commercial Car Journal* and *Fleet Owner, Research/Development* and *Science & Technology.*

To do so would enable too many partially informed advertising people to leap to too many partially-correct conclusions—as well as too many that have little relevancy to the "true facts" of the matter. Because the fact is using readership ratings to determine that one publication is more desirable than another has little or no place in the scheme of things.

Leading business publications can and do provide proof of readership for the doubters, however, by means of studies of the audiences they reach. This data is competitive only in that it tends to make the publication disseminating it appear desirable; and making yourself look desirable is the world's fastest way to make yourself looked at with raised eyebrows. This information does not compare readership scores of advertisements in one magazine versus another, although probabilities are rightfully discussed. Every advertising manager and agency man has the right to request such information from publications—and *should* request it so as to have all pertinent facts at hand prior to making a decision.

Basford, Incorporated recently made a Basford Ad Exposure Ratio study for *Research/Development* magazine; the study was performed as much for the edification of the magazine's editors and publisher as it was for promotional purposes.

The AER (Ad Exposure Ratio) for *Research/Development,* as determined by Basford's study, was found to be 62 percent. This is the chance of a particularly interesting advertisement being seen in this magazine, as reported by those who read it regularly.

The study demonstrated that *Research/Development* magazine enjoyed 2.2 pass-along recipients for each subscriber. It also revealed that R/D readers receive and read an average of 3.5 of the 11 other publications listed. They receive 2.1 of these publications as primary readers and 1.4 as pass-along readers.

The study also seemed to reinforce other research indicating that primary readers are somewhat more likely to see advertisements than pass-along readers. The actual comparison in this study was 63 percent for primary readers and 37 percent for pass-along readers. This is slightly higher than figures from earlier studies showing that primary readers have, on the average, a 64 percent better chance.

Such research by an independent organization is accepted as

valid and is convincing proof that the publication is read. Most leading business publications have had similar studies performed and are perfectly willing to show the results. Such studies are one more bit of hard information on which to base media selections.

Factors That Influence Readership

In preceding chapters when the creative process was discussed, many factors affecting readership were touched upon because they influence how the ad should be constructed in order to get the maximum return from it.

There are many others, however—actually enough to fill a book almost this size. At this time some of the more important ones bear looking into. This will involve the slaying of a few fearsome dragons that have long threatened the happiness of hapless advertising men who practically cringe when confronted with them. These are negative factors, of course.

Others, while perfectly valid, bear remembering because they exert a positive effect on readership of your ads.

Some that have been kicking around for decades were of unquestioned validity 'way back when—but today is not 'way back when. Tremendous changes have taken place in industrial advertising and in the media in which it appears. Today's business press is well-edited, helpful, interesting, and attractive. It is a far cry from the many drab publications that people in industry were supposed to read 25 years ago "because it is good for you."

Let's examine a few of these factors that influence readership—or that don't influence it.

Front of the Book vs. Back of the Book

Before business publications achieved their present degree of sophistication, advertisers clamored for positions "up front." It was felt that readership fell off rapidly once the halfway point was reached, and that advertisements in the second half of the magazine were, in effect, consigned to some sort of unspeakable oblivion due to their position.

Considerable justification for this belief existed at one time. Readership *did* fall off drastically toward the back of the book. But today more knowledgeable editing spreads interest—and editorial matter—throughout the magazine so the reader no longer lingers longer in the front and middle of the magazine than he does toward the tag end.

Marsteller Inc., in its internal house organ *Pubset,* has this to say on the subject:

ADVERTISING READERSHIP, FRONT VS. BACK OF ISSUE?

This question has frequently been asked, so we've checked our library and marketing files with the following results:

1. Several years ago, the Daniel Starch readership research organization searched through researched issues of publications like *Time, Life, Satevepost, Good Housekeeping,* and *McCall's* to find identical advertisements which had appeared at least once in each of three positions in the magazines—front, middle, and back. They found 144 such ads. An analysis was conducted whereby the "front of book" score for each ad was assigned an index value of 100, and that same ad's performance was calculated as above or below 100 in the other positions. The index values were then converted back to readership scores, with this result:

	Noted	Seen-Associated	Read Most
Front	48%	44%	10%
Middle	45	41	10
Back	44	41	11

These data indicate that (exclusive of cover positions) readership is fairly uniform from front to back, at least for the publications included in the test.

2. The Starch organization also did a major analysis of 12 million inquiries. This analysis concluded that "large or small numbers of people read an advertisement dependent on two factors: (1) the natural inherent product and subject interest to the reader and (2) the characteristics of the advertisement itself—what it says and how it says it." Dr. Starch reported "whether an advertisement is within the first dozen pages or the last dozen pages is of relatively minor importance. To be sure, cover positions and pages facing them do have decided attention advantages." He went on further to say that "the front 10 percent of pages show a slightly higher rate of (inquiry) returns, but the difference in position is completely overshadowed by the substance of layout and copy."

3. Audits & Surveys studied an issue of *Life* and an issue of *Look* on a similar basis, and came to the same conclusion in both cases.

4. Conover-Mast's *Purchasing* magazine was analyzed also. A representative issue of the publication had 51 full-page ads (black-and-white and two-color). The readership scores were separated for the first 17, the second 17, and back 17, by positions in the issue, with this result:

	Average Noted Score
1st 17 ads	22.2%
2nd 17 ads	21.1
3rd 17 ads	21.8

5. A contributing editor to *Media/Scope* treated this subject as follows:

"There is sufficient evidence to suggest that reader traffic does not start at its

highest point on the first page and decrease continually to the last. There are peaks and valleys which reflect the efforts of magazine editors to maintain good pacing and reader interest throughout the issue."

All of which goes to show that trade publications are read front to back, thus laying to rest another old wives' tale.

One fact that's often overlooked is that "position" cannot help a bad ad or hurt a good one. An advertisement that's inept and uninteresting will not receive high readership simply because it happens to be right up in the very front of the book. It will receive low readership because it doesn't deserve high readership.

And a good advertisement will be read and be read by a sizable portion of the buying influences you're trying to reach if it's *really* a good advertisement, whether it's on Page 2 or Page 176.

Preferred Positions

Preferred positions, such as the inside front cover, cover 3, and the back cover, invariably receive higher readership than do the so-called "inside" positions. That is why they are able to command a premium price.

According to Starch, the back cover (Cover 4, it's often called) of the typical business publication receives approximately 65 percent more readership than does an inside page. The second cover (inside front cover) attracts about 30 percent more readers than do pages in the middle of the book. The third cover (inside back cover) also receives approximately 30 percent more readership than do inside pages.

Starch undoubtedly has a mass of statistics as high as Chicago's John Hancock building to back up his observations. As far as the fourth cover and the second cover are concerned, he's undoubtedly right. However, most knowledgeable industrial advertising men scorn third covers as not worth the extra cost. And it has been the author's experience that this is a "dead" position—one that is not only *not* worth more money, but actually one to be avoided. Ads for my clients and companies have never done well on any third cover in some two decades. This is one man's opinion compared with statistics.

Certain preferred positions inside the book which usually command a preferred-position price *are* good buys and can be depended upon to deliver higher readership than run-of-book positions.

For instance, the first page in the book, the one facing the inside front cover, usually tallies up around 25-30 percent more readers than do random pages inside the publication. But you pay more, too.

Pages facing certain editorial matter inside the book, such as the editor's editorial, for example, are charged for at a premium rate in most instances. But they invariably deliver more readers to the advertisement than it would receive in a run-of-publication position.

In its Laboratory of Advertising Performance, McGraw-Hill reports on an analysis of 89 issues of two of its magazines after 8,900 personal interviews by Daniel Starch & Staff. Involved were nine different advertisers whose advertisements had appeared inside the book and on various covers. Here is the readership they received:

Company	Second Cover	Third Cover	Fourth Cover	Run-of-book
A	27.9%			17.3%
B	25.3			16.1
C	20.8			16.5
D	19.0			14.3
E	16.6			13.9
F		27.0%		19.2
G			28.5%	14.2
H			26.2	23.0
B*			26.0	16.1

Readership advantages for cover positions ranged from 14 percent to more than 100 percent above that received *for the same type of advertisements* inside the magazine. On a 12-time basis, the average cover costs somewhat more than one-third more than an inside page; depending on the ad and on the company that runs it, this extra cost is usually offset by more than that much additional readership.

Advertisers are extremely fond of good preferred positions, and heads-up advertising managers and agencies have more than their fair share of these positions that give increased exposure and readership.

A tip: Get as many second and fourth covers as you can—in the best publications in your field, of course. Even if management wields the ax on the budget at some time in the future, it can frequently be dissuaded from forcing you to relinquish the cover positions. Once abandoned, they're usually gone forever for all practical purposes.

Cover positions in the leading trade publications have a formal "waiting list" of advertisers who are panting with ill-concealed eagerness to sew them up. The old Diamond T Motor Truck Com-

*One advertiser, Company "B," had experience with second covers, fourth covers and run-of-book inside pages.

pany, for instance, had a "bid" in for almost 10 years for the fourth cover of *Commercial Car Journal* before it became available.

Right vs. Left

In politics right is right and left is wrong, but we're discussing here the age-old question of right-hand pages versus left-hand pages. This is so controversial that a heated discussion of politics or religion is considered noncontroversial in comparison. Even the experts—or those who claim to be experts—disagree with each other on this.

For example, Starch studies of some publications show that right-hand pages have at least a 10 percent advantage over left-hand pages. This is due, no doubt, to the fact that most of us are both right-handed and right-eyed. As a consequence we hold a magazine so that the right hand turns the pages. And because this is the page that is thumbed to get a grasp on it so it can be turned, the mind automatically tends to concentrate more attention on this page than on the opposite, left-hand page.

Readex ratings of some magazines bear out the conclusion that Starch has reached.

On the other hand, Mills Shepard studies of *Electrical World* indicate that left-hand pages receive 2 percent more readership than do right-hand pages.

And McGraw-Hill's Reader Feedback studies show left-hand pages in *Textile World* receive 1 percent more readership than right-hand pages.

Probably the truth of the matter is that there's very little difference. Given a choice, though, which you usually are not, take the right-hand page. You'll be ahead in the long run.

Fat vs. Thin

Size of issue also affects the readership an advertisement receives. Publishers are understandably anxious to poo-poo the idea that fat issues of books cut readership of individual advertisements, and much research has been done in an effort to produce reliable data to dispel this idea. Most of it is undoubtedly valid, all of it is truthful.

McGraw-Hill states unequivocally that larger issues do *not* limit readership of advertisements. Instead, the publisher contends, the larger issues, if anything, offer a better chance of getting an ad noticed, along with an equal chance of getting the ad read.

A check of 147 issues of *Power* magazine and an equal number of issues of *Factory* showed that larger issues offer equal readership for the advertising and somewhat higher attention-getting values. Ads in seven issues of *Power* that were over 350 pages in length—the book, not the ads—averaged the highest Noted scores (22.9 percent of any size-group of that publication, and they maintained a Read Most average of 8.7 percent. *Factory's* 10 issues over 400 pages in length scored the highest Noted average (23.4 percent) of any size-group of *Factory,* and maintained a Read Most average of 8.8 percent.

This is all well and good, but the fact remains that advertisements in fat issues of books have *less time spent on each individual ad* than do ads in thinner issues.

The competition in fat issues is greater, too, for there are just that many more ads clamoring for the attention of the reader. This makes the job harder for each individual advertisement in the issue.

And readers do not spend proportionately more time on fat issues than they do reading thin ones. The overall trend is to spend more time reading business publications than was spent, say, 10 years ago. Time spent on various publications differs greatly according to the field, although the average for all business publications would seem to be in the neighborhood of 1½ hours.

That's per issue, and it doesn't change very much whether fat or thin.

Continuity

On-again, off-again industrial advertisers—and there are many of them—accomplish just one thing: They throw away the money they spend on advertising. They don't *invest* it in continuous planned advertising; they *waste* it on sporadic advertising that's done by fits and starts at the whim of top management—or as sales start to decline.

American Business Press put it just about as well as anybody has in quite some time when it discussed continuity in an advertisement recently. Its ad read, in part:

> *In advertising, you have to be as relentless as a 30-year-old girl looking for a husband.*

That's because prospects simply do not remember your company. There's no earthly reason why they should. The prospect is, naturally enough, self-oriented, not your-company-oriented. You and your company are the farthest things from his mind—unless you deliberately inject yourself there somehow, such as by advertising.

"If there is one enterprise on earth that a 'quitter' should leave severely alone, it is advertising. To make a success of advertising, one must be prepared to stick like a barnacle on a boat's bottom," so said John Wanamaker, merchant, who made a success of his business due in large part to continuous advertising.

One study showed advertisers who appeared in every issue of two business publications averaged 21 percent higher readership than did those who used five issues or less. Advertisers in one monthly business magazine increased their readership scores after becoming 12-time advertisers.

Another study showed that a company increased recognition of its primary message 12 percent by upping its space from 7 one-third pages to 10 pages. A similar company cut its space from 13 to 7 pages and lost 6 percent in recognition.

The Laboratory of Advertising Performance reports on a study of several thousand advertisements and the massive difference continuity makes. Advertisers whose insertions amount to 12 or more pages a year get almost a fourth more readers at only three-quarters of the cost per reader than do those using six pages or less. The figures look like this, using a base of 100 at the low end:

Annual schedule	Scored ads	Readership	Cost per reader
1 - 6 pages	1,007	100	100
7 - 11 pages	871	109	87
12 or more pages	1,567	123	74

These ads appeared in 135 issues of 10 publications studied by Reader Feedback; all were one-page black-and-white run-of-publication ads. Ads were grouped according to the total number of pages used by the advertiser in the publication and in the year in which it appeared, and the average readership of scored advertisements was calculated. The annual schedule was figured on the basis of the total amount of space used in the publication in that year.

Readership averages are based on total advertisements scored and are *not* weighted to give each publication equal representation. Approximately 13,500 personal interviews were made to develop the readership figures.

"Repetition makes reputation," said editor Arthur Brisbane. Right he was, too, for nothing in advertising succeeds like repetition. *Nothing*. Repetition is the essential ingredient for advertising success. It's merely another way of saying continuity, of course.

A common fallacy harbored by many managements of industrial

companies is that "everybody knows about our company and the products we manufacture." The engineering-oriented, production-oriented throwbacks to the turn of the century who say this can usually be depended upon to add, "We don't really need to advertise. Why, we're the leader in the widget industry. Nobody will forget us if they need a new widget."

One advertising manager reports a company president who periodically asks him "for an alternative to advertising." A short, honest reply to that request could be: *Liquidate.*

Too often overlooked is the fact that prospects forget a company easily and fast. Readers of a publication in which a company advertises sporadically dismiss that company from their minds when its advertisements stop appearing regularly.

And there is no disputing that you advertise to a passing parade of buying influences, no matter what market. People you've sold move out. They retire. They die. They are promoted or transferred to another plant and/or another city. Stop advertising for a year and you've lost touch completely with at least one-third of the buying influences who "know your company and its products." Stop advertising for two years and more than half of all prospects are unaware of your company.

How efficient is your field sales force when that happens?

Proofs of Continuity's Value

The Scott Paper Company decided to test the effect of different levels of advertising on recognition for Scott as a manufacturer of paper towels for industrial washrooms. So Laboratory of Advertising Performance made a series of recognition surveys in three geographical areas of the country.

With the cooperation of *Business Week,* Scott ran about twice as many ads in one geographical area as in another. In a third area, no Scott towel advertisements appeared in the publication during the test period.

Recognition among subscribers to *Business Week*—all management people in business and industry, of course—was measured in all three areas before the advertising campaign started. It was measured again afterwards, using a sample of 1,000 names of individual subscribers to *Business Week* to represent a cross section of the audience for each geographical area; returns ran from 37 percent to 43.6 percent.

Using 100 as a base figure representing the level of recognition before the campaign started, it was found that recognition rose to

103 in the low-advertising area after four ads, and to 124 in the high advertising area after eight advertisements ran.

Another reason that continuity is so critically important is that not every issue of a business publication—even the very best ones in your field—is read by every one of your prospects.

A McGraw-Hill study on the subject showed that 95.1 percent of recipients of business magazines read one out of four issues. It also showed that 49.5 percent read all four issues. Furthermore, the study disclosed that 28.5 percent read three out of four issues. And 12.1 percent read two out of four issues. But more than 95 percent read only one issue out of four—that's the point.

Unless your advertisements appear continuously, there is an excellent chance they'll not be seen by the people who could be most important to you. This is a chance no prudent advertiser takes.

A fringe benefit of continuity is that it reinforces the opinion of current users of your products; through being continuously exposed to your advertising messages, they are *resold* on your products and the value they represent.

How much is this worth? Nobody yet has attached a price tag to this benefit, and it's doubtful if anybody ever can. But this is an intangible you certainly wouldn't care to throw lightly out the window.

Continuity of advertising is essential. It all depends on what you want your advertising to do. You can eschew continuity and let people forget, or you can get them to remember who you are and what you sell by advertising continuously. Advertising continuity in the best business publications serving your market literally keeps your firm name and your products uppermost in prospects' minds.

Readership

One of the best ways to boost readership of all of your advertisements is to *run more than one ad in an issue* of the magazine you've selected as best for your company.

Unfortunately, this highly productive tactic is little understood by the naive innocents who inhabit management chairs throughout typical industrial firms. Nor is its importance realized even dimly by engineers who fancy themselves "marketing men" in these backward companies.

One Chicago advertising executive tells of the two company presidents and one "marketing" vice-president— an excellent sales manager, he says—who practically throw up their hands in horror, emit little high-pitched squeaking noises and otherwise exhibit every symptom of having conniptions when faced with two company advertisements in one issue of a leading trade publication.

However, running two advertisements in the same issue obviously gives the advertiser twice the exposure that one provides. But it does much more.

Numerous studies have shown that the first ad in the book receives the same readership and Noted scores that it would if it ran alone, as would be expected. The second advertisement by the same advertiser, however, always receives *more* readership than the first ad did, and *more* readership than if it appeared unaccompanied by another ad. A cumulative effect results from having more than one advertisement in an issue.

This cumulative effect is greatly strengthened by the practice of a number of progressive advertisers of using consecutive right-hand pages, such as the Clark Equipment Company ads discussed in Chapter 9. Repetition is one of the pillars of advertising, and repetition of one-page ads on consecutive pages is one of the very best ways of creating tremendous impact in the reader's mind.

Even if multiple insertions do not follow each other on consecutive pages, each succeeding advertisement following the first one in the publication reinforces each of the others. The advertiser gains much in recognition and readership, and intangibly by creating the impression of a leader who dominates the magazine.

Dominating the magazine is translated in the reader's mind to dominating the industry. Such a positive attitude toward a company by its prospects is something everybody wants and only a few advertisers get.

Multiple insertions in the best business publications is a way to get it.

An Ad for All Seasons

Advertising, some "experts" would have it, is read when coyotes bark at the moon—only in certain months or at certain times of the year. This, too, is an old wives' tale. There's nothing to it.

The theory that advertising is not read in December because Christmas is at hand simply doesn't hold water—or snow, either. After all, the first of December rolls around every year and the world doesn't come to an end, nor does all of industry grind to a screaming halt.

But business still goes on. There is no automatic shut-down of production lines or offices.

The seasonal pattern, if one ever existed, has become a thing of the past. Publishers are understandably anxious to lay to rest the old saw that "nobody reads trade advertisements in December because of Christmas, or in June, July, and August because of vacations."

To help determine whether or not there actually are seasonal trends in reader interest, McGraw-Hill's research department analyzed the reader service response of 10 of the company's magazines for each month of the year.

This analysis compared (1) the number of readers responding to each publication month by month for a full year to determine if there are seasonal patterns to response, and (2) the monthly response in one year compared to the monthly response in the following year.

Results showed there is no general pattern of high interest in one season and low interest in another. Rate of response fluctuated widely between different publications. In one, for instance, April was above average in seven out of ten magazines—but January, June, August, and December showed six highs out of the 10 publications surveyed. And these are supposedly the nonproductive months of the year.

Since every season provides examples of high reader response, the only conclusion to be reached is that an advertisement or an article which offers real help to the industrial reader can and does get a good response in any month of the year. If any seasonal variations do exist, they are not great enough to affect the ability of an editor or an advertiser to get a good response from the publication's readers.

Space vs. Message

Size of space also affects readership of your advertisements, and there's one easily remembered rule of thumb that cannot be lightly dismissed—the larger the space unit, the larger the illustration the ad can have. And it's the illustration that stops the reader in almost every instance. Larger illustrations and higher readership are almost always inseparable.

Larger space means higher attention value. More space gives you room to stretch in, room to tell your story more completely. Larger space produces greater impact.

This is assuming that all factors are equal—which they generally are not. The story is much the same in advertising as it is in boxing. Fight fans are well aware of the truth of the old saying that "a good big man can whip a good little man every time."

In advertising, this holds equally true. However, there's another side of the coin. Dr. Joseph E. Bachelder, managing director of Center For Marketing Communications, recently said in *Media/scope:* "The message in the ad is so important that to a certain extent one is comparing apples and oranges when comparing ads of the same size. A quarter-page ad with a real message and exceedingly well done in a creative fashion can outdo a two-page spread which has nothing to say and uses four color."

Dr. Bachelder is quite right. But the qualifier—*all other factors being equal*—rules out violent fluctuations in the level of creative quality and level of communications thinking.

One study, for instance, indicated that advertisements of the same size had a disparity of readership up to 20 times, and "in one extreme case" the ratio was 50 to 1, *Media/scope* said.

The scintillating advertisements that are truly brilliant in concept and execution will always be with us and they will always receive outstanding readership; so, too, will inept, inane ads continue to clutter up trade magazines and continue to be ignored.

Media/scope drew up a table to show the relative effectiveness of different size space units on an index basis. This is:

1 page	100
1 page, bleed	116-137
¼ page	29
⅓ page	33
½ page	44
⅔ page	64-75
2 pages (spread)	132-150
2 page insert	211-241
3 pages	171
5 pages	163-186

Advantages of use of larger space are born out in McGraw-Hill studies. In its Laboratory of Advertising Performance the publisher states: "Larger advertisements get higher readership. The larger the advertisement, the more readers it attracts. In addition, reader comments indicate that larger space permits the advertiser to get across a more complete message and a better impression of the company."

By all means run the largest ads the budget will permit. However, if you are forced to make the difficult choice of having either continuity or larger size ads, choose continuity. You'll be ahead in the long run running two-thirds page ads every month, as opposed to running spreads three or four times a year.

Concentration

"Listen carefully," ABP said. "That sound you hear, a subdued, saddened wail, is your advertising budget dribbling away. All over the place. On uninhabited wastelands, far-off shores.

"And all the time you wanted your advertising to shout and stomp, grab and get action. What went wrong?

"You were probably playing the wrong game: Scatteration. You should have been playing *concentration*—especially in the leading business publications. Only it isn't really a game, it's smart business.

"Playing the field costs money—wastes it, too. You lose the discounts available to consistent advertisers. And you lose the *impact* of continuity."

And you don't really buy yourself anything by scattering advertisements through a series of marginal publications. Because of circulation duplication, secondary publications usually provide relatively few new readers—and they do so at a cost that is truly exorbitant when it's considered as applying only to the *additional* readers the secondary book enables you to reach.

One or two leading magazines serving a field of business or industry will, on the average, reach the great majority of men who can be reached by *five* magazines—and will reach them at a fraction of the cost of all five.

This principle is called "The Law of Diminishing Returns" by McGraw-Hill, who says it can be demonstrated by finding out what magazines a group of customers or prospects read. By ranking the publications they list in order of number of mentions and finding out how many new readers each succeeding publication adds, it is possible to determine the number of additional new readers and how much it costs to reach them.

The publisher conducted a study in nine fields to determine the cost of adding additional publications to secure unduplicated readers.

Combined cost and unduplicated coverage of five leading publications was:

	Cumulative unduplicated coverage	Cumulative Cost
Leading	66%	24%
Second	83%	44%
Third	93%	65%
Fourth	98%	84%
Fifth	100%	100%

Thus we see the leading publication secured about two-thirds of the coverage at about one-fourth of the cost. The fifth publication added to the schedule performed the ridiculous task of adding only 2 percent additional coverage at 17 percent of the cost of all five publications combined.

Unless your company has money to throw away, it behooves you to recognize that there comes a point where the cost of reaching a few new, unduplicated readers through an additional publication becomes prohibitive.

Repeat Ads

Industrial advertisers (and perhaps consumer advertisers, as well) are maladjusted in one respect. They are out of harmony with their environment from failure to reach a satisfactory adjustment between the desire to see an advertisement achieve complete success and the burning ambition to create a new advertisement that might do more.

Pointing this up is the fact that industrial advertisers get tired of their advertisements *long before readers do.* This applies both to campaigns and to individual ads and is a major reason for a shocking waste of money every year.

This waste occurs because good advertisements are not repeated, or are not repeated enough times. They are not repeated because (1) advertisers are tired of them, and (2) advertisers do not understand a basic principle that ads can be repeated time after time without loss of effectiveness.

One study measured these recognition scores for 70 ads running four times each in business publications: First appearance, 23.5 percent; second, 23.6 percent; third, 24 percent; fourth, 23.5 percent.

Another study zeroed in on inquiries produced by 31 repeated ads, American Business Press reported. First appearance of the ads generated 1,525 inquiries; second appearance, 1,217; third, 1,178; fourth, 1,067. So how do you explain the ads continuing to produce at better than two-thirds the rate as compared to their first time around if "everybody's seen them already?"

An account executive in a major Chicago agency tells of an advertising manager-client who received a terse memo from a product manager complaining on two scores—he ran two advertisements in the same issue of the best magazine to serve the field, and one ad had been run three times before, the other twice before.

This incredible dereliction of duty, according to the product manager, was only slightly less serious than that performed by one Benedict Arnold.

Sad part of the story is that when the advertising manager

memoed back to the effect that the company received *more than double* the exposure one ad would have produced due to the cumulative effect, that the medium was the best possible choice, and that repeat ads receive just as good readership as when they're virgin-pure, the vice-president of marketing got in the act. He called in the advertising manager, and in the true spirit of the engineering profession, sided with the product manager.

The Cold Facts

Center For Marketing Communications did a depth analysis of the performance of 80 ads which appeared four times in business publications under tightly controlled conditions. The ads ran in 23 publications during an 18-month period, with 65 advertisers involved.

The Center's conclusion is: "Industrial ads in general can be run *at least* four times in the same publication without material or necessary loss of effectiveness. This study indicates that readers of industrial publications look at and read each of the four appearances in virtually equal numbers. These findings hold true regardless of: (1) The readership service used. (2) The industry covered. (3) The publication in which the ad appears. (4) The type of question asked about readership. (5) The time interval between appearances of the ad. (6) Whether recognition or reading score is considered. (7) Whether the scores are based on personal interviews or mailed questionnaires."

Laboratory of Advertising Performance reports that "Four studies indicate little or no loss of readership for repeated advertisements, no matter what time elapses between the first and subsequent insertions."

Analysis of the readership of 1,600 repeated advertisements that ran up to four times each revealed the following, using an index of 100, according to LAP:

No. of Ads	Insertion	Readership
1,351	1st	100
1,351	2nd	100
197	1st	100
197	2nd	98
197	3rd	97
52	1st	100
52	2nd	103
52	3rd	103
52	4th	111

These and many other studies of multiple insertion advertising readership indicate that:

1. Little or no loss of readership as measured by Reader Feedback is indicated when advertisements are repeated once, twice, and three times.

2. Little or no change in thorough readership, as measured by Starch Read Most scores, is indicated for advertisements repeated once, twice, and three times.

3. Little or no shift in readership, as measured by Starch Noted scores, is indicated for advertisements repeated at intervals from one to 48 weeks between insertions in a weekly publication, or one to 12 months in a monthly magazine.

Now, let's look at the money side of the picture for a minute. In Denver at this writing the cost of production of a 7-by-10-inch black-and-white ad runs between $600 and $700. This means an advertiser who advertises in five separate markets and produces a dozen ads for each will spend $39,000 or more just for production.

Assuming the cost of space in the average leading business publication is $2,000 (just to have a nice, round figure), this would mean expenditure of $240,000 for space if only two publications per market are used.

However, if only half as many ads were produced and each one was repeated just once, an extra $19,500 would be available for more space. This could easily mean addition of an extra medium in a market where additional coverage is needed, or even two publications in two markets for a six-times schedule.

But if only four ads were produced for each of the markets and they were repeated three times each, an extra $26,000 would be available for space—where it would produce a return rather than inflate the company's ego by having so many different ads.

Unless the product line is extremely broad, and the decision has been made to advertise product by product—and if the line is *that* broad, there isn't enough money anyway—goodness knows the extra money will come in handy. More ads, more readership, more exposure, more impact, more economical coverage of the universe.

By repeating ads you pick up publication discounts, save on production, establish continuity, and boost total results. And you can do all of this within the budget, too, because one advertisement does the work of two—or three, or four, as far as that's concerned. And it does so just as effectively.

Chapter 16

DIRECT MAIL

DIRECT MAIL, according to the American Association of Advertising Agencies' Committee on Direct Mail, is "the use of mailed advertising to develop sales directly or indirectly, employing selected lists to achieve the desired circulation."

There are three separate and distinct forms of direct mail used today, the four A's claim. These are:

1. *Mail Media Advertising*—This is simply direct mail which produces sales *through established channels of distribution.* Examples of this form of direct mail advertising are: sales inquiry letters ("lead-getters"), credit-card offers, store-traffic builders, product couponing and sampling. Mail media advertising is directly competitive with magazines, newspapers, television, radio and other media for the advertising dollar.

2. *Mail Order Advertising*—This is direct mail which produces sales *directly with customers and prospects.* Examples are: sale of magazine and newspaper subscriptions, books, merchandise, correspondence courses, and other items sold directly by mail. Mail order advertising eliminates the use of a sales representative or middleman in the process of distribution. The important element is that completion of the sale is accomplished entirely by mail.

3. *Mail Sales Promotion*—Direct mail which stimulates or reinforces sales. Examples are: TV, radio, magazine, or newspaper advertising promotion. Others are: recipe books, instruction manuals, displays, coupons, annual reports, catalogs, external house organs, reference bulletins, etc.

By and large, the industrial advertising manager is primarily concerned with the first form—mail media advertising. Common usage of the term "direct mail" when it's applied to industrial mail programs mean mail media advertising, so in this chapter that is what is referred to henceforth unless otherwise noted.

Direct Mail Is Growing Up

Direct mail as an advertising medium is growing up; just a short time ago *Printer's Ink* quoted a direct mail veteran as having said: "Direct mail is currently going through the same metamorphosis that all advertising went through 50 or 60 years ago. It is emerging from its medicine man stage. Direct mail is becoming more and more a respectable and respected way of disseminating product information."

Without doubt direct mail has become a truly massive medium. Right now it is the *third largest* advertising medium in the country, right behind newspapers and television, and well ahead of consumer magazines. Ballpark volumes of the various media per year are: Newspapers, $5.5 billion; television, $4 billion; direct mail, $3.5 billion.

The "unseen medium," direct mail, is some $500 million ahead of consumer magazines in annual dollar volume, although consumer magazines are the next largest benefactor from the advertisers' dollars.

Direct Mail Is Misunderstood

More often than not, direct mail is misunderstood throughout industry. It is regarded either as a panacea for all that ails a company's sales, or as a vulgar pretender standing in the wings all ready and willing to siphon off the company's promotional dollars to no good end.

And direct mail is one of the easiest victims of the eager amateur who believes implicitly it is simple and easy to master because, after all, all you have to do is mail something to a prospect. This, of course, miraculously transforms him into a cherished customer who is practically panting with eagerness to part with his hard-earned money—preferably in very large sums.

Corporate management in many small to medium-size industrial companies are the amateurs hardest to ignore. Their intentions are good. Although they have only a dim understanding at best of *how* they can use the magic of direct mail, their objective is a valid one—more sales.

These amateurs who tamper with the promotional program are horribly prone to abandon formal marketing objectives (if the company has any) and formal communications objectives (if the company has any) and go blithely off on a wild tangent. Without thought of the consequences they'd scuttle a program when it's half-completed, thus wasting most of the money allocated for it originally, and committing at the same time the worst sin of all—waste of precious time. It can't be replaced.

Most industrial ad men are accustomed to encountering more or less difficulty—usually more—in persuading management to accept the fact there is a certain time lag in every form of advertising. During this period it's all outgo, nothing is income. If only the managements of industrial companies would realize that advertising (in all media) they do this year will affect *next* year's sales—and those of the year *after*. Remarkably little industrial advertising produces measurable results *this* year. If it did, life would be much easier for all advertising managers. And industry would maintain continuity of advertising so as to reap benefits to the fullest.

Unfortunately, such managements know that mail is delivered in a matter of days almost any place in the country, so they also "know" that direct mail "should be used to produce sales now."

It seldom works that way.

Another thing about direct mail is that it is seemingly so easy to measure, particularly when compared to space advertising. After all, it should be a question of arithmetic, shouldn't it? You mail so many pieces to so many prospects and you reap so many orders as a result. This is mail order-type thinking, not direct mail advertising thinking.

Happily, a large portion of the misguided management thinking that reflects this naive attitude has changed as more research has been conducted to place the medium of direct mail where it belongs in the marketing communications media mix.

A Chicago advertising manager recently told the author of a company president who called him into his office one afternoon and said, "I want an alternative to this advertising we're doing. How about direct mail—we can save some money."

This president was neither more nor less uninformed than his peers in other companies on this score. That direct mail is a "cheap" medium is a fallacy that's even more widespread than dandruff.

Robert Stone, prolific writer on the subject of direct mail, acknowledged expert in this fascinating specialty for decades, and an *Advertising Age* columnist, said: "Direct mail is expensive. One of the most popular misconceptions about direct mail advertising is that it is inexpensive. Nothing could be further from reality. Direct mail is one of the most expensive advertising mediums at the disposal of today's business executive."

Fact of the matter is, the three most expensive ways yet devised by mortal man to promote the sale of a product to industry are:

1. Television
2. Salesmen
3. Direct mail

This statement holds true since it is predicated upon the assumption that industry will continue to use direct mail, either in whole or in part, as a substitute or alternative for space advertising in trade publications. The advocate of direct mail, which is a very direct and highly personalized medium, who recommends it as the cure-all for all that ails a company's communications effort—and who recommends it to replace a mass medium—is on very wonky ground indeed. *Use of direct mail for this purpose is indefensible.*

A Most Personal Medium

In his monumental work, *The Dartnell Direct Mail and Mail Order Handbook,* Richard S. Hodgson advanced the thought that the greatest mistake made by industrial advertisers when using direct mail is the tendency to forget that their customers and prospects are people.

Instead, they tend to think of them only as engineers, purchasing agents, production supervisors, controllers, and so on. The fact that a prospect has a functional role in industry (otherwise, he wouldn't be there, of course) somehow obviates the necessity of approaching him as a thinking, feeling human being with his fair share of emotions, hopes, and aspirations.

This, in turn, leads to a gross misuse of direct mail, this most personal of mediums, by neophytes who want to "use up" all of those extra catalog sheets gathering dust in the back storeroom. They profess to see no need to "get fancy" in presenting a plain nuts-and-bolts story, they want to go pore-mouth (as we used to say in turnip-greens and hog-jowls country) about the task of cultivating a prospect's interest and convincing him *this* is the promised land as far as he's concerned, *this* is the company to do business with, *this* is the company that's service-minded, *this* is the product he needs to solve all of his problems large and small.

To do so is a gross error.

Direct mail tyros who adopt this attitude and who try to penny-pinch their way to a curve on the sales chart that would make even the most hard-nosed company controller in all of industry break out in ecstatic smiles are doomed before they start—doomed to failure.

They conveniently ignore the fact that the industrial buyer in whom they're interested is being courted assiduously by other companies selling the same kind of widget. In short, competition has reared its ugly head—even in direct mail.

Industrial buyers, particularly those in metropolitan areas, are barraged with some 1,500 advertising impressions a day from all media. Only a tiny fraction of those messages make a real impression, a positive, forceful impression that can in any way alter the prospect's mind about a company or its products.

Audiences for industrial direct mail are smaller, more easily defined, and hence ideal prospective recipients for effective mailings even when the budget is limited. And competition is encountered from less companies than in the consumer field, although it is no less vigorous.

For this reason many industrial advertising managers using direct mail make the same mistake about this medium as they do about space advertisements. They regard the competition as more direct mail—or space ads—from their competitors. This is a fallacy, and a dangerous one at that.

Never for an instant lose sight of the fact that your competition is the direct mail sent to your prospect by every other industrial advertiser who contacts him. Too, it is *every* advertiser—both industrial and consumer. Every individual has a limited amount of time. Each day contains just 24 hours. Each work day takes a bite of 8 or 9 or even 10 of those hours, no more. And in that given period of time the competition for the full attention of the individual you want to reach is intense.

Six Fundamental Principles of Direct Mail

Now that a few fallacies concerning direct mail have been exposed, let's look at some basic principles for successful industrial direct mail, as given by Edward N. Mayer, Jr., in his *Handbook of Industrial Direct Mail Advertising,* published by the Business/Professional Advertising Association. These principles are:

1. *There must be a need for the product or service being advertised.* However, it is quite possible to create a need by emphasizing a want, or an unfulfilled wish of the people you are trying to sell. But keep in mind that you can't sell electric blankets to people in the tropics; nor can you sell bottling machinery to a plant that manufactures canned goods exclusively.

2. *There must be a need for the product or service being advertised at the particular time it is being advertised.* Although there is very little seasonal appeal involved in the sale of most industrial products, it must be obvious that, even though you make the best snow-removal equipment available, you are not going to be able to arouse much interest for this equipment in the purchasing agent for a plant in Dallas, Texas, during the summer's hottest spell.

3. *The proposition you are making must be attractive to the potential buyer.* Even though your bottling machine or snow-removal equipment is the best available, unless you can find reasons—solid reasons—why your proposition is a fair and attractive one, and your prospect should buy your product rather than your competitor's—you will be wasting your direct mail advertising, and to some degree your salesman's efforts.

4. *The advertising must be prepared from the reader's viewpoint.* The fact that you have a product or service to sell, from which you are going to derive a profit, isn't interesting to your best prospect. However, the fact that he can either reduce his costs or make a greater profit through its usage is interesting to him. You must think of any direct mail advertising you do in the industrial marketing field in terms of how it can talk the reader's language—how it can present your sales story, whatever it may be, in a way that will appeal to the prospect and make him realize that he is the one who will benefit from following your suggestions.

5. *Direct mail advertising, to be effective, must be sent to good prospects.*

6. *The reputation of the advertiser must be good or at least not open to question among the people being solicited.* If there is anything in the history of your company which is detrimental, it will be extremely wise to straighten out your reputation and your market acceptance in the field, if your advertising is to be successful.

Seven Keys to Success

Along with his fundamental principles, Mr. Mayer has given "seven cardinal rules" which he says must be followed to achieve success in industrial direct mail advertising. They are:

1. *Know exactly what you want your mailing to do.* Do you want an order, an inquiry, a chance to have a salesman call? Are you trying to open up a new territory, introduce a new product, or announce a new use for an old one? Or do you want to do a goodwill or institutional job?

2. *Write your copy so that the recipient will know what your product will do for him!* Have you appealed to his selfish instincts or have you used all of your space talking about yourself, your president, and your beautiful new factory? Have you made your copy human and easy to read? Have you given all the information your prospect needs to take the action you desire?

3. *Make the layout and format of your mailing tie in with your overall plan and objective.* Many a potential success has turned into a dismal failure because someone forgot that appearance is an important part of the selling impression.

4. *Address each mailing piece (correctly) to an individual or company who can buy the product or service you have to sell.* The list is the absolute foundation of successful direct mail.

5. *Make it easy for your prospect to send you an inquiry.* Have you included a reply card or return envelope? If you are not looking for direct business, have you listed the places where your product is available?

6. *Tell your story over again.* Very few salesmen make a sale on their first call. It isn't reasonable to expect a single mailing to produce a large return.

7. *Research every mailing you make.* Never take anything for granted in industrial direct mail advertising. Don't even trust your own experience. You cannot rest on your knowledge. Times and results change. What worked last year may not work today.

Functions of Direct Mail

Definitions, rules and sins are all necessary to bear in mind, but just what are the basic functions of industrial direct mail advertising? According to the Direct Mail/Marketing Association—and they should know—there are just six primary functions. These are:

1. *Creating more effective personal sales contracts.* This includes direct mail advertising which creates a specific opportunity for salesmen to call by getting inquiries or leads for personal followup. It also means paving the way for salesmen by lessening resistance, arousing interest, educating and informing the prospect before intended sales calls, but without trying to get back an order or response from the prospect through the mail.

2. *Bringing the prospect to you.* This applies particularly to the retail field and to service businesses (like banks) which do not have sales forces. It has other applications, such as getting customers or prospects to visit new plants or special displays.

3. *Delivering background, sales, or public relations messages to customers, prospects, enployees, or other special groups.* This includes mailings that are designed as pure advertising. It also covers any prestige reminder or goodwill advertising, employee relations, or anything to influence selective groups along certain lines of thought or action, but without direct response being sought by mail or without any direct personal follow-up intended.

4. *Taking actual orders through the mail.* This function is direct mail selling, or mail order selling, where every step in the sales process, from the initial contact to the final sale, is done exclusively by mail. This applies to publications, business, investment, and news services, as well as to selling merchandise by mail. It also applies to raising funds by charitable and educational organizations.

5. *Securing action from the prospect by mail.* This covers any promotion intended to secure response or action by mail, but not designed to secure an order or result in a personal contact between the prospect and the advertiser. Included in this category would be getting entries in a competition or securing requests for general information literature.

6. *Conducting research and market surveys.* This covers every phase of research, investigation, and fact-finding by mail.

Incidentally, the Direct Mail/Marketing Association is a wonderful source for information of all types about the medium. It is, of course, the advertising trade association for the direct mail medium, hence is authoritative. Member companies of DMMA are usually direct mail practitioners and users, but also include creators, producers and suppliers, as well as many advertising agencies.

The address of the Direct Mail/Marketing Association is:

Direct Mail/Marketing Association
6 East 43rd Street
New York, New York 10017

DMMA's Advertising Agency Committee initiates projects which will assist agency media and account personnel in programming effective mail advertising campaigns for their clients.

A few of the helpful services the Direct Mail/Marketing Association makes available to the advertising community include:

Washington Newsletter. This is a twice-monthly publication of current information on postal and legislative matters which affect business users of the mail. Copies are available upon request.

Library. DMMA's vast library contains more than 2,000 successful direct mail campaigns covering almost all categories of both consumer and industrial advertising, and thousands of loose samples of material used in direct mail. These include such items as reply cards, house organs, annual reports, and so on and on.

Information Service. DMMA is a thoroughly reliable source of information on almost every phase of direct mail. This includes such necessities as reliable list brokers, supplies and services, postal regulations, research data, and so forth.

Direct Mail Institutes. These intensive cram courses in direct mail take from three to five days as a rule, and cover both basic and advanced areas of direct mail, as well as some specialized aspects of the medium. They are held 10 times a year at strategic locations throughout the country.

Annual Conference. Round-table discussions and panel sessions provide a sound source of information on current practices and developments of the art, as well as a report on new techniques.

Workshops. These one-day programs are concerned primarily with specialized interests such as circulation promotion and mail order.

Direct Mail Leaders Contest. This annual competition for superior direct mail campaigns attracts widespread interest and entries from the country's leading advertising agencies and direct mail agencies.

Placement Service Bulletin. This bi-monthly publication emphasizes positions that are open on the middle management level. A nominal charge is made for such listings.

Standards of Practice. The direct mail medium polices itself through the Direct Mail/Marketing Association's Standards of Ethical Business Practice.

The small-to-medium size industrial company is unique in American business today, although more often than not this is nothing to write home about.

With marketing sophistication and know-how at an undreamed of level, the *average* industrial manufacturing company still carries on by muddling through. The *average* company proceeds on hope and hunch and trusts that having good intentions and a firm faith that the world is round will suffice to see it safely through the perils of the sales jungle.

Such a lack of firm policy, it is innocently hoped, will offset failure to develop a written marketing plan and formal marketing objectives. Furthermore, there is the unexpressed but ever-present trust that it will also make up, somehow or other, for lack of written communications objectives and a planned program complete with step-by-step details of how they will be achieved.

Such an attitude is unrealistic and unforgivable when it concerns mass media. It is especially asinine when it concerns a very specific medium such as direct mail. Failure is invited with open arms and a welcoming smile.

Many of these smaller companies—say, up to $50-75 million in annual sales—are being rescued from themselves by larger corporations whose managements *force* their acquired divisions to think in terms of marketing their products, rather than selling them. The day of the hardware salesman is long past. He's a relic of the dim, dead past and never again will he see the light of day.

Direct mail is a highly selective medium. It uses the approach best described by the old cliché, the "rifle approach." The fact that direct mail is not a mass medium makes it all the more essential that adequate planning precede the actual start of a program.

A midwestern advertising manager in a medium-size industrial company who's an old friend of the author's recently wrote deploring the fuzzy-minded top management in his company. The president actually advocates "using direct mail because nobody reads trade publications."

Now, there are reasons aplenty—and good ones at that—for using direct mail. But this is not one of them.

Both mediums have their places. To expect one to be more productive than a well-balanced mixture of the two is naive in the extreme.

Balance Is the Answer

Effective marketing strategy for an industrial company almost invariably calls for a balanced use of *both* space advertising and direct mail. Seldom, if ever, can one medium alone—*either* medium alone—achieve the impact and the effectiveness as can a blend of the two.

What's more, use of each medium must be planned so the total effect is synergistic. That is, each medium must reinforce and augment the communications job done by the other so they build upon each other to create a stronger *total* communications impression in the minds of those prospects who have been exposed to the messages than either could produce alone, or even than the two could do if not carefully coordinated.

Involved, of course, is determining which medium is to be assigned certain specific objectives. Direct mail is called for when:

1. Sampling is to be done.
2. When the message is either too long or too complex to be disseminated efficiently in space advertising.
3. When a specific market is to be aimed at so that waste circulation is minimized.
4. When a highly selective, personalized approach is called for.
5. When a localized market area is to be saturated without disturbing the "balance of nature" in other markets or other areas.
6. When timing or frequency of communications is of critical importance.
7. When communications and market research are to be used simultaneously, such as in establishing demand, determining price structure, developing prospect profiles, and locating specific buying influences by title or job function.
8. When mail order technique is called for; this is to sell the product directly, without assistance of dealers, jobbers, or distributors.
9. When inquiries are wanted from carefully selected individuals.
10. When it is desired to build attendance at a trade show among certain qualified prospects.
11. When eliciting response to build a mailing list is the goal.
12. When merchandising the space advertising program to specific individuals.
13. When responding to inquiries generated by other media, such as space advertising.

Four Basic Types of Direct Mail Campaigns

Once you've established firm campaign objectives, you have something concrete to strive for. There's a very firm, definite goal and specific objectives which should be *measurable*. With measurable objectives, you can then show one and all how much over the target the campaign went, or under it. At this time you'll feel the need to pick one of four basic types of direct mail campaigns to help achieve your objectives. These are:

1. *Persuasive*. A direct mail campaign of this type is usually chosen to produce immediate results—such as mail orders, inquiries for salesmen to follow, or to build a mailing list. A strong bid for action is used and response is made as easy and simple for the recipient as possible.

2. *Informative*. This type of campaign is not developed to produce a large volume of returns, although a response is welcome. Instead, something of an educational nature, such as a catalog, product literature, price pages, or some other similar material are mailed; they are designed so the recipient will want to file them for future reference.

3. *Reminder*. Reminder direct mail is not expected to persuade the recipient to respond, nor is it developed to provide a great mass of background information about a company or product. Instead, it is a form of name-dropping by mail. Its purpose is to keep the company's name and products fresh in the mind of those who receive the communication.

4. *Utility*. Direct mail pieces of this type are often used with the other three forms; they consist of order forms, reply cards, and stamped or postage-paid envelopes, samples of the product, reference charts (such as a table of decimal equivalents and tap drill sizes), folders, three-ring binders in which to file product literature, and so forth.

Characteristics of Direct Mail

The fantastic degree of *selectivity* possible with direct mail distinguishes this massive medium from all others.

Direct mail is the only advertising medium which enables you to aim your message directly at one specific individual, or a group of very similar individuals who share certain necessary common denominators. Using direct mail, you can easily communicate with 33,000 works managers or directors of manufacturing in metalworking establishments, for instance, and not say a single word to anybody else in those organizations.

Almost every adult American has been defined, classified, sub-classified and tabulated as to a number of criteria. It's a very simple matter for you to reach any group geographically, by income, by occupation, by SIC, by sales territory, by educational level, by type of residence, or almost any other way you care to make a breakdown.

Computers have eliminated the trial and error and the drudgery formerly associated with direct mail. They spew out information formerly compiled and retrieved at the expense of untold man-hours, they address labels, continuous-form envelopes, and almost everything else except one thing—as yet they don't plan the program, and they don't make decisions.

Selectivity is the key that has led direct mail to come into its own as a vitally important medium for the industrial advertiser. With selective direct mail, there is absolutely no waste, no paying for putting your message in front of people who couldn't care less about the product—and it obviates a tendency to generalize in an effort to appeal to varying interests of various groups of readers. With direct mail you talk only to the group you're interested in.

As an example of the selectivity direct mail makes possible, the old Diamond T Motor Truck company used direct mail very aggressively in support of its nationwide dealer organization.

Basis of the program was the Polk Motor Vehicle Registration List which gave the name address, firm name, and type of motor truck operated by every user of commercial vehicles in the United States for which state license plates had been issued. The list contained no deadwood, no nixies, nobody except bona fide owners, lessors, and other users of heavy-duty motor trucks. These are, quite obviously, the best possible prospects for the sale of additional and replacement vehicles, as well as parts and service.

As could be anticipated, the most active, most aggressive, most successful dealers eagerly participated in the direct mail program on a co-op basis; most dealer-distributor programs are cooperatively financed, incidentally, with the manufacturer usually picking up the lion's share of the tab. As a rule, most manufacturers assume around two-thirds of the cost of a cooperative direct mail program, leaving the outlets to assume the balance.

Few Copy, Format Restrictions

Copy can be as long as necessary when you're using the direct mail medium; there is no arbitrary length which must be adhered to because there is no arbitrary format such as a one-page ad, a spread ad, and so forth.

Long copy is particularly well suited for direct mail, and the old saying "the more you tell, the more you sell" was never more true than when used in connection with this medium.

You have the prospect's *undivided attention* with direct mail. You're not clamoring for attention. You're not competing with an advertisement across the gutter from yours, and there's no editorial matter to distract the prospect from what you want to tell him about your product.

The *format* is not limited in direct mail. You're free and unconfined (except by the budget and certain postal restrictions) in the physical appearance of your direct mail pieces.

What's more, direct mail is the only medium that makes it easy and inexpensive to *test* copy, test appeals, test layouts, test type faces and various other elements of the program. All of this can be done with a small sample at very low cost.

For instance, if you're undecided about which of two—or even more, for that matter—copy appeals are more on target, it's a very simple matter to produce the mailer you have in mind just as you have it in mind. Use any complicated techniques you want; die-cuts, pop-ups, and what not. The only change involved is in a piece of type, or all of the type if you want. A split run can be made on the press to provide certain quantities of mailers with the different appeals. They will measure the interest, response, or return—whatever your program is geared to produce.

Flexibility of timetables is inherent in direct mail. After all, you control when it is going to be produced and mailed, and this can reflect any special seasonal needs, a tie-in with space advertising, or reinforcing local dealer advertising.

There is, however, a factor you cannot control. This is the service you receive from the post office. Often this can be predicted with sufficient accuracy in most instances so you won't encounter a problem once your material is mailed.

This doesn't always hold true, though, for it's common gossip that the post office is going from bad to worse. Rates go up in massive 20 percent jumps, while service deteriorates.

But—back to the pluses of direct mail—you can make it easy for the recipients of your mailings to *respond*. Enclosing a postage-paid business reply envelope, a postage-paid reply card, or (and this is best of all when it comes to producing a volume return) a stamped, self-addressed envelope.

Making this enclosure will undoubtedly not increase the weight enough to add to your postage bill. Recipients of direct mail advertising use the postpaid reply route to return order forms, request a salesman to call, ask for a sample, or whatever it is you've asked them to do. Direct mail advertising that goes out without one of these built-in response producers is pretty largely a mailing that's wasted, assuming a response is desired. Never try to save a few pennies here.

The List

Now that we've looked at this highly selective, highly specialized, highly personalized and highly productive medium from a generalized point of view, let's get into the mechanics of direct mail—and learn how to put it to work for an industrial company.

The list, as the mailing list is usually called, is basic and is entitled to very careful scrutiny.

Your list is a vitally important element and it is impossible to overemphasize the extreme care with which it should be compiled and/or selected and maintained.

No mailing list floats effortlessly in over the transom, to land all neatly zip coded and broken down by sales territory, on the advertising manager's desk. A mailing list comes from one of two sources: internal or external.

Internal sources are customers and prospects. They shouldn't be combined into one gigantic mailing list because more often than not mailings will be made to both groups, but the messages in most instances are entirely different. Put all names on one list and it is impossible to break them out for various communications specially suited to each specific group.

Actually, the average industrial company should have at least three mailing lists:

1. Customers
2. Prospects
3. Combination of both

Easiest to compile is the customer list. Every firm, almost without exception, has a master record in the sales department or accounts receivable department of all of the firms to which it has made sales.

Seldom, however, can you take the customer list and use it for a direct mail list as you receive it from one of the other departments. For one thing, as often as not the addresses are incomplete; often there'll be a firm name and city, but no individual's name or title, no street address, no state, no zip code. This is perfectly adequate for sales department records or accounts receivable people. They seldom need more.

Since direct mail is above all else a personal medium, though, you'll want to mail to specific individuals and address them by name, title, firm, street address, city, state and zip code.

Internal sources for names of *prospects* are many indeed. They include:

- General correspondence
- Telephone inquiries
- Salesmen's call reports
- Employee and stockholder lists
- Bingo cards
- Trade show registrants

External sources include that old standby, directories. Principle ones of interest to the industrial advertising manager are:

- Telephone directories
- Yellow pages
- Business or industrial directories
- Chamber of Commerce directories (local, state)
- Dun & Bradstreet Directory
- Poor's Register

An unusually complete and helpful source of names and addresses of business directories and associations is in the *Dartnell Sales Promotion Handbook;* it contains more than 50 pages of data, and lists every worthwhile directory in almost every industry.

Of the directories listed above, you'll find Poor's Register most helpful. With industry broken down by SIC's, and names of key executives listed for every firm, firms properly identified as to products, located, and zip coded, this massive directory is virtually indispensable to the ad manager planning a direct mail program.

List brokers are a common source of mailing lists. These brokers are really agents, for they do not own the lists themselves. They handle correspondence and negotiations between list owners and those who rent the lists.

The list broker is a specialist in direct mail. He is usually well qualified to judge the quality of a list, and to secure the best possible list for the purpose you have in mind. He knows what lists are available, so using a list broker saves much time and trouble. The DMMA describes a list broker as:

> List brokers can be defined as independent agents whose primary function is to arrange rental and addressing transactions between list users and list owners. Brokers represent the list owners, and the commission that they receive from them for their services usually is 20 percent of the amount the mailer pays. The commission is deducted by the broker before payment is forwarded to the list owner.
>
> Here it should be pointed out that often there is an overlapping of activity in the list business. Some brokers not only arrange for the rental of lists that are owned by other companies, but they also either do compilation work or buy outright certain lists which they can make available for rental.
>
> Although this may seem confusing, in the course of working with list organizations you are likely to find that each has its own particular specialty. And very often you may decide that it is wise to deal with certain organizations for specific type lists.

For the most part the user rents lists for one-time use through the broker; the broker is reimbursed for his efforts by the list owner who realizes a return from his investment in time and money spent in compiling the list originally. Most list brokers have capable staffs who are constantly on the lookout for "new" lists, additional information about existing lists and new wrinkles to help users of direct mail make their lists more profitable.

Most list brokers, like most other businessmen, are honest and aboveboard in their transactions and you will encounter no difficulty in dealing with them. However, as in any other business or industry there is an occasional bad apple; the list broker with a heart full of larceny has given this segment of the direct mail industry a reputation that "it pays to do business with a broker you *know* you can trust," for all the world as if most brokers were out to steal your gold inlays. This is not the case.

Renting Lists

Remember when renting your list that you always do so on a one-time only basis. Should the list prove productive for the mailer who rents it from you, he is charged each time he rents it; the fee does not vary with subsequent rentals unless agreed upon ahead of time. And there exist few reasons for reducing the price of a desirable property.

Assuming your list is clean and is made up of buyers—as opposed to prospects, suspects, hopefuls and so on—you can anticipate charging around 2½ cents per name, or $25 per thousand names.

On the other hand, if your list consists primarily of prospects, suspects, expires, or other less active names it is obviously less attractive to the mail user and so must be priced lower. Such lists usually rent for $15 to $20 per thousand names, and there is less demand for such lists, too.

List owners usually handle the addressing of material, or supply labels to the list renter. The physical work is seldom performed by the owner of the list; he customarily relies upon a letter shop with which he does business to handle this. Many list owners return the addressed envelopes, labels, cards or what have you to the mailer for further handling.

Perhaps even more, however, insist on handling the entire mailing; in this case, the cost of folding, collating, stuffing and so on are billed to the mailer in addition to the list rental fee. This is done through the broker. This way the list owner is certain that nobody is going to copy his list; if you operate on the principle that you trust your fellow man—but not much—it's best to go this route.

When preparing material to be mailed for a list user, make sure the necessary arrangements have been made for a postal permit, that indicia are printed correctly, and other minor details are handled ahead of time to avoid a last-minute, frantic stab at the panic button.

List compilers are specialists in creating high quality lists. Almost any conceivable list is usually available on relatively short notice from the compilers without your having to go to the trouble and expense of having one compiled especially for your company. However, if the exact list you need is not in existence, the compilers will quickly produce one that matches your requirements right down to the last dot on the last "i."

Many of the leading list compilers maintain previously compiled lists, marvelously complete and specialized in almost any category you'd need. Most of these lists are broken down by geographic location, and many by demographic characteristics.

The list of lists is so long it's virtually endless. For example, Fritz S. Hofheimer, Inc., 88 Third Ave., Mineola, N. Y. 11501, phone (212) 674-6420, is a leading source of high quality lists. This company is a member of the Direct Mail/Marketing Association, and of Mail Advertising Service Association. It is thoroughly reliable and reputable. Hofheimer publishes an annual catalog of lists it offers—more than 20,000 in all! Separate lists are offered for Canada.

Use of Hofheimer's catalog puts fantastic selectivity in the direct mail advertiser's hands. As an example, let's assume you've prepared a lavish, beautiful, and precisely-written brochure, and you want to mail it only to certain carefully selected buying influences. To show the selective reach of these lists, it would be easy for you to mail to the following, although this is a somewhat improbable collection of individuals:

No. of names on list	*Name of list*	*Price per M*
67,214	Advertising managers	$32.50
14,147	Bank presidents	30.00
638	Whiskey and brandy distillers	40.00*
470	Prisons and reformatories	25.00*
24,686	Agricultural implement dealers	28.50
5,696	Butter, cheese, and egg wholesalers	35.00
9,230	Dog breeders and kennels	40.00
3,653	Fertilizer manufacturers	35.00
4,863	Camps, logging	35.00
4,507	Gunsmiths and firearms dealers	32.50
42,000	Mobile home owners	30.00
3,862	Monument and memorial makers	35.00
59,800	Socialites	30.00
70,000	Treasurers and controllers, corporate	35.00
4,933	Tree surgeons	35.00
2,194	Venereal disease clinics	30.00
3,393	Water well drillers	32.50
13	Windmill manufacturers	12.50*
10	Yo-yo manufacturers	8.50*
167	Zoological gardens	20.00*
24	Zwieback manufacturers	10.50*

Hofheimer, in common with many other list sources, offers complete mailing facilities and services—folding, collating, inserting,

*A flat rate for a small list, not a price per thousand names.

sealing, metering and sorting, all at competitive prices. A sample of your mailing piece or a description of your requirements will bring a prompt quotation for handling an entire job for you.

Incidentally, Hofheimer *guarantees* its lists. This is relatively common practice among the better list purveyors. Statistically, every year more than 25 percent of the country's population undergoes some kind of a change—both individual and industrial. Individuals move, change jobs, get promoted, retire, die.

To protect the user of Hofheimer lists against an abnormal number of post office returns, the company guarantees 95 percent deliverability. It makes refunds at the rate of 10 cents per piece, regardless of the class of mail and actual postage carried, for all in excess of 5 percent of the addresses furnished, provided the returns reach the company within 30 days after purchase of the list.

Dun & Bradstreet, Inc. has detailed lists of 300,000 manufacturing establishments, 15,000 mining establishments, 44,000 contract construction establishments, 28,000 transportation, communication and public utility establishments; all are available from D&B on IBM punched cards, magnetic tape, Cheshire labels, pressure-sensitive labels, 3 by 5 cards, tabular listings, and printed tabulating cards.

These D&B lists identify the establishments, give SIC's, full names, addresses, state-county-city geographical code, area code and telephone number, name and title of chief executive, number of employees, sales volume, credit rating, and net worth. Names of other executives in the firm are also available if needed, including the executive vice-president, individual in charge of manufacturing, head purchasing executive, and the treasurer or controller.

SRDS Joins the Mail Media Parade

Something long expected has finally come to pass—SRDS (Standard Rate & Data Service, Inc.) has finally entered the direct mail field. SRDS' newest service, *Direct Mail List Rates and Data,* provides quick, convenient, accurate source information about mailing lists currently available. The three classifications covered are: Business, Consumer, Farm.

The publisher said that "*Direct Mail List Rates and Data* will enable you to select the best prospects quickly and determine immediately the reliability of the list, its source, its cost, and how it can be mailed mechanically."

Standard Rate & Data Service's 48 years of experience, plus full cooperation of the DMAA and the 4A's Direct Mail Committee, went into the production of this newest reference work. It contains approximately 9,000 list selections and is issued twice a year with up-dating bulletins between editions.

This authoritative guide to direct mail lists is priced at $50 for the year, which includes both editions and attendant bulletins. It is available from:

Standard Rate & Data Service, Inc.
5201 Old Orchard Road,
Skokie, Illinois 60076
(312) 966-8500

Major Pitfall in List Compilation

A camouflaged booby-trap for the unwary industrial advertising manager about to launch a direct mail campaign is using names supplied by the company's field salesmen and internal product people.

Salesmen and product managers are quite sincere in believing they actually know "all" of the buying influences to whom direct mail should be addressed.

When it's composed of names submitted or approved by the product people and the field sales force, a direct mail list will inevitably consist entirely of the names of people on whom they call, and whom they know. These names should be included, without doubt. But if your list is composed entirely of these names, your direct mail advertising cannot hope to achieve more than a mediocre success.

More than 60 percent of all industrial sales calls are misdirected. And industrial salesmen of capital equipment frequently cannot call on buying influences high enough up the corporate ladder, despite their protestations to the contrary; they claim to be able to "see anybody in the company they want to" because they actually believe it. Unknown, unidentified buying influences are not called on, however.

In addition to names supplied by your people, include the names of key executives you can get from your list source—Dun & Bradstreet, R. L. Polk, or whoever it might be. These prime buying influences quite often are men upon whom your salesmen do not call because they are unable to get to them because they do not receive salesmen.

What's more, salesmen and product people seldom appreciate the importance of developing as effective a mailing list as humanly possible, nor do they understand the advisability of including as many names of key buying influences as it is possible to secure. They tend to feel that one or two names within a prospect company is sufficient. Just the opposite is true.

This was strikingly apparent during a recent conversation with an advertising manager friend; he works for a Cleveland company that manufactures capital equipment sold to the foundry industry—and he had encountered this very same problem in his company, it developed. He sent the author a copy of a memo to his product people on this subject; with individual and firm names changed, the memo follows because it illustrates this point so well.

To: Mr. Roger Houston

SUBJECT: Mailing List

Dear Rog:

Last week Bob Morton and I talked on the phone about the mailing list for your new direct mail program.

We do not want superfluous names on the list, so we are going to use a list from the following SIC's:

33 21 Gray iron foundries
33 22 Malleable iron foundries
33 23 Steel foundries
33 61 Aluminum castings
33 62 Brass, bronze, copper, copper-base alloy castings
33 69 Nonferrous castings, n.e.c.

Roger, if we concentrate exclusively on these SIC's, where our market potential really lies, we end up with a net list of slightly more than 3,600 establishments. All have 20 or more employees. Included are both ferrous and nonferrous foundries.

Incidentally, I got a copy of *Penton's Foundry List* to evaluate, and I can see why you like it. It can be very valuable to field salesmen and to sales managers, since it locates and identifies establishments.

For use as a mailing list it is not too practical, however. Too much time and money would be spent identifying and qualifying buying influences. This is not to say we can't do it; we can with, I would estimate, a 75-80 percent correct return.

This would take several weeks, probably up to two months. Cost, I'd guess, would run in the neighborhood of $1,500 to $2,000. This would include questionnaires, followups, phone calls, and verification of returns with internal labor here in the department.

Penton's list is a list of *firms.* Firms are fine, but you do not mail to them. The mail boy always throws your material in the round file.

To be effective and productive, direct mail must be addressed to a specific individual. This is what we have done for other product lines, and is what I recommend we continue to do.

Field salesmen (in *most* companies) tend to denigrate direct mail—and the direct mail list itself—because they do not consider direct mail's objective.

The objective of our program, as established by marketing management, is to make a sales call, by mail, *on executives on whom our salesmen do not now call.* This is what this type of direct mail *should* do.

With the cost of the average industrial sales call at an all time high—now nearly $72 per call—a call by mail for pennies *on a top executive the salesmen do not see is* dirt cheap.

As we discussed the other day, recommendations for our equipment probably start on the operating level. But we must not lose sight of the fact that, when an expenditure of tens of thousands of dollars is involved, top management is going to get in on the act.

Top management must be thoroughly familiar with Smith Widget Manufacturing Company, they must have confidence in us. They will on both scores if we advertise consistently, and if we continue to call on them by mail.

Roger, we can reach them by mail *only* if we use their names on the envelopes.

I've checked our list, and it's highly accurate. I used normal verification methods, without a survey. Dun & Bradstreet's massive reference, *D & B's Metalworking Directory,* Standard & Poor's excellent book *(Poor's Register), Automotive Industries' Marketing Guide,* and so on.

The list is valid, and it's clean as a whistle when you consider that throughout industry average annual personnel turnover, in the class of people we want to reach, is on the order of one-third.

But our list will be even better within the next three weeks because I'm getting the latest revision from D&B; it was compiled within the past month.

I realize, as you do, that no list is 100 percent perfect, the minute it is compiled somebody quits his job, somebody dies, a firm goes out of business, a merger occurs, or a score of possibilities can change the quo of the status.

But the Dun & Bradstreet list is, in my opinion, and in that of our agency, the best there is. It is remarkably accurate. It is the best way to get the names of the four top executives in all of the foundries we want to reach, at a cost that is not prohibitive—and without wasting time.

We can cross-check the establishments against Penton's list, or any other you suggest if it will ease your mind.

But I feel very strongly, Rog, that we absolutely *must* mail to individuals, not simply to a firm. In good conscience I can't acquiesce with any other course, nor can I countenance mailing only to names supplied by product management and the sales force.

If there's real doubt in your mind, let's get together and Indian wrassle. I'll pop for lunch!

Cordially,
/s/
Bud Edwards
Advertising Manager

That advertising manager touched 'most all of the bases on this subject—and he's 110 percent right. He knows his subject.

List Maintenance

Without being iconoclastic about the matter, there are a number of ground rules the industrial advertising manager should follow as far as maintenance of the mailing list is concerned.

Average industrial lists change more than 30 percent per year. Considering a mailing list a static thing is a terrible tactical error. Reconcile yourself to constant maintenance, and budget for it.

Allocate approximately 10 percent of your direct mail budget to list development, procurement, and maintenance. This figure naturally varies considerably, depending upon the nature of your business and the breakdown of your promotional budget. The more you spend on direct mail, the smaller the percentage will be. Skimping here is the wrong place to try to save a dollar.

Rely on outside experts. Except for the giants of industry, very few companies have or can afford full-time list experts in their advertising departments. Rather than attempting to muddle through or make do with something almost right, you're much better off to rely on outside sources for lists—including compiling and maintenance. Cost will be less in the long run.

Too many spoons spoil the soup. Adopt and enforce a strict rule that everybody and his brother is *not* to get his hands on the mailing list, nor is just anybody permitted to add or delete names. Establish a firm policy as to why and when maintenance is to be performed, the kind of names that are to be added to the list, and the person who is to do the actual work, and who is to supervise it. Dilution of responsibility results in dilution of the value of the list.

Be a chronic list questioner. Refuse to accept at face value any list, including your own. The perfect list has never yet been compiled and chances are mighty small indeed that it ever will. The sooner you learn to be skeptical about *all* lists, the sooner you'll be in a position where you can't get burned by a poor one. Numerous good lists exist, of course, but numerous incredibly poor lists are used by mail advertisers who should know better. Make it standard operating procedure to analyze all lists thoroughly and accurately—including your own—before using them.

Lists are like teeth: They should be cleaned twice a year. Normal maintenance should be done continuously without stopping for anything, regardless of how busy the department is. But major cleanings should be scheduled every six months and the list should then be reviewed, analyzed, and checked to make absolutely sure it is as good as you can make it.

Six mailings a year over a sizable list call for mechanical addressing. Excepting First Day Covers and other special mailings, the economics of the situation dictates use of mechanical addressing, although you should analyze this to ascertain whether you're going the right route or not.

The mailing list is the key to success in direct mail advertising. Respect it, cherish it, nurture it. You can't put too much effort, time, or thought into keeping it clean and up to date. The better the list, the better the results. It's that simple. And this is a fundamental truth that cannot be avoided, ignored, or swept under the carpet—even temporarily.

Besides periodic maintenance, it is necessary that the mailing list be updated daily, or as often as mailings are made and returns return. Basis of corrections made this frequently are:

> *Nixies*—This is mail returned by the post office as undeliverable for one reason or another. Personnel changes, mergers, new plant locations, companies now out of business; all these reasons result in a certain percentage of nixies. The cleaner the list is, the fewer the nixies, of course, although there are always a few. They're like death and taxes.
>
> *Salesmen's call reports*—Many aggressive industrial companies have a policy that all new names showing up in salesmen's call reports are automatically bucked on to the advertising department to be put on the appropriate direct mail list. Furthermore, these companies have standing instructions to their salesmen to report all new names (plus changes, although this seldom gets done, salesmen despising paperwork as they do) to be added to the list.
>
> *Customer notifications*—It is not at all unusual for customers to accept the responsibility of sending you changes in their status, address, and so on as they receive mail from you. These notifications should, of course, be acted upon immediately; if these customers are interested enough to help you communicate with them, they're certainly customers you want to take good care of.

Easiest and best list cleaner yet devised is asking the recipients of your direct mail advertising to help you get the job done. Many industrial mail users routinely request change-of-address information in each mailing they make, while others include list cleaners at less frequent intervals—say, three or four times a year.

Other companies make special list-cleaning mailings to elicit information they need to maintain their mailing lists. This may well be the most effective way of handling the cleaning job, although it's also the most expensive way.

Your nearby post office will lend you a hand with a pair of special services designed to update your mailing lists. If you print *Address Correction Requested* on your outgoing mail, you will be notified of the addressee's new address when first-class mail is forwarded. A charge of 15 cents per piece will be made for this service.

Pieces of third- and fourth-class mail bearing the words *Return Postage Guaranteed* which are undeliverable as addressed will be returned to sender upon payment of return postage at the applicable rate. Reason for nondelivery or the new address of the addressee will be furnished for each such piece only when the 15-cent fee for a notice is paid in addition to the return postage.

Paying for returns, unless they number into the thousands, is good policy. It saves future postage, time, materials mailed, and prevents the illusion of accomplishing something constructive if the list is horribly inadequate. If the returns *should* be more than 25 percent of a mailing, the time has long since passed when the list should have been thoroughly cleaned and the time for immediate action is *right now.*

Formats

Direct mail is a highly personal medium. In fact, the personal letter from one person to another is the oldest form of direct mail—and it is still one of the most effective.

In a personal letter you can talk just as frankly and confidentially as if you were actually engaging in conversation with the individual you're trying to convert from prospect to customer.

Failure to personalize direct mail letters lessens their effectiveness very substantially. Even mass mailings are personal communications because they are received in privacy by one person; he regards the letter as a communication to himself and to nobody else.

Personalizing, via fill-ins of varying lengths (lines) is no longer prohibitively costly, nor is it too time-consuming for the typical direct mail advertiser to use. Today's techniques result in printed letters that look very much like the real thing; a close match on the fill-in of the address and salutation produces a letter that looks as if it had been individually typed. Cost is a fraction of the fully-typed letter, of course.

Auto-typed letters, if the quantity is no more than a thousand or so, are superior to the reproduced letter, although they cost more. They are produced by electric typewriters which produce letter after letter, error-free, and all exactly the same in every respect; the principle is much the same as that of the old player-piano. Letters are produced from a "master" tape or roll from a letter that was first individually typed and approved.

Once auto-typed, it is an easy matter to fill in the address and/or the salutation in matching type to personalize these letters. The auto-typed direct mail letter is the best of all forms of letters, it is the most productive; the recipient usually cannot tell it from an individually typed letter unless he inspects the fill-in with a magnifying glass—and who does?

Another kind of widely used direct mail letter is the printed letter with a signature cut in a contrasting color (usually, but not always blue) and with the salutation—Dear Friend, Dear Sir, Dear Customer. Frequently the salutation is in the contrasting color also to present the appearance of being hand written.

The public, and especially the business community, is well aware of rising costs and the urgent need to hold them in line wherever possible. Such letters are known to hold costs down, so are accepted and received without resentment despite the vague salutation.

The Chrysler Airtemp Program

Airtemp Division, Chrysler Corporation, is a large industrial marketer who uses direct mail created by Graphic Service, and does so to good effect. Airtemp's program, now well established, is designed to attract new dealers for the division's products—room air conditioners, packaged cooling and heating systems, and applied machinery and systems.

This direct mail advertising campaign is a continuing effort directed to target dealers; the company realizes the way to achieve a sizable sales increase is through expanded distribution. Each Airtemp distributor furnishes a list of target dealers in his locality and he constantly cleans and updates it.

When a new dealer is signed up to sell Airtemp products, he is removed from the target dealer list, of course, for any communications the company sends to him henceforth will be of a different character than the ones created to persuade him to handle the line.

Each of the two-color mailing pieces (blue and black) includes a photograph of Tom Kirby, vice-president, marketing, of the Airtemp Division. This "humanizes" the pieces and shows prospective dealers they are not going to have to transact business with a huge, impersonal corporation. Prospective dealers see a living, breathing person, obviously warm and friendly, a man they begin to feel they know as the series progresses.

Graphic Service imparted more immediacy and produced greater impact by personalizing each individual mailing piece for each individual recipient with a drop-in paragraph or P.S. which tells the prospect exactly who his distributor is, where he's located, and what his phone number is. Let's see what the copy says:

(Page 1)

This name holds
a promise for you . . .
A promise too big
and too important
to overlook

(Page 2)

(logos)

Let me ask you something.

If you were to name the one thing—above everything else—that keeps you in business, what would your answer be?

You bet. *Profit.*

Because nobody—you, us, or anyone—moves, grows, or *stays* in business very long without it. At least, that's what we believe at Airtemp . . . not only for ourselves, but for everyone who is part of us.

In fact, profit is the promise we hold for you as an Airtemp Dealer.

What makes us so sure?

Look at our sales. In the last three years alone sales have actually doubled in every phase of our business . . . in room air conditioners, in packaged cooling and heating units, and in applied machinery and systems. And our sales figures so far this year indicate that the current year will top everything we've done in the past.

Look at our products. Our entire line of equipment is second to none in the industry, and in many instances far more advanced. In packaged units, for example, we offer a broad range of "Pre-charged" models. In water chillers, we stand alone with the smallest, lightest, most compact new chillers ever designed or manufactured by anyone. And our furnace line offers a wide variety of gas and oil-fired units as well as all-electric furnaces.

(Page 3)

Look at our plans. Based on our equipment and its advanced engineering, our expanding sales in every area, *and dealers like you who've made it happen,* we've already completed a $40,000,000 capital expansion to meet what we believe will be our biggest production demands in history.

In short, there is no question in my mind or in the mind of anyone at Airtemp that *Airtemp is going up and we're going to stay.*

We can see it, we can feel it, we can taste it.

Let me repeat: As a dealer who can share in this growth and the *profit* it represents, Airtemp holds a promise for you that you can't afford to overlook, and I urge you, most sincerely, to take the time *now* to get the story for yourself.

W. L. Regan, your local Airtemp distributor, will be glad to meet with you at your convenience and discuss our lines and plans in detail and answer your questions in full.

His number is 786-8710; he's the kind of person you'll like doing business with; and there's no obligation in any way.

Come on. Make this *your* year to grow with Airtemp. We'd like to have you with us.

Sincerely,
T. W. Kirby
Vice-President, Marketing

TWK/gs

Mortal man has yet to devise a sounder approach when attempting to enlist new dealers than dangling profit in front of their faces. This this mailer did, and did exceptionally well. A mighty deft hand was guiding that typewriter. While it might initially appear Airtemp was bragging a bit on its sales gains, prospective dealers automatically translated this into retail sales with 40 percent markup.

This copy approach is sound and logical and persuasive.

Notice the next to last two paragraphs on page three; these are drop-ins. They make it easy for the prospective dealer to take immediate action by picking up his phone and calling the individual who can "close" him—the local Airtemp distributor. No waiting, no risking having a prospect who's very close to being sold get unsold by delay in contact. This is smart direct mail advertising because it strikes while the iron—the prospect—is hot.

Chrysler Airtemp had used the usual collection of trade shows, distributor salesmen's incentive programs, publicity, and space advertising to attract new dealers, all with a certain measure of success.

Addition of this personalized direct mail advertising campaign aimed directly at prospects judged hottest by aggressive, on-the-spot distributors *doubled* the number of new dealers signed up in the first 12 months this excellent program was employed. You don't have to be a mathametician to estimate what effect this many additional new dealers had on sales!

A Winner for Victor

Final example of the illustrated-letter mailing piece was also produced by Graphic Service, although this fine direct mail agency by no means limits itself to one format.

Victor Business Machines Group, according to James G. Johnson, Electrowriter sales manager, spends a lot of money on trade shows each year. He said, "When prospects visit our booth, we spend a great deal of time explaining the Electrowriter, what it does, and then point out its uses in the particular field being covered by the trade show.

"What we want is some way to pre-educate those attending the show so they will have a basic knowledge of the Electrowriter and how it can be applied in their business or industry."

It's axiomatic that every exhibitor at every trade show has a burning desire for lots and lots of traffic in his booth. An empty or mostly empty booth is a depressing thing, and it creates a terribly negative impression of attendees at trade shows. Victor wanted not only a heavy traffic flow, but wanted a *knowledgeable* group to see its wares at the International Association of Fire Chiefs convention, where Victor exhibited. The problem was put to Graphic Service.

Graphic Service folks realized instantly that the thing of prime importance was to interest fire chiefs in Victor's Electrowriter Alarm System so they'd be intrigued enough to search out Victor's booth to learn more about the product.

What was finally worked out was a four-page letter that graphically described Victor's amazing new alarm system, and went into quite a bit of detail on how it sends an immediate *written* message to selected fire stations, the police department and to public utilities.

3900 NORTH ROCKWELL STREET, CHICAGO, ILLINOIS 60618

At right, start of the four-page illustrated letter used by Victor Business Machines to arouse interest in product before trade show. It did the job—nine of every 10 of those who called mentioned piece or brought it with them.

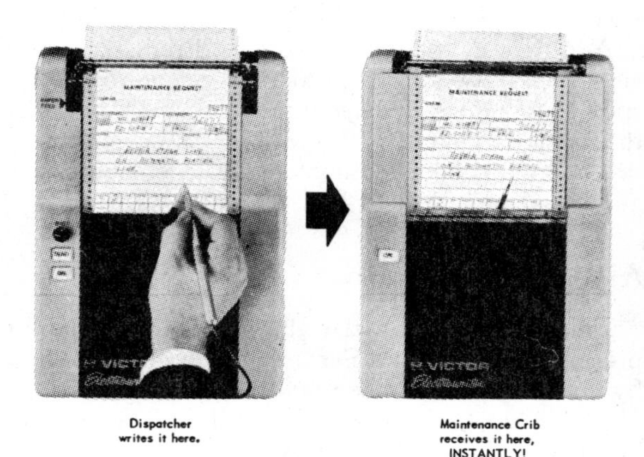

Dispatcher
writes it here.
Maintenance Crib
receives it here,
INSTANTLY!

HERE'S HOW YOU CAN IMPROVE
YOUR MAINTENANCE DISPATCHING
CONTROL WITH ELECTROWRITERS

The units you see above make up Victor's new Electrowriter Maintenance Dispatching System that you can use to transmit written "work orders" to any number of maintenance cribs in your plant in a matter of seconds.

Let me tell you how it works, and how it can benefit you.

It did the job.

Sales manager Johnson reported, "So often at conventions I've stood in a booth while people stroll by and look in with sort of a blank, hesitant expression, as though they were thinking, 'I wonder if there's anything worthwhile in there?'

"It was a real pleasure at the Fire Chief's convention to have men walk in *knowing where they were going and knowing what they wanted to learn.*

"On top of it all, we got much more traffic than we expected."

Victor has used this same kind of a pre-education program for the petroleum industry show, the Midwest Hotel-Motel Convention and the Armed Forces Communication Electrical Association Show. All were highly successful.

That the mail goes to the right people and that it accomplishes its objective isn't open to guesswork or interpretation at Victor. Sales manager Johnson said after the first couple of mailings prior to shows, "These pieces are really getting through. About nine out of 10 people visiting the booth either mentioned the mailing piece early in the conversation, or had it with them."

Self Mailers

Self mailers—pieces mailed sans envelope—are usually closed with a gummed "wafer" to prevent unfolding in the mail. Self mailers are considerably less costly to produce and mail since no envelope is required, and they can be mailed in bulk.

When an extra heavy stock is used, such as an 80-pound cover stock, a variety of shapes, sizes, folds, and other treatments may be used to catch the eye and add interest to the piece. And when either a colored stock or screenings of second colors are used overall, some truly outstanding self mailers can be produced at remarkably low cost.

The self mailer on page 1298 was created by Derse Advertising Company, Milwaukee, specialist in signs of all types and trade show exhibits. It is 8 inches square. On the outside this mailer looks as if it's printed on a light brown stock, although this is actually brown ink laid down solid on white stock. Colors are brown, black, and red. On the side opposite the address, the theme of the piece is splashed boldly across the mailer—that Derse Advertising Company provides all of the services listed on the other side, all tied up in one nice, neat package. The "string" tieing the package together is a nice touch, and the white wafer sealing the mailer seems to belong there.

Opening just the two flaps of the package gives Derse a generous area for copy space, four black-and-white halftones, and a strong, hard-sell bid for action.

When the top flaps of the package are opened up, there's a very strong and very convincing testimonial based on articles in Mil-

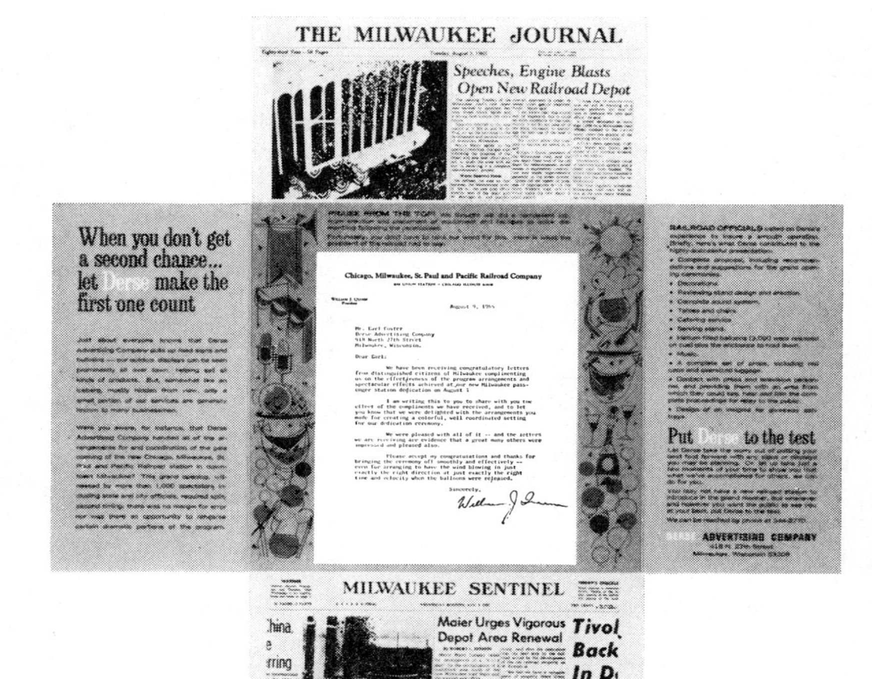

Chicago, Milwaukee, St. Paul and Pacific Railroad Company

August 9, 1965

Mr. Earl Foster
Derse Advertising Company
918 North 27th Street
Milwaukee, Wisconsin.

Dear Earl:

We have been receiving congratulatory letters from distinguished citizens of Milwaukee complimenting us on the effectiveness of the program arrangements and spectacular effects achieved at our new Milwaukee passenger station dedication on August 1.

I am writing this to you to share with you the effect of the compliments we have received, and to let you know that we were delighted with the arrangements you made for creating a colorful, well coordinated setting for our dedication ceremony.

We were pleased with all of it -- and the letters we are receiving are evidence that a great many others were impressed and pleased also.

Please accept my congratulations and thanks for bringing the ceremony off smoothly and effectively -- even for arranging to have the wind blowing in just exactly the right direction at just exactly the right time and velocity when the balloons were released.

Sincerely,

William J. Quinn

waukee's two leading newspapers, as well as an endorsement from the Chicago, Milwaukee, St. Paul and Pacific Railroad Company about how delighted William J. Quinn, president of the railroad, was with arrangements Derse made to create a "colorful, well coordinated setting" for the dedication of an imposing new three-story railroad depot.

Catalogs and Price Lists

Catalogs, product literature, and price lists have long been favorite mailing pieces for industrial direct mail advertisers. They're effective, for they put your selling message in front of the prospect just the way you want it presented. There's no deviation in presentation, as there is from salesman to salesman.

Mass mailings of catalogs and similar literature are no longer possible for many companies, however. Printing costs, paper costs, production costs, administrative costs—and even that for postage itself—have zoomed in recent years.

Catalogs, up-to-date literature, and prices are still excellent mailing pieces and can still be used without waste *if* your mailing list is clean and well maintained. If it isn't, you shouldn't be using it. When you mail with the assurance that those who will receive your mailings have been qualified, then it becomes obvious the investment may well pay off.

Literature about the company's products may range from lavish, four-color catalogs with hundreds, or even thousands, of pages—or it may be a single-sheet, front and back black-and-white technical story.

Mailing literature pays, and pays handsomely, in increased awareness of the product and the company, in heightened receptiveness to the salesman's story, and in occasional over-the-transom orders—*if* you put your literature in the right hands. If you're less than 100 percent sure on this score, forget it and put the money into a clean list for future mailings.

Promiscuous, helter-skelter mailing of literature alone, unaccompanied by a covering letter, order form, reply card or some other request for action is also a waste of money in most instances.

Showmanship Formats

One thing in life is as sure and certain as rising taxes: The oddball, the curious, and the unique can be depended upon to attract people's attention.

Human nature varies neither a whit nor a jot (find increments smaller than those!) from Portland, Maine to Portland, Oregon—or anywhere in between. And human nature being what it is, people *like* things and ideas and places that are strictly off the beaten path. They thoroughly enjoy being titillated by the unusual.

A word of caution, though. Showmanship mailings should be wisely chosen so they do not call so much attention to themselves that they obscure the sales message. As with every medium and every technique, there are pitfalls to be avoided. Dick Hodgson, author of *The Dartnell Direct Mail and Mail Order Handbook,* quotes Henry Hoke, editor of *The Reporter of Direct Mail Advertising,* on seven basic problems to avoid in developing showmanship in direct mail. These are:

1. Do not use any unusual or tricky format unless there is a real reason for it. Many advertisers are tempted to use so-called trick mailing pieces simply because they see something similarly clever used by someone else.

2. Be sure of your audience. Use the same good taste and judgment in selecting unusual mailing pieces as you would use in your copy writing to a given audience.

3. Do not use unusual or tricky pieces on the spur of the moment, just to be different. Plan your unusual pieces carefully in advance, along with the rest of your merchandising campaign.

4. Be sure the finished job will look right when it reaches each recipient. Many good ideas go wrong due to amateur handling. For example, in die-cutting, be sure you use the right weight of stock. With tip-ons, be sure they will stay on. In sampling, be sure they are packaged right.

5. Realize that only a limited number of producers are equipped with machinery and experience to handle intricate, unusual formats properly. Some printers have discouraged the use of die-cuts because they are not equipped, or do not know how to handle them. Avoid disappointments by employing experienced production facilities.

6. Appreciate the limitation of tricky forms and abide by those limitations. Follow the advice of experienced designers who usually know what can and cannot be done.

7. A final rule of warning should be printed in large letters, framed and hung in clear view of every planning desk: *Do not make your unusual mailing piece so clever that the recipient will remember your cleverness rather than your offer.*

Hodgson also noted that Kenneth Goode and Zenn Kaufman, in their book, *Profitable Showmanship,* have defined seven general principles about successful business showmanship. These are:

1. *Ideas are born right or wrong.* Showmanship calls for extremes—but the *right* extremes. Doing a thing differently may be doing it worse, no matter how differently! It does not help to be different when all the others are right.

2. *Find yourself a "natural."* The greatest danger in showmanship is the almost irresistible temptation to accept its traditional symbols—often threadbare and tawdry. Take hockey, for example, Red-white-and-blue uniforms look like showmanship. The idea of recruiting a whole Chicago team among American-born boys *is* showmanship.

3. *Think BIG.* Do not waste time on middle-sized elephants. There is no percentage in a "little-bigness," in second bests. If you cannot get a Jumbo, the biggest of them all, don't compromise on a near-Jumbo. Reverse your attack completely and get a *baby* elephant, the smallest of them all. Lacking a whale, turn completely about and exploit a minnow. Take a lesson from the little tourist restaurant buried deep in the Alabama woods which courageously called itself, "Swamp View."

4. *Do it surpassingly.* Sincerity in showmanship includes adequacy! Half a show is *not* better than none. It is worse! Don't ever feel that because you have done your best you have done everything.

5. *Don't compete with yourself.* Do it surpassingly. But do not have more than one *it.* Circuses have six rings to take care of 6,000 customers

simultaneously. When the ringmaster seeks the climax of attention, he turns off everything but the spotlight, and speaks alone—quite softly. Advertisers, as a rule, give themselves more competition than their competitors do. You cannot get 300-percent attention by combining three 100-percent features.

6. *Make it crystal clear.* Sincerity in showmanship also includes absolute clarity of meaning. To avoid ambiguity may, in fact, be the greatest function of showmanship. True meanings must explode themselves—immediately, unmistakably, energetically to every mind.
7. *Keep it a game.* The genius of showmanship expresses itself in apt and picturesque play, sometimes quite unconsciously. Make your work interesting to people—and people will make it important for you.

Almost everything is an adaptation. New ideas don't spring forth fullblown from nothing. Something always triggers an idea, something that has already transpired, something that somebody has already done. With thought, however, you can improve upon almost anything that's been done by others. And just because you can't seem to come up with something completely new and different doesn't mean that what you have come up with won't be effective.

Various audiences have been exposed to various ideas, but not every audience has been exposed to every idea.

Letter Gadgets

Something—almost anything, in fact—stuck to a letter attracts the attention of the recipient far faster than a plain letter. Tiny plastic reproductions of everyday items, for example, are ridiculously inexpensive, yet they provide a good place for copy to take off from.

Shown below are a miniature gold-colored hammer to hammer this point home, as well as scissors (which actually work), a crescent wrench, and a monkey wrench. To prove this is not monkey business, these items are placed alongside a penny to show size.

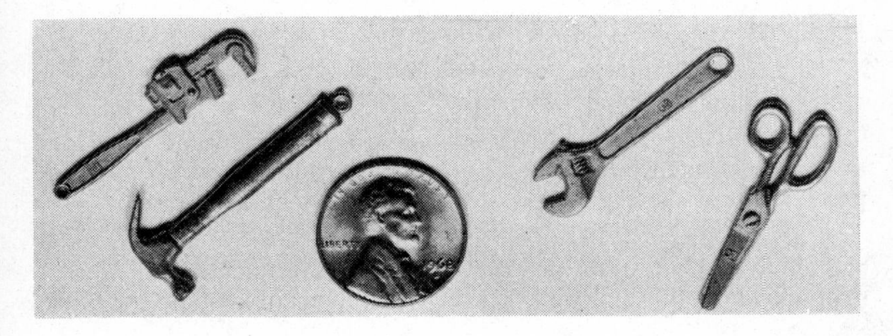

A good source for letter gadgets—and that's what they're called, incidentally—is:

Hewig Letter Gadgets
861 Manhattan Avenue
Brooklyn, New York 11222
(212) 383-2070

Other Tip-Ons

You're limited only by your imagination and that ever-present ogre, the budget, when it comes to tipping things onto your letters and mailing pieces.

Shown is a clever tip-on that really works—an abacus. If the office adding machine, calculator, or the controller's computer breaks down, the abacus could keep your business from going on the rocks. Nobody wants business on the rocks.

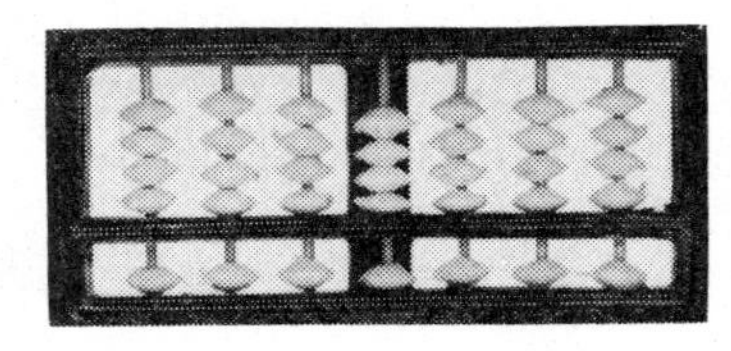

Plastic abacus that really works was used by the author as a direct-mail curiosity.

This particular abacus works so well it enables the author to handle the expense account without bothering a hard-working secretary. Other tip-ons might be keys, buttons, wrist watch calendars, and so on. All do what they're supposed to do, which is attract attention.

Abrasives, sandpaper, a message scratched on glass with a diamond, cloth, and so forth are all unusual enough to pique the curiosity and cause the recipient of a message on their surface to peek again at the mailer.

Magnification

Take a familiar object and blow it up to an absurd size and it automatically evokes amusement.

The ad manager of a prominent manufacturer of semiconductors had an integrated circuit made of plastic via the injection molding process.

Now, the original circuit is about half the size of a sugar cube and about 3/32nd of an inch thick. All of the recipients of his direct mail ads know this full well. What made this mailing stand out more vividly than a sore thumb was that it was 13 inches wide, 18 inches deep, and 4 inches thick! Selected buying influences in some 2,500 establishments received the giant integrated circuit and they practically howled. It was such good-natured fun poked at the industry for constantly trying to make its products smaller and smaller that the mailing won't be forgotten for years.

Miniaturization

Reductions in size always have appeal. One direct mail advertiser recently mailed a tiny telegram, hardly larger than an airmail stamp, complete with a tiny magnifying glass so the recipients could read it.

And stamp-sized books of hundreds of pages are available from dealers in advertising specialties; they invariably cause much comment and make a very strong impression.

Miniaturization is an excellent route to go because the impression the tiny items make is large, and also because of the kindly bite the post office takes due to the light weight of the items.

Unusual Shapes and Folds

Novel die cuts and unexpected folds are stoppers.

Almost nobody is able to discard a tightly folded oversize flyer, for example, without unfolding the thing just to see what's inside. This is akin to the big-game hunter's desire always to "glass just one more valley" and to go through just one more pass between two mountains to see what's on the other side. Everybody wants to find out what is hidden behind a mountain or an enticing fold or cut shape in a mailing piece.

Useful Items

When you're mailing to an industrial audience, these stout-hearted members of industry *who are businessmen first and people and consumers as a very close second.*

Here you can use ballpoint pen refills (available from many sources for 6 cents each for all-metal ones), golf tees, plastic hat covers, combs, folding umbrellas, toothbrushes, shoelaces, plastic raincoats, portfolios, tie bars, or what have you. But don't mail razor blades. Too many people have been badly cut, including a number of small fry. Congress has legislation pending to outlaw mailing of razor blades and assorted drugs, even including the ubiquitous aspirin. Children can become ill.

Advertising Specialties

Advertising specialties are really an extension of useful items; they can be imprinted or unimprinted. But why miss a chance to make another impression, not once but many times?

Ballpoint pens, matches, cigarette lighters for those who don't mind a little lung cancer, tie bars, cuff links, and so on are all attractive, useful and welcome. They can do double duty, too, serving as hand-out pieces as well as items to be mailed. Shown in a photograph are: Diamond T "Old No. 1" cuff links, Diamond T "Old No. 1" tie bar, pearl-handled scissors-knife, pearl-handled money-clip knife, Zippo lighter, stainless steel knife with case, and stainless steel Christy knife with case.

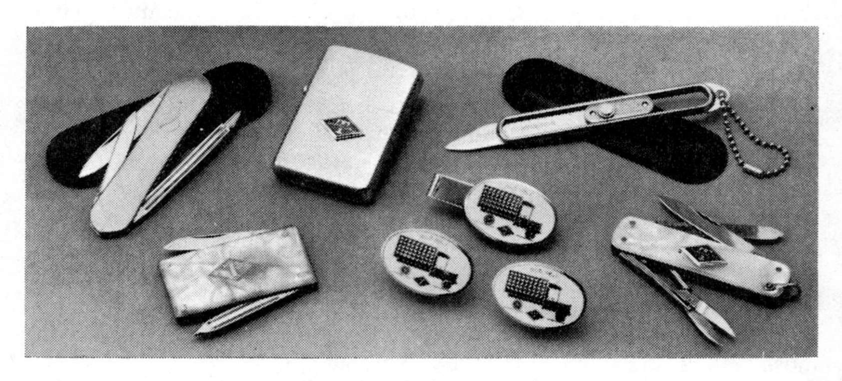

The jewelry, rhodium-plated or gold-plated, was used by Diamond T Motor Truck Company. It was purchased from Leavens Manufacturing Company, Summer Street, Attleboro, Massachusetts, and is of exceptionally high quality.

The money-clip knife was also used by Diamond T., and is available from a number of advertising specialty houses.

The Diamond T pearl-handled scissors-knife is a superb item; it's all stainless steel and brass bound. The author imported it directly from:

Viola and Company
Viale Coni Zugna 34
Milan, Italy

When you're importing, *always* engage a reliable customs broker to handle the paperwork connected with getting the shipment into the country and through customs. You pay for the merchandise with an irrevocable letter of credit in favor of the foreign manufacturer;

payment to his account is made when he presents shipping documents showing the merchandise is aboard a ship. This can be handled through your company's local bank.

Be absolutely *sure* to instruct your customs broker *in writing* to have your shipments insured. You can depend on having the boxes broken into and approximately 10 percent of the merchandise stolen.

Customs brokers handle shipments for a tiny fraction of the total value of the shipment, usually around 5 percent, and take all of the headaches and frustrations out of importing. They're intimately familiar with the government forms; they handle payment of the customs fee and bill you net on this.

Sources of domestic advertising specialties can be found in the *Thomas Register* and other directories, although you might save yourself some time by looking in the classified advertisements in the back of *The Reporter of Direct Mail Advertising.* This is a magazine you should be reading if you plan on doing any volume of direct mail advertising. Subscriptions are $7.50 per year. Address of the publication is:

> *The Reporter of Direct Mail Advertising*
> 224 Seventh Street
> Garden City,
> Long Island,
> New York 11530

Historical Items

For the past few years—in fact, since 1961 marked the 100th anniversary of the beginning of the War Between the States—there's been a noticeable upsurge in interest in things historical and in Americana in particular.

Full-sized reproductions of old newspapers, on "antiqued" paper so they look and feel properly old and yellowed, are popular mailing pieces. E. F. Houghton & Company celebrated its 100th anniversary with an exceptionally attractive and nicely bound portfolio of old newspapers, all historic editions such as the April 10, 1865 issue of The Philadelphia *Inquirer* announcing the end of the war with the headline, *Victory! Victory!*

Historical mailers not only attract attention, but they receive avid and thorough readership; and they're frequently taken home, passed around to members of the family, then taken to school by the youngsters. Such pieces are an excellent buy and are highly effective in terms of interest aroused.

First Day Covers

Philatelists and almost everybody else take an interest in First Day Covers—that is, stamps issued and canceled by a specially designated post office to commemorate an historical event.

The beauty of First Day Covers is that although the recipient may not be a philatelist—a stamp collector, that is—almost everybody knows somebody who *is*. Frequently it's one of the recipient's offspring. One sure way to become an instant hero is to present a First Day Cover to a dedicated collector.

You can use regular envelopes, but they lack the impact that specially prepared envelopes developed especially for this purpose have. These First Day Cover envelopes are called "cachets" and are available from a number of sources at a modest price. They are usually beautifully engraved, and often printed in two or three colors. For a source of cachets nearest you, contact your nearest coin and stamp dealer, look in the advertisements in *The Reporter of Direct Mail Advertising,* or order from:

Cover Craft Cachets
Paterson, New Jersey

The post office is the source of information about future First Day Cover stamps.

Caution: When mailing First Day Covers, do *not* seal the envelopes. Put your letter inside and tuck in the flap. Philatelists will *not* slit open a First Day Cover envelope; to do so destroys its desirability as a collector's item for them.

Handling a First Day Cover mailing program is easy. Simply order cachets from the source you've selected, have them shipped directly to your letter shop, assuming you use one, have them addressed and then have the letter shop ship them in ample time to the postmaster at the city of issue for the new stamp. A postal money order, bank draft or cashier's check for the proper amount of postage must accompany the covers; no company or personal checks are accepted. The post office makes no charge for affixing the stamps and mailing.

Unusual Postmarks

Mailings from odd-sounding places that tickle the fancy and stir the wanderlust are economical, as well as highly popular. They are received with enthusiasm even among those who are only casually interested. Attention is called to the postmark in copy inside the mailing piece, of course, although recipients catch on fast when a campaign is a continuing one, and they look forward to receiving future mailings.

The mechanics of making unusual postmark mailings is simplicity itself, although certain considerations should be borne in mind. You can get an alphabetical index of the *Directory of Post Offices* from the Superintendent of Documents, Washington, D.C. 20402. This manual lists post offices that lend themselves to almost any theme or scheme, whether it be Faith, Hope and Charity, Construction, Economy, Value, or what have you.

Prudence dictates that you verify the post office you've selected is still a going concern. Mortality rate among small post offices today is high.

Write to the postmaster at the town you've selected and request a sample of his postmark to be sure it's legible. Sometimes they're pretty badly worn. Then tell him of your plans and give him your timetable as closely as you can pinpoint it. This is frequently necessary to assure having sufficient labor available to handle your mailing. Your mailing may well be the largest the post office has handled in its entire history.

Be sure to purchase your stamps from the post office you're using. This is common courtesy and will be appreciated by the postmaster; he receives credit for stamp sales and wants to make as good a showing as possible. Stamps will have to be applied to your letters or mailers *before* they are shipped to the post office you've selected, however. Even if you buy them from Spotted Horse, Wyoming, the postmaster there will not affix them for you. First Day Covers are the only exception to this.

Although the post office is a government service, nonetheless you've asked a favor of the postmaster who handles your mailing. It's only decent to send a token of your appreciation to him after the job is done. And a nice touch is to send a sample of the mailing, along with a brief story about it, to the town's newspaper—or the one nearest the town from which your mail was sent. Give the postmaster a warm mention and you've made a friend for life.

Foreign Mailings

Foreign stamps and postmarks are conspicuously successful in attracting attention. They inject an aura of glamour and romance which produces high readership. Best practice is to use as many stamps as are required for the minimum postage; that is, use stamps of as low denomination as possible to add up to the correct total postage.

Doing this, you receive more stamps for the same amount of money and more attention when the mailing is received. This practice actually makes envelopes or mailing pieces real billboards for your message inside.

Foreign mailings are easy to arrange through any of the following firms which specialize in this end of the direct mail advertising field:

Adhan n.v., Algemeen Adressenbureau, Atjehstraat 12, 's—Gravenhage

Adv. Dist. of Am., Inc., 400 Madison Avenue, N. Y. C. 10017

Chadwick-Latz Ltd., Publicity House, Finsbury Square, London, EC 2, England

Dillon, Agnew & Marton, Inc., New York, Amsterdam, London
654 Madison Ave., N. Y., N. Y. 10021

Jock Falkson/Effective Letters, Box 4564, Johannesburg, South Africa

Han Snel NV, Prinsengracht 1025, Amsterdam C, The Netherlands

Han Snel NV, Avenue Concordia 62, Rotterdam, The Netherlands

Han Snel KG, Mittelstrasse 20.24, Koln, Germany

Robb Holland Limited, 86/88 Acre Lane, London S.W. 2, England

Indian Advertising Bureau, P.O. Box 10210, 55, Gariahat Road, Calcutta-19, India

Intercontinental Marketing Corp., GPO Box 1717, Tokyo, Japan

Intermail (Pty) Ltd., Box 23322 Joubert Park, Johannesburg, South Africa

Merchandising & Marketing, S.A. CV, Vallarta 1, Mexico 4, DF, Mexico

Mutator Intl. Mlgs., Willemsparkweg 112/114, Amsterdam Z., Netherlands

Publimer Around-the-World Direct Mail, Paris, London, New York,
5 Roosevelt Place, Scarsdale, New York

S/K Associates Advertising, I.P.O. Box 2301, Seoul, Korea

Money

This is a favorite subject of many people.

One of the most widely used tip-ons in direct mail is the penny. The penny has much going for it; it's legal tender, few of us can resist it, it attracts attention and causes the letter or mailer to assume much more importance in the eyes of the recipient than its negligible value warrants, it can be put in some parking meters, and it's inexpensive to use. What else can you ask of a penny?

Foreign coins are often available for even less than a penny, and they make an even stronger impression. Obsolete coins are also used with great success. McGraw-Hill made a series of mailings a year or so ago with authentic-looking reproductions of ancient Roman coins; accompanying each was a capsule description of the original coin, its worth when struck, and other tidbits of information. Numismatists were delighted.

Reproductions of Confederate money invariably do an exceptionally fine job of attracting and holding interest. Mailing good-quality antiqued reproductions in a window envelope so piques the curiosity it's safe to assume not one person in a thousand would throw away the envelope unopened.

Both of these items (in fact, a complete catalog of historic papers) are available from this source:

Historical Documents Company
8 North Preston Streeet
Philadelphia, Pennsylvania 19104
(215) 386-4268

Historical Documents Company offers a substantial list of high-grade documents and reproductions of important pieces of American history, such as the Declaration of Independence. Printed on parchment-like paper and appropriately yellow with "age," the antiqued documents are kept and framed and displayed by many who receive them; they are tasteful and of lasting interest, and they hang proudly in many offices and recreation rooms in homes.

Phonograph Records

Direct mail activity is making itself *heard* around the country these days!

This new direct mail tool is an all-vinyl "Soundsheet" which weighs just one-sixth of an ounce, yet provides an extremely fine quality high-fidelity phonograph record that can be played on any home or commercial record player at 33⅓ rpm—the ubiquitous LP (long playing) turntable speed.

Developed by Eva-Tone, Deerfield, Illinois, the Soundsheet "has not only proven to be highly flexible in adapting to marketing plans, but has also overcome the high cost of hard records, mailing costs, and handling costs."

A sales message can be put on a vinyl Soundsheet and mailed to prospects at a most reasonable cost. Sound fidelity is almost as good as on standard records, and there is no breakage and less shipping weight.

Szabo Food Service, Inc., Lyons, Illinois, used three Eva-Tone Soundsheets, bound into attractive "albums," with excellent success.

R. F. Neuzil, vice-president of communications, said the records produced a "tremendous increase in awareness of Szabo Food Service as the leader in the in-plant, hospital, and university feeding fields, and created an unexpectedly high volume of inquiries from top executives in leading companies in the industries to which we mailed them."

Dick Evans, president of Eva-Tone, is one of the most cooperative, helpful fellows you'll ever run across, and there's almost nothing he won't do to help you with your direct mail-sound program.

One thing, though: Dick says that while they make Soundsheets from tapes recorded by advertising managers, presidents, sales managers, order clerks, and assorted big butter and egg men, the fact remains that *this is a professional job for a professional narrator. And it should be done in a professional sound studio or radio station.*

Everybody is entranced with his own voice on tape or record, just as everybody delights in looking at pictures of themselves. But the ad manager and other executives in the company are just not cut out for this job of narration, despite personal opinions.

Narrators charge from $100 to $2,500 or more for a six-minute record, depending upon the narrator, how busy he happens to be at the moment, and how much he estimates the traffic will bear.

Eva-Tone will be happy to send you an Eva-Tone Soundsheet Idea Kit, complete with samples, price lists, suggestions, art-work aids, etc., if you'll make a letterhead request.

Eva-Tone
750 Central Avenue
Deerfield, Illinois 60015

Special Processes

Offbeat processes frequently make an impression that lasts and lasts—if they're well done.

An old stand-by is the 3-D message for which the reader dons a special pair of glasses accompanying the message. Actually, they're cardboard frames and special plastic lenses, readily mailable without danger of damage. Moreover, because they are not manufactured of the customary optical materials, the price is held down so the industrial direct mail advertiser can afford to buy them in quantity. Most printers can handle the job for you.

Day-Glo ink which fluoresces when viewed by either artificial room lights or by daylight has also been around for a long time now, but its impact, especially on large broadsides, is tremendous.

Vivid colors include orange, shocking pink, red, and chartreuse. Incidentally, printing with black ink on orange Day-Glo stock produces striking browns where the black is laid down, with Day-Glo highlights in the halftones. The effect is unusual, almost weird.

"Smellies" are mailing pieces printed with special perfumes. This is done by making another run through the press and applying perfume through the press fountain, instead of ink. Scents available include barbecue, pizza, grape, bourbon, gin, apricot, pickle, coffee, hickory, spruce, pine, rum, smoke (used with striking effectiveness by insurance companies making mailings about fire insurance), tobacco, and so on and on.

Other special processes include X-ray visuals, which use acetate overlays to expose the internal workings of a mechanical product; invisible ink, and others ad infinitum.

Hard Covers

Many industrial companies budget for reasonably large mailings of thick, comprehensive, expensive catalogs which are almost always paperbound. No valid reason exists, they feel, for a more expensive binding. After all, catalogs become outdated within a year at the most.

For a few prospects whom you're trying to impress, however, nothing can equal a fine binding job. People keep hardbound books.

For such special prospects the author had one client's catalog bound in genuine leather. Top quality cowhide, gold-stamped, was used with telling effect. The catalogs so bound had their tops, edges, and bottoms gold-edged. They were so impressive they paved the way to signing eight new dealers within the first three months after they were mailed. The psychological impression produced by that expensive binding (it *was* expensive, around $30 per catalog) made the recipients feel they were something special, and it did much to lower their sales resistance and to make them favorably disposed toward the advertiser.

Product Samples

Nothing, but nothing, sells as hard as making possible the laying on of the hands.

Chain store retailers found this out many decades ago when Woolworth and others stumbled onto the fact that goods displayed on open counters where shoppers could fondle and feel sold far faster than similar items kept behind glass.

Although the industrial purchase is made more logically and less emotionally than are consumer purchases, the basic principle of putting the product, or a part of it, in front of the prospect and letting him examine it cannot be questioned.

Unfortunately, this is not possible for a turret lathe, computer, road grader, bulldozer or similar large, heavy, expensive product. However, pieces of the product can be used in a direct mail campaign with excellent results. For instance, tip-on a tiny piece of a very large product onto a letter, then tell a strong quality story about this one little part. By inference at least, the recipient will receive the impression you want to give—that the entire product has had similar lavish care lavished onto it, all of which benefits the user.

One manufacturer of powdered metal parts—tiny, intricate, and forced to almost unbelievable precision and small tolerances—tipped on a miniature gear to mailings it made to prospective customers.

The letter, a four-pager, called attention to the complex shape of the part, the different surfaces which would have made machining prohibitively expensive, and to such features as the density and hardness. Finally, almost as an afterthought, the letter mentioned quite casually that the intricate part was quite inexpensive.

A series of these mailings resulted in a continuing flow of high-grade inquiries and requests to quote, or to have a sales engineer call. This advertiser acquired a number of new accounts with this direct mail advertising, and has an even larger number of suspects it is hopeful of closing eventually.

Split Mailings

The effect produced by split mailings, or cumulative mailings as some prefer to call them, is far greater than the impact of each mailing added together. Total impact is akin to that resulting from *squaring* each individual impact, rather than adding them together.

The Chicago office of Marsteller Inc. used the cumulative technique for its client, Clark Equipment Company, with outstanding results.

This $12,000 direct mail program triggered $3.5 million in sales and opened 50 new target accounts with a multimillion potential.

The direct mail campaign which Marsteller conceived was directed to 300 companies who were not buying Clark truck-trailers. One-sixth of the firms have become customers, placing initial orders for more than 700 semitrailers.

Called "Clark Cookout," the program involved six mailings of worthwhile items for backyard barbecues. Each mailing was associated with important product and service benefits of Clark trailers.

Marsteller selected dimensional direct mail for the Clark program for a very specific reason: A small, identifiable audience could be pinpointed, recipients would notice it, and the cost was reasonable for the sales potential involved.

Cost for dimensional direct mail is higher—in this instance $40 for each target account. Marsteller and Clark felt this was reasonable because average annual trailer purchases by these companies are ten units worth $55,000.

First mailing was made on July 1st. A chef's hat, representing both the cookout theme and the male aspects of barbecueing, introduced the program. The theme, "Hold on to your hat," emphasized that other cookout items were on the way. The hat also tells the Clark story that the man from Clark "wears many hats—equipment consultant, financier, used trailer specialist, and expediter."

As with all the program mailers, the salesman's card was attached. And, the mailer was personally addressed to the prospect at his place of business.

Five days later the second mailing was made. It was a set of barbecue tools and explained that Clark's full line offered "the right equipment to do the best job." Included were tongs, fork, spatula, and brush.

Four days afterward, a spice set emphasized the *quality* and *reputation* of Clark Trailers by pointing out that whether making trailers or grilling steaks, the little extras mean a better finished product. Copy explained that Clark's reputation resulted from careful attention to detail throughout the manufacturing process.

Mailing number four was also made four days later. It was a *Better Homes & Gardens* cookbook to keynote the theme, "There's no substitute for experience."

Speeding things up a bit, the fifth mailing was made three days later. It consisted of an apron and gloves specially designed for outdoor cooking—to provide prospects with "extra protection and handling ease."

Approximately a week after the prospect received the fifth mailer, his Clark salesman contacted him with the keystone of the entire campaign. Following his presentation, the salesman gave the customer a 14 oz. prime-cut porterhouse steak that had just been flown in from Milwaukee. The steak was packed in dry ice to preserve its flavor. Completing the series, the steak emphasized the personal service and attention that Clark provides its customers. And, it gave the salesman the perfect chance to talk to his prospect face to face.

Following the presentation many salesmen were asked to deliver quotes. Sales didn't materialize instantly, of course. Buying decision for trailers can take several months and many companies routinely purchase trailers at a specific time each year. However, by the end of the first quarter of the following year, 50 companies had placed first orders totaling $3,500,000.

Gag Mailings

Using gag items in a direct mail program is fun for all concerned, including the advertising manager. Recipients enjoy a chuckle when they open the mailings, and if they're tied in with the product, service, or selling proposition—as they should be—humor can do a job of making a positive impression.

For more than 20 years, Leo P. Bott, Jr. Advertising, an agency in Chicago, has mailed some wonderfully wild and wacky letters with gags, gimmicks, and guffaw-producing items attached, enclosed, tipped-on, inserted, and otherwise accompanying the letters.

Among Bott's gags have been a Mexican jumping bean, Spanish moss, excelsior, corset spring, detective badge, false mustache, mask, stereoptican picture, etc. The letters have caused many laughs, much comment, and incalculable good will.

Printers send out kooky scratch pads with gags, jokes, humorous drawings, and the recipient's name printed neatly at the top. This never hits the round file because it's personalized, as is all effective direct mail advertising.

Plastic "panic buttons" have been—and still are, for that matter—a popular item. Few and far between are the offices where some individual doesn't have a panic button epoxied to the wall over his desk. It's always good for a laugh.

Something, almost anything, should tie the gag in with your product, company, or proposition. It loses effectiveness and produces a "so what?" attitude if it doesn't. This is where the majority of gag-mailing industrial advertisers fumble the ball.

Teasers . . . The Case of Agent 3.1415

One of the cleverest teaser campaigns is one William T. Dyer, advertising manager of Electronic Products Division, Corning Glass Works, used for a highly refined mailing list of 200 prospects. Objectives of this campaign were to:

1. Isolate and communicate with a key list of specifying influences within the computer industry representing a potential for Corning's thin-film microcircuit business.
2. Identify Corning with the market.
3. Set forth the competitive advantages of Corning's product.
4. Motivate the prospect to take further action.

Electronics Products Division's mailing list was built through recommendations from the field sales force. *However, the list was screened by the division's microcircuit marketing groups for additions, deletions, and changes; they had the final say-so as to what names would be used, and properly so.*

Chances are this is one of the few industrial direct mail advertising campaigns that resulted in an investigation by the FBI. A special agent thought the campaign was exceptionally interesting, and asked for a copy to send to the late J. Edgar Hoover for use in the *FBI Newsletter.*

Twelve mailings were made over a three-month period; they included the following items:

1. Scribbled note—"you are being investigated . . ." This is on a torn piece of brown wrapping paper, "written" in black "ink" and with a stamped logo and signature, TOES, LTD.

2. Scribbled note—"So far, so good! Swallow this. Agent #3.1415 (logo) TOES, LTD."

3. Scribbled note—"You check out OK! Details will follow. Swallow this message. Agent #3.1415 (logo) TOES, LTD."

4. This was a 3-D mailing with shape and weight and form. It was a do-it-yourself Spy Kit containing such items as a water pistol—carefully labelled "Ray Gun"—a black mask, and a package of Tums for "relief of indigestion caused by swallowing all the previous messages." Also in the kit was a message telling the recipient that regular spy reports would follow. The stage was set. Recipients were hooked. After being teased like that, few could resist wondering what was next.

5. Special Report No. 1, containing a snapshot of the "secret research facility." The report read as follows:

TOES, LTD.

G
FROM: Special A ent #3.1415

ASSIGNMENT: The infiltration of all companies engaged in research and manufacture of micro-circuits for the purpose of obtaining daTa relating to the stability of organization and commitxment to micro-electronics field.

FINDINGS: Many cxxxxxx companies not firmly xxxxx committed to manufacture of micro-circuitry. Have wait-and-see attitude which could cause big problems for designers who must have a reliable source of micro-circuits. *However, hoave located one company which shows much* promise. Apparently has total commitment to micro-electronics field. Investment in new facilities totals millions of dollars. Reliable informatns say company was one of first in field and is determined to x continue leadership. Personal investigation indicates xxx conclusively that company is totally reliable and means to stay in micro-electronics. They have already developed highly automated processes which have consistently reduced costs for their customers. Company is in Raleigh, N.c. area. Its top xxxxx secret research facility is humming with activity. A photo of this facility is enclosed. Plan intensive undercover investigation of this company. A full report will follow.

G
Special xxxxx A ent # 3.1415

The tone of the copy in the "Special Report" is exactly right. The misspellings, strikeovers, and crossouts of the "typewritten" copy are deft touches that impart authenticity to the piece. Copy of this report reads:

TOES LTD.

FROM: Special Agent # 3.1415

ASSIGNMENT: Continuing undercover investigation of Corning Electronics in Raleigh, N.C. to gain information about the way company achieves such high reliability in manufacture of micro-circuits.

FINDINGS: Thexxx enclosed packet of information was intercepted by an accomplice in the Corning plant and turned over to this agent. Information is self-explanatory. Another report will follow.

agent #3.1415
(logo)
TOES, LTD.

FINAL REPORT

TO: All TOES, LTD. Members

FROM: National Headquarters
TOES, LTD.

Our mission is a complete success.

Special agents working under the auspices of the TOES, LTD. national organization have discovered that although there are some companies which are not totally committed to micro-electronics, Corning Electronics in Raleigh, North Carolina, plans to remain in micro-circuitry.

Investigation also reveals that the company understands designers' needs for high reliability micro-circuits and is qualified to meet all specifications.

Secret evidence accumulated from inspection of plants and questioning of reliable informants indicates conclusively that Corning plans to maintain leadership in micro-circuitry field and will be a reliable source of advanced micro-electronics indefinitely.

The advantage of materials used by Corning and company's experience in handling materials has also been proved conclusively.

This exhaustive undercover investigation was not achieved without some casualties. But they were minor, and all agents will recover. The only disappointment came with the desertion of Special Agent #3.1415 after a brilliant beginning. However, all members of TOES, LTD. have in their possession the special implement obtained for use if Special Agent #3.1415 should be encountered.

Remember that this organization may be reactivated at any time under the name Corning Electronics. This secret stuff has been fun, but now we've gotta let everybody in on the thin-film story.

So how did the FBI become involved?

It seems a night janitor at the Corning plant in New York found one of the roughly-typed messages in a wastebasket. The security man to whom he turned it over promptly called in the Federal Bureau of Investigation.

No telling how far it might have gone. TOES, LTD. *must* have been mighty elusive and hard to track down—if the FBI hadn't talked with Bill Dyer, Corning Electrics' ad manager. And the FBI agent had the Spy Kit in hand, so was aware it was some kind of a spoof by that time.

Effectiveness of this inspired direct mail campaign was not left to guesstimate. Corning conducted before-and-after attitude studies to measure results. Proven quite conclusively was that the company attained most of its objectives by enhancing Corning's reputation and brand preference in the industry.

3-D Spectaculars

Ever receive a tyrannosaur, stegosaur, pterodactyl, or any other species of hideously grinning dinosaur in your morning mail? A total of 750 prospects of Republic Flow Meters Company Division, Rockwell Manufacturing Company, did. Here's the story.

Republic has a reputation as a major supplier for designing and building instrumentation for steam boiler systems. However, this reputation was not enough to expand into such new markets as chemical plants, paper mills, refineries, etc. Salesmen were not too enthusiastic about making "cold calls" and preferred to sell known markets.

Because of the small, easily identified audience, direct mail became the medium. The direct mail campaign objectives were a directional strategy aimed at a defined group of prospects as an elaboration of the general advertising communications objectives and integrated within the marketing objectives.

Vehicle selected was a three-dimensional mail program; it was recommended by the company's agency, Marsteller Inc., to Republic's advertising manager, George W. Peak.

Although no three-dimensional program is low cost, the audience was small enough (750 engineers and technical executives) and the urgency of the marketing problem almost demanded a communications breakthrough in order to get immediate results.

Dinosaurs were a perfect, analogous series for Rockwell-Republic's new products. Theme of the campaign, "Wonders of the prehistoric world, for the men concerned with measurement and control." A stegosaur, for example, has been a success because of its mounted armor; and so is the Rockwell-Republic instrument today because of how it is mounted.

This campaign was designed so the salesmen could take immediate advantage of customer questions and inquiries it generated. The sales force was briefed about the 3-D mailers at their annual meeting two weeks before the campaign was launched. Each salesman's business card was enclosed in the last mailer, along with a note that he would call soon when he was next in the vicinity of the recipient of the mailing pieces. All 750 prospects were contacted by salesmen within 10 days after the last mailing was made.

First mailer in the campaign was a teaser which alerted the prospect that he would be "visited by seven dinosaurs." Seven metal dinosaurs followed with seven different sales messages attached to the creatures with red ribbon. (The bronze-like dinosaurs, 4 to 8 inches long, are not available commercially except at one or two of the country's museums with paleontological exhibits.)

The campaign spanned six weeks, and each mailer was ostensibly sent by Republic.

Efficiently executed, the dinosaur direct mail program fulfilled its objectives. The program brought immediate recognition to Rockwell and Republic. Although hardly considered the leading supplier to the process industries before the mailings, Republic was ranked at almost equal status with the leader, as shown by a later survey.

The promotion stirred much discussion within customer companies, generated many amusing stories, and brought favorable comment from publications. The dinos became conversation "openers" for Republic salesmen, who hailed this as the best foot-in-the-door campaign they had ever seen. This novel promotion helped build an image of a progressive Rockwell. Over 50 unsolicited letters were received from salesmen and recipients.

Direct Mail Copy

Much of what has already been said about copy in preceding chapters applies to direct mail just as much as it does to space advertising.

Copy must be written with the user—the buyer—in mind. It must be you-oriented, rather than advertiser oriented. And it is essential that it stress benefits, rather than product features.

In direct mail advertising, perhaps even more than in industrial space advertising, everyone concerned is firmly convinced he's a copywriter, possibly one of the great ones—although unrecognized as yet. The fact is, 99 percent of those in responsible positions in industry cannot write a literate letter. Typical letters from industrial executives are unbelievably verbose. And they ramble, digress, repeat, and repel.

Writers of these horrible-example letters are usually excellent *product* men and often strong personal salesmen. But they have no conception whatsoever of what marketing communications can and should do for the company, nor do they know how communications should be employed to best advantage.

Perhaps the oldest and most frequently used formula is "AIDA" —get *attention,* arouse *interest,* stimulate *desire,* ask for *action.*

Very similar to the AIDA formula is the AIDPPC formula developed by the late Robert Collier, one of direct mail advertising's great copywriters. He emphasized the proper sequence of thoughts in all direct mail sales copy as:

Attention	Persuasion
Interest	Proof
Description	Close

Most copy formulas are very similar, and there are literally dozens of them kicking around. Their proud creators have espoused them in everything from books to articles in the trade press to speeches at symposiums and association meetings. Among them are Victor Schwab's AAPPA Formula. These cryptic letters mean:

A—Get *Attention*

A—Show People an *Advantage*

P—*Prove* It

P—*Persuade* People to Grasp This Advantage

A—Ask for *Action*

Direct mail and mail order marketing expert Bob Stone, *Advertising Age* columnist and head of Stone & Adler, has used the following copy formula with success:

1. Promise a benefit in your headline or first paragraph—*your most important benefit.*
2. Immediately enlarge upon your most important benefit.
3. Tell the reader *specifically* what he is going to get.
4. Back up your statements with *proof* and *endorsements.*
5. Tell the reader what he might lose if he doesn't act.
6. Rephrase your prominent benefits in your closing offer.
7. Incite action—*now.*

Bob Stone also quoted 20 checklist points developed by Maxwell C. Ross, today a creative marketing consultant, back when he was director of advertising of Old American Insurance Company. This checklist is reprinted with permission from the March 25, 1968 issue of *Advertising Age,* copyright 1968 by Advertising Publications, Inc.

CHECKLIST FOR BETTER DIRECT MAIL COPY

Copy Technique

1. Does the lead sentence get in step with your reader at once?
2. Is your lead sentence more than two lines long?
3. Do your opening paragraphs promise a benefit to the reader?
4. Have you fired your biggest gun first?
5. Is there a *big idea* behind your letter?
6. Are your thoughts arranged in logical order?
7. Is what you say believable?
8. Is it clear how the reader is to order—and did you ask for the order?
9. Does the copy tie in with the order form—and have you directed attention to the order form in the letter?

Copy Editing

10. Does the letter have "you" attitude all the way through?
11. Does the letter have a conversational tone?
12. Have you formed a "bucket brigade" through your copy?
13. Does the letter score between 70 and 80 words of one syllable for every 100 words you write?
14. Are there any sentences which begin with an article—a, an, or the—where you might have avoided it?
15. Are there any places where you have strung together too many prepositional phrases?
16. Have you kept out "wandering" verbs?
17. Have you used action verbs instead of noun construction?
18. Are there any "thats" you do not need?
19. How does the copy rate on such letter craftsmanship points as (a) using active voice instead of passive, (b) periodic sentences instead of loose, (c) too many participles, (d) splitting infinitives, (e) repeating your company name too many times?
20. Does your letter look the way you want it to? (a) placement of page, (b) no paragraphs over six lines, (c) indentation and numbered paragraphs, (d) underscoring and capitalization used sparingly, (e) punctuation for reading ease.

Stone notes that nine of the points are devoted to the *technique* of writing, while 11 points are devoted to *editing*. He then calls attention to the fact that few amateurs even bother to edit their copy, and suggests this is where the men and the boys part company.

Significant is the fact the first four points of this checklist are given over to the lead. All of the professionals in direct mail advertising copy agree completely on one point: The lead and/or first paragraph determines whether the copy scores a resounding success, or is a gruesome failure and a waste of money.

It is there, right at the start of the sales call by mail, when your prospect decides to stay with you through the message until he's asked to take action, or he makes the decision to desert you.

As Elmer Wheeler said, "Your first 10 words are more important than your next 10,000."

Ross espoused a principle first stated by Richard Manville, now head of the advertising research firm which bears his name, but at that time an advertising consultant. Manville's principle is simply *to give people what they want in copy*—thus creating copy that out-pulls copy which presents things which people do not want as much, or do not want at all.

In his *Advertising Age* article, Bob Stone stressed the importance of having just one idea—which is actually one core idea, or one central idea, as discussed in the chapters on space advertising copy. In copy for direct mail advertising it is even more essential, if possible, that the copywriter should hew to a straight copy line based on one strong idea.

A disconnected series of little ideas, or even a well-connected series of little ideas, will invariably result in copy that fails to make much of an impression. Stone said, "Emphasize many ideas and you emphasize none."

Believability is, perhaps, even more important in direct mail than it is in space advertising copy. You can say, and be completely truthful, "This widget will reduce machining time 20 percent." But people have been bombarded by too many unsupported claims and glowing promises over the years to pay very much attention to such glittering generalities.

But if you say, "Don Olson, plant superintendent, General Steel Company, reduced machining time 20 percent with this widget," you're home free. This is a believable statement.

Just one unbelievable statement can shatter the impression the mailer can make. It can cancel out in one brief instant the effect produced by all the rest of the copy—which might be superb.

Attitude is critical. Direct mail advertising copy *must* be written with a "you" attitude. Direct mail is such a highly personal medium that copy written to a vast mass of recipients will be impersonal. And impersonal copy in a personal medium makes an impression exactly the opposite of the one you want and need.

It has been said that the first question the reader wants answered is: "What will you do for me if I listen to your story?"

To answer this question, direct mail copy must be you-oriented, not advertiser-oriented.

Use the "Bucket Brigade"

"The 'bucket-brigade' is a series of connectors," Stone said. "Connectors are transitional sentences or phrases which either end one paragraph or begin the next. Used properly, connectors give copy swing-movement, gliding the reader smoothly from one paragraph right into the next."

Examples are: *But that's not all, and in addition, moreover, so that is why, what's more, but there is just one thing, as I say, so mail your order today*—and so on.

Used with economy and taste, the bucket brigade can carry your story and your reader to the conclusion swiftly, smoothly, and as inevitably as night follows day.

When you next receive a dull, uninteresting direct mail piece, analyze it thoroughly. Chances are you'll find it doesn't contain enough of these connecting links to give the copy a fluid sense of movement; it will undoubtedly contain "island paragraphs"—paragraphs by themselves that are usually as dull as they look to the reader.

Too few writers bother to count the number of multisyllable words in their copy; you'll recall this was discussed at some length in an earlier chapter. Just because there's more room to use more words in direct mail copy than there is in space ad copy does *not* justify a long string of multisyllable words.

People to whom you're writing understand these words, of course, they can use them, *but they will not take the time to read them.* Boost the fog level of your copy and readership plummets. Fast.

Avoid starting sentences with articles (a, an, the). Steer clear of the prepositional phrase. Delete wandering verbs; keep them close to the subject rather than separated by a sea of other words. Use action verbs. Excite the reader, don't lull him to sleep. Use the active voice, not the passive. Do, don't talk about doing. Don't split infinitives. Many people don't care much, but among those who do you're hurting yourself unnecessarily. Keep your copy from being or looking soggy; open it up, let in some air, use short paragraphs, make it visually attractive.

Most reliable weapon with which to kill copy readability is repeating the company's name so many times and so often the reader is ready to scream.

Naturally, the company name should be mentioned. It's perfectly permissible to put it in display type, even across a spread, and it should be on both the front and back pages of the mailer. Signatures with addresses are proper and necessary.

But if you have even the slightest desire to have your copy read, do *not* for the love of all that's holy repeat the company name every sentence or two.

Copy route, chances are, follows a logical sales formula right through attention, interest desire and action. Then, the first draft written, the real pro applies a massive dose of self-discipline. He rewrites, polishes, and prunes until he's finally convinced the copy is the best he can do—that it's really copy he can be proud of. It is not at all unusual to rewrite a piece of copy three, four, six, a dozen times or more before it's finally just right.

Impose rigid self-discipline and then work—work hard. There's no other way to turn out copy that measures up to what you consider the very best you can write. No other copy is acceptable.

The Post Office

Only direct mail advertising is at the mercy of the vast, faceless, often capricious—and fantastically inefficient—army of bureaucrats which comprises the post office.

Some 30 years ago, the cost of a telephone call from New York to Los Angles was a fat $20.58. At that time, for this same $20.58, you could mail 2,058 first class letters anywhere in the country. Yet today, the federal government is investigating the telephone company —and first class postage has gone up 600 percent; today, for the price of that phone call back then, you can mail only 343 first class letters.

Rates for third class mail—the class used by business and industry for bulk mailings—were scheduled to increase quite sharply on the eve of the publishing of this handbook.

Offsetting such huge hikes in rates isn't easy for users of direct mail advertising. Many companies expect to become much more selective in mailing, and are looking for other ways to reduce costs.

One company with a $14 million annual postage bill, *Business Week* reported, schedules "postal cost reduction clinics" aimed at reducing expenditures while operating at normal levels. Some of the suggestions developed: Stationery of lighter stock, faster printing and paper handling, more self-mailers, and piggyback mailings (two or more messages in one envelope).

Meanwhile, the industry watched with interest progress of a

commercial postal service, the Independent Postal Service of America, which began operations in Oklahoma City and intended to expand services throughout the country. IPSA charged $25 per thousand for direct mail, *including addressing.*

Zip Code May Save the Day

Experience with the five-digit zip code now required to follow the name of the state on any addressed mail may permit sufficient mechanization and/or automation to enable the Post Office to pull itself up by its bootstraps.

Also, zip code is providing valuable clues to the potential of mailing lists. Westport, Connecticut, and Hibbing, Minnesota, for instance, are widely known as communities whose residents rank above the average in personal purchasing power. Research organizations are unearthing information about other communities identifiable by zip codes, as to their desirability or lack of it in providing good prospects for various products and services.

Direct mail advertisers are now required to do much of the work formerly done by the post office since the inception of zip code. Since regulations are constantly being changed or amended, the reader is advised to contact the post office he will be using for copies of manuals and bulletins containing up-to-the-minute material.

Chapter 17

TRADE SHOWS

THE trade show today is controversial. To some, the shows are well worthwhile. Others feel the trade show is the most unwieldy, most costly, most time-consuming, most ineffectual way to communicate product knowledge to others that has been devised since the Industrial Revolution.

Found at trade shows are fantastically advanced products that have become possible only due to the tremendous technological progress. Yet these products are still hauled to the fairs as their predecessors were centuries ago. Progress, massive and enthralling, on the one hand; a complete lack of progress on the other.

Nonetheless, the trade show is beloved by engineers and non-marketing marketing executives who can *see and talk with* honest-to-gosh prospects.

Many a marketing man fears that if this company does *not* exhibit in "key" trade shows throughout the year it will be forgotten by prospective customers and competitors will dominate the market.

Before the advent of the marketing concept, before mass communications, before the specialized business press, this fear might have had a valid reason for being.

It is completely unjustified today.

Such fear exists, however, and its existence should be recognized. It accounts for up to 85 percent of all trade show exhibits. At least 85 percent of all industrial companies in the country who regularly participate in these annual outings do so *because they are afraid not to.*

Company after company after company spends vast sums merely to haul its products to distant cities, to pull its sales force in from productive work in the field in order to talk with "prospects" *in one city.*

Trade shows are trying desperately to achieve respectability as more and more knowledgeable industrial advertising professionals seriously question their worth. The struggle is an uphill one because today's industrial advertising manager is privy to too much marketing knowledge; no longer does he merely write copy, make rough layouts, buy space, produce sales literature, and handle trade show exhibitions. His contribution to his company extends far beyond these functions, and part of this contribution is to point out the lack of productivity and to improve the quality of trade shows in which his company has traditionally exhibited.

It is very encouraging to know that *Industrial Marketing's* recent analysis of the source of inquiries shows that for the average industrial company, a scant 6 percent can be attributed to trade shows. This is a meager return for a much larger bite out of the total budget.

How to Select Trade Shows That Count

There's certainly no dearth of trade shows.

Just the opposite is true. The average industrial company can pick and choose and be as selective as it wants to be when it comes to exhibiting its products.

Speaking before a workshop conducted by the Association of National Advertisers at Oakbrook, Illinois, Homer Morrison, manager of the advertising department, Union Carbide Company, listed six criteria for selection of trade shows. If followed, they should help increase the return on your trade show investment. The criteria are:

1. The geographic area within a radius of 200 miles of the location of the show should be a fertile marketplace.
2. Determine that the show will provide a personal selling environment in which salesmen can make selling calls on a significant number of prospects who are in the marketplace, and who have some degree of buying influence.
3. Determine that the atmosphere of the show will be conducive to serious business discussion.
4. There should be products or processes that are new (or sufficiently improved) to the potential audience.
5. Total cost of show participation divided by the number of "sales calls" that can be expected to be made should compare favorably with the average cost of making a regular sales call.
6. Total amount to be spent on show participation must not be a disproportionally large share of the total promotional budget.

Firm, formal, written objectives are an absolute essential if a company is to benefit to any great extent from exhibiting at shows.

Enter a trade show without objectives and you're actually without a purpose. About all you can logically expect to accomplish is to prove to attendees of the show you're "still in the widget business." This startling communication can be made to an infinitely larger audience by using space advertising, and it can be accomplished at far less expense.

What's more, it can be communicated to a more highly selective audience composed only of prime prospects and major buying influences by using direct mail. This medium is also more effective and much less costly.

Unless your company has something in the product lineup that's truly new, truly improved, truly exciting, the trade show is a poor investment for it to make. This includes both time and money.

However, if you *do* happen to have a revolutionary new widget, then by all means exhibit at the National Widget Users Exposition and Congress.

So, since you're stuck with having the terrible tab for countless shows taken from the advertising budget, do everything possible to run a tight ship. This means, first of all, establishing firm objectives.

For obvious reasons it is impossible to give a generalized objective, or set of objectives, that would be applicable for every company. Valid objectives for one company might be something like these, which were used by a prominent manufacturer of widgets sold to the metalworking market:

1. Inform a minimum of 600 buying influences of the new automatic widget we now offer.
2. Show this automatic widget, in operation, to these influences.
3. Give each influence a piece of sales literature about the new widget.
4. Get names, titles, firms of those 600 influences for sales followup by the field force.
5. Make a name impression—the fact that Smith Widget Manufacturing Company exhibited—on an additional 1,000 attendees of the show. This could be accomplished by holding a daily raffle with three silver-plated working-model widgets holding two fountain pens as prizes. To be eligible, attendees must register and deposit their names in a barrel in the booth.
6. Make contact with 150 selected old customers, current hot prospects, and others whom marketing feels desirable, and give top management a chance to mingle with them. This can be accomplished by handing out printed invitations to a buffet dinner in the company's entertainment suite. Because attendance is controlled by printed invitations, cost is held in line and guests will be limited to those most important to the company. Invitations (R.S.V.P.) will have been mailed two weeks prior to the show's opening date, of course.

With such specific objectives, it is more likely than not that the company will realize some benefits from having exhibited at the show. Without objectives, everything would have been left to chance.

The Mechanics

Nothing entails so much advance planning as does a trade show.

Be sure to inform people in your company why shipments to the show must be made exactly when and how you specify. Work closely with traffic managers, truckers, airlines, freight forwarders, and others who will handle your equipment shipment en route from factory to show. Make certain they understand it is consigned to you *to be exhibited,* and that they know the dates of the show.

Have your traffic manager stay in close touch with the carriers during the time they have the shipment, and have him follow it from place to place with regular progress reports. This is especially essential if the shipment is interlined—handled by more than one trucking company. Trace, trace, trace. Instruct your traffic manager he's to live with that shipment every inch of the way, every hour of the day until it's delivered to the exhibition hall or to the official freight handlers for the show.

Finally, make certain that all concerned know you're to be kept fully informed of progress—or lack of progress. This latter is even more important because if something does go amiss you can take remedial action.

Exhibition halls are scenes of such chaotic confusion as to stagger the imagination when a major trade show is being set up. Easiest thing in the world is to lose your boxes and crates inside the hall itself, after they're safely out of the hands of the truckers. Aisles are virtually nonexistent, and trying to wend your way through boxes stacked 10 feet high and look for your lost ones among acres of others is enough to try the patience of a saint. Saintly advertising managers are scarce these days.

Smart exhibitors long ago figured out that the way around that problem is to paint their crates and boxes a distinctive color so they would stand out from all of the others. Naturally, red was used with great success. So was orange, yellow, blue, green, gray and black. Finally, though, everybody's boxes and crates were painted and everybody was back at the starting place.

So smart exhibitors again got the gun on their slower compatriots and took to leaving their crates and boxes unpainted. That raw wood really stood out from all of that painted wood. Trouble was, everybody else started doing this about the same time. Full circle.

Best way out of this labyrinth of colors and noncolors is to use something so offbeat nobody else would think of using it. Chartreuse.

Shocking pink. White. And, despite disliking the color as a matter of principle, the author used lavender with great success in recent years. Lavender boxes are just too too distinctive to like, but they really stand out and can be spotted the length of the Cow Palace.

Stripes and polka dots, carefully masked before spraying, can make crates clash frantically from those that are merely wildly colorful. Zigzag stripes of one color, with a background color entirely different, telegraph instantly that your lost crate is over in *that* dark corner.

The Exhibitors Manual

Every exhibitor at a trade show receives an exhibitors manual from show management. The manual becomes an extension of the advertising manager's person because it is checked and referred to so frequently. The volume provides a checklist of essential things to do and things not to do and serves as a second memory.

Almost every conceivable question that could come to mind is answered somewhere in this manual. The world of conventions and trade shows has many heads-up exhibit management organizations which have been in the business so long they can anticipate knotty questions even before some puzzled advertising manager can ask them.

Service contractors for the show are listed, along with addresses and telephone numbers to make it easy for advertising managers with special problems to contact the correct firms without having to go through exhibit management.

Having a checklist and referring to it daily during preparations for a trade show is an excellent way—in fact, the *only* way—to remember the myriad details you have to handle. Best possible checklist is one you make up yourself. List the things to be done, then in two ruled columns are spaces for dates—one the deadline date by which something must be handled, the other the date on which you concluded arrangements or took final action. This provides a fast, visual reference as to how things are progressing, and pinpoints any trouble areas before the trouble becomes serious.

It's a good idea to mark the deadline dates in a red squeakie, the dates each item was taken care of in blue or black. The color contrast makes your checklist graphic.

Arrangement of exhibits is specified by exhibit management. In general, specifications are quite uniform throughout the country, from show to show, and in all industries. Eight-foot backwalls (except for certain areas of the hall where the booth is erected immediately in front of an exterior wall), are standard. Nothing may project above this 8-foot height except equipment.

One critically important consideration when either planning a new booth or planning to use an existing one is to make absolutely certain it complies fully with all safety regulations and fire ordinances.

Your display house will see to it your exhibit meets established specifications, but be certain to check this. Fire marshals in all exhibition halls everywhere are extremely skittish since the disastrous fire which destroyed Chicago's magnificent lake-front McCormick Place the day before the National Housewares Show was scheduled to open. Fireproof buildings are a figment of the imagination; they do not exist. This tragic fire proved this once again.

So-called exhibitor package plans are proving highly popular with ad managers who have to exhibit at trade shows. What the package plan is, in essence, is having exhibit management combine almost all needed services into one neat bundle with one billing for services rendered.

So exhibit management will have at least a rough idea of what to expect—and what to make available—a form is provided in the manual for each exhibitor to estimate the approximate amount of labor he will require to set up his exhibit and his equipment. This makes it possible for the various unions involved to supply sufficient bodies to get the job done.

When an exhibitor pays for his floor space he is offered at no extra charge "standard booth equipment." This invariably consists of soiled draperies to form an 8-foot-tall backwall and 3-foot sidewalls. Using draperies at a show is really going poor-mouth, though. Almost every firm that has two nickels to jingle together has an exhibit booth designed and constructed by a professional display house.

Unless the company has its own furniture for the booth—tables, chairs, settees, smoking stands, coat racks, wastebaskets and so on—these must be rented. These items are delivered right to the exhibitor's booth and the ad manager signs to show he has received them. The renting firm picks them up immediately upon conclusion of the show.

Cost is high, of course, because this is trade show country. Furniture is usually of good quality and more than adequate for the purpose.

You'll be money ahead in the long run to rent furniture. If you buy your own there's always the chance you'll want to change color; color can be specified when you rent. What's more, if you buy furniture you have not only the original investment, you also have the cost of custom-built boxes to hold the furniture so it won't be battered to pieces in shipping. And then there's shipping, no inconsequential item in itself. By the time you pay all of this, you've invested more than the furniture is worth.

Return forms well before the show—the deadline is always given in the exhibitors manual—to get all company personnel properly registered. Nothing irritates product people, engineers, and others who normally do not man a booth as much as having to sweat out a massive line to get into a show where their company is exhibiting. Handle this detail well for all concerned, and you'll earn their gratitude.

Hotel rooms for all hands attending the show—booth personnel, visitors, and others from the company—are always a problem. Rooms are always doled out by a convention housing bureau. Check with your product people or whoever you most want to please in your company as to first, second, third, and fourth choices of hotels. Then get your application for room reservations in *immediately upon receiving your exhibitors manual. Fill out this form and mail it immediately if you want to get a hotel of your choosing.*

Housing bureaus always demand to know the names of individuals who will occupy the rooms you are reserving. But here's a tip. Get that reservation request in to the bureau with the *number* of rooms you want. Never mind listing the correct names of occupants—just put down names of people in your company regardless of whether they will attend the show or not. Names can be corrected later.

Booth Location

Maps of exhibit space supplied to each exhibitor by show management enable you to visualize the hall with all booths in place. Such maps make it easy for you to select a space that fits your budget and which stands every chance of attracting a good flow of traffic.

In general you're better off with space somewhat ahead of and to the left of the hall's registration area, restaurant, or central exhibit —whatever focal point exists. Peoeple tend on the whole to walk away from such an area, and they tend also to walk in a clockwise direction. Avoid dead ends and physical bottlenecks of any kind.

When you apply for space you're asked to give your first, second, third, and fourth choices. Try to select the space you want with the above in mind. You may want to block your choices together, with your first choice in the middle.

Something else to remember is that show managements always permit exhibitors to specify what companies they do *not* want to be near. This assures an exhibitor he won't have his bitterest competitor breathing down his neck from across the aisle, or next door. Such a situation would severely hamper both companies, of course.

The Booth

Very few companies use the background and sidewall draperies provided by show management. They make a poor impression. They make the company look like one that cannot afford to have a suitable booth built, and this can't help but reflect adversely on the company's products.

If your company has decided it can't live without exhibiting at trade shows, if there's no possible way you can prevent this squandering of money, it's important that you sell all concerned on one thing: *Going first class is the only way to go.*

Naturally, this means you'll eschew jerry-built displays whacked together in your plant's shipping room or carpenter shop.

Trade show booths are frightfully expensive things. Unless you *know* you're dealing with an honest, reputable display house, costs can creep up at an alarming rate.

Much of the cost of a booth, of course, is in the creative work. Concept, design, decorative treatment, and art are not inexpensive. Nor are the huge four-color translites, murals, special illustrations, attention-getting devices, special projection equipment, closed-circuit TV, "in booth" telephone systems and other specialty items.

Rule of thumb when having a new booth constructed is that you can expect to pay between $300 and $400 per running foot. Thus, a 50-foot booth should carry a price tag of somewhere between $15,000 and $20,000. However, it can run much higher if there's any great quantity of intricate and expensive electronic attention-grabbers built in. The figure can easily double itself. What's more, cost of island booths, finished on all four sides and often containing air-conditioned conference rooms and other niceties of life frequently run several times this figure.

When you're in process of having a new booth built, remember that it must serve two purposes—to be an attractive background for your products and equipment, and to attract prospects *into* your booth area.

The three best traffic stoppers at a trade show are light, motion, and sex.

Insist on having your booth *light, light, light.* It doesn't necessarily have to be painted a light color, although this is usually desirable, but it is absolutely necessary that it have a very high level of illumination. The booth should be lighter than the general surroundings in the hall, which itself is well lighted.

Motion—perhaps a lighted bulls-eye that revolves, flashing lights, blinking signs, moving machinery, a slide show, motion pictures, blowing streamers—all attract the eye of the show visitor and pull him into your booth. Still items are static and uninteresting; moving objects are vigorous, attractive, and appeal to the male desire to do something, to move things, to change things, to accomplish.

Individual trade shows have different rules and regulations about what constitutes a "nuisance" and what doesn't, so be sure to check your exhibitor's manual if there's any question in your mind about the legitimacy of what you're proposing to do. If the formal rules don't cover your particular situation, pick up the phone and call exhibit management.

Sex is attractive. Every study made points out that use of comely models in the booth results in higher traffic flow. Here again, use taste and don't be blatant about it. And don't make the mistake of having a bevy of beauties standing around doing nothing except showing how attractive they are.

Put your models to work. Give them a legitimate reason for being there. Have them answer the telephone, run the inquiry-card imprinter, handle registrations for door prizes, take care of requests for literature, demonstrate the product, run the projector, hand out giveaways, and keep literature supply neat and properly replenished. There is almost no end of tasks a pretty girl can legitimately handle at a trade show—and all the while she attracts the eye of your prospects. They're not immune to a pert face and shapely figure.

Going rate for capable models—those who are both a delight to look at and also have somewhat more than a bare minimum of intelligence—varies from city to city. New York is the highest. Models hired there through reputable agencies customarily get from $75 to $100 for an 8-hour day. In Cleveland, Detroit, Philadelphia, Los Angeles, Chicago, and other major centers, model services usually run from $65 to $90 a day.

You can get a free trade show booth in just about any size you want if you have it designed and constructed in 5-foot modules. Of course, you do have to pay the exhibit house for it, but a modular booth will save so much money during its life as compared to one that must be painstakingly bolted together by carpenters at every show that it's almost like getting it free of charge.

A booth built in 5-foot modules is the most flexible arrangement. Space at shows is sold in 10-foot increments as a rule. This means you can have, for instance, a half-dozen 5-foot modules for a 30-foot booth; but this also gives you a 10-foot booth, a 15, a 20, and a 25.

At the time your display house is building your new booth, instruct them to install electrical junction boxes in every module. This means the "electricians" at the halls merely have to plug in the lines running from the junction boxes—not an individual cord for each light, fixture, translite, or projector.

Having all of this work done by your display house so it becomes a permanent part of the booth is likely to save a minimum of $1,000 over the life of the booth if it's used three or four times a year for three or four years. In addition to saving labor, your booth will require fewer outlets in the halls, each of which has a price tag attached to it.

Following is an actual memo, with only the firm name and the ad manager's name changed, to illustrate the economics of trying to use an ailing trade show booth for too many years.

SMITH WIDGET MANUFACTURING COMPANY

Interoffice memo

TO: Mr. Carl Roberts

SUBJECT: Request for new trade show booth

Last fiscal year we exhibited at six trade shows.

We spent $9,546 to rebuild and refurbish our present obsolete booth. This is far too much, but with our antiquated booth—now some 7-8 years old—we had no other choice.

I recommend we have built a new, modern booth. Our present display house is well equipped to design and build it. I suggest it should be a 30-foot booth instead of a 55-foot unit such as we now have. Thirty feet is the amount of space we use most often; and marketing personnel from the metal treating market, which uses the most space, say this would be perfectly satisfactory.

A smaller booth at the Metal Show would reduce our rigging expense, which is very high. At the Metal Show in Detroit it was $5,700, and almost as much in Chicago. A 30-foot booth with less heavy equipment would reduce this to around $1,800.

The new booth could be amortized over a three or four-year period. It would require only minor refurbishing for each show. Our display house estimates refurbishing the new booth would cost less than $2,000 per year—and we have been spending almost this much for *each show.*

Also, we will save on labor cost at each show because the new booth would be built in easily-handled 5-foot modules. It would be easy and fast to erect, and could be used in 5-foot increments from 10 to 30 feet. Labor in halls is very inefficient and very costly. Estimated saving in setup and tear-down labor per year should be around $1,000-2,000 depending upon the number of shows in which we exhibit.

Booth cost includes necessary custom-built crates. We now need new crates for our old booth because they are worn out. Cost would be several hundred dollars.

A decision on this is needed quite soon; if we start construction within the next week or 10 days, the new booth will be ready for use at WESCON in August; otherwise, we will have another expensive rebuilding job to do on the old booth. Our display house has plans and designs ready for our approval.

RECAP:

Investment in new booth (approx.)	$5,500
Annual savings by investing in new booth:	
Refurbishing and rebuilding	$7,500
Rigging	4,000
Hall labor, setup and tear-down	1,500
Total *annual* savings resulting from new booth	$13,000

The new booth would pay for itself the first two or three times it is used, and we would realize significant savings for the next three years.

Not to be overlooked is the fact that a new booth would present a much better appearance, and make a better impression on our prospects and customers.

July 5 is the last day on which the new booth can be started if it is to be ready for WESCON.

Glen Travis
Advertising Manager

Evaluating Return From the $$$$$ Spent

Effectiveness of participation in a trade show can be measured only by the number of high-interest prospects to whom sales and marketing people in your company talked. Casual strollers through who entered the booth only out of idle curiosity or to ogle the models or to watch the card-sharp perform are worth little or nothing.

But your booth personnel should be instructed to take names of those who are considered genuine, livewire prospects, interested enough in your product to warrant a followup sales call.

These names should be guarded closely. The advertising manager will want to add them to the mailing list and ultimately forward them to the field salesman as soon as proper literature has been mailed. All of this should take place within two weeks of the end of the show. To procrastinate is to lose a possible prospect.

Incidentally, the advertising manager and his assistant are *not* booth personnel. Repeat: *The advertising manager and his assistant are not booth personnel.* Neither should be on the roster to do regularly scheduled duty. One or the other should be nearby—at least in the hall—during most show hours in case something arises that must be handled with hall labor or exhibit management. But they have no place standing there trying to sell the product or smile merrily at prospects and customers. This is the province of the sales or marketing executive in charge of the product line being exhibited, and he alone has the responsibility of establishing duty rosters with hours and dates.

Determining exactly how efficient your exhibit and your booth personnel were at the trade show in which you participated is simple enough. All that's necessary is to find out how many attendees at the show had an intense interest in your product, then find out how many of those interested individuals entered your booth.

The old reliable mail questionnaire is used to develop this information. Select a random sample of 2,000 names chosen on an every *nth* name basis from the roster of attendees who registered at the show. Show management can provide the list of registrants. Prepare a questionnaire and mail it to them while their memories are still fresh, say, not later than three weeks after the show closed. Data developed this way have proven to be projectable.

Sales Meetings magazine had this to say about evaluation of trade shows to make sure you're getting the biggest bang for the buck. The article in *Sales Meetings* was entitled, "How A. B. Dick Measures Trade Show Merit." It was written by J. W. Atkinson, sales promotion and advertising manager, A. B. Dick Company. It said:

"Sales promotion and advertising managers often fail to ask themselves and their companies what their trade show dollars are really buying.

"It's ironic that many of these same executives study and interpret advertising readership ratings with the diligence of a doctoral candidate—but are little more analytical about their trade show and convention exhibits than the housewife who enters her cake in the recipe contest at the country fair.

"At A. B. Dick Company, we evaluate trade shows as carefully as print advertising, direct mail, publicity, or any other element of our total communications program. We've evolved a trade show evaluation program that costs about 5 percent of our total trade show budget, a most reasonable figure considering that it tells us whether we're doing a selling job or merely going through the motions of an industry-wide ritual in the convention hall.

"THREE-STEP EVALUATION

"The evaluation program consists of three steps:

1. Definition of show's communications objectives.
2. Evaluation of facts to determine how completely objectives are achieved. (Here we have found depth interviewing of trade show visitors to be the most valuable single technique.)

3. Assignment of personnel unknown to demonstrators to "shop" our own and competitive exhibits.

"In addition, we make at least 12 other quantitative and qualitative measurements of general trade show effectiveness.

"One example of how this program is activated is provided by our experience at a recent Business Equipment Exposition. Our objective was to communicate A. B. Dick's ability to offer prospects and customers the most complete source of products and services to satisfy all their duplicating and copying needs.

"A. B. Dick originated the mimeographing process and still is mimeograph sales leader. Since 1950, the company also has developed equipment and supplies for offseet and fluid duplicating, electrostatic and diffusion transfer photocopying and the Videograph electronic data presentation system.

"With these products, we can employ the "broad line" marketing concept, as contrasted to many competitors' "single line" approach.

"However, until recently, subjective and statistical feedback indicated we were not getting this concept across at our exhibits. So we developed a full-line presentation to communicate the "complete source" philosophy and thoroughly briefed all booth personnel in its presentation.

"We set a specific objective to impress this advantage on at least 50 percent of all booth visitors. We deliberately made the goal modest because communicating a concept is always harder than telling a single product application story.

"To measure our effectiveness, we used shopper evaluation and other yardsticks, including the following:

- Total trade show attendance.
- Analysis of total audience by job title, geographical location, type and size of company, etc.
- Number of visitors who saw our exhibit.
- Number of visitors involved in our exhibit (those who asked questions, received personal demonstrations, etc.)
- Cost per personal demonstration.
- Cost per visitor stopped and involved.
- Number of sales leads.
- Number of visitors receiving a personal demonstration.
- Sales produced by show.
- Evaluation of competitors' effectiveness.
- Evaluation of our exhibit by our own personnel.

"Finally, at this show, we used depth interviews for the first time.

"Interviews were conducted by professional researchers who also knew office procedures, exhibit techniques and sales management. Aside from probing underlying attitudes and opinions of those interviewed, the interviews were unstructured.

"Instead of following a predetermined order of questioning, the interviewer asked questions in the order that seemed most logical, based on preceding responses. This helped insure spontaneity and avoid detection of the interviewer's motivation.

"Conducted with a statistically reliable sample of all exposition visitors, some of the interviews lasted up to 30 minutes. Each interviewer was so thoroughly briefed that he actually posed as an ordinary businessman attending the convention, engaging the respondent in what appeared to be a casual conversation between two visitors having similar interests.

"Out of the mass of information collected, we were able to make these firm determinations as to what our participation in this trade show had accomplished:

1. Of the 50,000 people who visited the exposition, 76 percent were prospects for A. B. Dick products.
2. Eighty-one percent of prospects spent at least two hours viewing duplicating and copying exhibits and 46 percent, at least half a day. (While this may seem like a lot of time, we are also aware of other studies that show the exhibit visitor spends only about six seconds for each 10 feet of booth unit to decide if that booth warrants his attention.)
3. Interviewers were asked to compare the A. B. Dick exhibit with those of three competitors. Although unaware that they were talking to an A. B. Dick representative, they rated our company's booth as the most interesting and informative of the four.
4. Finally, we analyzed how many of those interviewed knew that A.B. Dick offered all major duplicating and copying processes—the "complete source" concept around which the show had been built. Here are the results:

PERCENT OF ALL INTERVIEWED

	Knew concept	Didn't know
Visited booth	47%	38%
Didn't visit	1%	14%

PERCENT WHO VISITED BOOTH

Knew concept	Didn't know
55%	45%

"Thus, only 47 percent of all those interviewed—whether they had seen the booth or not—knew the "complete source" concept. However, of those who had seen the booth, 55 percent knew the concept and our goal was only 50 percent. By contrast, of those who had not seen the booth, only 7 percent knew the concept.

"While these figures alone indicated that the booth had accomplished its objective, we took the further step of dividing the total cost of the booth by the total number of prospects and customers who could "play back" the theme and adding a predetermined numerical factor representing the special advantage of a live demonstration. Result indicated that our Business Equipment Exposition effort was an effective tool in our total communications program.

"This type of evaluation continues to provide A. B. Dick with the perspective needed to properly allocate time and dollars to our trade show program."

Auditing Trade Shows

Most of the better trade shows are now audited either by firms of certified public accountants or by BPA—Business Publications Audit of Circulation, Inc.

According to *Clearing House,* publication of the Media Comparability Council, Business/Professional Advertising Association, the Audit Bureau of Circulation (ABC) during recent months has audited the registered attendance of a number of trade shows in conjunction with its new affiliate, Audit Bureau of Marketing Services. It is anticipated that this activity on the part of ABC will be stepped up significantly as time passes.

While exhibitors are more than pleased at having BPA and ABC audit trade show attendance, joy does not reign supreme among everybody concerned by any means.

More than a sneaking suspicion remains that most exhibit managements fear what the audits will disclose, fear the consequences of having this impartial, factual information in the hands of exhibitors, fear that facts revealed by the audits will severely hamper their selling activities. As far as trade shows are concerned, it's much easier to sell a pig in a poke than it is to peddle a questionable product.

Trade show auditing is in its infancy. With some 2,500 shows held annually and only a tiny handful audited, the room for improvement is large. Significant is that those shows which are the largest and most important are the ones that have been audited, much like the leading trade publications were quick to produce an A.I.A. form to present information about themselves. Several shows that were audited in Year One of The Audit—1965—actually *requested* an audit in 1966, which leads to the impression that show managements in those instances see an advantage to themselves in having the audit performed.

Equally significant, however, is that those managements requesting an audit in Year Two of The Audit run shows that are conceded to be of major importance; since no marginal shows, or shows other than those that are recognized as being major, are yet audited, this will undoubtedly result in giving the better shows an even larger sales edge over their competitors than they enjoyed before.

Costs of Trade Shows

Staggering, that's what they are—the direct cost of trade shows, that is. And usually these are the only costs considered. Indirect costs are more often than not several times as high, but equally often they're overlooked or conveniently ignored. Both types of costs will be discussed.

When management of an industrial company is struck with an inspiration to exhibit its wares in a trade show, it's usually after having received a promotional mailing from the show promoter.

This piece lovingly extolls the virtues of the trade show. It emphasizes the almost unbelievable number of board chairmen, presidents, executive vice-presidents, plain ordinary vice-presidents, research directors, chief engineers, plant superintendents, directors of manufacturing and others on that level of management who have been sitting around biting their nails all year long waiting impatiently until *THE DAY* finally arrives. *THE DAY*, of course, is the one on which this particular trade shows throws open its doors and admits these busy executives so that, once again, they can find out what has been happening in their field.

The promo piece points out that all an exhibitor has to spend is a thousand or two, give or take a little, depending on where in the hall he wants to be and how much space he requires.

A Typical Problem

Let's look at one company's expenses at the I.E.E.E. Show held in New York City in a recent year. We can assume it's typical for this size company and for the size space the company's exhibition used—30 feet. Best way to go into these costs is to quote the advertising manager's memo to the company president. It reads:

SMITH WIDGET MANUFACTURING COMPANY

Interoffice correspondence

TO: Mr. Carl Roberts

SUBJECT: I.E.E.E. Show cost

Dear Carl:

As you requested, I'm giving you a rundown on the costs of the recent I.E.E.E. Show held in New York in March.

Unfortunately, I'm able to give you only direct expenses. I have no way of knowing what indirect costs are; these would, of course, include salaries of individuals while they were at the show and en route, shop time spent readying equipment for the show, time spent in shipping and other plant departments. In addition, indirect costs should include the loss the company incurs from having field men in the booth instead of out selling; this can easily be determined by Sales as a fraction of each individual's annual productivity.

Space	$ 2,250.00
Al Miller studio, mounting literature	7.88
Models	320.00
Cleaning blazers worn by booth personnel	17.00
Expo decorating	67.20
Cleaning, waxing, mopping, chambermaiding	132.62
Shipping, outgoing	196.57
Shipping, incoming	160.00
Shipping, outgoing, laminar air-flow widget	98.00
Shipping literature and odds and ends	10.45
Booth photographs	10.00
Prepaid freight on booth by display house	186.91
Freight back to display house, check and store booth	214.39
Riggers, set up	397.88
Phone bill	93.62
Refurbishing of booth	1,436.17
New blazers and hats for booth personnel	58.29
Electrical service to booth	151.28
Movie film, extra print for safety's sake	28.00
Special literature on conveyor widget for show	375.00
Snap-out inquiry form	30.00
Printing district office listings on forms for handout	256.96
Literature and incidentals shipped to display house	12.31
Travel expenses, including plane tickets, of personnel	1,169.87
Travel expenses, on expense accounts	2,490.76
	$10,161.16

Several weeks go by before all invoices are received after a show, and before Accounting has all expense accounts, billings from the airlines and so forth—and before all costs are pulled together here in Advertising.

Cordially,
Joseph S. Nocco
Advertising Manager

This company did, in fact, pay only a trifling $2,250 for its 30 feet of corner space at this show in New York's Coliseum. That admittedly *isn't* a huge expenditure. And the company *could* afford it, just as the show promoter said.

What wasn't mentioned by the show promoter is that the rule of thumb commonly applied to trade show expense is that total direct costs customarily run between four and five times the cost of the space. This ratio holds for both large and small companies because large companies tend to purchase larger space, show more products, and have more bodies on booth duty, while smaller ones spend proportionately less.

Show expenses, though, are like an iceberg.

Only a tiny fraction of the total is visible above the surface. In this instance the advertising manager, although obviously not privy to individuals' salaries, could, nonetheless, make a reasoned guess-timate that was undoubtedly correct within plus or minus 7½ per-cent; this expense was put at $12,000.

Furthermore, there was the little matter of lost sales from having a large number of the field sales force in New York, as well as home office marketing personnel. This advertising manager checked on each salesman's annual sales for the preceding three years, divided this annual figure by 52 and came up with the conclusion the company probably lost a minimum of $100,000 in sales.

During this time under the searing lights and on the hard concrete, a total of 142 legitimate contacts were made by booth personnel. However, only *three* out of all those were with individuals on whom the sales force did not call at that time, and they turned out to be junior engineers a cut above the draftsmen level—hardly prime buying influences.

Thus, if we take *only* the direct costs and the indirect costs accounted for by salaries *and ignore lost sales,* we find this company spent a total of $22,161.16 to talk with 142 people to whom it talked frequently, both before and after the show—minus those three young engineers, of course. This figures out to more than $156 per contact —and the 16 cents was also ignored.

Proponents of trade shows, scarcer and scarcer these days, have always admitted when pinned right down to it that trade shows are a legitimate medium of communications *if the cost per sales contact at a show is approximately that of a contact made by a salesman in the normal course of events.*

Since the cost of the average industrial sales call is $71.27, Smith Widget Manufacturing Company spent some two and one-half times as much to make a contact at this trade show as it spends to call upon buying influences in their own offices.

This cost per contact of $156 per individual tallied up by Smith Widget obviously translates into a cost of $156,000 per thousand individuals. What advertising man in possession of even a tiny fraction of his faculties would advocate buying a medium with a cost of $156,000 per thousand?

Final consideration in trade show costs is: What percentage of the total communications budget does the company allocate for shows? If it approaches 10 percent, the time has long since passed when somebody should have taken a long, hard look at what the company has been getting for its money.

If trade shows siphon off more than 10 percent of the average industrial company's promotional dollar, chances are something is radically wrong with the emphasis placed on this communications medium. Consideration should be given to seminars, expanded direct mail advertising, and additional space advertising in trade publications. All do a better job, reach more buying influences and cost less.

How to Make It All Easier

You can lessen the pains and avoid a large share of the frustration of handling trade shows if you'll heed the following:

Fill out your "Empty" stickers before you leave for the show. These go on each and every crate, box, carton, container, case and so on that you'll use to pack up and reship your product, booth, furniture, floor tile and so on when the show closes and you tear down your exhibit. Write exhibit management and request that they be sent to you in your office—and at the same time, get your "Return" labels; these will usually be addressed to your display house, of course. Fill them out before you depart for the show.

Send all of the people in your home office, field force, and others in the company who will attend the show a machine copy of an area map showing the location of the exhibit hall and the hotel where they will stay. Circle the hotel and the hall. Everybody who receives this is grateful.

Send all of your people their copies of the hotel reservations. And you check personally when you get there ahead of them to make sure nothing has gone amiss.

Make copies of all bills of lading for all shipments—equipment, booth literature, and what have you. This makes tracing easier in case anything goes wrong—which it will.

Also have copies of all of the order forms you filled out and mailed to various suppliers of such stuff as furniture, water cooler, electricians, labor, carpenters, porter, janitor, and so on and on. Then, if you get any static in the hall (which you will), you'll be able to prove you ordered material and services as specified.

Check *immediately* upon arriving in the city where the show is to be held to see if your equipment and booth have arrived. If there's the slightest bit of doubt, get on the horn and start tracing *immediately*. Don't let anybody reassure you, don't take anybody's word that the shipment will show up tomorrow, or that it may be in the hall right now. Don't wait, don't hope, don't delay. Don't assume it will show up in time. If you do that, you can be morally certain of one thing—it won't.

Have handy the dimensions and weights of each individual crate, carton, box, case, container, drum and so forth. Your shipping department and that of your exhibit house will have compiled all of this data for you prior to shipping. Truck lines, airlines, and railroads are helpless unless you can supply this information.

Take phone numbers with you. Never does it fail but what something crops up that makes it necessary for you to call your boss, your assistant, your secretary, or somebody else. Take both office and *home* phone numbers. More likely than not whatever it is that makes it necessary for you to call long distance will happen on a weekend when everybody's office is closed.

Two last things: Lock your booth telephone at night.

Repeat: *Lock your booth telephone at night.* You can buy telephone locks at nearby drugstores, hardware stores, stationery stores, and often in the exhibit hall itself. These simple little locks cost a couple of dollars and have two keys. Tell the man in charge of your booth personnel that you have only *one* key. You keep it. Make the last thing you do at night to lock the phone.

Locking your booth telephone prevents all of those unexplained person-to-person calls to Willie Smith in Saigon or Frankfurt or London. They mount up amazingly. The author knows one hapless advertising manager who accumulated more than $700 worth of these calls, all made at night, all made to soldiers in far-flung cities throughout the world.

Final thing to remember: Don't blow your cool.

Chapter 18

LITERATURE

UNQUESTIONABLY one of the most important assignments handled by the industrial advertising department is the production of literature.

For the most part this is product sales literature. However, most advertising departments also create and produce a miscellaneous assortment of other print material including house organs, employee manuals, instruction manuals, company histories, annual reports, and so on.

When McGraw-Hill conducted a survey to determine what salesmen consider the most important selling tool with which they are provided, sales literature on the product won hands down, as reported by the Laboratory of Advertising Performance.

Salesmen of manufacturers selling machinery and equipment to the chemical process industry were singled out and asked the question:

> *Which sales aids are of greatest help in facilitating your general selling approach and in developing the confidence of present and potential customers?* (Check as many as are important to you.)

Predictably, manufacturer's literature breezed into a strong front-running position with a total of 95 percent of the vote. In second place was space advertising in trade and business publications; it had 70 percent of the vote. Considerably down the scale in importance in the salesmen's scheme of things came direct mail, which tallied up 45 percent of their favorable mentions.

Data for the report were developed with the cooperation of 101 manufacturers of machinery and equipment sold to the chemical processing industry. The sales managers of 46 companies cooperated with McGraw-Hill Research by distributing 2,091 questionnaires to their own salesmen. In addition, 55 other companies sent in 2,007 names of their salesmen so that they could be sent questionnaires. In the returns were those from direct salesmen, as well as manufacturer's representatives, so the results present a good cross-section of opinion of those selling industrial capital equipment.

What's more, according to LAP, industrial buyers, when asked to rate different information sources as to usefulness in supplying facts about products purchased for their companies, rated manufacturers' literature right at the top—63 percent of them stated literature was their number one source of help.

Thus, it's quite obvious there is unanimity of opinion as to the efficiency with which sales literature presents information, and from both sides of the desk at that—salesmen and buyers see eye to eye on this subject. This is indeed convincing.

Manufacturer's literature also serves another purpose which is seldom mentioned to salesmen, although they are, of course, fully aware of it. Collecting information of the three or four leading makes of widgets enables the prospective purchaser of a new widget to make an unhurried comparison of the merits and specifications of each, away from the blandishments and distractions and persuasive remarks of the salesman.

Actually, there are six primary objectives for sales literature. These are:

1. To support the salesmen.
2. To strengthen dealer relations.
3. To intensify the advertising.
4. To help hold old customers.
5. To help win new customers.
6. To help broaden the market.

Advertising Department Does Not Initiate Literature

Although the advertising department produces and frequently creates sales literature, advertising does not and cannot initiate it. To do so would be to assume the prerogative and function of a different department altogether.

Planning literature, that is, foreseeing the need for it, properly is part and parcel of marketing planning. Needs in this area should be spelled out in the marketing plan for the product line involved (or for the individual market, depending on how the company is structured) at the start of the fiscal year.

To expect the advertising manager to be able to "guesstimate" the number of different pieces of literature it will be necessary to produce during the year is absurd. Yet this happens most of the time in most companies.

In order to be able to plan a budget for the advertising department, the advertising manager must know the number of different pieces of literature to be produced, the degree of complexity of each, and the anticipated print run for each.

But it is the marketing and product people who are privy to plans for new products and revamped, renewed, renamed, and facelifted old products for which new sales literature will be needed in the forthcoming 12-month period. Too, they are conversant with thinking of top management on how hard specific products are to be promoted and the emphasis to be placed on all products.

Market management, product management, or sales management requests literature from advertising, usually with a requested needed-by date, guidelines as to how elaborate the piece is to be, any special photographs or artwork, slant of the copy, appeals to emphasize, and quantity needed. All of this must take place before the advertising department can do a good job.

How to Decide What Goes in the Literature

Assuming your company is like most industrial firms, you'll be subjected to pressure that's little short of ferocious to put everything that everybody and his brother can think of in the literature you produce.

The engineers, for instance, will lovingly dwell on the pitch of the thread of the bolts that hold the nickel-chrome, heat-treated steel of the frame of the widget together, and that the gears are helical and have faces that overobfuscate the retuddity with a bright linear kopacetic. And this is just the start of it.

Listen to them, keep on listening, mutter sweet nothings politely, smile toothily, and nod agreeably. But for the sake of sanity, *don't* put everything in the literature that they want. If you do this, nobody will wade through it because the copy will be so boring and tedious. Moreover, your literature will have missed its mark.

The product and marketing people also will talk features to you endlessly. You'd think that because this widget holds 8 cubic yards, or that it pumps 1,567 gallons per minute, nothing else mattered.

One sure way to determine exactly what should be in literature and what shouldn't, is to make an informal survey. Informal doesn't mean having lunch with a few friends or quizzing a few cohorts at the water fountain.

Instead, be a bit more formal than that. Go at the survey just as you would if you were doing some deep digging for market data. And indeed you are because you're determining what it is those in the marketplace want to know about your product. There's no necessity to invest a small fortune in printing, but by all means consider this thing carefully and draw up a questionnaire that's easy to answer, that has boxes to check off, and send a *stamped* envelope (not a postage-paid reply envelope) along with it. And write a covering letter asking for the recipient's help.

Explain in the letter that you're in the process of developing a new piece of literature on your new widget which is just about ready to be announced to a breathlessly awaiting world, and tell the recipient that you'd like to know what *he'd* like to know. His help, tell him, will enable you to produce a piece of literature to end all pieces of literature as far as answering questions he has about the product is concerned.

Send your questionnaire to:

1. Product and market people inside your company.
2. Your field sales force.
3. Your dealers, distributors, representatives, or jobbers.
4. Prospects and customers from those two mailing lists you have.

Don't make a big production out of the questionnaire. But it's best to mail at least 1,500; in addition to your own people and those who handle your product (presumably you can rely on a high percentage of returns from them), mailing to at least 250 customers and an equal number of prospects and dealers or distributors should be sufficient. Those who are really interested in your products will reply, and they're undoubtedly your best prospects anyway, so the chances are their thoughts would be most helpful.

Criticism may be leveled at you for using a questionnaire. You may hear the remark, "We never had a questionnaire before. Why all the fuss? Just put in everything about the widget and let it go at that."

Such thinking is commonplace throughout product-oriented companies with complex and highly-engineered products. They've used old-fashioned "bulletins" so long that nobody in the company actually realizes how poor the sales literature is.

Often overlooked, but a valuable source of information about what should be included in the piece of literature, is what is in your competitors' literature on the same product. Presumably they've given thought to this subject and have researched it. They may not be right, and circumstances certainly alter cases, but this viewpoint represents the combined thinking of dozens of individuals throughout your industry and it is not to be taken lightly.

Questions to ask yourself when planning a piece of literature are spelled out by S.D. Warren Company, manufacturers of fine papers, in its booklet, *The Sales Catalog.* The eight questions asked under the heading, Proper Preparation, are:

1. How are the products used by a potential customer? And how are they purchased?
2. How can the product and accompanying information best be presented and described so that prospective buyers can inform themselves fully? With pictures that display exteriors and interiors—with diagrams—with color? With installation photos?
3. How can the present literature be improved to make it more helpful to the user?
4. What products or models are most frequently purchased?
5. What are the different things that potential customers will want to know about the class of product—applications, ease of operation, construction specifications, economy, comfort, beauty?
6. What uses can be made of the product? Is it versatile? What are all of its advantages (major and minor)? Has the product features that are exclusive?
7. In what circumstances and environment will the literature be used? Will it be kept in a desk drawer or in an office file cabinet or on a shelf? Will it be used by shop mechanics? Should it conform to standards specified by a trade or professional association? What size will best suit the condition of use? What measure of protection is required?
8. What is the forecast on prices? Should price schedules be included, or should prices be issued in supplementary sections?

Since advertising managers as a breed are able to cut incisively to the crux of things rather than rehash trivialities for hours as the technical types are fond of doing, maybe you can save much time and conversation and effort by asking yourself (and maybe others) the following questions.

1. What information about the widget do your prospects and customers really want?
2. Is this the information they actually need to make a buying decision?
3. How should this information be organized to make the most persuasive case for your widget that can be made, and are you certain it is in logical order with nothing of consequence omitted?

4. How should you present your widget—photographically, line art, wash, scratchboard; black-and-white, four-color; product by itself, product in use, installation photographs, cutaway views, or what have you.
5. How detailed should your literature be? Should it be two pages (front and back), four pages, eight, or is it better to produce a complete catalog? What form should it take—loose pages, spiral bound, three-hole punched, side stitched, stapled, paperbound, hardbound?
6. When and to whom should the literature be distributed? How should it be distributed? Correct timing can affect sales and demand, as can the list of recipients and the method of distribution.

The literature you produce is a silent salesman. It continues to sell long after your prospects have forgotten your advertisements and have dismissed your salesmen from their minds. The power of the printed word in sales literature is mighty indeed.

Product Line Catalog Versus Individual Sales Literature

Perplexing many industrial advertising managers is the age-old question: Should I produce a complete, detailed catalog covering every widget we manufacture, or should I take the alternate approach and produce sales literature for each individual product as a separate item?

Answering that one is easy for many ad managers, especially those whose companies engage in high volume production of standardized items such as components to be incorporated into the end products of other manufacturers. Such products might be screw-machine products, nuts and bolts, fasteners, standard hardware, cotter pins, electric motors, pumps, hydraulic pistons, generators, tires, and other items for which there is a relatively stable demand and which do not undergo sweeping changes in approach very often.

For example, a full-line catalog of electric motors might well be in order and it could very easily be the most economical method of presenting a vast mass of product information about many different models to prospective customers. Such a catalog could have photographs and complete technical descriptions of each and every motor in the line, cutaway artwork, overlays, and four-color printing.

In short, the advertising manager for a company like this could logically make a major investment in a selling tool of high quality, secure in the knowledge that tomorrow or next week or next month the product would still look like the ones shown in the catalog. If new motors were developed, supplementary pages could be issued.

Volatility of the market and frequency of changes in the product are the big bugaboos confronting most advertising managers. They make investing in a full-line catalog, often to the tune of $50,000 or more, inadvisable.

In many companies the advertising manager is faced with the problem of producing a piece of literature for one product line only, when the company may manufacture a half-dozen different product lines or more, each for a different market.

All too often this hapless ad manager labors long and mightily, creates strong, succinct, swinging, selling copy; a beautiful, clean layout; and he uses superb photography or art; and then rides herd on his printer to assure a faultless job.

Then what happens? Somebody either changed one of the products, the sales manager dropped it from the line because it wasn't selling or there wasn't enough profit in it, or else some engineer developed a completely new widget—all without even a whisper to the unfortunate advertising manager.

Lack of internal communications causes this waste of time and effort and money too frequently in too many companies. Eliminating obsolescence in product sales literature is almost impossible in a fast-paced industry, especially when frequent product changes—such as occur in the electronics industry—create a built-in obsolescence in new literature even before the ink is dry.

You'll never live to see the day this problem doesn't exist, but much can be done to keep it fairly well under control. Most important thing to do is to lay down clear channels of information within your company—perhaps from marketing to sales to advertising to engineering to production, or however the sequence runs in your firm. Make sure, however, that you are on the route list for memos and other written matter concerning all new products and all revisions in existing products.

In many companies there's a product review committee, a new product committee, or some such group. Attend these meetings, or (better yet), get your name on the route list for a summary and save valuable time you can't afford to waste.

An exceptionally attractive and informative product-line booklet was produced by Electro-Motive Division, General Motors Corporation. The company's six-axle, six-motor mainline locomotive, the SD Series, is shown attractively in impressionistic art in color. It is identified on a separate page opposite the illustration. Flip this page and there are specifications for Model SD-45, components included in this model, and a tractive effort curve on the opposite page. All very tidy.

Continue flipping the half-pages and the same information is presented on the other models in the SD Series. Then there's a

Ringbinder catalog of GM locomotives has expensive art work on full pages by itself. Pages devoted to data are on half-pages (shown below) so that changes can be made fairly inexpensively.

striking night photograph, in black-and-white for a change of pace, of an SD Series locomotive in actual service.

This page is a fold-out. Printed in black against an olive-green background are line drawings of each model locomotive, with dimensions printed in a darker green. The effect is striking and very effective as well as providing necessary information for those in need of a locomotive.

If specifications were to change because the engineers got to doodling around with the product after literature has been printed—as usually happens—most of the expensive art, type, keylines and so

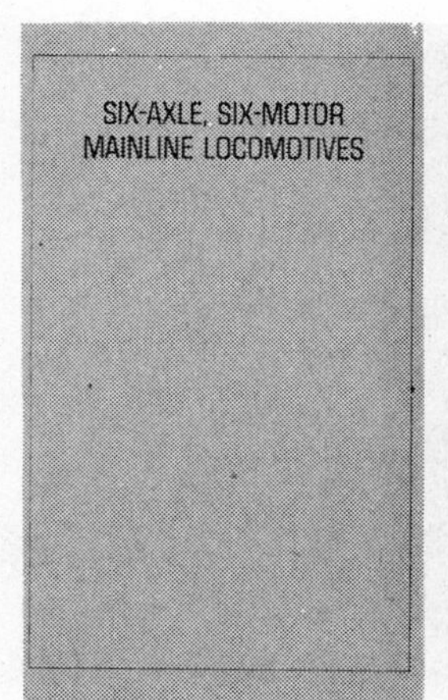

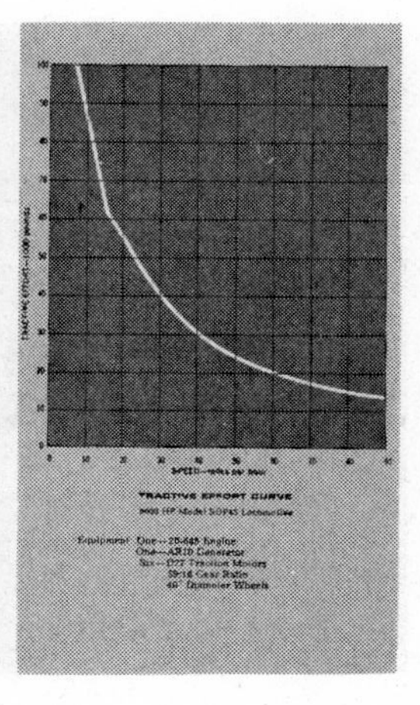

forth could be saved and reused in another printing. This is good planning. Much effort and thought went into this excellent booklet.

To negate literature obsolescence, many industrial advertising managers produce one or more prestige booklets of 12 or 16 pages to tell a corporate or divisional story.

Stress interesting or unique applications of your company's products. Tell about the achievements of your engineering staff, hit on the accomplishments of your research and development people, brag about the skill and depth of knowledge of the field sales force and the enviable position of your company in its industry. Emphasize the quality theme, the capability of your company, and its ability to solve prospects' problems.

Paul Marcott, advertising manager of Bell Helicopter Company, a Textron Company, took this tack with great success in his literature. He could do so because the company's choppers are sold in many versions in many diverse markets, both military and commercial. This made it impractical to invest in a full-line catalog suitable for every market and application.

A typical production is Bell Helicopter's attractive 28-page booklet; the cover is printed in four-color and shows small spot illustrations of various choppers in a wide variety of applications. Inside pages are printed in orange and black, while the halftones are mostly duotones, a combination of the two colors.

One thing Bell's booklet has going for it is that it's timeless. At the end of the Vietnamese War all that has been said remains just as compelling and just as arresting as the day it was written. Instead

Although the cover of this Bell Helicopter booklet shows military uses, it suggests civilian applications.

of a current document, the booklet discusses recent history. When it's both product- and company-oriented, there's nothing wrong with that.

This multipurpose type of literature makes prestige handout pieces that any company representative can present with pride to a prospect or customer. They dramatize the major role Bell Helicopter is playing in transportation, pipelining, construction, crop-dusting, oil fields, geological exploration, road building, ranching, rescue work, surveying, fire fighting, reforestation, and military service.

Quality can be emphasized, as Paul Marcott did, in photos and art and fine layout, as well as in words—and the obvious quality of the finished literature itself.

Supplementing a couple of basic pieces of prestige literature such as this can be sales literature on individual products. Thus, when a product becomes obsolete, there is no need to scrap an expensive catalog and start from scratch again; simply prepare a new piece of literature on the new or revised product and you're back in business without spending a small fortune.

This method may not be ideal, however, due simply to the fact your company wants to make a big splash. Perhaps the competitive situation dictates that to the broadest line goes the major portion of the spoils, a situation encountered with increasing frequency in bitterly competitive markets such as the automotive aftermarket.

If this is the case, the company undoubtedly feels the necessity of putting out a thick catalog to show prospective warehouse distributors, jobbers and dealers that it produces the right widget for every vehicle—and far more different widgets than the competition does. This is the "single source" concept, and it's a potent one.

Ideal solution to this problem is to do as Sealed Power Corporation did, which was to come up with an inch-thick, spiral-bound catalog. Although it's big and impressive and it hammers home to prospects the fact that Sealed Power markets an unusually comprehensive line of piston rings and internal engine parts, the catalog was nonetheless produced by advertising manager George Wickstrom without investing an inordinate amount of money.

This was possible because the catalog is, for the most part, a compilation of appropriate tabular information supplemented by individual pieces of product literature. Literature was produced one piece at a time, as needed. The entire thing was then collated, punched, and bound together.

An essential that musn't be overlooked if you want your catalog to be an effective, persuasive selling tool is a good index. Many companies think they are producing an effective catalog when they are, in fact, producing a pain in the neck for a busy purchasing agent by making it almost impossible to find anything without going through all the pages.

This holds especially true for companies that persist in hanging on a nonword name onto every product they produce. Products should be indexed by their generic names, then if pressure from the technical people forces you into it, you can get in the meaningless names to make them happy. But by all means make it easy for a person to find what he's looking for without wading through what is, to them, a bunch of gobbledegook.

Dividers, tabs, colors, even a simple printed index in the front listing the contents of the catalog, can all enable the user to locate what he's interested in without trying his temper and wasting his time.

Royal Typewriter, Inc., a division of Litton Industries, went this way on beautifully simple four-page, four-color literature on the Royal Model 660. Each feature (and benefit) of the Model 660 is covered with eye-arresting color photographs, and the clean, uncluttered layout makes this piece a thing of beauty.

Having prestige literature to sell company capability and the product line in general, then supplementing it with individual pieces of literature on each major product which warrants it is undoubtedly the soundest approach for the average industrial company.

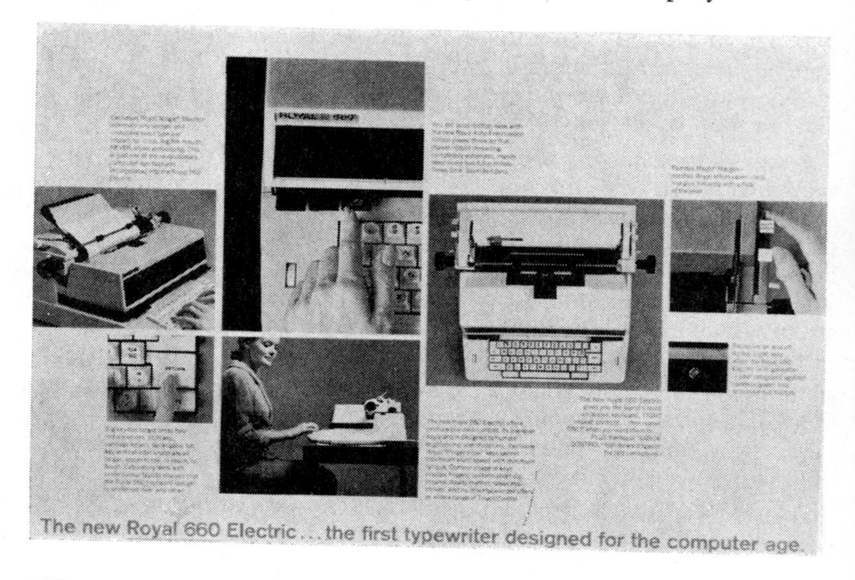

The new Royal 660 Electric . . . the first typewriter designed for the computer age.

Budgeting for Literature

Approximately 20 percent of the typical industrial advertising budget is earmarked to sales literature and catalogs, although in some companies—depending on method of distribution—the percentage goes much higher. Some companies regularly spend 50 percent or more of their promotional dollars this way.

Merely having attractive, accurate sales literature in his briefcase gives the salesman an important psychological boost. It makes him feel he is master of any situation he'll encounter, that the "factory" is backing him, and that he can cope with any questions a prospective buyer might throw at him. This one benefit alone may well be worth the total investment made in literature.

Buoying up the sales force's morale is using literature properly, and it is making effective use of the dollars allocated to produce it.

What is *not* using this portion of the budget to best advantage is the practice of producing a new piece of literature at the behest of one individual, or a group of people who want it merely to have—not because an objective is to be met.

When you're working on your annual budget you will, of course, query all of the product managers or market managers, the sales manager, vice-president of marketing, and any others in the company who initiate requests for literature. This will give you a good ball-park figure on how many individual pieces you will have to provide for in the budget. And if you discuss each piece with the individual, you can probably make a pretty close estimate of the cost involved.

It is routine for most ad managers to operate this way, of course. What most *do not* do, however, is to ask their people—in production or sales or marketing—for formal, written objectives for each piece of literature so that they can put it in its proper perspective as far as assigning dollars and cents is concerned.

There's no need to make a big production out of establishing the objective for the literature. A sentence or a short paragraph will do, just so long as it's logical and it represents an objective the literature can achieve.

Ask these questions:

1. What is the objective for this proposed new piece of literature? Just what do we expect from it?
2. What will it contribute to our total marketing program? Can a price tag be put on the contribution the literature or catalog will make?

3. Is the literature or catalog really necessary? Is there an alternative way of accomplishing the same objective, perhaps more effectively and more economically?

Based on past experience, an advertising manager can usually come quite close to the actual cost if he's told the company will require 47 pieces of new sales literature during the coming fiscal year, although he will require guidance from product or marketing people on whether each is to be a major effort, or if it is to fit into a pre-established format.

Inside or Outside?

Sooner or later the question arises: Should our sales literature be produced in the advertising department, or should it be done by outside specialists such as our advertising agency?

Before the question can be answered it's necessary to evaluate two factors as objectively as possible.

First of these is: Are you really equipped to handle the entire job inside?

Chances are you're exactly like most industrial ad managers. Ad managers are a capable breed. They are able administrators and they have more than a slight touch of genius when it comes to handling the company's money, for they are dollar-stretchers *par excellence.*

Furthermore, almost every ad manager, due to training and inclination, is a skillful editor who can pare and prune away the innocuous and the irrelevant to get to the heart of the company's story in all written matter, be it a space advertisement or a piece of sales literature.

Indisputable, though, is the fact that most advertising managers are not top writers. Nor do they really consider themselves writers despite their being the best word-mechanics in their companies. There is a vast difference in the *degree* of craftsmanship of any writing just as there is in the construction of any industrial product. The advertising manager has the perception and the training and the judgment to recognize this, although few others in the company do.

Besides the question of writing skill, there's a second factor—consideration of whether the average advertising manager *has the time* to spend writing literature. Most two-page, two-color pieces of sales literature require at least two days to write, considering the incessant telephone calls and other interruptions. This is after all reference material is on hand, of course.

Usually there's enough work to do on literature without writing it internally. For instance, there's directing the photographer, specifying type, buying type, making or buying layout, proofreading galleys, reading keylines and approving them, reviewing and approving retouching, reading and approving silverprints—all in addition to getting bids from three printers, plus other odds and ends.

Unless you can find an agency or studio that is in business for its health, having your literature produced by an outside source will always cost more—much more.

For example, if you write, lay out, and produce a reasonably simple two-color, two-page (front and back) piece of sales literature, you'll probably spend about $325 for the complete job—excluding original photography. Also, if any line or schematic drawings are included, these would have to be produced in your engineering department in order to get it under this price. The $325 does, however, include everything except writing and original photography and art; it includes layout, type, etch proofs, keyline, silverprint, and printing a quantity of 3,000 pieces.

Original photography of your widget on which you're producing literature can run from $25 to $10,000—although you'll probably lay out approximately $50 to $75 for it unless there's an unusual amount of setup time or travel involved. Include this and your sales literature ends up costing around $400.

However, if you had the same job done by your agency or by a studio, you could logically expect to be invoiced anywhere from 40 percent to 75 percent more, depending upon the markup the agency or studio customarily charges, how busy they happened to be at the moment, and whether they really wanted the business or not.

Some agencies and studios discourage small jobs such as this, unless there's a steady flow of them, to concentrate almost exclusively on higher-markup collateral material—four-color literature and catalogs, prestige booklets, films, and so on. Average price you can expect to pay for the two-page job in a metropolitan area is at least $500 to $600, and more if the agency supervises or supplies photography or art.

Final consideration when deciding whether to produce inside or go outside is that if you do the actual writing, or if your sales promotion manager or someone else within the department does, you're going to be locked into one man's viewpoint and one man's outlook on life.

What may well be the absolute living end in written persuasiveness and great style may easily be dated and dull tomorrow. And even if this doesn't happen, there is ample reason to question seriously the wisdom of having the stamp of one individual's personality on the company's sales literature year after year.

When an agency or studio creates some of your literature, you avoid this risk. Granted, one individual will write it, but that person is backstopped by other equally competent craftsmen in the agency.

Upshot of this is that the typical company gets, in most instances, a superior end product if it contracts out the writing, layout, and production of sales literature.

Striking a happy medium isn't difficult. You can stretch dollars by doing the simpler jobs internally, and retaining outside experts for those projects that are more demanding. This enables you to function as you should, as a manager; to use your abilities to make and save money for the company.

Copy for Sales Literature

Of primary importance is that copy written for sales literature be informative. When your prospect sits back with his feet on his desk to concentrate on a piece of your literature about your widget, the copy had better come through.

If it's been written with the prospect in mind, if it anticipates the questions he has in mind about your widget, if it gives him specifics on which he can base a buying decision, the literature has accomplished its purpose.

But if the literature fails on any of these scores the money you spent on it has been wasted and you've lost a prospect.

The copy in typical literature from the average company is poor. Much of it commits four cardinal sins:

1. Repeating the company name ad nauseam.
2. Bragging and boasting.
3. Boring hell out of the reader.
4. Not selling the product.

Of course, you've seen far too many examples of the first sin, literature wherein the company's name seemed to appear at least once in every sentence.

Repeating a firm name does *not* strengthen the firm in the reader's mind. It merely slows down his reading and dilutes the effectiveness of the copy.

And if you have to resort to brag and boast to describe your product there's one thing you'd better do even before you finish reading this page—look for a job with a company that manufactures better products.

Mull this one over for a minute, for instance. It's the actual lead-in paragraph in a three-color, 22-page booklet into which much money and time was poured. The company name has been changed, but the copy is verbatim otherwise.

> *Smith's Die Springs represent quality in design, in material, and in manufacturing. Quality controls are strict to assure you of an exceptional Die Spring—unmatched performance.*

Now change the name "Smith" to any other company name, and change the product from Die Springs to Widgets (even capitalized) or turret lathes or bulldozers, and there isn't a company in these United States that can't say the same thing about its products. Too many companies do just that.

And this lead-in on page 2 of an orange-and-black 8-page booklet really waves the company flag for all to salute:

> *Smith-Jones widgets are the end result of continuing research, skilled engineering, and precision manufacturing. This combination, unique with Smith-Jones, invariably produces widgets that instantly become the standard by which all others are judged. Smith-Jones widgets are acclaimed throughout the world as the finest it is possible to produce. Here at Smith-Jones we take great pride in the knowledge that Smith-Jones builds the best and has for more than 40 years. And we look resolutely to the future, determined to continue Smith-Jones' great traditions.*

Retain your lunch, anybody?

Copy *must* interest. Copy must make the product seem desirable by pointing out in a vivid, vital way the benefits the user derives from it. Copy must enable the reader to project himself and his company into the "you" that's in, or should be in, the sales literature copy.

Establish a rule of thumb in your advertising department that nobody ever, under any circumstances, starts writing copy with the words "New Horizons."

Twenty years or so ago, "New Horizons" and "New Directions" and similar vague generalities were the *in* thing. One company outdid all rivals and produced what it fondly hoped would be a prestige

48-page booklet titled: *New Directions and New Horizons.* It is cherished and preserved in the author's files. A carefully worded letter to the company requesting permission to reproduce the cover of that amazing booklet elicited an obviously suspicious response that can be summed up in one word: Why?

Organizing the Material

Half your battle is won if you can assist your product and engineering people in organizing their source material, so it's in the same sequence as information will be presented in the completed sales literature.

Following is a product literature source material outline suggested by James J. Hubbard, formerly an account executive at Marsteller Inc. The outline is logical and workable.

PRODUCT LITERATURE SOURCE OUTLINE

I. GENERIC NAME OF PRODUCT (widget, gadget, and so on).

II. PRODUCT BENEFITS (most important sales points, in order of importance—why the prospects should buy the product).

III. PRODUCT FEATURES (significant design points).

IV. APPLICATIONS (types of jobs and in what industries the product can be used, and why product is good for these applications).

V. PRODUCT DESCRIPTION (nuts-and-bolts description).

VI. DIMENSIONS AND SPECIFICATIONS (including drawings, tables, etc.).

Jim Hubbard then went on to suggest to the client the following sequence of material in the company's sales literature.

I. PRODUCT GENERIC NAME (avoid coined names, nonwords and similar inanities).

II. BENEFIT SUBHEAD (a short headline that tells what the widget will do for the buyer).

III. INTRODUCTION (capsule pitch on how this product can help the prospect, and why the product is good).

IV. APPLICATIONS (be specific, be factual, but be promotional; tell how well the product does the job, why it's better than competitive ones, stress advantages and savings).

V. FEATURES (here, again, be factual but promotional; stress uniqueness of features that actually are unique, emphasize exclusive features the product has).

VI. PRODUCT DESCRIPTION (describe product factually, but inject benefits into description—such as, "Stainless steel case prevents formation of algae which could contaminate the transmitter").

VII. DIMENSIONS AND SPECIFICATIONS (strictly nuts and bolts).

VIII. BID FOR ACTION (if your literature is to sell, it must do what every good salesman does—ask for the order. The bid for action might be to ask a salesman to call, phone the nearest district office, fill in and return a tipped-in reply card, ask for a free sample, write for more information and so on; it should be the last element in the literature except for the signature and address).

Make your sales literature copy pithy, punchy, and, above all, promotional. There's no getting around one thing: If literature sells, it's working for you. If it doesn't, it isn't.

Fitting Copy

When writing copy for sales literature, or for any other printed piece, for that matter, never write to fit a layout. Instead, make the layout after the copy is written. What this means, of course, is that copy length is not determined so it will be pleasing to some artist, but by what needs to be said to tell your product story.

Once copy is written, edited, and finish-typed, the layout artist then measures it, or makes a close estimate of how much space it will require after he has specced the type. He needs certain basic information to enable him to accomplish this, however, such as that given in Table I and Table II on page 1364.

Generally a writer starts by making a thumbnail layout, then proceeds to doodle a full-size rough.

Once satisfied with the rough layout, it's a simple matter to compute the amount of type you've selected required to fill each line. Then set your typewriter accordingly.

For instance, if a space 13 picas wide is to be filled with 10-point body type, cast on a 12-point linotype slug (2-point leaded), the table shows there are 2.5 ten-point characters to each pica of column width. Thus there will be 32.5 characters to the line.

Set the typewriter to start at 0 and to stop at 32 on the scale. Or, if you don't want to endure the aggravation of having to punch the margin release every time the carriage comes to the 32 and there are a couple of additional characters to go (which, of course, even out those lines that are a couple of characters short), you can draw a light pencil line down the right-hand margin. Or you can do as many copywriters do, hold down firmly on the period key and give the carriage a few quick turns, rolling the paper farther onto the roller.

TABLE I

Characters Per Pica

Type Size	*Average Characters Per Pica*
4 point	5
5 point	4
6 point	3.5
8 point	3
10 point	2.5
12 point	2
14 point	1.5
18 point	1

TABLE II

Average characters per one square pica with corresponding average type face required to fill space

Size of Average Type Face Required to Fill	*Characters Per One Square Pica*
4 point solid	15
4 point on 5 point	12

TABLE II *(Cont.)*

Size of Average Type Face Required to Fill	*Characters Per One Square Pica*
5 point solid	9.6
5 point on 6 point	8
6 point solid	7
6 point on 7 point	6
6 point on 8 point	5.3
8 point solid	4.5
8 point on 9 point	4
8 point on 10 point	3.6
10 point solid	3
10 point on 11 point	2.7
10 point on 12 point	2.5
12 point solid	2
12 point on 13 point	1.8
12 point on 14 point	1.7
14 point solid	1.4
14 point on 15 point	1.3
14 point on 16 point	1.2

This leaves a faint vertical line on the paper to show where the margin should be.

Determine the number of lines required to fill the space by measuring the vertical space with a line gauge. Most printers and typographers have a supply of 18-inch rulers especially made for measuring type; they are used as handout pieces to customers and prospects. Your printing or type salesman will give you one if asked.

This copy-fitting system will do for the average job. For more precise work, many tricky type-fitting systems have been developed. Some call for slide rules, others for IBM computers, and still others for an unbelievable expertise. This author likes the method developed by the International Typographical and Composition Association, 2233 Wisconsin Avenue, Washington, D.C. 20007.

Based on the most exhaustive study ever made of the frequency of use of the letters of the alphabet, the ITCA Copy-Fitting System is a landmark of progress in graphic arts technique. The results of this research, combined with an analysis of modern-day word spacing concepts, formed the basis of a computer program that delivered extremely accurate character-count information for the more than 15,000 sizes of type.

In sizes ranging from 4-point upward, every type face, old and new, used in the graphic arts was analyzed. This information has been organized into the simplest copy-fitting procedure ever devised. Using it enables the type user to perform any copy-fitting task easily and accurately. Every effort was made to supply a quick, precise solution to the stickiest problems.

Key to copy-fitting is based on what has come to be called The Gauge—with upper-case letters as a mark of respect and fond affection. This unbreakable gauge of sturdy vinyl has calibrated on it the ITCA numbers and their character counts per pica for all measures up to 42 picas. Also on The Gauge are typewriter-character counters for both elite and standard typewriters. You can get The Gauge from ITCA, or from a local typographer. The author's came from one of Chicago's leading type houses, The Adcrafters Commercial Typographers, Inc., 314 West Superior Street, Chicago 60610.

Approvals

Essentially the same logic prevails and the same techniques should be used in securing approvals of copy for sales literature as for space advertisements.

Certain additional problems crop up in copy written for sales literature, however. These problems occur merely because there is so much *more* copy in sales literature than there is in a space ad. So there's much more opportunity to put one's foot in the company's mouth. Lawsuits are viewed dimly indeed by most companies, as are advertising managers whose sales literature results in such suits being filed.

For that reason alone approval procedure is important, as we'll see. But first, though, let's consider briefly a few rather broad suggestions about the legality of the copy in your literature. These must necessarily be broad because of the tremendous differences in products and their applications; there's wide variance in considerations between copy written to promote sales of bulldozers and for caustic chemicals sold to industry.

About the only way to determine what legal pitfalls exist in your industry is to be guided by past experience, common and accepted practices, rules and regulations and restrictions established by your industry organization—and clearing any questions through channels with your company attorney. Many firms make it standard practice to clear all copy with an attorney before printing literature. They've either been burned before and are now gun-shy on the subject, or are overly cautious.

As in writing any advertising copy, avoid such words as *never, foolproof, fail-safe, can't fail, can't, won't, impossible, certain, positive, always, invariably, inevitably, and will* (consider "may" or "designed to").

There are many other similar words whose use can be inferred as putting the company in a position of making a flat statement, a guarantee, or failing to draw the user's attention to an inherent danger.

Better be safe than sorry about such terms. Perhaps they've been used for years by your company before you joined it. If so, chances are they've achieved acceptance in your industry and nothing untoward will occur from continuing to use them. Smart thing to do, though, is to draw this to management's attention in a memo; inquire about the desirability of requesting legal advice on these and similar terms.

Before submitting copy to those who must give it their blessing, make certain your own house is in order.

This includes, of course, having properly signed, witnessed releases from all identifiable people in the photographs you're using, having reproduction rights to such photographs and/or art, and that all company trademarks, slogans, and symbols are used properly. You'll find it is incumbent upon a company to use such identifying marks in interstate commerce in order to guarantee its exclusive right to the mark, slogan, or symbol.

Don't make the mistake of registering a trademark, using it a time or two and then retiring it only to bring it back into use months or years later and expecting it to be protected. Such marks must be used regularly to remain the exclusive property of the company. Have such trademarks, slogans, and symbols appear in sales literature which has an identifying printing date appearing somewhere in it; this constitutes use, although it is advisable also to use such marks in print advertisements from time to time.

When you discuss guarantees in your sales literature, and many companies do, spell out exactly what is guaranteed—the entire widget, certain component parts of it, the length of time for which it is guaranteed, what "lifetime" means if you use the term, details about who pays shipping expense and/or expense to get an expert into the customer's plant to perform examinations, diagnosis, and repairs; what percentage is charged back to the customer, if any.

Also state whether the guarantor (usually the manufacturer, but occasionally a distributor or dealer) is obligated to repair or replace.

Failure to spell out details fully and specifically could easily open the door to a Federal Trade Commission ruling that your company is engaging in unfair and deceptive practices. Moreover, it is not unknown for a company that did not spell out its guarantee to have been ruled to offer an *unconditional* guarantee—and few, mighty few, companies want to go that far.

Almost every warranty or guarantee has some limiting clauses and some conditions of use or maintenance or *something* that prevents manufacturers from being deluged with claims. Be wary about using lightly such terms as "money-back guarantee" or "satisfaction guaranteed" or "performance guaranteed." Such terminology should *always* be cleared with your legal department.

Repeat: *Such terminology should always be cleared with your legal counsel.*

If price of your product is mentioned, make absolutely certain it is correct and that your company is prepared to sell the product at that price. You can, of course, state that a given price is in effect for a specified period of time only. But if the product is not offered at the advertised price (in advertisements or in promotional literature), you are wide open for a bait-advertising or deceptive practices charge.

Not only must the price quoted for your product be an actual price at which the product can be purchased, but comparisons of your price with prices of competitive products must be accurate and must be stated correctly. If this is not the case it could be assumed there was an intent to deceive the prospective buyer.

To protect your department, get dated signatures of all persons who approve what you've done. A special form can be mimeographed for the purpose. This protects you if there's a major change in thinking after the money is spent and the piece is printed, and it protects you from those who shirk responsibility. A typical copy-approval form is shown on page 1368.

Never offer to let product or market or technical people review galleys, etch proofs, keylines, or silverprints. Inform your people that if, once they've approved the basic material, typos creep in, material is left out, lines are reversed, captions go on wrong photos, and so forth, it's strictly your baby. It's up to you to prevent these gremlins from sabotaging your literature, although the advertising manager doesn't live who hasn't had at least a few typographical errors in his time.

APPROVAL

Please review carefully the attached copy and other material to be used in printed matter No. ....

When you are satisfied that it is technically correct, sign your name and fill in the date in the blank by your title or job function.

Then phone me and I will pick up the material from you.

DATE	NAME	
________	______________________________	Application or market manager who requested this literature
________	______________________________	Product manager
________	______________________________	Market manager
________	______________________________	Research manager
________	______________________________	Engineering manager
________	______________________________	Sales manager
________	______________________________	V.P. marketing
________	______________________________	
________	______________________________	
________	______________________________	

R. H. Stansfield
Director of Advertising
and Sales Promotion

Proofreading

Because it is the ultimate responsibility of the advertising manager to eliminate all errors before literature is printed, proofreading is critically important. This refers to reading of galleys, type proofs, that is, for both context and for correctness. Best way to proofread is the team method, using a proofreader and a copyholder. If you do this with your secretary or your assistant, you read aloud the copy that has been set in type while the copyholder checks what you are reading, using the original typed copy as reference. Don't leave anything to chance or to interpretation.

When you read the type galleys aloud, read every word and every punctuation mark. With the copyholder-secretary (whom we'll call Kay) checking the correctness of what you read, you might say, for instance:

> *All upper-case letters for this subhead, Kay. AISI TYPE NUMBERS. Cap T The same stainless type can be made by a number of steel producers, period. Cap I In order to establish standards for comparison and specification comma, the American Iron cap A and cap I, Kay, Steel Institute cap S cap I has assigned numbers to the recognized standard types or analyses period. These cap T AISI all upper-case letters, Kay, types are sometimes given trade names by individual producers such as Republic cap R, Kay, "Enduro." Quotes cap E E-n-d-u-r-o period close quotes.*

That paragraph from one of Republic Steel Corporation's attractive booklets shows how proof is read. All numbers, fractions, and other tabular data are spoken out in full, just as they should appear in the printed piece, so they can be verified from the typed copy—which has, of course, itself been read and approved and certified as correct by your technical people.

Typographical errors made by the typographer or type house are reset at no charge, although according to trade custom *no financial responsibility other than this is accepted by typographers. Trade custom also dictates that the customer is responsible for reading all type proofs, or galleys, as well as all corrections that are made. Detecting errors is the responsibility of the customer, and this includes copy which has been accidentally omitted by the typesetter.*

Be especially alert for strictly mechanical errors: Misspellings, transposed letters, wrong fonts (wrong type face, although the letter or figure itself may be correct), bad letter spacing or bad word spacing or improper paragraph spacing. As noted above, these will be reset correctly by the typographer at no charge.

Look, too, for *widows* (type lines consisting of only *part* of a word); they should be fixed by adding a word or two of copy, although the copy doesn't have to be important. It can be merely a conjunction, or substitution of a longer word for a very short one—anything to add a few characters, or to delete a few to get that partial word into the line above.

Also be alert for several consecutive broken words at the end of lines; they detract greatly from the visual appearance of literature and are considered to be in very bad taste. Lines of type that are excessively loose due to improper word-spacing, or inability to break a word properly, should be corrected by minor rewriting.

Lines of type that are too tight—that have insufficient word-spacing—create an uncomfortable feeling in the reader and result in poor legibility. Let in some air by minor rewriting or deletion of an unimportant word or two—such as knocking out an "and" and substituting either a comma or a semicolon.

By themselves these are minor things, to be sure, but added together they are important because they contribute to an attractive, tasteful, professional piece of printed literature that you can be proud of—and that will reflect credit on both you and your company.

Something you'll have to watch with an eagle eye are omissions. Entire sentences or paragraphs are overlooked with remarkable ease by all concerned. For this reason the copyholder's function is critically important.

Another thing that must be checked carefully because it can't be anticipated in typed copy is how words are broken (divided) at the end of the line. Ligatures (characters consisting of two or more characters that are united) constitute another pitfall that should be avoided. For greater legibility and better letter-spacing where thin characters such as "i's" and "l's" and "f's" are concerned, typographic usage dictates that certain combinations should be run together in a single type character rather than be set individually. Thus, such combinations as "fi," "fl," "ffi," "ffl" and so on form single condensed characters, and the proofreader has to be careful that they don't appear as widely spaced individual characters.

Professional proofreaders' marks should be used in correcting type proofs; these marks constitute a language that is understood and used by all advertising people, typographers, and printers in the country. Short and succinct, these marks are a form of graphic arts shorthand used to convey specific instructions.

THE LANGUAGE OF PROOFREADING

MARK	EXPLANATION	EXAMPLE
ℓ	Take out character indicated.	ℓ The prooof.
^	Left out, insert.	h T^e proof.
#	Insert space.	# Theproof.
9	Turn inverted letter.	9 The p/oof.
x	Broken letter.	x /he proof.
⊥	Push down space.	⊥ The proof.
eq#	Even space.	eq# A good proof.
‿	Less space.	‿ The proof.
⊂	Close up; no space.	⊂ The pro of.
tr.	Transpose.	tr A proof good.
wf	Wrong font.	wf The proof.
lc	Lower case.	lc The Proof.
sc	Small capitals.	The proof. sc The proof.
c+sc	Capitals and small capitals.	The proof. c+sc The proof.
caps	Capitals.	The proof. caps The proof.
P	Capitalize.	P The proof.
ital	Italic.	The proof. ital The proof.
rom	Roman.	rom The proof.
bf	Bold face.	The proof. bf The proof.
stet	Let it stand.	The proof. stet The proof.
out sc	Out, see copy.	out sc He proof.
spell out	Spell out.	spell out King Geo.

MARK	EXPLANATION	EXAMPLE
¶	Start paragraph.	¶ read. The
no ¶	No paragraph; run in.	no ¶ marked. The proof.
⊓	Raise.	⊓ The proof.
⊔	Lower.	⊔ The proof.
⊏	Move left.	⊏ The proof.
⊐	Move right.	⊐ The proof.
‖	Align type.	‖ Three men. Two women.
═	Straighten line.	═ The proof.
⊙	Insert period.	⊙ The proof^
,/	Insert comma.	,/ The proof^
:/	Insert colon.	:/ The proof^
;/	Insert semicolon.	;/ The proof^
∨	Insert apostrophe.	∨ The boys proof.
∨ ∨	Insert quotation marks.	∨ ∨ Marked it proof.^
=/	Insert hyphen.	=/ A proofmark.
⩓	Insert inferior figure.	⩓ Water, HO
∨	Insert superior figure.	∨ A² + B² = C^
!	Insert exclamation mark.	! Prove it^
?	Insert question mark.	? Is it good^
(?)	Query for author.	(?) was The proof read by
[/]	Insert brackets.	[/] The Jones boy . . .
(/)	Insert parentheses.	(/) The proof 1
1/N	Insert 1-en dash.	1/N The proof^
1/M	Insert 1-em dash.	1/M The proof^
2/M	Insert 2-em dash.	2/M The proof^
□	Indent 1 em.	□ The proof.
□□	Indent 2 ems.	□□ The proof.
□□□	Indent 3 ems.	□□□ The proof.

Layout

Most of what should be said about layout for sales literature has already been said about layout for space advertisements in Chapter 11.

What cannot be overemphasized is an old homily: There is no substitute for taste.

Given a combination of a lack of good taste and a lack of a professional hand at the helm when sales literature is being created, and visual horrors are produced. They result in a negative impression of the company and its products.

Perhaps the best way to illustrate this, and to point out things to do and things to avoid, is to look at Horrible Example Number One. This is Lindberg Hevi-Duty's "Bulletin" on that company's semiconductor diffusion furnaces. Let's dissect it element by element and see just why it is so inept and just why it produces a poor impression of the company.

To start with, simplicity is next to godliness in layout for sales literature just as it is in layout for an advertisement. Poor layout can cripple sales literature just as fast as it can destroy an ad. Here again, the fewer the elements, the cleaner and simpler and more modern the layout is—and the more effective it is, too.

Reducing the number of elements per page to an absolute minimum, consistent with presenting all necessary information, always results in literature that's inviting to the eye and easy to read. Failure to limit the number of elements results in distracting clutter. It is impossible to generalize on just how many elements should be on one page, but somewhere between two and five are ideal. More than this is self-defeating.

Lindberg Hevi-Duty's bulletin has the following elements on the first page:

1. Name of company in display type.
2. Coined name of product in display type.
3. Unexplained symbol (not a logo or trademark) in the upper right-hand corner.
4. Model numbers of products, also in display type.
5. Generic name of products, also in display type.
6. Halftone of product, complete with a cute little black border around it (somebody was in mourning?).
7. Caption describing this product.
8. Halftone of the other product covered by this piece of literature.
9. Caption describing this other product.
10. A block of copy reversed out of solid blue.
11. Lindberg Hevi-Duty logo.
12. Attached box with initials and symbols in it.
13. Slogan.
14. Bulletin number.
15. Distracting little white line around the entire page.

In addition to being a nightmare of a layout, a jumble of clutter and clatter and a succession of distracting elements, this literature is virtually impossible to read. For some reason impossible to fathom the layout artist felt constrained to use a light sans serif type face that's not the easiest to read under favorable circumstances. When it's overprinted in black on a solid blue, as it is in the captions here, it is practically illegible unless a major effort is made.

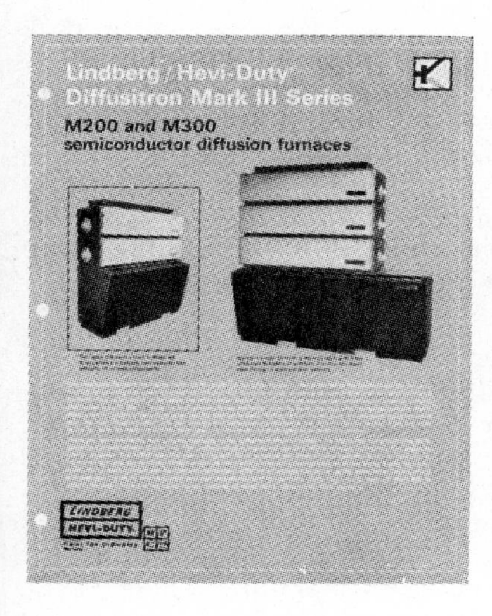

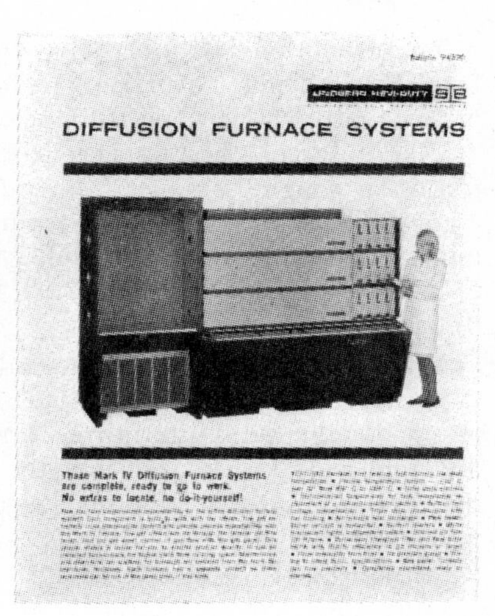

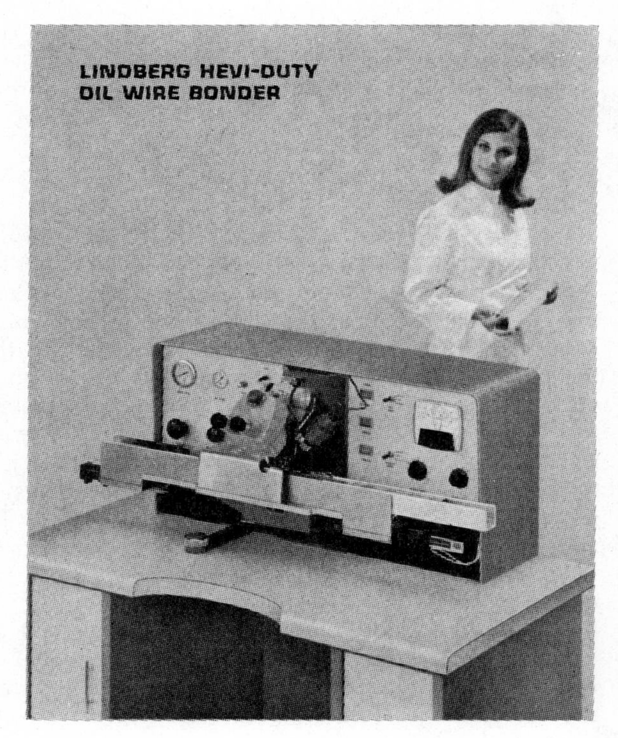

Evolution of a bulletin series. Above, left, an example of the earliest, heavy with clutter and reversed, hard-to-read type. Above, right, an intermediate stage, with better layout. Color is confined to two simple bars. At right, a yet newer bulletin. It marks the final steps toward the impact of simplicity.

These captions undoubtedly went unread by all except a hardy few. Professional advertising people know the one thing above all others that must be done is to make literature easy to read.

The body copy, set in two paragraphs, is another nightmare. It, too, is in a light sans serif face *and is a full 42 picas wide—seven inches.* There's practically no leading, and the wider the measure the more leading needed for legibility. Reversed out of a solid blue as it is, this type seems to "swim" or "float," and it is only with extreme difficulty that it can be read.

You can guess how hard this sales literature sold.

Shown on page 1373 (upper right) is Lindberg Hevi-Duty's newest two-color sales literature. The only color is in the two bars; different colors are used for the company's various product lines that are sold into specific markets. Color coding simplified collation, use and distribution of sales literature to the field sales force, and helped speed it to inquirers.

Note the clean appearance of this sales literature. There's eye-appealing white space. The company's logotype is shown prominently. Generic name of the product is in display type, not some nonsense word that means nothing to the prospect. This instantly identifies the literature for both company personnel and for prospects. No longer do they have to wonder what a "Diffusitron" is, or what various "Mark I's," "Mark II's," or "Mark III's" are.

Furthermore, there is no reverse type to strain the eyes and discourage reading of the message.

Lindberg Hevi-Duty literature continued to be refined and improved, as is apparent from the next example, also on page 1373.

Simplicity is the keynote of this strikingly attractive cover. Only two elements are present—the company name and product name appear in olive green in the upper left corner, and the photograph of the product, with its pretty "operator" softly out of focus, is the second. The photographic illustration bleeds from both sides, top and bottom. It is, incidentally, superb photography; creator is Spence Zog, ace photographer at Pohlman Studios, Milwaukee, Wis.

The layout (not shown), is airy and open. Tasteful white space, repetition of the olive-green bars that color-code this product line, and the outlined halftone illustrations of the product make the recipient of this piece of sales literature *want* to read what it has to say.

The copy is quoted here because it is a good example of what copy in sales literature should be—promotional and selling, yet factual and informative. It is the antithesis of the rambling copy the company had become accustomed to in its previous literature.

Lindberg Hevi-Duty Model 2212 DIL Wire Bonder

Here's a wire bonder for DIL strips . . . for high production, absolute control, and minimum handling. Companion die bonder available.

Just about everything's automatic that can *be automatic on this wire bonding system. You get high production with mechanical indexing and automatic wire feed. Saves time for the operator, of course. The needle is mounted in a low mass, frictionless bearing spindle so you get shockless bonding with no damaged parts. And there's no need to handle parts during processing; the in-line carrier and belt system takes care of storage. Making a setup, or making a changeover for different devices, is easy. Clean, functional design was developed with people in mind—for greater operator convenience, reduced operator fatigue. Easy access simplifies service.*

Features

Thermocompression bonding. Fast cycle time for high yield. In-line carrier and belt system for DIL strips and various flat pack configurations; special belts are available for TO series headers. Protective atmosphere. Multi-level belts. Mechanical indexing, automatic wire feed. Adjustable bonding force. Special tunnel to deliver DIL strips to the bonding station at precisely the right temperature. Pulsed flame cut-off. Optional tailpuller. Superior optical system—Bausch & Lomb stereo zoom. The bonder handles a wide range of wire sizes. It is easy to operate. Reduced operator fatigue.

How the Bonder Operates

Model 2212 console wire bonder has an in-line carrier and belt system for DIL strips and flat packs. It delivers parts to the work station through a heat tunnel which has a closely controlled heat profile. Parts arrive at precisely the right temperature. An inert gas atmosphere is preheated and delivered to the work station to protect parts during heat-up, bonding, and cooling.

Bonding is by thermocompression. When the bond is completed the belt is mechanically indexed. The carrier indexes vertically after each of the four belts of DIL strips is processed.

When the DIL strip is at the work station the operator uses a micro-manipulator to orient it to put the bonding point beneath the capillary. Then the operating lever is depressed to bring the wire into contact with the bonding area. Only very brief contact is required for a firm bond. Bonding force is adjusted with a precision vacuum gauge on the control panel.

A pulsed hydrogen flame severs the wire when the operator signals, producing a uniform ball for the next bond. A tailpuller is available as an option to remove the ball from the last bond immediately after the flame cut-off.

At no time does the operator have to take her eyes from the microscope during the assembly operation.

Wire is fed automatically to the capillary when the operator signals. Wire tension is variable and vacuum controlled. The bonder handles wire from .0007 to .003 in size.

Wrap-up of the product story is given neatly and quickly in a form that's highly readable for a busy man who wants to absorb information without fuss or folderol, without forbidding him to read by setting type 42 picas wide, then reversing it.

Credibility is lent to the whole story by having the model pose just as an ordinary operator would. And the company's logotype appears here, near the signature and the customary reminder that the company manufactures many other products in addition to the DIL bonder discussed. Even with all of the nuts and bolts information, the photo, the logo, the color-coding bars, and the signature, there is still plenty of clean white space to make the literature inviting to the eye.

Final example of good layout, and an example of the evolution of Lindberg Hevi-Duty's literature, is seen in a brochure promoting the company's semiconductor oven.

No nonsense words are thrown at the reader to cause him to wonder just what it is the company is trying to say. This brochure pulls no punches. It comes right out, straight from the shoulder, and tells the reader he is going to get helpful and interesting information about a semiconductor oven manufactured by Lindberg Hevi-Duty.

The spread is exceptionally appealing and attractive. Clean and simple and uncluttered, the major user benefit is given in the

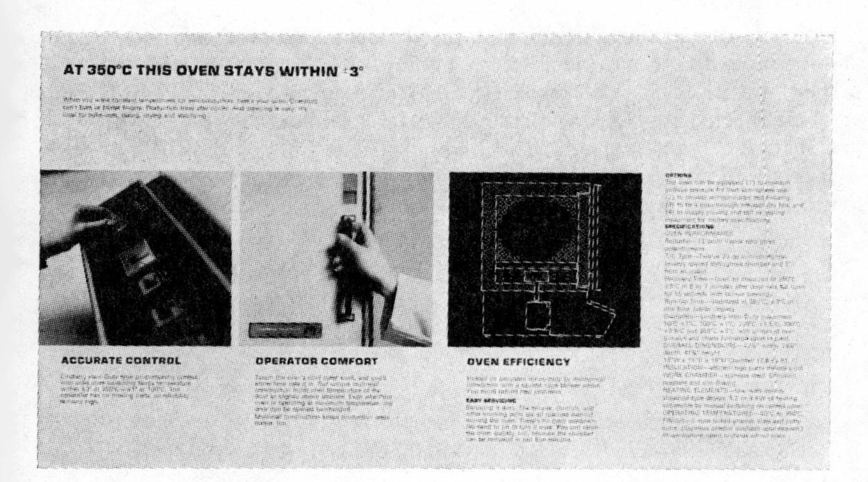

headline. In the copy block immediately below, set ragged-right, are additional user benefits spelled out in rapid-fire order.

The two photographic illustrations are duotones, a combination of blue and black. Options available to the buyer and the specifications of the standard semiconductor oven are given, neatly listed and logically arranged.

Page 4 is simple and functional and presents necessary performance information quickly and strikingly with two graphs showing recovery rate and heatup rate. Along with the logo and a kissoff, this winds up the company's message about this product.

Use a "Safe" Size?

First thing that pops to mind when planning a piece of literature for an industrial product is to make it that good old standard, accepted, approved, familiar, traditional, customary, usual "safe" size—8½ by 11 inches.

To be sure, three-ring binders, large envelopes in stock, salesmen's sample kits, literature jackets, proposal folders, presentation binders, and other items meant to contain or use literature are designed around this hoary old size. The size has been used for everything from the paper this manuscript is being typed on to the bond paper your outgoing letters are on. And so is most industrial literature in racks and on shelves throughout the country.

There's no law, though, that says that everything has to be this size. To deviate is not a felony, and it's not even an unwise course of action if deviation is done for a good reason. A good example of an unusually attractive piece of two-color sales literature took exactly the opposite tack: It is an 11 by 8½ inches (width always given first when discussing size of printed matter) booklet. *The Fine Art of Campus Food Service Management—A Vital Force in Modern Education* was produced by Szabo Food Service, Inc., a leader in the mass-feeding market.

STUDENT FACILITY SERVICES, A DYNAMIC CONCEPT

Campus food service is more than a matter of serving food on a timetable. It is the art of offering delicious and distinctive meals, captivatingly displayed, served in an attentive and friendly way.

This concept of providing rewarding meals in a relaxed atmosphere contributes to better education by helping promote a high level of health and morale among students and faculty.

To achieve this concept, Szabo Food Service knows that a campus food service must be skillfully programmed, actively supervised and efficiently executed. For this reason Szabo created its Student Facility Services Division, a specialized division offering colleges and universities complete food management services.

Student Facility Services Division relieves administrators of burdensome and time-consuming details connected with campus feeding. Food preparation and service, planning and design, staffing, training, supervision, purchasing, accounting—all these activities are performed by Szabo specialists. The result is campus food services far superior to standards which have been found acceptable by many administrators.

This brochure will acquaint you with the advantages of Szabo's dynamic concept of campus food services, and how its Student Facility Services Division benefits your administration, your faculty and your students.

ABOUT SZABO FOOD SERVICE, INC.

Szabo Food Service, Inc., is a publicly owned national food service management company. It was founded in 1946 by Joseph C. Szabo, its chairman. Principal offices are located in Lyons, Illinois, a western suburb of Chicago. Regional offices are strategically located in Chicago, Cincinnati, Denver, Indianapolis, Los Angeles, New York, Seattle and Winston-Salem.

Today, Szabo operates nearly 300 facilities in 24 states. We have served many of our clients continuously since 1946, applying Szabo management techniques to their individual needs.

Supported in depth by corporate staff departments, Szabo operates through five basic operating divisions: STUDENT FACILITY SERVICES DIVISION • HOSPITAL DIVISION • IN-PLANT DIVISION • PUBLIC RESTAURANT DIVISION • AUTOMATIC SERVICE DIVISION

Each division operates in an area of specialized food service programming, and has a long and successful record of accomplishments.

Depth in management, fiscal responsibility, ethical business methods and dedicated people—all these factors have made Szabo a leader in the field of food service management.

Type, most halftones and all solid areas are in a rich, chocolate brown; the second color, used in the logo, the decorative border and in occasional duotone illustrations inside the booklet, is an attractive, warm orange-red. The combination of the two colors has a connotation of friendship and hospitality and happy things in life.

Throughout, in pictures and words, the high quality and personalized service of Szabo's product, which is actually management service, not food, comes through strongly. Shown and described is the custom campus food service Szabo offers to colleges and universities, including candid shots of happy, smiling students who are obviously well fed. The booklet was produced when students went to school to study, rather than to riot. Photographs, incidentally, are by Bill Pease, president and *numero uno* photographer of Images West, Riverside, Illinois. They are excellent in every respect.

In addition to describing the high-caliber management service it offers, Szabo touched on the financial arrangements with institutions of higher learning. It is common practice for colleges and universities to show a profit on student feeding—a profit rebated by the food service holding the feeding contract. Szabo summed up its services on page 7, then listed directors and officers of the company, its transfer agent and its registrar; this quickly tells those who were not familiar with the company that it is large, stable, and reputable.

A fine source for excellent ideas in collateral material, including layout and illustrative techniques, is the better paper manufacturer. Good paper mills make regular mailings to customers and prospects just as all aggressive businesses do, and some of the printed matter they mail is of superb quality. Among the better paper houses are:

S. D. Warren Company
89 Broad Street
Boston, Massachusetts 02101

International Paper Company
220 East 42nd Street
New York, New York 10017

Hammermill Paper Company
1453 East Lake Road
Erie, Pennsylvania 16507

Mohawk Paper Mills, Inc.
465 Saratoga Street
Cohoes, New York 12047

Crown Zellerbach Corporation
One Bush Street
San Francisco, California 94104

Kimberly-Clark Corporation
North Lake Street
Neenah, Wisconsin 54965

Mead Corporation
118 West First Street
Dayton, Ohio 45402

Nekoosa-Edwards Paper Company
Port Edwards, Wisconsin 54469

House Organs

So-called house organs fall into one of three distinct categories:

1. An employee publication for internal distribution.
2. A sales publication produced for a company's sales force.
3. A customer publication, usually called an external house organ.

Again, the author acknowledges with gratitude the help of S. D. Warren Company, paper manufacturer, in permitting use of its excellent booklet, *The Company Publication,* as a good reference work for this portion of this chapter, as well as for quoting certain passages from it. This booklet of Warren's comes very close to being an in ol for an advertising manager tapped to create a com on, or house organ as we'll call it henceforth.

According ı ıny businesses have found that company publications c: : means of communication necessary to establish mutu: ıg between management and employees, between home offices and salesmen, between manufacturers and dealers, and between a business and its customers.

Many companies issue two publications—an internal house organ edited for persons within the organization, the other an external edited for people outside the company.

Internal house organs are designed expressly for plant and/or office people, of course; such publications are usually called "employee" publications. Ofttimes such publications are simple and unpretentious and are reproduced on a one-color printed masthead by either multilith or mimeograph. When this is the case, the personnel department usually does the writing or, at least, the information gathering. The advertising manager is much better off not to have a hand in such a publication. Advertising managers tend to be perfectionists, so devote far more time to such publications than they warrant.

The external house organ is directed toward the wholesaler, dealer, or jobber organization, including their salesmen, as well as to retailers and store people. This publication is usually slick, well illustrated, and generally either two-color or four-color, although it can take the form of a tabloid newspaper and be printed in black-and-white.

Still another audience for whom an external house organ is produced is customers. Examples of the latter are *Ford Times* and *Dodge News*. These are interesting, well-edited periodicals mailed regularly to owners and potential buyers.

W. A. Reedy, senior editor, advertising publications, Eastman Kodak Company, creates one of the finest external house organs being published today. It is an exceptionally beautiful printing job, and the quality never varies an iota from issue to issue. *Applied Photography* is printed in four-color process for the most part.

A typical cover of this quality external house organ features a superb cover shot of the sea, washed in gold by a setting sun. Jason Hailey, Los Angeles, was the photographer. Inside, the magazine specializes in clean layout and superb photography.

As with any other program, there must be an objective if a house organ—either internal or external—is to succeed. Mr. Reedy has his firmly in hand; following is information concerning *Applied Photography* and what it is to accomplish, as stated by Mr. Reedy.

1. The objective of *Applied Photography* is to promote the use of photography as a communications medium, mainly in advertising. Kodak seeks to present photographic ideas rather than information on how to make pictures.
2. *Applied Photography* is published four times a year.
3. The mailing list for the external house organ is 50,000 plus.
4. The mailing list is augmented by requests and through the use of mailing lists supplied by those who contributed photographs. Generally speaking, anyone employed in the art and advertising or publishing fields is eligible, as are those from the management end of advertising. (Advertising managers.)
5. *Applied Photography* is printed by letterpress, single color dry. (This means the most expensive printing process is used; to produce four-color illustrations, the paper is run through the press four times; ink is allowed to dry between press runs. Although the most costly, this method produces color illustrations that can only be called exquisite.)
6. Print run of *Applied Photography* is 60,000. An additional no-text edition of 25,000 is printed and later imprinted in six different languages for export use.
7. Cost per issue is more than $50,000.
8. Mr. Reedy does all of the work himself with the exception of preparation of layout mechanics, which is done by a printer.
9. Kodak regards *Applied Photography* as promotional in nature; it accompanies a companion publication, *Commercial Camera,* which is more of an advertising effort. Commercial photographers receive *Commercial Camera* and *Applied Photography,* while their customers receive only the latter publication. Both magazines are mailed to photographers in the same envelope, so Kodak is able to tailor its remarks in *Commercial Camera* to its companion publication.

Mr. Reedy added that "most magazine editors use photography to illustrate their subject matter. In Kodak's case, though, photography *is* the subject matter and considerable care must be taken in reproduction. This is the reason for single color dry letterpress, and also accounts for the rather high cost per copy." Well worth it it is, however, for such superb quality.

Steelways, published by American Iron and Steel Institute, is another outstanding external house organ, and also uses fine quality four-color printing for a prestige effect.

This magazine is distributed to more than 300,000 people in public and community life to foster a better understanding of the steel industry. To be added to the mailing list, write:

Steelways
American Iron and Steel Institute
150 East 42nd Street,
New York, New York 10017

Most external house organs fall into a pattern that is slick and professional. Photography is usually much above average and the writing is by full-time editors and reporters.

Internal house organs of many companies have a full-time editor on the staff, usually working under the advertising manager, who devotes most of his time to the publication.

Articles almost always have a company slant, as is to be expected, although most "house magazines" frequently use human-interest articles, travel articles and other mass-appeal material.

One thing to keep constantly in mind when writing and producing an employee publication is that people are interested first and foremost in themselves. Show plenty of pictures of people. People like pictures of themselves. And don't spare the verbal horsepower when describing the accomplishments of both individuals and departments. One of management's objectives in funding any employee publication is to build *esprit de corps,* to increase the feeling of belonging to one big, happy family.

You can turn out a nice looking house organ for employees without investing a fortune—and with a four-color cover, too, by using a *stock* four-color cover. Several firms offer four-color covers already printed, with pages 2, 3, and 4 blank. Your printer can imprint these blank pages in two-color, or in black-and-white. One such source is Monthly Cover Service, 2105 Merchandise Mart, Chicago, Illinois 60654.

Chapter 19

CORPORATE ADVERTISING

CORPORATE advertising has been around for decades—perhaps as long as product advertising. But it's not discussed very often. It's an unattractive stepchild that's kept hidden most of the time. Nonetheless, corporate advertising takes a very big bite out of the total promotional budget for industry.

Many esoteric articles filled with three-dollar words have been written about the long-predicted demise of product advertising. Seers who write these learned-sounding articles, many of which don't actually *say* anything, are very fast on the draw when it comes to predicting that corporate advertising will ultimately replace product advertising almost entirely. And they say it in the same tone they would use if promising you could rid yourself of athlete's foot or body odor.

The thing for you to do, if you're a devout man, is to pray that this indeed comes to pass; if you're not, next best thing is to cross all fingers and both arms and legs, then mutter an incantation or two, or go through some other personal ritual designed to bring about that which you greatly desire. For, just as surely as you're sitting there reading this, if your competitors all rush to jump on the corporate advertising bandwagon, that will leave only your company advertising its products.

About all you can look forward to then is cornering the market as your sales surge and your competitors' decline.

What Corporate Advertising Sells

Unlike product advertising, which obviously helps sell the product (or service), corporate advertising sells an intangible. It sells an idea, or, perhaps, a series of closely related ideas.

Call the idea "positive attributes" or whatever term you fancy, but corporate advertising is actually selling the advertiser's capabilities, the overall quality of its products, the depth of the company's research and development activities and what they're expected to lead to, the caliber of its personnel, its management, the problem-solving ability of the company's people, its ability to increase sales steadily and to earn a profit while doing so, its dominance of a market, its reliability and stability.

Corporate advertising, like any other advertising, tries to persuade the reader to accept the advertiser's viewpoint. It tries to persuade him to share the same favorable opinion of the company.

How much is invested in corporate advertising? That's a question that nobody yet has answered to anybody's satisfaction. But one thing is certain: In business publications edited for the top management "market" and the financial community "market," between 30 and 40 percent of all advertisements of one page or larger in size are *not* product advertisements. Call these by any name you want, but the fact remains they are definitely corporate advertising—advertising that is selling ideas, not products.

Ideas persuasively presented by corporate advertising are critically important because they influence every facet of the company's operations, both at the present time and well into the future. For instance, the "image" of the company in the minds of its many publics can influence the company's ability to function as it must in order to earn a profit. The financial community's opinion of the company determines whether needed financing is available at suitable interest rates and terms, or whether it is available at all in many instances.

The opinion people have of the company determines to a very large extent its ability to attract employees and executives of the caliber necessary for its continued progress. If the company's reputation in its community—and this includes the business community throughout the entire country—is such that it is considered an undesirable company to work for, the company is in deep, deep trouble. It cannot lure top-notch people into its fold. This obviously means the best people will work for competitors.

Furthermore, corporate advertising, while it is not created to sell products, nonetheless exerts great influence on future sales by making the company appear desirable from many viewpoints and making it a positive factor in the minds of its publics. Truly fine corporate advertising by a manufacturer of capital equipment, for example, cannot help but produce a significant effect on future sales by creating a receptive attitude toward both company and products in the minds of executives who will make buying decisions for that product in the years to come.

This is such a tremendously valuable asset that nobody, and no computer, as far as that's concerned, can assign a dollars-and-cents value to it.

Other protective campaigns are undertaken to protect a company or an industry from harassment by government; this is a problem that has become increasingly acute in modern times.

One thing to remember: There's an old saying to the effect that small minds discuss people, good minds discuss events, but great minds discuss *ideas.*

Your corporate advertising is aimed at the best minds in government and industry and finance. It discusses ideas. Make your discussion interesting and you'll plant your ideas in fertile ground—the best minds extant.

Objectives Are Absolutely Essential

Solid objectives that are well thought out and precisely defined are even more essential in corporate advertising than they are in product advertising.

There is no built-in interest in the product itself on which corporate advertising can lean for support. It has to cut the mustard all by itself.

The most common failing of much corporate advertising is that it rambles. It flits hither and yon, it tries hard to touch all bases, it attempts desperately to be all things to all men.

When vague, imprecise, enigmatic corporate advertising fails miserably to present an interesting message, a clear message, a message of importance to a carefully selected universe, you can be morally certain that no firm objectives were set before the ads were produced. Fuzzy thinking right at the start, even before a single word was written, before even a thumbnail layout was doodled out, even before a photograph was taken, doomed the campaign to waste the money invested in it right down to the last red cent.

Formal objectives are the one indispensable ingredient for success in a corporate advertising program.

Repeat: *Formal objectives are the one indispensable ingredient for success in a corporate advertising campaign.*

The objective(s) should be formulated only after very careful consideration. They should mesh neatly with the company's short-term marketing objectives, its profit objectives, its long-range goals. Moreover, objectives should be *attainable,* not some dreamy pie-in-the-sky idealistic wish. Objectives must reflect the company's needs *as determined by top management.* Unlike product advertising, corporate advertising should be based on bed-rock guidelines established by top management because only those executives up in the walnut-paneled corner offices with four windows have sufficient information to make this decision.

As advertising manager, it's up to you to help top management by advising what objectives can logically be expected to be attained, at what approximate cost, and through what methods.

Get the formal objective(s) *in writing*. Writing helps eliminate ambiguities, and it is lasting evidence that this is what management agreed the company needed. Having objectives in writing prevents future misunderstandings and attempts to weasel or hedge. And it permits *measurement of what advertising has accomplished.*

Assuming objectives are attainable through advertising and you accept them on that basis, you must be able to prove to management's satisfaction that advertising measured up to what was expected of it. This means measuring what was accomplished.

On the other hand, if management sets objectives—even though they're in writing—that are not attainable through advertising, it's incumbent on you to explain why the objectives are not acceptable to you and why they must be revised. Never make the biggest of all mistakes and let impossible objectives be foisted on you. That way lies management loss of confidence in advertising—and in you.

Once objectives are firmed up, they provide a foundation upon which to build the forthcoming campaign. Every question that arises during its creation will be considered just one way: In light of the objectives. You'll be able to explain to your agency exactly what your company must accomplish and why it needs to accomplish it. And the objectives will act as a road map to creative people at the agency, enabling them to devote their full time and attention to developing the best possible program to achieve those objectives.

How It's Done at Grumman Aircraft

The most meaningful way to consider the how's and why's of corporate advertising is to dissect what was done by a top-flight advertising professional in a leading company.

It's with sincere appreciation that the help of Norman G. MacKinnon, director of advertising, Grumman Aircraft Engineering Corporation, is acknowledged.

Norm's rationale of his company's outstanding corporate campaign in the aerospace market is so cogent that much of the analysis of Grumman's campaign is in his own words.

Before looking at one of Grumman's corporate ads, let's see what the man responsible for it has to say about the *raison d'etre* of his corporate advertising campaign. Norman MacKinnon had this to say:

"Corporate aerospace advertising is required to create an awareness of Grumman's corporate capabilities and to identify a company in all aspects of the industry.

"Today, the whole industry is faced with greater technological challenges than ever before, and there is greater competition for diminishing product lines.

"Aerospace, in my opinion, must make a greater selling effort, and advertising must be applied in greater intensity to support that sales effort in order to keep ahead in an extremely competitive market.

"Our corporate aerospace advertising is designed to create a better understanding and a friendlier attitude towards (the corporation) management and its philosophies. And insofar as Grumman is concerned, our advertising is designed to reflect Grumman management.

"More important is advertising's impact on the future of our company. It's like insurance . . . five, ten years from now, who knows what we might be producing? We must create acceptance for our products no matter what they are, or to whom we are selling.

"Again, if you will excuse another analogy, our advertising is like R&D: If you don't spend money on R&D today, you'll be nowhere tomorrow. The same holds true in the establishment of corporate identity—the company that spends for promotion and advertising shows, just as R&D fundings shows, that it's on the move.

"Aerospace advertising is primarily aimed at keeping the armed services, selection committees, and final arbiters in any defense system *aware*. Objective here is to remind this primary audience of the aerospace producer's capabilities in the systems area involved. Secondary audience is made up from government agencies, legislative bodies, business and finance, employees (morale factor), stockholders, and the tax-paying public in general who have a right to be informed on how his money is being spent in defense and space programs."

Mr. MacKinnon went on to analyze his corporate program as follows:

1. *The objective:*

Provide an umbrella for our total efforts. Identify our company as a complete independent aerospace producer—as a constantly growing leader in all aspects of aerospace, undersea technology, and commercial transportation.

Demonstrate our capabilities in areas of national defense policy such as:

a. Military and technological superiority over any potential enemy.

b. Attain greater technological reliability.

c. Reduce present cost of space operations.

d. Discover new and better ways of performing space missions.

2. *Strategy:*

Demonstrate total capability for designing, producing, and delivering such weapons systems and space products as spawned by, and as a result of, our individual capability and capacity which can be supported by demonstrable proof of our wide experience, record, and management and work force stability.

3. *Creative strategy:*

Such an objective as outlined above—total image development—product complex and individual capabilities and resources demands an overall thematic structure, a theme which transcends those individual capabilities, gives form and substance, and provides a base upon which to demonstrate and dramatize them.

Such a theme was required to voice past capability and, more important, to imply future capability.

Such a theme was required to be as applicable to management capabilities as it was to technical and production capabilities (we are selling "people" here).

Such a theme had to be believable, demonstrable, and rememberable.

The theme had to be easily grasped, easily understood, and easily translated by the audience to *its* needs.

And such a theme had to be promotable in areas other than advertising. The advertising campaign which grew out of the foregoing is:

MAN IS THE HEART
OF THE SYSTEM . . .
GRUMMAN NEVER FORGETS IT.

We created an advertising campaign which, through emotional appeal, lets the reader conclude for himself that our corporation has all the capabilities necessary to secure, and manage, major aerospace and other systems programs.

We introduced the human element into our advertising. Because our prime audience for our advertising had either flown, were flying, or had an emotional appeal towards flying, we took advantage of this emotional climate to get across the story of our total capabilities in aerospace.

We expressed a very real concern for the human element by showing that this was our *primary* concern. In other words, man is the *heart* of the system and Grumman never forgets it. This, then, was our attention getter and this theme carried through all of our advertising has gained recognition with similar format and continuity.

4. *Reaction:*

What is the reaction to our advertising? These are typical:

"One of the most outstanding examples of thoughtful, effective advertising that has ever appeared in the aerospace industry."

Robert W. Martin, Jr.
Publisher
Aviation Week & Space Technology

"Man is the heart of the system is one of the best advertisements I have seen in years."

Harry A. Bruno
H. A. Bruno & Associates
(Public Relations Counsel)

The highest readership score in a typical issue of *Armed Forces Management.*

Highest scoring advertisement in *Science & Technology.*

In two recent issues of *Business Week,* Starch readership research showed Grumman's ad was second among 100 studied ads in that issue, first in the other."

Shown nearby is one of Grumman's exciting, compelling ads—a four-color bleed spread. Skilful montage work shows a typical "pilot" and a military aircraft, both against the wild blue yonder.

Copy is reversed out of the dark blue sky; legibility is greatly helped by using a very readable serif type face. It reads:

A man is still the heart of the system. Grumman never forgets it.

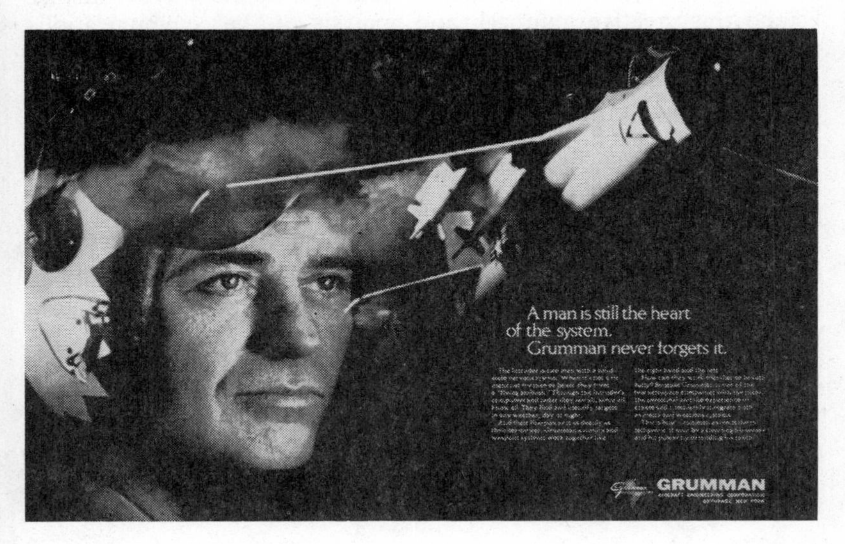

The Intruder is two men with a solid-state nervous system. When it's not a fit night out for man or beast, they form a "flying ambush." Through the Intruder's computers and radar they see all, sense all, know all. They find and identify targets in any weather, day, or night.

And their firepower is as deadly as their see-power. Grumman avionics and weapons systems work together like the right hand and the left.

How can they work together so beautifully? Because Grumman is one of the few aerospace companies with the plant, the personnel, and the experience to create and completely integrate both avionics and weapons systems.

This is how Grumman extends the intelligence of man by extending his senses, and his power by extending his reach.

This is an exceptionally powerful ad. Layout is clean, illustrative technique is gripping, copy is persuasive and convincing. Knowing a Grumman Intruder is up there enables the author to sleep better at night.

Grumman's approach is factual and objective, yet emotional and subjective at the same time. Humanizing the campaign, rather than presenting a mass of nuts and bolts and reasons why Grumman is the best buy, accomplished exactly that in a subtle way. Thinking behind this creative approach and analysis of the communications problems involved was first-rate.

Source of the Impetus Behind "Image" Advertising

So-called image advertising, in which the company itself is the product that's being sold, is due primarily to the fantastically fast-paced technological change in industry.

And mull this one over: More than half of the products that many companies manufacture today were unknown 10 years ago. Yet a handful of years from now most of these highly-touted new products on which all of the tender, loving care and all of those promotional dollars are being lavished will have disappeared from the scene.

Given reasonable success in the marketplace, though, the companies that make these less-than-successful products will still be in business—even if they haven't the foggiest idea of what they'll be producing a decade hence. All of which means that many managements have swung away from product advertising because the product is the thing that's not here to stay.

Hopefully, however, the company is.

And as companies expand and merge and acquire other firms, there is increased emphasis on advertising that enhances the company's image, that makes it more attractive to investors, that broadens its base of ownership, that makes security analysts go into rhapsodies over it, that make it well regarded by those who hold the business community's purse strings, that link its name with not only one product or market, but with a philosophy and an aura of success.

The image of the company in the minds of those diverse and widely separated publics is more than a mere intangible. It is solid and concrete and yes, Virginia, it really and truly exists. It is not merely imagined. You can almost inventory it at so many dollars and cents and list it as an asset in the annual report—or, if it's a sour image, as a liability.

Marketing Forum recently reported on how a strong image sells the financial community on a company. It said:

Strong "image" sells Wall St.: L&M

A study of "corporate image" as an influence in Wall Street, said to be the first of its kind, found evidence that it has a noticeable effect on price-earnings ratios, share prices, and buy-and-sell decisions of both private and professional investors. The study by Lippincott & Margulies, presented recently in its publication Design Sense, *also indicated that a favorable image has desirable effects in such areas as stock stability, corporate borrowing, and press exposure.*

Conclusions were based, in part, on opinions of Wall Street figures. Dan W. Lufkin, board chairman, Donaldson, Lufkin, and Jenrette, Inc., investment counselors, pointed out that in certain cases image actually outshines stock performance, notably among the giant food companies.

James H. Carey, vice-president, Chase Manhattan Bank, said that image alone was not enough. "It must be honest . . . must project a true picture of business experience, plus such things as quality control and extent of service."

The design firm compared price-earnings ratios of two leading companies in five industries to back up its case.

> *"Theoretically," said L&M, "companies in similar industries with similar general opportunities should have similar price-earnings ratios—if Wall Street did not give weight to the intangible value, or image, of a company." The P-E figures, covering 1961-65, showed superior performance by GE over Westinghouse, Scott vs. Kimberly-Clark, Du Pont compared with American Cyanamid, IBM over Sperry Rand and Sears, Roebuck vs Montgomery Ward.*

In commenting on this article, *Industrial Marketing* magazine quoted Lippincott & Margulies extensively, then went on to spot check a broad cross-section of paired companies in what are considered growth industries—such as electronics, chemicals, petroleum, and so on. In each pair, one company advertises heavily *to management,* while the other does little or no "image" advertising. *IM* quoted the following cost-earnings ratios:

Honeywell	23.9
Johnson Service	14.9
Union Carbide	13.09
Chemetron	9.21
Shell Oil Co.	16.02
Ashland Oil Co.	13.0
Kennecott Copper	10.98
Cerro Corp.	6.07
Square D Co.	16.5
ITE	12.08

In each example, the more highly valued stock represents the company that has projected its corporate image to other corporate leaders.

Although these pairs of companies are specific examples, they are *not* isolated instances. This list could go on and on and on. Every management is extremely interested in information of this type; gather it and use it to help justify budget requests.

In addition to communicating ideas that interest Wall Street, a company makes itself more attractive in the eyes of all beholders when it uses corporate advertising effectively. This could make the company more desirable as a merger partner, and strengthen its bargaining position.

One thing just as certain as the fact it will get dark tonight is that communicating ideas to maintain, change, or enhance the corporate image must be done deftly. Go at it heavy-handedly and you'll be preachy and pompous and pedantic. Your shirt will be considered to be very stuffed indeed. You cannot carp at the business and financial community, you cannot lecture to it, you cannot talk down to it.

Corporate advertising campaigns *must* be lively and interesting and the message they convey *must* be of genuine interest, free from gimmicks and cynical tricks designed only to get attention. There's room aplenty to be creative and fresh and to get off the beaten path, but do so with a good reason.

The surge in image—corporate, that is—advertising during recent years can be attributed also to expansion of the economy, to dawning realization that corporate advertising is an extra and mighty useful marketing tool, and to the vast changes that have taken place in the structure of industry itself.

Reaction to decades of laxity during which little or no formal attempt was made to communicate with industry's publics contributes to the ready acceptance of and intensity of feeling toward corporate advertising today.

Overreaction, though, can lead a company right down the primrose path of relying *entirely* on corporate advertising for all communications needs. If this route is chosen, sales will suffer as sure as God made little green apples.

A Successful Image Campaign

An excellent corporate advertising campaign, this one well known because it has been running in management publications for 10 years, is the famous Rockwell Report, created for the Rockwell Manufacturing Company by Marsteller Inc. One of these interesting, highly read ads is shown on page 1394.

Why the "Rockwell Report?" Because Rockwell Manufacturing Company had grown from a one-plant, one-product, one-market company to a diversified enterprise operating multiple plants making many products sold to a relatively large number of different markets.

Future plans called for further growth through diversification. Both the company and its agency, Marsteller Inc., felt the need for an overall corporate campaign that would help each division capitalize on the strength of the company as a whole.

Out of that broad need were crystallized these specific objectives:

1. Make Rockwell Manufacturing Company (whose shares

Rockwell Report

by A. C. Daugherty
President
ROCKWELL MANUFACTURING COMPANY

EXPENSE CONTROL is of vital concern to management these days. At every level, managers are being asked for action programs to maximize short-range profits by tighter controls on costs. The real challenge for a manager is to strike a balance between short-range *corrective* programs and continued long-range *constructive* plans. And further, to communicate this balance to people below him who may only see cause for pessimism in his actions.

For example, our managers have been working hard on controlling expenses this year. But we've invested in four new management development programs for supervisors instituted in 1967. We've been tough on marginal or inefficient producers as identified by a strengthened, improved performance appraisal system. At the same time, this system has provided a sound basis for salary increases and promotions that are comparable with last year's record.

So, while our employees know we take a tough line on inventory control of goods, they see we're putting just as much time and attention into building and improving our "people inventory." And that's the inventory on which the future of the business rests.

* * *

Colonel W. F. Rockwell has been awarded the Decoration of Francisco de Miranda, by decree of the President of Venezuela. The award has been made for his outstanding contribution in stimulating foreign investments for the industrial and economic development of the Republic of Venezuela. The award was presented to the Colonel at the Venezuelan Embassy in Washington, D.C., by the Venezuelan ambassador to the United States, Dr. Enrique Tejera-Paris. Colonel Rockwell has in the past received many distinguished international honors, including the title of "Commandeur de l'ordre de la Couronne" from King Leopold III, of Belgium; the "Cruzeiro do sul" of Brazil; and was knighted by the President of Italy in the order of "Al Merito della Repubblica."

* * *

Have you gotten a Rockwell power tool as a gift yet? If not, it won't be long, for the Premium & Incentive Department of our Power Tool Division reports sharply increased use of power tools as gifts, bonuses, and incentive prizes by business firms. (If you're on the business giving end, you may be interested in seeing a copy of our four-color Premium & Incentive Catalog: send us a note on your letterhead and we'll send one along.) But if you don't get a power tool in your business life, hint around: your wife can pick out your Christmas gift with the help of a knowledgeable Rockwell Power Tool dealer.

* * *

The Rockwell-Edward valves installed at an eastern utility may be the world's largest: 12 feet tall, they weigh 7 tons each, with steel walls over 5 inches thick. The Impactogear handwheels used to open and close them are 6 feet in diameter. Closing these valves during seat tests at elevated pressures required 1,175,000 pounds of thrust on the stem — a thrust equal to that developed by the Titan rocket boosters on the Gemini space flights.

* * *

This is one of a series of informal reports on Rockwell Manufacturing Company, Pittsburgh, Pa., makers of measurement and control devices, instruments, and power tools for 22 basic markets.

The Rockwell Report is a classic in the annals of corporate advertising. Shown here is a typical issue of the now-famous newsletter.

were not listed on any exchange) well known to professional investment and financial men.

2. Show customers, shareholders, investment and financial men the advantages inherent in Rockwell's particular kind of plant, product, and market diversification.
3. Create a corporate "character" or personality for the company by picturing it as a well managed, successful, healthy, enterprise growing soundly through carefully planned diversification.
4. Humanize management of the company by presenting management problems and solutions in terms of everyday experiences with which readers can identify themselves, and do it without bombast and bragging.
5. Capitalize on the prestige of any Rockwell product in any specific field by applying it to other products in other fields. A long-time user of Nordstrom Valves, for instance, is apt to have a higher regard for Delta Power Tools if he knows they are made by the same company.
6. Do all of the above at the lowest possible cost in order that the bulk of advertising money can be used for specific product advertising.

The Rockwell Report format, which has become familiar to so many millions of businessmen, was not created, full blown, out of thin air.

Once the objectives of the campaign were established, the big question had to be asked and answered: What kind of campaign would be most likely to achieve the objectives?

To answer that big question, many smaller ones had to be asked and answered. What copy approach and tone? What kind of layout treatment? Photographs or artwork—or nothing at all? Big space or small? Color or black and white?

Eventually, and after a lot of consideration, the "column" technique was selected. These are the reasons why:

Flexibility—several different and often unrelated subjects could be treated in each ad. This was important if the overall company story was to be told.

Informality—reflecting the essential personality of the company and its management.

Authenticity—by presenting each advertisement as a report by, and in the words of, the company president. This would also help to humanize and personalize the campaign.

Even after all of this thinking had been done and all of these decisions had been made, the thought cropped up: Is there enough legitimately interesting material about any company to support such a series over a long period? Won't we run dry?

Actually, the reverse is true. In a growing, dynamic company practically everything is grist for the mill. Every phase of management. Research. Production. Sales. Finance. Community relations. Industrial relations. New products and new uses for old products. There is, literally, no end of things to write about. The main problem is not one of getting material, but of selecting from the wealth that is always available.

Actual selecting is done in meetings between A. C. Daugherty, president of Rockwell, his advertising manager, and the agency account executive. In these conferences Rockwell Report subject matter is programmed several months ahead, but is deliberately kept flexible so that subjects of particular timeliness can be inserted as they arise. The account executive from Marsteller Inc. then writes copy around selected subjects; it is submitted to Mr. Daugherty and his advertising manager. Minor differences of viewpoint and expression are worked out, and the result is pretty much as Mr. Daugherty would have written it.

Two criteria must be met: First, have something interesting to say. Second, say it as interestingly as possible.

While the format and copy were being worked out, media selection was being made. Rockwell was interested, primarily, in reaching customers and potential customers; shareholders and potential shareholders. For Rockwell, most of this desired audience exists at the decision-making level in practically every segment of industry, business, and finance. From the beginning, the list has been built around a nucleus of management publications.

Readership Grew

When the first Rockwell Report appeared, everyone concerned thought it was sound, but at the same time, everyone realized that it had several possible weaknesses. No striking layout treatment. No dramatic illustrations. No color. Small size—just two-thirds of a page. And a great deal of copy for its size.

The big question was: *Will anybody read it?*

From the beginning, the agency had Starch and other organizations measure readership. From the vast mass of data compiled over the years, several interesting conclusions emerge. For instance, people *do* read the Rockwell Report. The Rockwell Report turns about twice as many "noters" into "readers" as the average ad in the books studied. Actual figures are: Average of all ads, 34 percent; Rockwell Report, 62 percent. That represents those who noted the ads and who also read most of the copy.

Cost Ratio figures are also impressive. In the Starch method, "cost ratios" compare the performance of ads in a given issue of a magazine by relating readership to the cost of the space used. The average of all ads in an issue is designated as 100, and each individual ad is related to this average. The Rockwell Report has always been above the average of ads in the same issues of publications studied. Rockwell Report ads produce about *three times more readers-per-dollar of space cost than average ads.*

Moreover, The Rockwell Report quickly went well above average in readership, and it has maintained its leadership position for many years. Apparently the series constantly develops and renews a large following of loyal readers much as newspaper and magazine columns do.

Incidentally, the highest "Read Most Cost Ratio" ever earned by a Rockwell Report was in the December 17, 1955 issue of *Business Week.* This was a fantastic 469, or 369 percent *more* readers per dollar than the average of all ads in that issue.

Readership is one thing, response is another. Readers respond to The Rockwell Report; they have ordered tens of thousands of reprints—security analysts, other financial people, management men, educators. Requests for additional information on subjects covered in Rockwell ads are received each time one appears. Finally, a number of direct sales resulted, even though this is corporate advertising.

How to Determine What Your Company Image Is

Top management, and even marketing management of many industrial companies cannot conceive of prospects and customers regarding their company in any way other than favorably. However, much as some outdated top management men would like to emulate an ostrich and keep their heads buried safely and comfortably in the sand, reports filtering in from the field through the sales manager often exert considerable pressure for remedial action. When this goes on long enough, even the engineers in top management and in marketing slots throughout the company can be led gently to accept the advisability of determining exactly *what* the company's image is.

Total image of the company is usually based on many factors; those that follow are the most important and will usually appear in any tabulation of factors influencing company image:

1. Prices
2. Sales contacts
3. Product specifications
4. Delivery
5. Service
6. Reliability of the product
7. Application engineering
8. Technical literature
9. Advertising
10. Manufacturing facilities
11. Breadth of product line
12. Research and development
13. Parts availability

How the company's universe feels about it in relationship to these 13 factors constitutes the company's image. Best way to get an objective analysis of the way the company is regarded is by undertaking a company image study. Personal interviews can be conducted throughout the country using teams of trained interviewers; this is an excellent method, but it is relatively slow and quite expensive. Best way to do an image study is to go the mail survey route.

Using mail to survey prospects and customers is a valid method of making a study *if the mailing list itself is valid.* Make certain your survey mailing goes to *both* prospects and customers.

One large company, which we'll call Smith Widget Manufacturing Company (SWMC) recently performed an image study quoted here because it is well thought out and obviously refers to a number of areas that are sensitive and need inquiring into by most industrial companies.

TO: Mr. Dave Carew — March 16

SUBJECT: Image Study, Widget Market

As a result of the meeting you attended on March 14, it was agreed that the study should be undertaken to develop information to satisfy the following objectives:

1. To identify areas of strength—and possible areas in which improvement can be attained—in the image of Smith Widget Manufacturing Company in the minds of those in the widget market.
2. To provide a basic framework around which a dynamic marketing program, designed to establish and/or maintain SWMC as the leading producer of widgets, can be developed and activated.
3. To develop specific communication goals, in line with SWMC's short- and long-term marketing plans, around which effective advertising and sales promotion programs can be designed.
4. To establish a bench mark against which the effect of the present advertising platform can be measured in future years.

The specific characteristics of the company to be evaluated by the study are segmented into five groups.

I. General Leadership Characteristics

A. Research and development (on new products).

B. Initiative.

C. Ability to keep abreast of market needs.

D. Contributions to the industry.

II. Product

A. Product quality.

B. Maintenance requirements.

C. Product price.

D. Ability to meet needs for widgets.

E. Improvement of existing products.

III. Marketing

A. *Sales*

1. Sales coverage (contact).
2. Salesman's knowledge of customer problems.
3. Technical capability of salesman.
4. Salesman's knowledge of SWMC's products.
5. Helpfulness of sales office.

IV. Service

A. Technical in-plant assistance.

B. Instructions in use of equipment.

C. Cooperation and efficiency shown during installation and setup of equipment.

D. Efficiency in solving equipment difficulties after setup.

E. Handling of complaints.

V. Advertising

A. Informative value of advertising relating to:

1. SWMC products.
2. Application of SWMC products.
3. Problem identification (customer's need for equipment).

B. Informative value of technical literature relating to:

1. SWMC Products.
2. Application of SWMC products.
3. Problem identification.

C. Amount of advertising.

D. Originality of advertising.

E. Persuasiveness of advertising.

These, then, are the areas that one company decided it needed information about in order to correct problems which had not been identified heretofore.

Always be certain that questions in the questionnaire are "open end" and that they do not identify any one company. Select recipients of the questionnaire from SIC's in which your company is most interested, and mail them to job titles or functions most important to you, although mailing by actual name is better.

Changing the Company Name

In a recent article, *Industrial Marketing* said, "The most expensive mania that modern business has fallen victim to is the compulsion to change the company name."

But *IM* tends to take a dim view of many goings on in the marketplace, especially if the changes are revolutionary, rather than evolutionary. Apparently tinkering with the company name falls into the first category and so incurred the magazine's editorial wrath.

Be that as it may, companies are changing their names at a faster rate than are lissome maidens in the month of June. Despite the complexities inherent in the process—and they range from new business cards and stationery to convincing stockholders of the necessity—more than 150 major firms listed by Standard & Poor's made a change in either firm name or trademark (or both) in a recent year. The trend continues.

The "world's greatest newspaper" (the Chicago *Tribune)* noted with some amazement in July, 1968, that a trickle of firms abandoning old, respected, long-established names for a series of initials had suddenly become a veritable deluge. The *Tribune* proceeded to call attention to the United Gas Improvement Company which suddenly became UGI Corporation, and to General Acceptance Corporation, which transformed itself into GAC Corporation.

Long ago Pittsburgh Plate Glass Company became PPG Industries, Inc., and General Aniline and Film Corporation (that's Ansco, you know) became GAF Corporation. The Thompson-Starret Company took the plunge and switched to TST Industries and Tractor Supply Company became TSC Industries. United Shoe Machinery Corporation, one of whose fine ads is discussed in Chapter 11, was transformed into USM Corporation.

The rush to clasp a bunch (usually three) of initials in a warm corporate embrace shows no signs of abating, although Wall Street and most individual investors are bewildered, confused, and dismayed. An information gap only slightly smaller than the Grand

Canyon has resulted from not being able to remember what the alphabet-soup initials stand for. And pity the poor devil who provides input for the stock ticker!

More than a score of the country's largest firms now use initials for their corporate names. One such is FMC Corporation, nee Food Machinery and Chemical Corporation, whose annual sales top the $1 billion mark.

Then there's TRW, Inc., formerly Thompson Ramo Wooldridge, Inc., also in the elite $1 billion class; interestingly, TRW engaged in a game of mixing up the alphabet when it acquired IRC, Inc., known at one time as International Resistance Company.

Regarded most fondly are three initials, although some of the name-changing companies modestly limit themselves to two—including GF Industries and G-L Industries—while other, brasher, firms take that somewhat inevitable extra step. Among those who took four initials are R.E.D.M. Corporation and BACM Industries. At least one company, UARCO, Inc., manufacturer of business forms, uses *five*.

Acronyms of initials of discarded company names have also found widespread, enthusiastic acceptance. The American-Bosch-Arma Corporation, for example, has recently become Arma Corporation; The Electric Bond and Share Company has become Ebasco Industries; and the Mid-America Pipeline Company is now known as Mapco, Inc.

More than half of the companies in *Fortune's 500* have initiated changeover programs in the past five years, involving the company name, trademark, or logotype. Some of these companies are reported to be reevaluating their approach for the *second* time, and at least one for the *third*. Management is vitally concerned with broadening the concept of their organizations, of not placing any sort of artificial, arbitrary hindrance in the path of orderly growth.

Let's look at some typical successful companies whose names have been changed, see why the change was made, and how advertising poured communications oil on the troubled waters of transition.

Most frequently encountered rationale for changing the company's name is that the old one was either irrelevant or misleading. What with the fantastic number of mergers which have taken place in the past couple of decades, many companies find themselves in businesses and markets they never dreamed of—and their old, familiar names which they've used for years reflect this.

Tennessee Gas Transmission Company is such a firm. The company's reason for wanting to change its name can be *seen* in one of the advertisements it ran when it found itself becoming bogged down in a bottomless morass when it attempted to explain just what it was the company did besides conveying natural gas through a pipeline. Shown below is a typical baby spread of the period, a four-color page and a one-third page in black-and-white.

While the advertisement itself is attractive, the art has strong emotional appeal, and the copy is crisp and well written, the fact remains that the one-third page opposite the full page is devoted to explaining what the company consists of and what it does.

Conrad H. Collier, director of advertising, said this "bird" ad is part of a campaign that was running before the company changed its name; the campaign was created to point up the fact Tennessee Gas Transmission Company was a significant factor in three other types of business besides the one highlighted by its name.

As long as the company was engaged solely in pipelining natural gas, its name couldn't be faulted.

But when growth occurred and the company expanded and diversified into areas far beyond its old boundaries, a different picture emerged. The company now has completely integrated oil operations; is a major supplier of packaging and manufactures industrial and agricultural chemicals.

So, as an ad in *Business Week* said, the company adopted a name "general enough to reflect our present . . . and fit our future." Tenneco Inc.—with "lots of elbow room"—was the choice.

One of the corporate advertisements (Mr. Collier prefers to call them "institutional" ads) announcing this landmark change for the company is shown below.

Hand caught in the act of changing letters was a dramatic way to introduce a new and meaningful name for an expanding, progressive company.

This interesting black-and-white bleed spread appeared in *Investment Dealers Digest, Financial Analysts Journal, and in Trusts & Estates;* the same ad in four color ran in a number of media chosen to reach management in business and industry.

Copy is so lucid and it does such an excellent job of explaining why the name of the company was changed that it is carried here. It reads:

Beginning a new era . . . under a new name

22 years ago, when we began as Tennessee Gas Transmission Company, our only business was transporting natural gas. And today, we operate one of America's largest pipe-

line networks, delivering billions of cubic feet of nature's finest fuel daily to utilities serving homes and industries in 24 states.

But, over the years, we have grown in other fields and are now active in four basic natural resource areas. In addition to our expanding pipelines, we're in every phase of petroleum as Tenneco Oil Company . . . exploration, producing, refining, and marketing. We're in chemicals as Tenneco Chemicals, Inc. . . . produce a host of chemicals and plastics for industry, farm, and home. We're in pulp and paper, as Packaging Corporation of America . . . from the forest to paperboard to versatile and colorful packages that merchandise the goods of our country.

As a result of these expanding activities we find our name "Tennessee Gas" too limiting. So we have changed it to . . . TENNECO INC.

We leave our old name with regret. It has served us and America well. But with the new comes the promise of even greater growth through four areas vital to the nation's economy—natural gas, oil, chemicals, and packaging.

Tenneco is on the move.

Tennessee Gas Transmission Company is now TENNECO INC. (new logo)

Following these name-changing advertisements, Tenneco Inc. launched a series of institutional ads designed to emphasize the company's new name, and to stress the company's success in four different types of major businesses. In sequence, the ads emphasize these four diversified businesses; the new name; and the new logotype. Divisions and subsidiary companies continue to run straight product advertisements, of course.

Shown nearby is a typical four-color Tenneco ad in the new series. Clean, simple, and dramatic, this illustration catches the reader's eye for obvious reasons—and while he's looking at the bikini-clad lass, he can't miss seeing the new Tenneco logo she's wearing.

It must be a tremendous relief not to have to run a full column of explanatory copy about what comprises the company.

Audience at which Tenneco aims with its new campaign is the broad mass of "influentials"—that is, the thought leaders and decision makers of the country. The company is particularly anxious to

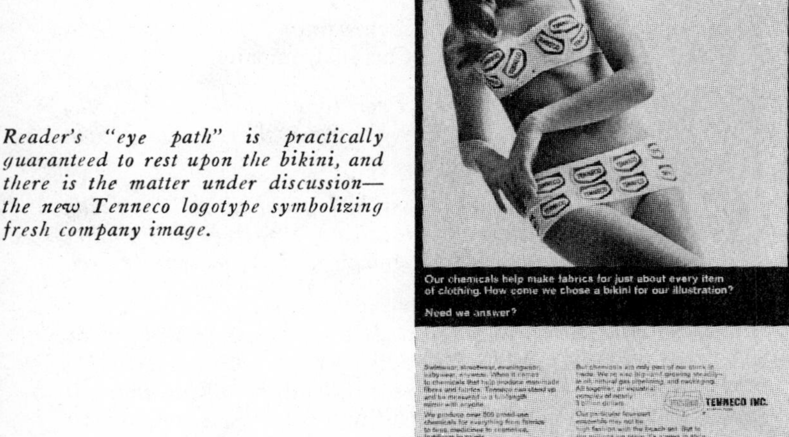

Reader's "eye path" is practically guaranteed to rest upon the bikini, and there is the matter under discussion—the new Tenneco logotype symbolizing fresh company image.

reach the broad financial fraternity of the nation so that the people who really count know who Tenneco is.

Ad director Collier stressed that these are not "marketing ads." Instead, he said, they are "image ads for lack of a better word." Media list for this campaign was: *U.S. News & World Report, Time, Newsweek, Business Week, Wall Street Journal, Forbes, Financial World, Barron's, Investment Dealers Digest, Financial Analysts Journal, Trusts & Estates, American Banker,* and the *Commercial & Financial Chronicle.* Media are listed in descending order of importance.

Incidentally, Tenneco's ads are extremely well read. The bikini ad topped all tested ads in a recent issue of *Business Week,* in addition to earning the highest efficiency levels among the 106 ads studied in that issue. In *Newsweek* the ad was the highest rated in the issue. And in *Time* it was "well above average."

Two More Classic Campaigns

Two communications programs stand out from 'most all others in the proliferation of name-change campaigns that have inundated business publications of the management genre of recent years. One is simple and was used by a smaller company; the other is more ambitious and was used by a giant.

Forbes magazine reports on the first of these and quotes the following delightful little ad which appeared in the *Wall Street Journal:*

> *The name we had was pretty confusing:*
> (The New Haven Board & Carton Company, Inc.)
>
> *By the time our telephone operators got it all out, the caller had hung up. If they tried to shorten it, people thought we were a railroad.*
>
> *Unfortunately, our competitors had grabbed all the really good names. (We thought of calling ourselves "Container & Packaging Corporation of America," but our lawyers felt somebody might sue.)*
>
> *So, we mulled it and mulled it. We ran contests and put all suggestions into the computer. Everything came up BLAH! Then one day our President, Lee Simkins, had an inspiration: "SIMKINS INDUSTRIES." He tried it out on his family and they all thought it was swell!*
>
> *A few Executives didn't like it much. After their employment was terminated, everybody else agreed it was really great. (Actually, we were all happy the Boss' name was not Weyerhaeuser, or Potlatch.)*
>
> *SIMKINS INDUSTRIES, INC.*
> *packaging*

Simkins Industries' modest little ad is a gem. It is as refreshing as dabbling a pair of tired feet in a crisp mountain stream, especially after wading through some of the pretentious, self-oriented, self-conscious copy ground out to explain why companies change their names.

This sparkling little ad required thought and tact and courage—all combined with a lively sense of humor, the ability to see an event in its proper perspective, and the candor needed not to take one's self too seriously. The last is rare indeed.

Signal Oil & Gas Becomes the Signal Companies

Much different and far more complex was the problem faced by Signal Oil and Gas Company, giant $1.5 billion Los Angeles-based conglomerate. Due to an aggressive program of planned growth and acquisition, the company had undergone radical changes. Its oil and gas operations, for example, formerly its life blood, accounted for less than half of the current dollar volume. As a result, the old name was simply outgrown. It applied to the company as it used to be, not as it now is.

Signal Oil and Gas Company's name-change advertising campaign is an exceptionally fine example of how such a program should be handled to arouse maximum interest in the change—both before the event occurred, as well as afterwards. Let's go into the nuts and bolts of the campaign itself, as well as the excellent thinking behind it.

The first step toward diversification was taken in 1952. At that time Signal Oil and Gas Company acquired a substantial stock interest in American President Lines, a leading Pacific Coast steamship company.

Even then, Signal Oil and Gas Company took to heart the aphorisms that to stand still is to fall behind—and that in diversification lies *both* stability and greater profitability. In 1964 Signal entered the booming aerospace field through a merger with The Garrett Corporation, one of its leaders. Then, in 1967, came simultaneous mergers with Mack Trucks, one of the oldest and most respected names in the automotive market, and with Arizona Bancorporation, a Phoenix holding company with profitable investments in a variety of areas, including banks and steel production. Hard on the heels of these desirable mergers came one with Dunham-Bush, Inc., an important factor in the design, manufacture, and distribution of systems and components for environmental comfort, and for food and materials preservation and processing in the commercial, industrial, and institutional markets.

That these mergers and acquisitions were both well chosen and highly successful is attested to by the fact that Signal's gross income more than tripled, and its earnings and assets have more than doubled.

In addition to these factors, management was well aware that continued identification of Signal as an "oil and gas" company was psychologically limiting. Moreover, such obsolete identification imposed an artificial handicap on the company's relationship with the financial community because the name inevitably conjured up an erroneous, incomplete image by failing to reflect the broad-based diversification which had taken place in the past decade and a half.

Worse yet, the "oil and gas" label stuck on there for all to see could be misinterpreted as a deliberate slighting of other important elements of the company, especially Garrett and Mack. The inference could be drawn that they did not loom large in management's plans for the future, when exactly the opposite is true.

The decision to change the name of a 45-year-old company isn't made as casually as choosing the necktie to harmonize with that day's suit, nor is it one that's rushed into. Signal management, in fact, had been considering making a name change for at least two years, although actual planning didn't begin to gel until mid-1967, which was about six months before the board of directors was asked to approve the new name.

First step, as with any other well-managed project, was to establish objectives. These were:

1. To adopt a parent company name which indicates broad diversification.

2. To develop a distinctive trademark or signature (logo) for the parent company.

3. To take full advantage of existing recognition and reputation of Signal and its subsidiaries.

4. To develop a consistent program for identifying subsidiaries and affiliates with the parent company in a way that does not conflict with their individual identities but supports and contributes to the broad recognition of the parent company, particularly in the financial community.

5. To build a parent company identification which adds to the strength and reputation of each affiliate in its respective field.

Responsibility for developing a recommended name—or names, that is—and logo was given to Signal's advertising and public relations agency, The Bowes Company, Los Angeles. Thus was avoided the pitfall of putting the company's future into the hands of one of the glib image merchants and design hotshots who specialize in extracting exorbitant fees from mesmerized managements in exchange for concocting brittle say-nothing names and highly contrived logos which also fail to communicate a single, solitary thing.

These "consultants" are responsible for many of the inanities which, for a fat fee, replaced well-known and highly respected firm names.

How many people in business don't know, for example, exactly what a Citgo is—or an Amex, an Abex, an Amax, for that matter—after untold millions of dollars have been spent to tell them? There are many more "A's," as well as 25 other letters of the alphabet involved in such ill-conceived foolishness.

All too often the name of the game seems to be change for the sake of change itself—and the greater the change and the more incomprehensible the new name is, the greater the fee for giving birth to it. (And the greater the confusion in the marketplace, among prospects, customers, security analysts, investors, brokerage houses, etc.)

Management of The Bowes Company determined to avoid such nonsense. The project began, logically enough, with an in-depth discussion between Bowes personnel (all of whom were intimately familiar with Signal's day-to-day operations and long-range objectives—unlike a strange image merchant) and Signal's top management.

Purpose was to clarify the objectives and all pertinent facts and make *sure* both teams were pulling in the same direction. Tugs-of-war are expensive and time-consuming. Resulting information was carefully documented by Bowes for study by the agency's account team and creative staff.

There was complete unanimity of thought on the subject at the agency. All agreed that the name ultimately selected should be easy to use and easy to remember. Furthermore, the chosen name should be one which indicated diversification while simultaneously representing the sum of the parts.

Consensus at the agency was that retention of the word "Signal" would be desirable because it would help maintain corporate recognition. Signal's publics wouldn't be presented with something foreign and unknown, so the task of creating awareness of the new name would be simplified.

Also among the advantages of retaining the word "Signal" in the new name were:

1. It was already well established.
2. The name was legally available.
3. "Signal" is a short name; it is easy to spell and pronounce (in fact, it can't be *mis*pronounced); it is not easily confused with any other commonly used name.
4. Meaning and connotations of "Signal" are both favorable and, coincidentally, have a fairly direct relationship to many of the products and services of the various affiliated companies—without creating any limitations. "Signal" has these various meanings: Sign for action; warning or command; object to be observed; way to transmit intelligence; messages; sounds; impulses; (as an adjective) notable; significant; outstanding; distinguished.

Scores of names were considered, tried on for fit, and ultimately rejected at the agency. Finally, all concerned agreed to recommend two alternatives:

1. Signal Industries, Inc.
2. The Signal Companies

These names were first submitted to Signal's top management, which chose The Signal Companies. Management then presented this name to the company's board of directors, who approved it.

"The Signal Companies" was preferred because it was considered more distinctive than "industries" (half of the cat-and-dog companies in business have renamed themselves Such-and-Such Industries). Moreover, "companies" is somewhat less confining than "industries"; banking, for example, is usually not considered an industry. Also, "companies" conveys a vivid word-picture of individual companies united in approach but individual in types of business and autonomous in managerial responsibility.

Specific reasons for the agency's recommending "The Signal Companies" as the new name for the parent company were:

1. The name is distinctive, yet simple, easy to remember, and not gimmicky or contrived. It rings true.
2. Plural "companies" carries the connotation of multiplicity, broad diversification, and continuing expansion.
3. No limitations as to kinds of companies—whether light industry, heavy industry, financial, service, transportation, or what have you—are inherent in the name.

Legality of the new name was checked prior to submission to Signal management; this included ascertaining whether or not "Companies" could be used alone—and it could not. To comply with Delaware law, the word "Inc." must be included after the name, wherever the full, official designation is required, such as on stock certificates, contracts, and similar legal documents. For the most part, though, the "Inc." could either be omitted or included in very small type.

In international situations, to help identify the company or any subsidiary as an indigenous operation, the customary designations can be added, such as "Ltd.," "GmbH," "S.A." and so on.

Also recommended by the agency was that affiliated companies be identified as "One of The Signal Companies." It was agreed that all subsidiaries should use this identification consistently and uniformly on letterheads, standard forms, and promotional material where appropriate. Continual repetition will have a synergistic effect in building and maintaining favorable recognition for the parent company and its various components.

To provide guidance and assure uniformity in usage of the parent company name and logo, the agency developed a comprehensive style manual with detailed instructions and examples of the identifying line in a wide variety of possible uses.

Signal's new logo, and an attractive one it is, was born in the creative department at The Bowes Company. Major considerations in developing the new trademark design for the parent company were:

1. It must be distinctive, easy to recognize and remember.
2. It should not be identified specifically with any type of operation.
3. It must be flexible enough to have dominance when used alone, but should not compete with identification of subsidiary companies, nor should it confuse the viewer.

The new corporate trademark or symbol or logo is shown above. It consists of two half circles, positioned to form a subtle initial "S," within a light-line square frame. The logo may be used in color (left half red, right half green), black and white, or blind embossed.

To summarize, The Bowes Company describes the logo as "simple, distinctive, subtle, contemporary and dynamic." And that's a pretty irrefutable assessment of the new logo, even if it is one of the agency's brainchildren—especially when it's mentally compared to some of the silly abominations hopefully embraced by other corporations in recent years.

Attributes of the new logo are:

Simple. It's free of frills, clean, highly visible, and perhaps best of all, it's not gimmicky.

Distinctive. No other logo is just like it, yet the component parts fit together so logically that it is very basic, easy to remember and to recognize.

Subtle. Signal's new logo avoids the well-worn cliché of an ordinary monogram or obvious initial. The "S" formed by the half circles is not gross or insulting; it arouses the viewer's curiosity and involves him by allowing him to "discover" the "S" for himself, and to relate to Signal on a more personal basis.

Contemporary. The simplicity of the symbol, together with the new corporate name, gives just the right amount of understatement to show corporate self-assurance and a feeling of the "today company." Yet it is not a faddish design that will be soon outdated, nor is it blatant and tasteless and vulgar as are many of the so-called "bolder" approaches which include screaming reverses and pseudo-cultural symbolism which enjoyed a brief vogue.

Unlimited. The logo is not symbolic of any specific type of business or industry, hence does not limit itself. It is readily adaptable to all present or future operations of Signal and its subsidiaries.

Dynamic. This logo is bold, solid, sharp, vigorous. It has substance. And it is easily and quickly read and absorbed and retained. In addition, it benefits from use of basic, familiar human-response colors—red and green. Colors and shapes work well together to attract and hold the eye. The colors, incidentally, might be described as "signal" colors!

Meaningful. The symbol, like The Signal Companies, is made up of separate elements, each well defined and self-sufficient, yet complementing each other as parts of a larger, orderly framework. Together the parts form an upward path between them, symbolic of progress. A feeling of positiveness, conciseness, confidence, and importance is imparted.

Reminiscent of the Signal heritage. The new logo is a logical evolvement from the way the company had been represented in the past. Colors are a soft suggestion of the old Signal stoplight and are retained in the new Signal trademark. They are all part of the subtle background, now incorporated in a new symbol for a new parent corporation.

Practical. The logo can be used in every size, in color, in black-and-white, in halftone and in line art; too, it can be lighted or painted. Economy is built in because it is simple to reproduce. And it's easy to control. Also pointed out by Signal's agency is that company typewriters could easily be equipped with a key to type the new "S" symbol, thus permitting broadest possible use.

At no time was there any doubt as to the advisability of changing Signal's name, nor was there any fear that such a change would result in dilution of the company's image or in reduced awareness of the company.

Need to make the change was manifest, and it was the consensus that the new name could not fail to strengthen the company—particularly since retention of the word "Signal" obviated the need to reestablish completely the company's identification. It's much better to start with something than with nothing.

Wisdom of retaining the word "Signal" is obvious upon examination of corporate advertising campaigns of companies who adopted a completely new name with no familiar element; many have spent into the seven-figure bracket in an attempt to build awareness of the company to former levels—with conspicuous lack of success. Signal didn't make this costly mistake.

Every step of Signal's name-change program was planned down to the last detail, and some sharp marketing thinking went into it.

Signal began the campaign with one of the most outstanding teaser ads to come down the pike in many a year. This tremendously stimulating and imaginative black-and-white one-page advertisement

Joining the conglomerate companies in one impossible combination was an effective way to demonstrate the need for a change in the corporate name, image of Signal Oil & Gas.

We've thought
of calling ourselves
Signalgarrettmacktruckarizonabancorporation

Our present name, Signal Oil and Gas Company, gives no hint of our diversification.

It doesn't remind you that we merged with Garrett in 1964, putting us not only in the aerospace business but into the development and production of gas turbines, heat transfer systems and life sciences research.

You may think of us as solid—"built like a Mack truck", in fact—but from our name you wouldn't know that we recently acquired that very company. Mack Trucks, Inc. is the nation's largest seller of trucks in many heavy duty lines.

And now, by adding Arizona Bancorporation to our action team, we're in banking, consumer financing, leasing, life insurance, prescription drugs and steel production.

For more information on our activities, write us at the address below. Of course our expanding petroleum production and marketing activities are of prime importance. So the "Oil and Gas Company" part still applies.

But "Signal" means a lot more these days.

Signal Oil and Gas Company

appeared in *Forbes, Fortune, Business Week* (Pacific Coast edition), four editions of *Time,* and three editions of *Wall Street Journal.* Insertions carried over into December.

If this headline isn't enough to titillate the fancy and pique the curiosity of even the staidest member of the business and financial community, nothing else would. Offhand, you probably can't name anybody who could read the headline and then not proceed on into the body copy. Copy reads:

We've thought of calling ourselves Signalgarrettmacktruckarizonabancorporation

Our present name, Signal Oil and Gas Company, gives no hint of our diversification.

It doesn't remind you that we merged with Garrett in 1964, putting us not only in the aerospace business but into the development and production of gas turbines, heat transfer systems and life sciences research.

You may think of us as solid—"built like a Mack truck," in fact—but from our name you wouldn't know that we recently acquired that very company. Mack Trucks, Inc. is the nation's largest seller of trucks in many heavy-duty lines.

And now, by adding Arizona Bancorporation to our action team, we're in banking, consumer financing, leasing, life insurance, prescription drugs, and steel production.

For more information on our activities, write us at the address below. Of course our expanding petroleum production and marketing activities are of prime importance. So the "Oil and Gas Company" part still applies.

But "Signal" means a lot more these days.

Signal Oil and Gas Company
1010 Wilshire Boulevard, Los Angeles, California 90017

That's stage-setting with a mighty sure hand.

Effectiveness of this ad was emphasized by the fact that it hit the editorial jackpot (which naturally warmed the cockles of many hearts at both Signal and its agency) because it was picked up as the lead in both *Time's* and *Newsweek's* stories about Signal's proposed acquisition of Allis-Chalmers Manufacturing Company, Milwaukee-based leader in electrical, construction, and farm machinery, whose annual sales are some $850 million. Publicity like this you can't buy.

Next ad in the campaign was a powerful all-type spread shown nearby. It makes impressive use of what appears to be *acres* of pristine white space to lure readers into the copy. Copy is doubly appealing because it's set in display type, all of it except one line.

We have decided against changing our name to
Signalgarrettmacktruckarizonabancorporation,
but because of continued diversification we are
definitely going to change our name to something
other than Signal Oil and Gas Company.

Typography is clean and attractive, set ragged-right, and well spaced. For a fast change of pace that reaches right out and grabs the reader, the "snapper" is set in very small type in the lower left hand corner of the spread; it delivered readers in droves to Signal's succinct statement about its continuing diversification. It reads:

> **We have decided against changing our name to Signalgarrettmacktruckarizonabancorporation, but because of continued diversification we are definitely going to change our name to *something* other than Signal Oil and Gas Company.**
>
> *Our diversification program includes recent acquisitions of Garrett, Mack Trucks, Inc., and Arizona Bancorporation. Signal Oil and Gas Company, Los Angeles, California.*

An unexpected advertising hiatus resulted from a proposed merger with Occidental Petroleum; the annual stockholders' meeting was postponed for one month, also. But the second part of Signal's name-change advertising campaign began as soon as possible thereafter.

First ad in the new series is reproduced nearby. It is highly dramatic. Only color on the left-hand page is the red-and-green Signal logo, while the right-hand page is in four color.

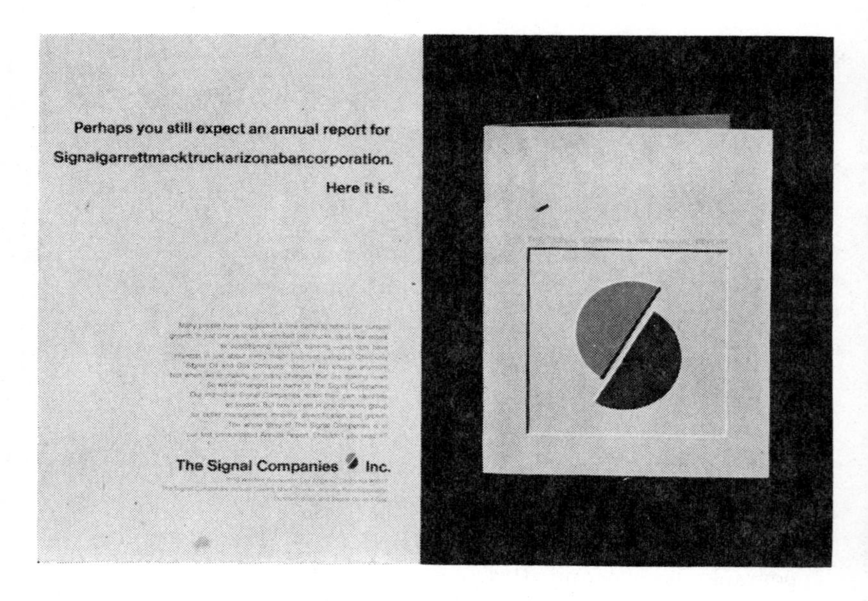

Copy is especially lucid, persuasive and "appropropiate." It says:

Perhaps you still expect an annual report for Signalgarrettmacktruckarizonabancorporation.

Here it is.

Many people have suggested a new name to reflect our current growth. In just one year, we diversified into trucks, steel, real estate, air conditioning systems, banking—and now have interests in just about every major business category. Obviously "Signal Oil and Gas Company" doesn't say enough anymore. Not when we're making so many changes that are making news. So we've changed our name to The Signal Companies. Our individual Signal Companies retain their own identities as leaders. But now all are in one dynamic group for better management, mobility, diversification, and growth. The whole story of The Signal Companies is in our first consolidated Annual Report. Shouldn't you read it?

The Signal Companies (logo) Inc.

Layout is simple and it takes full advantage of the known eye path of the reader. The combination of a four-color page and a three-color page—with the second and third colors used *functionally*—is sound thinking.

This spread not only announces the company's new name, but it illustrates and offers Signal's annual report. Investors, analysts, brokers, bankers, and others in the business and financial community couldn't help but notice this arresting ad, nor could many refrain from requesting their copy of the report. This spread appeared in the following media:

Fortune

Business Week

Time
- New York edition
- Chicago edition
- Los Angeles edition
- San Francisco edition
- Washington, D.C. edition

Forbes

Wall Street Journal

Barrons

U.S. News & World Report

Newsweek
- New York edition
- California edition
- Chicago edition

Dun's Review

American Banker

Financial Analysts Journal

Finance

Wall Street Transcript

Commercial & Financial Chronicle

Investment Dealer's Digest

Financial Executive

Financial World

Los Angeles *Times*

San Francisco *Chronicle-Examiner*

Phoenix *Republic & Gazette*

New York *Times*

Washington *Post*

Chicago *Tribune*

Additional ads are being developed to remind readers of Signal's new size and diversity; they will display the new name and logo prominently.

Media are selected to reach Signal's target audience in the business and financial community—people and institutions who regularly make investments, and people who influence the choice of investments. Business and financial publications were chosen on the basis of their coverage of all of these people. A few local newspapers (financial pages) also were chosen because of special local interests.

Cost of Signal's two stage-setting ads run over a two-year period reached a six-figure level for space alone. If all other elements of the program are included, the investment goes into the seven-figure bracket—about par for the course for a company of Signal's size.

The Bowes Company, Signal's agency, is developing a proposal for a name-change study to determine how much impact the campaign has actually produced. This survey would be designed to reveal both quantitative and qualitative recognition.

Important in the overall scheme of things is that the name-change campaign, while significant in its own right, is just one of several means to an end. In Signal's case, the end is a broad-scale awareness in the financial community of the new Signal.

This program includes extensive publicity, personal contacts with security analysts, a stockholder relations program, the annual report, other corporate documents, and media advertising which talks about the new Signal rather than about the new name.

The name change does have extra significance in Signal's case, however, because it not only reflects a very different corporate nature, but opens the way to disseminate just what that difference means to the company and to its many publics.

Radio Corporation of America's name change to RCA, Inc., for example, is much less meaningful because most people already knew that RCA is much more than a "radio" company—and also most people had already thought of RCA as RCA for years; this was like Coca Cola calling its product "Coke."

However, most people did not know that Signal is far more than an "oil and gas" company before the name change, so the new name not only properly identifies the company, but also serves notice the new Signal is a viable company, one that's on the move.

Signal's name-change advertising campaign is superb. It is well conceived and well executed, and it's tasteful. It evidences thoroughly professional thinking at the agency and within the company. Everybody who had a hand in it should be justifiably proud of the end product.

Happily it skillfully avoids the deadfall that has broken the back of many other campaigns designed to do the same job—boring the reader half to death by bragging and boasting and being too self-centered to present information in terms of *his* self-interest.

All in all, there's every reason to consider this campaign a signal success!

Sales—and the Corporate Name

What's in a name?

Look at it this way: If there's one word of paramount importance to business today, it's *change.* New products and processes are emerging at an accelerating rate—and, because of them, new and different markets.

The management "decision team," too, is on the move. There are many new faces to see, new people to be sold—and not all of them, by any means, accessible to salesmen.

These facts place an additional responsibility on advertising. Advertising's basic function is to help sell existing products, of course. But it must go beyond that. It must establish the importance and integrity of the *company name* (build an image, if you will) among all of those people who—now or in the future—can play an important part in a company's total successful operation.

Heart of the matter is that the name carry a separate identity all its own, that it produce an instantaneous recognition. It is the badge of identification, of course, but it is more. It is the touchstone of value.

Many companies have had the vision to foresee this technological revolution—the importance of change in our economy—and gear their advertising programs accordingly.

One such forward-looking firm is Cleveland-based Warner & Swasey Company. At the beginning of World War II, it recognized that a company's most important asset, an asset that would see it through any change in products or product lines, is a favorable company reputation.

It is with a great deal of pleasure and appreciation that the author acknowledges the help of B. T. Fullerton, director of marketing, Warner & Swasey Company, in preparing this case history of how advertising imparts prestige to a name.

Back at the start of World War II, Warner & Swasey's vice-president-sales stated, "I don't know what we are going to make when this war is over, but I want such a reputation for this company that even if it is baby carriages, the Warner & Swasey name will sell them."

Today, no baby carriages are in the Warner & Swasey line. But it does manufacture rugged earth-moving equipment, complex textile machinery, and sophisticated new automatic machine tools—and 75 percent of the company's shipments are in the new product lines.

And Warner & Swasey is selling them—last year *Poor's Register* listed the company as being in the $100-125 million sales bracket.

In order to achieve this volume and its place of leadership in its industry, Warner & Swasey developed a highly favorable corporate reputation among all of those countless unidentified people that a company touches or is affected by in one way or another. A consistent and well-conceived corporate advertising program produced greater public recognition, it is true, *but above all else it produced sales.*

Here is how the benefits of a consistent 30-year corporate advertising campaign have piled up and up and up at Warner & Swasey.

All of these years, Warner & Swasey has held fast to these basic purposes in this outstanding corporate advertising campaign—which is, incidentally, one of the best known, most admired, most respected, and most widely quoted campaigns ever to appear in publications edited for top management men:

> *A typical Warner & Swasey advertisement talks to a customer or prospect about business—the subject in which he is most interested. It talks about the profit-and-loss system, briefly, one point per advertisement, so that even the busiest businessman will read (as he* does, *in amazing numbers). Finally, the advertisement speaks clearly and convincingly as one businessman to another and is read and accepted in exactly that understanding way. In thus attracting the readership and attention of management men at all levels, it will stimulate the sale of Warner & Swasey products.*

One medium which has been on Warner & Swasey's schedule for more than a quarter-century is *U.S. News & World Report.* W&S runs 26 pages per year in this leading news weekly and considers it the key publication in its schedule because this magazine reaches more top management men in industry than do others in its field.

Now, newspaper editors are also readers, and they, too, read *U.S. News & World Report* as do many other upper-income, well-educated members of society in general. An uncounted, but very large, number of editors have seen Warner & Swasey's ads in the news magazine and have *reprinted them in their newspapers as editorials*—with proper credit, of course.

And a large percentage of readers of *U.S. News & World Report* who are corporation officials have published Warner & Swasey's advertisements in their companies' house magazines, or have them pinned to company bulletin boards.

Furthermore, members of Congress pass these messages out to a broader constituency by reprinting them in the *Congressional Record.*

There's no doubt that this unique campaign continues to meet the challenge of change by making new friends and reacquainting the old. Reports the company: "Even after more than 20 years of every-other-week appearance in *U.S. News & World Report,* the Warner & Swasey campaign still draws fan mail by the hundreds and thousands from readers of the magazine."

Warner & Swasey advertisements are quoted in full on the editorial pages of daily and weekly newspapers throughout the nation, throughout the year. It's not at all unusual to have 50, 60, 70 or more newspapers reprint the same advertisement at approximately the same time; this includes some of the leading dailies in important industrial cities, incidentally, which are prime markets for the company.

Executives at Warner & Swasey who have made a study of the situation estimate these editorials furnish at least an additional 30 *million* circulation to the campaign every year, although they stress that this is without doubt a very conservative estimate. Privately, the opinion is held that the actual figure is at least 60 million.

Not every letter received at Warner & Swasey is laudatory, by any means. Some are quite bitterly opposed to what they consider the ultraconservative nature of the ads.

Just what sort of pro-American corporate advertising campaign is it that does all of these things: Enhances Warner & Swasey's image, increases awareness of W&S as a leading manufacturer of sophisticated products, builds a reputation for integrity, recognizes the company's massive contribution toward Americanism, and sells the product?

Let's look.

Shown nearby is a typical advertisement from Warner & Swasey's classic corporate campaign which has been running in management-oriented publications for some three decades now.

Clean and simple and appealing, with plenty of attractive white space, superb typography, and an interesting in-use photographic illustration of the product, this ad does a tremendous job for Warner & Swasey—and for our country. Copy reads:

The bigger the government
the smaller the people

Everybody—labor union member, farmer, veteran, ship-owner, road builder, importer, sheep herder—everybody seems to want special "benefits" from the government. So

Typical Warner & Swasey ad, one of a long series pulling inquiries and orders in spite of taking a hard-hitting political stance.

they demand help, and get a law or regulation. That requires a bureau to enforce it, taxes to pay for it.

That is how Washington bureaucracy has grown to more than 2,000,000 and taxes have grown ruinously high.

Laws and regulations are written by government employees, and Americans are being drowned in laws they don't understand, bureaus they can't grasp, taxes they cannot afford.

Self-reliance (another name for self-respect) is like a muscle—unused, it soon becomes flabby. Our enemies know it, count on it. That is why every time we ask Government for something instead of doing it ourselves, we surrender, we lose, another bit of America.

High precision aircraft hydraulic
pump parts being machined
on a Warner & Swasey
1 AC Automatic Chucker.

YOU CAN PRODUCE IT BETTER, FASTER, FOR LESS WITH WARNER & SWASEY MACHINE TOOLS, TEXTILE MACHINERY, CONSTRUCTION MACHINERY

Warner & Swasey realizes that the company can prosper and grow and build for the future only if our country does, also. If the country goes down the drain, so does Warner & Swasey. It is that simple. That admirable philosophy led to an ad that said:

How do you get Obliterate on the ballot?

You vote for the best Republican or Democrat, sure he will work for what's best for the country, but somehow the bureaus and bureaucrats, the deficits and the debts, keep on mounting.

How do you get a place on the ballot where the American people can vote NO to hazy theories, NO to spending billions we haven't got for too many programs of questionable value, NO to courts more interested in kindness to criminals than laws and protection of decent citizens, NO to those many bureaucrats whose chief aim is to perpetuate their often-useless jobs.

Put places to mark these *on the ballot and you'd roll up the biggest patriots' landslide in history. And it's high time.*

Outdoor lift truck, a product of the Duplex Division of Warner & Swasey, hauling prepackaged lumber in outside storage area

Other powerful Warner & Swasey ads have been directed at government fiscal policies, foreign aid, domestic spending programs, and similar themes. Warner & Swasey is modest about the splendid contribution it has made toward preserving freedom in America. The vice-president-sales of the company said, "I have not referred to this as an 'institutional campaign,' because the purpose is very definitely to sell machines, and we know it is doing so. Let me put it this way: If an executive committee or board of directors has three proposals presented to it for the purpose of machine tools, and if they pick up the one with Warner & Swasey on the cover first, our advertising has been successful, because that's all we can ask for. *And we know by checking case after case that that has been happening.*

"We have even sold machines almost by mail from this campaign. A man walked into our Atlanta office one day and said he had never heard of our company except through our advertising, and he wanted to give us an order for a turret lathe.

"I believe that a casual purchase item like a tube of toothpaste is bought almost by reflex action. But capital goods like our products, which average more than $20,000 per unit, are very studied purchases. Everywhere we go we know that the men who control these studied purchases *know our company and know us favorably.*

"We have succeeded in reaching the very men our campaign was originally designed to reach—the top executive, the member of the executive committee, and the board of directors—whose favorable nod we must get.

"How do we know this? Through our sales managers and officers it is our business to be in touch with as many customers and prospective customers as we can. We all have the same experience—wherever we go and talk to key executives we are told that our product is being favorably considered or that the sale has actually been consummated *because of the reputation our advertising has built for our company.*

"Through this advertising Warner & Swasey has sat in thousands of directors' meetings, executive committee meetings, production executive meetings, where no Warner & Swasey man could ever sit —but Warner & Swasey, I repeat, has sat there and has spoken forcefully because our philosophy has spoken for us—our philosophy as expressed in our advertising."

Of the thousands of letters Warner & Swasey ads bring in to the company, an important part is from customers and prospects who have been turned into friends by the advertisements. A typical letter follows:

MANITOWOC ENGINEERING CORP.

John D. West
President

The Warner & Swasey Company
5701 Carnegie Avenue
Cleveland, Ohio 44103

Attn: Mr. W. K. Bailey, President

Dear Mr. Bailey:

Thank you for the copy of "More Precious than Gold" [an ad reprint] which you sent on August 10th.

For years I have read your advertising with a feeling of appreciation of your important contribution toward setting the record straight on many national economic issues.

No doubt you have had occasion to question whether this approach influenced the sale of your fine products. Let me assure you that in the recent case of our purchase of two of your machines, our awareness that we were dealing with a progressive company having strong convictions as to our free private enterprise system, somehow gave me added confidence in your company, and a feeling of sharing in your efforts.

I hasten to say, however, that the technical information supplied by your sales people and our superintendent's enlightening visit to your plant, actually sold the product.

I hope you plan to continue your advertising program along this most interesting and effective line.

Sincerely,

John D. West
President

This is one of the two ways advertising "sells"—by increasing the base of negotiations activity.

Warner & Swasey has received so many letters like this one from the president of a leading manufacturer of heavy crawler-type cranes, power shovels, and draglines that singling out one to quote was a difficult task. As might be expected, the same theme runs through almost all of them: *We bought Warner & Swasey machines because we know and respect your name as the result of your corporate advertising campaign.*

Also running through letters from top executives who gave the nod of approval to purchasing Warner & Swasey products is strong approbation for the company's splendid campaign—*and for Warner & Swasey as a company* for running it.

Chapter 20

MERCHANDISING

ALTHOUGH this is the shortest chapter in this book, it concerns a topic—merchandising—that is of vital importance to the success of your communications program.

Strangely enough, merchandising is usually either completely ignored or else given short shrift by most industrial advertising managers. This neglect may well be due to not understanding merchandising and what it can accomplish. (Would you believe many companies do *no* merchandising whatsoever?)

Just what is merchandising? In the context we're using it here, merchandising includes both the *internal* and *external* promotion of an advertisement and/or an advertising campaign. Let's look into these one at a time, although many techniques are applicable to both as will be seen.

Internal Promotion

Internal promotion sells the concept of the campaign—its strategy, audience, and media—to your salesman, product, and marketing people, to company management, agents, representatives, jobbers, distributors, and others in the channel of distribution.

Merchandising is an extremely effective technique for selling sound advertising. Because it does sell sound advertising it builds internal support for and understanding of advertising, and in turn increases the effectiveness of the sales effort externally.

Merchandising your advertising program internally means you are not content to sit idly by, twiddling your thumbs, and let nature take its course. You do more than merely hope that those with whom you work—*and through whom you sell*—will see your ads in various publications and, hopefully, regard them favorably. When you merchandise aggressively, you're taking positive action to make certain your advertising is seen and read and understood.

Actually, it's just as essential to merchandise your communications program internally as it is externally. So doing can help dispel the negative attitude towards advertising that's unbelievably prevalent in many less-than-progressive industrial companies. There's a widespread feeling in industry that advertising in some unexplained way is something that nice people don't talk about—like B.O., or an uncle who voted for F.D.R.

The woeful lack of understanding of the massive contribution industrial advertising makes, and how it does so, can be ameliorated to a great extent by merchandising your advertising program *and the rationale behind it.*

The following four questions raised by one industrial ad manager in a memo to his boss, a vice-president of marketing, point up the necessity to merchandise the advertising program:

1. How can the advertising department receive proper direction so as to operate efficiently if our people do not understand advertising's basic reason for being?

2. How can we establish realistic, concrete communications objectives when our marketing people have almost no concept of what advertising can—and cannot—do?

3. How can we measure the effectiveness of the advertising program unless we have communications objectives which reflect marketing objectives?

4. How can the advertising department expect our people to understand advertising's role in the marketing-communications mix unless we explain it to them?

These are pertinent questions that pinpoint the plight of many an industrial advertising manager. He's boxed in, can't move, can't plan; all due to a lack of understanding of the function he manages. The answer, of course, is a well-executed merchandising program. It should sell the current communications program, *as well as advertising per se,* by tactfully and persuasively educating your people in some of advertising's fundamentals.

Most efficient way to do this is to give examples and illustrations of the things you're talking about. Explain in nontechnical terms. Quote outside experts on various topics.

This is especially effective. Quoting recognized authorities from outside your company is an ideal way to provide basic education in advertising for those who count. Because the experts you quote are *not* in your department and are *not* associated with your company (but your agency *is*), their comments tend to be taken at face value. They encounter no credibility gap.

What's more, this is a custom-built solution to the problem of gathering suitable educational material. You can "borrow" it from any advertising publication you wish and reproduce it *within your company* without finding yourself on the inside looking out for copyright infringement.

And, because you are quoting a disinterested third party, you can present information you know is desirable without embarrassment. The following discussion, *Relating Advertising to Corporate Profits,* enlightened key personnel at Lindberg Hevi-Duty. Reproduced on an inexpensive, one-color (red) masthead designed specifically for the advertising department to use for its educational and merchandising program, the discussion quoted Alan G. St. George, associate market and research director, Meldrum & Fewsmith Inc., as follows:

According to a study done by *Business Management* among 108 company presidents, more than 80 percent felt that an immediate halt of advertising would have little or no effect on sales this year. More than two-thirds felt that an immediate halt would have little effect on next year's sales. These feelings lead to one conclusion—top management has little or no confidence in the ability of advertising to contribute to sales efforts or to increase profits.

The survey pointed to a paradox in the attitudes of presidents toward advertising. When respondents were asked, "How does your company measure the effectiveness of its advertising?" almost half named sales results.

This raises what may seem to be a rather academic question. Must advertising necessarily increase total sales volume to be considered effective? No! Of course all advertising has commercial reasons for being: advertising is a major factor in the reduction of selling costs, a reason that should be sufficient to convince management that it is worthwhile even if sales don't increase.

In another study, McGraw-Hill recorded the opinions of 646 top executives, sales managers, and advertising managers about what they felt were the objectives of business-press advertising. The results were as follows:

Task	*Percent who rated advertising as important*
Introducing new products	93
Creating favorable attitude toward firm	90
Contacting buying influences salesmen do not see	79
Paving the way for salesmen	79
Maintaining the market for established products	70
Reducing the cost of selling	43

Let's take as an example the highest-rated objective, that of introducing new products. Are there any critics of advertising who can deny the efficiency and the economy of introducing a new product to a large number of potential users through this medium? It can take months, if not years, to introduce many indus-

trial products by direct sales calls. In that time valuable sales have been lost, never to be regained.

This, in combination with the $71.27 cost of a direct sales call, should be enough to convince corporate management that advertising does reduce the cost of selling, thereby increasing profits.

Incidentally, there's a woeful lack of authoritative information on just how advertising affects corporate profits, but you can undoubtedly tell that by the fallacious opinions you encounter. Ignorance reigns supreme here. An educational effort in this areas is highly desirable in almost every company.

When your field salesmen are in your office periodically, make every effort to talk with them. Their help will be of inestimable value because they can clue you in about the sales resistance they encounter, tip you off to worthwhile case histories, and so on.

Get to know as many salesmen as possible. You'll find it easier to "sell" your communications program to them at the annual sales meeting if you do. Incidentally, this should be a major merchandising effort on your part, and that of your agency. Use slides, blown-up ads, banners, a flip-chart presentation, or whatever you feel best to dramatize your ad program and show how it will help the salesmen sell. Be sure *not* to put your foot in your mouth by claiming that advertising "sells." Stress, instead, that it helps salesmen sell, that it enables them to use their valuable time more productively, that it helps them ferret out prospects, that it saves time for them by letting them dispense with introducing company and product because advertising has already taken care of this for them.

Never hesitate to explain, but, heaven forbid, don't be patronizing. Although everybody *thinks* he understands industrial advertising, it is probable that you're the *only* person in the company who actually does—and this definitely includes your vice-president of marketing, especially if he's an ex-engineer.

Because advertising is not understood, it is distrusted. For the same illogical reason many in the company look askance at the advertising manager. For isn't he the character who spends all of that money; money which *could* have been pure profit?

One advertising manager tells the story of an unusually naive vice-president who reported he had had a complaint that the ad manager was "advertising the advertising department."

Seems that one of the company engineers had risen to the point where he was in charge of other engineers in marketing slots, hence qualified to receive the merchandising mailings. When he saw that it concerned advertising, that it discussed the company's campaign and the reasons why the copy platform was constructed as it was, he immediately lodged a vociferous protest with marketing brass, claiming that this was nobody's business except the advertising department's, and there was no need to bring anybody else in on advertising thinking.

Naturally, this occurred in a backward company unaccustomed to any merchandising. Unfortunately, though, this negative attitude is encountered all too frequently, especially in small to medium-size companies where the level of marketing sophistication is low and product complexity is high. The two seem to accompany each other.

Use of Preprints and Reprints

About the most dismaying position an industrial salesman can find himself in is to be in the office of a prospect and receive a comment about a product that his company is currently advertising in several magazines, and then realize that he does not know *what* product it is.

Keeping key people in the company, including the field sales force, dealers, and others informed about what advertising is doing to help them is one of the most important functions of a merchandising program.

There's no need, of course, to merchandise each ad individually unless it is a kick-off ad in a new campaign, or introduces the most revolutionary widget ever devised, or something equally sensational. Instead, mail either preprints or reprints (one is before the ad appears, the other after) each month of each ad that runs. It's desirable to capsulize each ad with a brief description, including communications objective, media used, and so on.

Something you can do to make this material more relevant to the salesman is to present it from his viewpoint; relate the advertising to his activities. You could say, for instance, that this single month's advertising makes 2,567,432 impressions on 78,964 individual buying influences, 6,123 of whom are in his *territory.* (Give territorial breakdowns in an attached sheet). Doing so enables salesmen to relate advertising to themselves—which is what they're most interested in.

Media Will Help You Merchandise

You can dramatize your advertising, make it come alive, and give it the full importance it deserves by employing creative merchandising techniques developed by media.

No publication can tell you how to merchandise, of course. You're the best judge of that. But the good ones, such as *Iron Age* and *Research/Development,* will gladly share their vast merchandising experience with you upon request, and assist in the production of certain merchandising pieces. Let's see just what these and other good magazines will do for advertisers.

The publication itself is a great merchandising tool. There's no better way to tell your own people about your campaign than with copies of the magazine itself—with your ad suitably spotlighted. You may order as many copies of the magazine as you need, but as with most publications, this must be done at least three weeks (preferably more) in advance of publication.

Your ad can be spotlighted with bookmarks which tell the recipient of the magazine to turn to page so-and-so to see your ad. *Iron Age,* for example, will imprint a bookmark with a short message and your company name.

Thumbcuts can index your advertisement, just as they do in a dictionary or other reference volume. Because they're unusual and not often encountered in a trade magazine, they're fine attention-grabbers.

Acetate overlays imprinted with your message and firm name in one or two colors, and hinged to the cover of your selected issue of the magazine also make a strong impression.

Plastic bags with a copy of the magazine inserted and heat-sealed may be imprinted with your sales message in one or two colors. This gets the magazine to recipients in first-class condition, incidentally.

Letters, Blowups, Covers

Letters from the publisher—personal letters—can enhance your internal merchandising program. You control the contents of the letters, of course, and the publication prints, signs, and addresses them. Letters are effective to presell in advance of the campaign. Or, you can attach them to copies of the magazine or cover reprints.

Advertising blowups produce tremendous impact. Take even the most unassuming advertisement and blow it up to single sheet size (up to 22 by 28 inches for full page ads, 34 by 22 inches for spreads) and it takes on an entirely new personality. You can't overlook it, and you can't help but read it. Advertisement blowups can carry an imprint such as, "as advertised in *Iron Age.*" Brightly colored mailing tubes and breezy explanatory letters can be an important part of the overall effect.

Various cover folders are available from media, designed primarily for carrying a reproduction of your advertisement with

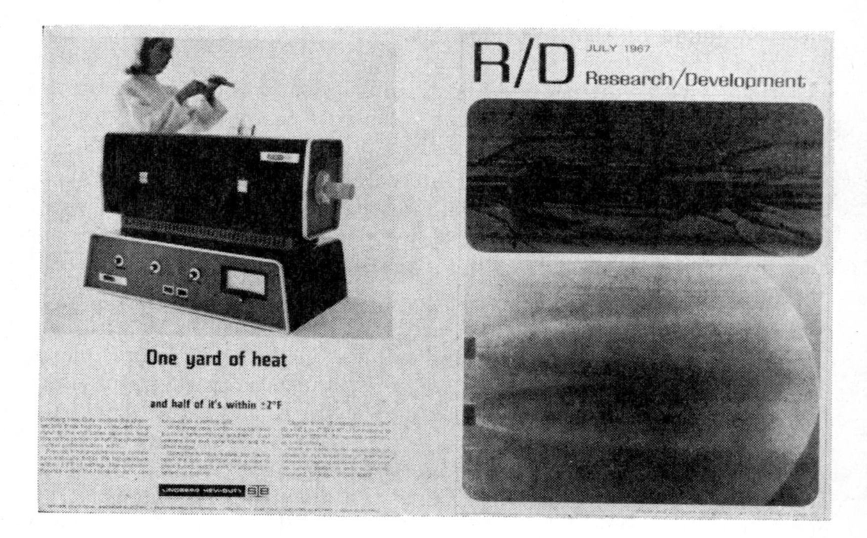

additional areas for your selling copy. The actual cover of the issue in which your advertisement appears may be used. Lindberg Hevi-Duty once used a cover of *Research/Development* with a four-color Lindberg Hevi-Duty ad on the back. The inside spread contained an editorial article on an exotic new piece of equipment Lindberg Hevi-Duty developed. This was a very hard-selling merchandising piece.

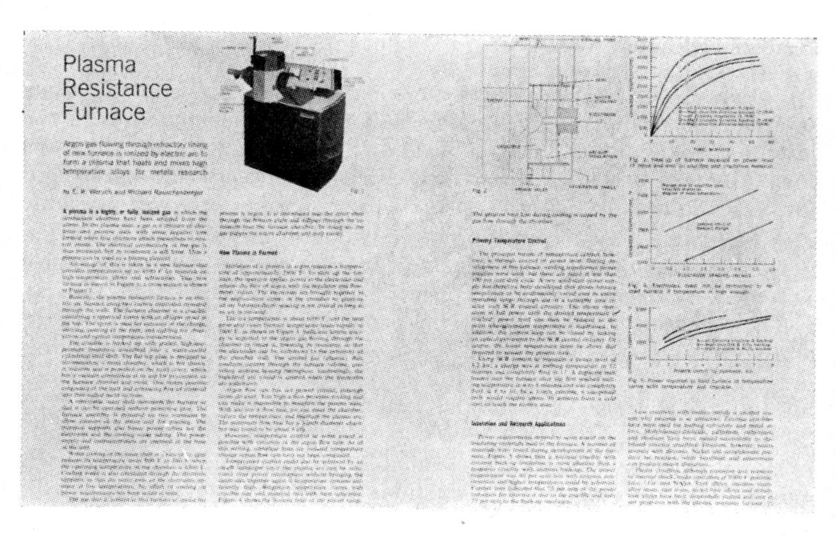

Jigsaw puzzles never lose their fascination. Your advertisement is seen often—each time the puzzle is put together. *Iron Age* has dies for making puzzles from full-page ads and spread ads. Both types are conveniently packaged in a brightly colored box.

Display cards are available, consisting of your advertisement laminated on chipboard, with an easel backing. They are ideal for displaying your message within view of everyone, and can also be put to good use in a trade-show booth. They also carry the "as advertised in" imprint.

Giant matchbooks are available from *Iron Age.* They are tremendously potent merchandisers that present your advertisement and your message and firm name forcefully, all the while attracting a fantastic amount of attention.

Another impressive merchandising tool is plaqued ads. There are almost as many different ways of dressing up an ad reprint to make a handsome presentation piece out of it as there are business publications that will help you with your merchandising. (*All* of the good ones will.)

A good example of the plaqued ads supplied may be seen in the illustration on page 1213. This happens to be an award, but is plaqued in the same way. These handsome pieces are designed to hang on the wall and come complete with all necessary hardware and attachments. They're obviously expensive (some are of solid walnut an inch thick). But if you run a decent schedule in a first-class magazine, they'll usually give you such items free of charge as long as you don't push a good thing too far by asking for too large a quantity, or asking too often. Best thing to do is to ask each magazine you use heavily just once a year, or twice at the most.

Incidentally an ad manager friend had publications he used mail out plaqued advertisements at the rate of one a month—that is, one publication mailed each month to a selected list of names. The plaqued ads were given to this advertiser at no charge, and the publications even packaged and mailed them, paying the postage. Yet several "marketing" people within that company who received these impressive merchandising pieces criticized him vociferously. One complained, "it cost 28 cents to mail this hunk of wood."

When it was explained that this merchandising cost the company not one red cent, these "marketing" people had the unmitigated temerity to suggest the ad manager try to get lower space rates instead of accepting merchandising from the publications. That ad manager said he muttered for days about the "bird-brained engineers who fancied themselves marketing men."

Plaqued ads make excellent displays to dress up district sales offices. They also look good in executive offices, and the reception room or lobby should contain several. Finally, the advertising department should display plaqued ads as part of a continuous program of putting its best foot forward.

Merchandising Allowance

For some reason or other, publication representatives don't offer pie in the sky to every advertiser. Fact is, most publications don't offer merchandising assistance of the no-charge variety *unless they're asked for it.*

Bear in mind the old bromide: The squeaking wheel gets the grease.

Almost every publication charges for extra copies of the magazine, reprints, overlays, blowups, and what have you, although this is not regarded as a profit center by media and every effort is made to hold costs down to a rock-bottom minimum.

Nonetheless, almost every publication you're likely to consider seriously will give you a "merchandising allowance" if you ask for it. Depending upon the volume of business you do with the book (which translates into how much space you use each year), your allowance can be sizable. Always check on just what you're entitled to in the way of a merchandise allowance before committing yourself when you're on the fence and two books appear to be a stand-off value. The merchandising can make all the difference.

One proposal that's received widespread comment in the advertising world was made by Keith Gallimore, ad director at Harnischfeger Corporation. *Media/scope* magazine recently reported that Mr. Gallimore had suggested to the American Business Press that the money rebated in the form of a cash discount (usually 2 percent) be given instead as a merchandising allowance. This would, in effect, lay on the line exactly what you could expect from media.

This is a sensible proposal, one with much merit because the 2 percent cash discount for paying bills on time almost always reverts back to the controller's dollar-hungry grasp. How many ad managers receive this 2 percent as part of their budgets?

Once taken, it's put back in the company till, gone forever from where it actually belongs—in the funds appropriated for the advertising budget. Incidentally, you can make a strong (but probably losing) case that this 2 percent is really your department's, that it does *not* belong to the controller, and that you should be entitled to get it back again.

Media/scope went on to say that in any event, "the 2 percent and its purpose should be written right into the advertising budget so that after the budget has been okayed, the controller won't expect to get his greedy hands around it later on."

This has been a contention of the author's for many years, and this is the first time the subject has been discussed in a major magazine.

External Merchandising

Since the objective of merchandising is to focus a bright spotlight on your advertising, thus increasing both its readership and its effectiveness, anything you can do to direct the attention of prospects and customers to it gives you that much more mileage from your promotional dollars.

Perhaps the major method of getting this additional mileage is to mail either preprints or reprints (the former produces more impact) of your advertisements to your customer-and-prospect mailing list. Some advertisers mail only the ad itself, although the smart ones use a professionally-written covering letter and include a postpaid business reply card; this is far more productive.

Your literature, catalogs, and other printed matter should retain the same general theme, graphic elements, and other distinctive features and devices used in your space advertising. Here, just as in advertising, constant repetition contributes immeasurably toward making a lasting impression.

Use publications in your external merchandising. Naturally, you can't afford to mail 19,000 copies of the magazine itself, nor would that be desirable. But it's a simple matter to isolate target accounts or key prospects and concentrate on them; investment won't be heavy when you do this, but returns—in sales—*will.* Chances are, depending on the type of business you're in, that your target accounts won't number more than a couple of dozen.

This is where the ducks are, so this is where to hunt them. Expend your merchandising ammunition here, don't scatter it all over the landscape so thinly it makes next to no impression. Concentration in merchandising, as in space advertising, pays off.

Dollars invested in merchandising probably won't total more than 5 percent of your total budget, but used wisely can increase the overall effectiveness of your program severalfold.

Chapter 21

THE BUDGET

ISOLATE one activity and hold it up for all to see as the one calculated to give an industrial advertising manager conniptions—it's the annual wrestling match in which he's pitted against that hideous ogre, the budget.

Most ad men regard it as like being in a rat race with the odds stacked in favor of the rats.

Ideally, budgeting should be done by politicians. They're born compromisers, whereas advertising men are essentially pragmatists. There simply isn't the necessary wherewithal to accomplish even a respectable portion of the really important things that need to be done in the communications area. Invariably something has to give, and the *what* is what makes life so miserable for an ad manager at budget time that he resembles a grizzly with a toothache.

Incidentally, let's clear the air as far as terminology is concerned. The words "appropriation" and "budget" are tossed around for all the world as if they meant the same thing. This is not the case.

"Appropriation," as any accountant or controller will be happy to tell you, actually means the maximum amount of dollars allocated for a specific purpose, whereas "budget" means the nuts-and-bolts details of *how* this sum of money will be used.

How Advertising Appropriations Are Determined

Industrial advertising appropriations (the *number* of dollars, not how they are to be used) are usually established in one of four ways in industry. Three of them are naive, unsophisticated, and ignore all sound principles of good management. Here is how industry does it:

1. By management fiat.
2. By percentage of sales.
3. By the competitive parity method.
4. By the task method.

The fiat, or edict, method of establishing the size of the advertising appropriation is used by almost half of all industrial companies. The company president, the sales manager, or the vice-president of marketing calls the ad manager into his office (or writes him a memo) and presents a *fait accompli.* The conversation usually goes like this: "Your 'budget' for the next fiscal year is $000,000. Let me know what you plan to do with it." No reply is needed.

On the surface this seems logical enough. After all, it is management's prerogative to manage, isn't it? And this certainly should include managing the lifeblood of the business—money.

Do a little digging, though, and find out the *reason why* this specific sum was allotted for advertising. Invariably you'll find it is the exact amount management feels it can "spare" and still meet profit objectives. This is negative thinking right out of the last century. *It completely ignores the fact that advertising contributes to company profits.*

Usually this situation is encountered in companies whose management is riddled with engineers and ex-engineers. Usually, too, there's a pathetic dearth of marketing savvy, although technical competence is high. This type of company is, above all else, dependable. It can be depended upon to have no formal marketing plan, no formal communications plan, and the terms "marketing objectives" and "communications objectives" are so much gobbledygook.

"Everyone Else" Advertises

These backward managements are somewhat less than enthusiastic about "sparing" this money to "spend" on advertising, but reluctantly go along with it because almost all other companies (including competitors) advertise. Not to advertise might make them look bad to their peers.

They don't understand advertising, but you can bet your sweet life they *claim* they do. They don't *want* to understand advertising, so don't bother them with facts; their little minds are already made up. They haven't the slightest inkling of what advertising could contribute to their companies, but then, everybody *knows* advertising doesn't produce anything—it's a cost item. Trying to plant an idea in such minds is not sowing in fertile soil.

Setting the advertising appropriation by fiat doesn't consider the needs of the company, or what advertising can and should accomplish—how it should contribute to company profit by reducing the cost of selling. It's an archaic practice, but one that's going to be around for a long time. If you have to, learn to live with it, but continue the educational program you've established.

The practice of setting an advertising appropriation by allotting a certain percentage of sales (usually anticipated sales for the coming year, but not infrequently last year's actual sales) is commonplace in industry.

What it actually is is an attempt to set aside an optimum amount of money for the advertising appropriation, hoping against hope that it will be sufficient to accomplish what needs to be done—*without knowing what needs to be done.*

Establishing an appropriation for advertising by percentage of sales is as unsophisticated as the management fiat route. It ignores company aims and policies, marketing objectives, sales objectives, communications objectives, the competitive situation, the economic outlook, and similar matters that should be analyzed thoroughly before arriving at a firm figure.

Roughly one out of four industrial companies determine the advertising appropriation by the antiquated percentage of sales method. It's a great way to avoid facing reality.

The competitive parity method is a monkey-see, monkey-do performance which should be discouraged vigorously and vociferously. It is nothing more than attempting to determine what major competitors are investing in their advertising programs, then matching them dollar for dollar.

Such a course of action ignores the fact that companies differ tremendously in products, marketing objectives, strengths and weaknesses in the market, rate of new product introductions, channels of distribution, size and efficiency of the field sales force, company image, and many other considerations.

Any attempt to allocate a so-called "industry average" sum for advertising—despite the fact that these figures are readily available for almost every industry—is a veiled attempt to be average rather than be a leader. How many companies have this as an objective?

Reacting to competitive advertising, rather than acting on your own initiative, is a sure road to failure. This applies just as much to appropriating a specific sum for advertising as it does to copy-catting campaigns and a basic advertising philosophy.

About 25 percent of all industrial companies are sophisticated enough and possess enough know-how to work up an advertising appropriation *by the only valid method*—using the task approach.

The task method is the only logical, sensible method of establishing an appropriation because it is based firmly on the premise that enough money must be appropriated to achieve desired objectives. Inherent in the task method is stating objectives.

In most industrial companies, management—or, more likely, sales management—defines the goals, be they a certain dollar volume of sales, introduction of a new product, increased penetration into a certain market, or what have you. Acting on these goals, the advertising manager then sets communications objectives and decides what program will be most likely to produce the desired results.

How the budget is created from the appropriation and how the money is used to achieve the objectives is where past experience and seasoned professional judgment come into play.

The easiest and best way is to budget by objective (task) and assign all necessary money to each objective *by priority assigned by management.* Only top management has enough information about the company as a whole to make this decision.

The most serious error that can possibly be made is that of diluting the pressure put on each objective. If management has a caviar appetite and approves a hot-dog appropriation, it's certain that *none* of the objectives will be achieved if an inadequate sum of money is spread so thin that no real push is put on any one objective. Dollars will stretch just so far. Dilute them too much and they aren't used, they're wasted.

It's critically important that management be made to realize that a weak, wishy-washy attempt to achieve too many objectives with too little money will result in inevitable failure to achieve *any* of them. Management *must* assign priorities to objectives and leave it to advertising management to determine what is needed to achieve them—how much money is required—starting with the most important and working down. When the money is exhausted and some objectives are not budgeted for, it is up to management to decide if it is desirable to appropriate additional dollars to achieve them, or to accept the fact they can't be reached.

How to Present A Budget to Management

Assuming you've taken the task approach to determining what the advertising appropriation should be, all that remains to be done is to budget the allotted number of dollars by objective.

In order to get a budget approved "as submitted," you have to be prepared to outline and define advertising's role and functions and to present the objectives that investment of this money will attain. Merely presenting a breakdown of dollars and where they go doesn't say much, but setting forth objectives does.

Following is the budget presentation used by J. M. Sheehan, director of advertising and sales promotion for General American Transportation Corporation—otherwise known as GATX. Jack Sheehan, working with various members of his company and its divisions and with Grady Boles, vice-president and account executive at Edward H. Weiss Company, the GATX advertising agency, prepared the following presentation for the company's program. It is complete, just as presented to GATX management, although various elements are not "priced out" for competitive reasons. Accumulating this information, including internal costs, and presenting them on a summary sheet, presents no problem, however.

In addition to this presentation, Mr. Sheehan prepared a slide presentation which highlighted the written portion and included layouts of proposed ads, a review of competitive activity, and a summary of results of past programs—along with a detailed dollar-by-dollar breakdown of his suggested budget.

His suggested program was so on-target and his method of explaining what the appropriation would buy was so clear and forceful that management approved it virtually as presented. A portion of that presentation follows:

Foreword

The development and subsequent implementation of an effective advertising, public relations and sales promotion program *must* start from a firm base of clearly defined, reasonably attainable objectives.

The following programs proposed by the Advertising, Public Relations, and Sales Promotion Department were developed from such a base.

Corporate Communications Objectives

I. To present GATX as . . .

a. The prime source for the lease or purchase of railroad cars with special emphasis on tank, covered hopper, and other special purpose cars.

b. The operator (lessor) of the nation's largest and most comprehensive systems of tank storage terminals.

c. The designer and builder of all types of freight cars—serving both shippers and the railroads.

d. The fabricator and erector of a wide range of steel vessels, and their attendant "environment," for liquids, gases and dry bulk materials.

e. The prime source for custom molding of plastics; as well as a marketer of a *quality* proprietary line of plastic products.

f. The designers, fabricators, and erectors of an extensive line of engineered equipment and systems used in mining, processing, manufacturing, and in the control of air and water pollution.

g. A company energetically involved in research and development work for both government and industry, along with R&D for its own products and services.

h. A *growth* company that has diversified and is diversifying along a carefully charted course that will afford the opportunity to better serve its customers and shareholders.

II. To deliver our Corporate "messages" the many audiences of importance to GATX via the most effective and efficient means at our disposal—publication advertising, public relations, direct mail, brochures, trade shows, company publications, and a variety of other sales promotion tools.

The "audiences" of GATX are defined, in descending order of importance as:

a. Present and future customers.

b. Key influences in the financial community.

c. Present and future stockholders.

d. Suppliers.

e. Government officials, educators, opinion molders, and thought leaders.

III. To make certain that our corporate messages are disseminated in a way that will enable us to reach, with greater efficiency and frequency, our present customers and prospects. This primary segment of our "audience" is defined by industry as:

a. Chemical.

b. Petroleum.

c. Petrochemical.

d. Food.

e. Cement and nonmetallic mining.

f. Railroads.

By job function as:

a. Top management.

b. Traffic and distribution management.

c. Engineering and operating management.

Corporate Media Plan

The following corporate advertising media plan was designed to give maximum coverage of our prime audience as defined by Communications Objective II and further spelled out in Objective III.

The media plan allows us, for the first time, to hit *directly* and with *force* our customers and prospects in those industries of importance to the present and future prosperity of GATX.

It will reach top and middle management people in the chemical, petrochemical, petroleum, food, mining and railroad industries. Plus, it will give coverage of traffic and distribution managers across all industries.

The plan is designed to provide frequency, continuity, and impact against the target audiences, at reasonable cost, consistent with our objective.

We recommend the use of the leading publication(s) in the specific industries of prime interest to GATX, to present our corporate messages to the buying influences by industry and/or job function.

Chemical Process Industry and Petrochemicals	*Chemical Week*
Petroleum and Hydrocarbon Processing Industry	*Oil & Gas Journal*
Food Processing Industry	*Food Engineering*
Mining and Cement	*Pit & Quarry* *Rock Products*
Railroads	*Modern Railroads* *Railroad Age*
Traffic and Managers	*Traffic World* *Traffic Management*

To *increase* the penetration of our corporate messages to the required specific industries, as well as give us needed coverage across the entire industrial spectrum, we recommend the continued use of a business management publication, *Business Week.*

Each of the recommended publications has been evaluated in terms of upper and middle management people reached, circulation delivered, editorial environment, and cost efficiency.

While the publications listed cover different industries, they share one thing in common . . . their proven ability to deliver a quality audience—the decision-makers that are of primary importance to GATX.

In essence, this plan is one of *high frequency* and *direction* based on carefully defined objectives.

PROPOSED CORPORATE ADVERTISING MEDIA PLAN

Business Week	13 color pages	
Chemical Week	6 color spreads—12 color pages	
Oil & Gas Journal	6 color spreads— 6 color pages	
Food Engineering	6 color spreads— 6 color pages	
Pit & Quarry	3 color spreads— 3 color pages	
Rock Products	3 color spreads— 3 color pages	
Traffic World	6 color spreads— 6 color pages	
Traffic Management	6 color spreads— 6 color pages	
Modern Railroads	6 color spreads— 6 color pages	
Railway Age	6 color spreads— 6 color pages	
Estimated Advertising Space		$370,000.00
Estimated Advertising Production		60,000.00
	Total	$430,000.00

The presentation continued with similar sections covering corporate publicity, financial public relations, etc.

On page 1444 are two ads from the great GATX campaign. They stress the service the company provides, and also emphasize how GATX can free capital for customers to use to better advantage elsewhere—rather than putting it into rolling stock and terminal handling facilities which, happily, can be leased from GATX.

These fine ads from this outstanding campaign have earned excellent readership ratings. They are doing the job assigned to them and then some.

The manager of the GATX Tank Car Division went on record in writing that Jack Sheehan's advertising program—and the direct mail program—"helped us maintain a very high lease/sale ratio."

What's more, the Chicago Chapter of the Association of Industrial Advertisers* awarded its coveted Silver Award (second place) for excellence for integrated advertising campaigns. GATX also won a Silver Spike Award from the Association of Railroad Advertising Managers, "to recognize those advertisers whose promotion of their own products and services augments the individual and collective efforts of railroad advertisers, thus creating a better understanding on the part of the public of the importance of railroads in the transportation system of America and encouraging the development of additional rail freight and passenger traffic."

Besides all of this, Jack Sheehan received yet another award that same week from *Chemical Week* through Reader Feedback. The GATX ad was "right up there" in the letter grade scores, receiving an A+ rating.

By all means when you have successes like these, mention them in your presentation; they show management how hard your advertising campaign is working, how much benefit it is providing the company.

How to Get Management to Look Favorably on a Budget

According to McGraw-Hill, there are an even half-dozen key points to remember when preparing a budget for submission to management:

1. Educate yourself about the marketing problems confronting management in today's economy.
2. Gather and present evidence to show how advertising can help solve these problems.
3. Help management formulate immediate and long-range marketing policies.

*Now Business/Professional Advertising Association.

Two of the great ads from the GATX campaign, a series which won several awards and a host of letters from industry people praising the general concept. The copy made great sense to railroad people and to people using railroads.

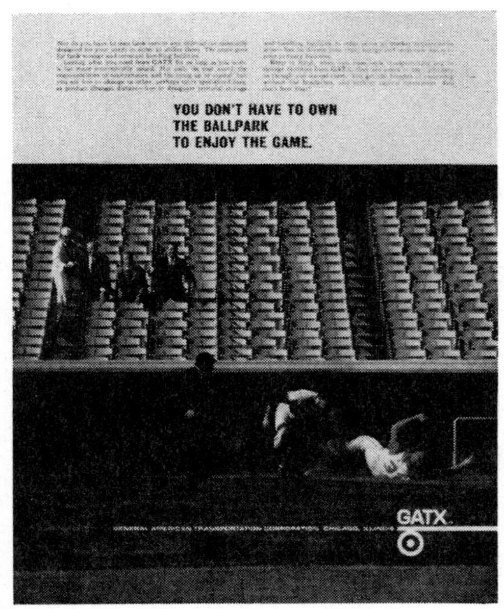

4. Use every opportunity to set forth the fundamental values of your company's advertising in reducing marketing costs, building customer preference and acceptance, protecting and improving market positions, increasing sales, and expanding profits.

5. Develop arguments to demonstrate that your company can't afford to stop or curtail effective product advertising, regardless of current, temporary conditions.

6. Know management objections to advertising—*and* the answers to them.

There are two final things which help assure having your budget accepted.

First, don't "go in high." Be forthright and honest. Tell management—probably your boss, the vice-president of marketing—that your budget is an honest one. Impress on him that you haven't deliberately padded it in anticipation of having the top brass take a whack at it with a meat ax. Stress that it is realistic and represents what is, in your considered opinion, the least dollars that can be expected to achieve the objectives.

If you submit an inflated budget in anticipation of having it cut, management will surely do so. Then, sooner or later, it will be apparent to the discerning that you're not *really* unhappy with the cut; furthermore, sooner of later, it will also be apparent that the objectives were achieved, or very nearly so. When this happens it's only a matter of time until you submit a budget, management cuts it; you resubmit, management recuts, you resubmit . . . and the game goes on and on. *You can't win it.*

Second thing to do is indicate an anticipated cash flow so that management knows approximately what to expect—that is, the timing of major expenditures. For instance, your production expense for producing ads will be heavy during the first quarter of the year, and probably completed in the first half. Merely knowing what to expect will make your controller happier and having his goodwill (or as good as you can expect to get) isn't to be regarded lightly. You don't have to tell exactly when each single last penny will be invoiced to the company, but give a good general idea of the *pattern* that's to be expected.

Finally, don't let every cat-and-dog expense in the company be foisted off on you. Stand up on your hind legs and fight against having miscellaneous charges against the advertising budget.

Don't let the company picnic, employee dances, labels and cartons, price lists, market research, the president's wife's flower gardens, sales meeting costs, salesmen's samples, the house organ, the annual report, nameplates, display signs, and so on and on be charged to advertising. This is a deceptive dodge that ultimately will cost the company dearly. Stop it before it becomes an entrenched practice—as it is in many companies today.

The Contingency Fund

One last thing you should budget for is the unexpected. Depending upon the size of your budget, approximately 2½ percent of the total should be earmarked "contingency fund."

The contingency fund makes available dollars to produce that unexpected piece of literature, that unexpected piece of research, that unexpected this or that. One thing you can predict with assurance is the unexpected. It always happens.

When you budget for it you're able to handle it without having to request a supplementary appropriation; always an undesirable thing to have to do.

Don't make the mistake, though, of "giving back" any unused portion of the contingency fund. The controller has no claim to it. Instead, plan ahead to use any unspent dollars where they will do the most good—a few extra pages for space ads for a product that's not moving as it should, an extra direct mail piece and mailing for an ailing product—anything constructive and productive.

ACKNOWLEDGEMENTS

(Continued from page 16)

Jim Hull, Sales Promotion, Magcobar, One of the Dresser Industries

Henry H. Hunter, Vice-President, Olin Mathieson Chemical Corporation

L. J. Iannuzzelli, Manager, Power Semiconductor Advertising, RCA Electronic Components and Devices, RCA, Inc.

Glenn F. Ihrig, President, Wellman Dynamics Corporation

James G. Johnson, Electrowriter Sales Manager, Victor Business Machines Group, Victor Comptometer Corporation

Laurence S. Johnson, Eva-Tone, Division of American Evatype Corporation

Richard C. Johnson, Advertising Director, H. B. Fuller Company

Edgar R. Jones, Publisher

Michael R. Kalbs, Advertising Manager, Brinkmann Instruments

C. G. Kennedy, Manager, Marketing Services, Clark Equipment Company

V. K. Kennedy, Vice-President, Sales, Omark-Winslow Aerospace Tool Company

Charles M. Kent, Advertising/Merchandising Manager, 3M Company

H. Keys, Unitron Instrument Company

James Kipps, Advertising and Sales Promotion Manager, Dura Business Machines, Division of Intercontinental Systems, Inc.

Leonard A. Kirsch, Director of Public Relations, Waldes Kohinoor, Inc.

Robert S. Knapp, Advertising Manager, Sperry Gyroscope Company

Miss Olga H. Knoepke, Argus Chemical Corporation

Walter P. Koval, Director, Advertising and Public Relations, Ametek, Inc.

R. Kral, Advertising Manager, Electric Motor Division, A. O. Smith Corporation

G. C. Kroening, Vice-President, Sales, Norplex Corporation

David A. Kurr, Director of Marketing, AMAX Aluminum Co., A Division of American Metal Climax, Inc.

Mrs. Joan R. Kurtz, Public Relations Department, Eastman Kodak Company

Bruce F. LaCentra, Director of Advertising, Friden, Inc., Division of The Singer Company

Floyd C. Lacy, Public Relations Supervisor, Dana Corporation

John W. Lambert, The Photography of H. Armstrong Roberts

Frank Linsenmeyer, Manager of Marketing Services, The Rotor Tool Company, A Division of Cooper Industries, Inc.

T. L. LaPin, Industrial Marketing Manager, Commercial Products, Kimberly-Clark Corporation

G. B. Leopard, Manager Corporate Communications, Brown Engineering, A Teledyne Company

Ralph Levine, Assistant Counsel, Carter-Wallace, Inc.

Leon Levitt, Manager, Advertising and Public Relations, Microdot Inc.

A. J. LIBERTY, Advertising Manager, American Optical Company

PAUL H. LOBIK, Advertising Manager, Coleman Instruments Corporation

M. L. LONG, Manager, Public Relations and Advertising, Air Products and Chemicals Inc.

ODIS A. LONG, Data Presentation Manager, Texas Instruments Incorporated

The Late THADDEUS J. LOPATKA, Vice-President, Diamond T Motor Truck Co.

NORMAN G. MACKINNON, Director of Advertising, Grumman Aircraft Engineering Corporation

DONALD G. MAIZE, Director, Advertising and Sales Promotion, Weyerhaeuser Company

DONALD R. MAKINS, Manager of Advertising, Austin-Western Division, Baldwin-Lima-Hamilton Corporation

PAUL MARCOTT, Advertising Manager, Bell Helicopter Company, A Textron Company

S. V. MARINO, Assistant Vice-President-Sales, Pinkerton's, Inc.

WILLIAM F. MAY, Chairman, American Can Company

LOWELL G. MCCLENNING, Marketing Services, Fairchild Semiconductor, A Division of Fairchild Camera and Instrument Corporation

WILLIAM E. MCKIE, Assistant Advertising Manager, Dennison Manufacturing Company

J. R. MCMENAMIN, Director of Advertising, Uniroyal, Inc.

GEORGE A. MENTZER, Manager, Advertising Services, The B. F. Goodrich Company

ELDREDGE MILLER, Advertising Manager, Johns-Manville

WALT MILLER, Advertising Director, Sloan Instrument Corporation

J. A. MOIR, Advertising & Sales Promotion, General Electric Company

ROBERT D. MOORE, Assistant Advertising Manager, American Air Filter Company, Inc.

CHARLES J. MOSS, Manager, Plastics Advertising, The Dow Chemical Company

WILLOUGHBY W. MOYER, Advertising Manager, Atlas Chemical Industries, Inc.

B. H. MUELLER, TRW Electro Insulation, TRW Inc.

JAMES H. MULLER, Sales Promotion Manager, Winchester Electronics Division, Litton Industries

DAVID L. NELSON, Marketing Manager, Micom Inc.

RAYMOND F. NEUZIL, Director of Corporate Communications, Szabo Food Service, Inc.

GAYNOR O'CORMAN, JR., Manager, Advertising Department, United Shoe Machinery Corporation

THOMAS A. O'GORMAN, Marketing Services Manager, Industrial Electronic Engineers, Inc.

R. F. OLSON, Director of Advertising, Rex Chainbelt, Inc.

WALTER J. O'NEILL, Advertising Manager, Standard Pressed Steel Company

RICHARD C. OSWANT, Advertising Manager, Chemical Division, PPG Industries, Inc.

JOHN E. OWENS, Assistant Advertising Manager, Lindberg Hevi-Duty, Division of Sola Basic Industries

FRED A. PAINE, Manager, Administration and Operations, A&SP—Marketing Services, Worthington Corporation

ROBERT M. PALMER, Vice-President—Marketing, Lindberg Hevi-Duty, Division of Sola Basic Industries

RICHARD R. PAPE, Manager, Nielsen Clearing House

R. S. PARKER, Advertising and Sales Promotion Manager, The Standard Register Company

A. K. PARRISH, Vice-President, Automotive Group of TRW Inc.

MISS DODE PENROD, Advertising Manager, The Flying Tiger Line Inc.

ROBERT C. PIERSON, Manager, Advertising and Sales Promotion, Fairchild-Davidson, A Division of Fairchild Camera and Instrument Corporation

ARNOLD I. PLANT, H. Klaff & Company

DICK POWELL, Hamlin, Inc.

MISS GEORGIA PRASSOS, Advertising and Sales Promotion, X-acto Precision Tools

W. S. PUNTON, Commercial Advertising Manager, Mobil Oil Corporation

F. J. RASKOPF, Director of Advertising, Collins Radio Company

R. J. REES, Divisional Advertising Supervisor, Wright Hoist Division, American Chain & Cable Company, Inc.

JOHN P. READING, Assistant Manager, Advertising and Sales Promotion, The Cincinnati Milling Machine Co.

W. A. REEDY, Senior Editor, Advertising Publications, Eastman Kodak Company

MISS ADRIANNE REICHEG, Alcan Sales Inc.

JAMES L. RICHARDSON, Director, Public Relations and Advertising, Combustion Engineering, Inc.

N. C. RICHARDSON, Advertising Manager, Waterbury Farrel, A Textron Company

G. M. ROBERTSON, Manager, Advertising Services and Measurement, General Electric Company

L. G. ROBLYER, Advertising Manager, Bendix Motor Components Division, The Bendix Corporation

RICHARD F. ROPER, Director, Public Relations and Advertising, Computer Sciences Corporation

A. M. RUNG, Director of Public Relations and Advertising, Chicago, Burlington & Quincy Railroad Company

GERALD J. RYAN, Senior Advertising Manager, Sylvania Electric Products, Inc.

W. J. ST. ONGE, JR., Advertising Manager, The Torrington Company

K. SAITOH, Executive Vice-President, Sharp Electronics Corporation

ROBERT A. SALAMONE, Director of Operations and Marketing, Dyna-Quip, A Division of Stile-Craft Manufacturers Inc.

RICHARD J. SANDRETTI, Public Relations Coordinator, Koehring Company

D. S. SAURMAN, Advertising Manager, Simonds Abrasive Company

H. K. SAXE, International Business Machines Corporation

FRED SCHAUB, Manager, Analytical Instruments Division, LKB Instruments, Inc.

CHAS. R. SHANK, Advertising Manager, T. B. Wood's Sons Company

E. M. SHANKS, Advertising Manager, Rust-Oleum Corporation

L. R. SHAULL, Manager—Public Relations, Airtemp Division, Chrysler Corp.

J. M. SHEEHAN, Director of Advertising and Public Relations, General American Transportation Corporation

R. R. SHEPHERD, Marketing Communications Manager, Westinghouse Electric Corporation

JOHN M. SHEVIAK, Director of Advertising, Parker-Hannifin Industrial Group

J. A. SHIELDS, Vice-President, Advertising, Shaw-Walker

SUKEHIRO SHIONOYA, OSG Tap and Die, Inc.

MORTON W. SIAS, Manager, Advertising and Public Relations, Brown Company

ROBERT SILVERT, Director of Customer Relations, Perrygraf Corporation

VIRGIL L. SIMPSON, Special Assistant, E. I. Du Pont de Nemours & Company Inc.

WILLIAM J. SIMS. Department Manager, Hog Chows Advertising and Sales Promotion, Ralston Purina Company

S. A. SKILNYK, Advertising Manager, Bourns Inc.

DONALD L. SMITH, Product Marketing Manager, Warner-Chilcott Laboratories Instruments Division

D. M. SMITH, Director, Advertising and Public Relations, Burroughs Corporation

ROBERT O. SNELLING, President, Snelling and Snelling

WILLIAM J. SPADA, Advertising Manager, Walter Kidde & Company, Inc.

JAMES D. SPIVEY, Vice-President—Marketing and Sales, True-Trace Corporation

S. G. SPRAGENS, Vice-President—Marketing, Pacific Plantronics, Inc.

ANTHONY STACHELCZYK, Sales Promotion Manager, The Echlin Manufacturing Company

J. WOOLSEY STANTON, President, Fancy Frozen Foods Company of Florida

LAWRENCE V. STAPLETON, Vice-President, Advertising & Sales Promotion, Trans World Airlines

J. E. STARBUCK, Director, Marketing Communications, Douglas Aircraft Company, Inc.

R. E. STAUFFER, JR., Advertising Manager, Grey-Rock, Division of Raybestos-Manhattan, Inc.

W. R. STERLING, Director of Advertising and Public Relations, Baker Division, Otis Elevator Company

NEIL P. STEWART, Divisional Manager, Advertising & Sales Promotion, Crown Zellerbach Corporation

PARKER STOUGH, Advertising/Sales Promotion Manager, I-T-E Circuit Breaker Company

DELISLE SUDDUTH, Sales Manager, Genisco Technology Corporation

BOB SUTPHEN, The Dick Sutphen Studio Inc.

DON TEER, Publications Advertising Coordinator, Hewlett-Packard

GEORGE E. TIBBALL, Advertising Coordinator, Princeton Applied Research Corp.

M. C. TOBIAS, General Advertising Manager, Reynolds Metals Company

JAMES E. TOBIN, Manager of Sales Promotion, Anaconda American Brass Co.

C. F. TOLL, General Manager, Advertising and Publicity, The Sherwin-Williams Company

ACKNOWLEDGEMENTS

B. S. TOOKER, Manager of Advertising, Fuller Transmission Division, Eaton Yale & Towne Inc.

WILLIAM C. TRACEY, Martin Marietta Corporation

C. S. TURPIN, Manager, Marketing Services, AVCO Bay State Abrasives

JUDD TUTTLE, Advertising Manager, American Monorail

JOHN W. TYHACZ, Advertising Manager, De Laval Separator Company

P. B. UTIGER, Advertising Manager, Sinclair Refining Company

WIM VAN DER GRAAF, Advertising Department, E. I. Du Pont de Nemours & Company

J. B. VANDERZEE, Advertising Manager, Autolite-Ford Parts Division, Ford Motor Company

THEODORE N. VOSS, Domestic Advertising Manager, Polaroid Corporation

L. G. WADDELL, Sales Manager, The Prime-Mover Company

ED WAHL, Gits Bros. Mfg. Co.

JOHN F. WALLACE, Manager, Machinery and Allied Industries, United States Steel Corporation

J. J. WARD, JR., Manager of Advertising, Pittsburgh Steel Company

S. D. WARREN COMPANY

HERBERT N. WASHBURN, Advertising and Sales Promotion Mgr., International Equipment Company

C. C. WEISS, The EIS Automotive Corporation

THOMAS R. WEISS, Manager, Advertising and Communications, Owens-Illinois

RICHARD D. WENTWORTH, Product Manager, Shooting Equipment, Inc.

BOB WHITE, Jennison-Wright Corporation

ROBERT M. WHITNEY, Director of Division Advertising, Eaton Yale & Towne

GEORGE WICKSTROM, Advertising Manager, Sealed Power Corporation

A. H. WIDOWIT, JR., Manager of Advertising, Universal Oil Products Company

R. N. WILKINSON, Advertising Manager, Caterpillar Tractor Co.

H. A. WILLIAMS, Vice-President and General Manager, Electronic Components Division, Stackpole Carbon Company

J. A. WILLIAMS, Manager, Advertising and Publicity, M&T Chemicals, Inc.

DOUGLAS WILLIAMSON, Advertising Manager, Handy & Harman

JOHN T. WILLOW, Manager, Advertising and Sales Promotion, Hammermill Paper Company

G. H. WILSON, Manager, Sales Promotion & Advertising, Federal Products Corporation

JAMES D. WOOD, Director, Press Relations and Advertising, Sperry Rand Corp.

ROBERT S. WOODBURY, Director, Public Relations, Mathatronics, A Division of Barry Wright Corporation

R. S. YATES, Advertising Assistant, The Timken Roller Bearing Company

ED YOTKA, Sales Manager, Compix, Commercial Photography Division of United Press International

JAMES L. YOUNG, Advertising Manager, Dempster Brothers Inc.

V. J. YUNKER, Assistant to the General Sales Manager, The Mechanex Corp.

NINON DE ZARA, Sales Promotion Manager, Amphenol RF Division

I'd like to thank the following advertising people—wonderful people, one and all—for their gracious help and encouragement in revising this book. Without them, I couldn't have done the job.

Dick Stansfield
Pueblo, Colorado
1976

THOMAS R. BRAMSON, President and Publisher, *Production*

HARRY B. DOYLE, JR., Advertising Sales, McGraw-Hill Publications, Denver

WILLIAM J. DWYER, Vice-President, Technical Publishing Company

HOWARD FISCHER, former Vice-President, Frye-Sills, Inc.

MYRA GISH, Secretary, CF&I Steel Corporation

BARBARA HANSON, Advertising and Sales Promotion Manager, Thomas Publishing Company

WAYNE JARVIS, General Manager, Kistler Graphics, Inc.

ELISABETH M. KITTREDGE, Secretary, Technical Publishing Company

RAYMOND D. LARSON, Vice-President, *MacRae's Blue Book*

THOMAS J. MCELHINNY, Regional Sales Manager, Buttenheim Publishing Corporation

WILLIAM H. NIMITZ, Advertising Department, E. I. Du Pont de Nemours, Inc.

JAMES T. QUILLINAN, President, Color Technique, Inc.

FRED STANLEY, Publisher, *Product Design & Development*

GENE WEYENETH, Publisher, *Engineering News-Record* and *Construction Methods & Equipment*

And my special thanks to two great guys who have done a lot for me, on this revision and over the years:

JACK KAY, Regional Vice-President, Chilton Company

WIM VAN DER GRAAF, Supervisor, Advertising Department, E. I. Du Pont de Nemours, Inc.

APPENDIX

GLOSSARY OF TERMS RELATING TO BUSINESS PUBLICATION AUDITS

Following is a glossary of terms relating to business publications auditing; it was developed by the Association of Industrial Advertisers and is used here with its permission.

ADDITIONS: New names, either of individuals or companies, added to a publication's mailing list.

ADVANCE RENEWAL: A subscription which has been renewed prior to the expiration of a previous subscription.

ADVERTISED PRICE: The basic price of publication. (See Basic Price.)

ARREARS: Subscribers whose names are retained on active subscription list after the period for which they are paid has expired.

ASSOCIATION SUBSCRIPTIONS:

a. Deductible association subscription.
   Individual subscription paid for out of association membership dues where the recipient has the option of deducting the subscription price from his dues if he does not wish to receive the publication.

b. Nondeductible association subscription.
   Individual subscription paid for out of association membership dues where the recipient does not have the option of deducting the subscription price from his dues and automatically receives the publication.

AUDIENCE: The total number of individuals exposed to any part of the content of a publication. Synonymous with total audience.

AUDIENCE, PASSALONG: Individuals, other than addressees, who are exposed to some part of the content of a publication.

AUDIENCE, PRIMARY: Individuals for whom a magazine is edited and who are exposed to some part of the content, and who receive it first in order of time.

AUDIENCE, TOTAL: See Audience.

AUDIT: Examination of publisher's records and corroborative data in order to check for correctness of the Publisher's Statements covering the period audited.

AUDIT REPORT: A document attesting to the accuracy and validity of a publisher's circulation claims, not to be confused with Publisher's Statement.

AVERAGE PAID: Average circulation, qualified as paid circulation, of all the issues, arrived at by dividing the total of all the paid copies during the period by the total number of issues.

BACK COPIES: Copies of periodicals of date prior to the current issue.

BASIC PRICE: The price at which a copy or a subscription may be purchased, as opposed to a special price.

BREAKDOWN: The division of circulation as to types of business or industry reached, the functions or titles of recipients, and/or their demographic characteristics or geographical location.

BULK SALES:

a. Definitions applicable to Audit Bureau of Circulations.

All copies or subscriptions purchased in quantities of five or more which promote the business or professional interests of the purchaser.

Single copy sales in bulk—sales of copies of a single issue of a publication in quantities of five or more to one purchaser.

Term Subscriptions in bulk—subscriptions for two or more consecutive issues of a publication sold in quantities of five or more to one purchaser.

b. Definitions applicable to Business Publication Audit of Circulation.

Two or more copies of a publication (whether or not individually wrapped or addressed) sent to a single addressee.

BUSINESS ANALYSIS: Breakdown of circulation by recipient's classification, by industry and/or occupation. (See Industry and Occupational Classification.)

BUSINESS PUBLICATION: A business publication is one dealing with management, manufacturing, sales or operation of industries or businesses, or some specific industry, occupation or profession, and which is published to interest and assist persons actively engaged in the field it covers.

CASH DISCOUNT: A discount not exceeding 5 percent of the basic subscription price, allowed to new or renewal subscribers of a publication.

CATEGORY: A category may refer to a division of recipients based on their industry or occupation. (See Industry and Occupational Classification.)

CENSUS: An enumeration of the individuals, or units, in a publication's universe.

CHECKING COPIES: Copies sent to advertisers and agencies for checking their advertisements. (Also see Promotion Copies and Sample Copies.)

CIRCULATION, BULK: See Bulk Sales.

CIRCULATION, CONTROLLED: A term used by the Canadian Circulation Audit Board and formerly used in the United States to describe the distribution of copies free of charge, but in accordance with a preconceived pattern of the recipients' eligibility. The Audit Bureau of Circulations does not use this term and the Business Publication Audit of Circulation has abandoned it for the term "Qualified Circulation." U.S. postal regulations define it as:

Copies of a publication circulated free or mainly free which contain at least 24 pages, contain at least 25 percent nonadvertising, issued four or more times a year and not owned or controlled by individuals or business concerns, and conducted as an auxiliary to and essentially for the advancement of the main business or calling of those who own or control them.

CIRCULATION, EFFECTIVE: That part of a publication's circulation received by individuals or establishments of interest to an advertiser.

CIRCULATION, FRANCHISE: That part of a publication's circulation which is obtained through contractual agreement with business firms who provide lists of their customers or prospective customers to whom copies of the publication are sent free of charge.

CIRCULATION, NONPAID: That circulation which meets the requirements of qualified circulation and which is distributed free of charge to the recipients in the field served.

CIRCULATION, PAID: Copies of publications which have been paid for by the purchasers, not for resale, and are distributed in the field served.

CIRCULATION, QUALIFIED: That circulation, paid or nonpaid, distributed to the field served, for which the mailing address, conformance to the field served, recipient qualification, and the correct business and/or occupational classifications are verified by auditable documentary evidence dated within 36 months. Qualified recipients must receive every issue of the publication, subject to normal removals and additions.

CIRCULATION, REQUEST:

a. Definition applicable to Audit Bureau of Circulations.

Number of recipients of a publication who do not pay for it, but receive copies upon request, when in the field served by the publication.

b. Definition applicable to Business Publication Audit of Circulation.

Number of recipients on a publication's circulation list who have completed a questionnaire specifically requesting receipt of the publication, or recipients who received a publication by virtue of their individually paid subscription.

CLASSIFICATION: See Breakdown.

CLUBS: Two or more subscriptions to the same publication obtained by solicitors, not part of publisher's organization, under plan of offering specific reward for sending in a specified number of subscriptions.

CLUB RAISER: Person who takes subscriptions in clubs. Differs from "group organizer" in that the club raiser may sell subscriptions at any price between the full basic price and 50 percent thereof. (See Group Organizer.)

COLLECTION STIMULANTS: Any inducement offered for prompt payment in excess of a 5 percent discount on subscriptions sold at the basic price subsequent to the receipt of a subscription order.

COMBINATION SALE: Subscriptions to two or more different publications sold at special combination price.

COMPARABILITY: The capability of a publication's circulation breakdowns to be compared with circulation breakdowns for other publications serving the same field.

COMPLIMENTARY COPIES: Free copies given as a courtesy.

CONTROLLED CIRCULATION: See Circulation, Controlled.

COPIES: See Checking, Promotion, Sample.

CORRESPONDENTS' COPIES: Copies of a publication given free to correspondents of the paper, reporters and editorial writers.

COVERAGE: The extent to which a publication is distributed to the individuals constituting the total universe whose interest it serves.

CREDIT SUBSCRIPTIONS: One upon which no payment is made at time of order.

DEDUCTIBLE FROM DUES: See Association Subscriptions-Deductible.

DEMOGRAPHIC EDITION: See Edition, Demographic.

DISTRIBUTION: The total number of copies distributed per issue, whether paid or nonpaid.

DISTRIBUTION, NONQUALIFIED: Those copies which fail to conform to the field served and definition of recipient qualification. Same as average other unpaid distribution.

DUPLICATE COVERAGE: The extent to which two or more competing publications are received by the same individuals.

EDITION: That portion of the total distribution of an issue of a periodical, which is unchanged, except for Replate or Split-Run. (Also see Replate and Split-Run.)

EDITION, DEMOGRAPHIC: That portion of a publication's circulation in which the editorial and/or advertising content is intended for recipients of a segment of the field served by the publication.

EDITION, GEOGRAPHIC: That portion of a publication's circulation in which the editorial and/or advertising content is intended for recipients in specific geographic areas.

EMPLOYEES' COPIES: Copies given free to employees of a publication.

ESTABLISHMENT: See Unit.

EXCHANGES: Free copies sent by a publication to other papers in mutual courtesy.

EXPIRATION: Termination of period for which subscription was paid.

EXPOSURE: The act of laying open. This occurs in a publication when one or more pages are seen by a recipient of the publication.

EXTENSION: Continuance by a publisher of a subscription beyond its original expiration date because of lowering of subscription price or reducing the frequency of issue.

FEATURE ISSUE SUBSCRIPTIONS: Subscriptions to periodic special feature issues only, such subscriptions being accepted at a price different from that made to those who subscribe for all issues of the year. Also known as "intermittent" subscriptions.

FIELD SERVED: The publisher's description of the market/markets or occupations to whose interest the publication's editorial content is directed.

FRANCHISE CIRCULATION: See Circulation, Franchise.

FREE PUBLICATION: Designating one which is distributed mainly free of charge to recipients in the field served.

FULFILLMENT: Procedures involved in delivering copies of publication to recipients.

FUNCTION: The type of work a recipient performs. It may or may not be the same as his title.

GEOGRAPHIC ANALYSIS: A breakdown of the publication's circulation, based on a single issue, by states, provinces, countries or other defined areas.

GEOGRAPHIC EDITION: See Edition, Geographic.

GIFT SUBSCRIPTION: Subscription paid for by other than the recipient or his employer. (Also see Bulk Sales.)

GROUP SUBSCRIPTION (MAIL SUBSCRIPTIONS SPECIAL): Subscriptions purchased in quantities of five or more, paid for by an employer for his employees and mailed by the publisher in bulk or to individual recipients.

GROUP ORGANIZER: A person who takes two or more subscriptions to the same publication from a group of individuals, collectively, and sends the order for all of the group at the same time, each member of the group thereby receiving a reduction from the regular subscription price.

INDUSTRY: A branch of business engaged in manufacturing or non-manufacturing activity.

INSTALLMENT SUBSCRIPTIONS: Subscriptions, collection of subscription price being made in installments within the subscription period.

INTERMITTENT SUBSCRIPTIONS: See Feature Issue Subscriptions.

LINEAR PROGRAMMING: A mathematical technique that optimizes a linear form subject to linear resraints, with the additional restraint that only non-negative results are permissible. It is used to allocate limited resources among alternative uses.

MAIL SUBSCRIPTIONS SPECIAL: See Group.

MONTHLY PAYMENT SUBSCRIPTIONS: Subscriptions for which the subscriber is not required to pay in advance for the whole term but in monthly installments within the subscription period.

NET PRESS RUN: Total of perfect copies printed suitable for distribution.

NEWSPAPER: For purposes of this glossary, a newspaper is defined as a publication with a tabloid format. See Business Publication.

NON-DEDUCTIBLE FROM DUES: See Association Subscriptions—Non-Deductible.

NONPAID DISTRIBUTION: See Circulation, Nonpaid.

NONPAID REQUEST: See Circulation, Request.

OCCUPATION: "One's occupation is that to which one's time is devoted or in which one is regularly or habitually engaged"—Webster's New International Dictionary. The name of one's occupation may be derived from the type of business in which the individual is engaged, as food processing or mining, or may describe the type of work he does, division, as design engineer or purchasing.

OCCUPATIONAL CLASSIFICATION: Division of recipients into groups according to their business or professional calling or according to the position they occupy in a business organization.

OFFICIAL ORGAN: A periodical which is owned by an association organized for other purposes than to publish the perodical or which is appointed as the official organ of an association in return for special privileges granted the association.

PAID CIRCULATION: See Circulation, Paid.

PAID PUBLICATION: Designating one which is distributed mainly to recipients who pay for their subscriptions.

PAID SUBSCRIBER: Purchaser of publication on a term contract, whose subscription qualifies as paid circulation in accordance with established rules.

Paid Subscription: A subscription paid in accordance with rules defining a paid subscriber. (Also see Subscription.)

Passalong Audience: See Audience, Passalong.

Penetration: The extent to which a publication's reach relates to the total of individuals and/or units in the field served.

Periodical: Publication of regular periodic issues, except newspapers.

Plant: An establishment engaged in producing or selling a product or service at a single location.

Premium: An inducement offered to a subscriber either free or at a price, with his own subscription.

Primary Audience: See Audience, Primary.

Promotion Copies: Copies sent to prospective advertisers and their agencies. (Also see Checking Copies and Sample Copies.)

Publication: See Periodical.

Publisher's Interim Statement: Certified circulation and distribution statement of publisher, made at the publisher's option for a period other than that of a regular six months' Publisher's Statement and issue unaudited, but subject to audit. Not applicable to BPA.

Publisher's Statement: Certified statement of circulation and distribution data six-months' period, made by a publisher and issued unaudited, but subject to audit.

Publisher's Statement, Sworn: A statement of a publication's circulation and distribution, sworn to by the publisher, whose publication is not affiliated with an audit bureau.

Qualified Circulation: See Circulation, Qualified.

Reach: The number of different individuals to whom a medium does (actual) or can (potential) expose an advertising message.

Reader: An individual who looks into the content of a publication.

Readership: A measure of the number of readers of a publication. This may be expressed in percentages representing various levels of reading, or it may be expressed in letter grades of A, B, C and so on.

Recipient: An individual or company to whom a publication is addressed, and whose existence as a recipient is reported in the Publisher's Statement and Audit Report.

Recipient Qualification: Verifiable evidence that the recipient of a publication is active in the field served by the publication.

Recipient, Qualified: Individuals who receive a publication and who conform to the recipient qualification requirements within the field served.

Reference Media: Books or publications of periodic issue giving statistical data and designed to be kept for reference.

Reliability: In sampling, the degree of stability any measure found within the sample is likely to have in the universe from which the sample was drawn.

Measures of reliability (the measures of the stability of the data) are used in market research to determine the point at which a sample is of adequate size to assure that a larger sample under the same procedures would not affect appreciably any values.

REMOVALS: Names of individuals or companies removed from the mailing list of a publication.

RENEWAL: A subscription which has been renewed prior to or at expiration or within six months thereafter.

RENEWAL PERCENTAGE: The ratio of subscription renewals to the total subscriptions possible of being renewed, during a specified period of time.

REPLATE: A change of one or more pages during the printing of an edition or issue of a newspaper or periodical. This procedure generally serves the purpose of adding late news items or of correcting an error in the original copy.

REPORT, AUDIT: See Audit Report.

REQUEST CIRCULATION: See Circulation, Request.

SAMPLE COPIES: Copies distributed free to prospective subscribers or prospective advertisers and copies distributed at shows, conventions or by publishers' salesmen for prospects.

SHORT TERM SUBSCRIPTION: Subscription for less than a year.

SINGLE COPY SALES IN BULK: See Bulk Sales.

SPLIT-RUN: The insertion or substitution of different advertising content for a portion of the distribution of an edition or of an issue for either a newspaper or periodical.

SPONSORED SUBSCRIPTIONS: Subscriptions obtained through cooperation between publisher and an organized local civic or charitable organization, members of schools, churches, fraternal or similar organizations, publisher donating a percentage of the subscription price to the organization involved.

STANDARD INDUSTRIAL CLASSIFICATION: A numerical coding system developed by the Bureau of the Budget used in the classification of business establishments according to the principal end-product made or service performed at that location.

STANDARDIZATION: A system for classifying recipients in terms of business or title or function that is uniform for all publications serving the same general field.

SUBSCRIBER: An individual, firm or corporation that orders and pays for a subscription to a publication. (See Subscription)

SUBSCRIPTION: Contractual agreement by an individual or firm to purchase one or more copies of a publication for a given period which conforms to established rules.

SUBSCRIPTION AGENCY: An individual, firm or corporation obtaining subscriptions for two or more publications. Subscriptions (except those resulting from a direct mail effort) produced for one publisher by another publisher are classed in Audit Bureau reports along with those obtained through agencies.

SUBSCRIPTIONS:
Association—See Association Subscriptions.
Bulk—See Bulk Sales.
Credit—See Credit Subscriptions.
Feature Issue—See Feature Issue Subscriptions.
Franchise—See Circulation, Franchise.
Gift—See Gift Subscriptions.
Group—See Group (Mail Subscriptions Special).
Installment—See Installment Subscriptions.
Intermittent—See Feature Issue Subscriptions.
Mail Subscriptions Special—See Group (Mail Subscriptions Special).
Monthly Payment—See Monthly Payment Subscriptions.
Paid—See Paid Subscriptions.
Short Term—See Short Term Subscription.
Sponsored—See Sponsored Subscriptions.
Term Bulk—See Bulk Sales.
Trial—See Short Term Subscriptions.

SUBSCRIPTION SALESMAN: One who, as a regular or temporary or part-time vocation, solicits subscriptions for publication. He may receive his compensation on either salary or commission basis or both.

SUBSCRIPTION SALESMAN'S COPIES: Copies of a publication carried by a subscription salesman to aid him in obtaining subscriptions. (See Sample Copies.)

TERM SUBSCRIPTIONS IN BULK: See Bulk Sales.

TITLE: An appellation given by a firm to certain of its personnel by virtue of their rank or function.

TOTAL AUDIENCE: See Audience.

TOTAL PAID: Total of all classes of a publication's distribution for which the purchasers have paid in accordance with the standards set by the rules.

TRAFFIC, READER: A measure of the number of readers who look at or are exposed to the different pages of an issue of a publication. Usually expressed as number of readers per page.

TRIAL SUBSCRIPTIONS: See Short Term Subscriptions.

TWO-PAY PLAN: Designation of sales plan under which the subscription solicitor collects from the subscriber a portion of the subscription price and the publisher or the subscription agency receives the balance direct from the subscriber. Some publishers refuse to start service until second payment is received.

UNIT: An establishment primarily engaged in one type of economic activity at a single physical location.

UNIT COUNT: The number of units included in a publication's circulation.

UNIVERSE: The total units or individuals under consideration.

UNPAID COPIES: Copies distributed either entirely free or at a price inadequate to qualify them as paid in accordance with established rules.

VALIDATE: To testify, as one in a position to know, to the truthfulness or reliability of evidence.

VERIFY: To prove to be true; to establish the correspondence between evidence and actual fact.

VOCATIONAL CLASSIFICATION: See Occupational Classification.

WASTE: That part of a publication's distribution considered to be valueless to the individual advertiser because of the absence of any relevance between the advertiser's proposition and the recipient's business interest.

Seven Deadly Sins

In his handbook on direct mail, Richard S. Hodgson quoted from the "Copy Chasers" who write a monthly column in *Industrial Marketing* magazine. The Copy Chasers' comments on the seven deadliest sins committed by industrial advertisers augment the cardinal rules and provide a checklist against which to measure a direct mail program. Sins are:

1. *The sin of being a braggart.* A lot of industrial advertising is like the blowhard—the man who interminably insists that he is better than the next guy. Claiming superiority, in itself, is not necessarily wrong—unless little or nothing is done to substantiate the claim in a friendly, persuasive, and convincing manner.

2. *The sin of talking to yourself*—instead of thinking of the other fellow. The most creative industrial advertising is that which directs its remarks to the interests of the readers—not to the interests of the company doing the talking.

3. *The sin of preaching.* Faced with white paper to fill, some advertisers get a compulsion to lecture. Looking down upon the reader from the high altitude of their superiority, they *tell* the reader—rather than *invite* him—to do what they want him to do.

4. *The sin of being noisy.* Everybody hates the bugler, but a good many advertisers believe they have to make a big noise in order to get readers to stand at attention. If you have something interesting to say about a subject of interest to readers, there is no need to set your hair on fire in order to catch their eye.

5. *The sin of being messy.* Nobody likes the man who is messy, dirty, or inconsiderate. A lot of advertising, unfortunately, can be so described.

6. *The sin of trying to be cute.* Don't be a smart-aleck in industrial advertising. Deliver your story in as straightforward a manner as possible—and you'll get more applause from your audience than if you put on an act.

7. *The sin of being dull.* Of all the deadly sins of industrial advertising, the worst by far is being dull. Almost all an advertising man is expected to do is to enliven the sales message with a crisp presentation of visual elements and some fast-moving copy.

How Industrial Direct Mail Should Be Used

Guidelines used and accepted by almost every successful practitioner of industrial direct mail advertising have been established by the Direct Mail/Marketing Association.

These guidelines have been proved effective, efficient, and well thought out through the years. Numerous organizations have organized numerous committees to consider and reconsider the subject of direct mail advertising, and to date none of them have either expanded or changed this comprehensive checklist.

DMMA has suggested that it be used to analyze direct mail programs in three main areas:

I. Checking the ways you are now using direct mail.

II. Marking the ways you are not now using direct mail but which could be profitable possibilities.

III. Double checking those direct mail applications you are now using that could be altered, improved, or increased—for greater results, effectiveness, and efficiency.

IN YOUR OWN ORGANIZATION:

1. *Building Morale of Employees*—A bulletin or house magazine published regularly, carrying announcements of company policy, stimulating ambition, encouraging thrift, promoting safety and efficiency, will make for greater loyalty among employees.

2. *Securing Data from Employees*—Letters or questionnaires occasionally directed to employees help cement a common interest in the organization and bring back practical ideas and much useful data.

3. *Stimulating Salesmen to Greater Efforts*—Interesting sales magazines, bulletins, or letters help in unifying a scattered selling organization, in speeding up sales, and in making better salesmen—by carrying success stories and sound ideas that have made sales.

4. *Paving the Way for Salesmen*—Forceful and intelligent direct mail, persistent and continuous, will create a field of prospective buyers who are live and ready to be sold.

5. *Securing Inquiries for Salesmen*—Direct mail can bring back actual inquiries from interested prospective customers—qualified prospects your salesmen can call upon and sell.

6. *Teaching Salesmen "How to Sell"*—A sales manual, or a series of messages, will help educate and stimulate salesmen to close more and bigger sales.

7. *Selling Stockholders and Others Interested in Your Company*—Enclosures with dividend checks and in pay envelopes, and other direct messages, will sell stockholders and employees on making a greater use of company products and services, and in suggesting their use to others.

8. *Keeping Contact with Customers Between Salesmen's Calls*—Messages to customers between salesmen's calls will help secure for your firm the maximum amount of business from each customer.

9. *Further Selling Prospective Customers After a Demonstration or Salesman's Call*—Direct mail emphasizing the superiorities of your product or service will help clinch sales and make it difficult for competition to gain a foothold.

10. *Acknowledging Orders or Payments*—An interesting letter, folder, or mailing card is a simple gesture which will cement a closer relationship between you and your customers.

11. *Welcoming New Customers*—A letter welcoming new customers can go a long way toward keeping them sold on your company, products and services.

12. *Collecting Accounts*—A series of diplomatic collection letters will bring and keep accounts up to date, leave the recipients in a friendly frame of mind, and hold them as customers.

BUILDING NEW BUSINESS

13. *Securing New Dealers*—Direct mail offers many concerns unlimited possibilities in lining up and selling new dealers.

14. *Securing Direct Orders*—Many organizations have built extremely profitable business through orders secured only with the help of direct mail. Many concerns not presently selling direct by mail can and should do so.

15. *Building Weak Territories*—Direct mail will provide intensified local sales stimulation wherever you may wish to apply it.

16. *Winning Back Inactive Customers*—A series of direct mail messages to "lost" customers often revives many of them.

17. *Developing Sales in Territories Not Covered By Salesmen*—Communities unapproachable because of distance(bad transportation schedules, or poor roads, offer the alert organization vast possibilities to increase its sales direct-by-mail.

18. *Developing Sales Among Specified Groups*—With direct mail you can direct your selling messages specifically to those you wish to sell, in the language they will understand, and in a form that will stimulate action.

19. *Following Inquiries Received from Direct Advertising or Other Forms of Advertising*—A series of messages outlining the "reasons why" your product or service should be bought will help you cash in on inquirers whose initial interest was aroused by other media—publications, radio, television, and so on.

20. *Driving Home Sales Arguments*—Several mailings, each planned to stress one or more selling points, will progressively educate your prospective customer on the many reasons why he should buy your product or service—and from you.

21. *Selling Other Items in Line*—Mailing pieces, package inserts, or handout folders will educate your customers on products and services other than those they are buying.

22. *Getting Product Prescribed or Specified*—Professional men, such as physicians and dentists, will prescribe a product for their patients if they are correctly educated on its merits and what it will accomplish. Likewise, consumers and dealers will ask for a product by name if they are thoroughly familiar with it. Direct advertising can be profitably used for this purpose.

23. *Selling New Type of Buyer*—Perhaps there are new outlets through which your product or service might be sold. Direct mail is a powerful tool in the development of new sales channels.

ASSISTING PRESENT DEALERS

24. *Bringing Buyer to Showroom*—Invitations through letter or printed announcements will bring prospective customers to your showroom or factory.

25. *Helping Present Dealer Sell More*—Assisting your dealer with direct mail and "point of purchase" helps will sell your product or service faster, step up turnover. The right kind of dealer helps will win his hearty cooperation.

26. *Merchandising Your Plans to Dealer*—Direct mail can forcefully present and explain your merchandising plans to the dealer, and show him how to put your promotion ideas and material to work as sales-builders.

27. *Educating Dealers on Superiorities of Your Product or Service*—Memories are short when it comes to remembering the other fellow's product or service and its superiorities, especially when you keep telling your dealers the benefits and advantages of your own.

28. *Educating Retail Clerks in the Selling of a Product*—Clerks are the neck of the retail selling bottle. If they believe in a company and a product, their influence is a powerful aid to sales. If indifferent, they lose their sales-making effectiveness. Direct mail that is friendly, understanding, helpful, and stimulating will enlist their cooperation and up the sales curve.

29. *Securing Information from Dealers or Dealer's Clerks*—Letters, printed messages, a bulletin, or a house magazine will bring back helpful data from the individuals who actually sell your product or your service—information you can pass along to other dealers or sales clerks to help them sell more.

30. *Referring Inquiries from Consumer Advertising to Local Dealers*—The manufacturer can use direct mail to refer an inquirer to his local dealer for prompt attention. At the same time, the dealer can be alerted with the details of the prospect's inquiry.

THE CONSUMER

31. *Creating a Need or a Demand for a Product*—Direct mail, consistently used, will stimulate the demand for your product or service, and will remind the customer to ask for it by name.

32. *Increasing Consumption of a Product Among Present Users*—Package inserts, booklets, etc. can be used to educate customers to the full use of the products they buy, especially new benefits and advantages.

33. *Bringing Customers into a Store to Buy*—This applies to retailers; personal, friendly, cordial, and interesting direct mail messages, telling about the merchandise, will bring back past customers, stimulate present patrons, and lure new people to you.

34. *Opening New Charge Accounts*—This also applies to retailers. There are many people in every community who pay their bills promptly and do the bulk of their buying where they have accounts. A careful compilation of such a list and a well-planned direct mail program inviting them to open charge accounts will bring new customers to your store.

35. *Capitalizing on Special Events*—Direct mail helps retailers to capitalize on such events as marriages, births, graduations, promotions, etc. Likewise, letters can be sent to select lists featuring private sales. Other lists and format can cover general sales.

OTHER USES

36. *Building Goodwill*—The possibilities of building goodwill and solidifying friendships through direct advertisng are unlmited. It's the little handshake through the mail that cements business relationships and holds your customers. Certain "reminder" forms also can help build goodwill.

37. *Capitalizing on Other Advertising*—Direct advertising is the salesmate of all other media. As the workhorse among advertising and promotion mediums, it helps the sponsor capitalize on his investment in all visual and audio advertising—especially when initial interest can be given a lift and converted into action and sales.

38. *As a "Leader" or "Hook" in Other Forms of Advertising*—Publication space, as well as radio and television commercials, is often too limited to tell enough of the story about a product or service to make a sale. Direct mail provides the leader or hook—in the form of booklets, folders, catalogs, instruction manuals—that other mediums of advertising can feature, to stimulate action as well as to satisfy the inquirer with full story of product or service.

39. *Breaking Down Resistance to a Product or Service*—Direct mail helps to overcome resistance in the minds of prospective customers.

40. *Stimulating Interest in Forthcoming Events*—A special "week" or "day" devoted to the greater use of a product; an anniversary, a new line launched by a dealer, special "openings," and scores of other happenings can all be promoted by direct mail to produce sales.

41. *Distribution of Samples*—There are thousands of logical prospects who could be converted into users of your product if you proved to them its merits. Direct mail can help you do this by letting prospects convince themselves by actual test . . . provided your product lends itself to sampling by mail.

42. *Announcing a New Product, New Policy, or New Addition*—There is no quicker way to make announcements to specific individuals or groups, to create interest and stimulate sales, than through the personal, action-producing medium —direct mail.

43. *Announcing a New Address or Change in Telephone Number*—When these important changes are made, a letter or printed announcement sent through the mail has a personal appeal that will register your message better than any other form of advertising.

44. *Keeping a Concern or Product "In Mind"*—Direct advertising includes many forms of "reminder" advertising—blotters, calendars, novelties. Regular mailings help keep you in the minds of customers and prospects.

45. *Research for New Ideas and Suggestions*—Direct advertising is a powerful force in building sales. Direct mail can be used to find market facts, cut sales fumbling, chart direct, profitable trails to sales. It furnishes all the important tools for sales research, to discover what, where, how, and to whom to sell—and at what price.

46. *Correcting Present Mailing Lists*—Householders have an average annual change rate of 22 percent; merchants of 23 percent; agents of 29 percent; advertising men of 37 percent. Keeping a mailing list up to date is a most important detail. Direct mail can be employed to keep your list accurate by asking your customer occasionally if his name and address is correct, or if there are others in his organization you should be reaching.

47. *Securing Names for Lists*—Direct mail can help you build mailing lists by securing names of customers and prospects from many sources—such as direct from distributors, salesmen, clerks, stockholders, employees; from people who have access to the names of individuals in specific groups; from recommendation of customers and friends; from special mail surveys, questionnaires, etc.

48. *Protecting Patients or Special Processes*—Shouting forth the ownership of such patents or processes by direct advertising can leave no question in the minds of your customers, present or prospective, as to who owns such a product or process. At the same time, it gives you greater protection from possible infringers.

49. *Raising Funds*—Direct advertising can afford an effective, economical method of raising funds for worthy causes.

Mail-Oriented Agencies

Here are some of the leading specialists in the country in the direct mail medium, and they are the creators of exceptionally fine campaigns—both consumer and industrial.

Shell Alpert Associates, Inc., 455 Mountainview Ave., Orange, N. J. 07050 — (212) 867-8978

Altheimer & Baer, Inc., 404 North Wells St., Chicago, Ill. 60610 — (312) 944-2100

American Mail Advertising Inc., 600 Winter St., Waltham, Mass. 02154 — (617) 899-2870

Ansa-Letter, 200 Hudson St., New York City 10013 — (212) 966-4500

Arau Associates, Inc., 15 East 48 St., New York City 10017 — (212) 421-6530

Leo P. Bott, Jr., Advertising, 64 East Jackson Blvd., Chicago, Ill. 60604 — (312) 427-9187

Buckley-Dement DM Advertising, 555 West Jackson Blvd., Chicago, Ill. 60606 — (312) 427-3862

Cabot-Letter, 411 South Sangamon St., Chicago, Ill. 60607 — (312) 666-9878
In New York City, Dial 211, ask for — Enterprise 6530

Lawrence G. Chait & Co., Inc., 641 Lexington Ave., New York City 10022 — (212) 751-7220

Computer Profile Marketing, Inc., 135 West 50th St., New York City 10020 — (212) 757-3313

Lional Day, 84 East Main St., Patchogue, N. Y. 11772 — (516) 475-4113

Dickie Raymond—A Metromedia Company, Columbia Park, Boston, Mass. 02101	(617) 288-1234
485 Lexington Ave., New York City 10017	(212) 682-9100
1 East Wacker Drive, Chicago, Ill. 60601	(312) 467-4367
3636 South Bronson Ave., Los Angeles, Calif. 90018	(213) 295-5545
DM Corp. of America, 703 North 16th St., St. Louis, Mo. 63103	(314) 436-1122
Franklin & Joseph, Inc., 641 Lexington Ave., New York City 10022	(212) 751-3151
Graphic Service, 846 South Main St., Dayton, Ohio 45402	(513) 222-8317
James Gray, Hoover Nahm Inc., 636-11 Ave., New York City 10036	(212) 765-4000
Idea Planning Associates, 1180 Ave. of Amer., New York City 10036	(212) 582-6447
Cliff Kelley, Inc., 1007 Washington Ave., St. Louis, Mo. 63101	(314) 231-6750
Nat Lazar, 1 Jane Street, New York City 10014	(212) 729-7068
Mail and Media Inc., 404 Park Ave. South, New York City 10016	(212) 685-4515
McVicker & Higginbotham, Inc., 76 Atlantic Ave., Brooklyn, N. Y. 11201	(212) 522-2940
R. L. Polk & Co., 431 Howard St., Detroit, Mich. 48231	(313) 961-9470
Radstone Adv. Publ., 6340 Coldwater, North Hollywood, Calif. 91606	(213) 769-1090
Reply-O-Letter: 1860 Broadway, New York City 10023	(212) 245-8118
664 North Mich. Ave., Chicago, Ill. 60611	(312) 642-2858
10 Post Office Square, Boston, Mass. 02109	(617) 426-1555
P.O.B. 4514, Cleveland, Ohio 44124	(216) 381-7733
818 The Queensway, Toronto, Canada	(416) 251-1521
93 Alfred St., Brisbane Valley, Australia	5-2151
26/32 Clifton, London E.C.2, England	BI-4377
Sales Letters, Inc., 153 West 23 St., New York City 10011	(212) 929-2680
Smith & Hemmings, 2000 Pasadena, Los Angeles, Calif. 90031	(213) 223-3241
The Smith Company, 47 Fremont St., San Francisco, Calif. 94105	(415) 781-6564
William Steiner Associates, Inc., 65 West 55 St., New York City 10022	(212) 688-7030

Sales Problems

According to Jim Smiley, vice-president of Graphic Service, sales problems are very much like construction problems. They fit into certain well-defined groups. These groups, he explains, are as different as sawing wood and pounding nails.

Once they're analyzed and understood, however, and the right kind of program for each is developed, the direct mail advertiser is well on the road to success. The 15 classes of programs Graphic has defined are:

1. *Assistant Salesman Program.* If you can identify your customers and prospects by name, but feel that your salesmen can't call on every prospect often enough—or if you need to increase the salesmen's effectiveness—this is the program you need.

2. *Favorable Opinion Program.* If your salesmen find it difficult to get prospects to be "open minded" toward your company or product—or if you want your prospects to say to themselves, "That's the kind of company I'd like to do business with . . ."—This fills the bill.

3. *Prospect Qualifying Program.* If you want prospects to identify themselves as warm (or hot) prospects for your particular product—or if you want to get leads for followup phone or personal calls—or if you want to supply leads to your distributors or dealers or retailers—this is the ticket.

4. *List Building Program:* If you'd like to promote your better prospects by mail, but have only a general idea of who they are, you need this program.

5. *Door Opener Program.* If you know who your best prospects are but your salesmen, branches, distributors or dealers have a difficult time getting in to see them (either because they are protected executives; are blocked behind a purchasing agent you can't "go around"; or are impatient when your man calls with "nothing new")—or if you want to make it easy for your salesmen to call on new prospects—this is for you.

6. *New Product Program.* If you have a new product to introduce to new markets, or a real change in your product to promote, or other real news to get to your prospects—or if you are moving your current products into new markets—this is the one to do the job.

7. *Traffic Builder Program.* If you have a retail store, or if you are a manufacturer or distributor with a relatively "big ticket" product, sold through retail stores—or if you are showing your product at an important show and want people to come to you—choose this program.

8. *Account Reactivator Program.* If sales to some distributors or dealers have fallen off sharply or stopped altogether, or if you have lost customers and know their names and addresses—or if charge account customers have stopped buying from you—you need this.

9. *Fact Finder Program.* If you want to know what your customers think of your product; what your distributors think of you; how your product is being used; why people have stopped buying; whether they'll buy the new product

you're thinking about; or any other kind of research or survey dealing with facts or opinions, go this route.

10. *"Pure Advertising" Program.* If you want to educate your prospects and customers about the benefits your product has to offer; or if you want them to be sure to think of you when they are ready to buy or to ask for bids—or if you want to make a strong company or brand impression—take this tack.

11. *"Salesman Stimulator" Program.* If you want your salesmen to work harder; or if you want your distributor, wholesaler, or retailer's salesmen to mention, demonstrate or sell your product more effectively—or if you want more dealers signed up, or want service men to sell your product—you need this program.

12. *"Sampling" Program.* If you have a product that "sells itself" to most users once they try it, and it's the kind of a product that can be sampled, or tried out, this program is tailor made.

13. *Mail Order Program.* If you want to open and stock retail outlets entirely by mail; or get industrial buyers to order direct from the factory; or cover those "open" territories where your distributors are weak or nonexistent—or get ultimate users to send in orders by mail—this program is made to order.

14. *Subscription Program.* If you're selling subscriptions to magazines, or plays, or book clubs, or records or anything else that goes on and on—this is a producer.

15. *Fund Raising Program.* If you are interested in an organization that depends on gifts, or on "memberships," for support, go this way to go over the top.

Each of these problems has a "best" kind of direct mail answer, and the techniques that work for one problem may fail on another. That's one reason why direct mail is so difficult for most people. They often "adapt" successful campaigns which look great and worked fine for somebody else, but don't fit their problems—hence don't do the job.

The analytical and creative thinking at Graphic Service is the product of more than a quarter-century of direct mail experience. Specialty of the house in the organization is ferreting out the problem, determining what it *really* is—sometimes the manufacturer or other client doesn't actually understand it, so an outside viewpoint is mandatory—and then developing the one best direct mail program to solve it. This Graphic Service does exceedingly well from its headquarters at 846 South Main Street, Dayton, Ohio 45402.

List Brokers

Following is a list of active mailing list brokers. Almost every conceivable list for both consumer and industrial direct mail advertising may be rented through these brokers, or your list may be offered through them.

Just as you don't necessarily buy your new automobile from the first dealer to whom you talk, neither should you leap at the first offer from the first broker you talk with. Time spent on writing a few letters, explaining in detail just what it is you need (or offer), on phone calls, or in personal visits, is well invested.

You'll find these brokers are knowledgeable professionals who are anxious to do business with you—and to help you.

Accredited Mlg. Lists, Inc., 15 East 40 St., New York City 10016	(212) 683-1356
Washington Office: 1875 Connecticut Ave., N.W. 20009	(202) 232-1177
Addresses Unlimited, 14744 Oxnard St., Van Nuys, Calif. 91401	(213) 873-4114
Allison Mlg. Lists Corp., 329 Park Ave. South, New York City 10010	(212) 254-8650
George Bryant & Staff, 71 Grand Ave., Englewood, N. J. 07631	(201) 567-3200
Richard Buehrer Associates (Natwick), 339 West 51, New York City 10019	(212) 246-2662
Catholic Lists, Inc., 381 Park Ave., South, New York City 10016	(212) 684-2908
The Coolidge Co., Inc., 11 West 42 St., New York City 10036	(212) 695-2010
Dependable Mlg. Lists, Inc., 381 Park Ave., South, New York City 10016	(212) 679-7160
Alan Drey Co., Inc., 333 North Michigan Ave., Chicago, Ill. 60601	(312) 346-7453
Walter Drey, Inc., 257 Park Ave., South, New York City 10016	(212) 674-7061
Sanford Evans Serv. Ltd., 501 Yonge St., Toronto 5, Ontario	924-3755
Guild Co., 160 Engle St., Englewood, N. J. 07631 N. Y.	(212) 279-0461
Leonard G. Holland Associates, Inc., Woodmere, N. Y. 11590	(516) 374-1624
Walter Karl, Inc., Armonk, N. Y. 10504	(212) 324-3336
Lewis Kleid, Inc., 230 Park Ave., New York City 10017	(212) 689-8711
Kogos, Inc., P.O. Box 814, Webster, Mass. 01571	(203) 935-5030
E. J. Krane, 640 North Broad St., Philadelphia, Pa. 19130	(215) 236-4141
C. Levine Screened Mailing Lists, 250 West 57, New York City 10019	(212) 586-2086
Willa Maddern, Inc., 215 Park Ave., South, New York City 10003	(212) 777-7460
Mail Dynamics, Inc., 11 West 42 St., New York City 10036	(212) 524-9930
Mosely MO List Serv., 38 Newbury, Boston, Mass. 02116	(617) 266-3380
Names in the News, Inc., 45 West 18 St., New York City 10011	(212) 242-1050

Names Unlimited, Inc., 352 Park Ave., South, New York City 10010 (212) 686-2454

People in Places, Inc., P.O. Box 1001, Morristown, N. J. 07960 (212) 477-3774

Peterson & Associates, Inc., 1925 Old York Rd., Abington, Pa. 19001 (215) 659-1191

Planned Circulation, 355 Route 46, Mountain Lakes, N. J. 07046 (212) 687-4158

Publishers Mailing Lists, 60 South Main St., New City, N. Y. 10956 (914) 634-8724

Reliable Mailing Lists, P.O. Box 7457, North Kansas City, Mo. 64116

RF List Rentals, Inc., 641 Lexington Ave., New York City 10022 (212) 751-3151

Russell Rose Associates, 339 West 51 St., New York City 10019 (212) 586-5739

Roskam Co., 800 West 47 St., Kansas City, Mo. 64112 (816) 561-2772

"Hank" Ruby & Co., Inc., 339 West 51 St., New York City 10019 (212) 586-5315

Wm. Stroh Inc., 568-54 St., West New York, N. J. 07093 (201) 864-4800

James E. True Associates, Inc., 830 Northern Blvd., Great Neck, N. Y. 11021 (516) 466-3222

Florence Wolf Inc., 211 East Chicago Ave., Chicago, Ill. 60611 (312) 944-4150

For the fun of it, here's a little question-and-answer session on readership; you'll probably find it's fun. It is reprinted with permission from the July 4, 1966 issue of *Advertising Age.* Copyright 1966 by Advertising Publications, Inc.

QUESTIONS

(Answers on page 1474)

1. Readership studies are a measure of how well an ad communicates its selling message.
☐ True ☐ False

2. Readership of magazine ads is substantially lower among non-users of a brand than users.
☐ True ☐ False

3. Half-page horizontal ads are not as effective as half-page vertical insertions.
☐ True ☐ False

4. Men tend to give more attention to pictures of men than they do to pictures of women.
☐ True ☐ False

5. Drawings generally achieve a higher noted score than photographs.
☐ True ☐ False

6. Multi-page ads attract correspondingly more readers than one-page or two-page ads.
☐ True ☐ False

7. In a weekly magazine, about one-quarter of all inquiries produced by an ad are received during the first week after the ad appears.
☐ True ☐ False

8. Generally, ads picturing the planning process or pre-trip activities are among the most successful travel ads.
☐ True ☐ False

9. Although the costs of reaching a reader have substantially increased in recent years, the increase has not outrun other business costs.
☐ True ☐ False

10. Food ads with recipes are usually better read than food ads without recipes.
☐ True ☐ **False**

11. It makes no difference in testimonial advertising whether the testimonial is by a celebrity or not.
☐ True ☐ False

12. Readership scores for half-page full-color ads are about 85 percent higher than for half-page black-and-white insertions.
☐ True ☐ False

13. One of the best ways to get maximum readership for a steamship line is to show lots of water.
☐ True ☐ False

14. Interests of farm magazine readers follow the same pattern as general consumer magazine readers.
☐ True ☐ False

15. The easier an advertiser makes it for a reader to send in an inquiry card, the more likely the reader will study the ad.
☐ True ☐ False

16. Single-column quarter-page ads have a distinct advantage over square-shaped quarter-pages.
☐ True ☐ False

17. Readership scores of half-page advertisements using black-and-white plus one color score about 25 percent better than half-page ads using no additional color.
☐ True ☐ False

18. Single-page advertisements separated by suitable intervals reach a larger number of readers than the same space used all at once.
☐ True ☐ False

ANSWERS

(Quiz on page 1473)

1. *False.* They are a quantitative study and not a qualitative one—they are intended to measure how many people see and read the ad. Much of the criticism of readership studies has stemmed from a failure to differentiate between these two types of studies.
2. *True.* Readership is about 40 percent higher among brand users.
3. *False.* Horizontal ads are slightly more successful in producing readership than are vertical ads.
4. *True.* Men also seem much more inclined to look at women than women are to look at men in ads.
5. *False.* Photographs generally score higher than drawings.
6. *False.* Although multi-page ads attract more attention than do one-page or two-page insertions, they do not attract correspondingly more readers. (In other words, three pages do not attract three times as many people as one page.)
7. *False.* About half of all inquiries produced by an ad appearing in a weekly publication should be received during the first week.
8. *False.* The highest attention goes to those travel ads which picture the travel destination.
9. *True.* Cost-per-reader has increased about 68 percent in the last decade, which is about the same as the increase for general business costs.
10. *True.* The use of recipes generally results in substantially higher readership of food ads.
11. *False.* Celebrity testimonials are far more effective than testimonials by non-celebrities.
12. *True.* Half-page full-color advertisements attract nearly twice as many readers as black-and-white units of the same size.
13. *True.* Many high-scoring ads show the ship itself out at sea.
14. *True.* Men are principally interested in forms of transportation and mechanical things. Women are interested in food, household furnishings, and clothes.
15. *False.* The easier an advertiser makes it for the reader to send in an inquiry card, the less likely the reader will bother to study the ad. Presumably, readers feel the literature would be more complete, and hence why read the ad?
16. *True.* A reader's eyes are more likely to sweep across the upper half of a page and so are more likely to be stopped by a quarter-page that occupies an entire column.
17. *False.* They score about the same. One color plus black-and-white does not attract any more readers than do plain black-and-white ads in magazines.
18. *True.* Except for special overriding reasons, single-page ads are more effective than multi-page or gatefolds using the same total amount of space.

APPENDIX

PUBLICATION IMAGE PROFILE TRAITS

TIMELY—provides information of recent developments and new ideas while they are still newsworthy.

HELPFUL—furnishes its readers with information which is useful for the accomplishment of their work.

INTERESTING—engages and holds the attention of its readers.

OUTSPOKEN—expresses its opinions frankly.

INFLUENTIAL—has a strong effect on the actions and ideas of its readers.

AUTHORITATIVE—has the stature or experience necessary to present ideas that carry weight.

RESPECTED—is widely recognized for its worth or stature in the business world.

SOUND—is strong and secure. It has a high degree of business health.

EXPERIENCED—has gained through actual experience a first-hand knowledge of its field.

LEADING—is ahead of almost all others in its field.

INTELLIGENT—is brilliant, resourceful and mentally keen.

RESEARCH-MINDED—studiously investigates the facts before writing its articles or reporting the news.

SCIENTIFIC—displays expert knowledge of its subject matter in the writing of its articles.

LEARNED—has unusually wide and deep knowledge of its field gained by study, research, or experience.

ALERT—watches for new ideas and new developments in its field.

MODERN—is up to date and belongs to the present time.

PROGRESSIVE—accepts and uses new ideas in order to move forward.

DYNAMIC—is energetic, forceful, and enthusiastic.

PIONEERING—has a reputation for being the first to explore and use new ideas and new developments.

PENETRATING—has the power to see below the surface and to understand and explain that which is not readily evident.

FAR-SIGHTED—has a reputation for seeing trends and predicting events before they are obvious to others.

PROPER—acts in strict accordance with the standards which are considered correct for a business magazine.

OPEN-MINDED—is happy to receive ideas or new arguments.

UNBIASED—is free from undue or improper influence.

RELIABLE—merits confidence or trust. It is believable, truthful and accurate.

WELL-ORGANIZED—arranges its material so that it is convenient to read.

COMPREHENSIVE—thoroughly covers all the subjects that are of importance to its readers.

SPECIALIZED—stresses one specific area of interest in particular.

DIVERSIFIED—covers a number of different areas of interest.

INDEX

A

B

C

D

E

F

G

H

I

J

K

L

M

Q

R

S

*Discontinued

T

U

V

W